THE CONFERENCE ON SECURITY AND CO-OPERATION IN EUROPE

ANALYSIS AND BASIC DOCUMENTS, 1972–1993

THE CONFERENCE ON SECURITY AND CO-OPERATION IN EUROPE

ANALYSIS AND BASIC DOCUMENTS, 1972–1993

Edited by

ARIE BLOED

Associate Professor of International Law,
University of Utrecht, The Netherlands

KLUWER ACADEMIC PUBLISHERS

DORDRECHT / BOSTON / LONDON

in co-operation with The Europa Institute,
Faculty of Law, University of Utrecht, The Netherlands

A C.I.P. Catalogue record for this book is available from the Library of Congress.

ISBN 0-7923-2593-1 (HB)

Published by Martinus Nijhoff Publishers,
P.O. Box 163, 3300 AD Dordrecht, The Netherlands.

Sold and distributed in the U.S.A. and Canada
by Kluwer Academic Publishers,
101 Philip Drive, Norwell, MA 02061, U.S.A.

In all other countries, sold and distributed
by Kluwer Academic Publishers Group,
P.O. Box 322, 3300 AH Dordrecht, The Netherlands.

Printed on acid-free paper

Printed in the Netherlands

TABLE OF CONTENTS

I. DOCUMENTS OF CSCE MEETINGS

---

[1] The full texts of the documents, adopted at the Geneva Meeting of Experts on Peaceful Settlement of Disputes (October 1992), have been included in the decisions of the Stockholm meeting of the CSCE Council (December 1992) and are, therefore, not reproduced here.

II. DOCUMENTS OF THE CSCE COUNCIL OF FOREIGN MINISTERS

III. DOCUMENTS OF THE COMMITTEE OF SENIOR OFFICIALS (excerpts)

---

[2] In conformity to the existing practice, both "Nagorno-Karabakh" and "Nagorny-Karabakh" is used in the present publication. CSCE documents usually use the term "Nagorno-Karabakh" or "Nagorno Karabakh".

PREFACE

In 1990 a first edition of the present collection of documents of the Conference on Security and Co-operation in Europe was published under the title *From Helsinki to Vienna: Basic Documents of the Helsinki Process*. It contained all the substantive official documents which had been signed or adopted by meetings within the framework of the CSCE up to the spring of 1990. In this second edition all substantive CSCE documents which have been adopted up to July 1993 are included. From the considerably increased size of this book it may be derived that the CSCE process has been quite 'productive' in the recent period. As a matter of fact, the greater part of this book is occupied by documents which were agreed upon after the revolutionary events in the countries of Central and Eastern Europe during the second half of 1989 and thereafter. This is a clear reflection of the growing significance of the CSCE in the recent period: the CSCE has become an increasingly important instrument of conflict prevention and crisis management in the turbulent Eurasian area which has unfortunately become the scene of a growing number of bloody conflicts, most of which are ethnic- or nationalistic-based. The CSCE has also maintained its traditional functions as 'the conscience of Europe', although it has to be observed that the relative weight of the human dimension within the whole of the CSCE process seems to have diminished to some extent. That does not detract from the fact that the CSCE gave birth to a number of very important documents in this area. All in all it has to be observed that the CSCE has developed into an institution which produces an increasing amount of paper.

The documents in this second edition are again preceded by a survey of the basic features of the CSCE and the CSCE process. This introduction is even more necessary in view of the fact that the CSCE is becoming an increasingly complicated phenomenon in international relations. Even many persons active in the CSCE area are nowadays hardly able to obtain a good survey of all its aspects. Moreover, a survey is given of the main developments at all summit and follow-up meetings and specialized conferences which have taken place within the framework of the CSCE since the signing of the Final Act of Helsinki in 1975. In view of the purpose of this introduction, it has a mainly descriptive character. The present author intends to publish a more extensive, analytical study of the CSCE process in the near future.

A new part of this second edition consists of the texts of a great number of interpretative statements and reservations which have been submitted by participating States upon the negotiation and/or adoption of CSCE documents. These interpretative statements and reservations, based on recommendation 79 of the so-called *Blue Book* which contains the main procedural rules of the CSCE process, have so far only been published in the journals of the day of the meetings concerned. These journals, however, were not published and are not accessible to the public; indeed, they were not even stored in the archives of the Foreign Offices of some CSCE States. Besides, the interpretative statements and reservations were not systematically registered nor were/are they printed with the documents concerned. Therefore, it is very difficult to obtain all these texts, although a number of them are quite important for the interpretation of the CSCE provisions concerned. I have succeeded in obtaining the texts of a great number of these recommendation 79-statements, also thanks to the invaluable help of several colleagues and friends in the Netherlands, several other CSCE States and the CSCE Secretariat in Prague (in particular Dr. Claude Altermatt). I am fully aware of the fact, however, that I did not succeed in obtaining all of these statements. I would be obliged if I could receive the texts of missing statements which may then be included in a possible third edition of this collection of documents.

Although quite some attention has recently been devoted to the CSCE, the publication of this collection of CSCE documents is even more necessary. Although a number of these documents are now more widely available than they were in the past - in the last two years most of them have been published, for instance, in the quarterly *Helsinki Monitor* (published by the Netherlands Helsinki Committee) -, this is certainly not the case with all CSCE documents. Some of them are hardly available for scholarly research. In particular the documents, adopted by the Committee of Senior Officials (CSO), may be considered to be almost completely inaccessible, although they contain important material. Moreover, a complete and up-to-date collection of these documents in the English language in a single volume is still wanting.

In this collection only the substantive CSCE documents are published, including the texts of meetings of the Council, the Committee of Senior Officials and the Parliamentary Assembly. Documents which only contain the organizational modalities - prepared by special preparatory meetings - are omitted. The only exceptions are (a) the Final Recommendations of the Helsinki Consultations (1973), which contain the main organizational and procedural rules which, except for some minor changes, have up until now been applied during all CSCE meetings, and (b) the organizational modalities of a number of specialized CSCE meetings, which have been added to the 1989 Concluding Document of Vienna and the Charter of Paris (1990) as annexes. However, the work programmes for these specialized meetings (determining the working hours) have been omitted, as they have now become obsolete.

As far as the documents of the CSO are concerned, it has to be observed that a selection has been made. A great number of CSO documents also contain many organizational and procedural decisions which have hardly any practical relevance for a larger audience and are therefore omitted. Although any selection is to some extent arbitrary, nevertheless I decided to include in the present volume only those parts of the CSO decisions which may be considered to remain relevant for the medium term. Only a few documents, adopted by the CSO Vienna Group, have been included. The texts of the Consultative Committee of the Conflict Prevention Centre have been omitted. In contrast, the recent reports and other texts of the CSCE High Commissioner on National Minorities have been included. The same holds true for reports of CSCE missions. In view of the increasing number of CSCE missions, however, a selection was necessary. The editor aimed at presenting an illustrative survey of the documents which resulted from these CSCE activities.

Although some of the older CSCE documents may have lost part of their practical significance in view of the new political situation in Europe, they are formally still fully applicable and may be invoked at any time in the future; therefore, all are included in the present volume.

In relation to the text of the CSCE documents it has to be noted that the texts of the original documents have been followed in all their sinuosities. Only clearly evident printing errors have been corrected.

The publication of this book would not have been possible without the help of a great number of colleagues and friends. Dr. Claude Altermatt (CSCE Secretariat), Dr. Thomas Buchsbaum (Austrian Foreign Ministry and presently Council of Europe), Dr. Alexis Heraclides (Greek Foreign Ministry) and Ms. Erika B. Schlager (Congressional Helsinki Commission in Washington, DC) have been very helpful in providing me with texts of documents. I also feel greatly indebted to Ms. Inge Hofstee for her tiresome proofreading of the texts of the documents and to Ms. Marieke Klap-Vreugdenhil in the preparation of the camera-ready texts of the present book. The assistance of Ms. Annemiek Goris is duly acknowledged as well. Mr. Peter Morris did a great job in 'polishing up' the English in the Introduction. Ms. Lindy Melman of Martinus Nijhoff Publishers took good care of the technical aspects of this publication. The staff of the ODIHR in Warsaw deserves my gratitude for providing me with the computer-files of the texts of some reports of CSCE missions. Last but not least, I want to express my gratitude to Mr. Rob W. Zaagman, presently assistant to the CSCE High Commissioner on National Minorities, who gave highly valuable comments to a draft of the introduction as well as useful further advice. He also provided me with a number of texts. The responsibility for the contents of the present publication, however, remains fully with the undersigned.

Maartensdijk, August 1993 Dr. Arie Bloed

ABBREVIATIONS

APELL	Awareness and Preparedness for Emergencies at the Local Level
CBM	Confidence-building Measure
CCEET	Centre for Co-operation with European Economies in Transition
CDE	Conference on Disarmament in Europe
CEDAW	Convention on the Elimination of all Forms of Discrimination against Women
CHD	Conference on the Human Dimension of the CSCE
CFE	Conventional Armed Forces in Europe
CiO	Chairman-in-Office
CIS	Commonwealth of Independent States
CMEA	Council for Mutual Economic Assistance
COMTRADE	UN Trade Data Bank
COST	European Co-operation in the field of Scientific and Technical Research
CPC	Conflict Prevention Centre
CPC/CC	Consultative Committee of the Conflict Prevention Centre
CSBM	Confidence- and Security-building Measure
CSCE	Conference on Security and Co-operation in Europe
'CSCM'	'Conference on Security and Co-operation in the Mediterranean'
CSO	Committee of Senior Officials
DG	Discussion Group
DMR	Dniester Moldovan Republic
DMSSR	Dniester Moldovan Soviet Socialist Republic
EBRD	European Bank for Reconstruction and Development
EC	European Community
ECE	United Nations Economic Commission for Europe
ECMM	European Community Monitoring Mission
EDC	European Disarmament Conference
EEA	European Economic Area
EEA	European Environment Agency
EFTA	European Free Trade Association
EIB	European Investment Bank
EMEP	Monitoring and Evaluation Programme of the Convention on Long-Range Transboundary Air Pollution in Europe
ESSR	Estonian Soviet Socialist Republic
FAO	Food and Agriculture Organization
FSC	Forum on Security Co-operation
FRG	Federal Republic of Germany

FYROM	Former Yugoslav Republic of Macedonia
GATT	General Agreement on Tariffs and Trade
GDR	German Democratic Republic
HCNM	CSCE High Commissioner on National Minorities
IAEA	International Atomic Energy Agency
ICC	International Chamber of Commerce
ICFY	International Conference on the Former Yugoslavia
ICRC	International Committee of the Red Cross
ICSU	International Council of Scientific Unions
IFC	International Finance Corporation
IIASA	International Institute for Applied Systems Analysis
ILC	International Law Commission
IMO	International Maritime Organization
INES	International Nuclear Events Scale
INTOR	International Fusion Project (carried out under the aegis of the IAEA)
IPCS	International Programme on Chemical Safety
IRPTC	UNEP International Register of Potentially Toxic Chemicals
ITU	International Telecommunications Union
IUCN	International Union for Conservation of Nature and Natural Resources
JNA	Yugoslav National Army
MAP	Mediterranean Action Plan
MBFR	Mutual and Balanced Force Reductions
MPT	Multilateral Preparatory Talks
MSSR	Moldovan Soviet Socialist Republic
MURFAAMCE	Mutual Reduction of Forces and Armaments and Associated Measures in Central Europe ('MBFR')
NACC	North Atlantic Co-operation Council
NATO	North Atlantic Treaty Organization
NGO	Non-governmental organization
NNA States	Neutral and Non-aligned States
NPT	Non-Proliferation Treaty
NUSS	Nuclear Safety Standards
ODIHR	Office for Democratic Institutions and Human Rights
OECD	Organization for Economic Co-operation and Development
OFE	Office for Free Elections
PL	Plenary Meeting
PrepCom	Preparatory Committee
REMPEC	Regional Marine Pollution Emergency Response Centre for the Mediterranean Sea
ROCC	Regional Oil Combating Centre

SCOPE	Scientific Committee on Problems of the Environment (of the ICSU)
SALT	Strategic Arms Limitation Talks
SAM	Sanctions Assistance Mission
SAMCOMM	SAM Communication Centre
SFRY	Socialist Federal Republic of Yugoslavia
SG	Study Group
SME	Small and medium-sized enterprise
SSR	Soviet Socialist Republic
SWB	Special Working Body
TDF	Territorial Defence Forces
TEM	Trans-European Motorway
TIR	Transport International Routier
UIC	Union International des Chemins de Fer (International Union of Railways)
UK	United Kingdom
UN	United Nations Organization
UNCED	United Nations Conference on Environment and Development
UNCITRAL	United Nations Commission on International Trade Law
UNDP	United Nations Development Programme
UNEP	United Nations Environment Programme
UNESCO	United Nations Educational, Scientific and Cultural Organization
UNHCR	United Nations High Commissioner for Refugees
UNIIMOG	UN Iran Iraq Observer Group
UNISIST	World scientific and technical information system of UNESCO
UNPA	United Nations Protected Area
UNPROFOR	United Nations Protection Force
UNTSO	UN Truce Supervision Organization
USA	United States of America
USSR	Union of Socialist Soviet Republics
WEU	Western European Union
WHO	World Health Organization
WPO	Warsaw Pact Organization

BRIEF CSCE CHRONOLOGY

Meetings of the Committee of Senior Officials are listed separately below.

22 November 1972-8 June 1973:	Multilateral Preparatory Talks (MPT) in Dipoli, near Helsinki.
3-7 July 1973:	Stage I of the Conference on Security and Co-operation (CSCE) in Helsinki.
18 September 1973-21 July 1975:	Stage II of the CSCE in Geneva.
30 July-1 August 1975:	Stage III of the CSCE: signing of the Final Act of the CSCE in Helsinki.
4 October 1977-9 March 1978:	Belgrade Follow-up Meeting
31 October-11 December 1978:	Montreux Meeting of Experts on Peaceful Settlement of Disputes.
13 February-26 March 1979:	Valletta Meeting of Experts on the Mediterranean.
18 February-3 March 1980:	Hamburg Scientific Forum.
11 November 1980-9 September 1983:	Madrid Follow-up Meeting
17 January 1984-19 September 1986:	Stockholm Conference on Confidence- and Security-building Measures and Disarmament in Europe.
21 March-30 April 1984:	Athens Meeting of Experts on Peaceful Settlement of Disputes.
16-26 October 1984:	Venice Seminar on the Mediterranean.
7 May-17 June 1985:	Ottawa Meeting of Experts on Human Rights and Fundamental Freedoms.

30 July-1 August 1985	Meeting of Foreign Ministers in Helsinki (Tenth Anniversary of Final Act of Helsinki)
15 October-25 November 1985:	Budapest Cultural Forum.
15 April-26 May 1986:	Bern Meeting of Experts on Human Contacts.
4 November 1986-19 January 1989:	Vienna Follow-up Meeting
9 March 1989-4 March 1992	CSBM Negotiations, Vienna
9 March 1989-10 July 1992	CFE Negotiations, Vienna
18 April-12 May 1989	Information Forum, London
30 May-23 June 1989	First meeting of the Conference on the Human Dimension of the CSCE, Paris
16 October-3 November 1989	Meeting on the Protection of the Environment, Sofia
16 January-5 February 1990	Seminar on Military Doctrine, Vienna
19 March-11 April 1990	Conference on Economic Co-operation, Bonn
5-29 June 1990	Second meeting of the Conference on the Human Dimension of the CSCE, Copenhagen
24 September-19 October 1990	Meeting of on the Mediterranean, Palma de Mallorca
1-2 October 1990	Meeting of Foreign Ministers of the CSCE States, New York
17 November 1990	Adoption of the first Vienna Document on CSBMs

19 November 1990	Signature of the CFE Treaty, Paris
19-21 November 1990	CSCE Summit Meeting, Paris
15 January-8 February 1991	Meeting of Experts on Peaceful Settlement of Disputes, Valletta
2-3 April 1991	Constituent meeting of the CSCE Parliamentary Assembly, Madrid
28 May-7 June 1991	Symposium on the Cultural Heritage, Cracow
19-20 June 1991	First meeting of the CSCE Council of Ministers, Berlin
1-19 July 1991	Meeting of Experts on National Minorities, Geneva
10 September 1991	Additional meeting of the CSCE Council, Moscow
10 September-4 October 1991	Third meeting of the Conference on the Human Dimension of the CSCE, Moscow
8-18 October 1991	Seminar on Military Doctrine, Vienna
4-15 November 1991	Seminar of Experts on Democratic Institutions, Oslo
30-31 January 1992	Second meeting of the CSCE Council of Ministers, Prague
19-21 February 1992	Seminar on Conversion of Military Industry to Civilian Production, Bratislava
4 March 1992	Adoption of the second Vienna Document on CSBMs

4-6 March 1992	Seminar on Armed Forces in Democratic Societies, Vienna
10-23 March 1992	Preparatory meeting of the Helsinki Follow-up Meeting, Helsinki
24 March 1992	Signature of the Treaty on Open Skies, Helsinki
24 March 1992	Additional meeting of the CSCE Council, Helsinki
24 March-8 July 1992	Follow-up Meeting, Helsinki
3-5 July 1992	First meeting of the CSCE Parliamentary Assembly, Budapest
9-10 July 1992	CSCE Summit Meeting, Helsinki
10 July 1992	Signature of the CFE-IA Agreement, Helsinki
Since 22 September 1992	Forum on Security Co-operation, Vienna
12-23 October 1992	Meeting of Experts on Peaceful Settlement of Disputes, Geneva
16-20 November 1992	CSCE Human Dimension Seminar on Tolerance, Warsaw
14-15 December 1992	Third meeting of the CSCE Council of Ministers, Stockholm
16-18 March 1993	Economic Forum, Prague
31 March-2 April 1993	Seminar on Defence Planning, Vienna
20-23 April 1993	CSCE Human Dimension Seminar on Migration, including

	Refugees and Displaced Persons, Warsaw
6-7 May 1993	Seminar on a Code of Conduct Governing Mutual Relations in the Field of Security, Vienna
17-21 May 1993	Mediterranean Seminar, Valletta
24-28 May 1993	CSCE Human Dimension Seminar on National Minorities, Warsaw
7-9 June 1993	Seminar on Peacekeeping, Vienna
6-9 July 1993	Second meeting of the CSCE Parliamentary Assembly, Helsinki
27 September-6 October 1993	Seminar of Experts on Sustainable Development of Boreal and Temperate Forests, Montreal (scheduled)
27 September-15 October 1993	CSCE Implementation Meeting on Human Dimension Issues, Warsaw (scheduled)
10 October-2 December 1994	CSCE Review Conference, Budapest (scheduled)
December 1994	CSCE Summit Meeting (scheduled)

MEETINGS OF THE COMMITTEE OF SENIOR OFFICIALS

28-29 January 1991	1st CSO meeting, Vienna
23-24 May 1991	2nd CSO meeting, Prague
17-20 June 1991	3rd CSO meeting, Berlin
3-4 July 1991	1st Emergency CSO meeting, Prague
8-9 August 1991	1st Additional Emergency CSO meeting, Prague
3-4 September 1991	2nd Additional Emergency CSO meeting, Prague
10 October 1991	3rd Additional Emergency CSO meeting, Prague
22-24 October 1991	4th CSO meeting, Prague
29 November 1991	4th Additional Emergency CSO meeting, Prague
8-11 January 1992	5th CSO meeting, Prague
27-30 January 1992	6th CSO meeting, Prague
27-28 February 1992	7th CSO meeting, Prague
13 March 1992	8th CSO meeting, Helsinki
19, 23-24 March 1992	9th CSO meeting, Helsinki
29 April-1 May 1992	10th CSO meeting, Helsinki
6-12 May 1992	2nd Emergency CSO meeting, Helsinki
18-21 May 1992	11th CSO meeting, Helsinki
8-11 June 1992	12th CSO meeting, Helsinki
29 June - 7 July 1992	13th CSO meeting, Helsinki

9 July 1992	14th CSO meeting, Helsinki
13-14 August 1992	15th CSO meeting, Prague
16-18 September 1992	16th CSO meeting, Prague
5-6 November 1992	17th CSO meeting, Prague
11-13 December 1992	18th CSO meeting, Stockholm
2-4 February 1993	19th CSO meeting, Prague
16-18 March 1993	1st Economic Forum meeting (20th CSO meeting), Prague
26-29 April 1993	3rd Emergency CSO meeting, Prague
26-28 April 1993	21st CSO meeting, Prague
29-30 June 1993	22nd CSO meeting, Prague
21-23 September 1993	23rd CSO meeting, Prague (scheduled)

TWO DECADES OF THE CSCE PROCESS: FROM CONFRONTATION TO CO-OPERATION

AN INTRODUCTION

by

Arie Bloed

1. INTRODUCTION

Since the Final Act of Helsinki of the Conference on Security and Co-operation in Europe (CSCE) was signed on 1 August 1975, the CSCE or Helsinki process has acquired its own momentum. Although from the perspective of the 1990s this may seem to have been a natural development, the opposite is true. At certain critical moments during the Cold War the further continuation of the process was seriously threatened. This threat was particularly serious at the beginning of the 1980s, when East-West relations seriously deteriorated due to, *inter alia*, the Soviet invasion of Afghanistan, the proclamation of martial law and the prohibition of Solidarity in Poland and serious violations of human rights in Eastern Europe. In spite of these negative developments, the CSCE process survived and could even achieve substantive further progress.

After the collapse of communism in the States of Central and Eastern Europe in the second half of 1989 and thereafter, the CSCE became the object of some euphoria. Several former socialist States, in particular Poland and Czechoslovakia, considered the CSCE as the institution that should develop into some kind of collective security organization for the whole of Europe, encompassing both the Warsaw Pact and NATO. Although these optimistic ideas about the future of the CSCE did not come true, the CSCE process underwent a fundamental change of character. Until the end of the 1980s it was mainly an international institution which had the character of a diplomatic conference which often convened at different places in the CSCE area. Its main aim was to negotiate norms which should govern the behaviour of the participating States, in particular in the areas of political and security co-operation, human rights and economic co-operation. In 1990 and 1991 the CSCE achieved its most impressive results in this area.

At the same time, the CSCE was confronted with a number of new problems in the field of conflict prevention and conflict management as a consequence of the unexpected occurrence of a great number of ethnic-based conflicts in the CSCE area, mainly in the former socialist states. In view of

A. Bloed (ed.), The Conference on Security and Co-operation in Europe, 1–118.

the fact that no international instruments were available to deal with these potential and actual conflicts, the CSCE was called upon to help solve these problems. As the former 'debating' institution, however, the CSCE had no instruments for that purpose. This resulted in a fast process of developing a great number of new procedures - which in CSCE jargon are often called 'mechanisms' - which all aim to deal with such problems. The presently available procedures include, for instance, a Berlin emergency mechanism (since June 1991), a Vienna mechanism on unusual military activities (since November 1990), mechanisms for the human dimension of the CSCE, procedures for the peaceful settlement of disputes, and recent instruments like the CSCE High Commissioner on National Minorities and CSCE peacekeeping operations. The proclamation of the CSCE as a regional arrangement in the sense of chapter VIII of the Charter of the United Nations in July 1992 was also part of this development.

During the two decades of the CSCE's existence its geographical scope hardly changed, except for the fact that Albania finally joined the CSCE in 1991. Although the geographical scope of the CSCE hardly changed, the fact that Japan was officially admitted as an observer in 1992 may also be considered as a certain extension of the geographical scope of the CSCE. Nevertheless, the number of CSCE States rose dramatically from 35 in 1973 to 53 in 1993 (the situation as of July 1993) as a result of the dissolution of the Soviet Union, Yugoslavia and Czechoslovakia. A further increase may be expected (in particular Macedonia). As a result the CSCE was transformed from a predominantly Euro-Atlantic institution into a Eurasian-Atlantic one, in which Central-Asian and Caucasian problems tend to occupy a not unimportant place.

All this has fundamentally changed the character of the CSCE. This explains why nowadays one could speak of an "old" CSCE which existed until the end of the 1980s[1] and a "new" CSCE since the beginning of the 1990s. To a great extent the "old" CSCE is characterized by a 'confrontational' approach by the participating States (in particular between the Western and East European States), whereas the emphasis in the "new" CSCE is on 'co-operation' between all CSCE States. This fundamental change is also clearly reflected in the institutionalization of the CSCE. The "old" CSCE consisted only of periodic follow-up meetings and *ad hoc* conferences on specific subjects; the "new" CSCE is characterized by the establishment of regularly convening political organs and a number of small permanent administrative bodies.

---

[1] Concerning the history of the 'old' CSCE an abundant literature exists. A good and extensive survey is offered by: V.-Y. Ghebali, *La diplomatie de la détente; la CSCE, 1973-1989* (Brussels 1989).

As a consequence the CSCE process has changed into a very complicated international institution. The "old" CSCE was already a remarkable and rather complex phenomenon in international relations with unique procedural and substantive features. This made it hardly comparable with any other international forum. This situation has been further complicated during the recent period in which the CSCE seems to be in a transitionary stage on the road towards a 'traditional' international organization, although this might still take a long period before its completion (if ever). This means that the present CSCE contains elements of both the "old" and the "new" CSCE which makes it a rather hybrid international institution. In institutional terms, this is reflected in the traditional, political and process-oriented character of the CSCE, whereas at the same time it increasingly encompasses elements of permanently functioning, 'bureaucratic' organs. In spite of all changes, however, at present the "Cold War origins" of the CSCE are still clearly visible in many respects and it may be expected that this will be the case in the foreseeable future as well.

In order to be able to place the documents in the present publication within its proper political and legal context, the basic features of the Helsinki process, including its institutional and legal aspects, will be described below (paragraphs 2.2 and 2.3). This description will be preceded by a survey of the origin of the CSCE process and by a brief description of the main results of the preparatory meeting which laid the basis for the CSCE and the ensuing Helsinki process (the so-called Multilateral Preparatory Talks in Helsinki) (paragraph 2.1). The concluding document of this preparatory meeting (the so-called *Blue Book*) is still of great practical importance for the functioning of the CSCE process at present. Thereupon, a survey will be given of the main developments at the Conference itself which took place between 1973 and 1975, including a brief description of the contents of the Final Act of Helsinki (paragraph 3.1). Subsequently, attention will be paid to the CSCE summit meetings and follow-up meetings (paragraph 3.2) and to the great number of specialized conferences and expert meetings which have taken place within the framework of the CSCE since the signing of the Final Act (chapters 4-5). A description of all official CSCE meetings will follow in a thematic order, grouped around the main issues which have so far been dealt with within the framework of the CSCE process: security issues (paragraph 4.1), peaceful settlement of disputes (paragraph 4.2), economic and scientific/technical co-operation and co-operation in the field of the environment (paragraph 4.3), the Mediterranean (paragraph 4.4), and the human dimension of the CSCE, including information and culture (paragraph

4.5).[2] Within these groups the description will follow a chronological order. Finally, attention will be paid to meetings of the CSCE (Council of) Foreign Ministers and the Committee of Senior Officials (chapters 5-6). In a concluding chapter (chapter 7), attention will be paid to the activities of parliamentarians within the CSCE process, in particular in the context of meetings of the recently established CSCE Parliamentary Assembly. As indicated above, this descriptive analysis of the Helsinki process mainly aims to provide the framework for the CSCE documents which are published in the second part of this book; therefore special attention will be given to the institutional aspects of the CSCE process.

2. THE CSCE PROCESS: ITS ORIGIN, DEVELOPMENT AND BASIC FEATURES

2.1. Origin and development of the CSCE Process

2.1.1. Origin of the CSCE

Although the Conference on Security and Co-operation in Europe itself dates back to the beginning of the 1970s, its roots extend much further back. Some authors even go back as far as Stalin, who submitted proposals for some kind of collective security system for Europe in the 1930s, although the connection between those proposals and the present CSCE is highly artificial. A more direct link may be established with developments at the beginning of the 1950s. During this period, the Soviet Union made efforts to establish some kind of European collective security system, the main purpose of which was to prevent the entry of the Federal Republic of Germany into the Western military alliances. The latter was the main reason for the Western refusal to respond positively to these proposals. Consequently, in 1954 and 1955, Soviet-initiated "European security conferences" were only attended by representatives of the East European States. The "European security conference" of May 1955 resulted in the conclusion of the Warsaw Treaty of Friendship, Co-operation and Mutual Assistance, the basis of the Warsaw Pact Organization (WPO).

---

[2] In the 1970s and 1980s, the term "third basket issues" was used to denote questions related to human rights and fundamental freedoms, humanitarian issues, information, culture and education, although from a formal perspective the issue of human rights belonged in the first basket (see *infra* section 3.1.2). The term "human dimension of the CSCE" was only officially introduced at the Vienna Follow-up Meeting (1986-1989). For a description of this concept, see *infra* section 2.3.2.1.

In the 1960s, the idea of a European security conference was again launched by the USSR, although formally the initiative was taken by the Warsaw Pact. In July 1966, the Political Consultative Committee, the supreme organ of the WPO, issued the so-called Declaration of Bucharest. This extensive declaration proposed a great number of measures for the strengthening of peace and security in Europe, *inter alia*, the convening of a European conference on security and co-operation. This was the green light for a protracted "communiqué dialogue" between the NATO and the WPO in which East and West gradually grew towards each other.

The difficulties which had to be solved were mainly connected with the very different aims which were pursued by the East European and the Western States. Although they had a great number of goals, the East European States mainly aimed at a formal recognition of the post-war territorial *status quo* in Europe. The West European States had thus far refused to recognize the course of certain frontiers, *inter alia*, the politically highly sensitive Oder-Neisse-frontier between Poland and the German Democratic Republic (GDR). Another important goal which the Warsaw Pact States pursued by organizing a European conference on security and co-operation was the further development of economic relations between Eastern Europe and the Western States. This was considered to be one of the instruments by which to solve certain problems in the economies of the East European States which were experiencing a serious decline.

The Western countries' interest in the convening of a European conference had a different background. They were not at all interested in granting the East European States the desired recognition of the territorial situation in Europe, unless the latter were prepared to yield to Western wishes. The West was mainly interested in achieving progress in the field of (military) security issues and in the field of humanitarian questions (more specifically a free flow of individuals, information and ideas between East and West). Especially the proposals in the latter field met with vehement East European protests, as the Warsaw Pact States formally considered these humanitarian issues to belong to the internal affairs of their States.

Gradually a compromise could be achieved, greatly stimulated by the relaxation of tension between East and West as a result of the West-German *Ostpolitik*, the new policy towards Eastern Europe pursued since 1969. This change of policy on the part of the Federal Republic of Germany resulted in the conclusion of four *Ostverträge* which normalized the relations of the Federal Republic of Germany (FRG) with the USSR, Poland, Czechoslovakia and the GDR. Moreover, in September 1971, the Four-Power-Agreement on Berlin was concluded. The final decision about the convening of a Conference on Security and Co-operation in Europe - which was agreed to be the official name of the conference - was taken in 1972 after the conclusion of the first SALT-agreement between the USA and the USSR (26

May). "In the light of these favourable developments, Ministers agreed to enter into multilateral conversations concerned with preparations for a Conference on Security and Co-operation in Europe", the Foreign Ministers of the fifteen NATO States stated in the final communiqué of the meeting of the NATO Council of 30 and 31 May 1972. At the same time, NATO Ministers repeated their proposal "that multilateral explorations on mutual and balanced force reductions be undertaken as soon as practicable, either before or in parallel with multilateral preparatory talks on a Conference on Security and Co-operation in Europe". In this way the NATO States once again stressed their opinion that an indissoluble link exists between military and political détente. In the course of 1972, this connection was also accepted by the East European States. This resulted in a parallel, but simultaneous start of two diplomatic conferences: the CSCE in Helsinki (see below section 2.1.2) and the negotiations on Mutual and Balanced Force Reductions (MBFR)[3] with a smaller number of participating States, which started in 1973. The MBFR negotiations dragged on in Vienna until the beginning of 1989 when the conference was formally dissolved. Its task was transferred to a new round of negotiations with a larger number of participating States (all NATO and Warsaw Pact States) and another mandate: the negotiations on Conventional Forces and Armaments in Europe (CFE), which started in Vienna in March 1989 and which were successfully concluded in November 1990. In contrast to the MBFR negotiations, the CSCE has been more successful, although agreement on its concluding document, the Final Act of Helsinki, could only be achieved in 1975 by the laborious and long-lasting efforts of a great number of diplomats and experts from all the (then) 35 participating States.

2.1.2. Multilateral Preparatory Talks in Helsinki 1972-1973

At the invitation of the Finnish government, Multilateral Preparatory Talks (MPT) started at the Dipoli conference centre (near Helsinki) on 22 November 1972. The heads of the diplomatic missions, accredited in Helsinki, of 32 European States, Canada and the USA were the participants at these MPT. Albania was the only European State which rejected the Finnish invitation to participate, claiming that "security in Europe cannot be arranged by a conference that is organized by the two super-powers" which

---

[3] The official name was Mutual Reduction of Forces and Armaments and Associated Measures in Central Europe (MURFAAMCE).

are trying to resolve major international problems "between themselves" and at the expense of other States and world public opinion.[4]

The MPT, usually referred to as the Helsinki Consultations, were held to solve the numerous preparatory aspects connected with the organization of the Conference (date, place, agenda, participation, financial questions, rules of procedure, etc.). However, the MPT actually far exceeded the scope of a meeting with a purely preparatory function. Not only were the strictly organizational and procedural aspects of the CSCE established at the MPT, but also the main lines of the substantive issues which were to be discussed at the Conference. This explains why the MPT appeared to be very complicated and took much more time than had been expected. The disagreements between East and West[5] about almost all aspects of the organization of the security conference were so fundamental that for a long time it was rather unlikely that there would ever be a CSCE. It was therefore a remarkable achievement that after more than half a year the 34 States nevertheless succeeded in reaching a compromise on all outstanding issues on 8 June 1973. This compromise consisted of the adoption of the "Final Recommendations of the Helsinki Consultations", usually referred to as the *Blue Book*.

In the *Blue Book* the blueprint for the Conference was established which has determined the essence and nature of the CSCE process to a great extent so far, both as far as its scope and its rules of procedure are concerned. However, it must be realized that this basic CSCE document also contained a great number of ambiguities due to its compromisory nature.

As far as the organization of the Conference is concerned, the *Blue Book* determined that it was to be held in three stages. The first stage was to be held in Helsinki at the ministerial level. The Ministers for Foreign Affairs should officially approve the Final Recommendations and present their governments' views on the problems at issue (recommendations 7 and 63). The second stage was to be the "working stage", to be held in Geneva. At this stage, a final CSCE document had to be negotiated (recommendations 8 and 63). At the third and last stage of the CSCE, again in Helsinki, a final document was to be adopted (recommendations 10-12 and 63).

---

4 *Hronika* 1972, p. 3154A, quoted in: L. Acimovic, *Problems of Security and Cooperation in Europe* (Alphen aan den Rijn/Rockville 1981), p. 116.

5 The neutral and non-aligned countries took a position somewhere in between East and West. Most of them were convinced of the desirability of a CSCE and some even wanted a permanent institutional structure (like the East European States), but they supported the Western view on the agenda and the thorough preparation of the CSCE at the MPT.

The major part of the *Blue Book* was dedicated to the agenda which encompassed a detailed enumeration of all the problems which had to be discussed in the second stage of the Conference (recommendations 13-53). In this agenda the main issues of the CSCE process were officially determined. It gave birth to the three main areas or 'baskets'[6] of the CSCE on substantive issues, whereas the (organizational) follow-up to the Conference is often referred to as the fourth CSCE 'basket':

I. Questions relating to security in Europe, encompassing both the basic principles guiding relations between the participating States and a number of confidence-building measures;
II. Co-operation in the fields of economics, science and technology, and the environment;
III. Co-operation in humanitarian and other fields;
IV. Follow-up to the conference.

In the *Blue Book* it was laid down that all European States, the United States and Canada were entitled to participate in the CSCE. In practice these were the 34 States which participated in the MPT, whereas Monaco decided to join the CSCE after the conclusion of the MPT. Albania therefore remained the only European State which definitively abstained from the Conference.[7] The *Blue Book* also provided for "contributions" to the CSCE by non-participating States and in particular by those States which are situated adjacent to Europe. This provision, which was inserted after strong pressure from Malta, referred specifically to Mediterranean States.

A very important part of the *Blue Book* is devoted to the rules of procedure of the Conference. It was laid down that all States would participate as "sovereign and independent States and in conditions of full equality". Moreover, it was specifically stated that the Conference "shall take place outside military alliances" (recommendation 65). The sovereign equality of all participating States was expressed in particular in the principle of consensus which was to govern the decision-making process of the CSCE

[6] The term *basket* was born out of the rather chaotic origin of the CSCE: in order to bring some order in the great number of very varying proposals, submitted by the 34 States, the latter were provisionally filed in three imaginary 'baskets'. Until now this term has remained the official CSCE jargon for its main substantive issues.

[7] Only in 1991, after the change of government in Albania, did this state also join the CSCE. Officially Albania was admitted to the CSCE at the first meeting of the CSCE Council of Ministers in Berlin in June 1991 (see the text of the Berlin Council decisions *infra* in the present publication).

(recommendation 69) and in a rotating chairmanship (recommendations 70-71).

As far as the structure of the Conference is concerned, the *Blue Book* determined that the Conference was to function through a number of working bodies: the central organ was to be the Co-ordinating Committee. In addition, committees and sub-committees were provided, which could set up their own working groups. All working bodies and working groups were to be open to all participating States: another expression of the sovereign equality of all CSCE States (recommendations 67-68). Except for some very specific occasions, all sessions of CSCE organs would be closed to the public (recommendation 80).

It was decided that the working languages of the CSCE would be English, French, German, Italian, Russian and Spanish (recommendation 81).

The *Blue Book* also provided for an Executive Secretary who was charged with "technical matters". The Executive Secretary was to be a national of the corresponding host country (recommendation 74). This implied that the Conference would have very limited administrative support. In line with this minimal secretariat service it was also stipulated that no official verbatim records would be taken except at the meetings of the first and third (ceremonial) stages (recommendation 77).

Finally, the *Blue Book* determined the follow-up to the Conference. From the very beginning, the participating states did not aim to organize a single Conference. In contrast, they aimed at a Conference which should be followed by a process. This follow-up should deal with the implementation of the decisions to be achieved at the CSCE and with the further promotion of "the process of improving security and developing co-operation in Europe" (recommendation 53).

On the basis of the *Blue Book*, the Conference on Security and Co-operation in Europe took place in three stages: an official opening phase at the level of Foreign Ministers in Helsinki from 3 to 7 July 1973; a second stage at expert level in Geneva from 18 September 1973 until 21 July 1975; and a third concluding stage at summit level in Helsinki from 30 July until 1 August 1975 which resulted in the solemn signing of the Final Act of Helsinki.

2.1.3. Development of the process

After the signature of the Final Act of Helsinki on 1 August 1975, the CSCE did not come to an end. The Final Act provided for a follow-up to the Conference which basically boiled down to the convening of periodic follow-up meetings for review and further development. The follow-up meetings which have so far taken place (Belgrade 1977-1978, Madrid 1980-1983,

Vienna 1986-1989 and Helsinki 1992), have also decided to organize expert meetings and *ad hoc* conferences on specific subjects. This has resulted in the situation that since 1975 pan-European negotiations on a great number of issues have taken place within the framework of the CSCE. This development has led to the fact that nowadays, as a rule, reference is made to the CSCE or Helsinki *process*. An important milestone in the development of the Helsinki process was the CSCE Summit Meeting in Paris in November 1990. This summit meeting, convened in order to set new guidelines for the process after the revolutionary events in the former socialist countries, adopted the *Charter of Paris for a New Europe*. The Paris Summit constituted the starting-point for a considerable institutional 'upgrading' of the CSCE process by establishing permanent political and administrative organs. This also resulted in a change to the functions of the follow-up meetings (in 1992 officially renamed *review conferences*). Since then the emphasis in CSCE policy-making, in particular, has shifted from the follow-up meetings to the newly established CSCE Council of Foreign Ministers and the Committee of Senior Officials, the Council's subsidiary body.

Within the framework of the Helsinki process an increasing number of official CSCE documents have been adopted (until now only the Final Act of Helsinki and the Charter of Paris have been *signed*[8]). The Final Act of 1975 has been succeeded by several substantive concluding documents. Of major importance are the concluding documents of the follow-up meetings of Madrid (1983), Vienna (1989) and Helsinki (1992). In addition, a number of specialized CSCE meetings have also resulted in the adoption of substantive concluding documents. Major examples are the subsequent documents on Confidence- and Security-Building Measures (adopted in 1986, 1990 and 1992 respectively) and the documents of the Conference on the Human Dimension of the CSCE (adopted in 1990 and 1991). As a rule, these substantive CSCE concluding documents are referred to as "the Helsinki agreements".

Since the signing of the Final Act of Helsinki the CSCE process has acquired its own momentum which has survived critical lows in East-West relations. After the collapse of communism in the States of Central and

---

[8] For the sake of completeness, reference has to be made to the treaties which have been negotiated and concluded in the framework of the CSCE. As a matter of fact, these documents have been signed as well. It concerns the Treaty on Conventional Armed Forces in Europe (CFE, 1990) and the Open Skies Treaty. The link with the CSCE, however, is of a rather *sui generis* nature (see *infra* sections 4.1.6 and 4.1.7). The mandate for the CFE-negotiations was laid down in the Vienna Concluding Document (1989) and separately signed by the NATO and Warsaw Pact States. In December 1992, the first CSCE treaty was adopted and signed by a number of CSCE states: the Convention on Conciliation and Arbitration within the CSCE (see *infra* 4.2.4 and 5.7).

Eastern Europe, the CSCE entered a new phase in its existence. As indicated above, this increasingly complex Helsinki process is characterized by remarkable and unique basic features, a number of which will now be dealt with.

2.2. The CSCE as a dynamic political process: basic features

Although the CSCE process has been subject to drastic changes in its character and powers over the last few years, in essence it is still the dynamic political process which it has been since its inception. This is reflected most particularly in its very light institutional structure and its strictly political character. After the collapse of communism, however, the institutional structure of the CSCE in particular has been fundamentally changed. Therefore, one may distinguish an 'old' CSCE which existed until 1990 and a 'new' CSCE which has developed on the basis of the 1990 Charter of Paris for a New Europe.[9] Although the 'new' CSCE is developing in the direction of a 'normal' international organization, it still has to be considered as a unique phenomenon in international relations which is hardly comparable with any other international institution.[10]

In order to substantiate this observation, some of the basic features of the CSCE process will now be dealt with:
the remarkably light institutional structure of the CSCE; the strict equality of all 53 participating states, most clearly reflected in the decision-making process; the (political) nature of CSCE commitments and documents; the pan-European and, since 1992, Eurasian character of the CSCE process; the interlinkage between the different main areas ('baskets') of the CSCE process; and the involvement of private citizens and non-governmental organizations in the process.

2.2.1. Institutional structure of the CSCE

A basic feature of the CSCE process is its remarkably light institutional structure. It is important, however, to make a clear distinction between the 'old' CSCE as it existed until 1990, and the 'new' CSCE which was based

---

9 See *infra* section 3.2.4.

10 A slightly comparable institution is the Council of the Baltic Sea States, established at a Conference of Foreign Ministers of the Baltic Sea States in Copenhagen in March 1992. See Mare Kukk, 'The Council of the Baltic Sea States', in: *Helsinki Monitor*, 1993, No. 3, pp. 5-12.

on the Charter of Paris for a New Europe, adopted by the CSCE Summit in Paris in November 1990.[11]

In essence the institutional structure of the 'old' CSCE only consisted of *ad hoc* follow-up meetings which are organized every two or three years and which are hosted by one of the CSCE States (so far Yugoslavia, Spain, Austria, Finland and in 1994 Hungary[12]). The host country was charged with providing modest administrative support in the form of an Executive Secretary, who has the nationality of the host country, supplemented with a modest staff (in particular interpreters, due to the six official languages of the CSCE). Apart from the periodic follow-up meetings, specialized conferences and expert meetings on specific subjects have been organized since 1978 on an *ad hoc* basis. In the course of the development of the CSCE process, the number and scope of such specialized conferences and expert meetings have steadily increased. In the 'old' CSCE permanent administrative or political bodies did not exist. In institutional terms, the CSCE had the character of a diplomatic conference which convened on various occasions.

The 'new' CSCE, as created in 1990, was largely the result of an intensive policy debate about the future of European security after the surprising collapse of communism in Central and Eastern Europe from the second half of 1989 onwards. The euphoric expectations concerning the development of the CSCE into some kind of collective security system, adhered to by several CSCE states, were not shared by all CSCE states, but there was a general opinion that the CSCE should be given a more firm institutional basis in order to be able to meet the demands of the new epoch in Europe. This resulted in the decisions, adopted at the Paris Summit in November 1990. The then adopted *Charter of Paris for a New Europe* created a new institutional structure for the CSCE, but it did so in a highly remarkable way. In general terms, the new institutional structure consists of three permanent administrative organs, two new political organs which convene at certain intervals, and certain *ad hoc* meetings. The *Charter* also expressed the desire to create a CSCE parliamentary body which was given concrete form at an inter-parliamentary meeting in the spring of 1992. The institutional structure of the CSCE was further elaborated at the Prague meeting of the CSCE Council (January 1992) and at the last CSCE Follow-up Meeting in Helsinki (March-July 1992), most notably by introducing the more or less permanently functioning Forum for Security Co-operation in Vienna and by the establishment of the new post of CSCE High

---

11 See *infra* section 3.2.4.

12 The Budapest meeting which is scheduled for October-December 1994 will be the first *review conference*, the new name for the former follow-up meetings.

Commissioner on National Minorities. Finally, apart from several smaller changes to the institutional structure, a recent innovation concerned the establishment of the function of a CSCE Secretary General who took office in June 1993. All in all, the institutional structure of the CSCE has become highly complex. In the following paragraphs only the main elements of this structure will be described.

The institutional structure nowadays consists of several components: political decision-making bodies; permanent administrative organs; high-ranking personalities; a parliamentary assembly; *ad hoc* bodies.

The system of political decision-making bodies is rather simple: the Council of Ministers for Foreign Affairs of the CSCE (hereafter: Council) and the Committee of Senior Officials (CSO). Moreover, every two years a review conference is to take place, concluded by a CSCE Summit Meeting (officially called Meetings of Heads of State or Government).

The Council as "the central forum for regular political consultations within the CSCE process"[13] will convene at least once a year. It is "the central decision-making and governing body of the CSCE", as stipulated in the Helsinki 1992 Document.[14] Between the meetings of the Council, "the CSO (...) will be responsible for overview, management and co-ordination and will act as the Council's agent in taking appropriate decisions".[15] The CSO has also been granted functions in the area of economic co-operation: it meets once a year as the Economic Forum.[16] As the tasks of the CSO increased considerably, the regular meetings of the CSO - which officially must convene at least four times a year, but in practice meets much more often - appeared to be insufficient. For that reason the CSCE Council established the so-called CSO Vienna Group which meets in Vienna as often as necessary between meetings of the CSO, as a rule once a week. The national delegates to the regular CSO meetings - which usually take place at the seat of the CSCE Secretariat in Prague - and the CSO Vienna Group are very often the same and this guarantees the continuity of CSO activities.[17] The Vienna Group, in combination with the CSCE Forum for Security Co-

---

13 Charter of Paris for a New Europe, Supplementary Document, chapter I, paragraph A.1.

14 Chapter I.6 of the Helsinki Decisions of the Helsinki 1992 Document. See *infra* section 3.2.5.

15 Idem, chapter I.9.

16 See *infra* section 4.3.4.

17 The delegates are often based in Vienna as the national representatives to the security talks in Vienna, among other things within the framework of the Forum for Security Co-operation (see *infra* section 4.1.4).

operation, developed into a more or less permanently functioning crisis management machinery, meeting very frequently. All this contributed to the fact that Vienna is increasingly becoming the focal point for CSCE activities.[18]

A new element in the structure of the 'new' CSCE is also the function of Chairman-in-Office. This function is fulfilled by the Foreign Minister of the state which occupies the chairmanship of the CSCE or by the Senior Official of that state. The chairmanship is on a rotation basis. In 1991 Germany held the first CSCE Chair, succeeded by Czechoslovakia in January 1992. In December 1992 the chairmanship was taken over by Sweden. This task will again be transferred to Italy at the meeting of the Council in Rome which is scheduled to take place at the end of 1993. The Chairman-in-Office may be considered to be the CSCE's 'super-co-ordinator': he/she is responsible for the co-ordination of and consultation on current CSCE business. In carrying out his/her tasks, the Chairman-in-Office may be assisted by the preceding and succeeding Chairmen, operating together as the CSCE *Troika*, by *ad hoc* steering groups, and by personal representatives. The function of personal representatives of the Chairman-in-Office has so far only been used in practice in certain crisis areas (e.g. Moldova, Georgia) so far: it is an instrument for the CSCE to investigate the situation in problem areas on the spot, resulting in concrete recommendations for further action.

In addition to the regular meetings of the Council and the CSCE, every two years a review conference will take place. The review conference, which is the successor of the former CSCE follow-up meetings, has a double task which highly resembles the functions of its predecessor: the review of all CSCE activities, including a thorough implementation debate, and the preparation of a "decision-oriented" document to be adopted at the CSCE Summit Meeting. The function of the Summit Meeting itself is rather vague: it should "set priorities and provide orientation at the highest political level". The next summit is planned to take place in Budapest in December 1994.

In 1992 a new institutional structure for the CSCE human dimension was established. This structure, succeeding the annual meetings of the Conference on the Human Dimension of the CSCE,[19] encompasses two types of expert meetings: human dimension seminars on specific subjects[20] and biennial implementation meetings which are scheduled for the years in which no review conference is to take place. Both Human Dimension

---

[18] See also *infra* chapter 6.

[19] See *infra* section 4.5.5.

[20] See *infra* section 4.5.9.

Seminars and Implementation Meetings are not entitled to adopt "negotiated documents".[21]

At the Paris Summit in November 1990 the decision was also taken to establish three permanent administrative organs: a Secretariat in Prague, a Conflict Prevention Centre (CPC) in Vienna and an Office for Free Elections (OFE) in Warsaw. In January 1991 the latter organ was transformed into the Office for Democratic Institutions and Human Rights (ODIHR). These three organs with a very modest size and mandate express most visibly the 'new' CSCE.

The establishment of these three administrative organs of the CSCE has been realized in a rather peculiar way which clearly reflects the fear among a number of CSCE participating States of creating a new bureaucracy which might even undermine existing international organizations (such as the Council of Europe or NATO). The desire to keep the 'administrative institutionalization' of the CSCE as modest as possible is reflected in the fragmentation of offices over three states (Austria, Poland and the Czech Republic), the limited mandate of a mainly administrative character for all three organs, and the minimal size of the staff. Moreover, the seconding system also aims at avoiding the creation of a new bureaucracy: the directors and officers in all three organs are seconded by their governments and remain in function at the CSCE bodies only for two or three years.

The mandate for all three administrative organs is rather modest. The CPC is charged with "assist[ing] the Council in reducing the risk of conflict". In practice, however, its tasks are mainly related to supporting the implementation of confidence- and security-building measures in the military sphere, such as the mechanism on unusual military activities[22] and the organization of annual implementation meetings. At a later stage, the CPC was granted additional tasks in the field of peaceful settlement of disputes[23] and in relation to the Forum on Security Co-operation.[24] The implementation of the functions of the CPC is entrusted to two bodies: the Consultative Committee in which all CSCE states are represented, and a small Secretariat.

---

[21] The first biennial implementation meeting on human dimension issues was scheduled to take place in Warsaw from 27 September to 15 October 1993. It will deal, among other things, with concrete problems concerning the implementation of human dimension commitments by CSCE states and a critical evaluation of the supervisory mechanisms which exist within the CSCE framework in the field of the human dimension.

[22] See *infra* section 2.3.1.2.

[23] See also *infra* section 2.3.1.3.

[24] See *infra* section 4.1.4.

The OFE was charged with facilitating contacts and the exchange of information on elections within CSCE states. Its functions increased considerably when the OFE was transferred into the ODIHR. The ODIHR is not only charged with the traditional tasks in the field of elections, but it is also responsible for a number of activities in all other areas covered by the human dimension of the CSCE. As such it has certain tasks in the application of the CSCE Human Dimension Mechanism and in the organization of human dimension seminars and implementation meetings. It also acts as a clearing-house for information on states of public emergency. A special ODIHR task is the maintenance of relations with the Council of Europe.

The CSCE Secretariat is charged with providing administrative support to the meetings of the Council and the CSO. It also maintains an archive of CSCE documentation, provides information to the public domain regarding the CSCE, and fulfils other related tasks. Since recently, the CSCE Secretariat in Prague and the CPC Secretariat in Vienna have been incorporated in a single organizational structure under the direction of the newly-established Secretary General.

The CSCE High Commissioner on National Minorities (HCNM) took office in January 1993. His mandate was laid down in the Helsinki 1992 Document of July 1992. The HCNM is the first independent, high-ranking personality within the CSCE process which was thus far characterized by a predominantly intergovernmental character. Mr. Max van der Stoel, a former Minister for Foreign Affairs of the Netherlands, was appointed as the first CSCE High Commissioner in December 1992. The post of High Commissioner has been designed as a conflict prevention instrument. According to the mandate, the HCNM provides 'early warning' and, as appropriate, 'early action' at the earliest possible stage with regard to tensions involving national minority issues that have the potential to develop into a conflict within the CSCE area.[25]

The second high-ranking personality within the CSCE process is the Secretary-General of the CSCE. This post was created by the CSCE Council in December 1992. Half a year later, in June 1993, the German Ambassador, Wilhelm Höynck, took office as the first CSCE Secretary-General with his seat in Vienna. Although this new post is considered to be the second high-ranking post within the CSCE, its status is not fully comparable with the High Commissioner. In relation to the High Commissioner it has been agreed that he should be "an eminent international personality with longstanding relevant experience from whom an impartial performance of the

---

[25] Chapter II.3 of the Helsinki Decisions of the Helsinki 1992 Document.

function may be expected".[26] Corresponding requirements for the post of Secretary-General have not been agreed upon. The latter post is clearly subordinated to the Chairman-in-Office.[27] Moreover, the Secretary-General is the CSCE's chief administrative officer, supervising the work of the three permanent administrative CSCE bodies.[28]

At the Paris Summit, decisions on the establishment of a CSCE Parliamentary Assembly appeared to be impossible. In April 1991 this vacuum was felt by delegations of the parliaments of the CSCE participating states themselves at a meeting in Madrid. Although a formal link with the CSCE process exists,[29] the CSCE Parliamentary Assembly is an independent body. Remarkable aspects of the CSCE Assembly are the proportional representation of the parliaments of the CSCE states and the system of weighted voting. The Assembly will meet once a year in one of the capitals of the CSCE states. The first 'regular' meeting took place in Budapest in July 1992. A small secretariat for the CSCE Assembly was created in Copenhagen.

Finally, the institutional structure of the CSCE process also encompasses an increasing number of *ad hoc* bodies. These *ad hoc* bodies are, in particular, missions of long duration in several trouble spots in the CSCE area. Such long-term missions are situated at several places in the former Yugoslavia (missions in Belgrade, Kosovo, Sandjak, and Vojvodina, and the spill-over monitor mission in Macedonia). In addition, the following missions have been established: in Georgia to deal with the disputes concerning, *inter alia*, Ossetia and Abkhazia, in that state; in Moldova, aimed at the conflict concerning Trans-Dniestria; and in Estonia, dealing with the serious problems with, in particular, the large Russian minority. In addition to the CSCE missions of long duration, the CSCE has also created a number of other *ad hoc* bodies, such as Sanctions Assistance Missions (in close co-operation with the EC) in order to assist states neighbouring the former Yugoslavia in implementing the UN-imposed sanctions on the former Yugoslavia; steering groups concerning specific conflicts; the Executive Secretariat for the Forum for Security Co-operation in Vienna; peace

---

26 Helsinki Decisions, chapter II.8.

27 See Annex 1 of the Summary of Conclusions of the Stockholm Meeting of the CSCE Council (15 December 1992).

28 See further *infra* section 2.3.1.4.

29 This is reflected, *inter alia*, in statements about meetings of the CSCE Assembly by the CSCE Council and in the concluding document of the Helsinki Summit in 1992.

conferences (such as the Conference on Nagorny-Karabakh and the related 'Minsk group'[30]); etc.

2.2.2. Decision-making process

Another basic feature of the CSCE process is the strict equality of all participating states. This basic principle is reflected in several elements within the CSCE, such as a rotating chairmanship at CSCE meetings and the rule that the CSCE was lacking in organs of limited composition. The new CSCE, however, indicates deviations from these CSCE principles: at certain CSCE meetings the chairmanship has been entrusted to directors of CSCE organs (for instance, the ODIHR Director at Human Dimension Seminars), whereas the proliferation of new CSCE bodies has resulted in the establishment of a number of organs with limited composition (such as steering groups or peace conferences).

The principle of equality of CSCE states is most clearly reflected in the decision-making process within the CSCE. Decision-making at meetings within the framework of the CSCE is only possible by consensus. This rule was laid down in the 1973 Final Recommendations of the Helsinki Consultations, the *Blue Book*, as follows: "Decisions of the Conference shall be taken by consensus. Consensus shall be understood to mean the absence of any objection expressed by a Representative and submitted by him as constituting an obstacle to the taking of the decision in question" (recommendation 69).

In CSCE practice the rule of consensus has sometimes led to surrealistic situations at CSCE follow-up meetings and has been of considerable influence to small CSCE States. States such as Malta have made ample use of this possibility. The rigidity of the rule of consensus was, to a certain extent, mitigated in two ways. In the first place, by defining the principle in negative terms: consensus is considered to be achieved if no State has expressed an *objection*. In this way, decision-making is sometimes possible, as no State wishes to block further progress, even though it would prefer another decision. In the second place, the rule of consensus is, to a certain extent, mitigated by the provision that States are allowed to make reservations or interpretative statements (recommendation 79 of the *Blue Book*). In this way, States may express their specific interpretations concerning certain CSCE decisions, although it is not clear which effects ensue from such statements. Although one might assume that reservations aim to avoid becoming bound to certain agreements without formally

---

30 The Belorussian capital Minsk was designated as the venue for the CSCE peace conference on Nagorny-Karabakh.

blocking the decision-making, there is no *communis opinio* on this issue. There is general agreement, however, that the submission of interpretative statements does not affect the binding force of the CSCE provisions concerned.

The right to make reservations has rarely been used in CSCE practice. At the conclusion of the Vienna Follow-up Meeting, in January 1989, Romania made use of this right in a very striking way. It stated, in the most general terms, that it would not be bound by any provision of the Concluding Document which it considered to be "inadequate". From the context of the Romanian statement it could be determined that this "reservation" concerned a number of human rights and humanitarian provisions, although it did not specify these clauses. The Western CSCE States strongly protested against Romania's behaviour and considered the Romanian reservation to be "absurd and void". In January 1990, after the revolution in Romania, the new leadership in that State officially withdrew this reservation which had been made by the former Ceausescu regime.

In contrast to formal reservations, CSCE states made ample use of their right to submit interpretative statements, both during a process of negotiations and at the formal adoption of concluding documents by consensus. Interpretative statements may be used for various reasons, such as for formally stating or clarifying the national policy on a certain issue or for expressing the reasons why the state concerned is less satisfied with the results of the CSCE meetings without blocking the decision-making process. In practice, interpretative statements and reservations play a rather limited role, which is partly due to the fact that the texts are only incorporated in the daily journals of the CSCE meetings concerned. They are not included in the official publications of the texts of the CSCE documents. This explains why it appears to be extremely difficult to lay one's hands on the text of these interpretative statements and reservations, in particular because the daily journals have never been officially published. Even the 'inner circles' of the CSCE process have difficulty in obtaining these texts.

The consensus principle very much determined the course of CSCE meetings: as a rule such meetings were time-consuming, as it took a considerable amount of time to achieve consensus on a final document. On the other hand, the principle guaranteed that all CSCE participating states felt bound by all CSCE decisions. However, in the new CSCE, after the collapse of communism, the function of the principle changed. In view of the increasingly operational tasks of the CSCE in the area of conflict prevention, crisis management and dispute settlement, the consensus principle to a certain extent became a liability. This resulted in discussions on amendments which would make the CSCE decision-making process more flexible and more in conformity with the changing circumstances which require quick actions by the CSCE. Progress on this path has proved to be rather difficult. The negotiations on the Paris Charter did not produce concrete results. Between 1990 and 1992, however, some measures were taken in the CSCE framework which mitigated the rigidity of the consensus principle to a certain extent.

The *first exception* was adopted in November 1990. The Vienna Document on Confidence- and Security-Building Measures provides for a "Mechanism for consultation and co-operation as regards unusual military activities". This mechanism provides, *inter alia*, for the possibility to convene special emergency meetings of all CSCE participating states at the request of only one CSCE state. Although consensus is no longer required for the convening of such a meeting decision-making at these meetings again requires unanimity. Therefore, this first exception to the consensus principle is of a mainly procedural nature.[31]

The *second exception* was agreed upon in June 1991 in the context of the so-called Berlin emergency mechanism. This mechanism has been designed to give the CSCE an instrument in situations of political crisis. The Berlin mechanism may be used by CSCE states to raise certain conflicts within the framework of the CSCE process. In order to apply the mechanism the consent of only 13 states is required, which means that only a small minority of the CSCE states have to support the initiative to apply the Berlin mechanism. It has to be taken into account, however, that the exception to the principle of consensus in the context of the Berlin mechanism only applies to the convening of a special meeting within the CSCE framework. The decision-making at that meeting, however, is governed by the consensus principle. Therefore, it has to be observed that this second exception to the principle of consensus is also of a mainly procedural nature.

A *third exception* to the rule was adopted in October 1991. At the third meeting of the Conference on the Human Dimension of the CSCE, which took place in September and October in Moscow, a so-called emergency mechanism for the human dimension[32] was agreed upon. This 'Moscow mechanism' boils down to the possibility that in cases of very serious violations of human rights[33] a total of at least ten CSCE states are entitled to send a special rapporteur mission to the country where massive and gross violations of CSCE commitments in the human dimension field have occurred. The most remarkable aspect of this so-called Moscow mechanism is the fact that these rapporteur missions may be sent not only

---

[31] See further *infra* section 2.3.1.2.

[32] Concerning the 'human dimension of the CSCE' concept, see *infra* section 2.3.2.

[33] Formally, the Moscow Document refers to "a particularly serious threat to the fulfilment of the provisions of the CSCE human dimension" (paragraph 12). See the text *infra*.

with the support of at least ten CSCE states, but also against the will of the state concerned. As a matter of principle, this second exception to the principle of consensus is much more remarkable than those mentioned above, as it concerns an important substantive issue.

A *fourth exception* to the consensus principle was adopted at the end of January 1992 by the CSCE Council of Ministers in Prague. At that meeting the Ministers decided on the adoption of the so-called consensus-minus-one principle. That means that in situations of massive and gross violations of human rights the CSCE is entitled to adopt political measures against the state in which the violations occur, without the consent of the latter state. However, the effect of the application of the consensus-minus-one principle is necessarily rather limited: only "political declarations or other political steps" on the basis of this principle may be taken, while another important limitation is constituted by the clause that these political measures may be applied only "outside the territory of the State concerned".[34] The consensus-minus-one principle has been the basis for suspending the former Yugoslavia (now Serbia-Montenegro) from the CSCE in 1992 because of the atrocities it has committed in other former Yugoslav republics (in particular in Bosnia-Herzegovina).[35]

All in all it may be concluded that the consensus principle has recently been mitigated to a quite considerable extent. So far, however, a 'consensus-minus-two' principle appears to be difficult to achieve. This suggestion has been put forward in order to enable decision-making in the CSCE in cases of conflicts between two states also without the consent of the two conflicting states. In practice it would boil down to a translation of the well-known principle that no one can be a judge in one's own case. Only in specific procedures concerning peaceful settlement of disputes ('directed conciliation')

---

[34] See the decisions adopted at the meeting of the CSCE Council in Prague in January 1992.

[35] At its meeting in Prague in January 1992, the CSCE Council of Ministers decided that "in cases of clear, gross and uncorrected violations of relevant CSCE commitments", if necessary, the consensus-minus-one principle may be applied "in order to develop further the CSCE's capability to safeguard human rights, democracy and the rule of law through peaceful means" (paragraph 16 of the Prague Document on further Development of CSCE Institutions and Structures). This decision was clearly aimed at enabling certain actions in cases of violations of commitments in the field of the human dimension of the CSCE only. The suspension of Yugoslavia-Serbia's rights as a participating State because of its responsibility for the civil war in the former Yugoslavia evidently went beyond the level of the CSCE human dimension. The effect is a *de facto* extension of the scope of the consensus-minus-one principle to the political and security field.

has the consensus-minus-two rule been introduced at the end of 1992.[36] This issue, as well as other options,[37] will undoubtedly be further discussed at future CSCE meetings.

2.2.3. Legal nature of CSCE commitments and documents

One of the most complicated aspects of the CSCE process is the legal characterization of CSCE commitments and of the CSCE's concluding documents. In legal doctrine the view generally adhered to is that the Final Act of Helsinki and the CSCE documents do not have the character of treaties. This was also explicitly stressed by the heads of state or government at the end of the Conference in 1975. Moreover, arguing that the Final Act would be a legally binding agreement on the basis of another source of international law would be futile. The intention of the parties, as expressed at the end of the Conference in Helsinki in 1975, clearly points to the fact that the Final Act has to be considered as a political, not as a legal document.

This observation should not, however, be taken to imply that the CSCE documents are not binding. The binding force of these documents is not seriously doubted. Van Dijk correctly states: "A commitment does not have to be legally binding in order to have binding force; the distinction between legal and non-legal binding force resides in the legal consequences attached to the binding force", not in the binding force as such.[38] Violation of politically, but not legally binding agreements is as inadmissible as any violation of norms of international law. In this respect there is no difference between politically and legally binding rules.

Although the Final Act of Helsinki and the other Helsinki agreements are not legally binding, they contain numerous clauses which can be traced to international agreements to which a great number or all of the CSCE States are bound. The main example in this respect is the Charter of the United Nations: the Helsinki agreements contain numerous references to the purposes and principles of this Charter (see in particular the first basket of the Final Act of Helsinki and the concluding documents of Madrid, Vienna and Helsinki). In addition, references are frequently made to more specific

---

36 See further *infra* at section 2.3.1.3.

37 Another option would be a 'consensus-minus-three' principle which would be applicable in situations of conflicts between two states in which a third state is heavily involved (for instance the conflict between Armenia and Azerbaijan about Nagorny-Karabakh with Turkey as the third state involved).

38 P. van Dijk, 'The Final Act of Helsinki - Basis for a Pan-European system?', in: *Netherlands Yearbook of International Law*, 1980, p. 110.

treaties, for instance the 1966 International Covenants on Human Rights (Principle VII of the first basket of the Final Act of Helsinki). Moreover, the Principles guiding the relations among the participating States contain several provisions which are binding upon States as fundamental principles of international law.

The fact that the Helsinki agreements are not legally binding agreements has not affected their political authority. The opposite is true. This becomes evident from the fact that the Helsinki agreements are very frequently invoked as an authoritative source of obligations in order to substantiate that the CSCE States are obliged to adopt certain behaviour or to refrain from certain actions. The great political authority of the Final Act of Helsinki also ensues from the fact that it has been signed by the highest political representatives of the 35 CSCE States.

In fact, the Helsinki agreements are so often invoked by the CSCE States as an authoritative source of obligations, that now and again the opinion is put forward that these agreements are in a process of developing into customary law. In other words, from this point of view the Helsinki agreements are international legal instruments *in statu nascendi* or *soft law*. Adherents to this view often refer to the way in which the Universal Declaration of Human Rights is considered to have gradually acquired binding legal force. Moreover, they point to the fact the CSCE States often enact specific legislation in order to fulfil their obligations ensuing from adopted Helsinki agreements. Whatever view one adheres to, the fact should not be overlooked that, so far, the CSCE States have explicitly chosen a non-legally binding form for the CSCE documents. This intention is of tremendous importance in a discussion about the legal character of the Helsinki agreements. At the same time, we should not ignore the fact that these agreements may be important elements in a process of law-making.

It has to be observed that during the recent period the nature of certain CSCE documents has changed considerably. In the 'new' CSCE, the emphasis in the decision-making process has shifted from the follow-up meetings and specialized conferences to the newly established and regularly meeting Council of Ministers and, in particular, to the CSO. This has resulted in the situation that other CSCE bodies, such as *ad hoc* meetings, are no longer entitled to adopt binding documents.[39] If they are entitled to

---

[39] In the decision-making process in the "old" CSCE in the period prior to the Paris Summit in 1990, the emphasis was on the periodic follow-up meetings. These meetings determined the nature and mandate of any specialized meeting which had to be held between two follow-up meetings. Detailed rules about the precise competences of these specialized meetings were lacking. In principle, the next follow-up meeting "welcomed" and/or "took note of" the results of the specialized meetings, but there was a common understanding that the commitments entered into at such specialized meetings were not

produce documents at all, these documents have to be endorsed by the Council or the CSO in order to obtain (politically) binding force. In addition, it has to be noted that recently a number of CSCE documents have been produced which explicitly state that they do "not purport to express any new commitments on the part of participating States".[40] It is, therefore, of great importance to take into account the specific clauses in each CSCE document and the corresponding decisions of the Council and/or CSO, when judging the binding force of CSCE commitments.

Although the political character of CSCE commitments and documents is still largely unaffected, a certain trend towards a 'legalization' of the CSCE process may be detected in the recent period. This is reflected in some far-reaching proposals to give the CSCE process a treaty basis or to 'legalize' CSCE commitments. In 1990 and 1991 such proposals were put forward, among others, by the French President, François Mitterrand, and the (then) Czechoslovak President, Vacláv Hável. This would result in a transformation of the CSCE into a 'traditional' international organization, based on a constituent treaty, and on the commencing of negotiations on the text of conventions which would contain CSCE commitments in legal terms. These proposals have so far been refuted. However, certain important developments in this respect have to be noticed. The fact that in the framework of the CSCE two treaties on disarmament and security issues have been negotiated - the Treaty on Conventional Armed Forces in Europe (CFE Treaty) in 1990 and the Open Skies Treaty in 1992 - is of little relevance in this respects, as the link between these negotiation processes and the CSCE was rather weak and clearly *sui generis*. More important, however, is the fact that the CSCE Council in Stockholm in December 1992 adopted the text of a Convention on Conciliation and Arbitration within the CSCE, and declared it open for signature by interested participating states. In the spring of 1993 the Convention was signed by more than half of the CSCE states. This is the first CSCE convention in the proper sense of the word. This constitutes an important element, as for the first time in CSCE history a CSCE document has been adopted to which not all CSCE states are bound. This forms an important deviation to the (so far) fundamental principle of the 'universalism' of CSCE commitments, which means that to

---

dependent upon the final approval of the subsequent follow-up meeting. Cf. E.B. Schlager, 'The Procedural Framework of the CSCE: From the Helsinki Consultations to the Paris Charter, 1972-1990', in: Human Rights Law Journal, Vol. 12, No. 6-7, July 1991, pp. 22-237 at p. 231.

[40] Quotation from the Report to the CSCE Council from the CSCE Seminar of Experts on Democratic Institutions, Oslo, November 1991. Similar clauses may be found in several other recent CSCE documents.

date all CSCE commitments are fully applicable to all CSCE states.[41] This was also one of the reasons why a number of CSCE states refused to join the convention (such as the USA, the United Kingdom, Turkey and the Netherlands).

Another significant development is the fact that a CSCE group of experts has been established "to consider the relevance of an agreement granting an internationally recognized status to the CSCE Secretariat, the Conflict Prevention Centre and the ODIHR".[42] This activity should lead to an agreement which would grant a certain legal capacity to the permanent administrative bodies of the CSCE which so far lack any formal legal status. A convention on the international legal status of the CSCE as a whole is not envisaged. It is expected that decisions will be taken at the end of 1993 by the CSCE Council in Rome.

2.2.4. Pan-European character

The Helsinki process is further characterized by the fact that the CSCE is the only European forum where all European States, the USA and Canada and presently five Central Asian republics periodically convene for consultations on almost all important issues concerning their mutual relations: political and security issues, economic and scientific/technical co-operation, protection of the environment and questions relating to the human dimension. In this context it is significant that the CSCE process focuses on the situation in Europe. Most other international institutions which constitute meeting places for the 53 CSCE States are universal organizations and are - with the exception of the United Nations - furthermore restricted to specific areas of co-operation.

Although the principle of equality granted equal rights and obligations to all individual CSCE states, the old CSCE undoubtedly had a predominantly East-West character. In fact, the CSCE states fell into three groups: the sixteen NATO states, the seven Warsaw Pact states, and twelve neutral and non-aligned states (as a rule referred to as NNA States).[43] In

---

41 The only exception to this principle are a number of confidence- and security-building measures (CSBMs) in the security area. Most of these CSBMs are not applicable on the territory of the Northern American CSCE States and on Russian territory behind the Urals (the CSBMs are fully applicable to the Central Asian states as a result of specific arrangements which were made when these states were admitted to the CSCE).

42 Stockholm Council, Summary of Conclusions, paragraph 7 (text see *infra*).

43 Moreover, the twelve EC states formed a separate group, which - except for Ireland - also belonged to the NATO alliance.

practice, the NNA States have played a highly important role at most CSCE meetings by their efforts to "build bridges" between East and West. This "bloc-to-bloc" character of the CSCE is also reflected in the fact that the different groups of CSCE States often acted as groups at CSCE meetings. Although *de facto* the East-West relationship has greatly dominated the CSCE, in theory this seemed to be contrary to the CSCE principles: in the *Blue Book* it was expressly stipulated that all States participating in the CSCE "shall do so as sovereign and independent States and in conditions of full equality. The Conference shall take place outside military alliances" (recommendation 65).

After the collapse of communism the "bloc-to-bloc" nature of the CSCE has disappeared to a great extent, resulting in a considerable fragmentation of the process which makes the achievement of any agreement even more difficult, as well as time- and energy-consuming. Only the Twelve and Sixteen (respectively the European Community and NATO states) still function as groups, although the coherence within these groups has seriously diminished as well. In addition to the traditional Western groups some new informal groups have emerged which co-ordinate their positions *en marge* of some CSCE meetings. To these groups belong the *Central European Initiative*[44] and the group of *Visegrad* states.[45] The Nordic states and Baltic countries sometimes formed informal CSCE groups as well.

An international institution which has a certain similarity with the CSCE is the North Atlantic Co-operation Council (NACC). The establishment of the NACC at the end of 1991 was the response of the NATO to the pressure from Central and Eastern European states to join it. The NACC provides an institutional framework for the former socialist states for close co-operation with the alliance without full membership but with the corresponding security guarantees. At present, all NATO states and former socialist states (including the former Soviet republics in Central Asia) belong to the NACC. However, the NNA countries have not been invited to join the NACC, although Finland has been granted observer status. NACC's activities aim at an enhancement of security in its area, *inter alia*, in the sphere of confidence- and security-building measures (training, contacts between defence staffs, preparation of peacekeeping operations etc.). So,

---

[44] The Central European Initiative was called *Hexagonale* until recently. It encompasses Poland, the Czech Republic, Slovakia, Hungary, Italy, Austria and some former Yugoslav republics. In the past this group was known as the Pentagonale, but with the increase of members the name had to be changed into Hexagonale. After the disintegration of the former Yugoslavia, the character of the group changed as well, as is also reflected in the new name.

[45] Poland, the Czech Republic, Slovakia and Hungary.

both in geographical scope and in terms of aims and activities, the NACC and the CSCE could overlap each other. Therefore, co-ordination between both institutions is crucial.

2.2.5. Interlinkage

An important feature of the CSCE process is the *interlinkage of the baskets*. This means that in principle progress in one field should be accompanied by more or less simultaneous progress in other CSCE baskets. In this way political and security issues, questions of economic co-operation and humanitarian issues are firmly interconnected. The Western states in particular have always emphasized this linkage in the CSCE process, which aims at preventing quick results in, for instance, the less controversial second basket (the economy) without simultaneous progress in other politically more sensitive baskets (e.g. human rights).

Recently, developments which tend to imply that this interlinkage is becoming much less important may be discerned. For instance, the increasing number of specialized CSCE meetings dealing with very specific issues points to a direction in which the interlinkage seems to lose its strength. On the other hand, it has to be observed that so far the CSCE states have not been prepared formally to abandon this interlinkage. In contrast, during the meeting of the Council of Ministers of the CSCE in Prague in January 1992 the interlinkage was explicitly reconfirmed.[46]

This view was reiterated in even stronger terms at the Helsinki Summit Meeting of the CSCE in July 1992. On this occasion, the Heads of State or Government declared: "Our approach is based on our comprehensive concept of security as initiated in the Final Act. This concept relates the maintenance of peace to the respect for human rights and fundamental freedoms. It links economic and environmental solidarity and co-operation with peaceful inter-State relations. This is equally valid in managing change as it was necessary in mitigating confrontation."[47]

This interlinkage was and remains not only important for tactical reasons, but it is also important in substantive terms. It has to be realized that the issues at stake in the Helsinki process often do have a close substantive relationship with each other. This may be illustrated by referring to questions of security and the protection of human rights. Both fields are

---

[46] The Ministers stressed "the CSCE's comprehensive concept of security and stability, which includes human rights, political, military, economic and environmental components" (paragraph 6 of the Summary Conclusions of the Prague Meeting of the CSCE Council, 30-31 January 1992 (text *infra*).

[47] Paragraph 21 of the Helsinki Summit Declaration (text *infra*).

closely interrelated as negative developments in one field will almost automatically have unfavourable effects on the other. The establishment of the post of CSCE High Commissioner on National Minorities in 1992 as a preventive diplomacy instrument[48] is a clear reflection of this close relationship between security issues and the human dimension of the CSCE.

The basis for the interlinkage may be found in the first basket of the Final Act of Helsinki: in its decalogue of principles, it is explicitly stated that "(a)ll the principles (...) are of primary significance and, accordingly, they will be equally and unreservedly applied, each of them being interpreted taking into account the others".[49] These principles deal both with security issues (e.g. the principles on refraining from the threat or use of force and the inviolability of frontiers) and human rights issues (e.g. the principle on respect for human rights and fundamental freedoms). In practice, this linkage is not restricted to only the declaration of principles, but encompasses the other CSCE areas as well.

It has to be observed that the basket structure of the CSCE process has also been the subject of change in the "new" CSCE. In fact, one might observe that the basket structure in its original form no longer exists as a result of the fact that gradually the former differences between the baskets of the CSCE have largely disappeared. In particular the human dimension of the CSCE - a concept which was introduced in the CSCE only in 1989 - overlaps all the former 'border lines', encompassing elements of both the first, and the second and third baskets. As a result, the three traditional baskets are becoming increasingly intertwined. Instead of an undermining of a traditional characteristic of the CSCE process, this tendency of increasing intertwining therefore strengthens rather than weakens the interlinkage of the CSCE baskets as a basic feature of the CSCE process.

2.2.6. Involvement of NGOs and private citizens

A final basic feature of the Helsinki process concerns the *involvement of private citizens*. Although the CSCE process is an intergovernmental process, it has to be taken into account that private citizens and non-governmental organizations have an important role to play in order to achieve the purposes of the CSCE. This aspect of the Helsinki process was officially enacted in the Helsinki agreements, although in the Cold War period the East European States tried to keep the corresponding clauses as vague as possible. The pertinent clause in the Final Act of Helsinki reads as follows: "They [the

---

48 See *infra* section 2.3.1.4.

49 First final clause of the Declaration on Principles Guiding Relations between Participating States in the Final Act of Helsinki.

participating States] confirm that governments, institutions, organizations and persons have a relevant and positive role to play in contributing toward the achievement of these aims of their co-operation" (Principle IX on Co-operation among States). Only in the period of *glasnost* and *perestroika* could further progress be achieved in this area. In 1989, in the Concluding Document of the Vienna Follow-up Meeting, the Warsaw Pact states accepted the Western ideas about the freedom of groups of private citizens which monitor the implementation of CSCE commitments by their governments. The pertinent provision reads as follows: "To that end they will respect the right of persons to observe and promote the implementation of CSCE provisions and to associate with others for this purpose. They will facilitate direct contacts and communication among these persons, organizations and institutions within and between participating States and remove, where they exist, legal and administrative impediments inconsistent with the CSCE provisions. They will also take effective measures to facilitate access to information on the implementation of CSCE provisions and to facilitate the free expression of views on these matters" (provision 26 of the first basket of the Concluding Document of Vienna).

After the collapse of communism further progress could be achieved at a rapid pace. In particular, in the field of the human dimension of the CSCE the importance of private citizens and non-governmental organizations (NGOs) is currently quite considerable. This is reflected in the fact that recently the status and position of NGOs within the CSCE process has been enhanced, *inter alia*, by decisions which have been taken at the Helsinki Follow-up Meeting (March-July 1992) as laid down in the Helsinki Summit document *The Challenges of Change*. In this document a number of new possibilities for NGO involvement in the CSCE process have been created. In particular, in the area of the human dimension of the CSCE the possibilities for participation by NGOs have been considerably enhanced. The most remarkable development in this respect is the right of the newly established CSCE High Commissioner on National Minorities to receive communications from individuals and non-governmental groups.

Although NGOs have been granted considerable access to CSCE meetings,[50] many limitations continue to exist. Meetings of the most important political CSCE bodies, for instance, remain closed for NGOs. Moreover, it has been laid down in the Helsinki 1992 Document that the rights granted to NGOs do not apply to "persons or organizations which resort to the use of violence or publicly condone terrorism or the use of

[50] In particular at CSCE Human Dimension Seminars NGOs have been granted the right to participate fully in the discussions, both in the discussion groups and at official plenary meetings.

violence".[51] So far, this compromise clause has not been applied in practice, but it may be invoked at any time by CSCE states to try to exclude certain groups from CSCE premises. Finally, it has to be noted that NGOs or private citizens do not have a formal status in the application of CSCE mechanisms.[52]

Although the possibilities for NGOs to monitor the implementation of CSCE commitments by participating states have greatly increased, recently some new participating states have hampered certain activities by private citizens or NGOs on their territory. This indicates that the pertinent CSCE commitments have certainly not yet become obsolete.

2.3. CSCE procedures and mechanisms

During the Cold War period the CSCE had the character of a diplomatic conference in more or less permanent session. The main 'operational' task of the CSCE was to monitor the implementation of CSCE commitments. For that purpose implementation debates took place at various CSCE meetings. The tasks facing the 'new' CSCE are of a very different character. In addition to the traditional standard-setting and review functions, the CSCE got substantive tasks in the area of early warning, conflict prevention, crisis management and dispute settlement. In order to be able to implement these new tasks, the CSCE was granted a number of new procedures and mechanisms. In view of the relatively short period of time, the record of the CSCE in this respect is quite impressive: in about two to three years the CSCE acquired a considerable number of specific mechanisms, both in the security and in the human dimension area. It can even be stated that the CSCE has been 'too' successful in this area, as the progress has resulted in a considerable proliferation of procedures, mechanisms and (permanent or *ad hoc*) bodies which are presently causing serious co-ordination problems.[53] The most important of these procedures, instruments and mechanisms will

---

51 Paragraph IV.16 of the Helsinki Decisions.

52 The only exceptions are the right of human dimension missions to communicate with (groups of) private persons (see paragraph 6 of the Document of the Moscow Meeting of the Conference on the Human Dimension of the CSCE of October 1991) and the right of the High Commissioner on National Minorities to receive communications from private persons or NGOs (see paragraph II.23-25 of the Helsinki Decisions of July 1992).

53 As far as the human dimension is concerned, see, e.g., A. Bloed, 'Monitoring the Human Dimension of the CSCE: In Search of its Effectiveness', in: A. Bloed a.o. (Eds.), *Monitoring Human Rights in Europe; Comparing International Procedures and Mechanisms* (Dordrecht-Boston-London 1993), pp. 45-91.

now be described briefly. In the first place the procedures and mechanisms for early warning, conflict prevention and crisis management will be presented, followed by the procedures in the area of the human dimension of the CSCE.

2.3.1. Procedures and instruments for security issues

2.3.1.1. Berlin emergency mechanism

At the first meeting of the CSCE Council of Foreign Ministers in Berlin in June 1991, a "mechanism for consultation and co-operation with regard to emergency situations" was adopted. This so-called 'Berlin mechanism' - also referred to as the 'CSCE emergency mechanism' - provides for procedures which may be used by CSCE States in crisis situations.

The adoption of the Berlin mechanism was the outcome of a long discussion that had already started during the preparations of the Paris Summit in 1990. At the Paris Summit, however, no substantial progress concerning a political crisis mechanism was possible. This was due to hesitations in both East European and Western states. The USSR, for instance, feared far-going international interference with the political problems within its empire, in particular, relating to the sensitive issue of the position of the Baltic states. In addition, Turkey was not very eager to support the adoption of a CSCE crisis mechanism, as it feared that it might be used by Greece to raise the Cyprus question. In 1990 the USA was also not yet in favour of a crisis mechanism. This was due, *inter alia*, to its fear that it might lead to a considerable upgrading of the CSCE to an organization with substantive powers in the area of European security. It also feared a potential abuse of a CSCE crisis mechanism.

As practice indicated, soon after the Paris Summit the sphere changed considerably, also due to the upheavals in the former Soviet bloc (in particular the violent actions of Soviet troops in the Baltics). At the Berlin Council meeting in June 1991, the USSR was only prepared to accept the emergency mechanism when it was accompanied by strict conditions. This explains the fact that the preamble of the relevant document explicitly refers to the full application of "all the Principles of the Final Act, including the Principle of non-intervention in internal affairs". At that time it was clear that the Soviet Union considered the Baltic question as such an "internal affair". All this explains why the time was not yet ripe for a really effective crisis mechanism.

The mechanism may be invoked in cases of "a serious emergency situation which may arise from a violation of one of the Principles of the Final Act or as the result of major disruptions endangering peace, security or stability". The Berlin mechanism consists of two phases. In the first phase, clarification may be sought by any CSCE state when it considers that an emergency situation "is developing". The information requested has to be provided within 48 hours. The request and the reply will be transmitted to all other CSCE states.

Should the situation remain unsolved, the initiating CSCE state or states with the support of at least twelve other participating states may request that an emergency meeting of the CSO be held. The powers of an emergency CSO meeting, which must be held within two or three days, are limited: it may agree on "recommendations or conclusions to arrive at a solution" and it may also decide to convene a special meeting of the Council. However, these decisions may only be taken by consensus. This latter condition highly restricts the possibilities for the CSCE to act in crisis situations. This was clearly reflected in the Yugoslav crisis: although the Yugoslav tragedy was discussed in the CSCE framework on the basis of the Berlin mechanism, the CSCE appeared to be unable to adopt effective measures in this case, also because of the need for Yugoslav consent on all measures to be adopted.

The Berlin emergency mechanism has so far been applied only rarely. In addition to the Yugoslav crisis, the mechanism was invoked by Hungary in relation to a conflict with Czechoslovakia concerning the Gabcikovo dam on the river Danube at the border between Hungary and Slovakia in October 1992. This application of the emergency mechanism, however, has halted after the first phase (request for clarification), partly due to the fact that Hungary did not succeed in raising the support of twelve other CSCE states to convene an emergency meeting of the CSO.

Although the Berlin mechanism is certainly not a very effective instrument for the prevention and management of crises in the CSCE area, it may be used to raise issues at a high political level. This may undoubtedly exert political pressure on CSCE States. In this sense it may be a useful instrument for the CSCE States.

2.3.1.2. Vienna mechanism on unusual military activities

The Vienna "mechanism for consultation and co-operation as regards unusual military activities" was established in November 1990 as part of a series of new confidence- and security-building measures (CSBMs) within the CSCE process.[54] The mechanism has been laid down in paragraph 17 of the Vienna Document on Confidence- and Security-Building Measures which was formally adopted at the CSCE Summit of Paris. It states that CSCE states "will (...) consult and co-operate with each other about any unusual and unscheduled activities of their military forces outside their normal peacetime

[54] On CSBMs see *infra* sections 2.3.1.7.

locations which are militarily significant, within the zone of application for CSBMs and about which a participating State expresses its security concern".

Like the Berlin mechanism, the Vienna mechanism on unusual military activities consists of two phases. In phase I any CSCE participating State is entitled to request clarification from another CSCE State in cases of "unusual military activities" in the latter state. The requested state is obliged to respond within 48 hours. Both the request and the response will be communicated to all other CSCE states without delay. If the clarification does not satisfy the initiating state, it may commence the second phase of the mechanism. This phase provides for two options: the initiating state may request a bilateral meeting or it may request an emergency meeting of the CSCE which will take place in the framework of the CPC. In practice this means a meeting of the Consultative Committee of the CPC (CPC/CC) in Vienna. Both the bilateral meeting and the emergency CPC/CC meeting has to take place within 48 hours of the request having been made. In June 1991 this mechanism was applied by Austria and Italy in the case of the Yugoslav conflict.[55]

A related procedure concerns "co-operation as regards hazardous incidents of a military nature". On this issue paragraph 18 the 1990 Vienna Document on CSBMs states that "(p)articipating States will co-operate by reporting and clarifying hazardous incidents of a military nature".[56]

2.3.1.3. Peaceful settlement of disputes

New procedures for the peaceful settlement of disputes have been on the agenda of the CSCE since its very inception. During the Cold War period only very slight progress could be achieved.[57] Only after the revolutionary changes in Central and Eastern Europe, did the CSCE states succeed in achieving major progress.

At an expert meeting in Valletta (Malta) in January and February 1991 the first substantive steps were taken with the adoption of a Report which contains principles for dispute settlement and provisions for a new CSCE Procedure for Peaceful Settlement of Disputes. A striking feature of this new procedure was the mandatory involvement of third parties, as so far the CSCE states had never been able to achieve progress beyond the strictly intergovernmental level. This Procedure, often referred to as the Valletta

---

55 See R.W. Zaagman, 'The CSCE and the Yugoslav Crisis', in: *Helsinki Monitor*, 1992, No. 1, pp. 43-50 at pp. 44-45.

56 See also *infra* section 4.1.2.

57 See *infra* the description of the expert meetings in Montreux and Athens in section 4.2.1 and 4.4.2 respectively.

Mechanism, may be applied in any dispute between CSCE states, with a few exceptions. The major exception - which at the same time is a major weakness of the Procedure - concerns disputes which one of the parties considers to raise "issues concerning its territorial integrity, or national defence, title to sovereignty over land territory, or competing claims with regard to the jurisdiction over other areas" (Section XII of the Provisions for a CSCE Procedure for Peaceful Settlement of Disputes). Any disagreement concerning the question whether a certain dispute touches upon such issues is decided by the relevant CSCE state itself. The Valletta Procedure provides for political instruments for the settlement of disputes between CSCE states in the form of the establishment of so-called CSCE Dispute Settlement Mechanisms. These "Mechanisms" consist of one or more independent members which may be selected from a resource list of experts. The powers of these "Mechanisms" are extremely limited. So far, the Valletta mechanism has not been used by any CSCE state.

At the end of 1992 further progress was achieved. In October a meeting of experts in Geneva achieved consensus on a package of measures. These measures contained a strengthening of the Valletta mechanism, *inter alia*, by adding a procedure for 'directed conciliation', and, on the other hand, a Convention on Conciliation and Arbitration within the CSCE. The texts were formally adopted by the CSCE Council of Ministers at its Stockholm meeting in December 1992.[58]

The new procedure for 'directed conciliation' aims to strengthen the possibilities for political settlement of disputes within the CSCE. It provides for the possibility that the Council of Ministers or the CSO may "direct any two participating states to seek conciliation to assist them in resolving a dispute". Decisions may be taken, if necessary, without the consent of the two parties to the dispute in question (the so-called consensus-minus-two rule).[59]

The Convention on Conciliation and Arbitration within the CSCE is the first CSCE instrument which goes beyond the strictly political level. It provides for general conciliation and for arbitration on the basis of agreements *ad hoc* or, in advance, on the basis of reciprocal declarations. It also provides for the establishment of a Court of Conciliation and Arbitration, composed of Conciliation Commissions and Arbitral Tribunals which will be created (if necessary) for each dispute. The Court will be established in Geneva. At its Stockholm meeting in December 1992, the

---

[58] The Council decided to open the Convention for signature. During the Stockholm meeting 29 CSCE states signed the Convention which will enter into force after ratification by twelve parties.

[59] See Article 1 of the Provisions for Directed Conciliation; text *infra*.

CSCE Council of Ministers declared the Convention open for signature by interested CSCE states. At the time of writing this study, the Convention has been signed by 32 CSCE states. The Convention will enter into force two months after the date of deposit of the twelfth instrument of ratification or accession. It is hard to assess whether this Convention will be effective. On the one hand, a number of CSCE states have categorically refused to join the Convention (such as the USA, the United Kingdom, Turkey and the Netherlands) and, on the other, it has to be observed that other European instruments for dispute settlement[60] are also not used.

The adoption of the new instruments concerning peaceful settlement of disputes by the Stockholm Council constituted a precedent within the CSCE: for the first time in the history of the CSCE a part[61] of an official CSCE document was adopted in a legally binding form.[62]

2.3.1.4. CSCE High Commissioner on National Minorities

The post of CSCE High Commissioner on National Minorities (HCNM) has already been mentioned in the section on the institutional structure of the CSCE. The establishment of this new post was agreed upon at the Helsinki Follow-up Meeting of the CSCE which took place from March to July 1992 and was formally adopted at the Helsinki Summit Meeting. It was a CSCE response to the growing potential for conflict in the CSCE area resulting from ethnic tensions. The High Commissioner, therefore, is not designed as a human rights instrument - although the identity of the High Commissioner might indicate otherwise - but as an instrument of conflict prevention at the earliest possible stage. According to his mandate, the High Commissioner "will provide 'early warning' and, as appropriate, 'early action' at the earliest possible state in regard to tensions involving national minority issues which have not yet developed beyond an early warning stage, but (...) have the potential to develop into a conflict within the CSCE area, affecting peace, stability or relations between participating States".

---

[60] Such as the European Convention on the Peaceful Settlement of Disputes (1957).

[61] The package concerning the peaceful settlement of disputes within the CSCE consisted of two parts: the non-treaty elements of the package are politically binding on all participating States, but the treaty itself will, after its entry into force, be legally binding only on those states which have ratified it. Thus, the CSCE commitments are bifurcated, for the first time, into different sets of standards for different CSCE States. The non-treaty elements of the dispute settlement package are the "Provisions for a CSCE Conciliation Commission" and the "Provisions for Directed Conciliation". See *infra*.

[62] See also *supra* the section on the legal character of CSCE commitments and documents (section 2.2.3).

It should be observed that the mandate is rather vague. Crucial concepts, such as "early warning" or "tensions" or "potential to develop into a conflict" have not been defined. Although the mandate is vague, nevertheless it is clear that the main role of the High Commissioner will be in the actual tension phase, preceding the phase of the outbreak of actual (violent) conflicts. The primary aim of the High Commissioner is to achieve a de-escalation of tensions by way of, *inter alia*, promoting dialogue, confidence and cooperation between all parties concerned. His main formal power is the issuance of a formal notice of 'early warning' in those instances where a de-escalation of tensions appears to be impossible. In practice, however, the main power of the High Commissioner is rather that he may raise the attention of the CSO to certain problems.

So far the HCNM has dealt with minorities situations in the Baltics, in Slovakia and in the Balkans (Romania, Macedonia and Albania). The first reports, including recommendations for further action were endorsed by the CSO at the end of April 1993.[63] Due to the limited time which has passed since the first High Commissioner, Mr. Max van der Stoel, took office, the effectiveness of this new CSCE instrument of preventive diplomacy is hard to assess. It is clear, however, that in the first six months of the High Commissioner's activities, there were many positive reactions by CSCE states, reflected, *inter alia*, in the positive CSO decisions upon the HCNM's recommendations.

Although the HCNM officially draws upon the facilities of the ODIHR in Warsaw, the office of the High Commissioner has been established in The Hague. The HCNM has been granted a small staff, consisting of three diplomats who are assigned to the HCNM on a secondment basis.

2.3.1.5. Peacekeeping operations and the Chapter VIII arrangement

At the Helsinki Follow-up Meeting (March-July 1992) the decision was taken that the CSCE may organize its own peacekeeping operations (PKOs) in cases of conflicts within or among CSCE States. This decision fits into the transformation of the CSCE into an institution which is active, in particular, in the area of conflict prevention and crisis management. The detailed rules on this issue have been laid down in chapter III of the Helsinki Decisions (the second part of the Helsinki 1992 Document). An essential element of these operations is its voluntary character: they may only be organized with the consent of the parties concerned. It has also been laid down explicitly that such operations "will not entail enforcement action". The CSCE will not create its own military infrastructure. The notion is that the CSCE should take the political decisions to start PKOs, but that thereupon it will request

---

[63] For the reports of the High Commissioner on the Baltics and Slovakia, see *infra*.

other institutions to implement them. Paragraph 52 of chapter III states the following: *The CSCE may benefit from resources and possible experience and expertise of existing organizations such as the EC, NATO and the WEU, and could therefore request them to make their resources available in order to support it in carrying out peacekeeping activities. Other institutions and mechanisms, including the peacekeeping mechanism of the Commonwealth of Independent States (CIS), may also be asked by the CSCE to support peacekeeping in the CSCE region*".

All this implies that first a decision (by consensus) has to taken by all CSCE States, and that subsequently the other institutions will decide whether they will comply with the CSCE requests. Practice will show whether this will be a viable basis for CSCE PKOs. After the adoption of the Helsinki 1992 Document, developments in the international arena went on at a fast pace. Less than one year later it seemed to be rather unlikely that the role of the CSCE in the area of peacekeeping will be substantial in view of the fact that, in particular, the NATO is developing its own potential in that area. This new NATO activity is being undertaken in close contact with the United Nations.

At the Helsinki Summit Meeting the decision was also taken to proclaim the CSCE as a regional arrangement in the sense of chapter VIII of the Charter of the United Nations. The pertinent paragraph 25 of the Helsinki Summit Declaration reads as follows:

> "*Reaffirming the commitments to the Charter of the United Nations as subscribed to by our States, we declare our understanding that the CSCE is a regional arrangement in the sense of Chapter VIII of the Charter of the United Nations. As such, it provides an important link between European and global security. The rights and responsibilities of the Security Council remain unaffected in their entirety. The CSCE will work together closely with the United Nations especially in preventing and settling conflicts.*"

This decision resulted in a political upgrading of the functions of the CSCE in maintaining and restoring peace and security in the CSCE area. In theory this decision could also entail the involvement of the CSCE in the implementation of enforcement measures which may be decided upon by the UN Security Council. In view of the lack of a military infrastructure within the CSCE framework, it may not be expected that this theoretical option will soon be realized in practice. Besides, as already noticed, the CSCE Helsinki Summit decided that "CSCE peacekeeping operations will not entail enforcement action" (paragraph III.22 of the Helsinki Decisions).

2.3.1.6. Ad hoc CSCE missions

Recently, the CSCE has established an increasing number of missions whose tasks are related to the prevention and management of conflicts in various

CSCE states. The proliferation of *ad hoc* missions which have been created for one specific task or for the longer term, has caused a rather complicated situation within the CSCE. Missions may be created on the basis of specific CSCE mechanisms (such as the Human Dimension Mechanism or the Mechanism on Unusual Military Activities) or by a decision of political CSCE organs. In the Helsinki 1992 Document it is laid down that the CSO or the Consultative Committee of the CPC may establish fact-finding and rapporteur missions as an instrument of conflict prevention and crisis management (paragraphs III.12-16). Such missions have been despatched to several trouble areas, such as the former Yugoslavia and various former Soviet republics. A special type of mission is the so-called Sanctions Assistance Missions (SAMs) which have been create in co-operation with the EC. Together with an EC/CSCE Sanctions Co-ordinator, these SAMs aim to assist the implementation of UN-imposed sanctions against Serbia-Montenegro.

2.3.1.7. Confidence- and Security-building Measures (CSBMs)

Confidence- and security-building measures have been on the CSCE agenda since its very inception, at first under the title confidence-building measures (CBMs). Although until the end of the 1980s issues of disarmament were dealt with outside the formal framework of the CSCE, the more political-military CSBMs have always been a traditional CSCE issue. It has become an area in which the CSCE has managed to achieve impressive results. The presently applicable CSBMs are laid down in a number of successive documents, partly elaborated by some specialized CSCE conferences.

The basis for the CSCE negotiations on CSBMs has been laid down in the *Blue Book*. In recommendation 23 the *Blue Book* describes CBMs as measures which have to be adopted "in order to strengthen confidence and to increase stability and security", such as the prior notification of major military manoeuvres or the exchange of observers to military exercises.

The first CBMs were laid down in the Final Act of Helsinki, although these measures were still of a largely voluntary character. In the 1980s further progress could be achieved. On the basis of the mandate of the Madrid Concluding Document (1983) which also contained further elaborations of the existing confidence-building measures, a special conference on CSBMs was convened in Stockholm. This Stockholm Conference on Confidence- and Security-building Measures and Disarmament in Europe (often less correctly referred to as Conference on Disarmament in Europe or CDE) primarily aimed at the adoption of a number of mutually complementary CSBMs which were designed to reduce the risk of military confrontation in Europe. The CDE succeeded in achieving considerable progress, laid down in the so-called Document of the Stockholm Conference

(1986).[64] After the Vienna Follow-up Meeting the CDE started a new round in Vienna, often referred to as 'CDE-bis' or 'CDE-IA'. A few days before the opening of the CSCE summit meeting in Paris in November 1990, these negotiations resulted in an intermediate result: the 1990 Vienna Document on CSBMs. In March 1992, a few days before the opening of the preparatory meeting for the Helsinki Follow-up Meeting, the final result was produced in the form of the 1992 Vienna Document on CSBMs. Both documents contain impressive results, such as the introduction of a mechanism on unusual military activities and a procedure on co-operation as regards hazardous incidents of a military nature.[65] Another innovative element was the introduction of a permanently functioning communications network between the capitals of all CSCE states.

An important aspect of the functioning of CSBMs is the fact that the zone of application differs from the normal CSCE area. In the Final Act of Helsinki, the zone of application was limited to Europe, but the Soviet territory was only covered in a zone of 250 miles along its Western borders. Thus, the Asian part of the USSR as well as a major part of its European territory were excluded. At the Madrid Follow-up Meeting the zone of application was extended to the whole of Europe, thus including the Soviet territory to the Urals, as well as the adjoining sea area and air space. The Asian part of the Soviet Union, therefore, was still exempt from the CSBM commitments as well as the North American states.

After the disintegration of the Soviet Union the zone of application changed as well. When the five newly-independent Central Asian states were still part of the Soviet Union, they were outside the scope of the CSBMs.[66] This would mean that under the existing rules the Central Asian states (except a small part of Kazakhstan) were thus exempt from almost all CSCE military commitments. This was unacceptable to other European states. Therefore, all former Soviet republics (except Russia as the successor of the Soviet Union) had to accept formally all CSCE commitments, specifically including CSBMs as a condition for joining the CSCE. This extension of the zone of application of CSBMs was officially confirmed in the 1992 Vienna Document on CSBMs.[67]

---

[64] See further *infra* section 4.1.1.

[65] See *supra* section 2.3.1.2.

[66] Only a limited part of the territory of Kazakhstan is situated on the European continent. This part, therefore, was already covered by the CSBM regime of the CSCE when the USSR still existed.

[67] On CSBMs see further *infra* sections 4.1.1 and 4.1.2.

2.3.2. Human dimension mechanisms and procedures

2.3.2.1. General

The term 'human dimension of the CSCE' was only officially introduced in 1989. In the Concluding Document of the Vienna Follow-up Meeting of the CSCE (January 1989) it was described as follows: "the undertakings entered into in the Final Act and in other CSCE documents concerning respect for all human rights and fundamental freedoms, human contacts and other issues of a related humanitarian character". After the collapse of communism, the concept of the 'human dimension of the CSCE' received a much broader content. Nowadays it is considered to encompass not only human rights and fundamental freedoms including the protection of national minorities, but also issues related to the rule of law and democracy. The human dimension may be considered to be the successor of the former "Third Basket" which deals with humanitarian and related issues. The human dimension has a much larger scope, transpassing the border-lines between the traditional CSCE baskets. As such it contains elements of the first basket (e.g., human rights in relation to security issues), the second basket (e.g., migration, migrant workers) and the third basket.[68]

The human dimension was the first area of the CSCE which saw the establishment of a specific monitoring machinery which presently is generally known as the 'Human Dimension Mechanism'. This mechanism consists of two main elements: the Vienna mechanism as established in the Vienna Concluding Document of 1989 and the Moscow mechanism which partly constitutes a further elaboration of the Vienna mechanism. The Moscow mechanism was agreed upon at the last meeting of the Conference on the Human Dimension of the CSCE in Moscow (September-October 1991). Together they constitute a sophisticated, permanent machinery for supervising the implementation of human dimension commitments.

Besides the Human Dimension Mechanism, other procedures and instruments have also been developed for monitoring the implementation of human dimension commitments, such as the biennial implementation meetings of the CSCE (the first in September-October 1993).[69] In the

---

68 On the Human Dimension of the CSCE, see, e.g., A. Heraclides, *Security and Co-operation in Europe: The Human Dimension* (London 1993).

69 For an extensive analysis of all monitoring procedures, instruments and mechanisms in the field of the CSCE human dimension, reference may be made to: A. Bloed, 'Monitoring the CSCE Human Dimension: In Search of its Effectiveness', in: A. Bloed, L. Leicht, M. Nowak & A. Rosas (Eds.), *Monitoring Human Rights in Europe: Comparing International Procedures and Mechanisms* (Dordrecht-Boston-London 1993), pp. 45-91.

following sections, only the main elements of the Human Dimension Mechanism will be described.

2.3.2.2. The Vienna mechanism

The *Vienna mechanism*, the basis of which has been laid down in the Vienna Concluding Document, consists of four phases. It has been further elaborated, in particular, at the meetings of the Conference on the Human Dimension in Copenhagen (1990) and Moscow (1991) and at the Helsinki Follow-up Meeting (1992). At present, the mechanism consists of the following elements:[70]

> (1) to exchange information and to provide in as short a time as possible but no later than ten days, a written response to requests for information and to representations made to CSCE states by other participating states on questions relating to the human dimension of the CSCE. Usually, such communications are forwarded through diplomatic channels;
> (2) to hold bilateral meetings with other participating states that so request, in order to examine questions relating to the human dimension of the CSCE, including situations and specific cases, with a view to resolving them. The date and place of such meetings will be arranged as soon as possible by mutual agreement through diplomatic channels, as a rule within one week of the date of the request. In the course of a bilateral meeting, the CSCE states shall refrain from raising situations and cases not connected with the subject of the meeting, unless both sides have agreed to do so. The ODIHR can serve as a venue for such bilateral meetings;
> (3) any participating State which deems it necessary may bring situations and cases in the human dimension of the CSCE, including those which have been raised at the bilateral meetings described in paragraph 2, to the attention of other participating States through diplomatic channels or through the ODIHR;
> (4) any participating State which deems it necessary may provide information on the exchanges of information and the responses to its requests for information and to representations (paragraph 1) and on the results of the bilateral meetings (paragraph 2), including information concerning situations and specific cases, at CSCE

[70] See the chapter on the Human Dimension of the CSCE in the Vienna Concluding Document, paragraphs 42.1 and 42.2 of the Copenhagen Report, paragraph 2 of the Moscow Document, and paragraphs VI.5 and 7 of the Helsinki Decisions.

meetings, in particular at meetings of the CSO, the biennial review conferences and at the biennial implementation meetings.

This mechanism - which resembles a system of inter-state complaints procedures - signified a major step forward in the area of CSCE supervision as it created a system of supervision which can function permanently, whenever any of the participating States thinks that there is reason for putting it into operation. Moreover, the mechanism is of a non-voluntary character. When faced with requests for information from any of the CSCE States within the framework of the mechanism, the State concerned is under an obligation to provide an answer. It must also comply with a subsequent request to hold a bilateral meeting.

A major shortcoming of the Vienna mechanism was the lack of an independent element: the mechanism functioned at a strictly intergovernmental level. This shortcoming was 'repaired' at the Moscow Meeting of the Conference on the Human Dimension of the CSCE (CHD) in September-October 1991. The Moscow CHD Meeting adopted a system of missions of independent experts or rapporteurs.[71] Another disadvantage is the lack of any sanctions in cases of proven violations of human dimension commitments.[72] The last phase consists of raising issues at CSCE meetings, but as decision making at these meetings requires consensus no actions against the will of the state(s) concerned are possible. The effectiveness of the Vienna mechanism was (and to a great extent still is) based on political pressure: the public application of the mechanism hopefully leads to positive changes of behaviour by the state which is approached under it.

In 1989 and 1990 the Vienna mechanism was invoked on many occasions. After the revolutionary changes in Central and Eastern Europe the mechanism is now only rarely invoked.

2.3.2.3. The Moscow Mechanism

At the Moscow CHD meeting (September-October 1991) the Vienna mechanism was supplemented by a system of missions of independent experts or rapporteurs in the field of the human dimension of the CSCE. This system - often referred to as the *Moscow mechanism* - is rather complicated. It encompasses five separate procedures which may be used independently of

---

[71] See *infra* section 2.3.2.3.

[72] Since January 1992 the consensus-minus-one principle may be used to introduce 'political' sanctions in cases of very serious violations (see *supra* section 2.2.2). In cases of violations which are not covered by this regime - and *de facto* this concerns the great majority of cases of violations which are raised within the CSCE - the lack of possible sanctions remains the same.

one another to set up missions of rapporteurs or experts. Two of these procedures are linked to the Vienna mechanism: a) after the first or second phase of the Vienna mechanism, the initiating state may suggest that the other state should invite a mission of experts; b) if the other state refuses to do so, the requesting state may also initiate the establishment of a mission of rapporteurs against the will of the other state, if it receives the support of five other CSCE states.[73] In this way the possibility of an independent investigation into violations of human dimension commitments was created within the Vienna mechanism. This implies a breakthrough in comparison to the previous strictly intergovernmental character of the mechanism.

Furthermore, the Moscow mechanism encompasses three other procedures which may be used to establish missions. These procedures, which are not linked to the application of the Vienna mechanism, are: a) the voluntary invitation of a mission of experts by a CSCE state; b) the decision by the CSO to establish a mission of experts or rapporteurs; c) the establishment of an 'emergency' mission of rapporteurs in cases of a "particularly serious threat" to the fulfilment of human dimension provisions.[74] These missions have to be composed of independent experts which are selected from a list which comprises the names of up to three experts appointed by each CSCE state.

The Moscow mechanism constituted major progress. The system of human dimension missions of independent experts or rapporteurs was a first major deviation from the hitherto strictly intergovernmental supervisory procedures.

The mandate of these missions may vary according to the procedure from which these missions arose. In general it may be noted that the powers of missions of experts go beyond those of missions of rapporteurs.[75] The powers of missions of rapporteurs are mainly related to fact-finding and the rendering of advice or proposals for the solution of the questions raised.[76] Missions of experts have a broader mandate: their mandate aims to facilitate "resolution of a particular question or problem relating to the human dimension of the CSCE". For that purpose they may gather information

---

[73] Paragraphs 8 and 9 of the Moscow Document.

[74] Paragraphs 4, 12 and 13 of the Moscow Document.

[75] Missions of experts are established in cases where the receiving CSCE state invites such missions. Missions of rapporteurs are established when the receiving state refuses to invite a mission. Moreover, missions under paragraph 12 of the Moscow Document (the so-called 'emergency missions') are also called missions of rapporteurs. The CSO may establish both types of missions.

[76] Paragraph 11 of the Moscow Document.

"and, as appropriate, use its good offices and mediation services to promote dialogue and co-operation among interested parties". The exact terms of reference for each mission of experts have to be settled on an *ad hoc* basis.[77] Only the CSO is entitled to decide on any follow-up action, but in these cases the consensus principle is applicable (with the consensus-minus-one principle as the only, largely theoretical exception).

The Moscow mechanism became operational in May 1992 after the registration of the names of 45 experts at the ODIHR in accordance with paragraph 3 of the Moscow Document. Since then it has been applied on only a few occasions: at the time of writing (spring 1993) only two missions of experts and one mission of rapporteurs have been established. At the invitation of the states concerned, the missions of experts visited Estonia (December 1992) and Moldova (January-February 1993). A mission of rapporteurs visited Croatia[78] (September-October 1992) under the so-called "emergency procedure" (paragraph 12 of the Moscow CHD Document). At the 22nd meeting of the CSO in June 1993, the CSCE states decided to apply paragraph 13 of the Moscow CHD Document[79] by establishing a mission of rapporteurs which was sent to Serbia. This mission was charged, in particular, with investigating reports about human rights violations in Serbia-Montenegro.[80]

---

77 Paragraph 5 of the Moscow Document.

78 A planned visit to Bosnia-Herzegovina could not take place because of security reasons.

79 On the basis of this clause, the CSO may establish missions of experts or rapporteurs.

80 22-CSO/Journal No. 2, Annex 3.

3. DEVELOPMENT OF THE CSCE PROCESS SINCE 1973

3.1 The Conference on Security and Co-operation in Europe (1973-1975)

3.1.1. The negotiations: Helsinki-Geneva-Helsinki

Soon after the successful ending of the Multilateral Preparatory Talks,[81] the first stage of the Conference started in Helsinki on 3 July 1973. This meeting, which took place at Foreign Minister level, lasted until 7 July. At this meeting the Ministers of the 35 CSCE States officially adopted the Final Recommendations of the Helsinki Consultations and presented their views on the problems which were to be negotiated at the Conference in the following stage.

In general, this first stage of the CSCE did not encounter serious problems, due to the fact that real negotiations did not take place. In essence, the meeting consisted of the delivery of official speeches, which also had the purpose of informing the press and the public at large, at the open sessions of this first stage. Disagreement arose only about the question of the access to the meeting by representatives of non-participating States. As no agreement could be achieved on this problem, the principle of consensus precluded the participation of any non-CSCE-State.

The main work was done at the second stage of the Conference at the expert level which started on 18 September 1973 in Geneva and lasted - with a few breaks - until 21 July 1975. This unexpectedly long duration was caused by the great complexity of the problems on the agenda and the highly differing views of the participating States on their solution. Progress was also hampered by the necessity to reach consensus on all questions.

Due to the somewhat less controversial nature of the co-operation in the field of economics, science and technology and the environment, the most rapid progress was achieved in the second basket. The most complicated negotiations were connected with the third basket (humanitarian questions) and the first basket (in particular in relation to the principles guiding the relations among the participating States). During the time-consuming negotiations, the presence of the European neutral and non-aligned States (NNA States) appeared to be useful, as these States could often act as "mediators" between East and West by submitting their own proposals for compromises. Finally, on 21 July 1975, after protracted negotiations, all CSCE States achieved agreement on the adoption of an extensive document.

---

[81] See *supra* section 2.1.2.

Its origin indicates that this Final Act is a masterpiece of diplomatic skill in the sense that a great number of problems between the participating States were "solved" by agreeing on compromissory clauses. This observation should not, however, create the impression that the Final Act does not contain a great number of agreements on which all parties are in clear concord.

As agreed during the MPT, the third stage of the Conference again took place in Helsinki. The great importance of this meeting was expressed by the fact that all 35 CSCE States were represented by their heads of state and/or government. After the delivery of solemn speeches they signed the Final Act of the CSCE on 1 August 1975. In this way the Conference was concluded after several years of negotiations in which a great number of diplomats of the 35 participating States had been involved.

3.1.2. The Final Act of Helsinki: A short survey

According to the main scheme for the CSCE which was settled during the MPT, the Final Act of Helsinki consists of four chapters ('baskets'): questions relating to security; economic, scientific and technological co-operation and co-operation in the field of the environment; humanitarian and other issues; and the follow-up to the Conference.

3.1.2.1. Basket I: Questions relating to Security in Europe

The first basket consists of two main parts. The first part is the 'Declaration on Principles Guiding Relations between Participating States' and the second part is the 'Document on confidence-building measures and certain aspects of security and disarmament'.

The Declaration on Principles is undoubtedly the most important part of this basket. It contains an elaboration of ten fundamental principles, focusing on the European context. Those ten principles are the following:

1. Sovereign equality, respect for the rights inherent in sovereignty;
2. Refraining from the threat or use of force;
3. Inviolability of frontiers;
4. Territorial integrity of States;
5. Peaceful settlement of disputes;
6. Non-intervention in internal affairs;
7. Respect for human rights and fundamental freedoms, including the freedom of thought, conscience, religion or belief;
8. Equal rights and self-determination of peoples;
9. Co-operation among States;
10. Fulfilment in good faith of obligations under international law.

The negotiations on the final text of this Declaration on Principles were extremely laborious and complicated. Both the East European and the Western and NNA States sought to realize their main policy purposes in the text of the Declaration. The East European States made great efforts to achieve the general recognition of the territorial *status quo* of Europe by including a well-elaborated text for the principle of the inviolability of frontiers. This purpose was realized, but for a long time the West insisted on the inclusion of a paragraph which would provide for the possibility of peaceful changes of frontiers. As the Warsaw Pact States refused to accept this clause under the heading of the principle of inviolability of frontiers, a compromise was achieved by inserting the pertinent provision in the text of the principle on sovereign equality. Although this was a rather illogical solution, it was acceptable for the Western CSCE States in view of the agreement, laid down in the Declaration, that all ten principles "are of primary significance and (that), accordingly, they will be equally and unreservedly applied, each of them being interpreted taking into account the others".

A major achievement in the Declaration on Principles was the insertion of principle VII: respect for human rights and fundamental freedoms. This actually meant that in the Final Act the human rights principle had become just as important as (other) fundamental principles of international law, such as the sovereign equality of States and non-intervention in internal affairs. It was the first time that the human rights principle had acquired such a ranking in fundamental intergovernmental documents.

The second part of the first basket contained the first confidence-building measures (CBMs). The scope of the agreements in this "military" part of the Final Act was very modest, not only because of the reluctance of the States concerned, but also because of the fact that disarmament questions for Central Europe were simultaneously discussed in the MBFR negotiations in Vienna.

The CBMs in the Final Act were mainly of a voluntary nature, as the States were not (yet) ready to accept firm obligations in this field. These measures concerned, *inter alia*, the obligatory prior notification of major military manoeuvres exceeding a total of 25,000 troops which take place in an area within 250 kilometres from common frontiers; the exchange of observers for military manoeuvres on a voluntary and bilateral basis; and the prior notification of major military manoeuvres "at their own discretion".

3.1.2.2. *Basket II: Co-operation in the Fields of Economics, Science and Technology and the Environment*

This basket formed an area of major interest for the East European States in particular, as one of their main purposes with the CSCE was to achieve progress in the field of economic relations between East and West. Nevertheless, it has to be taken into account, that the CSCE did not aim to agree on solutions for specific concrete problems, as other international institutions - and more specifically the UN Economic Commission for Europe (ECE) - were charged with such questions. Instead, the CSCE aimed at establishing a political framework for economic co-operation which greatly determined the nature of the final agreements laid down in the Final Act. Due to the less controversial nature of the issues at stake in the second basket and as many international treaties on these issues already existed, agreement on problems of the second basket could be achieved relatively "easily".

The second basket deals with the following issues: commercial exchanges; industrial co-operation and projects of common interest; provisions concerning trade and industrial co-operation (e.g., arbitration); science and technology; the environment; and co-operation in other areas (transport, tourism, migrant labour, training of personnel).

After the second basket, an "intermediate" chapter was inserted on "Questions relating to Security and Co-operation in the Mediterranean". Malta, in particular, had been pressing this issue.

3.1.2.3. *Basket III: Co-operation in Humanitarian and Other Fields*

The third CSCE basket was one of the most controversial areas of the CSCE. The often diametrically opposed opinions of the CSCE States made the finding of solutions extremely difficult. This resulted in a text which is often characterized by a certain vagueness and ambiguity. In contrast to the first basket, in which the many commitments entered into are described in clear "legal" terms, the third basket commitments are usually much more cautiously worded and have often only the character of solemn intentions. In many places, phrases are used such as: "they intend to facilitate ...."; "they will endeavour gradually ....."; "they express the hope ..."; "they will examine in a favourable spirit"; etc.

The third basket contains four areas: human contacts; information; co-operation and exchanges in the field of culture; co-operation and exchanges in the field of education. Problems of human contacts and information appeared to be politically the most sensitive. Although the East European States were not at all interested in the regulation of these issues in the Final Act of Helsinki, they had to accept it as their "price" for achieving agreements on other (political and economic) issues in which the Warsaw Pact States were highly interested. This resulted in carefully worded regulations which constituted the first detailed regulation of these issues in the East-West context.

In the paragraph on human contacts, agreements were laid down concerning, *inter alia*, (international) contacts and regular meetings on the basis of family ties, reunification of families, marriages between citizens of different States, tourism, meetings among young people, and sport. All the provisions concerned were aimed at an increase in contacts among the peoples of the CSCE States.

In the paragraph on information, the CSCE States recognize the importance of the dissemination of information from the other participating States. A central point of disagreement in this field, however, was the Western policy of ensuring a free flow of information, as the East European States aimed at (state-)controlled co-operation in this area. The result was a paragraph with a great number of carefully worded, compromissory clauses. One of the most remarkable provisions concerns transboundary radio broadcasts: "The participating States note the expansion in the dissemination of information broadcast by radio, and express the hope for the continuation of this process, so as to meet the interest of mutual understanding among peoples and the aims set forth by this Conference." This provision was the most that could be achieved by the West in its efforts to adopt a strict prohibition of jamming foreign radio broadcasts.

The provisions concerning culture and education are aimed at increasing co-operation between all CSCE States in these areas. The paragraphs concerned contain detailed recommendations.

3.1.2.4. Basket IV: Follow-up to the Conference

The fourth basket on the follow-up to the CSCE is the shortest part of the Final Act. It contains the final agreements on the institutional structure of the follow-up. On this subject a great number of ideas were put forward during the negotiations, ranging from preference for a very weak institutional structure to the establishment of a new permanent international organization for Security and Co-operation in Europe. The ultimate agreement, laid down in the Final Act, boils down to a weak structure. The Final Act determines that meetings of representatives of the CSCE States will be organized, "beginning with a meeting at the level of representatives appointed by the Ministers of Foreign Affairs". This first meeting was to define "the appropriate modalities for the holding of other meetings which could include similar meetings and the possibility of a new Conference". These follow-up meetings are charged with reviewing the implementation of the provisions of the Final Act as well as with negotiating new agreements. The fourth basket of the Final Act also referred to the possibility of implementing the Final Act on a multilateral basis by organizing meetings of experts of the CSCE States and by discussing CSCE issues within the framework of existing international organizations. In essence, this structure of the follow-up to the CSCE has remained unchanged until the end of the 1980s. Only from 1990 onwards has the institutional system of the CSCE changed fundamentally (see below).

3.2. CSCE Summit Meetings and Follow-up Meetings (1977-1992)

3.2.1. The Belgrade Follow-up Meeting (1977-1978)

The signing of the Helsinki Final Act in August 1975 has to be considered as a culmination point in the process of *détente* between East and West. Shortly afterwards, the international climate seriously deteriorated. This was partly due to the fact that in Eastern Europe an increasing number of independent groups were established which set themselves the task of monitoring the implementation of the CSCE commitments entered into by their governments, in particular in the field of human rights. All these groups invoked the Final Act of Helsinki in order to prove the admissibility of their activities. This development surprised the authorities of most East European States in a very negative way and they tried to suppress these groups as much as possible. This "wave" of emerging independent citizen groups in Eastern Europe and the harsh policies of the authorities towards them alerted the Western countries. After the signing of the Final Act of Helsinki, the Western governments sometimes felt somewhat embarrassed about the results of the CSCE: they had consented to the East European wish for the recognition of the territorial *status quo*, whereas the East European concessions in the field of human rights were mainly still on paper. After the emergence of oppositional groups in Eastern Europe, the Western States became much more strongly aware of the important function of the Final Act in this respect. Western accusations against the Eastern European States of violations of the human rights provisions of the Final Act became an increasingly important part of the policies of the West. Under the administration of the US President, Jimmy Carter, human rights received further emphasis. This resulted in a deteriorating international climate.

This international climate greatly determined the first follow-up meeting of the CSCE for which preparatory talks started in Belgrade on 15 June 1977. The main problem at this preparatory meeting - which was to decide on the date, duration, agenda and other modalities of the follow-up meeting - concerned the review by the CSCE States of the implementation of their CSCE commitments. This problem was further complicated by the fact that decisions on this point would undoubtedly form a model for future follow-up meetings. In general, the Western countries acted in favour of extensive possibilities to review the (non-)implementation of the Final Act. In contrast, the Warsaw Pact States wanted to focus on the future by entering into new agreements and to limit the discussions on the past as much as possible.

Finally, after eight weeks of often heated debates, an agreement was achieved which was laid down in the so-called *Yellow Book* (because of the colour of its cover): the "Decisions of the Preparatory Meeting to Organize the Belgrade Meeting...".[82] It was agreed that the Belgrade follow-up meeting would review the implementation of the Final Act in its first phase, consider new proposals for further development of the Helsinki process in its second phase, and draft a concluding document in its third phase. However, the *Yellow Book* did not determine a strict separation between the phases which was blocked by the West in order to have the opportunity for a full review of implementation of CSCE commitments at all stages of the follow-up meeting.

The Belgrade meeting started on 4 October 1977. The meeting was characterized by vehement clashes between East and West, in particular concerning human rights issues. Western countries raised numerous individual cases of (alleged) violations of human rights in the East European States, particularly in Czechoslovakia and the USSR. In their turn, the East European States accused the Western States of violations of the fundamental principle of non-interference in internal affairs: most human rights issues were considered to belong to the domestic jurisdiction of the CSCE States. At a later stage, the East European States also started to accuse Western countries of violations of human rights (e.g., racism).

In spite of the troubled atmosphere, more than 100 proposals for new commitments were put forward on which no agreement could be achieved before the initially fixed date of 22 December 1977 for the closure of the meeting. An important Western proposal concerned strengthening the role of private citizens in the process of *détente* in respect of human rights and humanitarian issues. In contrast, the East European States stressed the intergovernmental nature of *détente*. Because of the sharp differences of opinion the Belgrade meeting continued in 1978.

Finally, as no agreement on any substantive question could be achieved, the Belgrade meeting was closed on 9 March 1978 with the adoption of only a brief Concluding Document. This Document stated that the Belgrade meeting had been held, that a review of implementation had taken place, that different views as to the degree of implementation had been expressed and that the participating States had agreed to hold a second follow-up meeting in Madrid which should start in November 1980. Moreover, the Belgrade Document also contained the mandates for three meetings of experts which

---

[82] Because of its predominantly technical/organizational character, the *Yellow Book* is not reproduced in the present volume.

were to be held within the framework of the follow-up to the CSCE, two of which were already foreseen in the Final Act of Helsinki: a meeting of experts at Montreux in 1978 on peaceful settlement of disputes; a meeting of experts in Bonn in 1978 in order to prepare a Scientific Forum; and a meeting of experts on the Mediterranean, to be held in Valletta in 1979.

3.2.2. The Madrid Follow-up Meeting (1980-1983)

The period after the Belgrade follow-up meeting was characterized by a further deterioration of the international climate. In particular, the Soviet invasion of Afghanistan in December 1979 formed a serious set-back to the process of *détente*. In addition, the human rights record of the East European States - especially of the Soviet Union, the GDR and Czechoslovakia - increasingly deteriorated. All this constituted serious violations of commitments laid down in the Final Act of Helsinki. It resulted, *inter alia*, in an American boycott of grain exports to the USSR and in a widespread boycott of the Moscow Olympic Games.

In this complicated constellation the Madrid follow-up meeting was to convene. Preparations for the follow-up meeting, which started on 9 September 1980 in Madrid appeared to be extremely difficult. The East European States aimed in particular at organizational arrangements which would allow only a limited period for the review of the implementation of the CSCE commitments by the participating States. In contrast, the Western countries did not want to accept any limitation in this respect. This was the main obstacle during the preparatory meeting which failed to achieve any definitive agreement within the allotted time. On 10 November the meeting lasted until midnight without success. As the follow-up meeting was scheduled to start the next day, the remarkable situation arose that just before midnight the clock was stopped in order to continue the fiction that it was still 10 November. It again proved to be quite difficult to put an end to this grotesque situation. Finally, late on 11 November the Madrid Follow-up Meeting was officially opened and a few days later agreement was reached on the agenda. Although the latter provided for a six-week period for review at the beginning of the meeting, the Western States unilaterally reserved the right to raise any question of implementation at any other time which they should deem proper. The agenda and other organizational modalities were laid down in a document which became known as the *Purple Book.*[83]

The Madrid meeting appeared to be becoming unprecedented in CSCE history as far as the length of the meeting was concerned: it was only concluded almost three years later on 6 September 1983. This was due not

---

83 Not reproduced in the present volume. See the previous note.

only to the complexity of the problems at stake, but, in particular, to the bad relations between East and West. Nevertheless, as early as December 1981, a successful termination of the conference appeared to be within reach, when the group of neutral and non-aligned countries filed a substantial draft final declaration. In this declaration an attempt had been made to work out a compromise acceptable to all the parties, in which a balance was sought between security problems (specifically a mandate for a European conference on confidence- and security-building measures), on the one hand, and human rights problems, on the other. The chances that this draft document would be acceptable to all CSCE States disappeared completely when, almost simultaneously with the filing of the draft, martial law was proclaimed in Poland, which was accompanied by numerous violations of human rights. This caused an atmosphere of serious crisis in the conference rooms and even endangered the whole CSCE process. All this led the Western countries to propose a great many radical amendments to the draft final document, *inter alia*, in the field of trade union freedom in 1982.

Nevertheless, albeit with lengthy breaks, the negotiations continued and in March 1983 the NNA countries submitted a revised draft concluding document which was intended as a last attempt to break through the deadlock between East and West. The Western States, in particular, were not fully satisfied and proposed several amendments. Only after the personal intervention of the Spanish Prime Minister could a definitive agreement be reached at the end of July 1983. Only Malta continued to live up to its reputation of blocking an agreement by demanding further concessions on Mediterranean issues. When it became clear that the remaining CSCE States would close the follow-up meeting anyhow by adopting the concluding document with or without Malta, the Mediterranean island-state finally relented. The Concluding Document of Madrid was then adopted on 9 September 1983 by the Foreign Ministers of all 35 CSCE States. The adoption was overshadowed, but not blocked, by the dramatic shooting down of a South Korean civil aircraft with 260 people aboard by Soviet fighters when flying over Soviet territory.

The Concluding Document contains a large number of confirmations of and additions to the 1975 Final Act of Helsinki concerning all baskets. Notable progress was achieved in the first basket by the agreement to convene a multi-stage Conference on Confidence- and Security-Building Measures (CSBMs) and Disarmament in Europe in Stockholm.[84] This Conference aimed at the discussion and negotiation of early warning measures designed to diminish the threat of surprise military attacks. Major progress was achieved in this field by the territorial applicability of the

---

[84] See *infra* section 4.1.1.

CSBMs which were to be negotiated: they would be applicable to all of Europe, including the entire European part of Soviet territory up to the Ural Mountains. This extension of the area was a significant new step because the CBMs (the previous denomination) contained in the Final Act of Helsinki were only applicable to 250 kilometres of Soviet territory extending from the European borders of the USSR.

An important part of the Concluding Document of Madrid was devoted to human rights. The Western States successfully insisted on the adoption of a great number of provisions in this area as a counter-balance to the adoption of measures in the field of military security which were strongly pushed by the East European States. Although a great number of human rights and humanitarian provisions of the Final Act of Helsinki were explicitly reconfirmed, some new agreements were also laid down in the Concluding Document. These concerned, *inter alia*, the right of workers freely to establish and join trade unions - a cogent problem after the events in Poland concerning Solidarity -, some more detailed rules concerning the freedom of religion, measures against terrorism, better working conditions for foreign journalists, and improved procedures for family reunification. The Concluding Document also pointed to the use of bilateral round-table meetings between CSCE States to discuss human rights issues. Due to the voluntary character of such meetings, however, this provision has remained mainly on paper. For the first time in a CSCE document, the Madrid Concluding Document also laid down the principle of free access to embassies and consulates, albeit with the clause "with due regard to the necessary requirements of security of these missions".

Besides a mandate for the Stockholm Conference, the Concluding Document also made provision for five more specialized or expert meetings on a variety of subjects: a meeting on the peaceful settlement of disputes in Athens in 1984, a seminar on Mediterranean co-operation in Venice in 1984, a human rights meeting in Ottawa in 1985, a Cultural Forum in Budapest in 1985, and a meeting on human contacts in Bern in 1986. The Bern meeting, in particular, was highly controversial and resulted in a compromise not to include the mandate for the meeting in the text of the Concluding Document, but only as an annex. In addition, it was laid down in the Concluding Document that in 1985 a meeting was to be held in Helsinki to commemorate the tenth anniversary of the signing of the Final Act. Finally, the Document provided for a next CSCE follow-up meeting in Vienna which was to start in November 1986.

3.2.3. The Vienna Follow-up Meeting (1986-1989)

The third follow-up meeting of the CSCE, which started on 4 November 1986, took place in an international climate which was quite different from that of previous CSCE follow-up meetings. This was largely due to the rather fundamental changes which had taken place in the Soviet Union after the change in Soviet leadership in 1985: in March of that year Mikhail Gorbachev took over the post of Secretary-General of the Communist Party of the Soviet Union. The new party-chief initiated new policies of *glasnost*, *perestroika* and "new thinking" in the Soviet Union which also had far-reaching effects on the international relations of the USSR. In relation to a great number of issues, which had sharply divided East and West for a long time, the Soviet position gradually and increasingly became flexible, resulting in an increasing improvement in East-West relations.

These new developments had a positive effect on the course of the negotiations at the Vienna follow-up meeting, if not on the duration of the meeting, then in any case on the quality of the results.

This third CSCE follow-up meeting was preceded by a preparatory meeting from 23 September to 6 October 1986 in Vienna. It only took two weeks, as a result of the agreement reached at the previous CSCE follow-up meeting that the preparatory meeting for Vienna should only deal with "adjustments to the agenda, working programme and modalities of the main Madrid Meeting". This implied that the major organizational issues which had caused considerable problems in Belgrade and Madrid were considered to be settled. This meant that the structure of the CSCE follow-up meetings had gradually become more fixed. The organizational modalities were therefore similar to those of the Madrid Meeting: a review phase during which the implementation of previous CSCE commitments was to be discussed; a phase during which new proposals would be proposed; and a final phase for the drafting of a concluding document. The objective to close the follow-up meeting in the summer of 1987 appeared, however, to be too optimistic.

The Vienna Meeting was opened at the ministerial level. The Soviet Foreign Minister, Shevardnadze, drew a great deal of attention with his unexpected proposal to convene a specialized CSCE conference on human rights in Moscow: a proposal which was to become one of the main obstacles on the road to a successful conclusion of the meeting. The review phase was again characterized by frank statements by Western States on the unsatisfactory situation in the field of human rights in certain East European States. The latter appeared to have opted for the policy of suffering all sorts of charges from the West with equanimity, in order to be able to do business with each other after the implementation debates. The Vienna Meeting showed, however, striking differences with previous follow-up meetings in some respects. This was not only reflected in the remarkable Shevardnadze proposal, but also in the climate of discussions on human rights issues. Although the West again accused specific East European States of violations of human rights, the latter much less frequently resorted to invoking the principle of non-intervention in internal affairs in order to avoid any further-going discussion. In contrast, objective discussions on (alleged) violations of human rights were found to be possible much more often. In Vienna, Czechoslovakia and Romania, in particular, resorted to the old tactics.

At the beginning of the Vienna Meeting the prospects for a new extensive concluding document appeared to be minimal. The Western CSCE States opted for the policy of especially emphasizing compliance with the commitments already entered into. They did not seem to be very keen on concluding new agreements if so much was still amiss in the implementation of the existing agreements. This was reflected in the fact that the main purpose of the Vienna Meeting, in the view of the Western States, would be agreement on more detailed supervisory mechanisms. In the course of the meeting, however, Western States also tabled a great number of new proposals, which also concerned new substantive commitments. For the first time in CSCE history, some proposals on humanitarian issues were submitted both by Western and East European States. This concerned, *inter alia*, a proposal on the protection of national minorities which was supported by Hungary. This example touches upon another new phenomenon in CSCE history: the East European States no longer behaved as a close-knit group. On the contrary, some East European States appeared to have discovered that the CSCE process could be a forum for promoting their own national interests more than ever before.

Although several East European States showed an increasing flexibility in relation to a great number of traditionally sensitive CSCE issues, it again took about 26 months before a final agreement could be achieved. This long duration was caused by a number of problems. Due to sharp differences of opinion between certain Western States (in particular France and the United States), it took a long time before the substantive Western proposal for a mandate for negotiations on the reduction of conventional armaments in Europe could be put forward. Another main obstacle was the Soviet proposal to organize a conference on human rights in Moscow. The USA, the United Kingdom and Canada, in particular, feared that consenting to this Soviet proposal would be interpreted as a signal that the Western countries would fully support the present human rights record of the USSR. The visit of Gorbachev to the British Prime Minister, Margaret Thatcher, appeared to be the decisive turning-point in the standpoint of the three Western countries. Another cause of the long duration of the Vienna Meeting appeared to be the difference between the "flexibility" of the Soviet Union in public and in the conference rooms: the "new" Soviet policy of *glasnost* and *perestroika* was not always immediately translated in concrete policy measures.

Definitive agreement could only be reached in January 1989. One of the very last obstacles to be overcome was a quarrel between Greece and Turkey about the territorial scope of the mandate for the talks on conventional armaments in Europe. Greece insisted on the inclusion of the Turkish harbour Mersin - from which the military connections between Turkey and Turkish Cyprus are maintained - in the mandate. The question was "solved" by its postponement to the future armaments talks. The final stage of the Vienna Meeting was also overshadowed by Romania which declared that it would concur in the adoption of the concluding document, but that it made a reservation concerning provisions with which it could not agree, without explicitly indicating which provisions these were. From the context of the Romanian statement it could be assumed that it particularly concerned a number of provisions on human rights and humanitarian questions (the Vienna Meeting introduced the term "human dimension of the CSCE" for the latter issues). The Romanian reservation was so vague and extravagant that it only raised strong protests from the Western countries which refused to recognize the legality of the Romanian reservation.[85]

All this, however, did not prevent the adoption, on 19 January 1989, of the extensive Concluding Document of Vienna at ministerial level. This document constituted a major step forward in the Helsinki process: in all baskets, but in particular in security issues and in the human dimension of the CSCE, substantive progress was achieved.

The Concluding Document of Vienna is a rather complicated document in comparison to previous CSCE documents. This was the result of, *inter alia*, the decision to incorporate in the Document not only the mandate, but also all organizational and procedural modalities for a great number of expert meetings and specialized conferences, which are to be held between 1989 and 1991. The insertion of all these arrangements in the Vienna Document makes it no longer necessary to convene preparatory meetings for all these CSCE conferences. Another reason for the more complicated nature of the Vienna Document is the incorporation of the mandate for the Negotiation on Conventional Armed Forces in Europe (CFE talks) in its text. Although the CFE were placed in the CSCE framework, only the 23 CSCE States which are parties to NATO and the Warsaw Pact were participants in it. The CFE were therefore structured as an "autonomous" conference within the CSCE framework. This was reflected not only in the fact that the relationship with the CSCE itself was rather weak, but also in the fact that its mandate, as laid down in the Vienna Document, was rather an independent agreement

---

[85] In January 1990, the Romanian reservation was officially withdrawn after the collapse of the Ceausescu dictatorship in Romania in December 1989. See also *supra* section 4.2.2.

between the 23 participating NATO and Warsaw Pact States. The mandate was even signed separately by the representatives of the States concerned. The CFE constituted the first CSCE meeting in which only a limited number of CSCE States were allowed to participate. The NNA States were only informed about the progress of the negotiations. The incorporation of the CFE in the CSCE framework had long been controversial, but the benefit of this incorporation (for instance, negotiations which would apply "from the Atlantic to the Ural Mountains") became decisive.

The main achievements of the Vienna Concluding Document concern the human dimension of the CSCE. In this area the CSCE States succeeded in reaching agreement not only on the adoption of a great number of new substantive commitments, but also on the introduction of a more or less permanently functioning supervisory mechanism. New substantive commitments concern, *inter alia*, the right of everyone to leave his country and to return to it, a detailed elaboration of the freedom of religion, the rights of persons in detention (including a prohibition of the abuse of psychiatric practices), a further elaboration of the rights of monitoring groups, a considerable improvement regarding the formalities for travelling abroad, and a prohibition of jamming foreign radio broadcasts.

Apart from the many new commitments, the Vienna Concluding Document contains a far-reaching supervisory mechanism for the human dimension of the CSCE. This mechanism in essence constitutes a combination of the Western proposal for new supervisory procedures and the Soviet proposal to convene a human rights conference in Moscow. The multilateral mechanism, as laid down in the Vienna Document, contains four elements: exchange of information; bilateral meetings; notification of all CSCE States; and raising issues at certain CSCE meetings.[86] Practice indicates that the many questions, which could be raised in relation to the supervisory mechanism, have not prevented its functioning. States have resorted to its procedures on a great number of occasions in the first year of its operation.

The major achievement in the field of military security issues was undoubtedly the agreement on the mandate for the CFE talks. These negotiations started in Vienna on 9 March 1989 and were concluded in November 1990 before the CSCE Summit Meeting in Paris during that month. The CSCE States also agreed to resume the work of the Stockholm Conference by deciding to commence Negotiations on Confidence- and Security-Building Measures (the addition "and Disarmament" was abolished). These Negotiations, usually (less correctly) referred to as the "Conference on Disarmament in Europe II", started in Vienna on 9 March 1989, simultaneously with the CFE talks. Their aim was to elaborate and adopt a

---

[86] For a more extensive discussion of the Vienna Mechanism, see *supra* section 2.3.2.2.

new set of mutually complementary confidence- and security-building measures designed to reduce the risk of military confrontation in Europe. In November 1990, the Vienna Negotiations produced the first concrete results in the form of an extensive document.[87]

In the second basket (economic co-operation and the environment), new agreements were entered into concerning, *inter alia*, the status of joint ventures, the working conditions of foreign businessmen, and concerning the protection of the environment, more in particular the struggle against transboundary pollution. In the Vienna Concluding Document, the human dimension has also received a place in the second basket, as it contains a provision in which the CSCE States explicitly acknowledge the "importance of the contribution of persons and organizations dedicated to the protection and improvement of the environment, and will allow them to express their concerns".

The Vienna Concluding Document contained the mandates for a great number of expert meetings and specialized conferences which had to take place before the next follow-up meeting of the CSCE in Helsinki in 1992. All this indicated a certain strengthening of the institutionalization of the CSCE process. This was not only reflected in the increasing number of specialized CSCE meetings, but also in the fact that several CSCE meetings acquired a more or less permanent status. The latter meetings concerned, in particular, the security and disarmament negotiations in Vienna and the Conference on the Human Dimension of the CSCE which was scheduled to meet three times in 1989, 1990 and 1991.

3.2.4. The Paris Summit Meeting (1990)

The revolutionary year 1989 had fundamentally changed the political map of Europe. Against this background, at the end of 1989, Soviet President Gorbachev launched the idea of a special CSCE summit conference. It was proposed that this summit should deal with the new political situation in Europe after the revolutionary developments in Central and Eastern Europe. At this summit the main lines of a new political map of Europe should be drawn. It was Gorbachev's understanding that the CSCE should play a leading role in the new Europe. Although at first the reaction in other CSCE States was rather hesitative, gradually a certain consensus was reached.

In the summer of 1990 a Preparatory Committee (PrepCom) in Vienna started to prepare the CSCE summit which was to become the second CSCE

---

87 In March 1992, preceding the Helsinki Follow-up Meeting, this Vienna Document was succeeded by another Vienna Document which contains results going beyond the 1990 Document (see further *infra* section 6.1).

summit after the meeting in July-August 1975 at which the Final Act of Helsinki was signed.

At the PrepCom a great number of proposals for a strengthening of the role of the CSCE in the post-Cold War Europe were discussed. The views on the future role of the CSCE differed markedly. A number of states favoured a transformation of the CSCE into an effective collective security system, guided by a European Security Council. In this concept, which was strongly defended by states like Poland and Czechoslovakia, the CSCE would be transformed into a strong international organization on a legal basis. Other states, such as the USA, were in favour of maintaining the light and political character of the CSCE. The fear of undermining other international institutions, such as the NATO, was one of the factors behind this policy. In this view the CSCE should considerably strengthen its role in the field of political consultations for which a modest institutionalization of the CSCE process was required.

Gradually, consensus on a concluding document for the Paris summit emerged. An important milestone was the special meeting of the Foreign Ministers of the CSCE states in New York on 1 and 2 October 1990.[88] The pending successful outcome of the CFE negotiations as well as the successful conclusion of the "4-plus-2" negotiations on the reunification of Germany removed the last obstacles for the convening of the Paris Summit.

The Summit meeting was held in Paris from 19 to 21 November 1990. At this meeting, the heads of state or government signed a substantive concluding document which was given the title *Charter of Paris for a New Europe*. In addition to this document, the Paris Summit 'welcomed' the signature of the CFE Treaty *en marge* of the Paris Summit and 'endorsed' the Vienna 1990 Document on CSBMs. Moreover, the Summit 'noted with great satisfaction' the conclusion of the 'Treaty on the Final Settlement with respect to Germany' which was signed in Moscow on 12 September 1990.

The Paris Charter which was signed[89] on 21 November 1990 by all the heads of state or government is imbued with a spirit of optimism. It officially declared that the "era of confrontation and division of Europe has ended". It

---

88 See *infra* paragraph 5.2.

89 The Charter of Paris is the second CSCE document which has been signed. The first CSCE document which was solemnly signed was the Final Act of Helsinki in 1990. All other CSCE documents have been adopted without any signing ceremony. This was also the case with the Helsinki 1992 Document "The Challenges of Change". An exception to this rule was, to a certain extent, the signature of the Convention on Conciliation and Arbitration within the CSCE by 29 CSCE states in December 1992 during the meeting of the CSCE Council. The CFE and Open Skies treaties have been signed as well, but these documents may not be considered as purely CSCE documents (see also *supra* section 2.2.3 and *infra* sections 4.1.6 and 4.1.7).

continued by stating that "(o)urs is a time for fulfilling the hopes and expectations our peoples have cherished for decades". The degree of violent, ethnic-based conflicts that were soon to emerge in various places within the CSCE area, was evidently not expected at the time of the Paris Summit.

The Paris Charter consists of three chapters: an introductory chapter, entitled "A new era of Democracy, Peace and Unity"; a second chapter on "Guidelines for the future"; a third chapter on "New structures and institutions of the CSCE Process". Finally, the Charter encompasses a "Supplementary Document to give effect to certain provisions contained in the Charter of Paris for a New Europe".

The first chapter on "A new era of Democracy, Peace and Unity" enumerates a number of lofty principles which are at the basis of the CSCE community. In this chapter all CSCE states pledged themselves to "strengthen democracy as the only system of government of our nations". In strong terms, the heads of state and government confirm the great importance of human rights and fundamental freedoms as "an essential safeguard against an over-mighty State". It is further laid down that their "observance and full exercise are the foundation of freedom, justice and peace". Although this part of the Paris Charter contains highly important principles, in essence they reconfirm that which had already been established at the Bonn Conference on Economic Co-operation and the Copenhagen CHD meeting.[90] In the second chapter on "Guidelines for the future", agreements were laid down in order to give new impetus to CSCE co-operation concerning security, the human dimension, economic co-operation, the environment, culture, migrant workers, the Mediterranean, and non-governmental organizations. This part also included the decision to convene two more specialized CSCE meetings: a meeting of experts on national minorities in Geneva in July 1991 and a seminar of experts on democratic institutions in Oslo in November 1991.

The third chapter on institutional questions laid the basis for the institutional structure of the 'new' CSCE which is characterized by a modest institutionalization of the CSCE process which was required for the CSCE to be able to face its new tasks. This part provided for, *inter alia*, the establishment of two new CSCE political decision-making bodies (the Council and the Committee of Senior Officials) and the creation of three permanent administrative bodies (a Secretariat in Prague, an Office for Free Elections in Warsaw and a Conflict Prevention Centre in Vienna).[91] The Supplementary Document which was appended to the Charter contained the

---

[90] See *infra* sections 4.3.3 and 4.5.5.2 respectively.

[91] See further *supra* section 2.2.1.

most important institutional arrangements for all these new bodies. This Document also contained a paragraph with financial arrangements for the 'new' CSCE.

3.2.5. The Helsinki Follow-up and Summit Meeting (1992)

From 24 March to 8 July 1992, the fourth CSCE follow-up meeting took place in Helsinki, preceded by a two-week preparatory meeting. It was the first follow-up meeting in the 'new' CSCE. It resulted in the adoption of a lengthy concluding document which was given the title "The Challenges of Change". The new international climate of the post-Cold War era is eloquently reflected in this title. The document contains the results of a diplomatic effort which was mainly aimed at transforming the CSCE into an instrument which should be able to play a central role in the further promotion of security and co-operation in an increasingly unstable Eurasia. Some of the main results of this CSCE meeting were the decision to establish a High Commissioner on National Minorities and the introduction of the possibility of peacekeeping activities under the aegis of the CSCE in close co-operation with NATO, WEU or CIS. In addition, other instruments for early warning, conflict prevention and crisis management were considerably expanded as well.

The opening of the Helsinki Meeting was used for the signature of the Treaty on Open Skies by the Foreign Ministers of 25 CSCE States. At the same time, the Foreign Ministers of all CSCE states issued a CSCE Declaration on the Treaty on Open Skies.[92]

The character of the Helsinki meeting differed substantially from previous follow-up meetings (which took place in Belgrade in 1977/78, in Madrid from 1980 to 1983 and in Vienna from 1986 to 1989). Differences occurred both in organizational and in substantive terms. In the context of the institutional innovations within the CSCE, the follow-up meetings have acquired a quite different character, which is reflected, *inter alia*, in the relatively short duration of these meetings in the 'new' CSCE. The considerable increase in the number of participating States also had its impact on the course of the follow-up meeting. In substantive terms the Helsinki Follow-up Meeting differed from preceding follow-up meetings, *inter alia*, in the sense that operational issues took a great deal of time, in particular the conflicts in the former Yugoslavia and concerning Nagorny Karabakh. This was reflected in a number of meetings of the Committee of Senior Officials at the CSCE premises in Helsinki.

---

[92] See further *infra* section 4.1.7.

The disappearance of the traditional East-West conflict constituted another important factor which influenced the character of the meeting. This was reflected not only in the substance of the issues at stake, but also in the atmosphere of the meeting. The consequences of the dissolution of the old Soviet empire constitute, among other things, new issues on the CSCE agenda.[93] A remarkable fact was that the traditional East-West opposition was substituted by discord within the Western ranks. France, in particular, has played a striking role: it has tried in vain to bloc a number of measures, such as the involvement of NATO in CSCE peacekeeping operations and an enhanced involvement of non-governmental organizations in the CSCE process. The French efforts to 'legalize' the CSCE failed as well.

The Helsinki Document consists of two parts: the "Helsinki Summit Declaration" which is to a certain extent a political introduction to the second and main part of the document, the "Helsinki Decisions". In contrast to the decision of the heads of the 52 delegations to negotiate and adopt only a short concluding report, the Helsinki Document is of considerable length.

The atmosphere expressed by the Helsinki Summit Declaration differs remarkably from the Charter of Paris for a New Europe of November 1990. The Paris Charter was phrased in very optimistic terms, looking forward to a bright new future after the collapse of communism in Eastern Europe. However, the Helsinki Declaration reflects a quite different mood, referring to "serious difficulties and disappointments" (paragraph 3). The 51 heads of state or government (Yugoslavia was excluded from the summit meeting) noted with concern that "(g)ross violations of CSCE commitments in the field of human rights and fundamental freedoms, including those related to national minorities, pose a special threat to the peaceful development of society, in particular in new democracies" (paragraph 12).

Against this background it is understandable that the CSCE States aimed to adopt additional instruments which may be used by the CSCE to address tensions before violence erupts and to manage crises which may develop. Therefore, the emphasis in the Helsinki Decisions is on conflict prevention and conflict management. "Early warning" is a new major concept in the CSCE which has been substantiated at the Helsinki follow-up meeting. The decision to organize peacekeeping operations under the aegis of the CSCE has been one of the most important items of the Helsinki meeting.[94]

---

[93] This relates not only to violent ethnic conflicts, such as in and around Nagorny Karabakh, Georgia and Moldova, but also to the presence of Russian troops on the territory of former Soviet republics. The Baltic states, in particular, played the latter 'card' consistently, which is reflected, *inter alia*, in corresponding clauses in the Helsinki Document (see paragraph 15 of the Helsinki Summit Declaration).

[94] See *supra* section 2.3.1.5.

This situation appears to have had an important impact upon the human dimension of the CSCE as well. This is reflected in the fact that at present the human dimension of the CSCE is considered predominantly in terms of security issues. The establishment of the CSCE High Commissioner on National Minorities as an instrument of conflict prevention is an example of this shift.

The Helsinki Decisions are laid down in twelve chapters, dealing with all areas of the Helsinki process. The major chapters deal with security issues and a strengthening of the institutional structure of the CSCE. On the latter issue the decision was taken to strengthen the role of the CSO considerably. The function of the Chairman-in-Office of the CSCE which had already been developed on the basis of the Charter of Paris, has been formally regulated in the Helsinki Decisions. In general terms the Chairman-in-Office is responsible for "the co-ordination of and consultation on current CSCE business". In performing his tasks, the chairman may be assisted by the troika[95] and by *ad hoc* steering groups on specific conflicts or disputes. Moreover, the chairman may designate personal representatives to assist him in dealing with certain crises or conflicts. An important decision was also the establishment of the Forum on Security Co-operation as the successor to the negotiations on confidence- and security-building measures (CSBMs) and disarmament (in particular, the CFE talks).

The Helsinki meeting was the first CSCE follow-up meeting where human dimension issues did not occupy a primary position. Nevertheless, a certain progress could be achieved. Only minimal progress appeared to be possible in the area of standard-setting. The provisions on new commitments in the field of the human dimension cover a broad area, but as a whole they are rather modest. At the same time it has to be realized that the standard-setting activities of the CSCE in the past had, to a large extent, "exhausted" the possibilities for further steps as all major issues were settled in the period immediately following the collapse of communism in Eastern Europe. That does not detract, however, from the fact that important problems are still pending, in particular concerning issues such as the protection of national minorities, migration, and capital punishment.

The "enhanced commitments" encompass the following subjects: national minorities, indigenous populations, tolerance and non-discrimination, migrant workers, refugees and displaced persons, international humanitarian law, democracy at a local and regional level, nationality, capital punishment, free media, education, compilation of human dimension commitments and domestic implementation guidelines.

---

95 The *troika* consists of the acting Chairman-in-Office and the preceding and succeeding Chairmen.

The Helsinki meeting also decided on the future structure of the CSCE human dimension as a successor to the three meetings of the Conference on the Human Dimension of the CSCE (1989-1991). This structure consists of "implementation meetings on human dimension issues" which will be organized in every year in which a review conference does not take place,[96] and of human dimension seminars. The implementation meetings will be convened at expert level and will last for three weeks. The first implementation meeting was scheduled to take place in Warsaw in September-October 1993. Apart from the biennial implementation meetings, the CSCE states also decided on the introduction of human dimension seminars. These seminars will address specific questions "of particular relevance to the Human Dimension" and "of current political concern". Both the implementation meetings and the human dimension seminars are designed as expert meetings with considerable possibilities for non-governmental organizations to participate. In addition, human dimension issues will also be raised at the biennial review conferences which are charged with monitoring the implementation of CSCE commitments in all CSCE areas as well as achieving further progress.[97]

A major success of the Helsinki meeting was the establishment of the new post of CSCE High Commissioner on National Minorities. The negotiations were based on a Dutch proposal. Although the Dutch delegation succeeded in acquiring the support of a great number of CSCE States as co-sponsors, that did not constitute a guarantee for the adoption of the proposal. Some important CSCE states had reservations until the very end of the follow-up meeting. States like the United Kingdom, Turkey and Spain feared, among other things, that the institute of a High Commissioner might result in an undesirable enhancement of the status of terrorist movements. That fear could only be allayed by including clauses on this issue, such as paragraph 25: "*The High Commissioner will not communicate with and will not acknowledge communications from any person or organization which practises or publicly condones terrorism or violence*". The inherent risk of such clauses is that they may be used as a ground for unwarrantly limiting the HCNM's room for manoeuvre.

A remarkable fact is that the HCNM has not been introduced as a human dimension instrument. It has explicitly been labelled as "an instrument of conflict prevention at the earliest possible stage". This is clearly reflected in

---

[96] In the years in which review conferences take place the function of the implementation meetings will be performed by these conferences.

[97] See *supra* section 2.2.1.

the functions of the HCNM: he is charged not with the promotion and protection of the rights of national minorities, but with "early warning".[98]

As noted above, much time was devoted to conflicts in different CSCE areas at the Helsinki meeting, the delegates of which then convened in special CSO meetings. As far as the conflict in the former Yugoslavia is concerned, it took protracted negotiations before the CSO decided on 12 May to exclude Yugoslavia (in practice encompassing Serbia-Montenegro) from the decision-making in questions concerning the Yugoslav crisis until 1 July. This decision was based on the so-called consensus-minus-one principle, as adopted at the Prague Council meeting in January 1992.

It took several meetings to decide how to proceed after 1 July, due to discord among CSCE States. Finally, just before the opening of the Helsinki Summit, on 8 July the CSO decided "that no representative of Yugoslavia [Serbia and Montenegro] will be present at the CSCE Summit in Helsinki or at any subsequent meetings of the CSCE until 14 October 1992". This complete suspension of Yugoslavia's rights within the CSCE process was repeated on several occasions afterwards. The CSO also decided to establish a special Steering Group for the Yugoslav crisis, consisting of 11 CSCE States. This Group meets regularly in Vienna.

At the Helsinki Summit, after protracted negotiations *en marge* of the summit meetings, the negotiators of the CSCE States succeeded in achieving consensus on a special political declaration on Yugoslavia. This encompassed the decision to send CSCE observer missions to certain regions, such as Sandjak, Vojvodina and Kosovo. It appeared to be extremely difficult to reach an agreement on this issue, among other things because some delegations (Turkey and Azerbaijan) linked the adoption of a 'strong' declaration on the Yugoslav crisis to the adoption of a corresponding declaration on Nagorny Karabakh. A declaration on Nagorny Karabakh, which would have encompassed the despatch of CSCE observers to the conflict area, appeared to be totally unacceptable for certain CSCE States. At the very last moment, when some Foreign Ministers had already left Helsinki, consensus on a declaration concerning Yugoslavia could finally be achieved.

In Helsinki, *en marge* of the CSCE Summit, the second CFE agreement was signed on 10 July. This agreement, which follows on the CFE Treaty of November 1990 and is, therefore, often referred to as CFE-IA, was only signed by those CSCE states which are parties to the CFE Treaty.[99]

---

[98] See further *supra* section 2.3.1.4.

[99] See *infra* section 4.1.6.

4. SPECIALIZED CSCE MEETINGS AND CONFERENCES

4.1. Meetings on military security issues

4.1.1. Stockholm Conference on Confidence- and Security-building Measures and Disarmament in Europe (1984-1986)

On 17 January 1984 the first specialized conference on the basis of the Madrid Concluding Document was commenced in Stockholm: the Conference on Confidence- and Security-Building Measures and Disarmament in Europe. As a rule this conference is (less correctly) referred to as the CDE, the Conference on Disarmament in Europe. As a matter of fact, the Stockholm meeting hardly dealt with disarmament issues. The CDE was preceded by a preparatory meeting in Helsinki which commenced on 25 October and lasted until 11 November 1983.

The CDE aimed at undertaking new, effective and concrete actions designed to make progress in strengthening confidence and security and in achieving disarmament. The first stage of the CDE was devoted to the negotiation and adoption of a set of mutually complementary confidence- and security-building measures (CSBMs) designed to reduce the risk of military confrontation in Europe. It was agreed that these CSBMs would cover the whole of Europe (from the Atlantic to the Ural Mountains, including the adjoining sea area and air space) and would be of military significance, politically binding and provide adequate forms of verification. Because of the complexity and sensitivity of the issues at stake, this first stage of the CDE was expected to last a long time and to cover the period until the next CSCE follow-up meeting in Vienna in 1986. It was therefore agreed that the second stage of the CDE would be determined by the Vienna meeting.

During the time-consuming negotiations, disagreement on a great number of issues between East and West was apparent. The Western States aimed to achieve agreement on concrete CSBMs which should have led to a greater openness and predictability in the military sphere, thereby reducing the risk of a surprise attack in Europe. Concrete proposals concerned, *inter alia*, the exchange of information on the structure of the armies, an annual announcement of the programme for military exercises for the subsequent year and a timely announcement of these exercises, the invitation of observers to these military exercises, verification and an improvement in communications between the CSCE States.

The East European States considered the Western proposals by and large to be efforts to institute legalized espionage. They focused on a number of more "political" measures, *inter alia*, a non-aggression pact and a declaration not to use nuclear weapons first.

In contrast to other CSCE meetings, the NNA countries had difficulties in finding common positions, due to their very divergent security issues. Therefore, they could hardly play their "usual bridge-building" role between East and West at the CDE.

In spite of the very great differences of opinion among the CSCE States, a certain convergence of opinions gradually became noticeable. This finally resulted in the adoption of a substantive concluding document on 19 September 1986 (the closing date of the Stockholm Conference): the "Document of the Stockholm Conference on confidence- and security-building measures and disarmament in Europe convened in accordance with the relevant provisions of the Concluding Document of the Madrid Meeting of the Conference on Security and Co-operation in Europe".

The measures provided for in this document constituted substantial progress in comparison to the CBMs which were laid down in the 1975 Final Act of Helsinki. The major provisions of the Stockholm Document are the following:

a) Notification to all other CSCE States of certain military activities 42 days or more in advance. These activities encompass, *inter alia*, military manoeuvres in which at least 13,000 land troops or 300 battle tanks are involved. (In the Final Act of Helsinki a minimum of 25,000 had been determined.)

b) The invitation of observers to military exercises on a voluntary basis, as laid down in the Final Act, is transformed into an obligation. Whenever more than 17,000 troops (or more than 5,000 in case of amphibious landings or parachute operations) are involved, the CSCE States concerned are obliged to invite military observers from all other CSCE States.

c) Each CSCE State will exchange, with all other participating States, an annual calendar of its major military activities, which are planned for the subsequent calendar year. This has to be transmitted every year, no later than 15 November, for the following year.

d) Under certain conditions all CSCE States have the right to conduct inspections on the territory of any other participating State. No CSCE State, however, is obliged to accept more than three inspections per calendar year. Moreover, a State is not obliged to accept more than one inspection per year from one other CSCE State. This CSBM on inspections, in particular, paved the way for future disarmament and arms control agreements, such as the Treaty on Intermediate-Range Nuclear Forces (INF) and other subsequent intrusive verification regimes.

The Stockholm Document also contains an extensive chapter on "refraining from the threat or use of force" which constitutes a certain further elaboration of the corresponding principle in the first basket of the Final Act of Helsinki. Although the Western States did not consider this part of the document to be of paramount importance, as the corresponding rules of international law and of the Final Act were considered to be clear enough, the East European States insisted on its insertion.

It was laid down in the Stockholm Document that the measures contained in it are "politically binding". They entered into force on 1 January 1987.

The success of the Stockholm Conference was continued in practice, as the standard of compliance with the provisions of its Document exceeded the minimum level. For instance, observers have also been invited to attend military exercises in which less than the agreed-upon minimum number of troops were involved.

After the Vienna Follow-up Meeting, the CDE was succeeded by the Vienna Negotiations on Confidence- and Security-Building Measures, sometimes referred to as CDE-IA or CDE-II.[100]

4.1.2. Vienna Negotiations on Confidence- and Security-building Measures (1989-1992)

On 9 March 1989 the CSCE states started another round of negotiations on confidence- and security-building measures (CSBMs).[101] These negotiations took place in the *Hofburg* in Vienna, the same building where the NATO and Warsaw Pact negotiators met for their talks on conventional disarmament in Europe. The Vienna CSBM negotiations were officially a continuation of the Stockholm CDE and were, therefore, often referred to as CDE-IA or CDE-I*bis*.[102] On 17 November 1990, after seven rounds of negotiations, the CSCE states succeeded in achieving consensus on a lengthy, substantive agreement on new CSBMs or further elaborations of already existing ones. It was decided that the new commitments are politically binding; they entered into force on 1 January 1991. The Vienna Document was of an intermediate nature: it was adopted a few days before the CSCE Summit in Paris. At the Paris Summit the Vienna Document was officially endorsed. At the same time, the heads of state or government of the CSCE states decided to continue the CSBM negotiations with a view to achieving further results before the Helsinki Follow-up Meeting in 1992.

The Vienna Document contains some amendments to CSBMs which were already adopted at the Stockholm CDE. The prior notification of certain military activities and the invitation of observers, for instance, were supplemented by clauses on the invitation of journalists of all CSCE states to attend certain military manoeuvres as observers. An major innovation was

---

100 See *infra* section 4.1.2.

101 On CSBM, see *supra* section 2.3.1.7.

102 See, e.g., Ghebali, op.cit. (note 1), p. 205.

the introduction of an exchange of military information through a new network of direct communications between the capitals of the CSCE states. This network complements the existing use of diplomatic channels. It works on a 24-hour-a-day basis. The system is co-ordinated by the Netherlands.

A striking new element of the Vienna Document was the adoption of the so-called "mechanism for consultation and co-operation as regards unusual military activities". The Vienna mechanism was clearly inspired by the Vienna mechanism of the human dimension of the CSCE. It consists of a first, bilateral phase of exchange of information within 48 hours after the request. If the requesting state is not satisfied, it is entitled to request either a bilateral meeting or an emergency meeting of all CSCE states.[103] This was the first procedural deviation from the sacred principle of consensus in CSCE decision-making. The Vienna Document does not clearly define what "unusual military activities" exactly are, so that this concept has to be further clarified in the practical functioning of the mechanism.[104]

Another new CSBM concerned "co-operation as regards hazardous incidents of a military nature". The CSCE states agreed on a number of procedures which are aimed at co-operation "by reporting and clarifying hazardous incidents of a military nature within the zone of application for CSBMs in order to prevent possible misunderstandings and mitigate the effects on another participating State" (paragraph 18).[105] The initiative for co-operation in this area rests primarily with the state where hazardous incidents occur: it should inform the other CSCE states about such events. Other CSCE states, however, are also entitled to request information which has to be given promptly.

The Vienna Document further provides for other new CSBMs, such as the annual exchange of more detailed military information (paragraphs 10-16) and visits to air bases (paragraphs 19-34). An annual meeting was foreseen to review the implementation of the CSBMs.

After the adoption of the Vienna Document on CSBMs in November 1990, the negotiations continued in Vienna. These negotiations were successfully concluded on 4 March 1992 when all CSCE states consented to another

---

[103] See further *supra* section 2.3.1.2.

[104] In paragraph 17 the Vienna Document refers to "any unusual and unscheduled activities of their military forces outside their normal peacetime locations which are militarily significant, within the zone of application for CSBMs and about which a participating State expresses its security concern".

[105] This mechanism was invoked, *inter alia*, in 1992 after the shooting down of an unarmed helicopter containing EC monitors by an aircraft of the Yugoslav army. See R.W. Zaagman, 'The CSCE and the Yugoslav Crisis', in: *Helsinki Monitor*, 1992, No. 1, pp. 49-50.

Vienna Document on CSBMs. The Vienna 1992 Document integrated a set of new confidence- and security-building measures with measures previously adopted. Just as the CSBMs in the 1990 Document, it was again determined that the new measures are politically binding, and they entered into force on 1 May 1992. The date of adoption of the new Document was only a few days before the opening of the preparatory meeting for the Helsinki Follow-up Meeting. This was a result of the mandate for the CSBM negotiations which were charged with achieving substantive results before Helsinki. Besides, a great number of national delegates to the CSBM talks moved to Helsinki in order to participate in the follow-up meeting. The Vienna 1992 Document was officially presented to the Helsinki Follow-up Meeting.

The issues, regulated in the Vienna 1992 Document, may also be found in previous CSCE documents: annual exchange of military information, procedures for risk reduction (such as the mechanism on unusual military activities and co-operation as regards hazardous incidents of a military nature), contacts, prior notification and observation of certain military activities, annual calendars, compliance and verification, communications, and annual implementation assessment meetings. Although many provisions are of a repetitive nature in the light of previous CSBM documents, further progress could also be achieved. New elements are, *inter alia*, the voluntary hosting of visits to dispel concerns about military activities (paragraph 19) and the agreements on the demonstration of new types of major weapons and equipment systems (paragraph 35). The Vienna 1992 Document also confirms the enlarged zone of application of the CSBMs after the admittance of the former Soviet republics to the CSCE. This resulted in the fact that the CSBMs are also applicable on the territory of the Central Asian CSCE states (but not on the Russian territory behind the Urals).[106]

Although specific clauses on the relationship between both Vienna Documents are lacking, it may be assumed that the 1992 Document has to be considered as the final document, encompassing also the preliminary agreements which were laid down in the Vienna 1990 Document.

4.1.3. Seminars on Military Doctrines (1990-1991)

From 16 January to 5 February 1990 a first CSCE Seminar on Military Doctrines was held in Vienna. For the first time in the history of the CSCE, it brought together a number of high-ranking military officers from all CSCE states, including the NATO countries and the fading Warsaw Pact. The discussions at the seminar focused on the various military doctrines of the CSCE states and their alliances. In this context military issues concerning

---

[106] See further *supra* section 2.3.1.7.

conventional armed forces, their groupings, structures, budgeting and activities were discussed. The seminar did not reach any formal conclusions, nor did it adopt a concluding document.

A second CSCE Seminar on Military Doctrines took place in Vienna from 8 to 18 October 1991. This seminar, which was organized in relation to the CFE and CSBM negotiations in Vienna, clearly reflected the post-Cold War climate in Europe. To a certain extent, the seminar was evidence of the transition from confrontation to co-operation in Europe. The participating states informed each other about their efforts to reduce defence budgets. At the same time, the challenges of modern technology to the armed forces were discussed.

Other seminars on security issues have been organized in 1992 and 1993 under the auspices of the Conflict Prevention Centre and the Forum on Security Co-operation.[107]

4.1.4. Vienna Forum on Security Co-operation (since 1992)

At the Helsinki Follow-up Meeting (March-July 1992), the CSCE participating states continued their negotiations on a mandate for a new round of security talks. The new forum should be a successor to the previous CSBM talks and the CFE negotiations. In contrast to the past practice of CFE negotiations which encompassed only the NATO and Warsaw Pact states, all CSCE states should be entitled to participate in the new round of negotiations which were to be held in Vienna as well. The new Forum should bring together the different lines of security activity within the CSCE framework: CSBMs, disarmament, and the development of (new) security structures.

The mandate for the Forum for Security Co-operation, as agreed upon at the Helsinki Follow-up Meeting, is in some respects repetitive: most topics are mentioned in the mandate itself and then listed in the Programme for Immediate Action. The mandate addresses arms control, disarmament and confidence- and security-building; dialogue; and conflict prevention. The Security Forum works in close co-operation with the Conflict Prevention Centre, although the relationship between both CSCE bodies has remained unclear due to differences of opinion among the CSCE states. The Programme for Immediate Action, which is annexed to the mandate, enumerates a great number of issues which have to be discussed at the Forum without prioritizing these issues. One of them is the elaboration of a

---

107 On these seminars, see further *infra* section 4.1.5.

code of conduct on mutual relations in the field of security (in the Programme referred to as "security enhancement" consultations).[108]

According to its mandate, the Forum consists of two bodies which in principle are composed of the same delegates in order to ensure coherence: the *Special Committee* for, among other things, negotiations on CSBMs, arms control and disarmament; and a *Consultative Committee* which deals with the existing and future tasks of the Conflict Prevention Centre. The Security Forum commenced functioning in Vienna on 22 September 1992. It will continue without a fixed deadline, thus resulting in a more or less permanently meeting security organ for all North American and Eurasian states.

4.1.5. Seminars on Other Security Issues (1992-1993)

In addition to the two above-mentioned seminars on military doctrines,[109] seminars on specific aspects of security have taken place as well. These seminars have been organized under the auspices of the CPC or the Forum on Security Co-operation.

From 19 to 21 February 1992 a Seminar on Conversion of Military Industry to Civilian Production was held in Bratislava. The seminar, organized under the auspices of the CPC, aimed at a discussion of the economic, social, international and defence aspects of conversion. Another seminar under auspices of the CPC was held in Vienna from 4 to 6 March 1992. At this Seminar on Armed Forces in Democratic Societies, the legal, political and practical arrangements for ensuring democratic control over the armed forces were discussed.

In the framework of the Forum on Security Co-operation several seminars have been organized and planned as well. From 31 March to 2 April 1993 a CSCE Seminar on Defence Planning was organized in Vienna. The objective of the Seminar was to exchange information about national approaches to defence planning, including the roles of the institutions involved.

From 6-7 May 1993 a Seminar on a Code of Conduct Governing Mutual Relations in the Field of Security was held. The organization of this Seminar resulted from point 12 of the Programme for Immediate Action of the CSCE Helsinki Document 1992. It aimed to contribute to consultations, which the CSCE states have undertaken with a view to strengthen the role of the

---

108 On the Forum, see H. Hurlburt, 'The CSCE Forum on Security Cooperation: Creating an Arms Control Negotiation for Post-Arms Control Europe', in: *Helsinki Monitor*, 1992, No. 3, pp. 21-32.

109 See *supra* section 4.1.3.

CSCE, and to advance their work on establishing a code of conduct governing their mutual relations in the field of security.

From 7 to 9 June 1993 a CSCE Seminar on Peacekeeping took place in Vienna. The Seminar focused on the role of the CSCE in the area of peacekeeping operations. At the Helsinki Summit in July 1992, the CSCE was assigned the power to organize such peacekeeping operations in co-operation with international organizations such as NATO and WEU. So far, this mandate has largely remained unused. Only a number of CSCE missions of long duration (Georgia, Moldova, Estonia, former Yugoslavia) may be considered to contain elements of peacekeeping operations, albeit on a minimal scale. The seminar discussed the CSCE experiences so far and the possible developments in the future, including relationships with other international institutions. Representatives of the NATO, the North Atlantic Co-operation Council (NACC) and the WEU actively participated in the discussion. The UN was represented by a regional officer. Of particular interest was the discussion about peacekeeping operations in the framework of the CIS. The Russian representative presented CIS activities in this area in great detail, but his plea for CIS peacekeeping only received the support of Tajikistan. CIS peacekeeping raised a number of important questions, especially concerning the relationship with other international bodies (CSCE, UN) and concerning political control of CSCE mandated peacekeeping operations. An issue giving rise to discussion also concerned the fact that the differences between peacekeeping and peace-enforcement actions are at present diminishing.

All above-mentioned seminars did not produce a final document or a chairman's summary.

4.1.6. Excursus: Vienna Negotiations on Conventional Armed Forces in Europe (1989-1992)

For the sake of completeness, the negotiations on Conventional Armed Forces in Europe (CFE) have to be mentioned as well in this survey of CSCE meetings and negotiations, although the link between the CFE and the CSCE was a quite peculiar one.

The mandate for the CFE negotiations was negotiated in a separate forum of direct talks between representatives of the NATO and Warsaw Pact countries which took place *en marge* of the CSCE Follow-up Meeting in Vienna. As some participants insisted on a formal link with the larger CSCE as a whole, it was finally agreed to include the mandate in the Vienna Concluding Document. This was a remarkable development, as only a number of CSCE states (NATO and Warsaw Pact states) were allowed to participate in these negotiations. So far, all CSCE fora had been open to all CSCE states. The way in which the CFE mandate was included in the

Vienna Concluding Document as a separate annex was also remarkable: the "Mandate for Negotiation on Conventional Armed Forces in Europe" was - in full contrast to previous CSCE habits - separately signed by the representatives of the 23 states concerned. This procedure as well as the language used in the mandate gave the impression of a 'quasi-legal' text in a document which for the rest was strictly political.

The link with the CSCE, however, was quite peculiar. The 12 neutral and non-aligned CSCE states were only involved in the CFE negotiations when plenary meetings of all the 35 CSCE states were convened during the various negotiating rounds "in order to exchange views and substantive information" on the progress of the CFE negotiations.[110] Although the participating states in the CFE negotiations had accepted the obligation "to take into consideration the views expressed in such meetings by other CSCE participating States", they were under no obligation to adopt the views of any NNA state. This was stated expressly in the CFE mandate: "The results of the negotiation will be determined only by the participants".[111] All this resulted in the highly autonomous status of the CFE negotiations in the framework of the CSCE process.

The negotiations on conventional disarmament in Europe, which started in Vienna on 9 March 1989, were very complicated. The problems related not only to the quantitative aspects of disarmament measures, but also to the scope of the CFE negotiations. The latter problem concentrated on the question whether combat aircraft should also be part of the CFE agreement which was finally accepted. The reunification of Germany caused other serious difficulties.

In view of the huge problems, the period of approximately 22 months needed to achieve final agreement was certainly not that extensive. A positive influence on the outcome of the CFE negotiations was also exerted by the US pressure which made its consent to the convening of the CSCE summit in Paris in November 1990 dependent upon a successful conclusion of the CFE talks.

The CFE negotiations resulted in one of the most far-reaching disarmament agreements that had ever been concluded. Its full implementation would result in a drastic reduction of the levels of armed forces and armaments in

---

110 See the mandate for the CFE negotiations appended to the Concluding Document of Vienna as Annex III in the form of a 'chairman's statement'. Organizational questions relating to the information meetings with the NNA states were laid down in Annex 2 of the CFE mandate.

111 See also A. Bloed, 'Institutional Aspects of the Helsinki Process after the Follow-up Meeting of Vienna', in: *Netherlands International Law Review*, 1989, No. 3, pp. 342-363.

the CFE states.[112] On 19 November 1990, the treaty was signed in Paris *en marge* of the CSCE Summit Meeting. The lengthy CFE Treaty consists of 23 Articles, followed by eight Protocols which again include two Annexes.[113] The Treaty defines and enumerates armaments, such as battle tanks, armoured combat vehicles, artillery, combat aircraft, combat helicopters and attack helicopters.[114] A Joint Consultative Group, encompassing representatives of all CFE parties, has, as its function, to "promote the objectives and implementation" of the CFE Treaty. It is entitled to discuss and decide on any issue relating to the Treaty, including the updating of the list of armaments and equipment. Decision-making requires consensus (Article XVI).

The CFE Treaty provided for a sophisticated system of inspection and exchange of information. It furthermore established general and regional ceilings for conventional armaments. In addition, it laid down a rule of sufficiency with the objective of ensuring that no single state party possesses more than approximately one-third of the conventional armaments and equipment limited by the Treaty in the CFE area. This area of application was defined as being the territory of all CFE states in "Europe from the Atlantic Ocean to the Ural Mountains" (Article II, paragraph IB), covering the territory of the NATO and Warsaw Pact states.

After the conclusion of the CFE Treaty in November 1990, the negotiations continued on the exact determination of the personal limits of the armed forces of each CFE state party. These negotiations were seriously hindered, in particular, by the political developments in the Soviet Union and in its successor states after the disintegration of the USSR. Soon after the conclusion of the first CFE Treaty in Paris, problems arose as to the interpretation of the Treaty on the side of the Soviet Union concerning, *inter alia*, the question whether certain troops and armaments would be covered by the Treaty. The consequences of the disintegration of the Soviet Union were the subject of complicated diplomatic negotiations as well. The eight former Soviet republics, which have territory in the area of application of the

---

[112] It has to be observed, however, that the CFE Treaty was largely overtaken by the speedy political developments in Europe. At present, subsequent defence budget cuts in many CSCE states have often resulted in lower levels of armaments and personnel strengths than those allowed under the CFE agreements.

[113] The CFE Treaty was the first legally binding document which was negotiated within the framework of the CSCE process.

[114] See Article II of the CFE Treaty and its Protocol on Existing Types of Conventional Armaments and Equipment.

CFE Treaty,[115] achieved a definitive agreement on the distribution of the CFE obligations at a meeting in Tashkent on 15 May 1992. At an Extraordinary Conference of the CFE states parties in Oslo on 5 June 1992, this agreement was accepted. Final agreement on the personnel strength of the conventional armed forces of the CFE states parties could only be achieved in the summer of 1992. The result, laid down in the second CFE agreement which is often referred to as the CFE-IA agreement,[116] could be signed *en marge* of the CSCE Summit in Helsinki on 10 July 1992.[117]

The CFE-1A agreement specifies the maximum numbers of military personnel, based on land within the zone of application, for each CFE state party and are applied 40 months after entry into force of the agreement.[118] The CFE-1A agreement also contains a number of measures in the field of exchange of information and verification which have an important confidence-building effect as well.

Both the CFE Treaty and the CFE-1A agreement entered into force on 9 November 1992, but had already been applied in practice since 17 July 1992. In contrast to the CFE Treaty, the measures in the CFE-1A agreement are only politically binding.

Growing irritation among the (former) neutral and non-aligned CSCE states about the limited number of states which were allowed to participate in the CFE negotiations was one of the reasons for the decision to organize a new CSCE round on CSBMs and disarmament which is open to all CSCE

---

115 The Russian Federation, Belarus, the Ukraine, Moldova, Georgia, Armenia, Azerbaijan and Kazakhstan. The Baltic states do not consider themselves as successor states of the former Soviet Union and are, therefore, outside the scope of the CFE regime.

116 Officially called "Concluding Act of the Negotiation on Personnel Strength of Conventional Armed Forces in Europe", initialled in Vienna on 6 July 1992 and signed in Helsinki on 10 July 1992 at the Meeting of Heads of State or Government of the participating States.

117 The text of the CFE Treaty has been reproduced in the present volume without the appended protocols and annexes. The complete text was published in: *International Legal Materials*, 1991, No. 1, pp. 6-68.

118 The limits for Armenia, Azerbaijan and Moldova were left open at the time of concluding the agreement. Later on, Azerbaijan announced a limit of 70,000 and Moldova 20,000. At the time of writing, Armenia has not announced any number as yet. Officially, this is due to the fact that it has not yet decided on a military doctrine as a consequence of which it claims that it is not yet able to determine the necessary size of its conventional armed forces.

states. This new round, under the title of Forum on Security Co-operation, commenced in Vienna in September 1992.[119]

4.1.7. Excursus: Negotiations on the Treaty on Open Skies (1990-1992)

Another round of security negotiations with a certain link with the CSCE process concerned the *Open Skies* talks. Although only NATO and Warsaw Pact states were entitled to participate in the negotiations on the Open Skies Treaty and a formal link with the CSCE did not exist during the negotiations, the treaty itself was linked to the CSCE process.

The negotiations on an Open Skies agreement had already started at the beginning of 1990. The negotiations took place in three rounds in Ottawa, Budapest and Vienna and were successfully concluded in March 1992. On 24 March 1992, the day of the opening of the Helsinki Follow-up Meeting, the Open Skies Treaty was signed by 25 states *en marge* of the Helsinki meeting. Although it was originally the intention that the Open Skies agreement would be concluded only between the NATO and Warsaw Pact states, the final outcome was somewhat different due to the dissolution of the Warsaw Pact in 1990/91 and also due to the disintegration of the Soviet Union. Although it remained uncertain until the last moment which former Soviet Republics (in the European zone) would join the new treaty, it was signed in Helsinki by 25 states: all NATO states, the former Warsaw Pact states of Poland, Czechoslovakia, Hungary, Romania and Bulgaria, and finally Belarus, the Russian Federation, the Ukraine and Georgia. The Open Skies Treaty will enter into force as soon as twenty States (including the USA and Russia) have ratified the agreement.[120] A political declaration was adopted, calling upon all states parties to the treaty to allow the accession of other interested CSCE states to join the Open Skies agreement.[121] This declaration, adopted by all the Foreign Ministers of the CSCE participating states on the occasion of the signature of the Treaty on Open Skies, pointed to the fact that the treaty had lost its original bloc-to-bloc character. However, the text of the political declaration is rather ambiguous, as it explicitly refers to Article

[119] See *supra* section 4.1.4.

[120] In June 1993, only a few states parties had ratified the Open Skies Treaty. Its entry into force, therefore, is not expected before 1994.

[121] This 'CSCE Declaration on the Treaty on Open Skies' was issued by the Foreign Ministers of the CSCE states on the occasion of the signing ceremony. The acting chairman of the Helsinki Follow-up Meeting recalled this event in the 2nd plenary meeting of the Follow-up Meeting on the afternoon of 24 March 1992. The CSCE Declaration on the Treaty on Open Skies was annexed to Journal No. 1 of the Helsinki Follow-up Meeting of 24 March 1992.

XVII of the Open Skies Treaty. This Article regulates the accession of other CSCE states to the treaty in such a way that all parties to the treaty have a right to block the accession of any state which they want to refrain from joining. On this basis, for instance, Turkey might block the accession of (Greek) Cyprus to the treaty.[122]

The Open Skies Treaty provides for a system of mutual reconnaissance flights over the territories of the states concerned, aimed at enhancing military 'transparency'. The convention is a highly technical agreement which has to be considered as a substantive confidence-building measure, but it is also an instrument which may become important in terms of conflict prevention and conflict management. It has a highly intrusive character as it allows, albeit on strictly defined conditions, the participating states to make inspections of military sites above each other's territories. This is one of the most far-reaching inspection regimes which has so far been agreed upon.[123] In the spring of 1992, the first inspection flights of an experimental nature took place. Among others, there was a Polish inspection flight above the Benelux states.

4.2. Meetings on peaceful settlement of disputes

4.2.1. Montreux Meeting on Peaceful Settlement of Disputes (1978)

The first specialized CSCE meeting which was completely devoted to issues of peaceful settlement of disputes in the framework of the CSCE was held at Montreux (Switzerland) from 31 October to 11 December 1978. This meeting of experts was charged with pursuing the examination and elaboration of a generally acceptable method for peaceful settlement of disputes aimed at complementing existing methods. This issue had been pushed strongly by Switzerland at the second phase of the CSCE in Geneva (1973-1975), but in that time no agreement on this problem could be achieved. The only result was a mandate for a meeting of experts in the Final Act of Helsinki.

---

122 The question of Cyprus had been a sensitive issue during the negotiations concerning the Treaty, in particular the relations between Turkey and Greece. This resulted in the compromise text of Article XVII about future accessions which does not explicitly state, but rather implies a right of veto for each state party concerning any request for accession by third states.

123 The text of the Open Skies Treaty has been reproduced in the present volume without the technical annexes. The complete text was published in: *Tractatenblad* [Netherlands Treaties Series], 1992, No. 142.

At the meeting of experts a working paper based on a Swiss draft Convention on a European System for the Peaceful Settlement of Disputes was discussed, but no agreement could be achieved. The Swiss proposal encompassed a far-reaching CSCE system of compulsory settlement of international disputes by way of consultations, inquiry, mediation, conciliation and arbitration. The Western States were, in general, more in favour of a more gradual extension of the existing (mandatory) methods of peaceful dispute settlement. The socialist States were strongly against the Swiss proposals, *inter alia*, because it provided for a strong involvement of third parties and because they feared interference in their internal affairs. The East European States proposed a system which was based mainly on compulsory consultations in which third parties would only play a role with the consent of the parties to the dispute.

Although no consensus was reached on any specific method, the CSCE States agreed on a common approach to the elaboration of a method which should be based on eight criteria (e.g., flexibility, consistency with sovereign equality of States, acceptability to all CSCE States, etc.). Furthermore, the participants in the Montreux meeting recommended that the CSCE States consider the possibility of promoting and extending the existing practice of including, in appropriate treaties, provisions for the peaceful settlement of disputes. Finally, the Report of the Montreux meeting, adopted on 11 December 1978, suggested that the CSCE States should consider the possibility of convening another meeting of experts on this subject at the Madrid Follow-up Meeting.

4.2.2. Athens Meeting on Peaceful Settlement of Disputes (1984)

As recommended by the Montreux Meeting, in 1983 the Madrid Follow-up Meeting indeed decided to convene a second meeting of experts on peaceful settlement of disputes. This second meeting was held in Athens from 21 March to 30 April 1984. Just as the Montreux Meeting, it was convened in order to pursue, on the basis of the Final Act of Helsinki, a generally acceptable method for the peaceful settlement of disputes aimed at complementing existing methods. The Athens meeting of experts aimed at achieving agreement on concrete methods of settlement of disputes. Switzerland submitted a new proposal which contained less far-reaching methods than in its previous drafts. In the 1984 proposal Switzerland no longer aimed at the establishment of a standing court of arbitration. Instead, it only contained an enumeration of possible procedures, none of which was intended to become obligatory. Moreover, the possibilities for the involvement of third parties were highly restricted in the new Swiss proposal. However, no agreement on the basis of this proposal appeared to be possible. The socialist States submitted their own proposal which stressed the almost exclusive significance of consultations and the need for agreement between the parties in a dispute about the very existence of a dispute. This implied a rejection of the idea of third party involvement. Another negative influence on the outcome of the expert meeting was the US declaration on the restriction of the acceptance of the compulsory jurisdiction of the International Court of Justice (in connection with the *Nicaragua* case).[124]

The Athens expert meeting adopted a short report, which hardly contained any substance. It noted that "some progress" had been made in the examination of a generally acceptable method for the peaceful settlement of disputes and that particular emphasis was put "on ways and means of including a third party element". It also referred to the desire for further discussions on this subject in "an appropriate framework within the CSCE process", but it did not propose a third expert meeting.

4.2.3. Valletta Meeting of Experts on Peaceful Settlement of Disputes (1991)

At the Vienna Follow-up Meeting some progress in the area of peaceful dispute settlement had been achieved, due to the changing attitude of the socialist states in the area of *glasnost* and *perestroika*. One of the achievements was the agreement in principle to agree on mandatory involvement of third parties in the settlement of certain categories of disputes between CSCE states. Further progress was achieved at the Paris Summit in November 1990. Another meeting of experts was convened, on the basis of the Vienna Concluding Document, in order to elaborate, among other things, new dispute settlement procedures. This first CSCE meeting on peaceful settlement of disputes after the Cold War was held in Valletta (Malta) from 15 January to 8 February 1991. It succeeded in achieving considerable results.

At the Valletta meeting consensus could be achieved on a new CSCE Procedure for Dispute Settlement. The Valletta Report consists of two parts. The first part lists 'principles for dispute settlement', whereas the second part is devoted to 'provisions for a CSCE procedure for peaceful settlement of disputes'. The essence of the Valletta Report rests in the second part. This provides for the possibility to establish a 'CSCE Dispute Settlement Mechanism' by CSCE states. The establishment of such a 'mechanism' (which is rather a commission of independent experts) may be initiated by any CSCE state and is not dependent upon the consent of the other party.

---

124 Case Concerning Military and Paramilitary Activities in and against Nicaragua (Nicaragua v. USA), Judgment of 26 November 1984, in: *Reports of Judgments, Advisory Opinions and Orders of the International Court of Justice*, 1984, pp. 398 et seq.

The members of such *ad hoc* 'mechanisms' are selected by a rather complicated procedure from a register of qualified candidates; the register comprises the names of up to four experts nominated by each CSCE state desiring to do so. The 'mechanisms' are not entitled to settle disputes by binding decisions. They are only empowered to make comments or to give advice which is not binding. However, the major weaknesses of the Valletta Procedure are its escape clauses. The Valletta Procedure may not be applied in certain disputes. The main exception has been laid down in Section XII of the 'Provisions' which excludes disputes which raise "issues concerning its territorial integrity, or national defence, title to sovereignty over land territory, or competing claims with regard to the jurisdiction over other areas". Any disagreement on the question whether a certain dispute touches upon such issues is itself decided by the CSCE State concerned.

So far, due to its weaknesses, the Valletta mechanism has not been used by any CSCE State. In October 1992, the Valletta mechanism was strengthened to a certain extent.[125]

4.2.4. Geneva Meeting of Experts on Peaceful Settlement of Disputes (1992)

At the Helsinki Follow-up Meeting (1992), the issue of peaceful settlement of disputes was intensively discussed, in particular on the basis of a French-German proposal (the so-called Badinter plan). This proposal provided for the conclusion of a legally binding treaty on the establishment of a court conciliation and arbitration in the CSCE. At this meeting, however, no consensus could be achieved on this proposal. Neither was an agreement possible on proposals to improve the so-called Valletta Mechanism. Therefore, it was decided to continue the negotiations at a special meeting which was convened in Geneva from 12 to 23 October 1992.

On the basis of the Helsinki 1992 Document, the Geneva meeting was charged with negotiating "a comprehensive and coherent set of measures" in the field of the peaceful settlement of disputes. In the Helsinki Document it was laid down that the CSCE States "will take into account the ideas expressed regarding procedures for a compulsory element in conciliation, setting up of a court of conciliation and arbitration within the CSCE, and other means". At the Geneva meeting consensus could be achieved on an extensive document which provides for, among others, adaptations of and

---

125 See *infra* section 4.2.4.

additions to the Valletta mechanism.[126] Besides, the Geneva expert meeting agreed on the text of a draft "Convention on Conciliation and Arbitration within the CSCE". This Convention provides for general conciliation and for arbitration on the basis of agreements *ad hoc* or, in advance, on the basis of reciprocal declarations. The CSCE Council of Ministers at its Stockholm meeting in December 1992 declared this convention open for signature.[127] This resulted in the first CSCE document which was adopted in the form of a legally binding document. However, several CSCE states have so far refused to join the convention.[128]

4.3. Meetings on economic and scientific co-operation and the environment

4.3.1. Scientific Forum of Hamburg (1978/1980)[129]

On 20 June 1978 a meeting of experts convened in Bonn to prepare a Scientific Forum. On 28 July 1978 this meeting decided that the Forum was to take place in Hamburg in 1980. The Scientific Forum started on 18 February 1980 and was held in the form of a meeting of leading personalities in science from the participating States. The Forum was the first meeting in the framework of the CSCE which was attended by private scientists, as delegations to former CSCE meetings were only composed of State officials.

The Scientific Forum discussed problems of common interest concerning current and future developments in science and promoting the expansion of contacts, communications and the exchange of information between scientific institutions and among scientists. The discussion concerned, more in particular, alternative energy sources, food production, medicine, humanities and social sciences (e.g., urbanization, environmental quality).

---

126 These amendments and additions have been laid down in a draft decision, to be adopted at the Stockholm meeting of the CSCE Council (see *infra* section 5.7). As these texts are almost identical to the text, as finally approved by the Stockholm Council, they are not reproduced in the present volume.

127 See also *infra* paragraph 5.7.

128 See also *supra* section 2.3.1.3.

129 From a formal point of view the Scientific Forum was a Third Basket meeting: its mandate was laid down in the paragraph on "science" in the third basket of the Final Act of Helsinki. As the results of the Hamburg Forum rather belong to the area of scientific co-operation, however, the editor has decided to place the Forum in the category of CSCE Second Basket meetings in the present publication.

Although the Forum dealt with especially non-controversial issues, the East-West conflict also determined this meeting. This was reflected, in particular, in criticism of the treatment of dissident scientists in the Soviet Union. Nevertheless, the Forum succeeded in adopting a substantive Report with a number of concrete recommendations. One of the most remarkable conclusions of the Report concerned human rights: the Report states "that respect for human rights and fundamental freedoms by all States represents one of the foundations for a significant improvement in their mutual relations, and in international scientific co-operation at all levels".

4.3.2. Sofia Meeting on the Protection of the Environment (1989)

From 16 October to 3 November 1989 the first CSCE meeting completely devoted to the protection of the environment took place in Sofia. It dealt with three specific areas: prevention and control of the transboundary effects of industrial accidents; management of potentially hazardous chemicals; pollution of transboundary watercourses and international lakes.

The Sofia meeting took place at the moment when profound changes occurred in the political system of the socialist states. The greater freedom for citizens in some Warsaw Pact states was also tested in Sofia on the occasion of the Sofia meeting. This was evidenced in the efforts of non-governmental environmental groups which called upon the CSCE meeting to pay attention to their interests. Actions by the Bulgarian police to suppress these uncontrolled demonstrations were severely criticized in the conference rooms. In spite of the fact that the protection of the environment was the topic of the conference, the Sofia meeting did not take place in a vacuum which was reflected in the fact that several delegations raised human rights issues in their interventions. One of the topics raised was the position of the Turkish minority in Bulgaria which was the subject of suppressive government policy, leading to a mass exodus to Turkey.

At the meeting a concluding document was drafted, but consensus could not be achieved due to Romanian opposition. The Romanian objections focused, in particular, on the paragraphs in which the freedoms of expression and assembly for "individuals, groups and organizations concerned with environmental issues" were reaffirmed. Although the chairman at the concluding meeting could only take note of the lack of consensus, nevertheless he took a remarkable decision by including the text of the draft concluding document as an annex to the journal of the day. In this way the draft text could be officially transmitted to later CSCE meetings.

Although the draft Sofia Document could not be adopted at the meeting itself, one year later it nevertheless received binding force. After the overthrow of the Ceausescu regime, the Romanian authorities withdrew their objections. Therefore, the Sofia Document could be adopted at a special meeting in Vienna on 5 November 1990 *en marge* of the preparations for the Paris Summit Meeting of that same month.[130]

4.3.3. Bonn Conference on Economic Co-operation in Europe (1990)

From 19 March until 11 April 1990 the Conference on Economic Co-operation in Europe took place in the West German capital, Bonn. It was the first CSCE meeting fully devoted to issues of economic co-operation. The Bonn Conference was followed with great interest, as it was the first CSCE meeting after the revolutionary events in the former socialist states. In contrast to the CSCE meetings in 1989,[131] which all ended without concrete results due, *inter alia*, to the obstructive policy of the communist authorities in Romania, the Bonn Conference was a great success. At the Bonn Conference, consensus could be achieved on a substantive concluding document which contained a number of agreements which hitherto had been completely unimaginable. Not only were traditional Western values, such as multiparty democracy based on free elections and the rule of law, embraced by all the former socialist states as well, but all CSCE states now also recognized the system of market economy as the only viable economic system. The states also explicitly recognized the "relationship between political pluralism and market economies". As a matter of fact, the results of the Bonn Conference made the previously agreed upon commitments in the Second Basket more or less obsolete. These commitments were based on the assumption of the existence of two opposing socio-economic systems in the CSCE area.

4.3.4. Economic Forum (1993)

From 16 to 18 March 1993 the first Economic Forum was held at the seat of the CSCE Secretariat in Prague. Although at first sight the Economic Forum appears to have had the character of an independent CSCE meeting, it was, in fact, a special meeting of the Committee of Senior Officials. Its main aim was an exchange of views and experiences concerning key issues of the economic transition process to democratic market economies in order to give

---

[130] *Ad hoc* meeting in Vienna of Representatives of participating States of the CSCE on the Adoption of the Report of the Sofia Meeting on the Protection of the Environment on 5 November 1990.

[131] The London Information Forum, the Paris meeting of the Conference on the Human Dimension of the CSCE, the Sofia Meeting on the Protection of the Environment.

political stimulus to the dialogue on this issue.[132] In addition, the Forum was to suggest practical efforts for the development of free market systems and economic co-operation and encourage activities within international organizations. There is general agreement on the fact that the CSCE should not itself develop into an operational institution in the area of economic co-operation. Its main aim is restricted to political dialogue in this field which should preferably result in measures to be taken by other international economic bodies.

The Forum resulted in a substantive Chairman's Summary. It contains a brief description of the main items which were discussed. In accordance with the mandate, the discussions focused on "key elements of a favourable business climate", on "the human factors in the economic transition process" and on "integrating economic and environmental factors". The Chairman's Summary listed a considerable number of issues which were identified as being especially important for the process of economic transition to market economies. It was suggested that the CSO should organize seminars and expert meetings on these issues. It was agreed that the results of the first Economic Forum should be conveyed to the CSCE Parliamentary Assembly, "noting the prominent role of parliamentarians in the context of creating favourable conditions for economic transition".[133]

The next meeting of the Economic Forum is scheduled to take place in Prague from 15-17 March 1994.

4.4. Meetings on the Mediterranean

4.4.1. Valletta Meeting on Co-operation in the Mediterranean (1979)

From 13 February to 26 March 1979 a meeting of experts was held at the Maltese capital Valletta in order to discuss the possibilities for further promoting the co-operation among the Mediterranean States in the economic, scientific and cultural fields. This meeting was convened at the invitation of Malta which had strongly promoted Mediterranean co-operation at the Belgrade Follow-up Meeting. Its proposals, however, did not receive an enthusiastic response, as they envisaged a strong institutionalization of the CSCE process by establishing permanent CSCE organs. At Valletta these proposals were rejected and the CSCE States officially concluded in the Report, adopted on 26 March 1979, that the ECE, UNESCO and UNEP, in

---

[132] See chapter VIII of the Helsinki 1992 Document (Decisions).

[133] 1-EF(20-CSO)/Journal No. 3, Annex.

particular, provided a satisfactory framework for developing the pertinent co-operation among the CSCE States and the non-participating Mediterranean States. Consequently, the recommendations and conclusions of the Report of the Valletta Meeting are mainly addressed to these UN institutions.

4.4.2. Venice Seminar on Co-operation in the Mediterranean (1984)

From 16 to 26 October 1984, the Venice Seminar on economic, scientific and cultural co-operation in the Mediterranean took place as the follow-up of the Valletta meeting of experts on the same subject of 1979.[134] This Seminar aimed, *inter alia,* at the further development of co-operation between CSCE States and non-CSCE States in the Mediterranean. This aim was only partially realized, due to the refusal of States like Algeria, Lebanon, Libya, Morocco, Syria and Tunisia to participate in the Seminar. Only Egypt and Israel accepted the invitation which resulted in the realization of a rather extensive co-operation programme. Representatives of several international organizations and UN organs participated in the Seminar as well.

The protection of the Mediterranean environment was one of the main themes of discussion at the Seminar. In this field, in particular, the Seminar adopted recommendations to the governments of the participating States. These recommendations were laid down in the Report of the Venice Seminar which was adopted on 26 October 1984.

4.4.3. Palma de Mallorca Meeting on the Mediterranean (1990)

Just before the convening of the CSCE Summit in Paris, a specialized CSCE meeting was held in Palma de Mallorca from 24 September to 19 October 1990. This meeting was completely devoted to problems concerning the Mediterranean, in particular economic, social and environmental issues. One of the most striking events at this meeting was the proposal, submitted by Italy and Spain, to establish a Conference on Security and Cooperation in the Mediterranean along the same lines as the "mother" CSCE. Although several CSCE States expressed their (conditional) support for the Italian-Spanish initiative, it failed to acquire the necessary consensus. France, in particular, considered a CSCM consisting of about twenty Mediterranean States aiming to consider solutions for complicated problems such as the Arab-Israeli conflict, Lebanon, Cyprus etc. to be highly ambitious. Nevertheless, the concluding document of the Palma de Mallorca meeting contains a reference to the suggestion for a "CSCM" which had been made at the meeting.

---

[134] See *supra* section 4.4.1.

The Palma de Mallorca meeting officially aimed at widening the scope of co-operation with the non-participating Mediterranean states and strengthening confidence and security in that region. Representatives of non-participating Mediterranean states and of a number of relevant international organizations participated in the meeting. Albania participated as an observer.

The Meeting on the Mediterranean adopted a substantive concluding document which consists of two parts: a first part on specific aspects of co-operation, dealing with economic policy and development; the second part concerns the protection of Mediterranean ecosystems, dealing with the uses and pollution of the environment of the area.

4.4.4. Mediterranean Seminar in Valletta (1993)

From 17 to 21 May 1993 a CSCE 'Mediterranean Seminar' took place in the Maltese capital Valletta. After the expert meetings in Valletta (1979), Venice (1984) and Palma de Mallorca (1990), the Valletta Seminar was the fourth CSCE meeting on Mediterranean issues. The Valletta seminar was not entitled to produce a concluding document with commitments binding on the CSCE states. However, the results of the meeting were laid down in non-committal form in a Chairman's Summary, drafted by the Swedish Chairman-in-Office. After the presentation of this written summary at the CSO Vienna Group on 27 May 1993, the Chairman's Summary was officially circulated among the CSCE states, non-participating Mediterranean states and among interested international organizations. From a formal point of view, this summary was delivered by Sweden on its own initiative. However, its contents and the official means of presentation give it a standing which might go beyond the strictly 'personal' level.

At the Valletta Seminar a great number of issues were discussed, focusing on environmental problems and on demographical issues (including migration).

The number of CSCE states which participated in the Seminar was low: only 32 of the 53 states were represented. In particular the successor states of the former Soviet Union were missing: only the Russian Federation was present. On the other hand, the former Yugoslav Republic of Macedonia was present for the first time at a CSCE meeting as an observer.

4.5. Meetings on the Human Dimension of the CSCE (including information and culture)

4.5.1. Ottawa Meeting on Human Rights and Fundamental Freedoms (1985)

The first CSCE meeting which was completely devoted to questions of human rights took place in Ottawa from 7 May to 17 June 1985. The mandate for this meeting of experts - which was preceded by a preparatory meeting which lasted two weeks - encompassed not only a discussion on the respect of human rights and fundamental freedoms in all their aspects, as embodied in the Final Act of Helsinki and the Concluding Document of Madrid, but also the elaboration of conclusions and recommendations to be submitted to the governments of all participating States.

The review phase of this expert meeting was used by the Western States to express their concern about violations of human rights in certain CSCE States, especially East European countries. These violations, as put forward by the Western States, concerned, *inter alia*, the fate of Helsinki monitoring groups, the suppression of religious freedoms, the abuse of psychiatry for political purposes, the violation of rights of minorities and the freedom of movement, including the right of everyone to leave his country and to return to his country.

The East European States were not prepared to discuss these allegations and focused their attention on problems of mass unemployment and other drawbacks in the Western world. Moreover, they also aimed to introduce third generation rights (e.g., the right to live in peace) into the CSCE process. The disagreements remained so fundamental that the adoption of a concluding document appeared to be out of the question. The meeting ended without even an official communiqué.

4.5.2. Budapest Cultural Forum (1985)

From 15 October to 25 November 1985, a Cultural Forum took place in Budapest. This Forum was also preceded by a preparatory meeting which determined the agenda and the remaining organizational aspects. Not only did representatives of the governments of the CSCE States participate in this Forum, but also leading personalities in the field of culture from the participating States. Consequently the character of this meeting was similar to that of the Hamburg Scientific Forum of 1980.

The Cultural Forum was charged with discussing interrelated problems concerning "creation, dissemination and co-operation, including the promotion and expansion of contacts and exchanges in the different fields of culture".

The Forum showed the fundamental differences between East and West concerning the nature and function of culture. The East European States stressed the servitude of the artist towards the socialist state as well as the fact that the artist's works should primarily contribute to a more human and ethical world and to international peace. On the other hand Western States emphasized the individuality of the artist in a pluralistic society and his freedom of expression, dissemination and movement.

Although a great number of proposals were submitted to the Cultural Forum and the atmosphere at the conference as a rule appeared to be constructive, the 35 CSCE States did not succeed in achieving agreement on a concluding document. So the Cultural Forum appeared to be another CSCE expert meeting which failed to achieve results, not even the adoption of a brief official communiqué.

Nevertheless, the Cultural Forum was not considered to be a total failure. Its aim was to initiate a discussion about cultural life in order to promote understanding and closer relations between the CSCE countries. To a limited extent this is what it achieved.

4.5.3. Bern Meeting on Human Contacts (1986)

From 15 April to 26 May 1986 - subsequent to a two-week preparatory meeting -, the Meeting on Human Contacts was held in Bern. The mandate for this meeting was only agreed upon at the Madrid Follow-up Meeting of the CSCE after protracted negotiations, which were due to the fact that the subject constituted a highly sensitive issue for the East European States. This resulted in the compromise that the mandate was not included in the Madrid Concluding Document, but added to it as an annex in the form of a "chairman's statement". Although this sometimes raised the suspicion that the East European States might use this "lower rank" in order to abstain from the meeting, in practice the Bern meeting did not differ in any way from other CSCE expert meetings.

The Bern meeting indicated a certain flexibility on the part of the East European States. This concerned new commitments in respect of, *inter alia*, contacts on the basis of family ties and marriages between citizens of two CSCE States. It therefore appeared to be possible to conclude the Bern meeting with the adoption of a substantive final document. A draft document was elaborated and put forward by Switzerland on behalf of the NNA States which was acceptable to nearly all CSCE States. This document contained a great number of provisions in the field of human contacts, such as family visits and reunification, marriages of citizens of different CSCE States, tourism, contacts between religious institutions and the protection of postal and telephone services.

Only the USA, however, refused to concur in the adoption of the document. The leader of the US delegation motivated its far-reaching step by stating that the adoption of the draft concluding document would affect the credibility of the CSCE process: the compliance with the provisions of the third basket of the CSCE was so unsatisfactory, that only the adoption of a substantive final document with clear new commitments would suffice. As the draft document contained too many escape clauses, its rejection would serve the case of promoting human contacts better than its acceptance.[135] This was the first time in CSCE history that the adoption of a draft concluding document concerning the humanitarian aspects of the CSCE process was blocked by a single Western State.

The Soviet Union, however, repeatedly announced that despite the American veto, it considered itself to be bound by the provisions of the draft Bern document.

4.5.4. London Information Forum (1989)

The Information Forum in London was the first specialized CSCE meeting after the conclusion of the Vienna Follow-up Meeting. Only a few months after the Vienna meeting, it was held in London from 18 April to 12 May 1989. The Information Forum was "to discuss improvement of the circulation of, access to and exchange of information; co-operation in the field of information; and the improvement of working conditions for journalists".

The Information Forum had a quite particular character, due to the participation of a number of journalists who played a very independent role at the meeting. This resulted in a CSCE meeting which developed at two levels: an official, intergovernmental level composed of diplomats and a second, informal level of journalists which developed their own negotiation circuit. The informal circuit also resulted in a great number of proposals which were elaborated in negotiations between the journalists themselves.

Nevertheless, the Forum ended without a concluding document. Nevertheless, the Forum exerted a certain influence, as the great number of proposals which were submitted during the meeting, were taken up again at other CSCE meetings. However, the results of the London Forum soon became obsolete as a result of the revolutionary developments in Central and Eastern Europe.

---

[135] See on this event, in particular, W. Korey, *The Promises We Keep; Human Rights, the Helsinki Process, and American Foreign Policy* (New York 1993), pp. 202-212.

4.5.5. Conference on the Human Dimension of the CSCE (CHD)

4.5.5.1. CHD Meeting in Paris (1989)

Less than half a year after the conclusion of the CSCE Follow-up Meeting in Vienna, the first meeting of the Conference on the Human Dimension of the CSCE took place. From 30 May to 23 June 1989, delegates of the 35 CSCE states convened in Paris to discuss all issues concerning the CSCE human dimension which they deemed relevant. The CHD meeting was not only charged with reviewing the implementation of already existing CSCE commitments in this area, but it was also required to consider the adoption of new measures. A separate point of discussion was the evaluation and improvement of the Vienna mechanism for the human dimension, including the discussion of cases under the fourth paragraph of the mechanism.

At the meeting not less than 36 proposals were submitted. From the outset onwards, however, it was evident that it would be impossible to achieve consensus on a substantive concluding document. To a great extent, this was due to the position of Romania which was not even prepared to consent to an official reconfirmation of the achievements of the Vienna Concluding Document. It may be recalled that in this way Romania continued its policy, as it had submitted a heavily criticized reservation concerning the human dimension paragraphs at the conclusion of the Vienna Follow-up Meeting.[136] Another reason for the impossibility to achieve a concluding document was undoubtedly also the fact that the Paris meeting took place soon after the Vienna meeting where the same issues had been debated over a period from 1986 to 1989.

The Paris CHD meeting, however, was not a failure. It offered a forum for raising cases of alleged violations of human dimension commitments under the Vienna mechanism. These discussions, characterized by the Dutch head of delegation, Mr. Max van der Stoel, as "very frank and at times lively", concerned, *inter alia*, the mass flight of members of the Turkish minority in Bulgaria, the treatment of dissidents in Czechoslovakia, and the serious human rights situation in Romania. The proposals, submitted at the Paris meeting, were also not lost. As the Paris meeting was to be succeeded by two more CHD meetings, the 36 proposals were referred to the Copenhagen meeting for further discussion.

4.5.5.2. CHD Meeting in Copenhagen (1990)

In contrast to the first meeting of the Conference on the Human Dimension of the CSCE in Paris in May and June 1989, its second meeting in

---

136 See *supra* section 3.2.3.

Copenhagen from 5 to 29 June 1990 constituted a major step forward on the road to common European standards in the field of human rights. This Conference adopted an extensive concluding document which constituted the most remarkable human rights document adopted in the framework of the CSCE process since the signing of the Final Act of Helsinki in August 1975.

The Copenhagen meeting which was held shortly after the successful Bonn Conference on Economic Co-operation reflected the new political climate in Europe. The Warsaw Pact states had ceased to exist as a group. In addition to this fragmentation of the CSCE process, the disagreements within the group of Western states increased as well. Nevertheless, in no more than four weeks the Copenhagen meeting succeeded in achieving consensus on a far-reaching document which sometimes was referred to as a "European Constitution on Human Rights". The short time available for drafting is reflected in certain imperfections in the document itself.

The "Document of the Copenhagen Meeting of the Conference on the Human Dimension of the CSCE" consists of an introduction, five chapters of varying length (altogether 45 provisions) and a chairman's statement by way of an annex. The chapters concern 1) the rule of law, 2) individual rights and related issues, 3) the working of democratic institutions and the importance of co-operation in this area, 4) national minorities, and 5) the supervisory mechanism for the human dimension of the CSCE. The chairman's statement concerns the access of non-governmental organizations (NGOs) and the media to meetings of the CHD which has been annexed to the Document, in particular, in view of the Moscow meeting in September and October 1991.

The first chapter of the Document encompasses one of the main achievements of the Copenhagen meeting: a set of detailed provisions on the rule of law and democracy as an inherent element of the rule of law, in particular concerning the elements which are considered to be essential for democratic societies based on the rule of law. Moreover a detailed provision has been inserted concerning free elections. Chapter I of the Copenhagen Document also contains a detailed provision on free elections, according to which the CSCE States entered into the obligation, *inter alia*, to hold free elections by secret ballot or by equivalent free voting procedure at reasonable intervals (paragraphs 6 and 7). These clauses also contain commitments concerning the role of foreign and domestic observers.

The second chapter of the Copenhagen Document encompasses a significant number of separate human rights and fundamental freedoms, some of which have been elaborated in detail. The chapter contains provisions on, *inter alia*, the freedom of expression, the right of peaceful assembly and demonstration, the right of association, the freedom of thought, conscience and religion, the freedom of movement, rights of children, the prohibition of torture and other inhuman or degrading treatment, the right to have conscientious objections to military service, the rights of migrant workers, and a provision on derogations from human rights obligations during a state of public emergency. An interesting clause concerns the exceptions to the rights which have been agreed upon. This clause, which is seldomly seen in international documents, reads as follows: "Restrictions on this right will have the character of *very rare exceptions*, will be considered necessary only if they respond to a specific public need, pursue a legitimate aim and are proportionate to that aim, and will not be abused or applied in an arbitrary manner".

An important new provision concerns the consequences of the proclamation of a state of public emergency by a CSCE State (paragraph 25). This issue was promoted with great vigour by the Netherlands delegation. In essence the new provision refers to the regulations on the consequences of a state of public emergency as laid down in other international instruments.

The chapter on the protection of national minorities belongs to the major achievements of the Copenhagen CHD meeting. The CSCE states achieved consensus on a number of commitments which are so far unparalleled in international documents, despite the fact that CSCE States such as Bulgaria, Romania, France and Greece created a great number of obstacles on the road to a generally acceptable document. Nevertheless, the negotiations resulted in an extensive chapter, encompassing not less than eleven, partly quite extensive, paragraphs. In spite of its careful wording and escape clauses, this fourth chapter contains a number of agreements which constituted an important step forward on the difficult road to a *communis opinio* about the status of national minorities in international law and international relations. As a matter of fact, these commitments exerted a great influence on the drafting of the UN Declaration on the Rights of Persons Belonging to National or Ethnic, Religious and Linguistic Minorities which was adopted by the UN General Assembly in December 1992.

Although the CSCE states failed to achieve consensus on a definition of "national minorities", the question of who belongs to a national minority was solved in a very voluntaristic way: "To belong to a national minority is a matter of a person's individual choice and no disadvantage may arise from the exercise of such choice." In the same paragraph it has also been laid down that persons belonging to a national minority have the right "to establish and maintain unimpeded contacts among themselves within their country as well as contacts across frontiers with citizens of other States with whom they share a common ethnic or national origin, cultural heritage or religious beliefs" (paragraph 32.4). This agreement banned the 'traditional' East European practice of prohibiting contacts between members of national minorities across frontiers (e.g., contacts between the Hungarian minority in Romania with citizens of Hungary).

The Copenhagen Document bears clear signs of the most controversial issues which could be solved only by compromising on carefully formulated clauses. This resulted in the insertion of a great number of escape clauses which strongly affect the obligatory character of the provisions concerned. Often the CSCE States only pledge to "endeavour" or to "consider" and in one case they were only prepared to "note". Moreover, they could often only achieve agreement by referring to "national legislation" as another escape clause. The formula "to note" has been used for the very sensitive issue of possible autonomous administrations of minorities (paragraph 35).

Despite the great number of escape clauses incorporated in the text of the chapter on national minorities, two CSCE States felt obliged to submit interpretative statements, viz., Greece and Bulgaria. In the Greek statement the unlimited validity of the principle of territorial integrity of States was stressed. Besides, in the Bulgarian statement, the domestic jurisdiction of States in dealing with national minorities, "whenever they exist", was emphasized.

The chapter on the Vienna mechanism of the human dimension of the CSCE was the most disappointing part of the Copenhagen Document. Although a considerable number of proposals on this subject were submitted, agreement could only be achieved on a few minor questions. Even efforts only to mention the proposals for new measures in the Copenhagen Document were confronted with serious opposition from some CSCE States. Several CSCE States feared an institutionalization of the CSCE which might hamper its dynamic functioning. Agreement could only be achieved on some minor questions connected with the functioning of the mechanism. The "innovations", introduced by the Copenhagen Document, are related to certain time-limits and the form in which information must be provided by states under the mechanism. Also the decision was taken "to refrain, in the course of the bilateral meeting held under paragraph 2,[137] from raising situations and cases not connected with the subject of the meeting, unless both sides have agreed to do so". The latter decision definitively decided the question whether CSCE States are entitled to raise new questions, not connected with the original subject, at the bilateral meetings.

4.5.5.3. CHD Meeting in Moscow (1991)

The third and last CHD meeting which took place in Moscow from 10 September to 4 October 1991 resulted in the adoption of another substantive concluding document. It was the first CSCE meeting with the full participation of the three Baltic states.[138] The major achievement of the Moscow Meeting concerns the further development of the supervisory

---

137 This refers to the second phase of the Vienna human dimension mechanism (bilateral meetings).

138 See *infra* paragraph 5.4.

mechanism of the human dimension of the CSCE which encompassed deviations from the rigid principle of consensus. Another major achievement concerns a detailed clause concerning the existence of a state of emergency and the measures taken thereunder.

As far as standard setting is concerned, the Moscow Meeting clearly demonstrated that the limits have been reached. Nearly all major issues in the field of the human dimension of the CSCE have been more or less satisfactorily settled. Therefore, in Moscow only slight progress could be achieved, *inter alia*, by introducing clauses on the equality of men and women and on the freedom of artistic expression. No progress, however, was possible on the highly topical issue of the international protection of the rights of national minorities. In particular some Western delegations — e.g., France, Greece and Turkey — blocked any significant progress in this field.

The agreements concerning the existence of a state of emergency and the measures taken thereunder, as laid down in the Moscow Document, had mainly been influenced by the recent *coup d'état* attempt in the Soviet Union. At the Copenhagen CHD meeting, the issue had been intensively discussed for the first time. In Moscow the issue was again raised by the Soviet delegation which aimed at the adoption of a more detailed agreement in this field. This resulted in an extensive paragraph with a number of new provisions on this subject (paragraph 28, subdivided into ten subparagraphs). The relevant clause stipulates in greater detail that there are a number of rights from which no derogation is allowed, even during a state of public emergency. Moreover, CSCE States, which declare a state of public emergency, are under the obligation to inform the CSCE immediately. In comparison to the corresponding rules in international treaties on human rights, the Moscow Document has achieved slight progress. This concerns in particular the freedom of expression and the freedom of information. These are freedoms from which, according to international law, derogation is allowed under certain conditions. The Moscow Document, however, stipulates the agreement that the CSCE States "will endeavour to maintain freedom of expression and freedom of information, consistent with their international obligations and commitments, with a view to enabling public discussion on the observance of human rights and fundamental freedoms as well as on the lifting of the state of public emergency" (paragraph 28.9). It was further agreed in the same paragraph that the CSCE State "will, in conformity with international standards regarding the freedom of expression, take no measures aimed at barring journalists from the legitimate exercise of their profession other than those strictly required by the exigencies of the situation".

In the Moscow Document the CSCE States "emphasize that issues relating to human rights, fundamental freedoms, democracy and the rule of law are of international concern, as respect for these rights and freedoms constitutes one of the foundations of the international order."[139] The 38 States further "categorically and irrevocably declare that the commitments undertaken in the field of the human dimension of the CSCE are matters of direct and legitimate concern to all participating States and do not belong exclusively to the internal affairs of the State concerned" (preamble to the Moscow Document). In this way the traditional controversy between East and West on whether the implementation of human rights and fundamental freedoms belongs essentially to the internal affairs of the States concerned has been definitely settled: human rights issues are matters of direct and legitimate concern to all CSCE States.

Impressive results could be achieved in the field of the supervisory mechanism of the human dimension of the CSCE. The Vienna mechanism, which until that time had a strictly intergovernmental character, was supplemented by a rather complicated system of missions of independent rapporteurs or experts. The system provides for voluntary and compulsory missions. The most far-reaching, compulsory form of missions has been provided for as a so-called "emergency procedure". Paragraph 12 of the Moscow Document stipulates the following: "If a participating State considers that a particularly serious threat to the fulfilment of the provisions of the CSCE human dimension has arisen in another participating State, it may, with the support of at least nine other participating States, engage the procedure set forth in paragraph 10". This means that on the basis of this "emergency mechanism" ten CSCE States are entitled to send a mission of rapporteurs to another CSCE State, even against the will of the latter. This major deviation of the principle of consensus and at the same time a major limitation of state sovereignty was agreed upon only at the very last moment. The United Kingdom was fiercely opposed to the introduction of this new mechanism, but due to the overwhelming majority of CSCE States the British government decided to relent. Nevertheless, the UK delegation made an interpretative statement to the effect that "(i)n order to protect public safety or national security the United Kingdom might be obliged to decline or to regulate access at a particular time or to a particular place".[140]

---

139 This statement occurred for the first time in the Geneva Report on National Minorities; see further *infra* section 4.5.7.

140 Moscow CHD Meeting, Journal No. 18, paragraph 6.

4.5.6. Cracow Symposium on the Cultural Heritage (1991)

In the historical environment of the Polish town of Cracow, the CSCE Symposium on the Cultural Heritage took place from 28 May to 7 June 1991. The Cracow Symposium was the second CSCE meeting on cultural issues after the CSCE Cultural Forum in Budapest in 1985. The mandate for this symposium was laid down in the Vienna Concluding Document and it aimed at a discussion of common features of the cultural heritage of the peoples of the CSCE states "with due attention to the originality and diversity of their respective cultures". Two study groups were established. One of them dealt with questions related to increasing the awareness of the cultural heritage, whereas the second focused on the protection and preservation of the cultural heritage. The Cracow Symposium was attended by a great number of non-governmental personalities, who were all involved in cultural issues in a broad sense of the term.

The Cracow Symposium produced a rather lengthy concluding document. In the first paragraph of this document, the CSCE states stressed "that respect for human rights and fundamental freedoms is essential to the full development of cultural creativity". The Symposium as such had a rather technical character, focusing mainly on the preservation of the material cultural heritage.

Albania participated in the symposium as an observer. Representatives of the Baltic states were included in the national delegations of Poland and Denmark, due to the opposition of the Soviet delegation to having these representatives admitted as observers.

4.5.7. Geneva Meeting of Experts on National Minorities (1991)

From 1 to 19 July 1991 a CSCE meeting of experts on national minorities took place in Geneva. Due to the extremely sensitive nature of the subject concerned the meeting did not achieve any impressive results. Although at the very last moment the meeting achieved consensus on the adoption of a substantive concluding document, this could not detract from the fact that the major questions remained unsolved. The participating States did not achieve agreement on the question of how to define the concept of "national minorities". Moreover, the CSCE States could not reach agreement on the question whether national minorities should be granted collective rights. For a number of CSCE States this would have implied a danger of separation of their minorities from the state. Besides, proposals which aimed at the creation of a special supervisory mechanism for the protection of the rights of national minorities were blocked by lack of consensus. This boils down to the fact that only the normal mechanism of the human dimension of the CSCE is available for CSCE states to take action in cases of (alleged) violations of the rights of minorities. This was confirmed in the concluding document of the CHD meeting in Moscow.

It is no surprise that the conflict in Yugoslavia to a great extent determined the course of the discussions in Geneva. This caused a great number of collisions between Yugoslavia and the delegations of neighbouring States.

The result was a rather vague concluding document which enumerates a number of principles (e.g. non-discrimination) which should govern the treatment of national minorities. Moreover, the Geneva Report contains an enumeration of fourteen measures (the co-called *shopping list*) which have been taken by some CSCE States in order to promote the rights of minorities, such as representation in advisory and decision-making bodies, local and autonomous administration, measures in the field of education, and the establishment of permanent mixed commissions to facilitate dialogue between border regions concerned. An important achievement was the following statement: "Issues concerning national minorities, as well as compliance with international obligations and commitments concerning the rights of persons belonging to them, are matters of legitimate international concern and consequently do not constitute exclusively an internal affair of the respective State."

4.5.8. Oslo Seminar of Experts on Democratic Institutions (1991)

From 4 to 15 November 1991 a CSCE Seminar of Experts on Democratic Institutions took place in Oslo. The mandate of the Oslo Seminar, as it has been laid down in the Charter of Paris for a New Europe, stated that the purpose of the Seminar "is to hold discussions of ways and means of consolidating and strengthening viable democratic institutions in participating States, including comparative studies of legislation on human rights and fundamental freedoms". On the basis of this vague and broadly defined mandate the Seminar developed into a large gathering of a great number of often highly-qualified experts who discussed nearly all aspects of the functioning of a democratic society. Although the mandate of the Seminar was phrased in general terms, it was evident that its purpose was in particular to assist the "new democracies" in Central and Eastern Europe in the complicated process of building democratic societies. As such the Oslo Seminar was one of the first instances of the shifting emphasis within the human dimension of the CSCE. Due to the major successes in the area of standard setting, the emphasis within the CSCE shifted towards practical co-operation in the implementation of the CSCE norms which had previously been agreed upon.

The Oslo Seminar was not meant to produce new commitments. Nevertheless, partly due to the lack of experience with strictly expert meetings within the CSCE process, a time-consuming negotiation process on compiling a final report was started. The discussions concerning a report were seriously complicated by the question - which was raised by France time and again - whether a seminar of experts is entitled to make recommendations in the context of the new CSCE in which decision-making power is vested in the Council and the CSO. This procedural issue focused, in particular, on the question whether the Warsaw Office for Free Elections should be transformed into a broader designed Office for Democratic Institutions. The most complicated issue, however, was the relationship between the CSCE and the Council of Europe. At the very last moment, a compromise was achieved, recognizing the "relevant" role of the Council of Europe. France, disappointed that it did not succeed with the term "essential", made a long interpretative statement.

The different nature of the Oslo Seminar was also expressed in the nature of its final report, entitled "Report to the CSCE Council from the CSCE Seminar of Experts on Democratic Institutions". Instead of new commitments, the Report mainly contains a summary of the topics which had been raised at the meetings of the three study groups. The Oslo Report explicitly stated that it did not "purport to express any new commitments on the part of participating States".

4.5.9. Human Dimension Seminars (1992-1993)

4.5.9.1. General

Together with the biennial implementation meetings, CSCE Human Dimension Seminars have been introduced as a successor to the Conference on the Human Dimension of the CSCE. On the instruction of the CSCE Council which decided on the main structures of the human dimension at its Prague meeting (January 1992), the mandate and organizational modalities are laid down in the Helsinki 1992 Document. Human Dimension Seminars are intended to "address specific questions of particular relevance to the Human Dimension and of current political concern" (paragraph VI.17 of the Helsinki Decisions). Unless otherwise decided, seminars will be held at the seat of the ODIHR in Warsaw and will not exceed one week's duration. Their powers are very limited: seminars are not entitled to produce negotiated documents or follow-up programmes (paragraph VI.20 of the Helsinki Decisions). At the first seminars, a limited number of participating states even prevented the submission of summaries by the moderators of the discussion groups in their personal capacity. Only at the third seminar on national minorities was this obstacle overcome, albeit conditionally. The organization of the seminars is entrusted to the ODIHR. The director of the ODIHR acts as the chairman of the seminars.

4.5.9.2. Seminar on Tolerance (1992)

The first Human Dimension Seminar, devoted to tolerance, took place from 16 to 20 November 1992. Although its outcome may be considered to be questionable, the seminar itself set some precedents. One of them is the more or less unhindered access of non-governmental organizations and private citizens to the meetings. During the discussions in plenaries and discussion groups, they were even treated on an equal footing with members of the official national delegations. The expert character of the seminar was also reflected in the fact that several national delegations contained experts on specific issues.

The seminar encompassed three discussion groups. The first one focused on the role of educational and cultural institutions as well as the media in promoting tolerance. The second discussion group debated the role of local authorities in promoting tolerance, whereas the third group discussed legal issues and law enforcement.

The fact that the seminar was not entitled to produce a document, not even in the form of written summaries by the moderators, determined the significance of the meeting to a certain extent. It implied that the link with formal decision-making bodies within the CSCE was extremely weak.

4.5.9.3. Seminar on Migration (1993)

From 20 to 23 April 1993, the second CSCE Human Dimension Seminar took place in Warsaw. This seminar was devoted to the highly topical question of Migration, including Refugees and Displaced Persons. The seminar focused on the prevention of and protection against involuntary migration and the role of international organizations in this area. As already observed, the seminar was not entitled to adopt a negotiated concluding document. However, there was a strong conviction that the role of the CSCE should be enhanced in this field. The political mechanisms which have been developed in the framework of the CSCE were generally considered to be of great importance to prevent, in particular, possible situations of mass-flight, as is occurring at present in the former Yugoslavia.

In comparison to the first Human Dimension Seminar on Tolerance in November 1992, the Seminar on Migration had a much more CSCE-like character. It dealt with concrete and acute political problems which require a quick solution. Moreover, a great number of implementation issues were discussed in detail. In this respect the seminar constituted an important forum for dialogue between NGOs and governmental representatives.

4.5.9.4. Seminar on National Minorities (1993)

The third Human Dimension Seminar on 'Case Studies on National Minorities Issues: Positive Results' was held in Warsaw from 24 to 28 May 1993. As may be derived from its rather unusual title, the seminar focused on the positive solutions to national minority problems. This resulted in a somewhat unreal atmosphere as the serious problems which presently exist were hardly touched upon.

At the beginning of the seminar the High Commissioner on National Minorities, Mr. Max van der Stoel, held a keynote speech. The fact that the High Commissioner was present at this CSCE seminar once more confirmed that although the Commissioner's mandate has been formulated in terms of conflict prevention, a close link with the CSCE human dimension exists. The two discussion groups focused on participation in political, legal and judicial institutions, and on educational and cultural arrangements and confidence-building measures. At this seminar, both moderators were allowed for the first time to deliver their summaries of the two discussion groups in written form, albeit in their personal capacity.

One of the issues discussed at the seminar was the enhancement of the role of the CSCE in the area of the protection of national minorities in addition to the functions performed by other international bodies in this area, such as the UN and the Council of Europe. This discussion focused on the sophisticated political monitoring mechanisms of the CSCE and the ways in which the latter could be improved.

5. MEETINGS OF THE CSCE (COUNCIL OF) FOREIGN MINISTERS

5.1. CSCE Tenth Anniversary Meeting (1985)

The Ministers for Foreign Affairs of the 35 participating states of the CSCE met in Helsinki in 1985 for a ceremonial meeting in order to commemorate the tenth anniversary of the signature of the Final Act of Helsinki. This meeting, which was announced in the Concluding Document of Madrid, took place from 30 July to 1 August. The Helsinki meeting may be considered as the first meeting of Ministers for Foreign Affairs of the CSCE states.

This high-level meeting did not produce a concluding document or a communiqué. The ministers delivered speeches during the official sessions in which they presented their views on major achievements of the CSCE and problems which were still to be solved. The meeting, which was conducted in a constructive spirit, took place on the verge of the important policy changes which were to take place under the guidance of the newly elected Soviet President Gorbachev. The Helsinki meeting was also used for a great number of bilateral meetings between the Foreign Ministers.

5.2. Meeting of the Foreign Ministers of the CSCE participating States in New York (1990)

On 1 and 2 October 1990 the Ministers for Foreign Affairs of all CSCE States convened in New York in order to prepare the CSCE summit meeting which was scheduled to take place in Paris in November of that year.[141] At this first CSCE meeting on American soil general agreement was expressed about the need to strengthen the role of the CSCE and to elaborate new forms of co-operation. However, the Ministers could not yet reach agreement on how to give concrete form to this strengthening of the role of the CSCE. Officially only a convergence of points of view upon this issue could be discerned. The NATO States themselves also stuck to different opinions in certain respects. This disagreement concentrated on the question of which tasks should be assigned to the proposed CSCE Centre for the Prevention of Conflicts. The West German and Italian governments supported the East European views according to which this Centre should be granted a major role in the prevention of conflicts in Europe, whereas the other NATO States wanted to restrict its functions. In their view the Centre should, in particular, supervise the implementation of the so-called confidence- and security-building measures in the military field and constitute a forum for the discussion of any "unusual military activities". As practice showed, the latter view was decisive at the Paris Summit.

From a CSCE perspective, the New York meeting of Foreign Ministers was also interesting because of the fact that the Ministers issued a "Statement on the Crisis in the Gulf", calling upon Iraq to withdraw its troops from Kuwait. This Statement is remarkable because of the fact that it concerned a conflict which in principle was out of the geographical scope of the CSCE process. The issuance of the Statement indicated that 'out-of-area' problems are also relevant to the CSCE.

En marge of this CSCE meeting in New York the then Soviet Foreign Minister, Eduard Shevardnadze, and his US colleague, James Baker, succeeded in solving the main outstanding problems which had so far hampered the successful conclusion of the CFE negotiations. The major problem which could be solved concerned the status of land-based navy aircraft. The final problems could be solved at a lower level just preceding the Paris Summit.

The New York meeting of Foreign Ministers of CSCE states may be considered as a predecessor of the regular CSCE Council meetings which were to start in June 1991.

---

141 See *supra* section 3.2.4.

5.3. First Meeting of the Council in Berlin (June 1991)

On 19 and 20 June 1991, the newly established CSCE Council of (Foreign) Ministers convened for the first time. It was of symbolic significance that this first Council meeting was held in Berlin, the centre of East-West confrontation in the Cold War period. This first CSCE Council meeting was chaired by the German Foreign Minister, Hans-Dietrich Genscher, as the first chairman of the CSCE.

One of the major decisions, taken at the Berlin meeting, was the adoption of the "mechanism for consultation and co-operation with regard to emergency situations". This so-called 'Berlin mechanism' or 'emergency mechanism' provides for procedures which may be used by CSCE States in crisis situations.[142]

The Berlin Council meeting dealt intensively with the Yugoslav problems which threatened to become a civil war. It adopted a political declaration, the message of which was clearly aimed at Croatia and Slovenia not to threaten the territorial integrity of Yugoslavia. Although the Ministers recognized "that it is for the peoples of Yugoslavia themselves to decide on the country's future", they also "expressed their friendly concern and their support for democratic development, unity and territorial integrity of Yugoslavia". Although this was support for the policy of the Yugoslav government in Belgrade, the political declaration of the CSCE could not prevent Croatia and Slovenia from declaring their independence on 25 June. Two days later the Berlin emergency mechanism was applied, but without substantive results.

The Berlin Council also endorsed the Valletta Report on dispute settlement.[143] The Council decided to charge the CSCE Conflict Prevention Centre in Vienna with maintaining the register of qualified candidates from which list parties to a dispute may select members of a so-called 'dispute settlement mechanism'. The Council also recalled the experience of the Permanent Court of Arbitration in The Hague and its Secretary-General which may be drawn upon, if so agreed, in implementing the new CSCE dispute settlement procedure.

The Council welcomed the meeting of parliamentarians from CSCE participating states in Madrid on 2 and 3 April 1991 which resulted in the establishment of the CSCE Parliamentary Assembly. The Ministers, reaffirming "their commitment to strengthening democracy as the only system of government of their countries", looked forward "to the collective

---

[142] See also *supra* section 2.3.1.1.

[143] See *supra* section 4.2.3.

expression of the views of the CSCE Parliamentary Assembly on security and co-operation in Europe and on the future development of the CSCE".

At the Berlin Council meeting the number of participating states increased again to 35 with the admittance of Albania to the CSCE ranks. At the end of 1990 the unification of Germany, with the ensuing disappearance of the German Democratic Republic, had resulted in a decrease of the number of CSCE states to 34. The application of Albania was preceded by a visit of the acting Chairman of the CSCE, the German Minister Genscher, to Tirana. During that visit Albania declared itself to be prepared to accept all CSCE commitments. This was confirmed in the Albanian letter of application, in which the Albanian government declared that it would accept "in their entirety all commitments and responsibilities contained in those documents" (i.e. Helsinki Final Act, Paris Charter and all other CSCE documents). In the same letter, Albania invited a CSCE mission of rapporteurs to visit its country. This invitation, in fact, was a condition for the admittance of Albania to the CSCE, a practice that was also followed in future cases of admittance of states to the CSCE (with the exception of the three Baltic states). The mission to Albania, which took place from 16 to 19 September 1991, was charged with investigating the efforts undertaken by this Balkan state to implement the CSCE commitments.

The Berlin Council meeting had a rather modest significance. It implemented a number of guidelines, set by the Paris Summit in November 1990, in particular in the field of emergency situations. The scope of the decisions in that area, however, was not very impressive. Its decisions on the Yugoslav crisis had only historical value and had hardly any impact upon the developments, if any at all.

5.4. Additional Meeting of the Council in Moscow (September 1991)

On 10 September 1991, on the occasion of the opening of the last meeting of the Conference on the Human Dimension of the CSCE in Moscow, the Council of Ministers convened for an additional meeting. This meeting, which lasted only fifteen minutes, was necessary in order to decide on the applications for admission to the CSCE by some newly-independent states. The meeting, which took place soon after the failed *coup d'état* in the Soviet Union, decided to admit the three newly-independent Baltic states to the CSCE. This ended the practice of representatives of Estonia, Latvia and Lithuania participating in CSCE meetings only as members of delegations of other CSCE states. The latter procedure was an effort to circumvent the Soviet opposition which prevented the Baltic states from official participation in some form or another (observer or full 'membership').

Although other (informal) applications for admittance as a full participating state or for observer status at the CSCE were pending as well, these issues were not debated at the Council meeting. These applications originated, among others, from some Soviet republics. They were sometimes raised during the meeting of the CHD in the following weeks, albeit without concrete results.

5.5. Second Meeting of the Council in Prague (January 1992)

The second meeting of the Council of Ministers of the CSCE took place in Prague on 30 and 31 January 1992. Besides the admittance of ten CIS republics to the CSCE ranks, important decisions were taken in the fields of security issues and the human dimension of the CSCE. It was explicitly decided that the CSCE's "comprehensive concept of security and stability" has to be maintained. This means that the CSCE States stuck to the inter-linkage between the three baskets of the CSCE process.[144]

The Prague meeting took an important decision in the field of the human dimension of the CSCE which constituted a deviation from the fundamental principle of consensus: "The Council decided, in order to develop further the CSCE's capability to safeguard human rights, democracy and the rule of law through peaceful means, that appropriate action may be taken by the Council or the Committee of Senior Officials, if necessary in the absence of the consent of the State concerned, in cases of clear, gross and uncorrected violations of relevant CSCE commitments" (paragraph 16 of the Prague Document on Further Development of CSCE Institutions and Structures). The practical effect of this so-called "consensus-minus-one" principle is limited, however, as the "appropriate action" may only consist of "political declarations or other political steps to apply outside the territory of the State concerned". The principle was first applied by the Helsinki Follow-up Meeting on the basis of which Yugoslavia was suspended from further participation in the CSCE process.

The Council decided that "monitoring and promoting progress in the human dimension remains a key function of the CSCE. Issues related to the human dimension will therefore be considered by the Council or the Committee of Senior Officials (CSO) whenever necessary". In addition, it was laid down that meetings of a short duration may be convened to address clearly-defined issues. The Council decided on the general lines for the future of the human dimension of the CSCE. The Helsinki Follow-up Meeting was charged with elaborating these decisions in greater detail. In

---

[144] See *supra* section 2.2.5.

order to extend practical co-operation among the CSCE States in the human dimension, the Ministers decided to provide additional functions for the Office for Free Elections (with its seat in Warsaw) which will henceforth be called the Office for Democratic Institutions and Human Rights (ODIHR). The ODIHR was also designated as the CSCE institution charged with the tasks in connection with expert and rapporteur missions in the context of the human dimension mechanism. Moreover, it was laid down that the organization of biennial implementation meetings on human dimension issues will be one of the future tasks of the ODIHR.

An important issue in the field of the human dimension of the CSCE is its relationship with the Council of Europe. In general terms the Council of Ministers decided that the ODIHR should "work closely with other institutions active in the field of democratic institution-building and human rights, particularly the Council of Europe and the European Commission for Democracy through Law" in order to "avoid duplication of work".

The Prague Meeting of the Council of Ministers adopted, *inter alia*, a lengthy document containing a number of decisions on institutional questions and certain guidelines for the Helsinki Follow-up Meeting: the "Prague Document on Further Development of CSCE Institutions and Structures". In this document it was laid down that an 'Economic Forum' will be established within the framework of the CSO. This decision aims to give political stimulus to the dialogue on "the transition to and development of free-market economies as an essential contribution to the building of democracy".

The ministers also agreed that the capabilities of the CSCE to engage in crisis management and conflict prevention and resolution should be improved. To this end, the Helsinki Meeting was requested to study possibilities for improving the instruments of fact-finding and rapporteur missions, monitor missions, good offices, counselling and conciliation, and dispute settlement. In addition, peacekeeping was mentioned for the first time as a potential CSCE activity. The Ministers also decided to enlarge the functions of the Conflict Prevention Centre of the CSCE (with its seat in Vienna).

An important development at the Prague Meeting of the Council of Ministers was also the decision to establish official relations with a number of international organizations. At the Prague Meeting seven organizations and institutions were represented: the United Nations, the UN Economic Commission for Europe, the Council of Europe, the Western European Union, NATO, OECD and the European Bank for Reconstruction and Development. In this enumeration the EC is missing, due to the fact that in recent years the European Commission has always been represented at CSCE meetings as part of the delegation of the acting chairman of the EC. Relations may also be established with "other European and transatlantic organizations".

Besides the above-mentioned "Prague Document" and the lengthy Summary of Conclusions, the Council also adopted a Declaration on Non-Proliferation and Arms Transfers.

In comparison to the first Council meeting in Berlin, the Prague meeting was of a more substantive nature. It determined the future development of the CSCE process to a high extent, leaving the details for further elaboration to the subsequent follow-up meeting in Helsinki. This concerned, *inter alia*, the future structure of the human dimension of the CSCE. The decision on the consensus-minus-one principle was of rather limited practical significance, but of considerable symbolic value as it constituted an important deviation from the hitherto sacrosanct principle of consensus. In this way the CSCE is developing into an institution with greater operational powers. The admittance of most former Soviet republics to the CSCE highlighted a change in the character of the CSCE which since that time has become a truly Eurasian and North Atlantic institution.

5.6. Additional Meeting of the Council in Helsinki (March 1992)

The opening of the Follow-up Meeting in Helsinki was preceded by an additional meeting of the CSCE Council in Helsinki. At this meeting, which was held on 24 March 1992, the Council discussed the CSCE response to the tragic developments in and around Nagorny Karabakh. Previous appeals by the Committee of Senior Officials, which were based on the report of the CSCE rapporteur mission to that area of February, had not resulted in an effective cease-fire. Therefore, the Ministers "reiterated in the strongest terms the call for an immediate and effective cease-fire including an active commitment by responsible local commanders to its implementation". The ministers also "issued an appeal for the re-establishment of conditions for confidence and constructive dialogue, including the cessation of measures of economic and political constraint". The major decision of the Council in this respect concerned the establishment of a special peace conference on Nagorny Karabakh under the auspices of the CSCE. This conference "would provide an ongoing forum for negotiations towards a peaceful settlement of the crisis on the basis of the principles, commitments and provisions of the CSCE". The conference was to take place in Minsk with a limited number of participants: in addition to the directly involved states - Armenia and Azerbaijan - the conference would have Belarus, Czechoslovakia, France, Germany, Italy, Russia, Sweden, Turkey and the USA as participants. Representatives of Nagorny Karabakh should also have been involved. Soon after the Council meeting, the Chairman-in-Office (the then Czechoslovak

Foreign Minister, Dienstbier) appointed the Italian Ambassador, Mario Raffaelli, as chairman of the Conference on Nagorny Karabakh.[145]

At this additional Council meeting, the former Soviet republic of Georgia and the former Yugoslav republics of Slovenia and Croatia were admitted to the CSCE. This resulted in another increase in the number of CSCE states to 51 after the dramatic increase at the Prague Council Meeting from 38 to 48 CSCE participating state. During the course of the Helsinki Follow-up Meeting the number of CSCE States further increased to 52, when Bosnia-Herzegovina was admitted to the CSCE on 29 April.[146]

5.7. Third Meeting of the Council in Stockholm (December 1992)

The third meeting of the CSCE Council took place in Stockholm on 14 and 15 December 1992. The Stockholm Council was indicative of CSCE activities in the post-Cold War period, as it spent much time discussing the various bloody crises in the CSCE area, in particular in the former Yugoslavia and in various areas of the former Soviet Union. In addition, the Stockholm meeting dealt with a further development of the preventive diplomacy tools of the CSCE and its structures and institutions as well as its relations with other international bodies.

The Stockholm meeting of Ministers for Foreign Affairs was attended by delegates from only 49 CSCE states, since the former Yugoslavia has been suspended since July 1992 and Tajikistan and Uzbekistan did not send any representatives at all to Stockholm. From the remaining 49 CSCE states, only 43 were represented by their Foreign Ministers. Several other international bodies were represented as well, such as the EC Commission (represented by Commissioner Frans Andriessen as a member of the UK delegation), the WEU, the UN and the Council of Europe. Lord Owen, Co-Chairman of the International Conference on the former Yugoslavia, was present as well. At the meeting, the CSCE chairmanship was transferred from Czechoslovakia to Sweden. It was decided that Italy will succeed Sweden as Chairman-in-Office at the end of 1993.

---

145 Due to disagreements, in particular between Azerbaijan and Armenia, the protracted negotiations to prepare the Minsk Conference which took place in Rome did not yet produce concrete results. Nevertheless, as of summer 1993, the Minsk Group continued its efforts to find ways and means to end the bloody conflict in and around Nagorny Karabakh.

146 The decision to admit Bosnia-Herzegovina was taken by the Committee of Senior Officials at its tenth meeting in Helsinki on 29 April 1992. This decision was to be formally confirmed at the next session of the CSCE Council.

As at many previous CSCE meetings, the Yugoslav tragedy again required much time. In the relevant chapter of the Summary of Conclusions of the Stockholm Meeting, the Ministers stated explicitly that "primary responsibility for the conflict lies with the present leaders of Serbia and Montenegro and with the Serbian forces operating in Bosnia-Herzegovina". The new Chairman-in-Office, the Swedish Foreign Minister, Ms. Margaretha af Ugglas, assisted by the CSCE Troika, was requested to travel to Belgrade prior to the elections in Serbia-Montenegro "to underline to Serbian authorities the stark fate and the increased penalties with which they will be faced".[147] The Ministers did not achieve consensus on a request by some CSCE states (such as Bosnia-Herzegovina) to call upon the UN to lift the arms embargo against Bosnia-Herzegovina. This resulted in the non-committal clause that this issue "should continue to be considered as a matter of importance in the United Nations Security Council". The Ministers also discussed the results of the mission of rapporteurs on Croatia and Bosnia-Herzegovina under the Moscow Human Dimension Mechanism. They welcomed the offer from the rapporteurs to refine their proposals "on making the principle of personal accountability effective, including the possibility of the establishment of an *ad hoc* tribunal".

The Council also made statements on several other problem areas, such as the withdrawal of Russian troops from the territory of the Baltic states, the conflict in the Left-Bank Dniester Areas of Moldova, and the conflicts in and around Nagorny Karabakh, Georgia and Tajikistan. The Ministers welcomed the "visible CSCE presence" in Georgia and requested the parties to co-operate with the CSCE mission.[148] The Council also pointed to the decision to send a CSCE mission of long duration to Estonia as an instrument of preventive diplomacy, aimed at promoting "stability and dialogue between the Estonian- and Russian-speaking communities in Estonia".[149]

The gradual transformation of the CSCE in the direction of a 'normal' international organization was reflected in some organizational decisions. The Council decided to strengthen its contacts with relevant international organizations, in particular with the United Nations. In this context, the CSO

---

147 This visit took place on 17 and 18 December 1992, a few days after the conclusion of the Stockholm meeting.

148 The mission was decided upon at the 18th CSO meeting on 15 December 1992. The mandate of the Mission of the Personal Representative of the Chairman-in-Office for Georgia, led by the Hungarian Ambassador, Istvan Gyarmati, included establishing a framework for political negotiations in Georgia.

149 The mission, headed by the Finnish Ambassador, Klaus Törnudd, started functioning at the beginning of 1993 for a (renewable) period of six months.

was requested to examine the proposal by the UN Secretary-General to the CSCE to seek observer status at the UN. In turn, the CSCE Council decided that henceforth a representative of the UN Secretary-General will be invited to attend the meetings of the CSCE Council and of the CSO. Furthermore, the Council decided that the permanent mission to the UN of the CSCE state which holds the office of CSCE Chairman "will serve as a focal point of the CSCE at the United Nations". The Ministers were also in favour of a further involvement of NGOs in the activities of the CSCE.

Important decisions were also taken in relation to the CSCE structures and institutions. Although the Council stressed that the CSCE "should retain its flexibility and openness, avoiding the creation of a bureaucracy", it decided on the establishment of the post of Secretary General of the CSCE. The Secretary General, appointed by the Council for a period of three years, will act as the representative of the Chairman-in-Office. His tasks include the management of "CSCE structures and operations". This is most visibly reflected in the Council decision to establish a single organizational structure under the direction of the Secretary General for the CSCE bodies in Prague (the Secretariat) and Vienna (CPC). As the CSCE's chief administrative officer, the Secretary General will also oversee the work of the ODIHR in Warsaw. Another decision of the Council concerned regular meetings of representatives of the CSCE states in Vienna during periods between CSO sessions.[150]

At the Stockholm meeting, the Council decided to appoint Mr. Max van der Stoel as the first CSCE High Commissioner on National Minorities. The Ministers "encouraged the High Commissioner to analyse carefully potential areas of tension, to visit any participating State and to undertake wide-ranging discussions at all levels with parties directly involved in the issues".[151]

An important decision by the Council concerned the peaceful settlement of disputes. The Ministers endorsed the results of the Geneva meeting of experts on dispute settlement of October 1992.[152] These texts included amendments and additions to the Valletta Mechanism and the text of a draft Convention on Conciliation and Arbitration within the CSCE. At the Stockholm meeting, this Convention was signed by 29 CSCE states. This

---

150 See also *supra* section 2.2.1.

151 See further *supra* section 2.3.1.4.

152 See *supra* section 4.2.4.

meant that for the first time in the history of the CSCE a substantive CSCE document was adopted which was not applicable to all CSCE states.[153]

The Council also granted the CSCE its first official logo for which purpose the logotype of the Stockholm Council meeting was to be used.

The Council admitted the Czech Republic and the Slovak Republic as participating states from 1 January 1993. This decision was necessary as a result of the dissolution of the former Czechoslovakia into two new states. At first, Liechtenstein raised some problems concerning the admittance of both new states to the CSCE because of some outstanding problems between Liechtenstein and Czechoslovakia.[154] Finally, consensus was achieved, although the parties concerned made interpretative statements on the question. The request by Macedonia for admittance to the CSCE ranks, however, was not accepted due to the persistent Greek opposition to the use of the term "Macedonia" in the official name of the new state.

The significance of the Stockholm meeting was related, *inter alia*, to the institutional development of the CSCE. The establishment of the post of Secretary General and the further development of official relations with international organizations point to the transition of the CSCE into a more traditional international organization. The opening of the Convention on Conciliation and Arbitration for signature was another indication of this development. The relevance of the Council meeting for the solution of the increasing number of conflicts in the CSCE area, however, appears to be very limited.

6. MEETINGS OF THE COMMITTEE OF SENIOR OFFICIALS

Since its establishment at the Paris Summit Meeting in November 1990, the Committee of Senior Officials has developed into the real 'workshop' of the CSCE. Upon its establishment at the Paris Summit in November 1990, nothing had been arranged about the frequency of its meetings. It was only determined that the meetings will not exceed two days, unless otherwise agreed. At the Berlin Council meeting (June 1991), the CSCE emergency mechanism was adopted which provides for the possibility of special meetings of the CSCE in emergency situations.

The position of the CSO was further strengthened by the Council at its Prague meeting (January 1992). The Prague Council decided that between Council meetings the CSO "will be responsible for overview, management

---

153 See further *supra* section 2.3.1.3.

154 The problems concerned a dispute relating to Czechoslovakia's expropriation of Liechtenstein property after the Second World War.

and co-ordination and will act as the Council's agent in taking appropriate decisions". On that occasion it was determined that the CSO should meet at least every three months. In addition, the CSO was given the power to delegate tasks to other CSCE institutions or to open-ended *ad hoc* groups of CSCE states for specific purposes.[155] Also, the CSO was granted additional powers in relation to all CSCE areas and other CSCE bodies.

The Helsinki Follow-up Meeting also decided on a further enlargement of the powers of the CSO, in particular in the area of early warning, conflict prevention and crisis management. Concerning early warning and preventive action, the Helsinki Document (July 1992) determined that the CSO, "acting as the Council's agent, will have primary responsibility in this regard".[156] In December 1992, at the third Council meeting in Stockholm, the strong position of the CSO in the overall activities of the CSCE was confirmed. In addition, the Council instructed representatives of the CSCE states to meet regularly in Vienna during periods between CSO sessions. This was the basis for the creation of the very frequently-meeting CSO Vienna Group.[157] The CSO also has general supervision over activities in relation to the human dimension of the CSCE which is reflected, *inter alia*, in the decisions on the organizational modalities of all human dimension meetings, the CSO influence on the use of the Human Dimension Mechanism and the reports of missions under the mechanism.

As a result, the CSO has become the central policy- and decision-making body of the CSCE, not only in the area of conflict prevention and conflict management, but also in the area of the human dimension of the CSCE.

Since its first meeting on 28 and 29 January 1991, the frequency of CSO meetings has increased constantly. As a matter of fact, it has convened much more often than the minimum four times a year which was laid down in the Prague Council decisions. At these CSO meetings, characterized by a short duration (as a rule two days) but with night-long sessions as a result of the overloaded agendas, the CSO has discussed a great number of issues, ranging from minor organizational issues to the increasing number of violent conflicts in (and between) various CSCE states. On most of these issues, concrete decisions were taken.

An issue which has taken much time at CSO meetings is the Yugoslav tragedy since the outbreak of the hostilities in the summer of 1991. Although

---

155 Paragraphs 1-2 of the Prague Document on Further Development of CSCE Institutions and Structures.

156 Paragraph III.4 of the Helsinki Decisions of the Helsinki 1992 Document.

157 The CSO Vienna Group meets, as a rule, once a week. See further *supra* section 2.2.1.

the CSO - and the CSCE as a whole - could only dispose of instruments with a rather limited scope, it has made great efforts to contribute to stopping the violence and to finding ways and means to solve the conflict in peaceful ways. This has resulted in an impressive set of documents, adopted by the CSO on the crisis in the former Yugoslavia. These decisions concern, *inter alia*, appeals to the fighting parties to stop the bloodshed and to agree on a durable cease-fire, the establishment of long-term missions in certain areas in the former Yugoslavia (Sandjak, Kosovo, Vojvodina, Macedonia) and neighbouring countries, the establishment of Sanctions Assistance Missions and an EC/CSCE Sanctions Co-ordinator to help implement the UN-imposed embargoes against Serbia-Montenegro, the despatch of human rights missions of rapporteurs to certain areas, etc. Together with the relevant documents, adopted by other CSCE bodies, the size of the CSCE 'file' on the conflict in the former Yugoslavia has become considerable.

As a result of the outbreak of ever more (violent) conflicts, the CSO agenda has been enlarged as well. Efforts have been undertaken to help solve, in particular, the conflict in and around Nagorny-Karabakh. The Council decision to organize a CSCE peace conference on this conflict, known as the so-called 'Minsk Conference', could not yet be implemented. Many other efforts, undertaken by the CSO, aimed at solving the conflict (such as appeals for cease-fires, the establishment of humanitarian corridors, the despatch of military and civilian observers) were also not successful. On several occasions, the CSO also dealt with the conflicts in, *inter alia*, the Baltic states (in particular concerning the large Russian communities), Moldova (concerning the conflict in Trans-Dniestria), Georgia (concerning Ossetia and Abkhazia), Tajikistan and Azerbaijan (the internal constitutional crisis in June 1993). Other problem areas were dealt with as well. In a number of cases, the CSO decided to make use of the instruments of long-term missions, special *ad hoc* missions of rapporteurs, personal representatives of the Chairman-in-Office, and visits by the Chairman-in-Office him/herself on behalf of the CSCE.

All this has resulted in a situation which indicates that the CSO and its Vienna Group have become the focal point within the CSCE concerning conflict prevention and crisis management. In addition, the Vienna-based Conflict Prevention Centre and its Consultative Committee deal with the more technical military issues at stake. The CSO involvement also concerns the activities of new CSCE instruments such as the CSCE High Commissioner on National Minorities. In April 1993, the CSO welcomed and endorsed the conclusions and recommendations of the High Commissioner in relation to his first missions. These missions concerned the Baltic states and the Hungarian minority in Slovakia.

In the area of organizational issues, the CSO extensively discussed the administrative, financial and personnel arrangements for the various permanent CSCE bodies on several occasions. Time was also devoted to deciding on the organizational modalities of *ad hoc* meetings on specialized issues (human dimension seminars, Mediterranean Seminar, etc.). Once a year, the CSO also convenes as the Economic Forum, for the first time in March 1993. In addition, the CSO prepares the meetings of the CSCE Council.

'Membership'[158] issues have also been frequently discussed. In the spring of 1992, during the course of the Helsinki Follow-up Meeting, the status of the former Yugoslavia (Serbia-Montenegro) was often debated and this resulted first in the suspension of the Yugoslav rights concerning the decision-making on the Yugoslav conflict (May 1992) and finally in the complete suspension of Yugoslavia from participation in CSCE meetings (July 1993 and since then renewed several times). The application for admittance by Macedonia was also often discussed, but blocked because of Greek opposition to the name 'Macedonia' for the new State. In April 1993 Macedonia was granted observer status as "the Former Yugoslav Republic Macedonia".

As a rule, meetings of the CSO take place at the seat of the CSCE Secretariat in Prague, unless specific reasons point to another meeting place. Such reasons can be meetings of the CSCE Council or a Follow-up Meeting. Until the end of June 1993, 22 meetings of the CSO had taken place, most of which were in Prague. Other meetings of the CSO were held in Vienna, Berlin, Helsinki and Stockholm: the first CSO meeting took place in Vienna,[159] two CSO meetings took place in Berlin and Stockholm, prior to meetings of the CSCE Council, and several meetings took place in Helsinki *en marge* of the Follow-up Meeting (March-July 1992). On the basis of the Berlin emergency mechanism, some emergency meetings of the CSO were organized as well, all dealing with the Yugoslav crisis. The CSO Vienna Group met for the first time on 18 January 1993. Up to the end of June 1993, there have been 18 meetings of the CSO Vienna Group.

---

158 Formally the CSCE does not (yet) have any member states, as it is not yet a traditional international organization because of the lack of a legal basis. As a political process, the official terminology is still 'participating State of the CSCE'.

159 At that moment, January 1991, the CSCE Secretariat in Prague had not yet been established.

7. MEETINGS OF THE CSCE PARLIAMENTARY ASSEMBLY

7.1. Preparatory meeting in Madrid (1991)

As mentioned above (section 2.2.1), no agreement was possible on the establishment of a CSCE Parliamentary Assembly at the CSCE Summit Meeting in Paris in November 1990. This was due to disagreement about the possible role of the Parliamentary Assembly of the Council of Europe in relation to the new CSCE Assembly. An original idea was to base the new CSCE parliamentary body on the existing parliamentary assembly of the Council of Europe. This option had been agreed upon by the NATO states: at the NATO Summit Meeting in London in July 1990, the heads of state and government of the NATO Member States issued a "London Declaration on a transformed North Atlantic Alliance" in which this idea was explicitly mentioned. The suggestion was enthusiastically taken up by the Council of Europe with counter-productive effects. In contrast to the NATO Declaration, some CSCE states, in particular the USA, later on blocked any role of the Parliamentary Assembly of the Council of Europe.

The reasons for this change of mind in the US administration were obvious: the USA is not a member state of the Council of Europe which is a strictly European body and the Americans were not in favour of granting the Council of Europe an institutionalized place within the CSCE process. Another, less obvious reason for the American change of mind was the fact that apparently the American administration at the NATO meeting acted without consulting the American Congress which caused serious problems in relations with the parliament.

As the question could not be solved at the Paris Summit, the *Charter of Paris for a New Europe* referred the issue for further 'review' to the first meeting of the newly established CSCE Council.

However, the issue was settled before the first Council meeting. Delegations from the parliaments of the 34 CSCE states met in Madrid on 2 and 3 April 1991 which resulted in the decision to establish a CSCE Parliamentary Assembly which was to function independently from existing parliamentary bodies. It was decided that the new Assembly, which would have 245 members, would meet once a year for a one week session in one of the capitals of the CSCE states. Remarkable decisions concerned the composition of the body and its decision-making process. In contrast to existing CSCE practices, the parliaments of the CSCE states are represented according to the size of their states. This means that a state such as the USA received 17 seats in the Assembly, whereas, for instance, the Netherlands were granted 10 seats. In spite of objections from the Soviet representatives, who wanted to maintain the principle of consensus, the meeting decided that decisions by the new Assembly may be taken by majority vote. The task of the new Assembly would be to advise the CSCE Council and the CSCE participating states. From a formal perspective, the CSCE Parliamentary Assembly does not appear to be part of the formal CSCE process, but only an independent assembly of parliamentarians from the CSCE states. In this respect, the CSCE Assembly fully resembles the North Atlantic Assembly. In practice a close link with the CSCE process exists. It has to be noted, however, that this link has so far been is rather of a formal than of a substantive nature.

The decisions, taken at the Madrid meeting, were laid down in the Final Resolution Concerning the Establishment of the CSCE Parliamentary Assembly.

7.2. First meeting in Budapest (1992)

During the final days of the Helsinki Follow-up Meeting, the CSCE Parliamentary Assembly met for its inaugural session in Budapest from 3 to 5 July 1992. It adopted a 'Budapest Declaration', containing a number of recommendations for the Helsinki Summit which was to meet a few days later. The Assembly appeared to be in favour of a considerable strengthening of the role of the CSCE in the security field, which should also include a legal basis. The Budapest Declaration also favoured a more active role for parliaments and parliamentarians in the prevention, management and settlement of conflicts. In the field of the human dimension of the CSCE the Parliamentary Assembly expressed its concern "that existing CSCE mechanisms such as the improved Moscow Mechanism on the Human Dimension are not sufficiently used".

The tragic conflict in the former Yugoslavia constituted a subject of major concern at the meeting. The Assembly blamed all parties, although the leadership of Serbia and the Bosnian Serbs were considered to be the main instigators of the dirty war.

The Assembly decided to create a permanent secretariat which will be temporarily located in Copenhagen. Ilkka Suominen, the President of the Finnish parliament and the former Minister of Industry, was elected as the new President of the Parliamentary Assembly. Delegates from Canada, Denmark, Hungary, Russia and Turkey were elected as vice-presidents.

7.3. Second meeting in Helsinki (1993)

From 6 to 9 July 1993, the second meeting of the Parliamentary Assembly took place in Helsinki. The Assembly adopted a four-part declaration, dealing with human rights, disarmament, economic co-operation and the

Yugoslav crisis. In the last mentioned, the Assembly supports Macedonia's application for admittance to the CSCE.

A remarkable step was the Assembly recommendation that "the CSCE parliaments appoint and co-ordinate delegations in order to send them to Turkey with the purpose of establishing a permanent and close observation of the situation of the Kurdish population". This recommendation resulted from the serious concern of the Assembly about the wave of violence and terrorism by radical Kurdish groups in Turkey as well as about the treatment of minorities by the Turkish authorities.

On organizational issues, the Assembly recommended the introduction of decision-making by majority vote in the CSCE as well as the establishment of a security committee of limited composition, based on the model of the UN Security Council.

I

DOCUMENTS

OF

CSCE MEETINGS

FINAL RECOMMENDATIONS OF THE HELSINKI CONSULTATIONS

Helsinki, 8 June 1973

(1) The participants in the Helsinki Consultations on the question of the Conference on Security and Co-operation in Europe, representing the Governments of States listed in the annex, recommend to their Governments that this Conference should be convened under the conditions specified below, concerning its organization, agenda and the related instructions, participation, date, place, rules of procedure and financial arrangements.

(2) The participants expressed their collective agreement to these Recommendations on 8 June, 1973.

(3) Each State entitled to participate in the Conference will inform the Government of Finland, within the time limits laid down in Chapter 3, of its decision to take part in this Conference, thereby indicating its intention to do so on the basis of the Final Recommendations of the Helsinki Consultations. The Government of Finland will inform all States entitled to participate of the communications received in this respect.

(4) The Government of Finland will take the necessary measures, in accordance with the arrangements provided for in the Final Recommendations, to organize the first stage of the Conference.

(5) **Index of recommendations**

1. Organization of the Conference
2. Agenda and the Related Instructions
3. Participation, Contributions, Guests
4. Date
5. Place
6. Rules of Procedure
7. Financial Arrangements

Annex: List of Participating Countries

1. Organization of the Conference on Security and Co-operation in Europe

(6) The Conference on Security and Co-operation in Europe will take place in three stages:

(a) Stage I

(7) The first stage will consist of a meeting of the Ministers for Foreign Affairs of the participating States. In accordance with the recommendations of the Helsinki Consultations, the Ministers will adopt the rules of procedure, the agenda and the instructions of the working bodies of the Conference, together with the other arrangements relating to the conduct of the Conference. The Ministers will state the views of their Governments on the problems relating to security and co-operation in Europe. Should they so wish they will put forward, for consideration in the course of the second stage, proposals relating to the various topics on the agenda.

(b) Stage II

(8) The second stage will comprise the work of the specialized committees and sub-committees whose instructions are defined in Chapter 2 of these recommendations (points I, II and III of the agenda). Within this framework and on the basis of the proposals submitted either by the Ministers for Foreign Affairs, or subsequently by the delegations of the participating States, the committees and sub-committees will prepare drafts of declarations, recommendations, resolutions or any other final documents. The participating States will be represented in these bodies by such delegates and experts as they shall designate for the purpose.

(9) A Co-ordinating Committee, composed of representatives appointed by the Ministers for Foreign Affairs, will meet periodically during the second stage of the Conference. It will co-ordinate the activities of the committees and assemble the results of their work with a view to the final stage of the Conference. The Co-ordinating Committee shall also be entrusted with the execution of the tasks defined in point IV of the agenda, as stated in Chapter 2 of the present recommendations. It will furthermore, submit to the participating Governments such recommendations as it may consider useful regarding the conduct of the Conference, especially the organization of its third stage.

(c) Stage III

(10) In the light of the recommendations drawn up by the Co-ordinating Committee, the Conference will meet for its third stage.

(11) The level of representation at the third stage will be decided by the participating States during the Conference, before the end of the second stage.

(12) The Conference will adopt its final documents, in formal session, at the close of this third stage.

2. Agenda and the related instructions

I. Questions related to security in Europe

(13) In carrying out the instructions set out below, the Committee will bear in mind the wider objective of promoting better relations among participating States and ensuring conditions in which their people can live in peace free from any threat to or attempt against their security.

(14) In its work the Committee will proceed from the premise that the strengthening of security in Europe is not directed against any State or continent and should constitute an important contribution to world peace and security.

(15) In considering questions relating to security in Europe, the Committee will bear in mind the broader context of world security and in particular the relationship which exists between security in Europe and in the Mediterranean area.

(16) The Committee will be assisted in its tasks by the appropriate Sub-Committees.

1.

(17) (a) The Committee/Sub-Committee is charged with the task of considering and stating in conformity with the purposes and principles of the United Nations those basic principles which each participating State is to respect and apply in its relations with all other participating States, irrespective of their political, economic or social systems, in order to ensure the peace and security of all participating States.

(18) The principles to be stated shall be included in a document of appropriate form to be submitted by the Committee for adoption by the Conference. It shall express the determination of the participating States to respect and apply the principles equally and unreservedly in all aspects to their mutual relations and co-operation, in order to ensure to all participating States the benefits resulting from the application of these principles by all.

(19) The reaffirmation, with such clarifications and additions as may be deemed desirable, and the precise statement, in conformity with the purposes and principles of the United Nations, of the following principles of primary significance guiding the mutual relations of the participating States, are deemed to be of particular importance:

- sovereign equality, respect for the rights inherent in sovereignty;
- refraining from the threat or use of force;
- inviolability of frontiers;
- territorial integrity of States;
- peaceful settlement of disputes;
- non-intervention in internal affairs;
- respect for human rights and fundamental freedoms, including the freedom of thought, conscience, religion or belief;
- equal rights and self-determination of peoples;
- co-operation among States;
- fulfilment in good faith of obligations under international law.

(20) In discharging itself of these tasks, the Committee/Sub-Committee shall take into account in particular the Declaration on Principles of International Law concerning Friendly Relations and Co-operation among States in accordance with the Charter of the United Nations.

(21) (b) The Committee/Sub-Committee shall give expression to the idea that respect for the above-listed principles will encourage the development of normal and friendly relations among the participating States as well as of their political contacts which in turn would contribute to the furthering of their co-operation. It shall also consider proposals designed to give effect to refraining from the threat or use of force. In this context, it shall study proposals for and undertake the elaboration of a method for the peaceful settlement of disputes among participating States.

2.

(22) The Committee/Sub-Committee shall have regard to the fact that the participating States are desirous of eliminating any causes of tension that may exist among them and of contributing to the strengthening of peace and security in the world, bearing in mind the fact that efforts aimed at disarmament complement political détente and are essential elements in a process in which all participating States have a vital interest.

(23) In order to strengthen confidence and to increase stability and security, the Committee/Sub-Committee shall submit to the Conference appropriate proposals on confidence-building measures such as the prior notification of major military manoeuvres on a basis to be specified by the Conference, and the exchange of observers by invitation at military manoeuvres under mutually acceptable conditions. The Committee/Sub-Committee will also study the question of prior notification of major military movements and submit its conclusions.

(24) The Committee/Sub-Committee shall pay due attention to the views expressed by participating States on the various subjects mentioned in the preceding paragraphs, on the particular interest they attach thereto, especially from the point of view of their own security and of their desire to be informed about the relevant developments.

II. Co-operation in the fields of economics, of science and technology and of the environment

(25) The Committee shall be responsible for drawing up a draft final document/documents containing guidelines and concrete recommendations which could stimulate common efforts for increased co-operation in the fields of economics, science and technology and environment, which might guide the participating States in their mutual relations in these areas and which they might utilize in the conclusion of bilateral or multilateral agreements, as well as recommendations on specific measures for the development of co-operation which could be agreed by participating States.

(26) The Committee will bear in mind the contribution which such co-operation could make to the reinforcement of peace and security in Europe. It will also bear in mind the interests of developing countries and regions and the positive effects which the broadening of co-

operation among participating States could have on world economic relations.

(27) The Committee, having in mind the foregoing, shall study ways and means that would make it possible, by mutual agreement among participating States, to facilitate, with due regard for the diversity of economic and social systems and under conditions of reciprocity of advantages and obligations, the development of trade and cooperation in the various fields of economic activity, science, technology and in the field of the environment. In this regard, it will in particular take account of the work of the United Nations Economic Commission for Europe.

(28) In considering questions relating to co-operation in Europe covered by this mandate, the Committee will bear in mind the relationship which exists between such co-operation in Europe and in the Mediterranean area.

(29) The Committee in its final draft/drafts will formulate relevant proposals, based on full respect for the principles guiding relations among the participating States enumerated in the terms of reference for the Committee on item I of the agenda.

(30) The Committee, assisted by the appropriate Sub-Committees, will examine the following questions:

1. Commercial exchanges

(31) The Committee/Sub-Committee will examine general provisions designed to promote trade and the exchange of services between participating States. It could discuss general problems relating to most favoured nation treatment. It could also examine measures aiming at the reduction or progressive elimination of all kinds of obstacles to the development of trade.

(32) The Committee/Sub-Committee will examine specific measures designed to facilitate commercial transactions and the exchange of services, such as measures aiming at the improvement of

- business contacts and facilities
- the exchange of information on commercial opportunities and specific trading conditions
- provisions for the settlement of commercial disputes including various forms of arbitration.

2. Industrial co-operation and projects of common interest

(33) The Committee/Sub-Committee will study the forms and modalities of industrial co-operation and will examine the various measures by which participating States could encourage the development of this co-operation using, as appropriate, the framework of bilateral or multilateral intergovernmental agreements.

(34) The Committee/Sub-Committee will examine, in particular, the measures which governments could take to create conditions favourable to this co-operation between competent organizations, firms and enterprises of participating States. It will bear in mind that the specific forms of such co-operation should be settled bilaterally unless otherwise agreed upon by the participants. This examination could bear on the various forms of co-operation, such as co-operation in production and sales, on the exchange of information concerning the possibilities of industrial co-operation, on the improvement of conditions for setting up projects, and on other measures which could develop and facilitate various forms of industrial co-operation.

(35) The Committee/Sub-Committee will also examine the possibilities of encouraging projects of common interest and of working out, where relevant, recommendations in this respect.

(36) This examination could bear on the possibilities of implementing projects of common interest in the fields of energy resources, exploitation of raw materials and, when appropriate, of transport and communications.

3. Science and technology

(37) The Committee/Sub-Committee shall consider proposals for the development of co-operation in the field of science and technology, taking into account already existing or planned co-operation in this field, with a view to facilitating, through such means as the improvement of contacts and information, access to new developments in science and technology, and to contributing to the most effective solution of problems of common interest and to the betterment of the conditions of human life.

(38) These proposals, in particular, shall be concerned with the areas where there are the most favourable prerequisites for such co-operation, the forms and methods for its implementation, as well as with the obstacles that hinder such co-operation and measures for their removal. In the consideration of these questions, the Committee/Sub-Committee

will seek to build on existing practices and take into account the possibilities and capabilities of relevant existing international organizations.

4. Environment

(39) The Committee/Sub-Committee shall be responsible for discussing questions of environmental protection and improvement and in particular for determining the fields that are important for the participating States and can best lend themselves to the development of co-operation between them, such as: protection of the seas surrounding Europe, of the waters and of the atmosphere; improvement of environmental and living conditions, especially in towns; protection of nature and of its resources.

(40) The Committee/Sub-Committee shall examine and put forward the most appropriate bilateral and multilateral forms and methods of co-operation, including co-operation on a regional and subregional basis, for the various fields that have been determined. In the consideration of these questions, the Committee/Sub-Committee will seek to build on existing practices and take into account the possibilities and capabilities of the relevant existing international organizations.

5. Co-operation in other areas

(41) The Committee/Sub-Committee could examine the following questions:

- problems relating to the development of transport and communications between participating States;
- promotion of tourism by the exchange of information, techniques and the results of practical experience and by the study of appropriate measures;
- economic and social aspects of migrant labour;
- training of personnel in various fields of economic activity;
- such other questions as may be decided by common agreement.

III. Co-operation in humanitarian and other fields

(42) With the aim of contributing to the strengthening of peace and understanding among the peoples of the participating States and to the spiritual enrichment of the human personality, without distinction as to race, sex, language or religion and irrespective of their political, economic and social systems, the Committee, assisted by the appropriate Sub-Committees, shall be charged with examining all possibilities of co-operation conducive to creating better conditions for increased cultural and educational exchanges, for broader

dissemination of information, for contacts between people, and for the solution of humanitarian problems. In this connection, it shall not only draw upon existing forms of co-operation, but shall also work out new ways and means appropriate to these aims.

(43) The Committee in its final document will formulate relevant proposals, based on full respect for the principles guiding relations among the participating States enumerated in the terms of reference for the Committee on item I of the agenda.

(44) The Committee shall also consider to what extent existing institutions could be used to achieve these aims.

1. Human contacts

(45) The Committee/Sub-Committee shall prepare proposals to facilitate freer movement and contacts, individually or collectively, privately or officially, among persons, institutions and organizations of the participating States.

(46) With a view to contributing to the favourable examination and settlement of relevant matters by the States concerned under mutually acceptable conditions, it shall pay particular attention to:

(a) contacts and regular meetings on a basis of family ties; reunification of families; marriage between nationals of different States;

(b) travel for personal or professional reasons; improvement of conditions for tourism, on an individual or collective basis;

(c) meetings among young people; expansion of contacts and competitions, particularly in the field of sport.

2. Information

(47) The Committee/Sub-Committee shall prepare proposals to facilitate the freer and wider dissemination of information of all kinds. In doing so it shall pay particular attention to:

(a) improving the circulation of, and access to, oral, printed, filmed and broadcast information and extending the exchange of information;

(b) encouraging co-operation in these fields of information on a basis of short or long term agreements;

(c) improving conditions under which journalists from one participating State exercise their profession in another participating State.

3. Co-operation and exchanges in the field of culture

(48) The Committee/Sub-Committee shall prepare proposals aimed at extending and improving co-operation and exchanges in the various fields of culture and shall indicate the components and objectives of a consistent long-term development of such exchanges. In its work, it shall bear in mind the results of the Intergovernmental Conference on Cultural Policies in Europe, Helsinki, June 1972 including the broader concept of culture outlined by that Conference.

(49) The Committee/Sub-Committee shall consider in particular:

(a) Extension of relations among competent government agencies and non-governmental bodies dealing with matters of culture;

(b) Promotion of fuller mutual knowledge of and access to achievements in literature, art and other fields of cultural activity;

(c) Improvement of facilities for contacts and exchanges in the above-mentioned spheres;

(d) Extension of contacts and co-operation among creative artists and people engaged in cultural activities;

(e) Common search for new fields and forms of co-operation; co-operation in the investigation of the social aspects of culture;

(f) Encouragement of such forms of cultural co-operation as: international events in the fields of art, film, theatre, music, folklore, etc.; book fairs and exhibitions; joint projects in the field of protection of monuments and sites; co-production and exchange of films and of radio and television programmes.

(50) The Committee/Sub-Committee while considering the role of States in co-operation in the field of culture will bear in mind the contribution that national minorities or regional cultures could make to it within the framework of respect for principles referred to above.

4. Co-operation and exchanges in the field of education

(51) The Committee/Sub-Committee shall prepare proposals aimed at broadening co-operation and exchanges in the fields of education and

science on a short or long-term basis. These proposals shall be carried out bilaterally and multilaterally as appropriate, between participating States and non-governmental bodies. The Committee/Sub-Committee shall consider in particular:

(a) Expansion of links between State institutions and non-governmental bodies whose activities are concerned with questions of education and science.

(b) Improved access, under mutually acceptable conditions, for students, teachers and scholars from the participating States to each other's educational, cultural and scientific institutions, and a more exact assessment of the problems of comparison and equivalence between academic degrees and diplomas.

(c) Encouragement of the study of the languages and civilizations of other peoples for the purpose of creating favourable conditions for promoting wider acquaintance with the culture of each country.

(d) Exchange of experience in teaching methods in various fields including those used in adult education and exchanges in the field of teaching materials.

(52) The Committee/Sub-Committee while considering the role of States in co-operation in the field of education will bear in mind the contribution that national minorities or regional cultures could make to it within the framework of respect for principles referred to above.

IV. Follow-up to the conference

(53) The Co-ordinating Committee shall consider, on the basis of the progress made at the Conference such measures as may be required to give effect to the decisions of the Conference and to further the process of improving security and developing co-operation in Europe. Having considered proposals to this effect, including proposals of an organizational nature, it shall make any recommendations which it deems necessary. In examining the follow-up of the Conference, the Committee shall also consider the contributions which it believes could be asked from existing international organizations.

3. Participation, contributions, guests

(a) Participation

(54) All European States, the United States and Canada shall be entitled to take part in the Conference on Security and Co-operation in Europe. If any of these States wishes to attend as an observer it may do so. In that case, its representatives may attend all stages of the Conference and of its working bodies, but shall not participate in the taking of decisions. Such a State may decide later to accept these decisions or some of them under the conditions defined by the Conference.

(55) States referred to in the first sentence of the paragraph above wishing to participate in the Conference or to attend as observers must so inform the Finnish Government at the latest on 25 June 1973.

(b) Contributions

(56) The Conference and its working bodies will acquaint themselves, in such manner as they may determine, with the points of view held by non-participating States on the subject of the various agenda items.

(57) States situated in regions adjacent to Europe and to whom reference is made in the provisions of Chapter 2, and in particular those of the Mediterranean States which have already expressed their interest in stating their views to the Conference, are especially envisaged by this Chapter.

(58) The Co-ordinating Committee may decide, by consensus, the means by which the working bodies of the Conference may consult appropriate international organizations, on the subject of the various agenda items.

(c) Guests

(59) The Secretary-General of the United Nations will be invited as guest of honour to the inaugural session of the Conference.

4. Date

(60) 1. The Conference on Security and Co-operation in Europe shall be opened on 3 July 1973 at 11.30 a.m.

(61) 2. The date of the opening of the second stage shall be determined by the Ministers during the first stage.

(62) 3. The date of the opening of the third stage shall be decided during the second stage by agreement among the participating States on the basis of the recommendations of the Co-ordinating Committee.

5. Place of the conference

(63) Taking into account with appreciation the invitation by the Government of Finland, having in view practical considerations and rotation, the first stage of the Conference on Security and Co-operation in Europe will be held in Helsinki; the second stage will be held in Geneva; the third stage will be held in Helsinki.

6. Rules of procedure

(64) The States participating in the Conference on Security and Co-operation in Europe shall conduct their work as follows:

(65) 1. All States participating in the Conference shall do so as sovereign and independent States and in conditions of full equality. The Conference shall take place outside military alliances.

(66) 2. The representation of the participating States at each stage of the Conference shall be determined in accordance with the provisions laid down in Chapter 1 of these Final Recommendations.

(67) 3. The working bodies of the Conference shall be the Coordinating Committee, the Committees and the Sub-Committees. These working bodies will function during the second stage of the Conference. However, the Co-ordinating Committee will meet at the site of the second stage before the opening of the second stage in order to settle questions relating to the organization of that stage.

(68) The working bodies of the Conference may, if they so wish, set up such working groups as they may consider useful. The working bodies and working groups of the Conference shall be open to all participating States.

(69) 4. Decisions of the Conference shall be taken by consensus. Consensus shall be understood to mean the absence of any objection expressed by a Representative and submitted by him as constituting an obstacle to the taking of the decision in question.

5. Chairmanship

(70) A. The Chair at the inaugural and closing meetings of the first stage of the Conference shall be taken by the Minister for Foreign Affairs of the host country. The Chair at other meetings shall be taken on a basis of rotation, as follows:

(a) The Chair at each meeting shall be taken by the Minister for Foreign Affairs of a different participating State, in an order established in accordance with a list selected by lot country by country before the end of the Helsinki Consultations;

(b) If the Conference should meet both in the morning and in the afternoon of the same day, the two meetings shall be regarded as constituting two distinct meetings;

(c) In the interval between meetings of the Conference, the functions of the Chair shall be exercised by that Minister for Foreign Affairs who presided over the immediately preceding meeting of the Conference;

(d) Should a Minister for Foreign Affairs be prevented from taking the Chair, it shall be taken by the Minister for Foreign Affairs of the country next in the order established.

(71) B. The Chair at the inaugural meetings of the working bodies of the Conference shall be taken by the Representative of the host country. Thereafter, the office of Chairman shall be filled as follows:

(a) The Chairman of the Co-ordinating Committee and the Chairmen of the Committees shall be designated on a basis of daily rotation, in French alphabetical order, starting from a letter drawn by lot;

(b) The Chairmen of Sub-Committees and of other subsidiary bodies of the Conference shall be designated on a basis of rotation in accordance with practical arrangements to be established at the appropriate time by the bodies in question.

(72) Where necessary, a rapporteur shall be designated by consensus.

(73) C. The provisions laid down for the meetings of the first stage shall be applicable *mutatis mutandis* to the meetings of the third stage of the

Conference. They may be further defined by the Co-ordinating Committee.

74) 6. The Executive Secretary for technical matters at each stage of the Conference shall be a national of the corresponding host country. He is designated by the host country subject to agreement by the participating States.

(75) In organizing the services, the Executive Secretary of each stage will be responsible for the recruitment of his staff and assured of the collaboration of the Secretariats of the other stages.

(76) The Executive Secretaries will work under the authority of the Conference and report on their activities to the appropriate body of each stage of the Conference, especially on financial matters.

(77) 7. Official verbatim records shall be taken at the meetings of the first and third stages of the Conference.

(78) Proposals on matters of substance and amendments thereto shall be submitted in writing to the Chairman and circulated to all participants. The proposals adopted shall be registered by the Executive Secretary and circulated among the participants.

(79) Representatives of the States participating in the Conference may ask for their formal reservations or interpretative statements concerning given decisions to be duly registered by the Executive Secretary and circulated to the participating States. Such statements must be submitted in writing to the Executive Secretary.

(80) 8. The inaugural and closing sessions of the first stage of the Conference will be open. Other sessions of the first stage may be open if the Ministers so decide. The Co-ordinating Committee, the Committees and the Sub-Committees shall not, as a rule, meet in open sessions, unless the participants decide otherwise. Arrangements for the third stage will be similar to those for the first stage and may be further defined by the Co-ordinating Committee.

(81) 9. The working languages of the Conference and of its working bodies shall be: English, French, German, Italian, Russian and Spanish.

(82) Speeches made in any of the working languages shall be interpreted into the other working languages.

(83) 10. Any Representative may make a statement in a language other than the working languages. In this case, he shall himself provide for interpretation into one of the working languages.

(84) 11. Records and decisions of the Conference shall be issued and circulated to participants in the working languages.

(85) The participants shall decide by consensus whether it is desirable to make public, through the appropriate services of the Conference, certain documents or communiqués on the work of the Conference and if they decide in the affirmative shall specify the contents.

(86) 12. During the discussion of any matter, a Representative may raise a point of order and the Chairman shall give him the floor immediately. A Representative raising a point of order may not speak on the substance of the matter under discussion.

(87) 13. During the meeting the Chairman shall keep a list of speakers and may declare it closed with the consent of the meeting. He shall, however, accord the right of reply to any Representative if a speech after he has declared the list closed makes this desirable.

(88) 14. These procedural arrangements shall be adopted by consensus. Once adopted, they can only be altered by consensus.

7. Financial arrangements

A. Distribution of Expenses.

(89) The following scale of distribution has been agreed for the expenses of the Conference, subject to the reservation that the distribution in question concerns the Conference only and shall not be considered as a precedent which could be relied on in other circumstances:

(90)

France	8.80	per cent	
Federal Republic of Germany	8.80		
Italy	8.80		
Union of Soviet Socialist Republics	8.80		
United Kingdom	8.80		
United States of America	8.80	52.80	
Canada	5.52	5.52	
Belgium	3.48		
German Democratic Republic	3.48		
Netherlands	3.48		
Poland	3.48		
Spain	3.48		
Sweden	3.48	20.88	
Austria	2.00		
Czechoslovakia	2.00		
Denmark	2.00		
Finland	2.00		
Hungary	2.00		
Norway	2.00		
Switzerland	2.00	14.00	
Greece	0.80		
Romania	0.80		
Turkey	0.80		
Yugoslavia	0.80	3.20	
Bulgaria	0.60		
Ireland	0.60		
Luxembourg	0.60		
Portugal	0.60	2.40	
Cyprus	0.20		
Holy See	0.20		
Iceland	0.20		
Liechtenstein	0.20		
Malta	0.20		
San Marino	0.20	1.20	
	-----	-----	
	100	100	per cent

(91) Necessary alterations of the cost-sharing scale due to any possible modifications in the list of participating States above will be decided upon by consensus.*

---

* The cost-sharing scale (paragraph 90) has been altered by the following

B. System of financing

(92) 1. The monies needed to finance the Conference will be advanced by the host country of each stage subject to reimbursement out of the contributions of the participating States according to the agreed cost-sharing scale.

(93) 2. Payment of contributions by participating States shall be made to a special account of the Conference.

(94) 3. Payment shall be made in the currency of the host country.

(95) 4. Accounts will be rendered in respect of each stage or at intervals of three (3) months, as appropriate.

(96) 5. Accounts shall be expressed in the currency of the host country and shall be rendered as soon as technically possible after the termination of a billing period. They shall be payable within sixty (60) days of presentation.

---

decision of the Co-ordinating Committee, made in Geneva, 31st August 1973:

"**Decision No. 7:**

Monaco's share in the expenses of the Conference is fixed at 0.20 %; this percentage will be deducted from Canada's share, which will thus amount to 5.32 %."

ANNEX

Austria
Belgium
Bulgaria
Canada
Cyprus
Czechoslovakia
Denmark
Finland
France
German Democratic Republic
Federal Republic of Germany
Greece
Holy See
Hungary
Iceland
Ireland
Italy
Liechtenstein
Luxembourg
Malta
Netherlands
Norway
Poland
Portugal
Romania
San Marino
Spain
Sweden
Switzerland
Turkey
Union of Soviet Socialist Republics
United Kingdom
United States of America
Yugoslavia

INTERPRETATIVE STATEMENT[1]

Editor's note: On 29 November 1972, the delegation of the Holy See at the Helsinki Consultations made an interpretative statement on the definition of 'consensus' as laid down in the Final Recommendations of the Helsinki Consultations. The text of this statement reads as follows:

The delegation of the Holy See is in agreement with the definition of 'consensus' as expressed in paragraph 5 of Document CESC/HC/3.

However, in view of the special position arising from the nature of the Holy See - a position which will be explained by its Representative during the general debate - I consider it my duty to make an anticipatory *interpretative statement* here in respect of paragraph 5 on consensus.

Our purpose in doing so is not to request in any way the amendment of the text relating to the formation of the consensus as provided for in paragraph 5, but solely to envisage certain circumstances which might confront the Holy See in the course of these Consultations.

it is foreseeable, in fact, that discussions will arise on specific problems of a political nature, problems on which the Holy See - for reasons which will be very understandable - will be unable to take up a position; nor will it do so.

This attitude is not to be interpreted as either agreement or disagreement, nor should it prevent a consensus from being formed. The Holy See reserves the option of explaining, if need be, the reasons for its attitude, and of requesting that that explanation be incorporated in the documentation of the Consultations.

1 CESC/HC/5 of 29 November 1972. (Statement made by Joseph B. Zabkar on behalf of the Holy See.)

FINAL ACT OF HELSINKI

FINAL ACT OF THE CONFERENCE ON SECURITY AND CO-OPERATION IN EUROPE

Helsinki, 1 August 1975

The Conference on Security and Co-operation in Europe, which opened at Helsinki on 3 July 1973 and continued at Geneva from 18 September 1973 to 21 July 1975, was concluded at Helsinki on 1 August 1975 by the High Representatives of Austria, Belgium, Bulgaria, Canada, Cyprus, Czechoslovakia, Denmark, Finland, France, the German Democratic Republic, the Federal Republic of Germany, Greece, the Holy See, Hungary, Iceland, Ireland, Italy, Liechtenstein, Luxembourg, Malta, Monaco, the Netherlands, Norway, Poland, Portugal, Romania, San Marino, Spain, Sweden, Switzerland, Turkey, the Union of Soviet Socialist Republics, the United Kingdom, the United States of America and Yugoslavia.

During the opening and closing stages of the Conference the participants were addressed by the Secretary-General of the United Nations as their guest of honour. The Director-General of UNESCO and the Executive Secretary of the United Nations Economic Commission for Europe addressed the Conference during its second stage.

During the meetings of the second stage of the Conference, contributions were received, and statements heard, from the following non-participating Mediterranean States on various agenda items: the Democratic and Popular Republic of Algeria, the Arab Republic of Egypt, Israel, the Kingdom of Morocco, the Syrian Arab Republic, Tunisia.

Motivated by the political will, in the interest of peoples, to improve and intensify their relations and to contribute in Europe to peace, security, justice and co-operation as well as to rapprochement among themselves and with the other States of the world,

Determined, in consequence, to give full effect to the results of the Conference and to assure, among their States and throughout Europe, the benefits deriving from those results and thus to broaden, deepen and make continuing and lasting the process of détente,

The High Representatives of the participating States have solemnly adopted the following:

QUESTIONS RELATING TO SECURITY IN EUROPE

The States participating in the Conference on Security and Co-operation in Europe,

Reaffirming their objective of promoting better relations among themselves and ensuring conditions in which their people can live in true and lasting peace free from any threat to or attempt against their security;

Convinced of the need to exert efforts to make détente both a continuing and an increasingly viable and comprehensive process, universal in scope, and that the implementation of the results of the Conference on Security and Co-operation in Europe will be a major contribution to this process;

Considering that solidarity among peoples, as well as the common purpose of the participating States in achieving the aims as set forth by the Conference on Security and Co-operation in Europe, should lead to the development of better and closer relations among them in all fields and thus to overcoming the confrontation stemming from the character of their past relations, and to better mutual understanding;

Mindful of their common history and recognizing that the existence of elements common to their traditions and values can assist them in developing their relations, and desiring to search, fully taking into account the individuality and diversity of their positions and views, for possibilities of joining their efforts with a view to overcoming distrust and increasing confidence, solving the problems that separate them and co-operating in the interest of mankind;

Recognizing the indivisibility of security in Europe as well as their common interest in the development of co-operation throughout Europe and among themselves and expressing their intention to pursue efforts accordingly;

Recognizing the close link between peace and security in Europe and in the world as a whole and conscious of the need for each of them to make its contribution to the strengthening of world peace and security and to the promotion of fundamental rights, economic and social progress and well-being for all peoples;

Have adopted the following:

1.

(a) Declaration on principles guiding relations between participating States

The participating States,

Reaffirming their commitment to peace, security and justice and the continuing development of friendly relations and co-operation;

Recognizing that this commitment, which reflects the interest and aspirations of peoples, constitutes for each participating State a present and future responsibility, heightened by experience of the past;

Reaffirming, in conformity with their membership in the United Nations and in accordance with the purposes and principles of the United Nations, their full and active support for the United Nations and for the enhancement of its role and effectiveness in strengthening international peace, security and justice, and in promoting the solution of international problems, as well as the development of friendly relations and co-operation among States;

Expressing their common adherence to the principles which are set forth below and are in conformity with the Charter of the United Nations, as well as their common will to act, in the application of these principles, in conformity with the purposes and principles of the Charter of the United Nations;

Declare their determination to respect and put into practice, each of them in its relations with all other participating States, irrespective of their political, economic or social systems as well as of their size, geographical location or level of economic development, the following principles, which all are of primary significance, guiding their mutual relations:

I. Sovereign equality, respect for the rights inherent in sovereignty

The participating States will respect each other's sovereign equality and individuality as well as all the rights inherent in and encompassed by its sovereignty, including in particular the right of every State to juridical equality, to territorial integrity and to freedom and political independence. They will also respect each other's right freely to choose and develop its political, social, economic and cultural systems as well as its right to determine its laws and regulations.

Within the framework of international law, all the participating States have equal rights and duties. They will respect each other's right to define and conduct as it wishes its relations with other States in accordance with international law and in the spirit of the present Declaration. They consider that their frontiers can be changed, in accordance with international law, by peaceful means and by agreement. They also have the right to belong or not to belong to international organizations, to be or not to be a party to bilateral or multilateral treaties including the right to be or not to be a party to treaties of alliance; they also have the right to neutrality.

II. Refraining from the threat or use of force

The participating States will refrain in their mutual relations, as well as in their international relations in general, from the threat or use of force against the territorial integrity or political independence of any State, or in any other manner inconsistent with the purposes of the United Nations and with the present Declaration. No consideration may be invoked to serve to warrant resort to the threat or use of force in contravention of this principle.

Accordingly, the participating States will refrain from any acts constituting a threat of force or direct or indirect use of force against another participating State. Likewise they will refrain from any manifestation of force for the purpose of inducing another participating State to renounce the full exercise of its sovereign rights. Likewise they will also refrain in their mutual relations from any act of reprisal by force.

No such threat or use of force will be employed as a means of settling disputes, or questions likely to give rise to disputes, between them.

III. Inviolability of frontiers

The participating States regard as inviolable all one another's frontiers as well as the frontiers of all States in Europe and therefore they will refrain now and in the future from assaulting these frontiers.

Accordingly, they will also refrain from any demand for, or act of, seizure and usurpation of part or all of the territory of any participating State.

IV. Territorial integrity of States

The participating States will respect the territorial integrity of each of the participating States.

Accordingly, they will refrain from any action inconsistent with the purposes and principles of the Charter of the United Nations against the territorial integrity, political independence or the unity of any participating State, and in particular from any such action constituting a threat or use of force.

The participating States will likewise refrain from making each other's territory the object of military occupation or other direct or indirect measures of force in contravention of international law, or the object of acquisition by means of such measures or the threat of them. No such occupation or acquisition will be recognized as legal.

V. Peaceful settlement of disputes

The participating States will settle disputes among them by peaceful means in such a manner as not to endanger international peace and security, and justice.

They will endeavour in good faith and a spirit of co-operation to reach a rapid and equitable solution on the basis of international law.

For this purpose they will use such means as negotiation, enquiry, mediation, conciliation, arbitration, judicial settlement or other peaceful means of their own choice including any settlement procedure agreed to in advance of disputes to which they are parties.

In the event of failure to reach a solution by any of the above peaceful means, the parties to a dispute will continue to seek a mutually agreed way to settle the dispute peacefully.

Participating States, parties to a dispute among them, as well as other participating States, will refrain from any action which might aggravate the situation to such a degree as to endanger the maintenance of international peace and security and thereby make a peaceful settlement of the dispute more difficult.

VI. Non-intervention in internal affairs

The participating States will refrain from any intervention, direct or indirect, individual or collective, in the internal or external affairs falling within the domestic jurisdiction of another participating State, regardless of their mutual relations.

They will accordingly refrain from any form of armed intervention or threat of such intervention against another participating State.

They will likewise in all circumstances refrain from any other act of military, or of political, economic or other coercion designed to subordinate to their own interest the exercise by another participating State of the rights inherent in its sovereignty and thus to secure advantages of any kind.

Accordingly, they will, inter alia, refrain from direct or indirect assistance to terrorist activities, or to subversive or other activities directed towards the violent overthrow of the regime of another participating State.

VII. Respect for human rights and fundamental freedoms, including the freedom of thought, conscience, religion or belief

The participating States will respect human rights and fundamental freedoms, including the freedom of thought, conscience, religion or belief, for all without distinction as to race, sex, language or religion.

They will promote and encourage the effective exercise of civil, political, economic, social, cultural and other rights and freedoms all of which derive from the inherent dignity of the human person and are essential for his free and full development.

Within this framework the participating States will recognize and respect the freedom of the individual to profess and practise, alone or in community with others, religion or belief acting in accordance with the dictates of his own conscience.

The participating States on whose territory national minorities exist will respect the right of persons belonging to such minorities to equality before the law, will afford them the full opportunity for the actual enjoyment of human rights and fundamental freedoms and will, in this manner, protect their legitimate interests in this sphere.

The participating States recognize the universal significance of human rights and fundamental freedoms, respect for which is an essential factor for the peace, justice and well-being necessary to ensure the development of friendly relations and co-operation among themselves as among all States.

They will constantly respect these rights and freedoms in their mutual relations and will endeavour jointly and separately, including in co-operation with the United Nations, to promote universal and effective respect for them.

They confirm the right of the individual to know and act upon his rights and duties in this field.

In the field of human rights and fundamental freedoms, the participating States will act in conformity with the purposes and principles of the Charter of the United Nations and with the Universal Declaration of Human Rights. They will also fulfil their obligations as set forth in the international declarations and agreements in this field, including inter alia the International Covenants on Human Rights, by which they may be bound.

VIII. Equal rights and self-determination of peoples

The participating States will respect the equal rights of peoples and their right to self-determination, acting at all times in conformity with the purposes and principles of the Charter of the United Nations and with the relevant norms of international law, including those relating to territorial integrity of States.

By virtue of the principle of equal rights and self-determination of peoples, all peoples always have the right, in full freedom, to determine, when and as they wish, their internal and external political status, without external interference, and to pursue as they wish their political, economic, social and cultural development.

The participating States reaffirm the universal significance of respect for and effective exercise of equal rights and self-determination of peoples for the development of friendly relations among themselves as among all States; they also recall the importance of the elimination of any form of violation of this principle.

IX. Co-operation among States

The participating States will develop their co-operation with one another and with all States in all fields in accordance with the purposes and principles of the Charter of the United Nations. In developing their co-operation the participating States will place special emphasis on the fields as set forth within the framework of the Conference on Security and Co-operation in Europe, with each of them making its contribution in conditions of full equality.

They will endeavour, in developing their co-operation as equals, to promote mutual understanding and confidence, friendly and good-neighbourly relations among themselves, international peace, security and justice. They will equally endeavour, in developing their co-operation, to improve the well-being of peoples and contribute to the fulfilment of their aspirations through, inter alia, the benefits resulting from increased mutual knowledge and from progress and achievement in the economic, scientific, technological, social, cultural and humanitarian fields. They will take steps to promote conditions favourable to making these benefits available to all; they will take into account the interest of all in the narrowing of differences in the levels of economic development, and in particular the interest of developing countries throughout the world.

They confirm that governments, institutions, organizations and persons have a relevant and positive role to play in contributing toward the achievement of these aims of their co-operation.

They will strive, in increasing their co-operation as set forth above, to develop closer relations among themselves on an improved and more enduring basis for the benefit of peoples.

X. Fulfilment in good faith of obligations under international law

The participating States will fulfil in good faith their obligations under international law, both those obligations arising from the generally recognized principles and rules of international law and those obligations arising from treaties or other agreements, in conformity with international law, to which they are parties.

In exercising their sovereign rights, including the right to determine their laws and regulations, they will conform with their legal obligations under international law; they will furthermore pay due regard to and implement the provisions in the Final Act of the Conference on Security and Co-operation in Europe.

The participating States confirm that in the event of a conflict between the obligations of the members of the United Nations under the Charter of the

United Nations and their obligations under any treaty or other international agreement, their obligations under the Charter will prevail, in accordance with Article 103 of the Charter of the United Nations.

All the principles set forth above are of primary significance and, accordingly, they will be equally and unreservedly applied, each of them being interpreted taking into account the others.

The participating States express their determination fully to respect and apply these principles, as set forth in the present Declaration, in all aspects, to their mutual relations and co-operation in order to ensure to each participating State the benefits resulting from the respect and application of these principles by all.

The participating States, paying due regard to the principles above and, in particular, to the first sentence of the tenth principle, "Fulfilment in good faith of obligations under international law", note that the present Declaration does not affect their rights and obligations, nor the corresponding treaties and other agreements and arrangements.

The participating States express the conviction that respect for these principles will encourage the development of normal and friendly relations and the progress of co-operation among them in all fields. They also express the conviction that respect for these principles will encourage the development of political contacts among them which in turn would contribute to better mutual understanding of their positions and views.

The participating States declare their intention to conduct their relations with all other States in the spirit of the principles contained in the present Declaration.

(b) Matters related to giving effect to certain of the above principles

(i) The participating States,

Reaffirming that they will respect and give effect to refraining from the threat or use of force and convinced of the necessity to make it an effective norm of international life,

Declare that they are resolved to respect and carry out, in their relations with one another, inter alia, the following provisions which are in conformity with the Declaration on Principles Guiding Relations between Participating States:

- To give effect and expression, by all the ways and forms which they consider appropriate, to the duty to refrain from the threat or use of force in their relations with one another.

- To refrain from any use of armed forces inconsistent with the purposes and principles of the Charter of the United Nations and the provisions of the Declaration on Principles Guiding Relations between Participating States, against another participating State, in particular from invasion of or attack on its territory.

- To refrain from any manifestation of force for the purpose of inducing another participating State to renounce the full exercise of its sovereign rights.

- To refrain from any act of economic coercion designed to subordinate to their own interest the exercise by another participating State of the rights inherent in its sovereignty and thus to secure advantages of any kind.

- To take effective measures which by their scope and by their nature constitute steps towards the ultimate achievement of general and complete disarmament under strict and effective international control.

- To promote, by all means which each of them considers appropriate, a climate of confidence and respect among peoples consonant with their duty to refrain from propaganda for wars of aggression or for any threat or use of force inconsistent with the purposes of the United Nations and with the Declaration on Principles Guiding Relations between Participating States, against another participating State.

- To make every effort to settle exclusively by peaceful means any dispute between them, the continuance of which is likely to endanger the maintenance of international peace and security in Europe, and to seek, first of all, a solution through the peaceful means set forth in Article 33 of the United Nations Charter.
  To refrain from any action which could hinder the peaceful settlement of disputes between the participating States.

(ii) The participating States,

Reaffirming their determination to settle their disputes as set forth in the Principle of Peaceful Settlement of Disputes;

Convinced that the peaceful settlement of disputes is a complement to refraining from the threat or use of force, both being essential though not exclusive factors for the maintenance and consolidation of peace and security;

Desiring to reinforce and improve the methods at their disposal for the peaceful settlement of disputes;

1. Are resolved to pursue the examination and elaboration of a generally acceptable method for the peaceful settlement of disputes aimed at complementing existing methods, and to continue to this end to work upon the "Draft Convention on a European System for the Peaceful Settlement of Disputes" submitted by Switzerland during the second stage of the Conference on Security and Co-operation in Europe, as well as other proposals relating to it and directed towards the elaboration of such a method.

2. Decide that, on the invitation of Switzerland, a meeting of experts of all the participating States will be convoked in order to fulfil the mandate described in paragraph 1 above within the framework and under the procedures of the follow-up to the Conference laid down in the chapter "Follow-up to the Conference".

3. This meeting of experts will take place after the meeting of the representatives appointed by the Ministers of Foreign Affairs of the participating States, scheduled according to the chapter "Follow-up to the Conference" for 1977; the results of the work of this meeting of experts will be submitted to Governments.

2.

Document on confidence-building measures and certain aspects of security and disarmament

The participating States,

Desirous of eliminating the causes of tension that may exist among them and thus of contributing to the strengthening of peace and security in the world;

Determined to strengthen confidence among them and thus to contribute to increasing stability and security in Europe;

Determined further to refrain in their mutual relations, as well as in their international relations in general, from the threat or use of force against the territorial integrity or political independence of any State, or in any other manner inconsistent with the purposes of the United Nations and with the Declaration on Principles Guiding Relations between Participating States as adopted in this Final Act;

Recognizing the need to contribute to reducing the dangers of armed conflict and of misunderstanding or miscalculation of military activities which could give rise to apprehension, particularly in a situation where the participating States lack clear and timely information about the nature of such activities;

Taking into account considerations relevant to efforts aimed at lessening tension and promoting disarmament;

Recognizing that the exchange of observers by invitation at military manoeuvres will help to promote contacts and mutual understanding;

Having studied the question of prior notification of major military movements in the context of confidence-building;

Recognizing that there are other ways in which individual States can contribute further to their common objectives;

Convinced of the political importance of prior notification of major military manoeuvres for the promotion of mutual understanding and the strengthening of confidence, stability and security;

Accepting the responsibility of each of them to promote these objectives and to implement this measure, in accordance with the accepted criteria and modalities, as essentials for the realization of these objectives;

Recognizing that this measure deriving from political decision rests upon a voluntary basis;

Have adopted the following:

I

Prior notification of major military manoeuvres

They will notify their major military manoeuvres to all other participating States through usual diplomatic channels in accordance with the following provisions:

Notification will be given of major military manoeuvres exceeding a total of 25,000 troops, independently or combined with any possible air or naval components (in this context the word "troops" includes amphibious and airborne troops). In the case of independent manoeuvres of amphibious or airborne troops, or of combined manoeuvres involving them, these troops will be included in this total. Furthermore, in the case of combined manoeuvres which do not reach the above total but which involve land forces together with significant numbers of either amphibious or airborne troops, or both, notification can also be given.

Notification will be given of major military manoeuvres which take place on the territory, in Europe, of any participating State as well as, if applicable, in the adjoining sea area and air space.

In the case of a participating State whose territory extends beyond Europe, prior notification need be given only of manoeuvres which take place in an area within 250 kilometres from its frontier facing or shared with any other European participating State, the participating State need not, however, give notification in cases in which that area is also contiguous to the participating State's frontier facing or shared with a non-European non-participating State.

Notification will be given 21 days or more in advance of the start of the manoeuvre or in the case of a manoeuvre arranged at shorter notice at the earliest possible opportunity prior to its starting date.

Notification will contain information of the designation, if any, the general purpose of and the States involved in the manoeuvre, the type or types and numerical strength of the forces engaged, the area and estimated time-frame of its conduct. The participating States will also, if possible, provide additional relevant information, particularly that related to the components of the forces engaged and the period of involvement of these forces.

Prior notification of other military manoeuvres
The participating States recognize that they can contribute further to strengthening confidence and increasing security and stability, and to this end may also notify smaller-scale military manoeuvres to other participating States, with special regard for those near the area of such manoeuvres. To the same end, the participating States also recognize that they may notify other military manoeuvres conducted by them.

Exchange of observers
The participating States will invite other participating States, voluntarily and on a bilateral basis, in a spirit of reciprocity and goodwill towards all participating States, to send observers to attend military manoeuvres.

The inviting State will determine in each case the number of observers, the procedures and conditions of their participation, and give other information which it may consider useful. It will provide appropriate facilities and hospitality.

The invitation will be given as far ahead as is conveniently possible through usual diplomatic channels.

Prior notification of major military movements
In accordance with the Final Recommendations of the Helsinki Consultations the participating States studied the question of prior notification of major military movements as a measure to strengthen confidence.

Accordingly, the participating States recognize that they may, at their own discretion and with a view to contributing to confidence-building, notify their major military movements.

In the same spirit, further consideration will be given by the States participating in the Conference on Security and Co-operation in Europe to the question of prior notification of major military movements, bearing in mind, in particular, the experience gained by the implementation of the measures which are set forth in this document.

Other confidence-building measures
The participating States recognize that there are other means by which their common objectives can be promoted.
In particular, they will, with due regard to reciprocity and with a view to better mutual understanding, promote exchanges by invitation among their military personnel, including visits by military delegations.

***

In order to make a fuller contribution to their common objective of confidence-building, the participating States, when conducting their military activities in the area covered by the provisions for the prior notification of major military manoeuvres, will duly take into account and respect this objective.

They also recognize that the experience gained by the implementation of the provisions set forth above, together with further efforts, could lead to developing and enlarging measures aimed at strengthening confidence.

II

Questions relating to disarmament

The participating States recognize the interest of all of them in efforts aimed at lessening military confrontation and promoting disarmament which are designed to complement political détente in Europe and to strengthen their security. They are convinced of the necessity to take effective measures in these fields which by their scope and by their nature constitute steps towards the ultimate achievement of general and complete disarmament under strict and effective international control, and which should result in strengthening peace and security throughout the world.

III

General considerations

Having considered the views expressed on various subjects related to the strengthening of security in Europe through joint efforts aimed at promoting détente and disarmament, the participating States, when engaged in such efforts, will, in this context, proceed, in particular, from the following essential considerations:

- The complementary nature of the political and military aspects of security;

- The interrelation between the security of each participating State and security in Europe as a whole and the relationship which exists, in the broader context of world security, between security in Europe and security in the Mediterranean area;

- Respect for the security interests of all States participating in the Conference on Security and Co-operation in Europe inherent in their sovereign equality;

- The importance that participants in negotiating fora see to it that information about relevant developments, progress and results is provided on an appropriate basis to other States participating in the Conference on Security and Co-operation in Europe and, in return, the justified interest of any of those States in having their views considered.

CO-OPERATION IN THE FIELD OF ECONOMICS, OF SCIENCE AND TECHNOLOGY AND OF THE ENVIRONMENT

The participating States,

Convinced that their efforts to develop co-operation in the fields of trade, industry, science and technology, the environment and other areas of economic activity contribute to the reinforcement of peace and security in Europe and in the world as a whole,

Recognizing that co-operation in these fields would promote economic and social progress and the improvement of the conditions of life,

Aware of the diversity of their economic and social systems,

Reaffirming their will to intensify such co-operation between one another, irrespective of their systems,

Recognizing that such co-operation, with due regard for the different levels of economic development, can be developed, on the basis of equality and mutual satisfaction of the partners, and of reciprocity permitting, as a whole, an equitable distribution of advantages and obligations of comparable scale, with respect for bilateral and multilateral agreements,

Taking into account the interests of the developing countries throughout the world, including those among the participating countries as long as they are developing from the economic point of view; reaffirming their will to co-operate for the achievement of the aims and objectives established by the appropriate bodies of the United Nations in the pertinent documents concerning development, it being understood that each participating State maintains the positions it has taken on them; giving special attention to the least developed countries,

Convinced that the growing world-wide economic interdependence calls for increasing common and effective efforts towards the solution of major world economic problems such as food, energy, commodities, monetary and financial problems, and therefore emphasizes the need for promoting stable and equitable international economic relations, thus contributing to the continuous and diversified economic development of all countries,

Having taken into account the work already undertaken by relevant international organizations and wishing to take advantage of the possibilities offered by these organizations, in particular by the United Nations Economic

Commission for Europe, for giving effect to the provisions of the final documents of the Conference,

Considering that the guidelines and concrete recommendations contained in the following texts are aimed at promoting further development of their mutual economic relations, and convinced that their co-operation in this field should take place in full respect for the principles guiding relations among participating States as set forth in the relevant document,

Have adopted the following:

1. Commercial exchanges

General provisions

The participating States,

Conscious of the growing role of international trade as one of the most important factors in economic growth and social progress,

Recognizing that trade represents an essential sector of their co-operation, and bearing in mind that the provisions contained in the above preamble apply in particular to this sector,

Considering that the volume and structure of trade among the participating States do not in all cases correspond to the possibilities created by the current level of their economic, scientific and technological development,

are resolved to promote, on the basis of the modalities of their economic co-operation, the expansion of their mutual trade in goods and services, and to ensure conditions favourable to such development;

recognize the beneficial effects which can result for the development of trade from the application of most favoured nation treatment;

will encourage the expansion of trade on as broad a multilateral basis as possible, thereby endeavouring to utilize the various economic and commercial possibilities;

recognize the importance of bilateral and multilateral intergovernmental and other agreements for the long-term development of trade;

note the importance of monetary and financial questions for the development of international trade, and will endeavour to deal with them with a view to contributing to the continuous expansion of trade;

will endeavour to reduce or progressively eliminate all kinds of obstacles to the development of trade;

will foster a steady growth of trade while avoiding as far as possible abrupt fluctuations in their trade;

consider that their trade in various products should be conducted in such a way as not to cause or threaten to cause serious injury - and should the situation arise, market disruption - in domestic markets for these products and in particular to the detriment of domestic producers of like or directly competitive products; as regards the concept of market disruption, it is understood that it should not be invoked in a way inconsistent with the relevant provisions of their international agreements; if they resort to safeguard measures, they will do so in conformity with their commitments in this field arising from international agreements to which they are parties and will take account of the interests of the parties directly concerned;

will give due attention to measures for the promotion of trade and the diversification of its structure;

note that the growth and diversification of trade would contribute to widening the possibilities of choice of products;

consider it appropriate to create favourable conditions for the participation of firms, organizations and enterprises in the development of trade.

Business contacts and facilities

The participating States,

Conscious of the importance of the contribution which an improvement of business contacts, and the accompanying growth of confidence in business relationships, could make to the development of commercial and economic relations,

will take measures further to improve conditions for the expansion of contacts between representatives of official bodies, of the different organizations, enterprises, firms and banks concerned with foreign trade, in particular, where useful, between sellers and users of products and services for the purpose of studying commercial possibilities, concluding contracts, ensuring their implementation and providing after-sales services;

will encourage organizations, enterprises and firms concerned with foreign trade to take measures to accelerate the conduct of business negotiations;

will further take measures aimed at improving working conditions of representatives of foreign organizations, enterprises, firms and banks concerned with external trade, particularly as follows:

- by providing the necessary information, including information on legislation and procedures relating to the establishment and operation of permanent representation by the above mentioned bodies;

- by examining as favourably as possible requests for the establishment of permanent representation and of offices for this purpose, including, where appropriate, the opening of joint offices by two or more firms;

- by encouraging the provision, on conditions as favourable as possible and equal for all representatives of the above-mentioned bodies, of hotel accommodation, means of communication, and of other facilities normally required by them, as well as of suitable business and residential premises for purposes of permanent representation;

recognize the importance of such measures to encourage greater participation by small and medium sized firms in trade between participating States.

Economic and commercial information

The participating States,

Conscious of the growing role of economic and commercial information in the development of international trade,

Considering that economic information should be of such a nature as to allow adequate market analysis and to permit the preparation of medium and long term forecasts, thus contributing to the establishment of a continuing flow of trade and a better utilization of commercial possibilities,

Expressing their readiness to improve the quality and increase the quantity and supply of economic and relevant administrative information,

Considering that the value of statistical information on the international level depends to a considerable extent on the possibility of its comparability,

will promote the publication and dissemination of economic and commercial information at regular intervals and as quickly as possible, in particular:

- statistics concerning production, national income, budget, consumption and productivity;

- foreign trade statistics drawn up on the basis of comparable classification including breakdown by product with indication of volume and value, as well as country of origin or destination;

- laws and regulations concerning foreign trade;

- information allowing forecasts of development of the economy to assist in trade promotion, for example, information on the general orientation of national economic plans and programmes;

- other information to help businessmen in commercial contacts, for example, periodic directories, lists, and where possible, organizational charts of firms and organizations concerned with foreign trade;

will in addition to the above encourage the development of the exchange of economic and commercial information through, where appropriate, joint commissions for economic, scientific and technical co-operation, national and joint chambers of commerce, and other suitable bodies;

will support a study, in the framework of the United Nations Economic Commission for Europe, of the possibilities of creating a multilateral system of notification of laws and regulations concerning foreign trade and changes therein;

will encourage international work on the harmonization of statistical nomenclatures, notably in the United Nations Economic Commission for Europe.

Marketing

The participating States,

Recognizing the importance of adapting production to the requirements of foreign markets in order to ensure the expansion of international trade,

Conscious of the need of exporters to be as fully familiar as possible with and take account of the requirements of potential users,

will encourage organizations, enterprises and firms concerned with foreign trade to develop further the knowledge and techniques required for effective marketing;

will encourage the improvement of conditions for the implementation of measures to promote trade and to satisfy the needs of users in respect of imported products, in particular through market research and advertising measures as well as, where useful, the establishment of supply facilities, the furnishing of spare parts, the functioning of after sales services, and the training of the necessary local technical personnel;

will encourage international co-operation in the field of trade promotion, including marketing, and the work undertaken on these subjects within the international bodies, in particular the United Nations Economic Commission for Europe.

2. Industrial co-operation and projects of common interest

Industrial co-operation

The participating States,

Considering that industrial co-operation, being motivated by economic considerations, can

- create lasting ties thus strengthening long-term overall economic co-operation,
- contribute to economic growth as well as to the expansion and diversification of international trade and to a wider utilization of modern technology,
- lead to the mutually advantageous utilization of economic complementarities through better use of all factors of production, and
- accelerate the industrial development of all those who take part in such co-operation,

propose to encourage the development of industrial co-operation between the competent organizations, enterprises and firms of their countries;

consider that industrial co-operation may be facilitated by means of intergovernmental and other bilateral and multilateral agreements between the interested parties;

note that in promoting industrial co-operation they should bear in mind the economic structures and the development levels of their countries;

note that industrial co-operation is implemented by means of contracts concluded between competent organizations, enterprises and firms on the basis of economic considerations;

express their willingness to promote measures designed to create favourable conditions for industrial co-operation;

recognize that industrial co-operation covers a number of forms of economic relations going beyond the framework of conventional trade, and that in concluding contracts on industrial co-operation the partners will determine jointly the appropriate forms and conditions of co-operation, taking into account their mutual interests and capabilities;

recognize further that, if it is in their mutual interest, concrete forms such as the following may be useful for the development of industrial co-operation: joint production and sale, specialization in production and sale, construction, adaptation and modernization of industrial plants, co-operation for the setting up of complete industrial installations with a view to thus obtaining part of the resultant products, mixed companies, exchanges of "know-how", of technical information, of patents and of licenses, and joint industrial research within the framework of specific co-operation projects;

recognize that new forms of industrial co-operation can be applied with a view to meeting specific needs;

note the importance of economic, commercial, technical and administrative information such as to ensure the development of industrial co-operation;

Consider it desirable:

- to improve the quality and the quantity of information relevant to industrial co-operation, in particular the laws and regulations, including those relating to foreign exchange, general orientation of national economic plans and programmes as well as programme priorities and economic conditions of the market; and

- disseminate as quickly as possible published documentation thereon;

will encourage all forms of exchange of information and communication of experience relevant to industrial co-operation, including through contacts between potential partners and, where appropriate, through joint commissions for economic, industrial, scientific and technical co-operation, national and joint chambers of commerce, and other suitable bodies;

consider it desirable, with a view to expanding industrial co-operation, to encourage the exploration of co-operation possibilities and the implementation of co-operation projects and will take measures to this end, *inter alia*, by facilitating and increasing all forms of business contacts between competent organizations, enterprises and firms and between their respective qualified personnel;

note that the provisions adopted by the Conference relating to business contacts in the economic and commercial fields also apply to foreign organizations, enterprises and firms engaged in industrial co-operation, taking into account the specific conditions of this co-operation, and will endeavour to ensure, in particular, the existence of appropriate working conditions for personnel engaged in the implementation of co-operation projects;

consider it desirable that proposals for industrial co-operation projects should be sufficiently specific and should contain the necessary economic and technical data, in particular preliminary estimates of the cost of the project, information on the form of co-operation envisaged, and market possibilities, to enable potential partners to proceed with initial studies and to arrive at decisions in the shortest possible time;

will encourage the parties concerned with industrial co-operation to take measures to accelerate the conduct of negotiations for the conclusion of co-operation contracts;

recommend further the continued examination - for example within the framework of the United Nations Economic Commission for Europe - of means of improving the provision of information to those concerned on general conditions of industrial co-operation and guidance on the preparation of contracts in this field;

consider it desirable to further improve conditions for the implementation of industrial co-operation projects, in particular with respect to:

- the protection of the interests of the partners in industrial co-operation projects, including the legal protection of the various kinds of property involved;

- the consideration, in ways that are compatible with their economic systems, of the needs and possibilities of industrial co-operation within the framework of economic policy and particularly in national economic plans and programmes;

consider it desirable that the partners, when concluding industrial co-operation contracts, should devote due attention to provisions concerning the extension of the necessary mutual assistance and the provision of the necessary information during the implementation of these contracts, in particular with a view to attaining the required technical level and quality of the products resulting from such co-operation;

recognize the usefulness of an increased participation of small and medium sized firms in industrial co-operation projects.

Projects of common interest

The participating States,

Considering that their economic potential and their natural resources permit, through common efforts, long-term co-operation in the implementation, including at the regional or sub-regional level, of major projects of common interest, and that these may contribute to the speeding-up of the economic development of the countries participating therein,

Considering it desirable that the competent organizations, enterprises and firms of all countries should be given the possibility of indicating their interest in participating in such projects, and, in case of agreement, of taking part in their implementation,

Noting that the provisions adopted by the Conference relating to industrial co-operation are also applicable to projects of common interest,

regard it as necessary to encourage, where appropriate, the investigation by competent and interested organizations, enterprises and firms of the possibilities for the carrying out of projects of common interest in the fields of energy resources and of the exploitation of raw materials, as well as of transport and communications;

regard it as desirable that organizations, enterprises and firms exploring the possibilities of taking part in projects of common interest exchange with their potential partners, through the appropriate channels, the requisite economic, legal, financial and technical information pertaining to these projects;

consider that the fields of energy resources, in particular, petroleum, natural gas and coal, and the extraction and processing of mineral raw materials, in particular, iron ore and bauxite, are suitable ones for strengthening long-term economic co-operation and for the development of trade which could result;

consider that possibilities for projects of common interest with a view to long-term economic co-operation also exist in the following fields:

- exchanges of electrical energy within Europe with a view to utilizing the capacity of the electrical power stations as rationally as possible;

- co-operation in research for new sources of energy and, in particular, in the field of nuclear energy;

- development of road networks and co-operation aimed at establishing a coherent navigable network in Europe;

- co-operation in research and the perfecting of equipment for multi-modal transport operations and for the handling of containers;

recommend that the States interested in projects of common interest should consider under what conditions it would be possible to establish them, and if they so desire, create the necessary conditions for their actual implementation.

3. Provisions concerning trade and industrial co-operation

Harmonization of standards

The participating States,

Recognizing the development of international harmonization of standards and technical regulations and of international co-operation in the field of certification as an important means of eliminating technical obstacles to international trade and industrial co-operation, thereby facilitating their development and increasing productivity, reaffirm their interest to achieve the widest possible international harmonization of standards and technical regulations;

express their readiness to promote international agreements and other appropriate arrangements on acceptance of certificates of conformity with standards and technical regulations;

consider it desirable to increase international co-operation on standardization, in particular by supporting the activities of intergovernmental and other appropriate organizations in this field.

Arbitration

The participating States,

Considering that the prompt and equitable settlement of disputes which may arise from commercial transactions relating to goods and services and contracts for industrial co-operation would contribute to expanding and facilitating trade and co-operation,

Considering that arbitration is an appropriate means of settling such disputes,

recommend, where appropriate, to organizations, enterprises and firms in their countries, to include arbitration clauses in commercial contracts and industrial co-operation contracts, or in special agreements;

recommend that the provisions on arbitration should provide for arbitration under a mutually acceptable set of arbitration rules, and permit arbitration in a third country, taking into account existing intergovernmental and other agreements in this field.

Specific bilateral arrangements

The participating States,

Conscious of the need to facilitate trade and to promote the application of new forms of industrial co-operation,

will consider favourably the conclusion, in appropriate cases, of specific bilateral agreements concerning various problems of mutual interest in the fields of commercial exchanges and industrial co-operation, in particular with a view to avoiding double taxation and to facilitating the transfer of profits and the return of the value of the assets invested.

4. Science and technology

The participating States,

Convinced that scientific and technological co-operation constitutes an important contribution to the strengthening of security and co-operation among them, in that it assists the effective solution of problems of common interest and the improvement of the conditions of human life,

Considering that in developing such co-operation, it is important to promote the sharing of information and experience, facilitating the study and transfer of scientific and technological achievements, as well as the access to such achievements on a mutually advantageous basis and in fields of co-operation agreed between interested parties,

Considering that it is for the potential partners, i.e. the competent organizations, institutions, enterprises, scientists and technologists of the participating States to determine the opportunities for mutually beneficial co-operation and to develop its details,

Affirming that such co-operation can be developed and implemented bilaterally and multilaterally at the governmental and non-governmental levels, for example, through intergovernmental and other agreements, international programmes, co-operative projects and commercial channels, while utilizing also various forms of contacts, including direct and individual contacts,

Aware of the need to take measures further to improve scientific and technological co-operation between them,

Possibilities for improving co-operation

Recognize that possibilities exist for further improving scientific and technological co-operation, and to this end, express their intention to remove obstacles to such co-operation, in particular through:

- the improvement of opportunities for the exchange and dissemination of scientific and technological information among the parties interested in scientific and technological research and co-operation including information related to the organization and implementation of such co-operation;

- the expeditious implementation and improvement in organization, including programmes, of international visits of scientists and specialists in connexion with exchanges, conferences and co-operation;

- the wider use of commercial channels and activities for applied scientific and technological research and for the transfer of achievements obtained in this field while providing information on and protection of intellectual and industrial property rights;

Fields of co-operation
Consider that possibilities to expand co-operation exist within the areas given below as examples, noting that it is for potential partners in the participating countries to identify and develop projects and arrangements of mutual interest and benefit:

Agriculture
Research into new methods and technologies for increasing the productivity of crop cultivation and animal husbandry; the application of chemistry to agriculture; the design, construction and utilization of agricultural machinery; technologies of irrigation and other agricultural land improvement works;

Energy
New technologies of production, transport and distribution of energy aimed at improving the use of existing fuels and sources of hydroenergy, as well as research in the field of new energy sources, including nuclear, solar and geothermal energy;

New technologies, rational use of resources
Research on new technologies and equipment designed in particular to reduce energy consumption and to minimize or eliminate waste;

Transport technology
Research on the means of transport and the technology applied to the development and operation of international, national and urban transport networks including container transport as well as transport safety;

Physics
Study of problems in high energy physics and plasma physics; research in the field of theoretical and experimental nuclear physics;

Chemistry
Research on problems in electrochemistry and the chemistry of polymers, of natural products, and of metals and alloys, as well as the development of improved chemical technology, especially materials processing; practical application of the latest achievements of chemistry to industry, construction and other sectors of the economy;

Meteorology and hydrology
Meteorological and hydrological research, including methods of collection, evaluation and transmission of data and their utilization for weather forecasting and hydrology forecasting;

Oceanography
Oceanographic research, including the study of air/sea interactions;

Seismological research
Study and forecasting of earthquakes and associated geological changes; development and research of technology of seism-resisting constructions;

Research on glaciology, permafrost and problems of life under conditions of cold
Research on glaciology and permafrost; transportation and construction technologies; human adaptation to climatic extremes and changes in the living conditions of indigenous populations;

Computer, communication and information technologies
Development of computers as well as of telecommunications and information systems; technology associated with computers and telecommunications, including their use for management systems, for production processes, for automation, for the study of economic problems, in scientific research and for the collection, processing and dissemination of information;

Space research
Space exploration and the study of the earth's natural resources and the natural environment by remote sensing in particular with the assistance of satellites and rocket-probes;

Medicine and public health
Research on cardiovascular, tumour and virus diseases, molecular biology, neurophysiology; development and testing of new drugs; study of contemporary problems of pediatrics, gerontology and the organization and techniques of medical services;

Environmental research
Research on specific scientific and technological problems related to human environment.

Forms and methods of co-operation
Express their view that scientific and technological co-operation should, in particular, employ the following forms and methods:

- exchange and circulation of books, periodicals and other scientific and technological publications and papers among interested organizations, scientific and technological institutions, enterprises and scientists and technologists, as well as participation in international programmes for the abstracting and indexing of publications;

- exchanges and visits as well as other direct contacts and communications among scientists and technologists, on the basis of mutual agreement and other arrangements, for such purposes as consultations, lecturing and conducting research, including the use of laboratories, scientific libraries, and other documentation centres in connection therewith;

- holding of international and national conferences, symposia, seminars, courses and other meetings of a scientific and technological character, which would include the participation of foreign scientists and technologists;

- joint preparation and implementation of programmes and projects of mutual interest on the basis of consultation and agreement among all parties concerned, including, where possible and appropriate, exchanges of experience and research results, and correlation of research programmes, between scientific and technological research institutions and organizations;

- use of commercial channels and methods for identifying and transferring technological and scientific developments, including the conclusion of mutually beneficial co-operation arrangements between firms and enterprises in fields agreed upon between them and for carrying out, where appropriate, joint research and development programmes and projects;

consider it desirable that periodic exchanges of views and information take place on scientific policy, in particular on general problems of orientation and administration of research and the question of a better use of large-scale scientific and experimental equipment on a co-operative basis;

recommend that, in developing co-operation in the field of science and technology, full use be made of existing practices of bilateral and multilateral co-operation, including that of a regional or sub-regional character, together with the forms and methods of co-operation described in this document;

recommend further that more effective utilization be made of the possibilities and capabilities of existing international organizations, intergovernmental and non-governmental, concerned with science and technology, for improving exchanges of information and experience, as well as for developing other forms of co-operation in fields of common interest, for example:

- in the United Nations Economic Commission for Europe, study of possibilities for expanding multilateral co-operation, taking into account models for projects and research used in various international organizations; and for sponsoring conferences, symposia, and study and working groups such as those which would bring together younger scientists and technologists with eminent specialists in their field;

- through their participation in particular international scientific and technological co-operation programmes, including those of UNESCO and other international organizations, pursuit of continuing progress towards the objectives of such programmes, notably those of UNISIST with particular respect to information policy guidance, technical advice, information contributions and data processing.

5. Environment

The participating States,

Affirming that the protection and improvement of the environment, as well as the protection of nature and the rational utilization of its resources in the interests of present and future generations, is one of the tasks of major importance to the well-being of peoples and the economic development of all countries and that many environmental problems, particularly in Europe, can be solved effectively only through close co-operation,

Acknowledging that each of the participating States, in accordance with the principles of international law, ought to ensure, in a spirit of co-operation, that activities carried out on its territory do not cause degradation of the environment in another State or in areas lying beyond the limits of national jurisdiction,

Considering that the success of any environmental policy presupposes that all population groups and social forces, aware of their responsibilities, help to protect and improve the environment, which necessitates continued and thorough educative action, particularly with regard to youth,

Affirming that experience has shown that economic development and technological progress must be compatible with the protection of the environment and the preservation of historical and cultural values; that damage to the environment is best avoided by preventive measures; and that the ecological balance must be preserved in the exploitation and management of natural resources,

AIMS OF CO-OPERATION

Agree to the following aims of co-operation, in particular:

- to study, with a view to their solution, those environmental problems which, by their nature, are of a multilateral, bilateral, regional or sub-regional dimension; as well as to encourage the development of an interdisciplinary approach to environmental problems;

- to increase the effectiveness of national and international measures for the protection of the environment, by the comparison and, if appropriate, the harmonization of methods of gathering and analyzing facts, by improving the knowledge of pollution phenomena and rational utilization of natural resources, by the exchange of information, by the harmonization of definitions and the adoption, as far as possible, of a common terminology in the field of the environment;

- to take the necessary measures to bring environmental policies closer together and, where appropriate and possible, to harmonize them;

- to encourage, where possible and appropriate, national and international efforts by their interested organizations, enterprises and firms in the development, production and improvement of equipment designed for monitoring, protecting and enhancing the environment.

FIELDS OF CO-OPERATION

To attain these aims, the participating States will make use of every suitable opportunity to co-operate in the field of environment and, in particular, within the areas described below as examples:

Control of air pollution
Desulphurization of fossil fuels and exhaust gases; pollution control of heavy metals, particles, aerosols, nitrogen oxides, in particular those emitted by transport, power stations, and other industrial plants; systems and methods of

observation and control of air pollution and its effects, including long-range transport of air pollutants;

Water pollution control and fresh water utilization
Prevention and control of water pollution, in particular of transboundary rivers and international lakes; techniques for the improvement of the quality of water and further development of ways and means for industrial and municipal sewage effluent purification; methods of assessment of fresh water resources and the improvement of their utilization, in particular by developing methods of production which are less polluting and lead to less consumption of fresh water;

Protection of the marine environment
Protection of the marine environment of participating States, and especially the Mediterranean Sea, from pollutants emanating from land-based sources and those from ships and other vessels, notably the harmful substances listed in Annexes I and II to the London Convention on the Prevention of Marine Pollution by the Dumping of Wastes and Other Matters; problems of maintaining marine ecological balances and food chains, in particular such problems as may arise from the exploration and exploitation of biological and mineral resources of the seas and the sea-bed;

Land utilization and soils
Problems associated with more effective use of lands, including land amelioration, reclamation and recultivation; control of soil pollution, water and air erosion, as well as other forms of soil degradation; maintaining and increasing the productivity of soils with due regard for the possible negative effects of the application of chemical fertilizers and pesticides;

Nature conservation and nature reserves
Protection of nature and nature reserves; conservation and maintenance of existing genetic resources, especially rare animal and plant species; conservation of natural ecological systems; establishment of nature reserves and other protected landscapes and areas, including their use for research, tourism, recreation and other purposes;

Improvement of environmental conditions in areas of human settlement
Environmental conditions associated with transport, housing, working areas, urban development and planning, water supply and sewage disposal systems; assessment of harmful effects of noise, and noise control methods; collection, treatment and utilization of wastes, including the recovery and recycling of materials; research on substitutes for non-biodegradable substances;

Fundamental research, monitoring, forecasting and assessment of environmental changes
Study of changes in climate, landscapes and ecological balances under the impact of both natural factors and human activities; forecasting of possible genetic changes in flora and fauna as a result of environmental pollution; harmonization of statistical data, development of scientific concepts and systems of monitoring networks, standardized methods of observation, measurement and assessment of changes in the biosphere; assessment of the effects of environmental pollution levels and degradation of the environment upon human health; study and development of criteria and standards for various environmental pollutants and regulation regarding production and use of various products;

Legal and administrative measures
Legal and administrative measures for the protection of the environment including procedures for establishing environmental impact assessments.

FORMS AND METHODS OF CO-OPERATION

The participating States declare that problems relating to the protection and improvement of the environment will be solved on both a bilateral and a multilateral, including regional and sub-regional, basis, making full use of existing patterns and forms of co-operation. They will develop co-operation in the field of the environment in particular by taking into consideration the Stockholm Declaration on the Human Environment, relevant resolutions of the United Nations General Assembly and the United Nations Economic Commission for Europe Prague symposium on environmental problems.

The participating States are resolved that co-operation in the field of the environment will be implemented in particular through:

- exchanges of scientific and technical information, documentation and research results, including information on the means of determining the possible effects on the environment of technical and economic activities;

- organization of conferences, symposia and meetings of experts;

- exchanges of scientists, specialists and trainees;

- joint preparation and implementation of programmes and projects for the study and solution of various problems of environmental protection;

- harmonization, where appropriate and necessary, of environmental protection standards and norms, in particular with the object of avoiding possible difficulties in trade which may arise from efforts to resolve ecological problems of production processes and which relate to the achievement of certain environmental qualities in manufactured products;

- consultations on various aspects of environmental protection, as agreed upon among countries concerned, especially in connexion with problems which could have international consequences.

The participating States will further develop such co-operation by:

- promoting the progressive development, codification and implementation of international law as one means of preserving and enhancing the human environment, including principles and practices, as accepted by them, relating to pollution and other environmental damage caused by activities within the jurisdiction or control of their States affecting other countries and regions;

- supporting and promoting the implementation of relevant international Conventions to which they are parties, in particular those designed to prevent and combat marine and fresh water pollution, recommending States to ratify Conventions which have already been signed, as well as considering possibilities of accepting other appropriate Conventions to which they are not parties at present;

- advocating the inclusion, where appropriate and possible, of the various areas of co-operation into the programmes of work of the United Nations Economic Commission for Europe, supporting such co-operation within the framework of the Commission and of the United Nations Environment Programme, and taking into account the work of other competent international organizations of which they are members;

- making wider use, in all types of co-operation, of information already available from national and international sources, including internationally agreed criteria, and utilizing the possibilities and capabilities of various competent international organizations.

The participating States agree on the following recommendations on specific measures:

- to develop through international co-operation an extensive programme for the monitoring and evaluation of the long-range transport of air pollutants, starting with sulphur dioxide and with possible extension to other pollutants, and to this end to take into account basic elements of a co-operation programme which were identified by the experts who met in Oslo in December 1974 at the invitation of the Norwegian Institute of Air Research;

- to advocate that within the framework of the United Nations Economic Commission for Europe a study be carried out of procedures and relevant experience relating to the activities of Governments in developing the capabilities of their countries to predict adequately environmental consequences of economic activities and technological development.

6. Co-operation in other areas

Development of transport

The participating States,

Considering that the improvement of the conditions of transport constitutes one of the factors essential to the development of co-operation among them,

Considering that it is necessary to encourage the development of transport and the solution of existing problems by employing appropriate national and international means,

Taking into account the work being carried out on these subjects by existing international organizations, especially the Inland Transport Committee of the United Nations Economic Commission for Europe,

note that the speed of technical progress in the various fields of transport makes desirable a development of co-operation and an increase in exchanges of information among them;

declare themselves in favour of a simplification and a harmonization of administrative formalities in the field of international transport, in particular at frontiers;

consider it desirable to promote, while allowing for their particular national circumstances in this sector, the harmonization of administrative and technical provisions concerning safety in road, rail, river, air and sea transport;

express their intention to encourage the development of international inland transport of passengers and goods as well as the possibilities of adequate participation in such transport on the basis of reciprocal advantage;

declare themselves in favour, with due respect for their rights and international commitments, of the elimination of disparities arising from the legal provisions applied to traffic on inland waterways which are subject to international conventions and, in particular, of the disparity in the application of those provisions; and to this end invite the member States of the Central Commission for the Navigation of the Rhine, of the Danube Commission and of other bodies to develop the work and studies now being carried out, in particular within the United Nations Economic Commission for Europe;

express their willingness, with a view to improving international rail transport and with due respect for their rights and international commitments, to work towards the elimination of difficulties arising from disparities in existing international legal provisions governing the reciprocal railway transport of passengers and goods between their territories;

express the desire for intensification of the work being carried out by existing international organizations in the field of transport, especially that of the Inland Transport Committee of the United Nations Economic Commission for Europe, and express their intention to contribute thereto by their efforts;

consider that examination by the participating States of the possibilities of their accession to the different conventions or to membership of international organizations specializing in transport matters, as well as their efforts to implement conventions when ratified, could contribute to the strengthening of their co-operation in this field.

Promotion of tourism

The participating States,

Aware of the contribution made by international tourism to the development of mutual understanding among peoples, to increased knowledge of other countries' achievements in various fields, as well as to economic, social and cultural progress,

Recognizing the interrelationship between the development of tourism and measures taken in other areas of economic activity,

express their intention to encourage increased tourism on both an individual and group basis in particular by:

- encouraging the improvement of the tourist infrastructure and co-operation in this field;

- encouraging the carrying out of joint tourist projects including technical co-operation, particularly where this is suggested by territorial proximity and the convergence of tourist interests;

- encouraging the exchange of information, including relevant laws and regulations, studies, data and documentation relating to tourism, and by improving statistics with a view to facilitating their comparability;

- dealing in a positive spirit with questions connected with the allocation of financial means for tourist travel abroad, having regard to their economic possibilities, as well as with those connected with the formalities required for such travel, taking into account other provisions on tourism adopted by the Conference;

- facilitating the activities of foreign travel agencies and passenger transport companies in the promotion of international tourism;

- encouraging tourism outside the high season;

- examining the possibilities of exchanging specialists and students in the field of tourism, with a view to improving their qualifications;

- promoting conferences and symposia on the planning and development of tourism;

consider it desirable to carry out in the appropriate international framework, and with the co-operation of the relevant national bodies, detailed studies on tourism, in particular:

- a comparative study on the status and activities of travel agencies as well as on ways and means of achieving better co-operation among them;

- a study of the problems raised by the seasonal concentration of vacations, with the ultimate objective of encouraging tourism outside peak periods;

- studies of the problems arising in areas where tourism has injured the environment;

consider also that interested parties might wish to study the following questions:

- uniformity of hotel classification; and

- tourist routes comprising two or more countries;

will endeavour, where possible, to ensure that the development of tourism does not injure the environment and the artistic, historic and cultural heritage in their respective countries;

will pursue their co-operation in the field of tourism bilaterally and multilaterally with a view to attaining the above objectives.

Economic and social aspects of migrant labour

The participating States,

Considering that the movements of migrant workers in Europe have reached substantial proportions, and that they constitute an important economic, social and human factor for host countries as well as for countries of origin,

Recognizing that workers' migrations have also given rise to a number of economic, social, human and other problems in both the receiving countries and the countries of origin,

Taking due account of the activities of the competent international organizations, more particularly the International Labour Organisation, in this area,

are of the opinion that the problems arising bilaterally from the migration of workers in Europe as well as between the participating States should be dealt with by the parties directly concerned, in order to resolve these problems in their mutual interest, in the light of the concern of each State involved to take due account of the requirements resulting from its socio-economic situation, having regard to the obligation of each State to comply with the bilateral and multilateral agreements to which it is party, and with the following aims in view:

to encourage the efforts of the countries of origin directed towards increasing the possibilities of employment for their nationals in their own territories, in particular by developing economic co-operation appropriate for this purpose and suitable for the host countries and the countries of origin concerned;

to ensure, through collaboration between the host country and the country of origin, the conditions under which the orderly movement of workers might take place, while at the same time protecting their personal and social welfare and, if appropriate, to organize the recruitment of migrant workers and the provision of elementary language and vocational training;

to ensure equality of rights between migrant workers and nationals of the host countries with regard to conditions of employment and work and to social security, and to endeavour to ensure that migrant workers may enjoy satisfactory living conditions, especially housing conditions;

to endeavour to ensure, as far as possible, that migrant workers may enjoy the same opportunities as nationals of the host countries of finding other suitable employment in the event of unemployment;
to regard with favour the provision of vocational training to migrant workers and, as far as possible, free instruction in the language of the host country, in the framework of their employment;

to confirm the right of migrant workers to receive, as far as possible, regular information in their own language, covering both their country of origin and the host country;

to ensure that the children of migrant workers established in the host country have access to the education usually given there, under the same conditions as the children of that country and, furthermore, to permit them to receive supplementary education in their own language, national culture, history and geography;

to bear in mind that migrant workers, particularly those who have acquired qualifications, can by returning to their countries after a certain period of time help to remedy any deficiency of skilled labour in their country of origin;

to facilitate, as far as possible, the reuniting of migrant workers with their families;

to regard with favour the efforts of the countries of origin to attract the savings of migrant workers, with a view to increasing, within the framework of their economic development, appropriate opportunities for employment, thereby facilitating the reintegration of those workers on their return home.

Training of personnel

The participating States,

Conscious of the importance of the training and advanced training of professional staff and technicians for the economic development of every country,

declare themselves willing to encourage co-operation in this field notably by promoting exchange of information on the subject of institutions, programmes and methods of training and advanced training open to professional staff and technicians in the various sectors of economic activity and especially in those of management, public planning, agriculture and commercial and banking techniques;

consider that it is desirable to develop, under mutually acceptable conditions, exchanges of professional staff and technicians, particularly through training activities, of which it would be left to the competent and interested bodies in the participating States to discuss the modalities - duration, financing, education and qualification levels of potential participants;

declare themselves in favour of examining, through appropriate channels, the possibilities of co-operating on the organization and carrying out of vocational training on the job, more particularly in professions involving modern techniques.

QUESTIONS RELATING TO SECURITY AND CO-OPERATION IN THE MEDITERRANEAN

The participating States,

Conscious of the geographical, historical, cultural, economic and political aspects of their relationship with the non-participating Mediterranean States,

Convinced that security in Europe is to be considered in the broader context of world security and is closely linked with security in the Mediterranean area as a whole, and that accordingly the process of improving security should not be confined to Europe but should extend to other parts of the world, and in particular to the Mediterranean area,

Believing that the strengthening of security and the intensification of co-operation in Europe would stimulate positive processes in the Mediterranean region, and expressing their intention to contribute towards peace, security and justice in the region, in which ends the participating States and the non-participating Mediterranean States have a common interest,

Recognizing the importance of their mutual economic relations with the non-participating Mediterranean States, and conscious of their common interest in the further development of co-operation,

Noting with appreciation the interest expressed by the non-participating Mediterranean States in the Conference since its inception, and having duly taken their contributions into account,

Declare their intention:

- to promote the development of good-neighbourly relations with the non-participating Mediterranean States in conformity with the purposes and principles of the Charter of the United Nations, on which their relations are based, and with the United Nations Declaration on Principles of International Law concerning Friendly Relations and Co-operation among States and accordingly, in this context, to conduct their relations with the non-participating Mediterranean States in the spirit of the principles set forth in the Declaration on Principles Guiding Relations between Participating States;

- to seek, by further improving their relations with the non-participating Mediterranean States, to increase mutual confidence, so as to promote security and stability in the Mediterranean area as a whole;

- to encourage with the non-participating Mediterranean States the development of mutually beneficial co-operation in the various fields of economic activity, especially by expanding commercial exchanges, on the basis of a common awareness of the necessity for stability and progress in trade relations, of their mutual economic interests, and of differences in the levels of economic development, thereby promoting their economic advancement and well-being;

- to contribute to a diversified development of the economies of the non-participating Mediterranean countries, whilst taking due account of their national development objectives, and to co-operate with them, especially in the sectors of industry, science and technology, in their efforts to achieve a better utilization of their resources, thus promoting a more harmonious development of economic relations;

- to intensify their efforts and their co-operation on a bilateral and multilateral basis with the non-participating Mediterranean States directed towards the improvement of the environment of the Mediterranean, especially the safeguarding of the biological resources and ecological balance of the sea, by appropriate measures including the prevention and control of pollution; to this end, and in view of the present situation, to co-operate through competent international organizations and in particular within the United Nations Environment Programme (UNEP);

- to promote further contacts and co-operation with the non-participating Mediterranean States in other relevant fields.

In order to advance the objectives set forth above, the participating States also declare their intention of maintaining and amplifying the contacts and dialogue as initiated by the CSCE with the non-participating Mediterranean States to include all the States of the Mediterranean, with the purpose of contributing to peace, reducing armed forces in the region, strengthening security, lessening tensions in the region, and widening the scope of co-operation, ends in which all share a common interest, as well as with the purpose of defining further common objectives.

The participating States would seek, in the framework of their multilateral efforts, to encourage progress and appropriate initiatives and to proceed to an exchange of views on the attainment of the above purposes.

CO-OPERATION IN HUMANITARIAN AND OTHER FIELDS

The participating States,

Desiring to contribute to the strengthening of peace and understanding among peoples and to the spiritual enrichment of the human personality without distinction as to race, sex, language or religion,

Conscious that increased cultural and educational exchanges, broader dissemination of information, contacts between people, and the solution of humanitarian problems will contribute to the attainment of these aims,

Determined therefore to co-operate among themselves, irrespective of their political, economic and social systems, in order to create better conditions in the above fields, to develop and strengthen existing forms of co-operation and to work out new ways and means appropriate to these aims,

Convinced that this co-operation should take place in full respect for the principles guiding relations among participating States as set forth in the relevant document,

Have adopted the following:

1. Human contacts

The participating States,

Considering the development of contacts to be an important element in the strengthening of friendly relations and trust among peoples,

Affirming, in relation to their present effort to improve conditions in this area, the importance they attach to humanitarian considerations,

Desiring in this spirit to develop, with the continuance of détente, further efforts to achieve continuing progress in this field

And conscious that the questions relevant hereto must be settled by the States concerned under mutually acceptable conditions,

Make it their aim to facilitate freer movement and contacts, individually and collectively, whether privately or officially, among persons, institutions and organizations of the participating States, and to contribute to the solution of the humanitarian problems that arise in that connexion,

Declare their readiness to these ends to take measures which they consider appropriate and to conclude agreements or arrangements among themselves, as may be needed, and

Express their intention now to proceed to the implementation of the following:

(a) Contacts and Regular Meetings on the Basis of Family Ties
In order to promote further development of contacts on the basis of family ties the participating States will favourably consider applications for travel with the purpose of allowing persons to enter or leave their territory temporarily, and on a regular basis if desired, in order to visit members of their families.

Applications for temporary visits to meet members of their families will be dealt with without distinction as to the country of origin or destination: existing requirements for travel documents and visas will be applied in this spirit. The preparation and issue of such documents and visas will be effected within reasonable time limits; cases of urgent necessity - such as serious illness or death - will be given priority treatment. They will take such steps as may be necessary to ensure that the fees for official travel documents and visas are acceptable.

They confirm that the presentation of an application concerning contacts on the basis of family ties will not modify the rights and obligations of the applicant or of members of his family.

(b) Reunification of Families
The participating States will deal in a positive and humanitarian spirit with the applications of persons who wish to be reunited with members of their family, with special attention being given to requests of an urgent character - such as requests submitted by persons who are ill or old.

They will deal with applications in this field as expeditiously as possible.

They will lower where necessary the fees charged in connexion with these applications to ensure that they are at a moderate level.

Applications for the purpose of family reunification which are not granted may be renewed at the appropriate level and will be reconsidered at reasonably short intervals by the authorities of the country of residence or destination, whichever is concerned; under such circumstances fees will be charged only when applications are granted.

Persons whose applications for family reunification are granted may bring with them or ship their household and personal effects; to this end the participating States will use all possibilities provided by existing regulations.

Until members of the same family are reunited meetings and contacts between them may take place in accordance with the modalities for contacts on the basis of family ties.

The participating States will support the efforts of Red Cross and Red Crescent Societies concerned with the problems of family reunification.

They confirm that the presentation of an application concerning family reunification will not modify the rights and obligations of the applicant or of members of his family.

The receiving participating State will take appropriate care with regard to employment for persons from other participating States who take up permanent residence in that State in connexion with family reunification with its citizens and see that they are afforded opportunities equal to those enjoyed by its own citizens for education, medical assistance and social security.

(c) Marriage between Citizens of Different States

The participating States will examine favourably and on the basis of humanitarian considerations requests for exit or entry permits from persons who have decided to marry a citizen from another participating State.

The processing and issuing of the documents required for the above purposes and for the marriage will be in accordance with the provisions accepted for family reunification.

In dealing with requests from couples from different participating States, once married, to enable them and the minor children of their marriage to transfer their permanent residence to a State in which either one is normally a resident, the participating States will also apply the provisions accepted for family reunification.

(d) Travel for Personal or Professional Reasons

The participating States intend to facilitate wider travel by their citizens for personal or professional reasons and to this end they intend in particular:

- gradually to simplify and to administer flexibly the procedures for exit and entry;

- to ease regulations concerning movement of citizens from the other participating States in their territory, with due regard to security requirements.

They will endeavour gradually to lower, where necessary, the fees for visas and official travel documents.

They intend to consider, as necessary, means - including, in so far as appropriate, the conclusion of multilateral or bilateral consular conventions or other relevant agreements or understandings - for the improvement of arrangements to provide consular services, including legal and consular assistance.

* * *

They confirm that religious faiths, institutions and organizations, practising within the constitutional framework of the participating States, and their representatives can, in the field of their activities, have contacts and meetings among themselves and exchange information.

(e) Improvement of Conditions for Tourism on an Individual or Collective Basis

The participating States consider that tourism contributes to a fuller knowledge of the life, culture and history of other countries, to the growth of understanding among peoples, to the improvement of contacts and to the broader use of leisure. They intend to promote the development of tourism, on an individual or collective basis, and, in particular, they intend:

- to promote visits to their respective countries by encouraging the provisions of appropriate facilities and the simplification and expediting of necessary formalities relating to such visits;

- to increase, on the basis of appropriate agreements or arrangements where necessary, co-operation in the development of tourism, in particular by considering bilaterally possible ways to increase information relating to travel to other countries and to the reception and service of tourists, and other related questions of mutual interest.

(f) Meetings among Young People

The participating States intend to further the development of contacts and exchanges among young people by encouraging:

- increased exchanges and contacts on a short or long term basis among young people working, training or undergoing education through bilateral or multilateral agreements or regular programmes in all cases where it is possible;

- study by their youth organizations of the question of possible agreements relating to frameworks of multilateral youth co-operation;

- agreements or regular programmes relating to the organization of exchanges of students, of international youth seminars, of courses of professional training and foreign language study;

- the further development of youth tourism and the provision to this end of appropriate facilities;

- the development, where possible, of exchanges, contacts and co-operation on a bilateral or multilateral basis between their organizations which represent wide circles of young people working, training or undergoing education;

- awareness among youth of the importance of developing mutual understanding and of strengthening friendly relations and confidence among peoples.

(g) Sport
In order to expand existing links and co-operation in the field of sport the participating States will encourage contacts and exchanges of this kind, including sports meetings and competitions of all sorts, on the basis of the established international rules, regulations and practice.

(h) Expansion of Contacts
By way of further developing contacts among governmental institutions and non-governmental organizations and associations, including women's organizations, the participating States will facilitate the convening of meetings as well as travel by delegations, groups and individuals.

2. Information

The participating States,

Conscious of the need for an ever wider knowledge and understanding of the various aspects of life in other participating States,

Acknowledging the contribution of this process to the growth of confidence between peoples,

Desiring, with the development of mutual understanding between the participating States and with the further improvement of their relations, to continue further efforts towards progress in this field,

Recognizing the importance of the dissemination of information from the other participating States and of a better acquaintance with such information,

Emphasizing therefore the essential and influential role of the press, radio, television, cinema and news agencies and of the journalists working in these fields,

Make it their aim to facilitate the freer and wider dissemination of information of all kinds, to encourage co-operation in the field of information and the exchange of information with other countries, and to improve the conditions under which journalists from one participating State exercise their profession in another participating State, and

Express their intention in particular:

(a) Improvement of the Circulation of, Access to, and Exchange of Information

(i) Oral information

- To facilitate the dissemination of oral information through the encouragement of lectures and lecture tours by personalities and specialists from the other participating States, as well as exchanges of opinions at round table meetings, seminars, symposia, summer schools, congresses and other bilateral and multilateral meetings.

(ii) Printed information

- To facilitate the improvement of the dissemination, on their territory, of newspapers and printed publications, periodical and non-periodical, from the other participating States. For this purpose:

  they will encourage their competent firms and organizations to conclude agreements and contracts designed gradually to increase the quantities and the number of titles of newspapers and publications imported from the other participating States. These agreements and contracts should in particular mention the speediest conditions of delivery and the use of the normal channels existing in each country for the distribution of its own publications and newspapers, as well as forms and means of payment agreed between the parties making it possible to achieve the objectives aimed at by these agreements and contracts;

where necessary, they will take appropriate measures to achieve the above objectives and to implement the provisions contained in the agreements and contracts.

To contribute to the improvement of access by the public to periodical and non-periodical printed publications imported on the bases indicated above. In particular:

they will encourage an increase in the number of places where these publications are on sale;

they will facilitate the availability of these periodical publications during congresses, conferences, official visits and other international events and to tourists during the season;

they will develop the possibilities for taking out subscriptions according to the modalities particular to each country;

they will improve the opportunities for reading and borrowing these publications in large public libraries and their reading rooms as well as in university libraries.

They intend to improve the possibilities for acquaintance with bulletins of official information issued by diplomatic missions and distributed by those missions on the basis of arrangements acceptable to the interested parties.

(iii) Filmed and Broadcast Information

- To promote the improvement of the dissemination of filmed and broadcast information. To this end:

they will encourage the wider showing and broadcasting of a greater variety of recorded and filmed information from the other participating States, illustrating the various aspects of life in their countries and received on the basis of such agreements or arrangements as may be necessary between the organizations and firms directly concerned;

they will facilitate the import by competent organizations and firms of recorded audio-visual material from the other participating States.

The participating States note the expansion in the dissemination of information broadcast by radio, and express the hope for the continuation of this process, so as to meet the interest of mutual understanding among peoples and the aims set forth by this Conference.

(b) Co-operation in the Field of Information

- To encourage co-operation in the field of information on the basis of short or long term agreements or arrangements. In particular:

  they will favour increased co-operation among mass media organizations, including press agencies, as well as among publishing houses and organizations;

  they will favour co-operation among public or private, national or international radio and television organizations, in particular through the exchange of both live and recorded radio and television programmes, and through the joint production and the broadcasting and distribution of such programmes;

  they will encourage meetings and contacts both between journalists' organizations and between journalists from the participating States;

  they will view favourably the possibilities of arrangements between periodical publications as well as between newspapers from the participating States, for the purpose of exchanging and publishing articles;

  they will encourage the exchange of technical information as well as the organization of joint research and meetings devoted to the exchange of experience and views between experts in the field of the press, radio and television.

(c) Improvement of Working Conditions for Journalists

The participating States, desiring to improve the conditions under which journalists from one participating State exercise their profession in another participating State, intend in particular to:

- examine in a favourable spirit and within a suitable and reasonable time scale requests from journalists for visas;

- grant to permanently accredited journalists of the participating States, on the basis of arrangements, multiple entry and exit visas for specified periods;

- facilitate the issue to accredited journalists of the participating States of permits for stay in their country of temporary residence and, if and when these are necessary, of other official papers which it is appropriate for them to have;

- ease, on a basis of reciprocity, procedures for arranging travel by journalists of the participating States in the country where they are exercising their profession, and to provide progressively greater opportunities for such travel, subject to the observance of regulations relating to the existence of areas closed for security reasons;

- ensure that requests by such journalists for such travel receive, in so far as possible, an expeditious response, taking into account the time scale of the request;

- increase the opportunities for journalists of the participating States to communicate personally with their sources, including organizations and official institutions;

- grant to journalists of the participating States the right to import, subject only to its being taken out again, the technical equipment (photographic, cinematographic, tape recorder, radio and television) necessary for the exercise of their profession;*

- enable journalists of the other participating States, whether permanently or temporarily accredited, to transmit completely, normally and rapidly by means recognized by the participating States to the information organs which they represent, the results of their professional activity, including tape recordings and undeveloped film,

---

* While recognizing that appropriate local personnel are employed by foreign journalists in many instances, the participating States note that the above provisions would be applied, subject to the observance of the appropriate rules, to persons from the other participating States, who are regularly and professionally engaged as technicians, photographers or cameramen of the press, radio, television or cinema.

for the purpose of publication or of broadcasting on the radio or television.

The participating States reaffirm that the legitimate pursuit of their professional activity will neither render journalists liable to expulsion nor otherwise penalize them. If an accredited journalist is expelled, he will be informed of the reasons for this act and may submit an application for re-examination of his case.

3. Co-operation and exchanges in the field of culture

The participating States,

Considering that cultural exchanges and co-operation contribute to a better comprehension among people and among peoples, and thus promote a lasting understanding among States,

Confirming the conclusions already formulated in this field at the multilateral level, particularly at the Intergovernmental Conference on Cultural Policies in Europe, organized by UNESCO in Helsinki in June 1972, where interest was manifested in the active participation of the broadest possible social groups in an increasingly diversified cultural life,

Desiring, with the development of mutual confidence and the further improvement of relations between the participating States, to continue further efforts toward progress in this field,

Disposed in this spirit to increase substantially their cultural exchanges, with regard both to persons and to cultural works, and to develop among them an active co-operation, both at the bilateral and the multilateral level, in all the fields of culture,

Convinced that such a development of their mutual relations will contribute to the enrichment of the respective cultures, while respecting the originality of each, as well as to the reinforcement among them of a consciousness of common values, while continuing to develop cultural co-operation with other countries of the world,

Declare that they jointly set themselves the following objectives:

(a) to develop the mutual exchange of information with a view to a better knowledge of respective cultural achievements,

(b) to improve the facilities for the exchange and for the dissemination of cultural property,

(c) to promote access by all to respective cultural achievements,

(d) to develop contacts and co-operation among persons active in the field of culture,

(e) to seek new fields and forms of cultural co-operation,

Thus *give expression to* their common will to take progressive, coherent and long-term action in order to achieve the objectives of the present declaration; and

Express their intention now to proceed to the implementation of the following:

Extension of Relations

To expand and improve at the various levels co-operation and links in the field of culture, in particular by:

- concluding, where appropriate, agreements on a bilateral or multilateral basis, providing for the extension of relations among competent State institutions and non-governmental organizations in the field of culture, as well as among people engaged in cultural activities, taking into account the need both for flexibility and the fullest possible use of existing agreements, and bearing in mind that agreements and also other arrangements constitute important means of developing cultural co-operation and exchanges;

- contributing to the development of direct communication and co-operation among relevant State institutions and non-governmental organizations, including, where necessary, such communication and co-operation carried out on the basis of special agreements and arrangements;

- encouraging direct contacts and communications among persons engaged in cultural activities, including, where necessary, such contacts and communications carried out on the basis of special agreements and arrangements.

Mutual Knowledge

Within their competence to adopt, on a bilateral and multilateral level, appropriate measures which would give their peoples a more comprehensive and complete mutual knowledge of their achievements in the various fields of culture, and among them:

- to examine jointly, if necessary with the assistance of appropriate international organizations, the possible creation in Europe and the structure of a bank of cultural data, which would collect information from the participating countries and make it available to its correspondents on their request, and to convene for this purpose a meeting of experts from interested States;

- to consider, if necessary in conjunction with appropriate international organizations, ways of compiling in Europe an inventory of documentary films of a cultural or scientific nature from the participating States;

- to encourage more frequent book exhibitions and to examine the possibility of organizing periodically in Europe a large-scale exhibition of books from the participating States;

- to promote the systematic exchange, between the institutions concerned and publishing houses, of catalogues of available books as well as of pre-publication material which will include, as far as possible, all forthcoming publications; and also to promote the exchange of material between firms publishing encyclopaedias, with a view to improving the presentation of each country;

- to examine jointly questions of expanding and improving exchanges of information in the various fields of culture, such as theatre, music, library work as well as the conservation and restoration of cultural property.

Exchanges and Dissemination

To contribute to the improvement of facilities for exchanges and the dissemination of cultural property, by appropriate means, in particular by:

- studying the possibilities for harmonizing and reducing the charges relating to international commercial exchanges of books and other cultural materials, and also for new means of insuring works of art in foreign exhibitions and for reducing the risks of damage or loss to which these works are exposed by their movement;

- facilitating the formalities of customs clearance, in good time for programmes of artistic events, of the works of art, materials and accessories appearing on lists agreed upon by the organizers of these events;

- encouraging meetings among representatives of competent organizations and relevant firms to examine measures within their field of activity - such as the simplification of orders, time limits for sending supplies and modalities of payment - which might facilitate international commercial exchanges of books;

- promoting the loan and exchange of films among their film institutes and film libraries;

- encouraging the exchange of information among interested parties concerning events of a cultural character foreseen in the participating States, in fields where this is most appropriate, such as music, theatre and the plastic and graphic arts, with a view to contributing to the compilation and publication of a calendar of such events, with the assistance, where necessary, of the appropriate international organizations;

- encouraging a study of the impact which the foreseeable development, and a possible harmonization among interested parties, of the technical means used for the dissemination of culture might have on the development of cultural co-operation and exchanges, while keeping in view the preservation of the diversity and originality of their respective cultures;

- encouraging, in the way they deem appropriate, within their cultural policies, the further development of interest in the cultural heritage of the other participating States, conscious of the merits and the value of each culture;

- endeavouring to ensure the full and effective application of the international agreements and conventions on copyrights and on circulation of cultural property to which they are party or to which they may decide in the future to become party.

Access
To promote fuller mutual access by all to the achievements - works, experiences and performing arts - in the various fields of culture of their countries, and to that end to make the best possible efforts, in accordance with their competence, more particularly:

- to promote wider dissemination of books and artistic works, in particular by such means as:

  facilitating, while taking full account of the international copyright conventions to which they are party, international contacts and communications between authors and publishing houses as well as other cultural institutions, with a view to a more complete mutual access to cultural achievements;

  recommending that, in determining the size of editions, publishing houses take into account also the demand from the other participating States, and that rights of sale in other participating States be granted, where possible, to several sales organizations of the importing countries, by agreement between interested partners;

  encouraging competent organizations and relevant firms to conclude agreements and contracts and contributing, by this means, to a gradual increase in the number and diversity of works by authors from the other participating States available in the original and in translation in their libraries and bookshops;

  promoting, where deemed appropriate, an increase in the number of sales outlets where books by authors from the other participating States, imported in the original on the basis of agreements and contracts, and in translation, are for sale;

  promoting, on a wider scale, the translation of works in the sphere of literature and other fields of cultural activity, produced in the languages of the other participating States, especially from the less widely-spoken languages, and the publication and dissemination of the translated works by such measures as:

    encouraging more regular contacts between interested publishing houses;

    developing their efforts in the basic and advanced training of translators;

encouraging, by appropriate means, the publishing houses of their countries to publish translations;

facilitating the exchange between publishers and interested institutions of lists of books which might be translated;

promoting between their countries the professional activity and co-operation of translators;

carrying out joint studies on ways of further promoting translations and their dissemination;

improving and expanding exchanges of books, bibliographies and catalogue cards between libraries;

- to envisage other appropriate measures which would permit, where necessary by mutual agreement among interested parties, the facilitation of access to their respective cultural achievements, in particular in the field of books;

- to contribute by appropriate means to the wider use of the mass media in order to improve mutual acquaintance with the cultural life of each;

- to seek to develop the necessary conditions for migrant workers and their families to preserve their links with their national culture, and also to adapt themselves to their new cultural environment;

- to encourage the competent bodies and enterprises to make a wider choice and effect wider distribution of full-length and documentary films from the other participating States, and to promote more frequent non-commercial showings, such as premières, film weeks and festivals, giving due consideration to films from countries whose cinematographic works are less well known;

- to promote, by appropriate means, the extension of opportunities for specialists from the other participating States to work with materials of a cultural character from film and audio-visual archives, within the framework of the existing rules for work on such archival materials;

- to encourage a joint study by interested bodies, where appropriate with the assistance of the competent international organizations, of the expediency and the conditions for the establishment of a repertory of their recorded television programmes of a cultural nature, as well as of the means of viewing them rapidly in order to facilitate their selection and possible acquisition.

Contacts and Co-operation

To contribute, by appropriate means, to the development of contacts and co-operation in the various fields of culture, especially among creative artists and people engaged in cultural activities, in particular by making efforts to:

- promote for persons active in the field of culture, travel and meetings including, where necessary, those carried out on the basis of agreements, contracts or other special arrangements and which are relevant to their cultural co-operation;

- encourage in this way contacts among creative and performing artists and artistic groups with a view to their working together, making known their works in other participating States or exchanging views on topics relevant to their common activity;

- encourage, where necessary through appropriate arrangements, exchanges of trainees and specialists and the granting of scholarships for basic and advanced training in various fields of culture such as the arts and architecture, museums and libraries, literary studies and translation, and contribute to the creation of favourable conditions of reception in their respective institutions;

- encourage the exchange of experience in the training of organizers of cultural activities as well as of teachers and specialists in fields such as theatre, opera, ballet, music and fine arts;

- continue to encourage the organization of international meetings among creative artists, especially young creative artists, on current questions of artistic and literary creation which are of interest for joint study;

- study other possibilities for developing exchanges and co-operation among persons active in the field of culture, with a view to a better mutual knowledge of the cultural life of the participating States.

Fields and Forms of Co-operation

To encourage the search for new fields and forms of cultural co-operation, to these ends contributing to the conclusion among interested parties, where necessary, of appropriate agreements and arrangements, and in this context to promote:

- joint studies regarding cultural policies, in particular in their social aspects, and as they relate to planning, town-planning, educational and environmental policies, and the cultural aspects of tourism;

- the exchange of knowledge in the realm of cultural diversity, with a view to contributing thus to a better understanding by interested parties of such diversity where it occurs;

- the exchange of information, and as may be appropriate, meetings of experts, the elaboration and the execution of research programmes and projects, as well as their joint evaluation, and the dissemination of the results, on the subjects indicated above;

- such forms of cultural co-operation and the development of such joint projects as:

  international events in the fields of the plastic and graphic arts, cinema, theatre, ballet, music, folklore, etc.; book fairs and exhibitions, joint performances of operatic and dramatic works, as well as performances given by soloists, instrumental ensembles, orchestras, choirs and other artistic groups, including those composed of amateurs, paying due attention to the organization of international cultural youth events and the exchange of youth artists;

  the inclusion of works by writers and composers from the other participating States in the repertoires of soloists and artistic ensembles;

  the preparation, translation and publication of articles, studies and monographs, as well as of low-cost books and of artistic and literary collections, suited to making better known respective cultural achievements, envisaging for this purpose meetings among experts and representatives of publishing houses;

  the co-production and the exchange of films and of radio and television programmes, by promoting, in particular, meetings among producers, technicians and representatives of the public authorities with a view to working out favourable conditions for the execution of specific joint projects and by encouraging, in the field of co-production, the establishment of international filming teams;

  the organization of competitions for architects and town-planners, bearing in mind the possible implementation of the best projects and the formation, where possible, of international teams;

the implementation of joint projects for conserving, restoring and showing to advantage works of art, historical and archaeological monuments and sites of cultural interest, with the help, in appropriate cases, of international organizations of a governmental or non-governmental character as well as of private institutions - competent and active in these fields - envisaging for this purpose:

periodic meetings of experts of the interested parties to elaborate the necessary proposals, while bearing in mind the need to consider these questions in a wider social and economic context;

the publication in appropriate periodicals of articles designed to make known and to compare, among the participating States, the most significant achievements and innovations;

a joint study with a view to the improvement and possible harmonization of the different systems used to inventory and catalogue the historical monuments and places of cultural interest in their countries; the study of the possibilities for organizing international courses for the training of specialists in different disciplines relating to restoration.

* * *

National minorities or regional cultures. The participating States, recognizing the contribution that national minorities or regional cultures can make to co-operation among them in various fields of culture, intend, when such minorities or cultures exist within their territory, to facilitate this contribution, taking into account the legitimate interests of their members.

4. Co-operation and exchanges in the field of education

The participating States,

Conscious that the development of relations of an international character in the fields of education and science contributes to a better mutual understanding and is to the advantage of all peoples as well as to the benefit of future generations,

Prepared to facilitate, between organizations, institutions and persons engaged in education and science, the further development of exchanges of knowledge and experience as well as of contacts, on the basis of special arrangements where these are necessary,

Desiring to strengthen the links among educational and scientific establishments and also to encourage their co-operation in sectors of common interest, particularly where the levels of knowledge and resources require efforts to be concerted internationally, and

Convinced that progress in these fields should be accompanied and supported by a wider knowledge of foreign languages,

Express to these ends their intention in particular:

(a) Extension of Relations

To expand and improve at the various levels co-operation and links in the fields of education and science, in particular by:

- concluding, where appropriate, bilateral or multilateral agreements providing for co-operation and exchanges among State institutions, non-governmental bodies and persons engaged in activities in education and science, bearing in mind the need both for flexibility and the fuller use of existing agreements and arrangements;

- promoting the conclusion of direct arrangements between universities and other institutions of higher education and research, in the framework of agreements between governments where appropriate;

- encouraging among persons engaged in education and science direct contacts and communications, including those based on special agreements or arrangements where these are appropriate.

(b) Access and Exchanges

To improve access, under mutually acceptable conditions, for students, teachers and scholars of the participating States to each other's educational, cultural and scientific institutions, and to intensify exchanges among these institutions in all areas of common interest, in particular by:

- increasing the exchange of information on facilities for study and courses open to foreign participants, as well as on the conditions under which they will be admitted and received;

- facilitating travel between the participating States by scholars, teachers and students for purposes of study, teaching and research as well as for improving knowledge of each other's educational, cultural and scientific achievements;

- encouraging the award of scholarships for study, teaching and research in their countries to scholars, teachers and students of other participating States;

- establishing, developing or encouraging programmes providing for the broader exchange of scholars, teachers and students, including the organization of symposia, seminars and collaborative projects, and the exchanges of educational and scholarly information such as university publications and materials from libraries;

- promoting the efficient implementation of such arrangements and programmes by providing scholars, teachers and students in good time with more detailed information about their placing in universities and institutes and the programmes envisaged for them; by granting them the opportunity to use relevant scholarly, scientific and open archival materials; and by facilitating their travel within the receiving State for the purpose of study or research as well as in the form of vacation tours on the basis of the usual procedures;

- promoting a more exact assessment of the problems of comparison and equivalence of academic degrees and diplomas by fostering the exchange of information on the organization, duration and content of studies, the comparison of methods of assessing levels of knowledge and academic qualifications, and, where feasible, arriving at the mutual recognition of academic degrees and diplomas either through governmental agreements, where necessary, or direct arrangements between universities and other institutions of higher learning and research;

- recommending, moreover, to the appropriate international organizations that they should intensify their efforts to reach a generally acceptable solution to the problems of comparison and equivalence between academic degrees and diplomas.

(c) Science

Within their competence to broaden and improve co-operation and exchanges in the field of science, in particular:

To increase, on a bilateral or multilateral basis, the exchange and dissemination of scientific information and documentation by such means as:

- making this information more widely available to scientists and research workers of the other participating States through, for instance, participation in international information-sharing programmes or through other appropriate arrangements;

- broadening and facilitating the exchange of samples and other scientific materials used particularly for fundamental research in the fields of natural sciences and medicine;

- inviting scientific institutions and universities to keep each other more fully and regularly informed about their current and contemplated research work in fields of common interest.

To facilitate the extension of communications and direct contacts between universities, scientific institutions and associations as well as among scientists and research workers, including those based where necessary on special agreements or arrangements, by such means as:

- further developing exchanges of scientists and research workers and encouraging the organization of preparatory meetings or working groups on research topics of common interest;

- encouraging the creation of joint teams of scientists to pursue research projects under arrangements made by the scientific institutions of several countries;

- assisting the organization and successful functioning of international conferences and seminars and participation in them by their scientists and research workers;

- furthermore envisaging, in the near future, a "Scientific Forum" in the form of a meeting of leading personalities in science from the participating States to discuss interrelated problems of common interest concerning current and future developments in science, and to promote the expansion of contacts, communications and the exchange of information between scientific institutions and among scientists;

- foreseeing, at an early date, a meeting of experts representing the participating States and their national scientific institutions, in order to prepare such a "Scientific Forum" in consultation with appropriate international organizations, such as UNESCO and the ECE;

- considering in due course what further steps might be taken with respect to the "Scientific Forum".

To develop in the field of scientific research, on a bilateral or multilateral basis, the co-ordination of programmes carried out in the participating States and the organization of joint programmes, especially in the areas mentioned below, which may involve the combined efforts of scientists and in certain cases the use of costly or unique equipment. The list of subjects in these areas is illustrative; and specific projects would have to be determined subsequently by the potential partners in the participating States, taking account of the contribution which could be made by appropriate international organizations and scientific institutions:

- *exact and natural sciences*, in particular fundamental research in such fields as mathematics, physics, theoretical physics, geophysics, chemistry, biology, ecology and astronomy;

- *medicine*, in particular basic research into cancer and cardiovascular diseases, studies on the diseases endemic in the developing countries, as well as medico-social research with special emphasis on occupational diseases, the rehabilitation of the handicapped and the care of mothers, children and the elderly;

- *the humanities and social sciences*, such as history, geography, philosophy, psychology, pedagogical research, linguistics, sociology, the legal, political and economic sciences; comparative studies on social, socio-economic and cultural phenomena which are of common interest to the participating States, especially the problems of human environment and urban development; and scientific studies on the methods of conserving and restoring monuments and works of art.

(d) Foreign Languages and Civilizations

To encourage the study of foreign languages and civilizations as an important means of expanding communication among peoples for their better acquaintance with the culture of each country, as well as for the strengthening of international co-operation; to this end to stimulate, within their competence, the further development and improvement of foreign language teaching and the diversification of choice of languages taught at various levels, paying due attention to less widely-spread or studied languages, and in particular:

- to intensify co-operation aimed at improving the teaching of foreign languages through exchanges of information and experience concerning the development and application of effective modern teaching methods and technical aids, adapted to the needs of different categories of students, including methods of accelerated teaching; and to consider the possibility of conducting, on a bilateral or multilateral basis, studies of new methods of foreign language teaching;

- to encourage co-operation between institutions concerned, on a bilateral or multilateral basis, aimed at exploiting more fully the resources of modern educational technology in language teaching, for example through comparative studies by their specialists and, where agreed, through exchanges or transfers of audiovisual materials, of materials used for preparing textbooks, as well as of information about new types of technical equipment used for teaching languages;

- to promote the exchange of information on the experience acquired in the training of language teachers and to intensify exchanges on a bilateral basis of language teachers and students as well as to facilitate their participation in summer courses in languages and civilizations, wherever these are organized;

- to encourage co-operation among experts in the field of lexicography with the aim of defining the necessary terminological equivalents, particularly in the scientific and technical disciplines, in order to facilitate relations among scientific institutions and specialists;

- to promote the wider spread of foreign language study among the different types of secondary education establishments and greater possibilities of choice between an increased number of European languages; and in this context to consider, wherever appropriate, the possibilities for developing the recruitment and training of teachers as well as the organization of the student groups required;

- to favour, in higher education, a wider choice in the languages offered to language students and greater opportunities for other students to study various foreign languages; also to facilitate, where desirable, the organization of courses in languages and civilizations, on the basis of special arrangements as necessary, to be given by foreign lecturers, particularly from European countries having less widelyspread or studied languages;

- to promote, within the framework of adult education, the further development of specialized programmes, adapted to various needs and interests, for teaching foreign languages to their own inhabitants and the languages of host countries to interested adults from other countries; in this context to encourage interested institutions to co-operate, for example, in the elaboration of programmes for teaching by radio and television and by accelerated methods, and also, where desirable, in the definition of study objectives for such programmes, with a view to arriving at comparable levels of language proficiency;

- to encourage the association, where appropriate, of the teaching of foreign languages with the study of the corresponding civilizations and also to make further efforts to stimulate interest in the study of foreign languages, including relevant out-of-class activities.

(e) Teaching Methods

To promote the exchange of experience, on a bilateral or multilateral basis, in teaching methods at all levels of education, including those used in permanent and adult education, as well as the exchange of teaching materials, in particular by:

- further developing various forms of contacts and co-operation in the different fields of pedagogical science, for example through comparative or joint studies carried out by interested institutions or through exchanges of information on the results of teaching experiments;

- intensifying exchanges of information on teaching methods used in various educational systems and on results of research into the processes by which pupils and students acquire knowledge, taking account of relevant experience in different types of specialized education;

- facilitating exchanges of experience concerning the organization and functioning of education intended for adults and recurrent education, the relationships between these and other forms and levels of education, as well as concerning the means of adapting education, including vocational and technical training, to the needs of economic and social development in their countries;

- encouraging exchanges of experience in the education of youth and adults in international understanding, with particular reference to those major problems of mankind whose solution calls for a common approach and wider international co-operation;

- encouraging exchanges of teaching materials - including school textbooks, having in mind the possibility of promoting mutual knowledge and facilitating the presentation of each country in such books - as well as exchanges of information on technical innovations in the field of education.

***

National minorities or regional cultures. The participating States, recognizing the contribution that national minorities or regional cultures can make to co-operation among them in various fields of education, intend, when such minorities or cultures exist within their territory, to facilitate this contribution, taking into account the legitimate interests of their members.

FOLLOW-UP TO THE CONFERENCE

The participating States,

Having considered and evaluated the progress made at the Conference on Security and Co-operation in Europe,

Considering further that, within the broader context of the world, the Conference is an important part of the process of improving security and developing co-operation in Europe and that its results will contribute significantly to this process,

Intending to implement the provisions of the Final Act of the Conference in order to give full effect to its results and thus to further the process of improving security and developing co-operation in Europe,

Convinced that, in order to achieve the aims sought by the Conference, they should make further unilateral, bilateral and multilateral efforts and continue, in the appropriate forms set forth below, the multilateral process initiated by the Conference,

1. *Declare their resolve*, in the period following the Conference, to pay due regard to and implement the provisions of the Final Act of the Conference:

(a) unilaterally, in all cases which lend themselves to such action;

(b) bilaterally, by negotiations with other participating States;

(c) multilaterally, by meetings of experts of the participating States, and also within the framework of existing international organizations, such as the United Nations Economic Commission for Europe and UNESCO, with regard to educational, scientific and cultural co-operation;

2. *Declare furthermore their resolve* to continue the multilateral process initiated by the Conference:

(a) by proceeding to a thorough exchange of views both on the implementation of the provisions of the Final Act and of the tasks defined by the Conference, as well as, in the context of the questions dealt with by the latter, on the deepening of their mutual relations, the improvement of security and the development of co-operation in Europe, and the development of the process of détente in the future;

(b) by organizing to these ends meetings among their representatives, beginning with a meeting at the level of representatives appointed by the Ministers of Foreign Affairs. This meeting will define the appropriate modalities for the holding of other meetings which could include further similar meetings and the possibility of a new Conference;

3. The first of the meetings indicated above will be held at Belgrade in 1977. A preparatory meeting to organize this meeting will be held at Belgrade on 15 June 1977. The preparatory meeting will decide on the date, duration, agenda and other modalities of the meeting of representatives appointed by the Ministers of Foreign Affairs;

4. The rules of procedure, the working methods and the scale of distribution for the expenses of the Conference will, *mutatis mutandis*, be applied to the meetings envisaged in paragraphs 1(c), 2 and 3 above. All the above-mentioned meetings will be held in the participating States in rotation. The services of a technical secretariat will be provided by the host country.

The original of this Final Act, drawn up in English, French, German, Italian, Russian and Spanish, will be transmitted to the Government of the Republic of Finland, which will retain it in its archives. Each of the participating States will receive from the Government of the Republic of Finland a true copy of this Final Act.

The text of this Final Act will be published in each participating State, which will disseminate it and make it known as widely as possible.

The Government of the Republic of Finland is requested to transmit to the Secretary-General of the United Nations the text of this Final Act, which is not eligible for registration under Article 102 of the Charter of the United Nations, with a view to its circulation to all the members of the Organization as an official document of the United Nations.

The Government of the Republic of Finland is also requested to transmit the text of this Final Act to the Director-General of UNESCO and to the Executive Secretary of the United Nations Economic Commission for Europe.

Wherefore, the undersigned High Representatives of the participating States, mindful of the high political significance which they attach to the results of the Conference, and declaring their determination to act in accordance with the provisions contained in the above texts, have subscribed their signatures below:

Done at Helsinki,
on 1st August 1975,
in the name of
....

RESERVATIONS AND INTERPRETATIVE STATEMENTS

Statements concerning the Declaration on Principles
Editors note: On 19 July 1975, Sub-Committee 1 of Committee I, dealing with the First Basket of the (draft) Final Act of Helsinki, agreed on the text of the "Declaration on Principles Guiding Relations between Participating States". At this occasion, the following statements have been made:[1]

a) The Chairman [*Czechoslovakia; Ed.*] made the following Statement:
"Taking into account the fourth paragraph of the preamble to the 'Declaration on Principles Guiding Relations between Participating States', which reads as follows:

> "Expressing their common adherence to the principles which are set forth below and are in conformity with the Charter of the United Nations, as well as their common will to act, in the application of these principles, in conformity with the purposes and principles of the Charter of the United Nations;"

Taking into account the first operative paragraph of the document on relationship with the non-participating Mediterranean States, CSCE/CC/103;

Taking into account the wording of the last paragraph of the 'Declaration on Principles of International Law concerning Friendly Relations and Co-operation among States in accordance with the Charter of the United Nations' which says:

> "The principles of the Charter which are embodied in this Declaration ...";

It has been noted that the mention of conformity with the Charter is considered as covering a mention of conformity with the above mentioned 'Declaration'.

In these circumstances it has not been found indispensable to mention this 'Declaration' in the preambular part of the document on Principles."

No objection was raised.

* * *

b) The Representative of Romania made the following Statement:

"At the time of the adoption of the following text in the Principle of non-intervention in internal affairs:

---

1 Committee I, Sub-Committee 1, Journal No. 337 (19 July 1975), paragraph 4.

'They will accordingly refrain from any form of armed intervention or threat of such intervention against another participating State.'

the Representative of Romania made the following Statement:

1. The concept 'armed intervention' means, by definition, an unlawful act;

2. This text is linked to the preceding paragraph, which defines non-intervention as meaning refraining from any intervention in the internal or external affairs falling within the domestic jurisdiction of another participating State."

* * *

c) The Representative of the Federal Republic of Germany made the following Statement:

"We understand the words 'duties in this field' to refer to the limitations which are placed upon the exercise of human rights under the Universal Declaration of 1948 and the two United Nations Conventions of 1966, and of which the individual should be aware when exercising his rights."

* * *

d) The Representative of Italy made the following Statement:

"The Delegation of Italy is aware of the discrepancy existing in the formulation of the Tenth Principle between the expressions 'obligations under international law' in the first paragraph and the expression 'legal obligations under international law' in the second paragraph.

It is the opinion of the Italian Government that any obligation under International Law is automatically a legal obligation. This applies to all obligations deriving from provisions of International Law whatever the sources of those provisions.

We therefore interpret the two expressions at present existing side by side in the formulation of the Tenth Principle as entirely equivalent to one another in their political and juridical substance, notwithstanding the difference in wording.

The Delegation of Italy accordingly gives its agreement to the text in question, since it considers that such a difference in wording cannot be invoked in order to cast doubt upon or reduce in any way the binding character of any provision or principle of International Law and the consequent duty to conform to all the obligations deriving from it."

* * *

e) The Representatives of Canada and the United States of America associated themselves with the Statement of the Representative of Italy under point 4(d) above.

* * *

f) The Representative of Spain made the following Statement:

"The Delegation of Spain understands that in the text of the Final Clause of the principles, which states:

> "The participating States, paying due regard to the principles above and, in particular, to the first sentence of the Tenth Principle, "Fulfilment in good faith of obligations under international law", note that the present Declaration does not affect their rights and obligations, nor the corresponding treaties and other agreements and arrangements",

the rights, obligations, treaties, agreements and arrangements are those in conformity with international law."

* * *

g) The Representative of Sweden made the following Statement:

"Sub-Committee A has today, 19th July 1975, registered the following text:

> "The participating States, paying due regard to the principles above and, in particular, to the first sentence of the Tenth Principle, "Fulfilment in good faith of obligations under international law", note that the present Declaration does not affect their rights and obligations, nor the corresponding treaties and other agreements and arrangements".

The Swedish Delegation has raised no objections to the adoption of the above-quoted text on the assumption that the rights, obligations, treaties, agreements and arrangements referred to in it are those which are in force at the time of the adoption of the final document/documents of the Conference on Security and Co-operation in Europe and which are valid under international law."

* * *

h) The Representative of Romania made the following Statement:

"The Delegation of Romania to the Conference on Security and Co-operation in Europe states at the time of registration of the provision concerning the relationships between the Declaration of Principles on the one hand, and the corresponding rights and obligations, treaties, agreements and arrangements on the other, that it interprets this provision in the sense that it refers to treaties, agreements and arrangements which are in conformity with international law."

* * *

i) The Representative of Cyprus made the following Statement:

"The Delegation of Cyprus associates itself fully with the formal reservations and interpretative statements just made by the Representatives of Sweden, Spain and Romania."

* * *

j) The Representative of Portugal made the following Statement:

"The Delegation of Portugal supports the interpretative statements made by the Representatives of Spain and Romania."

* * * * *

Editor's note: The following reservation and interpretative statement have been made at the adoption of the final text of the Final Act of Helsinki on 31 July and 1 August 1975:

Formal Reservation by the Turkish Government relating to the decision to adopt the Final Act of Helsinki[2]

Formal Reservation by the Turkish Government regarding the State of Cyprus at the Conference on Security and Co-operation in Europe.

The Republic of Turkey adhere to all the provisions adopted at the Conference on Security and Co-operation in Europe. However, as the representation of the State of Cyprus in the Conference cannot be considered legal and therefore legitimate, Turkey deems it necessary to register its reserve as to the validity and applicability of these provisions as far as that particular State is concerned, on the following grounds:

Turkey,

CONSIDERING that the Constitution of the State of Cyprus being an integral part of the International Treaties by which the State was established is based upon two distinct national communities have flagrantly and continuously been violated by one of the communities since 1963 and totally collapsed by the coup of 15th July, 1974,

2 CSCE/III/1, Helsinki, 31 July 1975.

NOTING that the existence of the two communal "de facto" administrations in Cyprus have been clearly recognised by the three Guarantor States - Turkey, Greece and the United Kingdom - responsible for the constitutional order in Cyprus, by their declaration in Geneva on 30th July, 1974,

REGISTERING that intercommunal talks are taking place between the two communities on an "equal footing" for the purpose of reconciling their legitimate rights and for finding a political solution acceptable for both sides,

RECORDING that in the bi-communal State of Cyprus, it is legally impossible for either community to represent the whole State without the consent of the other,

REFERRING to the statement of the Turkish Cypriot Community that the provisions adopted at this Conference will not be binding on them since neither the presence of their representatives nor their consent for the representation has been sought for this Conference,

STRESSING therefore that the representation of Cyprus at this Conference is deprived of any legal ground,

CONCLUDING thereby that for the reasons given above, the State of Cyprus is not legitimately represented at the Conference,

STATES that the provisions of the Final Act of the Conference on Security and Co-operation in Europe, to which Turkey will become a party by its signature are not valid as regards the relations with the State of Cyprus, and consequently will have no effects until such time that a government legitimately representing the two national communities is established in Cyprus.

* * *

Interpretative Statement by the Government of the Republic of Cyprus relating to the Adoption of the Final Act of Helsinki[3]

The Republic of Cyprus referring to the formal reservation made by the Republic of Turkey on 31st July 1975, under reference CSCE/III/1, and stressing that the Turkish invasion of Cyprus does not give to Turkey any qualification to dispute the legitimacy of the Cyprus government, which is recognized in all international relations, wishes to make the following Interpretative Statement to be duly registered and circulated:

1. Article 65 of the Rules of Procedure provides that all States participating in the Conference shall do so as sovereign and independent States and in conditions of full equality

---

3 CSCE/III/2, Helsinki, 1 August 1975.

2. The Helsinki Recommendations and the Final Act do not provide for limited implementation of the results of the Conference

3. The Preamble to the Final Act underlines that the Participating States are determined to give full effect to the results of the Conference and to assure, among their States and throughout Europe the benefits deriving from those results

4. The Declaration of Principles provides for the equal and unreserved application of the principles and for ensuring to each participating State the benefits resulting from the respect and application of these principles by all.

Consequently, any reservation concerning the validity of the provisions of the Final Act in the relations of each participating State with all or any other participating State is of no effect. It also constitutes an a priori refusal to assume obligations which the participating States undertake by the signing of the Final Act.

CONCLUDING DOCUMENT OF BELGRADE

CONCLUDING DOCUMENT OF THE BELGRADE MEETING 1977 OF REPRESENTATIVES OF THE PARTICIPATING STATES OF THE CONFERENCE ON SECURITY AND CO-OPERATION IN EUROPE, HELD ON THE BASIS OF THE PROVISIONS OF THE FINAL ACT RELATING TO THE FOLLOW-UP TO THE CONFERENCE

Belgrade, 8 March 1978

The representatives of the participating States of the Conference on Security and Co-operation in Europe, appointed by the Ministers of Foreign Affairs of these States, met at Belgrade from 4 October 1977 to 9 March 1978 in accordance with the provisions of the Final Act relating to the Follow-up to the Conference.

The participants received a message from the President of the Socialist Federal Republic of Yugoslavia, Josip Broz Tito, and were addressed by Mr. Milos Minic, Vice-President of the Federal Executive Council and Federal Secretary for Foreign Affairs of the Socialist Federal Republic of Yugoslavia.

Contributions were made by the following non-participating Mediterranean States: Algeria, Egypt, Israel, Lebanon, Morocco, Syria and Tunisia.

The representatives of the participating States stressed the importance they attach to détente, which has continued since the adoption of the Final Act in spite of difficulties and obstacles encountered. In this context they underlined the role of the CSCE, the implementation of the provisions of the Final Act being essential for the development of this process.

The representatives of the participating States held a thorough exchange of views both on the implementation of the provisions of the Final Act and of the tasks defined by the Conference, as well as, in the context of the questions dealt with by the latter, on the deepening of their mutual relations, the improvement of security and the development of co-operation in Europe, and the development of the process of détente in the future.

The representatives of the participating States stressed the political importance of the Conference on Security and Co-operation in Europe and reaffirmed the resolve of their Governments, to implement fully, unilaterally, bilaterally and multilaterally, all the provisions of the Final Act.

It was recognized that the exchange of views constitutes in itself a valuable contribution towards the achievement of the aims set by the CSCE, although different views were expressed as to the degree of implementa-tion of the Final Act reached so far.

They also examined proposals concerning the above questions and the definition of the appropriate modalities for the holding of other meetings in conformity with the provisions of the chapter of the Final Act concerning the Follow-up to the Conference.

Consensus was not reached on a number of proposals submitted to the meeting.

In conformity with the relevant provisions of the Final Act and with their resolve to continue the multilateral process initiated by the CSCE, the participating States will hold further meetings among their representatives. The second of these meetings will be held in Madrid commencing Tuesday, 11 November 1980.

A preparatory meeting will be held in Madrid commencing Tuesday, 9 September 1980, to decide on appropriate modalities for the main Madrid Meeting. This will be done on the basis of the Final Act as well as of the other relevant documents adopted during the process of the CSCE.[1]

It was also agreed to hold, within the framework of the Follow-up to the CSCE, the meetings of experts of the participating States indicated below.

In conformity with the mandate contained in the Final Act and according to the proposals made to this effect by the Government of Switzerland a meeting of experts will be convened at Montreux on 31 October 1978, charged with pursuing the examination and elaboration of a generally acceptable method for peaceful settlement of disputes aimed at complementing existing methods.

Upon the invitation of the Government of the Federal Republic of Germany, the meeting of experts envisaged in the Final Act in order to prepare a

---

[1] The other relevant documents adopted during the process of the CSCE are: The Final Recommendations of the Helsinki Consulta-tions; the Decisions of the Preparatory Meeting to organize the Belgrade Meeting 1977; this Concluding Document.

"Scientific Forum" will take place in Bonn starting on 20 June 1978. Representatives of UNESCO and the United Nations Economic Commission for Europe shall be invited to state their views.

Upon the invitation of the Government of Malta, a meeting of experts on the Mediterranean will be convened on 13 February 1979 in Valletta. Its mandate will be, within the framework of the Mediterranean Chapter of the Final Act, to consider the possibilities and means of promoting concrete initiatives for mutually beneficial co-operation concerning various economic, scientific and cultural fields, in addition to other initiatives relating to the above subjects already under way. The non-participating Mediterranean States will be invited to contribute to the work of this meeting. Questions relating to security will be discussed at the Madrid Meeting.

The duration of the meetings of experts should not exceed 4-6 weeks. They will draw up conclusions and recommendations and send their reports to the Governments of the participating States. The results of these meetings will be taken into account, as appropriate, at the Madrid Meeting.

All the above-mentioned meetings will be held in conformity with paragraph 4 of the chapter on "Follow-up to the Conference" of the Final Act.

The Government of the Socialist Federal Republic of Yugoslavia is requested to transmit the present document to the Secretary-General of the United Nations, to the Director-General of UNESCO and to the Executive Secretary of the United Nations Economic Commission for Europe. The Government of the Socialist Federal Republic of Yugoslavia is also requested to transmit the present document to the governments of the Mediterranean non-participating States.

The representatives of the participating States expressed their profound gratitude to the people and Government of the Socialist Federal Republic of Yugoslavia for the excellent organization of the Belgrade Meeting and the warm hospitality extended to the delegations which participated in the Meeting.

RESERVATIONS AND INTERPRETATIVE STATEMENTS[2]

Reservation of Turkey:

Formal reservation of the Government of Turkey concerning the adoption of the Concluding Document of the Belgrade Meeting 1977.

The delegation of Turkey gives its consensus to the Concluding Document of the Belgrade Meeting 1977. However, since the representation of the State of Cyprus at the Meeting can be considered neither legal nor, consequently, legitimate, the Turkish Government deems it necessary to record its reservation regarding the validity and the applicability of the content of the said document in its relations with that State, for the reasons mentioned below:

Considering that the Constitution of the State of Cyprus, an integral part of the international treaties which gave birth to that State, had as its basis the existence of two distinct national entities,

Stressing the fact that this Constitution was, from 1963, subject to flagrant and continuous violations by the Greek Cypriot side, until it lost all executory force by the coup d'état of 15 July 1974,

Noting that this state of affairs was clearly recognized in the Declaration made at Geneva on 30 July 1974 by the three States guarantors of constitutional order in Cyprus,

Recalling the recent efforts of the Secretary-General of the United Nations and the need for the two parties concerned to begin negotiations "on an equal footing" with a view to reconciling their legitimate rights and to reaching an acceptable and durable political solution,

Referring to the statements of the leaders of the Turkish Federated State of Cyprus, who made it known publicly that the emissaries of the Greek Cypriot Administration are in no way qualified to represent the Turkish people of Cyprus at the Belgrade Meeting 1977, and that the latter cannot be bound by the decisions adopted by this Meeting, since neither the participation of its representatives nor its agreement concerning the representation of the State of Cyprus have been solicited for this Meeting,

Stressing the fact that the will of the State of Cyprus can in no case be expressed in this totality by only one of the two entities composing that State, and that

---

2 Journal No. 172, 8 March 1978.

consequently the representation of Cyprus at the present Meeting is devoid of all legal foundation,

CONCLUDING from this fact that, for the reasons set forth above, the State of Cyprus is not legitimately represented at the Meeting, its apparent consent being vitiated by an all too obvious unilateral action,

Reaffirming the maintenance of its position as set forth in detail in Journal No. 83 dated 21 July 1975 of the Co-ordinating Committee during the Second Phase of the CSCE, in document CSCE/III/1 dated 31 July 1975, during the Third Phase of the CSCE, and finally in Journal No. 66 dated 5 August 1977 of the Preparatory Meeting to organize the present Meeting, all these documents having been registered and circulated by the Executive Secretaries in office, in conformity with paragraph 79 of the Rules of Procedure of the Conference,

Declares that the Concluding Document of the Belgrade Meeting 1977, including the decisions contained in it, will have no validity with regard to relations with Cyprus and will remain without effect until such time as a government legitimately representing the Turkish and Greek Cypriots is constituted in Cyprus.

* * *

Interpretative statement by Cyprus

Interpretative statement by the Government of the Republic of Cyprus.

With reference to the "reservation" entered today by the Delegation of Turkey, the Delegation of the Republic of Cyprus wishes to make the following statement to be duly registered and circulated:

1. It reiterates and reaffirms the statement made by the Government of the Republic of Cyprus contained in document CSCE/III/2 dated 1 August 1975 and also reflected in the replies to a similar Turkish "reservation" made at the close of the Preparatory Meeting to organize the Belgrade Meeting 1977.

2. The "reservation" of Turkey which came as an afterthought following the invasion and occupation of part of Cyprus also challenges both the constitution and Rules of Procedure of the Conference and is incompatible with participation therein.

3. This untenable "reservation" is made in a vain attempt to justify the continued violation by Turkey of the Final Act in the case of Cyprus.

4. The Delegation of Turkey persists with its "reservation" undaunted by the fact that in this Conference as well as in all other international fora, it remains completely isolated on this matter.

5. The participation of Cyprus throughout the totality of the CSCE process in itself amounts to a complete answer to the Turkish challenge in addition to a succession of decisions at the United Nations as well as other international fora.

6. The Turkish "reservation" makes reference to the Constitution of the Republic of Cyprus as well as to a fictitious entity called "Turkish Federated State of Cyprus", which was proclaimed contrary to the former and was also deplored by United Nations Security Council Resolution No. 367(1975).

7. Note is taken of the fact that not only previous arguments based on the Constitution of Cyprus had to be abandoned by Turkey, ostensibly because of the aforesaid fictitious entity but also attempts to justify the Turkish invasion by reference to the "restoration" of the constitutional *status quo ante* have been dropped. Thus all pretexts for the violation of the Final Act have disappeared.

8. Reference in the Turkish "reservation" to the 1974 Geneva Declaration is misleading not only because it was merely an attempt to bring about a ceasefire which was violated by the second and major phase of the invasion, but also because it could not and did not affect the Cyprus Constitution, it was made in the absence of Cyprus and it was in any event superseded by subsequent events, in particular by a series of United Nations Resolutions and further Turkish unilateral actions.

9. The Government of the Republic of Cyprus calls upon the Government of Turkey to abandon its "reservations" and co-operate in the quest for a peaceful solution of the Cyprus problem in accordance with the Final Act through meaningful and constructive negotiations, the first step being the compliance with all United Nations General Assembly and Security Council Resolutions on Cyprus.

It is in the light of this statement and with particular reference to the reaffirmation of the resolve of the Governments of the participating States to implement fully, unilaterally, bilaterally and multilaterally, all the provisions of the Final Act, that the delegation of the Republic of Cyprus gives consensus to the Concluding Document which does not, as the Final Act does not, permit selectivity in its application.

* * *

Statement by the delegate of Greece

The position of my delegation with regard to the reservation of the distinguished delegate of Turkey is well known.

REPORT OF MONTREUX

REPORT OF THE MEETING OF EXPERTS REPRESENTING THE PARTICIPATING STATES OF THE CONFERENCE ON SECURITY AND CO-OPERATION IN EUROPE, FORESEEN BY THE FINAL ACT OF THE CSCE IN ORDER TO PURSUE THE EXAMINATION AND ELABORATION OF A GENERALLY ACCEPTABLE METHOD FOR PEACEFUL SETTLEMENT OF DISPUTES AIMED AT COMPLEMENTING EXISTING METHODS

Montreux, 11 December 1978

In accordance with the mandate of the Final Act of the Conference on Security and Co-operation in Europe and the relevant provisions of the Concluding Document of the Belgrade Meeting 1977, a Meeting of Experts representing the participating States took place at Montreux from 31 October to 11 December 1978 in order to pursue the examination and elaboration of a generally acceptable method for peaceful settlement of disputes aimed at complementing existing methods.

At the opening meeting the participants were addressed by Mr. Pierre Aubert, Head of the Federal Political Department, on behalf of the Government of Switzerland.

The participants adopted an agenda and proceeded to a general exchange of views after which several proposals aimed at complementing existing methods for peaceful settlement of disputes were submitted and discussed. A working paper based on the "Draft Convention on a European System for the Peaceful Settlement of Disputes" was submitted for consideration which put forward the following subsidiary and compulsory procedures: negotiation, inquiry, mediation, conciliation and arbitration. Another working paper was submitted for consideration which put forward a proposal of mandatory consultations as a possible method for peaceful settlement of disputes. A further paper was submitted which put forward the concept of a comprehensive method for peaceful settlement of disputes within specific subject areas, including appropriate mandatory features. Other proposals and ideas were put forward for consideration. Divergent views were expressed and no consensus was reached on specific methods.

The participants stressed the importance their governments attach to détente, which has continued since the adoption of the Final Act in spite of difficulties and obstacles encountered. In this context they underlined the role of the CSCE, the implementation of the provisions of the Final Act being essential for the development of this process.

The participants reaffirmed the adherence of their governments to the principle of peaceful settlement of disputes as enshrined in the Charter of the United Nations and in the Final Act of the CSCE. They also stressed the significance of elaborating, in accordance with the mandate contained in the Final Act, a method for peaceful settlement of disputes.

The participants agreed on a common approach to the elaboration of a method for peaceful settlement of disputes between or among the participating States which should be based on the following:

- consistency with the principles and the purposes of the Charter of the United Nations and with the Final Act of Helsinki, especially principle V of the latter document;

- consistency with sovereign equality of States and the free choice of means;

- experience and the treaty and diplomatic practice and the views of all the participating States in this field;

- acceptability to all participating States irrespective of their political, economic or social systems as well as of their size, geographical location or level of economic development;

- subsidiarity to existing methods and institutions for the peaceful settlement of international disputes;

- complementarity to existing methods so as to promote, in good faith and a spirit of co-operation, a rapid and equitable solution on the basis of international law;

- flexibility of the method;

- capacity for progressive development of the method.

The method to be elaborated should contribute to peace, security and justice in Europe, to the further development of détente and co-operation among the participating States.

The participants recommended that the participating States consider the possibility of promoting and extending the existing practice of including, in appropriate treaties among and between them, provisions for the peaceful settlement of disputes.

The participants recommended to the governments of States participating in the CSCE that they consider, at the Madrid Meeting, the possibility of convening another Meeting of Experts in order to pursue, on the basis of the Final Act, the examination and elaboration of a generally acceptable method for peaceful settlement of disputes aimed at complementing existing methods, taking into account the common approach set forth above, as well as the various proposals and ideas discussed at the Montreux Meeting.

The participants recommended that contacts between the governments of participating States continue in order better to acquaint themselves with each other's views on the subject of peaceful settlement of disputes.

The participants expressed their deep gratitude to the Government of Switzerland for the excellent organization of the Meeting and for the warm hospitality extended to them during their stay at Montreux.

REPORT OF VALLETTA

REPORT OF THE MEETING OF EXPERTS REPRESENTING THE PARTICIPATING STATES OF THE CONFERENCE ON SECURITY AND CO-OPERATION IN EUROPE, FORESEEN BY THE CONCLUDING DOCUMENT OF THE BELGRADE MEETING 1977 TO CONSIDER, WITHIN THE FRAMEWORK OF THE MEDITERRANEAN CHAPTER OF THE FINAL ACT, THE POSSIBILITIES AND MEANS OF PROMOTING CONCRETE INITIATIVES FOR MUTUALLY BENEFICIAL CO-OPERATION CONCERNING VARIOUS ECONOMIC, SCIENTIFIC AND CULTURAL FIELDS; IN ADDITION TO OTHER INITIATIVES RELATING TO THE ABOVE SUBJECTS ALREADY UNDER WAY.

Valletta, 26 March 1979

In accordance with the mandate of the Concluding Document of the Belgrade Meeting 1977, a Meeting of Experts representing the participating States took place at Valletta upon the invitation of the Government of Malta, from 13 February to 26 March 1979 in order to consider within the framework of the Mediterranean Chapter of the Final Act of the Conference on Security and Co-operation in Europe (CSCE), the possibilities and means of promoting concrete initiatives for mutually beneficial co-operation concerning various economic, scientific and cultural fields, in addition to other initiatives relating to the above subjects already under way.

During the opening session of the Meeting, a message was received from Dr. Anton Buttigieg, President of the Republic of Malta, and the participants were addressed by Mr. Wistin Abela, Minister of Development, Energy, Port and Telecommunications of the Republic of Malta.

The participants adopted an agenda and agreed on modalities appropriate to this Meeting.

The participants had a general exchange of views.

In accordance with the Concluding Document of the Belgrade Meeting 1977 all the non-participating Mediterranean States were invited to contribute to the work of the Meeting. Egypt and Israel accepted and made their contributions in plenary on 21 February. Syria addressed the plenary on 27 February. The representatives of the United Nations Economic Commission for Europe (ECE), UNESCO and the United Nations Environment Programme (UNEP) made contributions relating to the work of the Meeting.

Two working bodies concerned with co-operation in the economic and in the scientific and cultural fields respectively were established by the plenary and pursued their work under its guidance. The non-participating Mediterranean States which made contributions participated in the discussions of the working bodies. Upon the invitation of the plenary, the representatives of the ECE and UNESCO made additional contributions in the working bodies.

The participants stressed the will of their governments to promote the development of good-neighbourly relations and co-operation with the non-participating Mediterranean States and reaffirmed the importance their governments attach to the attainment of the objectives set forth in the Final Act of the CSCE by implementing all of its provisions, as well as their readiness to pursue their efforts accordingly.

The participants considered many measures and activities already under way or envisaged, both bilateral and multilateral, relating to mutually beneficial co-operation in the fields of economics, science and culture; in doing so, they drew attention to certain current problems in the above-mentioned fields and examined ways of solving them. The participants were of the opinion that the exchange of views which took place in this context was a useful outcome of the Meeting.

The Meeting of Experts noted that particularly useful and concrete work in the fields specified in the mandate of the Valletta Meeting is being done by competent international organisations, notably by ECE, UNESCO and UNEP.

In accordance with the mandate of the Meeting and taking into account the contributions made at the Meeting by non-participating Mediterranean States and by the representatives of ECE, UNESCO and UNEP, the participants considered ideas and proposals for further initiatives intended to promote mutually beneficial co-operation in sectors falling within the fields identified for consideration by the Meeting.

The Meeting of Experts concluded that for many of those sectors ECE, UNESCO and UNEP provided a framework for investigating and developping further co-operation among the participating States and the non-participating Mediterranean States, whereas in other sectors unilateral efforts, or bilateral or other forms of multilateral co-operation were more suitable.

Accordingly, the participants, having examined the ideas, considerations and proposals which had been submitted, recommended to Governments of the participating States that they envisage within their possibilities and interests, through their participation in international organisations and in their bilateral and multilateral relations with the participating States and with the non-participating Mediterranean States, the following:

Economics

Continuing their efforts to contribute to the diversified development of the economies of the States concerned, including the non-participating Mediterranean States, taking due account of their national development objectives.

Developing the exchange of statistical data, including with the non-participating Mediterranean States, among national statistical institutes, and considering the convening of a meeting of experts within the framework of ECE, with a view to drawing up an inventory of existing data and considering further actions in the fields of data concerning national accounts, labour, agricultural and industrial production, trade, transport, tourism, the environment, education and health.

Examining within the framework of UNEP, the possibilities of participating States being provided with information and advice on relevant environmental programmes and activities with a view to achieving better harmonization between Mediterranean and other international programmes; contributing to the efforts to reduce pollution of the Mediterranean; and considering the possibility of developing co-operation initiated within the framework of the Barcelona Convention.

Considering the holding of meetings at a technical level, within the framework of the appropriate international organisations, in order to determine the most suitable criteria for making the best possible use of tourist resources and promoting further co-operation among interested countries in the fields of vocational training, in-service training and scholarships.

Intensifying the exchange, bilaterally as well as in co-operation with the competent international organisations, of the results of studies on the conservation and rational use of energy and developing their co-operation in the area of solar energy, including with the non-participating Mediterranean States, by supporting the activities of UNEP and taking due account of the outcome of the CSCE "Scientific Forum".

Considering the expansion of trans-European and Mediterranean transport networks and promoting with a view to facilitating trade, the further application in these areas of the TIR Convention as well as other instruments and recommendations elaborated within the framework of ECE relating to international transport of goods.

Considering co-operative efforts, within the competent international organisations, to adapt agricultural production in the Mediterranean to meet existing needs.

Urging better co-operation among the participating States and the non-participating Mediterranean States in the field of fisheries in the Mediterranean, and supporting further studies within competent international organisations on fish processing.

Supporting the programme sponsored by UNEP for the development of aquaculture in the Mediterranean as a co-operative project between all interested countries.

Promoting co-operation in the field of telecommunications technology among appropriate institutions or firms of interested participating States and non-participating Mediterranean States through the carrying out of joint research, including on new equipment and current technology, the exchange of information, the organisation of training courses for specialists, in co-operation with the International Telecommunications Union. Studying the possibility of convening a meeting of experts of interested countries on telecommunications in the Mediterranean.

Recommending the host countries and the countries of origin to intensify their contacts with a view to finding solutions to the problems which exist in the field of migrant labour. While fully implementing the existing agreements to which they are parties, they should also continue, by all appropriate means, their efforts to improve the situation of migrant workers in conformity with the provisions of the Final Act on migrant labour, including the solution of the problems in the economic, social, human and other fields.

Science

Practising more widely the holding, within the framework of the competent international organisations mentioned in the Final Act, of conferences, symposia and meetings on the most pressing scientific and technical problems of the Mediterranean that are of general interest.

Reinforcing their co-operation in controlling and eradicating certain diseases prevalent in the Mediterranean (e.g. thalassaemia), facilitating studies and conferences, particularly under the aegis of the World Health Organisation, with a view to establishing programmes for the prevention, detection and treatment of these diseases and for the training of specialized personnel, on the basis of the expertise which some participating States could share with other countries.

Urging further exchanges of views within the competent international organisations, on co-operative studies on gerontology, including environmental geriatric care.

Considering the convening under the aegis of the competent international organisations of a scientific conference on the protection of the Mediterranean ecosystem, particularly with a view to studying co-operative projects in the fields of afforestation, forest management, management of water resources, reclamation of arid and semi-arid areas, and drawing up an inventory of the technical centres for research existing in these areas.

Developing co-operation in the field of seismology, increasing the exchange of information on seismic phenomena in the Mediterranean and adjacent areas, and considering the convening, under the aegis of UNESCO, of a symposium on seismicity in the Mediterranean and its repercussions in Europe and Africa.

Studying, in co-operation with other participating States and with non-participating Mediterranean States, the possibility of the drafting of a comprehensive history of the Mediterranean utilizing the valuable experience of UNESCO and under its aegis.

Encouraging studies relevant to the needs of the Mediterranean, particularly in the fields of science and technology.

Culture

Supporting the holding of congresses and conferences by existing international organisations in the field of culture, both in the participating States and in the non-participating Mediterranean States.

Increasing their co-operation, both at the bilateral and multilateral level, including within the competent international organisations in the field of scientific research and in the protection and preservation of the cultural and historical heritage of the Mediterranean, notably archaeological and architectural remains, with a view to developing in particular underwater archaeological research and harmonizing the legal and technical modalities for the protection and preservation of this heritage.

Considering the preparation of a study on the relationship between the development of tourism in the Mediterranean and the protection, preservation and presentation of the cultural and historical heritage, with the participation of interested participating and non-participating States, and in collaboration with competent international organizations.

Expanding their co-operation in the field of the dissemination of scientific and cultural knowledge through radio and television; increasing the exchanges of scientific and cultural radio and television programmes; studying the possibilities, in collaboration with the competent international organisations, of using radio and television for vocational and adult training.

Promoting the exchange of films among the film libraries of the participating States and the non-participating Mediterranean States and the holding of Film Weeks.

Encouraging the efforts of UNESCO to help Mediterranean countries establish a Mediterranean Cultural Centre.

The participants recommended to the Governments of the participating States of the CSCE that they take into account, as appropriate, at the Madrid Meeting, the results of the Valletta Meeting and that they be mindful in the interim of the outcome achieved by unilateral efforts and within the framework of competent international organisations and in bilateral or multilateral co-operation, in the fields of the mandate for the Valletta Meeting.

The participants expressed their deep gratitude to the Government and the people of Malta for the excellent organisation of the Meeting and for the warm hospitality extended to them during their stay in Valletta.

REPORT OF THE "SCIENTIFIC FORUM"

REPORT OF THE "SCIENTIFIC FORUM" OF THE CONFERENCE ON SECURITY AND CO-OPERATION IN EUROPE

Hamburg, 3 March 1980

In accordance with the provisions of the Final Act of the Conference on Security and Co-operation in Europe and of the report of the meeting of experts representing the participating States and their national scientific institutions held in Bonn from 20 June to 28 July 1978, the "Scientific Forum" took place in Hamburg, Federal Republic of Germany, from 18 February to 3 March 1980. It was held in the form of a meeting of leading personalities in science from the participating States.

During the opening session of the "Scientific Forum" the participants were welcomed by Hans-Ulrich Klose, Lord Mayor of the Free and Hanseatic City of Hamburg, and were addressed by Dr. Hildegard Hamm-Brücher, Minister of State, Ministry of Foreign Affairs, on behalf of the Government of the Federal Republic of Germany.

During the first working session of the Plenary representatives of UNESCO and the United Nations Economic Commission for Europe (ECE) made their contributions. Opening statements were made by representatives of delegations of the participating States.

Four subsidiary working bodies were established by the Plenary on alternative energy sources, food production, medicine, and the humanities and social sciences. Representatives of UNESCO and the ECE were invited to make additional contributions in these working bodies.

The "Scientific Forum" discussed interrelated problems of common interest concerning current and future developments in science, and promotion of expansion of contacts, communications and the exchange of information between scientific institutions and among scientists.

In this context the subsidiary working bodies considered the following areas and subjects:

Exact and natural sciences
Scientific research, in particular fundamental research, in the field of alternative energy sources

Exact and natural sciences
Scientific research, in particular fundamental research, in the field of food production

Medicine
Current trends in medical research, in particular in basic research and primarily on cardiovascular, tumour and virus diseases, taking into consideration the influence of the changing environment on human health

The humanities and social sciences
Comparative studies on the social, socio-economic and cultural phenomena, especially the problems of human environment and urban development.

The subsidiary working bodies also reviewed written contributions submitted to the "Scientific Forum".

On the basis of their deliberations they drew up reports which were reviewed by the Plenary and are included, as amended, in Annexes 1-4.

As a result of its proceedings the "Scientific Forum" concluded the following:

- Since the signing of the Final Act of the CSCE, there has been a significant expansion of international co-operation in research and training and in the exchange of information. Progress, however, has been greater in some areas than in others. It is observed that the present state of international scientific co-operation still requires improvements in various respects. Such improvements should be achieved bilaterally and multilaterally at governmental and non-governmental levels through intergovernmental and other agreements, international programmes and co-operative projects, and by providing equitable opportunities for scientific research and for wider communication and travel necessary for professional purposes.

- This goal can, however, be reached only by respect for all the principles and by full implementation of the relevant provisions of the Final Act. All participating States are, therefore, urged to observe the spirit and the letter of the Final Act, particularly with respect to conditions essential for international scientific co-operation.

- It is furthermore considered necessary to state that respect for human rights and fundamental freedoms by all States represents one of the foundations for a significant improvement in their mutual relations, and in international scientific co-operation at all levels.

- Appropriate support should be given to arrange advanced seminars and training courses for young scientists from participating and other States that would enable them to study new scientific methods for shorter or longer periods. Information about these activities and arrangements should be disseminated as widely as possible.

- The different levels of scientific development in particular fields in the participating States should be taken into account when pursuing scientific co-operation.

- It is recommended that the participating States study the possibility of convening a new "Scientific Forum", at a suitable date, depending on developments in science and in scientific co-operation among the participating States. The results of the "Scientific Forum" in Hamburg may be taken into account, as appropriate, by the participating States at the Madrid Meeting, scheduled for November 1980.

The participants expressed their deep gratitude to the Government of the Federal Republic of Germany for the excellent organization of the "Scientific Forum" and for the warm hospitality extended to them during their stay in Hamburg.

ANNEX 1: ALTERNATIVE ENERGY SOURCES

1. Introduction

The working body examined the problems created by the rapid dwindling of easily accessible reserves of fossil energy and reviewed alternative solutions provided by other energy sources.

During the discussions it became apparent that delegates from different countries interpreted the term "alternative energy" in different ways. However, it was agreed that the following four main categories should be discussed as energy options for the future:

Advanced utilization of fossil energy, nuclear energy (fission and fusion), solar energy (direct and indirect forms), and energy conservation. The working body made no attempt to give priorities to the different options.

2. Need for fundamental research on various alternative energy sources

2.0 General

The working body noted that the questions of developing energy resources are today of vital importance. The further development of civilization in the economic as well as in the political field depends on the possibility of satisfying demand for energy in industry, in the residential and service sectors, in transport, in food production, and in the mining and processing of minerals.

In spite of the necessity for and possibility of the more economical use of energy, the demand for energy will continue to rise. The problem demands especially urgent solutions because of the diminishing energy resource represented by oil and gas.

That is why the task of scientific research in the field of energy is to supply during the next decade a reliable scientific basis for planning and use of all basic resources of energy. Such a basis should include forecasts of the environmental effects of the various types of energy, and in particular improved assessments of the effects on the global and regional climate.

The working body recommends governments to use international co-operation for the fulfilling of this task.

It is not possible to give universal priorities for any research objectives, as many countries have already found and applied technological solutions to problems relevant to their situation, whose relevance for other countries has yet to be investigated.

2.1 Problems of utilization of fossil fuels: efficiency and safety

The urgent need to increase utilization of low-quality fossil energy resources - coal, brown coal, oil shale and tar sand, lignite, peat, etc. - as well as at the same time to tighten the environmental requirements, make it necessary to develop ever more advanced combustion methods, in spite of the heed for an intensified interest in more efficient and cleaner combustion methods, as well as in the use of synthetic liquid and gaseous fuel from coal, oil shale and tar sands, and considering that several large demonstration projects exist, synthetic fuel production is still on a rather narrow basis. Both fundamental and applied research are needed on a broad front before synthetic liquid or gaseous fuels are capable of substituting for natural hydrocarbons on a commercial scale.

Particular attention must be given to the problems of safety in deep mining and to the efficiency of production methods in both deep and open-cast mining.

2.2 Nuclear energy

The problem of energy supply for the majority of participating countries cannot be solved without using nuclear energy for producing electricity and heat. The economic efficiency of nuclear fission technology has been established, the reliability has been shown to be good, and the environmental aspects are becoming well understood. All aspects of the nuclear fuel cycle will require continuing efforts to assure its full reliability and safety, in order to ensure public acceptability.

For the guarantee of further nuclear prospects the development of breeder reactors is necessary.

The working body states that insufficient effort has so far been made in the development of unconventional types of reactors.

The working body notes that research in the field of controlled thermonuclear fusion is nearing the level of scientific demonstration. Great efforts are necessary, however, to demonstrate even more urgently the technological feasibility of fusion.

2.3 Solar energy and other renewable energy sources

Many ways exist for the wider application of solar energy through direct and indirect methods, and in decentralized and centralized forms. In the long term they could contribute significantly to the solution of energy problems. Some of these solar technologies are already in use, some are under development and some are still in the research stage. The same is true for geothermal and didal sources of energy.

Apart from the scientific and technical problems, however, there are also a number of other open questions pertaining to the wider application of solar energy. Among those questions are economic, infrastructural, environmental, legal and administrative considerations. It is important that these problems are treated together with the scientific problems within a common framework in order to ensure a balanced and optimal use of solar energy.

The tentative suggestions for promising solar energy research areas in the list below do not assign priorities. Further, the selection of areas to a certain extent reflects the specialities of individual scientists in the working body. The list is therefore only indicative and is subject to revision.

- Energy storage, crucial to the small and large-scale use of solar energy and also of great general importance.
- Solar heating, including systems for integration into local or district heating schemes.
- Energy from biosystems, especially production and conversion of fuels from wood, cultivated biomass, etc.
- Solar electricity based on the industrial development of existing photovoltaic or photothermal techniques and on research on novel approaches.
- Basic research in photochemistry and photobiology.
- Scientific evaluation of future solar energy prospects on a national or regional scale.
- Integration of solar energy into existing energy systems, for different forms of energy and end-use requirements.

2.4 Energy conservation

Energy consumption and economic activity are very closely related. The principal way to optimize this relationship is conservation. Conservation should be aimed at minimizing energy losses, elimination of ineffective energy use, recycling of materials as well as development of energy-saving processes and technologies. Much research and development activity is needed continuously for efforts in energy conservation in industry, in transportation, in buildings and in appliances and services of many kinds and in improvements in technology. This can be achieved through fundamental as well as applied research.

In this context the working body would stress the vital role of technological innovation.

3. International co-operation

Special attention must be paid to the problems of exchange and assessment of scientific and technical data. Individual and institutional scientific contacts are seen here as the best means. Strengthening of existing information centres is another, e.g. within the framework of ECE and UNESCO.

The working body supports the existing forms of international and regional co-operation, increased contacts amongst research organizations, including the United Nations special organization, e.g. International Atomic Energy Agency, UNESCO, Economic Commission for Europe etc., and non-governmental organizations, e.g. International Council of Scientific Unions.

Forms of co-operation can include the organization of international conferences, symposia, schools, exchange of scientists between different countries and bodies, discussion of research programmes on a regional or bilateral scale, and the working out and realization of joint international projects. The working body notes with approval examples of international activity such as INTOR, (International Fusion Project) carried out under the aegis of IAEA, and the energy project of IIASA.

The working body especially asks international organizations to take initiatives to promote co-operation in fields of advanced coal utilization technology, deep coal mining safety and solar energy.

The working body on alternative energy sources considers its meetings to have been useful. Since the energy problem is important and of a long-term nature, the working body proposes the continuation of this type of interdisciplinary scientific meeting.

The working body had a thorough discussion on all tasks on agenda item number 2. The content of these discussions is reflected both in this Annex and in the general conclusions contained in the Report of the "Scientific Forum".

ANNEX 2: FOOD PRODUCTION

The future demand, and for many the present demand, for food and feed in the world, emphasized by the "Scientific Forum" of the CSCE, requires sustained research and development efforts in all aspects of the food system.

The need became evident, during the discussions of the Working Body, for more integrated multidisciplinary research, training at undergraduate and post-graduate level, exchanges of scientists and their interaction. Although the Working Body recognised the limits of the mandate of the "Scientific Forum" it agreed that food production was of world importance.

In plant genetics and breeding there is a need for international co-opera-tion on the development of more productive plants with higher photosynthetic capacity, more efficient capability to use available mineral nutrients, and better ability to withstand environmental stresses. In this research, scientists should make effective use of modern plant-breeding techniques, including haploid breeding, and various tissue culture tech-niques in addition to standard methods to obtain crosses, noting the importance of wide crosses. In research on crop production, there is a need for co-operation on the development of energy-efficient management systems based on biological nitrogen fixation and other ecological means as well as the conservation and management of natural resources. The importance of plant protection was stressed as a means of reducing losses.

In the area of animal production, there is a need for more co-operative research on the genetic improvement of farm livestock; the control of infectious diseases, metabolic disorders and infertility; the increased use of non-protein nitrogen in the ruminant diet; animal housing, nutrition and improvement of the efficiency of management systems; and elimina-tion of stress susceptibility and improvement of products of animal origin.

Special attention is drawn to the need for international co-operation in identifying and preserving germ plasm of plants and animals in their natural ecosystems. This should include more, and more comprehensive, gene banks to preserve genetic materials for the benefit of plant and animal production in the future.

Fisheries contribute substantially to the food system. International attitudes should facilitate rather than hinder fisheries research. Continued international vigilance must be maintained on the effects on the stock of the size of catch and of pollution to ensure long-term benefits from this important natural resource.

Attention is drawn to the significant contribution that technology can make to the diminution of post-harvest losses and to the maintenance of the wholesomeness and nutritional quality of foods. More research is needed on alternative sources and economic production of basic food components such as proteins, essential amino acids, etc. Collective efforts should be expanded in the fight against all forms of malnutrition through the assurance of the natural quality of foods and protection against introduction of harmful contaminants during production, processing, storage and distribution. Intensified efforts are needed in the area of nutrition education both at academic and consumer levels and should include multidisciplinary behavioural studies on eating habits and food acceptance. In the final analysis, it is health and nutritional status that is the prerequisite for the well-being of all mankind.

The Working Body expressed confidence that existing governmental and non-governmental international organizations will be able to help in expanding research on the subject to which attention is drawn in this report.

The Working Body thus had a thorough discussion on all tasks on agenda item number 2. The content of these discussions is reflected both in this Annex and in the general conclusions contained in the Report of the "Scientific Forum".

ANNEX 3: MEDICINE

The outcome of the work of the subsidiary working body is presented in the following sections on cardiovascular, neoplastic and viral diseases. The working body had a thorough discussion on all tasks on agenda item number 2. The content of these discussions is reflected both in this Annex and in the general conclusions contained in the Report of the "Scientific Forum".

Cardiovascular diseases

The various reports presented to the "Scientific Forum", and other information available, underline that cardiovascular diseases, where atherosclerosis and/or hypertension are involved, are of major concern in most participating countries. These two main and interrelated ailments with their complications - ischemic heart disease, cerebrovascular disease and peripheral vascular disease together show a high level of incidence and account for a high death rate.

Therefore it seems imperative that special efforts of basic research should be focused on the mechanisms of atherogenesis and causal mechanisms in essential hypertension. On the other hand, it emerges from the reports that there is also great need for help from the behavioural sciences in order to improve compliance both of doctors and the public especially with respect to advice in the interest of prevention and treatment. Preventive measures in childhood are worth a special research effort.

From the various reports it is seen that marked and diverse research efforts are already being made in most countries towards illuminating the mechanisms that lie behind these groups of diseases. A main effort also appears to be directed towards their prevention and treatment.

Since the etiology and pathogenesis of these diseases are far from being fully understood and since these ailments dominate the disease pattern in so many countries, it appears that they must be looked upon as fields for international concern and that fruitful patterns of international co-operation should be encouraged. Such co-operation should be looked upon as an effort additional to the widespread research already going on in the different countries.

In order to identify projects and fields related to cardiovascular diseases where international co-operation might be fruitful one could use the following list of "indications".

'Indications' for making a bi- or multinational co-operative effort in the cardiovascular field.*

1. Co-operative research

1.1 international studies that exploit the transcultural differences in exposure to known or presumed risk factors (for instance in connexion with migration) to draw conclusions about causality either in a qualitative or a quantitative sense.

1.2 studies that require such large numbers of patients, in order to come to a conclusion, that these cannot be found in one single country. Large and complicated drug trials might be an example in point.

1.3 studies that are so costly that they can only be financed by a collaborative effort.

1.4 studies in which there is an abundance of patients of a certain kind, say with rheumatic heart disease, in one country and resources such as interested experts and/or financial support available in another country.

---

* Here efforts are meant that are distinct from research activities on a local or international co-operative basis, the results of which are then reported to audiences of scientific meetings and in the international literature.

1.5 study projects that can only succeed if expertise in different fields from different countries is pooled.

1.6 study of occurrence, natural history and/or treatment of uncommon cardiovascular diseases that necessitates pooling of observations from different countries.

2. Evaluation

Comparative studies of the efficiency and effectiveness of different health care systems and health care practices in the fields of prevention, clinical medicine and rehabilitation.

3. Co-operative surveillance

Examples:
- a co-operative early warning system for the side effects of drugs.
- a co-operative early warning system for failures of certain types of electronic pacemakers.

4. Standardization of nomenclature

Examples:
- coronary angiogram
- congenital heart disease
- level of rehabilitation after myocardial infarction and cerebrovascular disease.

5. Standardization of procedures

Examples:
- determination of all blood lipids and lipoproteins used in epidemiological research.
- determination of prostaglandins.
- collection of epidemiological data.

6. Transfer of techniques

Examples:

- a systematic programme of practical courses in new and/or difficult biochemical determinations with an updated listing of such courses that is made internationally available.
- exchange of computer software in the field of epidemiology and clinical cardiology.
- facilitation of transfer of new or difficult techniques in the cardiovascular field.

7. Co-operative moves by scientists in the field of prevention

Example:

- simultaneous urging against cigarette consumption or in favour of food habits that can promote prevention.

Cancer

The group stresses that international co-operation in cancer research is necessary in order to achieve progress in the cancer problem.

Such international co-operation exists in Europe and throughout the world, and is carried out by a variety of governmental and non-governmental organizations and societies.

The group urges governments and other appropriate bodies to increase support for such organizations, so that existing programmes of international co-operation can be continued and enlarged. Due care should be taken to avoid unnecessary duplication. Progress of international collaboration in cancer research should be monitored periodically by the appropriate bodies.

The group requests that special emphasis should be devoted to the following:

(1) Free dissemination of regional and local data on cancer and related etiological factors, and assistance for field studies.

(2) Extension of cancer registries to include new regions and countries.

(3) Extension of information exchange in cancer treatment, including data on screening, testing, toxicity, drug interactions and, where applicable, exchange of drugs. Elaboration of ethical principles.

(4) Standardization of reagents, diagnostic methods and test systems.

(5) Access to research facilities and data from health care systems.

(6) Training courses, especially for young scientists in oncology and appropriate basic biology, including new methods.

(7) Increased opportunities, especially for young scientists to learn new approaches in cancer research, by short-term and long-term fellowships.

(8) Direct and rapid contact between working scientists in collaborating laboratories, by all available means of communication.

Virology

In spite of great achievements in the prevention of some of the most severe virus diseases, the relative and absolute importance of viruses as causes of acute and chronic infectious diseases has increased.

For this reason, and being aware of the utmost importance of international co-operation, for example in the eradication of smallpox, the virologists feel that such co-operation is necessary in trying to solve some of the many important problems in virology. International co-operation exists already in the field of virology both in Europe and in the world and is carried out by several governmental and non-governmental organizations.

The virologists urge that the existing programmes in the field of virology should be continued and enlarged. Unnecessary duplication should be avoided.

Although partly covered by existing organizations and arrangements further international co-operation is required in the following:

- Rapid dissemination of information on epidemiology of virus diseases in the different regions.

- Some fields of molecular virology, as for example recombinant DNA, including safety regulations and evaluation of benefits.

- Promoting channels for information on new methods in diagnostic procedures, especially rapid diagnosis of virus diseases.

- Standardization of material for diagnostic tests as well as for materials used for prevention and treatment of virus diseases.

- Study and prevention of some of the common and especially important diseases such as respiratory infections and hepatitis.

- Obtaining access to research facilities in different institutions, especially for young scientists, including training courses, and long or short-term fellowships, for example in regional institutions prepared to give training in applied clinical and epidemiological virology.

- Direct and rapid contact between working scientists in collaborating laboratories by all available means of communication.

ANNEX 4: HUMANITIES AND SOCIAL SCIENCES

1. The main issues to be faced

A. General issues

The main issues to be faced include such general phenomena as rapid demographic, social, cultural and psychological changes, the impact of the increasing sophistication of technology, the shifting role of women in society, alterations of values concerning the environment, and limitations imposed by a growing energy shortage. (A more detailed list of the problems to be faced appears in the Appendix).

B. Urbanization

The process of urbanization has brought new possibilities and problems which have affected rural areas and open spaces as well as cities and their inhabitants. Among them are effects of internal and external migration, problems of crowding, disorder and crime, alterations to the natural environment, and pollution of the atmosphere, water resources and the land. All of this calls for an improved understanding of the processes of urbanization and their relationship to regional development.

C. Environmental quality

There has been a growing consciousness of the importance of environmental protection, but there are practical problems due to imperfect understanding of the environment. In addition, economic accounting should to an increasing extent take into consideration not only economic activity but also the social, cultural and ecological values of the environment.

D. Research methodology

The highly complex problems of urban development and environmental protection require the use of multidisciplinary approaches, comparative studies and the development of mathematical, simulation or other kinds of models. Some of the difficulties in research on these matters are due to differences in the collection, analysis of data and other materials in the various countries.

2. The tasks ahead

Based on the above considerations, six major areas of research were identified:

(1) Changes in population structures and characteristics.

(2) Present and future social, cultural, behavioural, economic and spatial problems of the process of urbanization.

(3) Preservation of national patrimony and environment.

(4) Impact of new technologies on human behaviour, natural environment and urban ecosystems.

(5) Organization of ecologically orientated urban and regional planning and management.

(6) Education, training, preparation and diffusion of information.

These areas were drawn from the detailed list of topics presented in the Appendix.

To ensure that such research is undertaken, and that its results will be put to use, two developments are needed. One is a larger allocation of funding than is presently characteristic in the social sciences and humanities, especially in the lesser developed countries with smaller resources. The other is the creation of closer co-operation between scientists, planners, the public and policy-makers.

It was emphasized that the necessary research efforts can be attained by existing institutions with the support of governments and administrative authorities. There was also agreement that promotion and expansion of international co-operation and collaboration are needed in research as well as in the training of scientists and in the exchange of information.

3. Recommendations

a) Scientific conferences and seminars should be organized during the coming years on the problems of urban development, cultural changes and the quality of the environment. These meetings could focus particularly upon problems in comparative studies and methodology in the interdisciplinary approach to investigations of social, socio-economic, ecological and cultural aspects of urban development and environmental change. These conferences or seminars could be organized by UNESCO or ECE, and where appropriate in co-operation with existing international scien-tific bodies including the European Co-ordination Centre for Research and Documentation in Social Sciences (known as the Vienna Centre) and the International Institute for Applied Systems Analysis (IIASA). A consultative body of experts should prepare the meetings on the basis of results of national studies. The latter might focus upon a number of special pilot projects on urban and/or environmental issues, the results of which would then be discussed in the international forum.

b) International, national and regional organizations operating in Europe should be encouraged by CSCE, within their field of competence, to arrange advanced training courses and seminars for scientists from states participating in the CSCE. In particular, provision should be made for young scientists to attend training courses arranged in participating states.

c) An inventory of recently completed and ongoing studies on the problems of urban development and of the human environment should be organized. A review of experience in international co-operation in research and in the exchange of information should be undertaken. These reviews could be compiled by one of the existing international bodies, for example through UNEP, ECE or UNESCO.

d) Eco-toxicological studies connected with relevant methods in the social and health sciences should be supported and improved on an international basis, especially within the relevant projects of the Scientific Committee on Problems of the Environment (SCOPE) of ICSU, and WHO.

e) A series of comparative studies should be strengthened on the procedure in integrated urban and regional planning and management in order to determine the most effective way to link research to the process of decision-making.

f) The impact of science and technology on society; the methodology of interdisciplinary studies with special reference to behavioural, social and natural sciences; research and policy-making in social fields; the decision-making process including the involvement of the public; research in political sciences relevant to the CSCE countries; science policy and improved and more efficient forms of co-operation including the institutional framework, are themes which should be further explored in future meetings.

The working body had a thorough discussion on all tasks on agenda item number 2. The content of these discussions is reflected both in this Annex and in the general conclusions contained in the Report of the "Scientific Forum".

APPENDIX

General issues

1. The impact of increasingly sophisticated technology on urban development, life-styles and the environment, compared with "appropriate" technology which may be less sophisticated but more closely adapted to the environment and the preservation of social values.

2. The impact of an ageing population on the economy; requirements for social services, housing and transportation.

3. The effects of the changing role of women in the work force.

4. The effects of shifts in social values on the role the individual plays in planning and policy-making.

5. The gap between the perceptions of various groups of professionals as to what society needs and how this should be provided, and the perceptions of the public at large.

6. Finding effective means for including in planning and policy-making the results of research on human dimensions of urbanization and environmental quality.

7. Problems of undertaking and implementing truly comprehensive planning.

8. How to make research in social sciences and the humanities more relevant for planning and policy-making.

Environmental issues

1. The impact of environment on human health.

2. How to tackle the problems of environmental hazards and technological risks.

3. How to develop comprehensive environmental plans into which plans for industrial, transportation, urban and social development might be fitted.

4. Determination of the values which individuals attach to particular environments, and the extent to which such values vary over space and time.

5. Impediments to the improvement of environmental quality.

6. How to investigate objectively changes in the quality of life.

7. How to develop a broader perspective in planning so that more intensive use may be made of existing resources rather than bringing in new supplies from elsewhere, e.g. the introduction of wastewater renovation and re-cycling as opposed to development of water supplies at progressively further distances from the city.

8. The impact of economic development on environmental quality.

9. Sustaining an interest in the environmental question at the political level.

Methodological Issues

1. The circumstances in which an interdisciplinary approach is especially appropriate, and the ways in which it can be most successfully pursued.

2. The integration of non-technical and non-economic factors in models relating to urban development and environmental quality management.

3. Problems of undertaking comparative studies, especially where cultural traits make data collection difficult, or where meanings and values attached to given phenomena are unique to a particular area.

4. How to take account of shifts in social values and new developments in technology in planning and policy-making.

5. Provision of opportunities for education on the environment.

6. How to cope with decision-making under uncertainty

7. Inclusion of predictions of shifts in social values and development of technologies in plans and policies.

Urban development and human environment

1. Social and cultural problems of urbanization

Changes in population structures and their impact on urban life and development. (Professional structure, the impact of women entering the work force, new family models, youth-adult correlations, increasing ratio of old people).

2. Urban migration and its consequences

Social effects of migration to and from cities and its impact on areas of immigration and emigration. Increasing diffusion of urban population from cities to countryside leading up to levelling of differences between urban and rural life. The role of small and medium-sized cities. The process of concentration and of deconcentration of urban activities.

3. The future of urbanization

Human adaptation to changes in urban life. The impact of technical progress on the functional and spatial structure of urbanization from the ecological point of view. Prognosis of new forms of urbanization. Environment and technology. Optimum size of cities. The "human scale" in urban development.

4. Technology and the economy confronted with human, social, cultural and ecological needs

Human perception of urban environment. Economic value of ecological and social factors. How to integrate ecological, social, cultural and economic criteria.

5. Preservation of national patrimony and environment

Interdisciplinary environmental research. Preservation of the national patrimony on a local and national scale (architectural and cultural and traditional values, urban structures). Adaptation of old cities to new needs. Revalorisation of old housing system.

6. Interrelation of urban and regional development

Correlation between urban and regional growth and national development. Urban and rural development. Structural forms of the net of settlements. Process of urban concentration and deconcentration.

7. Methods of ecologically-orientated integrated urban and regional planning

Principles of integrated planning. Methodology of long-term urban and regional planning presenting several strategies of development. How to compare them from economic and ecological points of view (mathematical models). The territorial integration of planning and implementation. Systems of urban management.

8. Problems of big cities and metropolitan areas

Comparison of various cities' growth. Internal structures of metropolia, their complex problems: housing, recreation, traffic, places of work, etc. Special problems of highly industrialized cities and regions, harbour cities and coastal urbanization.

9. Education, training and information

Methodology of comprehensive environmental training and education of undergraduate and postgraduate specialists. Special training of young scientists. Information on the importance of ecological, social and cultural aspects of urban development and environmental protection for decision-makers and the general public. New means: mass media, etc.

Public participation in planning and implementation decisions. Public control of the mode of complementation of the results of planning based on scientific research.

CONCLUDING DOCUMENT OF MADRID

CONCLUDING DOCUMENT OF THE MADRID MEETING OF REPRESENTATIVES OF THE PARTICIPATING STATES OF THE CONFERENCE ON SECURITY AND CO-OPERATION IN EUROPE, HELD ON THE BASIS OF THE PROVISIONS OF THE FINAL ACT RELATING TO THE FOLLOW-UP TO THE CONFERENCE

Madrid, 6 September 1983

The representatives of the participating States of the Conference on Security and Co-operation in Europe met in Madrid from 11 November 1980 to 9 September 1983 in accordance with the provisions of the Final Act relating to the Follow-up to the Conference, as well as on the basis of the other relevant documents adopted during the process of the CSCE.

The participants were addressed on 12 November 1980 by the Spanish Prime Minister.

Opening statements were made by all Heads of Delegations among whom were Ministers and Deputy Ministers of Foreign Affairs of a number of participating States. Some Ministers of Foreign Affairs addressed the Meeting also at later stages.

Contributions were made by representatives of the United Nations Economic Commission for Europe (ECE) and UNESCO.

Contributions were also made by the following non-participating Mediterranean States: Algeria, Egypt, Israel, Morocco and Tunisia.

The representatives of the participating States stressed the high political significance of the Conference on Security and Co-operation in Europe and of the process initiated by it as well as of the ways and means it provides for States to further their efforts to increase security, develop co-operation and enhance mutual understanding in Europe. They therefore reaffirmed their commitment to the process of the CSCE and emphasized the importance of the implementation of all the provisions and the respect for all the principles of the Final Act by each of them as being essential for the development of this process. Furthermore, they stressed the importance they attach to security and genuine détente, while deploring the deterioration of the international situation since the Belgrade Meeting 1977.

Accordingly, the participating States agreed that renewed efforts should be made to give full effect to the Final Act through concrete action, unilateral, bilateral and multilateral, in order to restore trust and confidence between the participating States which would permit a substantial improvement in their mutual relations. They considered that the future of the CSCE process required balanced progress in all sections of the Final Act.

In accordance with the mandate provided for in the Final Act and the Agenda of the Madrid Meeting, the representatives of the participating States held a thorough exchange of views both on the implementation of the provisions of the Final Act and of the tasks defined by the Conference, as well as, in the context of the questions dealt with by the latter, on the deepening of their mutual relations, the improvement of security and the development of co-operation in Europe, and the development of the process of détente in the future.
It was confirmed that the thorough exchange of views constitutes in itself a valuable contribution towards the achievement of the aims set by the CSCE. In this context, it was agreed that these aims can only be attained by continuous implementation, unilaterally, bilaterally and multilaterally, of all the provisions and by respect for all the principles of the Final Act.

During this exchange of views, different and at times contradictory opinions were expressed as to the degree of implementation of the Final Act reached so far by participating States. While certain progress was noted, concern was expressed at the serious deficiencies in the implementation on this document.

Critical assessments from different viewpoints were given as to the application of and respect for the principles of the Final Act. Serious violations of a number of these principles were deplored during these assessments. Therefore, the participating States, at times represented at a higher level, considered it necessary to state, at various stages of the Meeting, that strict application of and respect for these principles, in all their aspects, are essential for the improvement of mutual relations between the participating States.

The necessity was also stressed that the relations of the participating States with all other States should be conducted in the spirit of these principles.

Concern was expressed about the continued lack of confidence among participating States.

Concern was also expressed as to the spread of terrorism.

The implementation of the provisions of the Final Act concerning Confidence-Building Measures, Co-operation in the field of Economics, of Science and Technology and of Environment, as well as Co-operation in Humanitarian and other fields was thoroughly discussed. It was considered that the numerous possibilities offered by the Final Act had not been sufficiently utilized. Questions relating to Security and Co-operation in the Mediterranean were also discussed.

The participating States reaffirmed their commitment to the continuation of the CSCE process as agreed to in the chapter on the Follow-up to the Conference contained in the Final Act.

The representatives of the participating States took note of the reports of the meetings of experts and of the "Scientific Forum", and in the course of their deliberations took the results of these meetings into account.

The representatives of the participating States examined all the proposals submitted concerning the above questions and agreed on the following:

QUESTIONS RELATING TO SECURITY IN EUROPE

The participating States express their determination

- to exert new efforts to make détente an effective, as well as continuing increasingly viable and comprehensive process, universal in scope, as undertaken under the Final Act;

- to seek solutions to outstanding problems through peaceful means;

- to fulfil consistently all the provisions under the Final Act and, in particular, strictly and unreservedly to respect and put into practice all the ten principles contained in the Declaration on Principles Guiding Relations between Participating States, irrespective of their political, economic or social systems, as well as of their size, geographical location or level of economic development, including their commitment to conduct their relations with all other States in the spirit of these principles;

- to develop relations of mutual co-operation, friendship and confidence, refraining from any action which, being contrary to the Final Act, might impair such relations;

- to encourage genuine efforts to implement the Final Act;

- to exert genuine efforts towards containing an increasing arms build-up as well as towards strengthening confidence and security and promoting disarmament.

Principles

They reaffirm their determination fully to respect and apply these principles and accordingly, to promote by all means, both in law and practice, their increased effectiveness. They consider that one such means could be to give legislative expression - in forms appropriate to practices and procedures specific to each country - to the ten principles set forth in the Final Act.

They recognize it as important that treaties and agreements concluded by participating States reflect and be consonant with the relevant principles and, where appropriate, refer to them.

The participating States reaffirm the need that refraining from the threat or use of force, as a norm of international life, should be strictly and effectively observed. To this end they stress their duty, under the relevant provisions of the Final Act, to act accordingly.

The participating States condemn terrorism, including terrorism in international relations, as endangering or taking innocent human lives or otherwise jeopardizing human rights and fundamental freedoms, and emphasize the necessity to take resolute measures to combat it. They express their determination to take effective measures for the prevention and suppression of acts of terrorism, both at the national level and through international co-operation including appropriate bilateral and multilateral agreements, and accordingly to broaden and reinforce mutual co-operation to combat such acts. They agree to do so in conformity with the Charter of the United Nations, the United Nations Declaration on Principles of International Law concerning Friendly Relations and Co-operation among States and the Helsinki Final Act.

In the context of the combat against acts of terrorism, they will take all appropriate measures in preventing their respective territories from being used for the preparation, organization or commission of terrorist activities, including those directed against other participating States and their citizens. This also includes measures to prohibit on their territories illegal activities of persons, groups and organizations that instigate, organize or engage in the perpetration of acts of terrorism.

The participating States confirm that they will refrain from direct or indirect assistance to terrorist activities or to subversive or other activities directed towards the violent overthrow of the regime of another participating State. Accordingly, they will refrain, *inter alia*, from financing, encouraging, fomenting or tolerating any such activities.

They express their determination to do their utmost to assure necessary security to all official representatives and persons who participate on their territories in activities within the scope of diplomatic, consular or other official relations.

They emphasize that all the participating States recognize in the Final Act the universal significance of human rights and fundamental freedoms, respect for which is an essential factor for the peace, justice and well-being necessary to ensure the development of friendly relations and co-operation among themselves, as among all States.

The participating States stress their determination to promote and encourage the effective exercise of human rights and fundamental freedoms, all of which derive from the inherent dignity of the human person and are essential for his free and full development, and to ensure constant and tangible progress in accordance with the Final Act, aiming at further and steady development in this field in all participating States, irrespective of their political, economic and social systems.

They similarly stress their determination to develop their laws and regulations in the field of civil, political, economic, social, cultural and other human rights and fundamental freedoms; they also emphasize their determination to ensure the effective exercise of these rights and freedoms.

They recall the right of the individual to know and act upon his rights and duties in the field of human rights and fundamental freedoms, as embodied in the Final Act, and will take the necessary action in their respective countries to effectively ensure this right.

The participating States reaffirm that they will recognize, respect and furthermore agree to take the action necessary to ensure the freedom of the individual to profess and practise, alone or in community with others, religion or belief acting in accordance with the dictates of his own conscience.

In this context, they will consult, whenever necessary, the religious faiths, institutions and organizations, which act within the constitutional framework of their respective countries.

They will favourably consider applications by religious communities of believers practising or prepared to practise their faith within the constitutional framework of their States, to be granted the status provided for in their respective countries for religious faiths, institutions and organizations.

They stress also the importance of constant progress in ensuring the respect for and actual enjoyment of the rights of persons belonging to national minorities as well as protecting their legitimate interests as provided for in the Final Act.

They stress the importance of ensuring equal rights of men and women; accordingly, they agree to take all actions necessary to promote equally effective participation of men and women in political, economic, social and cultural life.

The participating States will ensure the right of workers freely to establish and join trade unions, the right of trade unions freely to exercise their activities and other rights as laid down in relevant international instruments. They note that these rights will be exercised in compliance with the law of the State and in conformity with the State's obligations under international law. They will encourage, as appropriate, direct contacts and communication among such trade unions and their representatives.

They reaffirm that governments, institutions, organizations and persons have a relevant and positive role to play in contributing toward the achievement of the above-mentioned aims of their co-operation.

They reaffirm the particular significance of the Universal Declaration of Human Rights, the International Covenants on Human Rights and other relevant international instruments of their joint and separate efforts to stimulate and develop universal respect for human rights and fundamental freedoms; they call on all participating States to act in conformity with those international instruments and on those participating States, which have not yet done so, to consider the possibility of acceding to the cove-nants.

They agree to give favourable consideration to the use of bilateral round-table meetings, held on a voluntary basis, between delegations composed by each participating State to discuss issues of human rights and fundamental freedoms in accordance with an agreed agenda in a spirit of mutual respect with a view to achieving greater understanding and co-operation based on the provisions of the Final Act.

They decide to convene a meeting of experts of the participating States on questions concerning respect, in their States, for human rights and fundamental freedoms, in all their aspects, as embodied in the Final Act.

Upon invitation of the Government of Canada, the meeting of experts will be held in Ottawa, beginning on 7 May 1985. It will draw up conclusions and recommendations to be submitted to the governments of all participating States.

The meeting will be preceded by a preparatory meeting which will be held in Ottawa upon the invitation of the Government of Canada, starting on 23 April 1985.

In conformity with the recommendation contained in the Report of the Montreux Meeting of Experts, another meeting of experts of the participating States will be convened, at the invitation of the Government of Greece. It will take place in Athens and will commence on 21 March 1984, with the purpose of pursuing, on the basis of the Final Act, the examination of a generally acceptable method for the peaceful settlement of disputes aimed at complementing existing methods. The meeting will take into account the common approach set forth in the above-mentioned report.

Recalling the right of any participating State to belong or not to belong to international organizations, to be or not to be a party to bilateral or multilateral treaties including the right to be or not to be a party to treaties of alliance, and also the right to neutrality, the participating States take note of the declaration of the Government of the Republic of Malta in which it stated that, as an effective contribution to détente, peace and security in the Mediterranean region, the Republic of Malta is a neutral State adhering to a policy of non-alignment. They call upon all States to respect that declaration.

CONFERENCE ON CONFIDENCE- AND SECURITY-BUILDING MEASURES AND DISARMAMENT IN EUROPE

The participating States,

Recalling the provisions of the Final Act according to which they recognize the interest of all of them in efforts aimed at lessening military confrontation and promoting disarmament,

Have agreed to convene a Conference on Confidence and Security-building Measures and Disarmament in Europe.

The aim of the Conference is, as a substantial and integral part of the multilateral process initiated by the Conference on Security and Co-operation in Europe, with the participation of all the States signatories of the Final Act, to undertake, in stages, new, effective and concrete actions designed to make progress in strengthening confidence and security and in achieving disarmament, so as to give effect and expression to the duty of States to refrain from the threat or use of force in their mutual relations.

Thus the Conference will begin a process of which the first stage will be devoted to the negotiation and adoption of a set of mutually complementary confidence- and security-building measures designed to reduce the risk of military confrontation in Europe.

The first stage of the Conference will be held in Stockholm commencing on 17 January 1984.

On the basis of equality of rights, balance and reciprocity, equal respect for the security interests of all CSCE participating States, and of their respective obligations concerning confidence- and security-building measures and disarmament in Europe, these confidence- and security-building measures will cover the whole of Europe as well as the adjoining sea area[*] and air space. They will be of military significance and politically binding and will be provided with adequate forms of verification which correspond to their content.

As far as the adjoining sea area[*] and air space is concerned, the measures will be applicable to the military activities of all the participating States taking place there whenever these activities affect security in Europe as well as constitute a part of activities taking place within the whole of Europe as referred to above, which they will agree to notify. Necessary specifications will be made through the negotiations on the confidence- and security-building measures at the Conference.

---

[*] In this context, the notion of adjoining sea area is understood to refer also to ocean areas adjoining Europe.

[*] In this context, the notion of adjoining sea area is understood to refer also to ocean areas adjoining Europe.

Nothing in the definition of the zone given above will diminish obligations already undertaken under the Final Act. The confidence- and security-building measures to be agreed upon at the Conference will also be applicable in all areas covered by any of the provisions in the Final Act relating to confidence-building measures and certain aspects of security and disarmament.

The provisions established by the negotiators will come into force in the forms and according to the procedure to be agreed upon by the Conference.

Taking into account the above-mentioned aim of the Conference, the next follow-up meeting of the participating States of the CSCE, to be held in Vienna, commencing on 4 November 1986, will assess the progress achieved during the first stage of the Conference.

Taking into account the relevant provisions of the Final Act, and having reviewed the results achieved by the first stage of the Conference, and also in the light of other relevant negotiations on security and disarmament affecting Europe, a future CSCE follow-up meeting will consider ways and appropriate means for the participating States to continue their efforts for security and disarmament in Europe, including the question of supplementing the present mandate for the next stage of the Conference on Confidence- and Security-building Measures and Disarmament in Europe.

A preparatory meeting, charged with establishing the agenda, time-table and other organizational modalities for the first stage of the Conference, will be held in Helsinki, commencing on 25 October 1983. Its duration shall not exceed three weeks.

The rules of procedure, the working methods and the scale of distribution for the expenses valid for the CSCE will, *mutatis mutandis*, be applied to the Conference and to the preparatory meeting referred to in the preceding paragraph. The services of a technical secretariat will be provided by the host country.

CO-OPERATION IN THE FIELD OF ECONOMICS, OF SCIENCE AND TECHNOLOGY AND OF THE ENVIRONMENT

The participating States consider that the implementation of all provisions of the Final Act and full respect for the principles guiding relations among them set out therein are an essential basis for the development of co-operation among them in the field of economics, of science and technology and of the environment. At the same time they reaffirm their conviction that co-operation in these fields contributes to the reinforcement of peace and security in Europe and in the world as a whole. In this spirit they reiterate their resolve to pursue and intensify such co-operation between one another, irrespective of their economic and social systems.

The participating States confirm their interest in promoting adequate, favourable conditions in order further to develop trade and industrial co-operation among them, in particular by fully implementing all provisions of the second chapter of the Final Act, so as to make greater use of the possibilities created by their economic, scientific and technical potential. In this context and taking into consideration the efforts already made unilaterally, bilaterally and multilaterally in order to overcome all kinds of obstacles to trade, they reaffirm their intention to make further efforts aimed at reducing or progressively eliminating all kinds of obstacles to the development of trade.

Taking account of the activities of the United Nations Economic Commission for Europe (ECE) already carried out in the field of all kinds of obstacles to trade, they recommend that further work on this subject be directed in particular towards identifying these obstacles and examining them with a view to finding means for their reduction or progressive elimination, in order to contribute to harmonious development of their economic relations.

On the basis of the provisions of the Final Act concerning business contacts and facilities the participating States declare their intention to make efforts to enable business negotiations and activities to be carried out more efficiently and expeditiously and further to create conditions facilitating closer contacts between representatives and experts of seller firms on the one hand and buyer as well as user firms on the other at all stages of transaction. They will also further other forms of operational contacts between sellers and users such as the holding of technical symposia and demonstrations and after-sales training or requalification courses for technical staff of user firms and organizations.

They also agree to take measures further to develop and improve facilities and working conditions for representatives of foreign firms and organizations on their territory, including telecommunications facilities for representatives of such firms and organizations, as well as to develop these and other amenities for temporarily resident staff including particularly site personnel. They will endeavour further to take measures to speed up as far as possible procedures for the registration of foreign firms' representations and offices as well as for granting entry visas to business representatives.

The participating States declare their intention to ensure the regular publication and dissemination, as rapidly as possible, of economic and commercial information compiled in such a way as to facilitate the appreciation of market opportunities and thus to contribute effectively to the process of developing international trade and industrial co-operation.
To this end and in order to make further progress in achieving the aims laid down in the relevant provisions of the Final Act they intend to intensify their efforts to improve the comparability, comprehensiveness and clarity of their economic and commercial statistics, in particular by adopting where necessary the following measures: by accompanying their economic and trade statistics by adequately defined summary indices based wherever possible on constant values; by publishing their interim statistics whenever technically possible at least on a quarterly basis; by publishing their statistical compilations in sufficient detail to achieve the aims referred to above, in particular by using for their foreign trade statistics a product breakdown permitting the identification of particular products for purposes of market analysis; by striving to have their economic and trade statistics no less comprehensive than those previously published by the State concerned.

They further express their willingness to co-operate towards the early completion of work in the appropriate United Nations bodies on the harmonization and alignment of statistical nomenclatures.

The participating States further recognize the usefulness of making economic and commercial information existing in other participating States readily available to enterprises and firms in their countries through appropriate channels.

The participating States, conscious of the need further to improve the conditions conducive to a more efficient functioning of institutions and firms acting in the field of marketing, will promote a more active exchange of knowledge and techniques required for effective marketing, and will encourage more intensive relations among such institutions and firms. They agree to make full use of the possibilities offered by the ECE to further their co-operation in this field.

The participating States note the increasing frequency in their economic relations of compensation transactions in all their forms. They recognize that a useful role can be played by such transactions, concluded on a mutually acceptable basis. At the same time they recognize that problems can be created by the linkage in such transactions between purchases and sales.

Taking account of the studies of the ECE already carried out in this field, they recommend that further work on this subject be directed in particular towards identifying such problems and examining ways of solving them in order to contribute to a harmonious development of their economic relations.

The participating States recognize that the expansion of industrial co-operation, on the basis of their mutual interest and motivated by economic considerations, can contribute to the further development and diversifi-cation of their economic relations and to a wider utilization of modern technology.

They note the useful role bilateral agreements on economic, industrial and technical co-operation, including where appropriate, those of a long-term nature can play. They also express their willingness to promote favourable conditions for the development of industrial co-operation among competent organizations, enterprises and firms. To this end and with a view to facilitating the identification of new possibilities for industrial co-operation projects they recognize the desirability of further developing and improving the conditions for business activities and the exchange of economic and commercial information among competent organizations, enterprises and firms including small and medium-sized enterprises.

They also note that, if it is in the mutual interest of potential partners, new forms of industrial co-operation can be envisaged, including those with organizations, institutions and firms of third countries.

They recommend that the ECE pursue and continue to pay particular attention to its activities in the field of industrial co-operation, *inter alia* by further directing its efforts towards examining ways of promoting favourable conditions for the development of co-operation in this field, including the organization of symposia and seminars.

The participating States declare their readiness to continue their efforts aiming at a wider participation by small and medium-size enterprises in trade and industrial co-operation. Aware of the problems particularly affecting such enterprises, the participating States will endeavour further to improve the conditions dealt with in the preceding paragraphs in order to facilitate the operations of these enterprises in the above-mentioned fields. The participating States further recommend that the ECE develop its special studies pertaining to these problems.

The participating States recognize the increasing importance of co-operation in the field of energy, *inter alia* that of a long-term nature, on both a bilateral and multilateral basis. Welcoming the results so far achieved through such endeavours and in particular the work carried out by the ECE they express their support for continuing the co-operation pursued by the Senior Advisers to ECE Governments on Energy aiming at the fulfilment of all parts of their mandate.

The participating States reaffirm their interest in reducing and preventing technical barriers to trade and welcome the increased co-operation in this field, *inter alia* the work of the Government Officials Responsible for Standardization Policies in the ECE. They will encourage the conclusion of international certification arrangements covering where appropriate the mutual acceptance of certification systems providing mutually satisfactory guarantees.

The participating States recommend that appropriate action be taken in order to facilitate the use and enlarge the scope of arbitration as an instrument for settling disputes in international trade and industrial co-operation. They recommend in particular the application of the provisions of the United Nations Convention on Recognition and Enforcement of Foreign Arbitral Awards of 1958 as well as a wider recourse to the arbitration rules elaborated by the United Nations Commission on International Trade Law. They also advocate that parties should, on the basis of the provisions of the Final Act, be allowed freedom in the choice of arbitrators and the place of arbitration, including the choice of arbitrators and the place of arbitration in a third country.

The participating States recognize the important role of scientific and technical progress in the economic and social development of all countries in particular those which are developing from an economic point of view. Taking into account the objectives which countries or institutions concerned pursue in their bilateral and multilateral relations they underline the importance of further developing, on the basis of reciprocal advantage and on the basis of mutual agreement and other arrangements, the forms and methods of co-operation in the field of science and technology provided for in the Final Act, for instance international programmes and co-operative projects, while utilizing also various forms of contacts, including direct and individual contacts among scientists and specialists as well as contacts and communications among interested organizations, scientific and technological institutions and enterprises.

In this context they recognize the value of an improved exchange and dissemination of information concerning scientific and technical developments as a means of facilitating, on the basis of mutual advantage, the study and the transfer of, as well as access to scientific and technical achievements in fields of co-operation agreed between interested parties.

The participating States recommend that in the field of science and technology the ECE should give due attention, through appropriate ways and means, to the elaboration of studies and practical projects for the development of co-operation among member countries.

Furthermore, the participating States, aware of the relevant part of the Report of the "Scientific Forum", agree to encourage the development of scientific co-operation in the field of agriculture at bilateral, multilateral and sub-regional levels, with aim, *inter alia*, of improving livestock and plant breeding and ensuring optimum use and conservation of water resources. To this end, they will promote further co-operation among research institutions and centres in their countries, through the exchange of information, the joint implementation of research programmes, the organization of meetings among scientists and specialists, and other methods.

The participating States invite the ECE and other competent international organizations to support the implementation of these activities and to examine the possibilities of providing a wider exchange of scientific and technological information in the field of agriculture.

The participating States welcome with satisfaction the important steps taken to strengthen co-operation within the framework of the ECE in the field of the environment, including the High-Level Meeting on the Protection of the Environment (13-16 November 1979). Taking due account of work undertaken or envisaged in other competent international organizations, they recommend the continuation of efforts in this field, including, *inter alia*,

- giving priority to the effective implementation of the provisions of the Resolution on Long-Range Transboundary Air Pollution adopted at the High-Level Meeting,

- the early ratification of the Convention on Long-Range Transboundary Air Pollution signed at the High-Level Meeting,

- implementation of the Recommendations contained in the Declaration on Low and Non-Waste Technology and Reutilization and Recycling of Wastes,

- implementation of Decision B and C of the thirty-fifth session of the ECE concerning the Declaration of Policy on Prevention and Control of Water Pollution, including transboundary pollution,

- support in carrying out the programme of work of the ECE concerning the protection of the environment, including, *inter alia*, the work under way in the field of the protection of flora and fauna.

In the context of the provisions of the Final Act concerning migrant labour in Europe, the participating States note that recent developments in the world economy have affected the situation of migrant workers. In this connection, the participating States express their wish that host countries and countries of origin, guided by a spirit of mutual interest and co-operation, intensify their contacts with a view to improving further the general situation of migrant workers and their families, *inter alia* the protection of their human rights including their economic, social and cultural rights while taking particularly into account the special problems of second generation migrants. They will also endeavour to provide or promote, where reasonable demand exists, adequate teaching of the language and culture of the countries of origin.

The participating States recommend that, among other measures for facilitating the social and economic reintegration of returning migrant labour, the payment of pensions as acquired or established under the social security system to which such workers have been admitted in the host country should be ensured by appropriate legislative means or reciprocal agreements.

The participating States further recognize the importance for their economic development of promoting the exchange of information and experience on training for management staff. To this end they recommend the organization, in an appropriate existing framework and with the help of interested organizations such as, for example, the ECE and the International Labour Organisation, of a symposium of persons responsible for services and institutions specializing in management training for admin-istrations and enterprises with a view to exchanging information on training problems and methods, comparing experiences and encouraging the development of relations among the centres concerned.

The participating States welcome the valuable contribution made by the ECE to the multilateral implementation of the provisions of the Final Act pertaining to co-operation in the fields of economics, of science and technology and of the environment. Aware of the potential of the ECE for intensifying co-operation in these fields, they recommend the fullest use of the existing mechanisms and resources in order to continue and consolidate the implementation of the relevant provisions of the Final Act in the interest of its member countries, including those within the ECE region which are developing from an economic point of view.

The participating States, bearing in mind their will expressed in the provisions of the Final Act, reiterate the determination of each of them to promote stable and equitable international economic relations in the mutual interest of all States and, in this spirit, to participate equitably in promoting and strengthening economic co-operation with the developing countries, in particular the least developed among them. They also note the usefulness, *inter alia*, of identifying and executing, in co-operation with developing countries, concrete projects, with a view to contributing to economic development in these countries.

They also declare their readiness to contribute to common efforts towards the establishment of a new international economic order and the implementation of the Strategy for the Third United Nations Development Decade, as adopted. They recognize the importance of the launching of mutually beneficial and adequately prepared global negotiations relating to international economic co-operation for development.

QUESTIONS RELATING TO SECURITY AND CO-OPERATION IN THE MEDITERRANEAN

The participating States, bearing in mind that security in Europe, considered in the broader context of world security, is closely linked to security in the Mediterranean area as a whole, reaffirm their intention to contribute to peace, security and justice in the Mediterranean region.

They further express their will

- to take positive steps towards lessening tensions and strengthening stability, security and peace in the Mediterranean and, to this end, to intensify efforts towards finding just, viable and lasting solutions, through peaceful means, to outstanding crucial problems, without resort to force or other means incompatible with the Principles of the Final Act, so as to promote confidence and security and make peace prevail in the region;

- to take measures designed to increase confidence and security;

- to develop good neighbourly relations with all States in the region, with due regard to reciprocity, and in the spirit of the principles contained in the Declaration on Principles Guiding Relations Between Participa-ting States of the Final Act;

- to study further the possibility of *ad hoc* meetings of Mediterranean States aimed at strengthening security and intensifying co-operation in the Mediterranean.

In addition the participating States will, within the framework of the implementation of the Valletta report, consider the possibilities offered by new transport infrastructure developments to facilitate new commercial and industrial exchanges, as well as by the improvement of existing transport networks, and by a wider co-ordination of transport investments between interested parties. In this context they recommend that a study be undertaken, within the framework of the ECE, in order to establish the current and potential transport flows in the Mediterranean involving the participating States and other States of this region taking account of the current work in this field. They will further consider the question of introducing or extending, in accordance with the existing IMO regulations, the use of suitable techniques for aids to maritime navigation, principally in straits.

They further note with satisfaction the results of the Meeting of Experts held in Valletta on the subject of economic, scientific and cultural co-operation within the framework of the Mediterranean Chapter of the Final Act. They reaffirm the conclusions and recommendations of the report of this Meeting and agree that they will be guided accordingly. They also take note of efforts under way aiming at implementing them as appropriate. To this end, the participating States agree to convene from 16 to 26 October 1984 a seminar to be held at Venice at the invitation of the Government of Italy, to review the initiatives already undertaken, or envisaged, in all the sectors outlined in the report of the Valletta Meeting and stimulate, where necessary, broader developments in these sectors.

Representatives of the competent international organizations and representatives of the non-participating Mediterranean States will be invited to this Seminar in accordance with the rules and practices adopted at the Valletta Meeting.*

---

* The organization of the Venice Seminar is set forth in the Chairman's statement of 6 September 1983 (see Annex I).

CO-OPERATION IN HUMANITARIAN AND OTHER FIELDS

The participating States,

Recalling the introductory sections of the Chapter on Co-operation in Humanitarian and other Fields of the Final Act including those concerning the development of mutual understanding between them and détente and those concerning progress in cultural and educational exchanges, broader dissemination of information, contacts between people and the solution of humanitarian problems,

Resolving to pursue and expand co-operation in these fields and to achieve a fuller utilization of the possibilities offered by the Final Act,

Agree now to implement the following:

Human Contacts

The participating States will favourably deal with applications relating to contacts and regular meetings on the basis of family ties, reunification of families and marriage between citizens of different States and will decide upon them in the same spirit.

They will decide upon these applications in emergency cases for family meetings as expeditiously as possible, for family reunification and for marriage between citizens of different States in normal practice within six months and for other family meetings within gradually decreasing time limits.

They confirm that the presentation or renewal of applications in these cases will not modify the rights and obligations of the applicants or of members of their families concerning *inter alia* employment, housing, residence status, family support, access to social, economic or educational benefits, as well as any other rights and obligations flowing from the laws and regulations of the respective participating State.

The participating States will provide the necessary information on the procedures to be followed by the applicants in these cases and on the regulations to be observed, as well as, upon the applicant's request, provide the relevant forms.

They will, where necessary, gradually reduce fees charged in connection with these applications, including those for visas and passports, in order to bring them to a moderate level in relation to the average monthly income in the respective participating States.

Applicants will be informed as expeditiously as possible of the decision that has been reached. In case of refusal applicants will also be informed of their right to renew applications after reasonably short intervals.

The participating States reaffirm their commitment fully to implement the provisions regarding diplomatic and other official missions and consular posts of other participating States contained in relevant multilateral or bilateral conventions, and to facilitate the normal functioning of those missions. Access by visitors to these missions will be assured with due regard to the necessary requirements of security of these missions.

They also reaffirm their willingness to take, within their competence, reasonable steps, including necessary security measures, when appropriate, to ensure satisfactory conditions for activities within the framework of mutual co-operation on their territory, such as sporting and cultural events, in which citizens of other participating States take part.

The participating States will endeavour, where appropriate, to improve the conditions relating to legal, consular and medical assistance for citizens of other participating States temporarily on their territory for personal or professional reasons, taking due account of relevant multilateral or bilateral conventions or agreements.

They will further implement the relevant provisions of the Final Act, so that religious faiths, institutions, organizations and their representatives can, in the field of their activity, develop contacts and meetings among themselves and exchange information.

The participating States will encourage contacts and exchanges among young people and foster the broadening of co-operation among their youth organizations. They will favour the holding among young people and youth organizations of educational, cultural and other comparable events and activities. They will also favour the study of problems relating to the younger generation. The participating States will further the development of individual or collective youth tourism, when necessary on the basis of arrangements, *inter alia* by encouraging the granting of suitable facilities by the transport authorities and tourist organizations of the participating States or such facilities as those offered by the railway authorities participating in the "Inter-Rail" system.

Information

The participating States will further encourage the freer and wider dissemination of printed matter, periodical and non-periodical, imported from other participating States, as well as an increase in the number of places where these publications are on public sale. These publications will also be accessible in reading rooms in large public libraries and similar institutions.

In particular, to facilitate the improvement of dissemination of printed information, the participating States will encourage contacts and negotiations between their competent firms and organizations with a view to concluding long-term agreements and contracts designed to increase the quantities and number of titles of newspapers and other publications imported from other participating States. They consider it desirable that the retail prices of foreign publications are not excessive in relation to prices in their country of origin.

They confirm their intention, according to the relevant provisions of the Final Act, to further extend the possibilities for the public to take out subscriptions.

They will favour the further expansion of co-operation among mass media and their representatives, especially between the editorial staffs of press agencies, newspapers, radio and television organizations as well as film companies. They will encourage a more regular exchange of news, articles, supplements and broadcasts as well as the exchange of editorial staff for better knowledge of respective practices. On the basis of reciprocity, they will improve the material and technical facilities provided for permanently or temporarily accredited television and radio reporters. Moreover, they will facilitate direct contacts among journalists as well as contacts within the framework of professional organizations.

They will decide without undue delay upon visa applications from journalists and re-examine within a reasonable time frame applications which have been refused. Moreover, journalists wishing to travel for personal reasons and not for the purpose of reporting shall enjoy the same treatment as other visitors from their country of origin.

They will grant permanent correspondents and members of their families living with them multiple entry and exit visas valid for one year.

The participating States will examine the possibility of granting, where necessary on the basis of bilateral arrangements, accreditation and related facilities to journalists from other participating States who are permanently accredited in third countries.

They will facilitate travel by journalists from other participating States within their territories, *inter alia* by taking concrete measures where necessary, to afford them opportunities to travel more extensively, with the exception of areas closed for security reasons. They will inform journalists in advance, whenever possible, if new areas are closed for security reasons.

They will further increase the possibilities and, when necessary, improve the conditions for journalists from other participating States to establish and maintain personal contacts and communication with their sources.

They will, as a rule, authorize radio and television journalists, at their request, to be accompanied by their own sound and film technicians and to use their own equipment.

Similarly, journalists may carry with them reference material, including personal notes and files, to be used strictly for their professional purposes.*

The participating States will, where necessary, facilitate the establishment and operation, in their capitals, of press centres or institutions performing the same functions, open to the national and foreign press with suitable working facilities for the latter.

They will also consider further ways and means to assist journalists from other participating States and thus to enable them to resolve practical problems they may encounter.

Co-operation and exchanges in the field of culture

They will endeavour, by taking appropriate steps, to make the relevant information concerning possibilities offered by bilateral cultural agreements and programmes available to interested persons, institutions and non-governmental organizations, thus facilitating their effective implementation.

The participating States will further encourage wider dissemination of and access to books, films and other forms and means of cultural expression

---

* In this context it is understood that import of printed matter may be subject to local regulations which will be applied with due regard to the journalists' need for adequate working material.

from other participating States, to this end improving by appropriate means, on bilateral and multilateral bases, the conditions for international commercial and non-commercial exchange of their cultural goods, *inter alia* by gradually lowering customs duties on these items.

The participating States will endeavour to encourage the translation, publication and dissemination of works in the sphere of literature and other fields of cultural activity from other participating States, especially those produced in less widely spoken languages, by facilitating co-operation between publishing houses, in particular through the exchange of lists of books which might be translated as well as of other relevant information.

They will contribute to the development of contacts, co-operation and joint projects among the participating States regarding the protection, preservation and recording of historical heritage and monuments and the relationship between man, environment and this heritage; they express their interest in the possibility of convening an inter-governmental conference on these matters within the framework of UNESCO.

The participating States will encourage their radio and television organizations to continue developing the presentation of the cultural and artistic achievements of other participating States on the basis of bilateral and multilateral arrangements between these organizations, providing *inter alia* for exchanges of information on productions, for the broadcasting of shows and programmes from other participating States, for co-productions, for the invitation of guest conductors and directors, as well as for the provision of mutual assistance to cultural film teams.

At the invitation of the Government of Hungary a "Cultural Forum" will take place in Budapest, commencing on 15 October 1985. It will be attended by leading personalities in the field of culture from the participating States. The "Forum" will discuss interrelated problems concerning creation, dissemination and co-operation, including the promotion and expansion of contacts and exchanges in the different fields of culture. A representative of UNESCO will be invited to present to the "Forum" the views of that organization. The "Forum" will be prepared by a meeting of experts, the duration of which will not exceed two weeks and which will be held upon the invitation of the Government of Hungary in Budapest, commencing 21 November 1984.

Co-operation and exchanges in the field of education

The participating States will promote the establishment of governmental and non-governmental arrangements and agreements in education and science, to be carried out with the participation of educational or other competent institutions.

The participating States will contribute to the further improvement of exchanges of students, teachers and scholars and their access to each other's educational, cultural and scientific institutions, and also their access to open information material in accordance with the laws and regulations prevailing in each country. In this context, they will facilitate travel by scholars, teachers and students within the receiving State, the establishment by them of contacts with their colleagues, and will also encourage libraries, higher education establishments and similar institutions in their territories to make catalogues and lists of open archival material available to scholars, teachers and students from other participa-ting States.

They will encourage a more regular exchange of information about scientific training programmes, courses and seminars for young scientists and facilitate a wider participation in these activities of young scientists from different participating States. They will call upon the appropriate national and international organizations and institutions to give support, where appropriate, to the realization of these training activities.

The representatives of the participating States noted the usefulness of the work done during the "Scientific Forum" held in Hamburg, Federal Republic of Germany, from 18 February to 3 March 1980. Taking into account the results of the "Scientific Forum", the participating States invited international organizations as well as the scientific organizations and scientists of the participating States to give due consideration to its conclusions and recommendations.

The participating States will favour widening the possibilities of teaching and studying less widely spread or studied European languages. They will, to this end, stimulate, within their competence, the organization of and attendance at summer university and other courses, the granting of scholarships for translators and the reinforcement of linguistic faculties including, in case of need, the provision of new facilities for studying these languages.

The participating States express their readiness to intensify the exchange, among them and within competent international organizations, of teaching materials, school textbooks, maps, bibliographies and other educational material, in order to promote better mutual knowledge and facilitate a fuller presentation of their respective countries.

FOLLOW-UP TO THE CONFERENCE

In conformity with the relevant provisions of the Final Act and with their resolve and commitment to continue the multilateral process initiated by the CSCE, the participating States will hold further meetings regularly among their representatives.

The third of these meetings will be held in Vienna commencing on 4 November 1986.

The agenda, working programme and modalities of the main Madrid Meeting will be applied *mutatis mutandis* to the main Vienna Meeting, unless other decisions on these questions are taken by the preparatory meeting mentioned below.

For the purpose of making the adjustments to the agenda, working programme and modalities of the main Madrid Meeting, a preparatory meeting will be held in Vienna commencing on 23 September 1986. It is understood that in this context adjustments concern those items requiring change as a result of the change in date and place, the drawing of lots, and the mention of the other meetings held in conformity with the decisions of the Madrid Meeting 1980. The duration of the preparatory meeting shall not exceed two weeks.

The participating States further decide that in 1985, the tenth Anniversary of the signature of the Final Act of the CSCE will be duly commemorated in Helsinki.

The duration of the meetings mentioned in this document, unless otherwise agreed, should not exceed six weeks. The results of these meetings will be taken into account, as appropriate, at the Vienna Follow-up Meeting.

All the above-mentioned meetings will be held in conformity with Paragraph 4 of the Chapter on "Follow-up to the Conference" of the Final Act.

The Government of Spain is requested to transmit the present document to the Secretary-General of the United Nations, to the Director-General of UNESCO and to the Executive Secretary of the United Nations Economic Commission for Europe. The Government of Spain is also requested to transmit the present document to the Governments of the non-participating Mediterranean States.

The text of this document will be published in each participating State, which will disseminate it and make it known as widely as possible.

The representatives of the participating States express their profound gratitude to the people and Government of Spain for the excellent organization of the Madrid Meeting and warm hospitality extended to the delegations which participated in the Meeting.

ANNEX I

CHAIRMAN'S STATEMENT

Venice Seminar on Economic, Scientific and Cultural Co-operation in the Mediterranean within the framework of the results of the Valletta Meeting of Eexperts

The Seminar will open on Tuesday, 16 October 1984 at 10 a.m. in Venice, Italy. It will close on Friday, 26 October 1984.

The work of the Seminar, guided by a Co-ordinating Committee composed of the delegations of the participating States, will be divided among three Study Groups devoted to Economics, Science and Culture respectively.

The first three days of the Seminar will be devoted to six sessions of the Committee.

The first session of the Committee will be public and will be devoted to the opening of the Seminar, to be followed by an address by a representative of the host country.

The second session of the Committee will decide whether to hold further sessions of the participating States to guide the work of the Study Groups and to take other decisions necessary for the Seminar.

The following four sessions of the Committee will be public and will be devoted to introductory statements by the representatives of the participating States which so desire (in an order selected by lot in advance) and to introductory statements by the representatives of the non-participating Mediterranean States and the international organizations invited. The statements should not exceed 10 minutes per delegation.

Beginning on the fourth day and for the following three and a half working days, simultaneous meetings of the three Study Groups will be held.

The last one and a half days will be devoted to three sessions of the Committee. Two sessions will decide upon the most appropriate use for the documentation presented in the course of the work concerning the specific sectors indicated in the Valletta Report, such as publication of the introductory statements and distribution of the studies to the relevant international organizations, and will take any other necessary decisions.

The final session of the Committee will be public and will be devoted to the official closing of the Seminar with an address by a representative of the host country.

The Chair at the opening and closing sessions of both the Committee and the Study Groups will be taken by a representative from the delegation of the host country. Selection of the successive chairmen by lot will then ensure daily rotation of the Chair, in French alphabetical order, among the representatives of the participating States.

Participation in the work of the Seminar by the non-participating Mediterranean States (Algeria, Egypt, Israel, Lebanon, Libya, Morocco, Syria and Tunisia) and the international organizations (UNESCO, ECE, UNEP, WHO, ITU) invited will follow the rules and practices adopted at Valletta. This means, *inter alia*, that they will take part in the work of the three Study Groups and of the four sessions of the Committee on the second and third day as well as its opening and closing sessions.

Contributions, on the subjects for consideration in one or more of the working languages of the CSCE, may be sent through the proper channels - preferably not later than three months before the opening of the Seminar - to the Executive Secretary, who will circulate them to the other participating States, and to the non-participating Mediterranean States and to the international organizations which have notified their intention of taking part.

The Italian Government will designate the Executive Secretary of the Seminar. This designation should be agreed to by the participating States. The services of a technical secretariat will be provided by the host country.

Other rules of procedure, working methods and the scale of distribution for the expenses of the CSCE will, *mutatis mutandis*, be applied to the Seminar.

The arrangements outlined above will not constitute a precedent for any other CSCE forum.

ANNEX II

CHAIRMAN'S STATEMENT

Bern Meeting of Experts on Human Contacts

The Chairman notes the absence of objection to the declaration made by the representative of Switzerland on 15 July 1983 extending an invitation by the Swiss Government to hold a meeting of experts on human contacts. Consequently, the Chairman notes that there is agreement to convene such a meeting to discuss the development of contacts among persons, institutions and organizations, with due account for the introductory part of the Chapter of the Final Act entitled *Co-operation in Humanitarian and Other Fields* and for the introductory part of section one (Human Contacts) of that Chapter, which reads *inter alia* as follows:

"The participating States,

Considering the development of contacts to be an important element in the strengthening of friendly relations and trust among peoples,

Affirming, in relation to their present effort to improve conditions in this area, the importance they attach to humanitarian considerations,

Desiring in this spirit to develop, with the continuance of détente, further efforts to achieve continuing progress in this field; ...."

The meeting will be convened in Bern, on 15 April 1986. Its duration will not exceed six weeks. The meeting will be preceded by preparatory consultations, which will be held in Bern commencing on 2 April 1986. The results of the meeting will be taken into account, as appropriate, at the Vienna Follow-up Meeting.

The Swiss Government will designate the Executive Secretary of the meeting. This designation should be agreed upon by the participating States. The services of a technical secretariat will be provided by the host country.

Other rules of procedure, working methods and the scale of distribution for the expenses of the CSCE will be applied *mutatis mutandis* to the Bern meeting.

The Chairman notes further that this statement will be an annex to the concluding document of the Madrid Meeting and will be published with it.

INTERPRETATIVE STATEMENTS

Statements by Austria[1]

The delegation of Austria stated that, with the aim of making at least a little progress in the Meeting - progress of a formal nature intended to complement the statements made on 15 July 1983 - they requested that, in accordance with Article 79 of the Final Recommendations of the Helsinki Consultations, three texts, which they would submit in writing, be appended to this Journal and circulated: these three texts are draft "Chairman's Statements", to be duly registered in the Journal of the day when general consensus is reached on them.

CHAIRMAN'S STATEMENT

In registering the section Principles of the Concluding Document of the Madrid Meeting, the Chairman notes the common understanding of the Meeting that the phrase

ispoveduiushchikh ili gotovykh ispovedovat'

in the Russian original of that document has the same meaning as the phrases

- "wirken oder zu wirken bereit sind",
- "practising or prepared to practise",
- "practican o desean practicar",
- "pratiquant ou disposés à pratiquer",
- "praticano o sono disposti a praticare",

in the originals of the Concluding Document in German, English, Spanish, French and Italian.

*

CHAIRMAN'S STATEMENT

The Chairman notes that in registering the provision on access to diplomatic and other official missions and consular posts in the section *Co-operation in Humanitarian and Other Fields* of the Concluding Document of the Madrid Meeting the understanding was reached that the phrase "access by visitors" refers to visitors who have an invitation as well as to visitors who have none.

---

[1] Journal No. 324, 166th Plenary Meeting (Madrid, 28 July 1983).

CHAIRMAN'S STATEMENT

The Chairman notes that, in paragraph 9 of the Preamble, the French expression "violations graves" is an adequate translation of:

- "ernsthafte Verletzungen" in German,
- "serious violations" in English,
- "graves violaciones" in Spanish,
- "gravi violazioni" in Italian,
- "ser'eznykh narushenii" in Russian.

* * *

Interpretative statement by Turkey[2]

In the course of negotiations in connection with Article 4 Paragraph 3 of the Conference on Confidence- and Security-building Measures and Disarmament in Europe of the document RM.39/Revised, we have noted with satisfaction the understanding, that the zone of application of the CDE, does include the area referred to under major Military manoeuvres Section of the Final Act. It was understood, without doubt, that all the CSBMs to be decided at the CDE Conference will also be applied in this area of the Zone. However, it has not been found possible to include this understanding with the same clarity in the written text of the Document that we are going to adopt. Therefore, my Government deems it necessary to unilaterally register this understanding in the Journal of the day.

---

[2] Idem.

STATEMENTS BY THE CHAIRMAN (USSR) AND AUSTRIA[3]

"There was general agreement that consensus had been achieved on the draft Concluding Document resulting from the Plenary meeting on 15 July 1983 together with the three Chairman's Statements that were registered in the Journal No. 324 of 28 July 1983.

On the question of Security in the Mediterranean the Chairman stated that the participating States had duly taken note of the proposals concerning questions relating to security in the Mediterranean as embodied in the Helsinki Final Act. The Chairman further noted that the participating States were ready to give support, when appropriate, to initiatives which Malta and other participating States concerned may launch in the post-Madrid period to maintain and amplify the contacts and dialogue of the participating States in terms of the Helsinki Final Act, as initiated by the CSCE with the non-participating Mediterranean States to include all the States of the Mediterranean, with the purpose of contributing to peace, reducing armed forces in the region, strengthening security, lessening tensions in the region, and widening the scope of co-operation, ends in which all share a common interest, as well as with the purpose of defining further common objectives.

The Delegation of Austria stated that it was the understanding of their Delegation that no initiative taken on the basis of the Chairman's Statement on the Security in the Mediterranean would be considered to be a CSCE meeting unless it had obtained the consensus of all 35 participating States.

It was agreed that the statement of Austria be registered in the Journal of the day."

---

[3] Journal No. 333, 175th Plenary Meeting (Madrid, 6 September 1983).

REPORT OF ATHENS

REPORT OF THE MEETING OF EXPERTS REPRESENTING THE PARTICIPATING STATES OF THE CONFERENCE ON SECURITY AND CO-OPERATION IN EUROPE, FORESEEN BY THE FINAL ACT OF THE CSCE AND THE CONCLUDING DOCUMENT OF THE MADRID MEETING, IN ORDER TO PURSUE, ON THE BASIS OF THE FINAL ACT, THE EXAMINATION OF A GENERALLY ACCEPTABLE METHOD FOR THE PEACEFUL SETTLEMENT OF DISPUTES AIMED AT COMPLEMENTING EXISTING METHODS.

Athens, 30 April 1984

In accordance with the mandate of the Final Act of the Conference on Security and Co-operation in Europe, in conformity with the recommendation contained in the Report of the Montreux Meeting of Experts, and in accordance with the relevant provisions of the Concluding Document of the Madrid Meeting 1980, a Meeting of Experts representing the participating States took place in Athens from 21 March to 30 April 1984 in order to pursue, on the basis of the Final Act, the examination of a generally acceptable method for the peaceful settlement of disputes aimed at complementing existing methods. The participants took into account the common approach set forth in the Report of the Montreux Meeting of Experts.

At the opening session the participants were addressed by Mr. Yiannis Capsis, Deputy Foreign Minister, on behalf of the Government of Greece.

The participants adopted an agenda and proceeded to a general exchange of views after which a number of proposals were submitted and discussed. A thorough discussion was held. Some progress was made in the examination of a generally acceptable method for the peaceful settlement of disputes aimed at complementing existing methods. Particular emphasis was put on ways and means of including a third party element in such a method. Divergent views were expressed and no consensus was reached on a method. It was recognized that further discussions should be pursued in an appropriate framework within the CSCE process.

The participants expressed their deep gratitude to the Government of Greece for the excellent organization of the Meeting and for the warm hospitality extended to them during their stay in Athens.

REPORT OF THE VENICE SEMINAR

REPORT OF THE CSCE VENICE SEMINAR ON ECONOMIC, SCIENTIFIC AND CULTURAL CO-OPERATION IN THE MEDITERRANEAN WITHIN THE FRAMEWORK OF THE RESULTS OF THE VALLETTA MEETING OF EXPERTS

Venice, 26 October 1984

In accordance with the mandate of the Concluding Document of the Madrid Meeting of Representatives of the participating States of the Conference on Security and Co-operation in Europe (CSCE), a Seminar was held at Venice, at the invitation of the Government of Italy, from 16 to 26 October 1984, to review the initiatives already undertaken, or envisaged, in all the sectors outlined in the report of the Valletta Meeting and to stimulate, where necessary, broader developments in these sectors.

Representatives of the participating States of the CSCE took part in the Seminar. Representatives of the non-participating Mediterranean States and of UNESCO, the Economic Commission for Europe (ECE), the United Nations Environment Programme (UNEP), the World Health Organization (WHO) and the International Telecommunication Union (ITU) were invited to participate in the Seminar in accordance with the Concluding Document of the Madrid Meeting.

Egypt and Israel accepted the invitation and participated in the work of the Seminar in the manner provided for in the above invitation. UNESCO, ECE, UNEP, WHO and ITU took part in the Seminar in the same manner.

The work of the Seminar was organized in accordance with the Chairman's statement at Annex I of the Madrid Concluding Document.

Written contributions to the Seminar, as provided for in the Chairman's statement, were submitted in advance.

The participants in the Seminar were addressed on 16 October 1984 by H.E. Mr. Giulio Andreotti, Minister of Foreign Affairs of Italy, on behalf of the host country.

The participants in the Seminar had a general exchange of views in the Co-ordinating Committee on questions relating to their economic, scientific and cultural co-operation within the framework of the Mediterranean Chapter of the Final Act.

Recalling their existing economic, scientific and cultural co-operation with the non-participating Mediterranean States, and the conclusions and recommendations of the Valletta Meeting of Experts, the representatives of the participating States of the CSCE reaffirmed their wish to develop further co-operation in these fields.

The representatives of the participating States of the CSCE stressed the importance attached by their Governments to the attainment of the objectives set forth in the Final Act by implementing all of its provisions, as well as their readiness to pursue their efforts accordingly.

The three Study Groups met to consider respectively the economic, scientific and cultural aspects of co-operation in the Mediterranean. The Groups reviewed the initiatives already undertaken, or envisaged, in these sectors aimed at implementing the conclusions and recommendations of the report of the Valletta Meeting of Experts.

The participants discussed certain current problems in the field of international economic co-operation. They acknowledged that such co-operation should take into account the interests of those countries which are developing from an economic point of view. In particular, co-operation should stimulate the production and marketing of goods and services of such countries. The representatives of the participating States of the CSCE reaffirmed the will of their Governments to intensify such co-operation.

The Seminar noted that as well as bilateral and multilateral co-operation, a constructive and positive role is played by the competent international organizations, notably UNESCO, ECE, UNEP, WHO and ITU, in carrying out useful and concrete work in the development of co-operation in the areas covered by the Valletta report.

The representatives of the participating States of the CSCE, having examined the ideas and proposals put forward in the course of the Seminar, decided to recommend to their Governments the following specific fields where broader developments could be envisaged, within their possibilities and interests, whether through their participation in international organizations or in bilateral and multilateral relations with the participating States and with the non-participating Mediterranean States:

The promotion of bilateral and multilateral co-operation among participating States and the non-participating Mediterranean States in the field of environment protection of the Mediterranean region within the appropriate frameworks, in order to contribute, in particular, to the implementation of the Mediterranean Action Plan (MAP), keeping in mind the provisions of the Final Act and the activities already included in the recommendations of the Meeting of Experts held at Valletta and the possibility of new initiatives in other fields of common interest, such as study programmes on jellyfish.

The strengthening, through the MAP, of actions aimed at better harmonization of national legislation on the protection of Mediterranean waters from pollution, in implementation in particular of the Barcelona Convention and its related protocols signed by the parties to the Convention.

The improvement of methodologies within the appropriate framework for evaluating economic damage caused by pollution in the Mediterranean and for determining means to protect the Mediterranean environment.

Co-operation in concrete actions aimed at ensuring compliance with standards laid down in the MARPOL Convention 73/78, for the prevention of pollution of the Mediterranean Sea resulting from maritime traffic.

Support for increasing efforts towards the preservation of the Mediterranean environment undertaken also within and beyond the framework of the Convention on Long-Range Transboundary Air Pollution and its Monitoring and Evaluation Programme (EMEP).

Co-operation among international organizations on the Mediterranean environment notably by the ECE and UNEP.

The promotion of a better cohesion between sea and land transport infrastructures and their methods of use, taking due account of new transport techniques; with this in view, giving due consideration to initiatives taken in the framework of the ECE related to: co-ordination of infrastructures, in connection with the Trans-European Motorway project (TEM) and studies on other European transport projects; harbour infrastructure and organization questions; and transport facilitation and training in the field of transport.

The encouragement of the more effective use of trans-shipment facilities with the aim of reducing costs, improving the timely distribution of goods, facilitating storage and thereby enhancing economic benefits.

The encouragement of more extensive participation by the countries bordering the Mediterranean in research and experiments aimed at providing coastal assistance to maritime navigation; and in joint studies on intra-Mediterranean maritime traffic and on the requirements of advanced types of maritime carriers.

The development and co-ordination of existing exchanges of statistical data, identification of the economic and social areas of priority interest for the further exchange of such data with due account taken of national legislation, and the promotion of research projects concerning social factors affecting economic development.

The continuation of efforts to solve problems in the field of migrant labour, bearing in mind the relevant provisions of the Final Act and the Madrid Concluding Document.

Participation in national programmes of theoretical and applied scientific research on topics of Mediterranean interest by teachers and students from as large a number of interested countries as possible.

Greater access to libraries and archives of scientific institutions for research workers engaged in research on problems of Mediterranean interest, taking into account national legislation regulating the conditions of such access.

The extension and improvement where appropriate of bilateral and multilateral co-operation in the scientific field, both at the intergovernmental level and between relevant institutions.

An increase in efforts to combat thalassaemia and other diseases in the Mediterranean; the encouragement of research including appropriate statistical research, particularly under the auspices of the WHO, with the objective of enhancing programmes for the prevention, diagnosis and treatment of those diseases prevalent in the Mediterranean region.

Joint research on the effects on human health of olive oil and leguminous plants, with particular reference to ascertaining the function of olive oil in the reduction of cholesterol.

Encouragement for the activities of the Community of Mediterranean Universities within which specific co-operation projects which appear to deserve support have been identified.

The identification of significant areas for cultural co-operation such as the conservation, protection, safeguarding and enhancement of the cultural heritage in the fields of archaeology, architecture, arts and crafts; the investigation of underwater archaeological remains; the training of professional staff and cultural personnel; cinematography; audiovisual media, with particular reference to their use in teaching activities; the dissemination of historical knowledge and the promotion of dialogue between historians of different traditions.

Recognition of the value and usefulness of instruments of cultural co-operation such as: cultural agreements; links between universities and institutes of higher education for the exchange of information and for the conduct of joint research projects; national and international cultural institutions, whether governmental or other, operating in the area; more contacts and co-operation among persons engaged in the field of culture from different countries.

Encouragement of efforts to deepen cultural co-operation in the Mediterranean, in particular through a broader use of radio, television and publications, and through the collection of material and the data required for these specialized activities, as well as the training of personnel.

The representatives of the participating States of the CSCE took note of the document of the United Nations Economic Commission for Europe detailing activities of co-operation which are of interest to the countries in the Mediterranean. It was agreed that such opportunities should be kept in mind.

The Seminar noted the opinion expressed by some Mediterranean participating States as to the desirability of ad hoc meetings of Mediterranean States on co-operation in the fields of economy, science and culture.

The participants expressed their deep gratitude to the Government and people of Italy for the excellent organization of the Seminar and the warm hospitality extended to them during their stay in Venice.

DOCUMENT OF THE STOCKHOLM CONFERENCE

ON CONFIDENCE- AND SECURITY-BUILDING MEASURES AND DISARMAMENT IN EUROPE CONVENED IN ACCORDANCE WITH THE RELEVANT PROVISIONS OF THE CONCLUDING DOCUMENT OF THE MADRID MEETING OF THE CONFERENCE ON SECURITY AND CO-OPERATION IN EUROPE

Stockholm, 19 September 1986

(1) The representatives of the participating States of the Conference on Security and Co-operation in Europe (CSCE), Austria, Belgium, Bulgaria, Canada, Cyprus, Czechoslovakia, Denmark, Finland, France, the German Democratic Republic, the Federal Republic of Germany, Greece, the Holy See, Hungary, Iceland, Ireland, Italy, Liechtenstein, Luxembourg, Malta, Monaco, the Netherlands, Norway, Poland, Portugal, Romania, San Marino, Spain, Sweden, Switzerland, Turkey, the Union of Soviet Socialist Republics, the United Kingdom, the United States of America and Yugoslavia, met in Stockholm from 17 January 1984 to 19 September 1986, in accordance with the provisions relating to the Conference on Confidence- and Security-Building Measures and Disarmament in Europe contained in the Concluding Document of the Madrid Follow-up Meeting of the CSCE.

(2) The participants were addressed by the Prime Minister of Sweden, the late Olof Palme, on 17 January 1984.

(3) Opening statements were made by the Ministers of Foreign Affairs and other Heads of Delegation. The Prime Minister of Spain as well as Ministers and senior officials of several other participating States addressed the Conference later. The Minister for Foreign Affairs of Sweden addressed the Conference on 19 September 1986.

(4) The Secretary-General of the United Nations addressed the Conference on 6 July 1984.

(5) Contributions were made by the following non-participating Mediterranean States: Algeria, Egypt, Israel, Lebanon, Libya, Morocco, Syria and Tunisia.

(6) The participating States recalled that the aim of the Conference on Confidence-and Security-Building Measures and Disarmament in Europe is, as a substantial and integral part of the multilateral process initiated by the Conference on Security and Co-operation in Europe, to undertake, in stages, new, effective and concrete actions designed to make progress in strengthening confidence and security and in achieving disarmament, so as to give effect and expression to the duty of States to refrain from the threat or use of force in their mutual relations as well as in their international relations in general.

(7) The participating States recognized that the set of mutually complementary confidence- and security-building measures which are adopted in the present document and which are in accordance with the Madrid mandate serve by their scope and nature and by their implementation to strengthen confidence and security in Europe and thus to give effect and expression to the duty of States to refrain from the threat or use of force.

(8) Consequently the participating States have declared the following:

Refraining from the threat or use of force

(9) The participating States, recalling their obligation to refrain, in their mutual relations as well as in their international relations in general, from the threat or use of force against the territorial integrity or political independence of any State, or in any other manner inconsistent with the purposes of the United Nations, accordingly reaffirm their commitment to respect and put into practice the principle of refraining from the threat or use of force, as laid down in the Final Act.

(10) No consideration may be invoked to serve to warrant resort to the threat or use of force in contravention of this principle.

(11) They recall the inherent right of individual or collective self-defence if an armed attack occurs, as set forth in the Charter of the United Nations.

(12) They will refrain from any manifestation of force for the purpose of inducing any other State to renounce the full exercise of its sovereign rights.

(13) As set forth in the Final Act, no occupation or acquisition of territory resulting from the threat or use of force in contravention of international law, will be recognized as legal.

(14) They recognize their commitment to peace and security. Accordingly they reaffirm that they will refrain from any use of armed forces inconsistent with the purposes and principles of the Charter of the United Nations and the provisions of the Declaration on Principles Guiding Relations between Participating States, against another participating State, in particular from invasion of or attack on its territory.

(15) They will abide by their commitment to refrain from the threat or use of force in their relations with any State, regardless of that State's political, social, economic or cultural system and irrespective of whether or not they maintain with that State relations of alliance.

(16) They stress that non-compliance with the obligation of refraining from the threat or use of force, as recalled above, constitutes a violation of international law.

(17) They stress their commitment to the principle of peaceful settlement of disputes as contained in the Final Act, convinced that it is an essential complement to the duty of States to refrain from the threat or use of force, both being essential factors for the maintenance and consolidation of peace and security. They recall their determination and the necessity to reinforce and to improve the methods at their disposal for the peaceful settlement of dis-putes. They reaffirm their resolve to make every effort to settle exclusively by peaceful means any dispute between them.

(18) The participating States stress their commitment to the Final Act and the need for full implementation of all its provisions, which will further the process of improving security and developing co-operation in Europe, thereby contributing to international peace and security in the world as a whole.

(19) They emphasize their commitment to all the principles of the Declaration on Principles Guiding Relations between Participating States and declare their determination to respect and put them into practice irrespective of their political, economic or social systems as well as of their size, geographical location or level of economic development.

(20) All these ten principles are of primary significance and, accordingly, they will be equally and unreservedly applied, each of them being interpreted taking into account the others.

(21) Respect for and the application of these principles will enhance the development of friendly relations and co-operation among the participating States in all fields covered by the provisions of the Final Act.

(22) They reconfirm their commitment to the basic principle of the sovereign equality of States and stress that all States have equal rights and duties within the framework of international law.

(23) They reaffirm the universal significance of human rights and fundamental freedoms. Respect for and the effective exercise of these rights and freedoms are essential factors for international peace, justice and security, as well as for the development of friendly relations and co-operation among themselves as among all States, as set forth in the Declaration on Principles Guiding Relations between Participating States.

(24) They reaffirm that, in the broader context of world security, security in Europe is closely linked with security in the Mediterranean area as a whole; in this context, they confirm their inten-tion to develop good neighbourly relations with all States in the region, with due regard to reciprocity, and in the spirit of the principles contained in the Declaration on Principles Guiding Relations between Participating States, so as to promote confi-dence and security and make peace prevail in the region in ac-cordance with the provisions contained in the Mediterranean chapter of the Final Act.

(25) They emphasize the necessity to take resolute measures to prevent and to combat terrorism, including terrorism in international relations. They express their determination to take effective measures, both at the national level and through

international co-operation, for the prevention and suppression of all acts of terrorism. They will take all appropriate measures in preventing their respective territories from being used for the preparation, organization or commission of terrorist activities. This also in-cludes measures to prohibit on their territories illegal activities, including subversive activities, of persons, groups and organiza-tions that instigate, organize or engage in the perpetration of acts of terrorism, including those directed against other States and their citizens.

(26) They will fulfil in good faith their obligations under international law; they also stress that strict compliance with their commitments within the framework of the CSCE is essential for building confidence and security.

(27) The participating States confirm that in the event of a conflict between the obligations of the members of the United Nations under the Charter of the United Nations and their obligations under any treaty or other international agreement, their obligations under the Charter will prevail, in accordance with Article 103 of the Charter of the United Nations.

(28) The participating States have adopted the following measures:

Prior notification of certain military activities

(29) The participating States will give notification in writing through diplomatic channels in an agreed form of content, to all other participating States 42 days or more in advance of the start of notifiable* military activities in the zone of application for confidence- and security-building measures (CSBMs).**

(30) Notification will be given by the participating State on whose territory the activity in question is planned to take place even if the forces of that State are not engaged in the activity or their strength is below the notifiable level. This will not relieve other participating States of their obligation to give notification, if

---

* In this document, the term notifiable means subject to notification.

** See Annex I.

their involvement in the planned military activity reaches the notifiable level.

(31) Each of the following military activities in the field conducted as a single activity in the zone of application for CSBMs at or above the levels defined below, will be notified:

(31.1) The engagement of formations of land forces*** of the participating States in the same exercise activity conducted under a single operational command independently or in combination with any possible air or naval components.

(31.1.1) This military activity will be subject to notification whenever it involves at any time during the activity:
- at least 13,000 troops, including the support troops, or
- at least 300 battle tanks
if organized into a divisional structure or at least two brigades/ regiments, not necessarily subordinate to the same division.

(31.1.2) The participation of air forces of the participating States will be included in the notification if it is foreseen that in the course of the activity 200 or more sorties by aircraft, excluding helicopters, will be flown.

(31.2) The engagement of military forces either in an amphibious landing or in a parachute assault by airborne forces in the zone of application for CSBMs.

(31.2.1) These military activities will be subject to notification whenever the amphibious landing involves at least 3,000 troops or whenever the parachute drop involves at least 3,000 troops.

(31.3) The engagement of formations of land forces of the participating States in a transfer from outside the zone of application for CSBMs to arrival points in the zone, or from inside the zone of application for CSBMs to points of concentration in the zone, to participate in a notifiable exercise activity or to be concentrated.

*** In this context, the term land forces includes amphibious, airmobile and airborne forces.

(31.3.1) The arrival or concentration of these forces will be subject to notification whenever it involves, at any time during the activity:
- at least 13,000 troops, including support troops, or
- at least 300 battle tanks

if organized into a divisional structure or at least two brigades/ regiments, not necessarily subordinate to the same division.

(31.3.2) Forces which have been transferred into the zone will be subject to all provisions of agreed CSBMs when they depart their arrival points to participate in a notifiable exercise activity or to be concentrated within the zone of application for CSBMs.

(32) Notifiable military activities carried out without advance notice to the troops involved, are exceptions to the requirement for prior notification to be made 42 days in advance.

(32.1) Notification of such activities, above the agreed thresholds, will be given at the time the troops involved commence such activities.

(33) Notification will be given in writing of each notifiable military activity in the following agreed form:

(34) **A - General Information**

(34.1) The designation of the military activity;

(34.2) The general purpose of the military activity;

(34.3) The names of the States involved in the military activity;

(34.4) The level of command, organizing and commanding the military activity;

(34.5) The start and end dates of the military activity.

(35) **B - Information on different types of notifiable military activities**

(35.1) The engagement of formations of land forces of the participating States in the same exercise activity conducted under a single operational command independently or in combination with any possible air or naval components:

(35.1.1) The total number of troops taking part in the military activity (i.e., ground troops, amphibious troops, airmobile and airborne troops) and the number of troops participating for each State involved, if applicable;

(35.1.2) Number and type of divisions participating for each State;

(35.1.3) The total number of battle tanks for each State and the total number of anti-tank guided missile launchers mounted on armoured vehicles;

(35.1.4) The total number of artillery pieces and multiple rocket launchers (100 mm calibre or above);

(35.1.5) The total number of helicopters, by category;

(35.1.6) Envisaged number of sorties by aircraft, excluding helicopters;

(35.1.7) Purpose of air missions;

(35.1.8) Categories of aircraft involved;

(35.1.9) The level of command, organizing and commanding the air force participation;

(35.1.10) Naval ship-to-shore gunfire;

(35.1.11) Indication of other naval ship-to-shore support;

(35.1.12) The level of command, organizing and commanding the naval force participation.

(35.2) The engagement of military forces either in an amphibious landing or in a parachute assault by airborne forces in the zone of application for CSBMs:

(35.2.1) The total number of amphibious troops involved in notifiable amphibious landings, and/or the total number of airborne troops involved in notifiable parachute assaults;

(35.2.2) In the case of a notifiable amphibious landing, the point or points of embarkation, if in the zone of application for CSBMs.

(35.3) The engagement of formations of land forces of the participating States in a transfer from outside the zone of application for CSBMs to arrival points in the zone, or from inside the zone of application for CSBMs to points of concentration in the zone, to participate in a notifiable exercise activity or to be concentrated:

(35.3.1) The total number of troops transferred;

(35.3.2) Number and type of divisions participating in the transfer;

(35.3.3) The total number of battle tanks participating in a notifiable arrival or concentration;

(35.3.4) Geographical co-ordinates for the points of arrival and for the points of concentration.

(36) **C - The envisaged area and timeframe of the activity**

(36.1) The area of the military activity delimited by geographic features together with geographic co-ordinates, as appropriate;

(36.2) The start and end dates of each phase (transfers, deployment, concentration of forces, active exercise phase, recovery phase) of activities in the zone of application for CSBMs of participating formations, the tactical purpose and corresponding geographical areas (delimited by geographical co-ordinates) for each phase;

(36.3) Brief description of each phase.

(37) **D - Other information**

(37.1) Changes, if any, in relation to information provided in the annual calendar regarding the activity;

(37.2) Relationship of the activity to other notifiable activities.

Observation of certain military activities

(38) The participating States will invite observers from all other participating States to the following notifiable military activities:

(38.1) - The engagement of formations of land forces**** of the participating States in the same exercise activity conducted under a single operational command independently or in combination with any possible air or naval components.

(38.2) - The engagement of military forces either in an amphibious landing or in a parachute assault by airborne forces in the zone of application for CSBMs.

(38.3) - In the case of the engagement of formations of land forces of the participating States in a transfer from outside the zone of application for CSBMs to arrival points in the zone, or from inside the zone of application for CSBMs to points of concentration in the zone, to participate in a notifiable exercise activity or to be concentrated, the concentration of these forces. Forces which have been transferred into the zone will be subject to all provisions of agreed confidence- and security-building measures when they depart their arrival points to participate in a notifiable exercise activity or to be concentrated within the zone of application for CSBMs.

(38.4) The above-mentioned activities will be subject to observation whenever the number of troops engaged meets or exceeds 17,000 troops, except in the case of either an amphibious landing or a parachute assault by airborne forces, which will be subject to observation whenever the number of troops engaged meets or exceeds 5,000 troops.

(39) The host State will extend the invitations in writing through diplomatic channels to all other participating States at the time of notification. The host State will be the participating State on whose territory the notified activity will take place.

(40) The host State may delegate some of its responsibilities as host to another participating State engaged in the military activity on the territory of the host State. In such cases, the host State will specify the allocation of responsibilities in its invitation to observe the activity.

**** In this context, the term land forces includes amphibious, airmobile and airborne forces.

(41) Each participating State may send up to two observers to the military activity to be observed.

(42) The invited State may decide whether to send military and/or civilian observers, including members of its personnel accredited to the host State. Military observers will, normally, wear their uniforms and insignia while performing their tasks.

(43) Replies to the invitation will be given in writing not later than 21 days after the issue of the invitation.

(44) The participating States accepting an invitation will provide the names and ranks of their observers in their reply to the invitation. If the invitation is not accepted in time, it will be assumed that no observers will be sent.

(45) Together with the invitation the host State will provide a general observation programme, including the following information:

(45.1) - the date, time and place of assembly of observers;

(45.2) - planned duration of the observation programme;

(45.3) - languages to be used in interpretation and/or translation;

(45.4) - arrangements for board, lodging and transportation of the observers;

(45.5) - arrangements for observation equipment which will be issued to the observers by the host State;

(45.6) - possible authorization by the host State of the use of special equipment that the observers may bring with them;

(45.7) - arrangements for special clothing to be issued to the observers because of weather or environmental factors.

(46) The observers may make requests with regard to the observation programme. The host State will, if possible, accede to them.

(47) The host State will determine a duration of observation which permits the observers to observe a notifiable military activity from the time that agreed thresholds for observation are met or

exceeded until, for the last time during the activity, the thresholds for observation are no longer met.

(48) The host State will provide the observers with transportation to the area of the notified activity and back. This transportation will be provided from either the capital or another suitable location to be announced in the invitation, so that the observers are in position before the start of the observation programme.

(49) The invited State will cover the travel expenses for its observers to the capital, or another suitable location specified in the invitation, of the host State, and back.

(50) The observers will be provided equal treatment and offered equal opportunities to carry out their functions.

(51) The observers will be granted, during their mission, the privileges and immunities accorded to diplomatic agents in the Vienna Convention on Diplomatic Relations.

(52) The host State will not be required to permit observation of restricted locations, installations or defence sites.

(53) In order to allow the observers to confirm that the notified activity is non-threatening in character and that it is carried out in conformity with the appropriate provisions of the notification, the host State will:

(53.1) - at the commencement of the observation programme give a briefing on the purpose, the basic situation, the phases of the activity and possible changes as compared with the notification and provide the observers with a map of the area of the military activity with a scale of 1 to not more than 500,000 and an observation programme with a daily schedule as well as a sketch indicating the basic situation;

(53.2) - provide the observers with appropriate observation equipment; however, the observers will be allowed to use their personal binoculars, which will be subject to examination and approval by the host State;

(53.3) - in the course of the observation programme give the observers daily briefings with the help of maps on the various phases of the military activity and their development and inform the observers about their positions geographically; in the case of a land force activity conducted in combination with air or naval components, briefings will be given by representatives of these forces;

(53.4) - provide opportunities to observe directly forces of the State/States engaged in the military activity so that the observers get an impression of the flow of the activity; to this end, the observers will be given the opportunity to observe major combat units of the participating formations of a divisional or equivalent level and, whenever possible, to visit some units and communicate with commanders and troops; commanders or other senior personnel of participating formations as well as of the visited units will inform the observers of the mission of their respective units;

(53.5) - guide the observers in the area of the military activity; the observers will follow the instructions issued by the host State in accordance with the provisions set out in this document;

(53.6) - provide the observers with appropriate means of transportation in the area of the military activity;

(53.7) - provide the observers with opportunities for timely communication with their embassies or other official missions and consular posts; the host State is not obliged to cover the communication expense of the observers;

(53.8) - provide the observers with appropriate board and lodging in a location suitable for carrying out the observation programme and, when necessary, medical care.

(54) The participating States need not invite observers to notifiable military activities which are carried out without advance notice to the troops involved unless these notifiable activities have a duration of more than 72 hours. The continuation of these activities beyond this time will be subject to observation while the agreed thresholds for observation are met or exceeded. The observation programme will follow as closely as practically possible all the provisions for observation set out in this document.

Annual calendars

(55) Each participating State will exchange, with all other participating States, an annual calendar of its military activities subject to prior notification,[*****] within the zone of application for CSBMs, forecast for the subsequent calendar year. It will be transmitted every year, in writing, through diplomatic channels, not later than 15 November for the following year.

(56) Each participating State will list the above-mentioned activities chronologically and will provide information on each activity in accordance with the following model:

(56.1) - type of military activity and its designation;

(56.2) - general characteristics and purpose of the military activity;

(56.3) - States involved in the military activity;

(56.4) - area of the military activity, indicated by appropriate geographic features and/or defined by geographic co-ordinates;

(56.5) - planned duration of the military activity and the 14-day period, indicated by dates, within which it is envisaged to start;

(56.6) - the envisaged total number of troops* engaged in the military activity;

(56.7) - the types of armed forces involved in the military activity;

(56.8) - the envisaged level of command, under which the military activity will take place;

(56.9) - the number and type of divisions whose participation in the military activity is envisaged;

***** as defined in the provisions on Prior Notification of Certain Military Activities.

(56.10) - any additional information concerning, *inter alia*, components of armed forces, which the participating State planning the military activity considers relevant.

(57) Should changes regarding the military activities in the annual calendar prove necessary, they will be communicated to all other participating States no later than in the appropriate notification.

(58) Information on military activities subject to prior notification not included in an annual calendar will be communicated to all participating States as soon as possible, in accordance with the model provided in the annual calendar.

Constraining provisions

(59) Each participating State will communicate, in writing, to all other participating States, by November 15 each year, information concerning military activities subject to prior notification* involving more than 40,000 troops*, which it plans to carry out in the second subsequent calendar year. Such communication will include preliminary information on each activity, as to its general purpose, timeframe and duration, area, size and States involved.

(60) Participating States will not carry out military activities subject to prior notification involving more than 75,000 troops, unless they have been the object of communication as defined above.

(61) Participating States will not carry out military activities subject to prior notification involving more than 40,000 troops unless they have been included in the annual calendar, not later than 15 November each year.

(62) If military activities subject to prior notification are carried out in addition to those contained in the annual calendar, they should be as few as possible.

---

* As defined in the provisions on Prior Notification of Certain Military Activities.

Compliance and verification

(63) According to the Madrid Mandate, the confidence- and security-building measures to be agreed upon "will be provided with adequate forms of verification which correspond to their content".

(64) The participating States recognize that national technical means can play a role in monitoring compliance with agreed confidence- and security-building measures.

(65) In accordance with the provisions contained in this document each participating State has the right to conduct inspections on the territory of any other participating State within the zone of application for CSBMs.

(66) Any participating State will be allowed to address a request for inspection to another participating State on whose territory, within the zone of application for CSBMs, compliance with the agreed confidence- and security-building measures is in doubt.

(67) No participating State will be obliged to accept on its territory within the zone of application for CSBMs, more than three inspections per calendar year.

(68) No participating State will be obliged to accept more than one inspection per calendar year from the same participating State.

(69) An inspection will not be counted if, due to *force majeure*, it cannot be carried out.

(70) The participating State which requests an inspection will state the reasons for such a request.

(71) The participating State which has received such a request will reply in the affirmative to the request within the agreed period of time, subject to the provisions contained in paragraphs (67) and (68).

(72) Any possible dispute as to the validity of the reasons for a request will not prevent or delay the conduct of an inspection.

(73) The participating State which requests an inspection will be permitted to designate for inspection on the territory of another State within the zone of application for CSBMs, a specific area. Such an area will be referred to as the "specified area". The specified area will comprise terrain where notifiable military activities are conducted or where another participating State believes a noti-fiable military activity is taking place. The specified area will be defined and limited by the scope and scale of notifiable military activities but will not exceed that required for an army level military activity.

(74) In the specified area the representatives of the inspecting State accompanied by the representatives of the receiving State will be permitted access, entry and unobstructed survey, except for areas or sensitive points to which access is normally denied or restricted, military and other defence installations, as well as naval vessels, military vehicles and aircraft. The number and extent of the restricted areas should be as limited as possible. Areas where notifiable military activities can take place will not be declared restricted areas, except for certain permanent or temporary military installations which, in territorial terms, should be as small as possible, and consequently those areas will not be used to prevent inspection of notifiable military activities. Restricted areas will not be employed in a way inconsistent with the agreed provisions on inspection.

(75) Within the specified area, the forces of participating States other than the receiving State will also be subject to the inspection conducted by the inspecting State.

(76) Inspection will be permitted on the ground, from the air, or both.

(77) The representatives of the receiving State will accompany the inspection team, including when it is in land vehicles and an aircraft from the time of their first employment until the time they are no longer in use for the purposes of inspection.

(78) In its request, the inspecting State will notify the receiving State of:

(78.1) - the reasons for the request;

(78.2) - the location of the specified area defined by geographical co-ordinates;

(78.3) - the preferred point(s) of entry for the inspection team;

(78.4) - mode of transport to and from the point(s) of entry and, if applicable, to and from the specified area;

(78.5) - where in the specified area the inspection will begin;

(78.6) - whether the inspection will be conducted from the ground, from the air, or both simultaneously;

(78.7) - whether aerial inspection will be conducted using an airplane, a helicopter, or both;

(78.8) - whether the inspection team will use land vehicles provided by the receiving State or, if mutually agreed, its own vehicles;

(78.9) - information for the issuance of diplomatic visas to inspectors entering the receiving State.

(79) The reply to the request will be given in the shortest possible period of time, but within not more than twenty-four hours. Within thirty-six hours after the issuance of the request, the inspection team will be permitted to enter the territory of the receiving State.

(80) Any request for inspection as well as the reply thereto will be communicated to all participating States without delay.

(81) The receiving State should designate the point(s) of entry as close as possible to the specified area. The receiving State will ensure that the inspection team will be able to reach the specified area without delay from the point(s) of entry.

(82) All participating States will facilitate the passage of the inspection teams through their territory.

(83) Within 48 hours after the arrival of the inspection team at the specified area, the inspection will be terminated.

(84) There will be no more than four inspectors in an inspection team. While conducting the inspection the inspection team may divide into two parts.

(85) The inspectors and, if applicable, auxiliary personnel, will be granted during their mission the privileges and immunities in accordance with the Vienna Convention on Diplomatic Relations.

(86) The receiving State will provide the inspection team with appropriate board and lodging in a location suitable for carrying out the inspection, and, when necessary, medical care; however this does not exclude the use by the inspection team of its own tents and rations.

(87) The inspection team will have use of its own maps, own photo cameras, own binoculars and own dictaphones, as well as own aeronautical charts.

(88) The inspection team will have access to appropriate telecommunications equipment of the receiving State, including the opportu-nity for continuous communication between the members of an inspection team in an aircraft and those in a land vehicle employed in the inspection.

(89) The inspecting State will specify whether aerial inspection will be conducted using an airplane, a helicopter or both. Aircraft for inspection will be chosen by mutual agreement between the inspecting and receiving States. Aircraft will be chosen which provide the inspection team a continuous view of the ground during the inspection.

(90) After the flight plan, specifying, *inter alia*, the inspection team's choice of flight path, speed and altitude in the specified area, has been filed with the competent air traffic control authority the inspection aircraft will be permitted to enter the specified area without delay. Within the specified area, the inspection team will, at its request, be permitted to deviate from the approved flight plan to make specific observations provided such deviation is consistent with paragraph (74) as well as flight safety and air traffic requirements. Directions to the crew will be given through a representative of the receiving State on board the aircraft involved in the inspection.

(91) One member of the inspection team will be permitted, if such a request is made, at any time to observe data on navigational equipment of the aircraft and to have access to maps and charts used by the flight crew for the purpose of determining the exact location of the aircraft during the inspection flight.

(92) Aerial and ground inspectors may return to the specified area as often as desired within the 48-hours inspection period.

(93) The receiving State will provide for inspection purposes land vehicles with cross country capability. Whenever mutually agreed taking into account the specific geography relating to the area to be inspected, the inspecting State will be permitted to use its own vehicles.

(94) If land vehicles or aircraft are provided by the inspecting State, there will be one accompanying driver for each land vehicle, or accompanying aircraft crew.

(95) The inspecting State will prepare a report of its inspection and will provide a copy of that report to all participating States without delay.

(96) The inspection expenses will be incurred by the receiving State except when the inspecting State uses its own aircraft and/or land vehicles. The travel expenses to and from the point(s) of entry will be borne by the inspecting State.

(97) Diplomatic channels will be used for communications concerning compliance and verification.

(98) Each participating State will be entitled to obtain timely clarification from any other participating State concerning the application of agreed confidence- and security-building measures. Communications in this context will, if appropriate, be transmitted to all other participating States.

***

(99) The participating States stress that these confidence- and security-building measures are designed to reduce the dangers of armed conflict and of misunderstanding or miscalculation of

military activities and emphasize that their implementation will contribute to these objectives.

(100) Reaffirming the relevant objectives of the Final Act, the participating States are determined to continue building confidence, to lessen military confrontation and to enhance security for all. They are also determined to achieve progress in disarmament.

(101) The measures adopted in this document are politically binding and will come into force on 1 January 1987.

(102) The Government of Sweden is requested to transmit the present document to the follow-up meeting of the CSCE in Vienna and to the Secretary-General of the United Nations. The Government of Sweden is also requested to transmit the present document to the Governments of the non-participating Mediterranean States.

(103) The text of this document will be published in each participating State, which will disseminate it and make it known as widely as possible.

(104) The representatives of the participating States express their profound gratitude to the Government and people of Sweden for the excellent arrangements made for the Stockholm Conference and the warm hospitality extended to the delegations which participated in the Conference.

ANNEX I

Under the terms of the Madrid mandate, the zone of application for CSBMs is defined as follows:

> "On the basis of equality of rights, balance and reciprocity, equal respect for the security interests of all CSCE participating States, and of their respective obligations concerning confidence- and security-building measures and disarmament in Europe, these confidence- and security-building measures will cover the whole of Europe as well as the adjoining sea area* and air space. They will be of military significance and politically binding and will be provided with adequate forms of verification which correspond to their content.
>
> As far as the adjoining sea area* and air space is concerned, the measures will be applicable to the military activities of all the participating States taking place there whenever these activities affect security in Europe as well as constitute a part of activities taking place within the whole of Europe as referred to above, which they will agree to notify. Necessary specifications will be made through the negotiations on the confidence- and security-building measures at the Conference.
>
> Nothing in the definition of the zone given above will diminish obligations already undertaken under the Final Act. The confi-dence- and security-building measures to be agreed upon at the Conference will also be applicable in all areas covered by any of the provisions in the Final Act relating to confidence-building measures and certain aspects of security and disarmament."

Wherever the term "the zone of application for CSBMs" is used in this document, the above definition will apply.

---

* In this context, the notion of adjoining sea area is understood to refer also to ocean areas adjoining Europe.

ANNEX II

CHAIRMAN'S STATEMENT

It is understood that, taking into account the agreed date of entry into force of the agreed confidence- and security-building measures and the provisions contained in them concerning the timeframes of certain advance notifications, and expressing their interest in an early transition to the full implementation of the provisions of this document, the participating States agree to the following:

The annual calendars concerning military activities subject to prior notification and forecast for 1987 will be exchanged not later than 15 December 1986.

Communications, in accordance with agreed provisions, concerning military activities involving more than 40,000 troops planned for the calendar year 1988 will be exchanged by 15 December 1986. Participating States may undertake activities involving more than 75,000 troops during the calendar year 1987 provided that they are included in the annual calendar exchanged by 15 December 1986.

Activities to begin during the first 42 days after 1 January 1987 will be subject to the relevant provisions of the Final Act of the CSCE. However, the participating States will make every effort to apply to them the provisions of this document to the maximum extent possible.

This statement will be an annex to the Document of the Stockholm Conference and will be published with it.

ANNEX III

CHAIRMAN'S STATEMENT

It is understood that each participating State can raise any question consistent with the mandate of the Conference on Confidence- and Security-Building Measures and Disarmament in Europe at any stage subsequent to the Vienna CSCE Follow-up Meeting.

This statement will be an annex to the Document of the Stockholm Conference and will be published with it.

ANNEX IV

CHAIRMAN'S STATEMENT

It is understood that the participating States recall that they have the right to belong or not to belong to international organizations, to be or not to be a party to bilateral or multilateral treaties including the right to be or not to be a party to treaties of alliance; they also have the right of neutrality. In this context, they will not take advantage of these rights to circumvent the purposes of the system of inspection, and in particular the provision that no participating State will be obliged to accept on its territory within the zone of application for CSBMs, more than three inspections per calendar year.

Appropriate understandings between participating States on this subject will be expressed in interpretative statements to be included in the journal of the day.

This statement will be an annex to the Document of the Stockholm Conference and will be published with it.

RESERVATIONS AND INTERPRETATIVE STATEMENTS*

Reservation by Turkey

The Government of Turkey had formally placed a reservation regarding the representation of Cyprus at the CSCE on 31 July 1975 (CSCE/III/1). The same reservation was placed at the Belgrade and Madrid Follow-up Meetings as well as at the Bern Meeting of Experts on Human Contacts.

There exist in Cyprus today two separate political entities. In the north, the Turkish Republic of Northern Cyprus is the exclusive, sole and legitimate authority and represents the Turkish people of Cyprus. In the south, the Greek Cypriot administration represents and has only the authority to speak on behalf of the Greek Cypriots. That is, there is not today a single authority representing the whole of Cyprus and its peoples.

The Turkish Republic of Northern Cyprus has already informed that the decisions adopted at this Conference will not be binding on them since they were not represented at the Conference.

The Republic of Turkey adheres to all the decisions reached by the CSCE. However, since for the reasons stated before, the representation of Cyprus at the CSCE is neither legal nor legitimate, the Government of the Republic of Turkey declares that the CSCE Stockholm decisions will have no validity or applicability as regards and in relation to Cyprus.

* * *

Interpretative statement by Cyprus

With reference to the reservation just made by the representative of Turkey, my Government wishes to make the following interpretative statement to be duly registered by the Executive Secretary and circulated to the participating States, in accordance with paragraph 79 of the Rules of Procedure of the Final Recommendations of the Helsinki Consultations:

It should be stressed that last year, in connection with a similar case concerning the representation of the Republic of Cyprus at this Conference, the Chairman of the plenary meeting of 14 June 1985 made a ruling recalling that the Rules of Procedure in paragraph 65 of the Final Recommendations of the Helsinki Consultations applied to the case and quoted the relevant part which reads as follows: "All States

* Journal No. 379/Rev. 2 (Stockholm, 19 September 1986).

participating in the Conference shall do so as sovereign and independent States and in conditions of full equality."

Moreover, the Government of the Republic of Cyprus wishes to reiterate its interpretative statement contained in document CSCE/III/2 of 1 August 1975 as well as all subsequent interpretative statements made in reply to "formal reservations" by the Government of Turkey at CSCE meetings following the adoption of the Helsinki Final Act.

The Turkish invasion of the Republic of Cyprus does not qualify Turkey to dispute the legitimacy of the Government of the Republic of Cyprus, which is recognized by the community of nations, the United Nations and the other international organizations as the sole and legitimate authority representing the whole of Cyprus.

The so-called "Turkish Republic of Northern Cyprus" is an entity which does not exist. The Security Council in its resolutions 541 (1983) and 550 (1984) has denounced, condemned and considered as legally invalid this non-existent entity.

Furthermore, it called upon all States not to recognize the purported "Turkish Republic of Northern Cyprus" set up by secessionist acts and not to facilitate or in any way assist the aforesaid entity.

The consensus given by the government of the Republic of Cyprus to the adoption of the Document of the Stockholm Conference is binding upon the whole of Cyprus, as it has been given by the representative of the legitimate Government of Cyprus.

Any reservation concerning the validity of the decisions of the Stockholm Conference on Confidence- and Security-Building Measures in relations of each participating State with all or any other participating State, or any kind of selectivity in implementing these decisions, is of no effect.

* * *

Interpretative statement by Greece

The delegation of Greece stated that it supported the interpretative statement by the delegation of Cyprus.

* * *

Interpretative statement by Switzerland

Given the peculiar character of the organization of the national defence of Switzerland, based essentially on a militia system and designed solely to ensure the defence of the national territory, the Swiss Government considers that no provision of the Document of the Stockholm Conference, to which it has just given its agreement, applies to the following activities of the Swiss armed forces:

- mobilization exercises
- partial mobilization
- general mobilization.

* * *

Interpretative statement by Italy

In the light of the Chairman's statement appearing in Annex IV of the Document of the Stockholm Conference, and on behalf of the authors of document CSCE/SC.1/Amplified, I wish to state that, in order not to circumvent the purposes of the inspection system, Belgium, Canada, Denmark, France, Federal Republic of Germany, Greece, Iceland, Italy, Luxembourg, Netherlands, Norway, Portugal, Spain, Turkey, United Kingdom and the United States of America will not use their right to inspect one another in the context of paragraph (67) of the Document of the Stockholm Conference.

* * *

Interpretative statement by Romania

In the light of the Chairman's statement in Annex IV of the Document of the Stockholm Conference and on behalf of the Romanian Delegation, I wish to state that, in order not to circumvent the purposes of the system of inspection, those States which are parties to a treaty of alliance will not use their right to inspect other States parties to the same treaty of alliance in the context of paragraph (67) of the Document of the Stockholm Conference.

* * *

Interpretative statement by Hungary

In the light of the Chairman's statement, in Annex IV of the Document of the Stockholm Conference, and on behalf of the Delegations of socialist States, which are parties to a treaty of alliance, I wish to state that, in order not to circumvent the purposes of the system of inspection, those States will not use their right to inspect other States, parties to the same treaty of alliance, in the context of paragraph (67) of the Document of the Stockholm Conference.

* * *

Interpretative statement by the Union of Soviet Socialist Republics

In connection with the Chairman's statement contained in Annex III, the Soviet Union intends in the future to raise at the Conference on Confidence- and Security-Building Measures and Disarmament in Europe questions regarding notification of independent manoeuvres of air and naval forces, limitation of the scale of military manoeuvres and coverage by notifications of the territories of all the participating States of the Conference.

* * *

Interpretative statement by Italy

In connection with certain remarks made a short time ago by the distinguished representative of the Delegation of the Soviet Union, I should like to state, on behalf of the sixteen countries who were the authors of document CSCE/SC.1/Amplified, that our interpretation of the Madrid Mandate, under which the CDE was convened, has been made clear on several occasions in the course of the work of this Conference and remains unchanged.

* * *

Interpretative statements by France

a) On behalf of the Governments of France, the United Kingdom and the United States of America, I wish to state that the points of agreement which have emerged during this Conference do not affect and can in no way affect the quadripartite rights and responsibilities relating to Berlin and to Germany as a whole.

*

b) It was agreed on the occasion of the adoption of the Madrid Mandate that the confidence-building measures adopted in the framework of the CDE should be "provided with forms of verification which correspond to their content".

The measures we have just adopted are verifiable.

The French Delegation wishes to recall on this occasion that the verification provisions adopted in the framework of the closing document of the Stockholm Conference do not necessarily constitute a precedent for other negotiations with a different object.

*

c) The French Delegation recalls that, for France, the first part of the "Document of the Stockholm Conference", which constitutes the political statement of the motives that prompted the adoption of concrete confidence-building measures, can in no way be interpreted as a complement or amendment to the texts already agreed upon within the CSCE. It can clearly not be placed on the same level as the "Declaration on Principles Guiding Relations between Participating States" of the Final Act, nor considered as altering the balance of the Final Act or of the Madrid Concluding Document.

It cannot, *a fortiori*, affect in any way the rights and obligations of the States Members of the United Nations under the Charter.

We recall, however, that the Final Act, notwithstanding the importance we attach to the observance and implementation of its provisions, has not the force of a treaty. It is in this spirit that we interpret the paragraph concerning non-compliance with the obligation of refraining from the threat or use of force as signifying that violations of the relevant provisions of the Charter constitute violations of international law.

* * *

Interpretative statement by the Union of Soviet Socialist Republics

In connection with the statement by the Delegations of France, the United Kingdom and the United States of America regarding quadripartite rights and responsibilities, the Delegation of the Union of Soviet Socialist Republics states that nothing in the Document of the Stockholm Conference affects the rights and responsibilities of the four powers and the relevant quadripartite agreements, decisions and practices, as well as the rights and duties of the participating States under the United Nations Charter, treaties and agreements previously concluded by them.

CONCLUDING DOCUMENT OF VIENNA

CONCLUDING DOCUMENT OF THE VIENNA MEETING 1986 OF REPRESENTATIVES OF THE PARTICIPATING STATES OF THE CONFERENCE ON SECURITY AND CO-OPERATION IN EUROPE, HELD ON THE BASIS OF THE PROVISIONS OF THE FINAL ACT RELATING TO THE FOLLOW-UP TO THE CONFERENCE

Vienna, 15 January 1989

The representatives of the participating States of the Conference on Security and Co-operation in Europe (CSCE), Austria, Belgium, Bulgaria, Canada, Cyprus, Czechoslovakia, Denmark, Finland, France, the German Democratic Republic, the Federal Republic of Germany, Greece, the Holy See, Hungary, Iceland, Ireland, Italy, Liechtenstein, Luxembourg, Malta, Monaco, the Netherlands, Norway, Poland, Portugal, Romania, San Marino, Spain, Sweden, Switzerland, Turkey, the Union of Soviet Socialist Republics, the United Kingdom, the United States of America and Yugoslavia, met in Vienna from 4 November 1986 to 19 January 1989 in accordance with the provisions of the Final Act relating to the Follow-up to the Conference, as well as on the basis of the other relevant CSCE documents.

The participants were addressed on 4 November 1986 by the Austrian Federal Chancellor.

Opening statements were made by all Heads of Delegations among whom were Ministers and Deputy Ministers of many participating States. Some Ministers of Foreign Affairs addressed the Meeting also at later stages.

The participants were addressed by a representative of the SecretaryGeneral of the United Nations. Contributions were made by representatives of the United Nations Economic Commission for Europe (ECE) and UNESCO.

Contributions were also made by the following non-participating Mediterranean States: Algeria, Egypt, Israel, Lebanon, Libya, Morocco, Syria and Tunisia.

The representatives of the participating States reaffirmed their commitment to the CSCE process and underlined its essential role in increasing confidence, in opening up new ways for co-operation, in promoting respect for human rights and fundamental freedoms and thus strengthening international security.

The participating States welcomed the favourable developments in the international situation since the conclusion of the Madrid Meeting in 1983 and expressed their satisfaction that the CSCE process has contributed to these developments. Noting the intensification of political dialogue among them and the important progress in negotiations on military security and disarmament, they agreed that renewed efforts should be undertaken to consolidate these positive trends and to achieve a substantial further improvement of their mutual relations. Accordingly, they reaffirmed their resolve fully to implement, unilaterally, bilaterally and multilaterally, all the provisions of the Final Act and of the other CSCE documents.

As provided for in the Agenda of the Vienna Meeting, the representatives of the participating States held a thorough exchange of views both on the implementation of the provisions of the Final Act and the Madrid Concluding Document and of the tasks defined by the Conference, as well as, in the context of the questions dealt with by the latter, on the deepening of their mutual relations, the improvement of security and the development of co-operation in Europe, and the development of the process of détente in the future.

During this exchange of views the participating States examined thoroughly and in detail the implementation of the Final Act and of the Madrid Concluding Document. Different and at times contradictory opinions were expressed about the extent of the realization of these commitments. While encouraging developments were noted in many areas, the participants criticized the continuing serious deficiencies in the implementation of these documents.

An open and frank discussion was held about the application of and respect for the principles of the Final Act. Concern was expressed about serious violations of a number of these principles. In particular, questions relating to respect for human rights and fundamental freedoms were the focus of intensive and controversial discussion. The participating States agreed that full respect for the principles, in all their aspects, is essential for the improvement of their mutual relations.

The implementation of the provisions of the Final Act concerning confidence-building measures, concerning co-operation in the field of economics, of science and technology and of the environment, concerning questions relating to security and co-operation in the Mediterranean as well as concerning co-operation in humanitarian and other fields was discussed. The implementation of the provisions of the Madrid Concluding Document and of other CSCE documents was also discussed. It was considered that the numerous possibilities offered by the Final Act had not been sufficiently realized.

The participating States also expressed concern about the spread of terrorism and condemned it unreservedly.

The discussion reflected the broader context of the CSCE process and confirmed the importance of taking into account its world dimension in implementing the provisions of the Final Act.

In their deliberations the representatives of the participating States took into account the results of

- the Stockholm Conference on Confidence- and Security-Building Measures and Disarmament in Europe;
- the Athens Meeting of Experts in order to pursue the examination and elaboration of a generally acceptable method for the peaceful settlement of disputes aimed at complementing existing methods;
- the Venice Seminar on Economic, Scientific and Cultural Co-operation in the Mediterranean;
- the Ottawa Meeting of Experts on Questions concerning Respect, in their States, for Human Rights and Fundamental Freedoms, in all their Aspects, as embodied in the Final Act;
- the Budapest "Cultural Forum";
- the Bern Meeting of Experts on Human Contacts.

The participating States moreover noted that the tenth anniversary of the signing of the Final Act had been commemorated at Helsinki on 1 August 1985.

The participating States reaffirmed their commitment to the continuation of the CSCE process as agreed to in the chapter on the Follow-up to the Conference contained in the Final Act. Recognizing the need for balanced progress covering all sections of the Final Act, they expressed their determination also to benefit from new opportunities for their co-operation and reached corresponding decisions concerning follow-up activities.

The representatives of the participating States examined all the proposals submitted to the Meeting and agreed on the following:

QUESTIONS RELATING TO SECURITY IN EUROPE

The participating States express their determination

- to build on the current positive developments in their relations in order to make détente a viable, comprehensive and genuine process, universal in scope;
- to assume their responsibility fully to implement the commitments contained in the Final Act and other CSCE documents;
- to intensify their efforts to seek solutions to problems burdening their relations and to strengthen safeguards for international peace and security;
- to promote co-operation and dialogue among them, to ensure the effective exercise of human rights and fundamental freedoms and to facilitate contacts and communication between people;
- to exert new efforts to make further progress to strengthen confidence and security and to promote disarmament.

Principles

(1) The participating States reaffirm their commitment to all ten principles of the Final Act's Declaration on Principles Guiding Relations between participating States and their determination to respect them and put them into practice. The participating States reaffirm that all these principles are of primary significance and, accordingly, will be equally and unreservedly applied, each of them being interpreted taking into account the others.

(2) They stress that respect for and full application of these principles as well as strict compliance with all CSCE commitments deriving from them are of great political importance and essential for building confidence and security as well as for the development of their friendly relations and of their co-operation in all fields.

(3) In this context, they confirm that they will respect each other's right freely to choose and develop their political, social, economic and cultural systems as well as their right to determine their laws, regulations, practices and policies. In exercising these rights, they will ensure that their laws, regulations, practices and policies conform with their obligations under international law and are brought into harmony with the provisions of the Declaration on Principles and other CSCE commitments.

(4) They also confirm that, by virtue of the principle of equal rights and self-determination of peoples and in conformity with the relevant provisions of the Final Act, all peoples always have the right, in full freedom, to determine, when and as they wish, their internal and external political status, without external interference, and to pursue as they wish their political, economic, social and cultural development.

(5) They confirm their commitment strictly and effectively to observe the principle of the territorial integrity of States. They will refrain from any violation of this principle and thus from any action aimed by direct or indirect means, in contravention of the purposes and principles of the Charter of the United Nations, other obligations under international law or the provisions of the Final Act, at violating the territorial integrity, political independence or the unity of a State. No actions or situations in contravention of this principle will be recognized as legal by the participating States.

(6) The participating States confirm their commitment to the principle of peaceful settlement of disputes, convinced that it is an essential complement to the duty of States to refrain from the threat or use of force, both being essential factors for the maintenance and consolidation of peace and security. They express their determination to pursue continuous efforts to examine and elaborate, on the basis of the relevant provisions of the Final Act and the Madrid Concluding Document and taking into account the reports of the meetings of experts in Montreux and Athens, a generally acceptable method for the peaceful settlement of disputes aimed at complementing existing methods. In this context they accept, in principle, the mandatory involvement of a third party when a dispute cannot be settled by other peaceful means.

(7) In order to ensure the progressive implementation of this commitment, including, as a first step, the mandatory involvement of a third party in the settlement of certain categories of disputes, they decide to convene a Meeting of Experts in Valletta from 15 January to 8 February 1991 to establish a list of such categories and the related procedures and mechanisms. This list would be subject to subsequent gradual extension. The Meeting will also consider the possibility of establishing mechanisms for arriving at binding third-party

decisions. The next CSCE Follow-up Meeting will assess the progress achieved at the Meeting of Experts. The agenda, timetable and other organizational modalities are set out in Annex I.

(8) The participating States unreservedly condemn, as criminal, all acts, methods and practices of terrorism, wherever and by whomever committed, including those which jeopardize friendly relations among States and their security, and agree that terrorism cannot be justified under any circumstances.

(9) They express their determination to work for the eradication of terrorism both bilaterally and through multilateral co-operation, particularly in such international fora as the United Nations, the International Civil Aviation Organization and the International Maritime Organization and in accordance with the relevant provisions of the Final Act and the Madrid Concluding Document.

(10) Convinced of the need to combine measures at a national level with reinforced international co-operation, the participating States express their intention

(10.1) - to pursue a policy of firmness in response to terrorist demands;

(10.2) - to reinforce and develop bilateral and multilateral co-operation among themselves in order to prevent and combat terrorism as well as to increase efficiency in existing co-operation at the bilateral level or in the framework of groups of States including, as appropriate, through the exchange of information;

(10.3) - to prevent on their territories illegal activities of persons, groups or organizations that instigate, organize or engage in the perpetration of acts of terrorism or subversive or other activities directed towards the violent overthrow of the regime of another participating State;

(10.4) - to take effective measures for the prevention and suppression of acts of terrorism directed at diplomatic or consular representatives and against terrorism involving violations of the Vienna Conventions on Diplomatic and Consular Relations, in particular their provisions relating to diplomatic and consular privileges and immunities;

(10.5) - to ensure the extradition or prosecution of persons implicated in terrorist acts and to co-operate closely in cases of conflict of jurisdiction where several States are concerned, acting in both respects in accordance with the relevant international agreements;

(10.6) - to consider becoming parties, if they have not yet done so, to the relevant international conventions relating to the suppression of acts of terrorism;

(10.7) - to continue to work in the appropriate international bodies in order to improve and extend measures against terrorism and to ensure that the relevant agreements are accepted and acted upon by as many States as possible.

(11) They confirm that they will respect human rights and fundamental freedoms, including the freedom of thought, conscience, religion or belief, for all without distinction as to race, sex, language or religion. They also confirm the universal significance of human rights and fundamental freedoms, respect for which is an essential factor for the peace, justice and security necessary to ensure the development of friendly relations and co-operation among themselves, as among all States.

(12) They express their determination to guarantee the effective exercise of human rights and fundamental freedoms, all of which derive from the inherent dignity of the human person and are essential for his free and full development. They recognize that civil, political, economic, social, cultural and other rights and freedoms are all of paramount importance and must be fully realized by all appropriate means.

(13) In this context they will

(13.1) - develop their laws, regulations and policies in the field of civil, political, economic, social, cultural and other human rights and fundamental freedoms and put them into practice in order to guarantee the effective exercise of these rights and freedoms;

(13.2) - consider acceding to the International Covenant on Civil and Political Rights, the International Covenant on Economic, Social and Cultural Rights, the Optional Protocol to the Covenant on

Civil and Political Rights and other relevant international instruments, if they have not yet done so;

(13.3) - publish and disseminate the text of the Final Act, of the Madrid Concluding Document and of the present Document as well as those of any relevant international instruments in the field of human rights, in order to ensure the availability of these documents in their entirety, to make them known as widely as possible and to render them accessible to all individuals in their countries, in particular through public library systems;

(13.4) - effectively ensure the right of the individual to know and act upon his rights and duties in this field, and to that end publish and make accessible all laws, regulations and procedures relating to human rights and fundamental freedoms;

(13.5) - respect the right of their citizens to contribute actively, individually or in association with others, to the promotion and protection of human rights and fundamental freedoms;

(13.6) - encourage in schools and other educational institutions consideration of the promotion and protection of human rights and fundamental freedoms;

(13.7) - ensure human rights and fundamental freedoms to everyone within their territory and subject to their jurisdiction, without distinction of any kind such as race, colour, sex, language, religion, political or other opinion, national or social origin, property, birth or other status;

(13.8) - ensure that no individual exercising, expressing the intention to exercise or seeking to exercise these rights and freedoms or any member of his family, will as a consequence be discriminated against in any manner;

(13.9) - ensure that effective remedies as well as full information about them are available to those who claim that their human rights and fundamental freedoms have been violated; they will, *inter alia*, effectively apply the following remedies:
- the right of the individual to appeal to executive, legislative, judicial or administrative organs;
- the right to a fair and public hearing within a reasonable time before an independent and impartial tribunal, including the right

to present legal arguments and to be represented by legal counsel of one's choice;
- the right to be promptly and officially informed of the decision taken on any appeal, including the legal grounds on which this decision was based. This information will be provided as a rule in writing and, in any event, in a way that will enable the individual to make effective use of further available remedies.

(14) The participating States recognize that the promotion of economic, social, cultural rights as well as of civil and political rights is of paramount importance for human dignity and for the attainment of the legitimate aspirations of every individual. They will therefore continue their efforts with a view to achieving progressively the full realization of economic, social and cultural rights by all appropriate means, including in particular by the adoption of legislative measures. In this context they will pay special attention to problems in the areas of employment, housing, social security, health, education and culture. They will promote constant progress in the realization of all rights and freedoms within their countries, as well as in the development of relations among themselves and with other States, so that everyone actually enjoys to the full his economic, social and cultural rights as well as his civil and political rights.

(15) The participating States confirm their determination to ensure equal rights of men and women. Accordingly, they will take all measures necessary, including legislative measures, to promote equally effective participation of men and women in political, economic, social and cultural life. They will consider the possibility of acceding to the Convention on the Elimination of All Forms of Discrimination Against Women, if they have not yet done so.

(16) In order to ensure the freedom of the individual to profess and practise religion or belief, the participating States will, *inter alia*,

(16.1) - take effective measures to prevent and eliminate discrimination against individuals or communities on the grounds of religion or belief in the recognition, exercise and enjoyment of human rights and fundamental freedoms in all fields of civil, political, economic, social and cultural life, and to ensure the effective equality between believers and non-believers;

(16.2) - foster a climate of mutual tolerance and respect between believers of different communities as well as between believers and non-believers;

(16.3) - grant upon their request to communities of believers, practising or prepared to practise their faith within the constitutional framework of their States, recognition of the status provided for them in their respective countries;

(16.4) - respect the right of these religious communities to
- establish and maintain freely accessible places of worship or assembly,
- organize themselves according to their own hierarchical and institutional structure,
- select, appoint and replace their personnel in accordance with their respective requirements and standards as well as with any freely accepted arrangement between them and their State,
- solicit and receive voluntary financial and other contributions;

(16.5) - engage in consultations with religious faiths, institutions and organizations in order to achieve a better understanding of the requirements of religious freedom;

(16.6) - respect the right of everyone to give and receive religious education in the language of his choice, whether individually or in association with others;

(16.7) - in this context respect, *inter alia*, the liberty of parents to ensure the religious and moral education of their children in conformity with their own convictions;

(16.8) - allow the training of religious personnel in appropriate institutions;

(16.9) - respect the right of individual believers and communities of believers to acquire, possess, and use sacred books, religious publications in the language of their choice and other articles and materials related to the practice of religion or belief;

(16.10) - allow religious faiths, institutions and organizations to produce, import and disseminate religious publications and materials;

(16.11) - favourably consider the interest of religious communities to participate in public dialogue, including through the mass media.

(17) The participating States recognize that the exercise of the above mentioned rights relating to the freedom of religion or belief may be subject only to such limitations as are provided by law and consistent with their obligations under international law and with their international commitments. They will ensure in their laws and regulations and in their application the full and effective exercise of the freedom of thought, conscience, religion or belief.

(18) The participating States will exert sustained efforts to implement the provisions of the Final Act and of the Madrid Concluding Document pertaining to national minorities. They will take all the necessary legislative, administrative, judicial and other measures and apply the relevant international instruments by which they may be bound, to ensure the protection of human rights and fundamental freedoms of persons belonging to national minorities within their territory. They will refrain from any discrimination against such persons and will contribute to the realization of their legitimate interests and aspirations in the field of human rights and fundamental freedoms.

(19) They will protect and create conditions for the promotion of the ethnic, cultural, linguistic and religious identity of national minorities on their territory. They will respect the free exercise of rights by persons belonging to such minorities and ensure their full equality with others.

(20) The participating States will respect fully the right of everyone
- to freedom of movement and residence within the borders of each State, and
- to leave any country, including his own, and to return to his country.

(21) The participating States will ensure that the exercise of the above-mentioned rights will not be subject to any restrictions except those which are provided by law and are consistent with their obligations under international law, in particular the International Covenant on Civil and Political Rights, and with their international commitments, in particular the Universal Declaration of Human Rights. These restrictions have the

character of exceptions. The participating States will ensure that these restrictions are not abused and are not applied in an arbitrary manner, but in such a way that the effective exercise of these rights is ensured.

(22) In this context they will allow all refugees who so desire to return in safety to their homes.

(23) The participating States will

(23.1) - ensure that no one will be subjected to arbitrary arrest, detention or exile;

(23.2) - ensure that all individuals in detention or incarceration will be treated with humanity and with respect for the inherent dignity of the human person;

(23.3) - observe the United Nations Standard Minimum Rules for the Treatment of Prisoners as well as the United Nations Code of Conduct for Law Enforcement Officials;

(23.4) - prohibit torture and other cruel, inhuman or degrading treatment or punishment and take effective legislative, administrative, judicial and other measures to prevent and punish such practices;

(23.5) - consider acceding to the Convention against Torture and other Cruel, Inhuman or Degrading Treatment or Punishment, if they have not yet done so;

(23.6) - protect individuals from any psychiatric or other medical practices that violate human rights and fundamental freedoms and take effective measures to prevent and punish such practices.

(24) With regard to the question of capital punishment, the participating States note that capital punishment has been abolished in a number of them. In participating States where capital punishment has not been abolished, sentence of death may be imposed only for the most serious crimes in accordance with the law in force at the time of the commission of the crime and not contrary to their international commitments. This question will be kept under consideration. In this context, the participating States will co-operate within relevant international organizations.

(25) With the aim of developing mutual understanding and confidence, promoting friendly and good neighbourly relations, strengthening international peace, security and justice and improving the implementation of their CSCE commitments, the participating States will further develop co-operation and promote dialogue between them in all fields and at all levels on the basis of full equality. They agree that full respect for and application of the principles and the fulfilment of the other CSCE provisions will improve their relations and advance the development of their co-operation. They will refrain from any action inconsistent with the provisions of the Final Act and other CSCE documents and recognize that any such action would impair relations between them and hinder the development of co-operation among them.

(26) They confirm that governments, institutions, organizations and persons have a relevant and positive role to play in contributing to the achievement of the aims of their co-operation and to the full realization of the Final Act. To that end they will respect the right of persons to observe and promote the implementation of CSCE provisions and to associate with others for this purpose. They will facilitate direct contacts and communication among these persons, organizations and institutions within and between participating States and remove, where they exist, legal and administrative impediments inconsistent with the CSCE provisions. They will also take effective measures to facilitate access to information on the implementation of CSCE provisions and to facilitate the free expression of views on these matters.

(27) The participating States heard accounts of the Meeting of Experts on Questions concerning Respect, in their States, for Human Rights and Fundamental Freedoms, in all their Aspects, as embodied in the Final Act, held in Ottawa from 7 May to 17 June 1985. They welcomed the fact that frank discussions had taken place of matters of key concern. Noting that these discussions had not led to agreed conclusions, they agreed that such thorough exchanges of views themselves constitute a valuable contribution to the CSCE process. In this respect it was noted in particular that proposals made at the Meeting had received further consideration at the Vienna Follow-up Meeting. They also welcomed the decision to allow public access to part of the Meeting and noted that this practice was further developed at later meetings.

Confidence- and security-building measures and certain aspects of security and disarmament in europe

Stockholm Conference: Assessment of progress achieved

The participating States,

In accordance with the relevant provisions of the Madrid Concluding Document, assessed progress achieved during the Conference on Confidence- and Security-building Measures and Disarmament in Europe, which met in Stockholm from 17 January 1984 to 19 September 1986.

They welcomed the adoption at Stockholm of a set of mutually complementary confidence- and security-building measures (CSBMs).

They noted that these measures are in accordance with the criteria of the Madrid mandate and constitute a substantial improvement and extension of the confidence-building measures adopted in the Final Act.

They noted that the adoption of the Stockholm Document was a politically significant achievement and that its measures are an important step in efforts aimed at reducing the risk of military confrontation in Europe. They agreed that the extent to which the measures will in practice contribute to greater confidence and security will depend on the record of implementation. They were encouraged by initial implementation and noted that further experience and detailed review will be required. They reaffirmed their determination to comply strictly with and apply in good faith all the provisions of the Document of the Stockholm Conference.

They reaffirmed their commitment to the provisions of the Madrid Concluding Document relating to the Conference on Confidence- and Security-building Measures and Disarmament in Europe and agreed to resume the work of the Conference with a view to achieving further progress towards its aim.

New efforts for security and disarmament in Europe

The participating States,

Recalling the relevant provisions of the Final Act and of the Madrid Concluding Document according to which they recognize the interest of all of them in efforts aimed at lessening military confrontation and promoting disarmament,

Reaffirming their determination expressed in the Final Act to strengthen confidence among them and thus to contribute to increasing stability and security in Europe,

Stressing the complementary nature of the efforts within the framework of the CSCE process aimed at building confidence and security and establishing stability and achieving progress in disarmament, in order to lessen military confrontation and to enhance security for all,

Stressing that in undertaking such efforts they will respect the security interests of all CSCE participating States inherent in their sovereign equality,
Having also considered ways and appropriate means to continue their efforts for security and disarmament in Europe,

Have reached the understanding that these efforts should be structured as set forth below:

Negotiations on Confidence- and Security-building Measures

The participating States have agreed that Negotiations on Confidence- and Security-building Measures will take place in order to build upon and expand the results already achieved at the Stockholm Conference with the aim of elaborating and adopting a new set of mutually complementary confidence- and security-building measures designed to reduce the risk of military confrontation in Europe.

These negotiations will take place in accordance with the Madrid mandate.

The decisions of the Preparatory Meeting held in Helsinki from 25 October to 11 November 1983 will be applied *mutatis mutandis* (see Annex II).

These negotiations will take place in Vienna, commencing in the week beginning on 6 March 1989.

The next Follow-up Meeting of the participating States of the CSCE, to be held in Helsinki, commencing on 24 March 1992, will assess the progress achieved in these negotiations.

Negotiation on Conventional Armed Forces in Europe

The Negotiation on Conventional Armed Forces in Europe will take place as agreed by those States named in the mandate contained in the Chairman's statement in Annex III of this document, who among themselves have determined the agenda, the rules of procedure and the organizational modalities of these negotiations, and will determine their timetable and results. These negotiations will be conducted within the framework of the CSCE process.

These negotiations will take place in Vienna, commencing in the week beginning on 6 March 1989.

The next Follow-up Meeting of the participating States of the CSCE, to be held in Helsinki, commencing on 24 March 1992, will exchange views on the progress achieved in these negotiations.

Meetings in order to Exchange Views and Information concerning the course of the Negotiation on Conventional Armed Forces in Europe

It has been agreed that the participating States will hold meetings in order to exchange views and information concerning the course of the Negotiation on Conventional Armed Forces in Europe.

These meetings will be held at least twice during each session of the Negotiation on Conventional Armed Forces in Europe.

Provisions on practical modalities relating to these meetings are contained in Annex IV of this Document.

At these meetings, substantive information will be provided by the participants in the Negotiation on Conventional Armed Forces in Europe on developments, progress and results in the negotiations with the aim of enabling each participating State to appraise their course.

The participants in these negotiations have undertaken to take into consideration, in the course of their negotiations, the views expressed at such meetings by other participating States concerning their own security.

Information will also be provided on a bilateral basis.

The next Follow-up Meeting of the participating States of the CSCE, to be held in Helsinki, commencing on 24 March 1992, will consider the functioning of these arrangements.

Taking into account the relevant provisions of the Final Act and of the Madrid Concluding Document, and having considered the results achieved in the two negotiations, and also in the light of other relevant negotiations on security and disarmament affecting Europe, a future CSCE follow-up meeting will consider ways and appropriate means for the participating States to continue their efforts for security and disarmament in Europe, including the question of supplementing the Madrid mandate for the next stage of the Conference on Confidence- and Security-building Measures and Disarmament in Europe.

CO-OPERATION IN THE FIELD OF ECONOMICS, OF SCIENCE AND TECHNOLOGY AND OF THE ENVIRONMENT

The participating States reaffirm their willingness to further their co-operation in the field of economics, of science and technology and of the environment, and to promote stable and equitable international economic relations in the interest of all States. They express their readiness to intensify the dialogue in the competent fora with a view to facilitating appropriate solutions for key interrelated economic issues such as money, finance, debt and trade. In this connection, they stress the importance of policies aimed at promoting structural adjustments, stimulating the growth of national economies and creating an international economic environment conducive to development.

The participating States recognize the important role of the United Nations Economic Commission for Europe (ECE) in fostering regional economic co-operation and in contributing to the implementation of the provisions of the Final Act and subsequent CSCE documents. They express their readiness to make further use of the existing framework, resources and experience of the ECE in areas which are of significance for the implementation of recommendations of the CSCE.

Trade and industrial co-operation

(1) In order to make better use of their economic potential, and to foster the expansion of their commercial exchanges, the participating States will make further efforts to promote favourable conditions for trade and industrial co-operation, taking into account all the relevant provisions of the Final Act and the Madrid Concluding Document.

(2) The participating States recognize the importance of favourable business conditions for the development of trade between them. They will facilitate direct contacts between business people, potential buyers and end-users, including on-site contacts relevant to the business intended or being transacted. They will take measures to improve working conditions for business people, regarding, among other things,

accreditation, accommodation, communications, and recruitment and management of personnel. They will also take measures to avoid unjustifiable delays in visa procedures and customs clearance. Further, they recognize the opportunities offered by trade fairs and exhibitions for developing commercial contacts and achieving concrete business results.

(3) The participating States will continue their efforts further to reduce or progressively eliminate obstacles of all kinds to trade, thus contributing to the expansion and diversification of their commercial relations. They express their support for the work done in this field in appropriate international fora.

(4) The participating States will encourage forms of trade compatible with the efficient conduct of international business relations and will also encourage business partners to decide independently upon their trading patterns. As to compensation transactions in all their forms, they recommend that proposals of this kind be addressed at the beginning of negotiations and, when agreed upon, dealt with in a flexible way, especially regarding the choice of products. In this connection, the special concerns of small and medium-sized enterprises should be taken into account. The participating States recognize the valuable role of the ECE in dealing with questions related to compensation transactions.

(5) The participating States recognize that, within their respective economies, increased autonomy for enterprises can help achieve a better response to market needs and thus contribute to the development of trade and co-operation among them.

(6) In order to facilitate the identification of market opportunities, the participating States will further promote the publication and availability of comprehensive, comparable and timely economic and commercial information. They will publish up-to-date macroeconomic information and statistics, and envisage making balance of payment figures available. They will also provide the United Nations trade databank, COMTRADE, with detailed data in a format relevant to the efficient conduct of foreign trade. They will encourage co-operation between their statistical services and within the framework of the ECE in order, *inter alia*, to facilitate the identification of disparities in foreign trade statistics and to improve the international comparability of such statistics. Furthermore, they consider it useful to increase the publication and exchange of statistics on such topics as demography, public health, agriculture, the environment and energy.

(7) Noting the growing importance of services in their mutual economic relations, the participating States will examine, in appropriate bodies, developments in this area and prospects for improved access to the services market.

(8) Affirming the importance of industrial co-operation in their long-term economic relations, the participating States will promote measures designed to create favourable conditions for the development of such co-operation. They will therefore examine, within the competent fora, the improvement of the legal, administrative and economic framework for industrial co-operation. Furthermore, they will encourage contacts between potential partners, develop exchanges of appropriate information and promote the participation of small and medium-sized enterprises in industrial co-operation.

(9) The participating States recognize that productive, competitive and profit-earning joint ventures can play a role in mutually beneficial industrial co-operation. They will improve the legal, administrative and financial conditions for investment in, and operation of, joint ventures. They will also promote the exchange of all information relevant to the establishment of joint ventures, including all necessary technical information, as well as information on management, labour conditions, accounting and taxation, repatriation of profits and the protection of investments, production conditions and access to domestic supplies and markets.

(10) The participating States stress the importance of their standardization policies and practices, and of related activities, for the facilitation of international trade, especially regarding products subject to compulsory certification. Accordingly, they will consider mutual recognition of their national testing and certification procedures and practices, and promote co-operation among relevant national bodies and within international organizations including the ECE.

(11) The participating States recognize the growing importance of effective marketing in the development of trade and industrial co-operation, in the production and promotion of new products and in meeting the needs of the consumer. Given the growth of marketing opportunities, they will seek to improve the conditions for firms and organizations engaging in research into domestic or foreign markets and in other marketing activities.

(12) The participating States affirm the usefulness for all enterprises, and especially for small and medium-sized ones, of flexible and mutually agreed arbitration provisions for ensuring the equitable settlement of disputes in international trade and industrial co-operation. Bearing in mind the relevant provisions of the Final Act and the Madrid Concluding Document, they attach particular importance to freedom in the choice of arbitrators, including the presiding arbitrator, and of the country of arbitration. They recommend that consideration be given to the adoption of the Model Law on international commercial arbitration of the United Nations Commission on International Trade Law (UNCITRAL). In addition, they recognize the value of agreements on co-operation in the field of commercial arbitration between Chambers of Commerce and other arbitration bodies.

(13) The participating States agree to convene a Conference on Economic Co-operation in Europe. This Conference will take place in Bonn from 19 March to 11 April 1990. The aim of the Conference is to provide new impulses for economic relations between participating States, in particular by improving business conditions for commercial exchanges and industrial co-operation and by considering new possibilities for, and ways of, economic co-operation. The Conference will be attended by representatives of the participating States and of the business community. The agenda, timetable and other organizational modalities are set out in Annex V. The next Follow-up Meeting, to be held in Helsinki, commencing on 24 March 1992, will assess the results achieved at the Conference.

Science and technology

(14) The participating States emphasize the important role of science and technology in their overall economic and social development, bearing in mind particularly those sciences and technologies which are of direct relevance to improving the quality of life.

(15) Recognizing the importance of scientific and technological co-operation, the participating States will develop further mutually advantageous co-operation in the fields already set forth in the Final Act, and will examine possibilities for co-operation in new areas of growing importance and common interest. Furthermore, they express their intention to improve conditions for such co-operation by fostering the exchange of information on, and experience with, scientific and technological achievements, having in mind especially the interests of

the countries of the region which are developing from the economic point of view.

(16) The participating States also reaffirm the role of general intergovernmental agreements as well as of bilateral agreements involving universities, scientific and technological institutions and industry, in developing mutually beneficial exchanges. Under-lining the importance of freedom of communication and exchange of views for progress in science and technology, they will promote and support direct and individual contacts between scientists, specialists and interested business people. Recalling the conclusions reached at the Hamburg Scientific Forum, they will respect human rights and fundamental freedoms, which represent one of the foundations for a significant improvement in international scientific co-operation at all levels. They will also endeavour to create conditions enabling interested partners to develop appropriate joint research programmes and projects on the basis of reciprocity and mutual advantage and, when appropriate, on a commercial basis.

(17) Given the depletion of natural resources, including non-renewable sources of energy, the participating States will promote co-operation in the rational use of such resources, and in the use of alternative sources of energy, including thermonuclear fusion.

(18) Taking note of the progress made in, and the new opportunities offered by, research and development in biotechnology, the participating States consider it desirable to enhance the exchange of information on laws and regulations relating to the safety aspects of genetic engineering. They will therefore facilitate consultation and exchange of information on safety guidelines. In this context, they emphasize the importance of ethical principles when dealing with genetic engineering and its application.

(19) The participating States will develop their co-operation in medical and related sciences by intensifying research and the exchange of information on drug abuse and on new or increasingly widespread diseases. They will co-operate in particular in combating the spread of AIDS, taking into account the Global AIDS Strategy of the World Health Organization (WHO). They will also co-operate in research concerning the long-term consequences of radiation.

(20) The participating States recognize the importance of scientific research, of environmentally sound technologies and, in particular, of improved

international co-operation in these fields, for the monitoring, prevention and reduction of pollution. They will therefore promote, *inter alia* within the relevant international fora, exchange of information on, and experience with, these technologies. In this respect they will also promote, on a commercial basis, exchanges in the fields of pollution-abatement technologies, technologies and products with less or no emission of ozone-depleting substances, processing and combustion techniques, new methods of waste treatment including recycling and disposal, and low- and non-waste technologies.

(21) The participating States will exchange appropriate information in specific fields of engineering industries and automation. They will do this on the basis of mutual advantage for potential partners, who will decide independently on the areas of co-operation and with due respect for bilateral and multilateral agreements. To this end they will, *inter alia*, develop statistics in fields of engineering industries of commercial importance.

(22) In the context of their scientific and technological co-operation, the participating States will consider the possibility of encouraging the development and use of alternatives to animal experimentation, including for product testing.

(23) In the important field of nuclear energy, the participating States recognize that, while individual States should assume full responsibility for the safety of their own nuclear facilities, nuclear safety requires closer international co-operation, especially within the International Atomic Energy Agency (IAEA). They note that it is essential to maintain the highest possible safety standards in the management and operation of nuclear facilities. They therefore support the work done within the IAEA in developing basic safety principles, and urge all States to use the revised Nuclear Safety Standards - NUSS codes - as a basis for regulating nuclear safety practices. They also recall the need further to improve the efficiency of the existing system of nuclear liability.

Environment

(24) Recognizing the need for preventive action, the participating States will strengthen their co-operation and intensify efforts aimed at protecting and improving the environment, bearing in mind the need to maintain and restore the ecological balance in air, water and soil. They will do this by, *inter alia*, developing their internal legislation and their

international commitments, and by applying the best available means, taking into account levels of development as well as economic and technical constraints. They underline the importance of the Regional Strategy for Environmental Protection and Rational Use of Natural Resources in ECE Member Countries Covering the Period up to the Year 2000 and Beyond. They welcome, and will take due account of, the report of the World Commission on Environment and Development and the Environmental Perspective to the Year 2000 and Beyond, as well as the work already undertaken within the competent international fora, in particular within the framework of the 1979 Convention on Long-Range Transboundary Air Pollution (hereafter called "the Convention").

(25) The participating States are convinced of the need for timely and effective reductions of sulphur emissions or their transboundary fluxes. They call upon Contracting Parties and Signatories to the Convention to become parties to the Protocol on the reduction of sulphur emissions or their transboundary fluxes by at least 30 per cent. They recommend that further steps to reduce sulphur emissions, in line with the objectives of the Protocol, be taken by those States which are not parties to the Protocol, and that those States where this goal is already accomplished continue to control their emissions. Recalling that the said Protocol provides for reductions of sulphur emissions at the latest by 1993, they will work within the framework of the Convention for the elaboration at an early date of an arrangement for further reductions of sulphur emissions beyond the level established by the Protocol.

(26) The participating States consider that control and reduction of nitrogen oxide emissions, or their transboundary fluxes, deserve high priority in their pollution abatement programmes. They welcome the elaboration and adoption of the Protocol on Control of Nitrogen Oxide Emissions.

(27) Furthermore, they recognize the need to develop, within the framework of the Convention, arrangements to reduce emissions of other relevant air pollutants such as hydrocarbons and those producing photochemical oxidants. They will strengthen their co-operation accordingly, including by collecting and processing the necessary information.

(28) The participating States agree to strengthen and develop the co-operative programme for the Monitoring and Evaluation of the Long-Range Transmission of Air Pollutants in Europe (EMEP), *inter alia*

through extending and improving the system of monitoring stations, providing EMEP with the necessary information regarding emissions of pollutants, further developing comparable methods of measurement, and expanding coverage to include other relevant air pollutants, in particular nitrogen oxides, hydrocarbons and photochemical oxidants. They also recommend that those countries which have not yet done so should become parties to the Protocol on the Long-Term Financing of EMEP.

(29) The participating States will make every effort to become parties, as soon as possible, to the Vienna Convention for the Protection of the Ozone Layer and to the Montreal Protocol on Substances that Deplete the Ozone Layer. Further, they will foster national action and international co-operation on the control and reduction of the emission of ozone-depleting substances.

(30) The participating States agree that further national and international research efforts should be made regarding the global warming phenomenon, and the role played therein by emissions of carbon dioxide and trace gases, in order to provide a scientific basis for mitigative action.

(31) In order to protect and improve freshwater resources and to reduce significantly the pollution of seas and coastal areas, transboundary watercourses and international lakes from all sources of pollution, the participating States will develop and intensify national efforts as well as bilateral and multilateral co-operation. They recommend the elaboration of a framework convention or specific conventions to improve the protection of transboundary watercourses and international lakes. They will reduce significantly discharges of toxic, persistent and potentially hazardous substances. Furthermore, they will devote special attention to the development of appropriate alternatives to sea disposal in order to decrease progressively and substantially the dumping of harmful wastes and the incineration of noxious liquid wastes at sea, with a view to the early termination of such methods.

(32) The participating States recognize the need to improve international co-operation on the transboundary movement of hazardous wastes. Taking into account the valuable work done in other international fora, they will encourage the elaboration of international agreements, including a global convention on the control of transboundary movements of hazardous wastes.

(33) The participating States will seek closer co-operation and greater exchange of information on the problems associated with potentially hazardous chemicals, including assessment of the risks to health and the environment. They will explore possibilities for closer harmonization of their legislation and regulations on the handling of these chemicals.

(34) The participating States will strengthen international co-operation on natural resources and flora and fauna. They will promote early accession to, and effective implementation of, relevant agreements. They will also develop further effective measures to combat soil degradation and to protect flora, fauna and their habitats on the basis of the Declaration on this subject adopted by the ECE. They will intensify their exchanges of views and experience on ways and means of achieving a more rational use of natural resources.

(35) The participating States acknowledge the importance of the contribution of persons and organizations dedicated to the protection and improvement of the environment, and will allow them to express their concerns. They will promote greater public awareness and understanding of environmental issues and will co-operate in the field of environmental education, *inter alia* through exchanges of experience and results of research studies, development of educational programmes and ecological training.

(36) The participating States will co-operate bilaterally and multilaterally with a view to improving and co-ordinating their arrangements for prevention, early warning, exchange of information and mutual assistance in cases of industrial accidents likely to cause transboundary damage to the environment. They will also initiate the examination of key elements related to the transboundary character of industrial accidents, such as clean-up, restoration and liability.

(37) The participating States agree to convene a Meeting on the protection of the environment. This Meeting will take place in Sofia from 16 October to 3 November 1989. The aim of the Meeting is to elaborate recommendations on principles and guidelines for further measures and co-operation in new and important areas of environmental protection. The agenda, timetable and other organizational modalities are set out in Annex VI. The next Follow-up Meeting, to be held in Helsinki, commencing on 24 March 1992, will assess the results achieved at the Meeting.

Co-operation in other areas

(38) The participating States recognize the important role of transport in economic and social development and the overall consequences of increased activity in the transport sector, including problems related to the environment. They will therefore encourage the elaboration of measures for achieving an economically more efficient transport system, taking into account the relative merits of different modes of transport and their potential effects on human health, safety and the environment. In this connection they will, through bilateral and multilateral means, give particular attention to questions concerning multimodal transport networks, combined transport, transit flows and the simplification of transport formalities and, in particular, of transport documents. They also welcome the work done by the ECE in this context.

(39) The participating States underline the economic importance of tourism and its contribution to the mutual understanding of peoples. They therefore favour the development of co-operation in this field and will facilitate normal contacts between tourists and the local population. To this end they will endeavour to improve the infrastructure for tourism, *inter alia* by diversifying accommodation and by developing facilities for low-budget and youth tourism, including small-scale private accommodation. They will also consider in a positive spirit the progressive phasing out, for foreign tourists, of minimum exchange requirements where they apply, allow the reconversion of legally acquired local currency, and, furthermore, encourage non-discriminatory pricing for all foreign tourists irrespective of their nationality. They will also reduce arrival and departure procedures to the necessary minimum. The participating States will create conditions conducive to the establishment of joint projects in the field of tourism, including joint ventures and personnel training programmes.

(40) The participating States emphasize the need for effective implementation of the provisions of the Final Act and the Madrid Concluding Document relating to migrant workers and their families in Europe. They invite host countries and countries of origin to make efforts to improve further the economic, social, cultural and other conditions of life for migrant workers and their families legally residing in the host countries. They recommend that host countries and countries of origin should promote their bilateral co-operation in relevant fields with a view to facilitating the reintegration of migrant workers and their families returning to their country of origin.

(41) The participating States will, in accordance with their relevant commitments undertaken in the Final Act and the Madrid Concluding Document, consider favourably applications for family reunification as well as family contacts and visits involving migrant workers from other participating States legally residing in the host countries.

(42) The participating States will ensure that migrant workers from other participating States, and their families, can freely enjoy and maintain their national culture and have access to the culture of the host country.

(43) Aiming at ensuring effective equality of opportunity between the children of migrant workers and the children of their own nationals regarding access to all forms and levels of education, the participating States affirm their readiness to take measures needed for the better use and improvement of educational opportunities. Furthermore, they will encourage or facilitate, where reasonable demand exists, supplementary teaching in their mother tongue for the children of migrant workers.

(44) The participating States recognize that issues of migrant workers have their human dimension.

(45) The participating States acknowledge that the impact of economic and technological change is being acutely felt in the work place. They underline their readiness to encourage co-operation in the field of vocational training policy through increased exchange of information and experience, with the aim of enhancing the educational standards, professional knowledge, skills and adaptability of personnel involved in industry and commerce.

(46) The participating States recognize the importance of facilitating the integration of young people into professional life. They will therefore continue their efforts to ensure the necessary conditions for the education and vocational training of young people and to promote youth employment opportunities in various sectors of the economy. They will continue their efforts to create conditions for developing the level of scientific and cultural knowledge of their citizens, especially young people, and for facilitating their access to achievements in the areas of natural and social sciences, as well as culture.

QUESTIONS RELATING TO SECURITY AND CO-OPERATION IN THE MEDITERRANEAN

The participating States

reaffirm their commitment to, and stress the continuing relevance of, the provisions of the Final Act and the Madrid Concluding Document concerning security and co-operation in the Mediterranean; in this context, they underline the relevance of the Mediterranean paragraph of the Stockholm Document.

They stress the importance of the CSCE process for increasing security and improving co-operation in the Mediterranean area.

They reiterate their conviction that security in Europe is to be considered in the broader context of world security and is closely linked with security in the Mediterranean area as a whole, and that accordingly the process of improving security should not be confined to Europe but should extend to other parts of the world, and in particular to the Mediterranean area.

They express their concern over the continuing tensions in the region and renew their willingness to intensify efforts towards finding just, viable and lasting solutions, through peaceful means, to outstanding crucial problems.

They consider that broader and more active co-operation could contribute to increased mutual understanding and enhanced confidence, thereby promoting stability, security and peace in the region.

They note the results of existing bilateral and multilateral forms of co-operation and express their readiness to increase efforts in the economic, scientific and cultural fields, and in the field of environment, taking due account of the interests of the developing countries in the region, and taking into consideration the work under way in these fields.

They note with satisfaction the positive outcome of the Seminar on economic, scientific and cultural co-operation in the Mediterranean within the framework of the results of the Valletta Meeting of 1979, held in Venice from 16 to 26 October 1984 in accordance with the relevant provisions and objectives of the Madrid Concluding Document. They welcome the concrete contribution of this Seminar to the development of co-operation in the Mediterranean area and they support continued efforts to implement its recommendations as well as those of the Valletta meeting.

They note the continuing interest of the non-participating Mediterranean States in the CSCE and in efforts with the participating States in strengthening security and promoting co-operation in the Mediterranean. They recognize to this end the need to maintain and amplify their contacts with the non-participating Mediterranean States as initiated by the CSCE and to develop good neighbourly relations with all of them, with due regard to reciprocity and in the spirit of the principles contained in the Declaration on Principles Guiding Relations between Participating States of the Final Act.

The participating States

in conformity with the provisions of the Mediterranean chapters of the Final Act and the Madrid Concluding Document, agree to convene a Meeting on the Mediterranean in order to consider ways and means of further enhancing various aspects of co-operation, including the protection and improvement of Mediterranean ecosystems, with the aim of widening the scope of their co-operation with the non-participating Mediterranean States and contributing to the strengthening of confidence and security in the region.

Representatives of the non-participating Mediterranean States (Algeria, Egypt, Israel, Lebanon, Libya, Morocco, Syria and Tunisia) and representatives of the competent international organizations (UNESCO, ECE, UNEP*, WHO, ITU, IMO) will be invited to this Meeting in accordance with the rules and practices adopted for the previous CSCE Mediterranean follow-up events.

The Meeting will be held in Palma de Mallorca from 24 September to 19 October 1990. The agenda, timetable and other organizational modalities are set out in Annex VII.

The next Follow-up Meeting, to be held in Helsinki, commencing on 24 March 1992, will assess the results achieved at this Meeting.

CO-OPERATION IN HUMANITARIAN AND OTHER FIELDS

The participating States,

Considering that co-operation in humanitarian and other fields is an essential factor for the development of their relations,

---

* It is understood that the invitation to UNEP includes ROCC (Regional Oil Combating Center) and MAP (Mediterranean Action Plan).

Agreeing that their co-operation in these fields should take place in full respect for the principles guiding relations between participating States as set forth in the Final Act as well as for the provisions in the Madrid Concluding Document and in the present Document pertaining to those principles,

Confirming that, in implementing the provisions concerning co-operation in humanitarian and other fields in the framework of their laws and regulations, they will ensure that those laws and regulations conform with their obligations under international law and are brought into harmony with their CSCE commitments,

Recognizing that the implementation of the relevant provisions of the Final Act and of the Madrid Concluding Document requires continuous and intensified efforts,

Have adopted and will implement the following:

Human Contacts

(1) In implementing the human contacts provisions of the Final Act, the Madrid Concluding Document and the present Document, they will fully respect their obligations under international law as referred to in the subchapter of the present Document devoted to principles, in particular that everyone shall be free to leave any country, including his own, and to return to his country, as well as their international commitments in this field.

(2) They will ensure that their policies concerning entry into their territories are fully consistent with the aims set out in the relevant provisions of the Final Act, the Madrid Concluding Document and the present Document.

(3) They will take the necessary steps to find solutions as expeditiously as possible, but in any case within six months, to all applications based on the human contacts provisions of the Final Act and the Madrid Concluding Document, outstanding at the conclusion of the Vienna Follow-up Meeting.

(4) Thereafter they will conduct regular reviews in order to ensure that all applications based on the human contacts provisions of the Final Act and of the other aforementioned CSCE documents are being dealt with in a manner consistent with those provisions.

(5) They will decide upon applications relating to family meetings in accordance with the Final Act and the other aforementioned CSCE documents in as short a time as possible and in normal practice within one month.

(6) In the same manner they will decide upon applications relating to family reunification or marriage between citizens of different States, in normal practice within three months.

(7) In dealing favourably with applications relating to family meetings, they will take due account of the wishes of the applicant, in particular on the timing and sufficiently long duration of such meetings, and on travelling together with other members of his family for joint family meetings.

(8) In dealing favourably with applications relating to family meetings, they will also allow visits to and from more distant relatives.

(9) In dealing favourably with applications relating to family reunification or marriage between citizens of different States, they will respect the wishes of the applicants on the country of destination ready to accept them.

(10) They will pay particular attention to the solution of problems involving the reunification of minor children with their parents. In this context and on the basis of the relevant provisions of the Final Act and of the other aforementioned CSCE documents, they will ensure
- that an application for this purpose submitted while the child is a minor will be dealt with favourably and expeditiously in order to effect the reunification without delay; and
- that adequate arrangements are made to protect the interests and welfare of the children concerned.

(11) They will consider the scope for gradually reducing and eventually eliminating any requirement which might exist for travellers to obtain local currency in excess of actual expenditure, giving priority to persons travelling for the purpose of family meetings. They will accord such persons the opportunity in practice to bring in or to take out with them personal possessions or gifts.

(12) They will pay immediate attention to applications for travel of an urgent humanitarian nature and deal with them favourably as follows:

- They will decide within three working days upon applications relating to visits to a seriously ill or dying family member, travel to attend the funeral of a family member or travel by those who have a proven need of urgent medical treatment or who can be shown to be critically or terminally ill.
- They will decide as expeditiously as possible upon applications relating to travel by those who are seriously ill or by the elderly, and other travel of an urgent humanitarian nature.

They will intensify efforts by their local, regional and central authorities concerned with the implementation of the above, and ensure that charges for giving priority treatment to such applications do not exceed costs actually incurred.

(13) In dealing with applications for travel for family meetings, family reunification or marriage between citizens of different States, they will ensure that acts or omissions by members of the applicant's family do not adversely affect the rights of the applicant as set forth in the relevant international instruments.

(14) They will ensure that all documents necessary for applications based on the human contacts provisions of the Final Act and of the other aforementioned CSCE documents are easily accessible to the applicant. The documents will remain valid throughout the application procedure. In the event of a renewed application the documents already submitted by the applicant in connection with previous applications will be taken into consideration.

(15) They will simplify practices and gradually reduce administrative requirements for applications based on the human contacts provisions of the Final Act and of the other aforementioned CSCE documents.

(16) They will ensure that, when applications based on the human contacts provisions of the Final Act and of the other aforementioned CSCE documents are refused for reasons specified in the relevant international instruments, the applicant is promptly provided in writing with an official notification of the grounds on which the decision was based. As a rule and in all cases where the applicant so requests, he will be given the necessary information about the procedure for making use of any effective administrative or judicial remedies against the decision available to him as envisaged in the above-mentioned international instruments. In cases where exit for permanent settlement abroad is involved, this information will be provided as part of the official notification foreseen above.

(17) If in this context an individual's application for travel abroad has been refused for reasons of national security, they will ensure that, within strictly warranted time limits, any restriction on that individual's travel is as short as possible and is not applied in an arbitrary manner. They will also ensure that the applicant can have the refusal reviewed within six months and, should the need arise, at regular intervals thereafter so that any changes in the circumstances surrounding the refusal, such as time elapsed since the applicant was last engaged in work or duties involving national security, are taken into account. Before individuals take up such work or duties they will be formally notified if and how this could affect applications they might submit for such travel.

(18) Within one year of the conclusion of the Vienna Follow-up Meeting they will publish and make easily accessible, where this has not already been done, all their laws and statutory regulations concerning movement by individuals within their territory and travel between States.

(19) In dealing favourably with applications based on the human contacts provisions of the Final Act and of the other aforementioned CSCE documents, they will ensure that these are dealt with in good time in order, *inter alia*, to take due account of important family, personal or professional considerations significant for the applicant.

(20) They will deal favourably with applications for travel abroad without distinction of any kind, such as race, colour, sex, language, religion, political or other opinion, national or social origin, property, birth, age or other status. They will ensure that any refusal does not affect applications submitted by other persons.

(21) They will further facilitate travel on an individual or collective basis for personal or professional reasons and for tourism, such as travel by delegations, groups and individuals. To this end they will reduce the time for the consideration of applications for such travel to a minimum.

(22) They will give serious consideration to proposals for concluding agreements on the issuing of multiple entry visas and the reciprocal easing of visa processing formalities, and consider possibilities for the reciprocal abolition of entry visas on the basis of agreements between them.

(23) They will consider adhering to the relevant multilateral instruments as well as concluding complementary or other bilateral agreements, if necessary, in order to improve arrangements for ensuring effective consular, legal and medical assistance for citizens of other participating States temporarily on their territory.

(24) They will take any necessary measures to ensure that citizens of other participating States temporarily on their territory for personal or professional reasons, *inter alia* for the purpose of participating in cultural, scientific and educational activities, are afforded appropriate personal safety, where this is not already the case.

(25) They will facilitate and encourage the establishment and maintenance of direct personal contacts between their citizens as well as between representatives of their institutions and organizations through travel between States and other means of communication.

(26) They will facilitate such contacts and co-operation among their peoples through such measures as direct sports exchanges on a local and regional level, the unimpeded establishment and implementation of town-twinning arrangements, as well as student and teacher exchanges.

(27) They will encourage the further development of direct contacts between young people, as well as between governmental and non-governmental youth and student organizations and institutions; the conclusion between such organizations and institutions of bilateral and multilateral arrangements and programmes; and the holding on a bilateral and multilateral basis of educational, cultural and other events and activities by and for young people.

(28) They will make further efforts to facilitate travel and tourism by young people, *inter alia* by recommending to those of their railway authorities which are members of the International Union of Railways (UIC) that they expand the Inter-Rail system to cover all their European networks and by recommending to those of their railway authorities which are not members of the UIC that they consider establishing similar facilities.

(29) In accordance with the Universal Postal Convention and the International Telecommunication Convention, they will

- guarantee the freedom of transit of postal communication;
- ensure the rapid and unhindered delivery of correspondence, including personal mail and parcels;

- respect the privacy and integrity of postal and telephone communications; and
- ensure the conditions necessary for rapid and uninterrupted telephone calls, including the use of international direct dialling systems, where they exist, and their development.

(30) They will encourage direct personal contacts between the citizens of their States, *inter alia* by facilitating individual travel within their countries and by allowing foreigners to meet their citizens as well as, when invited to do so, to stay in private homes.

(31) They will ensure that the status of persons belonging to national minorities or regional cultures on their territories is equal to that of other citizens with regard to human contacts under the Final Act and the other aforementioned CSCE documents and that these persons can establish and maintain such contacts through travel and other means of communication, including contacts with citizens of other States with whom they share a common national origin or cultural heritage.

(32) They will allow believers, religious faiths and their representatives, in groups or on an individual basis, to establish and maintain direct personal contacts and communication with each other, in their own and other countries, *inter alia* through travel, pilgrimages and participation in assemblies and other religious events. In this context and commensurate with such contacts and events, those concerned will be allowed to acquire, receive and carry with them religious publications and objects related to the practice of their religion or belief.

(33) They heard accounts of the Meeting of Experts on Human Contacts held in Bern from 15 April to 26 May 1986. Noting that no conclusions had been agreed upon at the Meeting, they regarded both the frankness of the discussion and the greater degree of openness in the exchanges as welcome developments. In this respect they noted the particular importance of the fact that proposals made at the Meeting had received further consideration at the Vienna Follow-up Meeting.

Information

(34) They will continue efforts to contribute to an ever wider knowledge and understanding of life in their States, thus promoting confidence between peoples.
They will make further efforts to facilitate the freer and wider dissemination of information of all kinds, to encourage co-operation in

the field of information and to improve the working conditions for journalists.

In this connection and in accordance with the International Covenant on Civil and Political Rights, the Universal Declaration of Human Rights and their relevant international commitments concerning seeking, receiving and imparting information of all kinds, they will ensure that individuals can freely choose their sources of information.

In this context they will

- ensure that radio services operating in accordance with the ITU Radio Regulations can be directly and normally received in their States; and
- allow individuals, institutions and organizations, while respecting intellectual property rights, including copyright, to obtain, possess, reproduce and distribute information material of all kinds.

To these ends they will remove any restrictions inconsistent with the above-mentioned obligations and commitments.

(35) They will take every opportunity offered by modern means of communication, including cable and satellites, to increase the freer and wider dissemination of information of all kinds. They will also encourage co-operation and exchanges between their relevant institutions, organizations and technical experts, and work towards the harmonization of technical standards and norms. They will bear in mind the effects of these modern means of communication on their mass media.

(36) They will ensure in practice that official information bulletins can be freely distributed on their territory by the diplomatic and other official missions and consular posts of the other participating States.

(37) They will encourage radio and television organizations, on the basis of arrangements between them, to broadcast live, especially in the organizing countries, programmes and discussions with participants from different States and to broadcast statements of and interviews with political and other personalities from the participating States.

(38) They will encourage radio and television organizations to report on different aspects of life in other participating States and to increase the number of telebridges between their countries.

(39) Recalling that the legitimate pursuit of journalists' professional activity will neither render them liable to expulsion nor otherwise penalize them, they will refrain from taking restrictive measures such as

withdrawing a journalist's accreditation or expelling him because of the content of the reporting of the journalist or of his information media.

(40) They will ensure that, in pursuing this activity, journalists, including those representing media from other participating States, are free to seek access to and maintain contacts with public and private sources of information and that their need for professional confidentiality is respected.

(41) They will respect the copyright of journalists.

(42) On the basis of arrangements between them, where necessary, and for the purpose of regular reporting, they will grant accreditation, where it is required, and multiple entry visas to journalists from other participating States, regardless of their domicile. On this basis they will reduce to a maximum of two months the period for issuing both accreditation and multiple entry visas to journalists.

(43) They will facilitate the work of foreign journalists by providing relevant information, on request, on matters of practical concern, such as import regulations, taxation and accommodation.

(44) They will ensure that official press conferences and, as appropriate, other similar official press events are also open to foreign journalists, upon accreditation, where this is required.

(45) They will ensure in practice that persons belonging to national minorities or regional cultures on their territories can disseminate, have access to, and exchange information in their mother tongue.

(46) They agree to convene an Information Forum to discuss improvement of the circulation of, access to and exchange of information; co-operation in the field of information; and the improvement of working conditions for journalists. The Forum will be held in London from 18 April to 12 May 1989. It will be attended by personalities from the participating States in the field of information. The agenda, timetable and other organizational modalities are set out in Annex VIII.

Co-operation and exchanges in the field of culture

(47) They will promote and give full effect to their cultural co-operation, *inter alia* through the implementation of any relevant bilateral and

multilateral agreements concluded among them in the various fields of culture.

(48) They will encourage non-governmental organizations interested in the field of culture to participate, together with State institutions, in the elaboration and implementation of these agreements and specific projects, as well as in the elaboration of practical measures concerning cultural exchange and co-operation.

(49) They will favour the establishment, by mutual agreement, of cultural institutes or centres of other participating States on their territory. Unhindered access by the public to such institutes or centres as well as their normal functioning will be assured.

(50) They will assure unhindered access by the public to cultural events organized on their territory by persons or institutions from other participating States and ensure that the organizers can use all means available in the host country to publicize such events.

(51) They will facilitate and encourage direct personal contacts in the field of culture, on both an individual and a collective basis, as well as contacts between cultural institutions, associations of creative and performing artists and other organizations in order to increase the opportunities for their citizens to acquaint themselves directly with the creative work in and from other participating States.

(52) They will ensure the unimpeded circulation of works of art and other cultural objects, subject only to those restrictions which are aimed at preserving their cultural heritage, are based on respect for intellectual and artistic property rights or derive from their international commitments on the circulation of cultural property.

(53) They will encourage co-operation between and joint artistic endeavours of persons from different participating States who are engaged in cultural activities; as appropriate, facilitate specific initiatives to this end by such persons, institutions and organizations and encourage the participation of young people in such initiatives. In this context they will encourage meetings and symposia, exhibitions, festivals and tours by ensembles or companies, and research and training programmes in which persons from the other participating States may also freely take part and make their contribution.

(54) The replacement of persons or groups invited to participate in a cultural activity will be exceptional and subject to prior agreement by the inviting party.

(55) They will encourage the holding of film weeks including, as appropriate, meetings of artists and experts as well as lectures on cinematographic art; facilitate and encourage direct contacts between film directors and producers with a view to co-producing films; and encourage co-operation in the protection of film material and the exchange of technical information and publications about the cinema.

(56) They will explore the scope for computerizing bibliographies and catalogues of cultural works and productions in a standard form and disseminating them.

(57) They will encourage museums and art galleries to develop direct contacts, *inter alia* with a view to organizing exhibitions, inclu-ding loans of works of art, and exchanging catalogues.

(58) They will renew their efforts to give effect to the provisions of the Final Act and the Madrid Concluding Document relating to less widely spoken languages. They will also encourage initiatives aimed at increasing the number of translations of literature from and into these languages and improving their quality, in particular by the holding of workshops involving translators, authors and publishers, by the publication of dictionaries and, where appropriate, by the exchange of translators through scholarships.

(59) They will ensure that persons belonging to national minorities or regional cultures on their territories can maintain and develop their own culture in all its aspects, including language, literature and religion; and that they can preserve their cultural and historical monuments and objects.

(60) They heard accounts of the work done and the ideas advanced during the Cultural Forum held in Budapest from 15 October to 25 November 1985. Noting that no conclusions had been agreed upon at the Forum, they welcomed the fact that many of the useful ideas and proposals put forward there had received renewed consideration at the Vienna Follow-up Meeting and that institutions and organizations in the participating States have based many activities on these ideas. They expressed their appreciation of the significant contributions made to the event by leading personalities in the field of culture, and noted, in the

light of the experience gained, the importance of securing, both inside and outside future meetings of this nature, arrangements which would permit a freer and more spontaneous discussion.

(61) Taking duly into account the originality and diversity of their respective cultures, they will encourage efforts to explore common features and to foster greater awareness of their cultural heritage. Accordingly they will encourage initiatives which may contribute to a better knowledge of the cultural heritage of the other participating States in all its forms, including regional aspects and folk art.

(62) They agree to convene a Symposium on the Cultural Heritage of the CSCE participating States. The Symposium will take place in Cracow from 28 May to 7 June 1991. It will be attended by scholars and other personalities from the participating States who are engaged in cultural activities. The agenda, timetable and other organizational modalities are set out in Annex IX.

Co-operation and exchanges in the field of education

(63) They will ensure access by all to the various types and levels of education without discrimination as to race, colour, sex, language, religion, political or other opinion, national or social origin, property, birth or other status.

(64) In order to encourage wider co-operation in science and education, they will facilitate unimpeded communication between universities and other institutions of higher education and research. They will also facilitate direct personal contacts, inclu-ding contacts through travel, between scholars, scientists and other persons active in these fields.

(65) They will also ensure unimpeded access by scholars, teachers and students from the other participating States to open information material available in public archives, libraries, research institutes and similar bodies.

(66) They will facilitate exchanges of schoolchildren between their countries on the basis of bilateral arrangements, where necessary, including meeting and staying with families of the host country in their homes, with the aim of acquainting schoolchildren with life, traditions and education in other participating States.

(67) They will encourage their relevant government agencies or educational institutions to include, as appropriate, the Final Act as a whole in the curricula of schools and universities.

(68) They will ensure that persons belonging to national minorities or regional cultures on their territories can give and receive instruction on their own culture, including instruction through parental transmission of language, religion and cultural identity to their children.

(69) They will encourage their radio and television organizations to inform each other of the educational programmes they produce and to consider exchanging such programmes.

(70) They will encourage direct contacts and co-operation between relevant governmental institutions or organizations in the field of education and science.

(71) They will encourage further co-operation and contacts between specialized institutions and experts in the field of education and rehabilitation of handicapped children.

Human dimension of the CSCE

The participating States,

Recalling the undertakings entered into in the Final Act and in other CSCE documents concerning respect for all human rights and fundamental freedoms, human contacts and other issues of a related humanitarian character,

Recognizing the need to improve the implementation of their CSCE commitments and their co-operation in these areas which are hereafter referred to as the human dimension of the CSCE,

Have, on the basis of the principles and provisions of the Final Act and of other relevant CSCE documents, decided:

1. to exchange information and respond to requests for information and to representations made to them by other participating States on questions relating to the human dimension of the CSCE. Such communications may be forwarded through diplomatic channels or be addressed to any agency designated for these purposes;
2. to hold bilateral meetings with other participating States that so request, in order to examine questions relating to the human dimension

of the CSCE, including situations and specific cases, with a view to resolving them. The date and place of such meetings will be arranged by mutual agreement through diplomatic channels;

3. that any participating State which deems it necessary may bring situations and cases in the human dimension of the CSCE, including those which have been raised at the bilateral meetings described in paragraph 2, to the attention of other participating States through diplomatic channels;
4. that any participating State which deems it necessary may provide information on the exchanges of information and the responses to its requests for information and to representations (paragraph 1) and on the results of the bilateral meetings (paragraph 2), including information concerning situations and specific cases, at the meetings of the Conference on the Human Dimension as well as at the main CSCE Follow-up Meetings.

The participating States decide further to convene a Conference on the Human Dimension of the CSCE in order to achieve further progress concerning respect for all human rights and fundamental freedoms, human contacts and other issues of a related humanitarian character. The Conference will hold three meetings before the next CSCE Follow-up Meeting.

The Conference will:

- review developments in the human dimension of the CSCE including the implementation of the relevant CSCE commitments;
- evaluate the functioning of the procedures described in paragraphs 1 to 4 and discuss the information provided according to paragraph 4;
- consider practical proposals for new measures aimed at improving the implementation of the commitments relating to the human dimension of the CSCE and enhancing the effectiveness of the procedures described in paragraphs 1 to 4.

On the basis of these proposals, the Conference will consider adopting new measures.

The first Meeting of the Conference will be held in Paris from 30 May to 23 June 1989.

The second Meeting of the Conference will be held in Copenhagen from 5 to 29 June 1990.

The third Meeting of the Conference will be held in Moscow from 10 September to 4 October 1991.

The agenda, timetable and other organizational modalities are set out in Annex X.

The next main CSCE Follow-up Meeting, to be held in Helsinki, commencing on 24 March 1992, will assess the functioning of the procedures set out in paragraphs 1 to 4 above and the progress made at the Meetings of the Conference on the Human Dimension of the CSCE. It will consider ways of further strengthening and improving these procedures and will take appropriate decisions.

FOLLOW-UP TO THE CONFERENCE

In conformity with the relevant provisions of the Final Act and with their resolve and commitment to continue the multilateral process initiated by the CSCE, the participating States will hold further meetings regularly among their representatives.

The fourth main Follow-up Meeting will be held in Helsinki, commencing on 24 March 1992.

The agenda, work programme and modalities of the main Vienna Meeting will be applied *mutatis mutandis* to the main Helsinki Meeting, unless other decisions on these questions are taken by the preparatory meeting mentioned below.

For the purpose of making the adjustments to the agenda, work programme and modalities applied at the main Vienna Meeting, a preparatory meeting will be held in Helsinki, commencing on 10 March 1992. It is understood that in this context adjustments concern those items requiring change as a result of the change in date and place, the drawing of lots, and the mention of the other meetings held in conformity with the decisions of the Vienna Meeting 1986. The duration of the preparatory meeting shall not exceed two weeks.

The agenda, work programme and modalities for CSCE follow-up meetings mentioned in this document have been prepared by the main Vienna Meeting. The results of these meetings will be taken into account, as appropriate, at the main Helsinki Meeting.

All the meetings referred to in this Chapter will be held in conformity with Paragraph 4 of the Chapter on "Follow-up to the Conference" of the Final Act.

The participating States examined the scope for rationalizing the modalities for future CSCE follow-up meetings, for enhancing their effectiveness and for ensuring the best possible use of resources. In the light of their examination and in connection with the steps taken at the main Vienna Meeting, including the drawing up of mandates annexed to this document, they decided:

- to dispense with preparatory meetings unless otherwise agreed;
- bearing in mind the purpose of the meeting, to limit the number of subsidiary working bodies meeting simultaneously to the lowest possible;
- to limit the duration of meetings, unless otherwise agreed, to a period not exceeding four weeks;
- in the case of meetings to which non-governmental participants are invited to contribute, to make maximum use of the possibility of having informal meetings in order to allow for a more spontaneous discussion;
- to observe to the same extent as the host country its national day.

The main Helsinki Meeting will review these arrangements and other modalities in the light of experience, with a view to making any improvements which may be necessary.

The Government of Austria is requested to transmit the present document to the Secretary-General of the United Nations, to the Director-General of UNESCO and to the Executive Secretary of the United Nations Economic Commission for Europe and to other international organizations mentioned in this document. The Government of Austria is also requested to transmit the present document to the Governments of the non-participating Mediterranean States.

The text of this document will be published in each participating State, which will disseminate it and make it known as widely as possible.

The representatives of the participating States express their profound gratitude to the people and Government of Austria for the excellent organization of the Vienna Meeting and the warm hospitality extended to the delegations which participated in the Meeting.

ANNEX I

AGENDA, TIMETABLE AND OTHER ORGANIZATIONAL MODALITIES OF THE MEETING OF EXPERTS ON PEACEFUL SETTLEMENT OF DISPUTES

I. Agenda

1. Formal opening of the Meeting. Address by a representative of the host country.
2. General exchange of views.
3. Examination of proposals submitted.
4. Preparation and adoption of the report of the Meeting.
5. Formal closure of the Meeting.

II. Timetable and other organizational modalities

1. The Meeting will open on Tuesday, 15 January 1991 at 10.30 a.m., in Valletta. It will close not later than Friday, 8 February 1991.
2. Participants may circulate written proposals or other contributions prior to the Meeting through diplomatic channels or through the Executive Secretary to all other participating States in order to allow for a thorough preparation of the Meeting.
3. The timetable of the Meeting will be the following:
   - from Tuesday, 15 January to Thursday, 17 January 1991, the Meeting will deal with Agenda item 2;
   - from Friday, 18 January to Friday, 8 February 1991, the Meeting will deal with Agenda items 3, 4 and 5.
4. The Chair at the opening and closing meetings will be taken by a representative of the host country. After the opening meeting, the Chair will be taken in daily rotation, in French alphabetical order, starting with a representative of Italy.
5. In conformity with paragraph 74 of the Final Recommendations of the Helsinki Consultations, the Government of Malta will designate an Executive Secretary. This designation will be subject to approval by the participating States.
6. The other rules of procedure, the working methods and the scale of distribution of the expenses of the CSCE will, *mutatis mutandis*, be applied to the Meeting.

ANNEX II

CHAIRMAN'S STATEMENT

NEGOTIATIONS ON CONFIDENCE- AND SECURITY-BUILDING MEASURES

With reference to the provision that the decisions of the Preparatory Meeting held in Helsinki from 25 October to 11 November 1983 will be applied *mutatis mutandis* to the Negotiations on Confidence- and Security-building Measures, which will take place according to the relevant provisions of the subchapter "Confidence- and Security-building Measures and certain Aspects of Security and Disarmament in Europe", it is understood that

- the meetings of the Plenary during the first two weeks will be held according to the work programme attached to this statement. The first Plenary will be held on 9 March 1989 at 10.30 a.m. The first session will end on 23 March 1989,
- subsequent work programmes will be adopted by the Plenary,
- in conformity with the rules of procedure, the Government of Austria will designate an Executive Secretary, the designation being subject to approval by the participating States,
- the Chair at the first Plenary meeting will be taken by the representative of the host country and thereafter in daily rotation, in French alphabetical order, starting with the representative of Greece.

This statement will be an Annex to the Concluding Document of the Vienna Meeting and will be published with it.

ANNEX III

CHAIRMAN'S STATEMENT

NEGOTIATION ON CONVENTIONAL ARMED FORCES IN EUROPE

It is understood that the following mandate has been agreed by the States participating in the future Negotiation on Conventional Armed Forces in Europe:

"Mandate for Negotiation on Conventional Armed Forces* in Europe

The representatives of Belgium, Bulgaria, Canada, Czechoslovakia, Denmark, France, the German Democratic Republic, the Federal Republic of Germany, Greece, Hungary, Iceland, Italy, Luxembourg, the Netherlands, Norway, Poland, Portugal, Romania, Spain, Turkey, the Union of Soviet Socialist Republics, the United Kingdom and the United States of America held consultations in Vienna from 17 February 1987 to 10 January 1989.

These States,

Conscious of the common responsibility which they all have for seeking to achieve greater stability and security in Europe;

Acknowledging that it is their armed forces which bear most immediately on the essential security relationship in Europe, in particular as they are signatories of the Treaties of Brussels (1948), Washington (1949) or Warsaw (1955), and accordingly are members of the North Atlantic Alliance or parties to the Warsaw Treaty;

Recalling that they are all participants in the CSCE process;

Recalling that, as reaffirmed in the Helsinki Final Act, they have the right to belong or not to belong to international organizations, to be or not to be a party to bilateral or multilateral treaties including the right to be or not to be a party to treaties of alliance;

Determined that a Negotiation on Conventional Armed Forces in Europe should take place in the framework of the CSCE process;

---

* Conventional Armed Forces include conventional armaments and equipment.

Reaffirming also that they participate in negotiations as sovereign and independent States and on the basis of full equality;

Have agreed on the following provisions:

Participants

The participants in this negotiation shall be the 23 above-listed States hereinafter referred to as "the participants".

Objectives and methods

The objectives of the negotiation shall be to strengthen stability and security in Europe through the establishment of a stable and secure balance of conventional armed forces, which include conventional armaments and equipment, at lower levels; the elimination of disparities prejudicial to stability and security; and the elimination, as a matter of priority, of the capability for launching surprise attack and for initiating large-scale offensive action. Each and every participant undertakes to contribute to the attainment of these objectives.

These objectives shall be achieved by the application of militarily significant measures such as reductions, limitations, redeployment provisions, equal ceilings, and related measures, among others.

In order to achieve the above objectives, measures should be pursued for the whole area of application with provisions, if and where appropriate, for regional differentiation to redress disparities within the area of application and in a way which precludes circumvention.

The process of strengthening stability and security should proceed step-by-step, in a manner which will ensure that the security of each participant is not affected adversely at any stage.

Scope and area of application

The subject of the negotiation shall be the conventional armed forces, which include conventional armaments and equipment, of the participants based on land within the territory of the participants in Europe from the Atlantic to the Urals.

The existence of multiple capabilities will not be a criterion for modifying the scope of the negotiation:

- No conventional armaments or equipment will be excluded from the subject of the negotiation because they may have other capabilities in addition to conventional ones. Such armaments or equipment will not be singled out in a separate category;
- Nuclear weapons will not be a subject of this negotiation.

Particular emphasis will initially be placed on those forces directly related to the achievement of the objectives of the negotiation set out above.

Naval forces and chemical weapons will not be addressed.

The area of application* shall be the entire land territory of the participants in Europe from the Atlantic to the Urals, which includes all the European island territories of the participants. In the case of the Soviet Union the area of application includes all the territory lying west of the Ural River and the Caspian Sea. In the case of Turkey the area of application includes the territory of Turkey north and west of the following line: the point of intersection of the border with the 39th parallel, Muradiye, Patnos, Karayazi, Tekman, Kemaliye, Feke, Ceyhan, Dogankent, Gözne and thence to the sea.

Exchange of information and verification

Compliance with the provisions of any agreement shall be verified through an effective and strict verification regime which, among other things, will include on-site inspections as a matter of right and exchanges of information.

Information shall be exchanged in sufficient detail so as to allow a meaningful comparison of the capabilities of the forces involved. Information shall also be exchanged in sufficient detail so as to provide a basis for the verification of compliance.

The specific modalities for verification and the exchange of information, including the degree of detail of the information and the order of its exchange, shall be agreed at the negotiation proper.

---

* The participants will be guided by the language on non-circumvention as set out in the section on Objectives and Methods.

Procedures and other arrangements

The procedures for the negotiation, including the agenda, work programme and timetable, working methods, financial issues and other organizational modalities, as agreed by the participants themselves, are set out in Annex 1 of this mandate. They can be changed only by consensus of the participants.

The participants decided to take part in meetings of the States signatories of the Helsinki Final Act to be held at least twice during each round of the Negotiation on Conventional Armed Forces in Europe in order to exchange views and substantive information concerning the course of the Negotiation on Conventional Armed Forces in Europe. Detailed modalities for these meetings are contained in Annex 2 to this mandate.

The participants will take into consideration the views expressed in such meetings by other CSCE participating States concerning their own security.

Participants will also provide information bilaterally.

The participants undertake to inform the next CSCE Follow-up Meeting of their work and possible results and to exchange views, at that meeting, with the other CSCE participating States on progress achieved in the negotiation.

The participants foresee that, in the light of circumstances at the time, they will provide in their timetable for a temporary suspension to permit this exchange of views. The appropriate time and duration of this suspension is their sole responsibility.

Any modification of this mandate is the sole responsibility of the participants, whether they modify it themselves or concur in its modification at a future CSCE Follow-up Meeting.

The results of the negotiation will be determined only by the participants.

Character of agreements

Agreements reached shall be internationally binding. Modalities for their entry into force will be decided at the negotiation.

Venue

The negotiation shall commence in Vienna no later than in the seventh week following the closure of the Vienna CSCE Meeting.

* * *

The representatives of the 23 participants, whose initials appear below, have concluded the foregoing mandate, which is equally authentic in the English, French, German, Italian, Russian and Spanish languages.

The representatives, recalling the commitment of their States to the achievement of a balanced outcome at the Vienna CSCE Meeting, have decided to transmit it to that Meeting with the recommendation that it be attached to its Concluding Document.

Palais Liechtenstein
Vienna, Austria,
the 10th day of January 1989

Here appear the initials of the representatives of Belgium, Bulgaria, Canada, Czechoslovakia, Denmark, France, the German Democratic Republic, the Federal Republic of Germany, Greece, Hungary, Iceland, Italy, Luxembourg, the Netherlands, Norway, Poland, Portugal, Romania, Spain, Turkey, the Union of Soviet Socialist Republics, the United Kingdom and the United States of America.

ANNEX 1

PROCEDURES FOR THE NEGOTIATION ON CONVENTIONAL ARMED FORCES IN EUROPE

The representatives of the 23 States listed in the mandate, hereinafter referred to as "the participants", held consultations in Vienna from 17 February 1987 to 10 January 1989, and agreed on the following procedural arrangements for the conduct of the Negotiation on Conventional Armed Forces in Europe.

These procedural arrangements have been adopted by the consensus of the participants. They can be changed only by consensus of the participants.

I. Agenda

1. Formal opening.
2. Negotiations, including presentation of proposals by the participants, elaboration of measures and procedures for their implementation, in

accordance with the provisions of the mandate of the Negotiation on Conventional Armed Forces in Europe.

II. Work programme

The first plenary of the Negotiation on Conventional Armed Forces in Europe will open in Vienna at 3 p.m. on the Thursday of the week referred to in the section of the mandate on Venue. A work programme for the meetings of the plenary during the first fourteen days of the round is attached. Thereafter, the plenary will agree further work programmes for the remainder of the first round, and for subsequent rounds. A decision on the date for conclusion of the round will be taken at the first plenary.

In 1989, there will in principle be four rounds.

The participants will, in setting their timetable, take due account of the practical needs of all delegations, including those participating in other negotiations within the framework of the CSCE process.

III. Working methods

With the exception of the formal opening, all business under the agenda will -unless otherwise agreed - be dealt with in closed plenary and in such subsidiary working bodies as are established by the plenary. The work of such subsidiary bodies will be guided by the plenary.

Decisions shall be taken by consensus of the participants. Consensus shall be understood to mean the absence of any objection by any participant to the taking of the decision in question.

The proceedings of the negotiation shall be confidential unless otherwise agreed at the negotiation.
Unless otherwise agreed, only accredited representatives of the participants shall have access to meetings.

During the plenary meetings all participants shall be seated in the French alphabetical order.

IV. Languages

The official languages of the negotiation shall be: English, French, German, Italian, Russian and Spanish. Statements made in any of these languages shall be interpreted into the other official languages.

V. Role of the chairman

The chairman of the first plenary will be the representative of Poland. The chair thereafter will rotate weekly according to the French alphabetical order.

The chairman of each meeting shall keep a list of speakers and may declare it closed with the consent of the meeting. The chairman shall, however, accord the right of reply to any representative if a speech made following closure of the list makes this desirable.

If any representative raises a point of order during a discussion, the chairman shall give that representative the floor immediately. A representative raising a point of order may not speak on the substance of the matter under discussion.

The chairman shall keep a journal which shall record the date of the plenary, and the names of the chairman of the plenary and of speakers in the plenary. The journal shall be handed from chairman to chairman. It shall be made available only to participants.

VI. Decisions, interpretative statements, and proposals and related documents on matters of substance

Decisions on matters of substance shall be attached to the journal. Interpretative statements, if any, shall be attached to the journal at the request of the originator.

Formal proposals and related documents on matters of substance and amendments thereto shall be submitted in writing to the chairman and shall be registered at the request of the originator. They shall be circulated in writing to the participants.

VII. Financial issues

The following scale of distribution has been agreed for the common expenses of the negotiation subject to the reservation that the distribution in question concerns only this negotiation and shall not be considered a precedent which could be relied on in other circumstances:

9.95% for	France, Federal Republic of Germany, Italy, Union of Soviet Socialist Republics, United Kingdom, United States of America
6.25% for	Canada
5.0% for	Spain
3.85% for	Belgium, German Democratic Republic, Netherlands, Poland
2.25% for	Czechoslovakia, Denmark, Hungary, Norway
0.85% for	Greece, Romania, Turkey
0.65% for	Bulgaria, Luxembourg, Portugal
0.15% for	Iceland

Payment of contributions by the participants shall be made into a special account of the negotiation. Accounts shall be rendered by the host country in respect of each round or at intervals of 3 months, as appropriate. Accounts shall be expressed in the currency of the host country and shall be rendered as soon as technically possible after the termination of a billing period. Accounts shall be payable within 60 days of presentation in the currency of the host country.

VIII. Host country support

The government of Austria shall provide security and other necessary support services for the negotiation.

The host country shall be asked to appoint an administrator, agreed by the participants, to make and manage arrangements for the negotiation. The administrator shall be a national of the host country. The task of the administrator shall include, in liaison with the appropriate host country authorities:

a. to arrange accreditation for the participants,
b. to manage the facilities of the negotiation,
c. to ensure the security of, and control access to, the facilities and meetings,
d. to employ and manage interpretation staff,
e. to make available appropriate technical equipment,
f. to ensure the availability of translation services in all official languages; the practical arrangements for their use being agreed at the negotiation,
g. to deal with financial matters,
h. to make available to participants as necessary facilities for press briefings and to arrange appropriate media accreditation.

The administrator shall act at all times in conformity with these rules of procedure. Liaison between the administrator and the plenary will be effected by the chairman.

ANNEX 2

MODALITIES FOR MEETINGS TO EXCHANGE VIEWS AND INFORMATION CONCERNING THE COURSE OF THE NEGOTIATION ON CONVENTIONAL ARMED FORCES IN EUROPE

The participants have, for their part, agreed the following modalities for the meetings which are to be held between participants in the Negotiation on Conventional Armed Forces in Europe and other CSCE participating States.

Unless otherwise agreed, meetings will take place at least twice in the course of each round of the negotiation.

Meetings will not be extended beyond the day on which they convene, unless otherwise agreed.

The chair at the first meeting will be taken by the delegation chosen for this purpose by lot. The chair will then rotate among the 35 States represented in alphabetical order according to the French alphabet.

Further practical arrangements may, if necessary, be agreed by consensus, taking due regard of relevant precedents.

Statement of the representative of Denmark

On behalf of the government of Denmark, I wish to confirm that the Faroe Islands are included in the area of application for the Negotiation on Conventional Armed Forces in Europe.

Statement of the representative of Norway

On behalf of the government of Norway, I confirm that Svalbard including Bear Island, is included in the area of application for the Negotiation on Conventional Armed Forces in Europe.

Statement of the representative of Portugal

The islands of Azores and Madeira have by right the status of European Islands. It has been agreed in the mandate that all the European island territories of the participants are included in the area of application. I can therefore state on behalf of my government that the Azores and Madeira are within the area of application for the Negotiation on Conventional Armed Forces in Europe.

Statement of the representative of Spain

On behalf of the government of Spain, I confirm that the Canary Islands are included in the area of application for the Negotiation on Conventional Armed Forces in Europe.

Statement of the representative of the Union of Soviet Socialist Republics

On behalf of the government of the Union of Soviet Socialist Republics, I confirm that Franz Josef Land and Novaya Zemlya are included in the area of application for the Negotiation on Conventional Armed Forces in Europe."

This statement will be an Annex to the Concluding Document of the Vienna Meeting and will be published with it.

ANNEX IV

CHAIRMAN'S STATEMENT

MEETINGS IN ORDER TO EXCHANGE VIEWS AND INFORMATION CONCERNING THE COURSE OF THE NEGOTIATION ON CONVENTIONAL ARMED FORCES IN EUROPE

The meetings to exchange views and information concerning the course of the Negotiation on Conventional Armed Forces in Europe will, unless otherwise agreed, be held as follows:

- on the second Tuesday of each session of the Negotiation on Conventional Armed Forces in Europe,
- on every fourth Tuesday thereafter unless it happens to be in the penultimate week of the session,
- on the Tuesday of the concluding week of each session.

Consequently, the first meeting will take place on 21 March 1989. It will commence at 10.30 a.m.

These meetings will not be extended beyond the day on which they convene, unless otherwise agreed.

The Chair will be taken in daily rotation, in French alphabetical order, starting with the representative of Sweden.

Further practical arrangements related to the procedure and working methods may, if necessary, be agreed to accord with the rules of procedure of the CSCE.

This statement will be an Annex to the Concluding Document of the Vienna Meeting and will be published with it.

ANNEX V

CONFERENCE ON ECONOMIC CO-OPERATION IN EUROPE

I. Agenda

1. Formal opening. Address by a representative of the host country.
2. Statements by delegations of the participating States.
3. Contributions by the Economic Commission for Europe (ECE) and the International Chamber of Commerce (ICC).
4. Consideration of the following items:
   A. Development and diversification of economic relations through practical measures regarding:
      (a) Business contacts
      (b) Working conditions for businesspeople
      (c) Economic and commercial information
      (d) Role of small and medium-sized enterprises
      (e) Marketing and product promotion.
   B. Industrial co-operation:
      Requirements for the establishment and operation, on a mutually advantageous basis, of joint ventures and other forms of industrial co-operation such as co-production, specialization and licensing:
      (a) Economic conditions and legal and administrative aspects
      (b) Investment-related matters.
   C. Co-operation in specific areas:
      (a) Energy and raw material saving techniques
      (b) Equipment for environmental protection
      (c) Techniques aimed at improving the quality of life
      (d) Agro-industry and food processing, including natural food production
      (e) Machinery for the production of durable and non-durable consumer goods
      (f) Urban development and town planning.
   D. Monetary and financial aspects of commercial exchanges and industrial co-operation, such as:
      (a) Currency convertibility and pricing, and their effects on international competition
      (b) Financial instruments and other support facilities offered by the financial services sector.
5. Concluding discussion and summing up.
6. Formal closure.

II. Organizational framework and other modalities

1. The Conference will be attended by delegations, which may include businesspeople and representatives of relevant organizations and institutions, from the participating States. At the concluding Plenary meetings, in the fourth week, delegations may also include leading members of the business community and of relevant organizations and institutions. The Conference will open on 19 March 1990, at 3 p.m., in Bonn. It will close on 11 April 1990.
2. The ECE and the ICC are invited to attend the Conference.
3. All Plenary meetings will be open. Unless otherwise agreed, all meetings of Subsidiary Working Bodies will be open.
4. Agenda items 1, 5 and 6 will be dealt with in the Plenary. Agenda item 4 will be dealt with in the Plenary and in the Subsidiary Working Bodies (SWBs), in a balanced and structured way. Contributions under Agenda items 2 and 3 may be made both in the Plenary and in the SWBs.
5. Subsidiary Working Bodies A, B, C and D will be set up and will deal with Agenda item 4, in the following manner:

   SWB A: Development and diversification of economic relations through practical measures regarding:
   - Business contacts
   - Working conditions for businesspeople
   - Economic and commercial information
   - Role of small and medium-sized enterprises

   SWB B: Industrial co-operation:
   Requirements for the establishment and operation, on a mutually advantageous basis, of joint ventures and other forms of industrial co-operation such as co-production, specialization and licensing:
   - Economic conditions and legal and administrative aspects
   - Investment-related matters
   - Marketing and product promotion

   SWB C: Co-operation in specific areas:
   - Energy and raw material saving techniques
   - Equipment for environmental protection
   - Techniques aimed at improving the quality of life
   - Agro-industry and food processing, including natural food production
   - Machinery for the production of durable and non-durable consumer goods
   - Urban development and town planning

SWB D: Monetary and financial aspects of commercial exchanges and industrial co-operation, such as:
- Currency convertibility and pricing, and their effects on international competition
- Financial instruments and other support facilities offered by the financial services sector.

6. The Plenary will decide upon working methods which may be required to deal with the specific topics of Agenda item 4 and with Agenda item 5.
7. Sessions of the Plenary and of the Subsidiary Working Bodies will be held according to the attached work programme.
8. The Chair at the opening and closing Plenary sessions will be taken by a representative of the host country. After the opening session, the Chair will be taken in daily rotation, in French alphabetical order, starting with a representative of Austria.
9. The Chair at the opening meetings of the SWBs will be taken by a representative of the host country. Selection of the next Chairman will be by lot. The Chair will then be taken in daily rotation among the representatives of the participating States in French alphabetical order.
10. In conformity with paragraph 74 of the Final Recommendations of the Helsinki Consultations, the Government of the Federal Republic of Germany will designate an Executive Secretary. This designation will be subject to approval by the participating States.
11. The other rules of procedure, the working methods and the scale of distribution of expenses of the CSCE will, *mutatis mutandis*, be applied to the Conference.

MEETING ON THE PROTECTION OF THE ENVIRONMENT

A. Agenda

1. Formal opening of the Meeting. Address by a representative of the host country.
2. Opening statements by representatives of the participating States.
3. Contributions by the Economic Commission for Europe (ECE), the United Nations Environment Programme (UNEP) and the International Union for Conservation of Nature and Natural Resources (IUCN).
4. Review of the work already done, or currently under way, in the fields of:
   (a) prevention and control of the transboundary effects of industrial accidents;
   (b) management of potentially hazardous chemicals;
   (c) pollution of transboundary watercourses and international lakes.
5. In the light of Agenda item 4, examination of possibilities for further measures and co-operation, including improved exchange of information. The discussion will focus on legal, practical, technical and technological aspects, as well as on educational matters and public awareness.
6. Drawing up of conclusions and recommendations.
7. Closing statements.
8. Formal closure.

B. Organizational framework and other modalities

1. The Meeting will open on 16 October 1989 at 10.30 a.m., in Sofia. It will close on 3 November 1989.
2. The ECE, UNEP and IUCN will be invited to attend the Meeting.
3. All Plenary meetings will be open.
4. Agenda items 1, 2, 3, 4, 6, 7 and 8 will be dealt with in the Plenary.
5. Agenda item 5 will be dealt with in the Plenary and in two Subsidiary Working Bodies (SWBs), which will cover the fields mentioned in Agenda item 4, in a balanced and structured way, as follows:
   - a general debate, including an exchange of views on educational matters and public awareness, will be held in the Plenary to initiate the work of the Subsidiary Working Bodies;
   - SWB I will deal with the legal, administrative and practical aspects of issues such as liability and restoration, systems of alert, assistance upon request, preventive measures, information flows and consultations;

- SWB II will deal with the scientific, technical and technological aspects of issues such as preventive measures, risk assessment, assessment of damage, clean-up, measurement and monitoring;
- the SWBs I and II will submit their reports to the Plenary.

6. The timetable of the Meeting will be the following:
   - from 16 to 19 October 1989 the Plenary will deal with Agenda items 1, 2, 3, 4 and the general debate related to Agenda item 5;
   - from 19 October to 1 November 1989 the two SWBs will meet to deal with Agenda item 5;
   - from 1 to 3 November 1989 the Plenary will consider reports by the SWBs and on this basis draw up conclusions and recommendations in the three fields listed in Agenda item 4, as provided for under Agenda item 6.
7. Prior to the Meeting, the participating States and international organizations attending are invited to circulate written contributions, through diplomatic channels or through the Executive Secretary, to all participating States in order to allow thorough preparation of the Meeting.
8. Meetings of the Plenary and the SWBs will be held according to the attached work programme.
9. The Chair at the opening and closing Plenary meetings will be taken by a representative of the host country. After the opening meeting, the Chair will be taken in daily rotation, in French alphabetical order starting with a representative of Turkey.
10. The Chair at the opening meetings of the SWBs will be taken by a representative of the host country. Selection of the next Chairman will be by lot. The Chair will then be taken in daily rotation among the representatives of the participating States in French alphabetical order.
11. In conformity with paragraph 74 of the Final Recommendations of the Helsinki Consultations, the Government of the host country will designate an Executive Secretary. This designation will be subject to approval by the participating States.
12. The other rules of procedure, the working methods and the scale of distribution of the expenses of the CSCE will, *mutatis mutandis*, be applied to the Meeting.

ANNEX VII

MEETING ON THE MEDITERRANEAN

I. Agenda

1. Formal opening of the Meeting. Address by a representative of the host country.
2. Opening statements by representatives of the participating States, the non-participating Mediterranean States, and the international organizations invited; opening statements should, as a rule, not exceed 15 minutes per delegation.
3. Exchange of views on issues raised in opening statements, taking into consideration the provisions of the Mediterranean chapters of the Final Act and the Madrid Concluding Document, and review of the existing practice of contacts and co-operation with the non-participating Mediterranean States.
4. Specific aspects of co-operation:
   - examination of the opportunities offered to contribute to the faster social and economic development of the countries of the region, in particular those which are developing from an economic point of view;
   - examination of possibilities for the harmonization of statistical methods;
   - encouragement of contacts at various levels (expert meetings, round tables, study visits) with a view to contributing to the implementation of concrete programmes for co-operation;
   - co-operation in the field of solar and wind energy;
   - consideration of questions relating to the conservation and restoration of historic centres and the preservation of cultural heritage including marine archaeology;
5. Protection of Mediterranean ecosystems:
   - urban, agricultural and industrial water uses and requirements in the Mediterranean countries;
   - pollution of surface and underground water and of the Mediterranean Sea;
   - national, bilateral and international action to control and prevent pollution by national and transboundary waterways flowing into the Mediterranean and pollution by ships;
   - recycling of waste water and the use of other new technologies to obtain water resources;
   - desertification and the struggle against it, including parameters and techniques; initiatives in international co-operation in this field; the role of forest conservation and reforestation;

- international co-operation in the Mediterranean in preventing and extinguishing forest fires; the role of meteorology and communication networks; traditional and other techniques in the struggle against forest fires, including the use and international co-ordination of aerial means, land techniques, and standardization of fire-fighting methods; information and awareness campaigns;
- atmospheric problems, in particular air quality in urban centres and the effects of air pollution on historical monuments and biological ecosystems; typical sources of air pollution in Mediterranean countries and Mediterranean share in long-range air pollution;
- the biosphere and related questions of ecology and human activities; nature conservation; study of coastal and island areas including urban development;
- environmental aspects of the development of tourism;
- review and improvement of exchanges of information relating to the protection of the environment.

6. Elaboration and adoption of the report of the Meeting, including conclusions and recommendations based on the reports of the Subsidiary Working Bodies.
7. Closing statements, address by a representative of the host country and formal closure of the Meeting.

II. Organizational framework and other modalities

1. The Meeting will open on Monday, 24 September 1990, at 3 p.m., in Palma de Mallorca; it will close not later than Friday, 19 October 1990.
2. Agenda items 1, 2, 3 and 7 will be dealt with in open Plenary.
3. Agenda item 6 will be dealt with in closed Plenary by the participating States.
4. Agenda item 4 will be dealt with in Subsidiary Working Body (SWB) I.
5. Agenda item 5 will be dealt with in SWB II.
6. The timetable of the Meeting will be the following:
   - from Monday, 24 September to Wednesday, 26 September, the Plenary will deal with Agenda items 1 and 2;
   - on Thursday, 27 September and Friday, 28 September, the Plenary will deal with Agenda item 3;
   - from Monday, 1 October, to Tuesday, 16 October, the two SWBs will meet alternately to deal with Agenda items 4 and 5;

- Tuesday, 16 October, will be devoted to the adoption of reports by the SWBs for submission to the Plenary;
- on Wednesday, 17 October, and Thursday, 18 October, the Plenary will deal with Agenda item 6;
- on Friday, 19 October, the Plenary will deal with Agenda item 7.

7. Meetings of the Plenary and of the SWBs will be held according to the work programme set forth on page 5 of this Annex.
8. Participants may circulate written contributions prior to the Meeting through diplomatic channels or through the Executive Secretary to all other participating States in order to allow a thorough preparation of the Meeting.
9. The Chair at the opening and closing Plenary meetings will be taken by a representative of the host country. After the opening meeting, the Chair will be taken in daily rotation among the representatives of the participating States, in French alphabetical order, starting with a representative of Italy.
10. The Chair at the opening meetings of the SWBs will be taken by a representative of the host country. Selection of the next Chairman will be by lot. The Chair will then be taken in daily rotation among the representatives of the participating States in French alphabetical order.
11. Opening statements under Agenda item 2 will be made in the following order: Liechtenstein, Cyprus, the United States of America, Italy, Norway, Bulgaria, the Netherlands, Turkey, the Holy See, the Union of Soviet Socialist Republics, Canada, Austria, Finland, Luxembourg, Malta, Belgium, Romania, the German Democratic Republic, Iceland, France, the Federal Republic of Germany, Sweden, Yugoslavia, Spain, Hungary, Denmark, Czechoslovakia, San Marino, the United Kingdom, Monaco, Ireland, Greece, Portugal, Switzerland, Poland.
12. In conformity with paragraph 74 of the Final Recommendations of the Helsinki Consultations, the Government of Spain will designate an Executive Secretary. This designation will be subject to the agreement of the participating States.
13. The other rules of procedure, the working methods, and the scale of distribution of the expenses of the CSCE will, *mutatis mutandis*, be applied to the Meeting.

ANNEX VIII

AGENDA, TIMETABLE AND OTHER ORGANIZATIONAL MODALITIES OF THE INFORMATION FORUM

I. Agenda

1. Formal opening of the Information Forum. Address by a representative of the host country.
2. Opening statements by representatives of the participating States; contributions by UNESCO and by the International Telecommunication Union (ITU).
3. Discussion of current and possible future problems and issues concerning
   - the improvement of the circulation of, access to and exchange of information;
   - co-operation in the field of information;
   - the improvement of working conditions for journalists.

   In dealing with these three main areas of the Final Act, the participants in the Information Forum, drawing on their professional experience, will review the present situation on the basis of the relevant CSCE provisions with the aim of indicating any necessary improvements or possible new developments in those fields. In so doing they will take into account the fields of oral information, printed information and filmed and broadcast information, as well as the aim, as laid down in the Final Act, to facilitate the freer and wider dissemination of information of all kinds, thus contributing to an ever wider knowledge and understanding of life in other participating States. Particular attention will also be paid to the latest achievements in the field of information gathering and transmission, including the prospects offered by new information and communication technology.
4. Closing statements by representatives of the participating States.
5. Formal closure of the Information Forum.

II. Timetable and other organizational modalities

1. The Information Forum will open on Tuesday, 18 April 1989, at 10.30 a.m., in London. It will close on Friday, 12 May 1989.
2. All Plenary meetings will be open.
3. Agenda items 1, 2, 4 and 5 will be dealt with in the Plenary.
4. Agenda item 3 will be dealt with in three Subsidiary Working Bodies, one on Printed Information (SWB A), one on Filmed, Broadcast and Oral Information (SWB B) and one on Communication (SWB C), in a structured and balanced way. Possible themes for discussion in the Subsidiary Working Bodies are set out below. Agenda item 3 will also

be dealt with in the Plenary sessions which are not devoted to Agenda items 1, 2, 4 and 5.

5. The timetable of the Forum will be the following:
   - The first three days will be devoted, as required, to opening statements by representatives of those participating States which so desire and to the contributions by UNESCO and by ITU. The opening statements should, as a rule, not exceed 20 minutes per delegation and will be held in the following order: the German Democratic Republic, Iceland, Luxembourg, Finland, Greece, Belgium, Portugal, Spain, Italy, the Holy See, Bulgaria, the Netherlands, France, Malta, Czechoslovakia, Ireland, the United Kingdom, Turkey, Denmark, San Marino, Norway, the Union of Soviet Socialist Republics, Romania, Switzerland, Austria, Canada, the United States of America, Yugoslavia, Liechtenstein, the Federal Republic of Germany, Poland, Hungary, Cyprus, Sweden, Monaco.
   - Beginning on Friday, 21 April and ending on Monday, 8 May, the three Subsidiary Working Bodies will meet concurrently.
   - Agenda items 4 and 5 shall be dealt with on the last three days of the Forum.
6. Participants may circulate written contributions on the subjects for consideration in one or more of the working languages of the CSCE prior to the Forum through the Executive Secretary to all other participating States in order to allow a thorough preparation of the relevant discussions.
7. If the Forum does not reach any agreed conclusions, proposals and projects submitted to the Forum will be forwarded to the next Follow-up Meeting by the Government of the host country.
8. Meetings of the Plenary and of the Subsidiary Working Bodies will be held according to the attached work programme.
9. At the opening and closing Plenary sessions, the Chair will be taken by a representative of the host country. After the opening session, the Chair will be taken in daily rotation, in French alphabetical order, starting with a representative of Sweden.
10. The Chair at the opening sessions of the Subsidiary Working Bodies will be taken by a representative of the host country. Selection of the next Chairman of each Subsidiary Working Body will be by lot. The Chair will then be taken in daily rotation in French alphabetical order.
11. In conformity with paragraph 74 of the Final Recommendations of the Helsinki Consultations, the Government of the United Kingdom will designate an Executive Secretary. This designation will be subject to approval by the participating States.

12. The other rules of procedure, the working methods and the scale of distribution of the expenses of the CSCE will, *mutatis mutandis*, be applied to the Forum.

III. Indicative list of themes for discussion in the subsidiary working bodies

SWB A: *Printed Information* with particular reference to

- Distribution of periodicals and other publications both commercially published and official, questions relating to the import of publications.
- Access to periodicals and other publications, e.g. in reading rooms and cultural information centres.
- Questions relating to printing and publishing including access to technical means.
- Contacts and exchanges between newspapers and periodicals, exchange of newspaper subscriptions.

SWB B: *Filmed, Broadcast and Oral Information* with particular reference to

- Access to new means of communication, including satellite and other cross-frontier broadcasting.
- Contacts and exchanges between broadcasting companies, e.g. telebridges, joint discussion or other programmes.
- Dissemination and use of recorded audio-visual material.
- Participation in international discussion fora.
- Public lectures, exchanges of study visits between officials and non-governmental organizations.
- Press conferences.

SWB A and SWB B

Both SWBs will also deal with general considerations concerning the exercise of the profession of journalists, in particular the improvement of working conditions for journalists and media personnel, including

- The role of journalists in all its aspects.
- Facilitation of travel.
- Facilitation of access to sources.
- Respect for confidentiality of sources and materials.
- Visas/accreditation for journalists and radio/television crews.
- Possibilities for accredited correspondents to employ local nationals of their choice.

SWB C: *Communication* with particular reference to

- The impact on a national and international level of new production techniques and broadcasting technologies such as

satellite and cable TV, telecommunications technology, use of computers, new telephonic communication.
- The legal, pedagogical, cultural and social implications of current and future developments in the field of communication.
- Role of journalists in the context of such developments.
- Questions of copyright of journalists, commercial aspects.

ANNEX IX

AGENDA, TIMETABLE AND OTHER ORGANIZATIONAL MODALITIES OF THE SYMPOSIUM ON THE CULTURAL HERITAGE

I. Agenda

1. Formal opening of the Symposium. Address by a representative of the host country.
2. Introductory statements by representatives of the participating States; contribution by UNESCO.
3. Discussion of common features of the cultural heritage of the peoples of the participating States, with due attention to the originality and diversity of their respective cultures; consideration of:
   (a) scope and measures necessary for increasing awareness and expanding mutual knowledge of this heritage;
   (b) scope for improving, *inter alia* through co-operation and joint efforts, the protection and preservation of this heritage, including historical, cultural and religious monuments and objects.

   In dealing with these items, the participants in the Symposium will review the implementation of the relevant CSCE provisions, thus facilitating the identification of the scope for further action in these fields.
4. Closing statements and summing up of the results of the Symposium.
5. Formal closure of the Symposium.

II. Timetable and other organizational modalities

1. The Symposium will open on Tuesday, 28 May 1991, at 10.30 a.m., in Cracow. It will close on Friday, 7 June 1991.
2. All Plenary meetings will be open.
3. Under the guidance of the Plenary, Study Group A, devoted to questions related to increasing the awareness of the cultural heritage, will deal with Agenda item 3(a) and Study Group B, devoted to the discussion of the protection and preservation of the cultural heritage, will deal with Agenda item 3(b).

   Under Agenda item 3(a), Study Group A will discuss in particular
   - sources and manifestations of the cultural heritage of the peoples of the participating States, including its contemporary aspects, and access to them;
   - interrelationship between regional and other features of the cultural heritage;
   - role of the sciences and humanities.

   Under Agenda item 3(b), Study Group B will discuss in particular

- implementation of co-operation programmes;
- preservation of the cultural heritage, including socio-economic aspects, and its interrelationship with the protection of the environment;
- use of modern technical methods and means in the preservation of the cultural heritage and in the dissemination of knowledge about it.

Both Study Group A and Study Group B will further deal with:

- scope for expanding contacts, communications and exchanges of information between institutions, experts and other interested persons in the field of culture;
- scope for creation, dissemination and co-operation.

4. The first one-and-a-half days of the Symposium will be devoted to Plenary meetings on Agenda items 1, 2 and 3. Introductory statements, as a rule, should not exceed 20 minutes per delegation and will be held in the following order: Poland, Spain, Norway, Hungary, the Federal Republic of Germany, San Marino, Portugal, Turkey, Ireland, Bulgaria, Austria, Monaco, Yugoslavia, Malta, Denmark, the United Kingdom, Belgium, Canada, Switzerland, Cyprus, France, the Holy See, Romania, Liechtenstein, Italy, the Netherlands, the German Democratic Republic, Finland, Greece, Luxembourg, Sweden, Iceland, Czechoslovakia, the Union of Soviet Socialist Republics, the United States of America.

   The last one-and-a-half days will be devoted to Plenary meetings on Agenda items 3, 4 and 5.

   The Symposium will proceed according to the attached work programme.

5. The Chair at the opening and closing meetings will be taken by a representative of the host country. After the opening Plenary meeting, the Chair at the Plenary meetings will be taken in daily rotation, in French alphabetical order, starting with a representative of Bulgaria.

   The Chair at the opening sessions of the two Study Groups will be taken by a representative of the host country. Selection of the next Chairman of each Study Group will be by lot. The Chair will then be taken in daily rotation, in French alphabetical order.

6. In conformity with paragraph 74 of the Final Recommendations of the Helsinki Consultations, the Government of Poland will designate an Executive Secretary. This designation will be subject to agreement by the participating States. The services of a technical secretariat will be provided by the host country.

7. Contributions on the subjects for consideration in one or more of the working languages of the CSCE may be sent through the proper channels - preferably not later than three months before the opening of

the Symposium - to the Executive Secretary, who will circulate them to the other participating States and to UNESCO.

8. If the Symposium does not reach any agreed conclusions, projects and proposals submitted to it will be forwarded by the Government of the host country to the next Follow-up Meeting.

9. The other rules of procedure, the working methods and the scale of distribution of the expenses of the CSCE will, *mutatis mutandis*, be applied to the Symposium.

ANNEX X

AGENDA, TIMETABLE AND OTHER ORGANIZATIONAL MODALITIES OF THE MEETINGS OF THE CONFERENCE ON THE HUMAN DIMENSION OF THE CSCE

I. Agenda

1. Formal opening. Address by a representative of the host country.
2. Opening statements by the representatives of the participating States.
3. Exchange of views on the situation in the participating States with regard to respect for all human rights and fundamental freedoms, human contacts and other issues of a related humanitarian character, including the implementation of relevant CSCE commitments.
4. Evaluation of the functioning of the procedures described in paragraphs 1 to 4 and discussion of the information provided according to paragraph 4 of the section dealing with the human dimension of the CSCE in the present Concluding Document.
5. Presentation and consideration of practical proposals for new measures aimed at improving implementation of commitments and co-operation in the human dimension of the CSCE and at enhancing the effectiveness of the above-mentioned procedures.
6. Closing statements by the representatives of the participating States.
7. Formal closure of the Meeting.

II. Timetable and other organizational modalities

1. The first Meeting of the Conference will open on 30 May 1989 at 10.30 a.m., in Paris. It will close on 23 June 1989.
   The second Meeting of the Conference will open on 5 June 1990 at 10.30 a.m., in Copenhagen. It will close on 29 June 1990.
   The third Meeting of the Conference will open on 10 September 1991 at 10.30 a.m., in Moscow. It will close on 4 October 1991.
2. Agenda items 1, 2, 3, 6 and 7 will be dealt with in Plenary meetings.
3. Agenda items 4 and 5 will be dealt with in Plenary meetings and in Subsidiary Working Bodies:
   Agenda item 4 will be dealt with in Subsidiary Working Body A;
   Agenda item 5 will be dealt with in Subsidiary Working Body B.
4. The meetings of the Plenary will be open unless otherwise decided. The meetings of the Subsidiary Working Bodies will be closed.
5. If it so decides in the Plenary, each Meeting may, on the basis of proposals introduced, consider elaborating and adopting new measures to be implemented upon closure of that Meeting.
6. The Chair at the opening and closing Plenary meetings of each Meeting of the Conference will be taken by a representative of the host

country. At the other Plenary meetings, the Chair will be taken in daily rotation, in French alphabetical order, starting at the first Meeting with a representative of the Netherlands and continuing at the two subsequent Meetings of the Conference.

7. Opening statements under Agenda item 2 will be made in the following order:
   - at the first Meeting: Liechtenstein, France, the German Democratic Republic, Norway, Italy, Malta, the Netherlands, Belgium, Switzerland, Bulgaria, Cyprus, the Union of Soviet Socialist Republics, Poland, Portugal, Turkey, Denmark, Iceland, Hungary, the Federal Republic of Germany, Czechoslovakia, Spain, Sweden, Ireland, the Holy See, Yugoslavia, Finland, Austria, Monaco, Canada, the United Kingdom, Romania, Greece, the United States of America, Luxembourg, San Marino
   - at the second Meeting: San Marino, Greece, Monaco, the Union of Soviet Socialist Republics, Yugoslavia, Czechoslovakia, Belgium, Turkey, Bulgaria, Cyprus, Switzerland, Iceland, the Netherlands, Finland, Luxembourg, Poland, Hungary, the United States of America, Canada, Norway, Portugal, Malta, Ireland, the Holy See, Spain, France, Sweden, the German Democratic Republic, Romania, Italy, the United Kingdom, Denmark, Austria, the Federal Republic of Germany, Liechtenstein
   - at the third Meeting: Luxembourg, Greece, Canada, Belgium, San Marino, the Union of Soviet Socialist Republics, Hungary, Iceland, the German Democratic Republic, Ireland, Bulgaria, Yugoslavia, the United Kingdom, the Netherlands, Denmark, Malta, Sweden, Monaco, Czechoslovakia, Portugal, Poland, Austria, Cyprus, Switzerland, the Holy See, the United States of America, Spain, Italy, Liechtenstein, France, the Federal Republic of Germany, Turkey, Finland, Romania, Norway

   The statements, as a rule, should not exceed 20 minutes per speaker.

8. In conformity with paragraph 74 of the Final Recommendations of the Helsinki Consultations, the Governments of France, Denmark, and the Union of Soviet Socialist Republics will designate the Executive Secretary of the respective Meeting. This designation will be subject to agreement by the participating States.

9. The other rules of procedure, the working methods and the scale of distribution of expenses of the CSCE will, *mutatis mutandis*, be applied to the Meetings of the Conference.

WORK PROGRAMME FOR THE FIRST MEETING OF THE CONFERENCE ON THE HUMAN DIMENSION OF THE CSCE

From 30 to 31 May 1989, the Plenary will deal with Agenda items 1 and 2.
From 1 June 1989, the Plenary will deal with Agenda items 3 and 4.
From 12 June 1989, the Plenary will deal with Agenda item 5.
From 22 to 23 June 1989, the Plenary will deal with Agenda items 6 and 7.
From 6 to 14 June 1989, Subsidiary Working Body A will deal with Agenda item 4.
From 13 to 21 June 1989, Subsidiary Working Body B will deal with Agenda item 5.

* * *

WORK PROGRAMME FOR THE SECOND MEETING OF THE CONFERENCE ON THE HUMAN DIMENSION OF THE CSCE

From 5 to 6 June 1990, the Plenary will deal with Agenda items 1 and 2.
From 7 June 1990, the Plenary will deal with Agenda items 3 and 4.
From 18 June 1990, the Plenary will deal with Agenda item 5.
From 28 to 29 June 1990, the Plenary will deal with Agenda items 6 and 7.
From 12 to 20 June 1990, Subsidiary Working Body A will deal with Agenda item 4.
From 19 to 27 June 1990, Subsidiary Working Body B will deal with Agenda item 5.

* * *

WORK PROGRAMME FOR THE THIRD MEETING OF THE CONFERENCE ON THE HUMAN DIMENSION OF THE CSCE

From 10 to 11 September 1991, the Plenary will deal with Agenda items 1 and 2.
From 12 September 1991, the Plenary will deal with Agenda items 3 and 4.
From 23 September 1991, the Plenary will deal with Agenda item 5.
From 3 to 4 October 1991, the Plenary will deal with Agenda items 6 and 7.
From 17 to 25 September 1991, Subsidiary Working Body A will deal with Agenda item 4.
From 24 September to 2 October 1991, Subsidiary Working Body B will deal with Agenda item 5.

ANNEX XI

CHAIRMAN'S STATEMENT ON THE OPENNESS AND ACCESS TO THE CSCE FOLLOW-UP MEETINGS MENTIONED IN THE VIENNA CONCLUDING DOCUMENT

The practices of openness and access to CSCE meetings based on the relevant provisions of the Final Act and applied by host countries have evolved in a positive way. These practices relate *inter alia* to access to the host State, to the venue and to open sessions of CSCE meetings for representatives of the media, representatives of non-governmental organizations or religious groups, and private individuals, both nationals and foreigners; unimpeded contacts between delegates or visitors and citizens of the host State; respect for CSCE-related activities, including the holding of peaceful gatherings, and for the freedom of journalists to report without hindrance as well as to pursue their professional activity in conformity with CSCE commitments. In the light of that experience, all participating States understand that Governments of host countries for the CSCE Follow-up Meetings mentioned in the Vienna Concluding Document will follow and build upon these practices as they were most recently applied at the Vienna Meeting.

RESERVATIONS AND INTERPRETATIVE STATEMENTS[1]

In the morning session of the 162nd Plenary Meeting on 15 January 1989 the following reservations and interpretative statements were made:

(a) The delegation of Romania made the following statement:

"Romania has taken part in the work of the Vienna Meeting organized as a follow-up to the Conference on Security and Co-operation in Europe, animated by the desire to make its contribution to the strengthening of confidence, security and co-operation in our continent, in order to give a new perspective to relations between the European countries in the spirit of, and in conformity with, the Helsinki Final Act. These relations must be founded on the principles of full equality of rights, respect for national independence and sovereignty, non-interference in internal affairs, and mutual advantage, and of the right of each people to decide independently on the path it takes for economic and social development.

With regard to the Concluding Document of the Meeting, the delegation of the Socialist Republic of Romania is authorized to make the following statement:

On the whole, the Concluding Document contains important provisions, the implementation of which will be able to contribute to better understanding and co-operation between our peoples and to strengthening confidence, peace and security in our continent and the whole world. In particular, Romania emphasizes the importance of the provisions of the Concluding Document concerning negotiations on the reduction of armed forces and conventional arms and considers that the latter should be carried on between independent and sovereign States, on the basis of full equality, in the framework of the CSCE process, adhering to the latter's democratic rules of procedure. We consider that it is necessary that all the European States be able to participate in these negotiations and that the measures agreed upon should take due account of the security interests of all these States.

Romania also considers that the Concluding Document, as regards the development of co-operation in the field of economics, of science and technology, the prevention of pollution and the protection of the environment, contains acceptable provisions although, in our opinion, they could have been even more binding and supported to a larger extent by the great achievements of science, knowledge and culture, in view of the level that has been reached in the development of productive forces.

---

[1] Journal No. 397, 162nd Plenary Meeting (Vienna, 15 January 1989).

As far as human rights are concerned, the Concluding Document of the Meeting contains a number of important provisions with which Romania is in agreement.

It is, however, regrettable that this document should not have incorporated, in an appropriate manner and as a firm commitment by States, certain proposals by Romania concerning a number of fundamental principles of human rights and humanitarian problems, such as: the commitment of the States to ensure employment for every citizen of their countries and the elimination of unemployment; vocational training, education and guaranteed employment and dignified living conditions for young people; the right to equal pay for equal work; the establishment of appropriate housing conditions for each family; wide access by the entire population to the achievements of modern science and technology; the guarantee of dignified and civilized living conditions for all citizens.

At the same time we note that - on the pretext of concern for human rights and religious freedom - provisions have been introduced and maintained in the Concluding Document that are not in conformity with the principles and spirit of the Helsinki Final Act or with the realities of the age in which we live, and that are not in agreement with the international norms and regulations to which the States have acceded. Such provisions may open the way to interference in the internal affairs of other States and to the violation of national independence and sovereignty, and can stimulate and encourage activities and manifestations of obscurantism that are retrograde. Similarly, provisions have been retained in it that in fact are capable of stimulating emigration and encouraging the brain-drain, harming the economic and social development interests of the peoples, primarily those that are less developed.

Romania has, during the work of the Meeting, submitted its observations and reservations, chapter by chapter, indicating in a concrete manner what were the problems for which an appropriate solution had not been found in the Document; they are observations and reservations that we still maintain.

In view of all the above, the Romanian delegation states that Romania assumes no commitment to implement those among the provisions of the Concluding Document regarding which it has presented observations and reservations that have not been accepted - provisions that it considers to be inadequate.

However, seeing that, on the whole, the Document contains important provisions aimed at strengthening security and developing co-operation in Europe, and on the basis of its desire to make its contribution to efforts designed to promote in the future the objectives to which our States have subscribed, the Romanian delegation is authorized to associate itself - subject to the reservations mentioned - with the consensus for the adoption of the Draft Concluding Document.

Romania reaffirms its position, which was also expressed in the course of our deliberations, that all the provisions of this Document should - as stated in the Document itself - be implemented in the constitutional framework of the internal legislation and regulations of each country, of its traditions and special conditions and, at the same time, in a spirit of co-operation and strict observance of the principles guiding relations between the participating States.

Romania has ensured and continues to ensure in a practical manner, in day-to-day life, the full exercise of the fundamental human rights and freedoms which are enshrined in the very Constitution of the country, and creates all the conditions needed to ensure that all citizens enjoy those rights and freedoms without any distinction, in a broad framework of real democracy that gives the entire people the possibility of participating directly in the management of all sectors of the economic and social life of the entire society.

Romania will make every effort to contribute, in the future also, to the development of co-operation and the strengthening of confidence and security in our continent, for a united Europe within the diversity of social systems, a Europe of free independent and sovereign States and of economic and social progress, co-operation and peace, with an ever more important role in the general development of the present-day world.

The Romanian delegation requests the Executive Secretary to take the necessary action, in conformity with Article 79 of the Rules of Procedure, to ensure that the present declaration is registered and circulated to the participating States as an interpretative statement of reservations concerning the acceptance as a whole of the Concluding Document of the Vienna Meeting."

(b) The delegation of the United Kingdom made the following statement:

"On behalf of the Governments of the United Kingdom, the United States of America and France, I wish to state that the points of agreement which have emerged at the Vienna talks in respect of the mandates for the Negotiation on Conventional Armed Forces in Europe and for the Negotiations on Confidence- and Security-building Measures do not and cannot in any way affect the Quadripartite rights and responsibilities relating to Berlin and Germany as a whole. I request that this statement be entered in the Journal of the Day."

(c) The delegation of the Union of Soviet Socialist Republics made the following statement:

"In connection with the statement by the delegation of the United Kingdom, the delegation of the Union of Soviet Socialist Republics states that it could only regard it as referring to the arrangements concerning the Negotiation on Conventional Armed Forces in Europe and the Negotiations on Confidence- and Security-building Measures in Europe.

In this sense, the delegation of the Union of Soviet Socialist Republics states that nothing in the aforementioned arrangements affects the rights and responsibilities of the Four Powers and the corresponding Quadripartite agreements, decisions and practices relating thereto, nor the rights and obligations of the participating States under the Charter of the United Nations and the treaties and agreements previously concluded by them.

With regard to the expression "Berlin and Germany as a whole" used in the statement by the delegation of the United Kingdom, the point of view of the Soviet Union on this subject is well known.

The delegation of the Union of Soviet Socialist Republics requests that this statement be entered in the Journal of the Day."

(d) The delegation of Poland made the following statement on behalf of the delegations of Bulgaria, Hungary, the German Democratic Republic, Poland, Romania, the Union of Soviet Socialist Republics and Czechoslovakia:

"In connection with the agreement, reflected in the appropriate subsection of the Concluding Document, on the holding in Vienna, commencing on 6 March 1989, of negotiations on confidence- and security-building measures in order to build upon and expand the results achieved at the Stockholm Conference, and also with the aim of elaborating and adopting a new set of mutually complementary confidence- and security-building measures, the delegation of Poland, on behalf of the delegations of Bulgaria, Hungary, the German Democratic Republic, Poland, Romania, the Union of Soviet Socialist Republics and Czechoslovakia, would like to state that the aforementioned States reaffirm their intention of raising in these negotiations questions regarding notification of independent manoeuvres of air and naval forces, limitation of the scale of military activities and also, in the future, coverage by notifications of the territories of all the participating States of the CSCE."

(e) The delegation of Denmark made the following statement:

"In connection with the remarks of the distinguished representative of Poland, I should like to state, on behalf of the sixteen delegations which introduced

WT.129, that the future negotiations on CSBMs will take place on the basis of the Madrid mandate. Our interpretation of this mandate regarding the subjects referred to by the distinguished representative of Poland has been made clear on several occasions in the course of the work of the Stockholm Conference and this Meeting.

I request that this statement be entered into the Journal of the Day."

* * *

In the afternoon session of the 162nd Plenary Meeting on 15 January 1989 the following reservations and interpretative statements were made:

(a) The delegation of Switzerland made the following statement:

"The Swiss Government recalls the interpretative statement made by its delegation at the Stockholm Conference and reproduced in the revised version of Journal No. 379 of the 178th Plenary meeting dated 19 September 1989, which statement it still maintains.

Depending on the possible results of the efforts in the field of confidence- and security-building measures and disarmament within the framework of the CSCE process, the Swiss Government reserves the right to reaffirm in due course and in an appropriate manner the validity of the above-mentioned statement."

(b) The delegation of Portugal made the following statement:

"The death penalty was abolished in Portugal in the last century. The 1976 Constitution of the Portuguese Republic prohibits the death penalty and extradition to a State in which the offence is punished by the death penalty.

It is for that reason that the Portuguese delegation must make the following reservation, which is identical with that formulated by my country to the European Convention on the suppression of terrorism. This reservation concerns paragraph 10.5 of the section on principles, on page 8 of the Concluding Document of the Vienna Meeting:

> 'Portugal cannot accept requests for extradition when the offences are punished by the death penalty or by penalties or security measures involving perpetual imprisonment in the requesting State.'[2]"

[2] Unofficial translation

(c) The delegation of Canada made the following statement:

"With respect to the statement made earlier in this meeting by the distinguished representative of Romania, the delegation of Canada wishes to draw attention to Rule 4 of the Rules of Procedure, which states as follows:

> '4. Decisions of the Conference shall be taken by consensus. Consensus shall be understood to mean the absence of any objection expressed by a Representative and submitted by him as constituting an obstacle to the taking of the decision in question.'

The Conference has now adopted by consensus the Concluding Document of the Vienna Meeting. The Canadian delegation considers that, in accordance with the practice and procedures of the Helsinki Final Act, and the Helsinki process as a whole, all provisions of the document are equally binding on all participating States.

I also request that, in accordance with paragraph 79 of the Rules of Procedure, this interpretative statement be duly registered by the Executive Secretary and circulated to the participating States by including in the Journal of the Day for this Plenary meeting."

(d) The delegation of Turkey made the following statement:

"On behalf of the delegation of Turkey, I would like to make the following statement regarding the Chapter of the Concluding Document on Follow-up to the Conference.

My delegation is among those who had reservations on increasing the number of follow-up meetings. We still believe that this number could have been reduced significantly if possibilities offered by other European fora were fully utilized.

A related aspect which I would like to dwell upon briefly is the relationship of those meetings with the CSCE process itself. It is the common understanding that they are not simply technical meetings which have to be assessed on their own merits, but they all have a political character, being part of the process.

In this context I would like to cite the follow-up Meeting on the Protection of the Environment which is going to be hosted by the Government of Bulgaria. As my delegation has on several occasions stated clearly, we are still unhappy, to say the least, about the way the Turkish Muslim minority in this participating State is treated and about the unforthcoming attitude adopted by the Bulgarian authorities on thousands of specific cases of family reunification, especially of minor children.

It is our sincere hope that in view of the provisions of the Concluding Document which we have adopted today this attitude will change and all outstanding cases will be solved in the meantime. Otherwise, my Government will face a strong opposition at home while taking its decision for sending a delegation to Sofia. My Government cannot ignore such an opposition. We would therefore urge the interested delegation to take into consideration the risks of such a situation, a situation which can easily be avoided if necessary steps are taken by their authorities.

I would also like to add that the degree of access to be achieved there in accordance with the standards set by the Vienna and other meetings will also have a bearing in that respect."

(e) The delegation of Bulgaria made the following statement:

"In connection with the statement by the delegation of Turkey, the delegation of the People's Republic of Bulgaria states the following:

1. As has been repeatedly stated in the past, there neither is nor has been in Bulgaria a Turkish national minority, and we therefore consider the statement by the Turkish delegation at today's Plenary meeting irrelevant.

2. Any actions that violate the rule of consensus and conflict with decisions already adopted in the CSCE will create a serious precedent and tend to undermine future events in the framework of the all-European process. The entire responsibility in such cases will rest with the State taking such a step.

3. The People's Republic of Bulgaria will do everything possible to ensure the necessary conditions for the successful holding of the Meeting on the Protection of the Environment in Sofia in 1989, in accordance with the generally accepted standards of the CSCE and with the Concluding Document of the Vienna Meeting.

We shall regard actions aimed at undermining the Sofia Meeting on the Protection of the Environment as indicating unwillingness to join in the all-European efforts for the protection of the environment. We shall also regard such actions as an evasion of the obligations already assumed in this sphere."

(f) The delegation of Austria made the following statement:

"The Austrian delegation, as the delegation of the country hosting the third CSCE Follow-up Meeting, expressed its gratification at the adoption of the Vienna Concluding Document by a consensus of all participating States.

With reference to the statement made by the Romanian delegation in today's Plenary meeting under Agenda item 8 and to statements by other delegations under Agenda item 9, the Austrian delegation associates itself with the statement of the Canadian delegation regarding the unrestricted politically binding nature of all provisions of the Vienna Concluding Document for all CSCE participating States."

Editor's note: After the revolution in Romania in December 1989, the new Romanian Government issued a statement concerning the withdrawal of its reservations and interpretative statements in relation to the Vienna Concluding Document. The Romanian delegation to the Negotiations on CSBMs in Vienna requested the Executive Secretary of these Negotiations to circulate this statement under paragraph 79 of the Final Recommendations of the Helsinki Consultations. The text of this statement - which was circulated on 15 January 1990 (CSCE/WV/Inf.14) - reads as follows:

STATEMENT

by the Ministry of Foreign Affairs of Romania

The victory of the revolution in Romania which led to the elimination of tyranny and the conquest of liberty is an event which represents an historic turning point for the Romanian people in the field of foreign policy as well.

Romania was and remains a European country. The Romanian people has always nourished the desire to develop friendly ties and co-operation with European countries, to which history and common civilization bound it so closely.

Voicing the will of the people for Romania's reconstruction and renewal, the Programme of the Council of the National Salvation Front provides that the foreign policy of the country should serve the promotion of good-neighbourliness, friendship and peace in the world, and should be integrated into the process aimed at building a united Europe, a Common Home for all peoples on the continent, through the observation by Romania of its international commitments.

Kept aside against its own will by the old regime from the process initiated by the Helsinki Final Act, the Romanian people, now free to decide on its destiny, is ready, in the new circumstances created by the establishment of a truly democratic society, to associate itself entirely with the all-European process.

The Ministry of Foreign Affairs is authorized to declare officially that Romania withdraws its "formal reservations and interpretative statements", presented on 15 January 1989 upon instruction by the old regime, in connection with the Concluding Document of the Vienna Meeting of the Conference on Security and Co-operation in Europe and confirms the acceptance by Romania of this Document in its entirety.

Romania will act towards the full implementation, in good faith, of all provisions of this Document and is determined to contribute, together with the other European States, to the establishment on the continent of a climate of peace and security, and of free co-operation among peoples in different fields.

Sergiu Celac
Minister of Foreign Affairs

REPORT ON THE PROTECTION OF THE ENVIRONMENT

REPORT ON CONCLUSIONS AND RECOMMENDATIONS OF THE MEETING ON THE PROTECTION OF THE ENVIRONMENT OF THE CONFERENCE ON THE SECURITY AND CO-OPERATION IN EUROPE[1]

Sofia 1989 - 1990

In accordance with the mandate of the Concluding Document of the Vienna Meeting of the representatives of the participating States of the Conference on Security and Co-operation in Europe, the Meeting on the Protection of the Environment took place in Sofia, Bulgaria, from 16 October to 3 November 1989.

During the formal opening of the Meeting on the Protection of the Environment, the participants were welcomed by Mr. Todor Zhivkov, President of the State Council of the People's Republic of Bulgaria. Opening

---

[1] Note of the editor: Adopted in Vienna on 5 November 1990 at an *ad hoc* meeting of the CSCE participating States (see also *supra* section 4.3.2. of the Introduction of the present book). The text adopted at the Vienna Meeting reads as follows:
"Ad hoc meeting in Vienna of representatives of the participating States of the CSCE on the adoption of the Report of the Sofia Meeting on the Protection of the Environment.
The representatives of Austria, Belgium, Bulgaria, Canada, Cyprus, the Czech and Slovak Federal Republic, Denmark, Finland, France, Germany, Greece, the Holy See, Hungary, Iceland, Ireland, Italy - European Community, Liechtenstein, Luxembourg, Malta, Monaco, the Netherlands, Norway, Poland, Portugal, Romania, San Marino, Spain, Sweden, Switzerland, Turkey, the Union of Soviet Socialist Republics, the United Kingdom, the United States of America and Yugoslavia,
Conscious of the new situation and of the development of security, stability and co-operation in Europe, and in the context of preparing a Summit Meeting in Paris,
Having taken into account document CSCE/SEM.36/Rev.1 of the Sofia Meeting on the Protection of the Environment and Journal No.2/Rev.1 of the Bonn Conference on Economic Co-operation in Europe,
Have adopted the attached Report on Conclusions and Recommendations of the Meeting on the Protection of the Environment of the Conference on Security and Co-operation in Europe.

Vienna, 5 November 1990"

statements were made by representatives of the participating States. The United Nations Economic Commission for Europe (ECE), the United Nations Environment Programme (UNEP) and the International Union for Conservation of Nature and Natural Resources (IUCN) made contributions to the Meeting.

The Meeting reviewed the work already done, or currently under way, in the fields of prevention and control of the transboundary effects of industrial accidents, management of potentially hazardous chemicals, and pollution of transboundary watercourses and international lakes, and examined possibilities for further measures and co-operation, including improved exchange of information.

A general debate in the Plenary included an exchange of views on items 4 and 5 of the agenda and on other relevant provisions of the Vienna Concluding Document.

Subsidiary Working Body I dealt with the legal, administrative and practical aspects of issues such as liability and restoration, systems of alert, assistance upon request, preventive measures, information flows and consultations.

Subsidiary Working Body II dealt with the scientific, technical and technological aspects of issues such as preventive measures, risk assessment, assessment of damage, clean-up, measurement and monitoring.

The participating States are aware of the opportunities, as they become apparent during the Meeting, for increased co-operation in the CSCE process, with regard to the protection of the environment. They reaffirm their will to strengthen their co-operation and intensify efforts aimed at protecting and improving the environment, bearing in mind the need to maintain and restore the ecological balance in air, water and soil. They also recall their commitment in the Vienna Concluding Document to acknowledge the importance of the contribution of persons and organizations dedicated to the protection and improvement of the environment, and to allow them to express their concerns. They reiterate their willingness to promote greater public awareness and understanding of environmental issues.

The participating States reaffirm their respect for the right of individuals, groups and organizations concerned with environmental issues to express freely their views, to associate with others, to peacefully assemble, as well as to obtain, publish and distribute information on these issues, without legal and administrative impediments inconsistent with the CSCE provisions. These individuals, groups and organizations have the right to participate in public debates on environmental issues, as well as to establish and maintain direct and independent contacts at national and international level.

The participating States will also encourage education and instruction on environmental protection, promote the reproduction, circulation and exchange of information and data, as well as of audiovisual and printed material, on environmental issues, and encourage public access to such information, data and material.

The participating States will also stimulate exchange of information and environmental data, and foster scientific and technological co-operation in order to prevent and reduce pollution.

On the basis of the discussions held during the Meeting, the participating States recommend

- that the ECE elaborate an international convention, code of practice or other appropriate legal instruments on the prevention and control of the transboundary effects of industrial accidents;

- the development of international exchange of information and the co-ordination of efforts in order to achieve closer harmonization concerning the management of hazardous chemicals;

- that the ECE elaborate a framework convention on the protection and use of transboundary watercourses and international lakes;

- the implementation of the above recommendations as soon as possible, bearing in mind that the results will be evaluated by the next Follow-up Meeting of the CSCE, to be held in Helsinki in 1992.

These recommendations are developed in parts I, II and III as follows:

I. Prevention and control of the transboundary effects of industrial accidents

The participating States recognize the importance of developing and applying commonly agreed policies and strategies for appropriate arrangements for the prevention of, and response to, industrial accidents, their consequences and their transboundary impact on man and the environment.

They give special emphasis to the reduction of the risk of accidents, thereby reducing or preventing their adverse transboundary effects; to increasing preparedness to control and cope with emergencies in a transboundary context; and to the examination of key elements for clean-up, restoration and liability.

They stress the importance of international co-operation, recognize the value of existing bilateral and multilateral agreements and take into account the work already done or currently under way by various international organizations, in particular the Process for Responding to Technological Accidents (APELL) developed by the United Nations Environment Programme (UNEP) and the Code of Conduct on Accidental Pollution of Transboundary Inland Waters of the United Nations Economic Commission for Europe (ECE) and the work done by the OECD as well as the work done by the European Community.

As a common objective they recognize the importance of establishing, or reinforcing, regional or subregional mechanisms for response, assistance and exchange of information in environmental emergencies. They emphasize the need for effective measures with a view to:

- limiting the frequency and severity of accidents caused by all industrial activities through better measures of prevention;

- preventing adverse effects from accidents through better land-use planning, and

- mitigating the consequences of accidents by developing adequate emergency plans.

In order to achieve these goals the participating States recommend:

- that the United Nations Economic Commission for Europe (ECE) elaborate an international convention, code of practice or other appropriate legal instruments which should be based essentially upon the objectives and principles mentioned below, avoiding redundancy and duplication of efforts and building upon work already under way in international organizations, and taking into account work achieved or in progress in other international fora, without prejudice to any existing or future bilateral or multilateral agreements, with due regard to the legislation and practices of participating States, recognizing that such legal instruments should provide for a high level of protection and safety, and develop, *inter alia*, a precise definition of the industrial activities to be covered;

- that the development of all appropriate measures of prevention, preparedness and response shall recognize the combined responsibilities of industry and competent authorities. In meeting them

  (i) full responsibility for safe industrial operation and for taking all appropriate measures to prevent accidents rests with the operator of the installation. This means that, *inter alia*, the operator has to implement the most appropriate technologies and measures to prevent accidents including on-site emergency planning, to ensure appropriate training facilities and managerial structures and to provide the public authorities with the necessary information to assess risks,

  (ii) the public authorities, with due regard to national legislation and practices, will take some combination of, amongst others, the following measures: setting safety objectives on the basis of a risk evaluation of the installation; applying a licensing system to certain installations; ensuring that, under land-use policies, a safe distance between the installation and the surrounding population is preserved; preparing off-site emergency plans;

- that consultation and exchange of information on the prevention and control of industrial accidents and their transboundary effects be facilitated, *inter alia*, by:

  (i) notifying each other of their initial points of contact for industrial accidents covering, as appropriate, regional and local authorities,

  (ii) establishing early warning systems and co-ordination on a bilateral and multilateral basis in order to ensure immediate notification of the competent authorities of the State likely to be affected, of the type and extent of an accident, and of its possible effects on man and the environment;

- that the potentially affected public be given adequate information, *inter alia*, on risks, safety measures, correct behaviour and protection measures and, whenever possible and appropriate, the opportunity to participate, by providing their views and concerns when decisions are being made by public authorities on prevention, preparedness and emergency planning;

- the development of bilateral and multilateral mechanisms for, and conditions of, mutual assistance, co-operation and co-ordination including emergency response for the implementation of measures to control the effects of industrial accidents including, *inter alia*, as appropriate, provision for appropriate privileges, immunities and facilities for the expeditious performance of assistance functions;

- the enhancement of scientific and technological co-operation, including the exchange of information on best available technologies, for improved environmental protection, industrial safety, and emergency response, including criteria for the monitoring and assessment of transboundary damage, and the promotion of research into less dangerous processes in order to limit environmental hazards;

- co-operation for the further development of on-site and off-site training;

- that the "polluter-pays" principle be applied to physical and juridical persons;

- the consideration of further appropriate ways and means of elaborating principles and guidelines on the nature and scope of liability;

- that disputes be settled peacefully in accordance with procedures to be established in conformity with international law.

II. Management of hazardous chemicals

The participating States agree on the need to facilitate international exchange of information and co-operation on chemicals. They recognize the effects of chemicals on human health and the environment as well as the effort to facilitate international trade of chemicals. They are also aware of the significance of international agreements and instruments with regard to the transboundary movement of hazardous waste, and for export notification on banned or severely restricted chemicals.

They will build upon the work of international organizations related to hazardous chemicals, in particular within the International Programme on Chemical Safety (IPCS), the UNEP International Register of Potentially Toxic Chemicals (IRPTC), the Food and Agriculture Organization of the United Nations (FAO) and the Economic Commission for Europe (ECE), and support the further development of their work. They will take into account the chemicals programmes of the European Community (EC), the

Council for Mutual Economic Assistance (CMEA) and the Organization for Economic Co-operation and Development (OECD).

In order to strengthen legal and institutional arrangements for the management of chemicals, at least the following elements will be taken into account by the participating States:

- to prevent danger to man and the environment, procedures enabling the identification of hazardous properties, in particular toxicological and ecotoxicological properties, of chemicals;

- a system for the classification and labelling of chemicals which may involve hazard to man or the environment;

- a notification procedure providing for the mandatory screening of new chemical substances for any hazardous properties;

- systematic investigation of chemicals already on the market, on the basis of priority criteria established with regard to the quantities produced, the suspected hazards, and the utilization of the substances concerned. This investigation would be most productively accomplished through co-operation between the countries involved;

- a comprehensive system for the control of hazardous chemicals, taking into account the risk of exposure, including substitution by non- or less hazardous chemicals and, if necessary, limitation or prohibition of their use;

- procedures to facilitate the international exchange of information on chemicals;

- procedures for the proper storage of chemicals to ensure the safety of man and the environment, including questions of location in order to minimize transboundary effects;

- further training in the field of toxicology and ecotoxicology and other relevant disciplines including an exchange of educational programmes.

International organizations with relevant experience and ongoing programmes will be invited to assist participating countries in implementing the above tasks and to co-ordinate efforts in a step-by-step approach, to achieve closer harmonization of legislation and existing practices with regard to chemicals on the basis of the most advanced systems of protection and management. The approach could contain *inter alia* the following elements:

- early and regular exchange of information on relevant national infrastructures, new legislation and regulations, scientific findings, monitoring and assessment procedures, etc.;

- harmonization of methods for chemicals testing and good laboratory practice to facilitate the mutual acceptance of data, and establishment of a minimum set of data for the assessment of chemicals;

- harmonization of classification and labelling systems for hazardous chemicals, especially for the purpose of facilitating the development of international trade and the protection of transit and importing countries;

- criteria for selection of chemicals for further assessment and management, taking into account *inter alia* the production volume, the suspected hazard and the utilization of chemicals;

- harmonization of notification procedures for new chemical substances, including identification of toxicological and ecotoxicological properties;

- recommendations for the substitution of hazardous chemicals by non-dangerous or less hazardous chemicals.

III. Pollution of transboundary watercourses and international lakes

The participating States agree on the need to define principles for a sustainable use of transboundary watercourses and international lakes as well as to elaborate arrangements to protect them from pollution. For this aim the participating States recommend that the ECE elaborate a framework convention, whereby existing bilateral and multilateral agreements on the protection and use of transboundary watercourses and international lakes, as well as ongoing activities and completed work in other fora, such as the ECE Senior Advisers on Environmental and Water Problems and the United Nations International Law Commission, should be taken into account. Such a framework convention should contain, in particular, the following elements:

Basic principles, such as:

- Pollution of transboundary watercourses and international lakes, contributing also to the pollution of seas, will be prevented or reduced with the aim of sustainable management, conservation of water resources and environmental protection.

- Effective prevention and pollution control measures will be applied at the source wherever possible.

- Regular consultations on issues of mutual interest and implementation of pollution abatement measures will be promoted.

- Warning and alarm systems and contingency plans will be introduced.

- With the aim of prevention, environmental impact assessment and other means of assessment will be developed, adopted and subsequently implemented.

- Water quality will be monitored and assessed and discharges of pollutants will be registered; methods of analysis, monitoring and assessment, including registration of discharges, will be harmonized.

- For transboundary watercourses and international lakes, parties will establish emission limits based, to the extent possible, on the best available technologies, specifically applicable to individual sectors or industries or to specific substances; for municipal waste water, at least biological treatment will be introduced; use of no- and low-waste technologies will be promoted.

- Parties will apply water quality objectives; the ecosystems approach will be promoted.

- Discharges will be subject to a prior licence by the competent authority; the approved discharges must be monitored and controlled.

- General water management policies covering transboundary waters including ecological and other impacts of water construction works and water regulation will be implemented.

- The 'polluter-pays' principle will be applied to physical and juridical persons.

- Responsibility and liability issues will be examined.

- Disputes will be settled peacefully in accordance with procedures to be established in conformity with international law.

- Scientific and technological information - including best available technologies - will be exchanged where necessary to achieve the goals of the framework convention in accordance with the national laws, regulations and practice.

- A reporting system concerning the implementation of the framework convention will be established.

Principles related to commissions and to other forms of co-operation

The States bordering transboundary watercourses and international lakes will conclude, where they do not yet exist, specific agreements on the establishment of bilateral or multilateral commissions or other forms of co-operation where appropriate. Their tasks to be described in the framework convention will be *inter alia* without prejudice to existing agreements the following:

- To carry out investigations on the components of the catchment areas of the water bodies concerned and to identify priority uses of waters;

- To carry out joint measuring programmes concerning water quality and quantity;

- To draw up inventories and exchange information on significant discharges;

- To set emission limits for waste water and evaluate effectiveness of control programmes;

- To set water quality objectives; to introduce the minimum obligation of maintaining at least the existing water quality;

- To develop concerted action programmes for the reduction of pollution loads discharged both from point-sources (municipal; industrial) and from diffuse sources (particularly agriculture);

- To establish alarm and warning procedures;

- To provide for consultations on existing and planned uses of water that are likely to have significant adverse transboundary effects, including water construction works and water regulation;

- To promote co-operation on the exchange of information and on the exchange of best available technologies in accordance with national laws, regulations and practice as well as to encourage co-operation in scientific research programmes.

In cases where a coastal State is directly and significantly affected by pollution from transboundary watercourses, the riparian States can, if they all so agree, invite that coastal State to be involved in the activities of the commission, where appropriate, or in other forms of co-operation.

States are encouraged to join such specific agreements (e.g. the Danube, the Elbe) parallel to the elaboration of a framework convention.

DOCUMENT OF THE BONN CONFERENCE

DOCUMENT OF THE BONN CONFERENCE ON ECONOMIC CO-OPERATION IN EUROPE CONVENED IN ACCORDANCE WITH THE RELEVANT PROVISIONS OF THE CONCLUDING DOCUMENT OF THE VIENNA MEETING OF THE CONFERENCE ON SECURITY AND CO-OPERATION IN EUROPE

Bonn, 11 April 1990

The representatives of the participating States of the Conference on Security and Co-operation in Europe (CSCE), Austria, Belgium, Bulgaria, Canada, Cyprus, Czechoslovakia, Denmark, Finland, France, the German Democratic Republic, the Federal Republic of Germany, Greece, the Holy See, Hungary, Iceland, Ireland, Italy, Liechtenstein, Luxembourg, Malta, Monaco, the Netherlands, Norway, Poland, Portugal, Romania, San Marino, Spain, Sweden, Switzerland, Turkey, the Union of Soviet Socialist Republics, the United Kingdom, the United States of America and Yugoslavia met in Bonn from 19 March to 11 April 1990, in accordance with the provisions relating to the Conference on Economic Co-operation in Europe contained in the Concluding Document of the Vienna Follow-up Meeting of the CSCE. Delegations included members of the business community.

The Conference was opened and closed by the Minister of Economics of the Federal Republic of Germany.

The President, the Chancellor and the Deputy Chancellor and Minister for Foreign Affairs of the Federal Republic of Germany addressed the Conference.

At the opening and concluding plenary meetings statements were made by delegates of the participating States, among them Prime Ministers, Vice Prime Ministers, Ministers, State Secretaries and the Vice-President of the Commission of the European Communities. Contributions were made by the Executive Secretary of the United Nations Economic Commission for Europe (ECE) and the Secretary General of the International Chamber of Commerce (ICC).

The participating States welcome the fact that members of the business community gave the Conference the benefit of their practical experience, thus contributing to its success.

Having in mind the aim of the Conference to provide new impulses for economic relations between participating States, in particular by improving business conditions for commercial exchanges and industrial co-operation and by considering new possibilities for, and ways of, economic co-operation;

Meeting at a time of profound and rapid change,

The participating States,

Confirm their intention to shape a new order of peace, stability and prosperity in Europe based on the comprehensive and balanced concept set out in the Helsinki Final Act and the subsequent documents of the CSCE, and resolve to respect all the principles of the Final Act and to implement all the provisions of the CSCE documents;

Reaffirm the fundamental role of the CSCE in the future of Europe;

Recognize that democratic institutions and economic freedom foster economic and social progress;

Share the common objectives of sustainable economic growth, a rising standard of living, an improved quality of life, expanding employment, efficient use of economic resources and protection of the environment;

Believe that co-operation in the field of economics, science and technology and the environment is an essential element in their overall relations, and that it should become even more prominent in the future;

Resolve to work together to expand their co-operation in that field and to enhance the growth of their economies;

Believe that the success of their co-operation will depend in large measure on prevailing political and economic conditions;

Stress the importance of the political and economic reforms taking place, and of a supportive international economic environment, recognize the particular economic interests and concerns of countries as they achieve a market economy, and acknowledge other difficulties, such as indebtedness, which are to be dealt with in the competent fora;

Consider that the process of economic reform and structural adjustment, with increased reliance on market forces, will enhance economic performance, improve efficiency of the public sector, respond better to the needs and wishes of consumers, improve the conditions for closer co-operation and contribute to a more open world trading system;

Believe that increased integration of all participating countries into the international economic and financial system, in accordance with the internationally recognized rules and involving the acceptance of disciplines as well as benefits, will also facilitate economic co-operation;

Value the important roles of existing multilateral economic institutions and mechanisms;
Consider that increased emphasis on economic co-operation within the CSCE process should take into account the interests of participating States that are developing from an economic point of view and should not detract from development co-operation with, including assistance to, developing countries;

Recognize that the performance of market-based economies relies primarily on the freedom of individual enterprise and the consequent economic growth;

Believe that economic freedom for the individual includes the right freely to own, buy, sell and otherwise utilize property;

Confirm that, while governments provide the overall framework for economic activity, business partners make their own decisions;

Consider that the progressive convergence of economic policies among the participating States opens new long-term perspectives for the strengthening of their economic relations.

Accordingly the participating States,

Recognizing the relationship between political pluralism and market economies, and being committed to the principles concerning:

- Multiparty democracy based on free, periodic and genuine elections;

- The rule of law and equal protection under the law for all, based on respect for human rights and effective, accessible and just legal systems;

- Economic activity that accordingly upholds human dignity and is free from forced labour, discrimination against workers on grounds of race, sex, language, political opinion or religion, or denial of the rights of workers freely to establish or join independent trade unions,

Will endeavour to achieve or maintain the following:

- Fiscal and monetary policies that promote balanced, sustainable economic growth and enhance the ability of markets to function efficiently;

- International and domestic policies aimed at expanding the free flow of trade, capital, investment and repatriation of profits in convertible currencies;

- Free and competitive market economies where prices are based on supply and demand;

- Policies that promote social justice and improve living and working conditions;

- Environmentally sustainable economic growth and development;

- Full recognition and protection of all types of property including private property, and the right of citizens to own and use them, as well as intellectual property rights;

- The right to prompt, just and effective compensation in the event private property is taken for public use;

- Direct contact between customers and suppliers in order to facilitate the exchange of goods and services among companies - whether private or state-owned - and individuals in both domestic and international markets,

Have come to the following conclusions:

A. Development and diversification of economic relations

1. The participating States wish to create favourable conditions for a harmonious development and diversification of their economic relations based on internationally agreed rules and practices. They therefore agree to improve business conditions, facilities and practices for each other's firms in their respective markets, based on freedom of establishment. They agree to permit and encourage direct contacts between businessmen at all levels of commerce and stages of industry and end-users. To that end they will, in accordance with their relevant commitments undertaken in the CSCE process, facilitate the prompt

entry, stay and free movement of businessmen in their territory; the participating States will facilitate, on a non-discriminatory basis, the establishment and operation of business offices and firms in their territory, including the renting and purchasing of commercial premises and housing, the acquisition of equipment and transport facilities, access to telecommunications, utilities and social services, the carrying out of audits as well as the unhindered recruitment of local staff required by firms. They encourage direct contacts between representatives of commercial and business organizations and economic institutions. The participating States stress that expeditious processing/treatment of goods and persons at international borders stimulates international trade and they will therefore make their borders more open for that purpose. They also stress the importance of trade facilitation and electronic data interchange for their trade relations.

2. The participating States resolve to publish and make available comprehensive, comparable and timely economic, commercial and demographic information as a basis for economic research, co-operation and efficient conduct of business relations. To that effect they will provide the United Nations Trade Data Bank (COMTRADE) with up-to-date trade figures to at least the three-digit level of the United Nations product classification (SITC-Rev.2). They will also publish detailed, comparable and up-to-date data on balance of payments and gross national product statistics on at least an annual basis as a step towards their integration in international economic activities. They stress the need for national statistics and accounting systems to conform with international standards.

3. The participating States will, in order to facilitate and promote economic co-operation, undertake comprehensive co-operation between their respective statistical services in the bilateral and multilateral context. The priority areas for such co-operation are the statistics on external trade, capital movements, employment, transport, foreign tourism, environment, energy and other raw materials such as forestry and mineral products and industrial production in addition to other major components of national production and national income accounting. The object of this co-operation is to exchange detailed and complete information on relevant statistical elements available and the techniques and methodology employed, and to correlate statistical data with the aim of achieving comparability of such statistics among participating States. In view of this aim, the participating States welcome a further development of the work of relevant organizations, notably the ECE, regarding statistics.

4. The participating States recognize the particular importance of small and medium-sized enterprises in their economic co-operation. These enterprises will benefit particularly from improvements in the business environment and the strengthening of market forces. Participating States will therefore pay special attention to the creation of a competitive business environment conducive to the development of SMEs. To that end they will endeavour to provide the appropriate economic, legal, banking and fiscal conditions that take account of the specific requirements of SMEs. They will strengthen information channels and networks and encourage dialogue and the exchange of expertise between the interested parties, including public authorities, representatives of business and other public and private agencies providing services to business.

5. The participating States are prepared, insofar as the appropriate conditions exist, to provide support for the SME sector by promoting: business co-operation networks, which facilitate the search for business partners; access to information services, including publications and databanks; management and expert training and information on availability of technical know-how and innovations.

6. The participating States confirm the importance they attach to marketing and product promotion as a means of developing trade and industrial and economic co-operation among themselves. They will therefore encourage trade promotion activities including advertising, consulting, factoring and other business services, and the organization of seminars, fairs and exhibitions. They favour the conduct of market research and other marketing activities by both domestic and foreign firms on their respective territories.

7. The participating States recognize the importance, for the economic process, of the development of the human potential. They therefore recognize the value of co-operation in training programmes for managers and specialists in marketing, product promotion and other fields. Insofar as the appropriate conditions exist, such programmes will be held both in host countries and in countries of origin, and under the aegis of vocational training establishments or of companies either in the context of industrial co-operation projects or within *ad hoc* programmes. They express the view that the operation of relevant bodies, e.g. the European Training Foundation, can contribute to improved co-operation in this field.

B. Industrial co-operation

1. The participating States note that the economic, fiscal, legal and social infrastructure and the political conditions in their countries determine the extent to which the various forms of industrial co-operation including joint ventures and other means of direct foreign investment can be envisaged. Each participating State will assess its possibilities and interests with a view to creating favourable conditions for industrial co-operation. They are aware that such co-operation, based on freedom of establishment and non-discriminatory treatment of different types of ownership including private property, will have a positive influence on managerial and technical know-how, the extent of investments, the quality of production, the exchange and application of technology and marketing opportunities.

2. The participating States recognize the importance of protecting industrial, commercial and intellectual property rights for their co-operation in both trade- and research-related aspects. They will ensure adequate and effective protection and enforcement of industrial, commercial and intellectual property rights, including by fully observing international commitments, and will encourage appropriate arrangements among themselves. They will provide natural and legal persons of other States with guarantees of these rights, including non-discriminatory procedures for their acquisition and access to their courts and appropriate administrative bodies.

3. Among the conditions for the development of industrial co-operation the participating States emphasize the need for market-oriented and stable economic policies, an appropriate and reliable legal and administrative framework, consisting of such elements as: fiscal, competition, bankruptcy, and insolvency legislation; company laws; arbitration procedures (taking due account of the UNCITRAL model law and other relevant arrangements); protection of industrial and intellectual property rights; investment protection in national legislation as well as in the framework of multilateral and bilateral agreements; free transfer of capital and profits in foreign currency; accounting systems; a free flow of economic data and market information; business facilities; and entrepreneurial autonomy.

4. Possible forms of industrial co-operation, such as co-production, specialization, subcontracting, licensing agreements, joint ventures and other forms of investment, will be decided by firms according to the

conditions existing and the nature and the objectives of the co-operation.

5. The participating States recognize the importance of comprehensive information on all legal provisions of host countries for foreign investment, joint ventures and other forms of co-operation, including those concerning foreign staff. They encourage host countries to make this information readily and widely available in an up-to-date form.

6. The participating States are prepared, insofar as the appropriate conditions exist, to foster a favourable climate for investment and the different forms of industrial co-operation, on a non-discriminatory basis, notably by concluding further agreements on avoidance of double taxation and bilateral and multilateral arrangements for investment promotion and protection, with particular reference to the transfer of profits and repatriation of invested capital. In this respect the establishment of measures to support economic development through investment (e.g. industrial parks developed by the host country, tax policies and practical assistance) may be of interest. They encourage a greater exchange of information on industrial co-operation opportunities for interested parties by such means as the holding of business weeks. The participating States agree on the importance of standardization and certification in improving their economic relations; to this end they envisage mutual exchange of information, greater co-operation within existing multilateral organizations and, where appropriate, technical assistance.

C. Co-operation in specific areas

1. The participating States, while acknowledging the role of governments in creating favourable framework conditions, recognize that the initiative of the enterprises directly concerned is of paramount importance in bringing about co-operation in the specific areas covered by this chapter.

2. The participating States consider that they should extend and deepen their co-operation in the field of energy and raw material saving techniques. To that end they favour the marketing of energy conservation and raw material saving technologies and will promote increased energy efficiency. The participating States will also co-operate bilaterally and multilaterally in the field of hydrocarbon technologies, solid fuels and renewable energies and processes for the separation of waste components and their recycling and upgrading.

They will also co-operate, e.g. through the International Atomic Energy Agency, in the field of nuclear energy and of the safety of nuclear installations in accordance with their energy policies.

3. The participating States are prepared to exchange information on energy and raw material saving techniques and, insofar as the appropriate conditions exist, to co-operate in the establishment, operation and utilization of European databases in the field of energy, to undertake joint projects to measure energy-combustion-related environmental pollution, to enhance energy efficiency by means of substitution of energy products and to promote professional training in energy-saving techniques.

4. The participating States note the increasing importance of environmental issues in the context of their economic co-operation. They recognize that it is vital to ensure the environmental sustainability of economic development. They acknowledge the significance of international economic co-operation aimed at securing a more efficient use of energy and raw materials. They will also endeavour to strengthen co-operation in the field of environmentally sound technology.

5. At the Sofia CSCE Meeting on the environment, the participating States agreed on enhancement of scientific and technological co-operation, including the exchange of information on best available technologies for improved environmental protection, industrial safety and emergency response. The participating States consider that among the areas for co-operation are pollution monitoring, major technological hazard and accident prevention, assessment of chemicals, treatment and disposal of toxic and dangerous waste, as well as prevention and reduction of air and water pollution, especially that of transboundary watercourses and international lakes, and transboundary pollution caused by energy production, conversion and consumption. The participating States recognize the importance of the ECE and UNEP for the promotion of co-operation in the field of the environment.

6. The participating States are prepared, insofar as the appropriate conditions exist, to take the necessary steps in order to stimulate the exchange of know-how, to promote the wider adoption of environmentally sound technologies and to create demonstration projects in the field of environment. Subsequent co-operation in environmental technology should, in principle, be carried out on a

commercial basis. Governments should encourage the application of such technology and set adequate emission standards and promote public awareness. The participating States would welcome improved arrangements for gathering and disseminating information on cleaner technologies. They note the important role which information networks for environmental technology transfer could play in promoting the development and application of environmental forecasting techniques and the exchange of information on the best technology available for preventing damage to the environment, the possibilities of overcoming hazards due to accidents in industrial works and the rational use of natural resources without disturbing the ecological balance. In this context they recognize the valuable contributions of global and regional organizations such as UNEP, ECE and the European Environment Agency.

7. With a view to improving the quality of life the participating States attach priority to techniques designed to promote the health and safety of their populations. They intend to co-operate in assessing the impact of environmental stress on the population by exchanging relevant data on the effects of environmental pollution. They also consider it important to create the conditions enabling the various elements which contribute to an improved quality of life to be developed.

8. The participating States affirm the importance of co-operation in agro-industry and food processing, including natural food production, and welcome increased commercial relations in this field. They will facilitate joint research, training and exchange of know-how as well as the promotion of contacts between potential partners, especially small and medium-sized enterprises.

9. The participating States welcome efforts to promote co-operation among business enterprises producing machinery for the production of consumer goods as a means of responding to the needs of consumers. They stress the importance of increasing co-operation in the consumer goods sector and will encourage greater access to potential consumers of products. In this context, they note that conversion from military to consumer production may give rise to new business opportunities.

10. The participating States recognize that effective town planning can help to redress urban problems causing a substantial deterioration in the quality of life by striking a balance between economic development and environmental protection as well as ensuring the possibility of citizens to freely take part in economic, political, social and cultural

life. They will promote closer co-operation, and encourage the exchange of information on town planning, including infrastructure (e.g. transport), housing construction, protection of monuments and restoration of the architectural heritage. They will also encourage the exchange of information on, and new approaches to, the economic adaptation of structurally weak regions and the alleviation of environmental damage in urban areas.

D. Monetary and financial aspects

1. The participating States consider that the introduction of undistorted internal pricing is essential to economic reform and a necessary step to currency convertibility. They recognize that both are important for economic development and for increased economic co-operation. They agree that progress towards full convertibility and efficient allocation of resources requires a functioning price mechanism which reflects market-determined and undistorted domestic costs, consumer preferences and international prices. The participating States affirm that currency convertibility forges an efficient link between domestic and foreign price systems capable of transmitting adequate price signals for the allocation of resources inside and outside the country, reflecting international competitiveness. Special attention will thus have to be given to the appropriate level of exchange rates in terms of market-determined prices and other convertible currencies. The success of currency convertibility depends largely on the timely and coherent implementation of measures aimed at developing a market economy which should be underpinned by sound fiscal and monetary policies.

2. The participating States are prepared, insofar as the appropriate conditions exist, to co-operate in establishing conditions for an efficient price mechanism and for progress towards convertibility. This could involve fields such as reform of the banking system, introducing a money market, reform of the investment laws, transformation of public enterprises, taxation, structural adjustment policy, organization of a labour and capital market as well as a foreign exchange market and setting up of the legal framework for introducing convertibility. It could also embrace the establishment of statistics which are essential for creating and maintaining stable monetary and financial conditions and for guiding economic policy.

3. The participating States acknowledge that a market-oriented financial system facilitates the expansion of economic co-operation and that financial instruments play an important role in that context. While, in

the period of transition to a market economy, public financial support to well-defined projects can serve as a multiplier in the framework of economic reforms, such intervention should not distort the emerging market mechanisms. The participating States agree that capital from private sources will progressively become the principal source of external finance.

4. The participating States look forward to the successful conclusion of negotiations to establish the European Bank for Reconstruction and Development (EBRD). They are prepared, insofar as the appropriate conditions exist, to co-operate through the EBRD and other multilateral financial institutions. Furthermore, they agree to foster a favourable climate for investment, notably by bilateral and multilateral arrangements for investment promotion and protection. They also agree to facilitate the provision of technical advice and expert training in improving management skills and setting up market-based financial mechanisms and credit rating systems.

* * * * *

In view of the profound and rapid changes taking place in Europe, and wishing to maintain the valuable momentum built up at the present Conference, the participating States are of the opinion that further ways to strengthen their co-operation in the field of economics, of science and technology and of the environment should be considered. They suggest that the next follow-up meeting or any other main CSCE meeting at the appropriate level examines the possibilities for expanding and intensifying economic co-operation, including through meetings within the CSCE aimed at periodic review of progress and providing new impulses for economic relations among participating States.

Furthermore, the participating States recognize the increasing importance of the different existing international economic institutions in promoting economic co-operation in their fields of competence. In this respect they see a need for discussion of the specificities and longer-term issues of economic changes and reforms in the participating States and related problems of co-operation among them and to share experiences. To this end, they invite the ECE, in view of its annual session, to develop practical measures in priority areas. They invite the OECD to consider hosting meetings of experts from the CSCE participating States and OECD member States to promote the process of economic reform. They recommend that the objective of such undertakings is full integration of the reforming countries into the international economic system. They also consider it important that the expertise and experience of the ICC be fully utilized. The participating States suggest co-ordination among the different existing international economic institutions to avoid duplication and to ensure the maximum effectiveness of their work.

As set out in the Concluding Document of the CSCE Vienna Meeting, the Conference on Economic Co-operation in Europe has been attended by representatives of the participating States and of the business community. The informal discussions held in the course of the Conference have led to comments and suggestions by representatives of the business community.
A summary of these comments and suggestions is to be found in the Journal of the day.

The representatives of the participating States express their profound gratitude to the Government of the Federal Republic of Germany for the excellent organization of the Conference and the warm hospitality extended to the delegations which participated in the Conference.

INTERPRETATIVE STATEMENTS[1]

Interpretative statement by San Marino

The delegation of the Republic of San Marino, while confirming its own full acceptance of the Document of the Bonn Conference on Economic Co-operation in Europe, wishes to point out that, in view of the limited dimensions of the territory of San Marino, the principle of freedom of establishment and the right of free acquisition of immovable property must be regarded as being guaranteed and applied within the context of the legal provisions in force in the Republic of San Marino.

* * *

Interpretative statement by Liechtenstein

States having accepted on their territory a considerable proportion of foreigners as residents may be considered as having largely acted in conformity with the principle of freedom of establishment.

---

[1] Journal No. 18.

DOCUMENT OF THE COPENHAGEN MEETING OF THE CONFERENCE ON THE HUMAN DIMENSION OF THE CSCE

Copenhagen, 29 June 1990

The representatives of the participating States of the Conference on Security and Co-operation in Europe (CSCE), Austria, Belgium, Bulgaria, Canada, Cyprus, Czechoslovakia, Denmark, Finland, France, the German Democratic Republic, the Federal Republic of Germany, Greece, the Holy See, Hungary, Iceland, Ireland, Italy, Liechtenstein, Luxembourg, Malta, Monaco, the Netherlands, Norway, Poland, Portugal, Romania, San Marino, Spain, Sweden, Switzerland, Turkey, the Union of Soviet Socialist Republics, the United Kingdom, the United States of America and Yugoslavia, met in Copenhagen from 5 to 29 June 1990, in accordance with the provisions relating to the Conference on the Human Dimension of the CSCE contained in the Concluding Document of the Vienna Follow-up Meeting of the CSCE.

The representative of Albania attended the Copenhagen Meeting as observer.

The first Meeting of the Conference was held in Paris from 30 May to 23 June 1989.

The Copenhagen Meeting was opened and closed by the Minister for Foreign Affairs of Denmark.

The formal opening of the Copenhagen Meeting was attended by Her Majesty the Queen of Denmark and His Royal Highness the Prince Consort.

Opening statements were made by Ministers and Deputy Ministers of the participating States.

At a special meeting of the Ministers for Foreign Affairs of the participating States of the CSCE on 5 June 1990, convened on the invitation of the Minister for Foreign Affairs of Denmark, it was agreed to convene a Preparatory Committee in Vienna on 10 July 1990 to prepare a Summit Meeting in Paris of their Heads of State or Government.

The participating States welcome with great satisfaction the fundamental political changes that have occurred in Europe since the first Meeting of the Conference on the Human Dimension of the CSCE in Paris in 1989. They note that the CSCE process has contributed significantly to bringing about these changes and that these developments in turn have greatly advanced the implementation of the provisions of the Final Act and of the other CSCE documents.

They recognize that pluralistic democracy and the rule of law are essential for ensuring respect for all human rights and fundamental freedoms, the development of human contacts and the resolution of other issues of a related humanitarian character. They therefore welcome the commitment expressed by all participating States to the ideals of democracy and political pluralism as well as their common determination to build democratic societies based on free elections and the rule of law.

At the Copenhagen Meeting the participating States held a review of the implementation of their commitments in the field of the human dimension. They considered that the degree of compliance with the commitments contained in the relevant provisions of the CSCE documents had shown a fundamental improvement since the Paris Meeting. They also expressed the view, however, that further steps are required for the full realization of their commitments relating to the human dimension.

The participating States express their conviction that full respect for human rights and fundamental freedoms and the development of societies based on pluralistic democracy and the rule of law are prerequisites for progress in setting up the lasting order of peace, security, justice and co-operation that they seek to establish in Europe. They therefore reaffirm their commitment to implement fully all provisions of the Final Act and of the other CSCE documents relating to the human dimension and undertake to build on the progress they have made.

They recognize that co-operation among themselves, as well as the active involvement of persons, groups, organizations and institutions, will be essential to ensure continuing progress towards their shared objectives.

In order to strengthen respect for, and enjoyment of, human rights and fundamental freedoms, to develop human contacts and to resolve issues of a related humanitarian character, the participating States agree on the following:

I

(1) The participating States express their conviction that the protection and promotion of human rights and fundamental freedoms is one of the basic purposes of government, and reaffirm that the recognition of these rights and freedoms constitutes the foundation of freedom, justice and peace.

(2) They are determined to support and advance those principles of justice which form the basis of the rule of law. They consider that the rule of law does not mean merely a formal legality which assures regularity and consistency in the achievement and enforcement of democratic order, but justice based on the recognition and full acceptance of the supreme value of the human personality and guaranteed by institutions providing a framework for its fullest expression.

(3) They reaffirm that democracy is an inherent element of the rule of law. They recognize the importance of pluralism with regard to political organizations.

(4) They confirm that they will respect each other's right freely to choose and develop, in accordance with international human rights standards, their political, social, economic and cultural systems. In exercising this right, they will ensure that their laws, regulations, practices and policies conform with their obligations under international law and are brought into harmony with the provisions of the Declaration on Principles and other CSCE commitments.

(5) They solemnly declare that among those elements of justice which are essential to the full expression of the inherent dignity and of the equal and inalienable rights of all human beings are the following:

(5.1) - free elections that will be held at reasonable intervals by secret ballot or by equivalent free voting procedure, under conditions which ensure in practice the free expression of the opinion of the electors in the choice of their representatives;

(5.2) - a form of government that is representative in character, in which the executive is accountable to the elected legislature or the electorate;

(5.3) - the duty of the government and public authorities to comply with the constitution and to act in a manner consistent with law;

(5.4) - a clear separation between the State and political parties; in particular, political parties will not be merged with the State;

(5.5) - the activity of the government and the administration as well as that of the judiciary will be exercised in accordance with the system established by law. Respect for that system must be ensured;

(5.6) - military forces and the police will be under the control of, and accountable to, the civil authorities;

(5.7) - human rights and fundamental freedoms will be guaranteed by law and in accordance with their obligations under international law;

(5.8) - legislation, adopted at the end of a public procedure, and regulations will be published, that being the condition for their applicability. Those texts will be accessible to everyone;

(5.9) - all persons are equal before the law and are entitled without any discrimination to the equal protection of the law. In this respect, the law will prohibit any discrimination and guarantee to all persons equal and effective protection against discrimination on any ground;

(5.10) - everyone will have an effective means of redress against administrative decisions, so as to guarantee respect for fundamental rights and ensure legal integrity;

(5.11) - administrative decisions against a person must be fully justifiable and must as a rule indicate the usual remedies available;

(5.12) - the independence of judges and the impartial operation of the public judicial service will be ensured;

(5.13) - the independence of legal practitioners will be recognized and protected, in particular as regards conditions for recruitment and practice;

(5.14) - the rules relating to criminal procedure will contain a clear definition of powers in relation to prosecution and the measures preceding and accompanying prosecution;

(5.15) - any person arrested or detained on a criminal charge will have the right, so that the lawfulness of his arrest or detention can be decided, to be brought promptly before a judge or other officer authorized by law to exercise this function;

(5.16) - in the determination of any criminal charge against him, or of his rights and obligations in a suit at law, everyone will be entitled to a fair and public hearing by a competent, independent and impartial tribunal established by law;

(5.17) - any person prosecuted will have the right to defend himself in person or through prompt legal assistance of his own choosing or, if he does not have sufficient means to pay for legal assistance, to be given it free when the interests of justice so require;

(5.18) - no one will be charged with, tried for or convicted of any criminal offence unless the offence is provided for by a law which defines the elements of the offence with clarity and precision;

(5.19) - everyone will be presumed innocent until proved guilty according to law;

(5.20) - considering the important contribution of international instruments in the field of human rights to the rule of law at a national level, the participating States reaffirm that they will consider acceding to the International Covenant on Civil and Political Rights, the International Covenant on Economic, Social and Cultural Rights and other relevant international instruments, if they have not yet done so;

(5.21) - in order to supplement domestic remedies and better to ensure that the participating States respect the international obligations they have undertaken, the participating States will consider acceding to a regional or global international convention concerning the protection of human rights, such as the European Convention on Human Rights or the Optional Protocol to the International Covenant on Civil and Political Rights, which provide for procedures of individual recourse to international bodies.

(6) The participating States declare that the will of the people, freely and fairly expressed through periodic and genuine elections, is the basis of the authority and legitimacy of all government. The participating States will accordingly respect the right of their citizens to take part in the governing of their country, either directly or through representatives freely chosen by them through fair electoral processes. They recognize their responsibility to defend and protect, in accordance with their laws, their international human rights obligations and their international commitments, the democratic order freely established through the will of the people against the activities of persons, groups or organizations that engage in or refuse to renounce terrorism or violence aimed at the overthrow of that order or of that of another participating State.

(7) To ensure that the will of the people serves as the basis of the authority of government, the participating States will

(7.1) - hold free elections at reasonable intervals, as established by law;

(7.2) - permit all seats in at least one chamber of the national legislature to be freely contested in a popular vote;

(7.3) - guarantee universal and equal suffrage to adult citizens;

(7.4) - ensure that votes are cast by secret ballot or by equivalent free voting procedure, and that they are counted and reported honestly with the official results made public;

(7.5) - respect the right of citizens to seek political or public office, individually or as representatives of political parties or organizations, without discrimination;

(7.6) - respect the right of individuals and groups to establish, in full freedom, their own political parties or other political organizations and provide such political parties and organizations with the necessary legal guarantees to enable them to compete with each other on a basis of equal treatment before the law and by the authorities;

(7.7) - ensure that law and public policy work to permit political campaigning to be conducted in a fair and free atmosphere in which neither administrative action, violence nor intimidation bars the parties and the candidates from freely presenting their views and qualifications, or prevents the voters from learning and discussing them or from casting their vote free of fear of retribution;

(7.8) - provide that no legal or administrative obstacle stands in the way of unimpeded access to the media on a non-discriminatory basis for all political groupings and individuals wishing to participate in the electoral process;

(7.9) - ensure that candidates who obtain the necessary number of votes required by law are duly installed in office and are permitted to remain in office until their term expires or is otherwise brought to an end in a manner that is regulated by law in conformity with democratic parliamentary and constitutional procedures.

(8) The participating States consider that the presence of observers, both foreign and domestic, can enhance the electoral process for States in which elections are taking place. They therefore invite observers from any other CSCE participating States and any appropriate private institutions and organizations who may wish to do so to observe the course of their national election proceedings, to the extent permitted by law. They will also endeavour to facilitate similar access for election proceedings held below the national level. Such observers will undertake not to interfere in the electoral proceedings.

II

(9) The participating States reaffirm that

(9.1) - everyone will have the right to freedom of expression including he right to communication. This right will include freedom to hold opinions and to receive and impart information and ideas without interference by public authority and regardless of frontiers. The exercise of this right may be subject only to such restrictions as are prescribed by law and are consistent with international standards. In particular, no limitation will be imposed on access to, and use of, means of reproducing documents of any kind, while respecting, however, rights relating to intellectual property, including copyright;

(9.2) - everyone will have the right of peaceful assembly and demonstration. Any restrictions which may be placed on the exercise of these rights will be prescribed by law and consistent with international standards;

(9.3) - the right of association will be guaranteed. The right to form and - subject to the general right of a trade union to determine its own membership - freely to join a trade union will be guaranteed. These rights will exclude any prior control. Freedom of association for workers, including the freedom to strike, will be guaranteed, subject to limitations prescribed by law and consistent with international standards;

(9.4) - everyone will have the right to freedom of thought, conscience and religion. This right includes freedom to change one's religion or belief and freedom to manifest one's religion or belief, either alone or in community with others, in public or in private, through worship, teaching, practice and observance. The exercise of these rights may be subject only to such restrictions as are prescribed by law and are consistent with international standards;

(9.5) - they will respect the right of everyone to leave any country, including his own, and to return to his country, consistent with a State's international obligations and CSCE commitments. Restrictions on this right will have the character of very rare exceptions, will be considered necessary only if they respond to a specific public need, pursue a legitimate aim and are proportionate to that aim, and will not be abused or applied in an arbitrary manner;

(9.6) - everyone has the right peacefully to enjoy his property either on his own or in common with others. No one may be deprived of his property except in the public interest and subject to the conditions provided for by law and consistent with international commitments and obligations.

(10) In reaffirming their commitment to ensure effectively the rights of the individual to know and act upon human rights and fundamental freedoms, and to contribute actively, individually or in association

with others, to their promotion and protection, the participating States express their commitment to

(10.1) - respect the right of everyone, individually or in association with others, to seek, receive and impart freely views and information on human rights and fundamental freedoms, including the rights to disseminate and publish such views and information;

(10.2) - respect the rights of everyone, individually or in association with others, to study and discuss the observance of human rights and fundamental freedoms and to develop and discuss ideas for improved protection of human rights and better means for ensuring compliance with international human rights standards;

(10.3) - ensure that individuals are permitted to exercise the right to association, including the right to form, join and participate effectively in non-governmental organizations which seek the promotion and protection of human rights and fundamental freedoms, including trade unions and human rights monitoring groups;

(10.4) - allow members of such groups and organizations to have unhindered access to and communication with similar bodies within and outside their countries and with international organizations, to engage in exchanges, contacts and co-operation with such groups and organizations and to solicit, receive and utilize for the purpose of promoting and protecting human rights and fundamental freedoms voluntary financial contributions from national and international sources as provided for by law.

(11) The participating States further affirm that, where violations of human rights and fundamental freedoms are alleged to have occurred, the effective remedies available include

(11.1) - the right of the individual to seek and receive adequate legal assistance;

(11.2) - the right of the individual to seek and receive assistance from others in defending human rights and fundamental freedoms, and to assist others in defending human rights and fundamental freedoms;

(11.3) - the right of individuals or groups acting on their behalf to communicate with international bodies with competence to receive and consider information concerning allegations of human rights abuses.

(12) The participating States, wishing to ensure greater transparency in the implementation of the commitments undertaken in the Vienna Concluding Document under the heading of the human dimension of the CSCE, decide to accept as a confidence-building measure the presence of observers sent by participating States and representatives of non-governmental organizations and other interested persons at proceedings before courts as provided for in national legislation and international law; it is understood that proceedings may only be held *in camera* in the circumstances prescribed by law and consistent with obligations under international law and international commitments.

(13) The participating States decide to accord particular attention to the recognition of the rights of the child, his civil rights and his individual freedoms, his economic, social and cultural rights, and his right to special protection against all forms of violence and exploitation. They will consider acceding to the Convention on the Rights of the Child, if they have not yet done so, which was opened for signature by States on 26 January 1990. They will recognize in their domestic legislation the rights of the child as affirmed in the international agreements to which they are Parties.

(14) The participating States agree to encourage the creation, within their countries, of conditions for the training of students and trainees from other participating States, including persons taking vocational and technical courses. They also agree to promote travel by young people from their countries for the purpose of obtaining education in other participating States and to that end to encourage the conclusion, where appropriate, of bilateral and multilateral agreements between their relevant governmental institutions, organizations and educational establishments.

(15) The participating States will act in such a way as to facilitate the transfer of sentenced persons and encourage those participating States which are not Parties to the Convention on the Transfer of Sentenced Persons, signed at Strasbourg on 21 November 1983, to consider acceding to the Convention.

(16) The participating States

(16.1) - reaffirm their commitment to prohibit torture and other cruel, inhuman or degrading treatment or punishment, to take effective legislative, administrative, judicial and other measures to prevent and punish such practices, to protect individuals from any psychiatric or other medical practices that violate human rights and fundamental freedoms and to take effective measures to prevent and punish such practices;

(16.2) - intend, as a matter of urgency, to consider acceding to the Convention against Torture and Other Cruel, Inhuman or Degrading Treatment or Punishment, if they have not yet done so, and recognizing the competences of the Committee against Torture under articles 21 and 22 of the Convention and withdrawing reservations regarding the competence of the Committee under article 20;

(16.3) - stress that no exceptional circumstances whatsoever, whether a state of war or a threat of war, internal political instability or any other public emergency, may be invoked as a justification of torture;

(16.4) - will ensure that education and information regarding the prohibition against torture are fully included in the training of law enforcement personnel, civil or military, medical personnel, public officials and other persons who may be involved in the custody, interrogation or treatment of any individual subjected to any form of arrest, detention or imprisonment;

(16.5) - will keep under systematic review interrogation rules, instructions, methods and practices as well as arrangements for the custody and treatment of persons subjected to any form of arrest, detention or imprisonment in any territory under their jurisdiction, with a view to preventing any cases of torture;

(16.6) - will take up with priority for consideration and for appropriate action, in accordance with the agreed measures and procedures for the effective implementation of the commitments relating to the human dimension of the CSCE, any cases of torture and other inhuman or degrading treatment or punishment made known to them through official channels or coming from any other reliable source of information;

(16.7) - will act upon the understanding that preserving and guaranteeing the life and security of any individual subjected to any form of torture and other inhuman or degrading treatment or punishment will be the sole criterion in determining the urgency and priorities to be accorded in taking appropriate remedial action; and, therefore, the consideration of any cases of torture and other inhuman or degrading treatment or punishment within the framework of any other international body or mechanism may not be invoked as a reason for refraining from consideration and appropriate action in accordance with the agreed measures and procedures for the effective implementation of the commitments relating to the human dimension of the CSCE.

(17) The participating States

(17.1) - recall the commitment undertaken in the Vienna Concluding Document to keep the question of capital punishment under consideration and to co-operate within relevant international organizations;

(17.2) - recall, in this context, the adoption by the General Assembly of the United Nations, on 15 December 1989, of the Second Optional Protocol to the International Covenant on Civil and Political Rights, aiming at the abolition of the death penalty;

(17.3) - note the restrictions and safeguards regarding the use of the death penalty which have been adopted by the international community, in particular article 6 of the International Covenant on Civil and Political Rights;

(17.4) - note the provisions of the Sixth Protocol to the European Convention for the Protection of Human Rights and Fundamental Freedoms, concerning the abolition of the death penalty;

(17.5) - note recent measures taken by a number of participating States towards the abolition of capital punishment;

(17.6) - note the activities of several non-governmental organizations on the question of the death penalty;

(17.7) - will exchange information within the framework of the Conference on the Human Dimension on the question of the abolition of the death penalty and keep that question under consideration;

(17.8) - will make available to the public information regarding the use of the death penalty.

(18) The participating States

(18.1) - note that the United Nations Commission on Human Rights has recognized the right of everyone to have conscientious objections to military service;

(18.2) - note recent measures taken by a number of participating States to permit exemption from compulsory military service on the basis of conscientious objections;

(18.3) - note the activities of several non-governmental organizations on the question of conscientious objections to compulsory military service;

(18.4) - agree to consider introducing, where this has not yet been done, various forms of alternative service, which are compatible with the reasons for conscientious objection, such forms of alternative service being in principle of a non-combatant or civilian nature, in the public interest and of a non-punitive nature;

(18.5) - will make available to the public information on this issue;

(18.6) - will keep under consideration, within the framework of the Conference on the Human Dimension, the relevant questions related to the exemption from compulsory military service, where it exists, of individuals on the basis of conscientious objections to armed service, and will exchange information on these questions.

(19) The participating States affirm that freer movement and contacts among their citizens are important in the context of the protection and promotion of human rights and fundamental freedoms. They will ensure that their policies concerning entry into their territories are fully consistent with the aims set out in the relevant provisions of the Final Act, the Madrid Concluding Document and the Vienna Concluding Document. While reaffirming their determination not to recede from the commitments contained in CSCE documents, they

undertake to implement fully and improve present commitments in the field of human contacts, including on a bilateral and multilateral basis. In this context they will

(19.1) - strive to implement the procedures for entry into their territories, including the issuing of visas and passport and customs control, in good faith and without unjustified delay. Where necessary, they will shorten the waiting time for visa decisions, as well as simplify practices and reduce administrative requirements for visa applications;

(19.2) - ensure, in dealing with visa applications, that these are processed as expeditiously as possible in order, *inter alia*, to take due account of important family, personal or professional considerations, especially in cases of an urgent, humanitarian nature;

(19.3) - endeavour, where necessary, to reduce fees charged in connection with visa applications to the lowest possible level.

(20) The participating States concerned will consult and, where appropriate, co-operate in dealing with problems that might emerge as a result of the increased movement of persons.

(21) The participating States recommend the consideration, at the next CSCE Follow-up Meeting in Helsinki, of the advisability of holding a meeting of experts on consular matters.

(22) The participating States reaffirm that the protection and promotion of the rights of migrant workers have their human dimension. In this context, they

(22.1) - agree that the protection and promotion of the rights of migrant workers are the concern of all participating States and that as such they should be addressed within the CSCE process;

(22.2) - reaffirm their commitment to implement fully in their domestic legislation the rights of migrant workers provided for in international agreements to which they are parties;

(22.3) - consider that, in future international instruments concerning the rights of migrant workers, they should take into account the fact that this issue is of importance for all of them;

(22.4) - express their readiness to examine, at future CSCE meetings, the relevant aspects of the further promotion of the rights of migrant workers and their families.

(23) The participating States reaffirm their conviction expressed in the Vienna Concluding Document that the promotion of economic, social and cultural rights as well as of civil and political rights is of paramount importance for human dignity and for the attainment of the legitimate aspirations of every individual. They also reaffirm their commitment taken in the Document of the Bonn Conference on Economic Co-operation in Europe to the promotion of social justice and the improvement of living and working conditions. In the context of continuing their efforts with a view to achieving progressively the full realization of economic, social and cultural rights by all appropriate means, they will pay special attention to problems in the areas of employment, housing, social security, health, education and culture.

(24) The participating States will ensure that the exercise of all the human rights and fundamental freedoms set out above will not be subject to any restrictions except those which are provided by law and are consistent with their obligations under international law, in particular the International Covenant on Civil and Political Rights, and with their international commitments, in particular the Universal Declaration of Human Rights. These restrictions have the character of exceptions. The participating States will ensure that these restrictions are not abused and are not applied in an arbitrary manner, but in such a way that the effective exercise of these rights is ensured.

Any restriction on rights and freedoms must, in a democratic society, relate to one of the objectives of the applicable law and be strictly proportionate to the aim of that law.

(25) The participating States confirm that any derogations from obligations relating to human rights and fundamental freedoms during a state of public emergency must remain strictly within the limits provided for by international law, in particular the relevant international instruments by which they are bound, especially with respect to rights from which there can be no derogation. They also reaffirm that

(25.1) - measures derogating from such obligations must be taken in strict conformity with the procedural requirements laid down in those instruments;

(25.2) - the imposition of a state of public emergency must be proclaimed officially, publicly, and in accordance with the provisions laid down by law;

(25.3) - measures derogating from obligations will be limited to the extent strictly required by the exigencies of the situation;

(25.4) - such measures will not discriminate solely on the grounds of race, colour, sex, language, religion, social origin or of belonging to a minority.

III

(26) The participating States recognize that vigorous democracy depends on the existence as an integral part of national life of democratic values and practices as well as an extensive range of democratic institutions. They will therefore encourage, facilitate and, where appropriate, support practical co-operative endeavours and the sharing of information, ideas and expertise among themselves and by direct contacts and co-operation between individuals, groups and organizations in areas including the following:

- constitutional law, reform and development,
- electoral legislation, administration and observation,
- establishment and management of courts and legal systems,
- the development of an impartial and effective public service where recruitment and advancement are based on a merit system,
- law enforcement,
- local government and decentralization,
- access to information and protection of privacy,
- developing political parties and their role in pluralistic societies,
- free and independent trade unions,
- co-operative movements,
- developing other forms of free associations and public interest groups,
- journalism, independent media, and intellectual and cultural life,

- the teaching of democratic values, institutions and practices in educational institutions and the fostering of an atmosphere of free enquiry.

Such endeavours may cover the range of co-operation encompassed in the human dimension of the CSCE, including training, exchange of information, books and instructional materials, co-operative programmes and projects, academic and professional exchanges and conferences, scholarships, research grants, provision of expertise and advice, business and scientific contacts and programmes.

(27) The participating States will also facilitate the establishment and strengthening of independent national institutions in the area of human rights and the rule of law, which may also serve as focal points for co-ordination and collaboration between such institutions in the participating States. They propose that co-operation be encouraged between parliamentarians from participating States, including through existing inter-parliamentary associations and, *inter alia*, through joint commissions, television debates involving parliamentarians, meetings and round-table discussions. They will also encourage existing institutions, such as organizations within the United Nations system and the Council of Europe, to continue and expand the work they have begun in this area.

(28) The participating States recognize the important expertise of the Council of Europe in the field of human rights and fundamental freedoms and agree to consider further ways and means to enable the Council of Europe to make a contribution to the human dimension of the CSCE. They agree that the nature of this contribution could be examined further in a future CSCE forum.

(29) The participating States will consider the idea of convening a meeting or seminar of experts to review and discuss co-operative measures designed to promote and sustain viable democratic institutions in participating States, including comparative studies of legislation in participating States in the area of human rights and fundamental freedoms, *inter alia* drawing upon the experience acquired in this area by the Council of Europe and the activities of the Commission "Democracy through Law".

IV

(30) The participating States recognize that the questions relating to national minorities can only be satisfactorily resolved in a democratic political framework based on the rule of law, with a functioning independent judiciary. This framework guarantees full respect for human rights and fundamental freedoms, equal rights and status for all citizens, the free expression of all their legitimate interests and aspirations, political pluralism, social tolerance and the implementation of legal rules that place effective restraints on the abuse of governmental power.

They also recognize the important role of non-governmental organizations, including political parties, trade unions, human rights organizations and religious groups, in the promotion of tolerance, cultural diversity and the resolution of questions relating to national minorities.

They further reaffirm that respect for the rights of persons belonging to national minorities as part of universally recognized human rights is an essential factor for peace, justice, stability and democracy in the participating States.

(31) Persons belonging to national minorities have the right to exercise fully and effectively their human rights and fundamental freedoms without any discrimination and in full equality before the law.

The participating States will adopt, where necessary, special measures for the purpose of ensuring to persons belonging to national minorities full equality with the other citizens in the exercise and enjoyment of human rights and fundamental freedoms.

(32) To belong to a national minority is a matter of a person's individual choice and no disadvantage may arise from the exercise of such choice.

Persons belonging to national minorities have the right freely to express, preserve and develop their ethnic, cultural, linguistic or religious identity and to maintain and develop their culture in all its aspects, free of any attempts at assimilation against their will. In particular, they have the right

(32.1) - to use freely their mother tongue in private as well as in public;

(32.2) - to establish and maintain their own educational, cultural and religious institutions, organizations or associations, which can seek voluntary financial and other contributions as well as public assistance, in conformity with national legislation;

(32.3) - to profess and practise their religion, including the acquisition, possession and use of religious materials, and to conduct religious educational activities in their mother tongue;

(32.4) - to establish and maintain unimpeded contacts among themselves within their country as well as contacts across frontiers with citizens of other States with whom they share a common ethnic or national origin, cultural heritage or religious beliefs;

(32.5) - to disseminate, have access to and exchange information in their mother tongue;

(32.6) - to establish and maintain organizations or associations within their country and to participate in international non-governmental organizations.

Persons belonging to national minorities can exercise and enjoy their rights individually as well as in community with other members of their group. No disadvantage may arise for a person belonging to a national minority on account of the exercise or non-exercise of any such rights.

(33) The participating States will protect the ethnic, cultural, linguistic and religious identity of national minorities on their territory and create conditions for the promotion of that identity. They will take the necessary measures to that effect after due consultations, including contacts with organizations or associations of such minorities, in accordance with the decision-making procedures of each State.
Any such measures will be in conformity with the principles of equality and non-discrimination with respect to the other citizens of the participating State concerned.

(34) The participating States will endeavour to ensure that persons belonging to national minorities, notwithstanding the need to learn the official language or languages of the State concerned, have adequate opportunities for instruction of their mother tongue or in their mother tongue, as well as, wherever possible and necessary, for its use before public authorities, in conformity with applicable national legislation.

In the context of the teaching of history and culture in educational establishments, they will also take account of the history and culture of national minorities.

(35) The participating States will respect the right of persons belonging to national minorities to effective participation in public affairs, including participation in the affairs relating to the protection and promotion of the identity of such minorities.
The participating States note the efforts undertaken to protect and create conditions for the promotion of the ethnic, cultural, linguistic and religious identity of certain national minorities by establishing, as one of the possible means to achieve these aims, appropriate local or autonomous administrations corresponding to the specific historical and territorial circumstances of such minorities and in accordance with the policies of the State concerned.

(36) The participating States recognize the particular importance of increasing constructive co-operation among themselves on questions relating to national minorities. Such co-operation seeks to promote mutual understanding and confidence, friendly and good-neighbourly relations, international peace, security and justice.
Every participating State will promote a climate of mutual respect, understanding, co-operation and solidarity among all persons living on its territory, without distinction as to ethnic or national origin or religion, and will encourage the solution of problems through dialogue based on the principles of the rule of law.

(37) None of these commitments may be interpreted as implying any right to engage in any activity or perform any action in contravention of the purposes and principles of the Charter of the United Nations, other obligations under international law or the provisions of the Final Act, including the principle of territorial integrity of States.

(38) The participating States, in their efforts to protect and promote the rights of persons belonging to national minorities, will fully respect their undertakings under existing human rights conventions and other relevant international instruments and consider adhering to the relevant conventions, if they have not yet done so, including those providing for a right of complaint by individuals.

(39) The participating States will co-operate closely in the competent international organizations to which they belong, including the

United Nations and, as appropriate, the Council of Europe, bearing in mind their on-going work with respect to questions relating to national minorities.

They will consider convening a meeting of experts for a thorough discussion of the issue of national minorities.

(40) The participating States clearly and unequivocally condemn totalitarianism, racial and ethnic hatred, anti-semitism, xenophobia and discrimination against anyone as well as persecution on religious and ideological grounds. In this context, they also recognize the particular problems of Roma (gypsies).

They declare their firm intention to intensify the efforts to combat these phenomena in all their forms and therefore will

(40.1) - take effective measures, including the adoption, in conformity with their constitutional systems and their international obligations, of such laws as may be necessary, to provide protection against any acts that constitute incitement to violence against persons or groups based on national, racial, ethnic or religious discrimination, hostility or hatred, including anti-semitism;

(40.2) - commit themselves to take appropriate and proportionate measures to protect persons or groups who may be subject to threats or acts of discrimination, hostility or violence as a result of their racial, ethnic, cultural, linguistic or religious identity, and to protect their property;

(40.3) - take effective measures, in conformity with their constitutional systems, at the national, regional and local levels to promote understanding and tolerance, particularly in the fields of education, culture and information;

(40.4) - endeavour to ensure that the objectives of education include special attention to the problem of racial prejudice and hatred and to the development of respect for different civilizations and cultures;

(40.5) - recognize the right of the individual to effective remedies and endeavour to recognize, in conformity with national legislation, the right of interested persons and groups to initiate and support complaints against acts of discrimination, including racist and xenophobic acts;

(40.6) - consider adhering, if they have not yet done so, to the international instruments which address the problem of discrimination and ensure full compliance with the obligations therein, including those relating to the submission of periodic reports;

(40.7) - consider, also, accepting those international mechanisms which allow States and individuals to bring communications relating to discrimination before international bodies.

V

(41) The participating States reaffirm their commitment to the human dimension of the CSCE and emphasize its importance as an integral part of a balanced approach to security and co-operation in Europe. They agree that the Conference on the Human Dimension of the CSCE and the human dimension mechanism described in the section on the human dimension of the CSCE of the Vienna Concluding Document have demonstrated their value as methods of furthering their dialogue and co-operation and assisting in the resolution of relevant specific questions. They express their conviction that these should be continued and developed as part of an expanding CSCE process.

(42) The participating States recognize the need to enhance further the effectiveness of the procedures described in paragraphs 1 to 4 of the section on the human dimension of the CSCE of the Vienna Concluding Document and with this aim decide

(42.1) - to provide in as short a time as possible, but no later than four weeks, a written response to requests for information and to representations made to them in writing by other participating States under paragraph 1;

(42.2) - that the bilateral meetings, as contained in paragraph 2, will take place as soon as possible, as a rule within three weeks of the date of the request;

(42.3) - to refrain, in the course of a bilateral meeting held under paragraph 2, from raising situations and cases not connected with the subject of the meeting, unless both sides have agreed to do so.

(43) The participating States examined practical proposals for new measures aimed at improving the implementation of the commitments relating to the human dimension of the CSCE. In this regard, they considered proposals related to the sending of observers to examine situations and specific cases, the appointment of rapporteurs to investigate and suggest appropriate solutions, the setting up of a Committee on the Human Dimension of the CSCE, greater involvement of persons, organizations and institutions in the human dimension mechanism and further bilateral and multilateral efforts to promote the resolution of relevant issues.
They decide to continue to discuss thoroughly in subsequent relevant CSCE fora these and other proposals designed to strengthen the human dimension mechanism, and to consider adopting, in the context of the further development of the CSCE process, appropriate new measures. They agree that these measures should contribute to achieving further effective progress, enhance conflict prevention and confidence in the field of the human dimension of the CSCE.

***

(44) The representatives of the participating States express their profound gratitude to the people and Government of Denmark for the excellent organization of the Copenhagen Meeting and the warm hospitality extended to the delegations which participated in the Meeting.

(45) In accordance with the provisions relating to the Conference on the Human Dimension of the CSCE contained in the Concluding Document of the Vienna Follow-up Meeting of the CSCE, the third Meeting of the Conference will take place in Moscow from 10 September to 4 October 1991.

ANNEX

CHAIRMAN'S STATEMENT

ON THE ACCESS OF NON-GOVERNMENTAL ORGANIZATIONS AND THE MEDIA TO MEETINGS OF THE CONFERENCE ON THE HUMAN DIMENSION

The Chairman notes that the practices of openness and access to the Meetings of the Conference on the Human Dimension, as they were applied at the Vienna Meeting and as contained in Annex XI of the Concluding Document of that Meeting, are of importance to all participating States. In order to follow and build upon those practices at forthcoming CSCE meetings of the Conference on the Human Dimension, the participating States agree that the following practices of openness and access should be respected:

- free movement by members of interested non-governmental organizations (NGOs) in the Conference premises, except for the areas restricted to delegations and to the services of the Executive Secretariat. Accordingly, badges will be issued to them, at their request, by the Executive Secretariat;
- unimpeded contacts between members of interested NGOs and delegates, as well as with accredited representatives of the media;
- access to official documents of the Conference in all the working languages and also to any document that delegates might wish to communicate to members of interested NGOs;
- the opportunity for members of interested NGOs to transmit to delegates communications relating to the human dimension of the CSCE. Mailboxes for each delegation will be accessible to them for this purpose;
- free access for delegates to all documents emanating from interested NGOs and addressed to the Executive Secretariat for the information of the Conference. Accordingly, the Executive Secretariat will make available to delegates a regularly updated collection of such documents;

They further undertake to guarantee to representatives of the media

- free movement in the Conference premises, except for the areas restricted to delegations and to the services of the Executive Secretariat. Accordingly, badges will be issued to them by the Executive Secretariat upon presentation of the requisite credentials;
- unimpeded contacts with delegates and with members of interested NGOs;

- access to official documents of the Conference in all the working languages.

The Chairman notes further that this statement will be an Annex to the Document of the Copenhagen Meeting and will be published with it.

INTERPRETATIVE STATEMENTS[1]

Interpretative statement by Greece

The Greek delegation welcomes the Document of the Copenhagen Meeting of the Conference on the Human Dimension of the CSCE adopted by consensus, containing important provisions which constitute a positive step along the road to a world based on the principles of the rule of law and democracy and aim at strengthening and more effectively protecting human rights and freedoms, to which Greece has always been firmly committed.

In view of all the above, it is the understanding of the Greek delegation that the exercise of the rights set forth in paragraphs 32.3, 32.4, 32.5 and 32.6 of this Document should be in accordance with the relevant provisions of international human rights law and should respect, *inter alia*, the rights and freedoms of others and the principle of territorial integrity of the States concerned.

The Greek delegation wishes this statement to be recorded in the journal of the day.

* * *

Interpretative statement by Bulgaria

Bulgaria welcomes and fully supports the adoption by the participating States of the Copenhagen Document as a major positive step forward in the further promotion of human rights and fundamental freedoms, in particular in the fields of the rule of law, free and democratic elections, respect for and protection of all individual rights and the development of appropriate implementation procedures.

In the absence of any definition, the use of the term 'national minorities', as well as any provisions related to the rights of persons belonging to such minorities, whenever they exist, and covering other similarly identifiable groups, cannot be construed either as exempting any participating State from compliance with the international standards on human rights and fundamental freedoms or as being contrary in any way to the relevant principles of sovereign equality, inviolability of frontiers and territorial integrity of States. In this respect Bulgaria maintains its previously recorded positions.

The applicability of those provisions on minorities, which are of a political rather than a humanitarian nature and are related to organizations or associations, the use before public authorities of languages other than the official languages, local or autonomous arrangements, financial and other contributions as well as public

---

[1] Journal No. 18 (Copenhagen, 28 June 1990).

assistance, etc. falls exclusively within the competence of each participating State, as it stems from the adopted Document.

While confirming its readiness to implement fully and effectively the agreed provisions on an equal footing with all participating States, Bulgaria declares that this shall not in any way prejudice the right of the freely and democratically elected Parliament in Bulgaria to consider those provisions and to determine the appropriate legal and other means for their implementation in accordance with the sovereign will of the Bulgarian people.

* * * * *

Editor's note: By communication of 28 June 1990 (No. CSCE/CHDC/Inf.7) the Executive Secretary of the Copenhagen Meeting of the Conference on the Human Dimension circulated the following text to the participating States, which had not been regularly submitted at the Plenary Meeting:

"The attached text has been submitted by the delegation of Turkey under paragraph 79 of the Final Recommendations of the Helsinki Consultations (Chapter 6, Rules of Procedure) for circulation to the participating States.

'I have the honour to inform you that the following text constitutes the interpretative statement by the Government of the Republic of Turkey under paragraph 79 of the Rules of Procedure (Chapter 6 of the Final Recommendations of the Helsinki Consultations) on document CSCE/CHDC.43, adopted today:

- 'In Turkey's concept, the term 'national minorities' only encompasses population groups whose status is subject to bilateral or multilateral international instruments.

- The provisions of the Document of the Copenhagen Meeting of the Conference on the Human Dimension of the CSCE shall be applied in conformity with its Constitution and national legislation.'

I hereby request that you communicate the above to the participating States.'"

REPORT OF THE MEETING ON THE MEDITERRANEAN OF THE CONFERENCE ON SECURITY AND CO-OPERATION IN EUROPE

Palma de Mallorca, 18 October 1990

The representatives of Austria, Belgium, Bulgaria, Canada, Cyprus, Czechoslovakia, Denmark, Finland, France, the German Democratic Republic, the Federal Republic of Germany, Greece, the Holy See, Hungary, Iceland, Ireland, Italy, Liechtenstein, Luxembourg, Malta, Monaco, the Netherlands, Norway, Poland, Portugal, Romania, San Marino, Spain, Sweden, Switzerland, Turkey, the Union of Soviet Socialist Republics, the United Kingdom, the United States of America and Yugoslavia met at the CSCE Meeting on the Mediterranean held in Palma de Mallorca from 24 September to 19 October in accordance with the relevant provisions contained in the Concluding Document of the Vienna CSCE Follow-up Meeting 1986.

The representative of the German Democratic Republic attended the Meeting until 2 October.

Representatives of the non-participating Mediterranean States (Algeria, Egypt, Israel, Lebanon, Libya, Morocco, Syria and Tunisia) and of the competent international organizations (UNESCO, ECE, UNEP, WHO, ITU and IMO) were invited to participate in the Meeting in accordance with the Concluding Document of the Vienna CSCE Follow-up Meeting 1986 and participated in the work of the Meeting under the procedure set out in the invitation.

The representative of Albania attended the Meeting as observer.

The formal opening was attended by H.M. the King of Spain. The Meeting was opened by the Spanish Foreign Minister and closed by the Spanish Minister of Public Works and Urban Development, also responsible for the environment.

At the plenary meetings, statements were made by delegates of the participating States, among them members of governments as well as a member of the Commission of the European Communities. Contributions were also made by representatives of Algeria, Egypt, Israel, Lebanon, Morocco, Syria, Tunisia, and of UNESCO, ECE and UNEP.

In the course of the Meeting, references were made to fundamental political changes that have occurred in Europe since the conclusion of the Vienna CSCE Meeting and to their positive relevance to the Mediterranean region.

The participating States recognized that the CSCE process had contributed significantly to bringing about these changes and that those developments had greatly advanced the implementation of the Final Act and of the other CSCE Documents.

The participating States reaffirmed their commitment to all ten principles of the Final Act's Declaration on Principles Guiding Relations between Participating States and their determination to respect them and put them into practice.

The participating States expressed their conviction that full respect for human rights and fundamental freedoms and the development of societies based on pluralistic democracy and the rule of law were prerequisites for progress in setting up a lasting order of peace, security, justice and co-operation.

They also supported continued efforts to implement the relevant recommendations of the CSCE Meetings on the Mediterranean held in Valletta in 1979 and in Venice in 1984.

The participating States reaffirmed their commitment to, and stressed the continuing relevance of, the provisions of the CSCE concerning security and co-operation in the Mediterranean. They reiterated their conviction that security in Europe was to be considered also in the broader context of world security and was closely linked with security in the Mediterranean area as a whole.

They expressed their concern over the continuing tensions in the region and renewed their determination to intensify efforts towards finding just, viable and lasting solutions, through peaceful means, to outstanding crucial problems, based on respect for the Principles of the Final Act.

In the course of the Meeting a suggestion was made that, when circumstances allowed, a meeting outside the CSCE could take place that, inspired by experiences of the CSCE process, could discuss a set of generally accepted rules and principles in the fields of stability, co-operation and the human dimension in the Mediterranean.

The participating States during their exchange of views on item 3 of the Agenda, reaffirmed their will to strengthen their co-operation and intensify efforts aimed at further enhancing various aspects of co-operation, including the protection and improvement of Mediterranean ecosystems, with the objective of widening the scope of their co-operation with the non-participating Mediterranean States and contributing to the strengthening of stability in the region.

The presence of the eight non-participating Mediterranean States and their contribution to the Meeting were a positive development.

The participating States expressed the wish to promote favourable conditions for a harmonious development and diversification of relations with the non-participating Mediterranean States. They expressed their intention to work together with the non-participating Mediterranean States to expand their co-operation in various fields in order to promote favourable political, cultural and economic conditions.

The importance of developing intra-Mediterranean relations and, in particular, trade and economic co-operation in this region was stressed. That perspective, as well as the promotion of sustainable development aimed at bringing the coastal countries closer, required national efforts in order to ensure the identification of adequate priorities, strengthen the trend towards market economies and underline human rights. Based on respect for the Helsinki principles, such efforts should rely on political, cultural, religious and economic conditions, leading to active co-operation between the participating States and the non-participating States.

The participating States noted the increasing significance of ecological issues in the context of their co-operation within the CSCE framework. They recognized the need to provide for ecological stability in the Mediterranean region. At the same time they underlined the importance of the global aspects, including the preparatory work for the 1992 United Nations Conference on the Environment and Development.

The marine environment and that of watercourses as well as terrestrial ecosystems in the Mediterranean region had today become so fragile that the future of the region and its socio-economic development required an increased effort in different fields: protection of the sea; conservation of water resources; air pollution prevention; sound waste management, especially for toxic waste; forest-fire fighting and policies against desertification; protection of biological diversity, particularly of ecosystems and species; and development of environmentally sound tourism. The deterioration of the environment including the cultural heritage would be an additional risk for the political, social and economic balance in the region.

The participating States recognized the work under way to tackle the major environmental problems facing the Mediterranean region. Since the adoption of the Mediterranean Action Plan co-ordinated by UNEP in 1975, a major international effort had been put in hand involving several United Nations agencies, including ECE, UNEP, UNESCO, WHO, ITU, IMO, UNDP and FAO, as well as the European Communities and major international institutions such as the World Bank and the European Investment Bank. A number of key international instruments, notably the Barcelona Convention and its protocols, had also been put in place. Those activities provided a solid platform for the proposals set out below, which are intended to support and, where necessary to augment them.

The participating States recognized that all sectors of society, including governments, the public and industry, bore a responsibility for integrating environmental considerations into economic and social policy- and decision-making, thereby contributing to sustainable development. Policies should be guided, *inter alia*, by the Polluter Pays Principle and the Precautionary Principle. The participating States found it necessary to promote greater environmental awareness in the countries concerned by means of educational and vocational training measures and by information campaigns. They also underlined the importance of the contribution of persons and organizations dedicated to the protection and improvement of the environment. They stressed the need to respect the right of such persons and organizations freely to express their concerns.

The participating States reaffirmed their willingness expressed at the Sofia CSCE Meeting on the Protection of the Environment to continue to promote exchanges of information and environmental data. Such co-operation should be of special significance for increasing the effectiveness of environmental protection measures in the Mediterranean region.

Mediterranean co-operation would benefit from closer relations between participating States and non-participating States and should include equally training, scientific and technological research, utilization of energy resources, statistical harmonization and environmentally sound technologies.

Subsidiary Working Body I dealt with item 4 of the Agenda: Specific aspects of co-operation.

Subsidiary Working Body II dealt with item 5 of the Agenda: Protection of Mediterranean ecosystems.

A. Specific aspects of co-operation

1. Examination of the opportunities offered to contribute to the faster social and economic development of the countries of the region, in particular those which are developing from an economic point of view

1.1 Positive political changes in Europe and economic dynamism, combined with improved market access, have been an important external factor for the economic, social and human rights development of the Mediterranean region. The participating States confirm their willingness to continue to co-operate, where appropriate, through a policy of friendly and open relations, with the non-participating Mediterranean States. It is also necessary that the non-participating Mediterranean States broadly liberalize intra-Mediterranean trade. Regional and subregional integration under way in the Mediterranean area among some non-participating Mediterranean States, especially if combined with an easing of political tensions, should lead to more intensive trade. Initiatives along those lines should be supported.

1.2 Co-operation projects and financial measures in this region should be co-ordinated, when appropriate, among and between donors and recipient States, and other relevant bodies, in order to avoid duplication. In some cases, projects should be carried out at the multilateral level to ensure maximum effectiveness. One of the main requirements for the creation of millions of jobs is the economic and political stability of the region. This in turn will only come about if there is a freer and more equitable political and economic environment, based on sustainable economic growth.

1.3 The participating States are prepared to co-operate with the non-participating Mediterranean States in meeting those challenges. To this end they will examine possibilities for achieving equitable market access and for improved financial, technical and economic co-operation, when considered appropriate by individual participating States. The guidelines for action in these fields in the Mediterranean should entail in particular:

- support for regional co-operation and integration among Mediterranean countries;

- intensified efforts regarding environmental projects in the countries concerned;

- further support for private investment and joint ventures as a means of creating new employment opportunities;

- effective use of forms of co-operation such as Mediterranean concerns, consortia, and trade and business associations;

- more intensive dialogue with Mediterranean partners on fundamental issues of economic policy in particular;

- the need for policies aimed at economic and social development to incorporate environmental considerations and thereby promote sustainable development.

1.4 Financial assistance and other forms of co-operation alone cannot constitute an adequate response. The solution to the problems of the Mediterranean region will be facilitated through far-reaching economic reforms, the introduction of market mechanisms, a real effort to tackle demographic problems, the promotion of political reforms aimed at achieving democracy and a multi-party system, and guarantees of human rights for all citizens. It is the economic, fiscal, legal and social infrastructure and political conditions that determine the extent to which economic operators are prepared to engage in economic and industrial co-operation. The Mediterranean countries are encouraged to assess their possibilities and interests in this regard.

1.5 The participating States emphasize that rational development of transport infrastructure is of importance for co-operation with and within the Mediterranean region. They believe it is useful to continue the analysis of the current and potential transport flows, in particular multimodal transport in the Mediterranean region. They note the fruitful work of the ECE and UNDP, and the appropriateness of continuing this activity.

1.6 The participating States note the importance of continued comprehensive discussion of issues relating to the social and economic development of the countries of the region and co-operation among them. With this purpose in mind, relying on the work of the United Nations and other relevant international organizations, they also believe it is useful to seek adequate fora (conferences, expert meetings, round tables, study visits) on economic co-operation of the Mediterranean and other States concerned.

1.7 The participating States welcome the Environmental Program for the Mediterranean initiated in 1990 by the World Bank and the European Investment Bank.

2. *Examination of possibilities for the harmonization of statistical methods*

The aim is the publication and availability of comprehensive, comparable and updated economic, commercial and demographic data as an instrument for co-operation and as a basis for efficient business relations. To this end, the participating States express their view that a meeting of statistical offices of the Mediterranean countries could be convened by an appropriate institution, such as the ECE Conference of European Statisticians, to discuss harmonization of statistical methods and to consider possible assistance in the field of statistics.

3. *Encouragement of contacts at various levels (expert meetings, round tables, study visits) with a view to contributing to the implementation of concrete programmes for co-operation*

Contacts and co-operation among all the Mediterranean countries should be systematically encouraged since they are a source of peace, stability and economic development in the region. Such contacts should take place at governmental, non-governmental and people-to-people levels. Contacts in the form of expert meetings, round tables and study visits could deal with cultural, religious, human-rights, demographic, environmental, agricultural, water-resources, transport, communication and economic subjects, including small and medium-sized enterprises. They have a special role in the development of economic infrastructure in the region. The need for establishing economic, legal, banking and other conditions that would take into account the requirements of such enterprises could also be discussed in this context together with arrangements providing these enterprises with appropriate conditions.

4. *Co-operation in the field of solar and wind energy*

The Mediterranean region offers excellent climatic conditions for the application of solar and wind energy. The uses of solar and wind energy as well as of other alternative and renewable energy sources, the adoption of energy savings measures and the setting up of pilot plants should be intensified. Consideration should be given to setting up - with suitable environmental precautions - solar, wind, biomass, geothermal and hydroelectric power plants to help solve the problems connected with environmental hazards and the depletion of fossil fuels. Exchange of information and regional co-operation in this field should thus be encouraged.

5. *Consideration of questions relating to the conservation and restoration of historic centres and the preservation of cultural heritage, including marine archeology*

The protection, conservation, restoration and preservation of the cultural heritage, including historic monuments and their environment, are of great importance for the balanced development of the Mediterranean countries. The participating States appreciate and encourage the efforts to achieve these aims, *inter alia*, within international organizations such as UNESCO or the programme within the Mediterranean Action Plan dealing with coastal historic sites of common interest. They appreciate and encourage contributions and expert co-operation towards the restoration of historic centres. The cultural, social and educational role of museums, the protection of submerged archeological remains, the scientific work in this respect and the fight against the illegal sale and illicit traffic of antiquities should also be encouraged. Meetings of experts from all countries concerned, including non-participating Mediterranean States, should be promoted for the exchange of views and information in the field of cultural heritage, including underwater archaeology and the illegal sale and illicit traffic of antiquities and, if deemed necessary, for the introduction of effective measures to reinforce co-operation in a practical way.

B. **Protection of Mediterranean ecosystems**

1. *Urban, agricultural and industrial water uses and requirements in the Mediterranean countries*

1.1 It is essential for all the Mediterranean countries to draw up and implement coherent long-term water supply policies which take into account not only of the actual needs of the population and the production sectors concerned, but also of the need to preserve the environment and, in particular, to ensure that the ecological potential of the Mediterranean wetlands is not lost. Such policies should promote the efficient use of water, avoiding needless waste, and be based on a thorough analysis of the quantity and quality of available water resources. Particular attention should also be paid to establishing appropriate means for assessing the environmental impact of dams, aqueducts and other water resource development works.

1.2 The participating States declare their readiness to:

- encourage the exchange of information on water resources in the Mediterranean Basin, taking advantage of the experiences of relevant organizations as well as the methodology of the CORINE programme of the European Community and other programmes;

- encourage consideration of the impact on the Mediterranean environment - including transboundary effects - of policies regarding water supply and the exploitation of water resources;

- promote research and exchange of experience regarding the assessment of the environmental impact of water supply works and the exploitation of water resources;

- support moves to ensure the efficient use and conservation of water resources, including awareness promotion campaigns.

2. *Pollution of surface and underground water and of the Mediterranean Sea*

2.1 Controlling water pollution in the Mediterranean Basin is both an environmental policy objective and an economic necessity. Pollution of surface and underground water not only damages the environment, it also destroys an extremely scarce resource. The preparation and implementation of effective measures to protect watercourses and aquifers against pollution is therefore an absolute priority for the Mediterranean countries and should form a fundamental part of an integrated water-management policy.

2.2 The participating States intend to:

- encourage the Mediterranean countries concerned to set up a legal and regulatory framework to help combat the pollution of surface and underground water and to set up appropriate administrative structures;

- promote exchanges of information, and the establishment of arrangements to facilitate appropriate transfer of environmentally sound technologies to prevent and reduce the pollution of surface and underground water;

- intensify international co-operation on the environmental protection of the Mediterranean, including co-operation among the participating States and non-participating Mediterranean States concerned.

2.3 Controlling the pollution of the Mediterranean is a key objective of the Barcelona Convention and the protocols on pollution from land-based sources, dumping at sea and measures to control pollution by oil and other harmful substances, as well as of the Mediterranean Action Plan. Broader international support for these agreements could contribute to their more effective realization. Parties to these agreements are encouraged to strengthen implementation based on a substance-oriented approach, focusing on individual sectors or industries, as well as on a source-oriented approach, in order to maintain the quality of the marine environment in the Mediterranean and guarantee sustainable development.

The Genoa Declaration and the Charter on Euro-Mediterranean Co-operation concerning the environment in the Mediterranean Basin, referred to as the Nicosia Charter, stressed the reduction of pollution from land-based sources, in particular by adopting concrete measures concerning urban sewage and waste treatment and disposal.

2.4 The participating States should:

- call on the Mediterranean coastal countries to continue implementation of the Barcelona Convention as well as the protocols on pollution from land-based sources and dumping at sea and on co-operation in combatting pollution by oil and other harmful substances;

- call on all States to terminate the dumping of harmful wastes, as well as incineration activities, at sea in accordance with appropriate global and regional agreements;

- encourage - taking into account, in particular, the Genoa Declaration and the guidelines proposed by the signatories to the Nicosia Charter - the setting-up of urban-sewage treatment plants with at least biological treatment, where possible and appropriate; the establishment of emission limits based, to the extent possible, on the best available technologies, not entailing excessive costs, specifically applicable to individual sectors or industries or to specific substances; the management, reduction and possible elimination of hazardous and toxic industrial waste; and the investment efforts undertaken in this respect;

- encourage the use of clean production methods in order to reduce the generation of waste at source and encourage appropriate technology transfers and the acquisition of means for the prevention and reduction of sea pollution and for the treatment and disposal of waste;

- urge the adoption of appropriate measures to apply the precautionary principle to waste management policy;

- call on all States which have not yet done so to accede to and/or ratify as soon as possible the Basel Convention on the control of the transboundary movements of hazardous wastes and their disposal, in order to reduce the transboundary movements of such wastes and ensure their disposal in an environmentally sound way;

- express their support for the work of the contracting parties of the Barcelona Convention on the monitoring of the transboundary movements of hazardous wastes in the Mediterranean region and on the elaboration of a regional agreement in accordance with the spirit of the Basel Convention;

- encourage the reduction of the negative impact on Mediterranean ecosystems of agricultural practices that are not environmentally sound.

3. National, bilateral and international action to control and prevent pollution by national and transboundary waterways flowing into the Mediterranean and pollution by ships

3.1 The prevention, reduction and control of polluting waste from land sources which reaches the Mediterranean via watercourses is one of the basic objectives of the Protocol for the protection of the Mediterranean Sea against pollution from land-based sources, However, in spite of the measures adopted by the Contracting Parties pursuant to the Protocol, they are still a long way from bringing this type of pollution completely under control, since more investment is needed to treat household and industrial wastes and waste water which are currently discharged without adequate treatment.

3.2 Pollution from ships and the danger of accidents at sea present a continuous hazard to the coastal States of the Mediterranean, many of which have invested heavily in industries that depend on a clean marine environment. Greater and more sustained efforts are required to implement various global and regional conventions aimed at preventing pollution from ships.

3.3 The participating States should therefore:

- call on the coastal States to continue the proceedings on the implementation of the Protocol on pollution from land-based sources;

- call on all States to prevent and phase out the discharges at sea from ships of oils and their mixtures and all noxious liquid substances, in accordance with global and appropriate regional standards and controls;

- reconfirm their support for the recommendations and conclusions elaborated in this field by the Vienna CSCE Follow-up Meeting 1986, the Bonn CSCE Conference and the Sofia CSCE Meeting, as well as the proceedings of the ECE, taking into account the work of the International Law Commission, with a view to drawing up conventions on the protection and use of trans-frontier watercourses and international lakes and on the prevention and control of the transboundary effects of industrial accidents that could supplement and enhance the effectiveness of the arrangements set up by the Protocol for the protection of the Mediterranean Sea against pollution from land-based sources, and also taking into account the ECE draft Convention on the application of environmental impact assessment in a transboundary context;

- encourage the efforts undertaken or under consideration by participating States and non-participating Mediterranean States to equip Mediterranean ports with reception facilities for ballast and bilge waters;

- promote the establishment of national surveillance systems to control pollution from ships in accordance with the relevant international conventions on marine pollution;

- encourage the Mediterranean States to adopt appropriate measures to establish the Mediterranean Sea as a special area with regard to garbage disposal at sea from ships, according to the principles established in the MARPOL Convention;

- encourage efforts to develop a co-ordination system among the existing structures to respond to emergency alerts occurring in the Mediterranean Sea which could involve serious consequences for the marine environment, taking into account the work in the ECE on elaboration of a legal instrument for the prevention and control of transboundary effects of industrial accidents and the Malta Regional Marine Pollution Emergency Response Centre for the Mediterranean Sea (REMPEC);

- call on the countries concerned to accede to and/or ratify the international conventions on marine pollution, particularly the International Convention for the Prevention of Pollution from ships, 1973, as modified by the 1978 Protocol, with Annexes I, II, III, IV and V (MARPOL 73/78), the Convention on the Prevention of Marine Pollution by Dumping of Wastes and Other Matter, 1972 (London Dumping Convention) and the Convention on the International Regulations for Preventing Collisions at Sea, 1972.

4. *Recycling of waste water and the use of other new technologies to obtain water resources*

4.1 In response to the growing needs of the population and of production sectors, the Mediterranean countries should take new measures to ensure the best possible use of available water resources. It is certainly time to step up the recycling of waste water.

4.2 Certain participating States and non-participating Mediterranean States have already developed techniques for the treatment and recycling of waste water - for agricultural and industrial purposes - the economic feasibility of which has been fully confirmed. Other treatment and desalination techniques for the supply of water to population groups suffering from severe shortage have also been developed.

4.3 The participating States should encourage:

- research into the development of new technologies for the recycling and re-use of waste water and the creation of additional water resources, and exchange of the results of such research;

- the implementation of demonstration projects in this field and the exchange of experience between countries concerned.

5. *Desertification and the struggle against it, including parameters and techniques; initiatives in international co-operation in this field; the role of forest conservation and reforestation*

5.1 Deforestation, soil erosion, inappropriate farming practices and unfavourable climatic conditions explain the scale of this problem in the Mediterranean Basin. Desertification control thus calls for the implementation of an overall strategy including reforestation and erosion control measures and the development of farming practices better suited to soil type and climatic conditions. Research in this area should also be stepped up in order to improve understanding of the causes of desertification, including increased information, training and incentives for the farmers concerned.

5.2 The participating States should:

- promote the objective of a positive balance between the regeneration of plant cover and forest clearance by 1995;

- promote campaigns to increase public awareness and demonstration projects to develop new farming practices compatible with soil protection;

- step up the implementation of programmes to combat desertification, erosion and deforestation, and intensify co-operation for the development of research activities in this field;

- encourage the establishment of programmes to prevent the erosion and degradation of limestone regions in view of their sensitivity and ecological fragility;

- promote the dissemination and optimum use of the results of research on these subjects through, for example, the work initiated by the Sahara and Sahel Observatory.

6. *International co-operation in the Mediterranean in preventing and extinguishing forest fires; the role of meteorology and communication networks; traditional and other techniques in the struggle against forest fires, including the use and international co-ordination of aerial means, land techniques, and standardization of fire-fighting methods; information and awareness campaigns*

6.1 Forest fires represent one of the most serious environmental problems for the Mediterranean countries, in which hundreds of thousands of hectares of forest are destroyed by fire each year.

6.2 Action in this area should be based on an overall approach which includes the identification of causes, prevention, surveillance, fire-fighting and the extension of co-operation in the field of research, particularly into the influence of climatic factors on the risk of fires, this being one aspect of the EPOCH programme.

6.3 The participating States should:

- promote the establishment of integrated strategies for the prevention, surveillance and control of forest fires;

- encourage regional co-operation for the creation of communication networks including the exchange of meteorological data enabling fire-fighting measures to be made more effective, taking into account the work done by the European Community;

- assist, where possible, the non-participating Mediterranean States in their efforts to acquire the adequate means to fight forest fires;

- step up research into the causes of forest fires and the dissemination and use of results;

- encourage public awareness promotion campaigns on the danger of forest fires;

- envisage the setting up of forms of co-operation with the participation of all Mediterranean countries.

7. *Atmospheric problems, in particular air quality in urban centres and the effects of air pollution on historical monuments and biological ecosystems; typical sources of air pollution in Mediterranean countries and the Mediterranean share in long-range air pollution*

7.1 In a number of Mediterranean towns and regions which have seen large-scale industrial development or very rapid population growth, atmospheric pollution levels are too high, in particular as a result of the increase in road traffic. This leads to excessive concentrations of various pollutants, including SO2, NOx, COx, VOC, dust and photochemical ozone, which can cause damage to the historical and architectural heritage, can lead to forest decline, threaten crops and natural vegetation and endanger human health.

7.2 The situation, moreover, could worsen if the Mediterranean countries do not adopt appropriate measures to prevent the deterioration of air quality which may result from economic and industrial development. It is also essential for the Mediterranean countries to take into consideration other requirements, in particular the need to contribute to the action to be taken to prevent global climatic change, which could have particularly dramatic effects on the Mediterranean Basin. It therefore appears necessary to implement co-ordinated policies to increase the use of renewable energy resources and the energy efficiency of non-renewable energy resources such as fossil fuels without thereby compromising economic development.

7.3 The participating States undertake to:

- promote, for example within the existing framework of activities such as the forthcoming Second World Climate Conference and the Mediterranean Action Plan, studies and the establishment of a monitoring network for the Mediterranean region on climate changes and on the effects of atmospheric pollutants and the elaboration of a programme to prevent adverse effects, and, in accordance with the 1979 Convention on Long-Range Transboundary Air Pollution, to reinforce co-operative activities on air quality problems, including those associated with photochemical ozone and other secondary pollutants;

- encourage measures to improve air quality in urban centres and surrounding areas;

- encourage efforts for the abatement of atmospheric pollution in living spaces (indoor pollution) through new housing design, clean appliances, and building and furniture materials which do not release atmospheric pollutants;

- encourage the exchange of information on improved technologies available for the reduction of air pollution and their application in existing plants and to the design of new industrial complexes as well as to the control of emissions from mobile sources;

- intensify efforts to exchange atmospheric-pollution reduction technologies;

- support the implementation of measures to improve energy efficiency, energy saving and the increased use of renewable energy sources;

- improve the dissemination and application of the results of research programmes into the effects of pollution on human health, historical and architectural heritage and ecosystems.

8. *The biosphere and related questions of ecology and human activities; nature conservation; study of coastal and island areas including urban development*

8.1 The Mediterranean coastal areas, which are among the richest in terms of the diversity of habitats, species and landscapes, are subject to growing pressure. Mediterranean coastal wetlands play an essential role in the maintenance of biological diversity; unfortunately, however, a significant proportion of them has disappeared as a result of human activities. For this reason the Genoa Declaration and the signatories to the Nicosia Charter attach special importance to the protection and management of the Mediterranean coast. A number of key international instruments aimed specifically at protecting internationally important species and their habitats have been introduced in recent years, including the Berne, Bonn and Ramsar Conventions, the Protocol to the Barcelona Convention concerning Mediterranean Specially Protected Areas and the ECE and EC legal instruments.

8.2 The participating States undertake to:

- co-operate with the non-participating Mediterranean States to encourage the establishment of more effective policies and appropriate instruments, such as environmental protection infrastructures for the integrated management of coastal areas;

- support work under way to identify sensitive coastal areas in need of protection and to set up a geographical database for the coastal zone also through remote sensing monitoring systems;

- support the work done by the General Council for Fisheries in the Mediterranean;

- encourage the establishment of procedures for the assessment of the environmental impact of development projects in order to prevent possible negative effects, including appropriate consultations in the spirit of good neighbourly relations with any State likely to be affected, taking into consideration the work of the ECE;

- give active support to the implementation of existing international instruments to protect key species and their habitats, in particular rare or endangered species;

- promote the establishment of monitoring and integrated management plans for the most endangered biotopes, especially in coastal wetlands;

- welcome the decision taken by, or under consideration in, some coastal States to ban pelagic drift-netting in the Mediterranean Sea;

- note the commitment by signatories to the Barcelona Convention to adopt all appropriate measures for the protection of *Posidonia oceanica* communities and all other marine phanerogams which are essential plants for the Mediterranean ecosystem and to undertake to control and to regulate trawling and other activities destructive to *Posidonia* bottoms and all other marine phanerogams.

9. *Environmental aspects of the development of tourism*

9.1 The development of tourism places severe stresses on the environment and on natural resources, particularly in the Mediterranean, where seasonal saturation, over-occupation of the coastline and the destruction of nature have already reached alarming proportions. The maintenance of environmental quality is a precondition for the establishment and development of tourism. Greater international co-operation aimed at a balanced development of tourism in the Mediterranean should be promoted.

9.2 For this reason, the Mediterranean countries - for which tourism is one of the most important economic activities - have compelling reasons for drawing up and applying more effective environmental protection policies and promoting environmentally sound tourism. In particular, in co-operation with all countries concerned, they ought to take appropriate steps to reduce seasonal tourist congestion on the coast, such as promoting cultural and low-season tourism and providing tourist facilities inland.

9.3 The participating States declare their readiness to:

- encourage the further development of integrated environmental-management programmes to assess in advance the environmental impact of tourist resorts;

- co-operate in the efforts of the Mediterranean countries to ensure better seasonal distribution and more balanced geographical distribution of tourism in order to reduce the pressure on the coastline through the encouragement of different kinds of tourism (culture, conferences, health spas, sports tourism, etc.);

- encourage the implementation of projects for the management and restoration of Mediterranean coastal areas damaged by tourism;

- promote exchanges of information aimed at ensuring a suitable quality of bathing waters;

- promote campaigns to inform tourists and make them aware of the need for responsible behaviour which respects the environment, using for this purpose, amongst other means, existing international organizations, such as the World Tourism Organization.

10. Review and improvement of exchanges of information relating to the protection of the environment

10.1 The setting up of a co-ordinated information system on the state of the environment and natural resources would facilitate the implementation of effective policies and the use of research and human resources in this field. Existing international organizations and institutions such as the ECE, MAP/UNEP and the newly established European Environment Agency, which is open to certain third countries, provide a basis for broadening and strengthening co-operation.

10.2 The exchange of information and experience relating to environmental protection between participating and non-participating Mediterranean States should be improved.

10.3 Co-operation and exchange of information on nuclear plant safety issues should be intensified.

10.4 The participating States should:

- seek opportunities to co-operate when appropriate among themselves and with the non-participating Mediterranean States in the creation of databases on the state of the environment and natural resources, especially in the priority areas listed in the Genoa Declaration and by the signatories to the Nicosia Charter;

- promote exchanges of information and experience acquired in drawing up and implementing environmental protection policies, drawing upon the experience of the ECE, in particular its monitoring programme EMEP, and of other relevant bodies such as UNEP;

- support the preparation of a document on the environmental rights of citizens as agreed in the Bergen Ministerial Declaration of 1990;

- encourage the dissemination of information on new, clean and pollution-control technologies, in particular through UNEP's Industry and Environment Office, the ECE, OECD, the newly established European Environment Agency and other appropriate bodies;

- support the continuation of the activities carried out in the framework of the Mediterranean Action Plan;

- encourage the exchange and dissemination of scientific information carried out through institutions such as the International Commission for Scientific Exploration of the Mediterranean Sea;

- support the organization, in co-operation with the non-participating Mediterranean States, of training programmes for environmental experts;

- encourage the examination of the possible establishment by participating and interested non-participating Mediterranean States of toxic emissions reporting programmes requiring that enterprises disclose to national and local officials information on the use, storage and routine or accidental release of toxic chemicals into the air, soil or water.

The representatives of the participating States express their profound gratitude to the people and government of Spain for the excellent organization of the Palma de Mallorca Meeting and the warm hospitality extended to the delegations which participated in the Meeting.

INTERPRETATIVE STATEMENTS[1]

Interpretative statement by the United States of America

The United States delegation can accept the mention, in the sixth paragraph of the final report, of a member of the Commission of the European Community, with the understanding that there is agreement that the acceptance of this wording shall not constitute a precedent for future CSCE Meetings.

* * *

Interpretative statement by Malta

The delegation of Malta interprets the paragraph dealing with the exchange of views on Agenda item 3 of the Report of the Meeting on the Mediterranean, held in Palma de Mallorca from 24 September to 19 October 1990, as only partially covering the ideas expressed in the debate on the question of security. Security was so widely discussed that it deserved, at least, an appropriate mention in the Report.

---

[1] Journal No. 19, 13th Plenary Meeting (18 October 1990).

VIENNA DOCUMENT 1990

OF THE NEGOTIATIONS ON CONFIDENCE- AND SECURITY-BUILDING MEASURES CONVENED IN ACCORDANCE WITH THE RELEVANT PROVISIONS OF THE CONCLUDING DOCUMENT OF THE VIENNA MEETING OF THE CONFERENCE ON SECURITY AND COOPERATION IN EUROPE

Vienna, 17 November 1990

(1) The representatives of the participating States of the Conference on Security and Co-operation in Europe (CSCE), Austria, Belgium, Bulgaria, Canada, Cyprus, Czech and Slovak Federal Republic, Denmark, Finland, France, Germany, Greece, the Holy See, Hungary, Iceland, Ireland, Italy, Liechtenstein, Luxembourg, Malta, Monaco, the Netherlands, Norway, Poland, Portugal, Romania, San Marino, Spain, Sweden, Switzerland, Turkey, the Union of Soviet Socialist Republics, the United Kingdom, the United States of America and Yugoslavia, met in Vienna from 9 March 1989, in accordance with the provisions relating to the Conference on Confidence- and Security-Building Measures and Disarmament in Europe contained in the Concluding Documents of the Madrid and Vienna Follow-up Meetings of the CSCE.

(2) The participating States recalled that the aim of the Conference on Confidence- and Security- Building Measures and Disarmament in Europe is, as a substantial and integral part of the multi-lateral process initiated by the Conference on Security and Co-operation in Europe, to undertake, in stages, new, effective and concrete actions designed to make progress in strengthening confidence and security and in achieving disarmament, so as to give effect and expression to the duty of States to refrain from the threat or use of force in their mutual relations as well as in their international relations in general.

(3) Opening statements were made by the Ministers of Foreign Affairs and other Heads of Delegation.

(4) From 16 January to 5 February 1990, the participating States held discussions in a seminar setting on military doctrine in relation to

the posture, structure and activities of conventional forces in the zone of application for confidence- and security-building measures*. Encouraged by the course of these discussions, the participating States decided to hold a second seminar on military doctrine in the spring of 1991 in Vienna.

(5) The participating States have adopted the present document which integrates a set of new confidence- and security-building measures with measures adopted in the Document of the Stockholm Conference which have been further developed in the light of experience gained.

(6) The participating States recognised that the mutually complementary confidence- and security-building measures which are adopted in the present document and which are in accordance with the mandates of the Madrid and Vienna Follow-up Meetings of the CSCE serve by their scope and nature and by their implementation to strengthen confidence and security in Europe.

(7) The participating States also recognised that the negotiations will continue in accordance with the mandates of the Madrid and Vienna Follow-up Meetings of the CSCE in order to further build upon and expand the results already achieved and that proposals which have been submitted remain subject to further negotiations.

(8) The participating States recalled the declaration on Refraining from the Threat or Use of Force contained in paragraphs (9) to (27) of the Document of the Stockholm Conference and stressed its continuing validity as seen in the light of the Charter of Paris for a New Europe.

(9) The participating States have adopted the following:

I. ANNUAL EXCHANGE OF MILITARY INFORMATION

Information on military forces

(10) The participating States will exchange annually information on their military forces concerning the military organization, manpower and major weapon and equipment systems, as specified below, in the

---

* Annex 1.

zone of application for confidence- and security-building measures (CSBMs).

(11) The information will be provided in an agreed format to all other participating States not later than 15 December of each year. It will be valid as of 1 January of the following year and will include:

(11.1) 1. Information on the command organisation of those military forces referred to under points 2 and 3 specifying the designation and subordination of all formations* and units** at each level of command down to and including brigade/regiment or equivalent level.

(11.2) 2. For each formation and combat unit*** of land forces down to and including brigade/regiment or equivalent level the information will indicate:

(11.2.1) - the designation and subordination;

(11.2.2) - whether it is active or non-active****;

(11.2.3) - the normal peacetime location of its headquarters indicated by exact geographic terms and/or co-ordinates;

(11.2.4) - the peacetime authorised personnel strength;

(11.2.5) - the major organic weapon and equipment systems, specifying the numbers of each type of:

(11.2.5.1) - battle tanks;

(11.2.5.2) - helicopters;

---

* In this context, formations are armies, corps and divisions and their equivalents.

** In this context, units are brigades, regiments and their equivalents.

*** In this context, combat units are infantry, armoured, mechanised, motorised rifle, artillery, combat engineer and army aviation units. Those combat units which are airmobile or airborne will also be included.

**** In this context, non-active formations or combat units are those manned from zero to fifteen per cent of their authorised combat strength. This term includes low strength formations and units.

(11.2.5.3) - armoured combat vehicles;

(11.2.5.4) - anti-tank guided missile launchers permanently/integrally mounted on armoured vehicles;

(11.2.5.5) - self-propelled and towed artillery pieces, mortars and multiple rocket launchers (100 mm calibre and above);

(11.2.5.6) - armoured vehicle launched bridges.

(11.3) For each amphibious formation and amphibious combat unit* permanently located in the zone of application down to and including brigade/regiment or equivalent level, the information will include the items as set out above.

(11.4) 3. For each air formation and air combat unit** of the air forces, air defence aviation and of naval aviation permanently based on land down to and including wing/air regiment or equivalent level the information will include:

(11.4.1) - the designation and subordination;

(11.4.2) - the normal peacetime location of the headquarters indicated by exact geographic terms and/or co-ordinates;

(11.4.3) - the normal peacetime location of the unit indicated by the air base or military airfield on which the unit is based, specifying:

(11.4.3.1) - the designation or, if applicable, name of the air base or military airfield and

(11.4.3.2) - its location indicated by exact geographic terms and/or co-ordinates;

(11.4.4) - the peacetime authorised personnel strength***;

---

* Combat unit as defined above.

** In this context, air combat units are units, the majority of whose organic aircraft are combat aircraft.

*** As an exception, this information need not be provided on air defence aviation units.

(11.4.5) - the numbers of each type of:

(11.4.5.1) - combat aircraft;

(11.4.5.2) - helicopters

organic to the formation or unit.

Information on plans for the deployment of major weapon and equipment systems

(12) The participating States will exchange annually information on their plans for the deployment of major weapon and equipment systems as specified in the provisions on Information on Military Forces within the zone of application for CSBMs.

(13) The information will be provided in an agreed format to all other participating States not later than 15 December of each year. It will cover plans for the following year and will include:

(13.1) - the type and name of the weapon/equipment systems to be deployed;

(13.2) - the total number of each weapon/equipment system;

(13.3) - whenever possible, the number of each weapon/equipment system planned to be allocated to each formation or unit;

(13.4) - the extent to which the deployment will add to or replace existing weapon/equipment systems.

Information on military budgets

(14) The participating States will exchange annually information on their military budgets for the forthcoming fiscal year, itemising defence expenditures on the basis of the categories set out in the United Nations "Instrument for Standardised International Reporting of Military Expenditures" adopted on 12 December 1980.

(15) The information will be provided to all other participating States not later than two months after the military budget has been approved by the competent national authorities.

(16) Each participating State may ask for clarification from any other participating State of the budgetary information provided. Questions should be submitted within a period of two months following the receipt of a participating State's budgetary information. Participating States will make every effort to answer such questions fully and promptly. The questions and replies may be transmitted to all other participating States.

II. RISK REDUCTION

Mechanism for consultation and co-operation as regards unusual military activities

(17) Participating States will, in accordance with the following provisions, consult and co-operate with each other about any unusual and unscheduled activities of their military forces outside their normal peacetime locations which are militarily significant, within the zone of application for CSBMs and about which a participating State expresses its security concern.

(17.1) The participating State which has concerns about such an activity may transmit a request for an explanation to another participating State where the activity is taking place.

(17.1.1) The request will state the cause, or causes, of the concern and, to the extent possible, the type and location, or area, of the activity.

(17.1.2) The reply will be transmitted within not more than 48 hours.

(17.1.3) The reply will give answers to questions raised, as well as any other relevant information which might help to clarify the activity giving rise to concern.

(17.1.4) The request and the reply will be transmitted to all other participating States without delay.

(17.2) The requesting State, after considering the reply provided, may then request a meeting to discuss the matter.

(17.2.1) The requesting State may ask for a meeting with the responding State.

(17.2.1.1) Such a meeting will be convened within not more than 48 hours.

(17.2.1.2) The request for such a meeting will be transmitted to all participating States without delay.

(17.2.1.3) The responding State is entitled to ask other interested participating States, in particular those which might be involved in the activity, to participate in the meeting.

(17.2.1.4) Such a meeting will be held at a venue to be mutually agreed upon by the requesting and the responding States. If there is no agreement, the meeting will be held at the Conflict Prevention Centre.

(17.2.1.5) The requesting and responding States will, jointly or separately, transmit a report of the meeting to all other participating States without delay.

(17.2.2) The requesting State may ask for a meeting of all participating States.

(17.2.2.1) Such a meeting will be convened within not more than 48 hours.

(17.2.2.2) The Conflict Prevention Centre will serve as the forum for such a meeting.

(17.2.2.3) Participating States involved in the matter to be discussed undertake to be represented at such a meeting.

(17.3) The communications between participating States provided for above will be transmitted preferably through the CSBM communications network.

Co-operation as regards hazardous incidents of a military nature

(18) Participating States will co-operate by reporting and clarifying hazardous incidents of a military nature within the zone of application for CSBMs in order to prevent possible misunderstandings and mitigate the effects on another participating State.

(18.1) Each participating State will designate a point to contact in case of such hazardous incidents and will so inform all other participating States. A list of such points will be kept available at the Conflict Prevention Centre.

(18.2) In the event of such a hazardous incident the participating State whose military forces are involved in the incident should provide the information available to other participating States in an expeditious manner. Any participating State affected by such an incident may also request clarification as appropriate. Such requests will receive a prompt response.

(18.3) Communications between participating States will be transmitted preferably through the CSBM communications network.

(18.4) Matters relating to information about such hazardous incidents may be discussed by participating States at the Conflict Prevention Centre, either at the annual implementation assessment meeting at the Centre, or at additional meetings convened there.

(18.5) These provisions will not affect the rights and obligations of participating States under any international agreement concerning hazardous incidents, nor will they preclude additional methods of reporting and clarifying hazardous incidents.

III. CONTACTS

Visits to air bases

(19) Each participating State with air combat units reported under paragraph (11) will arrange visits for representatives of all other participating States to one of its normal peacetime air bases* on which such units are located in order to provide the visitors with the opportunity to view activity at the air base, including preparations to carry out the functions of the air base and to gain an impression of the approximate number of air sorties and type of missions being flown.

(20) No participating State will be obliged to arrange more than one such visit in any five-year period.

---

* In this context, the term normal peacetime air base is understood to mean the normal peacetime location of the air combat unit indicated by the air base or military airfield on which the unit is based.

(21) Prior indications given by participating States of forthcoming schedules for such visits for the subsequent year(s) may be discussed at the annual implementation assessment meetings.

(22) As a rule, up to two visitors from each participating State will be invited.

(23) Invitations will be extended to all participating States 42 days or more in advance of the visit. The invitation will indicate a preliminary programme, including: place, date and time of assembly; planned duration; languages to be used; arrangements for board, lodging and transportation; equipment permitted to be used during the visit; and any other information that may be considered useful.

(24) When the air base to be visited is located on the territory of another participating State, the invitations will be issued by the participating State on whose territory the air base is located. In such cases, the responsibilities as host delegated by this State to the participating State arranging the visit will be specified in the invitation.

(25) Replies to the invitation, indicating the names and ranks of the visitors, will be given not later than 21 days after the issue of the invitation. If the invitation is not accepted in time, it will be assumed that no visitors will be sent.

(26) The visit to the air base will last for a minimum of 24 hours.

(27) In the course of the visit, the visitors will be given a briefing on the purpose and functions of the air base and on current activity at the air base. They will have the opportunity to communicate with commanders and troops, including those of support/logistic units located at the air base.

(28) The visitors will be provided with the opportunity to view all types of aircraft located at the air base.

(29) At the close of the visit, the host State will provide an opportunity for the visitors to meet together and with host State officials and senior air base personnel to discuss the course of the visit.

(30) The host State will determine the programme for the visit and access granted to visitors at the air base.

(31) The visitors will follow the instructions issued by the host State in accordance with the provisions set out in this document.

(32) The visitors will be provided with appropriate accommodation in a location suitable for carrying out the visit.

(33) The invited State will cover the travel expenses of its representatives to and from the place of assembly specified in the invitation.

(34) Participating States should, in due co-operation with the visitors, ensure that no action is taken which could be harmful to the safety of visitors.

Military contacts

(35) To improve further their mutual relations in the interest of strengthening the process of confidence and security building, the participating States will, as appropriate, promote and facilitate:

(35.1) - exchanges and visits between senior military/defence representatives;

(35.2) - contacts between relevant military institutions;

(35.3) - attendance by military representatives of other participating States at courses of instruction;

(35.4) - exchanges between military commanders and officers of commands down to brigade/regiment or equivalent level;

(35.5) - exchanges and contacts between academics and experts in military studies and related areas;

(35.6) - sporting and cultural events between members of their armed forces.

IV. PRIOR NOTIFICATION OF CERTAIN MILITARY ACTIVITIES

(36) The participating States will give notification in writing through diplomatic channels in an agreed form of content, to all other participating States 42 days or more in advance of the start of notifiable* military activities in the zone of application for confidence- and security-building measures (CSBMs).

(37) Notification will be given by the participating State on whose territory the activity in question is planned to take place even if the forces of that State are not engaged in the activity or their strength is below the notifiable level. This will not relieve other participating States of their obligation to give notification, if their involvement in the planned military activity reaches the notifiable level.

(38) Each of the following military activities in the field conducted as a single activity in the zone of application for CSBMs at or above the levels defined below, will be notified:

(38.1) The engagement of formations of land forces** of the participating States in the same exercise activity conducted under a single operational command independently or in combination with any possible air or naval components.

(38.1.1) This military activity will be subject to notification whenever it involves at any time during the activity:
- at least 13,000 troops, including support troops, or
- at least 300 battle tanks

if organized into a divisional structure or at least two brigades/regiments, not necessarily subordinate to the same division.

(38.1.2) The participation of air forces of the participating States will be included in the notification if it is foreseen that in the course of the activity 200 or more sorties by aircraft, excluding helicopters, will be flown.

---

* In this document, the term notifiable means subject to notification.

** In this context, the term land forces includes amphibious, airmobile and airborne forces.

(38.2) The engagement of military forces either in an amphibious landing or in a parachute assault by airborne forces in the zone of application for CSBMs.

(38.2.1) These military activities will be subject to notification whenever the amphibious landing involves at least 3,000 troops or whenever the parachute drop involves at least 3,000 troops.

(38.3) The engagement of formations of land forces of the participating States in a transfer from outside the zone of application for CSBMs to arrival points in the zone, or from inside the zone of application for CSBMs to points of concentration in the zone, to participate in a notifiable exercise activity or to be concentrated.

(38.3.1) The arrival or concentration of these forces will be subject to notification whenever it involves, at any time during the activity:
- at least 13,000 troops, including support troops, or
- at least 300 battle tanks

if organized into a divisional structure or at least two brigades/regiments, not necessarily subordinate to the same division.

(38.3.2) Forces which have been transferred into the zone will be subject to all provisions of agreed CSBMs when they depart their arrival points to participate in a notifiable exercise activity or to be concentrated within the zone of application for CSBMs.

(39) Notifiable military activities carried out without advance notice to the troops involved, are exceptions to the requirement for prior notification to be made 42 days in advance.

(39.1) Notification of such activities, above the agreed thresholds, will be given at the time the troops involved commence such activities.

(40) Notification will be given in writing of each notifiable military activity in the following agreed form:

(41) **A - General Information**

(41.1) The designation of the military activity;

(41.2) The general purpose of the military activity;

(41.3) The names of the States involved in the military activity;

(41.4) The level of command, organizing and commanding the military activity;

(41.5) The start and end dates of the military activity.

(42) **B - Information on different types of notifiable military activities**

(42.1) The engagement of formations of land forces of the participating States in the same exercise activity conducted under a single operational command independently or in combination with any possible air or naval components:

(42.1.1) The total number of troops taking part in the military activity (i.e. ground troops, amphibious troops, airmobile and airborne troops) and the number of troops participating for each State involved, if applicable;

(42.1.2) The designation, subordination, number and type of formations and units participating for each State down to and including brigade/regiment or equivalent level;

(42.1.3) The total number of battle tanks for each State and the total number of anti-tank guided missile launchers mounted on armoured vehicles;

(42.1.4) The total number of artillery pieces and multiple rocket launchers (100 mm calibre or above);

(42.1.5) The total number of helicopters, by category;

(42.1.6) Envisaged number of sorties by aircraft, excluding helicopters;

(42.1.7) Purpose of air missions;

(42.1.8) Categories of aircraft involved;

(42.1.9) The level of command, organizing and commanding the air force participation;

(42.1.10) Naval ship-to-shore gunfire;

(42.1.11) Indication of other naval ship-to-shore support;

(42.1.12) The level of command, organizing and commanding the naval force participation.

(42.2) The engagement of military forces either in an amphibious landing or in a parachute assault by airborne forces in the zone of application for CSBMs:

(42.2.1) The total number of amphibious troops involved in notifiable amphibious landings, and/or the total number of airborne troops involved in notifiable parachute assaults;

(42.2.2) In the case of a notifiable amphibious landing, the point or points of embarkation, if in the zone of application for CSBMs.

(42.3) The engagement of formations of land forces of the participating States in a transfer from outside the zone of application for CSBMs to arrival points in the zone, or from inside the zone of application for CSBMs to points of concentration in the zone, to participate in a notifiable exercise activity or to be concentrated:

(42.3.1) The total number of troops transferred;

(42.3.2) Number and type of divisions participating in the transfer;

(42.3.3) The total number of battle tanks participating in a notifiable arrival or concentration;

(42.3.4) Geographical co-ordinates for the points of arrival and for the points of concentration.

(43) **C - The envisaged area and timeframe of the activity**

(43.1) The area of the military activity delimited by geographic features together with geographic co-ordinates, as appropriate;

(43.2) The start and end dates of each phase (transfers, deployment, concentration of forces, active exercise phase, recovery phase) of activities in the zone of application for CSBMs of participating formations, the tactical purpose and corresponding geographical areas (delimited by geographical co-ordinates) for each phase;

(43.3) Brief description of each phase.

(44) **D - Other information**

(44.1) Changes, if any, in relation to information provided in the annual calendar regarding the activity;

(44.2) Relationship of the activity to other notifiable activities.

V. OBSERVATION OF CERTAIN MILITARY ACTIVITIES

(45) The participating States will invite observers from all other participating States to the following notifiable military activities:

(45.1) - The engagement of formations of land forces* of the participating States in the same exercise activity conducted under a single operational command independently or in combination with any possible air or naval components.

(45.2) - The engagement of military forces either in an amphibious landing or in a parachute assault by airborne forces in the zone of application for CSBMs.

(45.3) - In the case of the engagement of formations of land forces of the participating States in a transfer from outside the zone of application for CSBMs to arrival points in the zone, or from inside the zone of application for CSBMs to points of concentration in the zone, to participate in a notifiable exercise activity or to be concentrated, the concentration of these forces. Forces which have been transferred into the zone will be subject to all provisions of agreed confidence- and security-building measures when they depart their arrival points to participate in a notifiable exercise activity or to be concentrated within the zone of application for CSBMs.

---

* In this context, the term land forces includes amphibious, airmobile and airborne forces.

(45.4) The above-mentioned activities will be subject to observation whenever the number of troops engaged meets or exceeds 17,000 troops, except in the case of either an amphibious landing or a parachute assault by airborne forces, which will be subject to observation whenever the number of troops engaged meets or exceeds 5,000 troops.

(46) The host State will extend the invitations in writing through diplomatic channels to all other participating States at the time of notification. The host State will be the participating State on whose territory the notified activity will take place.

(47) The host State may delegate some of its responsibilities as host to another participating State engaged in the military activity on the territory of the host State. In such cases, the host State will specify the allocation of responsibilities in its invitation to observe the activity.

(48) Each participating State may send up to two observers to the military activity to be observed.

(49) The invited State may decide whether to send military and/or civilian observers, including members of its personnel accredited to the host State. Military observers will, normally, wear their uniforms and insignia while performing their tasks.

(50) Replies to the invitation will be given in writing not later than 21 days after the issue of the invitation.

(51) The participating States accepting an invitation will provide the names and ranks of their observers in their reply to the invitation. If the invitation is not accepted in time, it will be assumed that no observers will be sent.

(52) Together with the invitation the host State will provide a general observation programme, including, the following information:

(52.1) - the date, time and place of assembly of observers;

(52.2) - planned duration of the observation programme;

(52.3) - languages to be used in interpretation and/or translation;

(52.4) - arrangements for board, lodging and transportation of the observers;

(52.5) - arrangements for observation equipment which will be issued to the observers by the host State;

(52.6) - possible authorization by the host State of the use of special equipment that the observers may bring with them;

(52.7) - arrangements for special clothing to be issued to the observers because of weather or environmental factors;

(53) The observers may make requests with regard to the observation programme. The host State will, if possible, accede to them.

(54) The host State will determine a duration of observation which permits the observers to observe a notifiable military activity from the time that agreed thresholds for observation are met or exceeded until, for the last time during the activity, the thresholds for observation are no longer met.

(55) The host State will provide the observers with transportation to the area of the notified activity and back. This transportation will be provided from either the capital or another suitable location to be announced in the invitation, so that the observers are in position before the start of the observation programme.

(56) The invited State will cover the travel expenses for its observers to the capital, or another suitable location specified in the invitation, of the host State, and back.

(57) The observers will be provided equal treatment and offered equal opportunities to carry out their functions.

(58) The observers will be granted, during their mission, the privileges and immunities accorded to diplomatic agents in the Vienna Convention on Diplomatic Relations.

(59) The participating States will ensure that official personnel and troops taking part in an observed military activity, as well as other armed personnel located in the area of the military activity, are adequately informed regarding the presence, status and functions of observers. Participating States should, in due co-operation with

the observers, ensure that no action is taken which could be harmful to the safety of observers.

(60) The host State will not be required to permit observation of restricted locations, installations or defence sites.

(61) In order to allow the observers to confirm that the notified activity is non-threatening in character and that it is carried out in conformity with the appropriate provisions of the notification, the host State will:

(61.1) - at the commencement of the observation programme give a briefing on the purpose, the basic situation, the phases of the activity and possible changes as compared with the notification and provide the observers with an observation programme with a daily schedule;

(61.2) - provide the observers with a map with a scale of 1 to not more than 250,000 depicting the area of the notified military activity and the initial tactical situation in this area. To depict the entire area of the notified military activity, smaller-scale maps may be additionally provided;

(61.3) - provide the observers with appropriate observation equipment; in addition, the observers will be permitted to use their own binoculars, maps, photo and video cameras, dictaphones and hand-held passive night-vision devices. The above-mentioned equipment will be subject to examination and approval by the host State. It is understood that the host State may limit the use of certain equipment in restricted locations, installations or defence sites;

(61.4) - be encouraged, whenever feasible and with due consideration for the security of the observers, to provide an aerial survey, preferably by helicopter, of the area of the military activity. If carried out, such a survey should provide the observers with the opportunity to observe from the air the disposition of forces engaged in the activity in order to help them gain a general impression of its scope and scale. At least one observer from each participating State represented at the observation should be given the opportunity to participate in the survey. Helicopters and/or aircraft may be provided by the host State or by another participating State at the request of and in agreement with the host State;

(61.5) - in the course of the observation programme give the observers daily briefings with the help of maps on the various phases of the military activity and their development and inform the observers about their positions geographically; in the case of a land force activity conducted in combination with air or naval components, briefings will be given by representatives of these forces;

(61.6) - provide opportunities to observe directly forces of the State(s) engaged in the military activity so that the observers get an impression of the flow of the entire activity; to this end, the observers will be given the opportunity to observe combat and support units of all participating formations of a divisional or equivalent level and, whenever possible, to visit units below divisional or equivalent level and communicate with commanders and troops. Commanders and other senior personnel of the participating formations as well as of the visited units will inform the observers of the mission and disposition of their respective units;

(61.7) - guide the observers in the area of the military activity; the observers will follow the instructions issued by the host State in accordance with the provisions set out in this document;

(61.8) - provide the observers with appropriate means of transportation in the area of the military activity;

(61.9) - provide the observers with opportunities for timely communication with their embassies or other official missions and consular posts; the host State is not obligated to cover the communication expense of the observers;

(61.10) - provide the observers with appropriate board and lodging in a location suitable for carrying out the observation programme and, when necessary, medical care;

(61.11) - at the close of each observation, provide an opportunity for the observers to meet together and with host State officials to discuss the course of the observed activity. Where States other than the host State have been engaged in the activity, military representatives of those States will also be invited to take part in this discussion.

(62) The participating States need not invite observers to notifiable military activities which are carried out without advance notice to the troops involved unless these notifiable activities have a duration of more than 72 hours. The continuation of these activities beyond this time will be subject to observation while the agreed thresholds for observation are met or exceeded. The observation programme will follow as closely as practically possible all the provisions for observation set out in this document.

(63) The participating States are encouraged to permit media representatives from all participating States to attend observed military activities in accordance with accreditation procedures set down by the host State. In such instances, media representatives from all participating States will be treated without discrimination and given equal access to those facets of the activity open to media representatives.

(64) The presence of media representatives will not interfere with the observers carrying out their functions nor with the flow of the military activity.

VI. ANNUAL CALENDARS

(65) Each participating State will exchange, with all other participating States, an annual calendar of its military activities subject to prior notification*, within the zone of application for CSBMs, forecast for the subsequent calendar year. A participating State which is to host military activities subject to prior notification conducted by any other participating State(s) will include these activities in its annual calendar. It will be transmitted every year, in writing, through diplomatic channels, not later than 15 November for the following year.

(66) If a participating State does not forecast any military activity subject to prior notification it will so inform all other participating States in the same manner as prescribed for the exchange of annual calendars.

---

* as defined in the provisions on Prior Notification of Certain Military Activities.

(67) Each participating State will list the above-mentioned activities chronologically and will provide information on each activity in accordance with the following model:

(67.1) - type of military activity and its designation;

(67.2) - general characteristics and purpose of the military activity;

(67.3) - States involved in the military activity;

(67.4) - area of the military activity, indicated by geographic features where appropriate and defined by geographic co-ordinates;

(67.5) - planned duration of the military activity, indicated by envisaged start and end dates;

(67.6) - the envisaged total number of troops engaged in the military activity. For activities involving more than one State, the host State will provide such information for each State involved;

(67.7) - the types of armed forces involved in the military activity;

(67.8) - the envisaged level of the military activity and designation of direct operational command, under which this military activity will take place.

(67.9) - the number and type of divisions whose participation in the military activity is envisaged;

(67.10) - any additional information concerning, *inter alia*, components of armed forces, which the participating State planning the military activity considers relevant.

(68) Should changes regarding the military activities in the annual calendar prove necessary, they will be communicated to all other participating States no later than in the appropriate notification.

(69) Should a participating State cancel a military activity included in its annual calendar or reduce it to a level below notification thresholds, that State will inform the other participating States immediately.

(70) Information on military activities subject to prior notification not included in an annual calendar will be communicated to all participating States as soon as possible, in accordance with the model provided in the annual calendar.

VII. CONSTRAINING PROVISIONS

(71) Each participating State will communicate, in writing, to all other participating States, by 15 November each year, information concerning military activities subject to prior notification* involving more than 40,000 troops**, which it plans to carry out or host in the second subsequent calendar year. Such communication will include preliminary information on each activity, as to its general purpose, timeframe and duration, area, size and States involved.

(72) Participating States will not carry out military activities subject to prior notification involving more than 40,000 troops, unless they have been the object of communication as defined above.

(73) Participating States will not carry out military activities subject to prior notification involving more than 40,000 troops unless they have been included in the annual calendar, not later than 15 November each year.

(74) If military activities subject to prior notification are carried out in addition to those contained in the annual calendar, they should be as few as possible.

VIII. COMPLIANCE AND VERIFICATION

(75) According to the Madrid Mandate, the confidence- and security-building measures to be agreed upon "will be provided with adequate forms of verification which correspond to their content".

---

* as defined in the provisions on Prior Notification of Certain Military Activities.

** as defined in the provisions on Prior Notification of Certain Military Activities.

(76) The participating States recognize that national technical means can play a role in monitoring compliance with agreed confidence- and security-building measures.

INSPECTION

(77) In accordance with the provisions contained in this document each participating State has the right to conduct inspections on the territory of any other participating State within the zone of application for CSBMs.

(78) Any participating State will be allowed to address a request for inspection to another participating State on whose territory, within the zone of application for CSBMs, compliance with the agreed confidence- and security-building measures is in doubt.

(79) No participating State will be obliged to accept on its territory within the zone of application for CSBMs, more than three inspections per calendar year.

(80) No participating State will be obliged to accept more than one inspection per calendar year from the same participating State.

(81) An inspection will not be counted if, due to force majeure, it cannot be carried out.

(82) The participating State which requests an inspection will state the reasons for such a request.

(83) The participating State which has received such a request will reply in the affirmative to the request within the agreed period of time, subject to the provisions contained in paragraphs (79) and (80).

(84) Any possible dispute as to the validity of the reasons for a request will not prevent or delay the conduct of an inspection.

(85) The participating State which requests an inspection will be permitted to designate for inspection on the territory of another State within the zone of application for CSBMs, a specific area. Such an area will be referred to as the "specified area". The specified area will comprise terrain where notifiable military activities are conducted or where another participating State believes a notifiable military activity is taking place. The specified

area will be defined and limited by the scope and scale of notifiable military activities but will not exceed that required for an army level military activity.

(86) In the specified area the representatives of the inspecting State accompanied by the representatives of the receiving State will be permitted access, entry and unobstructed survey, except for areas or sensitive points to which access is normally denied or restricted, military and other defence installations, as well as naval vessels, military vehicles and aircraft. The number and extent of the restricted areas should be as limited as possible. Areas where notifiable military activities can take place will not be declared restricted areas, except for certain permanent or temporary military installations which, in territorial terms, should be as small as possible, and consequently those areas will not be used to prevent inspection of notifiable military activities. Restricted areas will not be employed in a way inconsistent with the agreed provisions on inspection.

(87) Within the specified area, the forces of participating States other than the receiving State will also be subject to the inspection conducted by the inspecting State.

(88) Inspection will be permitted on the ground, from the air, or both.

(89) The representatives of the receiving State will accompany the inspection team, including when it is in land vehicles and an aircraft from the time of their first employment until the time they are no longer in use for the purposes of inspection.

(90) In its request, the inspecting State will notify the receiving State of:

(90.1) - the reasons for the request;

(90.2) - the location of the specified area defined by geographical co-ordinates;

(90.3) - the preferred point(s) of entry for the inspection team;

(90.4) - mode of transport to and from the point(s) of entry and, if applicable, to and from the specified area;

(90.5) - where in the specified area the inspection will begin;

(90.6) - whether the inspection will be conducted from the ground, from the air, or both simultaneously;

(90.7) - whether aerial inspection will be conducted using an airplane, a helicopter, or both;

(90.8) - whether the inspection team will use land vehicles provided by the receiving State or, if mutually agreed, its own vehicles;

(90.9) - information for the issuance of diplomatic visas to inspectors entering the receiving State.

(91) The reply to the request will be given in the shortest possible period of time, but within not more than twenty-four hours. Within thirty-six hours after the issuance of the request, the inspection team will be permitted to enter the territory of the receiving State.

(92) Any request for inspection as well as the reply thereto will be communicated to all participating States without delay.

(93) The receiving State should designate the point(s) of entry as close as possible to the specified area. The receiving State will ensure that the inspection team will be able to reach the specified area without delay from the point(s) of entry.

(94) All participating States will facilitate the passage of the inspection teams through their territory.

(95) Within 48 hours after the arrival of the inspection team at the specified area, the inspection will be terminated.

(96) There will be no more than four inspectors in an inspection team. While conducting the inspection the inspection team may divide into two parts.

(97) The inspectors and, if applicable, auxiliary personnel, will be granted during their mission the privileges and immunities in accordance with the Vienna Convention on Diplomatic Relations.

(98) The participating States will ensure that troops, other armed personnel and officials in the specified area are adequately informed regarding the presence, status and functions of inspectors and, if applicable, auxiliary personnel. The receiving State will

ensure that no action is taken by its representatives which could endanger inspectors and, if applicable, auxiliary personnel. In carrying out their duties, inspectors and, if applicable, auxiliary personnel will take into account safety concerns expressed by representatives of the receiving State.

(99) The receiving State will provide the inspection team with appropriate board and lodging in a location suitable for carrying out the inspection, and, when necessary, medical care; however this does not exclude the use by the inspection team of its own tents and rations.

(100) The inspection team will have use of its own maps and charts, photo and video cameras, binoculars, hand-held passive night-vision devices and dictaphones. Upon arrival in the specified area the inspection team will show the equipment to the representatives of the receiving State.

(101) The inspection team will have access to appropriate telecommunications equipment of the receiving State for the purpose of communicating with its embassy or other official missions and consular posts accredited to the receiving State.

(102) The receiving State will provide the inspection team with access to appropriate telecommunications equipment for the purpose of continuous communication between the sub-teams.

(103) Inspectors will be entitled to request and to receive briefings at agreed times by military representatives of the receiving State. At the inspectors' request, such briefings will be given by commanders of formations or units in the specified area. Suggestions of the receiving State as to the briefings will be taken into consideration.

(104) The inspecting State will specify whether aerial inspection will be conducted using an airplane, a helicopter or both. Aircraft for inspection will be chosen by mutual agreement between the inspecting and receiving States. Aircraft will be chosen which provide the inspection team a continuous view of the ground during the inspection.

(105) After the flight plan, specifying, *inter alia*, the inspection team's choice of flight path, speed and altitude in the specified area, has been filed with the competent air traffic control authority the inspection aircraft will be permitted to enter the specified area without delay. Within the specified area, the inspection team will, at its request, be permitted to deviate from

the approved flight plan to make specific observations provided such deviation is consistent with paragraph (86) as well as flight safety and air traffic requirements. Directions to the crew will be given through a representative of the receiving State on board the aircraft involved in the inspection.

(106) One member of the inspection team will be permitted, if such a request is made, at any time to observe data on navigational equipment of the aircraft and to have access to maps and charts used by the flight crew for the purpose of determining the exact location of the aircraft during the inspection flight.

(107) Aerial and ground inspectors may return to the specified area as often as desired within the 48-hour inspection period.

(108) The receiving State will provide for inspection purposes land vehicles with cross country capability. Whenever mutually agreed taking into account the specific geography relating to the area to be inspected, the inspecting State will be permitted to use its own vehicles.

(109) If land vehicles or aircraft are provided by the inspecting State, there will be one accompanying driver for each land vehicle, or accompanying aircraft crew.

(110) The inspecting State will prepare a report of its inspection and will provide a copy of that report to all participating States without delay.

(111) The inspection expenses will be incurred by the receiving State except when the inspecting State uses its own aircraft and/or land vehicles. The travel expenses to and from the point(s) of entry will be borne by the inspecting State.

EVALUATION

(112) Information provided under the provisions on Information on Military Forces and on Information on Plans for the Deployment of Major Weapon and Equipment Systems will be subject to evaluation.

(113) Subject to the provisions below each participating State will provide the opportunity to visit active formations and units in their normal peacetime locations as specified in point 2 and 3 of the provisions on Information on Military Forces to allow the other participating States to evaluate the information provided.

(114) Each participating State will be obliged to accept a quota of one evaluation visit per calendar year for every sixty units, or portion thereof, reported under paragraph (11). However, no participating State will be obliged to accept more than fifteen visits per calendar year. No participating State will be obliged to accept more than one fifth of its quota of visits from the same participating State; a participating State with a quota of less than five visits will not be obliged to accept more than one visit from the same participating State during a calendar year. No formation or unit may be visited more than twice during a calendar year and more than once by the same participating State during a calendar year.

(115) No participating State will be obliged to accept more than one visit at any given time on its territory.

(116) If a participating State has formations or units stationed on the territory of other participating States (host States) in the zone of application for CSBMs, the maximum number of evaluation visits permitted to its forces in each of the States concerned will be proportional to the number of its units in each State. The application of this provision will not alter the number of visits this participating State (stationing State) will have to accept under paragraph (114).

(117) Requests for such visits will be submitted giving 5 days notice.

(118) The request will specify:

(118.1) - the formation or unit to be visited;

(118.2) - the proposed date of the visit;

(118.3) - the preferred point(s) of entry as well as the date and estimated time of arrival for the evaluation team;

(118.4) - the mode of transport to and from the point(s) of entry and, if applicable, to and from the formation or unit to be visited;

(118.5) - the names and ranks of the members of the team and, if applicable, information for the issue of diplomatic visas.

(119) If a formation or unit of a participating State is stationed on the territory of another participating State, the request will be addressed to the host State and sent simultaneously to the stationing State.

(120) The reply to the request will be given within 48 hours after the receipt of the request.

(121) In the case of formations or units of a participating State stationed on the territory of another participating State, the reply will be given by the host State in consultation with the stationing State. After consultation between the host State and the stationing State, the host State will specify in its reply any of its responsibilities which it agrees to delegate to the stationing State.

(122) The reply will indicate whether the formation or unit will be available for evaluation at the proposed date at its normal peacetime location.

(123) Formations or units may be in their normal peacetime location but be unavailable for evaluation. Each participating State will be entitled in such cases not to accept a visit; the reasons for the non-acceptance and the number of days that the formation or unit will be unavailable for evaluation will be stated in the reply. Each participating State will be entitled to invoke this provision up to a total of five times for an aggregate of no more than 30 days per calendar year.

(124) If the formation or unit is absent from its normal peacetime location, the reply will indicate the reasons for and the duration of its absence. The requested State may offer the possibility of a visit to the formation or unit outside its normal peacetime location. If the requested State does not offer this possibility, the requesting State will be able to visit the normal peacetime location of the formation or unit. The requesting State may however refrain in either case from the visit.

(125) Visits will not be counted against the quotas of receiving States, if they are not carried out. Likewise, if visits are not carried out, due to force majeure, they will not be counted.

(126) The reply will designate the point(s) of entry and indicate, if applicable, the time and place of assembly of the team. The point(s) of entry and, if applicable, the place of assembly will be designated as close as possible to the formation or unit to be visited. The receiving State will ensure that the team will be able to reach the formation or unit without delay.

(127) The request and the reply will be communicated to all participating States without delay.

(128) Participating States will facilitate the passage of teams through their territory.

(129) The team will have no more than two members. It may be accompanied by an interpreter as auxiliary personnel.

(130) The members of the team and, if applicable, auxiliary personnel, will be granted during their mission the privileges and immunities in accordance with the Vienna Convention on Diplomatic Relations.

(131) The visit will take place in the course of a single working day and last up to 12 hours.

(132) The visit will begin with a briefing by the officer commanding the formation or unit, or his deputy, in the headquarters of the formation or unit, concerning the personnel as well as the major weapon and equipment systems reported under paragraph (11).

(132.1) In the case of a visit to a formation, the receiving State may provide the possibility to see personnel and major weapon and equipment systems reported under paragraph (11) for that formation, but not for any of its formations or units, in their normal locations.

(132.2) In the case of a visit to a unit, the receiving State will provide the possibility to see the personnel and the major weapon and equipment systems of the unit reported under paragraph (11) in their normal locations.

(133) Access will not have to be granted to sensitive points, facilities and equipment.

(134) The team will be accompanied at all times by representatives of the receiving State.

(135) The receiving State will provide the team with appropriate transportation during the visit to the formation or unit.

(136) Personal binoculars and dictaphones may be used by the team.

(137) The visit will not interfere with activities of the formation or unit.

(138) The participating States will ensure that troops, other armed personnel and officials in the formation or unit are adequately informed regarding the presence, status and functions of members of teams and, if applicable, auxiliary personnel. Participating States will also ensure that no action is taken by their representatives which could endanger the members of teams and, if applicable, auxiliary personnel. In carrying out their duties, members of teams and, if applicable, auxiliary personnel will take into account safety concerns expressed by representatives of the receiving State.

(139) The travel expenses to and from the point(s) of entry will be borne by the visiting State.

(140) The visiting State will prepare a report of its visit which will be communicated to all participating States expeditiously.

(141) Each participating State will be entitled to obtain timely clarification from any other participating State concerning the application of agreed confidence- and security-building measures. Communications in this context will, if appropriate, be transmitted to all other participating States.

(142) The communications concerning compliance and verification will be transmitted preferably through the CSBM communications network.

IX. COMMUNICATIONS

(143) The participating States will establish a network of direct communications between their capitals for the transmission of messages relating to agreed measures. The network will complement the existing use of diplomatic channels. Participating States undertake to use the network flexibly, efficiently and in a cost-effective way.

(144) Each participating State will designate a point of contact capable of transmitting and receiving such messages from other participating States on a 24-hour-a-day basis. Each participating State will notify this designation in writing to other participating States not later than 15 April 1991 and will notify in advance any change in this designation.

(145) The technical characteristics of the network are set out in Annex II.

(146) Communications may be in any one of the six working languages of the CSCE.

(147) Details on the use of these six languages are set out in Annex III. The provisions of this annex have been elaborated for the practical purposes of the communication system only. They are not intended to change the existing use of all six working languages of the CSCE according to established rules and practice as set out in the Final Recommendations of the Helsinki Consultations.

(148) Messages will be considered official communications of the sending State. If the content of a message is not related to an agreed measure, the receiving State has the right to reject it by so informing the other participating States.

(149) Participating States may agree among themselves to use the network for other purposes.

(150) All aspects of the implementation of the network may be discussed at the annual implementation assessment meeting.

X. ANNUAL IMPLEMENTATION ASSESSMENT MEETING

(151) The participating States will hold each year a meeting to discuss the present and future implementation of agreed CSBMs. Discussion may extend to:

(151.1) - clarification of questions arising from such implementation;

(151.2) - operation of agreed measures;

(151.3) - implications of all information originating from the implementation of any agreed measures for the process of confidence and security building in the framework of the CSCE.

(152) Before the conclusion of each year's meeting the participating States will normally agree upon the agenda and dates for the subsequent year's meeting. Lack of agreement will not constitute sufficient reason to extend a meeting, unless otherwise agreed. Agenda and dates may, if necessary, be agreed between meetings.

(153) The Conflict Prevention Centre will serve as the forum for such meetings.

(154) The first annual implementation assessment meeting will be held in 1991.

(155) The participating States stress that this new set of mutually complementary confidence- and security-building measures builds upon and expands the results already achieved at the Stockholm Conference and is designed to reduce the risk of military confrontation in Europe and emphasize that its implementation will contribute to these objectives.

(156) Reaffirming the relevant objectives of the Final Act, the participating States are determined to continue building confidence, to lessen military confrontation and to enhance security for all.

(157) The measures adopted in this document are politically binding and will come into force on 1 January 1991.

(158) The Government of Austria is requested to transmit the present document to the Meeting of the Heads of State or Government of the CSCE participating States in Paris and to the Helsinki Follow-up Meeting of the CSCE. The Government of Austria is also requested to transmit the present document to the Secretary-General of the United Nations and to the Governments of the non-participating Mediterranean States.

(159) The text of this document will be published in each participating State, which will disseminate it and make it known as widely as possible.

(160) The representatives of the participating States express their profound gratitude to the Government and people of Austria for the excellent arrangements they are making for the Vienna CSBM Negotiations and the warm hospitality they are extending to the delegations which are participating in the Negotiations.

Vienna, 17 November 1990

ANNEX I

Under the terms of the Madrid mandate, the zone of application for CSBMs is defined as follows:

> "On the basis of equality of rights, balance and reciprocity, equal respect for the security interests of all CSCE participating States, and of their respective obligations concerning confidence- and security-building measures and disarmament in Europe, these confidence- and security-building measures will cover the whole of Europe as well as the adjoining sea area* and air space. They will be of military significance and politically binding and will be provided with adequate forms of verification which correspond to their content.
>
> As far as the adjoining sea area* and air space is concerned, the measures will be applicable to the military activities of all the participating States taking place there whenever these activities affect security in Europe as well as constitute a part of activities taking place within the whole of Europe as referred to above, which they will agree to notify. Necessary specifications will be made through the negotiations on the confidence- and security-building measures at the Conference.
>
> Nothing in the definition of the zone given above will diminish obligations already undertaken under the Final Act. The confidence- and security-building measures to be agreed upon at the Conference will also be applicable in all areas covered by any of the provisions in the Final Act relating to confidence-building measures and certain aspects of security and disarmament.
>
> Wherever the term "the zone of application for CSBMs" is used in this document, the above definition will apply.

---

* In this context, the notion of adjoining sea area is understood to refer also to ocean areas adjoining Europe."

ANNEX II

Technical characteristics of the communications network

1. The communications network will be based on a Packet Switched Data Network (PSDN) set up according to the X.25 protocol.

2. It will use public PSDN services wherever possible.

3. The message handling switch will be centralized in one location.

4. The message transfer system will need only a capacity to store and forward in order to perform its traffic management role.

5. The communications software could be based on the X.400 recommendations.

6. The minimum hardware requirement for the end point systems in the capitals will be PC-compatible.

7. Address codes will be used in order to ensure the privacy of the communications.

8. No encryption is required.

9. The integrity of messages should be protected.

ANNEX III

Use of the six CSCE working languages

Messages will, wherever possible, be transmitted in formats with headings in all six CSCE working languages.

Such formats will be elaborated and agreed among the participating States with a view to making transmitted messages immediately understandable by reducing the language element to a minimum. The participating States agree to co-operate in this respect. This would include repeating entries in the agreed formats in Latin letters.

Any narrative text, to the extent it is required in such formats, and messages that do not lend themselves to formatting will be transmitted in the CSCE working language chosen by the transmitting State.

Each participating State has the right to ask for clarification of messages in cases of doubt.

ANNEX IV

Chairman's Statement

The participating States, in order to facilitate an efficient use of the communications network, will give due consideration to practical needs of rapid transmission of their messages and of immediate understandability. A translation into another CSCE working language will be added where needed to meet that principle. The participating States have indicated at least two CSCE working languages in which they would prefer to receive the translation.

These provisions do not prejudice in any way the future continued use of all six working languages of the CSCE according to established rules and practice as set out in the Final Recommendations of the Helsinki Consultations.

This statement will be an annex to the Vienna Document 1990 and will be published with it.

Vienna, 17 November 1990

ANNEX V

Chairman's Statement

Bearing in mind that the Madrid mandate states that the CSBMs will be provided with adequate forms of verification it is understood that in the continuing negotiations an adequate solution will be found to evaluate non-active formations and units which are activated for routine training purposes.

This statement will be an annex to the Vienna Document 1990 and will be published with it.

Vienna, 17 November 1990

ANNEX VI

Chairman's Statement

It is understood that the question of costs during evaluation visits will be addressed in the course of further negotiations.

This statement will be an annex to the Vienna Document 1990 and will be published with it.

Vienna, 17 November 1990

ANNEX VII

Chairman's Statement

It is understood that, taking into account the agreed date of entry into force of the agreed confidence- and security-building measures and the provisions contained in them concerning constraining provisions, the annual exchange of military information and its evaluation, and expressing their interest in an early transition to the full implementation of the provisions of this document, the participating States agree to the following:

Communications, in accordance with agreed provisions, concerning military activities involving more than 40,000 troops planned for the calendar year 1992 will be exchanged by 15 December 1990.

The information on military forces will be exchanged not later than 15 April 1991 and valid as of 1 May 1991. The information on plans for the deployment of major weapon and equipment systems will be exchanged not later than 15 April, 1991.

The provisions on evaluation will be effective as of 1 July 1991. Therefore, for 1991 no participating State will be obliged to receive more than half the number of the evaluation visits it would otherwise according to this document be obliged to receive.

This statement will be an annex to the Vienna Document 1990 and will be published with it.

INTERPRETATIVE STATEMENTS[1]

Interpretative statement by Hungary on behalf of Czechoslovakia, Hungary and Poland

The Czech and Slovak Federal Republic, the Republic of Hungary and the Republic of Poland hereby state that each of them has the right to carry out inspections and evaluation visits on the territory of any other participating State and is ready to accept on its territory such inspections and evaluation visits under the 1990 Vienna Document of the Negotiations on Confidence- and Security-building Measures.

The Czech and Slovak Federal Republic, the Republic of Hungary and the Republic of Poland hereby state that they will not use their rights for circumventing the purposes of the system of inspections and evaluation and will continue to support the effective functioning of that system.

* * *

Interpretative statement by the Union of Soviet Socialist Republics

In accordance with the rules of procedure I request that the following interpretative statement of the Soviet delegation be registered.

The delegation of the Union of Soviet Socialist Republics, recalling that paragraph 7 of the introduction to the Document notes that the negotiations will continue and that proposals which have been submitted remain subject to further negotiations, reiterates its position that questions of extending confidence-building measures to the activities of naval and air forces will be considered among these proposals.

* * *

Interpretative statement by Turkey

The Government of Turkey had formally placed a reservation regarding the representation of Cyprus at the CSCE on 31 July 1975 (CSCE/III/1). The same reservation has been placed at subsequent meetings within the context of CSCE and in particular at the Stockholm Conference on Confidence- and Security-Building Measures and Disarmament in Europe (see Journal No. 379).

'The Republic of Cyprus' which was established, in accordance with international treaties, on the basis of a partnership between the two peoples of the Island, has ceased to exist as such after its constitution was unilaterally and unlawfully abrogated in 1963

---

[1] Journal No. 241/Rev.2, 66th Plenary Meeting (17 November 1990).

by the Greek Cypriot side by the use of force, despite the protestations and resistance of the Turkish Cypriot side. The Greek Cypriot Administration has ever since represented exclusively the Greek Cypriots and their interests. As a guarantor power under the 1960 Treaty of Guarantee, Turkey does not recognize this administration or any of its illegitimate claims.

There is no single authority which, in fact or in law, jointly represents or is competent to represent the Turkish Cypriots and the Greek Cypriots, and consequently Cyprus as a whole. This is the reason why a negotiating process is being pursued between the Turkish Cypriot and the Greek Cypriot leaders on the basis of equality.

The Turkish Cypriot people are represented by the Government of the Turkish Republic of Northern Cyprus which was recognized by Turkey in 1983.

The Republic of Turkey adheres to all the decisions reached by the CSCE. However, due to the reasons stated above, the representation of Cyprus by the Greek Cypriot administration at the CSCE is neither legal nor legitimate. Therefore, the Government of the Republic of Turkey declares that CSCE Vienna decisions concerning, *inter alia*, the confidence- and security-building measures will have no validity or applicability as regards and in relation to Cyprus.

* * *

Interpretative statement by Greece

With regard to the reservation placed by the Representative of Turkey, on the representation of the Republic of Cyprus, I should like to recall paragraph 65 of the Rules of Procedure of the Final Recommendations of the Helsinki Consultations which reads as follows:

> 'All States participating in the Conference shall do so as sovereign and independent States and in conditions of full equality.'

I would like also to state that the Republic of Cyprus and its Government enjoy worldwide recognition as this is explicitly reflected in United Nations Resolutions, including Security Council 541/83, 550/84 and the most recent one, 634 of 9 June 1989, and repeatedly reaffirmed by decisions and statements from the whole spectrum of Governments, groups of States and other international organizations.

* * *

The Chairman informed delegates that the representative of Cyprus, who was absent from the meeting, was communicating a letter to the Executive Secretary, containing an interpretative statement and a request to enter its text in the Journal of the day.

* * *

Interpretative statement by Cyprus

Given the gross violations of human rights and fundamental freedoms by Turkey, both on its territory and in the occupied part of Cyprus, in disregard to Turkey's obligations under the Helsinki Final Act, the United Nations Charter and International Law, Cyprus considers and shares the view that Turkey renders itself ineligible in participating in the CSCE process as long as these violations continue.

In particular, Principles 1, 2, 3, 4, 5 and 6 are grossly violated by Turkey in occupying part of the territory of the Republic of Cyprus, since July 1974, and in refusing to enter into a dialogue with the Government of Cyprus for the peaceful settlement of the problem. Principle 7 is violated both in the occupied part of Cyprus and in Turkey by denying human rights and fundamental freedoms to its own citizens such as freedom of association, freedom of expression, religious freedom, freedom of the press and also by applying torture and other inhuman and degrading treatment or punishment to political and other detainees and prisoners. Principle 8 is violated against the Kurdish national minority. Principles 9 and 10 are also violated in the case of Cyprus.

Turkey had all the necessary time available to change its policies so that they conform with commitments Turkey has undertaken under the Helsinki Final Act, other CSCE documents and the United Nations Charter and International Law.

In view of the fact that Turkey has so far failed to do so and has not even expressed any sign of willingness to do so, Cyprus deems it appropriate that the CSCE participating States take a decision at the appropriate level to suspend the participation of Turkey to the CSCE process, until such time that Turkey implements its obligations and follows the rules of civilised behaviour.

With regard to the statement made by the representative of Turkey, the delegation of Cyprus wishes to draw attention to Rule 4 of the Rules of Procedure, which states as follows:

> 'Decisions of the Conference shall be taken by consensus. Consensus shall be understood to mean the absence of any objection expressed by a representative and submitted by him as constituting an obstacle to the taking of the decision in question.'

Therefore, the Turkish statement is void *ab initio* and offending to the very Principles of the Final Act.

The Conference has adopted by consensus the Vienna Document on CSBMs. The Cyprus delegation considers that, in accordance with the practice and procedures of the Final Act, and the CSCE process as a whole, all provisions of the document are equally binding on all participating States.

Consequently, any reservation concerning the validity of the decisions of this Meeting in the relations of each participating State with all or any other participating State, or any kind of selectivity in implementing these decisions, is void and of no effect.

It is time for Turkey to stop its obstructive behaviour, accept and implement its own obligations, as well as the decisions of the international community and fora, and be party to the historic changes of our times.

* * *

Interpretative statement of the United States of America

The subject matter of the CSBM Information Exchange parallels in many ways the information exchange provided for in the CFE Treaty. In order to harmonize these two information exchanges to the maximum extent possible, it is our intention to use, wherever applicable, the definitions contained in the Protocol on Existing Types of Conventional Armaments and Equipment of the CFE Treaty as our guideline in implementing the exchange of military information under the CSBM Document.

* * *

Interpretative statement of Germany

As regards the agreed exchange of military information, it turns out that there is a certain parallelism with the CFE information exchange. We intend, in the framework of the CSBM information exchange on major weapon and equipment systems, to include in any case the types contained in the CFE Protocol on Existing Types of Conventional Armaments and Equipment.

COMMUNIQUE OF THE NEW YORK MEETING OF CSCE FOREIGN MINISTERS

New York, 2 October 1990

(1) Foreign Ministers of the thirty-five states participating in the Conference on Security and Co-operation in Europe met in New York October 1-2, 1990 to review progress on preparations for a meeting of their heads of state and government in Paris. This was the first meeting of the CSCE ever held in the United States.

(2) Ministers attached great importance to the comprehensive nature of the CSCE process, which brings together the peoples and governments of Europe, the United States, and Canada. The CSCE process proved its vitality in the difficult years of East/West confrontation and mistrust, and has developed into an important foundation for the new Europe. In the new era of relations among CSCE states, the objectives set out in Helsinki in 1975 have been realized to a degree unforeseen even a few years ago. Ministers agreed that the role of the CSCE must be enhanced to respond to new opportunities for co-operation.

(3) In that connection, Ministers discussed the work of the CSCE Summit Preparatory Committee, which has been meeting in Vienna since July 10. Their discussion reflected a convergence of views regarding the scope and objectives of the Paris Summit Meeting, and the major new steps which are now possible for the CSCE process. They expressed the hope that through the elimination of tension and the growth of co-operation the CSCE countries will be able to make an even greater contribution to the lessening of tensions in other parts of the world.

(4) Ministers approved the Agenda for the Paris Summit, which is annexed to this communique. They agreed that the Summit would take place as planned on November 19-21, 1990. However, they recognized that it was considered essential that a Treaty on Conventional Armed Forces in Europe be ready for signature at that time. They also expressed the hope that the Summit would endorse a set of substantial confidence- and security-building measures.

(5) Ministers welcomed the treaty on the final settlement with respect to Germany, noting it as a historic step toward a Europe whole and free. Ministers were unanimous in acknowledging that German unification is

an important contribution to stability, co-operation, and unity in Europe.

(6) Ministers expressed their profound gratitude to the people and Government of the United States for the excellent organization of the New York Meeting and the warm hospitality extended to the participants in the Meeting.

***

ANNEX

Agenda for the Paris CSCE summit meeting 1990[1]

1. Formal opening of the Conference
   Address by the Head of State of the host country
   Address by the Secretary-General of the United Nations

2. Statements and exchange of views by the Heads of State or Government of the participating States regarding the new situation in Europe and the action to be taken in the further development of security, stability and co-operation, including the enhancement of the CSCE process

3. Contribution by the Secretary-General of the Council of Europe[2]

4. Adoption and signature of the Summit document(s)

5. Formal closure of the Conference

---

1 Arrangements for the signing of a CFE treaty will be agreed among the countries concerned.

2 The modalities of this contribution will be subject to further clarification.

STATEMENT ON THE CRISIS IN THE GULF

Consistent with the principles contained in the Helsinki Final Act, which guide our mutual relations, we, the Foreign Ministers of the Participating States of the Conference on Security and Co-operation in Europe (CSCE), meeting in New York, join the United Nations in condemning Iraq's invasion and occupation of Kuwait. These actions jeopardize the just and peaceful world order to which more co-operative European relations are making an important contribution.

We call upon the Government of Iraq to withdraw from Kuwait immediately and without conditions. Seeking a peaceful solution, we support fully all of the relevant resolutions adopted by the United Nations Security Council and are determined to ensure their full and effective implementation.

We express our support for those countries that have particularly suffered because of the crisis created by Iraq and reaffirm our determination to work together to ensure that the burdens of standing against aggression are shouldered equitably by all.

We wish to contribute to the security and welfare in the area, in order to foster peace, tolerance, stability, and economic co-operation and development, and therefore we are determined to support efforts aimed at resolving the conflicts there and attaining a just, comprehensive, and lasting peace in compliance with the relevant resolutions of the United Nations Security Council.

CHARTER OF PARIS FOR A NEW EUROPE

Paris, 21 November 1990

A NEW ERA OF DEMOCRACY, PEACE AND UNITY

We, the Heads of State or Government of the States participating in the Conference on Security and Co-operation in Europe, have assembled in Paris at a time of profound change and historic expectations. The era of confrontation and division of Europe has ended. We declare that henceforth our relations will be founded on respect and co-operation.

Europe is liberating itself from the legacy of the past. The courage of men and women, the strength of the will of the peoples and the power of the ideas of the Helsinki Final Act have opened a new era of democracy, peace and unity in Europe.

Ours is a time for fulfilling the hopes and expectations our peoples have cherished for decades: steadfast commitment to democracy based on human rights and fundamental freedoms; prosperity through economic liberty and social justice; and equal security for all our countries.

The Ten Principles of the Final Act will guide us towards this ambitious future, just as they have lighted our way towards better relations for the past fifteen years. Full implementation of all CSCE commitments must form the basis for the initiatives we are now taking to enable our nations to live in accordance with their aspirations.

Human Rights, Democracy and Rule of Law

We undertake to build, consolidate and strengthen democracy as the only system of government of our nations. In this endeavour, we will abide by the following:

Human rights and fundamental freedoms are the birthright of all human beings, are inalienable and are guaranteed by law. Their protection and promotion is the first responsibility of government. Respect for them is an essential safeguard against an over-mighty State. Their observance and full exercise are the foundation of freedom, justice and peace.

Democratic government is based on the will of the people, expressed regularly through free and fair elections. Democracy has as its foundation respect for the human person and the rule of law. Democracy is the best safeguard of freedom of expression, tolerance of all groups of society, and equality of opportunity for each person.

Democracy, with its representative and pluralist character, entails accountability to the electorate, the obligation of public authorities to comply with the law and justice administered impartially. No one will be above the law.

We affirm that, without discrimination, every individual has the right to:
- freedom of thought, conscience and religion or belief,
- freedom of expression,
- freedom of association and peaceful assembly,
- freedom of movement;

no one will be:
- subject to arbitrary arrest or detention,
- subject to torture or other cruel, inhuman or degrading treatment or punishment;

everyone also has the right:
- to know and act upon his rights,
- to participate in free and fair elections,
- to fair and public trial if charged with an offence,
- to own property alone or in association and to exercise individual enterprise,
- to enjoy his economic, social and cultural rights.

We affirm that the ethnic, cultural, linguistic and religious identity of national minorities will be protected and that persons belonging to national minorities have the right freely to express, preserve and develop that identity without any discrimination and in full equality before the law.

We will ensure that everyone will enjoy recourse to effective remedies, national or international, against any violation of his rights.

Full respect for these precepts is the bedrock on which we will seek to construct the new Europe.

Our States will co-operate and support each other with the aim of making democratic gains irreversible.

Economic Liberty and Responsibility

Economic liberty, social justice and environmental responsibility are indispensable for prosperity.

The free will of the individual, exercised in democracy and protected by the rule of law, forms the necessary basis for successful economic and social development. We will promote economic activity which respects and upholds human dignity.

Freedom and political pluralism are necessary elements in our common objective of developing market economies towards sustainable economic growth, prosperity, social justice, expanding employment and efficient use of economic resources. The success of the transition to market economy by countries making efforts to this effect is important and in the interest of us all. It will enable us to share a higher level of prosperity which is our common objective. We will co-operate to this end.

Preservation of the environment is a shared responsibility of all our nations. While supporting national and regional efforts in this field, we must also look to the pressing need for joint action on a wider scale.

Friendly Relations among Participating States

Now that a new era is dawning in Europe, we are determined to expand and strengthen friendly relations and co-operation among the States of Europe, the United States of America and Canada, and to promote friendship among our peoples.

To uphold and promote democracy, peace and unity in Europe, we solemnly pledge our full commitment to the Ten Principles of the Helsinki Final Act. We affirm the continuing validity of the Ten Principles and our determination to put them into practice. All the Principles apply equally and unreservedly, each of them being interpreted taking into account the others. They form the basis for our relations.

In accordance with our obligations under the Charter of the United Nations and commitments under the Helsinki Final Act, we renew our pledge to refrain from the threat or use of force against the territorial integrity or political independence of any State, or from acting in any other manner inconsistent with the principles or purposes of those documents. We recall that non-compliance with obligations under the Charter of the United Nations constitutes a violation of international law.

We reaffirm our commitment to settle disputes by peaceful means. We decide to develop mechanisms for the prevention and resolution of conflicts among the participating States.

With the ending of the division of Europe, we still strive for a new quality in our security relations while fully respecting each other's freedom of choice in that respect. Security is indivisible and the security of every participating State is inseparably linked to that of all the others. We therefore pledge to co-operate in strengthening confidence and security among us and in promoting arms control and disarmament.

We welcome the Joint Declaration of Twenty-Two States on the improvement of their relations.

Our relations will rest on our common adherence to democratic values and to human rights and fundamental freedoms. We are convinced that in order to strengthen peace and security among our States, the advancement of democracy, and respect for and effective exercise of human rights, are indispensable. We reaffirm the equal rights of peoples and their right to self-determination in conformity with the Charter of the United Nations and with the relevant norms of international law, including those relating to territorial integrity of States.

We are determined to enhance political consultation and to widen co-operation to solve economic, social, environmental, cultural and humanitarian problems. This common resolve and our growing interdependence will help to overcome the mistrust of decades, to increase stability and to build a united Europe.

We want Europe to be a source of peace, open to dialogue and to co-operation with other countries, welcoming exchanges and involved in the search for common responses to the challenges of the future.

Security

Friendly relations among us will benefit from the consolidation of democracy and improved security.

We welcome the signature of the Treaty on Conventional Armed Forces in Europe by twenty-two participating States, which will lead to lower levels of armed forces. We endorse the adoption of a substantial new set of Confidence- and Security-building Measures which will lead to increased transparency and confidence among all participating States. These are important steps towards enhanced stability and security in Europe.

The unprecedented reduction in armed forces resulting from the Treaty on Conventional Armed Forces in Europe, together with new approaches to security and co-operation within the CSCE process, will lead to a new perception of security in Europe and a new dimension in our relations. In this context we fully recognize the freedom of States to choose their own security arrangements.

Unity

Europe whole and free is calling for a new beginning. We invite our peoples to join in this great endeavour.

We note with great satisfaction the Treaty on the Final Settlement with respect to Germany signed in Moscow on 12 September 1990 and sincerely welcome the fact that the German people have united to become one State in accordance with the principles of the Final Act of the Conference on Security and Co-operation in Europe and in full accord with their neighbours. The establishment of the national unity of Germany is an important contribution to a just and lasting order of peace for a united, democratic Europe aware of its responsibility for stability, peace and co-operation.

The participation of both North American and European States is a fundamental characteristic of the CSCE; it underlies its past achievements and is essential to the future of the CSCE process. An abiding adherence to shared values and our common heritage are the ties which bind us together. With all the rich diversity of our nations, we are united in our commitment to expand our co-operation in all fields. The challenges confronting us can only be met by common action, co-operation and solidarity.

The CSCE and the World

The destiny of our nations is linked to that of all other nations. We support fully the United Nations and the enhancement of its role in promoting international peace, security and justice. We reaffirm our commitment to the principles and purposes of the United Nations as enshrined in the Charter and condemn all violations of these principles. We recognize with satisfaction the growing role of the United Nations in world affairs and its increasing effectiveness, fostered by the improvement in relations among our States.

Aware of the dire needs of a great part of the world, we commit ourselves to solidarity with all other countries. Therefore, we issue a call from Paris today to all the nations of the world. We stand ready to join with any and all States in common efforts to protect and advance the community of fundamental human values.

GUIDELINES FOR THE FUTURE

Proceeding from our firm commitment to the full implementation of all CSCE principles and provisions, we now resolve to give a new impetus to a balanced and comprehensive development of our co-operation in order to address the needs and aspirations of our peoples.

Human Dimension

We declare our respect for human rights and fundamental freedoms to be irrevocable. We will fully implement and build upon the provisions relating to the human dimension of the CSCE.

Proceeding from the Document of the Copenhagen Meeting of the Conference on the Human Dimension, we will co-operate to strengthen democratic institutions and to promote the application of the rule of law. To that end, we decide to convene a seminar of experts in Oslo from 4 to 15 November 1991.

Determined to foster the rich contribution of national minorities to the life of our societies, we undertake further to improve their situation. We reaffirm our deep conviction that friendly relations among our peoples, as well as peace, justice, stability and democracy, require that the ethnic, cultural, linguistic and religious identity of national minorities be protected and conditions for the promotion of that identity be created. We declare that questions related to national minorities can only be satisfactorily resolved in a democratic political framework. We further acknowledge that the rights of persons belonging to national minorities must be fully respected as part of universal human rights. Being aware of the urgent need for increased co-operation on, as well as better protection of, national minorities, we decide to convene a meeting of experts on national minorities to be held in Geneva from 1 to 19 July 1991.

We express our determination to combat all forms of racial and ethnic hatred, anti-semitism, xenophobia and discrimination against anyone as well as persecution on religious and ideological grounds.

In accordance with our CSCE commitments, we stress that free movement and contacts among our citizens as well as the free flow of information and ideas are crucial for the maintenance and development of free societies and flourishing cultures. We welcome increased tourism and visits among our countries.

The human dimension mechanism has proved its usefulness, and we are consequently determined to expand it to include new procedures involving, *inter alia*, the services of experts or a roster of eminent persons experienced in human rights issues which could be raised under the mechanism. We shall provide, in the context of the mechanism, for individuals to be involved in the protection of their rights. Therefore, we undertake to develop further our commitments in this respect, in particular at the Moscow Meeting of the Conference on the Human Dimension, without prejudice to obligations under existing international instruments to which our States may be parties.

We recognize the important contribution of the Council of Europe to the promotion of human rights and the principles of democracy and the rule of law as well as to the development of cultural co-operation. We welcome moves by several participating States to join the Council of Europe and adhere to its European Convention on Human Rights. We welcome as well the readiness of the Council of Europe to make its experience available to the CSCE.

Security

The changing political and military environment in Europe opens new possibilities for common efforts in the field of military security. We will build on the important achievements attained in the Treaty on Conventional Armed Forces in Europe and in the Negotiations on Confidence- and Security-building Measures. We undertake to continue the CSBM negotiations under the same mandate, and to seek to conclude them no later than the Follow-up Meeting of the CSCE to be held in Helsinki in 1992. We also welcome the decision of the participating States concerned to continue the CFE negotiation under the same mandate and to seek to conclude it no later than the Helsinki Follow-up Meeting. Following a period for national preparations, we look forward to a more structured co-operation among all participating States on security matters, and to discussions and consultations among the thirty-four participating States aimed at establishing by 1992, from the conclusion of the Helsinki Follow-up Meeting, new negotiations on disarmament and confidence and security building open to all participating States.

We call for the earliest possible conclusion of the Convention on an effectively verifiable, global and comprehensive ban on chemical weapons, and we intend to be original signatories to it.

We reaffirm the importance of the Open Skies initiative and call for the successful conclusion of the negotiations as soon as possible.

Although the threat of conflict in Europe has diminished, other dangers threaten the stability of our societies. We are determined to co-operate in defending democratic institutions against activities which violate the independence, sovereign equality or territorial integrity of the participating States. These include illegal activities involving outside pressure, coercion and subversion.

We unreservedly condemn, as criminal, all acts, methods and practices of terrorism and express our determination to work for its eradication both bilaterally and through multilateral co-operation. We will also join together in combating illicit trafficking in drugs.

Being aware that an essential complement to the duty of States to refrain from the threat or use of force is the peaceful settlement of disputes, both being essential factors for the maintenance and consolidation of international peace and security, we will not only seek effective ways of preventing, through political means, conflicts which may yet emerge, but also define, in conformity with international law, appropriate mechanisms for the peaceful resolution of any disputes which may arise. Accordingly, we undertake to seek new forms of co-operation in this area, in particular a range of methods for the peaceful settlement of disputes, including mandatory third-party involvement. We stress that full use should be made in this context of the opportunity of the Meeting on the Peaceful Settlement of Disputes which will be convened in Valletta at the beginning of 1991. The Council of Ministers for Foreign Affairs will take into account the Report of the Valletta Meeting.

Economic Co-operation

We stress that economic co-operation based on market economy constitutes an essential element of our relations and will be instrumental in the construction of a prosperous and united Europe. Democratic institutions and economic liberty foster economic and social progress, as recognized in the Document of the Bonn Conference on Economic Co-operation, the results of which we strongly support.

We underline that co-operation in the economic field, science and technology is now an important pillar of the CSCE. The participating States should periodically review progress and give new impulses in these fields.

We are convinced that our overall economic co-operation should be expanded, free enterprise encouraged and trade increased and diversified according to GATT rules. We will promote social justice and progress and further the welfare of our peoples. We recognize in this context the importance of effective policies to address the problem of unemployment.

We reaffirm the need to continue to support democratic countries in transition towards the establishment of market economy and the creation of the basis for self-sustained economic and social growth, as already undertaken by the Group of twenty-four countries. We further underline the necessity of their increased integration, involving the acceptance of disciplines as well as benefits, into the international economic and financial system.

We consider that increased emphasis on economic co-operation within the CSCE process should take into account the interests of developing participating States.

We recall the link between respect for and promotion of human rights and fundamental freedoms and scientific progress. Co-operation in the field of science and technology will play an essential role in economic and social development. Therefore, it must evolve towards a greater sharing of appropriate scientific and technological information and knowledge with a view to overcoming the technological gap which exists among the participating States. We further encourage the participating States to work together in order to develop human potential and the spirit of free enterprise.

We are determined to give the necessary impetus to co-operation among our States in the fields of energy, transport and tourism for economic and social development. We welcome, in particular, practical steps to create optimal conditions for the economic and rational development of energy resources, with due regard for environmental considerations.

We recognize the important role of the European Community in the political and economic development of Europe. International economic organizations such as the United Nations Economic Commission for Europe (ECE), the Bretton Woods Institutions, the Organisation for Economic Co-operation and Development (OECD), the European Free Trade Association (EFTA) and the International Chamber of Commerce (ICC) also have a significant task in promoting economic co-operation, which will be further enhanced by the establishment of the European Bank for Reconstruction and Development (EBRD). In order to pursue our objectives, we stress the necessity for effective co-ordination of the activities of these organizations and emphasize the need to find methods for all our States to take part in these activities.

Environment

We recognize the urgent need to tackle the problems of the environment and the importance of individual and co-operative efforts in this area. We pledge to intensify our endeavours to protect and improve our environment in order to restore and maintain a sound ecological balance in air, water and soil. Therefore, we are determined to make full use of the CSCE as a framework for the formulation of common environmental commitments and objectives, and thus to pursue the work reflected in the Report of the Sofia Meeting on the Protection of the Environment.

We emphasize the significant role of a well-informed society in enabling the public and individuals to take initiatives to improve the environment. To this end, we commit ourselves to promoting public awareness and education on the environment as well as the public reporting of the environmental impact of policies, projects and programmes.

We attach priority to the introduction of clean and low-waste technology, being aware of the need to support countries which do not yet have their own means for appropriate measures.

We underline that environmental policies should be supported by appropriate legislative measures and administrative structures to ensure their effective implementation.

We stress the need for new measures providing for the systematic evaluation of compliance with the existing commitments and, moreover, for the development of more ambitious commitments with regard to notification and exchange of information about the state of the environment and potential environmental hazards. We also welcome the creation of the European Environment Agency (EEA).

We welcome the operational activities, problem-oriented studies and policy reviews in various existing international organizations engaged in the protection of the environment, such as the United Nations Environment Programme (UNEP), the United Nations Economic Commission for Europe (ECE) and the Organisation for Economic Co-operation and Development

(OECD). We emphasize the need for strengthening their co-operation and for their efficient co-ordination.

Culture

We recognize the essential contribution of our common European culture and our shared values in overcoming the division of the continent. Therefore, we underline our attachment to creative freedom and to the protection and promotion of our cultural and spiritual heritage, in all its richness and diversity.

In view of the recent changes in Europe, we stress the increased importance of the Cracow Symposium and we look forward to its consideration of guidelines for intensified co-operation in the field of culture. We invite the Council of Europe to contribute to this Symposium.

In order to promote greater familiarity amongst our peoples, we favour the establishment of cultural centres in cities of other participating States as well as increased co-operation in the audio-visual field and wider exchange in music, theatre, literature and the arts.

We resolve to make special efforts in our national policies to promote better understanding, in particular among young people, through cultural exchanges, co-operation in all fields of education and, more specifically, through teaching and training in the languages of other participating States. We intend to consider first results of this action at the Helsinki Follow-up Meeting in 1992.

Migrant Workers

We recognize that the issues of migrant workers and their families legally residing in host countries have economic, cultural and social aspects as well as their human dimension. We reaffirm that the protection and promotion of their rights, as well as the implementation of relevant international obligations, is our common concern.

Mediterranean

We consider that the fundamental political changes that have occurred in Europe have a positive relevance to the Mediterranean region. Thus, we will continue efforts to strengthen security and co-operation in the Mediterranean as an important factor for stability in Europe. We welcome the Report of the

Palma de Mallorca Meeting on the Mediterranean, the results of which we all support.

We are concerned with the continuing tensions in the region, and renew our determination to intensify efforts towards finding just, viable and lasting solutions, through peaceful means, to outstanding crucial problems, based on respect for the principles of the Final Act.

We wish to promote favourable conditions for a harmonious development and diversification of relations with the non-participating Mediterranean States. Enhanced co-operation with these States will be pursued with the aim of promoting economic and social development and thereby enhancing stability in the region. To this end, we will strive together with these countries towards a substantial narrowing of the prosperity gap between Europe and its Mediterranean neighbours.

Non-governmental Organizations

We recall the major role that non-governmental organizations, religious and other groups and individuals have played in the achievement of the objectives of the CSCE and will further facilitate their activities for the implementation of the CSCE commitments by the participating States. These organizations, groups and individuals must be involved in an appropriate way in the activities and new structures of the CSCE in order to fulfil their important tasks.

NEW STRUCTURES AND INSTITUTIONS OF THE CSCE PROCESS

Our common efforts to consolidate respect for human rights, democracy and the rule of law, to strengthen peace and to promote unity in Europe require a new quality of political dialogue and co-operation and thus development of the structures of the CSCE.

The intensification of our consultations at all levels is of prime importance in shaping our future relations. To this end, we decide on the following:

> We, the Heads of State or Government, shall meet next time in Helsinki on the occasion of the CSCE Follow-up Meeting 1992. Thereafter, we will meet on the occasion of subsequent follow-up meetings.
>
> Our Ministers for Foreign Affairs will meet, as a Council, regularly and at least once a year. These meetings will provide the central forum for political consultations within the CSCE process. The

Council will consider issues relevant to the Conference on Security and Co-operation in Europe and take appropriate decisions.

The first meeting of the Council will take place in Berlin.

A Committee of Senior Officials will prepare the meetings of the Council and carry out its decisions. The Committee will review current issues and may take appropriate decisions, including in the form of recommendations to the Council.

Additional meetings of the representatives of the participating States may be agreed upon to discuss questions of urgent concern.

The Council will examine the development of provisions for convening meetings of the Committee of Senior Officials in emergency situations.

Meetings of other Ministers may also be agreed by the participating States.

In order to provide administrative support for these consultations we establish a Secretariat in Prague.

Follow-up meetings of the participating States will be held, as a rule, every two years to allow the participating States to take stock of developments, review the implementation of their commitments and consider further steps in the CSCE process.

We decide to create a Conflict Prevention Centre in Vienna to assist the Council in reducing the risk of conflict.

We decide to establish an Office for Free Elections in Warsaw to facilitate contacts and the exchange of information on elections within participating States.

Recognizing the important role parliamentarians can play in the CSCE process, we call for greater parliamentary involvement in the CSCE, in particular through the creation of a CSCE parliamentary assembly, involving members of parliaments from all participating States. To this end, we urge that contacts be pursued at parliamentary level to discuss the field of activities, working methods and rules of procedure of such a CSCE parliamentary structure, drawing on existing experience and work already undertaken in this field.

We ask our Ministers for Foreign Affairs to review this matter on the occasion of their first meeting as a Council.

* * *

Procedural and organizational modalities relating to certain provisions contained in the Charter of Paris for a New Europe are set out in the Supplementary Document which is adopted together with the Charter of Paris.

We entrust to the Council the further steps which may be required to ensure the implementation of decisions contained in the present document, as well as in the Supplementary Document, and to consider further efforts for the strengthening of security and co-operation in Europe. The Council may adopt any amendment to the supplementary document which it may deem appropriate.

* * *

The original of the Charter of Paris for a New Europe, drawn up in English, French, German, Italian, Russian and Spanish, will be transmitted to the Government of the French Republic, which will retain it in its archives. Each of the participating States will receive from the Government of the French Republic a true copy of the Charter of Paris.

The text of the Charter of Paris will be published in each participating State, which will disseminate it and make it known as widely as possible.

The Government of the French Republic is requested to transmit to the Secretary-General of the United Nations the text of the Charter of Paris for a New Europe which is not eligible for registration under Article 102 of the Charter of the United Nations, with a view to its circulation to all the members of the Organization as an official document of the United Nations.

The Government of the French Republic is also requested to transmit the text of the Charter of Paris to all the other international organizations mentioned in the text.

Wherefore, we, the undersigned High Representatives of the participating States, mindful of the high political significance we attach to the results of the Summit Meeting, and declaring our determination to act in accordance with the provisions we have adopted, have subscribed our signatures below.

SUPPLEMENTARY DOCUMENT TO GIVE EFFECT TO CERTAIN PROVISIONS CONTAINED IN THE CHARTER OF PARIS FOR A NEW EUROPE

Procedures and organizational modalities relating to certain provisions contained in the Charter of Paris for a New Europe, signed in Paris on 21 November 1990, are set out below.

I. INSTITUTIONAL ARRANGEMENTS

A. THE COUNCIL

1. The Council, consisting of Ministers for Foreign Affairs of the participating States, provides the central forum for regular political consultations within the CSCE process.
2. The Council will:
   - consider issues relevant to the Conference on Security and Co-operation in Europe and take appropriate decisions;
   - prepare the meetings of Heads of State or Government of the participating States and implement tasks defined and decisions taken by these meetings.
3. The Council will hold meetings regularly and at least once a year.
4. The participating States may agree to hold additional meetings of the Council.
5. The Chair throughout each meeting of the Council will be taken by the representative of the host country.
6. An agenda for the meetings of the Council, including proposals for the venue - on a basis of rotation - and date of the next meeting, will be prepared by the Committee of Senior Officials.

B. THE COMMITTEE OF SENIOR OFFICIALS

1. A Committee of Senior Officials will prepare the work of the Council, carry out its decisions, review current issues and consider future work of the CSCE including its relations with other international fora.
2. In order to prepare the agenda of the meetings of the Council, the Committee will identify the issues for discussion on the basis of suggestions submitted by the participating States. The Committee will finalize a draft agenda shortly before the meeting of the Council.
3. Each participating State will establish a point of contact which will be used to transmit suggestions for the work of the Committee to the

Secretariat for collection and circulation and to facilitate communication between the Secretariat and each participating State.

4. Each meeting of the Committee will be chaired by a representative of the State whose Foreign Minister had been Chairman at the preceding Council meeting. Meetings will be convened by the Chairman of the Committee after consultation with the participating States.
   Meetings of the Committee will be held at the seat of the Secretariat and will not exceed two days, unless otherwise agreed. Meetings immediately preceding a meeting of the Council will be held at the venue of the Council meeting.
5. Due to practical considerations, the first meeting of the Committee will be held in Vienna from 28 to 29 January 1991. It will be chaired by the representative of Yugoslavia.

C. EMERGENCY MECHANISM

The Council will discuss the possibility of establishing a mechanism for convening meetings of the Committee of Senior Officials in emergency situations.

D. FOLLOW-UP MEETINGS

Follow-up meetings of the participating States will be held as a rule every two years. Their duration will not exceed three months, unless otherwise agreed.

E. THE CSCE SECRETARIAT

1. The Secretariat will:
   - provide administrative support to the meetings of the Council and of the Committee of Senior Officials;
   - maintain an archive of CSCE documentation and circulate documents as requested by the participating States;
   - provide information in the public domain regarding the CSCE to individuals, NGOs, international organizations and non-participating States;
   - provide support as appropriate to the Executive Secretaries of CSCE summit meetings, follow-up meetings and inter-sessional meetings.
2. The Secretariat will carry out other tasks assigned to it by the Council or the Committee of Senior Officials.

3. In order to carry out the tasks specified above, the Secretariat will consist of the following staff:
   - a Director, responsible to the Council through the Committee of Senior Officials;
   - three Officers who will be in charge of organization of meetings (including protocol and security), documentation and information, financial and administrative matters. In addition to these functions, the Director may assign other duties within the framework of the tasks of the Secretariat;
   - administrative and technical personnel, recruited by the Director.

F. THE CONFLICT PREVENTION CENTRE (CPC)

1. The Conflict Prevention Centre (CPC) will assist the Council in reducing the risk of conflict. The Centre's functions and structure are described below.
2. During its initial stage of operations the Centre's role will consist in giving support to the implementation of CSBMs such as:
   - mechanism for consultation and co-operation as regards unusual military activities;
   - annual exchange of military information;
   - communications network;
   - annual implementation assessment meetings;
   - co-operation as regards hazardous incidents of a military nature.
3. The Centre might assume other functions and the above tasks are without prejudice to any additional tasks concerning a procedure for the conciliation of disputes as well as broader tasks relating to dispute settlement, which may be assigned to it in the future by the Council of the Foreign Ministers.

Consultative Committee

4. The Consultative Committee, composed of representatives from all participating States, will be responsible to the Council. As a rule, these representatives will be the Heads of Delegation to the CSBM negotiations until the Helsinki Follow-up Meeting. The Consultative Committee will:
   - hold the meetings of the participating States which may be convened under the mechanism on unusual military activities;
   - hold the annual implementation assessment meetings;
   - prepare seminars on military doctrine and such other seminars as may be agreed by the participating States;
   - supervise the Secretariat of the Centre;

- provide the forum for discussion and clarification, as necessary, of information exchanged under agreed CSBMs;
- have overall responsibility for the communications network within the mandate of the CPC.

5. The Consultative Committee will work according to CSCE procedures. It will determine its own work programme and may decide to hold additional meetings. Meetings of the participating States, convened at the request of one or more participating States according to the procedures concerning unusual military activities, will be organized by the Director of the CPC Secretariat. Until the appointment of the Director this function will be carried out by the Executive Secretary of the CSBM negotiations.

Secretariat

6. The Secretariat will carry out the tasks assigned to it by the Consultative Committee to which it will be responsible. In particular, it will establish and maintain a data bank, for the use of all participating States, compiled on the basis of exchanged military information under agreed CSBMs and will publish Yearbooks on that basis.
7. The Secretariat will consist of the following staff:
   - a Director;
   - two officers in charge of organization of meetings (including protocol and security), communication, documentation and information, financial and administrative matters;
   - administrative and technical personnel, recruited by the Director.

* * *

8. The first meeting of the Consultative Committee of the Conflict Prevention Centre will be convened on 3 December 1990 and chaired by Yugoslavia.

G. THE OFFICE FOR FREE ELECTIONS

1. The function of the Office for Free Elections will be to facilitate contacts and the exchange of information on elections within participating States. The Office will thus foster the implementation of paragraphs 6, 7 and 8 of the Document of the Copenhagen Meeting of the Conference on the Human Dimension of the CSCE (the relevant provisions are contained in Annex I).

2. To this end, the Office will:
   - compile information, including information provided by the competent authorities of the participating States, on the dates, procedures and official results of scheduled national elections within participating States, as well as reports of election observations, and provide these on request to governments, parliaments and interested private organizations;
   - serve to facilitate contact among governments, parliaments or private organizations wishing to observe elections and competent authorities of the States in which elections are to take place;
   - organize and serve as the venue for seminars or other meetings related to election procedures and democratic institutions at the request of the participating States.
3. The Office will take into account the work of and co-operate with other institutions active in this field.
4. The Office will carry out other tasks assigned to it by the Council.
5. The Office's personnel will be composed of:
   - a Director, who will be responsible to the Council through the Committee of Senior Officials;
   - an Officer;
   - administrative and technical personnel, recruited by the Director of the Office.

H. PROCEDURES AND MODALITIES CONCERNING CSCE INSTITUTIONS

Staffing arrangements

1. The director of each institution will be of senior rank, seconded by his/her government, and appointed by the Council to a three-year, non-renewable term, on a basis of rotation.
2. In the event that the director can no longer fulfil his functions, the Chairman of the Council will, after consultation with the participating States, appoint a temporary director until the next meeting of the Council.
3. The officers will be seconded by their governments. Their terms of office will normally last two years. An extension of one year may be agreed upon by the director and the participating State seconding the officer.
4. The appointment of officers will be based on a system of rotation which will follow the French alphabetical order. The beginning of the rotation will be determined by lot for each position in the

institution. Vacant positions will be offered to the participating States following this order until the position is filled.

5. No participating State will have its nationals occupy more than one seconded position in the CSCE institutions, unless no other participating State is willing to second its national to a vacant position.

6. Each officer will be nominated by the participating State concerned after consultation with the director who will then make the appointment.

7. Administrative and technical personnel will be contracted by the director of the institution. Arrangements will be made, as required, for interpretation and translation services.

8. The director of each institution will determine its working arrangements.

9. Staff will be accredited by the seconding State to the host country where they will enjoy full diplomatic status.

Costs

10. The costs:
- of seconded personnel will be borne by the seconding country;
- of installation of the CSCE institutions will be shared according to CSCE procedures;
- of operation, including cost of official travel of staff once appointed, will be shared according to CSCE procedures;
- of the premises of the institution as well as the necessary security arrangements including those for meetings held at the seat of the institution, will be borne by the host country.

* * *

11. The host countries undertake to enable the institutions to function fully and enter into contractual and financial obligations and to accord them appropriate diplomatic status.

* * *

12. In order to function effectively, CSCE institutional structures created by the Summit will require agreed administrative, financial and personnel arrangements.

13. To this end a panel, chaired by the Executive Secretary of the Preparatory Committee and composed of the Executive Secretaries

of the Paris Summit and of the New York Meeting of Foreign Ministers, as well as the representatives of the host countries of the new CSCE institutions, will submit a report and proposals to participating States by the end of December 1990. This report and these proposals will be considered by an *ad hoc* group of experts of the participating States who will meet in Vienna under the responsibility of the Committee of Senior Officials from 14 to 18 January 1991 and make final recommendations on the above. This meeting will be convened and chaired by the representative of the State chairing the Committee of Senior Officials.

14. The Committee of Senior Officials will consider these recommendations and take the necessary decisions at its first meeting.
The first director of each institution will be nominated by the first meeting of the Committee of Senior Officials and confirmed by the Council through a silence procedure within one week. The Executive Secretariat of the CSBM negotiations in Vienna will provide services for the first meeting of the Consultative Committee of the CPC and for the first meeting of the Committee of Senior Officials.

15. The CSCE Secretariat, the Conflict Prevention Centre and the Office for Free Elections are accountable to the Council which is empowered to determine their tasks and methods of operation. Arrangements relating to the procedures, modalities and the locations of these institutions may be reviewed at the Helsinki Follow-up Meeting.

I. COMMUNICATIONS

The Council, acting upon recommendation of the Consultative Committee and of the Committee of Senior Officials, as appropriate, may decide that the communication network, established as part of the agreement on additional CSBMs, be used for other CSCE-related purposes.

J. APPLICATION OF CSCE RULES OF PROCEDURE

The rules of procedure, working methods, the scale of distribution of expenses and other modalities of the CSCE will be applied *mutatis mutandis*, unless otherwise decided.

II. MEETINGS OF EXPERTS

A. SEMINAR OF EXPERTS ON DEMOCRATIC INSTITUTIONS

The Seminar of Experts on Democratic Institutions will be held in Oslo from Monday, 4 November 1991 to Friday, 15 November 1991. Its purpose is to hold discussions of ways and means of consolidating and strengthening viable democratic institutions in participating States, including comparative studies of legislation on human rights and fundamental freedoms, drawing *inter alia* upon the experience acquired by the Council of Europe and the activities of the Commission "Democracy through Law".

The agenda, timetable and other organizational modalities are set out in Annex II.

B. MEETING OF EXPERTS ON NATIONAL MINORITIES

The Meeting of Experts on National Minorities will be held in Geneva from Monday, 1 July 1991 to Friday, 19 July 1991. Its purpose is to hold a thorough discussion on the issue of national minorities and of the rights of persons belonging to them, with due attention to the diversity of situations and to the legal, historical, political and economic backgrounds. It will include:

- an exchange of views on practical experience, in particular on national legislation, democratic institutions, international instruments, and other possible forms of co-operation;
- a review of the implementation of the relevant CSCE commitments and consideration of the scope for the improvement of relevant standards;
- a consideration of new measures aimed at improving the implementation of the aforementioned commitments.

The agenda, timetable and other organizational modalities are set out in Annex III.

III. FINANCIAL ARRANGEMENTS OF THE CSCE AND COST-EFFECTIVENESS

1. The Committee of Senior Officials will keep the cost-effectiveness of CSCE institutions, activities and personnel under review and report to the Council.
2. The following scale of distribution will be effective as of 22 November 1990:

Country	**Per cent**
France	9.1
Germany	9.1
Italy	9.1
Union of Soviet Socialist Republics	9.1
United Kingdom	9.1
United States of America	9.1
Canada	5.5
Belgium	3.6
Netherlands	3.6
Poland	3.6
Spain	3.6
Sweden	3.6
Austria	2.1
Czech and Slovak Federal Republic	2.1
Denmark	2.1
Finland	2.1
Hungary	2.1
Norway	2.1
Switzerland	2.1
Greece	0.83
Romania	0.83
Turkey	0.83
Yugoslavia	0.83
Bulgaria	0.62
Ireland	0.62
Luxembourg	0.62
Portugal	0.62
Cyprus	0.20
Holy See	0.20
Iceland	0.20
Liechtenstein	0.20
Malta	0.20
Monaco	0.20
San Marino	0.20
	100.00

ANNEX I

"(6) The participating States declare that the will of the people, freely and fairly expressed through periodic and genuine elections, is the basis of the authority and legitimacy of all government. The participating States will accordingly respect the right of their citizens to take part in the governing of their country, either directly or through representatives freely chosen by them through fair electoral processes. They recognize their responsibility to defend and protect, in accordance with their laws, their international human rights obligations and their international commitments, the democratic order freely established through the will of the people against the activities of persons, groups or organizations that engage in or refuse to renounce terrorism or violence aimed at the overthrow of that order or of that of another participating State.

(7) To ensure that the will of the people serves as the basis of the authority of government, the participating States will

(7.1) - hold free elections at reasonable intervals, as established by law;

(7.2) - permit all seats in at least one chamber of the national legislature to be freely contested in a popular vote;

(7.3) - guarantee universal and equal suffrage to adult citizens;

(7.4) - ensure that votes are cast by secret ballot or by equivalent free voting procedure, and that they are counted and reported honestly with the official results made public;

(7.5) - respect the rights of citizens to seek political or public office, individually or as representatives of political parties or organizations, without discrimination;

(7.6) - respect the right of individuals and groups to establish, in full freedom, their own political parties or other political organizations and provide such political parties and organizations with the necessary legal guarantees to enable them to compete with each other on a basis of equal treatment before the law and by the authorities;

(7.7) - ensure that law and public policy work to permit political campaigning to be conducted in a fair and free atmosphere in which neither administrative action, violence nor intimidation bars the parties and the candidates from freely presenting their views and qualifications, or prevents the voters from learning and discussing them or from casting their vote free of fear of retribution;

(7.8) - provide that no legal or administrative obstacle stands in the way of unimpeded access to the media on a non-discriminatory basis for all political groupings and individuals wishing to participate in the electoral process;

(7.9) - ensure that candidates who obtain the necessary number of votes required by law are duly installed in office and are permitted to remain in office until their term expires or is otherwise brought to an end in a manner that is regulated by law in conformity with democratic parliamentary and constitutional procedures.

(8) The participating States consider that the presence of observers, both foreign and domestic, can enhance the electoral process for States in which elections are taking place. They therefore invite observers from any other CSCE participating States and any appropriate private institutions and organizations who may wish to do so to observe the course of their national election proceedings, to the extent permitted by law. They will also endeavour to facilitate similar access for election proceedings held below the national level. Such observers will undertake not to interfere in the electoral proceedings."

ANNEX II

Seminar of experts on democratic institutions

I. *Agenda*

1. Formal opening of the Seminar.
Address by a representative of the host country.

2. Opening statements by representatives of the participating States.

3. Contributions by the Council of Europe and the Commission "Democracy through law".

4. Discussion of ways and means of consolidating and strengthening viable democratic institutions in participating States, including comparative studies of legislation on human rights and fundamental freedoms, drawing *inter alia* upon the experience acquired by the Council of Europe and the activities of the Commission "Democracy through law".

5. Closing statements by representatives of the participating States and summing up.

6. Formal closure of the Seminar.

II. *Timetable and other organizational modalities*

1. The Seminar will open on Monday, 4 November 1991, at 3 p.m., in Oslo. It will close on Friday, 15 November 1991.

2. All Plenary meetings will be open. The meetings of the Study Groups will be closed.

3. Agenda items 1, 2, 3, 5 and 6 will be dealt with in the Plenary.

4. Agenda item 4 will be dealt with in the Plenary as well as in the following three Study Groups:

**Study Group A*:
- Constitutional reforms
- The rule of law and independent courts
- Division of power between legislative, executive and judicial authorities

***Study Group B*:
- The organization of elections
- The organization of political parties

- The organization of independent non-governmental organizations (trade unions, employers organizations)
- The role of the media

****Study Group C*:
- Comparative studies of legislation in the area of human rights and fundamental freedoms.

5. Meetings of the Plenary and of the Study Groups will be held according to the attached work programme. The work programme may be modified by consensus.
Opening statements by representatives of the participating States should, as a rule, not exceed 12 minutes per delegation and will be held in the following order: Switzerland, Iceland, Sweden, Poland, Portugal, Holy See, Finland, Austria, Bulgaria, Cyprus, Turkey, Germany, United States of America, San Marino, Monaco, Czech and Slovak Federal Republic, Luxembourg, Romania, Ireland, Liechtenstein, United Kingdom, Greece, France, Denmark, Belgium, Yugoslavia, Canada, Norway, Malta, Spain, Union of Soviet Socialist Republics, Netherlands, Italy, Hungary.

6. Prior to the opening of the Seminar, delegations are encouraged to circulate through the Executive Secretariat written contributions on the issues to be dealt with in the Study Groups.

7. The Council of Ministers will take into account the summing up carried out under item 5 of the agenda.

8. At the opening and closing Plenary meetings, the Chair will be taken by a representative of the host country. After the opening Plenary meeting, the Chair will be taken in daily rotation, in French alphabetical order, starting with a representative of the United States of America.

9. The Chair at the opening meetings of the Study Groups will be taken by a representative of the host country. Thereafter, the Chair will be taken in daily rotation, in French alphabetical order starting

   - in Study Group A with a representative of Monaco;
   - in Study Group B with a representative of Romania;
   - in Study Group C with a representative of Malta.

10. In conformity with paragraph 74 of the Final Recommendations of the Helsinki Consultations, the Government of Norway will designate an Executive Secretary. This designation will be subject to approval by the participating States.

11. The other rules of procedure, the working methods and the scale of distribution of the expenses of the CSCE will, *mutatis mutandis*, be applied to the Seminar.

ANNEX III

Meeting of experts on national minorities

I. *Agenda*

1. Formal opening of the Meeting.
Address by a representative of the host country.

2. Opening statements by representatives of the participating States.

3. Contribution by the Council of Europe.

4. Thorough discussion on the issue of national minorities and of the rights of persons belonging to them, with due attention to the diversity of situations and to the legal, historical, political and economic backgrounds:

   a) exchange of views on practical experience, in particular on national legislation, democratic institutions, international instruments and other possible forms of co-operation;
   b) review of the implementation of the relevant CSCE commitments and consideration of the scope for the improvement of relevant standards;
   c) consideration of new measures aimed at improving the implementation of the aforementioned commitments.

5. Closing statements by representatives of the participating States and summing up.

6. Formal closure of the Meeting.

II. *Timetable and other organizational modalities*

1. The Meeting will open on Monday, 1 July 1991, at 3 p.m., in Geneva. It will close on Friday, 19 July 1991.

2. The meetings of the Plenary will be open. The meetings of the Subsidiary Working Bodies will be closed.

3. Agenda items 1, 2, 3, 5 and 6 will be dealt with in the Plenary.

4. Agenda item 4 will be dealt with in three Subsidiary Working Bodies (established according to the 3 sub-items) in a structured and balanced way. Agenda item 4 will also be dealt with in the Plenary meetings.

5. Meetings of the Plenary and of the Subsidiary Working Bodies will be held according to the attached work programme.

6. Opening statements by representatives of the participating States should, as a rule, not exceed 15 minutes per delegation and will be held in the following order: Yugoslavia, Iceland, Hungary, Bulgaria, San Marino, Cyprus, United Kingdom, United States of America, Malta, Belgium, Netherlands, Romania, Holy See, Ireland, Poland, Sweden, Italy, Portugal, Spain, Turkey, Czech and Slovak Federal Republic, Germany, Canada, Monaco, Luxembourg, Greece, Austria, Switzerland, Union of Soviet Socialist Republics, France, Finland, Liechtenstein, Norway, Denmark.

7. Participants are encouraged to circulate written contributions on the subjects for consideration in one or more of the working languages of the CSCE prior to the Meeting through the Executive Secretary to all other participating States in order to allow a thorough preparation of the relevant discussions.

8. The Council of Ministers will take into account the summing up carried out under Agenda item 5.

9. At the opening and closing Plenary meetings, the Chair will be taken by a representative of the host country. After the opening meeting, the Chair will be taken in daily rotation, in French alphabetical order of the participating States, starting with a representative of Ireland.

10. The Chair at the opening meetings of the Subsidiary Working Bodies will be taken by a representative of the host country. Thereafter, the Chair will be taken in daily rotation, in French alphabetical order starting: in Subsidiary Working Body A with a representative of Switzerland;
   - in Subsidiary Working Body B with a representative of France;
   - in Subsidiary Working Body C with a representative of Romania.

11. In conformity with paragraph 74 of the Final Recommendations of the Helsinki Consultations, the Government of Switzerland will designate an Executive Secretary. This designation will be subject to approval by the participating States.

12. The other rules of procedure, the working methods and the scale of distribution of the expenses of the CSCE will, *mutatis mutandis*, be applied to the Meeting of Experts on National Minorities.

REPORT OF THE CSCE MEETING OF EXPERTS ON PEACEFUL SETTLEMENT OF DISPUTES

Valletta, 8 February 1991

The representatives of Austria, Belgium, Bulgaria, Canada, Cyprus, the Czech and Slovak Federal Republic, Denmark, Finland, France, Germany, Greece, the Holy See, Hungary, Iceland, Ireland, Italy, Liechtenstein, Luxembourg - European Community, Malta, Monaco, the Netherlands, Norway, Poland, Portugal, Romania, San Marino, Spain, Sweden, Switzerland, Turkey, the Union of Soviet Socialist Republics, the United Kingdom, the United States of America and Yugoslavia met in Valletta from 15 January to 8 February 1991 in accordance with the relevant provisions of the Concluding Document of the Vienna CSCE Meeting 1986 and the Charter of Paris for a New Europe, to consider the question of Peaceful Settlement of Disputes.

The representative of Albania attended the Meeting as observer.

The formal opening was attended by H.E. Dr. Censu Tabone, President of Malta, who gave an address of welcome. The Meeting was opened by the Hon. Professor Guido de Marco, Deputy Prime Minister and Minister of Foreign Affairs and Justice of Malta, who delivered the opening address on behalf of the host country. He also closed the Meeting.

Opening statements were made by Heads of Delegation of the participating States.

The Hon. Gianni de Michelis, Minister of Foreign Affairs of Italy, addressed the meeting.

A number of proposals were submitted for consideration by the Meeting.

The representatives of the participating States held a general exchange of views on the peaceful settlement of disputes. It was observed that developments in Europe and the world since the Vienna Follow-up Meeting had enhanced the importance of the Meeting, and that this was also reflected in the Charter of Paris for a New Europe, signed by the Heads of State or Government of the participating States on 21 November 1990.

During their deliberations, the representatives of the participating States took note of the fact that the States were already bound by a number of agreements containing various methods for a peaceful settlement of disputes, and that, in practice, they made use of an even greater variety of such methods. It was noted in particular that many participating States have devised innovative approaches to dispute settlement designed to suit the characteristics of particular disputes, as well as developed arrangements aimed at preventing or managing disputes, such as notification and consultation arrangements, and the establishment of *ad hoc* and permanent joint commissions. It was also noted that many participating States were parties to the 1899 and/or 1907 Hague Conventions for the Pacific Settlement of International Disputes, and that many of them have accepted the jurisdiction of the International Court of Justice, in accordance with the Statute of the Court.

Following their deliberations, the representatives of the participating States adopted this Report.

PRINCIPLES FOR DISPUTE SETTLEMENT AND PROVISIONS FOR A CSCE PROCEDURE FOR PEACEFUL SETTLEMENT OF DISPUTES

Introduction

The commitment of the participating States in the Conference on Security and Co-operation in Europe (CSCE), laid down in principle V of the Helsinki Final Act, to settle disputes among them by peaceful means represents one of the cornerstones of the CSCE process. This commitment is reaffirmed in the Vienna Concluding Document and the Charter of Paris for a New Europe.

In accordance with the Helsinki Final Act, all ten principles of the Declaration on Principles Guiding Relations between Participating States are of primary significance and, accordingly, apply equally and unreservedly, each of them being interpreted taking into account the others.

In the Charter of Paris for a New Europe the participating States solemnly pledged their full commitment to these ten principles, in order to uphold and promote democracy, peace and unity in Europe. They expressed their conviction that in order to strengthen peace and security among the participating States, the advancement of democracy, and respect for and effective exercise of human rights, are indispensable. They also reaffirmed the equal rights of peoples and their right to self-determination in conformity with the Charter of the United Nations and with the relevant norms of international law, including those relating to territorial integrity of States.

Full implementation of all CSCE principles and commitments constitutes in itself an essential element in preventing disputes among the participating States.

In accordance with international law and in particular the Charter of the United Nations, and also in accordance with the relevant principles of the Helsinki Final Act, threat or use of force must not be resorted to in order to settle disputes between States. Such disputes must be settled through peaceful means in accordance with international law. All States must comply in good faith with their obligations under the generally recognized principles and rules of international law with respect to the maintenance of international peace and security.

The existence of appropriate dispute settlement procedures is indispensable for the implementation of the principle that all disputes should be settled exclusively by peaceful means. Such procedures are an essential contribution to the strengthening of the rule of law at the international level and of international peace and security, and justice.

International disputes are to be settled on the basis of the sovereign equality of States and in accordance with the principles of the free choice of means in conformity with international obligations and commitments and with the principles of justice and international law.

Agreement, whether *ad hoc* or given in advance, between the parties to a dispute upon procedures for its settlement, appropriate for the parties concerned and the characteristics of the dispute, is essential for an effective and lasting system for the peaceful settlement of disputes.

Compliance with binding decisions reached through procedures for the peaceful settlement of disputes is an essential element in any overall structure for the peaceful settlement of disputes.

PRINCIPLES FOR DISPUTE SETTLEMENT

General

1. The participating States reaffirm their commitment to abide by international law and their determination to respect and fully implement all CSCE principles and provisions.
2. In conformity with international law, including the Charter of the United Nations, and in accordance with the relevant CSCE principles and provisions, the participating States will refrain from resorting to the threat or use of force to settle their disputes, and will seek a peaceful settlement thereof.
3. The participating States recognize that recourse to, or acceptance of, a settlement procedure freely agreed to by States with regard to existing or future disputes to which they are parties is not incompatible with the sovereign equality of States. A request to have recourse to a settlement procedure does not constitute an unfriendly act.

Dispute prevention

4. The participating States will seek to prevent disputes and to develop, utilize, and improve mechanisms designed to prevent disputes from occurring, including, as appropriate, arrangements and procedures for prior notification and consultation regarding actions by one State likely to affect significantly the interests of another State.

Dispute management

5. Should disputes nevertheless occur, the participating States will take particular care not to let any dispute among them develop in such a way that it will endanger international peace and security, and justice. They will take appropriate steps to manage their disputes pending their settlement. To that end, the participating States will:
   a. address disputes at an early stage;
   b. refrain throughout the course of a dispute from any action which may aggravate the situation and make more difficult or impede the peaceful settlement of the dispute;
   c. seek by all appropriate means to make arrangements enabling the maintenance of good relations between them, including, where appropriate, the adoption of interim measures which are without prejudice to their legal positions in the dispute.

Dispute solution

6. As laid down in the Helsinki Final Act and subsequent relevant documents, the participating States will endeavour in good faith and in a spirit of co-operation to reach a rapid and equitable solution of their disputes on the basis of international law, and will for this purpose use such means as negotiation, enquiry, good offices, mediation, conciliation, arbitration, judicial settlement or other peaceful means of their own choice, including any settlement procedure agreed to in advance of disputes to which they are parties. To that end, the participating States concerned will in particular:
   a. consult with each other at as early a stage as possible;
   b. in case they cannot settle the dispute among themselves, endeavour to agree upon a settlement procedure suited to the nature and characteristics of the particular dispute;
   c. where a dispute is subject to a dispute settlement procedure agreed upon between the parties, settle the dispute through such procedure, unless they agree otherwise;
   d. accept, in the context of the CSCE Procedure for Peaceful Settlement of Disputes and its scope of applicability, the mandatory involvement of a third party when a dispute cannot be settled by other peaceful means.

Information from participating States

7. The participating States will, upon request from a participating State involved in a dispute, make best efforts to provide information regarding appropriate methods for the settlement of such dispute.

Continued efforts

8. In the event of failure to reach a solution within a reasonable time through the method agreed upon, the participating States parties to the dispute will continue to seek a way to settle the dispute peacefully.

Strengthening of commitments

9. The participating States will strengthen their commitments relating to the peaceful settlement of disputes. To that end, they will in particular:

a. endeavour to include, in their future treaties, clauses providing for the settlement of disputes arising from the interpretation or application of those treaties, and to consider whether or not there is an appropriate role for a third party, be it mandatory or non-mandatory;
b. refrain to the extent possible from making reservations to dispute settlement procedures;
c. consider withdrawing reservations they may have made regarding dispute settlement procedures embodied in multilateral treaties;
d. consider accepting the compulsory jurisdiction of the International Court of Justice, either by treaty or by unilateral declaration under Article 36, paragraph 2, of the Statute of the Court, and minimizing, where possible, any reservations attached to such a declaration;
e. if they have made such a declaration accompanied by one or more reservations or if they do so in the future, consider withdrawing such reservations;
f. consider submitting by special agreement to the International Court of Justice or to arbitration, using the Permanent Court of Arbitration, as appropriate, those disputes which lend themselves to such procedures;
g. to the extent feasible, become party to other appropriate treaties, and other international agreements on dispute settlement;
h. make wider use of international dispute settlement institutions;
i. consider accepting the jurisdiction of international bodies for the peaceful settlement of disputes or control mechanisms, established by multilateral treaties pertaining, *inter alia*, to the protection of human rights, or, as the case may be, withdrawing existing reservations in respect of such mechanisms;
j. examine means of establishing and strengthening mechanisms for securing compliance with binding decisions taken in the framework of the peaceful settlement of disputes;
k. work actively within the international community for the advancement of methods for the peaceful settlement of disputes.

Information to natural or legal persons

10. In relation to disputes between them that are of special relevance to particular natural or legal persons, the participating States will, as they deem appropriate, provide information to those persons and hear their views.

PROVISIONS FOR A CSCE PROCEDURE FOR PEACEFUL SETTLEMENT OF DISPUTES

Section I

If a dispute arises between participating States, they will, without undue delay and in good faith, seek to settle the dispute through a process of direct consultation and negotiation, or seek to agree upon an appropriate alternative procedure of settling the dispute.

Section II

Without prejudice to the right of any participating State to raise an issue within the CSCE process, a dispute of importance to peace, security, or stability among the participating States may be brought before the Committee of Senior Officials by any party to the dispute.

Section III

The procedure described below will not apply if the dispute has previously been dealt with, or is being addressed, under some other procedure for the settlement of disputes, as referred to in section VIII, or is covered by any other process which parties to the dispute have accepted.

Section IV

If the parties are unable, within a reasonable period of time, in the light of all circumstances of the dispute, to settle the dispute in direct consultation or negotiation, or to agree upon an appropriate procedure for settling the dispute, any party to the dispute may request the establishment of a CSCE Dispute Settlement Mechanism by notifying the other party or parties to the dispute.

Section V

1. A CSCE Dispute Settlement Mechanism consists of one or more members, selected by common agreement of the parties to a dispute from a register of qualified candidates maintained by the nominating institution. The register comprises the names of up to four persons nominated by each participating State desiring to do so. No member of a Mechanism may be a national of, or permanently resident in the territory of any State involved in the dispute. By agreement between the parties, a Mechanism may include members whose names are not included in the register.
2. If the parties to a dispute have not reached agreement on the composition of a Mechanism within three months from the initial request of a party for the establishment of a Mechanism, the Senior Official of the nominating institution will, in consultation with the parties to the dispute, select from the register a number of names less than six. If the Senior Official of the nominating institution is a national of any of the States involved in the dispute, his functions will be performed by the next most senior official who is not such a national.
3. Each party[1] to the dispute has the right to reject up to three of the nominees. The parties will inform the nominating institution of the rejections, if any, within one month of having been informed of the nominations. This information will be confidential. After one month from the date of informing the parties of the nominations, the nominating institution will notify the parties of the composition of the Mechanism.
4. If the result of the above process is that all the nominees have been rejected, the nominating institution will select from the register an additional five names which have not been included in the initial nominations.
5. Each party to the dispute has now the right to reject one nominee. The parties will inform the nominating institution of the rejections, if any, within fourteen days of having been informed of the nominations. This information will be confidential. After the expiry of fourteen days from the date of informing the parties of the nominations, the nominating institution will notify the parties of the composition of the Mechanism.

---

1 The problems arising when the parties are more than two will require further consideration.

Section VI

1. When the Mechanism has been established, it will seek appropriate contact with the parties to the dispute, separately or jointly. The Mechanism will adopt its methods of work, proceeding in such informal and flexible manner as it may deem practical.
2. Unless the parties agree otherwise, the proceedings of the Mechanism and any comment or advice offered by it will be confidential, although the fact that the Mechanism has been established may be acknowledged publicly.
3. The Mechanism may, if the parties so agree, use the premises and facilities of the International Bureau of the Permanent Court of Arbitration.

Section VII

The Mechanism will seek such information and comments from the parties as will enable it to assist the parties in identifying suitable procedures for the settlement of the dispute. The Mechanism may offer general or specific comment or advice.

Section VIII

The comment or advice of the Mechanism may relate to the inception or resumption of a process of negotiation among the parties, or to the adoption of any other dispute settlement procedure, such as fact-finding, conciliation, mediation, good offices, arbitration or adjudication or any adaptation of any such procedure or combination thereof, or any other procedure which it may indicate in relation to the circumstances of the dispute, or to any aspect of any such procedure.

Section IX

The parties will consider in good faith and in a spirit of co-operation any comment or advice of the Mechanism. If, on the basis of the proceedings of the Mechanism and of any comment or advice offered, the parties are nevertheless unable, within a reasonable time, to settle the dispute or to agree upon a procedure for its settlement, any party to the dispute may so notify the Mechanism and the other party to the dispute. Any party may thereupon, consistently with the provisions of Section VI, paragraph 2, bring that circumstance to the attention of the Committee of Senior Officials.

Section X

The failure of a party to act upon any comment or advice of the Mechanism with regard to a procedure for the settlement of a dispute does not relieve any of the parties of the duty to pursue its efforts to settle the dispute by peaceful means.

Section XI

In the event referred to in the second sentence of Section IX, any party to the dispute may, within a period of three months from any notification, request the Mechanism to provide general or specific comment or advice on the substance of the dispute, in order to assist the parties in finding a settlement in accordance with international law and their CSCE commitments. The parties will consider in good faith and in a spirit of co-operation any such comment or advice of the Mechanism.

Section XII

1. Notwithstanding a request by a party under either Section IV or Section XI, the Mechanism will not be established or continued, as the case may be, if another party to the dispute considers that because the dispute raises issues concerning its territorial integrity, or national defence, title to sovereignty over land territory, or competing claims with regard to the jurisdiction over other areas, the Mechanism should not be established or continued.
2. In that event, any other party to the dispute may bring that circumstance to the attention of the Committee of Senior Officials.

Section XIII

The parties to a dispute may at any time by mutual agreement modify or adapt the present procedure as they may consider appropriate to facilitate the settlement of their dispute, *inter alia*, by agreeing:

a. to authorize the Mechanism either to conduct a process of fact-finding, or to entrust one or more persons, one or more participating States, or any competent CSCE institution, or any other body, with a fact-finding mission;
b. to request the Mechanism to undertake or organize any expert function in regard to the subject-matter of the dispute;
c. to request the Mechanism to report in any other form than provided in the foregoing;

d. to accept any comment or advice of the Mechanism as binding, in part or in full, with regard to the settlement of the dispute.

Section XIV

Any expenses incurred in utilizing the CSCE Dispute Settlement Mechanism, other than those incurred by the parties to the dispute for the conduct of the proceedings, will be shared equally between the parties to the dispute unless they agree otherwise.

Section XV

Nothing stated in the foregoing will in any way affect the unity of the CSCE principles, or the right of participating States to raise within the CSCE process any issue relating to the implementation of any CSCE commitment concerning the principle of the peaceful settlement of disputes, or relating to any other CSCE commitment or provision.

Section XVI

All parties to a dispute will implement meaningfully and in good faith the CSCE Dispute Settlement Procedure.

* * *

The representatives of the participating States noted that the Council of Ministers for Foreign Affairs will take into account the Report of the Valletta Meeting at its first meeting in Berlin. In this context, the representatives of the participating States recommend that the Council establish the necessary arrangements in accordance with the Charter of Paris for a New Europe. They, furthermore, noted that the next CSCE Follow-up Meeting in Helsinki will assess the progress achieved at the Valletta Meeting. In this context, the representatives of the participating States consider that the commitments contained in the present Report as well as their implementation should be kept under review, bearing in mind the importance of enhancing the effectiveness of the procedure.

The representatives of the participating States expressed their deep gratitude to the people and the Government of Malta for the excellent organization of the Meeting and for the warm hospitality extended to them during their stay in Malta.

INTERPRETATIVE STATEMENTS

Interpretative statement by Luxembourg

Statement made by the head of the delegation of Luxembourg on behalf of the European Community and its member States:

I should like to make an interpretative statement on the use of the term 'participating State', which appears in the various texts adopted during this Meeting on Peaceful Settlement of Disputes.

The European Community and its member States consider that the term 'participating State' does not exclude the participation of the European Community in the procedure for the settlement of disputes to be drawn up in the present framework, alongside a member State, when the dispute concerns a matter falling within Community competence. If this were not ensured, all disputes concerning matters for which the Community is competent would be excluded from the field of application of the different methods proposed.

* * *

Interpretative statement by Greece

Greece believes that recourse of States to the CSCE mechanism for dispute settlement should not be subject to exceptions of any sort and that, consequently, exceptions should not have found their way in the Report of the Valletta Meeting (Section XII, paragraph 1) as they reduce the possibility of using the mechanism effectively.

As far as the phrase "competing claims with regard to the jurisdiction over other areas" contained in Section XII, paragraph 1, is concerned, the delegation of Greece accepted it in the terms it is written and solely in those, without any further qualification.

* * *

Interpretative statement by Turkey

The Turkish delegation wishes to express that it consents to the Section, which deals with exceptions to the CSCE Procedure for Peaceful Settlement of Disputes, containing the phraseology "...the jurisdiction over other areas" subject to the condition that it is construed by definition to comprise the areas listed hereinbelow: internal waters, territorial sea, all kinds of contiguous zone, continental shelf, exclusive economic zone, other areas of this kind as well as national airspace.

Editor's note: The following communication has been submitted by the delegation of Turkey under paragraph 79 of the Final Recommendations of the Helsinki Consultations and has been circulated by the Executive Secretary on 17 January 1991 (CSCE/PSDV/Inf.1).

The Government of Turkey had formally placed a reservation regarding the representation of Cyprus at the CSCE on 31 July 1975 (CSCE/III/I). The same reservation has been placed at subsequent meetings within the context of the CSCE.

"The Republic of Cyprus" which was established, in accordance with international treaties, on the basis of a partnership between the two peoples of the Island, has ceased to exist as such after its constitution was unilaterally and unlawfully abrogated in 1963 by the Greek Cypriot side by the use of force, despite the protestations and resistance of the Turkish Cypriot side. The Greek Cypriot Administration has ever since represented exclusively the Greek Cypriots and their interests. As a guarantor power under the 1960 Treaty of Guarantee, Turkey does not recognize this administration or any of its illegitimate claims.

There is no single authority which, in fact or in law, jointly represents or is competent to represent the Turkish Cypriots and the Greek Cypriots, and consequently Cyprus as a whole. This is the reason why a negotiating process is being pursued between the Turkish Cypriot and Greek Cypriot leaders on the basis of equality.

The Turkish Cypriot people are represented by the Government of the Turkish Republic of Northern Cyprus which was recognized by Turkey in 1983. President Denktas has formally expressed the desire of the Turkish Cypriot people to be associated with the CSCE process and its structures. Only when that becomes a reality, the Turkish Cypriots will have a chance to voice their own views on an equal footing with the Greek Cypriots.

Due to the reasons stated above, the representation of Cyprus by the Greek Cypriot administration at the CSCE is neither legal nor legitimate. Therefore, the Government of the Republic of Turkey declares that the Report of the Valletta Meeting and the conclusions therein will have no validity or applicability as regards and in relation to the Turkish Republic of Northern Cyprus and Turkish Cypriots.

Similarly, the commitments assumed by the Republic of Turkey under this Report will have no validity or applicability as regards and in relation to Cyprus.

(...)

* * *

Editor's note: The following communication has been submitted by the delegation of Cyprus under paragraph 79 of the Final Recommendations of the Helsinki Consultations and has been circulated by the Executive Secretary on 18 January 1991 (CSCE/PSDV/Inf. 2).

Interpretative statement by the delegation of Cyprus

With reference to the reservation of Turkey in Document CSCE/PSDV/Inf. 1, dated 17 January 1991, my Government wishes to make the following interpretative statement to be duly registered by the Executive Secretary and circulated to the participating States in accordance with paragraph 79 of the Rules of Procedure.

The Statement is to be included in the Journal of the day.

"With respect to the reservation of Turkey concerning the participation of Cyprus in the CSCE Meeting on the Peaceful Settlement of Disputes, the delegation of Cyprus wishes to draw attention to rule 4 of our Rules of Procedure which states as follows:

> "Decisions of the Conference shall be taken by consensus. Consensus shall be understood to mean the absence of any objection expressed by a Representative and submitted by him as constituting an obstacle to the taking of the decision in question".

The Conference has adopted by consensus the Document of the Paris Summit. The Cyprus delegation considers that, in accordance with the practice and procedures of the Final Act and the CSCE process as a whole, all provisions of the document are equally binding on all participating States.

Consequently, any reservation concerning the validity of the decisions of this Meeting in relations of each participating State with all or any other participating State, or any kind of selecting in implementing these decisions, is of no effect.

Furthermore, the delegation of Cyprus wishes also to state the following:

Given the gross violations of human rights and fundamental freedoms by Turkey, both on its territory and in the Turkish occupied part of Cyprus, Cyprus considers that Turkey is not eligible in participating in the CSCE process as long as these violations continue.

In particular, principles 1, 2, 3, 4, 5 and 6 are violated by Turkey in occupying part of the territory of Cyprus and in denying to enter into a dialogue with the Government of Cyprus for the settlement of the problem. Principle 7 is violated both in the occupied part of Cyprus and in Turkey by denying human rights and fundamental freedoms to its own citizens such as freedom of association, freedom of expression, religious freedom, freedom of the press and also by applying torture and other inhuman and degrading treatment or punishment to political and other detainees and prisoners. Principle 8 is violated against the Kurdish national Minority. Principles 9 and 10 are also violated in the case of Cyprus.

Turkey had all the necessary time available to change its policies so that they conform with commitments Turkey has undertaken under the Helsinki Final Act and other CSCE Documents.

In view of the fact that Turkey has so far failed to do so and has not even expressed any sign of willingness to do so, Cyprus deems it appropriate that the CSCE participating States take a decision at the appropriate level to suspend the participation of Turkey to the CSCE process.

As to the representation of Cyprus the delegation of Cyprus wishes to state that the Republic of Cyprus and its Government have been consistently recognized by all international organizations and in all international fora. Cyprus is a member State of the United Nations, the Commonwealth, the Council of Europe, the Non-Aligned Movement and other International Organizations and its Government is fully recognized by all members of these organizations, with the sole exception of Turkey *i.e.* the power occupying 38 % of the territory of the Republic.

The independence and sovereignty of the Republic of Cyprus as well as the legality of the Government of the Republic of Cyprus have been recognized in a series of resolutions of the United Nations Security Council, notably Resolutions 541 (1983), 550 (1984) and the most recent one 657 of June 15, 1990.

The Government of the Republic of Cyprus is its lawful Government, despite of the arbitrary and unilateral declaration of November 1983 purporting to create a separate Turkish Cypriot "State". It should be recalled in this respect that the Security Council condemned the attempted secession of part of the Republic of Cyprus, considered such declaration as legally invalid and called for its withdrawal, called upon all states not to recognize any Cypriot State other than the Republic of Cyprus and not to facilitate or in any way assist the secessionist entity.

18th January 1991

CRACOW SYMPOSIUM ON THE CULTURAL HERITAGE

DOCUMENT OF THE CRACOW SYMPOSIUM ON THE CULTURAL HERITAGE OF THE CSCE PARTICIPATING STATES

Cracow, 6 June 1991

The representatives of the participating States of the Conference on Security and Co-operation in Europe (CSCE), Austria, Belgium, Bulgaria, Canada, Cyprus, Czech and Slovak Federal Republic, Denmark, Finland, France, Germany, Greece, the Holy See, Hungary, Iceland, Ireland, Italy, Liechtenstein, Luxembourg - European Community, Malta, Monaco, the Netherlands, Norway, Poland, Portugal, Romania, San Marino, Spain, Sweden, Switzerland, Turkey, the Union of Soviet Socialist Republics, the United Kingdom, the United States of America and Yugoslavia met in Cracow from 28 May to 7 June 1991, in accordance with the relevant provisions of the Agenda and organizational modalities of the Symposium, as set forth in the Vienna Concluding Document, and with the provisions of the Charter of Paris for a new Europe. Albania attended the Symposium as an observer. Contributions were made in accordance with the above-mentioned documents by UNESCO and the Council of Europe.

The symposium was opened and closed by the Minister of Culture and Fine Arts of Poland and was addressed by the Prime Minister of Poland.

Opening statements were made by all Heads of Delegation among whom were Ministers of Culture of a number of participating States.

The participating States welcome with great satisfaction the profound political changes that have occurred in Europe. They underline the contribution made by culture in overcoming the divisions of the past and in strengthening co-operation among the participating States.

The participating States express their deeply held conviction that they share common values forged by history and based, *inter alia*, on respect for the individual, freedom of conscience, religion or belief, freedom of expression, recognition of the importance of spiritual and cultural values, commitment to the rule of law, tolerance and openness to dialogue with other cultures.

They take note of the interrelationship between cultural life and the well-being of their peoples, and the special importance that this has for democratic countries in transition towards a market economy. They encourage support, as already undertaken, afforded and the on-going assistance to those countries in preserving and protecting their cultural heritage.

The participating States respect the irreplaceable uniqueness of all their cultures and will endeavour to promote continued cultural dialogue among themselves and with the rest of the world. They reaffirm their belief that respect for cultural diversity promotes understanding and tolerance among individuals and groups.

They consider that the regional aspects of culture should in themselves constitute a factor in the understanding between peoples.

Regional cultural diversity is an expression of the richness of the common cultural identity of the participating States. Its preservation and protection contribute to building a democratic, peaceful and united Europe.

Reaffirming their commitment to the full implementation of the provisions relating to the cultural dimension in the Helsinki Final Act and other CSCE documents, the participating States agree on the following:

I. Culture and freedom

1. The participating States emphasize that respect for human rights and fundamental freedoms is essential to the full development of cultural creativity.

2. The State and the public authorities will refrain from infringing upon the freedom of artistic creation.

3. The participating States undertake to promote and protect the free and unhindered development of artistic creativity; they recognize the important role of the individual artist in society and will respect and protect the integrity of creative work.

4. They recognize the need for governments to strike a balance between their dual responsibility of acting in support of, and ensuring the freedom of, cultural activity.

5. They further acknowledge that, given the variety of cultural activity in the participating States, there are many ways in which governments might choose to respond effectively to concerns relating to the cultural heritage.

6. The participating States recall their respect for freedom of expression and, in connection with the exercise of that freedom in the artistic and cultural fields, state as follows:

6.1 The publication of written works, the performance and broadcasting of musical, theatrical and audiovisual works, and the exhibition of pictorial or sculptural works will not be subject to restriction or interference by the State save such restrictions as are prescribed by domestic legislation and are fully consistent with international standards.

6.2 They express their conviction that the existence, in the artistic and cultural fields, of a diversity of means of dissemination independent of the State, such as publishing houses, radio broadcasting, cinema and television enterprises, theatres and galleries, helps to ensure pluralism and the freedom of artistic and cultural expression.

7. The participating States recall their commitments to unhindered access to culture, and agree as follows:

7.1 While duly respecting intellectual property rights, any person or independent organization has the right to own privately, use and reproduce all kinds of cultural materials, such as books, publications and audiovisual recordings, and the means of reproducing them.

8. The participating States are resolved to promote the mutual knowledge of their respective cultures. Accordingly, they will encourage co-operation and exchanges in all fields of culture and creative work.

9. The participating States are convinced of the enrichment which regional and local cultures, including those connected with national minorities, bring to cultural life.

II. Culture and heritage

10. The participating States express their deeply-held conviction that the cultural heritage of each one of them constitutes an inalienable part of

their civilization, their memory and their common history, to be transmitted to future generations.

11. The participating States take note of the definitions of archaeological property, of the cultural heritage and the architectural heritage in the relevant international documents of the Council of Europe and UNESCO.

12. The complete and lasting documentation of sites, structures, cultural landscapes, objects and cultural systems, including historical, religious and cultural monuments, as they presently exist, is one of the most important legacies to the cultural heritage that can be provided for future generations.

13. The participating States also recognize as vital elements of their common cultural heritage, the heritage of those cultures which, because of language barriers, climate and geographical distance, limited population or turns of history and political circumstances, have not been widely accessible.

14. The participating States will endeavour to protect the cultural heritage, in compliance with relevant international agreements and with their domestic legislation.

15. The participating States will pay heed to the preservation, enhancement and restoration of the cultural heritage when drawing up cultural, environmental and regional and urban planning policies. They further note the importance of relating individual conservation projects to their authentic urban or rural environment, where appropriate and whenever possible.

16. The participating States recognize the importance of making their cultural heritage as widely accessible as possible. In doing so, they will pay particular attention to the needs of the handicapped.

16.1 They will endeavour to safeguard the heritage from damage which may be caused by management of and public access to it.

16.2 They will promote public awareness of the value of the heritage and the need to protect it.

16.3 They will seek, wherever possible, to facilitate access for researchers and scholars to relevant primary documents and archive materials.

17. The participating States note favourably the role of non-governmental associations in promoting awareness of the heritage and the need for its protection.

18. Partnerships among diverse groups at the local, regional and national level, from both the private and the public sector, are valuable for ensuring the effective and representative preservation of the cultural heritage. The preservation and interpretation of the values and the cultural heritage of diverse groups will be enhanced with the involvement of those groups, which is conducive to the tolerance and respect for different cultures which are of paramount importance.

19. The participating States recognize the usefulness and importance of exchanging information on preserving the cultural heritage and acknowledge that the use of data banks, on a national and multilateral level, could make a useful contribution to this work.

III. Principal areas of preservation and co-operation

20. The participating States will encourage training, at the initial and advanced levels, for the various professions and crafts involved in preserving and restoring the cultural heritage, as well as in administering it. They agree to keep one another informed of any important developments in this field and to co-operate with one another.

20.1 The dissemination of knowledge and skills, especially vanishing skills related to the cultural heritage, through training, the exchange of personnel, research and technical publication, is necessary to ensure continuity in cultural preservation. They therefore reaffirm their commitments to encourage bilateral and multilateral exchanges of trainees and specialists.

20.2 The participating States should invite the appropriate professional organizations to set up a national register of skilled craftspersons competent in the field of the protection and preservation of the cultural heritage, in order to facilitate contacts between such persons and the users of their services both nationally and internationally.

21. The participating States will exchange data on their cultural heritage policies, particularly regarding the methods, means and possibilities provided by new technologies.

22. The participating States will strive to share their knowledge and experience in the area of publishing and distribution of printed and audiovisual material.

22.1 With a view to increasing public awareness regarding the preservation of the cultural heritage, the participating States will make information available that will assist radio and television stations, as well as the print media, to promote information in this area.

23. They will endeavour to improve storage conditions for perishable cultural goods such as paper, film tapes and recorded sound materials, to establish national programmes for the preservation of the perishable cultural heritage and to set commonly accepted standards for all types of carriers of cultural products in order to safeguard the permanence of such items of culture.

24. The participating States will encourage the establishment of links between resource centres and data banks in cultural fields so as to facilitate the exchange of information between them.

25. With a view to a better understanding of the cultural values of the countries whose languages are less widely spoken, the participating States welcome the dissemination of knowledge about and of such languages, in particular through the translation and publication of literary works from these countries. The organization of international training courses for media and cultural personnel involved in promoting the understanding of less-spoken languages and less widely-known cultures should also be considered.

26. Acknowledging the important contribution of religious faiths, institutions and organizations to the cultural heritage, the participating States will co-operate closely with them regarding the preservation of the cultural heritage and pay due attention to monuments and objects of religious origin whose original communities no longer use them or no longer exist in the particular region.

27. Bearing in mind the important role that regional aspects of culture may play in linking people across national borders, the participating States will favour regional co-operation at the level of local and national authorities as well as non-governmental organizations with a view to fostering good-neighbourly relations.

28. The participating States will accord due attention to strengthening the heritage of popular culture of the past, including indigenous and vernacular cultures, and to encouraging a contemporary popular culture within the framework of their overall efforts for the preservation, study, protection and promotion of mutual awareness of their cultural heritage. The participating States note the importance of research into various forms of expression of past and present cultures - symbolic practices, technical objects and knowledge, folk art, languages - and the importance of doing what is necessary to highlight them.

29. The participating States will also pay attention to more recent contributions to the cultural heritage (art, including architectural works, of the 20th century).

30. The participating States will co-operate in preventing the illegal circulation of cultural objects, for example by considering adhering to the relevant international instruments.

31. The participating States will strive to preserve and protect those monuments and sites of remembrance, including most notably extermination camps, and the related archives, which are themselves testimonials to tragic experiences in their common past. Such steps need to be taken in order that those experiences may be remembered, may help to teach present and future generations of these events, and thus ensure that they are never repeated.

32. The interpretation of sensitive sites of remembrance can serve as a valuable means of promoting tolerance and understanding among people and will take into account social and cultural diversity.

33. The participating States recognize that, in defining priorities for preservation, it is important to take into account both intrinsic value of the cultural heritage, its relative state of deterioration and its historic cultural content. To this effect they will, as appropriate, endeavour to promote the use of risk charts, the exchange of information and the organization of on-site workshops, ideal also for the involvement of younger generations.

34. The participating States bear in mind that the preservation of the status of monuments and sites related to their history and culture, wherever they are located, constitutes an integral part of the overall efforts

within the CSCE for the preservation and protection of the common cultural heritage.

35. The participating States believe that taking concerted measures to protect the common cultural heritage from environmental damage is necessary. To this end they will consider establishing or joining networks for the collection of data and co-ordination of research. They will endeavour to co-ordinate policy decisions and undertake direct measures to reduce the impact of air pollution and other degradation on the common cultural heritage.

36. With a view to protecting cultural sites in urban environments, measures will be taken by the participating States to counteract the effects of pollution on the architectural complexes of threatened cities; to restore, preserve and revitalize historical urban centres; and to safeguard sites and protect them from damage due to the increasing flow of tourists.

37. The participating States note the importance of protecting the cultural landscape, particularly in villages and rural areas, from the danger inherent in changes in the pattern of economic activities and in the impact of pollution, with a special view to protecting dwellings and coherent ensembles of the everyday living environment.

38. In view of the contribution which natural history can make to our understanding of the world of today and its evolution in the future, the participating States will endeavour to foster the preservation and interpretation of natural history sites and collections.

39. The participating States note the importance of safeguarding public and private parks and historical gardens, as works of humanity and nature, due to their historical, botanical and social interest, including their decorative and architectural elements.

40. The participating States will endeavour to safeguard and protect the archaeological sites located on their territories, including sites located under water. They will bear this aspect in mind during regional development operations which are likely to be a threat to sites which have not yet been scientifically surveyed, excavated or restored.

41. They stress the need for co-ordination of the activities of international organizations and institutions, such as the Council of Europe and the UNESCO, in order to contribute to the full development of cultural

co-operation among the participating States. Bearing in mind the need to avoid duplication of effort, the participating States will co-operate closely within the competent international organizations to which they belong.

* * *

42. The participating States welcome the positive contribution made by the representatives of UNESCO and the Council of Europe to the proceedings of the Cracow Symposium on the Cultural Heritage. They note that the work and activities of UNESCO will be of continuing relevance to the CSCE's consideration of cultural issues. They further acknowledge the Council of Europe's rich experience and expertise in cultural matters, in particular in protecting the European cultural heritage, and agree to consider appropriate ways in which the participating States might make use of the Council of Europe in the context of the CSCE's work in this area.

43. In the two Study Groups many experts from the participating States spoke on national experiences, and put forward ideas of co-operation in the fields of cultural exchange and the preservation of cultural heritage, in particular on those aspects outlined in the mandate assigned to the respective groups. These contributions, copies of which will be deposited with the CSCE Secretariat, greatly contributed to the success of the Symposium. The participating States expressed their intention to pursue further these initiatives in appropriate international fora.

44. The representatives of the participating States expressed their profound gratitude to the people and Government of Poland for the excellent organization of the Symposium and the warm hospitality extended to the delegations which participated in the Symposium.

INTERPRETATIVE STATEMENT[1]

Interpretative statement by Italy on behalf of the delegations of Hungary and Italy

Paragraph 43 of the Document of the Cracow Symposium on the Cultural Heritage refers to 'contributions' by experts from the participating States. In the opinion of the Hungarian and Italian delegations, this expression refers in the first instance to the proposals submitted by the delegations of the participating States, which were translated and distributed by the Executive Secretariat with a number corresponding to the order in which they were submitted.

In this connection, the Hungarian and Italian delegations would like to confirm that each and every CSCE document should be translated and made available in all of the working languages of the CSCE. Any text, document, contribution etc. which is not translated and circulated in all of the CSCE languages cannot under any circumstances be considered as forming part of the CSCE documentation, nor as reflecting its procedures and/or decisions.

---

1 Journal No. 8, 5th Plenary Meeting (6 June 1991).

REPORT OF THE CSCE MEETING OF EXPERTS ON NATIONAL MINORITIES

Geneva, 19 July 1991

The representatives of Albania, Austria, Belgium, Bulgaria, Canada, Cyprus, the Czech and Slovak Federal Republic, Denmark, Finland, France, Germany, Greece, the Holy See, Hungary, Iceland, Ireland, Italy, Liechtenstein, Luxembourg, Malta, Monaco, the Netherlands-European Community, Norway, Poland, Portugal, Romania, San Marino, Spain, Sweden, Switzerland, Turkey, the Union of Soviet Socialist Republics, the United Kingdom, the United States of America and Yugoslavia met in Geneva from 1 to 19 July 1991 in accordance with the relevant provisions of the Charter of Paris for a New Europe.

An opening address to the Meeting was delivered by H.E. Rene Felber, Federal Councillor, Head of the Federal Department of Foreign Affairs of Switzerland, on behalf of the host country. Opening statements were made by H.E. Catharina Dales, Minister of the Interior of the Netherlands on behalf of the Netherlands-European Community, and by Heads of Delegation of the participating States. Contributions to the Meeting were made by Ms. Catherine Lalumiere, Secretary General of the Council of Europe, and Mr. Jan Martenson, Under-Secretary-General in charge of the United Nations Centre for Human Rights in Geneva. The State Secretary for Foreign Affairs of the host country, Mr. Klaus Jacobi, delivered a closing address to the Meeting.

In accordance with the relevant provisions of the Charter of Paris, the representatives of the participating States had a thorough discussion on the issues of national minorities and of the rights of persons belonging to them that reflected the diversity of situations and of the legal, historical, political and economic backgrounds. They had an exchange of views on practical experience with national minorities, in particular on national legislation, democratic institutions, international instruments and other possible forms of co-operation. Views were expressed on the implementation of the relevant CSCE commitments, and the representatives of the participating States also considered the scope for the improvement of relevant standards. They also considered new measures aimed at improving the implementation of the aforementioned commitments.

A number of proposals were submitted for consideration by the Meeting and, following their deliberations, the representatives of the participating States adopted this Report.

The text of the Report of the Geneva Meeting of Experts on National Minorities will be published in each participating State, which will disseminate it and make it known as widely as possible.

The representatives of the participating States note that the Council will take into account the summing up of the Meeting, in accordance with the Charter of Paris for a New Europe.

I.

Recognizing that their observance and full exercise of human rights and fundamental freedoms, including those of persons belonging to national minorities, are the foundation of the New Europe,

Reaffirming their deep conviction that friendly relations among their peoples, as well as peace, justice, stability and democracy, require that the ethnic, cultural, linguistic and religious identity of national minorities be protected, and conditions for the promotion of that identity be created,

Convinced that, in States with national minorities, democracy requires that all persons, including those belonging to national minorities, enjoy full and effective equality of rights and fundamental freedoms and benefit from the rule of law and democratic institutions,

Aware of the diversity of situations and constitutional systems in their countries, and therefore recognizing that various approaches to the implementation of CSCE commitments regarding national minorities are appropriate,

Mindful of the importance of exerting efforts to address national minorities issues, particularly in areas where democratic institutions are being consolidated and questions relating to national minorities are of special concern,

Aware that national minorities form an integral part of the society of the States in which they live and that they are a factor of enrichment of each respective State and society,

Confirming the need to respect and implement fully and fairly their undertakings in the field of human rights and fundamental freedoms as set forth in the international instruments by which they may be bound,

Reaffirming their strong determination to respect and apply, to their full extent, all their commitments relating to national minorities and persons belonging to them in the Helsinki Final Act, the Madrid Concluding Document and the Vienna Concluding Document, the Document of the Copenhagen Meeting of the Conference on the Human Dimension of the CSCE, the Document of the Cracow Symposium on the Cultural Heritage as well as the Charter of Paris for a New Europe, the participating States present below the summary of their conclusions.

The representatives of the participating States took as the fundamental basis of their work the commitments undertaken by them with respect to national minorities as contained in the relevant adopted CSCE documents, in particular those in the Charter of Paris for a New Europe and the Document of the Copenhagen Meeting of the Conference on the Human Dimension of the CSCE, which they fully reaffirmed.

II.

The participating States stress the continued importance of a thorough review of implementation of their CSCE commitments relating to persons belonging to national minorities.

They emphasize that human rights and fundamental freedoms are the basis for the protection and promotion of rights of persons belonging to national minorities. They further recognize that questions relating to national minorities can only be satisfactorily resolved in a democratic political framework based on the rule of law, with a functioning independent judiciary. This framework guarantees full respect for human rights and fundamental freedoms, equal rights and status for all citizens, including persons belonging to national minorities, the free expression of all their legitimate interests and aspirations, political pluralism, social tolerance and the implementation of legal rules that place effective restraints on the abuse of governmental power.

Issues concerning national minorities, as well as compliance with international obligations and commitments concerning the rights of persons belonging to them, are matters of legitimate international concern and consequently do not constitute exclusively an internal affair of the respective State.

They note that not all ethnic, cultural, linguistic or religious differences necessarily lead to the creation of national minorities.

III.

Respecting the right of persons belonging to national minorities to effective participation in public affairs, the participating States consider that when issues relating to the situation of national minorities are discussed within their countries, they themselves should have the effective opportunity to be involved, in accordance with the decision-making procedures of each State. They further consider that appropriate democratic participation of persons belonging to national minorities or their representatives in decision-making or consultative bodies constitutes an important element of effective participation in public affairs.

They consider that special efforts must be made to resolve specific problems in a constructive manner and through dialogue by means of negotiations and consultations with a view to improving the situation of persons belonging to national minorities. They recognize that the promotion of dialogue between States, and between States and persons belonging to national minorities, will be most successful when there is a free flow of information and ideas between all parties. They encourage unilateral, bilateral and multilateral efforts by governments to explore avenues for enhancing the effectiveness of their implementation of CSCE commitments relating to national minorities.

The participating States further consider that respect for human rights and fundamental freedoms must be accorded on a non-discriminatory basis throughout society. In areas inhabited mainly by persons belonging to a national minority, the human rights and fundamental freedoms of persons belonging to that minority, of persons belonging to the majority population of the respective State, and of persons belonging to other national minorities residing in these areas will be equally protected.

They reconfirm that persons belonging to national minorities have the right freely to express, preserve and develop their ethnic, cultural, linguistic or religious identity and to maintain and develop their culture in all its aspects, free of any attempts at assimilation against their will.

They will permit the competent authorities to inform the Office for Free Elections of all scheduled public elections on their territories, including those held below national level. The participating States will consider favourably, to the extent permitted by law, the presence of observers at elections held below the national level, including in areas inhabited by national minorities, and will endeavour to facilitate their access.

IV.

The participating States will create conditions for persons belonging to national minorities to have equal opportunity to be effectively involved in the public life, economic activities, and building of their societies.

In accordance with paragraph 31 of the Copenhagen Document, the participating States will take the necessary measures to prevent discrimination against individuals, particularly in respect of employment, housing and education, on the grounds of belonging or not belonging to a national minority. In that context, they will make provision, if they have not yet done so, for effective recourse to redress for individuals who have experienced discriminatory treatment on the grounds of their belonging or not belonging to a national minority, including by making available to individual victims of discrimination a broad array of administrative and judicial remedies.

The participating States are convinced that the preservation of the values and of the cultural heritage of national minorities requires the involvement of persons belonging to such minorities and that tolerance and respect for different cultures are of paramount importance in this regard. Accordingly, they confirm the importance of refraining from hindering the production of cultural materials concerning national minorities, including by persons belonging to them.

The participating States affirm that persons belonging to a national minority will enjoy the same rights and have the same duties of citizenship as the rest of the population.

The participating States reconfirm the importance of adopting, where necessary, special measures for the purpose of ensuring to persons belonging to national minorities full equality with the other citizens in the exercise and enjoyment of human rights and fundamental freedoms. They further recall the need to take the necessary measures to protect the ethnic, cultural, linguistic and religious identity of national minorities on their territory and create conditions for the promotion of that identity; any such measures will be in conformity with the principles of equality and non-discrimination with respect to the other citizens of the participating State concerned.

They recognize that such measures, which take into account, *inter alia*, historical and territorial circumstances of national minorities, are particularly important in areas where democratic institutions are being consolidated and national minorities issues are of special concern.

Aware of the diversity and varying constitutional systems among them, which make no single approach necessarily generally applicable, the participating States note with interest that positive results have been obtained by some of them in an appropriate democratic manner by, *inter alia*:

- advisory and decision-making bodies in which minorities are represented, in particular with regard to education, culture and religion;

- elected bodies and assemblies of national minority affairs;

- local and autonomous administration, as well as autonomy on a territorial basis, including the existence of consultative, legislative and executive bodies chosen through free and periodic elections;

- self-administration by a national minority of aspects concerning its identity in situations where autonomy on a territorial basis does not apply;

- decentralized or local forms of government;

- bilateral and multilateral agreements and other arrangements regarding national minorities;

- for persons belonging to national minorities, provision of adequate types and levels of education in their mother tongue with due regard to the number, geographic settlement patterns and cultural traditions of national minorities;

- funding the teaching of minority languages to the general public, as well as the inclusion of minority languages in teacher-training institutions, in particular in regions inhabited by persons belonging to national minorities;

- in cases where instruction in a particular subject is not provided in their territory in the minority language at all levels, taking the necessary measures to find means of recognizing diplomas issued abroad for a course of study completed in that language;

- creation of government research agencies to review legislation and disseminate information related to equal rights and non-discrimination;

- provision of financial and technical assistance to persons belonging to national minorities who so wish to exercise their right to establish and maintain their own educational, cultural and religious institutions, organizations and associations;

- governmental assistance for addressing local difficulties relating to discriminatory practices (e.g. a citizens relations service);

- encouragement of grassroots community relations efforts between minority communities, between majority and minority communities, and between neighbouring communities sharing borders, aimed at helping to prevent local tensions from arising and address conflicts peacefully should they arise; and

- encouragement of the establishment of permanent mixed commissions, either inter-State or regional, to facilitate continuing dialogue between the border regions concerned.

The participating States are of the view that these or other approaches, individually or in combination, could be helpful in improving the situation of national minorities on their territories.

V.

The participating States respect the right of persons belonging to national minorities to exercise and enjoy their rights alone or in community with others, to establish and maintain organizations and associations within their country, and to participate in international non-governmental organizations.

The participating States reaffirm, and will not hinder the exercise of, the right of persons belonging to national minorities to establish and maintain their own educational, cultural and religious institutions, organizations and associations.

In this regard, they recognize the major and vital role that individuals, non-governmental organizations, and religious and other groups play in fostering cross-cultural understanding and improving relations at all levels of society, as well as across international frontiers.

They believe that the first-hand observations and experience of such organizations, groups, and individuals can be of great value in promoting the implementation of CSCE commitments relating to persons belonging to national minorities. They therefore will encourage and not hinder the work of such organizations, groups and individuals and welcome their contributions in this area.

VI.

The participating States, concerned by the proliferation of acts of racial, ethnic and religious hatred, anti-semitism, xenophobia and discrimination, stress their determination to condemn, on a continuing basis, such acts against anyone.

In this context, they reaffirm their recognition of the particular problems of Roma (gypsies). They are ready to undertake effective measures in order to achieve full equality of opportunity between persons belonging to Roma ordinarily resident in their State and the rest of the resident population. They will also encourage research and studies regarding Roma and the particular problems they face.

They will take effective measures to promote tolerance, understanding, equality of opportunity and good relations between individuals of different origins within their country.

Further, the participating States will take effective measures, including the adoption, in conformity with their constitutional law and their international obligations, if they have not already done so, of laws that would prohibit acts that constitute incitement to violence based on national, racial, ethnic or religious discrimination, hostility or hatred, including anti-semitism, and policies to enforce such laws.

Moreover, in order to heighten public awareness of prejudice and hatred, to improve enforcement of laws against hate-related crime and otherwise to further efforts to address hatred and prejudice in society, they will make efforts to collect, publish on a regular basis, and make available to the public, data about crimes on their respective territories that are based on prejudice as to race, ethnic identity or religion, including the guidelines used for the collection of such data. These data should not contain any personal information.

They will consult and exchange views and information at the international level, including at future meetings of the CSCE, on crimes that manifest evidence of prejudice and hate.

VII.

Convinced that the protection of the rights of persons belonging to national minorities necessitates free flow of information and exchange of ideas, the participating States emphasize the importance of communication between persons belonging to national minorities without interference by public authorities and regardless of frontiers. The exercise of such rights may be subject only to such restrictions as are prescribed by law and are consistent with international standards. They reaffirm that no one belonging to a national minority, simply by virtue of belonging to such a minority, will be subject to penal or administrative sanctions for having had contacts within or outside his/her own country.

In access to the media, they will not discriminate against anyone based on ethnic, cultural, linguistic or religious grounds. They will make information available that will assist the electronic mass media in taking into account, in their programmes, the ethnic, cultural, linguistic and religious identity of national minorities.

They reaffirm that establishment and maintenance of unimpeded contacts among persons belonging to a national minority, as well as contacts across frontiers by persons belonging to a national minority with persons with whom they share a common ethnic or national origin, cultural heritage or religious belief, contributes to mutual understanding and promotes good-neighbourly relations.

They therefore encourage transfrontier co-operation arrangements on a national, regional and local level, *inter alia*, on local border crossings, the preservation of and visits to cultural and historical monuments and sites, tourism, the improvement of traffic, the economy, youth exchange, the protection of the environment and the establishment of regional commissions.

They will also encourage the creation of informal working arrangements (e.g. workshops, committees both within and between the participating States) where national minorities live, to discuss issues of, exchange experience on, and present proposals on, issues related to national minorities.

With a view to improving their information about the actual situation of national minorities, the participating States will, on a voluntary basis distribute, through the CSCE Secretariat, information to other participating States about the situation of national minorities in their respective territories, as well as statements of national policy in that respect.

The participating States will deposit with the CSCE Secretariat copies of the contributions made in the Plenary of the CSCE Meeting of Experts on National Minorities which they wish to be available to the public.

VIII.

The participating States welcome the positive contribution made by the representatives of the United Nations and the Council of Europe to the proceedings of the Geneva Meeting of Experts on National Minorities. They note that the work and activities of these organizations will be of continuing relevance to the CSCE's consideration of national minorities issues.

The participating States note that appropriate CSCE mechanisms may be of relevance in addressing questions relating to national minorities. Further, they recommend that the third Meeting of the Conference on the Human Dimension of the CSCE consider expanding the Human Dimension Mechanism. They will promote the involvement of individuals in the protection of their rights, including the rights of persons belonging to national minorities.

Finally, the representatives of the participating States request the Executive Secretary of the Meeting to transmit this Report to the third Meeting of the Conference on the Human Dimension of the CSCE.

The representatives of the participating States express their profound gratitude to the people and Government of Switzerland for the excellent organization of the Geneva Meeting and the warm hospitality extended to the delegations that participated in the Meeting.

INTERPRETATIVE STATEMENTS[1]

Interpretative statement by the Netherlands

I refer to the statement made by the head of the delegation of the United States of America and recorded in the Journal of 18 July on the use of the formulation 'The European Community and its Member States' in documents of this Meeting.

The European Community and its Member States hold that the term 'on behalf of the Netherlands-European Community', which appears in the second paragraph of the Report of our Meeting, should have read 'on behalf of the European Community and its Member States'.

In our view, wherever the term 'participating States' appear in our Report it implies that the European Community is involved. In this context I draw your attention to the text of the Single European Act adopted in 1987 by the Member States of the European Community, which confirms the will of the Member States to:

> 'work together to promote democracy on the basis of the fundamental rights recognized in the constitutions and laws of the Member States, in the Convention for the Protection of Human Rights and Fundamental Freedoms and in the European Social Charter, notably freedom, equality and social justice.'

* * *

Interpretative statement by Albania

The Albanian delegation joins in the consensus on this document on the understanding that it refers solely to national minorities and hence does not concern the question of the Albanian population in Kosovo and Yugoslavia.

In the view of the Albanian delegation, the question of that population, which is the third largest in the Yugoslav multinational State, is by no means a national-minority question but rather a national question.

* * *

---

[1] Journal No. 15 (Geneva, 19 July 1991).

Interpretative statement by Poland on behalf of the delegations of Austria, the Czech and Slovak Federal Republic, Hungary, Norway, Poland, Sweden and Yugoslavia

It is the understanding of the delegations of Austria, the Czech and Slovak Federal Republic, Hungary, Norway, Poland, Sweden and Yugoslavia that the paragraph of the Report of the CSCE Meeting of Experts on National Minorities reading:

> 'They note that all ethnic, cultural, linguistic or religious differences necessarily lead to the creation of national minorities.'

may not limit the right of the individual to choose to belong or not to belong to a national minority as laid down in paragraph 32 of the Document of the Copenhagen Meeting of the Conference on the Human Dimension of the CSCE.

* * *

Interpretative statement by Yugoslavia

I regret that the Report does not reflect a very important issue raised in the debate, namely, the separatist behaviour of a part of one national minority in my country and its claim to the right of self-determination. The only objective of the proposal of my delegation was to reaffirm the crystal-clear principle of the Helsinki Final Act stating that only peoples, and not national minorities, have the right to self-determination. In failing to do this, the Meeting did not meet its responsibility, and hence it contributed to the defining of a dangerous precedent, whose boomerang may tomorrow hit other participating States, threatening their territorial integrity, stability and peace. The manifestations and toleration of an aggressive separatism are in no way an activity that can help the further promotion of the rights of national minorities, nor can they, in particular, encourage reflections on guaranteeing national minorities various kinds of autonomies.

DOCUMENT OF THE MOSCOW MEETING OF THE CONFERENCE ON THE HUMAN DIMENSION OF THE CSCE

Moscow, 3 October 1991

The representatives of the participating States of the Conference on Security and Co-operation in Europe (CSCE), Albania, Austria, Belgium, Bulgaria, Canada, Cyprus, the Czech and Slovak Federal Republic, Denmark, Estonia, Finland, France, Germany, Greece, the Holy See, Hungary, Iceland, Ireland, Italy, Latvia, Liechtenstein, Lithuania, Luxembourg, Malta, Monaco, the Netherlands-European Community, Norway, Poland, Portugal, Romania, San Marino, Spain, Sweden, Switzerland, Turkey, the USSR, the United Kingdom, the United States of America and Yugoslavia, met in Moscow from 10 September to 4 October 1991, in accordance with the provisions relating to the Conference on the Human Dimension of the CSCE contained in the Concluding Document of the Vienna Follow-up Meeting of the CSCE.

They welcomed the admission as participating States of Estonia, Latvia and Lithuania decided at an additional Meeting at ministerial level of the representatives of the participating States in Moscow on 10 September 1991, convened by the Federal Minister for Foreign Affairs of the Federal Republic of Germany, Chairman-in-Office of the CSCE Council, prior to the opening of the Moscow Meeting.

The first Meeting of the Conference was held in Paris from 30 May to 23 June 1989. The second Meeting of the Conference was held in Copenhagen from 5 to 29 June 1990.

The Moscow Meeting was opened by the Minister for Foreign Affairs of the USSR. An opening address was delivered by the President of the USSR on behalf of the host country.

Opening statements were made by delegates of the participating States, among them Ministers, Deputy Ministers and the Vice-President of the Commission of the European Communities. A contribution to the Meeting was made by the Secretary General of the Council of Europe.

The participating States renew their commitment to implement fully all the principles and provisions of the Final Act of the Conference on Security and Co-operation in Europe, of the Charter of Paris for a New Europe and of the other CSCE documents relating to the human dimension, including, in particular, the Document of the Copenhagen Meeting of the Conference on the Human Dimension of the CSCE, and are determined to achieve still further progress in the implementation of these provisions, as full respect for human rights and fundamental freedoms and the development of societies based on pluralistic democracy and the rule of law are prerequisites for a lasting order of peace, security, justice and co-operation in Europe.

In this context, the participating States underlined that, in accordance with the Final Act of the Conference on Security and Co-operation in Europe and the Charter of Paris for a New Europe, the equal rights of peoples and their right to self-determination are to be respected in conformity with the Charter of the United Nations and the relevant norms of international law, including those relating to territorial integrity of States.

At the Moscow Meeting views were expressed by the participating States on the implementation of their commitments in the field of the human dimension. They considered that the degree of compliance with the commitments contained in the relevant provisions of the CSCE documents had shown further substantial improvement since the Copenhagen Meeting. They also considered that, in spite of the significant progress made, serious threats to and violations of CSCE principles and provisions continue to exist and have a sobering effect on the assessment of the over all situation in Europe. In particular, they deplored acts of discrimination, hostility and violence against persons or groups on national, ethnic or religious grounds. The participating States therefore expressed the view that, for the full realization of their commitments relating to the human dimension, continued efforts are still required which should benefit substantially from the profound political changes that have occurred.

The participating States emphasize that issues relating to human rights, fundamental freedoms, democracy and the rule of law are of international concern, as respect for these rights and freedoms constitutes one of the foundations of the international order. They categorically and irrevocably declare that the commitments undertaken in the field of the human dimension of the CSCE are matters of direct and legitimate concern to all participating States and do not belong exclusively to the internal affairs of the State concerned. They express their determination to fulfil all of their human dimension commitments and to resolve by peaceful means any related issue, individually and collectively, on the basis of mutual respect and co-operation. In this context they recognize that the active involvement of persons, groups, organizations and institutions is essential to ensure continuing progress in this direction.

The participating States express their collective determination to further safeguard human rights and fundamental freedoms and to consolidate democratic advances in their territories. They also recognize a compelling need to increase the CSCE's effectiveness in addressing human rights concerns that arise in their territories at this time of profound change in Europe.

In order to strengthen and expand the human dimension mechanism described in the section on the human dimension of the CSCE in the Concluding Document of the Vienna Meeting and to build upon and deepen the commitments set forth in the Document of the Copenhagen Meeting of the Conference on the Human Dimension of the CSCE, the participating States adopt the following:

I

1. The participating States emphasize that the human dimension mechanism described in paragraphs 1 to 4 of the section on the human dimension of the CSCE in the Vienna Concluding Document constitutes an essential achievement of the CSCE process, having demonstrated its value as a method of furthering respect for human rights, fundamental freedoms, democracy and the rule of law through dialogue and co-operation and assisting in the resolution of specific relevant questions. In order to improve further the implementation of the CSCE commitments in the human dimension, they decide to enhance the effectiveness of this mechanism and to strengthen and expand it as outlined in the following paragraphs.

2. The participating States amend paragraphs 42.1 and 42.2 of the Document of the Copenhagen Meeting to the effect that they will provide in the shortest possible time, but no later than ten days, a written response to requests for information and to representations made to them in writing by other participating States under paragraph 1 of the human dimension mechanism. Bilateral meetings, as referred to in paragraph 2 of the human dimension mechanism, will take place as soon as possible, and as a rule within one week of the date of the request.

3. A resource list comprising up to three experts appointed by each participating State will be established without delay at the CSCE

Institution.[1] The experts will be eminent persons, preferably experienced in the field of the human dimension, from whom an impartial performance of their functions may be expected.
The experts will be appointed for a period of three to six years at the discretion of the appointing State, no expert serving more than two consecutive terms. Within four weeks after notification by the CSCE Institution of the appointment, any participating State may make reservations regarding no more than two experts to be appointed by another participating State. In such case, the appointing State may, within four weeks of being notified of such reservations, reconsider its decision and appoint another expert or experts; if it confirms the appointment originally intended, the expert concerned cannot take part in any procedure with respect to the State having made the reservation without the latter's express consent.
The resource list will become operational as soon as 45 experts have been appointed.

4. A participating State may invite the assistance of a CSCE mission, consisting of up to three experts, to address or contribute to the resolution of questions in its territory relating to the human dimension of the CSCE. In such case, the State will select the person or persons concerned from the resource list. The mission of experts will not include the participating State's own nationals or residents or any of the persons it appointed to the resource list or more than one national or resident of any particular State.
The inviting State will inform without delay the CSCE Institution when a mission of experts is established, which in turn will notify all participating States. The CSCE institutions will also, whenever necessary, provide appropriate support to such a mission.

5. The purpose of a mission of experts is to facilitate resolution of a particular question or problem relating to the human dimension of the CSCE. Such mission may gather the information necessary for carrying out its tasks and, as appropriate, use its good offices and mediation services to promote dialogue and co-operation among interested parties. The State concerned will agree with the mission on the precise terms of reference and may thus assign any further functions to the mission of experts, *inter alia* fact-finding and advisory services, in order to suggest ways and means of facilitating the observance of CSCE commitments.

---

[1] The Council will take the decision on the institution.

6. The inviting State will co-operate fully with the mission of experts and facilitate its work. It will grant the mission all the facilities necessary for the independent exercise of its functions. It will, *inter alia*, allow the mission, for the purpose of carrying out its tasks, to enter its territory without delay, to hold discussions and to travel freely therein, to meet freely with officials, non-governmental organizations and any group or person from whom it wishes to receive information. The mission may also receive information in confidence from any individual, group or organization on questions it is addressing. The members of such missions will respect the confidential nature of their task.
The participating States will refrain from any action against persons, organizations or institutions on account of their contact with the mission of experts or of any publicly available information transmitted to it. The inviting State will comply with any request from a mission of experts to be accompanied by officials of that State if the mission considers this to be necessary to facilitate its work or guarantee its safety.

7. The mission of experts will submit its observations to the inviting State as soon as possible, preferably within three weeks after the mission has been established. The inviting State will transmit the observations of the mission, together with a description of any action it has taken or intends to take upon it, to the other participating States via the CSCE Institution no later than three weeks after the submission of the observations.
These observations and any comments by the inviting State may be discussed by the Committee of Senior Officials, which may consider any possible follow-up action. The observations and comments will remain confidential until brought to the attention of the Senior Officials. Before the circulation of the observations and any comments, no other mission of experts may be appointed for the same issue.

8. Furthermore, one or more participating States, having put into effect paragraphs 1 or 2 of the human dimension mechanism, may request that the CSCE Institution inquire of another participating State whether it would agree to invite a mission of experts to address a particular, clearly defined question on its territory relating to the human dimension of the CSCE. If the other participating State agrees to invite a mission of experts for the purpose indicated, the procedure set forth in paragraphs 4 to 7 will apply.

9. If a participating State (a) has directed an enquiry under paragraph 8 to another participating State and that State has not established a mission of experts within a period of ten days after the enquiry has been made, or (b) judges that the issue in question has not been resolved as a result of a mission of experts, it may, with the support of at least five other participating States, initiate the establishment of a mission of up to three CSCE rapporteurs. Such a decision will be addressed to the CSCE Institution, which will notify without delay the State concerned as well as all the other participating States.

10. The requesting State or States may appoint one person from the resource list to serve as a CSCE rapporteur. The requested State may, if it so chooses, appoint a further rapporteur from the resource list within six days after notification by the CSCE Institution of the appointment of the rapporteur. In such case the two designated rapporteurs, who will not be nationals or residents of, or persons appointed to the resource list by any of the States concerned, will by common agreement and without delay appoint a third rapporteur from the resource list. In case they fail to reach agreement within eight days, a third rapporteur who will not be a national or resident of, or a person appointed to the resource list by any of the States concerned, will be appointed from the resource list by the ranking official of the CSCE body designated by the Council. The provisions of the second part of paragraph 4 and the whole of paragraph 6 also apply to a mission of rapporteurs.

11. The CSCE rapporteur(s) will establish the facts, report on them and may give advice on possible solutions to the question raised. The report of the rapporteur(s), containing observations of facts, proposals or advice, will be submitted to the participating State or States concerned and, unless all the States concerned agree otherwise, to the CSCE Institution no later than three weeks after the last rapporteur has been appointed. The requested State will submit any observations on the report to the CSCE Institution, unless all the States concerned agree otherwise, no later than three weeks after the submission of the report.
The CSCE Institution will transmit the report, as well as any observations by the requested State or any other participating State, to all participating States without delay. The report may be placed on the agenda of the next regular meeting of the Committee of Senior Officials, which may decide on any possible follow-up action. The report will remain confidential until after that meeting of the

Committee. Before the circulation of the report no other rapporteur may be appointed for the same issue.

12. If a participating State considers that a particularly serious threat to the fulfilment of the provisions of the CSCE human dimension has arisen in another participating State, it may, with the support of at least nine other participating States, engage the procedure set forth in paragraph 10. The provisions of paragraph 11 will apply.

13. Upon the request of any participating State the Committee of Senior Officials may decide to establish a mission of experts or of CSCE rapporteurs. In such case the Committee will also determine whether to apply the appropriate provisions of the preceding paragraphs.

14. The participating State or States that have requested the establishment of a mission of experts or rapporteurs will cover the expenses of that mission. In case of the appointment of experts or rapporteurs pursuant to a decision of the Committee of Senior Officials, the expenses will be covered by the participating States in accordance with the usual scale of distribution of expenses. These procedures will be reviewed by the Helsinki Follow-up Meeting of the CSCE.

15. Nothing in the foregoing will in any way affect the right of participating States to raise within the CSCE process any issue relating to the implementation of any CSCE commitment, including any commitment relating to the human dimension of the CSCE.

16. In considering whether to invoke the procedures in paragraphs 9 and 10 or 12 regarding the case of an individual, participating States should pay due regard to whether that individual's case is already *sub judice* in an international judicial procedure.

Any reference to the Committee of Senior Officials in this document is subject to the decision of that Committee and the Council.

II

17. The participating States

17.1 - condemn unreservedly forces which seek to take power from a representative government of a participating State against the will of the people as expressed in free and fair elections and contrary to the justly established constitutional order;

17.2 - will support vigorously, in accordance with the Charter of the United Nations, in case of overthrow or attempted overthrow of a legitimately elected government of a participating State by undemocratic means, the legitimate organs of that State upholding human rights, democracy and the rule of law, recognizing their common commitment to countering any attempt to curb these basic values;

17.3 - recognize the need to make further peaceful efforts concerning human rights, democracy and the rule of law within the context of security and co-operation in Europe, individually and collectively, to make democratic advances irreversible and prevent any falling below the standards laid down in the principles and provisions of the Final Act, the Vienna Concluding Document, the Document of the Copenhagen Meeting, the Charter of Paris for a New Europe and the present document.

18. The participating States recall their commitment to the rule of law in the Document of the Copenhagen Meeting and affirm their dedication to supporting and advancing those principles of justice which form the basis of the rule of law. In particular, they again reaffirm that democracy is an inherent element in the rule of law and that pluralism is important in regard to political organizations.

18.1 Legislation will be formulated and adopted as the result of an open process reflecting the will of the people, either directly or through their elected representatives.

18.2 Everyone will have an effective means of redress against administrative decisions, so as to guarantee respect for fundamental rights and ensure legal integrity.

18.3 To the same end, there will be effective means of redress against administrative regulations for individuals affected thereby.

18.4 The participating States will endeavour to provide for judicial review of such regulations and decisions.

19. The participating States

19.1 - will respect the internationally recognized standards that relate to the independence of judges and legal practitioners and the impartial operation of the public judicial service including, *inter alia*, the Universal Declaration of Human Rights and the International Covenant on Civil and Political Rights;

19.2 - will, in implementing the relevant standards and commitments, ensure that the independence of the judiciary is guaranteed and enshrined in the constitution or the law of the country and is respected in practice, paying particular attention to the Basic Principles on the Independence of the Judiciary, which, *inter alia*, provide for

i. prohibiting improper influence on judges;

ii. preventing revision of judicial decisions by administrative authorities, except for the rights of the competent authorities to mitigate or commute sentences imposed by judges, in conformity with the law;

iii. protecting the judiciary's freedom of expression and association, subject only to such restrictions as are consistent with its functions;

iv. ensuring that judges are properly qualified, trained and selected on a non-discriminatory basis;

v. guaranteeing tenure and appropriate conditions of service, including on the matter of promotion of judges, where applicable;

vi. respecting conditions of immunity;

vii. ensuring that the disciplining, suspension and removal of judges are determined according to law.

20. For the promotion of the independence of the judiciary, the participating States will

20.1 - recognize the important function national and international associations of judges and lawyers can perform in strengthening respect for the independence of their members and in providing education and training on the role of the judiciary and the legal profession in society;

20.2 - promote and facilitate dialogue, exchanges and co-operation among national associations and other groups interested in ensuring respect for the independence of the judiciary and the protection of lawyers;

20.3 - co-operate among themselves through, *inter alia*, dialogue, contacts and exchanges in order to identify where problem areas exist concerning the protection of the independence of judges and legal practitioners and to develop ways and means to address and resolve such problems;

20.4 - co-operate on an ongoing basis in such areas as the education and training of judges and legal practitioners, as well as the preparation and enactment of legislation intended to strengthen respect for their independence and the impartial operation of the public judicial service.

21. The participating States will

21.1 - take all necessary measures to ensure that law enforcement personnel, when enforcing public order, will act in the public interest, respond to a specific need and pursue a legitimate aim, as well as use ways and means commensurate with the circumstances, which will not exceed the needs of enforcement;

21.2 - ensure that law enforcement acts are subject to judicial control, that law enforcement personnel are held accountable for such acts, and that due compensation may be sought, according to domestic law, by the victims of acts found to be in violation of the above commitments.

22. The participating States will take appropriate measures to ensure that education and information regarding the prohibition of excess force by law enforcement personnel as well as relevant international and domestic codes of conduct are included in the training of such personnel.

23. The participating States will treat all persons deprived of their liberty with humanity and with respect for the inherent dignity of the human person and will respect the internationally recognized standards that relate to the administration of justice and the human rights of detainees.

23.1 The participating States will ensure that

i. no one will be deprived of his liberty except on such grounds and in accordance with such procedures as are established by law;

ii. anyone who is arrested will be informed promptly in a language which he understands of the reason for his arrest, and will be informed of any charges against him;

iii. any person who has been deprived of his liberty will be promptly informed about his rights according to domestic law;

iv. any person arrested or detained will have the right to be brought promptly before a judge or other officer authorized by law to determine the lawfulness of his arrest or detention, and will be released without delay if it is unlawful;

v. anyone charged with a criminal offence will have the right to defend himself in person or through legal assistance of his own choosing or, if he has not sufficient means to pay for legal assistance, to be given it free when the interests of justice so require;

vi. any person arrested or detained will have the right, without undue delay, to notify or to require the competent authority to notify appropriate persons of his choice of his arrest, detention, imprisonment and whereabouts; any restriction in the exercise of this right will be prescribed by law and in accordance with international standards;

vii. effective measures will be adopted, if this has not already been done, to provide that law enforcement bodies do not take undue advantage of the situation of a detained or imprisoned person for the purpose of compelling him to confess, or otherwise to incriminate himself, or to force him to testify against any other person;

viii. the duration of any interrogation and the intervals between them will be recorded and certified, consistent with domestic law;

ix. a detained person or his counsel will have the right to make a request or complaint regarding his treatment, in particular when torture or other cruel, inhuman or degrading treatment has been applied, to the authorities responsible for the administration of the place of detention and to higher authorities, and when necessary, to appropriate authorities vested with reviewing or remedial power;

x. such request or complaint will be promptly dealt with and replied to without undue delay; if the request or complaint is rejected or in case of inordinate delay, the complainant will be entitled to bring it before a judicial or other authority; neither the detained or imprisoned person nor any complainant will suffer prejudice for making a request or complaint.

xi. anyone who has been the victim of an unlawful arrest or detention will have a legally enforceable right to seek compensation.

23.2 The participating States will

i. endeavour to take measures, as necessary, to improve the conditions of individuals in detention or imprisonment;

ii. pay particular attention to the question of alternatives to imprisonment.

24. The participating States reconfirm the right to the protection of private and family life, domicile, correspondence and electronic communications. In order to avoid any improper or arbitrary intrusion by the State in the realm of the individual, which would be harmful to any democratic society, the exercise of this right will be subject only to such restrictions as are prescribed by law and are consistent with internationally recognized human rights standards. In particular, the participating States will ensure that searches and seizures of persons and private premises and property will take place only in accordance with standards that are judicially enforceable.

25. The participating States will

25.1 - ensure that their military and paramilitary forces, internal security and intelligence services, and the police are subject to the effective direction and control of the appropriate civil authorities;

25.2 - maintain and, where necessary, strengthen executive control over the use of military and paramilitary forces as well as the activities of the internal security and intelligence services and the police;

25.3 - take appropriate steps to create, wherever they do not already exist, and maintain effective arrangements for legislative supervision of all such forces, services and activities.

26. The participating States reaffirm the right to freedom of expression, including the right to communication and the right of the media to collect, report and disseminate information, news and opinions. Any restriction in the exercise of this right will be prescribed by law and in accordance with international standards. They further recognize that independent media are essential to a free and open society and accountable systems of government and are of particular importance in safeguarding human rights and fundamental freedoms.

26.1 They consider that the print and broadcast media in their territory should enjoy unrestricted access to foreign news and information services. The public will enjoy similar freedom to receive and impart information and ideas without interference by public authority regardless of frontiers, including through foreign publications and foreign broadcasts. Any restriction in the exercise of this right will be prescribed by law and in accordance with international standards.

26.2 The participating States will not discriminate against independent media with respect to affording access to information, material and facilities.

27. The participating States

27.1 - express their intention to co-operate in the field of constitutional, administrative, commercial, civil and social welfare laws and other relevant areas, in order to develop, particularly in States where they do not yet exist, legal systems based on respect for human rights, the rule of law and democracy;

27.2 - to this end, envisage the continuation and enhancement of bilateral and multilateral legal and administrative co-operation, *inter alia*, in the following fields:
- development of an efficient administrative system;
- assistance in formulating law and regulations;
- training of administrative and legal staff;
- exchange of legal works and periodicals.

28. The participating States consider it important to protect human rights and fundamental freedoms during a state of public emergency, to take into account the relevant provisions of the Document of the Copenhagen Meeting, and to observe the international conventions to which they are parties.

28.1 The participating States reaffirm that a state of public emergency is justified only by the most exceptional and grave circumstances, consistent with the State's international obligations and CSCE commitments. A state of public emergency may not be used to subvert the democratic constitutional order, nor aim at the destruction of internationally recognized human rights and fundamental freedoms. If recourse to force cannot be avoided, its use must be reasonable and limited as far as possible.

28.2 A state of public emergency may be proclaimed only by a constitutionally lawful body, duly empowered to do so. In cases where the decision to impose a state of public emergency may be lawfully taken by the executive authorities, that decision should be subject to approval in the shortest possible time or to control by the legislature.

28.3 The decision to impose a state of public emergency will be proclaimed officially, publicly, and in accordance with provisions laid down by law. The decision will, where possible, lay down territorial limits of a state of public emergency. The State concerned will make available to its citizens information, without delay, about which measures have been taken. The state of public emergency will be lifted as soon as possible and will not remain in force longer than strictly required by the exigencies of the situation.

28.4 A *de facto* imposition or continuation of a state of public emergency not in accordance with provisions laid down by law is not permissible.

28.5 The participating States will endeavour to ensure that the normal functioning of the legislative bodies will be guaranteed to the highest possible extent during a state of public emergency.

28.6 The participating States confirm that any derogation from obligations relating to human rights and fundamental freedoms during a state of public emergency must remain strictly within the limits provided for by international law, in particular the relevant international instruments by which they are bound, especially with respect to rights from which there can be no derogation.

28.7 The participating States will endeavour to refrain from making derogations from those obligations from which, according to international conventions to which they are parties, derogation is possible under a state of public emergency. Measures derogating from such obligations must be taken in strict conformity with the procedural requirements laid down in those instruments. Such measures will neither go further nor remain in force longer than strictly required by the exigencies of the situation; they are by nature exceptional and should be interpreted and applied with restraint. Such measures will not discriminate solely on the grounds of race, colour, sex, language, religion, social origin or of belonging to a minority.

28.8 The participating States will endeavour to ensure that the legal guarantees necessary to uphold the rule of law will remain in force during a state of public emergency. They will endeavour to provide in their law for control over the regulations related to the state of public emergency, as well as the implementation of such regulations.

28.9 The participating States will endeavour to maintain freedom of expression and freedom of information, consistent with their international obligations and commitments, with a view to enabling public discussion on the observance of human rights and fundamental freedoms as well as on the lifting of the state of public emergency. They will, in conformity with international standards regarding the freedom of expression, take no measures aimed at barring journalists from the legitimate exercise of their profession other than those strictly required by the exigencies of the situation.

28.10 When a state of public emergency is declared or lifted in a participating State, the State concerned will immediately inform the CSCE Institution[2] of this decision, as well as of any derogation made from the State's international human rights obligations. The Institution will inform the other participating States without delay.

29. The participating States, recognizing their common interest in promoting contacts and the exchange of information amongst Ombudsmen and other institutions entrusted with similar functions of investigating individual complaints of citizens against public authorities, note with appreciation an offer by Spain to host a meeting of Ombudsmen.

30. The participating States suggest that the appropriate CSCE fora consider expanding the functions of the Office for Free Elections to enable it to assist in strengthening democratic institutions within the participating States.

31. The participating States acknowledge the extensive experience and expertise of the Council of Europe in the field of human rights. They welcome its contribution to strengthening democracy in Europe, including its readiness to make its experience available to the CSCE.

III

32. The participating States reaffirm their enduring commitment to the principles and provisions of the Final Act, the Vienna Concluding Document, and other relevant CSCE documents in which they undertook, *inter alia*, to respect human rights and fundamental

---

[2] The Council will take the decision on the institution.

freedoms and to ensure that they are guaranteed for all without distinction of any kind.

33. The participating States will remove all legal and other restrictions with respect to travel within their territories for their own nationals and foreigners, and with respect to residence for those entitled to permanent residence, except those restrictions which may be necessary and officially declared for military, safety, ecological or other legitimate government interests, in accordance with their national laws, consistent with CSCE commitments and international human rights obligations. The participating States undertake to keep such restrictions to a minimum.

34. The participating States will adopt, where appropriate, all feasible measures to protect journalists engaged in dangerous professional missions, particularly in cases of armed conflict, and will co-operate to that effect. These measures will include tracing missing journalists, ascertaining their fate, providing appropriate assistance and facilitating their return to their families.

35. The participating States reaffirm that guaranteeing the freedom of artistic creation and preserving the cultural heritage form part of the human dimension of the CSCE. They consider that independent intellectual and cultural life is crucial for the maintenance of free societies and democratic institutions. They will implement their commitments in the cultural field, as laid down in the Document of the Cracow Symposium on the Cultural Heritage, and express the view that cultural issues, including cultural freedom, creativity and co-operation, should be further considered in the CSCE.

36. The participating States recall their commitment in the Vienna Concluding Document to keep the question of capital punishment under consideration and reaffirm their undertakings in the Document of the Copenhagen Meeting to exchange information on the question of the abolition of the death penalty and to make available to the public information regarding the use of the death penalty.

36.1 They note

i. that the Second Optional Protocol to the International Covenant on Civil and Political Rights aiming at the abolition of the death penalty entered into force on 11 July 1991;

ii. that a number of participating States have recently taken steps towards the abolition of capital punishment;

iii. the activities of several non-governmental organizations concerning the question of the death penalty.

37. The participating States confirm the provisions and commitments of all CSCE documents, in particular the Document of the Copenhagen Meeting of the Conference on the Human Dimension of the CSCE, concerning questions relating to national minorities and the rights of persons belonging to them, and the Report of the Geneva CSCE Meeting of Experts on National Minorities, and call for their full and early implementation. They believe that, in particular, the use of the new and expanded CSCE mechanisms and procedures will contribute to further protection and promotion of the rights of persons belonging to national minorities.

38. The participating States recognize the need to ensure that the rights of migrant workers and their families lawfully residing in the participating States are respected and underline their right to express freely their ethnic, cultural, religious and linguistic characteristics. The exercise of such rights may be subject to such restrictions as are prescribed by law and are consistent with international standards.

38.1 They condemn all acts of discrimination on the ground of race, colour and ethnic origin, intolerance and xenophobia against migrant workers. They will, in conformity with domestic law and international obligations, take effective measures to promote tolerance, understanding, equality of opportunity and respect for the fundamental human rights of migrant workers and adopt, if they have not already done so, measures that would prohibit acts that constitute incitement to violence based on national, racial, ethnic or religious discrimination, hostility or hatred.

38.2 They will adopt appropriate measures that would enable migrant workers to participate in the life of the society of the participating States.

38.3 They note that issues which concern the human dimension of migrant workers residing on their territory could, as any other issue of the human dimension, be raised under the human dimension mechanism.

38.4 They recommend that the CSCE in its future work on the human dimension consider appropriate means to hold focused discussions on all issues regarding migrant workers, including *inter alia*, familiarization with the language and social life of the country concerned.

39. The participating States will

39.1 - increase their preparedness and co-operate fully to enable humanitarian relief operations to be undertaken speedily and effectively;

39.2 - take all necessary steps to facilitate speedy and unhindered access to the affected areas for such relief operations;

39.3 - make the necessary arrangements for those relief operations to be carried out.

40. The participating States recognize that full and true equality between men and women is a fundamental aspect of a just and democratic society based on the rule of law. They recognize that the full development of society and the welfare of all its members require equal opportunity for full and equal participation of men and women. In this context they will

40.1 - ensure that all CSCE commitments relating to the protection and promotion of human rights and fundamental freedoms are applied fully and without discrimination with regard to sex;

40.2 - comply with the Convention on the Elimination of All Forms of Discrimination against Women (CEDAW), if they are parties, and, if they have not already done so, consider ratifying or acceding to this Convention; States that have ratified or acceded to this Convention with reservations will consider withdrawing them;

40.3 - effectively implement the obligations in international instruments to which they are parties and take appropriate measures to implement the United Nations Nairobi Forward-looking Strategies for the Advancement of Women (FLS);

40.4 - affirm that it is their goal to achieve not only *de jure* but *de facto* equality of opportunity between men and women and to promote effective measures to that end;

40.5 - establish or strengthen national machinery, as appropriate, for the advancement of women in order to ensure that programmes and policies are assessed for their impact on women;

40.6 - encourage measures effectively to ensure full economic opportunity for women, including non-discriminatory employment policies and practices, equal access to education and training, and measures to facilitate combining employment with family responsibilities for female and male workers; and will seek to ensure that any structural adjustment policies or programmes do not have an adversely discriminatory effect on women;

40.7 - seek to eliminate all forms of violence against women, and all forms of traffic in women and exploitation of prostitution of women including by ensuring adequate legal prohibitions against such acts and other appropriate measures;

40.8 - encourage and promote equal opportunity for full participation by women in all aspects of political and public life, in decision-making processes and in international co-operation in general;

40.9 - recognize the vital role women and women's organizations play in national and international efforts to promote and enhance women's rights by providing, *inter alia*, direct services and support to women and encouraging a meaningful partnership between governments and these organizations for the purpose of advancing equality for women;

40.10 - recognize the rich contribution of women to all aspects of political, cultural, social and economic life and promote a broad understanding of these contributions, including those made in the informal and unpaid sectors;

40.11 - take measures to encourage that information regarding women and women's rights under international and domestic law is easily accessible;

40.12 - develop educational policies, consistent with their constitutional systems, to support the participation of women in all areas of study and work, including non-traditional areas, and encourage and promote a greater understanding of issues relating to equality between men and women;

40.13 - ensure the collection and analysis of data to assess adequately, monitor and improve the situation of women; these data should not contain any personal information.

41. The participating States decide

41.1 - to ensure protection of the human rights of persons with disabilities;

41.2 - to take steps to ensure the equal opportunity of such persons to participate fully in the life of their society;

41.3 - to promote the appropriate participation of such persons in decision-making in fields concerning them;

41.4 - to encourage services and training of social workers for the vocational and social rehabilitation of persons with disabilities;

41.5 - to encourage favourable conditions for the access of persons with disabilities to public buildings and services, housing, transport, and cultural and recreational activities.

42. The participating States

42.1 - affirm that human rights education is fundamental and that it is therefore essential that their citizens are educated on human rights and fundamental freedoms and the commitment to respect such rights and freedoms in domestic legislation and international instruments to which they may be parties;

42.2 - recognize that effective human rights education contributes to combating intolerance, religious, racial and ethnic prejudice and hatred, including against Roma, xenophobia and anti-semitism;

42.3 - will encourage their competent authorities responsible for education programmes to design effective human rights related curricula and courses for students at all levels, particularly students of law, administration and social sciences as well as those attending military, police and public service schools;

42.4 - will make information on all CSCE human dimension provisions available to their educators;

42.5 - will encourage organizations and educational establishments to co-operate in drawing up and exchanging human rights programmes at the national as well as the international level;

42.6 - will seek to ensure that activities undertaken with a view to promoting human rights education in the broader sense take into account experience, programmes and forms of co-operation within existing international governmental and non-governmental bodies, such as the United Nations and the Council of Europe.

43. The participating States will recognize as NGOs those which declare themselves as such, according to existing national procedures, and will facilitate the ability of such organizations to conduct their activities freely on their territories; to that effect they will

43.1 - endeavour to seek ways of further strengthening modalities for contacts and exchanges of views between NGOs and relevant national authorities and governmental institutions;

43.2 - endeavour to facilitate visits to their countries by NGOs from within any of the participating States in order to observe human dimension conditions;

43.3 - welcome NGO activities, including, *inter alia*, observing compliance with CSCE commitments in the field of the human dimension;

43.4 - allow NGOs, in view of their important function within the human dimension of the CSCE, to convey their views to their own governments and the governments of all the other participating States during the future work of the CSCE on the human dimension.

43.5 During the future work of the CSCE on the human dimension, NGOs will have the opportunity to distribute written contributions on specific issues of the human dimension of the CSCE to all delegations.

43.6 The CSCE Secretariat will, within the framework of the resources at its disposal, respond favourably to requests by NGOs for non-restricted documents of the CSCE.

43.7 Guidelines for the participation of NGOs in the future work of the CSCE on the human dimension might, *inter alia*, include the following:

i. NGOs should be allotted common space at such meeting sites or in their immediate vicinity for their use as well as reasonable access, at their own expense, to technical facilities, including photocopying machines, telephones and fax machines,

ii. NGOs should be informed and briefed on openness and access procedures in a timely manner,

iii. delegations to CSCE meetings should be further encouraged to include or invite NGO members.

The participating States recommend that the Helsinki Follow-up Meeting consider establishing such guidelines.

* * *

44. The representatives of the participating States express their profound gratitude to the people and Government of the USSR for the excellent organization of the Moscow Meeting and the warm hospitality extended to the delegations which participated in the Meeting.

INTERPRETATIVE STATEMENTS[1]

The delegation of Germany made the following interpretative statement:

The German Government will interpret the term 'migrant workers' as used in the Moscow Document in the sense given it in paragraph 38, namely 'migrant workers and their families lawfully residing in the participating States'.

* * *

The delegation of Belgium made the following interpretative statement on behalf of the delegations of Belgium, France, Spain and the United Kingdom:

Belgium, France, Spain and the United Kingdom interpret paragraph 16 of the present Document as implying that the procedures in paragraphs 9 and 10 or 12 will not be invoked in cases relating to an individual which have already been submitted to an international judicial procedure.

* * *

The delegation of Belgium made the following interpretative statement:

Belgium interprets its commitments under paragraph 37 of this Document as coming exclusively within the field of human rights. As regards persons coming within its jurisdiction and whatever designation they claim for their community, Belgium intends to comply with the international commitments to which it subscribed regarding the rights of the human person, including the collective exercise of these rights.

* * *

The delegation of Spain made the following interpretative statement, on behalf of the delegations of Italy, Poland and Spain:

I would like to express my satisfaction with the fact that the above-mentioned paragraph 29 notes with appreciation the offer by the Government of the Kingdom of Spain to host a meeting of Ombudsmen. During the preparation of this meeting, the Spanish authorities will take into account and welcome any co-operation which might be provided by the CSCE Office for Free Elections in Warsaw.

* * *

---

[1] Journal No. 18 (Moscow, 3 October 1991).

The delegation of France made the following interpretative statement:

France considers that institutional problems as a whole are a matter for the main Helsinki II Follow-up Meeting and that the text of the Document that has just been adopted, in particular paragraph (30), does not prejudge its future position in that regard.

* * *

The delegation of the United Kingdom made the following interpretative statement:

The United Kingdom welcomes the Document of the Moscow Meeting of the Conference on the Human Dimension of the CSCE adopted by consensus, and in particular its provisions for the expansion of the human dimension mechanism to include new procedures involving the services of experts experienced in human rights issues as foreseen in the Charter of Paris for a New Europe.

In this context, and if the services of experts are required in the territory of the United Kingdom, the United Kingdom wishes to state that it would act in accordance with the following interpretation of paragraph 6 of the Procedures. In order to protect public safety or national security the United Kingdom might be obliged to decline or to regulate access at a particular time or to a particular place proposed by the mission. The United Kingdom states that such action would be taken only when absolutely necessary and would have effect only for so long as is required.

The United Kingdom further states that, in such circumstances, it will immediately enter into consultations with the mission in order to clarify the situation and seek agreement on arrangements to enable the mission to obtain so much information as is practicable, and that, if such agreement cannot be reached, it will bring the matter at the earliest opportunity to the attention of the Committee of Senior Officials.

* * *

The delegation of Hungary made the following interpretative statement:

The Charter of Paris for a New Europe clearly emphasizes the need for increased co-operation and better protection of national minorities and warns us that although the threat of conflict in Europe has diminished, other dangers threaten the stability of our societies. At the opening of the Moscow Meeting of the Conference on the Human Dimension, High Representatives of the participating States expressed the view that the problems relating to national minorities acquire a burning character and require urgent actions in Europe so that security and stability could be maintained and strengthened in the continent. That approach and the pressing need for measures to be taken did not find its place in the Document of the Moscow Meeting.

In view of the aforementioned reasons Hungary would reiterate its position that

- the right of peoples to self-determination should be exercised in accordance with the principles of the Helsinki Final Act as well as with the precept enshrined in the Charter of Paris for a New Europe, taking into account the protection of minority rights;

- problems relating to national minorities should be settled in an appropriate democratic manner, by peaceful means and through dialogue among all parties concerned, through negotiation and consultation;

- concrete measures are to be taken to protect and promote the identity of national minorities. Such measures could be drawn from the relevant CSCE documents, containing a summing-up of the positive experience gained in minority protection;

- appropriate forms of self-government as well as their actual exercise would constitute an effective instrument to ensure national minorities the protection and promotion of their identity;

- the use and teaching of the languages of minorities and the establishment and maintenance of adequate cultural and educational institutions, as well as the reflection of minorities' views and languages in the media are further instruments to preserve the identity of national minorities.

REPORT TO THE CSCE COUNCIL FROM THE CSCE SEMINAR OF EXPERTS ON DEMOCRATIC INSTITUTIONS

Oslo, 15 November 1991

Representatives and experts of the participating States, Albania, Austria, Belgium, Bulgaria, Canada, Cyprus, Czech and Slovak Federal Republic, Denmark, Estonia, Finland, France, Germany, Greece, Holy See, Hungary, Iceland, Ireland, Italy, Latvia, Liechtenstein, Lithuania, Luxembourg, Malta, Monaco, Netherlands-European Community, Norway, Poland, Portugal, Romania, San Marino, Spain, Sweden, Switzerland, Turkey, Union of Soviet Socialist Republics, United Kingdom, United States of America and Yugoslavia, met in Oslo from 4 to 15 November 1991, in accordance with the provisions relating to the CSCE Seminar of Experts on Democratic Institutions contained in the Charter of Paris for a New Europe.

An opening address to the Seminar was delivered by H.E. Gro Harlem Brundtland, Prime Minister of Norway, on behalf of the host country.

Opening statements were made by representatives of the participating States. Contributions to the Seminar were made by the Secretary General of the Council of Europe and the President of the European Commission for Democracy through Law. The Foreign Minister of the host country, Mr. Thorvald Stoltenberg, delivered a closing address to the Seminar.

The participating States recalled their commitment to implement fully the provisions relating to human rights, democracy and the rule of law in the Final Act of the Conference on Security and Co-operation in Europe, the Charter of Paris for a New Europe and other CSCE documents, including, in particular, the Documents of the Copenhagen and Moscow Meetings of the Conference on the Human Dimension.

Proceeding from the commitments contained in these documents, experts had a thorough discussion of ways and means of consolidating and strengthening viable democratic institutions in participating States, including comparative studies of legislation on human rights and fundamental freedoms.

The representatives of the participating States expressed their profound gratitude to the people and Government of Norway for the excellent organization of the Seminar and the warm hospitality extended to the delegations which participated in the Seminar.

* * * * *

Representatives recalled that the mandate of the Oslo Seminar, as set out in Annex II of the Charter of Paris, required the Seminar to provide a summing up of its discussions for transmittal to the Council. They took account of the participation in the Seminar of experts not representing governments, and of the fact that the contributions of these experts were of particular value to all participants. In order to provide an adequate record of discussions, and to ensure that all views were adequately reflected, this Report, which does not purport to express any new commitments on the part of participating States, sets out the following Summary of Discussions as a record of its work:

I

In the discussions of experts, suggestions for practical measures to strengthen democratic institutions and the rule of law were set out. Experts also formulated their assessments of the political, economic, social and legal factors which influence the operation and effectiveness of democratic government and its institutions.

In this context, it was recalled that the participating States have already accepted high standards of human rights, fundamental freedoms, pluralistic democracy based on periodic and free elections by universal and equal suffrage, and the rule of law. It was broadly recognized that democratic government depended on the ability of democratic institutions to function effectively. In order to do so, the structure and authority of institutions needed to be backed by informed and active public support and broadly based acceptance in the society which they serve. A democratic culture was a necessary element for the functioning of all democratic governments, and required permanent encouragement. Where a democratic tradition of long duration has not had the chance to develop, or had been interrupted, it would be necessary to develop a democratic culture, on the local, regional and national level, in order to sustain new democratic institutions. It was noted that the reciprocal relationship between international human rights norms and national practices was important in this regard. The growth of a democratic culture can be fostered by society at many levels: in basic civic education, in the media, within religious and civic movements and organizations, in political parties, in the professions, notably the legal profession, in the judiciary, in public administration, within the armed forces and the police by securing the absolute allegiance to the civil power and democratic government.

It was also broadly recognized that the independence and authority of the judiciary was a crucial element in safeguarding the rule of law and securing effective implementation of human rights and fundamental freedoms. An independent judiciary serves to uphold the integrity of other democratic institutions, reinforce their effectiveness, and prevent abuse of power.

It was also broadly recognized that, along with the development of democratic institutions and political procedures, the reform of private law was essential in States where radical democratic reforms are being introduced. A legal foundation had to be provided for a functioning economy, securing the rights of the individual to engage in constructive economic activity, including the right to own property and to dispose of it under the law, alone or in association with others.

It was likewise broadly recognized that the ability of a society to satisfy the basic material needs of its population was important for the development of the democratic political process, and of a democratic culture based on shared values and goals.

II

In discussing the question of constitutional reforms, experts drew on national experiences. They noted that States choose different means for the implementation of democratic government, in response to their particular characteristics and traditions and to the circumstances of their constitutional history. As long as the core values of democratic government were assured, no single overall approach to the institutions and procedures of democratic government could be considered as having universal validity.

The issue of constitutional reforms was discussed from a variety of points of view, covering the technical aspects of the reform process as well as questions of substance. On matters of substance, exchanges concentrated on the separation of powers, and on constitutional or statutory guarantees for human rights and fundamental freedoms.

Particular emphasis was given in the discussions of the meeting to the ongoing efforts of the new democracies to create a political and legal infrastructure assuring the realization of pluralist democracy, human rights and the rule of law. In that context, a number of requirements, often conflicting, were identified.

It was a central theme that the new democracies are faced contemporaneously with an urgent need to mark the break with the former non-democratic system in an appropriate legal form, to assure stability in institutions, and effective implementation of policies as well as sound and fair administrative practices.

It was recognized that sweeping constitutional reforms touch the very foundations of a nation, and therefore warrant thorough analysis and discussion. On the other hand, fundamental political changes called for a swift follow-up in terms of constitutional reform. A decision on a definitive new constitution, adopted before a society has fully clarified and developed its vision of democratic government, might have to be reconsidered before long. Experts considered that in such a situation, a balance might be found, by providing for constitutional amendment procedures that allow for modifications, while entrenching certain basic provisions such as those relating to human rights, fundamental freedoms and the rule of law.

Experts discussed the composition and nature of the body empowered to draft a new constitution and the modalities for its adoption. A general view emerged to the effect that the drafting body must reflect the views of the political forces in order to bring about a national consensus. A new constitution should be adopted in a manner to ensure legitimacy.

The utility or admissibility of granting exceptional powers to the executive branch during a period of transition, in order to carry out unpopular but necessary economic reforms, was also considered. While some experts felt that such exceptional powers might be justified in order to create the long-term conditions for a stable, viable democracy, others were of the opinion that such measures would weaken the development of a democratic culture. In any event, conditions for granting exceptional powers should be defined, and their exercise subject to control as appropriate.

Direct participation of the people in important political decisions through plebiscites or referenda was highlighted as a means of enhancing the interest and involvement of the electorate in public affairs. As with any democratic process, popular consultation should be carried out with appropriate safeguards.

The extent to which institutions of the old totalitarian regime could be adapted to serve in a new democratic framework gave rise to diverging views. While the need for some continuity was recognized it was underlined that the identification of institutions with totalitarian rule might undermine their legitimacy even after a restructuring of such bodies had taken place.

In the discussion of the division of power between the legislative, executive and judicial authorities, it was noted that, although the classical doctrine of the separation of powers in its pure form was implemented mainly in presidential systems, its essence was also reflected in the practices of many other political systems.

It was also emphasized that separation of functions between the trial judge and the prosecuting authority was essential and required adequate guarantees. The strengthening of the role of the judiciary, and the creation of a well-trained and independent body of judges, was particularly important in those participating States emerging from a totalitarian past. Appointment procedures, remuneration and security of office were characterized as important factors.

In the context of constitutional reform, reference was made to the utility of vertical decentralization and division of the functions of government on a federal, regional and local basis for a wide range of purposes. Numerous forms were available to take account of historical, regional, linguistic or ethnic distinctions. Administrative decentralization, development of governmental functions on a regional basis, and reinforcement and reform of local government institutions might in varying ways respond to the needs of groups, including national minorities.

Attention was drawn to the difficulties that arise when coalition governments change frequently, due to a fragmented parliament. One way of avoiding instability was to admit no-confidence votes only when the parties behind such a vote are in a position to offer an alternative government.

Experts discussed the relationship between the organization of elections and of political parties, and the functioning of democratic institutions. They saw a dilemma between an ideal of representation of parties in Parliament directly on the basis of voting figures, and the need for stable and effective government.

Proportional election systems were well suited to ensure mathematically correct representation of the electorate. At the same time such systems entailed the possibility of a proliferation of political parties and ensuing difficulties in establishing parliamentary majorities. This in turn might lead to weak and unstable governments. The introduction of thresholds and the adjustment of mathematical methods applied in determining representation could help alleviate this problem. Electoral systems based on single-seat constituencies were seen as more likely to produce stable parliamentary majorities, but at the risk of leaving segments of the population unrepresented.

It was pointed out that rules relating to the organization of elections are also important for the resolution of electoral disputes and drawing or redrawing of electoral constituencies. Participating States apply different systems in this respect, some recognizing the authority of their legislature while others accept the competence of the judiciary. A third system referred to was the establishment of a special judicial body with sufficient expertise in electoral matters and completely immune from the influence of the legislative and executive branches.

It was underlined that representative government now confronted a situation where the media, interest groups, spontaneous social movements and single-issue pressure groups have taken over some of the functions previously performed by political parties. At the same time, the level of electoral participation in many established democracies had diminished. There were differing views on the implications of such changes for the environment in which democratic institutions operated. It was noted that non-governmental organizations and new approaches by the media to the political process might play a constructive role, by activating voters and by making the political parties aware of the concerns of voters.

Reference was made to the necessity for democracies to deal with the anti-democratic forces in society without doing violence to democratic procedures and the ideology on which democratic culture depended.

Extensive reference was made to the leading role played in many emerging democracies by broad, heterogeneous mass movements, united and inspired by their experience in confronting totalitarian regimes. The point was made that such movements may have to adjust in order to continue to play an active political role in post-revolutionary transition to democracy.

It was suggested that the process towards pluralism in former one-party States might require a codification of the role of political parties. Legislation was required to determine the conditions under which political parties were to operate, seek financial support and meet certain requirements, e.g. the readiness to contest elections. It was noted that members of political parties should not be barred from serving as judges or in public administration.

It was noted that while voluntary organizations present themselves under a variety of forms, they have many features in common. They are set up by groups of individuals pursuing common interests of a professional, economic or non-profit nature. Distinctions between them could be on the basis of criteria such as the degree of organization, size, complexity and the functions performed.

Although voluntary organizations might not primarily aim at exercising political responsibilities, they could help articulate citizens' demands on specific issues. They could serve to encourage diversity and the growth of different opinions and facilitate the integration of groups. It was underlined that voluntary organizations provided democratic societies with early-warning systems against government interference and anti-democratic activities. Many voluntary organizations played a prominent role in economic life, providing in some cases a complement to market forces. Many experts pointed out that public authorities should refrain from bureaucratic control.

Some pitfalls for voluntary organizations were pointed out: centralization of decision-making and co-option by State authorities. Reference was also made to the fact that narrow, well-defined interests are more likely to form the basis for voluntary organizations than more general ones.

Experts identified some trends in modern society which influence the working conditions for voluntary organizations and trade unions. In some countries, one could observe a certain tendency of voluntary organizations to withdraw from participation in consultative State organs, and the loosening of ties between trade unions and political parties. The effects thereof on civil society were not yet clear.

While noting the vital role of voluntary organizations for the functioning of democratic institutions, experts also referred to the question of their democratic legitimacy. Only direct, secret and universal suffrage could guarantee a democratic process. But openness and democratic control could not always be taken for granted in voluntary organizations. As the role of political parties had diminished in many countries, the relationship between parliaments and voluntary organizations had become more important.

It was emphasized that a democratic form of government requires freedom of expression, without which its citizens cannot obtain the information necessary for participation in political and public life. A diverse and independent press and broadcasting system has a vital role to play in any democracy. The question of imposing certain regulations on the media was discussed. It was pointed out that some protection was required against excesses of the press. At the same time, it was underlined that freedom of expression should only be subject to such restrictions as are prescribed by law and are necessary in a democratic society. Some participants pointed to the need for high ethical standards in the media and related this to the system of recruitment and training of journalists. It was, however, underlined that both elitist and popular newspapers had the right to exist.

Ideally, economic conditions should guarantee complete editorial independence. It was, however, pointed out that State intervention could sometimes become necessary in order to protect the diversity of the press. In this context, it was mentioned that one should also take into account that the press and broadcasting systems are parts of the cultural identity of a country.

In considering comparative studies of legislation in the area of human rights and fundamental freedoms, attention was drawn to the interrelationship between the protection of those rights, and the effective functioning of democratic political and judicial institutions.

Particular attention was given to the question of national implementation of international human rights instruments. Direct incorporation of such instruments as national legislation was mentioned as one form of national implementation. Another option would be to transform the provisions of international instruments into national legislation. It was pointed out that in some participating States this was already being realized by the jurisprudence of the national judiciary. In this connection, it was emphasized that it was the responsibility of each State to give full domestic effect to its international human rights obligations, irrespective of the means of implementation chosen.

The view was expressed that the national implementation of international human rights obligations requires the existence of effective domestic legal remedies and instruments for controlling public administration.

There was a discussion of the role of national institutions for the promotion and protection of human rights. It was pointed out that, in addition to the ordinary court system, including administrative courts, such institutions could comprise constitutional courts, national human rights commissions, complaints commissions, Ombudsmen or mediators.

In the experience of many experts, the institution of Ombudsman has proved useful in dealing with administrative abuse. By examining the legality of administrative acts, it has a complementary function to the courts. In this way, confidence in the rule of law is strengthened. The supervisory functions of the Ombudsman institution promote fair administrative practices and encourage confidence in government.

Reference was made to the importance of openness in public administration including access to information and documents, and adequate complaints procedures. Recourse to international human rights bodies was mentioned as complementing national complaints and review procedures. Provisions for legal assistance at all levels would be an important element in securing the successful operation of such complaints and review procedures.

The importance of an adequate code of criminal procedure was emphasized as a means of implementing human rights. In particular, attention was drawn to international standards for treatment during detention. It was considered that practical forms of international co-operation in this field could be of direct utility in the reorganization of prison services and penal institutions. Particular attention should be given to national implementation of international instruments against torture or inhuman and degrading treatment. The importance of training those responsible for dealing with detained persons, in particular police, prison officials and personnel, was also pointed out in this connection.

Economic and social rights were discussed. The point was made that there is a need to make a distinction between those rights which are enforceable before the courts, and provisions which should be regarded as expressing policy goals. It was also pointed out that the effective functioning of a market economy would not be incompatible with regulation of the economy or State provision for basic material needs for its citizens, and environmental safeguards.

It was pointed out that modern society would in some way have to deal with problems arising out of changes in technology, particularly in the fields of data processing and bio-technology. This was an area where international exchanges of information, policy studies, and proposed and adopted legislation for regulation to prevent misuse would be useful.

Reference was also made to the need to ensure adequate opportunity for participation of both men and women in all aspects of political and public life, through appropriate legislation and supervisory agencies.

III

The experts recognized that there is a need to strengthen CSCE co-operation in the fields of human rights, democratic institutions and the rule of law.

A widely held view among the experts was that one of the most important functions of CSCE co-operation in these fields would be to establish contacts between governments, institutions and organizations seeking expertise or assistance and counterparts that are in a position to provide such resources. The need to assure co-ordination of activities with a view to strengthening democratic institutions was underlined.

Participants noted in this context the support that has been expressed for the proposal of transforming the CSCE Office for Free Elections into a broadly focused office of democratic institutions. Paragraph 30 of the Document of the Moscow Meeting of the Conference on the Human Dimension was referred to in this connection.

Participants, while noting that any revision of the mandate of the Office for Free Elections would have to be decided by the appropriate body, expressed views to indicate possible additional functions a CSCE office of democratic institutions could serve. At this stage, certain experts made the following points:

- an office of democratic institutions could serve as the institutional framework for sharing and exchanging information on available technical assistance, expertise and national and international programmes aimed at assisting the new democracies in their institution-building;

- it could facilitate contacts between those offering such resources and those wishing to make use of them, thereby serving as a clearing-house and contact point and a facilitator for co-operative projects;

- it could establish and maintain a data-base of such resources and services;

- it could establish contacts with non-governmental organizations active in the field of democratic institution-building, with a view to enabling interested participating States to make use of their extensive resources and expertise;

- it could facilitate co-operation in training and education in disciplines relevant to democratic institutions;

- it could organize meetings and seminars on subjects related to the building and revitalization of democratic institutions, at the request of participating States.

The point was made by many participants that an office of democratic institutions should work closely with other institutions active in the field of democratic institution-building in order to avoid duplication of work. In this connection, certain experts underlined the relevant character of the role of the Council of Europe in the areas of the rule of law and the defence of human rights and the importance of taking account of its work, experience and extensive resources, particularly in the provision of expertise on democratic institutions, in the arrangement of seminars and programmes on democratic practice, and as a source of information about activities, resources and needs in participating States, as well as that of the European Commission for Democracy through Law. Effective liaison between a CSCE office of democratic institutions and these institutions should be ensured.

It was suggested that the establishment of national centres for democratic institutions could facilitate the further strengthening of such democracy, especially in countries carrying out radical democratic reforms. Such national centres might maintain links to a CSCE office of democratic institutions.

IV

In the course of the Seminar a number of practical proposals for future co-operation with a view to strengthening democratic institutions were made. The hope was expressed that these could become the object of follow-up action in a bilateral or multilateral context, as appropriate. In this connection, reference was also made to programmes within the framework of the Council of Europe.

The following specific possibilities were mentioned, bearing in mind the need to develop them further:

- Training programmes and exchanges of personnel
- Co-operation on education for democracy and human rights
- Resource list of experts on democratic institutions
- Seminars, informal workshops and round tables on democratic institutions
- Scholarship programmes for students and instructors
- Funding of higher education

- Ombudsmen's meetings and seminars

- Co-operation between local and regional authorities

- Involving NGOs in practical co-operation

- Co-operation in the training of personnel dealing with detained individuals

- Exchanges on modalities for free legal aid.

INTERPRETATIVE STATEMENTS[1]

Interpretative statements by France

1. France considers that the Report before you (document CSCE/SEDIO.3) is of a particular nature and corresponds to the specific character of the Seminar which met in Oslo from 4 to 15 November 1991.

   Accordingly, it interprets the paragraph at the top of page 3 of the English version of document CSCE/SEDIO.3 which is before you and, in particular, the phrase which reads as follows:

   '... this Report, which does not purport to express any new commitments on the part of participating States,'

   as meaning that this text is not a text negotiated by the participating States in the traditional meaning of this term.

2. France considers that, in the penultimate paragraph on page 6 of document CSCE/SEDIO.3, which reads as follows:

   '... it was noted that, although the classical doctrine of the separation of powers in its pure form was implemented mainly in presidential systems, its essence was also reflected in the practices of many other political systems,'

   the word 'mainly' reflects the opinions only of some experts. Other experts simply consider that the implementation of the separation of powers is more important in the case of presidential systems.

3. France considers that the last sentence of the second paragraph on page 7 of document CSCE/SEDIO.3, which reads as follows:

   'Administrative decentralization, development of governmental functions on a regional basis and reinforcement and reform of local government institutions might in varying ways respond to the needs of groups, including national minorities,'

   is not in conformity with the views expressed by several experts. For these experts, nationals belonging to national minorities must enjoy full equality, the same rights and have the same duties as other nationals in the countries where these national minorities live.

---

[1] Journal No. 10 (Oslo, 15 November 1991).

For these same experts, the word 'group' is meaningless.

4. France considers that the last sentence of the second paragraph on page 7 of document CSCE/SEDIO.3, which reads as follows:

'One way of avoiding instability was to admit no-confidence votes only when the parties behind such a vote are in a position to offer an alternative government'

simply expresses the opinion of certain experts. In the opinion of other experts, there are several other ways of ensuring governmental stability.

5. France considers that the reference in section III of document CSCE/SEDIO.3 to the role of the Council of Europe concerning the rule of law and human rights totally fails to reflect the essential role this organization plays in its fields of competence.

It regrets that the opinions of experts on this point have not been reflected in a more balanced manner.

It takes the opportunity to reaffirm that, in its view, it was not appropriate for the Seminar of Experts on Democratic Institutions to draw up a list of the possible future functions of the Office for Free Elections, and that the list in the above-mentioned document reflects only - as is indicated therein - the opinions of certain experts.

VIENNA DOCUMENT 1992

OF THE NEGOTIATIONS ON CONFIDENCE- AND SECURITY-BUILDING MEASURES CONVENED IN ACCORDANCE WITH THE RELEVANT PROVISIONS OF THE CONCLUDING DOCUMENT OF THE VIENNA MEETING OF THE CONFERENCE ON SECURITY AND CO-OPERATION IN EUROPE

Vienna, 4 March 1992

(1) Representatives of the participating States of the Conference on Security and Co-operation in Europe (CSCE), Albania, Armenia Austria, Azerbaijan, Belarus, Belgium, Bulgaria, Canada, Cyprus, the Czech and Slovak Federal Republic, Denmark, Estonia, Finland, France, Germany, Greece, the Holy See, Hungary, Iceland, Ireland, Italy, Kazakhstan, Kyrgyzstan, Latvia, Liechtenstein, Lithuania, Luxembourg, Malta, Moldova, Monaco, the Netherlands, Norway, Poland, Portugal, Romania, the Russian Federation, San Marino, Spain, Sweden, Switzerland, Tajikistan, Turkey, Turkmenistan, Ukraine, the United Kingdom, the United States of America, Uzbekistan and Yugoslavia, met in Vienna in accordance with the provisions relating to the Conference on Confidence- and Security-Building Measures and Disarmament in Europe contained in the Concluding Documents of the Madrid and Vienna Follow-up Meetings of the CSCE.

(2) The Negotiations were conducted from 9 March 1989 to 4 March 1992.

(3) The participating States recalled that the aim of the Conference on Confidence- and Security-Building Measures and Disarmament in Europe is, as a substantial and integral part of the multilateral process initiated by the Conference on Security and Co-operation in Europe, to undertake, in stages, new, effective and concrete actions designed to make progress in strengthening confidence and security and in achieving disarmament, so as to give effect and expression to the duty of States to refrain from the threat or use of force in their mutual relations as well as in their international relations in general.

(4) The participating States recognized that the mutually complementary confidence- and security-building measures which are adopted in the present document and which are in accordance with the mandates of the Madrid and Vienna Follow-up Meetings of the CSCE serve by their scope and nature and by their implementation to strengthen confidence and security among the participating States.

(5) The participating States recalled the declaration on Refraining from the Threat or Use of Force contained in paragraphs (9) to (27) of the Document of the Stockholm Conference and stressed its continuing validity as seen in the light of the Charter of Paris for a New Europe.

(6) From 8 to 18 October 1991, the participating States held discussions in a seminar setting on military doctrine in relation to the posture, structure and activities of conventional forces in the zone of application for confidence- and security-building measures[1]. The discussions built on the results of the first such seminar, which had been held in Vienna from 16 January to 5 February 1990.

(7) On 17 November 1990, the participating States adopted the Vienna Document 1990, which built upon and added to the confidence- and security-building measures contained in the Document of the Stockholm Conference 1986.

(8) In fulfilment of the Charter of Paris for a New Europe of November 1990, they continued the CSBM negotiations under the same mandate, and have adopted the present document which integrates a set of new confidence- and security-building measures with measures previously adopted.

---

1. Annex I

(9) The participating States have adopted the following:

I. Annual exchange of military information

Information on military forces

(10) The participating States will exchange annually information on their military forces concerning the military organization, manpower and major weapon and equipment systems, as specified below, in the zone of application for confidence- and security-building measures (CSBMs).

(11) The information will be provided in an agreed format to all other participating States not later than 15 December of each year. It will be valid as of 1 January of the following year and will include:

(11.1) 1. Information on the command organization of those military forces referred to under points 2 and 3 specifying the designation and subordination of all formations[2] and units[3] at each level of command down to and including brigade/regiment or equivalent level.

(11.1.1) Each participating State providing information on military forces will include a statement indicating the total number of units contained therein and the resultant annual evaluation quota as provided for in paragraph (114).

(11.2) 2. For each formation and combat unit[4] of land forces down to and including brigade/regiment or equivalent level the information will indicate:

(11.2.1) - the designation and subordination;

(11.2.2) - whether it is active or non-active[5];

---

2. In this context, formations are armies, corps and divisions and their equivalents.
3. In this context, units are brigades, regiments and their equivalents.
4. In this context, combat units are infantry, armoured, mechanized, motorized rifle, artillery, combat engineer and army aviation units. Those combat units which are airmobile or airborne will also be included.
5. In this context, non-active formations or combat units are those manned from zero to fifteen per cent of their authorized combat strength. This term includes low strength formations and units.

(11.2.3) - the normal peacetime location of its headquarters indicated by exact geographic terms and/or co-ordinates;

(11.2.4) - the peacetime authorized personnel strength;

(11.2.5) - the major organic weapon and equipment systems, specifying the numbers of each type of:

(11.2.5.1) - battle tanks;

(11.2.5.2) - helicopters;

(11.2.5.3) - armoured combat vehicles (armoured personnel carriers, armoured infantry fighting vehicles, heavy armament combat vehicles);

(11.2.5.4.) - armoured personnel carrier look-alikes and armoured infantry fighting vehicle look-alikes;

(11.2.5.5) - anti-tank guided missile launchers permanently/integrally mounted on armoured vehicles;

(11.2.5.6) - self-propelled and towed artillery pieces, mortars and multiple rocket launchers (100 mm calibre and above);

(11.2.5.7) - armoured vehicle launched bridges.

(11.3.1) For planned increases in personnel strength above that reported under paragraph (11.2.4) for more than 21 days by more than 1,500 troops for each active combat unit and by more than 5,000 troops for each active formation, excluding personnel increases in the formation's subordinate formations and/or combat units subject to separate reporting under paragraph (11.2); as well as

(11.3.2) for each non-active formation and non-active combat unit which is planned to be temporarily activated for routine military activities or for any other purpose with more than 2,000 troops for more than 21 days

(11.3.3) the following additional information will be provided in the annual exchange of military information:

(11.3.3.1) - designation and subordination of the formation or combat unit;

(11.3.3.2) - purpose of the increase or activation;

(11.3.3.3) - for active formations and combat units the planned number of troops exceeding the personnel strength indicated under paragraph (11.2.4) or for non-active formations and combat units the number of troops involved during the period of activation;

(11.3.3.4) - start and end dates of the envisaged increase in personnel strength or activation;

(11.3.3.5) - planned location/area of activation;

(11.3.3.6) - the numbers of each type of the major weapon and equipment systems as listed in paragraphs (11.2.5.1) to (11.2.5.7) which are planned to be used during the period of the personnel increase or activation.

(11.3.4) In cases where the information required under paragraphs (11.3.1) to (11.3.3.6) cannot be provided in the annual exchange of military information, or in cases of changes in the information already provided, the required information will be communicated at least 42 days prior to such a personnel increase or temporary activation taking effect or, in cases when the personnel increase or temporary activation is carried out without advance notice to the troops involved, at the latest at the time the increase or the activation has taken effect.

(11.4) For each amphibious formation and amphibious combat unit[6] permanently located in the zone of application down to and including brigade/regiment or equivalent level, the information will include the items as set out above.

(11.5) 3. For each air formation and air combat unit[7] of the air forces, air defence aviation and of naval aviation permanently based on land down to and including wing/air regiment or equivalent level the information will include:

(11.5.1) - the designation and subordination;

---

6. Combat units as defined above.
7. In this context, air combat units are units, the majority of whose organic aircraft are combat aircraft.

(11.5.2) - the normal peacetime location of the headquarters indicated by exact geographic terms and/or co-ordinates;

(11.5.3) - the normal peacetime location of the unit indicated by the air base or military airfield on which the unit is based, specifying:

(11.5.3.1) - the designation or, if applicable, name of the air base or military airfield and

(11.5.3.2) - its location indicated by exact geographic terms and/or co-ordinates;

(11.5.4) - the peacetime authorized personnel strength[8];

(11.5.5) - the numbers of each type of:

(11.5.5.1) - combat aircraft;

(11.5.5.2) - helicopters

organic to the formation or unit.

Data relating to major weapon and equipment systems

(12) The participating States will exchange data relating to their major weapon and equipment systems as specified in the provisions on Information on Military Forces within the zone of application for CSBMs.

(12.1) Data on existing weapon and equipment systems will be provided once to all other participating States not later than 15 December 1992.

(12.2) Data on new types or versions of major weapon and equipment systems will be provided by each State when its deployment plans for the systems concerned are provided for the first time in accordance with paragraphs (14) and (15) below or, at the latest, when it deploys the systems concerned for the first time in the zone of application for CSBMs. If a participating State has already provided data on the same new type or version, other participating

8. As an exception, this information need not be provided on air defence aviation units.

States may, if appropriate, certify the validity of those data as far as their system is concerned.

(13) The following data will be provided for each type or version of major weapon and equipment systems:

(13.1) BATTLE TANKS

(13.1.1) Type

(13.1.2) National Nomenclature/Name

(13.1.3) Main Gun Calibre

(13.1.4) Unladen Weight

(13.1.5) Data on new types or versions will, in addition, include:

(13.1.5.1) Night Vision Capability yes/no

(13.1.5.2) Additional Armour yes/no

(13.1.5.3) Track Width cm

(13.1.5.4) Floating Capability yes/no

(13.1.5.5) Snorkelling Equipment yes/no

(13.2) ARMOURED COMBAT VEHICLES

(13.2.1) Armoured Personnel Carriers

(13.2.1.1) Type

(13.2.1.2) National Nomenclature/Name

(13.2.1.3) Type and Calibre of Armaments, if any

(13.2.1.4) Data on new types or versions will, in addition, include:

(13.2.1.4.1) Night Vision Capability yes/no

(13.2.1.4.2) Seating Capacity

(13.2.1.4.3)	Floating Capability	yes/no
(13.2.1.4.4)	Snorkelling Equipment	yes/no
(13.2.2)	Armoured Infantry Fighting Vehicles	
(13.2.2.1)	Type	
(13.2.2.2)	National Nomenclature/Name	
(13.2.2.3)	Type and Calibre of Armaments	
(13.2.2.4)	Data on new types or versions will, in addition, include:	
(13.2.2.4.1)	Night Vision Capability	yes/no
(13.2.2.4.2)	Additional Armour	yes/no
(13.2.2.4.3)	Floating Capability	yes/no
(13.2.2.4.4)	Snorkelling Equipment	yes/no
(13.2.3)	Heavy Armament Combat Vehicles	
(13.2.3.1)	Type	
(13.2.3.2)	National Nomenclature/Name	
(13.2.3.3)	Main Gun Calibre	
(13.2.3.4)	Unladen Weight	
(13.2.3.5)	Data on new types or versions will, in addition, include:	
(13.2.3.5.1)	Night Vision Capability	yes/no
(13.2.3.5.2)	Additional Armour	yes/no
(13.2.3.5.3)	Floating Capability	yes/no
(13.2.3.5.4)	Snorkelling Equipment	yes/no

(13.3) ARMOURED PERSONNEL CARRIER LOOK-ALIKES AND ARMOURED INFANTRY FIGHTING VEHICLE LOOK-ALIKES

(13.3.1) Armoured Personnel Carrier Look-Alikes

(13.3.1.1) Type

(13.3.1.2) National Nomenclature/Name

(13.3.1.3) Type and Calibre of Armaments, if any

(13.3.2) Armoured Infantry Fighting Vehicle Look-Alikes

(13.3.2.1) Type

(13.3.2.2) National Nomenclature/Name

(13.3.2.3) Type and Calibre of Armaments, if any

(13.4) ANTI-TANK GUIDED MISSILE LAUNCHERS PERMANENTLY/INTEGRALLY MOUNTED ON ARMOURED VEHICLES

(13.4.1) Type

(13.4.2) National Nomenclature/Name

(13.5) SELF-PROPELLED AND TOWED ARTILLERY PIECES, MORTARS AND MULTIPLE ROCKET LAUNCHERS (100 mm CALIBRE AND ABOVE)

(13.5.1) Artillery pieces

(13.5.1.1) Type

(13.5.1.2) National Nomenclature/Name

(13.5.1.3) Calibre

(13.5.2) Mortars

(13.5.2.1) Type

(13.5.2.2) National Nomenclature/Name

(13.5.2.3) Calibre

(13.5.3) Multiple Launch Rocket Systems

(13.5.3.1) Type

(13.5.3.2) National Nomenclature/Name

(13.5.3.3) Calibre

(13.5.3.4) Data on new types or versions will, in addition, include:

(13.5.3.4.1) Number of Tubes

(13.6) ARMOURED VEHICLE LAUNCHED BRIDGES

(13.6.1) Type

(13.6.2) National Nomenclature/Name

(13.6.3) Data on new types or versions will, in addition, include:

(13.6.3.1) Span of the bridge ---- m

(13.6.3.2) Carrying Capacity/Load Classification ---- metric tons

(13.7) COMBAT AIRCRAFT

(13.7.1) Type

(13.7.2) National Nomenclature/Name

(13.7.3) Data on new types or versions will, in addition, include:

(13.7.3.1) Type of Integrally Mounted Armaments, if any

(13.8) HELICOPTERS

(13.8.1) Type

(13.8.2) National Nomenclature/Name

(13.8.3) Data on new types or versions will, in addition, include:

(13.8.3.1) Primary Role (e.g. specialized attack, multi-purpose attack, combat support, transport)

(13.8.3.2) Type of Integrally Mounted Armaments, if any

(13.9) Each participating State will, at the time the data are presented, ensure that other participating States are provided with photographs presenting the right or left side, top and front views for each of the types of major weapon and equipment systems concerned.

(13.10) Photographs of armoured personnel carrier look-alikes and armoured infantry fighting vehicle look-alikes will include a view of such vehicles so as to show clearly their internal configuration illustrating the specific characteristic which distinguishes each particular vehicle as a look-alike.

(13.11) The photographs of each type will be accompanied by a note giving the type designation and national nomenclature for all models and versions of the type which the photographs represent. The photographs of a type will contain an annotation of the data for that type.

Information on plans for the deployment of major weapon and equipment systems

(14) The participating States will exchange annually information on their plans for the deployment of major weapon and equipment systems as specified in the provisions on Information on Military Forces within the zone of application for CSBMs.

(15) The information will be provided in an agreed format to all other participating States not later than 15 December of each year. It will cover plans for the following year and will include:

(15.1) - the type and name of the weapon/equipment systems to be deployed;

(15.2) - the total number of each weapon/equipment system;

(15.3) - whenever possible, the number of each weapon/equipment system planned to be allocated to each formation or unit;

(15.4) - the extent to which the deployment will add to or replace existing weapon/equipment systems.

Information on military budgets

(16) The participating States will exchange annually information on their military budgets for the forthcoming fiscal year, itemising defence expenditures on the basis of the categories set out in the United Nations "Instrument for Standardised International Reporting of Military Expenditures" adopted on 12 December 1980.

(16.1) The information will be provided to all other participating States not later than two months after the military budget has been approved by the competent national authorities.

(16.2) Each participating State may ask for clarification from any other participating State of the budgetary information provided. Questions should be submitted within a period of two months following the receipt of a participating State's budgetary information. Participating States will make every effort to answer such questions fully and promptly. The questions and replies may be transmitted to all other participating States.

II. Risk reduction

Mechanism for consultation and co-operation as regards unusual military activities

(17) Participating States will, in accordance with the following provisions, consult and co-operate with each other about any unusual and unscheduled activities of their military forces outside their normal peacetime locations which are militarily significant, within the zone of application for CSBMs and about which a participating State expresses its security concern.

(17.1) The participating State which has concerns about such an activity may transmit a request for an explanation to another participating State where the activity is taking place.

(17.1.1) The request will state the cause, or causes, of the concern and, to the extent possible, the type and location, or area, of the activity.

(17.1.2) The reply will be transmitted within not more than 48 hours.

(17.1.3) The reply will give answers to questions raised, as well as any other relevant information which might help to clarify the activity giving rise to concern.

(17.1.4) The request and the reply will be transmitted to all other participating States without delay.

(17.2) The requesting State, after considering the reply provided, may then request a meeting to discuss the matter.

(17.2.1) The requesting State may ask for a meeting with the responding State.

(17.2.1.1) Such a meeting will be convened within not more than 48 hours.

(17.2.1.2) The request for such a meeting will be transmitted to all participating States without delay.

(17.2.1.3) The responding State is entitled to ask other interested participating States, in particular those which might be involved in the activity, to participate in the meeting.

(17.2.1.4) Such a meeting will be held at a venue to be mutually agreed upon by the requesting and the responding States. If there is no agreement, the meeting will be held at the Conflict Prevention Centre.

(17.2.1.5) The requesting and responding States will, jointly or separately, transmit a report of the meeting to all other participating States without delay.

(17.2.2) The requesting State may ask for a meeting of all participating States.

(17.2.2.1) Such a meeting will be convened within not more than 48 hours.

(17.2.2.2) The Conflict Prevention Centre will serve as the forum for such a meeting.

(17.2.2.3) Participating States involved in the matter to be discussed undertake to be represented at such a meeting.

(17.3) The communications between participating States provided for above will be transmitted preferably through the CSBM communications network.

Co-operation as regards hazardous incidents of a military nature

(18) Participating States will co-operate by reporting and clarifying hazardous incidents of a military nature within the zone of application for CSBMs in order to prevent possible misunderstandings and mitigate the effects on another participating State.

(18.1) Each participating State will designate a point to contact in case of such hazardous incidents and will so inform all other participating States. A list of such points will be kept available at the Conflict Prevention Centre.

(18.2) In the event of such a hazardous incident the participating State whose military forces are involved in the incident should provide the information available to other participating States in an expeditious manner. Any participating State affected by such an incident may also request clarification as appropriate. Such requests will receive a prompt response.

(18.3) Communications between participating States will be transmitted preferably through the CSBM communications network.

(18.4) Matters relating to information about such hazardous incidents may be discussed by participating States at the Conflict Prevention Centre, either at the annual implementation assessment meeting at the Centre, or at additional meetings convened there.

(18.5) These provisions will not affect the rights and obligations of participating States under any international agreement concerning hazardous incidents, nor will they preclude additional methods of reporting and clarifying hazardous incidents.

Voluntary hosting of visits to dispel concerns about military activities

(19) In order to help to dispel concerns about military activities in the zone of application for CSBMs, participating States are encouraged to invite, at their discretion, other participating States to designate personnel accredited to the host State or other representatives to

take part in visits to areas on the territory of the host State in which there may be cause for such concerns. Such invitations will be without prejudice to any action taken under paragraphs (17) to (17.3).

(19.1) States invited to participate in such visits will include those which are understood to have concerns. At the time invitations are issued, the host State will communicate to all other participating States its intention to conduct the visit, indicating the reasons for the visit, the area to be visited, the States invited and the general arrangements to be adopted.

(19.2) Arrangements for such visits, including the number of the representatives from other participating States to be invited, will be at the discretion of the host State, which will bear the in-country costs. However, the host State should take appropriate account of the need to ensure the effectiveness of the visit, the maximum amount of openness and transparency and the safety and security of the invited representatives. It should also take account, as far as practicable, of the wishes of visiting representatives as regards the itinerary of the visit. The host State and the States which provide visiting personnel may circulate joint or individual comments on the visit to all other participating States.

III. Contacts

Visits to air bases

(20) Each participating State with air combat units reported under paragraph (11) will arrange visits for representatives of all other participating States to one of its normal peacetime air bases[9] on which such units are located in order to provide the visitors with the opportunity to view activity at the air base, including preparations to carry out the functions of the air base and to gain an impression of the approximate number of air sorties and type of missions being flown.

(21) No participating State will be obliged to arrange more than one such visit in any five-year period. Prior indications given by

9. In this context, the term normal peacetime air base is understood to mean the normal peacetime location of the air combat unit indicated by the air base or military airfield on which the unit is based.

participating States of forthcoming schedules for such visits for the subsequent year(s) may be discussed at the annual implementation assessment meetings.

(22) As a rule, up to two visitors from each participating State will be invited.

(23) Invitations will be extended to all participating States 42 days or more in advance of the visit. The invitation will indicate a preliminary programme, including: place, date and time of assembly; planned duration; languages to be used; arrangements for board, lodging and transportation; equipment permitted to be used during the visit; and any other information that may be considered useful.

(24) When the air base to be visited is located on the territory of another participating State, the invitations will be issued by the participating State on whose territory the air base is located. In such cases, the responsibilities as host delegated by this State to the participating State arranging the visit will be specified in the invitation.

(25) The invited State may decide whether to send military and/or civilian visitors, including personnel accredited to the host State. Military visitors will normally wear their uniforms and insignia during the visit.

(26) Replies, indicating whether or not the invitation is accepted, will be given not later than 21 days after the issue of the invitation. Participating States accepting an invitation will provide the names and ranks of the visitors in their replies. If the invitation is not accepted in time, it will be assumed that no visitors will be sent.

(27) The visit to the air base will last for a minimum of 24 hours.
In the course of the visit, the visitors will be given a briefing on the purpose and functions of the air base and on current activity at the air base. They will have the opportunity to communicate with commanders and troops, including those of support/logistic units located at the air base.

(28) The visitors will be provided with the opportunity to view all types of aircraft located at the air base.

(29) At the close of the visit, the host State will provide an opportunity for the visitors to meet together and also with host State officials and senior air base personnel to discuss the course of the visit.

(30) The host State will determine the programme for the visit and access granted to visitors at the air base. The visitors will follow the instructions issued by the host State in accordance with the provisions set out in this document.

(31) The visitors will be provided with appropriate accommodation in a location suitable for carrying out the visit.

(32) The invited State will cover the travel expenses of its representatives to and from the place of assembly specified in the invitation.

(33) Participating States should, in due co-operation with the visitors, ensure that no action is taken which could be harmful to the safety of visitors.

Military contacts

(34) To improve further their mutual relations in the interest of strengthening the process of confidence- and security-building, the participating States will, as appropriate, promote and facilitate:

(34.1) - exchanges and visits between senior military/defence representatives;

(34.2) - contacts between relevant military institutions;

(34.3) - attendance by military representatives of other participating States at courses of instruction;

(34.4) - exchanges between military commanders and officers of commands down to brigade/regiment or equivalent level;

(34.5) - exchanges and contacts between academics and experts in military studies and related areas;

(34.6) - sporting and cultural events between members of their armed forces.

Demonstration of new types of major weapon and equipment systems

(35) The first participating State which deploys with its military forces in the zone of application a new type of major weapon and equipment system as specified in the provisions on Information on Military Forces will arrange at the earliest opportunity (e.g. during an observation) a demonstration for representatives of all other participating States.[10]

(35.1) The host State will determine the duration, the programme and other modalities of the demonstration.

(35.2) Invitations will be extended to all participating States 42 days or more in advance of visits. The invitation will indicate a preliminary programme, including: the number of visitors invited from each participating State; the type(s) of major weapon and equipment system(s) to be viewed; place, date and time of assembly; planned duration; languages to be used; arrangements for board, lodging and transportation, where necessary; equipment permitted to be used during the visit; and any other information that may be considered useful.

(35.3) Replies, indicating whether or not the invitation is accepted, will be given not later than 21 days after the issue of the invitation. Participating States accepting an invitation will provide the names and ranks of the visitors in their replies. If the invitation is not accepted in time, it will be assumed that no visitors will be sent.

(35.4) The invited State will cover the travel expenses of its representatives to and from the place of assembly and, if applicable, costs for accommodation during the visit.

---

10. This provision will not apply if another participating State has already arranged a demonstration of the same type of major weapon and equipment system.

IV. Prior notification of certain military activities

(36) The participating States will give notification in writing through diplomatic channels in an agreed form of content, to all other participating States 42 days or more in advance of the start of notifiable[11] military activities in the zone of application for CSBMs.

(37) Notification will be given by the participating State on whose territory the activity in question is planned to take place even if the forces of that State are not engaged in the activity or their strength is below the notifiable level. This will not relieve other participating States of their obligation to give notification, if their involvement in the planned military activity reaches the notifiable level.

(38) Each of the following military activities in the field conducted as a single activity in the zone of application for CSBMs at or above the levels defined below, will be notified:

(38.1) The engagement of formations of land forces[12] of the participating States in the same exercise activity conducted under a single operational command independently or in combination with any possible air or naval components.

(38.1.1) This military activity will be subject to notification whenever it involves at any time during the activity:
- at least 9,000 troops, including support troops, or
- at least 250 battle tanks

if organized into a divisional structure or at least two brigades/regiments, not necessarily subordinate to the same division.

(38.1.2) The participation of air forces of the participating States will be included in the notification if it is foreseen that in the course of the activity 200 or more sorties by aircraft, excluding helicopters, will be flown.

---

11. In this document, the term notifiable means subject to notification.
12. In this context, the term land forces includes amphibious, airmobile and airborne forces.

(38.2) The engagement of military forces either in an amphibious landing or in a parachute assault by airborne forces in the zone of application for CSBMs.

(38.2.1) These military activities will be subject to notification whenever the amphibious landing involves at least 3,000 troops or whenever the parachute drop involves at least 3,000 troops.

(38.3) The engagement of formations of land forces of the participating States in a transfer from outside the zone of application for CSBMs to arrival points in the zone, or from inside the zone of application for CSBMs to points of concentration in the zone, to participate in a notifiable exercise activity or to be concentrated.

(38.3.1) The arrival or concentration of these forces will be subject to notification whenever it involves, at any time during the activity:
- at least 9,000 troops, including support troops, or
- at least 250 battle tanks

if organized into a divisional structure or at least two brigades/regiments, not necessarily subordinate to the same division.

(38.3.2) Forces which have been transferred into the zone will be subject to all provisions of agreed CSBMs when they depart their arrival points to participate in a notifiable exercise activity or to be concentrated within the zone of application for CSBMs.

(39) Notifiable military activities carried out without advance notice to the troops involved, are exceptions to the requirement for prior notification to be made 42 days in advance.

(39.1) Notification of such activities, above the agreed thresholds, will be given at the time the troops involved commence such activities.

(40) Notification will be given in writing of each notifiable military activity in the following agreed form:

(41) **A - General Information**

(41.1) The designation of the military activity;

(41.2) The general purpose of the military activity;

(41.3) The names of the States involved in the military activity;

(41.4) The level of command, organizing and commanding the military activity;

(41.5) The start and end dates of the military activity.

(42) **B - Information on different types of notifiable military activities**

(42.1) The engagement of formations of land forces of the participating States in the same exercise activity conducted under a single operational command independently or in combination with any possible air or naval components:

(42.1.1) The total number of troops taking part in the military activity (i.e. ground troops, amphibious troops, airmobile and airborne troops) and the number of troops participating for each State involved, if applicable;

(42.1.2) The designation, subordination, number and type of formations and units participating for each State down to and including brigade/regiment or equivalent level;

(42.1.3) The total number of battle tanks for each State and the total number of anti-tank guided missile launchers mounted on armoured vehicles;

(42.1.4) The total number of artillery pieces and multiple rocket launchers (100 mm calibre or above);

(42.1.5) The total number of helicopters, by category;

(42.1.6) Envisaged number of sorties by aircraft, excluding helicopters;

(42.1.7) Purpose of air missions;

(42.1.8) Categories of aircraft involved;

(42.1.9) The level of command, organizing and commanding the air force participation;

(42.1.10) Naval ship-to-shore gunfire;

(42.1.11) Indication of other naval ship-to-shore support;

(42.1.12) The level of command, organizing and commanding the naval force participation.

(42.2) The engagement of military forces either in an amphibious landing or in a parachute assault by airborne forces in the zone of application for CSBMs:

(42.2.1) The total number of amphibious troops involved in notifiable amphibious landings, and/or the total number of airborne troops involved in notifiable parachute assaults;

(42.2.2) In the case of a notifiable amphibious landing, the point or points of embarkation, if in the zone of application for CSBMs.

(42.3) The engagement of formations of land forces of the participating States in a transfer from outside the zone of application for CSBMs to arrival points in the zone, or from inside the zone of application for CSBMs to points of concentration in the zone, to participate in a notifiable exercise activity or to be concentrated:

(42.3.1) The total number of troops transferred;

(42.3.2) Number and type of divisions participating in the transfer;

(42.3.3) The total number of battle tanks participating in a notifiable arrival or concentration;

(42.3.4) Geographical co-ordinates for the points of arrival and for the points of concentration.

(43) **C - The envisaged area and timeframe of the activity**

(43.1) The area of the military activity delimited by geographic features together with geographic co-ordinates, as appropriate;

(43.2) The start and end dates of each phase (transfers, deployment, concentration of forces, active exercise phase, recovery phase) of activities in the zone of application for CSBMs of participating formations, the tactical purpose and corresponding geographical areas (delimited by geographical co-ordinates) for each phase;

(43.3) Brief description of each phase.

(44) **D - Other information**

(44.1) Changes, if any, in relation to information provided in the annual calendar regarding the activity;

(44.2) Relationship of the activity to other notifiable activities.

V. Observation of certain military activities

(45) The participating States will invite observers from all other participating States to the following notifiable military activities:

(45.1) - The engagement of formations of land forces[13] of the participating States in the same exercise activity conducted under a single operational command independently or in combination with any possible air or naval components.

(45.2) - The engagement of military forces either in an amphibious landing or in a parachute assault by airborne forces in the zone of application for CSBMs

(45.3) - In the case of the engagement of formations of land forces of the participating States in a transfer from outside the zone of application for CSBMs to arrival points in the zone, or from inside the zone of application for CSBMs to points of concentration in the zone, to participate in a notifiable exercise activity or to be concentrated, the concentration of these forces. Forces which have been transferred into the zone will be subject to all provisions of agreed confidence- and security-building measures when they depart their arrival points to participate in a notifiable exercise activity or to be concentrated within the zone of application for CSBMs.

(45.4) The above-mentioned activities will be subject to observation whenever the number of troops engaged meets or exceeds 13,000 or where the number of battle tanks engaged meets or exceeds 300, except in the case of either an amphibious landing or a parachute

---

13. In this context, the term land forces includes amphibious, airmobile and airborne forces.

assault by airborne forces, which will be subject to observation whenever the number of troops engaged meets or exceeds 3,500.

(46) The host State will extend the invitations in writing through diplomatic channels to all other participating States at the time of notification. The host State will be the participating State on whose territory the notified activity will take place.

(47) The host State may delegate some of its responsibilities as host to another participating State engaged in the military activity on the territory of the host State. In such cases, the host State will specify the allocation of responsibilities in its invitation to observe the activity.

(48) Each participating State may send up to two observers to the military activity to be observed.

(49) The invited State may decide whether to send military and/or civilian observers, including personnel accredited to the host State. Military observers will normally wear their uniforms and insignia while performing their tasks.

(50) Replies, indicating whether or not the invitation is accepted, will be given in writing not later than 21 days after the issue of the invitation.

(51) The participating States accepting an invitation will provide the names and ranks of their observers in their reply to the invitation. If the invitation is not accepted in time, it will be assumed that no observers will be sent.

(52) Together with the invitation the host State will provide a general observation programme, including, the following information:

(52.1) - the date, time and place of assembly of observers;

(52.2) - planned duration of the observation programme;

(52.3) - languages to be used in interpretation and/or translation;

(52.4) - arrangements for board, lodging and transportation of the observers;

(52.5) - arrangements for observation equipment which will be issued to the observers by the host State;

(52.6) - possible authorization by the host State of the use of special equipment that the observers may bring with them;

(52.7) - arrangements for special clothing to be issued to the observers because of weather or environmental factors;

(53) The observers may make requests with regard to the observation programme. The host State will, if possible, accede to them.

(54) The host State will determine a duration of observation which permits the observers to observe a notifiable military activity from the time that agreed thresholds for observation are met or exceeded until, for the last time during the activity, the thresholds for observation are no longer met.

(55) The host State will provide the observers with transportation to the area of the notified activity and back. This transportation will be provided from either the capital or another suitable location to be announced in the invitation, so that the observers are in position before the start of the observation programme.

(56) The invited State will cover the travel expenses for its observers to the capital, or another suitable location specified in the invitation, of the host State, and back.

(57) The observers will be provided equal treatment and offered equal opportunities to carry out their functions.

(58) The observers will be granted, during their mission, the privileges and immunities accorded to diplomatic agents in the Vienna Convention on Diplomatic Relations.

(59) The participating States will ensure that official personnel and troops taking part in an observed military activity, as well as other armed personnel located in the area of the military activity, are adequately informed regarding the presence, status and functions of observers. Participating States should, in due co-operation with the observers, ensure that no action is taken which could be harmful to the safety of observers.

(60) The host State will not be required to permit observation of restricted locations, installations or defence sites.

(61) In order to allow the observers to confirm that the notified activity is non-threatening in character and that it is carried out in conformity with the appropriate provisions of the notification, the host State will:

(61.1) - at the commencement of the observation programme give a briefing on the purpose, the basic situation, the phases of the activity and possible changes as compared with the notification and provide the observers with an observation programme with a daily schedule;

(61.2) - provide the observers with a map with a scale of 1 to not more than 250,000 depicting the area of the notified military activity and the initial tactical situation in this area. To depict the entire area of the notified military activity, smaller-scale maps may be additionally provided;

(61.3) - provide the observers with appropriate observation equipment; in addition, the observers will be permitted to use their own binoculars, maps, photo and video cameras, dictaphones and hand-held passive night-vision devices. The above-mentioned equipment will be subject to examination and approval by the host State. It is understood that the host State may limit the use of certain equipment in restricted locations, installations or defence sites;

(61.4) be encouraged, whenever feasible and with due consideration for the security of the observers, to provide an aerial survey, preferably by helicopter, of the area of the military activity. If carried out, such a survey should provide the observers with the opportunity to observe from the air the disposition of forces engaged in the activity in order to help them gain a general impression of its scope and scale. At least one observer from each participating State represented at the observation should be given the opportunity to participate in the survey. Helicopters and/or aircraft may be provided by the host State or by another participating State at the request of and in agreement with the host State;

(61.5) - in the course of the observation programme give the observers daily briefings with the help of maps on the various phases of the military activity and their development and inform the observers about their positions geographically; in the case of a land force activity conducted in combination with air or naval components, briefings will be given by representatives of these forces;

(61.6) - provide opportunities to observe directly forces of the State(s) engaged in the military activity so that the observers get an impression of the flow of the entire activity; to this end, the observers will be given the opportunity to observe combat and support units of all participating formations of a divisional or equivalent level and, whenever possible, to visit units below divisional or equivalent level and communicate with commanders and troops. Commanders and other senior personnel of the participating formations as well as of the visited units will inform the observers of the mission and disposition of their respective units;

(61.7) - guide the observers in the area of the military activity; the observers will follow the instructions issued by the host State in accordance with the provisions set out in this document;

(61.8) - provide the observers with appropriate means of transportation in the area of the military activity;

(61.9) - provide the observers with opportunities for timely communication with their embassies or other official missions and consular posts; the host State is not obligated to cover the communication expense of the observers;

(61.10) - provide the observers with appropriate board and lodging in a location suitable for carrying out the observation programme and, when necessary, medical care;

(61.11) - at the close of each observation, provide an opportunity for the observers to meet together and also with host State officials to discuss the course of the observed activity. Where States other than the host State have been engaged in the activity, military representatives of those States will also be invited to take part in this discussion.

(62) The participating States need not invite observers to notifiable military activities which are carried out without advance notice to the troops involved unless these notifiable activities have a duration of more than 72 hours. The continuation of these activities beyond this time will be subject to observation while the agreed thresholds for observation are met or exceeded. The observation programme will follow as closely as practically possible all the provisions for observation set out in this document.

(63) The participating States are encouraged to permit media representatives from all participating States to attend observed military activities in accordance with accreditation procedures set down by the host State. In such instances, media representatives from all participating States will be treated without discrimination and given equal access to those facets of the activity open to media representatives.

(64) The presence of media representatives will not interfere with the observers carrying out their functions nor with the flow of the military activity.

VI. Annual calendars

(65) Each participating State will exchange, with all other participating States, an annual calendar of its military activities subject to prior notification[14], within the zone of application for CSBMs, forecast for the subsequent calendar year. A participating State which is to host military activities subject to prior notification conducted by any other participating State(s) will include these activities in its annual calendar. It will be transmitted every year, in writing, through diplomatic channels, not later than 15 November for the following year.

(66) If a participating State does not forecast any military activity subject to prior notification it will so inform all other participating States in the same manner as prescribed for the exchange of annual calendars.

---

14. as defined in the provisions on Prior Notification of Certain Military Activities.

(67) Each participating State will list the above-mentioned activities chronologically and will provide information on each activity in accordance with the following model:

(67.1) - type of military activity and its designation;

(67.2) - general characteristics and purpose of the military activity;

(67.3) - States involved in the military activity;

(67.4) - area of the military activity, indicated by geographic features where appropriate and defined by geographic co-ordinates;

(67.5) - planned duration of the military activity, indicated by envisaged start and end dates;

(67.6) - the envisaged total number of troops[15] engaged in the military activity. For activities involving more than one State, the host State will provide such information for each State involved;

(67.7) - the types of armed forces involved in the military activity;

(67.8) - the envisaged level of the military activity and designation of direct operational command, under which this military activity will take place;

(67.9) - the number and type of divisions whose participation in the military activity is envisaged;

(67.10) - any additional information concerning, *inter alia*, components of armed forces, which the participating State planning the military activity considers relevant;

(68) Should changes regarding the military activities in the annual calendar prove necessary, they will be communicated to all other participating States no later than in the appropriate notification.

(69) Should a participating State cancel a military activity included in its annual calendar or reduce it to a level below notification

---

15. as defined in the provisions on Prior Notification of Certain Military Activities.

thresholds, that State will inform the other participating States immediately.

(70) Information on military activities subject to prior notification not included in an annual calendar will be communicated to all participating States as soon as possible, in accordance with the model provided in the annual calendar.

VII. Constraining provisions

(71.1) No participating State will carry out within two calendar years more than one military activity subject to prior notification[16] involving more than 40,000 troops or 900 battle tanks.

(71.2) No participating State will carry out within a calendar year more than six military activities subject to prior notification[16] each one involving more than 13,000 troops or 300 battle tanks but not more than 40,000 troops or 900 battle tanks.

(71.2.1) Of these six military activities no participating State will carry out within a calendar year more than three military activities subject to prior notification[16] each one involving more than 25,000 troops of 400 battle tanks.

(71.3) No participating State will carry out simultaneously more than three military activities subject to prior notification[16] each one involving more than 13,000 troops or 300 battle tanks.

(72) Each participating State will communicate, in writing, to all other participating States, by 15 November each year, information concerning military activities subject to prior notification[17] involving more than 40,000 troops or 900 battle tanks, which it plans to carry out or host in the second subsequent calendar year. Such communication will include preliminary information on the activity, as to its general purpose, timeframe and duration, area, size and States involved.

(73) No participating State will carry out a military activity subject to prior notification[17] involving more than 40,000 troops or 900 battle

---

16. as defined in the provisions on Prior Notification of Certain Military Activities.
17. as defined in the provisions on Prior Notification of Certain Military Activities.

tanks, unless it has been the object of a communication as defined above and unless it has been included in the annual calendar, not later than 15 November each year.

(74) If military activities subject to prior notification[17] are carried out in addition to those contained in the annual calendar, they should be as few as possible.

VIII. Compliance and verification

(75) According to the Madrid Mandate, the confidence- and security-building measures to be agreed upon "will be provided with adequate forms of verification which correspond to their content".

(76) The participating States recognize that national technical means can play a role in monitoring compliance with agreed confidence- and security-building measures.

Inspection

(77) In accordance with the provisions contained in this document each participating State has the right to conduct inspections on the territory of any other participating State within the zone of application for CSBMs. The inspecting State may invite other participating States to participate in an inspection.

(78) Any participating State will be allowed to address a request for inspection to another participating State on whose territory, within the zone of application for CSBMs, compliance with the agreed confidence- and security-building measures is in doubt.

(79) No participating State will be obliged to accept on its territory within the zone of application for CSBMs, more than three inspections per calendar year.

(80) No participating State will be obliged to accept more than one inspection per calendar year from the same participating State.

(81) An inspection will not be counted if, due to force majeure, it cannot be carried out.

(82) The participating State which requests an inspection will state the reasons for such a request.

(83) The participating State which has received such a request will reply in the affirmative to the request within the agreed period of time, subject to the provisions contained in paragraphs (79) and (80).

(84) Any possible dispute as to the validity of the reasons for a request will not prevent or delay the conduct of an inspection.

(85) The participating State which requests an inspection will be permitted to designate for inspection on the territory of another State within the zone of application for CSBMs, a specific area. Such an area will be referred to as the "specified area". The specified area will comprise terrain where notifiable military activities are conducted or where another participating State believes a notifiable military activity is taking place. The specified area will be defined and limited by the scope and scale of notifiable military activities but will not exceed that required for an army level military activity.

(86) In the specified area the inspection team accompanied by the representatives of the receiving State will be permitted access, entry and unobstructed survey, except for areas or sensitive points to which access is normally denied or restricted, military and other defence installations, as well as naval vessels, military vehicles and aircraft. The number and extent of the restricted areas should be as limited as possible. Areas where notifiable military activities can take place will not be declared restricted areas, except for certain permanent or temporary military installations which, in territorial terms, should be as small as possible, and consequently those areas will not be used to prevent inspection of notifiable military activities. Restricted areas will not be employed in a way inconsistent with the agreed provisions on inspection.

(87) Within the specified area, the forces of participating States other than the receiving State will also be subject to the inspection.

(88) Inspection will be permitted on the ground, from the air, or both.

(89) The representatives of the receiving State will accompany the inspection team, including when it is in land vehicles and an

aircraft from the time of their first employment until the time they are no longer in use for the purposes of inspection.

(90) In its request, the inspecting State will notify the receiving State of:

(90.1) - the reasons for the request;

(90.2) - the location of the specified area defined by geographical co-ordinates;

(90.3) - the preferred point(s) of entry for the inspection team;

(90.4) - mode of transport to and from the point(s) of entry and, if applicable, to and from the specified area;

(90.5) - where in the specified area the inspection will begin;

(90.6) - whether the inspection will be conducted from the ground, from the air, or both simultaneously;

(90.7) - whether aerial inspection will be conducted using an airplane, a helicopter, or both;

(90.8) - whether the inspection team will use land vehicles provided by the receiving State or, if mutually agreed, its own vehicles;

(90.9) - other participating States participating in the inspection, if applicable;

(90.10) - information for the issuance of diplomatic visas to inspectors entering the receiving State.

(91) The reply to the request will be given in the shortest possible period of time, but within not more than twenty-four hours. Within thirty-six hours after the issuance of the request, the inspection team will be permitted to enter the territory of the receiving State.

(92) Any request for inspection as well as the reply thereto will be communicated to all participating States without delay.

(93) The receiving State should designate the point(s) of entry as close as possible to the specified area. The receiving State will ensure

that the inspection team will be able to reach the specified area without delay from the point(s) of entry.

(94) All participating States will facilitate the passage of the inspection teams through their territory.

(95) Within 48 hours after the arrival of the inspection team at the specified area, the inspection will be terminated.

(96) There will be no more than four inspectors in an inspection team. The inspecting State may invite other participating States to participate in an inspection. The inspection team will be headed by a national of the inspection State, which will have at least as many inspectors in the team as any invited State. The inspection team will be under the responsibility of the inspection State, against whose quota the inspection is counted. While conducting the inspection the inspection team may divide into two sub-teams.

(97) The inspectors and, if applicable, auxiliary personnel, will be granted during their mission the privileges and immunities in accordance with the Vienna Convention on Diplomatic Relations.

(98) The participating States will ensure that troops, other armed personnel and officials in the specified area are adequately informed regarding the presence, status and functions of inspectors and, if applicable, auxiliary personnel. The receiving State will ensure that no action is taken by its representatives which could endanger inspectors and, if applicable, auxiliary personnel. In carrying out their duties, inspectors and, if applicable, auxiliary personnel will take into account safety concerns expressed by representatives of the receiving State.

(99) The receiving State will provide the inspection team with appropriate board and lodging in a location suitable for carrying out the inspection, and, when necessary, medical care; however this does not exclude the use by the inspection team of its own tents and rations.

(100) The inspection team will have use of its own maps and charts, photo and video cameras, binoculars, hand-held passive night-vision devices and dictaphones. Upon arrival in the specified area the inspection team will show the equipment to the representatives of the receiving State. In addition, the receiving

State may provide the inspection team with a map depicting the area specified for the inspection.

(101) The inspection team will have access to appropriate telecommunications equipment of the receiving State for the purpose of communicating with its embassy or other official missions and consular posts of the inspecting State accredited to the receiving State.

(102) The receiving State will provide the inspection team with access to appropriate telecommunications equipment for the purpose of continuous communication between the sub-teams.

(103) Inspectors will be entitled to request and to receive briefings at agreed times by military representatives of the receiving State. At the inspectors' request, such briefings will be given by commanders of formations or units in the specified area. Suggestions of the receiving State as to the briefings will be taken into consideration.

(104) The inspecting State will specify whether aerial inspection will be conducted using an airplane, a helicopter or both. Aircraft for inspection will be chosen by mutual agreement between the inspecting and receiving States. Aircraft will be chosen which provide the inspection team a continuous view of the ground during the inspection.

(105) After the flight plan, specifying, *inter alia,* the inspection team's choice of flight path, speed and altitude in the specified area, has been filed with the competent air traffic control authority the inspection aircraft will be permitted to enter the specified area without delay. Within the specified area, the inspection team will, at its request, be permitted to deviate from the approved flight plan to make specific observations provided such deviation is consistent with paragraph (86) as well as flight safety and air traffic requirements. Directions to the crew will be given through a representative of the receiving State on board the aircraft involved in the inspection.

(106) One member of the inspection team will be permitted, if such a request is made, at any time to observe data on navigational equipment of the aircraft and to have access to maps and charts

used by the flight crew for the purpose of determining the exact location of the aircraft during the inspection flight.

(107) Aerial and ground inspectors may return to the specified area as often as desired within the 48-hour inspection period.

(108) The receiving State will provide for inspection purposes land vehicles with cross country capability. Whenever mutually agreed taking into account the specific geography relating to the area to be inspected, the inspecting State will be permitted to use its own vehicles.

(109) If land vehicles or aircraft are provided by the inspecting State, there will be one accompanying driver for each land vehicle, or accompanying aircraft crew.

(110) The inspecting State will prepare a report of its inspection and will provide a copy of that report to all participating States without delay.

(111) The inspection expenses will be incurred by the receiving State except when the inspecting State uses its own aircraft and/or land vehicles. The inspecting State will be responsible for travel expenses to and from the point(s) of entry.

Evaluation

(112) Information provided under the provisions on Information on Military Forces and on Information on Plans for the Deployment of Major Weapon and Equipment Systems will be subject to evaluation.

(113) Subject to the provisions below each participating State will provide the opportunity to visit active formations and units in their normal peacetime locations as specified in point 2 and 3 of the provisions on Information on Military Forces to allow the other participating States to evaluate the information provided.

(113.1) Non-active formations and combat units temporarily activated will be made available for evaluation during the period of temporary activation and in the area/location of activation indicated under paragraph (11.3.3). In such cases the provisions for the evaluation of active formations and units will be applicable, *mutatis mutandis*.

Evaluation visits conducted under this provision will count against the quotas established under paragraph (114).

(114) Each participating State will be obliged to accept a quota of one evaluation visit per calendar year for every sixty units, or portion thereof, reported under paragraph (11). However, no participating State will be obliged to accept more than fifteen visits per calendar year. No participating State will be obliged to accept more than one fifth of its quota of visits from the same participating State; a participating State with a quota of less than five visits will not be obliged to accept more than one visit from the same participating State during a calendar year. No formation or unit may be visited more than twice during a calendar year and more than once by the same participating State during a calendar year.

(115) No participating State will be obliged to accept more than one visit at any given time on its territory.

(116) If a participating State has formations or units stationed on the territory of other participating States (host States) in the zone of application for CSBMs, the maximum number of evaluation visits permitted to its forces in each of the States concerned will be proportional to the number of its units in each State. The application of this provision will not alter the number of visits this participating State (stationing State) will have to accept under paragraph (114).

(117) Requests for such visits will be submitted giving 5 days notice.

(118) The request will specify:

(118.1) - the formation or unit to be visited;

(118.2) - the proposed date of the visit;

(118.3) - the preferred point(s) of entry as well as the date and estimated time of arrival for the evaluation team;

(118.4) - the mode of transport to and from the point(s) of entry and, if applicable, to and from the formation or unit to be visited;

(118.5) - the names and ranks of the members of the team and, if applicable, information for the issue of diplomatic visas.

(119) If a formation or unit of a participating State is stationed on the territory of another participating State, the request will be addressed to the host State and sent simultaneously to the stationing State.

(120) The reply to the request will be given within 48 hours after the receipt of the request.

(121) In the case of formations or units of a participating State stationed on the territory of another participating State, the reply will be given by the host State in consultation with the stationing State. After consultation between the host State and the stationing State, the host State will specify in its reply any of its responsibilities which it agrees to delegate to the stationing State.

(122) The reply will indicate whether the formation or unit will be available for evaluation at the proposed date at its normal peacetime location.

(123) Formations or units may be in their normal peacetime location but be unavailable for evaluation. Each participating State will be entitled in such cases not to accept a visit; the reasons for the non-acceptance and the number of days that the formation or unit will be unavailable for evaluation will be stated in the reply. Each participating State will be entitled to invoke this provision up to a total of five times for an aggregate of no more than 30 days per calendar year.

(124) If the formation or unit is absent from its normal peacetime location, the reply will indicate the reasons for and the duration of its absence. The requested State may offer the possibility of a visit to the formation or unit outside its normal peacetime location. If the requested State does not offer this possibility, the requesting State will be able to visit the normal peacetime location of the formation or unit. The requesting State may however refrain in either case from the visit.

(125) Visits will not be counted against the quotas of receiving States, if they are not carried out. Likewise, if visits are not carried out, due to force majeure, they will not be counted.

(126) The reply will designate the point(s) of entry and indicate, if applicable, the time and place of assembly of the team. The

point(s) of entry and, if applicable, the place of assembly will be designated as close as possible to the formation or unit to be visited. The receiving State will ensure that the team will be able to reach the formation or unit without delay.

(127) The request and the reply will be communicated to all participating States without delay.

(128) Participating States will facilitate the passage of teams through their territory.

(129) The team will have no more than two members. It may be accompanied by an interpreter as auxiliary personnel.

(130) The members of the team and, if applicable, auxiliary personnel, will be granted during their mission the privileges and immunities in accordance with the Vienna Convention on Diplomatic Relations.

(131) The visit will take place in the course of a single working day and last up to 12 hours.

(132) The visit will begin with a briefing by the officer commanding the formation or unit, or his deputy, in the headquarters of the formation or unit, concerning the personnel as well as the major weapon and equipment systems reported under paragraph (11).

(132.1) In the case of a visit to a formation, the receiving State may provide the possibility to see personnel and major weapon and equipment systems reported under paragraph (11) for that formation, but not for any of its formations or units, in their normal locations.

(132.2) In the case of a visit to a unit, the receiving State will provide the possibility to see the personnel and the major weapon and equipment systems of the unit reported under paragraph (11) in their normal locations.

(133) Access will not have to be granted to sensitive points, facilities and equipment.

(134) The team will be accompanied at all times by representatives of the receiving State.

(135) The receiving State will provide the team with appropriate transportation during the visit to the formation or unit.

(136) Personal binoculars and dictaphones may be used by the team.

(137) The visit will not interfere with activities of the formation or unit.

(138) The participating States will ensure that troops, other armed personnel and officials in the formation or unit are adequately informed regarding the presence, status and functions of members of teams and, if applicable, auxiliary personnel. Participating States will also ensure that no action is taken by their representatives which could endanger the members of teams and, if applicable, auxiliary personnel. In carrying out their duties, members of teams and, if applicable, auxiliary personnel will take into account safety concerns expressed by representatives of the receiving State.

(139) The travel expenses to and from the point(s) of entry, including expenses for refuelling, maintenance and parking of aircraft and/or land vehicles of the visiting State, will be borne by the visiting State according to existing practices established under the CSBM inspection provisions.

(139.1) Expenses for evaluation visits incurred beyond the point(s) of entry will be borne by the receiving State, except when the visiting State uses its own aircraft and/or land vehicles in accordance with paragraph (118.4).

(139.2) The receiving State will provide appropriate board and, when necessary, lodging in a location suitable for carrying out the evaluation as well as any urgent medical care which may be required.

(139.3) In the case of visits to formations or units of a participating State stationed on the territory of another participating State, the stationing State will bear the costs for the discharge of those responsibilities which have been delegated to it by the host State under the terms of paragraph (121).

(140) The visiting State will prepare a report of its visit which will be communicated to all participating States expeditiously.

(141) Each participating State will be entitled to obtain timely clarification from any other participating State concerning the application of agreed confidence- and security-building measures. Communications in this context will, if appropriate, be transmitted to all other participating States.

(142) The communications concerning compliance and verification will be transmitted preferably through the CSBM communications network.

IX. Communications

(143) The participating States will establish a network of direct communications between their capitals for the transmission of messages relating to agreed measures. The network will complement the existing use of diplomatic channels. Participating States undertake to use the network flexibly, efficiently and in a cost-effective way.

(144) Each participating State will designate a point of contact capable of transmitting and receiving such messages from other participating States on a 24-hour-a-day basis and will notify in advance any change in this designation.

(145) Cost-sharing arrangements are set out in documents CSCE/WV/Dec.2 and CSCE/WV/Dec.4.

(146) Communications may be in any one of the six working languages of the CSCE.

(147) Details on the use of these six languages are set out in Annex II. The provisions of this annex have been elaborated for the practical purposes of the communication system only. They are not intended to change the existing use of all six working languages of the CSCE according to established rules and practice as set out in the Final Recommendations of the Helsinki Consultations.

(148) Messages will be considered official communications of the sending State. If the content of a message is not related to an agreed measure, the receiving State has the right to reject it by so informing the other participating States.

(149) Participating States may agree among themselves to use the network for other purposes.

(150) All aspects of the implementation of the network may be discussed at the annual implementation assessment meeting.

X. Annual implementation assessment meeting

(151) The participating States will hold each year a meeting to discuss the present and future implementation of agreed CSBMs. Discussion may extend to:

(151.1) - clarification of questions arising from such implementation;

(151.2) - operation of agreed measures;

(151.3) - implications of all information originating from the implementation of any agreed measures for the process of confidence- and security-building in the framework of the CSCE.

(152) Before the conclusion of each year's meeting the participating States will normally agree upon the agenda and dates for the subsequent year's meeting. Lack of agreement will not constitute sufficient reason to extend a meeting, unless otherwise agreed. Agenda and dates may, if necessary, be agreed between meetings.

(153) The Conflict Prevention Centre will serve as the forum for such meetings.

(154) The participating States will implement this new set of mutually complementary confidence- and security-building measures in order to promote security co-operation and to reduce the risk of military conflict.

(155) Reaffirming the relevant objectives of the Final Act and the Charter of Paris, the participating States are determined to continue building confidence and to enhance security for all.

(156) The measures adopted in this document are politically binding and will come into force on 1 May 1992.

(157) The Government of Austria is requested to transmit the present document to the Helsinki Follow-up Meeting of the CSCE. The

Government of Austria is also requested to transmit the present document to the Secretary-General of the United Nations and to the Governments of the non-participating Mediterranean States.

(158) The text of this document will be published in each participating State, which will disseminate it and make it known as widely as possible.

(159) The representatives of the participating States express their profound gratitude to the Government and people of Austria for the excellent arrangements they are making for the Vienna CSBM Negotiations and the warm hospitality they have extended to the delegations which participated in the Negotiations.

ANNEX I

Under the terms of the Madrid mandate, the zone of application for CSBMs is defined as follows:

> "On the basis of equality of rights, balance and reciprocity, equal respect for the security interests of all CSCE participating States, and of their respective obligations concerning confidence- and security-building measures and disarmament in Europe, these confidence- and security-building measures will cover the whole of Europe as well as the adjoining sea area[18] and air space. They will be of military significance and politically binding and will be provided with adequate forms of verification which correspond to their content.
>
> As far as the adjoining sea area[18] and air space is concerned, the measures will be applicable to the military activities of all the participating States taking place there whenever these activities affect security in Europe as well as constitute a part of activities taking place within the whole of Europe as referred to above, which they will agree to notify. Necessary specifications will be made through the negotiations on the confidence- and security-building measures at the Conference.
>
> Nothing in the definition of the zone given above will diminish obligations already undertaken under the Final Act. The confidence- and security-building measures to be agreed upon at the Conference will also be applicable in all areas covered by any of the provisions in the Final Act relating to confidence-building measures and certain aspects of security and disarmament.

Wherever the term "the zone of application for CSBMs" is used in this document, the above definition will apply. The following understanding will apply as well:

> The commitments undertaken in letters to the Chairman-in-Office of the CSCE Council by Armenia, Azerbaijan, Belarus, Kazakhstan, Kyrgyzstan, Moldova, Tajikistan, Turkmenistan, Ukraine and Uzbekistan on 29 January 1992 have the effect of extending the application of CSBMs in the Vienna Document 1992 to the territories of the above-mentioned States insofar as their territories were not covered already by the above.

---

18. In this context, the notion of adjoining sea area is understood to refer also to ocean areas adjoining Europe.

ANNEX II

Use of the six CSCE working languages

Messages will, wherever possible, be transmitted in formats with headings in all six CSCE working languages.

Such formats, agreed among the participating States with a view to making transmitted messages immediately understandable by reducing the language element to a minimum are annexed to document CSCE/WV/Dec.4. The formats may be subject to agreed modifications as required. Participating States will co-operate in this respect.

Any narrative text, to the extent it is required in such formats, and messages that do not lend themselves to formatting will be transmitted in the CSCE working language chosen by the transmitting State.

Each participating State has the right to ask for clarification of messages in cases of doubt.

ANNEX III

Chairman's Statement

The participating States, in order to facilitate an efficient use of the communications network, will give due consideration to practical needs of rapid transmission of their messages and of immediate understandability. A translation into another CSCE working language will be added where needed to meet that principle. The participating States have indicated at least two CSCE working languages in which they would prefer to receive the translation.

These provisions do not prejudice in any way the future continued use of all six working languages of the CSCE according to established rules and practice as set out in the Final Recommendations of the Helsinki Consultations.

This statement will be an annex to the Vienna Document 1992 and will be published with it.

Vienna, 4 March 1992

ANNEX V

Chairman's Statement

It is understood that the implementation aspects of CSBMs in the case of contiguous areas of participating States specified in the understanding of Annex I which share frontiers with non-European non-participating States may be discussed at future Annual Implementation Assessment Meetings.

This statement will be an annex to the Vienna Document 1992 and will be published with it.

Vienna, 4 March 1992

ANNEX VI

Chairman's Statement

It is understood that the participating States will take into consideration practical problems which may arise at an initial stage in implementing CSBMs on the territories of new participating States.

This statement will not constitute a precedent.

This statement will be an annex to the Vienna Document 1992 and will be published with it.

INTERPRETATIVE STATEMENTS[1]

Interpretative statement by Turkey

The Government of Turkey had formally placed a reservation regarding the representation of Cyprus at the CSCE on 31 July 1975 (CSCE/III/1). The same reservation has been placed at subsequent meetings within the context of CSCE and in particular at the Stockholm Conference on Confidence- and Security-building Measures and Disarmament in Europe (see Journal No. 379), and at the adoption of the Vienna Document 1990 (see Journal No. 241).

On the occasion of the adoption of the Vienna Document 1992, the Delegation of the Republic of Turkey makes the following reservation to be registered in the Journal of the day:

The Republic of Cyprus was established in 1960 in accordance with international treaties, on the basis of a partnership between the two peoples of the Island. Its constitution, guaranteed by the said agreements, was based on the equality of political rights and status of the Turkish and Greek peoples of the Island. This state of affairs and therefore "the Republic of Cyprus" has ceased to exist as such after its constitution has been unilaterally abrogated in 1963 by the Greek Cypriot side by use of force. The Turkish Cypriot side and Turkey have never accepted this illegal and illegitimate situation which amounted to the deprivation of the Turkish Cypriot people of the use of their rights as equal partners of the State established in 1960.

There is no single authority which in law or in fact is competent to represent jointly the Turkish Cypriots and the Greek Cypriots, consequently Cyprus as a whole.

The Greek Cypriot Administration has, since 1963, represented exclusively the Greek Cypriots and their interests. Therefore, as a guarantor power under the 1960 Treaty of Guarantee, Turkey does not recognize this administration or any of its illegitimate claims.

The Turkish Cypriot people are represented by the Government of the Turkish Republic of Northern Cyprus which carries all the prerequisites of statehood required by international norms. This State, democratically formed by the free will of the Turkish Cypriot people, is recognized by Turkey as having full jurisdiction over its territory and therefore, as the sole authority which can assume international obligations in that respect.

The Republic of Turkey adheres to all decisions so far reached in the CSCE and commits itself to implementing the Vienna Document 1992 on its territory.

---

1. Journal No. 315, 107th Plenary Meeting (4 March 1992), paragraph 6.

However, due to the reasons and positions stated above, the Government of the Republic of Turkey declares that the Vienna Document 1992 as well as the Annexes and statements contained therein have no validity, applicability or binding effect as regards and in relation to Cyprus and they do not create any obligations for Turkey in that respect.

The Vienna Document 1992 is negotiated and adopted on the basis of the commitments undertaken in the Helsinki Final Act and the ten principles contained therein, among them the principle X on the "fulfilment in good faith of obligations under international law".

Therefore, the implementation of the Vienna Document 1992 has to be carried out in full conformity with this principle, including respect for the relevant provisions of the international agreements and treaties regarding the demilitarized status of specific territories. Consequently, any notification or acts of implementation carried out under the provisions of the Vienna Document 1992 cannot in any way affect the demilitarized status of such territories as described in the relevant instruments as well as the international obligations related to this status arising from these international instruments.

* * *

Interpretative statement by Greece

With reference to the reservation just made by the representative of Turkey on the representation of the Republic of Cyprus, I should like to recall paragraph 65 of the Rules of Procedure of the Final Recommendations of the Helsinki Consultations which reads as follows: "All States participating in the Conference shall do so as sovereign and independent States and in conditions of full equality". Cyprus is of course one of them, indeed, a founding one.

I would like also to state that the Republic of Cyprus and its Government enjoy worldwide recognition as this is explicitly reflected in all relevant United Nations resolutions and repeatedly reaffirmed by decisions and statements from the whole spectrum of governments, groups of States and other international organizations.

This recognition is further reflected in multilateral and bilateral agreements, both legally and politically binding, signed between the Republic of Cyprus and a host of other States, among which, in the remoter and more recent past, with Turkey.

Furthermore, Greece firmly believes that the fact that Turkey persists in its refusal to implement its obligations towards a participating State (or refuses to recognize a participating State) is no justification for either not providing information on its military forces in northern Cyprus or providing it in a manner not consistent with the provisions of the Vienna Document. The entire territory of the Republic of Cyprus is within the zone of application for the confidence- and security-building measures.

The Turkish refusal to provide information about its occupation forces stationed in norther areas of the Republic of Cyprus constitutes, in essence, practice and form, a unilateral and arbitrary change of the zone of application. Hence, a serious breach of obligations that we hope will not be used in the future as a dangerous precedent.

With regard to the issue of the so-called demilitarized status of some of the Greek islands in the eastern Aegean, my delegation wishes to state that the Turkish statement is not only based on an interpretation of treaties, obligations and conditions which is unilateral and not shared by Greece, but is out of place and has been made in the framework of a totally inappropriate forum.

There is no connection whatsoever between the adoption of the Vienna Document 1992, on confidence and security-building measures and the Turkish statement referring to Greece.

Ironically speaking, Greece is being reproached for fully complying with its obligations. Greece has provided its military data in accordance with the relevant provisions of the Vienna Document 1990 and political commitments undertaken therein, by which it fully abides and will continue to abide in the future.

* * *

Interpretative statement by Cyprus

Mr. Chairman,

It is to say the least regrettable that the Turkish Delegate has opted, once again, to question the representation of the Republic of Cyprus to these Negotiations.

The attitude of Turkey, the country which has invaded and still occupies 37 % of the territory of Cyprus in gross violation of every rule of International Law and in breach of each one and all of the obligations under the Helsinki Final Act, the Paris Charter and all relevant documents, attempts to play the accuser and the judge, a role not compatible with her actions, the reports of International Organizations and the UN Resolutions, on Cyprus.

In particular, principles 1, 2, 3, 4, 5 and 6 are grossly violated by Turkey in occupying part of the territory of the Republic of Cyprus, since July 1974, and in refusing to enter into a dialogue with the Government of Cyprus for the peaceful settlement of the problem. Principle 7 is violated both in the occupied part of Cyprus and in Turkey by denying human rights and fundamental freedoms to its own citizens such as freedom of association, freedom of expression, religious freedom, freedom of the press and also by applying torture and other inhuman and degrading treatment or punishment to political and other detainees and prisoners. Principle 8 is violated against the Kurdish National minority. Principles 9 and 10 are also violated in the case of Cyprus.

With regard to the statement made by the Representative of Turkey, the delegation of Cyprus wishes to draw attention to Rules 69 and 65 of the Rules of Procedure, which respectively state as follows:

> "Decisions of the Conference shall be taken by consensus. Consensus shall be understood to mean the absence of any objection expressed by a Representative and submitted by him as constituting an obstacle to the taking of the decision in question."
>
> "All States participating in the Conference shall do so as sovereign and independent States and in conditions of full equality...".

Thus, this Turkish statement is void *ab initio* and offending to the very principles of the Final Act.

The Meeting has adopted by consensus the Vienna Document 1992. In accordance with the practice and procedures of the Final Act, and the CSCE process as a whole, all provisions of the document are equally binding on all participating States.

Consequently, any reservation concerning the validity of the decisions of this Meeting in the relations of each participating State with all or any other participating State, or any kind of selectivity in implementing these decisions, is void and of no effect.

The Republic of Cyprus is a Member State of the United Nations, the Council of Europe, the Commonwealth of Nations and other International Organizations, is associated with an Agreement with the European Economic Community and has diplomatic relations with all countries in the world, except Turkey. Numerous UN and Resolutions of other International Organizations do reiterate that the Government of the Republic of Cyprus is representing the whole of Cyprus and all Cypriots, Turks and Greeks alike.

It has been argued by the Turkish Representative that my delegation cannot possibly represent the Turkish Cypriot Community in Cyprus, and that there should be separate representation for the Turkish Cypriots.

My delegation does not represent either the Greek or the Turkish Community of Cyprus. This delegation represents the Government and people of Cyprus as a whole. Indeed if the reasoning of the Turkish delegation were to be followed, then many participating States here should have more than one delegation, since they have more than one ethnic community in their territory. Turkey, herself, would need to have at least one more delegation to represent the Community of Kurds living in Turkey, which numbers 12 million. But even in the case of countries having federal systems, the reasoning of the Turkish delegation is not and cannot be followed.

It is time for Turkey to stop its obstructive behaviour, accept and implement her own obligations, as well as the decisions of the International Community and fora, especially the latest UN Resolutions 649 and 716, and be party to the historic changes of our times, withdraw her occupation forces from the territory of the Republic of Cyprus, a participating State in the CSCE process, and leave the people of Cyprus, as a whole, to chart their peaceful future.

The CSCE principles prescribe that and the UN Resolutions call upon Turkey to do so.

It is to be questioned for how long Turkey will feel safe with its arrogant solitude.

In accordance with the Rules of Procedure, paragraph 79, I kindly request the Executive Secretary to duly register this statement and circulate it to the participating States by inclusion in the Journal of the day for this Plenary.

* * *

Interpretative statement by Germany

With reference to the Russian translation of the Vienna Document 1992 the German delegation draws attention to the fact that for the formulation "Aktivierung/Aktivieren" (in the English original "activation/activate") in paragraph 11.3.2 and in particular in paragraph 11.3.3.2 and subsequent paragraphs, the formulation "razvertyvanie" is proposed in Russian.

The delegation of the Federal Republic of Germany assumes that this Russian translation means, as in all the other language versions, the conversion of armed forces from a non-active (reserve) state to an active state, without necessarily at the same time bringing about combat-readiness. The linguistic problem of the Russian translation of the formulation "activation/activate", which we are interested in solving in a co-operative and constructive fashion, must not lead to application of the measure only when combat-readiness is also brought about. On the contrary it must always take effect as soon as non-active forces become active.

* * *

Interpretative statement by Portugal - European Community

The European Community and its Member States would like to record the importance they attach to the full implementation by all CSCE participating States of the obligations contained in the Vienna Document 1992 on Confidence- and Security-building Measures, and their determination to fulfil these obligations themselves in as forthcoming and transparent a way as possible.

* * *

Interpretative statement by Belarus

The Republic of Belarus and Ukraine note that the amendments to Annex I of the Vienna Document are intended solely to reflect arrangements emerging from the CSCE Council Meeting in Prague on 29 January 1992 and do not constitute a precedent in respect of other CSCE matters.

* * *

LETTER FROM TURKMENISTAN[2]

Dear Mr. Chairman,

I have received the letter of the representative of Ireland, Ambassador Declan Connolly, dated 12 February 1992, addressed to our Government in his capacity as Chairman of the Plenary Meeting of the Negotiations on Confidence- and Security-building Measures, with respect to giving effect to the undertaking in the third paragraph of my Government's Letter of Accession to the CSCE regarding the negotiation of specific provisions on the 1992 Vienna document's geographic scope, of which the content has been fully taken note of.

I would like to confirm, hereby, my Government's agreement to apply all the provisions of the Vienna Document 1992 on the CSBMs. I would also like to emphasize, as a part of this agreement, our readiness to take part in the forthcoming meetings which a revised geographic scope of application of the said document will be negotiated.

My Government reiterates its strong wish, that this issue which we attach great importance, will be finalized in stages with the formal participation of our delegation in the CSBM Negotiations.

In our view, the principles of equality of rights and mutual respect for security interests should play a cardinal role in the revision of the geographic scope of application of the Vienna Document 1990.

The relevant principles of the Helsinki Final Act dealing with the geographic scope of application must constitute the sole guidance to all of us, in taking into consideration this important matter. The zone of application of the CSBMs within the territory of Turkmenistan must be established on the basis of such principles, with specific provisions that will apply in case where our State has a frontier facing or shared with a non-participating State or a zone not covered by CSBMs within the territory of a CSCE participating State.

---

2. Journal No. 315, Annex.

We are in the opinion that the Helsinki Follow-up Meeting which is due to open in March 1992 is the most appropriate occasion to start considering these specific provisions of the zone of application that will apply in the cases of newly participating States.

I kindly request you, Mr. Chairman, to record this letter in the Journal of the day and convey it to the delegations taking part in the CSBM Negotiations in Vienna.

Please accept, Mr. Chairman, the assurances of my highest consideration.

Avdy Kuliev
Minister of Foreign Affairs of Turkmenistan

CSCE HELSINKI DOCUMENT 1992: THE CHALLENGES OF CHANGE

Helsinki, 10 July 1992

Helsinki Summit Declaration

Promises and problems of change

1. We, the Heads of State or Government of the States participating in the Conference on Security and Co-operation in Europe, have returned to the birthplace of the Helsinki process, to give new impetus to our common endeavour.

2. The Charter of Paris for a New Europe, signed at the last Summit, defined a common democratic foundation, established institutions for co-operation and set forth guidelines for realization of a community of free and democratic States from Vancouver to Vladivostok.

3. We have witnessed the end of the cold war, the fall of totalitarian regimes and the demise of the ideology on which they were based. All our countries now take democracy as the basis for their political, social and economic life. The CSCE has played a key role in these positive changes. Still, the legacy of the past remains strong. We are faced with challenges and opportunities, but also with serious difficulties and disappointments.

4. We have met here to review recent developments, to consolidate the achievements of the CSCE and to set its future direction. To meet new challenges we are approving here today a programme to enhance our capabilities for concerted action and to intensify our co-operation for democracy, prosperity and equal rights of security.

5. The aspirations of peoples freely to determine their internal and external political status have led to the spread of democracy and have recently found expression in the emergence of a number of sovereign States. Their full participation brings a new dimension to the CSCE.

6. We welcome the commitment of all participating States to our shared values. Respect for human rights and fundamental freedoms, including the rights of persons belonging to national minorities, democracy, the rule of law, economic liberty, social justice and environmental

responsibility are our common aims. They are immutable. Adherence to our commitments provides the basis for participation and co-operation in the CSCE and a cornerstone for further development of our societies.

7. We reaffirm the validity of the guiding principles and common values of the Helsinki Final Act and the Charter of Paris, embodying responsibilities of States towards each other and of governments towards their people. These are the collective conscience of our community. We recognize our accountability to each other for complying with them. We underline the democratic rights of citizens to demand from their governments respect for these values and standards.

8. We emphasize that the commitments undertaken in the field of the human dimension of the CSCE are matters of direct and legitimate concern to all participating States and do not belong exclusively to the internal affairs of the State concerned. The protection and promotion of human rights and fundamental freedoms and the strengthening of democratic institutions continue to be a vital basis for our comprehensive security.

9. The transition to and development of democracy and market economy by the new democracies is being carried forward with determination amidst difficulties and varying conditions. We offer our support and solidarity to participating States undergoing transformation to democracy and market economy. We welcome their efforts to become fully integrated into the wider community of States. Making this transition irreversible will ensure the security and prosperity of us all.

10. Encouragement of this sense of wider community remains one of our fundamental goals. We welcome in this connection the rapid adaptation of European and transatlantic institutions and organizations which are increasingly working together to face up to the challenges before us and to provide a solid foundation for peace and prosperity.

The European Community (EC), fulfilling its important role in the political and economic development of Europe, is moving towards a union and has decided to broaden its membership. It is closely involved in CSCE activities.

The North Atlantic Treaty Organization (NATO), one of the essential transatlantic links, has adopted a new strategic concept and strengthened its role as an integral aspect for security in Europe. Through establishment of the North Atlantic Co-operation Council (NACC) it has established patterns of co-operation with new partners in harmony with the goals of the CSCE. It has also offered practical support for the work of the CSCE.

The Western European Union (WEU) is an integral part of the development of the European Union; it is also the means to strengthen the European pillar of the Atlantic Alliance; it is developing an operational capacity; it is opening itself to additional co-operation with new partners and has offered to provide resources in support of the CSCE.

The Council of Europe is elaborating its own programmes for new democracies, opening up to new members and is co-operating with the CSCE in the human dimension.

The Group of Seven and the Group of Twenty-Four are deeply engaged in assistance to countries in transition.

The Organisation for Economic Co-operation and Development (OECD), United Nations Economic Commission for Europe (ECE) and the European Bank for Reconstruction and Development (EBRD) have a key role to play in the construction of a new Europe.

The Commonwealth of Independent States (CIS) has stated its readiness to assist the CSCE in pursuit of its objectives.

These and the other forms of regional and sub-regional co-operation which continue to develop, such as the Council of the Baltic Sea States, the Visegrad Triangle, the Black Sea Economic Co-operation and the Central European Initiative, multiply the links uniting CSCE participating States.

11. We welcome the adoption of the Vienna 1992 Document on Confidence- and Security-building Measures and the signature of the Treaty on Open Skies, with the adoption of the Declaration on the Treaty on Open Skies. We also welcome the imminent entry into force of the Treaty on Conventional Armed Forces in Europe (CFE) and the Concluding Act of the Negotiation on Personnel Strength of Conventional Armed Forces in Europe. These agreements provide a solid foundation for our further security co-operation. We welcome the recent United States-Russian joint understanding on Strategic Offensive Arms. We reaffirm our commitment to become original signatories to the forthcoming convention on the prohibition of the development, production, stockpiling and use of chemical weapons and on their destruction, and urge other States to do so.

12. This is a time of promise but also a time of instability and insecurity. Economic decline, social tension, aggressive nationalism, intolerance, xenophobia and ethnic conflicts threaten stability in the CSCE area. Gross violations of CSCE commitments in the field of human rights

and fundamental freedoms, including those related to national minorities, pose a special threat to the peaceful development of society, in particular in new democracies.

There is still much work to be done in building democratic and pluralistic societies, where diversity is fully protected and respected in practice. Consequently, we reject racial, ethnic and religious discrimination in any form. Freedom and tolerance must be taught and practised.

13. For the first time in decades we are facing warfare in the CSCE region. New armed conflicts and massive use of force to achieve hegemony and territorial expansion continue to occur. The loss of life, human misery, involving huge numbers of refugees have been the worst since the Second World War. Damage to our cultural heritage and the destruction of property have been appalling.

Our community is deeply concerned by these developments. Individually and jointly within the CSCE and the United Nations and other international organizations, we have sought to alleviate suffering and seek long-term solutions to the crises which have arisen.

With the Helsinki decisions, we have put in place a comprehensive programme of co-ordinated action which will provide additional tools for the CSCE to address tensions before violence erupts and to manage crises which may regrettably develop. The Council and the Committee of Senior Officials have already established for the CSCE an important role in dealing with crises which have developed within our area.

No international effort can be successful if those engaged in conflicts do not reaffirm their will to seek peaceful solutions to their differences. We stress our determination to hold parties to conflicts accountable for their actions.

14. In times of conflict the fulfilment of basic human needs is most at risk. We will exert every effort to ensure that they are met and that humanitarian commitments are respected. We will strive to relieve suffering by humanitarian cease-fires and to facilitate the delivery of assistance under international supervision, including its safe passage. We recognize that the refugee problems resulting from these conflicts require the co-operation of all of us. We express our support for and solidarity with those countries which bear the brunt of the refugee problems resulting from these conflicts. In this context we recognize the need for co-operation and concerted action.

15. Even where violence has been contained, the sovereignty and independence of some States still needs to be upheld. We express support for efforts by CSCE participating States to remove, in a peaceful manner and through negotiations, the problems that remain from the past, like the stationing of foreign armed forces on the territories of the Baltic States without the required consent of those countries.

    Therefore, in line with basic principles of international law and in order to prevent any possible conflict, we call on the participating States concerned to conclude, without delay, appropriate bilateral agreements, including timetables, for the early, orderly and complete withdrawal of such foreign troops from the territories of the Baltic States.

16. The degradation of the environment over many years threatens us all. The danger of nuclear accidents is a pressing concern. So are, in several parts of the CSCE area, defence-related hazards for the environment.

17. The present proliferation of weapons increases the danger of conflict and is an urgent challenge. Effective export controls on nuclear materials, conventional weapons and other sensitive goods and technologies are a pressing need.

The CSCE and the management of change

18. The CSCE has been instrumental in promoting changes; now it must adapt to the task of managing them. Our decisions in Helsinki are making the CSCE more operational and effective. We are determined to fully use consultations and concerted action to enable a common response to the challenges facing us.

19. In approaching these tasks, we emphasize the central role of the CSCE in fostering and managing change in our region. In this era of transition, the CSCE is crucial to our efforts to forestall aggression and violence by addressing the root causes of problems and to prevent, manage and settle conflicts peacefully by appropriate means.

20. To this end, we have further developed structures to ensure political management of crises and created new instruments of conflict prevention and crisis management. We have strengthened the Council and the Committee of Senior Officials (CSO) and devised means to assist them. The CSCE capacities in the field of early warning will be

strengthened in particular by the activities of the newly established High Commissioner on National Minorities.

We have provided for CSCE peacekeeping according to agreed modalities. CSCE peacekeeping activities may be undertaken in cases of conflict within or among participating States to help maintain peace and stability in support of an ongoing effort at a political solution. In this respect, we are also prepared to seek, on a case-by-case basis, the support of international institutions and organizations, such as the EC, NATO and WEU, as well as other institutions and mechanisms, including the peacekeeping mechanism of the CIS. We welcome their readiness to support CSCE peacekeeping activities, including by making available their resources.

We are further developing our possibilities for peaceful settlement of disputes.

21. Our approach is based on our comprehensive concept of security as initiated in the Final Act. This concept relates the maintenance of peace to the respect for human rights and fundamental freedoms. It links economic and environmental solidarity and co-operation with peaceful inter-State relations. This is equally valid in managing change as it was necessary in mitigating confrontation.

22. The CSCE is a forum for dialogue, negotiation and co-operation, providing direction and giving impulse to the shaping of the new Europe. We are determined to use it to give new impetus to the process of arms control, disarmament and confidence- and security-building, to the enhancement of consultation and co-operation on security matters and to furthering the process of reducing the risk of conflict. In this context, we will also consider new steps to further strengthen norms of behaviour on politico-military aspects of security. We will ensure that our efforts in these fields are coherent, interrelated and complementary.

23. We remain convinced that security is indivisible. No State in our CSCE community will strengthen its security at the expense of the security of other States. This is our resolute message to States which resort to the threat or use of force to achieve their objectives in flagrant violation of CSCE commitments.

24. Essential to the success of our efforts to foster democratic change within the CSCE framework will be increased co-operation with other European and transatlantic organizations and institutions. Therefore, we are convinced that a lasting and peaceful order for our community

of States will be built on mutually reinforcing institutions, each with its own area of action and responsibility.

25. Reaffirming the commitments to the Charter of the United Nations as subscribed to by our states, we declare our understanding that the CSCE is a regional arrangement in the sense of Chapter VIII of the Charter of the United Nations. As such, it provides an important link between European and global security. The rights and responsibilities of the Security Council remain unaffected in their entirety. The CSCE will work together closely with the United Nations especially in preventing and settling conflicts.

26. We restate our unreserved condemnation of all acts, methods and practices of terrorism. We are determined to enhance our co-operation to eliminate this threat to security, democracy and human rights. To this end, we will take measures to prevent in our territories criminal activities that support acts of terrorism in other States. We will encourage exchange of information concerning terrorist activities. We will seek further effective avenues for co-operation as appropriate. We will also take the necessary steps at a national level to fulfil our international obligations in this field.

27. Illicit trafficking in drugs represents a danger to the stability of our societies and democratic institutions. We will act together to strengthen all forms of bilateral and multilateral co-operation in the fight against illicit trafficking in drugs and other forms of international organized crime.

28. We will work to reinforce the close link which exists between political pluralism and the operation of a market economy. Enhanced co-operation in the field of economy, science and technology has a crucial role to play in strengthening security and stability in the CSCE region.

29. Economic co-operation remains an essential element of the CSCE. We will continue to support the transformations under way to introduce market economies as the means to enhance economic performance and increased integration into the international economic and financial systems.

30. We will also facilitate expanded economic co-operation which must take account of the prevailing political and economic conditions. We welcome the contribution of economic, financial and technical assistance programmes of the Group of Seven and the Group of

Twenty-Four to the transition process. In the framework of our co-operation we fully support the further development of the European Energy Charter which is of particular importance in the period of transition.

31. We will work together to help facilitate means of transportation and communication in order to deepen co-operation among us.

32. We renew our commitment to co-operate in protecting and improving the environment for present and future generations. We stress in particular the importance of co-operation to effectively ensure the safety of nuclear installations and to bring defence-related hazards for the environment under control.

We emphasize the need for greater public awareness and understanding of environmental issues and for public involvement in the planning and decision-making process.

We welcome the important outcome of the United Nations Conference on Environment and Development (UNCED) held in Rio de Janeiro in June 1992. We emphasize the need for effective and sustained implementation of UNCED decisions.

33. Further steps must be taken to stop the proliferation of weapons. It remains vital to ensure non-proliferation of nuclear weapons and the relevant technology and expertise. We urge all States which have not acceded to the Treaty on Non-proliferation of Nuclear Weapons to do so as non-nuclear weapons States and to conclude safeguards agreements with the International Atomic Energy Agency (IAEA). We commit ourselves to intensify our co-operation in the field of effective export controls applicable to nuclear materials, conventional weapons and other sensitive goods and technologies.

34. We welcome the development of regional co-operation among CSCE participating States as a valuable means of promoting pluralistic structures of stability. Based on the CSCE principles and commitments, regional co-operative activities serve the purpose of uniting us and promoting comprehensive security.

35. We encourage wide-ranging transfrontier co-operation, including human contacts, involving local and regional communities and authorities. This co-operation contributes to overcoming economic and social inequalities and enhancing ethnic understanding, fostering good-neighbourly relations among States and peoples.

36. In order to ensure full participation and co-operation by recently admitted participating States we are initiating a programme of co-ordinated support.

37. We reaffirm our conviction that strengthening security and co-operation in the Mediterranean is important for stability in the CSCE region. We recognize that the changes which have taken place in Europe are relevant to the Mediterranean region and that, conversely, economic, social, political and security developments in that region have a direct bearing on Europe.

38. We will therefore widen our co-operation and enlarge our dialogue with the non-participating Mediterranean States as a means to promote social and economic development, thereby enhancing stability in the region, in order to narrow the prosperity gap between Europe and its Mediterranean neighbours and protect the Mediterranean ecosystems. We stress the importance of intra-Mediterranean relations and the need for increased co-operation within the region.

39. We welcome and encourage the continuation of initiatives and negotiations aimed at finding just, lasting and viable solutions, through peaceful means, to the outstanding crucial problems of the Mediterranean region.

40. We have expanded dialogue with non-participating States, inviting them to take part in our activities on a selective basis when they can make a contribution.

41. We welcome the establishment of the CSCE Parliamentary Assembly which held its first meeting in Budapest on 3 to 5 July and look forward to the active participation of parliamentarians in the CSCE process.

42. We attach particular importance to the active involvement of our publics in the CSCE. We will expand the opportunities for contributions by and co-operation with individuals and non-governmental organizations in our work.

43. In order to foster our partnership, and to better manage change, we have today in Helsinki adopted an agenda for a strengthened and effective CSCE through the Helsinki Decisions. These decisions will be implemented fully and in good faith.

44. We entrust the Council with the further steps which may be required to implement them. The Council may adopt any amendment to the decisions which it may deem appropriate.

45. The full text of the Helsinki Document will be published in each participating State, which will make it known as widely as possible.

46. The Government of Finland is requested to transmit to the Secretary-General of the United Nations the text of the Helsinki Document, which is not eligible for registration under Article 102 of the Charter of the United Nations, with a view to this circulation to all the members of the Organization as an official document of the United Nations.

47. The next review conference will be held in Budapest in 1994 on the basis of modalities of the Helsinki Follow-up Meeting, *mutatis mutandis*, to be further specified by the CSO which may decide to organize a special preparatory meeting.

Helsinki, 10 July 1992

Helsinki Decisions

I

STRENGTHENING CSCE INSTITUTIONS AND STRUCTURES

(1) In order to enhance the coherence of their consultations and the efficiency of their concerted action based on their joint political will, as well as to further develop the practical aspects of co-operation among them, the participating States have decided to reaffirm and develop the decisions on CSCE structures and institutions set forth in the Charter of Paris and the Prague Document on Further Development of CSCE Institutions and Structures.

To this end, they have agreed as follows:

Meetings of Heads of State or Government

(2) Meetings of Heads of State or Government, as laid down in the Charter of Paris, will take place, as a rule, every two years on the occasion of review conferences.

(3) They will set priorities and provide orientation at the highest political level.

Review conferences

(4) Review conferences will precede the meetings of Heads of State or Government. They will be operational and of short duration. They will:

- review the entire range of activities within the CSCE, including a thorough implementation debate, and consider further steps to strengthen the CSCE process;
- prepare a decision-oriented document to be adopted at the meeting.

(5) Preparation of review conferences, including the agenda and modalities, will be carried out by the Committee of Senior Officials (CSO), which may decide to organize a special preparatory meeting.

CSCE Council

(6) The Council constitutes the central decision-making and governing body of the CSCE.

(7) The Council will ensure that the various CSCE activities relate closely to the central political goals of the CSCE.

(8) The participating States have agreed to enhance the working methods of the Council and promote effective consultations at its meetings.

Committee of Senior Officials

(9) Further to the decisions contained in the Charter of Paris and as set forth in the Prague Document, the CSO, between the meetings of the CSCE Council, will be responsible for overview, management and co-ordination and will act as the Council's agent in taking appropriate decisions. Additional responsibilities are described in Chapter III of this document.

(10) Greater use will be made of the points of contact and communications network in order to manage the flow of information more efficiently.

(11) The functions of the CSO convening as the Economic Forum are set out in Chapter VII of this document.

Chairman-in-Office

(12) The Chairman-in-Office will be responsible on behalf of the Council/CSO for the co-ordination of and consultation on current CSCE business.

(13) The Chairman-in-Office will be requested to communicate Council and CSO decisions to the CSCE institutions and to give them such advice regarding those decisions as may be required.

(14) In carrying out entrusted tasks, the Chairman-in-Office may be assisted, *inter alia*, by:
- the preceding and succeeding Chairmen, operating together as a Troika;
- *ad hoc* steering groups;
- personal representatives, if necessary.

Assistance to the Chairman-in-Office

Troika

(15) The Chairman-in-Office may be assisted by the preceding and succeeding Chairmen, operating together as a Troika, in carrying out entrusted tasks. The Chairman-in-Office will retain the responsibility for such tasks and for reporting on Troika activities to the Council/CSO.

Ad hoc steering groups

(16) *Ad hoc* steering groups may be established on a case-by-case basis in order to further assist the Chairman-in-Office, in particular in the field of conflict prevention, crisis management and dispute resolution.

(17) The decision of the Council/CSO to establish an *ad hoc* steering group will, in principle, be taken upon recommendation of the Chairman-in-Office and will include a description of its composition and mandate which will set out the specific tasks and objectives and specify the duration.

(18) If the matter is urgent, the Chairman-in-Office may consult the participating States to propose the establishment of an *ad hoc* steering group under a silence procedure. If objections to the proposal are voiced within five days and if further consultations by the Chairman-in-Office have not led to consensus, the CSO must address the question.

(19) In order to ensure efficiency, an *ad hoc* steering group will be composed of a restricted number of participating States which will include the Troika. Its composition and size will be decided taking into account the need for impartiality and efficiency.

(20) The council/CSO may decide to terminate or extend for a specific period of time the term of the activities of an *ad hoc* steering group as well as to amend the mandate, composition and instructions given to a steering group.

(21) The Chairman-in-Office will report comprehensively and on a regular basis to the CSO on the activities of the *ad hoc* steering group and on related developments.

Personal representatives

(22) When dealing with a crisis or a conflict, the Chairman-in-Office may, on his/her own responsibility, designate a personal representative with a clear and precise mandate in order to provide support. The Chairman-in-Office will inform the CSO of the intention to appoint a personal representative and of the mandate. In reports to the Council/CSO, the Chairman will include information on the activities of the personal representative as well as any observations or advice submitted by the latter.

High Commissioner on National Minorities

(23) The Council will appoint a High Commissioner on National Minorities. The High Commissioner provides 'early warning' and, as appropriate, 'early action' at the earliest possible stage in regard to tensions involving national minority issues that have the potential to develop into a conflict within the CSCE area, affecting peace, stability, or relations between participating States. The High Commissioner will draw upon the facilities of the Office for Democratic Institutions and Human Rights (ODIHR) in Warsaw.

Other institutions and structures

(24) Further to the Charter of Paris and the Prague Document, additional functions of the other CSCE institutions and structures are described in Chapters II, III, IV, V and VI of this document.

(25) The participating States mandate the CSO to study ways and means which would enable the three CSCE institutional arrangements to better accomplish their functions. In this regard they will consider the relevance of an agreement granting an internationally recognized status to the CSCE Secretariat, the Conflict Prevention Centre (CPC) and the ODIHR.

Implementation reviews

(26) Thorough review of the implementation of CSCE commitments will continue to play a prominent role in CSCE activities, thus enhancing co-operation among participating States.

(27) Reviews of implementation will be held regularly at review conferences as well as at special meetings convened for this purpose at

the ODIHR and the CPC, and when the CSO convenes as the Economic Forum as provided for in the relevant CSCE documents.

(28) These reviews of implementation will be of a co-operative nature, comprehensive in scope and at the same time able to address specific issues.

(29) The participating States will be invited to offer contributions on their implementation experience, with particular reference to difficulties encountered, and to provide their views of implementation throughout the CSCE area. Participating States are encouraged to circulate descriptions of contributions in advance of the meeting.

(30) Reviews should offer the opportunity to identify action which may be required to address problems. Meetings at which reviews of implementation take place may draw to the attention of the CSO any suggestions for measures to improve implementation which they deem advisable.

Communications

(31) The CSCE communications network is an important instrument for the implementation of the Vienna Document 1992 and other documents and agreements. As the CSCE's capacity to deal with emergency situations is being developed, the network is assuming a new and vital role in providing the participating States with up-to-date means for urgent communications. In this respect, it is essential that all participating states be connected to the system. The Consultative Committee of the CPC will monitor progress and, if necessary, recommend solutions for technical problems.

II

CSCE HIGH COMMISSIONER ON NATIONAL MINORITIES

(1) The participating States decide to establish a High Commissioner on National Minorities.

Mandate

(2) The High Commissioner will act under the aegis of the CSO and will thus be an instrument of conflict prevention at the earliest possible stage.

(3) The High Commissioner will provide 'early warning' and, as appropriate, 'early action' at the earliest possible stage in regard to tensions involving national minority issues which have not yet developed beyond an early warning stage, but, in the judgement of the High Commissioner, have the potential to develop into a conflict within the CSCE area, affecting peace, stability or relations between participating States, requiring the attention of and action by the Council or the CSO.

(4) Within the mandate, based on CSCE principles and commitments, the High Commissioner will work in confidence and will act independently of all parties directly involved in the tensions.

(5a) The High Commissioner will consider national minority issues occurring in the State of which the High Commissioner is a national or a resident, or involving a national minority to which the High Commissioner belongs, only if all parties directly involved agree, including the State concerned.

(5b) The High Commissioner will not consider national minority issues in situations involving organized acts of terrorism.

(5c) Nor will the High Commissioner consider violations of CSCE commitments with regard to an individual person belonging to a national minority.

(6) In considering a situation, the High Commissioner will take fully into account the availability of democratic means and international instruments to respond to it, and their utilization by the parties involved.

(7) When a particular national minority issue has been brought to the attention of the CSO, the involvement of the High Commissioner will require a request and a specific mandate from the CSO.

Profile, appointment, support

(8) The High Commissioner will be an eminent international personality with long-standing relevant experience from whom an impartial performance of the function may be expected.

(9) The High Commissioner will be appointed by the Council by consensus upon the recommendation of the CSO for a period of three years, which may be extended for one further term of three years only.

(10) The High Commissioner will draw upon the facilities of the ODIHR in Warsaw, and in particular upon the information relevant to all aspects of national minority questions available at the ODIHR.

Early warning

(11) The High Commissioner will:

(11a) collect and receive information regarding national minority issues from sources described below (see Supplement paragraphs (23)-(25));

(11b) assess at the earliest possible stage the role of the parties directly concerned, the nature of the tensions and recent developments therein and, where possible, the potential consequences for peace and stability within the CSCE area;

(11c) to this end, be able to pay a visit, in accordance with paragraph (17) and Supplement paragraphs (27)-(30), to any participating State and communicate in person, subject to the provisions of paragraph (25), with parties directly concerned to obtain first-hand information about the situation of national minorities.

(12) The High Commissioner may during a visit to a participating State, while obtaining first-hand information from all parties directly involved, discuss the questions with the parties, and where appropriate promote dialogue, confidence and co-operation between them.

Provision of early warning

(13) If, on the basis of exchanges of communications and contacts with relevant parties, the High Commissioner concludes that there is a *prima facie* risk of potential conflict (as set out in paragraph (3)) he/she may issue an early warning, which will be communicated promptly by the Chairman-in-Office to the CSO.

(14) The Chairman-in-Office will include this early warning in the agenda for the next meeting of the CSO. If a State believes that such an early warning merits prompt consultation, it may initiate the procedure set

out in Annex 2 of the Summary of Conclusions of the Berlin Meeting of the Council ('Emergency Mechanism').

(15) The High Commissioner will explain to the CSO the reasons for issuing the early warning.

Early action

(16) The High Commissioner may recommend that he/she be authorized to enter into further contact and closer consultations with the parties concerned with a view to possible solutions, according to a mandate to be decided by the CSO. The CSO may decide accordingly.

Accountability

(17) The High Commissioner will consult the Chairman-in-Office prior to a departure for a participating State to address a tension involving national minorities. The Chairman-in-Office will consult, in confidence, the participating State(s) concerned and may consult more widely.

(18) After a visit to a participating State, the High Commissioner will provide strictly confidential reports to the Chairman-in-Office on the findings and progress of the High Commissioner's involvement in a particular question.

(19) After termination of the involvement of the High Commissioner in a particular issue, the High Commissioner will report to the Chairman-in-Office on the findings, results and conclusions. Within a period of one month, the Chairman-in-Office will consult, in confidence, on the findings, results and conclusions the participating State(s) concerned and may consult more widely. Thereafter the report, together with possible comments, will be transmitted to the CSO.

(20) Should the High Commissioner conclude that the situation is escalating into a conflict, or if the High Commissioner deems that the scope for action by the High Commissioner is exhausted, the High Commissioner shall, through the Chairman-in-Office, so inform the CSO.

(21) Should the CSO become involved in a particular issue, the High Commissioner will provide information and, on request, advice to the CSO, or to any other institution or organization which the CSO may

invite, in accordance with the provisions of Chapter III of this document, to take action with regard to the tensions or conflict.

(22) The High Commissioner, if so requested by the CSO and with due regard to the requirement of confidentiality in his/her mandate, will provide information about his/her activities at CSCE implementation meetings on Human Dimension issues.

Supplement

Sources of information about national minority issues

(23) The High Commissioner may:

(23a) collect and receive information regarding the situation of national minorities and the role of parties involved therein from any source, including the media and non-governmental organizations with the exception referred to in paragraph (25);

(23b) receive specific reports from parties directly involved regarding developments concerning national minority issues. These may include reports on violations of CSCE commitments with respect to national minorities as well as other violations in the context of national minority issues.

(24) Such specific reports to the High Commissioner should meet the following requirements:

- they should be in writing, addressed to the High Commissioner as such and signed with full names and addresses;
- they should contain a factual account of the developments which are relevant to the situation of persons belonging to national minorities and the role of the parties involved therein, and which have taken place recently, in principle not more than 12 months previously. The reports should contain information which can be sufficiently substantiated.

(25) The High Commissioner will not communicate with and will not acknowledge communications from any person or organization which practises or publicly condones terrorism or violence.

Parties directly concerned

(26) Parties directly concerned in tensions who can provide specific reports to the High Commissioner and with whom the High Commissioner will seek to communicate in person during a visit to a participating State are the following:

(26a) governments of participating States, including, if appropriate, regional and local authorities in areas in which national minorities reside;

(26b) representatives of associations, non-governmental organizations, religious and other groups of national minorities directly concerned and in the area of tension, which are authorized by the persons belonging to those national minorities to represent them.

Conditions for travel by the High Commissioner

(27) Prior to an intended visit, the High Commissioner will submit to the participating State concerned specific information regarding the intended purpose of that visit. Within two weeks the State(s) concerned will consult with the High Commissioner on the objectives of the visit, which may include the promotion of dialogue, confidence and co-operation between the parties. After entry the State concerned will facilitate free travel and communication of the High Commissioner subject to the provisions of paragraph (25) above.

(28) If the State concerned does not allow the High Commissioner to enter the country and to travel and communicate freely, the High Commissioner will so inform the CSO.

(29) In the course of such a visit, subject to the provision of paragraph (25) the High Commissioner may consult the parties involved, and may receive information in confidence from any individual, group or organization directly concerned on questions the High Commissioner is addressing. The High Commissioner will respect the confidential nature of the information.

(30) The participating States will refrain from taking any action against persons, organizations or institutions on account of their contact with the High Commissioner.

High Commissioner and involvement of experts

(31) The High Commissioner may decide to request assistance from not more than three experts with relevant expertise in specific matters on which brief, specialized investigation and advice are required.

(32) If the High Commissioner decides to call on experts, the High Commissioner will set a clearly defined mandate and time-frame for the activities of the experts.

(33) Experts will only visit a participating State at the same time as the High Commissioner. Their mandate will be an integral part of the mandate of the High Commissioner and the same conditions for travel will apply.

(34) The advice and recommendations requested from the experts will be submitted in confidence to the High Commissioner, who will be responsible for the activities and for the reports of the experts and who will decide whether and in what form the advice and recommendations will be communicated to the parties concerned. They will be non-binding. If the High Commissioner decides to make the advice and recommendations available, the State(s) concerned will be given the opportunity to comment.

(35) The experts will be selected by the High Commissioner with the assistance of the ODIHR from the resource list established at the ODIHR as laid down in the Document of the Moscow Meeting.

(36) The experts will not include nationals or residents of the participating State concerned, or any person appointed by the State concerned, or any expert against whom the participating State has previously entered reservations. The experts will not include the participating State's own nationals or residents or any of the persons it appointed to the resource list, or more than one national or resident of any particular State.

Budget

(37) A separate budget will be determined at the ODIHR, which will provide, as appropriate, logistical support for travel and communication. The budget will be funded by the participating States according to the established CSCE scale of distribution. Details will be worked out by the Financial Committee and approved by the CSO.

III

Early Warning, Conflict Prevention and Crisis Management (including Fact-finding and Rapporteur Missions and CSCE Peacekeeping), Peaceful Settlement of Disputes

Early warning, conflict prevention and crisis management (including fact-finding and rapporteur missions and CSCE peacekeeping)

(1) The participating States have decided to strengthen the structure of their political consultations and increase their frequency, and to provide for more flexible and active dialogue and better early warning and dispute settlement, resulting in a more effective role in conflict prevention and resolution, complemented, when necessary, by peacekeeping operations.

(2) The participating States have decided to enhance their capability to identify the root causes of tensions through a more rigorous review of implementation to be conducted both through the ODIHR and the CPC. They have also decided to improve their capability to gather information and to monitor developments, as well as their ability to implement decisions about further steps. They have recommitted themselves to co-operating constructively in using the full range of possibilities within the CSCE to prevent and resolve conflicts.

Early warning and preventive action

(3) In order to have early warning of situations within the CSCE area which have the potential to develop into crises, including armed conflicts, the participating States will make intensive use of regular, in-depth political consultations, within the structures and institutions of the CSCE, including implementation review meetings.

(4) The CSO, acting as the Council's agent, will have primary responsibility in this regard.

(5) Without prejudice to the right of any State to raise any issue, the attention of the CSO may be drawn to such situations through the Chairman-in-Office, *inter alia*, by:
- any State directly involved in a dispute;
- a group of 11 States not directly involved in the dispute;

- the High Commissioner on National Minorities in situations he/she deems escalating into a conflict or exceeding the scope of his/her action;
- the Consultative Committee of the CPC in accordance with paragraph 33 of the Prague Document;
- the Consultative Committee of the CPC following the use of the mechanism for consultations and co-operation as regards unusual military activities;
- the use of the Human Dimension Mechanism or the Valletta Principles for Dispute Settlement and Provisions for a CSCE Procedure for Peaceful Settlement of Disputes.

Political management of crisis

(6) The CSO will promote steps by the State or States concerned to avoid any action which could aggravate the situation and, if appropriate, recommend other procedures and mechanisms to resolve the dispute peacefully.

(7) In order to facilitate its consideration of the situation, it may seek independent advice and counsel from relevant experts, institutions and international organizations.

(8) If the CSO concludes that concerted CSCE action is required, it will determine the procedure to be employed in the light of the nature of the situation. It will have, acting on behalf of the Council, overall CSCE responsibility for managing the crisis with a view to its resolution. It may, *inter alia*, decide to set up a framework for a negotiated settlement, or to dispatch a rapporteur or fact-finding mission. The CSO may also initiate or promote the exercise of good offices, mediation or conciliation.

(9) In this context the CSO may delegate tasks to:

- the Chairman-in-Office, who may designate a personal representative to carry out certain tasks, as defined in paragraph (22) of Chapter I of this document;
- the Chairman-in-Office, assisted by the preceding and succeeding Chairmen-in-Office operating together as a Troika, as defined in paragraph (15) of Chapter I of this document;
- an *ad hoc* steering group of participating States, as defined in paragraphs (16) to (21) of Chapter I of this document;
- the Consultative Committee of the CPC, or other CSCE institutions.

(10) Once the CSO has determined the procedure to be applied, it will establish a precise mandate for action, including provisions for reporting back within an agreed period. Within the limits of that mandate, those to whom the CSO has delegated tasks under the preceding paragraph will retain the freedom to determine how to proceed, with whom to consult, and the nature of any recommendations to be made.

(11) All participating States concerned in the situation will fully co-operate with the CSO and the agents it has designated.

Instruments of conflict prevention and crisis management

FACT-FINDING AND RAPPORTEUR MISSIONS

(12) Fact-finding and rapporteur missions can be used as an instrument of conflict prevention and crisis management.

(13) Without prejudice to the provisions of paragraph 13 of the Moscow Document in respect of Human Dimension issues, and paragraph 29 of the Prague Document in respect of Unusual Military Activities, the CSO or the Consultative Committee of the CPC may decide, by consensus, to establish such missions. Such decisions will in every case contain a clear mandate.

(14) The participating State(s) will co-operate fully with the mission on its territory in pursuance of the mandate and facilitate its work.

(15) Reports of fact-finding and rapporteur missions will be submitted for discussion to the CSO or the Consultative Committee of the CPC as applicable. Such reports and any observations submitted by the State(s) visited will remain confidential until they are discussed. The reports will normally be made public. If, however, the mission or the participating State(s) visited request that they should be kept confidential, they will not be made public, unless otherwise decided by the participating States.

(16) Except where provided on a voluntary basis, the expenses of fact-finding and rapporteur missions will be borne by all participating States in accordance with the scale of distribution.

CSCE PEACEKEEPING

(17) Peacekeeping constitutes an important operational element of the overall capability of the CSCE for conflict prevention and crisis management intended to complement the political process of dispute resolution. CSCE peacekeeping activities may be undertaken in cases of conflict within or among participating States to help maintain peace and stability in support of an ongoing effort at a political solution.

(18) A CSCE peacekeeping operation, according to its mandate, will involve civilian and/or military personnel, may range from small-scale to large-scale, and may assume a variety of forms including observer and monitor missions and larger deployments of forces. Peacekeeping activities could be used, *inter alia*, to supervise and help maintain cease-fires, to monitor troop withdrawals, to support the maintenance of law and order, to provide humanitarian and medical aid and to assist refugees.

(19) CSCE peacekeeping will be undertaken with due regard to the responsibilities of the United Nations in this field and will at all times be carried out in conformity with the Purposes and Principles of the Charter of the United Nations. CSCE peacekeeping will take place in particular within the framework of Chapter VIII of the Charter of the United Nations. The CSCE, in planning and carrying out peacekeeping operations, may draw upon the experience and expertise of the United Nations.

(20) The Chairman-in-Office will keep the United Nations Security Council fully informed of CSCE peacekeeping activities.

(21) The Council, or the CSO acting as its agent, may conclude because of the specific character of an operation and its envisaged size that the matter should be referred by the participating States to the United Nations Security Council.

(22) CSCE peacekeeping operations will not entail enforcement action.

(23) Peacekeeping operations require the consent of the parties directly concerned.

(24) Peacekeeping operations will be conducted impartially.

(25) Peacekeeping operations cannot be considered a substitute for a negotiated settlement and therefore must be understood to be limited in time.

(26) Requests to initiate peacekeeping operations by the CSCE may be addressed by one or more participating States to the CSO through the Chairman-in-Office.

(27) The CSO may request the Consultative Committee of the CPC to consider which peacekeeping activities might be most appropriate to the situation and to submit its recommendations to the CSO for decision.

(28) The CSO will exercise overall political control and guidance of a peacekeeping operation.

(29) Decisions to initiate and dispatch peacekeeping operations will be taken by consensus by the Council or the CSO acting as its agent.

(30) The Council/CSO will only take such decisions when all parties concerned have demonstrated their commitment to creating favourable conditions for the execution of the operation, *inter alia*, through a process of peaceful settlement and their willingness to co-operate. Before the decision to dispatch a mission is taken, the following conditions must be fulfilled:

- establishment of an effective and durable cease-fire;
- agreement on the necessary Memoranda of Understanding with the parties concerned, and
- provision of guarantees for the safety at all times of personnel involved.

(31) Missions will be dispatched as soon as possible following such a decision.

(32) Decisions by the CSO to establish a peacekeeping operation will include the adoption of a clear and precise mandate.

(33) When establishing a mission, the CSO will take into account the financial implications involved.

(34) The terms of reference of a peacekeeping operation will define practical modalities and determine requirements for personnel and other resources. Preparation of the terms of reference will be carried

out, as appropriate, by the Consultative Committee of the CPC. They will be adopted by the CSO unless it has agreed otherwise.

(35) All participating States are eligible to take part in CSCE peacekeeping operations. Appropriate consultations by the Chairman-in-Office will take place. Participating States will be invited by the Chairman-in-Office of the CSO to contribute, on an individual basis, to an operation case by case.

(36) Personnel will be provided by individual participating States.

(37) Parties concerned will be consulted about which participating States will contribute personnel to the operation.

(38) The Council/CSO will regularly review an operation and make any necessary decision related to its conduct, taking into account political developments and developments in the field.

Chain of Command

(39) The Council/CSO will assign overall operational guidance of an operation to the Chairman-in-Office assisted by an *ad hoc* group established at the CPC. The Chairman-in-Office will chair the *ad hoc* group and, in this capacity, be accountable to it, and will receive, on behalf of the *ad hoc* group, the reports of the Head of Mission. The *ad hoc* group will, as a rule, consist of representatives of the preceding and succeeding Chairmen-in-Office, of the participating States providing personnel for the mission and of participating States making other significant practical contributions to the operation.

(40) The *ad hoc* group will provide overall operational support for the mission and will monitor it. It will act as a 24-hour point of contact for the Head of Mission and assist the Head of Mission as required.

(41) Continuous liaison between the operation and all participating States will be ensured by the Consultative Committee of the CPC through the regular provision of information to it by the *ad hoc* group.

(42) In all cases where the CSO assigns tasks related to peacekeeping to the CPC, the Consultative Committee of the CPC will be responsible to the CSO for the execution of those tasks.

Head of Mission

(43) The Chairman-in-Office, after appropriate consultations, will nominate a Head of Mission for endorsement by the CSO.

(44) The Head of Mission will be responsible to the Chairman-in-Office. The Head of Mission will consult and be guided by the *ad hoc* group.

(45) The Head of Mission will have operational command in the mission area.

Financial Arrangements

(46) Peacekeeping operations require a sound financial basis and must be planned with maximum efficiency and cost-effectiveness on the basis of clear cost projections.

(47) Costs of CSCE peacekeeping activities will be borne by all CSCE participating States. At the beginning of each calendar year, the CSO will establish a reasonable ceiling for the cost of peacekeeping operations to which the CSCE scale of distribution will be applied. Beyond that limit, other special arrangements will be negotiated and agreed to by consensus. Full and timely payments will be required.

(48) Additional contributions could be provided by participating States on a voluntary basis.

(49) Financial accountability will be ensured by the Chairman-in-Office through regular reports to the participating States.

(50) A start-up fund will, if appropriate, be established to cover the initial costs of an operation. Contributions by a participating State to the start-up fund will be deducted from that State's regular assessed share of the costs relating to the operation.

(51) The Consultative Committee of the CPC is charged to submit to the CSO by the end of 1992 a recommendation with regard to financial modalities of CSCE peacekeeping operations, specifying, *inter alia*, the costs to be shared among participating States in accordance with the preceding paragraphs.

Co-operation with regional and transatlantic organizations

(52) The CSCE may benefit from resources and possible experience and expertise of existing organizations such as the EC, NATO and the WEU, and could therefore request them to make their resources available in order to support it in carrying out peacekeeping activities. Other institutions and mechanisms, including the peacekeeping mechanism of the Commonwealth of Independent States (CIS), may also be asked by the CSCE to support peacekeeping in the CSCE region.

(53) Decisions by the CSCE to seek the support of any such organization will be made on a case-by-case basis, having allowed for prior consultations with the participating States which belong to the organization concerned. The CSCE participating States will also take into account the consultations by the Chairman-in-Office regarding prospective participation in the mission, in light of the envisaged size of the operation and the specific character of the conflict.

(54) Contributions by such organizations will not affect the procedures for the establishment, conduct and command of CSCE peacekeeping operations as set out in paragraphs (17) to (51) above, nor does the involvement of any such organization affect the principle that all participating States are eligible to take part in CSCE peacekeeping operations as set out in paragraph (35) above.

(55) Organizations contributing to CSCE peacekeeping would carry out defined and mutually agreed tasks in connection with the practical implementation of a CSCE mandate.

(56) The *ad hoc* group will establish and maintain effective communication with any organization whose resources may be drawn upon in connection with CSCE peacekeeping activities.

Peaceful settlement of disputes

(57) The participating States consider their commitment to settle disputes among themselves by peaceful means to form a cornerstone of the CSCE process. In their view, the peaceful settlement of disputes is an essential component of the CSCE's overall ability to manage change effectively and to contribute to the maintenance of international peace and security.

(58) The participating States welcome the work done to this end by the Helsinki Follow-up Meeting. In particular they were encouraged by significant progress made on issues relating to creating a conciliation and arbitration court within the CSCE, enhancing the Valletta mechanism and establishing a CSCE procedure for conciliation including directed conciliation, for which proposals were submitted.

(59) In the light of the important subject matter and of the discussions held here in Helsinki, they have decided to continue to develop a comprehensive set of measures to expand the options available within the CSCE to assist States to resolve their disputes peacefully.

(60) In this respect, the Council of Ministers and the CSO could play an important role, in particular by encouraging wider use of conciliation.

(61) Accordingly, intending to reach early results, they have decided to convene a CSCE meeting in Geneva, with a first round from 12 to 23 October 1992, to negotiate a comprehensive and coherent set of measures as mentioned above. They will take into account the ideas expressed regarding procedures for a compulsory element in conciliation, setting up of a court of conciliation and arbitration within the CSCE, and other means.

(62) The results of the meeting will be submitted to the Council of Ministers at the Stockholm Meeting on 14 and 15 December 1992 for approval and, as appropriate, opening for signature.

IV

Relations with International Organizations, Relations with Non-participating States, Role of Non-governmental Organizations (NGOs)

(1) The new tasks before the CSCE require clearer relations and closer contacts with international organizations, in particular with the United Nations, and non-participating States. The CSCE remains at the same time a process whose activities go far beyond formal relations among governments to involve citizens and societies of the participating States. Successful efforts to build a lasting peaceful and democratic order and to manage the process of change require more structured and substantive input from groups, individuals, States and organizations outside the CSCE process.

To this end, the participating States have decided as follows:

Relations with international organizations

(2) The participating States, reaffirming their commitments to the Charter of the United Nations as subscribed to by them, declare their understanding that the CSCE is a regional arrangement in the sense of Chapter VIII of the Charter of the United Nations and as such provides an important link between European and global security. The rights and responsibilities of the United Nations Security Council remain unaffected in their entirety.

(3) Recalling the relevant decisions of the Prague Document, the participating States will improve contact and practical co-operation with appropriate international organizations.

(4) They may accordingly agree to invite presentations by those international organizations and institutions mentioned in the Prague Document and others, as appropriate.

(5) Those organizations, institutions and others as agreed may be invited to attend CSCE meetings and seminars as guests of honour with appropriate name-plates.

(6) They will make full use of the information exchange under paragraph 44 of the Prague Document.

Relations with non-participating Mediterranean States

(7) Recalling the provisions of the Final Act and other CSCE relevant documents and consistent with established practice, the non-participating Mediterranean States will continue to be invited to contribute to CSCE activities.

(8) Measures to widen the scope of co-operation with non-participating Mediterranean States are set forth in Chapter X.

Relations with non-participating States

(9) In accordance with paragraph 45 of the Prague Document, the participating States intend to deepen their co-operation and develop a substantial relationship with non-participating States, such as Japan, which display an interest in the CSCE, share its principles and

objectives, and are actively engaged in European co-operation through relevant organizations.

(10) To this end, Japan will be invited to attend CSCE meetings, including those of Heads of State and Government, the CSCE Council, the Committee of Senior Officials and other appropriate CSCE bodies which consider specific topics of expanded consultation and co-operation.

(11) Representatives of Japan may contribute to such meetings, without participating in the preparation and adoption of decisions, on subjects in which Japan has a direct interest and/or wishes to co-operate actively with the CSCE.

Increasing openness of CSCE activities, promoting understanding of the CSCE, expanding the role of NGOs

(12) The participating States will increase the openness of the CSCE institutions and structures and ensure wide dissemination of information on the CSCE.

(13) To this end:
- the Chairman-in-Office assisted by the CSCE Secretariat will arrange briefings on the political consultation process;
- the CSCE institutions will, within existing budgets, provide information to the public and organize public briefings on their activities;
- the Secretariat will facilitate the flow of information to and contact with the media, bearing in mind that CSCE policy issues remain the responsibility of participating States.

(14) The participating States will provide opportunities for the increased involvement of non-governmental organizations in CSCE activities.

(15) They will, accordingly:
- apply to all CSCE meetings the guidelines previously agreed for NGO access to certain CSCE meetings;
- make open to NGOs all plenary meetings of review conferences, ODIHR seminars, workshops and meetings, the CSO when meeting as the Economic Forum, and human rights implementation meetings, as well as other expert meetings. In addition each meeting may decide to open some other sessions to attendance by NGOs;

- instruct Directors of CSCE institutions and Executive Secretaries of CSCE meetings to designate an 'NGO liaison person' from among their staff;
- designate, as appropriate, one member of their Foreign Ministries and a member of their delegations to CSCE meetings to be responsible for NGO liaison;
- promote contacts and exchanges of views between NGOs and relevant national authorities and governmental institutions between CSCE meetings;
- facilitate during CSCE meetings informal discussion meetings between representatives of participating States and of NGOs;
- encourage written presentations by NGOs to CSCE institutions and meetings, titles of which may be kept and provided to the participating States upon request;
- provide encouragement to NGOs organizing seminars on CSCE-related issues;
- notify NGOs through the CSCE institutions of the dates of future CSCE meetings, together with an indication, when possible, of the subjects to be addressed, as well as, upon request, the activations of CSCE mechanisms which have been made known to all participating States.

(16) The above provisions will not be applied to persons or organizations which resort to the use of violence or publicly condone terrorism or the use of violence.

(17) The participating States will use all appropriate means to disseminate as widely as possible within their societies knowledge of the CSCE, its principles, commitments and activities.

(18) The concept of a CSCE Prize will be considered.

V

CSCE FORUM FOR SECURITY CO-OPERATION

The participating States of the Conference on Security and Co-operation in Europe,

(1) Reaffirming their commitments undertaken in the Charter of Paris for a New Europe and, in particular, their determination to establish new negotiations on disarmament and confidence- and security-building open to all participating States,

(2) Encouraged by the opportunities for the co-operative approaches to strengthening security offered by the historic changes and by the process of consolidation of democracy in the CSCE community of States,

(3) Welcoming the adoption of the Vienna Document 1992 on Confidence- and Security-building Measures, the conclusion of the Treaty on Open Skies and the adoption of the CSCE Declaration on the Treaty on Open skies and the Concluding Act of the Negotiation on Personnel Strength of Conventional Armed Forces in Europe as well as the imminent entry into force of the Treaty on Conventional Armed Forces in Europe (CFE),

(4) Determined to build upon those important achievements and to give a new impetus to arms control, disarmament and confidence- and security-building, security co-operation and conflict prevention in order to better contribute to the strengthening of security and stability and the establishment of a just and lasting peace within the CSCE community of States,

(5) Underlining the equality of rights and the equal respect for the security interests of all CSCE participating States,

(6) Reaffirming their right to choose their own security arrangements,

(7) Recognizing that security is indivisible and that the security of every participating State is inseparably linked to that of all others,

(8) Have decided

- to start a new negotiation on arms control, disarmament and confidence- and security-building,
- to enhance regular consultation and to intensify co-operation among them on matters related to security, and
- to further the process of reducing the risk of conflict.

(9) To carry out these tasks the participating States have decided to establish a new CSCE Forum for Security Co-operation, with a strengthened Conflict Prevention Centre, as an integral part of the CSCE.

(10) The participating States will ensure that their efforts in the Forum towards arms control, disarmament and confidence- and security-

building, security co-operation and conflict prevention are coherent, interrelated and complementary.

Objectives

(11) The participating States will strengthen security and stability through the negotiation of concrete measures aimed at keeping or achieving the levels of armed forces to a minimum commensurate with common or individual legitimate security needs within Europe and beyond. These new measures may entail reductions of and limitations on conventional armed forces and may, as appropriate, include measures of a regional character.

(12) They will address the question of the harmonization of obligations agreed among participating States under the various existing instruments concerning arms control, disarmament and confidence- and security-building.

(13) They will develop the Vienna Document 1992 on the basis of a review of its implementation.

(14) They will negotiate new stabilizing measures in respect of military forces and new confidence- and security-building measures designed to ensure greater transparency in the military field. Such measures may be of a regional character and/or may apply in relation to certain border areas.

* * *

(15) The participating States will aim at establishing among themselves new security relations based upon co-operative and common approaches to security. To this end, they will develop consultation, goal-oriented continuing dialogue and co-operation in the field of security.

(16) They will promote increased predictability about their military plans, programmes and capabilities, including the introduction of major new weapons systems.

(17) They will support and enhance regimes on non-proliferation and arms transfers.

(18) They will enhance contacts, liaison, exchanges and co-operation between their armed forces.

(19) They will promote consultation and co-operation in respect of challenges to their security from outside their territories.

(20) They will also consider other measures to foster security among the participating States in order to contribute to a just and lasting peace among them, including the possibility of further strengthening the norms of behaviour among them through the elaboration of additional security instruments.

* * *

(21) They will make every effort to prevent conflict and give full effect to relevant provisions.

(22) They will further enhance the capability of the CPC to reduce the risks of such conflicts through relevant conflict prevention techniques.

(23) They will foster their co-operation in the field of the implementation and verification of existing and future arms control, disarmament and confidence- and security-building agreements.

* * *

(24) The negotiations on new measures of arms control, disarmament and confidence- and security-building will proceed in distinct phases, taking into account progress made in the implementation of existing arms control agreements. They will also take into consideration ongoing reduction, restructuring and redeployment processes regarding armed forces as well as further relevant political and military developments. Such new measures will build upon the achievements of existing agreements and will be effective, concrete and militarily significant.

(25) All measures negotiated in the Forum will be developed in a way which precludes circumvention.

Programme for immediate action

(26) A Programme for Immediate Action is set out in the Annex. It can be amended, supplemented or extended by consensus. It will be reviewed, together with the progress and results obtained, at the review conference preceding the next meeting of CSCE Heads of State or Government.

(27) Additional proposals can be tabled and discussed at any time.

Area of application

(28) Each measure to be negotiated in the Forum will have an area of application according to its nature. The areas of application for negotiations under the Programme for Immediate Action are set out therein in relation to its relevant elements. This is without prejudice to subsequent negotiations on arms control, disarmament and confidence- and security-building or security co-operation in the Forum. Consideration of decisions concerning the area of application will take into account existing agreements and the need for greater transparency.

Constitution and organization of the forum

(29) The arrangements for the Forum will be as follows:

(30) *The Special Committee* meeting either:
- (a) for negotiations on arms control, disarmament and confidence- and security-building, or
- (b) for consideration of, goal-oriented dialogue on and, as appropriate, elaboration or negotiation of proposals for security enhancement and co-operation.

(31) *The Consultative Committee* in respect of the existing and future tasks of the CPC.

(32) In order to ensure coherence the representation of the participating States on the Special Committee and the Consultative Committee will in principle be assured by the same delegation. Appropriate meetings will be held as necessary for organizational purposes.

Procedures

(33) The Forum will, unless otherwise agreed below, work according to the CSCE procedures.

1. The Special Committee

(34) The Special Committee may establish under its authority subsidiary working bodies open to all participating States. They will work on an *ad referendum* basis and report regularly to the Special Committee.

Any question under consideration by such subsidiary working bodies may at any time be raised before the Special Committee.

(35) Consideration and negotiation of regional measures undertaken within the CSCE framework will form an integral part of the activity of the Forum.

(36) They will be dealt with in open-ended working groups established by the Special Committee.

(37) Alternatively, the Special Committee may decide, on the initiative of a limited number of participating States, and on the basis of information provided by them on the nature and the scope of the measures envisaged, that these States form a working group in order to consider, negotiate or develop among themselves certain regional measures. Such working groups will on a regular basis provide appropriate information on their activities to the Special Committee and will submit to it the results.

(38) Any question under consideration by such working groups may at any time be raised before the Special Committee.

(39) This is without prejudice to the right of States to consider, negotiate or develop measures among themselves outside the framework of the CSCE. In such cases they are invited to inform the Forum about progress and results of their work.

2. The Consultative Committee

(40) The procedures of the Consultative Committee will be based on the relevant decisions of the CSCE Council.

Form of commitments

(41) The results of the negotiations of the Forum will be expressed in international commitments. The nature of obligations will be determined by the character of the measures agreed. They will enter into force in the forms and according to the procedures to be agreed by the negotiators.

Verification

(42) Measures will, if appropriate, be provided with suitable forms of verification according to their nature.

Conference services

(43) Common conference services for the Special Committee and the Consultative Committee as well as for all their subsidiary bodies (including seminars) will be provided by an Executive Secretary to be nominated by the host country. The Executive Secretary may also, if so decided by those concerned, provide conference services for meetings of the CFE Joint Consultative Group and the Open Skies Consultative Commission. The Executive Secretary will assume full responsibility for the organization of all the relevant meetings as well as for all related administrative and budgeting arrangements, for which he will be accountable to the participating States according to procedures to be agreed.

(44) The Special Committee and the Consultative Committee will use the same premises.

(45) The new CSCE Forum for Security Co-operation shall commence in Vienna on 22 September 1992.

Annex

PROGRAMME FOR IMMEDIATE ACTION

(46) The participating States have decided to give early attention to the following:

A. ARMS CONTROL, DISARMAMENT AND CONFIDENCE- AND SECURITY-BUILDING

Measures to be negotiated under paragraphs 1-3 will apply to the territory of the participating States in Europe or in Asia as defined below in relation to the area of application of each measure. Measures to be negotiated under paragraphs 4 and 5 will apply to the conventional armed forces and facilities of the participating States both on the territory of all the participating States and beyond. Measures to be negotiated under paragraph 6 will apply to the territory or part thereof of the participating States involved in the measures. Exceptions to these rules on the area of application may be agreed by consensus.

1. Harmonization of obligations concerning arms control, disarmament and confidence- and security-building

An appropriate harmonization of the obligations of participating States under existing international instruments applicable to conventional armed forces in Europe, in particular of those concerning the exchange of information, verification and force levels. The harmonization of obligations concerning arms control, disarmament and confidence- and security-building will apply to the areas of application in respect of which the obligations have been undertaken.

2. Development of the Vienna Document 1992.

Improvement and further development of confidence- and security-building measures contained in this document. The area of application will be as set out in the Vienna Document 1992.

3. The further enhancement of stability and confidence

The negotiation of new stabilizing measures and confidence-building measures related to conventional armed forces, including, with due regard to the specific characteristics of the armed forces of individual participating States, measures to address force generation capabilities of active and non-active forces. These measures may be of a constraining kind. They will apply within the area of application set out in the Vienna document 1992. This is without prejudice to the possibility that participating States may, if they so choose, decide to offer certain assurances in respect of their conventional armed forces in parts of their territory adjacent to this area of application if they consider such forces relevant to the security of other CSCE participating States.

4. Global exchange of military information

The negotiation of further transparency by means of a global annual appropriately aggregated or disaggregated exchange of information encompassing armaments and equipment, including information on armaments and equipment categories limited by the CFE Treaty, and personnel in the conventional armed forces of the participating States. The regime will also include information on the production of military equipment. The regime will be separate from other information exchange regimes and, because of its special nature, will not involve limitations, constraints or verification.

5. Co-operation in respect of non-proliferation

Co-operation in respect of the strengthening of multilateral non-proliferation regimes, including the transfer of sensitive expertise, and the establishment of a responsible approach to international armaments transfers.

6. Regional measures

The negotiation by the participating States of suitable measures, including, where appropriate, reductions or limitations in accordance with the objectives set out above, for example in relation to certain regions or border areas. The area of application will be the territory or part thereof of the participating States' territories involved in a regional measure.

B. SECURITY ENHANCEMENT AND CO-OPERATION

Proposals for and dialogue on measures and activities under paragraphs 7-12 will apply to all participating States, unless otherwise agreed or specified below.

7. Force planning

The elaboration of provisions to provide transparency about each CSCE participating State's intentions in the medium to long term as regards the size, structure, training and equipment of its armed forces, as well as defence policy, doctrines and budgets related thereto. Such a system should be based on each participating State's national practice, and should provide the background for a dialogue among the participating States.

8. Co-operation in defence conversion

The development of a programme of exchanges, co-operation and the sharing of expertise in the field of defence conversion throughout all the territory of the participating States.

9. Co-operation in respect of non-proliferation

Co-operation in respect of the strengthening of multilateral non-proliferation regimes, including the transfer of sensitive expertise, and the establishment of a responsible approach to international armaments transfers.

10. Development of provisions on military co-operation and contacts

The development of a programme of military contacts, liaison arrangements, co-operation and exchanges, particularly in the fields of the training and organization of armed forces. Participation in this programme will be open to all CSCE participating States in respect of all their armed forces and territory.

11. Regional security issues

Discussion and clarification of regional security issues or specific security problems for example in relation to border areas.

12. Security enhancement consultations

Goal-oriented dialogue and consultations aimed at enhancing security co-operation, including through the further encouragement of responsible and co-operative norms of behaviour on politico-military aspects of security. The participating States will undertake consultations with a view to strengthening the role of the CSCE, by establishing a code of conduct governing their mutual relations in the field of security.

CONFLICT PREVENTION

Consistent with and further to the decisions taken in Paris, Prague and Helsinki about the tasks of the CPC, the following parts of this work programme will be undertaken in the CPC:

13. Relevant techniques

Without prejudice to other tasks of the CPC or to the competence of the Committee of Senior Officials in the field of conflict prevention and crisis management, the Consultative Committee will, particularly in the light of experience gained in the execution of its own tasks, maintain under consideration the need for improvements in relevant techniques.

14. Co-operation in the field of verification

The encouragement of practical co-operation, through training, exchanges and participating in evaluation and inspection teams, in the implementation of the verification provisions of arms control, disarmament and confidence- and security-building agreements among CSCE participants who are parties to such agreements. The area of application will correspond to that of the relevant agreements.

VI

THE HUMAN DIMENSION

(1) The participating States conducted a useful review of implementation of CSCE commitments in the Human Dimension. They based their discussion on the new community of values established among them, as set forth by the Charter of Paris for a New Europe and developed by the new standards created within the CSCE in recent years. They noted major progress in complying with Human Dimension commitments, but recognized developments of serious concern and thus the need for further improvement.

(2) The participating States express their strong determination to ensure full respect for human rights and fundamental freedoms, to abide by the rule of law, to promote the principles of democracy and, in this regard, to build, strengthen and protect democratic institutions, as well as to promote tolerance throughout society. To these ends, they will broaden the operational framework of the CSCE, including by further enhancing the ODIHR, so that information, ideas, and concerns can be exchanged in a more concrete and meaningful way, including as an early warning of tension and potential conflict. In doing so, they will focus their attention on topics in the Human Dimension of particular importance. They will therefore keep the strengthening of the Human Dimension under constant consideration, especially in a time of change.

(3) In this regard, the participating States adopt the following:

Framework for monitoring compliance with CSCE commitments and for promoting co-operation in the human dimension

(4) In order to strengthen and monitor compliance with CSCE commitments as well as to promote progress in the Human Dimension, the participating States agree to enhance the framework of their co-operation and to this end decide the following:

Enhanced role of the ODIHR

(5) Under the general guidance of the CSO and in addition to its existing tasks as set out in the Charter of Paris for a New Europe and in the Prague Document on Further Development of CSCE Institutions and Structures, the ODIHR will, as the main institution of the Human Dimension:

(5a) assist the monitoring of implementation of commitments in the Human Dimension by:

- serving as a venue for bilateral meetings under paragraph 2 and as a channel for information under paragraph 3 of the Human Dimension Mechanism as set out in the Vienna Concluding Document;
- receiving any comments from States visited by CSCE missions of relevance to the Human Dimension other than those under the Human Dimension Mechanism; it will transmit the report of those missions as well as eventual comments to all participating States with a view to discussion at the next implementation meeting or review conference;
- participating in or undertaking missions when instructed by the Council or the CSO;

(5b) act as a clearing-house for information on:

- a state of public emergency according to paragraph 28.10 of the Document of the Moscow Meeting of the Conference on the Human Dimension;
- resource lists, and assistance, e.g. in the field of censuses or on democracy at a local and regional level, and the holding of national seminars on such issues;

(5c) assist other activities in the field of the Human Dimension, including the building of democratic institutions by:

- fulfilling the tasks as defined in the 'Programme of co-ordinated support to recently admitted participating States';
- arranging 'Seminars on the democratic process' at the request of participating States. The same procedural provisions as set out in the 'Programme of co-ordinated support for recently admitted participating States' will also apply to these seminars;
- contributing, within the resources at its disposal, to the preparation of seminars at the request of one or more participating States;

- providing, as appropriate, facilities to the High Commissioner on National Minorities;
- communicating, as appropriate, with relevant international and non-governmental organizations;
- consulting and co-operating with relevant bodies of the Council of Europe and those associated with it, and examining how they can contribute, as appropriate, to the ODIHR's activities. The ODIHR will also, at the request of participating States, supply them with information about programmes within the framework of the Council of Europe which are open to all participating States.

(6) The activities on Human Dimension issues undertaken by the ODIHR may, *inter alia*, contribute to early warning in the prevention of conflicts.

Human dimension mechanism

(7) In order to align the Human Dimension Mechanism with present CSCE structures and institutions the participating States decide that:

Any participating State which deems it necessary may provide information on situations and cases which have been the subject of requests under paragraphs 1 or 2 of the chapter entitled the 'Human Dimension of the CSCE' of the Vienna Concluding Document or on the results of those procedures, to the participating States through the ODIHR — which can equally serve as a venue for bilateral meetings under paragraph 2 — or diplomatic channels. Such information may be discussed at meetings of the CSO, at implementation meetings on Human Dimension issues and review conferences.

(8) Procedures concerning the covering of expenses of expert and rapporteur missions of the Human Dimension Mechanism may be considered by the next review conference in the light of experience gained.

Implementation

Implementation Meetings on Human Dimension Issues

(9) Every year in which a review conference does not take place, the ODIHR will organize a three-weeks meeting at expert-level of all participating States at its seat to review implementation of CSCE

Human Dimension commitments. The meeting will perform the following tasks:

(9a) a thorough exchange of views on the implementation of Human Dimension commitments, including discussion on the information provided in accordance with paragraph 4 of the Human Dimension Mechanism and on the Human Dimension aspects of the reports of CSCE missions, as well as the consideration of ways and means of improving implementation;

(9b) an evaluation of the procedures for monitoring compliance with commitments.

(10) The implementation meeting may draw to the attention of the CSO measures to improve implementation which it deems necessary.

(11) The implementation meeting will not produce a negotiated document.

(12) Written contributions and information material will be of a non-restricted or restricted character as indicated by the submitting State.

(13) Implementation meetings will be organized to meet in formal and informal sessions. All formal sessions will be open. In addition, the participating States may decide, on a case-by-case basis, to open informal sessions.

(14) The Council of Europe, the European Commission for Democracy through Law and the European Bank for Reconstruction and Development (EBRD), as well as other relevant international organizations and institutions, will be encouraged by the implementation meeting to attend and make contributions.

(15) Non-governmental organizations having relevant experience in the field of the Human Dimension are invited to make written presentations to the implementation meeting, e.g. through the ODIHR, and may be invited by the implementation meeting, on the basis of their written presentations, to address specific questions orally as appropriate.

(16) During two half days in the course of the implementation meeting no formal session will be scheduled in order to provide better opportunities for possible contacts with NGOs. To this purpose, a hall at the meeting site will be placed at the disposal of NGOs.

CSCE Human Dimension Seminars

(17) Under the general guidance of the CSO, the ODIHR will organize CSCE Human Dimension seminars which will address specific questions of particular relevance to the Human Dimension and of current political concern. The CSO will establish an annual work programme including the titles and dates of such seminars. The agenda and modalities of each seminar will be approved by the CSO at the latest three months before the seminar. In doing so, the CSO will take into account views expressed by the ODIHR. Unless otherwise decided, seminars will be held at the seat of the ODIHR and will not exceed one week. The work programme will take into account work by relevant international organizations and institutions.

(18) These seminars will be organized in an open and flexible manner. Relevant international organizations and institutions may be invited to attend and to make contributions. So may NGOs with relevant experience. Independent experts attending the seminar as members of national delegations will also be free to speak in their own capacity.

(19) CSCE seminars will be organized to meet in formal and informal sessions. All formal sessions will be open. In addition, the participating States may decide, on a case-by-case basis, to open informal sessions.

(20) CSCE seminars will not produce a negotiated document or follow-up programmes.

(21) Contributions by independent experts will be of a non-restricted character.

(22) In order to launch the new CSCE Human Dimension Seminars without delay, the participating States decide now at the Helsinki Follow-up Meeting that the ODIHR will organize the following four seminars:

- Migration
- Case Studies on National Minorities Issues: Positive Results
- Tolerance
- Free Media

These seminars will be held before 31 December 1993. The agenda and modalities of the seminars will be decided by the CSO. Seminars on migrant workers and on local democracy will be included in the first annual work programme of seminars. The financial implications of the seminar programme will be kept under consideration by the CSO.

Enhanced commitments and co-operation in the human dimension

National minorities

The participating States

(23) Reaffirm in the strongest terms their determination to implement in a prompt and faithful manner all their CSCE commitments, including those contained in the Vienna Concluding Document, the Copenhagen Document and the Geneva Report, regarding questions relating to national minorities and rights of persons belonging to them;

(24) Will intensify in this context their efforts to ensure the free exercise by persons belonging to national minorities, individually or in community with others, of their human rights and fundamental freedoms, including the right to participate fully, in accordance with the democratic decision-making procedures of each State, in the political, economic, social and cultural life of their countries including through democratic participation in decision-making and consultative bodies at the national, regional and local level, *inter alia*, through political parties and associations;

(25) Will continue through unilateral, bilateral and multilateral efforts to explore further avenues for more effective implementation of their relevant CSCE commitments, including those related to the protection and the creation of conditions for the promotion of the ethnic, cultural, linguistic and religious identity of national minorities;

(26) Will address national minority issues in a constructive manner, by peaceful means and through dialogue among all parties concerned on the basis of CSCE principles and commitments;

(27) Will refrain from resettling and condemn all attempts, by the threat or use of force, to resettle persons with the aim of changing the ethnic composition of areas within their territories;

(28) Direct the ODIHR to organize, in spring 1993, a CSCE Human Dimension Seminar on Case Studies on National Minorities Issues: Positive Results.

Indigenous populations

The participating States

(29) Noting that persons belonging to indigenous populations may have special problems in exercising their rights, agree that their CSCE commitments regarding human rights and fundamental freedoms apply fully and without discrimination to such persons.

Tolerance and non-discrimination

The participating States

(30) Express their concern over recent and flagrant manifestations of intolerance, discrimination, aggressive nationalism, xenophobia, anti-semitism and racism and stress the vital role of tolerance, understanding and co-operation in the achievement and preservation of stable democratic societies;

(31) Direct the ODIHR to organize, in autumn 1992, a CSCE Human Dimension Seminar on Tolerance;

(32) Will consider adhering to the International Convention on the Elimination of All Forms of Racial Discrimination, if they have not already done so;

(33) Will consider taking appropriate measures within their constitutional framework and in conformity with their international obligations to assure to everyone on their territory protection against discrimination on racial, ethnic and religious grounds, as well as to protect all individuals, including foreigners, against acts of violence, including on any of these grounds. Moreover, they will make full use of their domestic legal processes, including enforcement of existing laws in this regard;

(34) Will consider developing programmes to create the conditions for promoting non-discrimination and cross-cultural understanding which will focus on human rights education, grass-roots action, cross-cultural training and research;

(35) Reaffirm, in this context, the need to develop appropriate programmes addressing problems of their respective nationals belonging to Roma and other groups traditionally identified as Gypsies and to create

conditions for them to have equal opportunities to participate fully in the life of society, and will consider how to co-operate to this end.

Migrant workers

The participating States

(36) Restate that human rights and fundamental freedoms are universal, that they are also enjoyed by migrant workers wherever they live and stress the importance of implementing all CSCE commitments on migrant workers and their families lawfully residing in the participating States;

(37) Will encourage the creation of conditions to foster greater harmony in relations between migrant workers and the rest of the society of the participating State in which they lawfully reside. To this end, they will seek to offer, *inter alia*, measures to facilitate the familiarization of migrant workers and their families with the languages and social life of the respective participating State in which they lawfully reside so as to enable them to participate in the life of the society of the host country;

(38) Will, in accordance with their domestic policies, laws and international obligations, seek, as appropriate, to create the conditions for promoting equality of opportunity in respect of working conditions, education, social security and health services, housing, access to trade unions as well as cultural rights for lawfully residing and working migrant workers.

Refugees and displaced persons

The participating States

(39) Express their concern over the problem of refugees and displaced persons;

(40) Emphasize the importance of preventing situations that may result in mass flows of refugees and displaced persons and stress the need to identify and address the root causes of displacement and involuntary migration;

(41) Recognize the need for international co-operation in dealing with mass flows of refugees and displaced persons;

(42) Recognize that displacement is often a result of violations of CSCE commitments, including those relating to the Human Dimension;

(43) Reaffirm the importance of existing international standards and instruments related to the protection of and assistance to refugees and will consider acceding to the Convention relating to the Status of Refugees and the Protocol, if they have not already done so;

(44) Recognize the importance of the United Nations High Commissioner for Refugees and the International Committee of the Red Cross, as well as of non-governmental organizations involved in relief work, for the protection of and assistance to refugees and displaced persons;

(45) Welcome and support unilateral, bilateral and multilateral efforts to ensure protection of and assistance to refugees and displaced persons with the aim of finding durable solutions;

(46) Direct the ODIHR to organize, in early 1993, a CSCE Human Dimension Seminar on Migration, Including Refugees and Displaced Persons.

International humanitarian law

The participating States

(47) Recall that international humanitarian law is based upon the inherent dignity of the human person;

(48) Will in all circumstances respect and ensure respect for international humanitarian law including the protection of the civilian population;

(49) Recall that those who violate international humanitarian law are held personally accountable;

(50) Acknowledge the essential role of the International Committee of the Red Cross in promoting the implementation and development of international humanitarian law, including the Geneva Conventions and their relevant Protocols;

(51) Reaffirm their commitment to extend full support to the International Committee of the Red Cross, as well as to the Red Cross and Red Crescent Societies, and to the United Nations organizations, particularly in times of armed conflict, respect their protective

emblems, prevent the misuse of these emblems and, as appropriate, exert all efforts to ensure access to the areas concerned;

(52) Commit themselves to fulfilling their obligation to teach and disseminate information about their obligations under international humanitarian law.

Democracy at a local and regional level

The participating States

(53) Will endeavour, in order to strengthen democratic participation and institution building and in developing co-operation among them, to share their respective experience on the functioning of democracy at a local and regional level, and welcome against this background the Council of Europe information and education network in this field;

(54) Will facilitate contacts and encourage various forms of co-operation between bodies at a local and regional level.

Nationality

The participating States

(55) Recognize that everyone has the right to a nationality and that no one should be deprived of his/her nationality arbitrarily;

(56) Underline that all aspects of nationality will be governed by the process of law. They will, as appropriate, take measures, consistent with their constitutional framework, not to increase statelessness;

(57) Will continue within the CSCE the discussion on these issues.

Capital punishment

The participating States

(58) Confirm their commitments in the Copenhagen and Moscow Documents concerning the question of capital punishment.

Free media

The participating States

(59) Direct the ODIHR to organize a CSCE Human Dimension Seminar on Free Media, to be held in 1993. The goal of the Seminar will be to encourage the discussion, demonstration, establishment of contacts and exchange of information between governmental representatives and media practitioners.

Education

The participating States

(60) Would welcome, in view of the importance of education as to the dissemination of the ideas of democracy, human rights and democratic institutions, especially in a period of change, the organization to this end of a seminar entitled 'Education: Structures, Policies and Strategies' by the Council of Europe, open to all participating States.

Compilation of human dimension commitments

The participating States

(61) Welcome the drawing up of compilations of existing CSCE Human Dimension commitments in order to promote greater understanding for the implementation of these commitments.

Domestic implementation guidelines

The participating States

(62) Will promote, where appropriate, the drawing up of guidelines to assist the effective implementation of domestic legislation on human rights issues related to CSCE commitments.

VII

ECONOMIC CO-OPERATION

(1) The participating States will intensify co-operation among them in order to achieve sustainable economic development. They will continue

to co-operate in supporting those participating States which are engaged in the transition process to market economies.

(2) The participating States welcome the fact that, in response to the Document of the Bonn Conference on Economic Co-operation and the Charter of Paris for a New Europe, the United Nations Economic Commission for Europe (ECE) has identified priority areas for its activities and considers the promotion of the process of reform in economies in transition important in the preparation of its work programme. They also welcome the establishment within OECD of the Centre for Co-operation with European Economies in Transition (CCEET), through which countries in transition have access to the expertise of that organization. They express their satisfaction that the EBRD is now in a position to provide substantial support for the restructuring and modernization of the economies in transition.

(3) The participating states invite these and other international economic and financial organizations to pursue their work, so as to facilitate the integration of the economies in transition into the international economic and financial system and to promote economic co-operation in the CSCE area. They call for increased co-ordination among them in order to ensure greater coherence and effectiveness of action and to avoid duplication.

(4) The participating States will work to ensure the further implementation of their existing commitments. They agree to give renewed impetus in particular in the areas of human resources, industrial co-operation, trade, statistics, infrastructure, energy, defence conversion, agriculture, tourism and science and technology.

(5) The participating States emphasize the need for continuing co-operation and investment in human resources development in order to cope with problems of transition to market economies, rapid technological changes and the evolution of society. Recognizing the importance of education and training, including management and vocational training at all levels, they will intensify their dialogue on education and training systems and promote further co-operation in this area.

(6) The participating States will enhance opportunities for industrial co-operation by providing an appropriate legal and economic environment for business, particularly with the aim of strengthening the private sector and developing small and medium-sized enterprises. They will create favourable conditions for business by progressively reducing

obstacles to trade, to freedom of establishment and to contacts among business communities. They will, if appropriate, improve legislation in particular with regard to customs, standardization, competition, property and intellectual property rights, banking, accounting and company law, capital movement and investment protection.

(7) The participating States recognize that the maintenance of an open multilateral trading system based on General Agreement on Tariffs and Trade (GATT) rules is an essential element in stimulating economic development. They will intensify their efforts to help economies in transition through increased market access.

(8) The participating States stress the importance of comprehensive, transparent and reliable statistics and commercial and administrative information as a basis for policy making and, in particular, for economic decision making, as well as for the efficient operation of a market economy. They will further improve the quality, timeliness and availability of this information. They recognize the valuable role of the ECE in this field, as well as the contribution by OECD of related fundamental analysis and information.

(9) The participating States emphasize the importance of the development of infrastructure, especially in the transport and telecommunication sectors, for a successful transition period and a greater share in international trade.

(10) In view of the impact of increasing transport activities on transport capacity, the environment and safety, they will co-operate in order to improve the efficiency and quality of transport by land, water and air. They will also co-operate in developing an efficient transport system within the CSCE area based on the principles of the market economy, safety and transparent and fully competitive conditions among operators and different modes of transport, with due consideration for the environment and social aspects. They stress the importance of further development and early completion of joint road and rail infrastructure projects, including those being undertaken by the ECE and United Nations Development Programme (UNDP).

(11) Taking into account the impact on the environment, they will pay particular attention to the development of low-emission transport systems, notably rail, inland waterways and combined transport operations.

(12) They will co-operate in creating an integrated telecommunications market, paying particular attention to the development of modern telecommunications infrastructure and related service capabilities, the establishment and expansion of telecommunications networks throughout the CSCE region, technical co-operation and the facilitation of the free flow of information.

(13) The participating States fully support the further development of the European Energy Charter and stress the importance of completing work on and implementing the Basic Agreement and the protocols. They consider these documents of particular importance for the period of transition and, recognizing their mutual interests in this field, they will co-operate to take advantage of the available opportunities.

(14) They emphasize the need for further energy sector co-operation with the objective of improving the security of energy supply, maximizing the efficiency of the production, conversion, transport, distribution and use of energy, enhancing safety and minimizing environmental problems, on an acceptable economic basis. In this context they also recognize the importance of existing international programmes, such as Energy Efficiency 2000 under the auspices of the ECE. The participating States underline the need for close co-operation in related areas such as commercial development of and research into renewable energy sources, as well as the free movement of energy products.

(15) The participating States stress the social and economic importance of the conversion of military production to civilian purposes. They support co-operation in the conversion of military production with interested participating States on a bilateral level, as well as within the framework of international organizations.

(16) The participating States stress the importance of agricultural reforms carried out in certain economies in transition. They will expand co-operation in sharing agricultural production expertise, including issues of privatization, co-operation and training in the agricultural and food industries.

(17) In order to take advantage of the enhanced opportunities for tourism since the opening of borders, the participating States will co-operate in improving, *inter alia*, infrastructure, services and harmonization of definitions and indicators, while giving due consideration to the impact of tourism on the environment. They will enhance their co-operation in the field of training and education in this sector and encourage the

exchange of know-how and relevant information and the setting up of joint operations.

(18) Reaffirming the essential role of science and technology in the process of sustainable economic and social development, the participating States will enhance their co-operation in this field giving priority to areas which are of direct concern to their populations and to their production systems. This will include areas such as environmental research, biomedicine and health research, nuclear safety, energy and raw material saving techniques, agro- and food-processing technologies as well as measurement and testing techniques in order to facilitate the progressive introduction of international standards and codes of good practice to support the development of trade.

(19) They will take steps towards a greater sharing, where appropriate, of scientific and technological information and knowledge to overcome the technological gap, and recognize that the transfer of technology and exchange of up-to-date know-how should be consistent with non-proliferation obligations and the protection of intellectual property rights.

(20) Recognizing the need to develop human resources in the field of science and technology, they welcome the opportunity for further collaboration within appropriate international organizations and in research programmes such as COST and EUREKA, as well as the recent establishment of the International Centre for Science and Technology with centres in the Russian Federation and Ukraine. They will work towards the development of scientific networks and joint research projects.

Economic Forum

Mandate

(21) The CSCE Ministers agreed at the Prague Council Meeting (30 January 1992) to establish an Economic Forum within the framework of the CSO.

(22) The CSO will convene as the Economic Forum to give political stimulus to the dialogue on the transition to and development of free-market economies as an essential contribution to the building of democracy, to suggest practical efforts for the development of free-market systems and economic co-operation, and to encourage activities

already under way within organizations such as the Organisation for Economic Co-operation and Development (OECD), the European Investment Bank (EIB), the EBRD and the ECE.

Organization

(23) The CSO will convene as the Economic Forum. The Economic Forum will thus be governed by the same arrangements as those applying to all regular CSO meetings.

(24) The Forum can invite contributions to its work by those European and transatlantic organizations relevant to the subject under discussion.

(25) The work of the Forum should be so structured as to avoid duplication of the work of international organizations and over-commitment of scarce resources.

(26) The Economic Forum will meet on an annual basis as a rule. The meeting will last for two to three days, and the discussion will focus on two to three specific subjects.

(27) The Economic Forum will consider topics and subjects that may require further study by experts. This will take the form of open-ended seminars on specific subjects during the course of the year. These meetings of experts may, with the agreement of the Forum, be organized and financed by one or more CSCE States and/or by international organizations, possibly in co-operation with private organizations.

(28) These meetings of experts can bring together economic policy makers, parliamentary leaders and representatives of non-governmental organizations and the private sector in a positive dialogue on co-operation and the transition to market economies.

(29) The Forum will welcome reports of meetings of expert groups and encourages their distribution to all CSCE States. However, these groups of experts will not produce documents with commitments binding on CSCE States.

Functions

(30) The Economic Forum will permit the exchange of views and experiences concerning key issues of the transition process, as well as on the work of relevant international organizations.

(31) The Economic Forum should serve as an important mechanism for reviewing the implementation of CSCE commitments in the areas of economics, the environment and science and technology. The Forum should disseminate information, help to identify structural problems and suggest practical efforts for the development of economic co-operation in these areas during the period of transition.

(32) The political impulses which the Economic Forum is mandated to give to the discussion on the economic, environmental and science and technology aspects of the transition process will complement and support work in the international economic and environmental organizations that are addressing these problems at an operational level.

Indicative agenda for the first meeting of the Economic Forum
Prague
16-18 March 1993

1. Opening

2. Discussion items

   Exchange of views and experiences concerning key issues of the transition process, and in this respect an implementation review, with particular focus on the following three areas, with an eye to the possibility for further co-operation:
   - key elements of a favourable business climate in the light of the provisions of the Document of the Bonn Conference, including the protection of all types of property and with particular emphasis on the place and role of public policy;
   - the human factors of the economic transition process, with emphasis on the development of human capital, including vocational and professional training and technical training, the development of managerial skills, fostering an entrepreneurial spirit, and working conditions;

- integrating economic and environmental factors during the transition to market economies.

3. Consideration of proposals for topics for seminars in 1993

4. Dates and agenda for the next meeting of the economic forum

VIII

ENVIRONMENT

(1) The participating States will intensify the existing and growing co-operation between them in order to restore and maintain a sound ecological balance in air, water and soil and they recognize their individual and common commitment towards achieving these goals.

(2) The participating States stress the need to develop, in the appropriate fora, efficient systems for monitoring and evaluating compliance with existing environmental commitments. They are looking forward to the results of environmental policy performance reviews being carried out in co-operation between OECD and the ECE. They encourage the ECE and other international organizations to consider ways of enabling all CSCE participating States to adhere to relevant conventions.

(3) The participating States underline that the integration of environmental protection in other policies and in the economic decision-making process is an essential condition both for the creation of sustainable economic development and for a prudent use of natural resources. In this respect, the use of economic and fiscal instruments in addition to regulatory instruments is important in order to implement, at national level, the 'polluter-pays' principle, as well as the precautionary approach.

(4) They emphasize that environmental protection should be a major consideration in international co-operation among them. They encourage work towards elaborating an Action Programme for Central and Eastern Europe, as well as elements for an Environmental Programme for the whole of Europe, in the follow-up to the 1991 ministerial conference 'Environment for Europe'.

(5) The participating States will support intensified work within the relevant international organizations to make liberalized international trade and the protection of the environment mutually supportive.

(6) The participating States stress the need to ensure effectively the safety of all nuclear installations, in order to protect the population and the environment. They will co-operate in the appropriate international fora on defining and establishing nuclear safety objectives.

(7) They recommend the widest possible adherence to the IAEA Conventions on Early Notification of a Nuclear Accident and on Assistance in the Case of a Nuclear Accident or Radiological Emergency and express their support for active work on the early elaboration of an international convention on nuclear safety in the framework of IAEA. The participating States welcome the International Nuclear Events Scale (INES) and Incident Reporting System.

(8) They will work to support the technical co-operation programmes of IAEA aimed at enhancing nuclear safety. They will support other international efforts in this direction aimed at, *inter alia*, upgrading the safety of nuclear installations where technically feasible, and where not feasible by developing and implementing plans, as soon as practically possible, to substitute them with facilities using environmentally sound energy production processes and through the improvement of energy efficiency.

(9) The participating States should ascertain that their military establishments conform to their nationally applicable environmental norms in the treatment and disposal of hazardous wastes.

(10) The participating States express their concern about the illegal international transport and disposal of toxic and hazardous wastes. They will co-operate to prevent the illegal movement and disposal of such wastes and to prohibit their export to and import by countries that do not have the technical means to process and dispose of them in an environmentally sound manner, in the context of the Basel Convention on the Control of Transboundary Movements of Hazardous Wastes and Their Disposal. With regard to international transport of radioactive waste they will take into account the IAEA Code of Practice on International Transboundary Movement of Radioactive Waste.

(11) The participating States will work towards the development of policies aimed at increasing environmental awareness and educating citizens to reduce the risks of natural and technological disasters, as well as preparing appropriate actions when such disasters occur. To this end, the participating States recognize the important work under way

through the United Nations Environment Programme (UNEP) Awareness and Preparedness for Emergencies at the Local Level (APELL) programme. The participating States will take appropriate steps to enhance public participation in environmental planning and decision making.

(12) The participating States urge the implementation of principles regarding the exchange of information on the state of the environment, consultation, early warning and assistance in environmental emergencies contained in the OECD Guiding Principles for Chemical Accident Prevention, Preparedness and Response, and in the ECE Convention on the Transboundary Effects of Industrial Accidents.

(13) They encourage the designation of national environmental arrangements, such as task forces, which could co-ordinate the dissemination of relevant information on expertise and equipment to countries facing emergencies, to the United Nations Centre for Urgent Environmental Assistance, and to other relevant international organizations. These arrangements will take into account the ECE Conventions on the Transboundary Effects of Industrial Accidents and on Environmental Impact Assessment in a Transboundary Context, as well as other relevant agreements.

(14) They would welcome the designation by the United Nations Centre for Urgent Environmental Assistance of one of its staff as liaison officer for the CSCE region, and recommend that the Centre be connected to the CSCE communications network, which could serve as a supplementary information system in emergency situations, taking into account the fact that the Centre will be subject to evaluation by the UNEP Governing Council in June 1993.

(15) The participating States will encourage in the appropriate fora the development of a network of protection areas in the CSCE region to conserve and safeguard the large-scale natural and near-natural biotopes and ecosystems still in existence, as part of their natural heritage, as well as further development of the protection and conservation of animals.

(16) Encouraging early implementation of the forest principles adopted at UNCED and recognizing the importance of sustaining the forest ecosystems of the CSCE region, the participating States decide to give impetus to this issue through practical discussions. In this regard, a Seminar of CSCE Experts on the subject of 'Sustainable Development

of Boreal and Temperate Forests', will be convened in Montreal from 27 September to 6 October 1993. A proposal outlining the budget, agenda and modalities of this seminar will be presented by Canada for approval by the CSO before the end of 1992.

IX

THE CSCE AND REGIONAL AND TRANSFRONTIER CO-OPERATION

(1) The participating States welcome the various regional co-operation activities among the CSCE participating States as well as transfrontier co-operation and consider them an effective form of promoting CSCE principles and objectives as well as implementing and developing CSCE commitments.

(2) The participating States will encourage appropriate links among the various forms of regional co-operation as well as steps to provide the CSCE with relevant information on their activities in the framework of regional co-operation, including future work plans.

(3) The participating States will encourage and promote, both bilaterally and, as appropriate, multilaterally, including through initiatives in European and other international organizations, transfrontier co-operation between territorial communities or authorities, involving border areas of two or more participating States with the aim of promoting friendly relations between States.

(4) The development of transfrontier co-operation should involve governments, regional and local authorities and communities.

(5) Transfrontier co-operation should be as comprehensive as possible, promoting increased contacts at all levels, including contacts among persons sharing a common origin, cultural heritage and religious belief.

(6) Special attention should be paid, *inter alia*, to co-operative infrastructural development, joint economic activity, ecology, tourism and administrative co-operation.

X

MEDITERRANEAN

(1) The participating States recognize that the changes which have taken place in Europe are relevant to the Mediterranean region and that, conversely, economic, social, political and security developments in that region can have a bearing on Europe. In this context, the CSO will seek to relate issues regarding co-operation in the Mediterranean to the goals of the CSCE process and will examine, as appropriate, practical modalities for possible contributions to the CSCE by non-participating Mediterranean States.

(2) The Chairman-in-Office of the CSO is encouraged to foster contacts with non-participating Mediterranean States in order to establish an effective information exchange.

(3) Non-participating Mediterranean States will be invited to future review conferences to make contributions concerning security and co-operation in the Mediterranean.

(4) A CSCE Mediterranean Seminar will be convened under the auspices of the CSO in the course of the year following this Follow-up Meeting. It will meet for a duration of no more than five working days. The date, location and agenda will be decided upon by the CSO.

(5) The Seminar can be attended by non-participating Mediterranean States, to which invitations will be extended.

(6) The agenda of the Seminar may comprise topics such as the environment, demographic trends or economic development and other areas of bilateral and multilateral co-operation between CSCE participating States and non-participating Mediterranean States reflecting the general framework of principles of co-operation in the Mediterranean region as provided for in the Final Act and other CSCE documents. The Seminar will not produce a document with commitments binding on CSCE participating States.

XI

PROGRAMME OF CO-ORDINATED SUPPORT FOR RECENTLY ADMITTED PARTICIPATING STATES

Further to paragraph 19 of the Summary of Conclusions of the Prague Meeting of the Council, the participating States decide to establish a programme of co-ordinated support for those participating States which have been admitted to the CSCE since 1991. Through the programme, *inter alia*, diplomatic, academic, legal and administrative expertise and advice on CSCE matters will be made available as follows.

(1) The programme will be co-ordinated by the ODIHR under the overall guidance of the CSO. The ODIHR will act as a centre of information for relevant activities of the CSCE and the participating States as well as international organizations, including the Council of Europe, as provided for in the mandate of the ODIHR. The ODIHR will make the information received available on request by the participating States.

(2) Subject to the approval of the CSO, the ODIHR will arrange meetings and seminars on CSCE matters, specially designed for recently admitted participating States. Such meetings and seminars will, where possible, be held in the recently admitted participating States. They will be focused on enhancing knowledge on matters dealt with in the CSCE among, *inter alia*, civil servants, the media and the public at large.

(3) Within its field of competence the CPC will arrange meetings and seminars on CSCE matters, specially designed for the recently admitted participating States. Such meetings and seminars will, where possible, be held in those States.

(4) The CSCE Secretariat will devote special attention to distributing CSCE documents to the recently admitted participating States.

(5) The officers of the CSCE Secretariat, the CPC Secretariat and the ODIHR will, when on missions to recently admitted participating States, make themselves available, to the extent possible to share their expertise in a relevant manner.

(6) Participating States may make available to the ODIHR any national inventories of CSCE expertise available within the diplomatic, academic, legal, administrative and other relevant fields. Persons,

institutions and organizations thus listed could, through national initiatives and following requests from the recently admitted participating States, be invited for, *inter alia*, lectures, seminars, courses and advisory services on CSCE matters in the recently admitted participating States. Such persons, institutions and organizations may also be invited to the seminars arranged by the ODIHR on CSCE matters for recently admitted States, in order to provide expertise in various areas of the democratic process.

(7) The participating States are encouraged to include representatives of the recently admitted participating States in government-sponsored internships, study and training programmes.

(8) Costs ensuing from national initiatives will be borne by the participating States providing the support in question. Costs of the CSCE institutions will be covered within their regular budgets. The provision of accommodation and full board, as well as of interpreters and meeting facilities, by those recently admitted participating States where activities take place will be welcomed as contributions to the costs of the programme of co-ordinated support. The participating States will be invited to contribute financially on a voluntary basis to the seminars and meetings envisaged.

(9) The next review conference will assess the results of this programme.

XII

ADMINISTRATIVE DECISIONS

Financial arrangements of the CSCE and cost-effectiveness

(1) An informal Financial Committee of Experts of the CSO is established to deal, *inter alia*, with the issues of budgets, cost savings and staffing. The Committee will meet quarterly, in conjunction with but prior to meetings of the CSO.

(2) The Committee will also consider rationalizing procedures concerning meetings and language staff as well as address a systematic way of handling arrears in CSCE payments by investigating the practice in international organizations, with a view to improving practices in the CSCE. The Committee will report and submit recommendations to the CSO for adoption.

(3) The following scale of distribution is effective as of 1 July 1992:*

Country	*Per cent*
France	9.00
Germany	9.00
Italy	9.00
Russian Federation	9.00
United Kingdom	9.00
United States	9.00
Canada	5.45
Spain	3.65
Belgium	3.55
Netherlands	3.55
Sweden	3.55
Switzerland	2.30
Austria	2.05
Denmark	2.05
Finland	2.05
Norway	2.05
Ukraine	1.75
Poland	1.40
Czech and Slovak Federal Republic	1.00
Turkey	1.00
Belarus	0.70
Greece	0.70
Hungary	0.70
Romania	0.70
Bulgaria	0.55

---

*. This decision is made on the understanding that the scale of distribution effective until 1 July 1992 will be applied to all costs related to the Helsinki Follow-up Meeting.

Ireland	0.55
Kazakhstan	0.55
Luxembourg	0.55
Portugal	0.55
Uzbekistan	0.55
Yugoslavia	0.55
Albania	0.20
Armenia	0.20
Azerbaijan	0.20
Bosnia and Herzegovina	0.20
Croatia	0.20
Cyprus	0.20
Estonia	0.20
Georgia	0.20
Iceland	0.20
Kyrgyzstan	0.20
Latvia	0.20
Lithuania	0.20
Moldova	0.20
Slovenia	0.20
Tajikistan	0.20
Turkmenistan	0.20
Holy See	0.15
Liechtenstein	0.15
Malta	0.15
Monaco	0.15
San Marino	0.15

(4) The question of reviewing the scale periodically, as well as questions relating to the criteria forming the basis of the scale, will be further discussed at an appropriate time by the CSO through the Financial Committee of Experts.

Financial arrangements for CSCE meetings

(5) The financial arrangements set out below do not apply to meetings covered by the budgets of the CSCE Secretariat or the ODIHR.

(6) Any participating State which offers to provide the venue and to organize a CSCE meeting not mentioned in paragraph (5) will ensure cost-effectiveness and financial discipline as regards the expenses of

such meetings. The host government will at the same time submit a cost estimate for the premises accompanied by sufficient information to enable the participating States to assess the adequacy and cost-effectiveness of the facilities offered. As soon as the work programme has been decided by the participating States, the host government will submit, if necessary with the help of the CSCE Secretariat, a projection of those expenses subject to reimbursement by the participating States in accordance with the CSCE scale of distribution, including estimated costs of personnel, language services and administration.

(7) One month before the start of the meeting in question, the organizing authority appointed by the host government will distribute to all participating States a more precise financial forecast, following, where applicable, the structure of the budgets of the CSCE institutions.

(8) The organizing authority will ensure that appropriate records and accounts are kept of transactions and that all payments are properly authorized. A complete account of expenses subject to reimbursement by the participating States in accordance with the CSCE scale of distribution will be presented to the CSO within 60 days of the closure of the meeting or on a quarterly basis for long-running meetings.

(9) The participating States will contribute promptly to the expenses incurred in accordance with the CSCE scale of distribution. The organizing authority/host government may present lists of arrears to the Financial Committee of Experts.

(10) Within 30 days of receiving the account of the meeting, participating States may transmit requests for further information or raise objections to the organizing authority if the account significantly exceeds the financial forecast.

(11) The accounts of such CSCE meetings will be subject to external auditing. The audit report will be submitted to the Financial Committee of Experts.

(12) The Consultative Committee of the CPC, in co-ordination with the host country, is requested to prepare modalities for the cost-effective provision of conference services through a joint Executive Secretary for all appropriate Vienna-based fora for deliberation or negotiation, including meetings of the Consultative Committee itself, the Special Committee of the Forum for Security Co-operation, CPC seminars,

and — if so agreed by those concerned — the CFE Joint Consultative Group and the Open Skies Consultative Commission.

INTERPRETATIVE STATEMENTS[1]

Interpretative statement by Kyrgyzstan

The Republic of Kyrgyzstan, recalling the definition of the zone of application set out in the Vienna Document 1992, proceeds on the understanding that references to the area of application in the mandate of the CSCE Forum for Security Co-operation do not prejudice the right of the Republic of Kyrgyzstan to determine its zone of application in respect of the Vienna Document 1992 and of the new measures under paragraphs 1 to 3 of the Programme for Immediate Action in the areas adjacent to the territories of non-participating States in accordance with the provisions of the Helsinki Final Act of 1975, and to discuss these issues at the relevant negotiations within the framework of the Forum.

* * *

Interpretative statement by Kazakhstan

We have been following closely and with interest the discussion on the mandate for a Forum for security negotiations. The new security environment in Europe as well as in Eurasia will to a large extent be influenced by the new negotiations and any results that may be reached in the Forum.

My country, as was stated in our letter to the Chairman of the Prague Meeting, is ready to comply with all its commitments deriving from various CSCE documents including the Vienna Document 1990 on confidence- and security-building measures.

In this context I would like to make a reference to Annexes I and V of the Vienna Document 1992 on the zone of application and how the temporary difficulties could be dealt with.

Having followed this last phase of deliberations in Working Group 2, we have realized that the matter of the area of application of the new or improved measures which will be developed in the Forum still remains to be settled. I would like to state that this issue is of importance for my country. To what extent our territory will be included in the area of application will depend on the principles in the Helsinki Final Act of 1975, the Madrid mandate, the Vienna Document 1992 and the language we will formulate in the mandate for a Forum. This language should be in line with the principle of the indivisibility of security and respect for the rights of all States under the relevant CSCE documents.

* * *

---

1. Journal No. 50 (Helsinki, 8 July 1992).

Interpretative statement by Turkey

On the occasion of the adoption of the Helsinki Decisions of the CSCE, the delegation of the Republic of Turkey wishes to refer to its statement at the Copenhagen and Moscow Meetings on the Human Dimension to the effect that, according to the Turkish constitutional system, the word "minorities" encompasses only groups of persons defined and recognized as such on the basis of multilateral or bilateral instruments to which Turkey is a party.

This is without prejudice to the constitutional principle that all citizens are equal before the law, enjoy the same rights and have the same obligations without discrimination, regardless of their sex, religion, race or ethnic origin.

* * *

Interpretative statement by Cyprus

In reply to the interpretative statement made by the delegation of Turkey, the delegation of Cyprus wishes to reiterate the following:

The decisions of the CSCE Helsinki Meeting adopted by consensus today according to Rule 69 of the Rules of Procedure are equally binding on all participating States without exception or selectivity.

The interpretative statement of the delegation of Turkey is therefore of no effect.

* * *

Interpretative statement by Austria, on behalf of the delegations of Austria, Germany, Denmark, Finland, Slovenia, Sweden and Switzerland

With regard to paragraph (5b) of the provisions concerning the High Commissioner on National Minorities, Austria as well as Germany, Denmark, Finland, Slovenia, Sweden and Switzerland make the following interpretative statement:

This provision does not prejudice in any way the possibility for the participating States to raise, comprehensively consider and deal with national minorities issues in the CSCE on the basis of CSCE principles and commitments.

We understand that this provision will be applied in such a way that the effective exercise of the functions of the High Commissioner is ensured.

* * *

Interpretative statement by Switzerland

The delegation of Switzerland makes the following interpretative statement in regard to paragraph 25 of the Helsinki Summit Declaration and Chapter IV, paragraph (2) of the Decisions in the Helsinki Document 1992 just adopted.

Switzerland, although not a Member of the United Nations, pursues a foreign policy which is consistent with the Purposes and Principles of the United Nations. Switzerland consequently fully supports the statement that the CSCE is a regional arrangement within the meaning of Chapter VIII of the Charter of the United Nations. However, should the Security Council, on the basis of article 53 of the Charter of the United Nations, call on the CSCE to take enforcement action under its authority, Switzerland, as a non-Member State of the United Nations, would have to decide on a case-by-case basis whether and in what manner it will take part in such action.

* * *

Interpretative statement by the Russian Federation

The adoption of the new CSCE scale of distribution will not serve as a precedent, including in relation to international organizations, for settling the issue of apportioning the USSR's external debt and assets among the States concerned.

* * *

Interpretative statement by the Ukraine

As a result of the discussions held in the working organs of the Helsinki Meeting on the distribution of the expenses of the CSCE among the participating States, it was decided, as is known, to assess Ukraine at 1.75 per cent. In view of the current extremely difficult economic position of Ukraine, of which we have spoken more than once, our delegation considered this rate to be too high. Nevertheless, we agreed with the rate set, not wishing to stand in the way of the consensus.

There is no doubt that Ukraine has considerable economic potential and we are convinced that its capacities will be fulfilled in time in the interests of the Ukrainian people and the development of multilateral co-operation with foreign countries. However, we cannot fail to take into account the current acute crisis in the economic situation of Ukraine. We cannot fail to take into account that, in the past, the economic indicators of Ukraine were deliberately set too high while heavy capital investments in military production were passed over in silence.

Today Ukraine is experiencing a sharp decrease in its national income, and in the volume of production. Considerable resources are being channelled towards the conversion of production and to changing its structure and also to dealing with heightened social problems.

Both the current task of mitigating the consequences of the Chernobyl disaster and the efforts to restore justice in relation to the peoples who were unlawfully deported during the Stalin era call for the expenditure of huge resources.

A very important factor to be taken into account is Ukraine's solvency, which is very limited and is even further constrained by the need to contribute considerable sums as Ukraine's share of servicing the former USSR's foreign debt (16.4 per cent).

The present Government of Ukraine is conducting a realistic assessment of the country's economic indicators, in accordance with international standards, and this will provide a true picture of our capacities.

In this connection, our delegation would like to state that Ukraine reserves the right to raise the question, in the relevant CSCE fora, of the review of the rate of its contribution, taking into account its current economic situation and solvency.

* * *

Interpretative statement by Poland

In connection with the section in the Helsinki Decisions document "Framework for monitoring compliance with CSCE commitments and for promoting co-operation in the Human Dimension", the delegation of Poland would like to recall the statement it made on 10 January 1992 at the CSO on the obligations of the host country with regard to the premises of the ODIHR, which do not entail bearing the costs of the premises for the implementation meetings on Human Dimension issues. It is the understanding of the Polish delegation that the same interpretation applies, *mutatis mutandis*, to the costs of premises for the Human Dimension seminars to be held at the seat of the ODIHR.

* * *

Interpretative statement by the United Kingdom

The United Kingdom welcomes the adoption by consensus of the Helsinki Document 1992 including those provisions in the Helsinki Decisions relating to the establishment of the High Commissioner on National Minorities and to the dispatch of fact-finding and rapporteur missions.

In this context, and if the services of the High Commissioner on National Minorities, or fact-finding and/or rapporteur missions, are required in the territory of the United

Kingdom, the United Kingdom wishes to state that it would act in accordance with the following interpretation of paragraphs (11c), (12), (27), (29) and (33) of Chapter II and paragraph (14) of Chapter III of the Helsinki Decisions. In order to protect public safety or national security, the United Kingdom might be obliged to decline or to regulate access at a particular time or to a particular place proposed by the High Commissioner or the mission. The United Kingdom states that such action would be taken only when absolutely necessary and would have effect only for so long as is required.

The United Kingdom further states that, in such circumstances, it will immediately enter into consultations with the High Commissioner or the mission in order to clarify the situation and seek agreement on arrangements to enable the High Commissioner or the mission to obtain as much information as is practicable, and that, if such agreement cannot be reached, it will bring he matter at the earliest opportunity to the attention of the Committee of Senior Officials.

* * *

Interpretative statement by Moldova

I would like to make an interpretative statement in connection with the Summit Declaration just adopted by the Plenary:

Paragraph 15 of the Declaration refers to the "stationing of foreign armed forces on the territories of the Baltic States without the required consent of those countries".

Furthermore, the Declaration states that "in line with basic principles of international law and in order to prevent any possible conflict, ... the participating States concerned [must] conclude, without delay, appropriate bilateral agreements, including timetables, for the early, orderly and complete withdrawal of such foreign troops ...".

I should like to state that these provisions are equally applicable to the Republic of Moldova. My country is faced with a similar situation and the withdrawal of foreign troops from its territory is an essential prerequisite for the peaceful settlement of the conflict in the eastern part of my country.

* * *

Interpretative statements by Armenia

(a) With regard to Chapter II, paragraph (5b) of the provisions concerning the High Commissioner on National Minorities, Armenia makes the following interpretative statement:

Our understanding is that the provision that the High Commissioner will not consider national minority issues in situations involving organized acts of terrorism reflects the unanimous condemnation of terrorism, but does not prejudice in any way the possibility for a comprehensive consideration of minorities issues in the CSCE. Paragraph (5b) is to be read in relation to the function of the High Commissioner as an instrument of "early warning" and "early action" and in recognition of the fact that situations involving organized acts of terrorism will as a rule have developed beyond an early warning stage.

(b) The fight against organized crime, including terrorism, is one of the priority activities of the domestic and foreign policy of the Republic of Armenia. In this connection, I would like to point out that we consider paragraph 26 of the Helsinki Summit Declaration regarding the fight against terrorism to be inadequate. Bearing in mind in particular that the aspiration of peoples to exercise their inalienable right to national self-determination is frequently described by those who oppose this movement as 'terrorism", it must be noted that paragraph 26 of the Declaration fails to draw a sufficiently clear legal and political distinction between these two concepts.

In an effort to contribute to the successful conclusion of work on the Helsinki Summit Declaration, the delegation of Armenia refrained from hindering the inclusion in the document of paragraph 26 in its present form.

It is our understanding that the provisions contained in paragraph 26 will be implemented in conformity with the generally applicable norms of international law and with all the fundamental principles of the Helsinki Final Act, including those concerning respect for the right of peoples to self-determination.

* * *

Interpretative statements by France

(a) France interprets the provisions of paragraphs (28) and (46)A.3 of Chapter V of the Document concerning the CSCE Forum for Security Co-operation as meaning that the assurances that the participating States choose to offer in respect of their conventional forces located outside the area of the Treaty on Conventional Armed Forces in Europe will be determining factors to be taken into account in the negotiation and possible adoption of new stabilizing and confidence-building measures. It is in the light of the assurances that it will have received in this field and to the extent that these offer sufficient guarantees of non-circumvention that it will, for its part, envisage joining the consensus for the adoption of new measures.

(b) The delegation of France points out that France's thinking on human rights issues is based in particular on a universal principle: all human beings are born free and equal in dignity and rights. The French Constitution draws on this principle and provides in article 2 that france is an indivisible Republic and ensures the equality of all its citizens without distinction as to origin, race or religion. It is in this light that the French Government has interpreted article 27 of the United Nations International Covenant on Civil and Political Rights and that it will interpret the provisions of the final document concerning the High Commissioner on National Minorities.

* * *

Interpretative statement by Turkey

The Government of Turkey had formally placed a reservation regarding the representation of Cyprus at the CSCE on 31 July 1975 (CSCE/III/I). The same reservation has been placed at subsequent meetings within the context of the CSCE. We wish to make a similar statement on the occasion of the adoption of the 'CSCE Helsinki Document 1992 - The Challenges of Change'.

'The Republic of Cyprus', which was established in accordance with international treaties on the basis of a partnership between the two peoples of the Island, ceased to exist as such after its Constitution was unilaterally and unlawfully abrogated in 1963 by the Greek Cypriot side by the use of force, despite the protestations and resistance of the Turkish Cypriot side. The Greek Cypriot Administration has ever since represented exclusively the Greek Cypriots and their interests. As a guarantor power under the 1960 Treaty of Guarantee, Turkey does not recognize this administration or its claims for legitimacy.

There is no single authority which, in fact or in law, jointly represents or is competent to represent the Turkish Cypriots and the Greek Cypriots, and consequently Cyprus as a whole. This is one of the main issues which has to be settled by the negotiating process which is being pursued between the Turkish Cypriot and the Greek Cypriot leaders on the basis of equality.

The Turkish Cypriot people are represented by the Government of the Turkish Republic of Northern Cyprus which was recognized by Turkey in 1983.

Due to the reasons stated above, the representation of Cyprus by the Greek Cypriot administration at the CSCE is neither legal nor legitimate. Therefore, the Government of the Republic of Turkey declares that the 'CSCE Helsinki Document 1992 - The Challenges of Change' will have no validity or applicability as regards and in relation to the Turkish Republic of Northern Cyprus and Turkish Cypriots.

Similar, the commitments assumed by the Republic of Turkey under these documents will have no validity or applicability as regards and in relation to Cyprus and they do not create obligations for Turkey in that respect.

FIRST MEETING OF THE ECONOMIC FORUM

Prague, 16-18 March 1993

CHAIRMAN'S SUMMARY[1]

According to its mandate, the Economic Forum should give political stimulus to the dialogue on the economic transition and suggest practical efforts for the development of free market systems and economic co-operation and encourage activities within relevant international organizations.

The First Meeting of the Economic Forum conducted a free and stimulating dialogue on key issues of the transition process to democratic market economies. Pursuant to the Helsinki Document 1992 representatives of international organizations were invited to participate. Representatives from OECD, EIB, EBRD and ECE as well as from UNEP, the Council of Europe, IBRD, IMF, ICC and ILO participated in the meeting and made oral and written contributions. This participation is especially important in order to deepen co-operation with these organizations, to ensure the broadest possible exchange of information and experience, and in order to avoid duplication.

Representatives of national NGOs and the business community were included in national delegations and participated actively in the discussions. The CSCE offers a unique forum for such a dialogue as it permits a discussion of the transition process on the basis of the links between human rights, individual freedom and democratic values.

The discussion was based on the principles of the Charter of Paris of a common conviction that freedom and political pluralism are necessary elements for sustainable economic growth, prosperity and efficient use of economic resources and that preservation of the environment is a shared interest and responsibility of all nations.

Against this background we have exchanged experiences of progress made and problems encountered so far and the progress in economic reform achieved by the countries in transition were welcomed. We have been

---

[1] 1-EF(20-CSO)/Journal No. 3, Annex.

reminded that economic reforms presuppose and must be the result of the mobilization of all internal possibilities and resources in a country but also that external assistance can and must play an important supportive role in a successful implementation of these reforms. The participants in the Economic Forum confirmed their support of the strong effects towards market reforms in Russia aimed at the creation of relevant conditions for its integration into the system of modern economic co-operation and partnership.

The transition process is complex, lengthy and contains difficult political choices. It was stressed that the Bonn principles and commitments are still valid and crucial for continued progress. In particular, they stressed the responsibility of each participating State to apply these principles fully both internally and externally.

The participating States and the relevant international organizations were to increase their efforts to remove obstacles and support measures for the creation of a favourable business climate and stimulate production, trade and investments in the transition countries.

It was suggested that the CSCE Secretariat, on the basis of information provided by the international organizations invited to the Economic Forum, should circulate details of ongoing programmes which could be relevant to the process of economic transformation and, on a quarterly basis, issue a calendar of activities carried out by such organizations and by individual participating States.

During the discussions of the First Meeting of the Economic Forum the following points were highlighted:

Key elements of a favourable business climate

- The interdependence of economic and political factors in the process of social change was stressed and it was pointed out that economic policies with a view to enhancing economic liberty, growth and prosperity constitute a prerequisite for a politically stable and secure Europe;

- the Economic Forum should actively support and contribute to a sustained dialogue on matters pertaining to the successful implementation of economic transition towards free-market economies, in particular emphasizing the involvement of the countries in transition, relevant international organizations and the private sector;

- the development of national policies establishing clearly defined macro-economic and structural priorities, including appropriate legislation, with a view to sustainability and transparency, is of fundamental importance for the successful pursuance of the process of economic and political transition. In this context, participants underlined the vital importance and motivation and an entrepreneurial spirit as well as understanding of the priorities and means of the transition process;

- the development of the private sector is a key element in the process of transition, calling for particular attention to the role of privatization and the creation of small and medium-sized enterprises. In this context, the need for structural reforms, including of the financial sector, and for protection of all types of property was emphasized;

- the discussion manifested broad interest in establishing more regular contacts between representatives of business and entrepreneur circles of the CSCE area;

- the catalytic role of foreign direct investments as a vehicle for economic development and transfer of know-how was underlined and participants pointed to the complementary roles of the three parties involved, host and home countries and enterprises;

- the fundamental importance of trade for the transition process and the need to facilitate trade in the CSCE region.

The human factors in the economic transition process

- Special attention should be paid to the overall social impact of measures of transition, particularly sharing of its costs and benefits, as well as to labour market effects;

- participants emphasized the importance of programmes for vocational, technical and professional training and retraining at different levels and for all segments of society, including training of trainers and training of disadvantaged groups, with a view to furthering the development of human resources and the capacity to meet the requirements of the transition process both in the private and public sectors;

- all actors in the transition process - governments, enterprises, employers, trade unions and international organizations - have an essential role to play in this regard.

Integrating economic and environmental factors

- Economic and environmental policies cannot be made and implemented in isolation as sustainable economic growth is not possible without environmental considerations being brought into economic policy making. Such environmental consideration should be implemented by both economic and regulatory instruments;

- the ecological crisis was in many countries in transition seen to be as grave as the economic crisis. Problems are considered to be particularly serious in the areas of nuclear energy, air and water pollution and hazardous waste. The need for financial and technical assistance as well as foreign investment and joint ventures was underlined. It was acknowledged that anticipatory measures are preferable to reactive response;

- the process of structural change in the economies of transition offers a unique opportunity to improve the environmental situation. This opportunity should be fully used and supplemented *inter alia* by an appropriate tax system and implementation of the polluter pays principle. Participating States looked forward to the successful outcome of the Financing Conference in Gdansk and the post-Dobris Ministerial Conference in Lucerne.

* * *

It was agreed that the results of the first Economic Forum should be conveyed to the CSCE Parliamentary Assembly, noting the prominent role of parliamentarians in the context of creating favourable conditions for economic transition.

Topics for seminars

In accordance with paragraph 27 of Chapter VII of the Helsinki Document, participants in the Economic Forum identified the following issues as being especially important for the process of economic transition to market economies:

1. Business climate development

For example:

- creation of favourable conditions for investment in countries in transition, including legislation, role of incentives and taxation policy;
- the 'business incubator' concept;
- efforts to support small and medium-sized businesses, including legal and institutional frameworks;
- Business, Education and Transition (BET) points network;

- increased co-operation between domestic entrepreneurs in countries in transition to market economy and foreign entrepreneurs active in those countries;
- means of promoting regular contact among business representatives, as well as researchers and academics, to discuss the process of economic transition.

2. Restructuring of economy and privatization
For example:
- legal framework for privatization;
- privatization and direct foreign investment;
- promotion of investment under limited financial resources;
- financing of conversion of military-industrial complexes.

3. Training/Retraining
For example:
- retraining of workforce in industries being phased out in economies in transition.

4. Unemployment, including the development of the labour market and efforts to resolve long-term unemployment.

5. Environmental policies
For example:
- recycling and destruction of industrial waste;
- organization and financing of community environmental projects.

6. Infrastructure
For example:
- transport;
- telecommunications;
- energy sector.

These areas may require further attention in accordance with paragraph 27 to 29 of the Helsinki Document. Pursuant to these paragraphs, the participants in the Economic Forum urged CSCE States and the international organizations invited to the Forum to seek funds to organize and finance seminars and meetings of expert groups on the issues listed above or other related topics authorized by the CSO. They furthermore agreed that the Committee of Senior Officials should encourage financing from other external sources.

* * *

Indicative agenda for the Second Meeting of the CSCE Economic Forum Prague, 15-17 March 1994

1. Opening

2. Discussion items

   Exchange of views and experiences concerning key issues of the transition process, and in this respect an implementation review, with particular focus on the following four areas, with an eye to the possibility for further co-operation, by governments and other actors:

   (a) further consideration of key elements in a favourable business climate, in particular the human factor, as well as legal and institutional frameworks, and the role of public administration in their implementation;

   (b) favourable conditions for mutual trade and investments in the CSCE area;

   (c) the role of infrastructures as key elements in the transition process;

   (d) co-operation in the area of science and technology for the development of industry and for the strengthening of its international competitiveness.

3. Reports from seminars and consideration of proposals for topics for 1994.

4. Dates and agenda for the next Meeting of the Economic Forum

5. Closure

MEDITERRANEAN SEMINAR

Valletta, 17-21 May 1993

CHAIRMAN'S SUMMARY[1]

The CSCE Mediterranean Seminar has been held here at the Mediterranean Conference Centre, Valletta, Malta on 17-21 May 1993 in accordance with the provisions of the Helsinki Document 1992 (The Challenges of Change) and the decisions adopted by the 21st Meeting of the Committee of Senior Officials. It is the aim of this Summary to highlight the discussion of the five-day Seminar and in no way to characterize the suggestions as binding commitments.

Representatives of CSCE participating States[2] have attended the Seminar. The representative of the Former Yugoslav Republic of Macedonia has attended the Seminar as an observer. Representatives of non-participating Mediterranean States and of the competent international organizations were invited to participate in the Seminar[3]. The work of the Seminar has been conducted in accordance with the procedures set out in the invitations, the aim being to stimulate an informal exchange of views.

The CSCE Mediterranean Seminar has, furthermore, been attended by the Directors of the CSCE Secretariat in Prague and of the Office of Democratic Institutions and Human Rights (ODIHR) in Warsaw.

The Deputy Prime Minister and Minister of Foreign Affairs of Malta, Professor Guido de Marco, delivered an opening statement to the Seminar.

In accordance with the mandate for the Seminar, the opening Plenary, following established CSCE practice, was chaired by a representative of the host country.

---

1 MSO5EW1/1 p.m./21.5.93.

2 Germany, United States of America, Austria, Belgium, Bulgaria, Canada, Cyprus, Croatia, Denmark-European Community, Spain, Finland, France, United Kingdom, Greece, Hungary, Ireland, Italy, Malta, Monaco, Norway, Netherlands, Poland, Portugal, Romania, Russian Federation, San Marino, Holy See, Slovak Republic, Slovenia, Sweden, Switzerland and Turkey.

3 Egypt, Israel, Lebanon, Libya, Morocco, Tunisia, UN/ECE, UNEP, WHO, IMO and the Council of Europe, attended.

The Seminar has met in open Plenary meetings, with statements made by delegates of participating States and by a representative of the Commission of the European Communities. Contributions have also been made by representatives of Egypt, Israel, Morocco and Tunisia, and of UNEP, WHO, ECE, IMO and the Council of Europe.

Delegations expressed the desirability of a more active presence of non-governmental organizations in future similar activities.

In his address to the Seminar, the Deputy Prime Minister of Malta referred to the attention which the CSCE had devoted to the Mediterranean region since the start of the process. He underlined the importance of co-operation and dialogue with the non-participating Mediterranean States in seeking solutions to the difficult issues which abound in the region and welcomed those initiatives and negotiations which aimed at finding just, lasting and viable solutions, through peaceful means, to the outstanding crucial problems of the Mediterranean region.

More vigorous action in protecting the Mediterranean environment in the light of the commitments undertaken at the CSCE Palma Meeting in 1990 was called for. Demographic trends and migration in the region provided the best example of the urgent and complex nature of Mediterranean issues. Referring to practical ways of co-operation, the Deputy Prime Minister of Malta spoke of the need for a more permanent working method for identifying, defining and addressing Mediterranean issues and outlined Malta's proposal for the setting up of a Council of the Mediterranean.

A representative of Germany, the Slovak Republic and of Italy, respectively, chaired the Plenary meetings dedicated to items 2(a): Environment. Follow-up to the results of the Palma Meeting. Identification of possible areas of co-operation; 2(b): Demographic trends. Migration. Social and economic background to these issues; and 2(c): Practical ways of co-operation between the non-participating Mediterranean States and the CSCE in the light of the Helsinki Document.

In considering practical ways of co-operation between the non-participating Mediterranean States and the CSCE in the light of the Helsinki Document, it was pointed out by delegations that this item gave a new and broader perspective to the agenda of the Seminar, as compared with previous CSCE Mediterranean Meetings devoted to more specific fields of co-operation.

Delegations have stressed that the changes which have taken place in Europe are relevant to the Mediterranean region and that, conversely, economic, social, political and security developments in that region have a direct bearing on Europe. In that context, the hope was expressed that the pressures of transition problems in the CSCE area would not divert attention from Mediterranean issues. At the same time, delegates have observed that the end of East-West confrontation may have the effect of widening the scope for dialogue between CSCE and non-participating Mediterranean States, eliminating some inhibitions stemming from that confrontation. Delegations have expressed the view that the time has come to give fresh impetus to an active CSCE-Mediterranean dialogue, in line with the guidelines contained in the Helsinki Decisions.

A number of participating States, for their part, have suggested practical ways for a wider and more regular political dialogue. It has been stated that this should be done, as appropriate, on a pragmatic basis. Suggestions include the possibility of inviting representatives of non-participating Mediterranean States to Council Meetings, and new modalities for more active participation by these countries in the deliberations on Mediterranean issues at the CSCE Review Meetings, without involving them in the CSCE decision-making process. Finally, it has been suggested that political dialogue between the CSCE and the non-participating Mediterranean States might be extended to the CSCE Troika and that the exchange of information could be increased between these States and the Chairman-in-Office, the CSCE Troika and the Secretary General of the CSCE. Other participating States believed that the existing framework for co-operation with the non-participating Mediterranean States reflects accurately the role that the CSCE can play in the Mediterranean issues.

The presence of delegations of non-participating Mediterranean States in the Seminar has followed the pattern of previous Mediterranean meetings. Their active participation in the debate has shown that a significant number of Mediterranean non-European countries maintain a marked interest in keeping the links, dialogue and co-operation with Europe active within the framework of the CSCE. Requests for more regular consultations have been put forward and an interest has been expressed in being associated with the CSCE in a more permanent and structured relationship. Non-participating Mediterranean States have expressed a wish to share the principles and objectives of the CSCE, which include the assertion of democratic institutions, the rule of law and respect for human rights as the solid foundation for positive and stable prospects of security and co-operation. The Seminar has shown that this interest is highly appreciated and reciprocated by CSCE participating States.

The debate in this Seminar has also touched upon ways of stimulating autonomous developments which might take shape outside the CSCE context, within a specifically Mediterranean framework of co-operation. Mention has been made in this context of some initiatives along those lines, pertaining, *inter alia*, to stability, co-operation and the human dimension in the Mediterranean.

Delegations have addressed political, social, economic and humanitarian factors behind demographic trends and migration, and have stressed the relevance of these issues to stability and security in the CSCE area.

Demographic trends and migration need to be analyzed in terms of their social and economic background and the continued influence of such factors on patterns of development. Attention has been drawn to increasing demographic imbalances between the northern and southern shores of the Mediterranean. The root causes of these phenomena encompass substantial population growth, alarming unemployment rates, socio-economic problems and environmental degradation. Inter-Mediterranean migratory flows also involve issues pertaining to ethnic minorities, who are at times subject to the xenophobia of certain isolated groups in the recipient countries.

It has been recognized that there are no easy, clear-cut solutions to these issues and that measures should address the factors behind these problems. In this regard it has been suggested that economic co-operation has to be intensified and enhanced in order to prevent people from leaving their countries. All bilateral and multilateral development programmes have great relevance in this context. Delegations have also pointed to the significance of development co-operation in support of measures to control population growth.

Among the examples of accelerated economic co-operation to which reference has been made, mention could be made of a further opening up of European markets to exports of manufactured goods; financing of projects and programmes in the field of agriculture; support for private sector operations through the encouragement of joint ventures between European companies and companies in the non-participating Mediterranean States; and support to macro-economic and sectoral reforms in these countries. The participants in the Seminar expressed the belief that human society should be the focal point of all socio-economic development.

It has been suggested that thought should be given to providing protection to those in need of it, with special reference to women, children and elderly people; examining further the relationship between development and international migration; developing channels for orderly legal migration;

supporting social diversity and cultural pluralism; and aiming for the goal of offering naturalization to long-stay legal immigrants.

It has been stressed that governmental migration policies should be further developed in both sending and receiving countries. Furthermore, it has been recognized that international migration is not in and of itself a negative phenomenon; the voluntary movement of people across borders can bring economic benefit to both sending and receiving countries. To achieve progress in moving towards a comprehensive approach in tackling migration questions, international organizations are considered a vital component of the multilateral response to migration challenges. The links with the CSCE and the Mediterranean community of States, as well as relevant international organizations, should be maintained and strengthened in this context.

In the field of the environment some important initiatives and projects were under way and it was important to take these into account in order to avoid duplication of effort. Even bold and innovative initiatives require greater co-ordination, if the efforts on a multilateral and bilateral basis were to come to full fruition.

The pressure on Mediterranean ecosystems has continued to increase in the last few years. "Business as usual" scenarios are, in the views expressed by delegations, perpetuating current developmental trends which tend to accelerate environmental degradation and depletion of natural resources and might, as a result, dramatically worsen social and economic conditions in all Mediterranean countries. Only alternative scenarios requiring substantial changes in such trends will be capable of reconciling economic growth with the protection of the Mediterranean environment in the long term.

Delegations have, therefore, stressed the necessity of establishing and implementing practical measures aimed at promoting the transition towards a sustainable future. In accordance with the recommendations of Agenda 21 of the United Nations Conference on Environment and Development (UNCED), held in Rio de Janeiro, all countries in the region should adopt national strategies for sustainable development. Several proposals of the CSCE Palma Meeting still provide a valid platform for defining actions within a national strategy.

Delegations have highlighted some actions which could be taken into account within national strategies, such as establishing and implementing the legal instruments of environmental impact assessment; strengthening national institutional capacity to integrate social, economic, developmental and environmental issues at all levels of decision-making and implementation;

promoting the rapid introduction of solar and wind energy; establishing economic instruments with a view to integrating environmental costs in all economic activities and to ensuring that prices reflect the relative scarcity and total value of resources: energy/CO_2-tax, water supply and waste water pricing, packaging charges, etc.

Although the definition and implementation of these sustainable development strategies have been considered by delegations to be first and foremost a national responsibility, regional co-operation and co-ordination, as recognized in Agenda 21, are regarded as playing an essential role in numerous areas in supporting and supplementing national efforts and actions.

The full range of international legal instruments relevant to the Mediterranean region has been addressed by the Seminar. Instruments to protect and to restore Mediterranean ecosystems that have been referred to as crucial in this context are, for example, the Mediterranean Action Plan and the Barcelona Convention, a need having been identified for the latter to be reviewed and reinforced in the light of the results of the Rio de Janeiro Conference.

The view was expressed that other legal instruments, such as the Conventions on Climate and on Biodiversity, the Barcelona Convention on a global level and the ECE Conventions on a European level, should be ratified, acceded to and implemented by all Mediterranean countries in a position to do so. The elaboration of new conventions and protocols such as the convention on desertification should, as stated by these delegations, be accelerated. Furthermore, delegates have called for consideration of the possibilities for providing assistance to governments lacking technical or financial means.

Delegations have stressed the priority that should be attached in international co-operation to cross-sectoral requirements such as institution-building, development of endogenous capacities and technology transfer, taking into account that in many countries of the region the fight against poverty and population growth and the improvement of the living conditions of the population are preconditions for the success of sustainable development and environmental protection strategies. Other preconditions referred to are awareness-raising, environmental education, access of the public to administrative information and public participation in decision-making.

HUMAN DIMENSION SEMINAR ON NATIONAL MINORITIES

CSCE HUMAN DIMENSION SEMINAR ON CASE STUDIES ON NATIONAL MINORITIES ISSUES: POSITIVE RESULTS

Warsaw, 24-28 May 1993

REPORT OF DISCUSSION GROUP 1[1]

In terms of the CSCE provisions on national minorities, Discussion Group 1 of the CSCE Human Dimension Seminar on Case-Studies of National Minorities: Positive Results may be seen as seeking to concretize the right of persons belonging to national minorities to effective participation in public affairs formulated in paragraph 35 of the Document of the Copenhagen Meeting of the Conference on the Human Dimension of the CSCE (1990) and to contextualize what some participants called the 'shopping list' of approaches yielding positive results contained in the Report of the Expert Meeting on National Minorities (Geneva 1991).

The purpose of Discussion Group 1 was to examine, through the presentation and discussion of positive results achieved in particular cases, how the institutional design of the state and interstate relations can respond to the concerns of national minorities.

This topic was divided by the level of institutional design or interstate relations, and further subdivided by type of institution or relations. In addition, a subgroup on National Minorities With Dispersed Settlement Patterns and Special Cases: Positive Results (chaired by Denmark), an informal group on technical aspects of national minority participation (chaired by Belgium), and an informal consultation on strengthening the role of the CSCE (chaired by Sweden) met separately and reported back to Discussion Group 1. This report makes reference to the conclusions of these three groups, while distinguishing them from the conclusions of Discussion Group 1 as a whole.

OUTLINE OF REPORT

1. National institutions

---

[1] Report by Karen Knop, Moderator DG1, 28 May 1993. Not an official CSCE negotiated document. The views expressed in this report are those of the Moderator alone.

a. Common Political Institutions
  i. Legislative
  ii. Administrative
b. Separate Political Institutions
c. Judicial Institutions [including informal group report]

2. Regional Relations
  a. National Minorities with Dispersed Settlement Patterns and Special Cases [sub-group report]
  b. Transfrontier Co-operation

3. International Relations
  a. Generally
  b. Strengthening the role of the CSCE [including informal consultation report]

1. NATIONAL INSTITUTIONS

The case-studies presented indicate the range of ways that participation and representation of national minorities may be ensured in national (intra-state) institutions.

A number of participants saw the division of powers in federal systems as potentially responsive to national minorities issues. In some federal examples, the compact settlement pattern of national minorities enables them to form a *de facto* majority in particular federal subunits and thereby to exercise the powers belonging to that subunit. At the same time, individual and minority rights guarantees protect members of other groups within the subunit where the national minority exercises majority control (*e.g.* Switzerland, Canada). The case of Belgium, where there are both linguistically-defined Communities and geographically-defined Regions, provides an example of a federal structure relevant to national minorities with a compact and/or a dispersed settlement pattern.

Some participants questioned the strict relevance of federalism to national minority issues, while others emphasized that decentralization of powers may respond to national minority concerns, regardless of whether the state is federal (*e.g.* the regions of Trentino-Alto Adige and Valle d'Aosta in Italy).

a. Common political institutions

i. Legislative

In the legislature itself, the representation of national minorities may be realized in a variety of ways.

First, persons belonging to national minorities may enjoy the same right of participation in the democratic process as all other individuals (*e.g.* United States). It was suggested that in such systems, the periodic redrawing of electoral boundaries may reflect ongoing democratic changes and thereby promote national minority representation (United States).
Second, certain states promote representation of national minorities in the legislature by lowering the number of votes needed for election in the case of candidates from national minorities (*e.g.* the Danish minority in Germany, national and ethnic minorities in Hungary), or, *third*, reserve a minimum number of seats for the national minority (*e.g.* Rumania).
Some participants expressed the concern that these types of arrangements might foster 'ethnic' parties focused solely on ethnic interests, while failing - except in very fragmented legislatures - to give minorities a sufficient number of seats to affect decision-making in the legislature. These speakers felt that in contrast, under a system of equal treatment, national minority members of state-wide parties would be more inclined to consider issues in a wider context, although their national minority interests would not necessarily be taken into account by the party. Other participants commented that collective representation of national minorities risked permanently marginalizing these minorities. The need to stress individual rights was also mentioned.
Fourth, the idea of 'consociational democracy' was introduced. Consociational democracy envisages plural societies as a coalition of groups where each group has a certain degree of self-administration, power is shared between them, and decisions are taken by 'grand coalition'.
Fifth, where national minorities are represented in the common legislature, the constitution may safeguard their identity by requiring a special majority for the passage of certain types of laws or providing an 'alarm bell' procedure that enables the linguistic group to suspend the adoption of a bill under certain conditions (*e.g.* Belgium).
The issue of citizenship laws that exclude members of minorities from participation in the political process was also raised.

Alternatively, a *legislative committee* may be formed to deal with national minorities issues.
In a number of states, *independent advisory bodies* composed of elected representatives of national minorities provide advice to the legislature (*e.g.* Sami Assembly in Norway, Sami parliaments in Finland and Sweden). In some cases, a limited decision-making role is also assumed. It was suggested that these bodies might serve as a model for non-territorial representation of national minorities, applying both to compact and dispersed minorities. The issue of how these bodies reconcile their dependence on the state for

resources, as well as information, with their independent advisory role was raised.
National minority participation in legislative decision-making is also addressed by a process of consultation with the national minorities concerned, such as that required by International Labour Organisation Convention No. 169 Concerning Indigenous and Tribal Peoples or the Norwegian Planning Act.

ii. Administrative
Where a minority is too small or too dispersed to win a seat in the legislature, its interests may be represented by a *body within the administration* (*e.g.* Contact Committee for the German minority in Denmark, Foundation for the Sorbian People in Germany, Polish National Minorities Bureau).
In some cases, the national minority may be *proportionally represented at certain levels of the administration* (*e.g.* German and Italian-speakers in the provincial administration of Bolzano, Italy).
Outside the administration, *independent advisory bodies* may advise the government (as opposed to the legislature) and must be consulted in matters that affect the interests of the relevant national minority (*e.g.* Austrian Ethnic Advisory Council).
Although the office of *Ombudsman* does not deal specifically with national minorities issues, it was offered as another example of an institution outside the administration of potential use to national minorities (*e.g.* Sweden, Poland).

b. Separate political institutions

Several case-studies were introduced as positive examples of a transition to some form of territorial autonomy for a compact minority. The canton of Jura in Switzerland, carved out of the territory of existing cantons through a series of plebiscites, was presented as a case where minority aspirations could be realized within a federal structure by peaceful and democratic means. Among the other positive examples were Greenland and Nunavut in northern Canada, although it was stressed in these two cases that the indigenous groups in question neither regard themselves nor are regarded by their government as minorities.

c. Judicial institutions [including informal group report]

Judicial institutions may protect the right of national minorities to participate in the decision-making process in a number of ways. This topic was discussed in both Discussion Group 1 and an informal group on technical aspects of national minority participation (chaired by Belgium).

The informal group noted that constitutional protection of national minorities could be achieved through general individual rights and/or special status for certain national minorities. It further noted that effective protection of rights requires an independent and impartial judiciary, as well as the official dissemination of information on national and international human rights standards to national minorities. Impartiality was seen as requiring a representative judiciary, whether representativeness is achieved through guaranteed representation on the bench or the encouragement of judges belonging to national minorities.

In the discussion of the report of the informal group in Discussion Group 1 as a whole, the importance of non-governmental organizations in funding cases before the courts was raised, as was the important role played by NGOs in institution-building in Eastern and Central Europe more generally, and their need for adequate financial resources.

In the discussion on judicial institutions in Discussion Group 1 as a whole, the American Fourteenth Amendment was presented as a tool that members of minorities could use to maximise their participation in public life. Apart from the two types of rights protection discussed by the informal group, a third type of judicial protection for national minorities was referred to in Discussion Group 1 as a whole; namely, the role of constitutional courts in protecting the powers exercised by a national minority with some degree of territorial autonomy.

2. REGIONAL RELATIONS

a. National Minorities With Dispersed Settlement Patterns and Special Cases [sub-group report]

The Sub-Group on National Minorities With Dispersed Settlement Patterns and Special Cases: Positive Results (chaired by Denmark) noted that although national minorities with and without compact settlement patterns share certain traits, the latter require a different approach. Their lack of a compact settlement pattern means that the identity of these national minorities is in greater danger of disintegration, as evidenced by loss of language, lack of knowledge of their own history, lack of programs designed to protect and promote cultural awareness, lack of political structures, and lack of specific economic programs. The Sub-Group observed that the Roma people are among the most pressing of these cases.

The Sub-Group noted that any solution to the problems of minorities dispersed throughout several states would benefit from a co-ordinated approach that transcends the individual state. Such an approach might include a human rights supervision mechanism, coordination of research programmes, international conferences of dispersed minorities and adequate financial assistance.

Among the positive results reported by the Sub-Group were the establishment of a Roma Council by Austria; the recognition of the Roma as a national minority, with the concomitant legal rights, by the Czech Republic; the creation of a Romanian network of municipalities to coordinate the resettlement of repatriated Roma; and a number of Council of Europe initiatives.

In the general discussion of the Sub-Group's report by Discussion Group 1, a number of participants were of the view that the positive results reported in the case of the Roma might serve as a precedent for other national minorities without a compact settlement pattern.

b. Transfrontier co-operation

Several participants noted that the relatively high degree of economic centralization in many European states has resulted in a high rate of unemployment for national minorities concentrated in border regions. For this reason, it was observed, economic agreements between these border regions may have a positive impact on the minorities settled there. Speakers introduced a number of examples of economic co-operation between border regions, with the Council of Europe drawing the Discussion Group's attention to its model agreements for transfrontier co-operation at the state and local levels.

Cases of transfrontier co-operation relating to the preservation of national minority ways of life were presented by Sweden (Sami, and the recently established state-level and provincial-level Euroarctic Barents Councils) and Norway (bilateral agreements preserving reindeer-grazing rights of the Sami across Norway's border with Sweden and Finland).

3. INTERNATIONAL RELATIONS

a. Generally

The cases presented by participants exhibited a number of different international dimensions. Examples were given of bilateral agreements for the protection of national minorities (*e.g.* Hungary). The example of the Aaland Islands highlighted the role of the League of Nations in the 'cementing' of the status of the Aaland Islands, namely their autonomy, the guarantees of their Swedish character, demilitarization and neutralization.

b. Strengthening the Role of the CSCE [including informal consultation report]

The Netherlands stressed the importance of the CSCE in both setting and implementing standards for the protection of national minorities.
On improving the implementation of CSCE commitments, the Netherlands proposed that:

* official and unofficial channels be found to convey the results of CSCE human dimension seminars and implementation meetings to the political decision-making bodies of the CSCE, including channels to convey the results of this seminar on national minorities to the implementation meeting scheduled for the fall;
* the list of experts available to participate in CSCE missions be expanded;
* co-ordination between CSCE bodies, in particular those involved with minority issues, be improved and CSCE co-operation with other international bodies be enhanced;
* the increasingly numerous and complex CSCE monitoring mechanisms be streamlined;
* increased financial and other resources for ODIHR and the High Commissioner on National Minorities be considered.

Second, in the area of standard-setting on the protection of national minorities, the Netherlands recommended that the impressive results achieved within the CSCE be co-ordinated with the work of the Council of Europe and the United Nations. For instance, the UN Declaration on the Rights of Persons Belonging to National or Ethnic, Religious and Linguistic Minorities contains standards not found in CSCE documents, notably the provision that national policies and programmes be planned and implemented with due regard for the legitimate interests of persons belonging to minorities. It was observed that activities in other fora should stimulate, rather than hamper, further development within the CSCE. The CSCE should give consideration to convening another special expert meeting on standard-setting. Another option would be a special working group on the protection of national minorities to be held at the forthcoming implementation meeting, as well as at the 1994 review conference in Budapest.
The informal consultation on strengthening the role of the CSCE (chaired by Sweden) raised the additional issues of how minority issues relate to the three baskets of the CSCE, the human dimension mechanisms being seen as central; the need for NGOs to play a greater role in a number of aspects of the CSCE process, including information-gathering, provision of expertise, participation in missions concerning national minorities and in the upcoming implementation meeting, bearing in mind the Council of Europe's more

established relationship with NGOs; and the need to translate and make available CSCE documents into a greater number of languages.

In Discussion Group 1 as a whole, the idea of a CSCE ombudsman was raised, as was the question of national minorities that fall outside the mandate of the High Commissioner. The Council of Europe recommended the inclusion of other organizations in the working group proposed by the Netherlands. The Discussion Group's attention was drawn to the proposed office of a sub-regional ombudsman (Baltic region), an idea which attracted some support from other participants, and to the need in the future to co-ordinate the activities of the CSCE High Commissioner with any sub-regional ombudsmen and national ombudsmen. The issue of whether NGOs would participate in the determination of their role in processes such as the CSCE and the issue of research into complementary methods of minority protection in the widest sense of the work, including general monitoring, conflict prevention and general purpose missions, were raised.

REPORT OF DISCUSSION GROUP 2[2]

In spite of unavoidable difficulties, our discussion group was truly productive.

1. There were three kinds of difficulties that had to be overcome before a dynamic and free exchange of personal opinions and experiences could take place (notwithstanding the size of the group and the shape of the room).

1.1 D.G.1 was assigned the responsibility of discussing institutional arrangements designed to share political power with minorities at the local, regional, national and international levels, while D.G.2 was to discuss matters relating to everyday life in a multicultural society — *i.e.* 'confidence building' and 'special' measures to implement international and CSCE commitments, language and educational policies, respect for cultural and religious identity and promotion of mutual understanding and exchanges, etc.

Such a 'division of labour' made some members of our group uncomfortable as they felt, with good reason, that no mutual confidence, understanding and exchange could develop in every day life without adequate guarantees in the political arena. This problem had to be discussed before the group agreed to concentrate on its specific task.

1.2 The second difficulty came from the nature of such a seminar which is neither a diplomatic meeting aiming at negotiating some form of an agreement, nor an academic conference aiming at a free exchange of ideas and experiences in order to expand the knowledge and personal wisdom of the participants.

This seminar is somewhere in the middle. Because it wanted to achieve the end product of the second kind in the framework of the first type, discussions often proceeded slowly and laboriously.

1.3 Finally, a more serious difficulty came from the differing situations among participating countries with regard to building multi-ethnic and multicultural democracies.

Some countries have a long established democracy, no external nor serious internal threat to their integrity and many years at experimenting ways of managing their ethnic, cultural, linguistic

---

[2] Report by Jean-Pierre Worms, Moderator of DG2. Not an official CSCE negotiated document. The views expressed in this report are those of the Moderator alone.

and/or religious diversity. Their experiences in this field are therefore quite sophisticated in their institutional arrangements and conceptual framework.

When asked to compare their endeavours with those of such long established democracies, the moderator constantly wondered if the new democracies were not put at an unfair disadvantage. They are involved in building their institutions and societies in the midst of incredible economic hardship and constant threat to their integrity from inside and outside. They necessarily feel less assured in the way they deal with their diversity and the concepts that guide their approach. They deserve all the more credit for moving forward in the difficult, but crucial, path of building pluralist multicultural democracies.

2. In spite of these difficulties the discussion group was unquestionably a positive experience. We were able to identify a set of essential principles to tackle such complex situations. We also managed to detect clearly what were the most important problems to be faced and needs to be met and thus contributed to opening the way to important follow-up activities for the CSCE and other international bodies (Council of Europe, NGOs, etc.).

2.1 The following principles are to guide local, national and international approaches to minority problems.

2.1.1 Problems should be clearly identified and analyzed in all their specificities in order to chose and adapt the right approach and judge of its efficiency. In particular one should be clear about the deep psychological mechanisms that give rise to misunderstanding and intolerance, hate and potential violence among communities, in order to devise efficient, preventive and confidence building measures.

2.1.2 All measures and policies at all levels should aim at striking the right balance between recognising, respecting and promoting the specific identities of the different peoples of a country, and on the other hand, building mutual understanding and a sense of belonging and actively participating in the life of their common country.

Integration is neither separation nor assimilation. 'Common' interest in modern, pluralist and democratic societies should be based not on the concept of a fair negotiated compromise between majority and minority and the dynamics of intercultural communication. Recognising the legitimacy of a minority's interests is the best way to ensure its sense of belonging and its loyalty to its country.

Such a dynamic and progressive concept of a pluralist democratic order, where the achievement of common good does not imply the abdication of specific identities and interest, was seen as particularly relevant with regard to the building of a new Europe. Europe is both a means and an end for such a new and more advanced democratic order.

2.1.3 There is no single model for striking such a delicate balance. Each country, each minority represent a different case and each case requires different ways of implementing common principles. What is more, unique arrangements have to be worked out at different levels of a society (local, regional, national) according to different patterns for each specific situation. Particular attention was called to the situation of dispersed minorities, notably the Roma and the very small minorities whose specific culture and identity could disappear in time. However, this diversity of existing situations was not described as an obstacle but as a call for imaginative, diverse and adaptable solutions, open to constant reappraisal.

2.1.4 No general management of a multicultural society and elaboration of special institutions and measures should be undergone without promoting participation of all parties concerned. Relationships between majority and minority should be conceived in terms of a constructive partnership. When a particular measure explicitly takes into account the desires and interests of a minority, it is a sure way of ensuring the positive involvement of that minority and the success of the measure.

2.2 Our discussion group also identified specific needs and problems of minorities which require urgent attention.

2.2.1 First and foremost two prerequisites to particular measures and policies regarding minorities:

a) an active policy of the state to redress social and economic discrepancies that discriminate along ethnic lines. No positive attitude towards minority policies can be expected from a minority who suffers from blatant economic and social disadvantage.

b) a clear political will to implement international commitments and national legislation. There is no good legislation if it is not applied. Moreover lip-service to good principles with no concrete implementation discredits any public authority and impedes any future positive action.

2.2.2 Minorities urgently need financial and technical aid to enable them to take into their own hands the elaboration and implementation of minority policies.
Their organisations need national and international recognition and support. Information should be made available for them to compare how they manage to fulfil this need in their respective countries and to whom they can turn should they need help.

2.2.3 Special attention was granted by the group to educational problems, particularly to learning of and in minority languages.
The great diversity of situations was noted as well as the common risk that only learning the language of the minority could put the members of that minority at a disadvantage for participating in all institutions and structures of their country: respect for a minority's culture and language should not lead its members to become second rate citizens. "Separate but equal" policies have proved elsewhere to be the surest way to breed inequality ... and ethnic conflicts.
Another point about education stressed the importance that should be given to the content of school curricula and books in order to fight prejudices and promote positive attitudes in a multicultural society.

2.2.4 The role of the media in educating the general public to values of a multicultural society was also stressed by the group. It was agreed that the best way such a role could be fulfilled, apart from minorities owning and running their own media, was through granting them access and full participation in the general media of their country.
Here again, participation of a minority in a common institution, but under its own colours, seemed the best way to ensure its constructive and dynamic integration in society.

3. The discussions in the group considered also the role of international organisations. It was recommended that they conform to the following principle: rather than being themselves actively operating at grassroot level, they should *help others* to do so. International organisations should function as a forum for grassroot structures and organisations so that they can build their own networks and benefit from European and worldwide exchanges of experiences and ideas. International organisations can play a critical role in he dissemination of case studies and positive results of actions and policies. They could also act as a

pool of information on support provisions and mechanisms for grassroot initiatives.
At intergovernmental level, policies concerning national minorities should continue to be developed and should include the following three interdependent elements:

- the definition of legal standards and protection mechanisms. The CSCE and the Council of Europe are the most appropriate international fora and supplement one another to reach this aim: at CSCE level political agreements and commitments are reached which can then be worked into international legal obligations within the Council of Europe. In this context, an appeal was made to the participating states to rapidly proceed to signing and ratifying the European Charter for Regional or Minority Languages and adopting an additional protocol to the European Convention on Human Rights on minority rights,

- setting up of mechanisms for mediation and preventive diplomacy,

- promoting confidence building measures through providing support to practical and innovative projects and initiatives at grassroot level by the people concerned: minority communities and NGOs.

II

DOCUMENTS

OF THE

CSCE COUNCIL

BERLIN MEETING OF THE CSCE COUNCIL

19-20 June 1991

Summary of Conclusions

I.

1. The Council of the CSCE held its first Meeting in Berlin on 19 and 20 June 1991.

2. The Ministers welcomed the Republic of Albania as a participating State of the CSCE following receipt of a letter accepting all CSCE commitments and responsibilities from the Minister for Foreign Affairs of the Republic of Albania, Mr. Kapllani, to the Chairman-in-Office of the Council, Federal Minister of Foreign Affairs, Mr. Genscher (Annex 1).

II.

3. The Ministers had political consultations on the European architecture and the strengthening of security in Europe as well as the consolidation of human rights, democracy and the rule of law, on prospects for economic transition and social change in Europe, on current issues and on the future work of the CSCE.

   In the framework of these consultations the Ministers came to the following conclusions:

4. They reaffirmed the importance of continued political and economic transformation in the democratic countries in transition towards a market economy. They stressed the necessity to continue support to these countries in their efforts to consolidate democracy and transform their economies.

5. They reaffirmed that co-operation in the fields of economy, science, technology and the environment remains an important pillar of the CSCE.

6. They adopted a mechanism for consultation and co-operation with regard to emergency situations (Annex 2).

7. They decided that the communication network, to be established under the provisions of the Vienna CSBM Document 1990, will be preferably used for all communications foreseen in the procedures in emergency situations. In this connection the CSCE Secretariat will be integrated into this communication network.

8. They endorsed the report of the Valletta Meeting on Peaceful Settlement of Disputes and agreed to designate the Conflict Prevention Centre as the nominating institution for the CSCE Dispute Settlement Mechanism under the provisions of the recommendations thereto of the Committee of Senior Officials (Annex 3).

9. They welcomed the establishment of the CSCE Parliamentary Assembly (Annex 4).

10. They noted with satisfaction the results of the Cracow Symposium on the Cultural Heritage of the CSCE participating States.

11. They invited the United Nations Centre for Human Rights to contribute to the Geneva Meeting of Experts on National Minorities.

12. They decided to invite the Council of Europe to make a contribution at the Moscow Meeting of the Conference on the Human Dimension.

13. They encouraged the exchange of information and relevant documents among CSCE and the main European and transatlantic institutions, such as the European Community, Council of Europe, ECE, NATO and WEU. The procedure concerning the CSCE's participation in this exchange should be considered at the next Meeting of the Committee of Senior Officials and reviewed after six months.

14. They requested the Committee of Senior Officials to prepare recommendations for the next Meeting of the Council on the further development of the CSCE institutions and structures, taking into account the debate at the First Council Meeting. The Consultative Committee of the Conflict Prevention Centre would contribute those sections of the recommendations which concern the enhancement of the role of the Conflict Prevention Centre.

15. They looked forward to a range of informal discussions and consultations on new negotiations on disarmament and confidence and security building open to all CSCE participating States. In this context they requested their representatives in Vienna, as a rule their representatives to the Consultative Committee of the Conflict Prevention Centre, to start informal preparatory consultations in September this year aimed at establishing by 1992, from the conclusion of the Helsinki Follow-up Meeting, new negotiations on disarmament and confidence and security building open to all participating States as set out in the Charter of Paris. They decided that formal preparatory negotiations for the new forum will be carried out at the Helsinki Follow-up Meeting.

16. They welcomed the fact that a further seminar on military doctrine would be held within the context of the Conflict Prevention Centre in Vienna, from 8 to 18 October 1991, and also welcomed the possibility of future seminars as may be agreed by the participating States.

17. In the light of the recent experience in the Gulf region, the Ministers see a need to halt the spread of weapons of mass destruction and for restraint and transparency in the transfer of conventional weapons and weapons technologies, particularly to regions of tension. This should be a priority of CSCE governments, and Ministers agreed to maintain a dialogue on these issues among CSCE countries.

18. They recalled the links of solidarity and of co-operation that unite their countries with the developing countries as well as the importance they attach, in this context, to respect for human rights and to the promotion of the fundamental values of the CSCE. They underlined the usefulness of an increasing co-operation among their countries on these questions in the appropriate fora.

19. They agreed that the next Meeting of the Council will be held in Prague on 30 and 31 January 1992.

ANNEX 1

Tirana, 18 June 1991

Mr. Minister,

The Government of the Republic of Albania hereby adopts the Helsinki Final Act, the Charter of Paris for a New Europe and all other documents of the Conference on Security and Co-operation in Europe.

The Government of the Republic of Albania accepts in their entirety all commitments and responsibilities contained in those documents, and declares its determination to act in accordance with their provisions.

The Government of the Republic of Albania welcomes a visit of a Rapporteur Mission to be arranged by the Chairman of the Council of Ministers of the Conference on Security and Co-operation in Europe. The Government of Albania will do everything possible to facilitate and assist this mission. The Government of Albania is confident that this mission will inform the participating States of progress in Albania towards full implementation of CSCE commitments as well as assist Albania towards that objective. The Government of Albania understands that this mission will draw upon the expertise of persons from participating States, CSCE institutions and other relevant organizations.

The Government of Albania expresses its readiness for signature of the Helsinki Final Act and the Charter of Paris by the Head of State or Government of the Republic of Albania at the earliest opportunity.

I kindly ask you, Mr. Minister, to circulate copies of this letter to all representatives of the participating States at the CSCE Council of Ministers.

Please accept, Mr. Minister, the assurances of my highest consideration.

Muhamet Kapllani

H.E. Hans-Dietrich GENSCHER
Chairman-in-Office of the
CSCE Council of Ministers,
Federal Minister of Foreign Affairs,
BONN

ANNEX 2

Mechanism for consultation and co-operation with regard to emergency situations

Participating States will in accordance with the following provisions, consult and co-operate with each other concerning a serious emergency situation which may arise from a violation of one of the Principles of the Final Act or as the result of major disruptions endangering peace, security or stability. In applying the mechanism for consultation and co-operation with regard to emergency situations all the Principles of the Final Act, including the Principle of non-intervention in internal affairs, and those of the Charter of Paris, are of primary significance and accordingly will be equally and unreservedly applied each of them being interpreted taking into account the others.

1. If any participating State concludes that an emergency situation, as described above, is developing, it may seek clarification from the State or States involved. The request will state the cause, or causes, of the concern.

1.1 The requested State or States will provide within 48 hours all relevant information in order to clarify the situation giving rise to the request.

1.2 The request and the reply will be transmitted to all other participating States without delay.

2. Should the situation remain unresolved, any of the States involved in the procedure described under point 1 above may address to the Chairman-in-Office of the Committee of Senior Officials a request that an emergency meeting of the Committee be held.

2.1 Any request addressed by the same State on an identical subject between two regular meetings of the Committee of Senior Officials will be inadmissible.

2.2 Any request should state the reasons why the matter is urgent and why the emergency mechanism is the most appropriate.

2.3 Any request should be accompanied by the texts of the request for clarification and of the reply provided for under point 1 above.

2.4 On receipt of the request, the Chairman-in-Office of the Committee of Senior Officials will immediately inform all participating States and the CSCE Secretariat and submit the relevant documentation.

2.5 The Chairman will also enter into contact with the States involved within a period of 24 hours following receipt of the request.

2.6 As soon as 12 or more participating States have seconded the request within a maximum period of 48 hours by addressing their support to the Chairman, he will immediately notify all participating States of the date and time of the meeting, which will be held at the earliest 48 hours and at the latest three days after this notification. The notification will also include the reason for, and the agenda of, the meeting.

2.7 Subject to the conditions set out in paragraphs 2.1 and 2.6 above, no judgement as to the facts nor any possible dispute as to the validity of the reasons offered for requesting the emergency convening of a meeting may be invoked for postponing or preventing the holding of an emergency meeting.

2.8 The meeting will be held at the seat of the Secretariat and last no more than two days, unless otherwise agreed.

2.9 The agenda of the emergency meeting will consist of a single item. Its formulation will be identical to that contained in the notification provided for in paragraph 2.6 above. It will not be open to amendment. The Chairman of the meeting will ensure that discussions do not depart from the subject on the agenda.

2.10 The meeting will be chaired by the representative of the State holding the chairmanship of the Committee of Senior Officials.

2.11 If the Chairman of the Committee of Senior Officials is a national of one of the States involved, as defined under point 1 above, the meeting will be chaired by the representative of the next State, in French alphabetical order, which is not involved in the situation.

2.12 The proceedings will be introduced by a short statement by the Chairman recalling the facts and stages of development of the situation. He will then indicate the number of speakers who have asked for the floor and will open the debate.

2.13 In the light of its assessment of the situation, the meeting may agree on recommendations or conclusions to arrive at a solution. It may also decide to convene a meeting at ministerial level.

2.14 The procedures for convening meetings under this mechanism do not affect the rule of consensus in other circumstances.

3. The procedures defined above will not be used in place of the mechanism concerning unusual military activities.

4. The communications between participating States provided for above will be transmitted preferably through the CSBM communications network.

The above procedures will be reviewed and, if necessary, revised at the Helsinki Follow-up Meeting.

ANNEX 3

Peaceful settlement of disputes

Taking into account the Report of the Valletta 1991 Meeting on Peaceful Settlement of Disputes, containing the Principles for Dispute Settlement and the Provisions for a CSCE Procedure for Peaceful Settlement of Disputes, the Council establishes the following arrangements in accordance with the Charter of Paris.

The Council

1. designates the Conflict Prevention Centre (CPC) to act as the nominating institution in accordance with Section V of the said Provisions, and requests the Director of the Secretariat of the CPC to assume his functions accordingly under the overall responsibility of the Council;

2. invites each participating State desiring to do so to communicate as soon as possible and preferably by 30 August 1991 the names of up to four persons to be entered into the register of qualified candidates to be maintained by the nominating institution in accordance with section V of said Provisions;

3. decides that the mechanism will come into force as soon as forty nominations have been received by the Director;

4. instructs the Director of the Secretariat of the CPC to notify the full list of nominations as soon as the fortieth nomination is received and subsequently to notify any additions or revisions which may be made;

5. recalls the experience of the Permanent Court of Arbitration and its Secretary-General which should be drawn upon, if so agreed, when the CSCE Procedure for Peaceful Settlement of Disputes is implemented;

6. notes that appropriate use can be made of the premises and facilities of the International Bureau of the Permanent Court of Arbitration.

ANNEX 4

The Council welcomes the successful outcome of the meeting in Madrid on 2 and 3 April 1991 of parliamentarians from CSCE participating States.

They note with satisfaction the consensus reached to adopt the "Final Resolution concerning the establishment of the CSCE Parliamentary Assembly". The Council considers that this Resolution represents an important step forward for the development of the Charter of Paris for a New Europe regarding greater parliamentary involvement in the CSCE.

Reaffirming their commitment to strengthening democracy as the only system of government of their countries, the Ministers look forward to the collective expression of the views of the CSCE Parliamentary Assembly on security and co-operation in Europe and on the future development of the CSCE.

Guidelines concerning the procedures governing Meetings of the Council of Ministers[1]

The Council of Ministers of Foreign Affairs of the CSCE participating States conducts its business in accordance with the provisions set out below. The rules of procedure contained in the Final Recommendations of the Helsinki Consultations will, *mutatis mutandis*, be applied to the Council Meetings.

1. **Agenda**

1.0 The Meeting of the Committee of Senior Officials which immediately precedes the Meeting of the Council submits a draft agenda to the Council of Ministers for approval.

1.1 In order to facilitate the work of the Council, the participating States are encouraged - on the subjects which lend themselves to this - to make available to the Secretariat written contributions on the items which are proposed for the agenda. The Secretariat circulates these contributions to the other participating States.

2. **Conduct of Business**

2.0 The opening and closing meetings of the Council are open. There should be only one address during the opening meeting. This should be by a representative of the host country. The work of the Council of Ministers is conducted in closed session.

2.1 At the beginning of the meeting in closed session, the current Chairman of the Council submits the agenda for formal adoption by the Council.

2.2 Once the agenda has been adopted, the Chairman of the Council of Ministers declares open the exchange of views on the first agenda item, without a prior general discussion.

2.3 In the course of the debate, he takes into account the following recommendations:

---

[1] Journal No. 2, Annex 1 (Berlin, 19 June 1991).

- He suggests a fixed period of time which it would be appropriate to allow for dealing with this point and indicates the number of speakers having already asked for the floor.

- Having allowed a reasonable period of time for discussion, he submits for the approval of the Council a proposal to close the debate on the first item, and proceeds in the same way regarding the other items on the agenda.

2.4 At meetings of the Council each delegation has two seats at the table.

3. **Results of the Council's work**

3.0 A brief factual summary of the conclusions reached in the course of the Council's work is prepared under the responsibility of the Council Chairman, assisted, if considered necessary, by a drafting group.

3.1 At the closing meeting, the Chairman of the Council reads out his summary as approved by the Council.

3.2 The Secretariat is responsible for transmitting the results of the Council's work to the participating States.

3.3 These guidelines may be reviewed, and if necessary revised, in the light of experience.

Statement on the situation in Yugoslavia[2]

Ministers discussed the situation in Yugoslavia.

They were informed by H.E. the Federal Secretary for Foreign Affairs of Yugoslavia, Budimir Loncar, about the latest developments in Yugoslavia.

The Ministers expressed their friendly concern and their support for democratic development, unity and territorial integrity of Yugoslavia, based on economic reforms, full application of human rights in all parts of Yugoslavia, including the rights of minorities, and the peaceful solution of the current crisis in the country. They called for continued progress in these fields.

Ministers stressed that it is only for the peoples of Yugoslavia themselves to decide on the country's future. Ministers therefore called for a continued dialogue among all parties concerned and confirmed their view that the possibilities for such a dialogue were not yet exhausted.

They expressed their belief that the existing constitutional disputes should be remedied, and that the way out of the present difficult impasse should be found without recourse to the use of force and in conformity with legal and constitutional procedures. They urged all parties concerned to redouble their efforts to resolve their differences peacefully through negotiations.

Ministers expressed their confidence that on this basis the international community would stand ready to assist Yugoslavia's efforts to transform itself economically and politically.

---

[2] Journal No. 2, Annex 3 (Berlin, 19 June 1991).

MOSCOW ADDITIONAL MEETING OF THE CSCE COUNCIL

Moscow, 10 September 1991

Decision[1]

On the basis of the letters from the Minister of Foreign Affairs of Estonia, H.E. Mr. Lennart Meri, dated 5 September 1991, the Minister of Foreign Affairs of Latvia, H.E. Mr. Janis Jurkans, dated 6 September 1991, and the Minister of Foreign Affairs of Lithuania, H.E. Mr. Algirdas Saudargas, dated 6 September 1991, to the chairman of the Council, Federal Minister for Foreign Affairs of Germany, H.E. Mr. Hans-Dietrich Genscher (see Annex)[2], the Republic of Estonia, Latvia and Lithuania were admitted as participating States of the CSCE process, in virtue of paragraph 54 of the Final Recommendations of the Helsinki Consultations.

---

1 Additional meeting of the Council, Journal (Moscow, 10 September 1991) paragraph 4.

2 Editor's note: Not reproduced in the present volume.

PRAGUE MEETING OF THE CSCE COUNCIL

30-31 January 1992

SUMMARY OF CONCLUSIONS

I

1. The Council of the CSCE held its second Meeting in Prague on 30 and 31 January 1992.

2. The Ministers welcomed Armenia, Azerbaijan, Belarus, Kazakhstan, Kirgistan, Moldova, Tajikistan, Turkmenistan, Ukraine and Uzbekistan as participating States, following receipt of letters accepting CSCE commitments and responsibilities from each of them (Annex).

3. The Ministers granted observer status to Croatia and Slovenia in the CSCE process.

4. They welcomed as guests of honour the representatives of the heads of the following international institutions and organizations: United Nations; United Nations Economic Commission for Europe; Council of Europe; Western European Union; North Atlantic Treaty Organization; Organization for Economic Co-operation and Development; European Bank for Reconstruction and Development.

II

5. The Ministers had political consultations on the transformation in Europe — the role of the CSCE and the contribution of European and other institutions, and on the strengthening of CSCE institutions and structures and orientations for the Helsinki Follow-up Meeting. They adopted with immediate effect the Prague Document on the further development of the CSCE institutions and structures.

III

6. The Ministers agreed that the Helsinki Follow-up Meeting should be an important milestone in the development of the CSCE process and should provide a clear vision for its future course. Representatives to the Follow-up Meeting should, in particular, be guided by:

- the CSCE's comprehensive concept of security and stability, which includes human rights, political, military, economic and environmental components;
- the important role of the CSCE in fostering democratic development and fully integrating participating States into the network of shared CSCE values, principles and norms and its role in promoting a stable security environment in Europe;
- the importance of a thorough implementation review, particularly in the area of human rights and fundamental freedoms, which will take account of the new situation in Europe and the enlarged number of CSCE participating States;
- the objective of the CSCE to prevent conflict and consolidate peace through eliminating the root causes of tensions, by attaining in particular full respect for human rights, including those inscribed in the CSCE provisions on national minorities, by building democratic institutions and by fostering economic and social progress;
- the need to strengthen the capacity of the CSCE to contribute, in accordance with CSCE principles, to a peaceful solution of problems involving national minorities which could lead to tensions and conflict — both within and between States — including possibilities for 'early warning';
- the need for further development of the CSCE's capability for conflict prevention, crisis management and peaceful settlement of disputes;
- the need to strengthen the effectiveness of CSCE institutions by matching their functions more closely to the achievement of these objectives.

IV

7. The Ministers had a comprehensive discussion on the Yugoslav crisis. They welcomed the cease-fire agreements reached under the auspices of the United Nations, which are in the process of implementation, and renewed their strong appeal for strict compliance with those agreements.

The Ministers also warned against any extension of the present conflict.

They reaffirmed their support for the efforts undertaken by the Secretary-General and the Security Council of the United Nations, and reiterated the need to create the conditions for an early deployment of United Nations peace-keeping forces on the basis of resolution 727 of the United Nations Security Council on Yugoslavia. They endorsed the concept of the United Nations peace-keeping operation and expressed their hope that it would facilitate the political settlement of the Yugoslav crisis.

The Ministers reiterated the commitment of the participating States to seek a peaceful and lasting settlement of the crisis, in accordance with the commitments and provisions of the CSCE and the equal legitimate aspirations of all the peoples concerned. The Ministers agreed that this requires from all the concerned parties:

- respect for international obligations with regard to the rule of law, democracy and human rights;
- guarantees for the rights of ethnic and national communities and minorities, in accordance with the commitments subscribed to in the framework of the CSCE;
- respect for the inviolability of all borders, whether internal or external, which can only be changed by peaceful means and by common agreement;
- commitment to settle by agreement all questions concerning State succession and regional disputes;
- guarantees for the absence of territorial claims towards any neighbouring State, including abstention from hostile propaganda activities that would, *inter alia*, promote such territorial claims.

The Ministers reiterated the determination of their States to co-operate closely in the search for a comprehensive solution to the crisis, in particular to refrain from any action impeding these goals. They stressed the special need for dialogue and enhanced co-operation between neighbouring States to this end.

The Ministers expressed their profound concern about the humanitarian aspects of the crisis. They insisted that all parties involved allow emergency aid to reach all people and communities in need. They declared their support for all efforts, in particular those by the humanitarian agencies of the United Nations, to facilitate the return to their homes of all persons displaced by the hostilities who desire to do so.

They reminded all those responsible for acts of violence and for violations of cease-fire agreements that under international law they are personally accountable for their actions that are in contravention of relevant norms of international humanitarian law.

The Ministers fully endorsed the efforts of the Committee of Senior Officials, including those undertaken within the framework of the mechanism for consultation and co-operation with regard to emergency situations.

The Ministers expressed their appreciation for the activities of the Monitor Mission and recalled their support for the Conference on

Yugoslavia, and its Chairman, taking place under the sponsorship of the European Community and its member States, expressing the hope that agreement on a global settlement of the Yugoslav crisis, including all issues under consideration by the Conference, will soon be reached. A CSCE Human Rights Rapporteur Mission visited Yugoslavia and submitted its report. Taking into account the conclusions of this report, the Ministers expressed their view that the human rights situation in Yugoslavia, including the situation of national minorities, should be kept under review by the CSCE, and that full use should be made to that end of the various CSCE mechanisms, including, if necessary, other missions. They requested the Committee of Senior Officials at its next meeting to examine the need for further action.

V

8. The Ministers expressed their concern over new signs of intolerance, aggressive nationalism, xenophobia and racism. They recalled the importance of non-discrimination and stressed the need to build their societies according to the basic values of the CSCE.

The Ministers requested the Helsinki Follow-up Meeting to address the need to ensure full compliance through appropriate means with commitments to protect individuals and groups from racial, ethnic and religious discrimination.

VI

The Ministers also came to the following conclusions:

9. The Ministers reaffirmed that the CSCE has a vital role to play in the building and consolidation of a new Europe. The contribution that the CSCE has to make to the fostering of political stability and security is indispensable. The CSCE, with its comprehensive mandate and wide participation, constitutes a unique forum for security negotiations.

10. The Ministers stressed that the CSCE also has a prominent role to play in the evolving European architecture and that the challenges facing Europe call for multi-faceted forms of co-operation, and a close relationship among European, transatlantic and other international institutions and organizations, drawing as appropriate upon their respective competences.

They requested their representatives at the Helsinki Follow-up Meeting to study further ways and means of fostering such co-operation with a view to enhancing its effectiveness and to avoid duplication.

VII

11. The Ministers adopted the Declaration on Non-Proliferation and Arms Transfers.

12. They stressed that the establishment, by 1992, from the conclusion of the Helsinki Follow-up Meeting, of new negotiations on disarmament and confidence- and security-building open to all participating States — as well as of a broader security dialogue and of effective mechanisms for conflict prevention — will mark an important step in consolidating a new co-operative order in Europe. They assessed the progress made so far in the informal consultations in Vienna for the new forum. They requested that these consultations be accelerated and that their conclusions be transmitted to the Helsinki Follow-up Meeting at its beginning.

13. They agreed that the CFE Treaty forms an important element for stability and security in Europe. They called upon all signatories and all relevant newly independent Stats to take all the necessary steps to ensure the early entry into force of the Treaty.

14. They assessed the progress made so far in the negotiations in Vienna.
They instructed their representatives at the Negotiations on Confidence- and Security-building Measures to conclude them prior to the opening of the Helsinki Follow-up Meeting with a substantial new CSBM package.
They expressed the hope that an Open Skies Agreement will be ready for conclusion in time for the opening of the Helsinki Follow-up Meeting.
They welcomed the determination of the participants in the Negotiation on Conventional Armed Forces in Europe to conclude, in connection with the entry into force of the CFE Treaty, an agreement limiting the personnel strength of their conventional armed forces within the area of application in time for the Helsinki Follow-up Meeting. In this context they stressed the need for the early participation of the relevant newly independent States in these negotiations.

15. They took note of the discussion at the Second Seminar on Military Doctrine held within the framework of the Conflict Prevention Centre.

VIII

16. They took note and endorsed, as appropriate, the results of:
- the Geneva Meeting of Experts on National Minorities;
- the Moscow Meeting of the Conference on the Human Dimension of the CSCE;
- the Oslo Seminar of Experts on Democratic Institutions.

17. They noted the Report of the Rapporteur Mission to Albania.

18. They noted with satisfaction that the CSCE communications network is now operational and they expressed their expectations that full use will be made of it. They expressed special thanks to the Netherlands for the key role which that country had played in establishing this network.

19. The Ministers agreed that, in the light of the conclusions of the rapporteur missions to new CSCE States and of any requests received from them, and from other States recently admitted to the CSCE process, informal consultations under the direction of the Chairman of the CSO should take place at Helsinki, during the Follow-up Meeting, in order to establish the modalities for a programme of co-ordinated support to such States, through which appropriate diplomatic, academic, legal and administrative expertise and advice on CSCE matters could be made available.

20. The Ministers encouraged the establishment and strengthening of independent chambers of commerce in countries in transition to open market economies, to function as a point of contact for private business and financial interests, and to encourage entrepreneurial activity. The Ministers would welcome the development and expansion of the activities of the International Chamber of Commerce in this area in co-operation with other institutions undertaking similar work.

21. The Ministers took note of a proposal to invite a high-level group of legal experts from CSCE participating States to elaborate a draft statute for a CSCE conciliation and arbitration body, taking into account the work already done within the CSCE. They welcomed the intention to submit this draft to the Helsinki Follow-up Meeting.

22. They agreed that the next Meeting of the Council will be held in Stockholm in early December 1992. They will seek to confirm the specific days for this Meeting at the opening of the Helsinki Follow-up

Meeting based on the proposal of the host country (3-4 December 1992).

23. Recalling that the Heads of State or Government decided in the Charter of Paris to meet on the occasion of the CSCE Helsinki Follow-up Meeting, the Council proposed that the Summit Meeting should be held over two days beginning on 9 July 1992.

* * *

ANNEX

Wording of letters of accession, accepting CSCE commitments and responsibilities, submitted by:

- Mr. Raffi K. Hovannisian, Minister of Foreign Affairs of the Republic of Armenia
- Mr. G.M. Sadihov, Minister of Foreign Affairs of Azerbaijan
- Mr. Pyotr K. Kravchanka, Minister of Foreign Affairs of the Republic of Belarus
- Mr. Tuleutai Suleimenov, Minister of Foreign Affairs of the Republic of Kazakhstan
- Mr. M. Imanaliev, Minister of Foreign Affairs, Republic of Kirgistan
- Mr. Nicolae Tiu, Minister of Foreign Affairs of the Republic of Moldova
- Lakim Kayumov, Minister of Foreign Affairs of the Republic of Tajikistan
- Mr. Avdi Kuliev, Minister of Foreign Affairs of the Republic of Turkmenistan
- Mr. Anatoly Zlenko, Minister of Foreign Affairs of Ukraine
- Fatih G. Teshabayev, First Deputy Minister of Foreign Affairs, Republic of Uzbekistan

Dear Mr. Minister,

The Government of [name of the State] hereby adopts the Helsinki Final Act, the Charter of Paris for a New Europe, and all other documents of the Conference on Security and Co-operation in Europe.

The Government of [name of the State] accepts in their entirety all commitments and responsibilities contained in those documents, and declares its determination to act in accordance with their provisions.

Concerning the Vienna Document on Confidence- and Security-building Measures, the Government of [name of the State] agrees to apply all the provisions of the Vienna Document on CSBMs, and to an understanding that the geographic scope of its application should be revised as soon as possible in order to ensure full effect of the rules of transparency, predictability and conflict prevention on its territory. Specific provisions on the above matter will be negotiated in the CSBM Negotiations and included in the Vienna Document 1992.

The Government [name of the State] recognizes the requirement for prompt entry into force of the Treaty on Conventional Armed Forces in Europe. To that end, the Government of [name of the State] underlines the need for States with territory in the CFE area of application to undertake to move forward promptly with the ratification of the CFE Treaty and to assume, in co-operation with other relevant newly independent States, all CFE obligations of the former Soviet Union.

The Government of [name of the State] invites and will fully facilitate the visit of a Rapporteur Mission to be arranged by the chairman of the Council of Ministers of the CSCE. This Mission will report to the participating States on progress in [name of the State] toward full implementation of CSCE commitments and provide assistance toward that objective.

The Government of [name of the State] will concur in the admission of all other States established on the territory of the former Soviet Union as full participating States.

The Government of [name of the State] expressed its readiness for signature of the Helsinki Final Act and the Charter of Paris by the Head of State or Government of [name of the State] at the earliest convenience.

I kindly ask you, Mr. Minister, to circulate copies of this letter to all representatives of the participating States of the CSCE Council of Ministers.

Please accept, Mr. Minister, the assurances of my highest consideration.

Sincerely,

Prague Document on Further Development of CSCE Institutions and Structures

1. The Ministers reaffirmed their commitment to pursue actively all the objectives set out in the Charter of Paris for a New Europe, and their determination to further strengthen CSCE institutions and structures for this purpose. To this end they took the following decisions and established certain guidelines for the discussions at the Helsinki Follow-up Meeting.

I

Overview and co-ordination

2. Between meetings of the CSCE Council, the Committee of Senior Officials will be responsible for overview, management and co-ordination and will act as the Council's agent in taking appropriate decisions.

3. In order to increase its effectiveness, the Committee of Senior Officials will meet more regularly, at least every three months. In conformity with the Charter of Paris and building on established practice, the Committee of Senior Officials may delegate tasks to other CSCE institutions or to open-ended *ad hoc* groups of participating States with a precise mandate.

II

Political consultations

4. In order to further strengthen the political consultation process, the Committee of Senior Officials may set aside certain meetings, or parts thereof, for addressing previously agreed specific issues. Other relevant policy-level officials could attend such meetings.

5. The facilities of the CSCE communications network will be made available to the Chairman-in-Office of the Committee of Senior Officials for transmission of urgent messages related to the work of the Committee.

III

Human dimension

6. The Ministers agreed that monitoring and promoting progress in the human dimension remains a key function of the CSCE.

7. Issues related to the human dimension will therefore be considered by the Council or the Committee of Senior Officials whenever necessary.

8. In addition, meetings of a short duration may also be decided upon by the Committee of Senior Officials to address clearly defined issues. Results of such meetings will be submitted to the Council through the Committee of Senior Officials for consideration or decisions as required.

9. In order to extend practical co-operation among participating States in the human dimension, the Ministers decided to give additional functions to the Office for Free Elections which will henceforth be called the Office for Democratic Institutions and Human Rights.

10. Under the general guidance of the CSO, the office should, *inter alia*:
    - organize a short CSCE Meeting at the seat of the Office for Democratic Institutions and Human Rights to address implementation of CSCE human dimension commitments every year in which a follow-up meeting does not take place. The Helsinki Follow-up Meeting will work out the organizational modalities for such meetings;
    - serve as an institutional framework for sharing and exchanging information on available technical assistance, expertise, and national and international programmes aimed at assisting the new democracies in their institution-building;
    - facilitate contacts between those offering such resources and those wishing to make use of them;
    - develop co-operation with the Council of Europe in order to make use of its database of such resources and services;
    - establish contacts with non-governmental organizations active in the field of democratic institution-building, with a view to enabling interested participating States to make use of their extensive resources and expertise;
    - facilitate co-operation in training and education in disciplines relevant to democratic institutions;

- organize meetings and seminars among all participating States on subjects related to the building and revitalization of democratic institutions, such as a short seminar on free media and, at an appropriate time, one on migration. These meetings and seminars will be held in Warsaw unless otherwise decided.

11. In order to avoid duplication of work specially in the fields enumerated above, the Ministers directed the Office to work closely with other institutions active in the field of democratic institution-building and human rights, particularly the Council of Europe and the European Commission for Democracy through Law.

12. The CSO will on an annual basis examine the need for meetings and seminars on the human dimension and democratic institutions and will establish a work programme.

13. The Ministers requested the Helsinki Follow-up Meeting to further specify the task of the Warsaw Office and to decide how the human dimension activities of the CSCE may be further carried forward.

14. The Office for Democratic Institutions and Human Rights is designated as the CSCE institution charged with the tasks in connection with expert and rapporteur missions according to the Document of the Moscow Meeting of the Conference on the Human Dimension of the CSCE.

15. The Office for Democratic Institutions and Human Rights will be connected to the CSCE communications network.

IV

Safeguarding human rights, democracy and the rule of law

16. The Council decided, in order to develop further the CSCE's capability to safeguard human rights, democracy and the rule of law through peaceful means, that appropriate action may be taken by the Council or the Committee of Senior Officials, if necessary in the absence of the consent of the State concerned, in cases of clear, gross and uncorrected violations of relevant CSCE commitments. Such actions would consist of political declarations or other political steps to apply outside the territory of the State concerned. This decision is without prejudice to existing CSCE mechanisms.

17. The Council requested the Helsinki Follow-up Meeting to consider further modalities in applying this decision.

V

Economic Co-operation

18. The Ministers agreed on the need to continue their efforts to strengthen the focus of CSCE on the transition to and development of free-market economies as an essential contribution to the building of democracy.

19. To this end, they agreed to establish an Economic Forum within the framework of the CSO. The CSO would convene as the economic forum to give political stimulus to the dialogue on these topics, to suggest practical efforts for the development of free-market systems and economic co-operation, and to encourage activities already underway within organizations such as the Organization for Economic Co-operation and Development (OECD), the European Investment Bank (EIB), the European Bank for Reconstruction and Development (EBRD) and the United Nations Economic Commission for Europe (ECE). The Forum will meet periodically in Prague and can invite contributions to its meetings by those European and transatlantic organizations relevant to the subject under discussion. It was agreed that the first meeting of the Economic Forum would be in early 1993.

20. The Ministers agreed that the Helsinki Follow-up Meeting will consider appropriate further measures to promote discussions in the framework of the CSCE on economic co-operation and related topics.

VI

Crisis management and conflict prevention instruments

21. The Council agreed that the capabilities of the CSCE to engage in crisis management and conflict prevention and resolution should be improved.

22. To this end, the Council requested the Helsinki Follow-up Meeting to study possibilities for improving the following instruments:
- fact finding and rapporteur missions;
- monitor missions;
- good offices;
- counselling and conciliation;

- dispute settlement.

23. In this context the Helsinki Follow-up Meeting should also give careful consideration to possibilities for CSCE peacekeeping or a CSCE role in peacekeeping.

24. Provision should be made for the further operational implementation within the CSCE of decisions by the Council or the Committee of Senior Officials.

25. Tasks may be delegated to the Chairman-in-Office of the Committee of Senior Officials, to the Consultative Committee of the Conflict Prevention Centre or to open-ended groups of participating States of an *ad hoc* character. In each case a precise mandate and arrangements for reporting back should be established.

Conflict Prevention Centre

26. In addition to the tasks already given to the Conflict Prevention Centre in the Supplementary Document of the Paris Charter and in the Summary of Conclusions of the Berlin Meeting of the CSCE Council, the functions and working methods of the CPC are enhanced as follows:

27. The Consultative Committee will serve as a forum in the security field wherein the CSCE participating States will conduct comprehensive and regular consultations on security issues with politico-military implications. In this context, any participating State may, in order to reduce the risk of conflict, promptly raise an issue which in its view has such implications. This is without prejudice to later decisions on the structure of a new security/arms control forum and the relationship it may have to the CPC.

28. The Consultative Committee will serve as a forum for consultation and co-operation in conflict prevention and for co-operation in the implementation of decisions on crisis management taken by the Council or by the CSO acting as its agent.

29. The Consultative Committee has the authority to initiate and, with the assistance of the CPC Secretariat, execute fact-finding and monitor missions in connection with paragraph 17 of the Vienna Document 1990 (Mechanism for Consultation and Co-operation as regards Unusual Military Activities).

30. The Consultative Committee, with the assistance of the CPC Secretariat, will execute any additional tasks assigned to it by the Council, or by the Committee of Senior Officials acting as its agent. This will include full responsibility in the implementation of such tasks. The Consultative Committee will report in an appropriate manner on the implementation of these tasks to the Committee of Senior Officials.

31. The Consultative Committee will develop general guidelines for the implementation of its operational tasks including, in due time, those that may be assigned to it by the Helsinki Follow-up Meeting and in the future.

32. In addition to the existing support to the implementation of CSBMs, the CPC will fulfil other functions as regards the implementation and verification of agreements in the field of disarmament and arms control, if so requested by the parties to those agreements and agreed upon by the Consultative Committee.

33. The Consultative Committee may at any time draw the attention of the Committee of Senior Officials to a situation which it considers requires the consideration of the Committee of Senior Officials.

34. The Consultative Committee will meet regularly, as a rule at least once a month. Working schedules should be flexible and additional meetings may be held, in the light of circumstances and future requirements.

35. The Consultative Committee may establish subsidiary working bodies, including open-ended *ad hoc* groups entrusted with specific tasks.

36. The regular meetings of the Consultative Committee will be chaired in alphabetical rotation. The Chairmanship will rotate immediately after the last regular meeting in every month.

37. The Chairman of the Consultative Committee and the Chairman of the Committee of Senior Officials will maintain contact with each other.

38. The Chairman of the Consultative Committee or his representative will attend meetings of the Committee of Senior Officials which are relevant to the tasks of the CPC.

39. In accordance with the paragraph on 'CSCE Relationship with International Organizations', European, Transatlantic and other

international organizations, such as the North Atlantic Treaty Organization (NATO), the Western European Union (WEU) and relevant United Nations bodies, will be invited to make appropriate contributions to future seminars organized by the CPC.

* * * * *

40. The Helsinki Follow-up Meeting should also examine further how the CSCE could co-operate with other international organizations in these fields.

VII

Parliamentary Assembly

41. In the interest of encouraging an active dialogue with the CSCE Parliamentary Assembly, the Chairman-in-Office of the Council will be in contact with the Chairman of the Committee of Heads of Delegation of the Assembly in order to explore possible interest in the presence of the Chairman of the Council at the Budapest Meeting of the Assembly in July 1992. The Chairman of the Council will be prepared to make himself available to report on the work of the CSCE; to answer parliamentarians' questions in this regard; and to take note of parliamentarians' views for subsequent transmission to the Council.

VIII

Non-Governmental Organizations

42. The Council requests the Helsinki Follow-up Meeting to strengthen relations between the CSCE and non-governmental organizations, in order to increase the role of non-governmental organizations in implementing CSCE goals and commitments. In particular, the Follow-up Meeting will develop opportunities and procedures for meaningful non-governmental organization involvement in the CSCE and possibilities for non-governmental organizations to communicate with CSCE structures and institutions, recalling *inter alia* the texts on non-governmental organizations agreed by the Sofia and Moscow Meetings and by the Oslo Seminar.

IX

CSCE relationship with international organizations

43. The Council of Europe, ECE, NATO, the Western European Union, OECD, EBRD, EIB and other European and transatlantic organizations which may be agreed will be invited to make contributions on the basis of CSCE precedent and practice to specialized CSCE Meetings where they have relevant expertise.

44. To ensure full co-ordination, the Ministers would welcome it if the above organizations would inform the CSCE Secretariat annually of their current work programme and of the facilities available for work relevant to the CSCE.

X

Relations with non-participating States

45. The Council requests the Helsinki Follow-up Meeting to recommend practical ways to establish a flexible dialogue between the CSCE and interested non-participating States or groups of States, for example through contacts between the said States and the Chairman-in-Office of the Council or of the Committee of Senior Officials.

XI

Financial arrangements of the CSCE and cost-effectiveness

46. The Council requested the Helsinki Follow-up Meeting to develop procedures which would ensure greater predictability and transparency of the costs of CSCE meetings and other activities. Measures to provide for increased cost-effectiveness should also be examined.

47. States proposing to host future CSCE meetings will present draft budgets along with their proposals. Detailed provisions in this respect will be developed at the Helsinki Follow-up Meeting.

INTERPRETATIVE STATEMENTS[1]

Interpretative statement by Romania

In connection with the adoption of the Prague Document on Further Development of CSCE Institutions and Structures, the delegation of Romania stated:

The Romanian delegation joined the other delegations in agreeing to a departure from the consensus rule in cases of clear and gross violations of CSCE commitments regarding human rights, democracy and the rule of law (section IV, paragraph 16 of the document).

We did so because the hypothesis of resorting to this procedure preoccupies us to the same extent like the other CSCE participating States. In fact, what is at stake are human rights and democracy, and those values are too dear to us, after so many decades of communist dictatorship, not to uphold them in every conceivable way.

However, we believe that through a future joint effort to clarify - at the Helsinki Follow-up Meeting - the conditions and the modalities of implementing this procedure, we should try to prevent the risks that resorting to it might become a stimulus for those who may be tempted to use the issues of human rights, including in particular the rights of persons belonging to minorities, as a substitute for promoting a revisionist policy, through incitation from outside of tensions, unrest and even conflicts in another country. In their turn, such tensions, unrest or conflicts would then be invoked as a device of politically stigmatizing and make vulnerable a country, in order to serve that policy.

Therefore, such risks that might affect also stability and security in Europe as a whole should be avoided, through a process of consultation during the preparatory stage of the Helsinki Follow-up Meeting and during the Meeting itself, in order to work out detailed rules and modalities of implementing this procedure, including guidelines to define the concept of 'clear, gross and uncorrected violation' of human rights, democracy and rule of law, and which is the forum that establishes that such violations are occurring, in such a way as to make sure that resort to it would be exceptional and in extreme situations, when none of the other possibilities of action through the CSCE mechanism has produced results, or was practicable.

---

1 2-C/Journal No. 1 (Prague, 30 January 1992).

Declaration of the CSCE Council on Non-Proliferation and Arms Transfers

The Ministers reiterated the commitment of their Governments to the prevention of the proliferation of weapons of mass destruction and the control of missile technology. They underlined their willingness to contribute to the ongoing efforts and international co-operation to this end. In this context, they expressed their support for the Treaty on the Non-Proliferation of Nuclear Weapons and for universal adherence to it. They welcomed the intention of all those CSCE-States not yet party to the NPT to accede to it and urged other States, who are not yet party to it, to do so as well. They also renewed their support for a global, comprehensive and effectively verifiable chemical weapons convention to be concluded in 1992. They also reaffirmed their support for the biological weapons convention, welcomed the results of the September 1991 review conference and called for universal adherence to it.

They expressed their view that excessive build-ups of conventional weapons beyond legitimate defensive needs pose a threat to international peace and security in particular in regions of tension. Based on the principles of transparency, consultation and restraint, they declared their commitment to address the threat of exercise responsibility, in particular with regard to arms transfers to States engaging in such excessive accumulations and to regions of tension.

They confirmed their support for and firmly committed themselves to provide full information to the United Nations Register of Conventional Arms. They called upon all other States to take the same action.

They agreed that effective national control of weapons and equipment transfer is acquiring the greatest importance. They declared their readiness to exchange views and to provide mutual assistance in the establishment of efficient national control mechanisms.

They agreed that in this connection the conversion of arms production to civilian production is also acquiring special importance.

The Ministers decided that the question of non-proliferation, including the transfer of sensitive expertise, and the establishment of a responsible approach to international armaments transfers should be included as a matter of priority in the work programme for the post Helsinki arms control process.

Helsinki Additional Meeting of the CSCE Council

24 March 1992

Summary of Conclusions

I

1. The Council of the CSCE held its First Additional Meeting in Helsinki on 24 March 1992

2. The Ministers welcomed Croatia, Georgia and Slovenia as participating States, following receipt of letters accepting CSCE commitments and responsibilities from each of them (Annexes 1-3)[1]. The Ministers do not consider that the admission of Croatia and Slovenia affects in any way the Conference on Yugoslavia nor prejudges the results of this Conference. The Ministers support the efforts of the Brussels Conference on Yugoslavia in search of an overall political settlement of the Yugoslav crisis.

II

3. The Ministers expressed their deep concern about the continuing escalation of the armed conflict in and around Nagorno-Karabakh and the resulting increased suffering and loss of life of the inhabitants. They held an extensive discussion of ways and means to end the conflict, bearing in mind the implications for regional and international security which could result from its continuation and further extension. They called upon all parties to exercise restraint.

4. The Ministers reiterated in the strongest terms the call for an immediate and effective cease-fire including an active commitment by responsible local commanders to its implementation. They issued an appeal for the re-establishment of conditions for confidence and constructive dialogue, including the cessation of measures of economic and political constraint.

---

[1] Editor's note: Not reproduced in the present volume.

5. The Ministers reviewed the ongoing action within the CSCE framework and endorsed in their entirety the decisions taken by the Committee of Senior Officials. They expressed their appreciation for the activities of the Chairman-in-Office of the CSCE undertaken in this connection and stressed their willingness to extend all possible assistance to him whenever it is needed.

6. The Ministers welcomed the complementary efforts made by the European Community and its member States, by the member States of the Commonwealth of Independent States, by the members of the North Atlantic Co-operation Council, and, in particular, the efforts made by the United Nations Secretary-General.
They requested the Chairman-in-Office of the CSCE to keep in close contact with the United Nations in this respect and to arrange for regular exchanges of information.
The Ministers agreed that the CSCE must play a major role in promoting a peace process relating to the conflict. They agreed that the situation in and around Nagorno-Karabakh requires further CSCE action.

7. The Ministers mandated the Chairman-in-Office of the CSCE Council of Ministers, Mr. Jirí Dienstbier, to visit the region shortly in order to contribute, in particular, to the establishment and maintenance of an effective cease-fire as well as to the establishment of a framework for an overall peaceful settlement.

8. The Ministers expressed their firm conviction that a conference on Nagorno-Karabakh under the auspices of the CSCE would provide an ongoing forum for negotiations towards a peaceful settlement of the crisis on the basis of the principles, commitments and provisions of the CSCE. The Ministers therefore requested the Chairman-in-Office of the CSCE Council of Ministers to convene such a conference as soon as possible.

9. The Ministers furthermore agreed that this Conference, which will take place in Minsk, will have as participants Armenia, Azerbaijan, Belarus, Czech and Slovak Federal Republic, France, Germany, Italy, Russian Federation, Sweden, Turkey and United States of America. Elected and other representatives of Nagorno-Karabakh will be invited to the Conference as interested parties by the Chairman of the Conference after consultation with the States participating at the Conference. The Chairman-in-Office of the CSCE Council will appoint

the Chairman of the Conference on Nagorno-Karabakh under the auspices of the CSCE.

10. The Ministers urged all CSCE participating States and all concerned parties to take all necessary steps to ensure that humanitarian assistance is provided to all those in need through rapid and effective means including safe corridors under international control.

11. The Ministers noted the commitment of Armenia and Azerbaijan to fully support the mission of the Chairman-in-Office of the CSCE Council to the region as well as other actions on which the CSCE Council has agreed and appeal to these two countries to pursue actively this commitment to reach a lasting, peaceful solution.

III

12. The Ministers agreed that the Stockholm Council Meeting will be held on 14-15 December 1992.

INTERPRETATIVE STATEMENT[1]

Interpretative statement by Azerbaijan

The Delegation of the Azerbaijan Republic, accepting the Summary of Conclusions of the Helsinki Additional Meeting of the CSCE Council and particularly paragraph 9, would like to reaffirm that Nagorno-Karabakh is an integral part of the Azerbaijan Republic and any representation of its inhabitants would not in any way prejudice that fact.

---

[1] C/1-AM/Journal (Helsinki, 24 March 1992), paragraph 6.

STOCKHOLM MEETING OF THE CSCE COUNCIL

Stockholm, 15 December 1992

SUMMARY OF CONCLUSIONS

Shaping a new Europe - the role of the CSCE

The CSCE Council held its Third Meeting in Stockholm on 14-15 December 1992.

The Ministers consulted on a broad range of issues, in particular the aggression in Bosnia-Herzegovina and Croatia, the crisis in parts of the former Yugoslavia, other regional crises and issues together with the strategy and structure of the CSCE.

In the light of serious threats to peace and security in the CSCE area the Ministers agreed to pursue a strategy of active diplomacy. They will provide the necessary resources.

The Ministers expressed their continuing commitment to use the CSCE to consolidate human rights, democracy, the rule of law and economic freedom as the foundation for peace, security and stability and to prevent, manage and solve conflicts in the CSCE area.

The Ministers condemned the extended use of force in Europe which has bred ever more violence and hatred. They strongly rejected continuing flagrant violations of human rights. They committed themselves to act to counter the growing manifestations of racism, anti-semitism and all forms of intolerance in the CSCE area.

The Ministers agreed to improve co-operation with relevant international organizations. They decided, in particular, to increase co-ordination with the United Nations.

Important aspects of the CSCE strategy include:

- Strengthening the CSCE's operational capabilities through structural reforms and the appointment of a Secretary General;

- Emphasizing the CSCE's ability to provide early warning through the appointment of a High Commissioner on National Minorities who will enjoy the full political support of all participating States;

- Active use of missions and representatives as part of preventive diplomacy to promote dialogue, stability and provide for early warning;

- Enhancing opportunities for the peaceful settlement of disputes through the approval of a comprehensive set of measures to this end. The Ministers stressed their expectations that participating States will avail themselves increasingly of these mechanisms;

- Effective use of missions and representatives in crisis areas as part of a strategy of consultation, negotiation and concerted action to limit conflicts before they become violent;

- Co-operating, as appropriate, with international organizations and with individual participating States to ensure that the broad spectrum of CSCE mechanisms and procedures, including peacekeeping, can be applied;

- Increased efforts at treating the root causes of conflicts by applying all aspects of the human dimension of the CSCE and by involving non-governmental organizations and individual citizens more directly in the work of the CSCE;

- Making all governments accountable to each other for their behaviour towards their citizens and towards neighbouring States and holding individuals personally accountable for war crimes and acts in violation of international humanitarian law;

- Greater use of the Forum for Security and Co-operation as a place for negotiation and dialogue which can ensure continued progress in reducing the risks of military conflict and enhancing stability in Europe;

- An active programme to help newly-admitted participating States to participate fully in the structures and work of the CSCE.

DECISIONS

1. Regional issues

Former Yugoslavia

1. The CSCE has given early and special attention to the tragic conflict in the former Yugoslavia which has led to all-out war and immense human suffering and which poses a growing threat to peace in the region.

2. Primary responsibility for the conflict lies with the present leaders of Serbia and Montenegro and with the Serbian forces operating in Bosnia-Herzegovina. In defiance of all efforts by the entire international community, these authorities continue to pursue territorial gain through the use of force and to violate basic human standards through the odious practice of 'ethnic cleansing', and other brutalities affecting many parts of the former Yugoslavia. All this must stop immediately.

3. The Ministers expressed their collective and individual determination to pursue all efforts to restore peace in former Yugoslavia. They did so on the basis of the special moral and political authority represented by the principles and commitments of the CSCE. They presented the leaders of Serbia and Montenegro with a clear choice. If there is a radical change of their policy towards their neighbours and their own people and genuine co-operation in the peace process, Serbia will be gradually readmitted to the international community; if, on the other hand, the Belgrade regime continues its present policies, the international community will take sterner action to ensure compliance with the relevant United Nations Security Council resolutions and the decisions of the International Conference on Former Yugoslavia.

4. The Ministers are using the means available to the CSCE to contribute to international efforts to end the fighting and prevent spillover of the conflict. They are working towards several immediate objectives:

- An end to systematic aggression in Bosnia-Herzegovina and Croatia, exemplified by recent stepped-up attacks against Sarajevo and other cities and villages in other parts of Bosnia-Herzegovina by Serb forces, and the prevention of a further expansion of the conflict to other areas of the former Yugoslavia and to countries neighbouring on Serbia and Montenegro.

- Cessation of violations of human rights and international humanitarian law, specifically the policy of 'ethnic cleansing' in particular in

Bosnia-Herzegovina as well as in Kosovo, Sandjak and Vojvodina and the systematic rape of Muslim women, and steps to ensure prosecution of those personally accountable.

- Expansion of humanitarian assistance to ease current suffering and measures to assure its rapid delivery to those most in need.

- An end to the systematic destruction of mosques, Catholic churches, synagogues and other religious monuments as well as other sites of cultural heritage in areas under Serbian control.

- A negotiated political settlement to the current conflict that preserves the integrity of Bosnia-Herzegovina, denies any gain through the seizure of territory by force and provides for the safe return of refugees and displaced persons to their homes.

- Effective fulfilment of the UNPROFOR mandate in the UNPA zones in Croatia and full implementation of the Vance Plan.

5. The Ministers requested the Chairman-in-Office, assisted by the Troika, to report to the Steering Committee of the International Conference on Former Yugoslavia on 16 December 1992, and to work to ensure closer co-ordination between the CSCE and the ICFY.

6. They requested her, assisted by the Troika, to travel to Belgrade prior to the elections on 20 December 1992 to underline to Serbian authorities the stark fate and the increased penalties with which they will be faced. She is requested also to visit as soon as possible CSCE missions in former Yugoslavia to highlight their importance and enhanced role.

7. The war in Bosnia-Herzegovina must stop. The sovereignty and territorial integrity of that country must be respected. The war must not be allowed to spread into other parts of the former Yugoslavia. This would have even more serious implications for the region.

8. The Ministers stressed the importance of the work of the CSCE missions of long duration in Kosovo, Sandjak and Vojvodina. They expressed their satisfaction with the work of the CSCE Spillover Mission to the former Yugoslav Republic of Macedonia, established in the Republic with the full co-operation of its governmental authorities, further to the initiative of the CSCE. They are determined to give all necessary support to these efforts. The CSCE presence there should be maintained and expanded; the missions should increasingly focus on helping to resolve specific local differences. In

particular, the Ministers agreed to increase substantially the size of the missions of long duration, with particular emphasis on Kosovo, and to take the necessary steps accordingly. They undertook to contribute urgently to these missions.

9. The Ministers, referring to the calls from some States for the United Nations to consider lifting the arms embargo against the Government of Bosnia-Herzegovina, recalled United Nations Security Council resolution 713 and recommended that this issue should continue to be considered as a matter of importance in the United Nations Security Council.

10. The Ministers welcomed the decision of the United Nations Security Council to place peacekeeping forces on the borders of the former Yugoslav Republic of Macedonia with Albania and Serbia and Montenegro. The present active role of the CSCE in seeking to prevent the spillover of conflict and tension will be substantially reinforced.

11. They supported the efforts of those political forces in Serbia that are striving to bring about full co-operation with the peace process. The Office for Democratic Institutions and Human Rights will assist participating States in the monitoring of the elections in Yugoslavia (Serbia and Montenegro). The participating States will draw the appropriate conclusions if the present authorities do not follow fair and just procedures.

12. All CSCE participating States committed themselves to scrupulous implementation of all United Nations Security Council resolutions on sanctions against Serbia-Montenegro. The Ministers recognized that countries of the region should not bear alone the unintended negative consequences of United Nations sanctions against Serbia-Montenegro. They urged the competent international organizations to provide appropriate financial and technical assistance to those countries in order to diminish the adverse effect. Efforts of the Government of Serbia-Montenegro to circumvent the sanctions need to be combated. They approved the deployment of Sanctions Assistance Missions to all States neighbouring Serbia and Montenegro and the expansion of their size. They welcomed the co-operation extended to the missions and called on participating States to provide technical assistance on enforcing sanctions to host countries. The mandate of the missions was extended for a further six months from 1 January 1993.

13. The Ministers reiterated their horror and dismay at the massive and systematic violations of human rights and international humanitarian law in the territory of the Republic of Bosnia-Herzegovina and other parts of the former Yugoslavia. They supported United Nations Security Council

resolutions 780 (1992) and 787 (1992) which emphasize that those responsible for such crimes will be held personally accountable. They are determined to implement these resolutions and to see to it that those responsible are brought to justice and asked the Chairman-in-Office to consult on this issue with the United Nations, especially the International Law Commission, and with the Co-Chairmen of the ICFY.

14. The Ministers welcomed the offer of the rapporteurs on Croatia and Bosnia-Herzegovina under the Moscow Human Dimension Mechanism to refine their proposals on making the principle of personal accountability effective, including the possibility of the establishment of an *ad hoc* tribunal, and to do so through continuing consultations with the Commission of Experts established pursuant to Security Council resolution 780 (1992).

15. The Ministers strongly supported the ICFY process and the efforts of the Co-Chairmen; they would like to see early results. They endorsed the constitutional arrangements for Bosnia-Herzegovina proposed by the Co-Chairmen in Geneva on 27 October 1992 as a basis for agreement. They hoped that at the meeting on 16 December 1992, participants will discuss the measures necessary to intensify pressure on the Serbian side in order to end the bloodshed. They called on all parties to negotiate constructively on a Bosnian constitution, as well as on the other problems under relevant working groups of the Geneva Conference, including the future status of Kosovo. Safeguards for the rights of national minorities within Serbia, including autonomy where appropriate, must be ensured.

16. The Ministers demanded full compliance by all parties with United Nations Security Council resolutions and with all decisions of the ICFY. Observers should be placed on the border of Bosnia-Herzegovina and Serbia and Montenegro without further delay. In view of the many violations of the no-fly zone, they believed that the Security Council should urgently consider taking the relevant decisions in the light of paragraph 6 of resolution 786.

17. The human rights and fundamental freedoms of the inhabitants of Kosovo must be respected. The Ministers called upon all parties, notably the Serbian authorities, to show the necessary restraint. They believed that a United Nations presence in Kosovo would be a positive step.

18. The Ministers paid tribute to UNHCR, ICRC and UNPROFOR and agreed to do more to ease suffering. They endorsed efforts under United Nations Security Council resolution 787 to ensure the safe delivery of humanitarian assistance, including the use of military means. They called on all parties to allow convoys safe passage, noting that interference in

humanitarian relief missions is an international crime for which the individuals responsible will be held personally accountable. They called for the urgent opening of the airports at Tuzla and Bihac in Bosnia-Herzegovina for the receipt of humanitarian aid. Given the importance of the work being undertaken by UNPROFOR II, they called on all CSCE participating States to support fully a broader financial burden-sharing.

19. More action is needed to provide safety and protection to the civilian population through the development of safe areas and the provision of refuge for particularly vulnerable categories of refugees. The Ministers were concerned by the increasing problem of refugees and displaced persons and called upon all participating States to do more to share economic and other burdens of States receiving refugees.

The Baltic States

The Ministers reviewed the implementation of paragraph 15 of the Helsinki Summit Declaration 1992.

Notwithstanding certain progress achieved, they expressed their concern that relevant agreements on the early, orderly and complete withdrawal of foreign troops from the territories of the Baltic States have yet to be concluded, and noted that the withdrawal of these troops should take place in full accordance with the basic principles of international law.

The CSCE will remain engaged therefore in the implementation of these provisions.

To that end, the Baltic States and the Russian Federation undertake regularly to submit information to relevant CSCE bodies about the implementation of paragraph 15 of the Helsinki Summit Declaration 1992, necessary for further review of this issue.

Moldova

The Ministers welcomed the easing of tension in the Left-Bank Dniester Areas of the Republic of Moldova, noting at the same time that a final political settlement of the conflict should be reached in order to establish durable peace in the region.

The Ministers noted with appreciation the activities of the Personal Representative of the Chairman-in-Office of the CSCE Council on the conflict in the Left-Bank Dniester Areas of the Republic of Moldova. They took note also of the interest of all parties involved in a CSCE role in efforts to settle the conflict. They requested all parties to the conflict to co-operate closely with the Personal Representative of the Chairman-in-Office. They called for the soonest possible conclusion of the work of the Personal Representative. They expected the final report and recommendations to be available at the next session of the CSO with a view to further CSCE involvement.

In this context, the Ministers expressed support for efforts to remove, in a peaceful manner and through negotiations, the problems that remain from the past, such as the stationing of foreign armed forces on the territory of the Republic of Moldova. They called on the participating States concerned to conclude, without delay, an appropriate bilateral agreement on the status and the early, orderly and complete withdrawal of foreign troops.

Georgia

1. The Ministers reiterated their commitment to support the stabilization of the situation within Georgia and the development of democracy and a market economy, which would create favourable conditions for the peaceful resolution of the conflict. In this context they welcomed the progress of democracy with the election of a legitimate government and hoped that the election process would soon be completed in a satisfactory manner.

2. The Ministers were pleased to note that the cease-fire between Georgians and Ossetians in the area of conflict continued to hold. They were concerned however that no progress had been made towards a political settlement of this dispute. They welcomed the establishment of a visible CSCE presence in the area. They were pleased that first contacts had been established with representatives of both conflicting parties, the trilateral peacekeeping forces and local military commanders. They likewise called upon the parties to co-operate fully with the Personal Representative of the Chairman-in-Office in his efforts to establish the framework for a peaceful and lasting solution, as stipulated by the provisions of the Sochi Agreement of 24 June 1992.

3. The Ministers remained deeply concerned at the recent upsurge in fighting in Abkhazia and at reports of heavy loss of life and lack of discipline and moderation among the armed forces of the protagonists. They urged all parties to the dispute in Abkhazia to renew their efforts to find a peaceful settlement in conformity with CSCE principles and the Charter of the United Nations, based on the provisions of the Moscow agreement of 3 September 1992. They requested the parties to co-operate with the CSCE Mission, led

by Ambassador Gyarmati, whose mandate included establishing a framework for political negotiations.

4. They requested the Chairman-in-Office and the Personal Representative of the Chairman-in-Office in Georgia to work out, in co-operation with the United Nations, practical modalities for co-ordination of efforts in order to ensure maximum efficiency through a rational division of labour. The participating States will be kept informed.

Conflict dealt with by the Conference on Nagorno-Karabakh

The Ministers asked the Chairman of the CSCE Conference on Nagorno-Karabakh, Hon. Mario Raffaelli, and the 'Minsk Group' to continue their tireless efforts to advance the peace process.

The Republic of Tajikistan

The Ministers expressed their deep concern about the crisis situation in the Republic of Tajikistan.

They urged all the conflicting parties to cease fighting and to start a constructive dialogue, which is the only basis for a political settlement in Tajikistan.

They encouraged participating States to contribute to humanitarian efforts in Tajikistan, especially in the light of that country's refugee crisis.

The Ministers noted the peace-making efforts of Russia, Kazakhstan, Kyrgyzstan and Uzbekistan aimed at the ending of bloodshed and the promotion of the negotiation process.

The Ministers considered that this issue should be studied by the CSO on a priority basis, bearing in mind the need for close co-operation with the efforts of the United Nations.

2. The CSCE as a Community of Values

The CSCE's comprehensive concept of security relates peace, security and prosperity directly to the observance of human rights and democratic freedoms. Many of the present problems are linked to the failure to observe CSCE commitments and principles.

The human dimension mechanisms of the CSCE are being used increasingly as a major foundation for the CSCE's efforts at early warning and conflict prevention. Their further elaboration and utilization will strengthen considerably the CSCE's ability to pursue the root causes of tensions and to refine its mechanisms for early warning on potentially dangerous situations.

The Ministers welcomed the strengthened role of the Office for Democratic Institutions and Human Rights and the appointment of the High Commissioner on National Minorities as especially useful steps towards integrating the human dimension more fully into the political consultations and concerted action of the participating States. They also decided to consider ways of using the 1993 Implementation Meeting on Human Dimension Issues to investigate possible new means of utilizing human rights mechanisms for these purposes. They expressed the hope that newly-admitted participating States would make particular use of the opportunities provided by these institutions.

Compliance with CSCE commitments is of fundamental importance. Monitoring of compliance provides governments of participating States with crucial information on which they can formulate policy. The Implementation Meeting on Human Dimension Issues to be held in 1993 offers an opportunity to improve the monitoring of compliance with Human Dimension commitments.

The Ministers expressed their profound concern at the recent manifestations of aggressive nationalism, xenophobia, anti-semitism, racism and other violations of human rights. Violations of international humanitarian law and CSCE principles and commitments, such as 'ethnic cleansing', or mass deportation, endangered the maintenance of peace, security and democracy and will not be tolerated. They were convinced that increased attention should be paid by the CSCE, and in particular by the Committee of Senior Officials and the High Commissioner on National Minorities, to these threats to human rights and fundamental freedoms. The CSO will report on this issue to the Council of Ministers at its next Meeting, when the Council will consider developments.

The Ministers also stressed the important role the Human Dimension of the CSCE should play in longer-term conflict prevention. They underlined the need for positive action aimed at fostering understanding, tolerance and national and local preventive action. They emphasized the importance of direct contact between experts, governmental and non-governmental, through the series of Human Dimension seminars successfully begun by the CSCE

Seminar on Tolerance and to be followed in 1993 by seminars on national minorities, migration and free media.

The increasing problem of refugees and displaced persons is an issue of major concern to all participating States, particularly in conflicts where the fulfilment of basic human needs is most at risk. The Ministers deplored the plight of civil populations most affected in such conflicts and called on all participating States to contribute to a concerted effort to share the common burden. All Governments are accountable to each other for their behaviour towards their citizens and towards their neighbours. Individuals are to be held personally accountable for war crimes and acts in violation of international humanitarian law.

The Ministers welcomed the rapid convening of the Human Dimension Seminar on Migration as an important contribution to pursuing better understanding of the underlying causes of uncontrolled migration. Another important step towards furthering implementation of existing human rights standards, including CSCE principles and commitments, will be the United Nations Conference on Human Rights, to be held in Vienna in June 1993. The Ministers expressed their support for the Conference and asked the Chairman-in-Office to represent them there.

The CSCE will continue to give political stimulus to the development of market economies by facilitating, through the March 1993 meeting of the Economic Forum, dialogue and co-operation among participating States and international organizations. The Ministers expressed the view that the Forum's initial meeting would continue the process of co-operation on these issues within the CSCE.

3. High Commissioner on National Minorities

The Council appointed Mr. Max van der Stoel as CSCE High Commissioner on National Minorities (HCNM) to strengthen the CSCE's capacity for early warning and preventive diplomacy. The High Commissioner will act within the mandate laid down in the Helsinki Document. The Ministers expressed their support for the High Commissioner and their readiness to co-operate with him in the execution of his complex but crucial task of identifying and containing at the earliest possible stage tensions involving national minority issues which have the potential to develop into a conflict within the CSCE area.

The Ministers encouraged the High Commissioner to analyse carefully potential areas of tension, to visit any participating State and to undertake wide-ranging discussions at all levels with parties directly involved in the issues. In this context, the High Commissioner may discuss the questions with the parties and, where appropriate, promote dialogue, confidence and co-operation between them at all levels, to enhance political solutions in line with CSCE principles and commitments.

The Ministers undertook to provide the High Commissioner with relevant information at their disposal on national minority issues, fully respecting the independence of the High Commissioner in accordance with the mandate.

4. Peaceful settlement of disputes

The Ministers considered the recommendations made by the CSCE Meeting on Peaceful Settlement of Disputes held in Geneva from 12 to 23 October 1992.

The Ministers reaffirmed the vital importance of the commitment of all participating States, under Principle V of the Helsinki Final Act, to settle their disputes by peaceful means. In this connection, they recalled other CSCE documents relating to the peaceful settlement of disputes, in particular the Concluding Document of the Vienna Follow-up Meeting, the Charter of Paris for a New Europe, the Report on Peaceful Settlement of Disputes adopted at Valletta and endorsed at the Berlin Meeting of 19 and 20 June 1991, and the Helsinki Document 1992.

The Ministers noted the variety of existing dispute settlement procedures, both within and outside the CSCE. They recalled the important contribution that the potential involvement of an impartial third party can make to the peaceful settlement of disputes and the fact that the Valletta Mechanism enables a participating State, under certain conditions, to seek the mandatory involvement of such a party.

The Ministers agreed that in the present circumstances, the principle of the peaceful settlement of disputes assumes particular relevance to problems facing participating States, and that the framework of the CSCE provides a unique opportunity to give impetus to this central aspect of CSCE commitments.

In order to further and strengthen their commitment to settle disputes exclusively by peaceful means, and in accordance with paragraphs (57) to (62) of Chapter III of the Helsinki Decisions of 1992 to develop a comprehensive and coherent set of measures available within the CSCE for the peaceful settlement of disputes, the Ministers have:

(a) Adopted measures to enhance the Valletta Provisions through modification of the procedure for selecting Dispute Settlement Mechanisms;

(b) Adopted the text of a Convention on Conciliation and Arbitration within the CSCE providing for general conciliation and for arbitration on the basis of agreements *ad hoc* or, in advance, on the basis of reciprocal declarations, and declared it open for signature by interested participating States;

(c) Adopted a conciliation procedure as an option available to participating States on the basis of agreements *ad hoc* or, in advance, on the basis of reciprocal declarations;

(d) Decided that the Council or the Committee of Senior Officials of the CSCE may direct any two participating States to seek conciliation to assist them in resolving a dispute that they have not been able to settle within a reasonable period of time and adopted provisions related thereto.

The Ministers recalled that nothing stated in the foregoing will in any way affect the unity of the CSCE principles, or the right of participating States to raise within the CSCE process any issue relating to the implementation of any CSCE commitment concerning the principle of the peaceful settlement of disputes, or relating to any other CSCE commitment or provision.

Procedures for the peaceful settlement of disputes within the CSCE will be reviewed during the review conference to be held at Budapest in 1994 and periodically thereafter as appropriate.

5. The CSCE Forum for Security Co-operation and Non-Proliferation

The Ministers welcomed the constructive work begun in the CSCE Forum for Security Co-operation. They stressed the importance of the contribution to security made by dialogue and negotiations in the Forum and their expectation that further significant progress on the Programme for Immediate Action adopted by the Helsinki Summit should be achieved by the next Meeting of the Council of Ministers. They reaffirmed the importance of full implementation of existing arms control, disarmament and confidence- and security-building provisions agreed within the framework of the CSCE, by all States concerned, including those recently admitted.

Resolved to fully implement the Declaration of the CSCE Council on Non-Proliferation and Arms Transfers adopted at the Prague Council Meeting 30-31 January 1992 and fully committed to CSCE co-operation in respect of non-proliferation, the Ministers agreed as a first step that their States will become original signatories to the Convention on the Prohibition of the Development, Production, Stockpiling and Use of Chemical Weapons and on their Destruction, which will be opened for signature in Paris on 13 January 1993. They also agreed to seek its timely ratification in order for it to enter into force at the earliest date provided for by the Convention. To this end they call upon all other States to sign and ratify the Convention as soon as possible.

They expressed their satisfaction that the Ministers of participating States not yet Parties to the Convention on Bacteriological (Biological) and Toxin Weapons declared that their States intend to become Parties to that Convention as well as to the 1925 Geneva Protocol on the prohibition of the use in war of chemical and biological weapons.

They welcomed that the Ministers of those participating States that are not Parties to the Treaty on the Non-Proliferation of Nuclear Weapons pledged that their States intend to become Parties to that Treaty as non-nuclear weapon States in the shortest time possible. Furthermore, they agreed that the Treaty should be extended indefinitely and urged all States that have not yet done so to become Parties to the Treaty.

6. Preventive diplomacy and peacekeeping

Consistent with the concept of preventive diplomacy, and while no conflict exists in Estonia, the CSCE is sending a mission to the country, to promote stability and dialogue between the Estonian- and Russian-speaking communities in Estonia.

The Ministers discussed the conflicts that have arisen within the CSCE area, including those in the former Soviet Union, and stressed that they should be resolved by peaceful means.

They reviewed experience with the instruments for early warning, conflict prevention and crisis management, in particular in the field of preventive diplomacy. They noted that, in association with efforts to bring about political solutions, stability can be enhanced by armed contingents for peacekeeping purposes. The deployment and conduct of such operations must be in accordance with the norms of international law and CSCE principles.

The Ministers concluded that the CSCE can play an especially important role in co-operation with mutually reinforcing European and transatlantic organizations by further developing relevant CSCE instruments in the field of preventive diplomacy and peacekeeping.

They requested relevant CSCE institutions, in particular the ODIHR and the CPC, to organize seminars to help share experience and increase knowledge of issues and techniques in the fields of early warning and peacekeeping. Furthermore, they requested the CSO to examine the issues involved in enhancing the capability of all the CSCE instruments.

7. Evolution of CSCE structures and institutions

To meet new challenges, the Ministers decided to add further to the improvements in the operational capacity of the CSCE agreed in Paris and Helsinki.

In doing so, they confirmed that the CSCE should retain its flexibility and openness, avoiding the creation of a bureaucracy. Further evolution in CSCE institutions and procedures should be based on the CSCE's democratic rules. It should preserve the strength and diversity afforded by the basic political structure established by the Paris Summit, and should improve the effectiveness of the CSCE's daily work.

Ministers tasked the CSO to conduct a wide ranging review of CSCE structures and operations with a view to establishing organizational arrangements to meet these needs.

As a first step, Ministers have decided to improve further CSCE operations and institutions by establishing the post of Secretary General of the CSCE (Annex 1).

The Ministers also decided to enhance the ability of the CSO to act as their agent and, pending completion of the review mandated above, instructed representatives of the participating States to meet regularly in Vienna in periods between sessions of the CSO. Under the Chairmanship of the Chairman-in-Office, these representatives will conduct consultations on all issues pertinent to the CSCE and undertake preliminary discussion of items suggested for the agenda of the CSO by the Chairman-in-Office. They will decide on matters necessary to ensure prompt and effective implementation of the decisions of the CSO.

To increase the efficiency of the work of the CSCE, the Ministers decided to establish for the Secretariats in Prague and Vienna a single organizational structure under the direction of the Secretary General. The Ministers decided that the CSO should agree the financial and administrative implications of this decision and should adjust staffing, budgets and procedures accordingly.

The implementation of the decision taken by the Heads of Government in Helsinki that the CSO should consider the relevance of an agreement granting an internationally recognized status to the CSCE Secretariat, the Conflict Prevention Centre and the ODIHR, the Ministers instructed the CSO to establish a group of legal and other experts to report through the Committee for decision at the Rome Council Meeting.

The Ministers tasked the Conflict Prevention Centre to take rapid steps to strengthen its ability to provide operational support for CSCE preventive diplomacy missions and peacekeeping activities. The Director of the CPC should present, for approval by the CSO, a proposal setting forth the staffing and budget implications of this decision.

The Ministers emphasized the vital importance of the efficient management of CSCE resources. To this end they instructed the CSO to draw up rules and procedures. They approved the attached Terms of Reference (Annex 2). The Ministers will note progress and take decisions, as necessary, at the Rome Council Meeting.

The Ministers noted that cost-efficiency may also be ensured through seeking new sources of financing CSCE activities. As one innovative possibility they requested the Director of the ODIHR to examine the establishment of a Foundation for Promoting Human Rights in the CSCE.

The Ministers noted that the commitments entered into in Helsinki to expand the role of NGOs have already shown their value. They asked the Chairman-in-Office to examine proposals put forward by NGOs on co-operation between NGOs and the CSCE, and, when appropriate, to submit them to the CSO for consideration.

8. Improved co-operation and contacts with international organizations, in particular the United Nations

The new challenges in the CSCE area require improved co-operation and close contacts with relevant international organizations, in accordance with the Helsinki Document. The Ministers expressed their intention to strengthen co-operation in particular with the United Nations.

The CSCE has entered a new phase in its relationship with the United Nations which should be developed further. The Ministers requested the CSO to examine the practical implications of the understanding, expressed in the Helsinki Document, that the CSCE is a regional arrangement in the sense of Chapter VIII of the Charter of the United Nations. In its examination the CSO should also examine the proposal by the United Nations Secretary-General to the CSCE to seek observer status at the United Nations.

The Ministers emphasized that the Chairman-in-Office should keep close contacts with the United Nations in order to promote regular exchanges of information, co-operation and co-ordination and avoid duplication of effort.

They instructed the Chairman-in-Office of the CSO to establish without delay regular contact with the United Nations Secretary-General to ensure that both the United Nations and CSCE participating States are kept informed of relevant activity, especially in the fields of early warning, conflict prevention, management and resolution of conflicts as well as the promotion of democratic values and human rights.

The Ministers decided that a representative of the United Nations Secretary-General will be invited to the meetings of the Council and the Committee of Senior Officials of the CSCE. Furthermore, they decided that the Permanent Mission to the United Nations of the participating State holding the Office of Chairman will serve as a focal point of the CSCE at the United Nations.

9. Integration of new participating States

The Ministers decided to intensify their support in conjunction with other institutions, notably the Council of Europe, for the building of democratic institutions to meet the needs identified by newly admitted participating States. They entrusted the Chairman-in-Office, assisted by the CSCE Troika, to consult with newly admitted participating States on useful steps under the Programme of Co-ordinated Support agreed at Helsinki.

The Chairman-in-Office, accompanied by a team of CSCE experts, will conduct a programme of visits to the newly admitted participating States to discuss the CSCE in all its aspects and to explore means of promoting the full involvement of those States in the work and activities of the CSCE. Experts will continue discussions and make an inventory of possible points for further action including ways of promoting information on the CSCE. The Ministers expressed their support for the expansion of CSCE activities in and visits to these States.

10. Admission of new participating States

The Ministers agreed that the Czech Republic and the Slovak Republic would be welcomed as participating States from 1 January 1993 following receipt of letters accepting CSCE commitments and responsibilities from each of them according to the draft in Annex 3.

11. Date and venue of the next Council Meeting

They agreed that the next meeting of the Council will be held in Rome in November/December 1993. They will confirm the specific days for this meeting by silence procedure following the proposal of the host country and recommendation by the CSO not later than March 1993.

ANNEX 1

The Secretary General of the CSCE

1. The Ministers decide to establish the post of Secretary General of the Conference on Security and Co-operation in Europe. The Secretary General will derive his/her authority from the collective decisions of the participating States and will act under the guidance of the Chairman-in-Office.

2. The Secretary General will be appointed by the Council by consensus upon recommendation of the CSO and Chairman-in-Office for a period of three years. This period may be extended for one further term of two years.

3. The Chairman-in-Office will be assisted by an open-ended *ad hoc* group in preparing his/her recommendation on the appointment to the CSO and Council.

4. The open-ended *ad hoc* group will assist the Chairman-in-Office in preparing recommendations to the CSO and the Council on the administrative and financial implications of the appointment of a Secretary General, including accommodation, staff requirements and budget.

5. The Ministers agreed on the following mandate for the Secretary General.

Mandate

(1) The Secretary General will act as the representative of the Chairman-in-Office and will support him/her in all activities aimed at fulfilling the goals of the CSCE. The Secretary General's tasks will also include the management of CSCE structures and operations; working closely with the Chairman-in-Office in the preparation and guidance of CSCE meetings; and ensuring the implementation of the decisions of the CSCE.

(ii) The Secretary General will oversee the work of the CSCE Secretariat, the CPC Secretariat and the ODIHR. The Secretary General will answer for the effective performance of CSCE staff to the Chairman-in-Office, the Council of Ministers and the CSO.

(iii) The Secretary General will assist the Chairman-in-Office in publicizing CSCE policy and practices internationally, including maintaining contacts with international organizations.

(iv) As the CSCE's Chief Administrative Officer, the Secretary General will advise on the financial implications of proposals and ensure economy in the staff and support services of the institutions.

(v) The Secretary General will prepare an annual report to the CSCE Council.

(vi) The Secretary General will perform such other functions as are entrusted to him/her by the Council or the CSO.

ANNEX 2

Management of resources

The Ministers instructed the CSO to draw up rules and procedures covering the following areas:

- Steps to increase the cost-effectiveness of CSCE activities;
- Effective management of funds and property, including funds allocated to particular activities;
- Procedures for timely presentation of budget proposals of CSCE institutions;
- Measures for adequate scrutiny of the financial implications of proposals including procedures for the authorization of expenditure;
- Effective CSCE auditing and ways and means of minimizing arrears in the payment of assessed contributions, bearing in mind the experience of other international organizations.

ANNEX 3

Bratislava/Prague, 1 January 1993

Your Excellency,

The Government of the Slovak/Czech Republic hereby adopts the Helsinki Final Act, the Charter of Paris for a New Europe and all other documents of the Conference on Security and Co-operation in Europe.

The Government of the Slovak/Czech Republic accepts in their entirety all commitments and responsibilities contained in these documents and declares its determination to act in accordance with their provisions. It will assume, in co-operation with the Czech/Slovak Republic as the other successor State to the Czech and Slovak Federal Republic, all CFE obligations of the Czech and Slovak Federal Republic.

The Government of the Slovak/Czech Republic invites and will fully facilitate the visit of a Rapporteur Mission to be arranged by the Chairman of the CSCE Council. This Mission will report to the CSCE participating States on the fulfilment by the Slovak/Czech Republic of CSCE commitments and provide assistance towards their fullest implementation.

The Government of the Slovak/Czech Republic expresses its readiness for signature of the Helsinki Final Act and the Charter of Paris by the Head of State or Government of the Slovak/Czech Republic at the earliest convenience.

I kindly ask Your Excellency to circulate copies of this letter to all CSCE participating States.

Please accept, Your Excellency, the assurances of my highest consideration.

Her Excellency
Margaretha af Ugglas
Chairman-in-Office of the
CSCE Council
Minister of Foreign Affairs
Kingdom of Sweden
Stockholm

DECISION ON PEACEFUL SETTLEMENT OF DISPUTES

1. At its Stockholm meeting of 14 and 15 December 1992, the CSCE Council considered the recommendations made by the CSCE Meeting on Peaceful Settlement of Disputes held in Geneva from 12 to 23 October 1992.

2. The Ministers reaffirmed the vital importance of the commitment of all participating States, under Principle V of the Helsinki Final Act, to settle their disputes by peaceful means. In this connection, they recalled other CSCE documents relating to the peaceful settlement of disputes, in particular the Concluding Document of the Vienna Follow-up Meeting, the Charter of Paris for a New Europe, the Report on Peaceful Settlement of Disputes adopted at Valletta and endorsed at the Berlin Meeting of 19 and 20 June 1991, and the Helsinki Document of 1992.

3. The Ministers noted the variety of existing dispute settlement procedures, both within and outside the CSCE. They recalled the important contribution that the potential involvement of an impartial third party can make to the peaceful settlement of disputes and the fact that the Valletta Mechanism enables a participating State, under certain conditions, to seek the mandatory involvement of such a party.

4. The Ministers agreed that in the present circumstances, the principle of the peaceful settlement of disputes assumes particular relevance to problems facing participating States, and that the framework of the CSCE provides a unique opportunity to give impetus to this central aspect of CSCE commitments.

5. In order to further and strengthen their commitment of settle disputes exclusively by peaceful means, and in accordance with paragraphs 57 to 62 of Chapter III of the Helsinki Decisions of 1992 to develop a comprehensive and coherent set of measures available within the CSCE for the peaceful settlement of disputes, the Ministers have:

   (a) Adopted measures to enhance the Valletta Provisions through modification of the procedure for selecting Dispute Settlement Mechanisms. This modification is set forth in *Annex 1*;

   (b) Adopted the text of a Convention on Conciliation and Arbitration within the CSCE providing for general conciliation and for arbitration on the basis of agreements *ad hoc* or, in advance, on the basis of reciprocal declarations, and declared it open for signature by interested participating States. This text is contained in *Annex 2*;

(c) Adopted a conciliation procedure as an option available to participating States on the basis of agreements *ad hoc* or, in advance, on the basis of reciprocal declarations. This procedure is set forth in *Annex 3*;

(d) Decided that the Council or the Committee of Senior Officials of the CSCE may direct any two participating States to seek conciliation to assist them in resolving a dispute that they have not been able to settle within a reasonable period of time. The provisions relating thereto are set forth in *Annex 4*.

6. The Ministers recalled that nothing stated in the foregoing will in any way affect the unity of the CSCE principles, or the right of participating States to raise within the CSCE process any issue relating to the implementation of any CSCE commitment concerning the principle of the peaceful settlement of disputes, or relating to any other CSCE commitment or provision.

7. Procedures for the peaceful settlement of disputes within the CSCE will be reviewed during the review conference to be held at Budapest in 1994 and periodically thereafter as appropriate.

Annex 1

Modification to Section V of the Valletta Provisions for a CSCE Procedure for Peaceful Settlement of Disputes

Section V of the Valletta Provisions for a CSCE Procedure for Peaceful Settlement of Disputes should read as follows:

Section V

1. A CSCE Dispute Settlement Mechanism consists of one or more members, selected by common agreement of the parties to a dispute from a register of qualified candidates maintained by the nominating institution. The register comprises the names of up to four persons nominated by each participating State desiring to do so. No member of a Mechanism may be a national of, or permanently resident in the territory of any State involved in the dispute. By agreement between the parties, a Mechanism may include members whose names are not included in the register.
2. If the parties to a dispute have not reached agreement on the composition of a Mechanism within two months from the initial request of a party for the establishment of a Mechanism, the Senior Official of the nominating institution will, in consultation with the parties to the dispute, select seven names from the register. If the Senior Official of the nominating institution is a national of any of the States involved in the dispute, his functions will be performed by the next most senior official who is not such a national.
3. Each party* to the dispute has the right to reject up to three of the nominees. The parties will inform the nominating institution of the rejections, if any, within one month of having been informed of the nominations. This information will be confidential. After one month from the date of informing the parties of the nominations, the nominating institution will notify the parties of the composition of the Mechanism.

Note: The modification means that the time period under paragraph 2 is shortened by one month, that seven names should be selected instead of "less than six", and that paragraphs 4 and 5 will no longer apply.

---

* The problems arising when the parties are more than two will require further consideration.

Annex 2

CONVENTION ON CONCILIATION AND ARBITRATION WITHIN THE CSCE

The States parties to this Convention, being States participating in the Conference on Security and Co-operation in Europe,

Conscious of their obligation, as provided for in Article 2, paragraph 3, and Article 33 of the Charter of the United Nations, to settle their disputes peacefully;

Emphasizing that they do not in any way intend to impair other existing institutions or mechanisms, including the International Court of Justice, the European Court of Human Rights, the Court of Justice of the European Communities and the Permanent Court of Arbitration;

Reaffirming their solemn commitment to settle their disputes through peaceful means and their decision to develop mechanisms to settle disputes between participating States;

Recalling that full implementation of all CSCE principles and commitments constitutes in itself an essential element in preventing disputes between the CSCE participating States;

Concerned to further and strengthen the commitments stated, in particular, in the Report of the Meeting of Experts on Peaceful settlement of Disputes adopted at Valletta and endorsed by the CSCE Council of Ministers of Foreign Affairs at its meeting in Berlin on 19 and 20 June 1991,

Have agreed as follows:

CHAPTER 1 - GENERAL PROVISIONS

Article 1
Establishment of the Court

A Court of Conciliation and Arbitration shall be established to settle, by means of conciliation and, where appropriate, arbitration, disputes which are submitted to it in accordance with the provisions of this Convention.

Article 2
Conciliation Commissions and Arbitral Tribunals

1. Conciliation shall be undertaken by a Conciliation Commission constituted for each dispute. The Commission shall be made up of conciliators drawn from a list established in accordance with the provisions of Article 3.

2. Arbitration shall be undertaken by an Arbitral Tribunal constituted for each dispute. The Tribunal shall be made up of arbitrators drawn from a list established in accordance with the provisions of Article 4.

3. Together, the conciliators and arbitrators shall constitute the Court of Conciliation and Arbitration within the CSCE, hereinafter referred to as "the Court".

Article 3
Appointment of Conciliators

1. Each State party to this Convention shall appoint, within two months following its entry into force, two conciliators of whom at least one is a national of that State. The other may be a national of another CSCE participating State. A State which becomes party to this Convention after its entry into force shall appoint its conciliators within two months following the entry into force of this Convention for the State concerned.

2. The conciliators must be persons holding or having held senior national or international positions and possessing recognized qualifications in international law, international relations, or the settlement of disputes.

3. Conciliators shall be appointed for a renewable period of six years. Their functions may not be terminated by the appointing State during their term of office. In the event of death, resignation or inability to attend recognized by the Bureau, the State concerned shall appoint a new conciliator; the term of office of the new conciliator shall be the remainder of the term of office of the predecessor.

4. Upon termination of their period of office, conciliators shall continue to hear any cases that they are already dealing with.

5. The names of the conciliators shall be notified to the Registrar, who shall enter them into a list, which shall be communicated to the CSCE Secretariat for transmission to the CSCE participating States.

Article 4
Appointment of Arbitrators

1. Each State party to this Convention shall appoint, within two months following its entry into force, one arbitrator and one alternate, who may be its nationals or nationals of any other CSCE participating State. A State which becomes Party to this Convention after its entry into force shall appoint its arbitrator and the alternate within two months of the entry into force of this Convention for that State.

2. Arbitrators and their alternates must possess the qualifications required in their respective countries for appointment to the highest judicial offices or must be jurisconsult of recognized competence in international law.

3. Arbitrators and their alternates are appointed for a period of six years, which may be renewed once. Their functions may not be terminated by the appointing State party during their term of office. In the event of death, resignation or inability to attend, recognized by the Bureau, the arbitrator shall be replaced by his or her alternate.

4. If an arbitrator and his or her alternate die, resign or are both unable to attend, the fact being recognized by the Bureau, new appointments will be made in accordance with paragraph 1. The new arbitrator and his or her alternate shall complete the term of office of their predecessors.

5. The Rules of the Court may provide for a partial renewal of the arbitrators and their alternates.

6. Upon expiry of their term of office, arbitrators shall continue to hear any cases that they are already dealing with.

7. The names of the arbitrators shall be notified to the Registrar, who shall enter them into a list, which shall be communicated to the CSCE Secretariat for transmission to the CSCE participating States.

Article 5
Independence of the Members of the Court and of the Registrar

The conciliators, the arbitrators and the Registrar shall perform their functions in full independence. Before taking up their duties, they shall make a declaration that they will exercise their powers impartially and conscientiously.

Article 6
Privileges and Immunities

The conciliators, the arbitrators, the Registrar and the agents and counsel of the parties to a dispute shall enjoy, while performing their functions in the territory of the States parties to this Convention, the privileges and immunities accorded to persons connected with the International Court of Justice.

Article 7
Bureau of the Court

1. The Bureau of the Court shall consist of a President, a Vice-President and three other members.

2. The President of the Court shall be elected by the members of the Court from among their number. The President presides over the Bureau.

3. The conciliators and the arbitrators shall each elect from among their number two members of the Bureau and their alternates.

4. The Bureau shall elect its Vice-President from among its members. The Vice-President shall be a conciliator if the President is an arbitrator, and an arbitrator if the President is a conciliator.

5. The Rules of the Court shall establish the procedures for the election of the President as well as of the other members of the Bureau and their alternates.

Article 8
Decision-making Procedure

1. The decisions of the Court shall be taken by a majority of the members participating in the vote. Those abstaining shall not be considered participating in the vote.

2. The decisions of the Bureau shall be taken by a majority of its members.

3. The decisions of the Conciliation Commissions and the Arbitral Tribunals shall be taken by a majority of their members, who may not abstain from voting.

4. In the event of a tied vote, the vote of the presiding officer shall prevail.

Article 9
Registrar

The Court shall appoint its Registrar and may provide for the appointment of such other officers as may be necessary. The staff regulations of the Registry shall be drawn up by the Bureau and adopted by the States parties to this Convention.

Article 10
Seat

1. The seat of the Court shall be established in Geneva.

2. At the request of the parties to the dispute and in agreement with the Bureau, a Conciliation Commission or an Arbitral Tribunal may meet at another location.

Article 11
Rules of the Court

1. The Court shall adopt its own Rules, which shall be subject to approval by States parties to this Convention.

2. The Rules of the Court shall establish, in particular, the rules of procedure to be followed by the Conciliation Commissions and Arbitral Tribunals constituted pursuant to this Convention. They shall

state which of these rules may not be waived by agreement between the parties to the dispute.

Article 12
Working Languages

The Rules of the Court shall establish rules on the use of languages.

Article 13
Financial Protocol

Subject to the provisions of Article 17, all the costs of the Court shall be met by the States parties to this Convention. The provisions for the calculation of the costs; for the drawing up and approval of the annual budget of the Court; for the distribution of the costs among the States parties to this Convention; for the audit of the accounts of the Court; and for related matters, shall be contained in a Financial Protocol to be adopted by the Committee of Senior Officials. A State becomes bound by the Protocol on becoming a party to this Convention.**

Article 14
Periodic Report

The Bureau shall annually present to the CSCE Council through the Committee of Senior Officials a report on the activities under this Convention.

Article 15
Notice of Requests for Conciliation or Arbitration

The Registrar of the Court shall give notice to the CSCE Secretariat of all requests for conciliation or arbitration, for immediate transmission to the CSCE participating States.

** Editor's note: The Financial Protocol has been adopted by the CSO at its twenty-first meeting in April 1993 (21-CSO/Journal No. 3, Annex 4). See *infra* the section on CSO Documents, pp. 1008-1015.

Article 16
Conduct of Parties - Interim Measures

1. During the proceedings, the parties to the dispute shall refrain from any action which may aggravate the situation or further impede or prevent the settlement of the dispute.

2. The Conciliation Commission may draw the attention of the parties to the dispute submitted to it to the measures the parties could take in order to prevent the dispute from being aggravated or its settlement made more difficult.

3. The Arbitral Tribunal constituted for a dispute may indicate the interim measures that ought to be taken by the parties to the dispute in accordance with the provisions of Article 26, paragraph 4.

Article 17
Procedural Costs

The parties to a dispute and any intervening party shall each bear their own costs.

CHAPTER II - COMPETENCE

Article 18
Competence of the Commission and of the Tribunal

1. Any State party to this Convention may submit to a Conciliation Commission any dispute with another State party which has not been settled within a reasonable period of time through negotiation.

2. Disputes may be submitted to an Arbitral Tribunal under the conditions stipulated in Article 26.

Article 19
Safeguarding the Existing Means of Settlement

1. A Conciliation Commission or an Arbitral Tribunal constituted for a dispute shall take no further action in the case:

(a) If, prior to being submitted to the Commission or the Tribunal, the dispute has been submitted to a court or tribunal whose jurisdiction in respect of the dispute the parties thereto are under a legal obligation to accept, or if such a body has already given a decision on the merit of the dispute;

(b) If the parties to the dispute have accepted in advance the exclusive jurisdiction of a jurisdictional body other than a Tribunal in accordance with this Convention which has jurisdiction to decide, with binding force, on the dispute submitted to it, or if the parties thereto have agreed to seek to settle the dispute exclusively by other means.

2. A Conciliation Commission constituted for a dispute shall take no further action if, even after the dispute has been submitted to it, one or all of the parties refer the dispute to a court or tribunal whose jurisdiction in respect of the dispute the parties thereto are under a legal obligation to accept.

3. A Conciliation Commission shall postpone examining a dispute if this dispute has been submitted to another body which has competence to formulate proposals with respect to this dispute. If those prior efforts do not lead to a settlement of the dispute, the Commission shall resume its work at the request of the parties or one of the parties to the dispute, subject to the provisions of Article 26, paragraph 1.

4. A State may, at the time of signing, ratifying or acceding to this Convention, make a reservation in order to ensure the compatibility of the mechanism of dispute settlement that this Convention establishes with other means of dispute settlement resulting from international undertakings applicable to that State.

5. If, at any time, the parties arrive at a settlement of their dispute, the Commission or Tribunal shall remove the dispute from its list, on receiving written confirmation from all the parties thereto that they have reached a settlement of the dispute.

6. In the event of disagreement between the parties to the dispute with regard to the competence of the Commission or the Tribunal, the decision in the matter shall rest with the Commission or the Tribunal.

CHAPTER III - CONCILIATION

Article 20
Request for the Constitution of a Conciliation Commission

1. Any State party to this Convention may lodge an application with the Registrar requesting the constitution of a Conciliation Commission for a dispute between it and one or more other States parties. Two or more States parties may also jointly lodge an application with the Registrar.

2. The constitution of a Conciliation Commission may also be requested by agreement between two or more States parties or between one or more States parties and one or more other CSCE participating States. The agreement shall be notified to the Registrar.

Article 21
Constitution of the Conciliation Commission

1. Each party to the dispute shall appoint, from the list of conciliators established in accordance with Article 3, one conciliator to sit on the Commission.

2. When more than two States are parties to the same dispute, the States asserting the same interest may agree to appoint one single conciliator. If they do not so agree, each of the two sides to the dispute shall appoint the same number of conciliators up to a maximum decided by the Bureau.

3. Any State which is a party to a dispute submitted to a Conciliation Commission and which is not a party to this Convention, may appoint a person to sit on the Commission, either from the list of conciliators established in accordance with Article 3, or from among other persons who are nationals of a CSCE participating State. In this event, for the purpose of examining the dispute, such persons shall have the same rights and the same obligations as the other members of the Commission. They shall perform their functions in full independence and shall make the declaration required by Article 5 before taking their seats on the Commission.

4. As soon as the application or the agreement whereby the parties to a dispute have requested the constitution of a Conciliation Commission is

received, the President of the Court shall consult the parties to the dispute as to the composition of the rest of the Commission.

5. The Bureau shall appoint three further conciliators to sit on the Commission. This number can be increased or decreased by the Bureau, provided it is uneven. Members of the Bureau and their alternates, who are on the list of conciliators, shall be eligible for appointment to the Commission.

6. The Commission shall elect its Chairman from among the members appointed by the Bureau.

7. The Rules of the Court shall stipulate the procedures applicable if an objection is raised to one of the members appointed to sit on the Commission or if that member is unable to or refuses to sit at the commencement or in the course of the proceedings.

8. Any question as to the application of this article shall be decided by the Bureau as a preliminary matter.

Article 22
Procedure for the Constitution of a Conciliation Commission

1. If the constitution of a Conciliation Commission is requested by means of an application, the application shall state the subject of the dispute, the name of the party or parties against which the application is directed, and the name of the conciliator or conciliators appointed by the requesting party or parties to the dispute. The application shall also briefly indicate the means of settlement previously resorted to.

2. As soon as an application has been received, the Registrar shall notify the other party or parties to the dispute mentioned in the application. Within a period of fifteen days from the notification, the other party or parties to the dispute shall appoint the conciliator or conciliators of their choice to sit on the Commission. If, within this period, one or more parties to the dispute have not appointed the member or members of the Commission whom they are entitled to appoint, the Bureau shall appoint the appropriate number of conciliators. Such appointment shall be made from among the conciliators appointed in accordance with Article 3 by the party or each of the parties involved or, if those parties have not yet appointed conciliators, from among the other conciliators not appointed by the other party or parties to the dispute.

3. If the constitution of a Conciliation Commission is requested by means of an agreement, the agreement shall state the subject of the dispute. If there is no agreement, in whole or in part, concerning the subject of the dispute, each party thereto may formulate its own position in respect of such subject.

4. At the same time as the parties request the constitution of a Conciliation Commission by agreement, each party shall notify the Registrar of the name of the conciliator or conciliators whom it has appointed to sit on the Commission.

Article 23
Conciliation Procedure

1. The conciliation proceedings shall be confidential and all parties to the dispute shall have the right to be heard. Subject to the provisions of Articles 10 and 11 and the Rules of the Court, the Conciliation Commission shall, after consultation with the parties to the dispute, determine the procedure.

2. If the parties to the dispute agree thereon, the Conciliation Commission may invite any State party to this Convention which has an interest in the settlement of the dispute to participate in the proceedings.

Article 24
Objective of Conciliation

The Conciliation Commission shall assist the parties to the dispute in finding a settlement in accordance with international law and their CSCE commitments.

Article 25
Result of the Conciliation

1. If, during the proceedings, the parties to the dispute, with the help of the Conciliation Commission, reach a mutually acceptable settlement, they shall record the terms of this settlement in a summary of conclusions signed by their representatives and by the members of the Commission. The signing of the document shall conclude the proceedings. The CSCE Council shall be informed through the Committee of Senior Officials of the success of the conciliation.

2. When the Conciliation Commission considers that all the aspects of the dispute and all the possibilities of finding a solution have been explored, it shall draw up a final report. The report shall contain the proposals of the Commission for the peaceful settlement of the dispute.

3. The report of the Conciliation Commission shall be notified to the parties to the dispute, which shall have a period of thirty days in which to examine it and inform the Chairman of the Commission whether they are willing to accept the proposed settlement.

4. If a party to the dispute does not accept the proposed settlement, the other party or parties are no longer bound by their own acceptance thereof.

5. If, within the period prescribed in paragraph 3, the parties to the dispute have not accepted the proposed settlement, the report shall be forwarded to the CSCE Council through the Committee of Senior Officials.

6. A report shall also be drawn up which provides immediate notification to the CSCE Council through the Committee of Senior Officials of circumstances where a party fails to appear for conciliation or leaves a procedure after it has begun.

CHAPTER IV - ARBITRATION

Article 26
Request for the Constitution of an Arbitral Tribunal

1. A request for arbitration may be made at any time by agreement between two or more States parties to this Convention or between one or more States parties to this Convention and one or more other CSCE participating States.

2. The States parties to this Convention may at any time by a notice addressed to the Depositary declare that they recognize as compulsory, *ipso facto* and without special agreement, the jurisdiction of an Arbitral Tribunal, subject to reciprocity. Such a declaration may be made for an unlimited period or for a specified time. It may cover all disputes or exclude disputes concerning a State's territorial integrity, national defence, title to sovereignty over land territory, or competing claims with regard to jurisdiction over other areas.

3. A request for arbitration against a State party to this Convention which has made the declaration specified in paragraph 2 may be made by means of an application to the Registrar only after a period of thirty days after the report of the Conciliation Commission which has dealt with the dispute has been transmitted to the CSCE Council in accordance with the provisions of Article 25, paragraph 5.

4. When a dispute is submitted to an Arbitral Tribunal in accordance with this article, the Tribunal may, on its own authority or at the request of one or all of the parties to the dispute, indicate interim measures that ought to be taken by the parties to the dispute to avoid an aggravation of the dispute, greater difficulty in reaching a solution, or the possibility of a future award of the Tribunal becoming unenforceable owing to the conduct of one or more of the parties to the dispute.

Article 27
Cases brought before an Arbitral Tribunal

1. If a request for arbitration is made by means of an agreement, it shall indicate the subject of the dispute. If there is no agreement, in whole or in part, concerning the subject of the dispute, each party thereto may formulate its own position in respect of such subject.

2. If a request for arbitration is made by means of an application, it shall indicate the subject of the dispute, the States party or parties to this Convention against which it is directed, and the main elements of fact and law on which it is grounded. As soon as the application is received, the Registrar shall notify the other States party or parties mentioned in the application.

Article 28
Constitution of the Arbitral Tribunal

1. When a request for arbitration is submitted, an Arbitral Tribunal shall be constituted.

2. The arbitrators appointed by the parties to the dispute in accordance with Article 4 are *ex officio* members of the Tribunal. When more than two States are parties to the same dispute, the States asserting the same interest may agree to appoint one single arbitrator.

3. The Bureau shall appoint, from among the arbitrators, a number of members to sit on the Tribunal so that the members appointed by the

Bureau total at least one more than the *ex officio* members. Members of the Bureau and their alternates, who are on the list of arbitrators, shall be eligible for appointment to the Tribunal.

4. If an *ex officio* member is unable to attend or has previously taken part in any capacity in the hearings of the case arising from the dispute submitted to the Tribunal, that member shall be replaced by his or her alternate. If the alternate is in the same situation, the State involved shall appoint a member to examine the dispute pursuant to the terms and conditions specified in paragraph 5. In the event of a question arising as to the capacity of a member or of his or her alternate to sit on the tribunal, the matter shall be decided by the Bureau.

5. Any State, which is a party to a dispute submitted to an Arbitral Tribunal and which is not party to this Convention, may appoint a person of its choice to sit on the Tribunal, either from the list of arbitrators established in accordance with Article 4 or from among other persons who are nationals of a CSCE participating State. Any person thus appointed must meet the conditions specified in Article 4, paragraph 2, and for the purpose of examining the dispute, shall have the same rights and obligations as the other members of the Tribunal. The person shall perform his or her functions in full independence and shall make the declaration required by Article 5 before sitting on the Tribunal.

6. The Tribunal shall appoint its Chairman from among the members appointed by the Bureau.

7. In the event that one of the members of the Tribunal appointed by the Bureau is unable to attend the proceedings, that member shall not be replaced unless the number of members appointed by the Bureau falls below the number of *ex officio* members, or members appointed by the parties to the dispute in accordance with paragraph 5. In this event, one or more new members shall be appointed by the Bureau pursuant to paragraphs 3 and 4 of this article. A new Chairman will not be elected if one or more new members are appointed, unless the member unable to attend is the Chairman of the Tribunal.

Article 29
Arbitration Procedure

1. All the parties to the dispute shall have the right to be heard during the arbitration proceedings, which shall conform to the principles of a fair trial. The proceedings shall consist of a written part and an oral part.

2. The Arbitral Tribunal shall have, in relation to the parties to the dispute, the necessary fact-finding and investigative powers to carry out its tasks.

3. Any CSCE participating State which considers that it has a particular interest of a legal nature likely to be affected by the ruling of the Tribunal may, within fifteen days of the transmission of the notification by the CSCE Secretariat as specified in Article 15, address to the Registrar a request to intervene. This request shall be immediately transmitted to the parties to the dispute and to the Tribunal constituted for the dispute.

4. If the intervening State establishes that it has such an interest, it shall be authorized to participate in the proceedings in so far as may be required for the protection of this interest. The relevant part of the ruling of the Tribunal is binding upon the intervening State.

5. The parties to the dispute have a period of thirty days in which to address their observations regarding the request for intervention to the Tribunal. The Tribunal shall render its decision on the admissibility of the request.

6. The hearings in the Tribunal shall be held *in camera*, unless the Tribunal decides otherwise at the request of the parties to the dispute.

7. In the event that one or more parties to the dispute fail to appear, the other party or parties thereto may request the Tribunal to decide in favour of its or their claim. Before doing so, the Tribunal must satisfy itself that it is competent and that the claims of the party or parties taking part in the proceedings are well-founded.

Article 30
Function of the Arbitral Tribunal

The function of the Arbitral Tribunal shall be to decide, in accordance with international law, such disputes as are submitted to it. This provision shall not prejudice the power of the Tribunal to decide a case *ex aequo et bono*, if the parties to the dispute so agree.

Article 31
Arbitral Award

1. The award of the Arbitral Tribunal shall state the reasons on which it is based. If it does not represent in whole or in part the unanimous opinion of the members of the Arbitral Tribunal, any member shall be entitled to deliver a separate or dissenting opinion.

2. Subject to Article 29, paragraph 4, the award of the Tribunal shall have binding force only between the parties to the dispute and in respect of the case to which it relates.

3. The award shall be final and not subject to appeal. However, the parties to the dispute or one of them may request that the Tribunal interpret its award as to the meaning or scope. Unless the parties to the dispute agree otherwise, such request shall be made at the latest within six months after the communication of the award. After receiving the observations of the parties to the dispute, the Tribunal shall render its interpretation as soon as possible.

4. An application for revision of the award may be made only when it is based upon the discovery of some fact which is of such a nature as to be a decisive factor and which, when the award was rendered, was unknown to the Tribunal and to the party or parties to the dispute claiming revision. The application for revision must be made at the latest within six months of the discovery of the new fact. No application for revision may be made after the lapse of ten years from the date of the award.

5. As far as possible, the examination of a request for interpretation or an application for revision should be carried out by the Tribunal which made the award in question. If the Bureau should find this to be impossible, another Tribunal shall be constituted in accordance with the provisions of Article 28.

Article 32
Publication of the arbitral award

The award shall be published by the Registrar. A certified copy shall be communicated to the parties to the dispute and to the CSCE Council through the Committee of Senior Officials.

CHAPTER V - FINAL PROVISIONS

Article 33
Signature and entry into force

1. This Convention shall be open for signature with the Government of Sweden by the CSCE participating States until 31 March 1993. It shall be subject to ratification.

2. The CSCE participating States which have not signed this Convention may subsequently accede thereto.

3. This Convention shall enter into force two months after the date of deposit of the twelfth instrument of ratification or accession.

4. For every State which ratifies or accedes to this Convention after the deposit of the twelfth instrument of ratification or accession, the Convention shall enter into force two months after its instrument of ratification or accession has been deposited.

5. The Government of Sweden shall serve as depositary of this Convention.

Article 34
Reservations

This Convention may not be the subject of any reservation that it does not expressly authorize.

Article 35
Amendments

1. Amendments to this Convention must be adopted in accordance with the following paragraphs.

2. Amendments to this Convention may be proposed by any State party thereto, and shall be communicated by the Depositary to the CSCE Secretariat for transmission to the CSCE participating States.

3. If the CSCE Council adopts the proposed text of the amendment, the text shall be forwarded by the Depositary to States parties to this Convention for acceptance in accordance with their respective constitutional requirements.

4. Any such amendment shall come into force on the thirtieth day after all States parties to this Convention have informed the Depositary of their acceptance thereof.

Article 36
Denunciation

1. Any State party to this Convention may, at any time, denounce this Convention by means of a notification addressed to the Depositary.

2. Such denunciation shall become effective one year after the date of receipt of the notification by the Depositary.

3. This Convention shall, however, continue to apply for the denouncing party with respect to proceedings which are under way at the time the denunciation enters into force. Such proceedings shall be pursued to their conclusion.

Article 37
Notifications and communications

The notifications and communications to be made by the Depositary shall be transmitted to the Registrar and to the CSCE Secretariat for further transmission to the CSCE participating States.

Article 38
Non-Parties

In conformity with international law, it is confirmed that nothing in this Convention shall be interpreted to establish any obligations or commitments for CSCE participating States that are not parties to this Convention if not expressly provided for and expressly accepted by such States in writing.

Article 39
Transitional Provisions

1. The Court shall proceed, within four months of the entry into force of this Convention, to elect the Bureau, to adopt its rules and to appoint the Registrar in accordance with the provisions of Articles 7, 9 and 11. The host Government of the Court shall, in co-operation with the Depositary, make the arrangements required.

2. Until a Registrar is appointed, the duties of the Registrar under Article 3, paragraph 5, and Article 4, paragraph 7 shall be performed by the Depositary.

Done at
in the English, French, German, Italian, Russian and Spanish languages,
all six language versions being equally authentic, on

Annex 3

Provisions for a CSCE Conciliation Commission

The participating States in the Conference on Security and Co-operation in Europe (CSCE) hereby establish a procedure to complement the Valletta Procedure for the Peaceful Settlement of Dispute endorsed by the Berlin Meeting, by the establishment of a Conciliation Commission ("the Commission") in accordance with the following provisions.

Section I

A dispute between two CSCE participating States may be brought before the Commission if the parties to it so agree.

Section II

A participating State may at any time declare that it will accept, on condition of reciprocity, conciliation by the Commission for disputes between it and other participating States. The declaration may not include conditions which would affect the procedures described in Sections III to XVII below. The declaration will be deposited with the Secretary of the Commission ("the Secretary") who will transmit copies to all the participating States.

Section III

1. Where the parties to a dispute have agreed to bring it before the Commission, the procedure will be invoked by a joint written request by the parties to the Secretary.

2. Where both parties to a dispute have made declarations under Section II which apply to that dispute, the procedure may be invoked by a written request by either party to the other and to the Secretary.

Section IV

1. As soon as the Secretary has received a request made in accordance with Section III, the Commission will be constituted in accordance with Section V.

2. Any question as to the application of Section II with respect to the dispute, and in particular as to reciprocity of the declarations made thereunder, will be decided by the commission as a preliminary

question. For this purpose the parties will proceed directly to the appointment of the conciliators.

Section V

1. The parties to the dispute will, within 20 days of the receipt by the Secretary of a written request under Section III, appoint one conciliator from the Register maintained for the purposes of the Valletta Procedure for the Peaceful Settlement of Disputes ("the Valletta Register"). A party which invokes the procedure in accordance with Section III, paragraph 2, should name its conciliator in its written request.

2. The conciliators will, within 20 days of the date of the second of their own appointments, appoint a third conciliator chosen from the Valletta Register, who will act as Chairman of the Commission. He will not be a national of either of the parties or have been nominated by either of them to the Register.

3. If the appointment of the Chairman, or of any of the other conciliators, has not been made within the prescribed period, it will be made within 20 days of the expiry of the relevant period by the Secretary General of the Permanent Court of Arbitration, after consultations with the parties.

4. Any vacancies will be filled in the manner prescribed for the initial appointment.

Section VI

1. The Commission will consult the parties on the procedure to be followed in the exercise of its responsibilities as described herein. The Commission will give effect to any agreement between the parties on procedure. In the absence of agreement on any point, the Commission may decide the matter.

2. Decisions and recommendations of the Commission will be made by a majority vote of the members.

Section VII

The Commission may, with the consent of the parties, invite any participating State to submit its views orally or in writing.

Section VIII

The parties will refrain throughout the course of the procedure from any action which may aggravate the situation and make more difficult or impede the peaceful settlement of the dispute. In this connection, the Commission may draw the attention of the parties to any measures which it considers might facilitate an amicable settlement.

Section IX

The Commission will seek to clarify the points in dispute between the parties and endeavour to bring about a resolution of the dispute on mutually agreeable terms.

Section X

If the Commission considers that to do so will facilitate an amicable settlement of the dispute, it may suggest possible terms of settlement and set a time limit within which the parties should inform the Commission whether they accept such recommendations.

Section XI

Each party will, within the time limits set under Section X, inform the Secretary and the other party whether or not it accepts the proposed terms of settlement. If both parties have not notified such acceptance within such time limit the Secretary will forward a report from the Commission to the Committee of Senior Officials of the CSCE. The report will not include the matters referred to in Section XII.

Section XII

Any measures recommended under Section VIII, and any information and comments provided to the Commission by the parties in confidence, will remain confidential unless the parties agree otherwise.

Section XIII

Each party to the dispute will bear its own costs and the costs of the conciliator appointed by it. The rest of the costs of the Commission will be shared equally by the parties.

Section XIV

A participating State may at any time, whether before or after a dispute has been referred to the Commission, declare, either generally or in relation to a particular dispute, that it will accept as binding, on condition of reciprocity, any terms of settlement proposed by the Commission. Such declaration will be deposited with the Secretary who will transmit copies to all the participating States.

Section XV

A declaration made under Section II or Section XIV may be withdrawn or modified by written notification to the Secretary who will transmit copies to all the participating States. A declaration made under Section II or Section XIV may not be withdrawn or modified in relation to a dispute to which it applies once a written request for conciliation of the dispute has been made under Section III, and the other party to the dispute has already made such declaration.

Section XVI

The parties may agree to modify the procedure set out in the preceding sections with respect to their particular dispute.

Section XVII

The Director of the Conflict Prevention Centre will act as Secretary of the Commission. In carrying out his functions the Director may consult the Committee of Senior Officials as and when he deems necessary. If the Director is a national of one of the parties to a dispute, his functions in respect of that dispute will be performed by the next most senior official of the Conflict Prevention Centre who is not such a national.

Annex 4

Provisions for Directed Conciliation

1. The Council of Ministers or the Committee of Senior Officials (CSO) may direct any two participating States to seek conciliation to assist them in resolving a dispute that they have not been able to settle within a reasonable period of time.

2. In using this authority, the Council or the CSO may direct that the parties to the dispute use the provisions for conciliation described in Annex 3, on the same basis as if the parties had made a joint written request to bring the dispute before the Conciliation Commission established by that Annex. However, in such situations:

   (a) the Council or the CSO may decide, in view of the nature of the particular dispute or other relevant factors, either to increase or to decrease any of the twenty-day periods for appointment by the parties of the two members of the Conciliation Commission or for selection of the Chairman; and

   (b) the work of the Commission will not be conducted in public, unless the parties agree otherwise.

3. Moreover, in cases involving disputes between two parties to the Convention on Conciliation and Arbitration within the CSCE, the Council or the CSO may direct that the parties use the provisions for conciliation established under that Convention, once that Convention enters into force.

4. The parties to the dispute may exercise any rights they otherwise have to participate in all discussions within the Council or CSO regarding the dispute, but they will not take part in the decision by the Council or the CSO directing the parties to conciliation, or in decisions described in paragraph 2(a).

5. The Council or the CSO will not direct parties to a dispute to seek conciliation under this Annex:

   (a) if the dispute is being addressed under some other procedure for the peaceful settlement of disputes;

(b) if the dispute is covered by any process outside the CSCE which the parties to the dispute have accepted, including under an agreement in which the parties have undertaken to address certain disputes only through negotiations; or

(c) if either party to the dispute considers that, because the dispute raises issues concerning its territorial integrity, or national defence, title to sovereignty over land territory, or competing claims with regard to the jurisdiction over other areas, the provisions of this Annex should not be applied.

6. The parties to the dispute will bear their own expenses. Except for disputes covered in paragraph 3, any other expenses incurred under the procedure will be shared by all participating States in accordance with the CSCE scale of distribution, subject to any procedures that the CSO may adopt to ensure that expenses are limited to those reasonable. With respect to disputes covered by paragraph 3, responsibility for such other expenses will be borne in accordance with the provisions of the Convention on Conciliation and Arbitration within the CSCE.

7. In addition to any reports otherwise provided for under the conciliation provisions described in paragraphs 2 and 3, the Council or the CSO may request the Commission to report on the results of the conciliation. The report will not reflect matters that are considered confidential under the applicable provisions, unless the parties agree otherwise.

INTERPRETATIVE STATEMENTS

Interpretative statements by Turkey[1]

(a) On the occasion of the adoption of the decision on peaceful settlement of disputes, Turkey would like to reconfirm her statement contained in Journal No. 10 of the CSCE Meeting on Peaceful Settlement of Disputes (Geneva, 12-23 October 1992).

Moreover, in connection with the statement of the delegation of the United Kingdom-European Community recorded in Journal No. 10 of the CSCE Meeting on Peaceful Settlement of Disputes (Geneva, 12-23 October 1992), we would like to state the following:

The European Community is not a participating State. Therefore members of the European Community can only take part in the CSCE procedures for peaceful settlement of disputes on an individual basis, that is to say, on an equal footing with other participating States in the CSCE. Turkey cannot accept that membership in the European Community be construed as having a privileged position in making use of CSCE procedures for peaceful settlement of disputes.

(b) With regard to paragraph 5 (c) of the 'Provisions for Directed Conciliation', we would like to make the following statement:

According to the understanding of Turkey, the term '... the jurisdiction over other areas' means '... the jurisdiction over maritime areas'.

* * *

Interpretative statement by Cyprus[2]

Referring to the adoption on 14 December 1992, on the first day of the Third Council Meeting, of the text of the Convention on Conciliation and Arbitration within the CSCE, the delegation of Cyprus made the following statement:

"In connection with the interpretative statement made by the delegation of Turkey on the occasion of the adoption by the CSCE Council of the decision on peaceful settlement of disputes, the delegation of Cyprus reconfirms its statement registered in Journal No. 10 of the CSCE Meeting on Peaceful Settlement of Disputes held in Geneva, 12-23 October 1992."

---

[1] Journal No. 1 (Stockholm, 14 December 1992).

[2] Journal No. 2 (Stockholm, 15 December 1992).

* * *

Interpretative statement by Liechtenstein

In connection with the adoption of agenda item 8 'Requests for admission to the CSCE as participating States', it is the understanding of the delegation of the Principality of Liechtenstein that outstanding issues between the Czech and Slovak Federal Republic and the Czech Republic and the Slovak Republic do encompass nationalization of property of Liechtenstein nationals seized without compensation in the years 1945 and thereafter.

* * *

Interpretative statement by the Czech and Slovak Federal Republic

In connection with the adoption of agenda 8 'Requests for admission to the CSCE as participating states', it is the understanding of the delegation of the Czech and Slovak Federal Republic and of its successor States that any informative talks, consultations or negotiations which might be conducted with the Principality of Liechtenstein cannot include the claims of property rights of the citizens of Liechtenstein, since Czechoslovak law does not recognize these claims as juridically founded.

* * *

Editor's note: At the Geneva Experts Meeting on Peaceful Settlement of Disputes (October 1992), the text of the Stockholm decisions on peaceful settlement of disputes has been prepared. At that meeting, the following interpretative statements in relation to the subject matter have been made.[3]

Interpretative statement by Turkey

The Government of Turkey had formally entered a reservation regarding the representation of Cyprus at the CSCE on 31 July 1975 (CSCE/III/I). The same reservation has been entered at subsequent meetings within the context of the CSCE. We wish to make a similar statement on the occasion of the Geneva Meeting on Peaceful Settlement of Disputes.

'The Republic of Cyprus' which was established, in accordance with international treaties, on the basis of a partnership between the two peoples of the Island, ceased to exist as such after its Constitution was unilaterally and unlawfully abrogated in

---

[3] Text in: RPDG/Journal No. 10 (Geneva, 23 October 1992).

1963 by the Greek Cypriot side by the use of force, despite the protestations and resistance of the Turkish Cypriot side. The Greek Cypriot administration has ever since represented exclusively the Greek Cypriot side. The Greek Cypriot adminstration has ever since represented exclusively the Greek Cypriot and their interests. As a guarantor Power under the 1960 Treaty of Guarantee, Turkey does not recognize this administration or its claims for legitimacy.

There is no single authority which, in fact or in law, jointly represents or is competent to represent the Turkish Cypriots and the Greek Cypriots, and consequently Cyprus as a whole. This is one of the main issues which has to be settled by the negotiating process which is being pursued between the Turkish Cypriot and Greek Cypriot leaders on the basis of equality.

The Turkish Cypriot people are represented by the Government of the Turkish Republic of Northern Cyprus, which was recognized by Turkey in 1983.

Due to the reasons stated above, the representation of Cyprus by the Greek Cypriot administration at the CSCE is neither legal not legitimate. Therefore, the Government of the Republic of Turkey declares that the decisions and the documents adopted by the CSCE Geneva Meeting on Peaceful Settlement of Disputes will have no validity or applicability as regards and in relation to the Turkish Republic of Northern Cyprus and Turkish Cypriots.

Similarly, the commitments assumed by the Republic of Turkey under these decisions and documents will have no validity or applicability as regards and in relation to Cyprus and they do not create obligations for Turkey in that respect.

* * *

Interpretative statement by Cyprus

The delegation of Cyprus would like to refer to the reservation made by the Turkish delegation with regard to Cyprus and observe the following:

Turkey is well known for its violations of all principles of the CSCE. Its record vis-a-vis Cyprus, is a clear example of the fact that, in reality, Turkey pays lipservice to the commitments of the CSCE, and its behaviour is guided by motives which are not only anachronistic but totally foreign to the very concept of the CSCE itself.

We would have expected that in a meeting on the peaceful settlement of disputes, Turkey would, at least for once, have put aside its vicious designs against Cyprus, a small and defenceless neighbour, and appeared to be up to the expectations of the Meeting. Unfortunately, this has not been the case.

The delegation of Cyprus wishes to state that in accordance with the principles and procedures of the CSCE, all decisions are equally binding on all participating States.

Consequently, any reservation with regard to the validity of the decisions of this Meeting as concerns the relations of each participating State with any other participating State or with all other participating States, or any kind of selectivity in implementing these decisions, is of no effect.

* * *

Interpretative statement by Greece

The content of the interpretative statement sent by the Turkish delegation with regard to the Republic of Cyprus refers to and reminds us all of the continuing flagrant violation of all the CSCE principles and commitments by Turkey with respect to the Republic of Cyprus, a full CSCE participating State which has been duly invited to take part in the Meeting, just like all other States present here.

We are convinced that the CSCE would be taking a great step forward if it ensured full respect for its own principles and commitments.

However, we must note in this respect that the violation of the CSCE principles and commitments by Turkey comes only second to the flagrant violation of a peremptory norm of public international law committed by her with regard to Cyprus, namely the principle of the non-use of force in international relations (Article 2, paragraph 4, of the United Nations Charter). This violation, unfortunately, continues to this day, since a great part of Cyprus is still under illegal foreign military occupation. It is to be hoped that meetings such as the one we have been having will contribute, in the present world situation, to the strengthening of the principle of international legality, permitting its effective and prompt application in the case of Cyprus as well.

* * *

Interpretative statement by the United Kingdom - European Community

It concerns the use of the term 'participating State' in the various texts agreed at this Meeting on Peaceful Settlement of Disputes.

The European Community and its Member States consider that the term 'participating State' does not exclude the participation of the European Community in any of the procedures for Peaceful Settlement of Disputes elaborated at the present Meeting alongside a Member State in so far as the dispute concerns an area falling within Community competence. If this were not the case, then all disputes concerning matters for which the Community is competent would be left outside the scope of application of the different procedures on which we have agreed.

* * *

Interpretative statement by the United States of America

In connection with the interpretative statement made by the delegation of the United Kingdom - European Community, the United States fully recognizes and appreciates the important contributions the European Community and its member States have made to the CSCE process.

We point out, however, that the Community, per se, is not a participating State in the CSCE under the provisions of the Helsinki Final Act.

We could not accept an interpretation of the EC statement which could be construed to reduce the requirements and commitments of individual EC States to the CSCE.

III

DOCUMENTS

OF THE

COMMITTEE OF SENIOR OFFICIALS

(excerpts)

FIRST EMERGENCY MEETING OF THE CSO

Prague, 3-4 July 1991

Urgent Appeal for a Cease-fire[1]

Recalling the statement on the situation in Yugoslavia issued by the Council of Ministers in Berlin on 19 June 1992, the CSO makes an urgent appeal that any recourse to the use of force in the present crisis in Yugoslavia continues to be absolutely inadmissible.

The CSO also reiterates the appeal issued at the end of the meeting of the Consultative Committee of the CPC on 1 July 1991 stressing the importance of an immediate and complete cessation of hostilities by all parties involved. A prompt implementation of the commitments undertaken by all concerned Yugoslav parties remains mandatory.

The CSO calls upon all relevant authorities in Yugoslavia to comply with these appeals and fulfil all commitments under the Charter of Paris and the Ten Principles of the Helsinki Final Act, in particular the unequivocal renunciation of the use of force. All fighting has to stop immediately. There must be political control over all armed forces. These forces have to return to their barracks and stay there. Hostile actions against these barracks must stop. Prisoners taken during the hostilities have to be released immediately.

All parties involved in this conflict are called upon to comply with this appeal immediately. The CSO offers its assistance in order to help restore peace in the area and is examining urgently relevant practical steps it can take, in particular the despatch of observers to Yugoslavia, in consultation and agreement with Yugoslav authorities.

---

[1] First Emergency CSO Meeting, Journal No. 1, Annex.

FIRST ADDITIONAL CSO MEETING

agreed at the first CSO emergency meeting

Prague, 8-9 August 1991

Appeal for a Cease-fire[1]

The Committee of Senior Officials,

Greatly disturbed by the appalling losses of human lives that have occurred in Yugoslavia after the urgent appeal for a cease-fire issued by the CSO on 3 July 1991,

Emphasizing the importance of a permanent, complete and effective cease-fire accepted and fully respected by all parties involved,

Welcomes the cease-fire proclaimed by the Federal Presidency of Yugoslavia on 6 August 1991, and urges that it will be fully maintained,

Therefore, urges all concerned parties to stabilize the cease-fire by separating their forces and withdrawing them from areas of conflict,

Reiterates this strong condemnation of any recourse to the use of force,

Alerts all parties to their responsibility to exercise the necessary political control over their regular or irregular armed forces,

Welcomes the offer by the EC to continue all their efforts to monitor an effective cease-fire and include other CSCE participating States invited by Yugoslavia.

* * *

---

1 Additional Meeting of the CSO agreed at the First Emergency Meeting of the Committee, Journal No. 1, Annex.

Monitor Mission to Yugoslavia[2]

The Committee of Senior Officials,

Reaffirming its decision on a "Mission to Yugoslavia" adopted at its First Emergency Meeting on 3 and 4 July 1991,

Welcomes the activities of the Monitor Mission to Yugoslavia, based upon the Memorandum of Understanding which was signed by representatives of the European Community and its Member States, the Federal Authorities of Yugoslavia, the Republic of Croatia and the Republic of Slovenia in Belgrade on 13 July 1991;

Appreciates the reports on the activities of the Mission provided by the EC Presidency and welcomes the progress made in the implementation of the Brioni Agreement of 7 July 1991, which they reflect;

Appeals to all parties concerned in Yugoslavia to co-operate in maintaining a permanent and effective cease-fire and welcomes EC readiness to extend their monitoring activities, through appropriate arrangements with Yugoslavia;

Supports an enlargement of the Mission, in agreement with the Yugoslav authorities, through the inclusion of members of other CSCE participating States on the basis of arrangements between the European Community and Yugoslav authorities;

Requests the European Community and its Member States and other interested CSCE participating States to continue their efforts towards a peaceful solution of the Yugoslav crisis;

Request the Mission to continue to report to the Committee on the progress of its activities on a regular basis.

---

[2] Idem, Journal No. 2, Annex 1.

Assistance to Negotiations on the Future of Yugoslavia[3]

The Committee of Senior Officials,

Underlines the urgent necessity that all parties concerned immediately begin negotiations on the future of Yugoslavia;

Supports strongly the intention of the Yugoslav authorities to begin these negotiations as soon as possible and not later than 15 August 1991;

Noting the Statement on the Situation in Yugoslavia of the CSCE Council in Berlin on 19 June 1991, urges the parties concerned to seek a peaceful settlement based on all the principles and commitments agreed upon in the CSCE process and to abstain from all acts of force or violence or other acts prejudicing the outcome of negotiations which must be acceptable to all people in Yugoslavia;

Stresses that the use of force to achieve political objectives is inadmissible and insists strongly that all parties act in full respect for all human rights, including the rights of national minorities;

Expresses its hope that the process of negotiations will lead to positive results and in this context reaffirms the offer of a CSCE Good Offices Mission, as decided at the First Emergency Meeting on 3 and 4 July 1991, and invites Yugoslavia to make use of this offer, if necessary, in order to facilitate dialogue and negotiations on the future of Yugoslavia;

Notes with satisfaction that the Yugoslav authorities, as an initial step to this end, have extended an invitation to the European Community and its Member States to assist the process of negotiations, as agreed at Brioni;

Supports the readiness of the European Community and its Member States, expressed in their declaration of 6 August 1991, as well as of other interested CSCE participating States, to facilitate and assist these negotiations, at a time and under conditions to be agreed with Yugoslavia;

Emphasizes its resolve to remain seized of this matter. The Committee will be convened by the Chairman for an additional meeting whenever the situation requires, and in any event no later than the first week of September 1991.

---

[3] Idem, Journal No. 2, Annex 2.

SECOND ADDITIONAL CSO MEETING[1]

Prague, 3-4 September 1991

Statement on the Cease-Fire in Yugoslavia[2]

The Committee of Senior Officials of the CSCE,

Greatly disturbed by the appalling losses of human lives that have occurred in spite of the urgent calls for a cease-fire issued on 3 July and 8 August 1991,

Stressing that no territorial gains or changes within Yugoslavia brought about by violence are acceptable,

Welcomes the cease-fire agreed in Belgrade on 1 September 1991 and insists upon strict implementation of and compliance with all its provisions;

Strongly endorses the agreement reached between the European Community and its Member States and Yugoslav parties on 1 September 1991 in Belgrade on the extension of the activities in Croatia of the Monitor Mission to Yugoslavia, enlarged to include members of other CSCE participating States, which is fully in accordance with the statements by the Committee of Senior Officials of 4 July and 9 August 1991;

Stresses the need for full respect for all provisions contained in the Memorandum of Understanding on the Extension of Monitoring Activities of the Monitor Mission to Yugoslavia, including the commitments by the Yugoslav parties concerned regarding the monitoring of the cease-fire;

Demands strongly that all political and military authorities in Yugoslavia co-operate fully and without restrictions with the Monitor Mission and guarantee the personal safety of the members of the Monitor Mission as indispensable prerequisites for successful extension of its monitoring activities;

Stresses that any body responsible for any violation of these provisions will bear the full consequences of its action;

---

[1] Editor's note: Meeting convened on the basis of the CSO decision, laid down in Annex 2 of Journal No. 2 of the Additional Meeting of the CSO of 8-9 August 1991.

[2] Second Additional CSO Meeting, Journal No. 1, Annex.

Warmly supports the initiative by the European Community and its Member States to convene the Conference on Yugoslavia.

* * *

Text on Armaments[3]

The CSCE Committee of Senior Officials, aiming to prevent military escalation of the conflict in Yugoslavia and wishing to contribute to its peaceful settlement,

Calls upon all States to stop and refrain - for the duration of the crisis in Yugoslavia - from supplying arms and military equipment to all Yugoslav parties concerned. This should include taking necessary measures to prevent any transfer of weapons.

Requests all CSCE participating States to submit to the Conflict Prevention Centre appropriate information outlining their Governments' policies on this subject.

* * *

Negotiations on the Future of Yugoslavia[4]

The Committee of Senior Officials of the CSCE,

Gravely concerned about the deteriorating situation in Yugoslavia, and insisting on the immediate implementation of the agreed cease-fire,

Underlines the necessity that the negotiations on the future of Yugoslavia begin immediately, with the view to achieving an outcome of the negotiations which must be acceptable to all people in Yugoslavia,

Fully endorses the decision taken by the European Community and its Member States to convene a Conference on Yugoslavia in the Peace Palace

---

[3] Editor's note: The following text concerning the halting, for the duration of the crisis in Yugoslavia, of the supply of arms and military equipment to all Yugoslav parties was adopted by the CSO on 4 September 1991; Second Additional Meeting of the CSO, Journal No. 2, Annex 1. (Title of the Resolution added by the Editor.)

[4] Second Additional Meeting of the CSO, Journal No. 2, Annex 2.

in The Hague on 7 September 1991, to be chaired by Lord Carrington, and at the same time set up an arbitration procedure,

Urges the political and military authorities to restore and maintain full control over all military actions, thus contributing to the success of the Conference,

Urges the parties concerned to seek a peaceful settlement based on all the principles and commitments agreed upon in the CSCE process and to abstain from all acts of force or violence or other acts,

Recalling the Committee's statement of 9 August on assistance to negotiations on the future of Yugoslavia, welcomes the readiness of other interested CSCE participating States to assist the peace process,

Stresses once again that the use of force to achieve political objectives is inadmissible and insists strongly that all parties act in full respect for all human rights, including the rights of national minorities,

Considers that all refugees who so wish must be allowed to return to their homes in safety,

Notes with satisfaction the preparedness of the European Community and its Member States and other CSCE participating States to continue their monitoring activities, as long as will be needed for the conference to be successful, and emphasizes the need that the Yugoslav parties fulfil their obligations accordingly,

Welcomes the decision of the European Community and its Member States to keep the other CSCE participating States fully informed of the proceedings of the Conference on Yugoslavia, through the Chairman of the Committee of Senior Officials and the CSCE Secretariat.

THIRD ADDITIONAL CSO MEETING

Prague, 10 October 1991

The Situation in Yugoslavia[1]

The Committee of Senior Officials of the CSCE,

Reaffirming its earlier resolutions on Yugoslavia and deeply concerned about the lack of respect therefor,

Deeply disturbed by the recent escalation of violence in Yugoslavia, causing loss of life and human suffering,

Appalled by the irresponsible behaviour of different Yugoslav parties which calls into doubt their willingness to settle their disputes by peaceful means,

Reiterating the determination of all participating States never to recognize any changes of borders, whether external or internal, brought about by force,

Deeply concerned about the increasing destruction and loss of life,

Noting that most delegations expressed their unreserved condemnation of the usurpation of power by the representatives of two republics in the Yugoslav Federal Presidency contrary to the established constitutional order of Yugoslavia as well as the Charter of Paris,

Recalling the Document of the Moscow Meeting of the Conference on the Human Dimension of the CSCE which emphasizes that issues relating to human rights, fundamental freedoms, national minorities, democracy and the rule of law do not belong exclusively to the internal affairs of the State concerned,

Recalling Un Security Council resolution 713/91,

Welcomes the conclusions reached at the meeting held in The Hague on 4 October 1991 which was chaired by the EC Presidency, with the participation of the President of Croatia, the President of Serbia and the Federal Minister of Defence, on the principles which should guide a solution

---

[1] Third Additional Meeting of the CSO, Journal, Annex . This meeting was a follow-up to the first emergency meeting of the CSO.

for the Yugoslav crisis, notably the principle that a political solution should be sought on the basis of the perspective of recognition of the independence of those republics in Yugoslavia wishing it, at the end of a negotiating process conducted in good faith and involving all parties;

Welcomes the Memorandum of Understanding, which was signed on 8 October 1991 in Zagreb under the auspices of the European Community by representatives for the Federal Secretary for National Defence of the SFRY and for the Republic of Croatia, on a general cease-fire in the territory of Croatia, and urges all parties concerned fully to abide by this agreement, particularly the renunciation of the use of major weapons systems;

Warmly commends both the collective and individual efforts of the men and women of the Monitor Mission to Yugoslavia;

Strongly supports the activities of the Monitor Mission and welcomes the extension and strengthening of these activities in Croatia and Bosnia-Herzegovina and recommends that consideration be given to the extension of activities to other areas as appropriate;

Welcomes the protocol on the Monitor Mission signed by the representatives of Hungary and the EC;

Condemns any acts endangering the security of members of the Monitor Mission and its equipment and demands that all Yugoslav parties comply fully with their obligation to protect and ensure the safety of the Mission and its members;

Takes note of the fact that the Western European Union is exploring ways in which the activities of the monitors could be supported so as to make their work a more effective contribution to the peace-keeping effort, the possibilities of which have not been exhausted;

Insists on compliance with the commitment, accepted by participating States at the Moscow Meeting of the Conference on the Human Dimension, to ensure that military and paramilitary forces be subject to the effective direction and control of appropriate democratically elected civilian authorities and to maintain and strengthen executive control over such forces so that their participation in acts of violence and warfare be ended once and for all. The Committee furthermore insists on the immediate cessation of mobilization on all sides;

Condemns all violations of relevant norms of international law applicable to non-international armed conflict which have occurred during the escalation of violence in Yugoslavia;

Expresses its conviction that those responsible for the unprecedented violence against people in Yugoslavia, with its ever-increasing loss of life, should be held personally accountable under international law for their actions;

Takes note of the support of many other participating States for the intention expressed on 6 October 1991 by the European Community and its Member States to apply restrictive measures to those parties continuing to flout the desire of the other Yugoslav parties as well as the international community for a successful outcome of the Conference on Yugoslavia;

Welcomes the continued engagement by all parties to the Yugoslav crisis in the Conference on Yugoslavia;

Urges all Yugoslav parties to take an active and constructive part without delay in the Conference on Yugoslavia which provides the essential framework for finding a peaceful solution to the Yugoslav crisis which respects the rights of all who live in Yugoslavia, including minorities;

Welcomes the progress which has been made at the Conference on Yugoslavia on 10 October 1991;

Welcomes the fact that parties which are not participating in its proceedings have been given access to the Conference and recommends that such access be granted to other parties concerned;

Considers that the unsettled issue of national minorities perpetuates the tension and instability and considers that the conflict must not be used for forcible change in the ethnic composition of the different areas;

Agrees that a successful outcome of the Conference on Yugoslavia should contain international guarantees for the protection of the rights of national minorities in accordance with the standards and commitments of the CSCE;

Underlines the importance of the immediate and full implementation of resolution 713/91 of the United Nations Security Council and welcomes the appointment of Mr. Cyrus Vance as the special representative of the UN Secretary-General;

Will examine ways in which the institutions of the CSCE, including the CPC, could further assist in the implementation of the provisions of this resolution.

FOURTH CSO MEETING

Prague, 22-24 October 1991

CSCE Human Rights Rapporteur Mission to Yugoslavia[1]

Recalling the Document of the Moscow Meeting, the CSCE Committee of Senior Officials agreed to form a human rights rapporteur mission. The mission will visit Bosnia-Herzegovina, Croatia, Macedonia, Montenegro, Serbia and Slovenia at a time to be agreed through consultation with Yugoslavia. It will inform itself of the situation with respect to human rights, including the rights of minorities, and will report to the Committee. Its report will be circulated by the CSCE Secretariat through the CSCE points of contact and will be considered by the Committee at a future meeting. The report will be made available to the Chairman of the Conference on Yugoslavia.

The mission will be led by the designated representative of the Chairman of the CSCE Council of Ministers. A representative from the CSCE Office for Free Elections will serve as secretary for the mission. The mission will also include, *inter alia*, a representative from the European Community and a representative of the Chairman of the Conference on Yugoslavia.

* * *

The Situation in Yugoslavia[2]

The Committee of Senior Officials of the CSCE,

1. Reaffirming its earlier resolutions on Yugoslavia,

2. Deeply concerned by the continuing violence and bloodshed in Yugoslavia, and by the obstacles encountered by the monitor mission to Yugoslavia,

3. Strongly condemns the constant and blatant violations of all cease-fire agreements concluded until the present day, and any attempt to bring about changes by force. No such change will be recognized as legal;

---

[1] 4-CSO/Journal No. 1, Annex 2.

[2] 4-CSO/Journal No. 1, Annex 3.

4. Welcomes the agreement reached on 14 October 1991 to continue the activities of the monitor mission to Yugoslavia, and reiterates its demand that all Yugoslav parties comply fully with their obligation to protect and ensure the safety of the mission and its members;

5. Underlines the importance of concerting all efforts made by CSCE participating States to solve the crisis in Yugoslavia and in this spirit endorses the Declaration on Yugoslavia adopted by the European Community and its member States, the United States of America and the Union of Soviet Socialist Republics of 18 October 1991 and it supports the continuing efforts by the Secretary-General of the United Nations;

6. Welcomes the fact that on 18 October 1991 the Chairman of the Conference on Yugoslavia presented arrangements for a general settlement of the Yugoslav crisis, and notes with great interest that it covers *inter alia* general principles, guidelines with regard to the implementation of human rights and rights of ethnic and national groups, other areas of co-operation and institutional aspects;

7. Urges all Yugoslav parties to continue their co-operation in the framework of the Conference on Yugoslavia;

8. Insists that the agreement reached in The Hague on 18 October 1991 at which the collective Presidency of the Socialist Federal Republic of Yugoslavia and President Tudjman, in the presence of President Milosevic, agreed to give their respective forces instructions to abide by the terms of a new cease-fire agreement, be immediately and fully implemented;

9. Calls upon all Yugoslav parties to strictly observe these terms and expresses grave concern about recent violations of these terms;

10. Reiterates its conviction that those responsible for the acts of unprecedented violence against people in Yugoslavia and for violations of cease-fire agreements be held personally accountable under international law for their actions, including those in contravention of relevant norms of international humanitarian law;

11. Calls upon all Yugoslav parties to strive to ensure the free movement of individuals and the free circulation of goods among different parts of Europe, transiting Yugoslavia by land, air and water;

12. Decides to continue to keep the crisis in Yugoslavia under closest consideration and invites the Chairman-in-Office of the Committee of Senior Officials to convene the Committee at a time he deems appropriate.

FOURTH ADDITIONAL CSO MEETING

Prague, 29 November 1991

Support for United Nations Action on Yugoslavia[1]

The Committee of Senior Officials of the CSCE,

1. Reaffirming its earlier resolutions on the conflict in Yugoslavia,

2. Recalling its strong support for the activities undertaken by the European Community and its member States, in particular the mandate given to them to organize a monitoring mission, including other interested CSCE participating States,

3. Stating that the conflict in Yugoslavia has led to a situation where principles and provisions of CSCE documents and the Charter of the United Nations are constantly violated and international peace and security threatened,

4. Stressing the need for complementary action by all organizations which can make a contribution to solving the crisis in Yugoslavia,

5. Recalling its resolution "The situation in Yugoslavia" adopted on 22 October 1991 stating its support for the continuing efforts by the Secretary-General of the United Nations,

6. Notes with satisfaction that all parties in Yugoslavia have called for the deployment of a United Nations peacekeeping operation as soon as possible;

7. Warmly welcomes the activities of the Secretary-General and his special representative;

8. Strongly supports Security Council resolution 721 unanimously adopted on 27 November 1991;

---

[1] Fourth Additional meeting of the CSO, Annex. This meeting was a follow-up meeting of the First Emergency Meeting of the CSO.

9. Calls upon all participating States to support and, where possible, to participate in the establishment of a United Nations peacekeeping operation once agreed upon by the Security Council;

10. Emphasizes that the stationing of peacekeeping forces must not in any way endorse the seizure of territory by force;

11. Welcomes the undertaking by the Security Council to examine and take appropriate action without delay upon the recommendations of the Secretary-General;

12. Strongly appeals to all parties in Yugoslavia to fully comply with the cease-fire agreed upon on 23 November 1991 in Geneva as one of the prerequisites for the establishment of a United Nations peacekeeping operation;

13. Expresses the hope that the Security Council will consider taking further measures to promote a swift solution of the conflict in Yugoslavia;

14. Reiterates its strong commitment to the continuation of the Conference on Yugoslavia, as the forum where the Yugoslav crisis will have to be solved;

15. Decides to continue to keep the crisis in Yugoslavia under closest consideration and invites the Chairman-in-Office of the Committee of Senior Officials to convene the Committee at a time he deems appropriate;

16. Requests the Chairman to transmit this text to the Secretary-General of the United Nations in order to inform the Security Council in accordance with resolution 713/91.

FIFTH CSO MEETING

Prague, 8-11 January 1991

Statements on the seat of the Russian Federation[1]

"Before opening the meeting the Chairman welcomed the delegation of the Russian Federation, referring to the letter from the Foreign Minister of the Russian Federation to the Chairman-in-Office of the CSCE Council (...). In this connection the Head of the Hungarian delegation stated: "I would like to join you in welcoming the delegation of the Russian Federation who takes over the seat of the former Soviet Union in the CSCE. I would like to state that the Hungarian Government's wish is that all States emerging on the territory of the former Soviet Union who wish to do so would be admitted as participating States of the CSCE as soon as possible, provided that they meet the standards of the CSCE and undertake to abide by the commitments contained in all documents of the CSCE. I request that this statement be recorded in the Journal of the day".

* * *

Declaration on Yugoslavia[2]

The Committee of Senior Officials of the CSCE,

1. Profoundly distressed over the dramatic events that occurred in Yugoslavia as a result of the inadmissible use of totally unwarranted force, particularly that which yesterday caused the death of five members of the Monitoring Mission,

2. Condemns in the strongest possible terms those responsible for shooting down an unarmed helicopter of the Monitoring Mission, requests an immediate and exhaustive evaluation of responsibility and expects those responsible to be held accountable for these and other equally unacceptable acts;

---

[1] 5-CSO/Journal No. 1, paragraph 2. (Title added by the Editor.)

[2] 5-CSO/Journal No. 1, Annex 2.

3. Strongly urges all parties in Yugoslavia, without exception, to fully co-operate with the efforts which have been ordered and are already underway aiming at a thorough investigation of this tragic occurrence;

4. Reaffirms its support and solidarity towards the members of the Monitor Mission, whose actions and courage deserve to be praised;

5. Urges all parties to take the necessary steps to ensure the safety of the Monitor Mission and of personnel sent by the United Nations;

* * *

6. Reiterating its firm commitment to seek a peaceful and lasting settlement of the crisis in Yugoslavia, in accordance with the principles and commitments of the CSCE,

7. Condemns in particular any use of major weapon systems in this conflict;

8. Strongly supports Resolution 724, adopted by the Security Council of the United Nations on 15 December 1991;

9. Takes note of the statement of the representative of the European Community and its member States referring to their Declaration of 16 December 1991;

10. Welcomes the Accord reached in Sarajevo on 2 January 1992 under the auspices of the special representative of the Secretary-General of the United Nations, Mr. Cyrus Vance, establishing modalities for the implementation of the cease-fire agreement of 23 November 1991, and underlines the importance of a strict compliance, by all parties, of the dispositions of the above-mentioned Agreements;

11. Urges the Security Council of the United Nations to take a decision on an early deployment of United Nations peace-keeping forces in Yugoslavia insisting that all parties concerned effectively implement all relevant conditions therefor;

12. Welcomes the decision taken by the Chairman of the Conference on Yugoslavia, Lord Carrington, to reconvene the Conference, which remains the appropriate forum for reaching a durable and comprehensive settlement of the crisis;

13. Warns against any extension of the present conflict and calls upon all parties to adopt a constructive participation in the Conference;

14. Recalls in this context its repeated affirmation to reject the use of force to change established borders, whether internal or external;

15. Decides to keep the situation in Yugoslavia under close consideration.

* * *

Exchange of Information and Documents[3]

1. It was agreed to initiate the exchange of information and relevant documents, as encouraged by the Council at their Berlin Meeting in June 1991, as a first concrete step towards increased contacts and co-operation, between the CSCE and the main European and transatlantic institutions, such as the European Community, the Council of Europe, the United Nations Economic Commission for Europe, the North Atlantic Treaty Organization, and the Western European Union, as well as the Organisation for Economic Co-operation and Development, the European Bank for Reconstruction and Development and the European Investment Bank.

2. The Director of the CSCE Secretariat is asked to enter into contact with the above-mentioned institutions to offer to provide them with CSCE documents and express interest in receiving similar documents from them. The list of relevant documents would be agreed between the CSCE Secretariat and the institutions concerned and could include concluding documents, conclusions, communiqués and similar public documents, calendars of anticipated meetings and conferences. The Director will establish modalities for such exchanges with appropriate officials of these institutions, including a definition of what documents might be included. The CSCE Secretariat will be responsible for the exchange of information and documents with all the CSCE institutions.

3. It is foreseen that documents will be offered in one or, if possible, several of the languages in which they are issued, but that no additional translation will be requested for the purpose of the exchange.

---

[3] 5-CSO/Journal No. 3, Annex 2.

4. The Director of the Secretariat will circulate a list of documents received to all participating States every month. Documents received will be made available upon request to those participating States not members of the institution in question.

5. The procedure will be reviewed by the Committee of Senior Officials six months after the first list of documents has been exchanged.

6. In addition to the above provisions for the exchange of documents, information will be exchanged with these organizations through their contributions to specialized CSCE Meetings, as provided for in the Prague Document on the further development of CSCE institutions and structures.

SEVENTH CSO MEETING

Prague, 27-28 January 1992

Decisions based on the Interim Report on Nagorno-Karabakh[1]

(1) The Committee of Senior Officials noted the "Interim Report of the Rapporteur Mission on the situation in Nagorno-Karabakh".

The Committee of Senior Officials:

(2) - urges the interested parties to impose an immediate cease-fire on all forces in the Nagorno-Karabakh area of the Azerbaijan Republic, the population of which expresses their will to enjoy all their rights including all those contained in the Principles of the Helsinki Final Act, and to implement fully their undertakings in the Communiqué issued by the Foreign Ministers of Armenia, Azerbaijan, and the Russian Federation in Moscow on 20 February 1992;

(3) - underlines the fact that the presence in the area of groups of eminent persons from CSCE participating States will contribute to the establishment of an effective cease-fire and urges concerned parties to guarantee their safety and to take all necessary steps to this end;

(4) - requests that all participating States and all states in the region impose an immediate embargo on all deliveries of weapons and munitions to forces engaged in combat in the Nagorno-Karabakh area, and inform the Conflict Prevention Centre of steps taken in this respect;

(5) - urgently requests the Chairman-in-Office of the CSCE to contact international and voluntary organizations with appropriate resources to provide humanitarian assistance, and to encourage them to provide such assistance, both to the inhabitants of Nagorno-Karabakh, and to the refugees and displaced persons on both sides of this conflict, including those from the Republics of Armenia and Azerbaijan;

---

[1] 7-CSO/Journal No. 2, Annex 1. (Title of the Resolution added by the Editor.)

(6) - requests that the Chairman-in-Office of the CSCE convene representatives of the States concerned with a view to immediately establishing safe corridors for the delivery of humanitarian assistance to the inhabitants of Nagorno-Karabakh;

(7) - requests the Chairman-in-Office of the CSCE, in contact with the authorities of Armenia and Azerbaijan, as well as local authorities and representatives in Nagorno-Karabakh, to promote, if necessary under the auspices of the International Committee of the Red Cross, the immediate exchange of hostages;

(8) - requests the Chairman-in-Office of the CSCE, in conjunction with the authorities of Armenia and Azerbaijan, as well as local authorities and representatives in Nagorno-Karabakh, to promote, if necessary under the auspices of the International Committee of the Red Cross, the immediate return of remains of all the dead to their families for respectful burial.

* * *

(9) The Committee of Senior Officials, seeking a peaceful and lasting settlement to the situation in Nagorno-Karabakh in accordance with the Principles, commitments and provisions of the CSCE and the equal legitimate aspirations of all peoples concerned, agreed that this requires from all the concerned parties:

(10) - respect for international obligations with regard to the rule of law, democracy and human rights including all those based on the Principles, commitments and provisions of the CSCE;

(11) - guarantees for the rights of ethnic and national communities and minorities, in accordance with the commitments subscribed to in the framework of the CSCE;

(12) - respect for the inviolability of all borders, whether internal or external, which can only be changed by peaceful means and by common agreement;

(13) - commitment to settle by agreement all questions concerning regional disputes;

(14) - guarantees for the absence of territorial claims towards any neighbouring state, including abstention from hostile propaganda activities that would, *inter alia*, promote such territorial claims.

* * *

The Committee of Senior Officials:

(15) - requests participating States in the region, in particular Kazakhstan and the Russian Federation, to continue their efforts to achieve a final and complete cease-fire and to promote negotiation among the parties in the framework of the CSCE and on the basis of CSCE principles;

(16) - strongly urges the continuation of the dialogue among all interested parties, including local authorities from Nagorno-Karabakh and representatives of Armenian and Azeri inhabitants from Nagorno-Karabakh. Among the first issues to be discussed in this dialogue should be the question of observers to monitor the cease-fire, the immediate needs of the refugees and displaced persons, the re-establishment of normal trade relations, and the establishment of an independent commission, including third parties, to review further problems relating to the refugees and displaced persons;

(17) - requests the Chairman-in-Office of the CSCE to stand ready to participate in this dialogue, and, if requested by the parties, to pursue it under the auspices of the CSCE;

(18) - requests the Chairman-in-Office of the CSCE to contact the governments of CSCE participating States to determine whether it would be possible to provide a group of observers to monitor a cease-fire when it is established, and to make recommendations on this subject;

(19) - calls the attention of the interested parties to the possibility of using the various CSCE mechanisms to facilitate progress toward a solution to the Nagorno-Karabakh problem, and, in this connection, the possibility of requesting the Chairman-in-Office of the CSCE to form an international advisory commission on constitutional questions;

* * *

(20) - requests the CSCE participating States which may be able positively to influence the situation to report on progress toward a peaceful settlement at subsequent CSO meetings, in particular on the elements mentioned above;

(21) - agrees that the possibility of additional missions to Nagorno-Karabakh to monitor the evolving situation will be considered whenever useful.

*

Interpretative statement by Armenia[2]

Armenia has no territorial dispute with Azerbaijan.

The Government of the Republic of Armenia considers that the question of Nagorno-Karabakh must be resolved in conformity with the principles of respect for human rights and self-determination of peoples, which are among the ten principles of the Final Act of Helsinki.

Armenia, as an interested third party, considers that the opening of negotiations between the representatives of the democratically elected authorities of Nagorno-Karabakh and those of the Government of Azerbaijan is the only route to the solution of this problem.

Armenia will support, to this end, all initiatives aimed at establishing such a dialogue and will make every effort to ensure that the negotiations are successful.

* * *

CSCE Human Rights Rapporteur Mission to Yugoslavia: Follow-up Mission[3]

Referring to the Summary of Conclusions of the Prague Meeting of the CSCE Council, the CSCE Committee of Senior Officials examined the need for further action concerning the human rights situation in Yugoslavia. The

---

[2] 7-CSO/Journal No.2, (Corrigendum), paragraph 6. Editor's note: This interpretative statement was made by Armenia in relation to the CSO decisions on the Interim Report of the Rapporteur Mission to Nagorno-Karabakh.

[3] 7-CSO/Journal No. 2, Annex 2.

Committee agreed that the human rights situation, including the situation of national minorities, requires further consideration and follow-up action by the CSCE. To that end, the Committee decided to send a follow-up mission to the Human Rights Rapporteur Mission to Yugoslavia as established by decision of the Committee on October 22, 1991 in Prague. The follow-up mission will examine further the situation in the previously visited Republics and give particular attention to the subjects mentioned for consecutive action in the first report.

The mission will not take place before the end of April and it will report to the Committee. The report will be circulated by the CSCE Secretariat through the CSCE points of contact and will be considered by the Committee at a future meeting. The report will be made available to the Chairman of the Conference on Yugoslavia.

EIGHTH CSO MEETING

Helsinki, 13 March 1992

Text concerning the situation in Nagorny-Karabakh[1]

The Committee of Senior Officials of the Conference on Security and Co-operation in Europe,

Deeply concerned by the escalation of the armed conflict in and around Nagorno-Karabakh resulting in greater loss of life and increased suffering of the inhabitants,

Reiterating its support for the goals of the mediation effort of the Russian Federation as embodied in the communiqué issued on 20 February 1992 in Moscow by the Foreign Ministers of Armenia, Azerbaijan and the Russian Federation,

Welcoming the complementary efforts taken by the European Community and its member states, by members of the North Atlantic Co-operation Council and by the Secretary-General of the United Nations through his recent decision to send a personal representative to the area,

* * *

1. *Reaffirms* its decisions of 28 February 1992 under the heading "Interim Report of the CSCE Rapporteur Mission to Nagorno-Karabakh" (7-CSO/Journal No. 2/Annex 1), and its determination to have their provisions implemented as soon as possible;

2. *Reiterates*, in the strongest terms, its call for an immediate and effective cease-fire, to include an active commitment by responsible local commanders to its implementation;

3. *Agrees* to convene an additional meeting of the Council in Helsinki on 24 March 1992;

4. *Recommends* that the Council request the CSCE Chairman-in-Office to convene as soon as possible a conference on Nagorno-Karabakh under the auspices of the CSCE, to provide an ongoing forum for

---

[1] 8-CSO/Journal, Annex 2. (Title added by the Editor.)

negotiations towards a peaceful settlement of the crisis in accordance with the principles, commitments and provisions of the CSCE;

5. *Welcomes* the intention of Foreign Minister Dienstbier, in his capacity as Chairman-in-Office of the CSCE Council, to visit the region shortly in order to contribute to the establishment and maintenance of an effective cease-fire and the achieving of a peaceful settlement;

6. *Requests* the Chairman-in-Office of the CSCE to organize and despatch without delay a second CSCE Mission to the region to examine the modalities of:

   - the negotiation and implementation of an immediate and effective cease-fire as an essential element of a long-term process leading to a political settlement;

   - the establishment of conditions conducive to the visit of the Chairman-in-Office;

   - the deployment of observers to monitor the cease-fire as soon as it is firmly established, including political and organizational aspects;

   and report as soon as possible to the Chairman-in-Office of the Council in preparation for his visit, the report to be circulated to the participating States;

7. *Notes* the commitment of Armenia and Azerbaijan to fully support the visits of this second Mission and of the Chairman-in-Office of the Council in the realization of their tasks;

8. *Stresses* once again the urgent need to ensure the provision of humanitarian assistance, and for efforts to establish safe corridors as foreshadowed in paragraphs 5 and 6 of its decision of 28 February 1992, including, in particular, convening a meeting of the States concerned; and encourages the Chairman-in-Office in the activities he undertakes to implement his corresponding mandate;

9. *Reiterates* its request that all participating States and all States in the region impose an immediate embargo on all deliveries of weapons and munitions to forces engaged in combat in the Nagorno-Karabakh area, and that all participating States inform the Conflict Prevention Centre of steps taken in this respect;

10. *Welcomes* the activities of the International Committee of the Red Cross, and endorses its appeal for respect by all concerned for international humanitarian law in armed conflict.

TENTH CSO MEETING

Helsinki, 29 April - 1 May 1992

Declaration on Bosnia-Herzegovina[1]

1. The statement adopted at the 15 April Plenary session of the Helsinki Follow-up Meeting expressed serious concern of the CSCE participating States over the situation in Bosnia-Herzegovina. This statement condemned the use of force and the violation of Bosnia-Herzegovina's territorial integrity and called upon all parties, in particular the leaders of Serbia and of the Yugoslav National Army (JNA), to take concrete steps to end the hostilities.

2. In the intervening two weeks, several steps have been taken. A ceasefire has been agreed, and there have been repeated promises to end the violence and respect the sovereignty and territorial integrity of all States concerned.

3. Despite these promises, the situation has deteriorated further. There has been an apparent extension of fighting in and around the capital of Bosnia-Herzegovina and in various parts of the country. Violations of territorial integrity of Bosnia-Herzegovina continue, towns are under siege, human suffering and material destruction continue on an unprecedented scale and there are growing numbers of refugees and displaced persons. In this connection, CSCE participating States note with concern the remarks contained in the reports by the Secretary-General of the United Nations prepared in conformity with Security Council resolution 749 (1992).

4. The CSCE participating States express their most urgent concern about the disregard for CSCE principles and commitments. They call upon all parties to the conflict to end the violence and co-operate fully in efforts to achieve a stable and lasting peace.

5. They reiterate, in particular, their demand that all parties to the conflict refrain from violence, intimidation or the threat or use of force and that the agreed ceasefire be strictly observed.

---

[1] 10-CSO/Journal, Annex 4.

6. The crisis has entered a critical phase. The CSCE participating States consider it essential to redouble their efforts to gain implementation of commitments to help to stop the aggression.

7. To this end, the Committee of Senior Officials concluded the following:

   (a) The objectives of the 15 April statement have not been attained. There is clear evidence of gross violations of CSCE commitments, which remain uncorrected. In particular, the authority of the legitimate government of Bosnia-Herzegovina is violated through continuing aggression by the JNA and by irregular forces which it supports. This aggression must fully and immediately cease.

   (b) The best vehicle for a peaceful solution remains the peace process instituted by the European Community and supported by the United Nations. The participating States urgently request the parties to the tripartite negotiations in Lisbon to reach an agreement in favour of co-existence between the communities and promoting the restoration of peace and stability throughout the Republic, while recalling that a comprehensive and negotiated settlement can only be obtained also with the commitment and full co-operation of the authorities of the neighbouring States of Bosnia-Herzegovina.

   (c) Furthermore, they request the parties concerned to ensure that the Monitor Mission instituted by the European Community is able to perform fully its tasks in Bosnia-Herzegovina.

   (d) The participating States call upon all parties to co-operate with the mission of the United Nations Secretary-General which is entrusted with the task of investigating the feasibility of a peacekeeping operation in Bosnia-Herzegovina.

   (e) As a prerequisite for the success of these efforts, regular and paramilitary forces in Bosnia-Herzegovina, in particular the JNA, should be subjected to the authorities of that Republic. Otherwise, they should be immediately withdrawn or disarmed and dissolved. Participating States urge immediate results from the negotiations currently under way to that end.

(f) Participating States noted with deep concern the growing flow of refugees from Bosnia-Herzegovina and expressed appreciation for the efforts of countries which receive them. Financial and humanitarian aid to these countries must increase. Arrangements for the rapid return of refugees to their homes are an essential element of a lasting solution to the problem.

(g) Participating States stressed the importance of unrestricted access for humanitarian aid to Bosnia-Herzegovina by land, sea and air. They rejected efforts to hinder the transport of such aid through use of blockades or other impediments and called upon controlling authorities to facilitate this vital traffic.

8. To facilitate the above developments, the participating States will intensify their consultations and detailed review of the situation in Bosnia-Herzegovina, proceeding from commitments undertaken and utilizing this review as a means of impressing upon those guilty of aggression their determination to bring it to a halt.

9. They have decided to continue their examination of the situation in Bosnia-Herzegovina and in the other parts of the former Socialist Federal Republic of Yugoslavia at the next meeting of the CSO to be convened by the Chairman-in-Office not later than 18 May 1992.

* * *

Decision concerning the Conference on Nagorny-Karabakh[2]

The Committee of Senior Officials

Decides that:

1. the Conference on Nagorno-Karabakh, a conference under the auspices of the CSCE will, *mutatis mutandis*, be guided by the rules of procedure of the CSCE;

2. the Chairman of the Conference will work in close contact with the relevant CSCE institutions and structures. In particular, he will regularly and fully report, directly or through his representatives, to the Council/CSO through the Chairman-in-Office on the activities of

---

[2] Idem, Annex 5. (Title added by the Editor.)

the Conference in order to enable the Council/CSO to consider the progress of the Conference;

3. as agreed by the Council of Ministers, the Conference shall meet in Minsk. Some sessions may be held in other localities if so decided by the Conference for practical reasons or cost-related considerations;

4. the host State will designate an Executive Secretary of the Conference;

5. the costs of the Conference will be borne by all the CSCE participating States in accordance with the CSCE scale of contribution. The Executive Secretary will present financial reports on a quarterly basis to the Council or the CSO as its agent and revised versions when the need arises. Auditing will be undertaken in a way similar to that with regard to the CSCE institutions;

6. the Conference will conduct its work through plenaries and working groups. The number of working groups and issues of negotiations will be decided by the participants to the Conference. The Chairman of the Conference, after consultations with the participants to the Conference, will decide on the frequency and the agenda of the plenaries;

7. representatives of the United Nations and of the International Committee of the Red Cross will be invited to observe proceedings of the Conference. The Chairman of the Conference, upon agreement by the participants to the Conference, can invite others to observe proceedings;

8. all decisions concerning the organizational modalities, financing and other arrangements for the Conference will not constitute a precedent and will be without prejudice to decisions which may be reached in these areas by the Helsinki Follow-up Meeting.

* * *

Text concerning a Monitor Mission to Nagorny-Karabakh[3]

1. In order to provide favourable conditions for the peaceful resolution of the armed conflict in and around Nagorno-Karabakh, in particular by the CSCE Conference on Nagorno-Karabakh, and to help stabilize the

---

[3] Idem, Annex 6. (Title added by the Editor.)

situation in the region, the Committee of Senior Officials agrees to establish a Mission to monitor the cease-fire.

2. The decision to despatch the Mission will be made as soon as the following conditions are fulfilled:

   (a) the establishment of an effective and durable cease-fire;

   (b) the consent and co-operation of all the parties concerned;

   (c) the conclusion of the necessary Memoranda of Understanding on the modalities and security of the Mission.

3. The cost of the Monitor Mission will be borne by all the CSCE participating States in accordance with the CSCE scale of contribution. Furthermore, additional voluntary contributions, including contributions in kind, would be welcomed.

4. The Committee of Senior Officials recommends the early appointment, by the Chairman-in-Office, of a Head of Mission with long-standing experience in peace-keeping operations. The Head of Mission should, to the extent possible, participate in the elaboration of the terms of reference of the Mission.

5. The CSO has decided that in advance of the decision to despatch the Mission, agreement must be reached on the terms of reference of the Mission, *inter alia*, the objectives of the Mission and the estimated duration, the size and composition of the Mission, the Mission area, the financial and other modalities, the chain of command and the tasks and accountability of the Head of Mission. For this purpose an informal *ad hoc* drafting group will be convened at the venue of the Helsinki Follow-up Meeting under the guidance of a representative of the Chairman-in-Office of the CSCE Council of Ministers and open to all interested participating States entrusted with working out modalities for the CSCE Monitor Mission. This decision is without prejudice to relevant paragraphs of the Prague Document on Further Development of CSCE Institutions and Structures or to the outcome of the Helsinki Follow-up Meeting. The *ad hoc* drafting group will take into account conclusions submitted by the advance team despatched to Transcaucasia by the Chairman-in-Office of the CSCE Council on 24 April 1992. It will submit the draft modalities for the CSCE Monitor Mission to the Committee of Senior Officials at its Eleventh Meeting.

* * *

Statements concerning the status of Nagorny-Karabakh[4]

'The delegation of Azerbaijan made the following statement:
"On behalf of the delegation of the Republic of Azerbaijan I should like to make an official statement, which I request to have recorded in the Journal of the day.

On 16 April this year the Chairman of the CSCE Council, Deputy Prime Minister of the Czech and Slovak Federal Republic and Minister of Foreign Affairs, Jiri Dienstbier addressed a letter to Mr. O. Sesaian, whom he referred to as 'Head of the Government of Nagorno-Karabakh'. Reference is also made in the letter to a post entitled 'President of the Supreme Soviet of Nagorno-Karabakh'.

In this connection I consider it necessary to state the following: the Nagorny region of Karabakh is an integral part of the Republic of Azerbaijan and this territory falls within the scope of application of the laws of the Azerbaijan State.

The authorities which existed in this region and were directing a campaign of armed separatism against the legitimate government of sovereign Azerbaijan have been dissolved by decree of the Supreme Soviet of the Republic of Azerbaijan.

Authorities of any kind in the Nagorny region of Karabakh similar to those referred to in the letter and proclaimed without the appropriate decisions of the Republic of Azerbaijan are illegal from the point of view of both the Azerbaijan Constitution and international law. They are not recognized and cannot be recognized by any State or international organization.

The disregard for this fact displayed in the letter from the Chairman of the CSCE Council constitutes a violation of the sovereignty of the Republic of Azerbaijan which is a member of the United Nations and the CSCE, and cannot be regarded in any other way than as interference in its internal affairs, threatening the disruption of the efforts of the CSCE towards peace.

In this connection I have to express my serious concern and register a strong protest.

---

4 10-CSO/Journal, paragraph 4.

I request the distinguished Chairman of the Committee of Senior Officials to provide an explanation in this regard and to have it recorded in the Journal of the day. If for any reason such an explanation cannot be provided at present, I request it to be provided at the next Meeting."

The delegation of the Czech and Slovak Federal Republic made the following statement:

"The fact of sending the letter of condolences to representatives of Nagorno-Karabakh in connection with the decease of Mr. Mkrtchian was and should be understood in its purely humanitarian sense.

Using any kind of titles and addresses bears no consequences as far as political position is concerned, does not prejudge in any way any political solution, which, *inter alia*, might be an outcome of the Conference on Nagorno-Karabakh.

In this sense the communication has a technical character and should be interpreted exactly in the same manner as visits and missions to the region and negotiations with representatives of Nagorno-Karabakh, conducted by a number of countries and different international bodies and their representatives, including the CSCE and the United Nations."

SECOND EMERGENCY MEETING OF THE CSO

Helsinki, 6-12 May 1992

Declaration on Bosnia-Herzegovina[1]

1. The statement adopted on 15 April by the representatives of the States participating in the CSCE Follow-up Meeting and the Declaration on Bosnia-Herzegovina adopted by the CSO on 1 May 1992 condemned the use of force and the violation of Bosnia-Herzegovina's territorial integrity and called upon all parties to take concrete steps to end the hostilities.

2. The aggression against Bosnia-Herzegovina continues and the objectives set on 15 April and 1 May still remain unattained. Despite a new agreement on a cease-fire, there has been a continuous extension of the conflict on an unprecedented scale including to other parts of the territory of the former Yugoslavia and involving different parties. In particular, there has been a relentless attack on Sarajevo and continuous fighting elsewhere with the use of air force and heavy weaponry by the Yugoslav National Army (JNA). An EC observer was killed and the EC Monitor Mission had to suspend its activity on the ground.

3. The CSCE participating States extend their condolences to the relatives of all who have died in this senseless conflict. They extend their particular sympathy to the family of Major Borrey and to the people of the Kingdom of Belgium on the tragic death of yet another member of the EC Monitor Mission. This service in the cause of peace deserves the gratitude of all CSCE participating States.

4. The pattern of clear, gross and uncorrected violations of CSCE commitments by the authorities in Belgrade and by the JNA is now unmistakably established. Those leaders have driven themselves into isolation. It is they who bear the prime responsibility for the escalation of bloodshed and destruction.

5. The CSO condemns all these acts and, having considered the situation in its Emergency Meeting, has thus come to the following conclusions:

---

[1] CSO/2-EM/Journal, Annex. *Editor's note: This Declaration was the result of a six days' CSO meeting (from 6 to 12 May) and adopted on the basis of the consensus-minus-one principle.*

The CSO:

(i) reiterates its demand that all parties to the conflict refrain from violence or the threat or use of force and that the agreed cease-fire be strictly and immediately observed;

(ii) expresses its strong condemnation of the shelling of Sarajevo and other cities by the JNA and emphasizes the need for the JNA to end its aggression;

(iii) insists that those elements of the JNA now in Bosnia-Herzegovina must either be subject to the authority of the Government of Bosnia-Herzegovina or else withdrawn or disarmed and disbanded, and until this is achieved will hold the authorities in Belgrade responsible for their actions;

(iv) insists also on the request for the immediate withdrawal of all military forces to their barracks and the dissolution of paramilitary forces currently in Bosnia-Herzegovina, and calls for the establishment of full control by the legitimate Government of Bosnia-Herzegovina over all its territory and over all the armed forces on it;

(v) demands that the JNA refrain from destroying the historical, religious and cultural heritage of Bosnia-Herzegovina;

(vi) demands that the responsible authorities promptly set up an inquiry that will enable to hold personally accountable and to punish all those responsible for the tragic deaths of Major Borrey;

(vii) urges all parties to co-operate with the representative of the United Nations Secretary General, Mr. Goulding, in his current mission in the area to investigate the feasibility of a peacekeeping operation in Bosnia-Herzegovina;

(viii) stresses, once again, in the light of the increasing violence in the country, the urgent need in Croatia, Slovenia and other countries for humanitarian assistance, material and financial, taking into account the high number of refugees and displaced persons, and fully supports the current efforts to deliver humanitarian aid to all the victims of the conflict in Bosnia-Herzegovina, in particular through the establishment of an air bridge. It calls in this connection for a safe and secure access under international supervision to airports in Bosnia-Herzegovina for the effective and unhindered delivery of humanitarian assistance;

(ix) decides, in application of paragraph 16 of the Prague Document on Further Development of CSCE Institutions and Structures, that in view of clear, gross and uncorrected violations of CSCE commitments appropriate action on matters relating to the crisis will until 30 June be taken in the absence of the consent of the delegation of Yugoslavia. The CSO will decide on 29 June, in the light of information provided by the European Community about the situation on the ground and about progress at the EC Peace Conference, whether to extend the application of this decision.

6. The CSO expresses its strongest support for the ceaseless efforts towards a peaceful solution to the crisis situation through the peace process instituted by the European Community and supported by the United Nations, and in particular the endeavours undertaken within the framework of the Conference on Yugoslavia, including the Lisbon Talks on the future constitutional arrangements for Bosnia-Herzegovina. The CSO calls in particular upon the Government of Serbia to accept Chapter 1 of the Draft Convention presented by the Chairman of the Brussels Conference without reservations and to co-operate fully in the resolution of all issues, including State succession.

7. The CSO will continue its examination of the situation in Bosnia-Herzegovina and in the other parts of the former Socialist Federal Republic of Yugoslavia at its next meeting to be convened by the Chairman-in-Office no later than 18 May 1992, and will consider on that occasion what further decisions may be necessary.

*

Interpretative statement by Yugoslavia[2]

The Yugoslav delegation cannot give its consent to the text of the Declaration on Bosnia-Herzegovina, but cannot prevent its adoption due to the application of paragraph 16 of the Prague Document on Further Development of CSCE Institutions and Structures.

---

[2] CSO/2-EM/Journal, paragraph 6.

ELEVENTH CSO MEETING

Helsinki, 18-21 May 1992

Interpretative statement by the Holy See[1]

In connection with the adoption of agenda item 5(b) and prior to any consideration of the question of arrangements for sending a CSCE Monitor Mission to Nagorno-Karabakh, the delegation of the Holy See would again like to draw the Committee's attention to its position of principle on this matter, as set forth in the reply of H.E. Monsignor Jean-Louis Tauran, Secretary for Relations of the Holy See with States, to H.E. Mr. Jirí Dienstbier in his capacity as Chairman-in-Office of the CSCE Council of Ministers. The participating States were informed of that letter by Communication No. 158, of 28 April 1992.

The position of the Holy See remains unchanged. Its specificity does not allow it to participate directly in the initiative in question, as regards either its political or financial consequences. The spiritual nature of the Holy See's universal mission and its humanitarian role require it to remain totally independent. That is why the delegation of the Holy See will not participate directly in the adoption of a decision on the proposal in question and consequently it will not make any objection to the consensus resulting from consultations.

Such a position by the Holy See in the CSCE is not new since it is based on the interpretative statement of 28 November 1972 made in connection with the adoption of the definition of consensus (see document CESC/HC/5). That interpretative statement says, *inter alia*, that the Holy See would not take up a position on concrete problems of a political nature and that 'this attitude is not to be interpreted as either agreement or disagreement, nor should it prevent a consensus from being formed'.

* * *

Situation in the Left-Bank Dniester Areas of the Republic of Moldova[2]

The Committee of Senior Officials takes note of the information on the efforts undertaken by the Ministers for Foreign Affairs of the Republic of Moldova, the Russian Federation, Romania and Ukraine, in particular

---

[1] 11-CSO/Journal No. 1, paragraph 6.

[2] 11-CSO/Journal No. 2, Annex.

pursuant to their Helsinki Declaration of 23 March 1992, to resolve the situation in the Left-Bank Dniester areas of the Republic of Moldova, and calls upon them to continue their peacemaking activities. The Committee of Senior Officials welcomes the understanding reached that the Committee would be kept informed about further steps to resolve the situation in the Left-Bank Dniester areas of the Republic of Moldova.

* * *

Statement on the former Yugoslavia[3]

The Committee of Senior Officials met on 18-20 May 1992 to continue its review of the situation on the territory of the former Socialist Federal Republic of Yugoslavia. The discussion was conducted within the framework of decisions taken in its declaration on 12 May 1992.

The Committee of Senior Officials noted with concern the further deteriorating situation in the former Socialist Federal Republic of Yugoslavia and the continued violation of CSCE commitments by authorities of Serbia and the JNA. It called again for fulfilment of all provisions set forth in recent statements of the CSCE on the issue.

It received with concern reports of continued fighting in the area and of continued destruction and human suffering which are resulting from the conflict and which are aggravated by the continued obstruction to delivery of humanitarian assistance.

The CSO also discussed reports of the grave situation of ethnic Albanians in Kosovo and the denial of fundamental freedoms to them and to Hungarian, Muslim and other ethnic minorities as well as reports that the preparations for elections on 31 May 1992 failed to provide the basis for free and fair elections, and stressed the responsibility of the authorities of Belgrade for these situations.

In view of these developments the CSO decided that:

1. Urgent and immediate steps must be taken to ensure humanitarian assistance through safe and secure access under international supervision to airports in Bosnia-Herzegovina. The city of Sarajevo

---

[3] 11-CSO/Journal No. 3, Annex 2. (Title added by the Editor.)

and its airport must be recognized by all parties to the conflict as a security zone.

2. All international efforts aimed at a lasting solution to the serious refugee problem, including the international high-level meeting convened for 21 May 1992 in Vienna and the International Conference on Refugees proposed by the Governments of Croatia and Slovenia, are to be encouraged.

3. The CSCE Office for Democratic Institutions and Human Rights shall submit by 25 May 1992 its report to the Chairman-in-Office of the Council of the CSCE about the preparation of elections to the Chamber of Citizens of the new Federal Assembly in Belgrade scheduled for 31 May 1992.

4. The Consultative Committee of the CSCE Conflict Prevention Centre is entrusted with the dispatch of a fact-finding mission as soon as possible with a view to determining the military situation in Kosovo. All parties should co-operate with the mission. The Consultative Committee should submit the report of the fact-finding mission to the next Meeting of the Committee of Senior Officials.

In view of the gravity of recent developments the Chairman-in-Office will convene the next Meeting of the Committee of Senior Officials, as appropriate, no later than 8 June 1992, to review the situation in the light of its decisions and take whatever action may be necessary.

*

Interpretative statement by Yugoslavia[4]

Editor's note: Concerning, inter alia, the decision taken by the CSO on the former Yugoslavia (11-CSO/Journal No. 3, Annex 2), the Yugoslav delegation submitted the following interpretative statement:

The Yugoslav delegation would like to stress again the full support and readiness of the Yugoslav authorities to help within their possibilities and responsibilities the free access of humanitarian aid.

---

[4] 11-CSO/Journal No. 3, paragraph 7.

The Yugoslav delegation is fully in favour of all efforts aimed at the lasting solution to the serious refugee problem, including the proposed international high-level meeting convened for 21 May. Having in mind the very serious problems, with over 500,000 refugees, Yugoslavia is ready to participate actively in any international meeting.

Concerning the ongoing mission of the CSCE Office for Democratic Institutions and Human Rights and its expected report, Yugoslavia remains co-operative, open and ready for further deliberations on the preparation of elections scheduled for 31 May.

The Yugoslav delegation cannot accept the *a priori* judgement that the preparations for the elections failed to provide the basis for free and fair elections, as indicated in the proposed text.

The Yugoslav delegation is fully ready to respect all CSCE commitments, including those of the Vienna Document 1990 of the Negotiations on Confidence- and Security-building Measures and the Prague Document 1992 on Further Development of CSCE Institutions and Structures, with regard to the right of the Consultative Committee of the CSCE Conflict Prevention Centre to dispatch a fact-finding mission.

The Yugoslav delegation cannot agree with the one-sided and unacceptable approach on the so-called "military situation in Kosovo" and deeply believes that it is only an artificially added new element to the complexity of the Yugoslav crisis. Otherwise, it is very well known that Yugoslavia has never rejected any mission sent by the CSCE and has shown full and open co-operation with those missions.

The general approach in the proposed text of the declaration is obviously one-sided, particularly in references to the use of force and violence and to the continued violation of CSCE commitments.

The approach is neither just nor objective, and does not reflect at all the actual situation in Bosnia-Herzegovina; it is not a contribution to a peaceful settlement based on an equal and just solution.

The Yugoslav delegation expresses its formal reservation to the declaration as well as to the Chairman's statement[5], and states that it cannot give its consent to the proposed text of the declaration on the Yugoslav crisis or to

---

[5] Not reproduced (Editor).

the Chairman's statement, but it cannot prevent their adoption owing to the application of paragraph 16 of the Prague Document on Further Development of CSCE Institutions and Structures.

* * *

Text on Nagorny-Karabakh[6]

The Committee of Senior Officials received with deep concern reports of recent developments in the crisis between Armenia and Azerbaijan.

Despite repeated efforts to arrange a lasting cease-fire and despite continued statements by all parties of their intention to seek a peaceful solution, the fighting has escalated. Recent heavy exchanges of fire have resulted in expansion of the crisis on the territory of Azerbaijan. Major cities have been subjected to bombardment and military occupation. Prospects for a negotiated settlement to the crisis have been damaged severely.

The CSCE participating States remain determined to pursue all efforts to ensure progress towards such a peaceful settlement based on CSCE principles. They cannot accept the continuing destruction and the tragic loss of human life which results from continuation of the violence. They are concerned that, left unchecked, this conflict could tear the fabric of hard-won democratic development, which has only recently begun in the countries of the area. If this were allowed to occur, our efforts to secure a stable and lasting peace throughout Europe would be endangered.

The new situation required extraordinary steps. As stated in the decision of the Council of Ministers of 24 March 1992, CSCE participating States call on all parties to the conflict to renounce the use of force as a means of settling the dispute. Participating States condemn, in particular, expansion of the conflict into other areas of Azerbaijan, and reject implications that *faits accomplis* may be created by military means. They state in the strongest terms their demand for respect of the territorial integrity of Azerbaijan and call for the immediate cessation of hostilities. There should be immediate withdrawal and the disarming of all forces involved in the hostilities.

In light of the urgent need for action to stop the fighting, the participating States have decided to call an emergency meeting of the States taking part in the Conference on Nagorno-Karabakh agreed by the Council of Ministers on

---

[6] 11-CSO/Journal No. 4, Annex. (Title added by the Editor.)

24 March 1992. The meeting will be under the responsibility of Signor Mario Raffaelli, who is Chairman of the Conference. Its goal should be to explore urgently all aspects of the situation, with a view to reopening the dialogue among parties to the conflict. The meeting should be scheduled as soon as possible. Signor Raffaelli should present an assessment and recommendations for further actions to a Meeting of the Committee of Senior Officials to be held in the first week of June.

TWELFTH CSO MEETING

Helsinki, 8-11 June 1992

Decisions of the Committee of Senior Officials[1]

1. The CSO met on 8-10 June 1992 to continue its examination of the situation in Bosnia-Herzegovina and in other parts of the former Socialist Federal Republic of Yugoslavia. The participating States focused in particular on the continued deterioration of the situation in Bosnia-Herzegovina and on arrangements for further decisions pertaining to the crisis as required by the statement of the CSO of 12 May 1992.

2. The CSO heard a moving description of the situation in Bosnia-Herzegovina and call to action by the Foreign Minister of that country, His Excellency Haris Silajdzic. His comments underscored the desperate humanitarian situation in Bosnia-Herzegovina and documented the continuing aggression which is destroying the fabric of his nation.

3. This continuing aggression has led to the deepening diplomatic and physical isolation of Serbia and its leaders. United Nations Security Council resolution 757 is a dramatic example of the determination of the world community not to tolerate the continued disregard by Serbia and the JNA for CSCE commitments and basic human standards. The participating States welcomed the Security Council action as an important concrete ratification of the political message the CSCE has been seeking to impress upon the leaders of Serbia.

4. The participating States expressed their determination to abide fully by the provisions of resolution 757 and to implement carefully the sanctions which it contains. They recalled also the ongoing process of examination of Belgrade's role in international organizations now under way in the United Nations and agreed to follow closely its implications for the CSCE.

5. The participating States expressed their dismay at the continuing hindrance of humanitarian aid to the people of Bosnia-Herzegovina. They called for the immediate facilitation of secure transport to areas of need. In particular, they stressed the importance of establishing a

---

[1] 12-CSO/Journal No. 3, Annex.

security zone in and around Sarajevo, including its airport, as envisaged in United Nations Security Council resolution 758, and called for support of the efforts undertaken by the participating States within the United Nations to secure such a zone.

6. They also drew attention to the human and environmental catastrophe which could result from continued shelling of the city of Tuzla, which is home to one of the largest chemical complexes in the Balkans. This plant contains large amounts of toxic and potentially hazardous chemicals. Fire or explosion could result in a serious threat to human health and to the environment.

7. The Committee of Senior Officials also decided on the following specific steps:

   (a) In accordance with its decision of 12 May 1992, the CSO will decide on 29 June 1992 further action to be taken in the light of the information provided by the EC about the situation on the ground and about progress at the EC Peace Conference. To facilitate this decision, the Chairman-in-Office, after consultations with delegations, has invited representatives of Austria, Canada, the Czech and Slovak Federal Republic, Germany, Greece, Portugal-European Community, the Russian Federation, Sweden, Switzerland, Turkey and the United States of America to form a task force. This task force will commence its work by 22 June 1992 at the latest and will consider the assessment provided by the EC and the conclusions of the review to be conducted by the United Nations. The task force will present its recommendations for further action to the CSO by 29 June 1992, including those on the question of the participation of the delegation of Yugoslavia in the CSCE, particularly with a view to the arrangements for the forthcoming Helsinki Summit.

   (b) The task force will also prepare recommendations, for consideration by the CSO at its Meeting on 29 June 1992, on the role that further CSCE missions, of either short or long duration, might play in promoting peace, averting violence and restoring respect for human rights and fundamental freedoms in Kosovo, Vojvodina and Sandjak and in support of the efforts of the EC Peace Conference. To help prepare such a recommendation the CSO has decided to send an exploratory mission to the above regions within the next two weeks.

* * *

Statements on the adoption of the "Decisions"[2]

"Following the adoption of the text entitled "Decisions of the Committee of Senior Officials" (...), the Chairman made the following announcement:

"The Chairman-in-Office will continue his efforts, outside this CSO Meeting, to create conditions enabling the fulfilment of the CSO decision on an exploratory mission. He also urges all the participating States to contribute to these efforts.

In this connection, he would like to point out that in his view the Helsinki Follow-up Meeting should adopt appropriate decisions as far as practical modalities, including logistic support and the question of financing such missions as CSCE operations, are concerned".

In connection with the adoption of the text entitled "Decisions of the Committee of Senior Officials" (...), statements were made by the following delegations with the request that they should be recorded in the Journal:

By the Russian Federation:

The delegation of the Russian Federation understands that the missions referred to in paragraph 7(b) are being sent to the specified regions of the Federal Republic of Yugoslavia.

By Yugoslavia:

Referring to the statement of the Chairman that he will contact the authorities of the regions mentioned in order to send missions, my delegation would like to say that those local authorities are not authorized to give consent to the proposed missions and under these circumstances Yugoslavia is not ready to receive them.

---

[2] 12-CSO/Journal No. 3, paragraph 4.

THIRTEENTH CSO MEETING

Helsinki, 29 June - 7 July 1992

Situation in the Left-Bank Dniester Areas of the Republic of Moldova[1]

The CSO notes with growing alarm the aggravation of the situation in the left-bank Dniester areas of the Republic of Moldova. In the light of this, we appeal urgently and pressingly to the parties involved in the conflict for an immediate and total cease-fire.

The CSO welcomes the efforts to bring peace to the area undertaken by the Republic of Moldova, Romania, the Russian Federation and Ukraine, in particular the joint decisions of the Presidents of these States, adopted in Istanbul, and notes their appeal to the CSCE that it should contribute to the settlement of the conflict through mediation and a constant review of the human rights situation. The CSO invites the Chairman-in-Office to examine this appeal and, after consultations with the interested parties, to submit to the Committee appropriate proposals as to how the CSCE might best be able to help.

* * *

Text on the Georgian-Ossetian conflict[2]

The Committee of Senior Officials

- notes its growing concern over the development of the Georgian-Ossetian conflict,

- welcomes the efforts of the leaders of the Russian Federation and Georgia which resulted in signing at Sochi of the Agreement on the Principles of the Settlement of the Georgian-Ossetian Conflict,

- takes note of the request by the Government of Georgia to dispatch a CSCE Fact-Finding Mission to the region of conflict,

---

1 13-CSO/Journal No. 4, Annex.

2 13-CSO/Journal No. 5, Annex. (Title added by the Editor.)

- invites the Chairman-in-Office to dispatch a Fact-Finding Mission to the region of conflict as soon as possible and, on the basis of its report as well as on the basis of the report of the CSCE Rapporteur Mission to Georgia, to submit to the Committee proposals on further possible action to be taken by the CSCE.

* * *

Decisions of the Committee of Senior Officials[3]

1. With reference to the decision of the CSO of 12 May 1992, (Serbia and Montenegro) and in the light of the statement by the authorities of Yugoslavia (Serbia and Montenegro), it is decided that no representative of Yugoslavia will be present at the CSCE Summit in Helsinki or at any subsequent meetings of the CSCE until 14 October 1992.

2. This decision will be reviewed by the CSO at its meeting to be held not later than 13 October 1992, in the light of the compliance of Yugoslavia (Serbia and Montenegro) with the principles, commitments and provisions of the CSCE.

3. As a part of its review on compliance, the CSO will take into account the acceptance by, and co-operation of, Yugoslavia (Serbia and Montenegro) with CSCE missions to Kosovo, Vojvodina and Sandjak as reflected in its decision of 10 June 1992, as well as any other missions to Yugoslavia (Serbia and Montenegro) that the CSO might decide.

4. This decision is not directed in any way against the peoples of Serbia and Montenegro.

5. The above decisions are without prejudice to the question of the future status of Yugoslavia (Serbia and Montenegro) which will be considered by the CSO as soon as possible. It is noted that the CSO will have available on that occasion information on deliberations within the United Nations and the legal opinion of the Arbitration Commission of the EC Conference on Yugoslavia.

---

[3] 13-CSO/Journal No. 7, Annex. *Editor's note: This text on Yugoslavia (Serbia-Montenegro) was adopted by the CSO on the basis of the consensus-minus-one principle.*

6. The nameplate "Yugoslavia" will be kept at CSCE meetings for the time being.

7. The exploratory mission decided by the CSO at its Twelfth Meeting will be dispatched as soon as possible to prepare recommendations, for consideration by the CSO, on the role that further CSCE missions, of either short or long duration, might play in promoting peace, averting violence and restoring respect for human rights and fundamental freedoms in Kosovo, Vojvodina and Sandjak and in support of the efforts of the EC Peace Conference. The report of this mission will be considered by the CSO as soon as possible.

8. A Steering Group is established, consisting of Austria, Canada, the Czech and Slovak Federal Republic, Germany, Greece, the Russian Federation, Sweden, Switzerland, Turkey, the United Kingdom-European Community and the United States of America, to submit recommendations to the CSO in respect of points 2, 5 and 7 above.

FOURTEENTH CSO MEETING

Helsinki, 9 July 1992

Statement by Italy on Nagorny-Karabakh[1]

The Italian delegation, speaking also in its capacity as Chairman of the CSCE Conference on Nagorno-Karabakh, must unfortunately note the impossibility, at this Meeting of the Committee of Senior Officials, of reaching consensus on a declaration by the Heads of State or Government meeting in Helsinki on the conflict in and around Nagorno-Karabakh, as well as on the activities carried out by the Minsk Group and its Chairman in accordance with the mandate adopted by the CSCE Council of Ministers on 24 March this year.

The Italian delegation has listened attentively to the positions expressed here and respects them. It must, however, observe that opposing interests and divergent aims do not allow compromise to be reached on any text, and this confirms the existence of a serious difficulty in the current phase of the process of seeking a negotiated settlement of the crisis.

The Italian delegation, as Chairman of the Minsk Conference, expresses its deep regret at this situation. It will vigorously pursue its own efforts with a view to fulfilling the mandate conferred on it. It must, however, point out that this mandate can only be successfully carried out if all the interested parties are able, in a spirit of constructive co-operation and with the flexibility required, to address the problems with whose solution the Minsk Conference is concerned.

The Italian delegation is firmly convinced that the use of force is unacceptable and incompatible with negotiation. There are no alternatives to the negotiating process other than further fighting and destruction, and the continuing deterioration of the situation on the ground strengthens its conviction in this regard.

Holding this conviction as it does, the Italian delegation considers it necessary to further reaffirm the common will of all the parties to commit themselves to pursuing the process of negotiating a peaceful solution to the crisis, which alone will enable the Minsk Group to work constructively and the CSCE to fulfil with due effectiveness the responsibility it directly and collectively assumed, on 24 March, for settling this conflict.

---

[1] 14-CSO/Journal, paragraph 4. (Title added by the Editor.)

FIFTEENTH CSO MEETING

Prague, 13-14 August 1992

Decisions of the Committee of Senior Officials[1]

1. The Committee of Senior Officials met on 13 and 14 August 1992 at an urgently called meeting to consider further steps required to deal with the worsening aggression against Bosnia-Herzegovina and other critical aspects of the crisis in other parts of the former Yugoslavia.

2. There was consensus among participating States that the worsening crisis requires greater action within the context of the CSCE. They expressed their determination to fully apply the decisions of the Helsinki Summit in order to help alleviate humanitarian problems and support the search for peace. In particular they agreed to despatch a rapporteur mission to Bosnia-Herzegovina to investigate the humanitarian situation with special reference to detention camps and to send long-duration missions to Kosovo, Sandjak and Vojvodina. They also agreed that the presence of observers in neighbouring countries would help to avoid a spillover of tension to their territories and would help oversee the fulfilment of United Nations sanctions.

3. The discussions reflected the alarming developments which have occurred since approval of the Declaration on the Yugoslav crisis by Heads of State and Government at the Helsinki Summit on 10 July 1992.

   - Despite repeated promises by Serbian authorities, a lasting ceasefire has not been possible. Humanitarian convoys are regularly subject to military attack; heavy artillery continues to bombard Sarajevo and other cities of Bosnia-Herzegovina and some bordering cities in Croatia.

   - Evidence has continued to mount that Serbian authorities are using the conflict to carry out disgraceful policies of so-called "ethnic cleansing" and detention of innocent civilians. Cases of human rights and international humanitarian law violations have been registered on all sides of the conflict. Treatment of those

[1] 15-CSO/Journal No. 2, Annex 1.

held in detention camps violates all standards of decency. The number of refugees continues to rise to tragic levels.

- Human rights abuses by Serbian authorities continue at a high level. Serbian Government-controlled media subject the Serbian population to a constant barrage of hate and xenophobia. Repression of the non-Serbian population in Kosovo, Sandjak and Vojvodina and elsewhere continues. Tensions in these areas are high and the danger of the spread of armed conflict continues to grow.

- Continued conflict in Bosnia-Herzegovina raises the danger of spillover of tensions to neighbouring countries. Serbia continues to seek avenues for evasion of United Nations sanctions.

4. The participating States agreed that the crisis has entered a new phase which will require even more co-operation and concerted action throughout the international community. They reiterated their rejection of any aspiration of Serbia and Montenegro, or of any other party involved, to change borders or ethnic composition by force or intimidation. They reaffirmed the need to respect the sovereignty, territorial integrity and political independence of Bosnia-Herzegovina.

5. The outrage that resulted from revelations about detention camps underlines the sense of anger felt everywhere about the catastrophe which is taking place.

6. Serbian authorities must understand that they are isolating themselves increasingly from the democratic community of States represented by the CSCE. Continued violation of the basic norms of international humanitarian law can lead only to disaster for themselves and their people.

7. The participating States welcomed the intention of the United Nations to expand its activities in the former Yugoslavia. They expressed strong support for United Nations Security Council resolution 770 which foresees the use of all necessary measures to guarantee humanitarian assistance and for United Nations Security Council resolution 771 on war crimes, which holds Serbian leaders and others personally responsible for their behaviour. They intend to co-operate closely with the United Nations and to provide assistance to the fulfilment of United Nations goals wherever possible. They request the Chairman-in-Office to reply in that spirit to the letter of the Secretary-

General of the United Nations of 31 July 1992. They decided to start consultations on matters referred to in the letter of the Secretary-General of the United Nations in an open-ended *ad hoc* group established in Vienna.

8. They underlined once again the imperative need for an urgent negotiated political solution in the former Yugoslavia. In that respect they welcomed the Conference hosted by the European Community and the United Nations in London on 26 August 1992 as a means of carrying forward negotiation and achieving a lasting settlement to the crisis. They requested the Chairman-in-Office to present decisions of the CSCE at this meeting and to determine how the CSCE process can be used to further the goals of this Conference.

9. The Meeting was preceded by a working session of the Steering Group on the Yugoslav crisis of 11 participating States established at the 13th Meeting of the Committee of Senior Officials on 8 July 1992. The participating States agree that more detailed work is now necessary and that more frequent meetings of the Steering Group are needed. To this end they decided that the Steering Group should meet in Vienna as from now until the next CSO Meeting scheduled to be held in Prague on 16-18 September 1992. The Steering Group will assist the Chairman-in-Office in the implementation of today's decisions further to the tasks already assigned to it on 8 July 1992. While operating in Vienna the Steering Group will maintain a liaison with the Consultative Committee of the Conflict Prevention Centre.

10. The participating States also welcomed the intention of the Chairman-in-Office, accompanied by representatives of the Troika, to travel to the former Yugoslavia within the next few days. They asked him to transmit the strong political message contained in this decision document to Serbian authorities and to undertake any discussion that may expedite its implementation.

* * *

Decision on Human Rights Situation[2]

The Committee of Senior Officials,

Remaining very deeply concerned about the failure by the Serbian authorities to observe human rights and international humanitarian law, and especially by the disgraceful practice of "ethnic cleansing",

Outraged by the existence of detention camps, which is completely unacceptable,

Aware of the acute danger of an even more rapid increase in the number of refugees and displaced persons, which is already approaching two million,

Welcoming the adoption of United Nations Security Council resolution 771, and the decision by the United Nations Commission on Human Rights to appoint a special rapporteur on this issue,

Underlines the importance of observing international humanitarian law;

Demands an end to the practice of "ethnic cleansing";

Demands the immediate disbandment of any detention camps, and the release of the innocent civilian population held there;

Reminds all responsible for the administration of such camps that, in the meantime, they must ensure that such places of detention are run humanely, in full respect for the Geneva Conventions;

Reminds all those who commit or order the commission of breaches of the Conventions that they bear individual responsibility for such breaches;

Calls on the Serbian authorities to create all necessary conditions to enable the earliest possible return of the refugees and displaced persons to their original homes in conditions of safety and dignity, including the adoption of an amnesty law for those having refused to fight, and an end to the call-up;

Considers that an initial step in this direction could be the establishment of safe havens in Bosnia-Herzegovina, under international control;

---

[2] Idem.

Decides, further to United Nations Security Council resolutions 770 and 771, to request that the Chairman-in-Office establish contact with the United Nations and other relevant international organizations to undertake an urgent examination of conditions for possible establishment of safe havens for refugees and displaced persons in Bosnia-Herzegovina;

Decides to establish a rapporteur mission to investigate allegations of human rights abuses; its primary task should be, in close co-ordination with the International Committee of the Red Cross and the United Nations Commission on Human Rights, to ensure that all alleged places of detention are inspected within the shortest possible time; the CSCE rapporteur mission, in common with other international bodies, should be guaranteed immediate, free and continuous access to all such places of detention;

Requests the Chairman-in-Office to establish the rapporteur mission as soon as possible; its first report should be available to the Committee of Senior Officials at its next meeting in September.

* * *

Decision on Missions of Long Duration[3]

The Committee of Senior Officials,

With reference to:

- the Declaration on Yugoslavia adopted by the Helsinki Summit;

- the Committee of Senior Officials' Decision of 10 June 1992 to send an exploratory mission to Kosovo, Sandjak and Vojvodina;

- the conclusions and recommendations in the report submitted to the Committee of Senior Officials by this mission;

- Chapter III, paragraphs 6-11, in the Helsinki Decisions on the political management of crises, and

In support of the efforts of the Conference on Yugoslavia,

---

[3] Idem

Decides to establish, in co-operation with the relevant authorities, a continuous presence in Kosovo, Sandjak and Vojvodina, in the form of missions of long duration.

The missions will:

- promote dialogues between the authorities concerned and representatives of the populations and communities in the three regions;

- collect information on all aspects relevant to violations of human rights and fundamental freedoms and promote solutions to such problems;

- establish contact points for solving problems that might be identified;

- assist in providing information on relevant legislation on human rights, protection of minorities, free media and democratic elections.

The missions should be sent out as soon as possible in accordance with paragraphs 9 and 10 of Chapter III of the Helsinki Decisions. Further elaboration of modalities is delegated to the Steering Group on Yugoslavia established by the Committee of Senior Officials on 8 July 1992.

The operational control of the missions will be maintained by the Chairman-in-Office assisted by the other members of the CSCE Troika and with practical support from the appropriate CSCE institution(s).

Except where provided on a voluntary basis, the expenses of the missions will be borne by all participating States in accordance with the scale of distribution.

Developments regarding the missions will be reported to the Committee of Senior Officials not later than at its regular September 1992 Meeting.

* * *

Decision on the Presence of Observers in Countries Bordering on Serbia and Montenegro[4]

The CSO welcomes the efforts under way to extend the European Community Monitoring Mission to neighbouring countries of Serbia and Montenegro to help avoid the spread of tension to their territory. It decided to examine possibilities for contribution of material support to this effort. It welcomed the agreement with the authorities in Budapest to extend EC Monitoring Mission activities to Hungarian territory. It looks forward to the agreement on memoranda of understanding with authorities in Sofia and Tirana. Such missions can contribute to enhancing stability in the region. In this context, it decided to explore with authorities in Skopje the possibility of despatch of similar missions under CSCE auspices.

A further important task is to strengthen mechanisms to ensure full compliance with UN sanctions. The Chairman-in-Office is requested to undertake discussions to examine means of assisting appropriate States bordering on Serbia and Montenegro in this task, including through the placement of experts on their territories. The CSO will review the decision at its next meeting.

* * *

Draft reply to United Nations Secretary-General's letter[5]

In response to your letter dated 31 July 1992, I requested the CSO to meet on an urgent basis for preliminary consultations on 13 and 14 August 1992. Following these consultations, I have the pleasure to communicate to you that the CSCE is willing to help the United Nations in carrying out peacekeeping activities including the establishing and managing of a mechanism for supervising the heavy weapons of the Parties in Bosnia-Herzegovina. In particular, the CSCE is prepared to co-ordinate individual or collective contributions by its participating States to these efforts.

The Helsinki Decisions provide the capability for the CSCE itself to establish and manage such a mechanism, although the possibility for the CSCE to act is dependent upon contributions from participating States, individually or collectively. To ensure an effective and co-ordinated response, the CSCE has

---

[4] Idem

[5] Idem, Annex 2. Editor's note: The CSO agreed on the wording of this letter in response to a letter from the UN Secretary-General.

established an *ad hoc* group which will examine relevant issues closely and report its conclusions to me.

I will inform you as soon as possible of the results of these consultations.

SIXTEENTH CSO MEETING

Prague, 16-18 September 1992

Text on Nagorny-Karabakh[1]

The Committee of Senior Officials

1. *Takes note* of the report of Mr. Mario Raffaelli, Chairman of the Conference on Nagorno-Karabakh, and expresses appreciation for his efforts aimed at finding a solution to the problems still standing in the way of convening the Minsk Conference;

2. *Expresses* its deep concern at the present impasse in the Minsk process;

3. *Invites* the Chairman-in-Office and the Chairman of the Minsk Conference, within their respective competence, to continue their contacts with a view to removing the obstacles and achieving the conditions which could provide new impetus to the Minsk process.

* * *

Decisions of the Committee of Senior Officials[2]

At its sixteenth regular Meeting from 16 to 18 September the Committee of Senior Officials reviewed the situation in Bosnia-Herzegovina and other parts of former Yugoslavia.

Regardless of the appeals of the London Conference the war in Bosnia-Herzegovina continues on an unabated scale. Although the heavy weapons of all parties should have been put under the supervision of UNPROFOR, the shelling of Sarajevo goes on, as well as fighting in other parts of the country, causing heavy human losses and material damage. The CSO, therefore, recalls to all parties to the conflict in Bosnia-Herzegovina their obligations to place all their heavy weapons, mortars and anti-aircraft weapons included, under international monitoring.

---

1 16-CSO/Journal No. 3. (Title added by the Editor.)

2 16-CSO/Journal No. 3, Annex 1.

The participating States reiterated their deep concern for the tragic events unfolding day by day and the growing danger that war might spread. They condemned attacks on international relief staff and on UNPROFOR. They expressed condolences to the participating States whose personnel have lost their lives in the service of the international community and the peoples of former Yugoslavia.

The CSO recalls its previous decision and recommends that the relevant working bodies of the London Conference give urgent consideration to the problem of safe havens.

The CSO also welcomes the decision of the United Nations Security Council to reinforce UNPROFOR in order to provide it with the capability to protect humanitarian transport in Bosnia-Herzegovina.

The CSO supports efforts by the United Nations Security Council to increase the safety of humanitarian aid and to pave the way to an end to the armed conflict in Bosnia-Herzegovina by imposing a ban on military flights in the airspace of Bosnia-Herzegovina and by deploying monitors along the border between Bosnia-Herzegovina and Serbia and Montenegro.

The CSO decides to maintain in force its decision of 8 July on the participation of Yugoslavia (Serbia and Montenegro) in meetings of the CSCE and to review it not later than November 1992. It will take account of the evolution of the situation and the decisions of the United Nations Security Council and General Assembly.

The participating States welcome the process begun at the London Conference and expressed their support for the statement of principles, specific decisions and the other agreements reached there. They also welcome the recent decisions of the United Nations Security Council and underline the need to implement fully the United Nations Security Council sanctions.

CSCE activities will be carried out in close co-ordination with other international bodies including the United Nations, European Community, the Council of Europe, UNHCR and ICRC. The CSCE Troika will promote such co-ordination. Participating States welcomed the information received from the CSCE Troika on its activities in connection with the crisis and requested the Troika to keep them fully informed on its activities.

The participating States insist that CSCE values should be respected and will endeavour to secure compliance with the commitments freely entered into by all States on the territory of former Yugoslavia.

In this regard the CSO will:

- decide to dispatch, should circumstances warrant it, further rapporteur missions on humanitarian aspects of the crisis, in particular the urgent closure of detention camps, and in co-ordination with the activities of the United Nations, the Council of Europe, UNHCR and ICRC;

- undertake preventive diplomacy through long-duration missions to Kosovo, Sandjak and Vojvodina and by fact-finding activities as appropriate;

- dispatch the CSCE Mission to Skopje to avoid the spillover of the conflict and welcomes progress in negotiations in establishing European Community Monitoring Missions with authorities in Budapest, Sofia and Tirana;

- promote in conjunction with the European Community Presidency the establishment and co-ordinate the activities of sanctions assistance missions to the countries neighbouring Serbia and Montenegro.

To ensure operational efficiency, it is decided to extend the mandate of the Steering Group established on 8 July 1992, in accordance with paragraph 20 of Chapter I of the Helsinki Decisions, until the next meeting of the CSO and to continue meetings of the group in Vienna. Mandate and composition of the group will also be reviewed at that meeting.

Liaison between the Steering Group and other participating States will be accomplished through the open-ended *ad hoc* group established by the CSO on 14 August 1992, which will also continue to meet in Vienna on dates immediately following Steering Group meetings.

Accordingly, the Committee took the following decisions on:

- humanitarian questions;

- missions of long duration;

- presence of observers in countries bordering Serbia and Montenegro; and

- sanctions monitoring.

* * *

Decision on humanitarian questions[3]

The Committee of Senior Officials reviewed further the urgent humanitarian problems that have resulted form the continuing conflict in former Yugoslavia. They recalled their decision of 14 August 1992, which set forth human rights criteria that the participating States expect to be upheld by all parties to the conflict, regardless of the continuation of hostilities.

The CSO noted in particular the urgent need for humanitarian assistance for those affected by the conflict. With winter approaching there must be a major effort to deal with major needs of persons whose lives have been disrupted.

In this connection, it underlined the high standards set by CSCE commitments and respect for humanitarian law in defining acceptable humanitarian conditions in time of conflict as well as during peace. It recalls the commitments to humanitarian law including the protection of the civilian population. The Committee of Senior Officials underlined the determination of participating States to utilize CSCE's special experience in the field of human rights to help in finding durable solutions, as a basis for assessing behaviour of parties to the conflict, for defining necessary solutions and for pursuing the personal accountability of those responsible for violations.

CSCE participating States intend to utilize this experience as an important aspect of their contribution to the search for a lasting solution to the conflict. They will pay special attention to the human rights situation in the former Yugoslavia. By mobilizing their joint political will and utilizing the tools available to us, they intend to maintain continuous observation and pressure for improvement of the situation. They will apply their efforts directly and in close co-operation with the Geneva follow-up of the London Conference.

As set forth in the decision of 14 August 1992, CSCE participating States intend to pursue with special vigour evidence of severe human rights abuses in several regions of the former Yugoslavia. In this connection, the CSO expressed special gratitude for the service performed by the rapporteur mission, headed by Ambassador Sir John Thomson, which was authorized at

---

[3] 16-CSO/Journal No. 3, Annex 1.

the meeting of 14 August 1992. They welcomed the presence of Ambassador Kenneth Blackwell, deputy chief of the mission, who described the observations of the mission and presented its recommendations.

This mission and previous missions of the CSCE as well as the mission of the United Nations Special Rapporteur on Human Rights and Detention Camps, Mr. Tadeusz Mazowiecki, have made possible a detailed documentation of the conditions that exist in Bosnia-Herzegovina. The description of the situation in detention camps and of the existence of practices such as ethnic cleansing confirmed fears that the situation in Bosnia-Herzegovina represents the most severe violation of human rights and disregard for international humanitarian law.

The Committee of Senior Officials approved public release of the descriptive sections of the report by Sir John Thomson's Mission[4] as an important contribution to better understanding of the conditions that have developed in Bosnia-Herzegovina.

Based on the conclusions of the rapporteur mission and on the results of the London Conference, the Committee of Senior Officials agreed the following:

- The CSCE participating States have documented evidence of the existence of policies of ethnic separation, cleansing and forced resettlement. Persons detained in camps are guiltless civilians; the number of genuine prisoners of war in these centres is minimal. The CSO expresses its abhorrence of this practices. All prisoners should be unilaterally released at the earliest moment once their safety is assured. This process will require broad international support.

- The participating States declare null and void the enforced sale or donation of property which has occurred in areas of conflict. They reaffirm their rejection of forced changes in borders or the ethnic composition of regions of Bosnia-Herzegovina and other parts of former Yugoslavia which have taken place during the conflict.

- The mission organized under the Moscow mechanism should leave for the area as soon as possible. Mission members are requested to consult with members of the Thomson Mission.

---

[4] Not reproduced in the present volume.

CSCE participating States will continue to place special emphasis on establishing personal accountability for the crimes which have been committed during the war. This responsibility should also extend to those in command of the detention centres as well as to those exercising political control. They renewed their support for the goals of United Nations Security Council resolution 771 and committed themselves to active assistance in implementation of provisions calling for collection of documentation of crimes. They requested the Chairman-in-Office to communicate this readiness, along with a copy of the report of the rapporteur mission, to the Secretary-General of the United Nations and Co-Chairmen of the London Conference.

To ensure closest possible co-ordination with the Geneva follow-up to the London Conference, the CSO asked Ambassador Blackwell to help facilitate contacts between the CSCE and the humanitarian working group in Geneva.

The CSO also requested that other members of the team remain ready to undertake further tasks in the humanitarian field, as appropriate, to support the goals set forth in their report.

The CSO welcomes the offer of the Council of Europe at the Meeting of the Committee of Ministers in Istanbul to work out details on its contribution to the various aspects of the crisis. This could include the study of the creation of an international criminal court, contribution to the CSCE missions on human rights and a contribution that the Council of Europe could make in the fields of its competence to the work of the international conference on peace in ex-Yugoslavia concerning the creation of a legal framework for the strict implementation of all human rights commitments and the elaboration of the constitutional framework necessary for a lasting solution of the problems related to the situation of nationalities and national minorities on the territory of former Yugoslavia.

* * *

Decision on missions of long duration[5]

The Committee of Senior Officials with reference to:

- its decision of 10 June 1992 to send an exploratory mission to Kosovo, Sandjak and Vojvodina and to the conclusions and recommendations in

---

[5] 16-CSO/Journal No. 3, Annex 1.

the report of 9 August 1992[6] submitted by this exploratory mission to the Committee of Senior Officials;

- the letter of 24 June 1992 from the Belgrade authorities accepting in principle missions of long duration to the three regions;

- its decision on 14 August 1992 that the missions of long duration establishing a continuous presence in Kosovo, Sandjak and Vojvodina will:

  promote dialogues between the authorities concerned and representatives of the populations and communities in the three regions;

  collect information on all aspects of violations of human rights and fundamental freedoms and promote solutions to such problems;

  establish contact points for solving problems that might be identified;

  assist in providing information on relevant legislation on human rights, protection of minorities, free media and democratic elections;

- the oral report presented to the CSO by the Head of the Missions, Ambassador Tore Bögh, concerning the reconnaissance trip carried out by him from 2 to 8 September 1992;

- the conclusions and recommendations dated 16 September 1992 of the Steering Group established on 8 July 1992;

- the urgency to deploy missions in the three regions;

Requests the Head of Missions to:

- begin immediately with the establishment of a continuous presence in the three regions;

---

[6] Not reproduced in the present volume.

- recruit, without delay, in close consultation with the Chairman-in-Office, upon recommendation by the Steering Group, a first contingent of personnel, and to dispatch it to the three regions;

- elaborate the organization of the missions including personnel requirements;

- elaborate on a priority basis draft modalities in co-operation with the Head of the Exploratory Mission, Ambassador Jan af Sillén, in consultation with the representatives of the relevant populations and communities and minorities in the three regions and the Belgrade authorities.

These modalities will include provisions concerning *inter alia*:

- the safety and freedom of movement for the members of the missions
- access to local populations, communities, minorities and authorities
- privileges and immunities
- locations
- duration

- submit these draft modalities and financial implications within a period of three weeks to the Steering Group for consideration and recommendation to the next CSO Meeting for its approval. In view of the urgency of the matter, the open-ended *ad hoc* group established in Vienna may, if necessary, consider and approve them on a preliminary basis.

All participating States will be eligible to take part in the missions. In the elaboration of the list of composition of full-scale missions, as well as the rotation of its members by the Steering Group, appropriate consultations will be held with the participating States.

The missions will be carried out in support of the International Conference on the former Yugoslavia and in co-operation with the Ethnic and National Communities and Minorities Working Group of that Conference. The missions will co-ordinate with the EC Monitor Mission. Co-operation will be sought with relevant humanitarian endeavours of the United Nations and other agencies.

* * *

Presence of observers in the countries bordering Serbia and Montenegro[7]

The CSO welcomes progress made in the negotiation of Memoranda of Understanding with the authorities in Budapest, Sofia, and Tirana to establish European Community Monitoring Missions on the territories of Hungary, Bulgaria and Albania. The CSO notes that the ECMM has already dispatched reconnaissance teams and aims to have the first monitors in place within two weeks from the signing of the Memoranda of Understanding. The CSO welcomes the signing today of the Memorandum of Understanding with the authorities in Sofia.

The CSO welcomes progress achieved in the effort to establish a Monitoring Mission in Skopje to avoid the spillover of the conflict and supports efforts to commence mission operations in the immediate future. It takes note of the report of the mission based on its initial visit of 10-14 September.

It will intensify efforts to resolve questions relating to material support for this mission. Further elaboration of modalities is delegated to the Steering Group established by the Committee of Senior Officials on 8 July 1992. Operational control of the mission in Skopje will be maintained by the Chairman-in-Office assisted by other members of the CSCE Troika and with practical support from the appropriate CSCE institutions."

* * *

Decision on Sanctions Monitoring[8]

The Committee of Senior Officials notes with satisfaction the steps taken by the international community to implement United Nations Security Council resolutions 713 imposing an arms embargo against all the republics of the former Yugoslavia and 757 imposing mandatory sanctions against Serbia and Montenegro.

The CSO welcomes the efforts undertaken by States neighbouring Serbia and Montenegro to enforce these United Nations Security Council resolutions. However, practical problems are being encountered by the neighbouring States in the enforcement of these sanctions, particularly transit traffic. In

---

[7] Idem.

[8] 16-CSO/Journal No. 3, Annex 1.

order to assist the neighbouring States in overcoming these special problems, the CSO urges all participating States to take necessary measures to ensure strict compliance with the sanctions in this respect.

The CSO takes note of the decisions of the London Conference on the former Yugoslavia concerning the implementation of sanctions and endorses the establishment of Sanctions Assistance Missions in all States neighbouring Serbia and Montenegro. The London Conference has invited the EC and the CSCE to co-ordinate these activities.

The Governments of Bulgaria, Hungary and Romania have invited experts to provide advice on ways of overcoming difficulties in the application of the sanctions. Officials from the EC Presidency and other CSCE States have participated in preliminary fact-finding missions to these countries. The CSO welcomes the intention of participating States to organize similar fact-finding missions to the other neighbouring States.

The CSO decides to endorse the plan drawn up by the United Kingdom/European Community in close co-ordination with the United States of America and other CSCE participating States. This plan calls for the establishment initially in Bulgaria, Hungary and Romania as early as possible of Sanctions Assistance Missions to assist the governments of these States in the implementation of sanctions. The status of these missions will be defined in Memoranda of Understanding agreed with the host governments as soon as possible. Similar sanctions assistance missions will be established in countries neighbouring Serbia and Montenegro that may also be experiencing problems in the implementation of sanctions.

The CSO applauds the decisions of some CSCE States to contribute experts to these missions and to meet their direct costs, and invites further contributions. Any remaining costs should be met according to the CSCE scale of distribution.

In order to facilitate co-ordination and enhance the possibilities for participation by additional CSCE States, the CSO requests that liaison is maintained by the countries involved and information emanating from the missions is passed to the EC Presidency and CSCE Chairman-in-Office, who will in turn inform CSCE participating States. To provide overall guidance, the States participating in the missions and the host countries will establish a Liaison Group in Vienna as soon as possible. The meetings of the group could be attended by the CSCE Troika and the EC Presidency. This Liaison Group will assist the EC Presidency and the CSCE Chairman-in-Office in their co-ordination responsibilities. Day-to-day operational co-ordination will be exercised by the mission leaders.

In accordance with the decision of the London Conference, the CSO requests the Chairman-in-Office to keep the United Nations Sanctions Committee and the representatives of the Co-Chairmen of the London Conference in Geneva informed on a regular basis about the actions taken by the CSCE to enforce the sanctions rigorously, including any problems that may be encountered.

* * *

Decision on the Georgian-Ossetian conflict[9]

The Committee of Senior Officials,

With reference to its decisions of 3 July 1992 and to the reports of the CSCE rapporteur mission to Georgia and of the CSCE fact-finding mission to the region of the Georgian-Ossetian conflict,

1. Underlines the importance of the Sochi Agreement on the principles of settlement of the Georgian-Ossetian conflict of 24 June 1992;

2. Recommends the Chairman-in-Office to appoint his personal representative who would undertake, as soon as possible, a fact-finding visit to Georgia.

   Upon receipt of the information gathered, the Consultative Committee of the Conflict Prevention Centre is requested to:

   - work out the terms of reference, the financial estimates and a Memorandum of Understanding for a mission of military experts who would monitor the cease-fire in close co-operation with the Mixed Control Commission established by the Sochi Agreement;

   - submit its recommendations to the next meeting of the Committee of Senior Officials for decision;

3. Taking note of the preparations made by the Council of Europe and the ODIHR in responding to the request by the Central Election Commission of the Republic of Georgia regarding the dispatch of

---

[9] 16-CSO/Journal No. 3, Annex 2.

observers to the forthcoming parliamentary elections, recommends that the ODIHR, in consultation with organizations such as the Council of Europe, co-ordinate the monitoring of the elections;

4. Invites the Chairman-in-Office to draw the attention of the appropriate international organizations to the concerns expressed on the issues of humanitarian aid and refugees, economic recovery and renovation of the infrastructure in the region of the conflict.

* * *

Guidelines for Financing of CSCE Missions[10]

Short-term missions
Short-term and exploratory missions frequently need to be undertaken at very short notice. When missions are decided by consensus these will be financed from the budgets of the appropriate CSCE institution, which will be allocated a sum for this purpose. This would include fact-finding and rapporteur missions under paragraphs (12)-(16) of Chapter III of the Helsinki Document. Urgent missions undertaken at the request of the Chairman-in-Office within the exercise of his responsibility, including urgent missions of personal representatives, will be financed from the budget of the CSCE Secretariat. Where the costs of such missions have been pre-paid by one or several of the participating States, these will be refunded from the corresponding budget sub-heading.

Funds to cover costs for rapporteur missions to be financed by some participating States under the Moscow mechanism will be advanced, in the first instance, by the ODIHR and subsequently refunded by the participating States concerned.

Long-term missions
In order to ensure the speedy dispatch of the long-term missions agreed at the Sixteenth Meeting of the CSO, the CSO decides that pending decisions on agreed general guidelines for financing long-term missions, the start-up costs for these missions will be met through the use of funds available in the CPC Secretariat following revision of the 1992 CPC budget (1,465,000 ATS). This amount will be transferred to the 1992 revised budget of the CSCE Secretariat entered under budget subitems 7.2 and 7.3 to the amount of 732,500 ATS respectively.

---

[10] 16-CSO/Journal No. 3, Annex 3.

Following the establishment of approved financial implications for these missions, the CSCE Secretariat will notify the participating States of their assessed share of the total costs for each mission, following deduction, according to the applicable scale of distribution, of the advanced start-up costs, and request payment. Costs for reimbursement according to the CSCE scale of distribution which have been prepaid by one or more participating States will be deducted from their assessed share of the total mission costs. Voluntary contributions will be welcomed.

Contributions to cover the costs of the Monitoring Mission to Skopje to avoid the spillover of the conflict will be made as follows:

- at least 900,000 ATS (30 % of the approved financial estimate) distributed according to the scale of distribution payable by 1 December 1992;

- the balance payable by 1 February 1993.

The participating States are encouraged where possible to make payment in full by 1 December.

The Steering Group will draw up a precise schedule of payments for the long-term missions to Kosovo, Sandjak and Vojvodina following elaboration of the total financial implications, for approval by the CSO.

For practical purposes the CSCE Secretariat will open bank accounts in Vienna for the financing of the missions. These accounts will be kept and administered by the CPC Secretariat on behalf of the CSCE Secretariat under the responsibility of the Chairman-in-Office. Procedures for the authorization of funds will be further elaborated by the informal Financial Committee of Experts of the CSO for the approval of the CSO.

The CSO instructs the informal Financial Committee of Experts to continue work on the structure for the financing of long-term missions, with particular attention to the establishment of a start-up fund for such missions. The informal Financial Committee of Experts of the CSO will hold *ad hoc* meetings in Vienna to be scheduled immediately before or after the meetings of the Steering/*Ad hoc* Group in order to prepare draft recommendations for the CSO at its next meeting.

SEVENTEENTH CSO MEETING

Prague, 5-6 November 1992

Text on Nagorny-Karabakh[1]

The Committee of Senior Officials

1. Calls upon the parties to the conflict dealt with by the Conference on Nagorno-Karabakh under the auspices of the CSCE to commit themselves actively to a peaceful settlement, in accordance with the CSCE principles and decisions;

2. Takes note of the interim report of Mr. Mario Raffaelli, Chairman of the Conference on Nagorno-Karabakh, and invites him to pursue his contacts with the interested parties with a view to providing new impetus to the Minsk process;

3. Decides to establish an open-ended *ad hoc* group in Vienna and authorizes it to consider and approve, on a preliminary basis pending confirmation by the CSO, terms of reference and financial modalities for the despatch of an Advance Monitoring Group, including any reconnaissance, to the area of conflict. The Chairman-in-Office will chair the *ad hoc* group. The Chairman-in-Office is authorized to call an additional meeting of the CSO to consider the deployment of the Advance Monitoring Group if the necessary conditions have been met;

4. Calls upon all CSCE participating States to co-ordinate their efforts, aimed at promoting a negotiated settlement, with the activities of the Minsk Group;

5. Urges those CSCE participating States which have sent observers to the region, or are proposing to do so, to integrate them into the CSCE Advance Monitoring Group, by placing them under the same chain of command, as soon as the group is deployed in the area, and asks the *ad hoc* group mentioned in point 3 to work out the modalities of this integration;

6. Instructs the *ad hoc* group to consider the report of the expert group led by Col. Happonen, as the appointed Head of the Advance

---

[1] 17-CSO/Journal No. 2, Annex 1. (Title added by the Editor.)

Monitoring Group, outlining a technical deployment plan for the Group;

7. Calls upon the participating States to respond urgently to the appeal by the Chairman-in-Office for contributions to the Advance Monitoring Group in personnel and other resources.

* * *

Personal Representative of the CSCE Chairman-in-Office for Georgia[2]

The Committee of Senior Officials,

Welcoming the cease-fire based on the Agreement on Principles of Settlement of the Georgian-Ossetian Conflict signed on 24 June 1992 in Sochi,

Being concerned by the possibility of a deterioration of the situation in the region and the risk of renewed conflict,

Noting the Appeal of the Ministry of Foreign Affairs of the Republic of Georgia for CSCE Observers in the region,

Taking into consideration its decision of 18 September 1992,

Noting the report of the Personal Representative of the Chairman-in-Office, the statement of the representative of Georgia and the recommendations of the Consultative Committee of the Conflict Prevention Centre,

1.Mandates the Personal Representative of the Chairman-in-Office to Georgia, to be assisted by a staff of two diplomatic advisers and a military team of four officers, headed by a senior military officer, and requests the Mission to

- begin discussions immediately with all parties to the Georgian-Ossetian conflict to identify and seek to eliminate sources of tension with the aim of extending civil order and political reconciliation beyond the immediate cease-fire zone to the surrounding towns and countryside;

---

[2] 17-CSO/Journal No. 2, Annex 2.

- initiate a visible CSCE presence in the region and establish contact with local authorities and representatives of the population;

- in support of the existing cease-fire, liaise with local military commanders of the trilateral peace-keeping forces established by the Sochi Agreement and establish appropriate forms of contact with them within the overall context of the CSCE political efforts, establish regular contacts with local military commanders, gather information on the military situation, investigate violent incidents and call local commanders' attention to possible political implications of specific military actions;

- facilitate the creation of a broader political framework, in which a lasting political conciliation an be achieved on the basis of CSCE principles and commitments;

2. Also requests the Personal Representative of the Chairman-in-Office to help establish a negotiating framework between the parties to the conflict in Abkhazia with the aim of establishing a stable cease-fire and to work out a political solution to the conflict;

3. Requests the Consultative Committee of the Conflict Prevention Centre to elaborate by 25 November, upon the recommendation of the Personal Representative of the Chairman-in-Office, modalities and financial implications for the Mission to allow the Mission to be despatched immediately. Between sessions of the CSO, overall guidance to the Personal Representative of the Chairman-in-Office will be provided by the Vienna *Ad Hoc* Group, the mandate of which is extended for this purpose.

   The Personal Representative of the Chairman-in-Office will be responsible for regular exchange of information and co-ordination with the United Nations and other international organizations, which are or may be involved in the future in the conflict;

4. Tasks the Personal Representative of the Chairman-in-Office to report to the Chairman-in-Office on a regular basis about his activities in Georgia, consider further possibilities for their extension and submit appropriate recommendations to the next meeting of the CSO.

   Asks the Chairman-in-Office to keep the *Ad Hoc* Group informed about the progress of the Mission;

5. Opens a separate budget line for the Mission with the CSCE Secretariat of an initial amount of 800,000 ATS and requests the Director of the CSCE Secretariat to inform the participating States of their contribution, according to the CSCE scale of distribution, to be paid, if possible, by the end of November.

The CSO will decide on the duration of the Mission and its budget at its next regular meeting.

* * *

Decisions on former Yugoslavia[3]

1. The participating States expressed their deep dismay at the continued violation of the territorial integrity and acts against the population of the Republic of Bosnia-Herzegovina. They will not tolerate the aggression against Bosnia-Herzegovina. They condemn the barbarous practice of "ethnic cleansing", the cowardly assaults on fleeing refugees as in Jajce and the consistent pattern of clear, gross and uncorrected violations of fundamental human rights, international humanitarian law and the CSCE principles and commitments. All this must be stopped as should hostilities in other parts of former Yugoslavia. Efforts should be actively pursued to prevent the spread of conflict to other parts of former Yugoslavia. Those who commit or order war crimes will be held personally accountable.

2. The Committee of Senior Officials confirms its support for the efforts of the Co-Chairmen of the Steering Committee of the International Conference on former Yugoslavia. It welcomes the progress made so far within the framework of the Conference, in particular the agreement of the three parties in Bosnia to begin talks on the cessation of hostilities and the demilitarisation of Sarajevo, and the withdrawal of the Yugoslav army from the Prevlaka peninsula.

3. The participating States also expressed their support for the outline of a constitutional structure for Bosnia-Herzegovina presented by the Co-Chairmen of the Steering Committee of the International Conference on 27 October 1992. This outline should serve as the basis for negotiations towards a peaceful settlement between the parties concerned.

---

[3] 17-CSO/Journal No. 2, Annex 3.

4. The scale of the humanitarian crisis continues to widen. The CSO calls upon all involved to intensify their efforts to bring relief, by protecting humanitarian relief deliveries as agreed within the framework of the International Conference on the former Yugoslavia. It welcomes the work of UNPROFOR in providing protection for the delivery of humanitarian assistance in Bosnia-Herzegovina and appeals to all parties to co-operate fully with UNPROFOR in this important task. It welcomes the deployment of additional United Nations forces. Given the importance of the work being undertaken by UNPROFOR II, the CSO urges all CSCE participating States to support fully a broader financial burdensharing. The CSO expresses its full support for the work of ICRC and UNHCR on behalf of detainees and prisoners. It renews its call for their safe release as early as possible. It calls on all parties concerned to notify detention camps and permit international inspection.

   Of highest importance, also in view of the forthcoming winter, is co-operation in accommodating refugees, thus enabling the release of detainees and the closing of camps to proceed. The CSO calls on all participating States to contribute to a concerted effort in order to share the common burden. The Committee expressed its support for the co-ordination of these efforts by competent international organizations such as the UNHCR.

   The CSO strongly supports action already under way to provide zones of safety in Bosnia-Herzegovina, particularly in those areas where there is the largest concentration of displaced persons, thus also facilitating the safe return of refugees.

5. The CSO condemns the continuing policy of ethnic discrimination and oppression in a number of parts of former Yugoslavia, including in Kosovo, Sandjak and Vojvodina, as well as the forceful changing of ethnic composition through expulsion and resettling. The CSO urges all parties involved to intensify their efforts to prevent the spread of conflict to other parts of former Yugoslavia.

6. The CSO supports the deployment of international observers to monitor the borders between Yugoslavia (Serbia and Montenegro) and Bosnia-Herzegovina, as decided by the London Conference.

7. The CSO notes the importance of effective use of the railway link between Ploce and Sarajevo. The unhindered delivery of humanitarian goods to the people in need in Bosnia-Herzegovina is of utmost

importance. New ways should be found to solve the transport problems connected with the humanitarian relief.

8. The CSO calls for the full implementation of the non-fly zone in Bosnia-Herzegovina, including the discontinuation of flights of combat helicopters.

9. The CSO decides to maintain in force its decision of 8 July 1992 to suspend the participation of Yugoslavia in the CSCE, and will review the subject at the next CSO Meeting.

10. The CSO decides to establish a Steering Group of restricted membership tasked with the operational support of CSCE activities in former Yugoslavia. The Steering Group will be composed of representatives of the CSCE Troika and participating states contributing personnel. The Chairman-in-Office, assisted by the Troika, may invite other countries to participate. The Steering Group will be chaired by the Chairman-in-Office and will report regularly to all participating States through the open-ended *ad hoc* group in Vienna. The composition of the Steering Group may vary in accordance with the composition of Missions.

11. The duration and the mandate of the Steering Group will be reviewed regularly by the CSO, in the light of developments.

12. The CSO heard a report from ECMM which comprises the 12 member States of the European Community and the Commission of the European Communities, plus Poland, the Czech and Slovak Federal Republic, Sweden and Canada, on its activities in former Yugoslavia and noted the invitation of the ECMM to include other participating States in the Monitor Mission.

* * *

Monitoring of Elections in Yugoslavia (Serbia and Montenegro)[4]

The CSO considers that the elections to be held in Yugoslavia (Serbia and Montenegro) on 20 December 1992 will be a major test of the political will to respect democratic processes and the popular will to move towards a settlement of the Yugoslav crisis. It expects the ODIHR to facilitate

[4] Idem.

international observation of the elections in Yugoslavia (Serbia and Montenegro). The CSO instructs it to co-operate with other governmental and non-governmental observers from CSCE participating States. The CSO considers it essential that the observers monitor the entire electoral process. Monitors should be especially sensitive to, *inter alia*, problems concerning the use of the media, particularly television, and questions of equitable financing for all participants in the process.

* * *

Missions of Long Duration to Kosovo, Sandjak and Vojvodina and Monitor Mission to Skopje[5]

The Committee of Senior Officials

1. Notes with appreciation the reports of Ambassadors Boegh and Frowick. It welcomes the establishment of the continuous CSCE presence in the three regions, decided at the Sixteenth Meeting of the CSO. It approves the modalities and financial provisions agreed for these missions by the *ad hoc* group;

2. Welcomes and accepts the offer of Japan, as a participant in the London Conference, to provide a member of the Missions of long duration;

3. Also welcomes the offer of the ECMM to second five officers to the Missions of long duration;

4. Authorises Ambassador Boegh to increase the size of his missions to twenty. The financial implications accompanying this increase will be assessed by the Informal Financial Committee of Experts of the CSO and approved on a provisional basis as soon as possible by the *ad hoc* group in Vienna;

5. Requests participating States to pay their assessed contributions to the costs of the Missions as a matter of urgency.

* * *

---

[5] Idem.

Sanctions Assistance Missions[6]

The Committee of Senior Officials heard an account of the establishment of Sanctions Assistance Missions in Bulgaria, Hungary and Romania and welcomed this development. It applauded the measures taken by these three countries to strengthen enforcement of the sanctions against Yugoslavia (Serbia and Montenegro).

The Committee called on all CSCE participating States to apply sanctions faithfully and stringently. It noted that despite the sanctions, key goods - especially oil and petroleum products - continue to reach Yugoslavia (Serbia and Montenegro) in large quantities. It considers necessary the urgent adoption of stringent new measures to counter this continuing haemorrhage in the embargo system and recommended that the EC/CSCE Sanctions Liaison Group co-operate closely with efforts of the United Nations Sanctions Committee towards this end.

The Committee welcomed the willingness expressed by the Government of Canada to supply a mission leader and one two-person team to a new Sanctions Assistance Mission to be established in the former Yugoslav Republic of Macedonia. It called for other interested CSCE participating States to provide personnel for this mission. It also considered that additional missions should be set up in the other States bordering Yugoslavia (Serbia and Montenegro).

* * *

CSO Decision on Personal Accountability for Crimes committed in former Yugoslavia[7]

The Committee of Senior Officials,

Recalling its previous decisions, in particular the decision taken by the Sixteenth Meeting of the CSO on 18 September 1992 stating *inter alia* that CSCE participating States will continue to place special emphasis on establishing personal accountability for the crimes which have been committed during the war on the territory of former Yugoslavia,

---

[6] Idem.

[7] Idem.

Reiterating the determination of participating States to utilize the CSCE's special experience in the field of human rights to help in finding durable solutions, as a basis for assessing behaviour of parties to the conflict, for defining necessary solutions and for pursuing the personal accountability of those responsible for violations,

Keeping in mind the findings and observations of the CSCE rapporteur mission, headed by Ambassador Sir John Thomson, on the human rights situation in Bosnia-Herzegovina,

Taking note of a report of the Rapporteurs under the Moscow Human Dimension Mechanism, Ambassador Corell, Ambassador Türk and Mrs. Thune, on the initial part of their mission, i.e., to Croatia from 30 September to 5 October 1992,[8]

Expressing its gratitude to the Rapporteurs, Ambassador Corell, Ambassador Türk and Mrs. Thune, for their comprehensive presentation and the wide range of recommendations and suggestions,

Expressing its most serious concern regarding the reported grave violations of human rights and norms of international humanitarian law on the territory of the Republic of Croatia, including atrocities perpetrated against unarmed civilians as well as the practice of "ethnic cleansing', the main responsibility for these violations to be attributed to the Serbian side,

Expressing, as well, its most serious concern regarding disturbing reports on continuous and serious violations of human rights and international humanitarian law on the territory of the Republic of Bosnia-Herzegovina and other parts of former Yugoslavia,

Recognizing the common responsibility of the members of the international community, and in particular of the participating States, to investigate gross violations of human rights and norms of international humanitarian law, including war crimes and crimes against humanity, and to see to it that those who have committed such crimes are brought to justice,

Highly appreciating in this context the valuable efforts of data collection by the Special Rapporteur of the United Nations Commission on Human Rights, Mr. Tadeusz Mazowiecki,

---

[8] Reproduced in section VI.1 of the Documents, *infra*.

Taking note of United Nations Security Council resolution 780 establishing an impartial Commission of Experts,

Recalling the readiness of the CSCE participating States (Sixteenth Meeting of the CSO) to support the goals of United Nations Security Council resolution 771 and their commitment to active assistance in implementation of provisions calling for collection of documentations of crimes,

Expressing its appreciation to the Government of the Republic of Croatia for the attitude of co-operation expressed with respect to the investigation and punishment of such crimes under international law and its willingness to provide full evidence of all alleged violations of human rights on its territory,

Decides that the mission of the Rapporteurs, Ambassador Corell, Ambassador Türk and Mrs. Thune, should be completed as soon as possible, bearing in mind the need to assure the safety of the Rapporteurs;

Asks the Chairman-in-Office to release the report to the public and to transmit it to the Committee of Experts drawn up by United Nations Security Council resolution 780;

Welcomes the report's recommendations and invites the rapporteurs to report on their findings to the appropriate United Nations bodies.

The CSO asks the Chairman-in-Office to draw the attention of the United Nations Secretary-General to the report's recommendation and particularly to the urgency of its implementation within the appropriate international framework. The United Nations Commission of Experts should give particular attention to the principle of personal responsibility for war crimes and examine how this principle could be put into practice by an *ad hoc* tribunal;

Endorses the urgency of the exhumation of mass graves in United Nations Protected Area Sector East and strongly calls on the Belgrade authorities to fully co-operate in providing conditions for the safe exhumation of the mass graves in the United Nations Protected Area Sector East of Croatia. Having noted also the activities and resources of United Nations Special Rapporteur Mazowiecki in this respect, the CSO considers that the recommendation should be referred to the Special Rapporteur and the Security Council resolution 780 Commission of Experts, via the United Nations Secretary-General, for follow-up action;

Welcomes Recommendations 4 and 6 relating to the provision of expert assistance to the Croatian Government in the interpretation of international legal norms, and the promotion of an effective, modern and democratic system for the administration of justice. The CSO sees these recommendations as fitting well into the concept of increased co-operation between the CSCE and the Council of Europe, and invites the Chairman-in-Office to seek the assistance of the Secretary General of the Council of Europe in implementing them;

Invites the Chairman-in-Office to ask the Croatian Government to publish the results of its investigations into the alleged executions at the village of Kip.

* * *

Thomson Mission[9]

The CSO recalled the recommendation in the report of the mission led by Sir John Thomson that allegations of the detention of Muslim prisoners in Serbia should be investigated. The CSO requests Sir John Thomson to nominate two or three of his colleagues to visit Serbia once more in order to carry out this work.

---

[9] 17-CSO/Journal No. 2, Annex 3.

EIGHTEENTH CSO MEETING

Stockholm, 11-13 December 1992

Decision on Estonia[1]

The Committee of Senior Officials,

Consistent with the concept of preventive diplomacy and in order to promote stability and dialogue between the Estonian- and Russian-speaking communities in Estonia,

With reference to its decision of 6 November 1992, and to the report of the Personal Representative of the Chairman-in-Office on the modalities of a possible mission to Estonia,

1. Decided to establish a small CSCE Mission in Estonia for a period of six months, to be launched no later than 15 February 1993, in order to further promote integration and better understanding between the communities in Estonia. It is expected that the Mission will contribute to the efforts of the Estonian national and local authorities to re-create a civic society, *inter alia* through the promotion of local mechanisms to facilitate dialogue;

2. Recognized the specific problems which exist in northeastern Estonia, in addition to misunderstandings and resentments caused by the implementation of the citizenship and language laws;

3. Authorized the Chairman-in-Office, after appropriate consultation, to appoint a Head of Mission. The Head of Mission will work out a proposal for terms of reference, based on the recommendations of the Personal Representative of the Chairman-in-Office, taking into consideration the findings of the CSCE/ODIHR Expert Mission to Estonia, and a proposal for a preliminary budget. Both will be submitted to the representatives of the participating States who are to meet regularly in Vienna for consideration and approval on a preliminary basis and to the Committee of Senior Officials for final approval at its next meeting;

---

[1] 19-CSO/Journal No.3, Annex 2.

4. Requested the Head of Mission to exchange information and co-operate on relevant questions with the High Commissioner on National Minorities and the Office for Democratic Institutions and Human Rights and other CSCE institutions during the preparation and operation of the Mission.

* * *

Identifying logo for the CSCE[2]

The Committee decided to adopt as the logo for the CSCE the letters CSCE in the blue and white block design above. This logo could be supplemented as appropriate by the letters abbreviating the words "Conference on Security and Co-operation in Europe" in another language or languages in the same style. This logo could be displayed to identify CSCE institutions, activities, personnel or property wherever appropriate. The blue and white colours symbolize the connection of the CSCE with the United Nations by may be varied for local or national purposes.

---

[2] 18-CSO/Journal No.3, Annex 3.

NINETEENTH CSO MEETING

Prague, 2-4 February 1993

Terms of reference for the CSCE Mission to Estonia[1]

Objective of the Mission

The objective of the Mission is to promote stability, dialogue and understanding between the communities in Estonia.

Mission activities

To this end the Mission will:

- establish and maintain contacts with competent authorities on both the national and the local level, in particular with those responsible for citizenship, migration, language questions, social services and employment;

- establish and maintain contacts with relevant non-governmental institutions and organizations, including political parties, trade unions and mass media organizations;

- collect information and serve as a clearing-house for information, technical assistance and advice on matters relating to the status of the communities in Estonia and the rights and duties of their members;

- contribute to the efforts of Estonian national and local authorities to re-create a civic society, *inter alia* through the promotion of local mechanisms to facilitate dialogue and understanding;

- keeping in mind the temporary nature of the Mission, consider ways and means of transferring its responsibilities to institutions or organizations representing the local population.

In its work the Mission will take into account the findings of the CSCE/ODIHR Mission to Estonia.

---

[1] CSCE/19-CSO/Journal No. 2, Annex 1.

Size and Composition

The Mission will number initially six members. All participating States are eligible to participate in the Mission.

Mission Area

The Mission will operate in the whole territory of the Republic of Estonia, but its activities will focus on the northern and north-eastern parts of the country. The Mission will establish its headquarters in Tallinn and other offices in Narva and Kohtla-Järve.

Co-ordination

The Mission will exchange information and co-operate on relevant questions with the Office for Democratic Institutions and Human Rights and, in questions falling within his competence, with the High Commissioner on National Minorities.

The Mission will exchange information and co-ordinate, as necessary, with representatives of the United Nation, of other international organizations and of CSCE participating States in Estonia.

Reports

The Head of Mission will submit regular reports to the Chairman-in-Office.

Conditions of Service

Provisions ensuring the safety and freedom of movement of the members of the Mission, access to the local population, communities and authorities, privileges and immunities will be included in the Memorandum of Understanding to be signed by the Head of Mission and the Government of Estonia.

Duration and Review Procedures

The Mission will operate for a period of six months. The operation, duration and other modalities of the Mission will be reviewed, as appropriate, by the Committee of Senior Officials.[2]

* * *

Text concerning the CPC and preventive diplomacy[3]

The CPC was tasked by the CSCE Council in Stockholm "to take rapid steps to strengthen its ability to provide operational support for CSCE preventive diplomacy missions and peacekeeping activities". The Director of the CPC was asked by the Council to present "for approval by the CSO, a proposal setting forth the staffing and budget implications of this decision".

This paper describes in part A first steps to strengthen the CPC's ability to provide support, sets out in part B a proposal on staffing and accommodation and outlines in part C the financial implications.

It is understood that what is set out below presents an urgent but preliminary set of general measures which need to be developed by the CPC and be kept under regular review; it is without prejudice to the restructuring of the CSCE with which Ministers have tasked the CSO.

A. To strengthen the ability of the CPC an operational section is established to provide operational support for CSCE preventive diplomacy missions and peacekeeping activities.

1. Missions need operational support before they deploy, during deployment and on recovery. This might include assistance with planning, accounting, transportation, communications, accommodation and logistics, as well as the normal staff work associated with operational missions.

2. The precise nature and scope of CPC operational support will vary according to the needs and circumstances of each mission and will be implemented in close consultation with the individual Heads of

---

[2] Editor's note: At its 18th meeting on 24 June 1992, the CSO Vienna Group decided to prolong the mandate with six months till February 1994.

[3] CSCE/19-CSO/Journal No. 2, Annex 2. (Title added by the Editor.)

Missions and as necessary the Chairman-in-Office. The CPC will give operational support to the missions in the following fields:

(a) Planning and Operations, such as:

(1) providing information on mission area and briefing or arranging for briefings of team members;

(2) developing standardized formats for financial modalities and memoranda of understanding;

(3) supporting and participating in advance teams to mission areas to make preparations, and providing necessary assistance in planning and establishing mission operations, including logistics;

(4) co-ordination of mission support;

(5) security measures and contingency planning.

(b) Logistics, Transport and Communications, such as:

(1) acquisition, control, storage and disposal of any equipment;

(2) acquisition and issue of consumable supplies;

(3) movement of personnel and equipment to and from mission areas, including travel arrangements;

(4) ensuring proper repair and maintenance of vehicles and equipment;

(5) establishment and maintenance of reliable communication links with and within the mission;

(6) ensuring prompt response to mission requests for administrative/logistic support.

(c) Administration, such as:

(1) budgeting, accounting, financial planning and disbursement of funds, management of resources;

(2) billing of participating States;

(3) register of presence and availability of mission members and candidates for missions;

(4) routine staff work (secretarial and archival functions).

Implicit in the above is that these functions are carried out on the basis of sound commercial practice.

(...)

* * *

Sanctions Co-ordinator[4]

1. Pursuant to its decision of 18 September 1992 to establish Sanctions Assistance Missions (SAMs) to assist with the implementation of sanctions against Serbia-Montenegro, the CSO recognizes the need for co-ordination of the activity of the SAMs, national authorities and regional or international organizations on sanctions, and therefore decides to establish the post of EC/CSCE Sanctions Co-ordinator.

2. The Sanctions Co-ordinator will oversee the operation of the implementation of sanctions, co-ordinate with SAMs and SAMCOMM, liaise with and between countries in the region on the implementation of sanctions, advise States and relevant international bodies on how sanctions should be implemented more effectively and provide basic direction and co-ordination between all levels and participants involved with sanctions, including liaison with and reports to the United Nations Sanctions Committee. The CSO invites the United Nations Security Council to take appropriate steps to ensure that the Sanctions Co-ordinator has the full support and co-operation of the appropriate United Nations bodies. The CSO urges the United Nations Security Council and Sanctions Committee to address and examine as a matter of urgency the issue of direct losses of the countries in the region resulting from the implementation of sanctions.

3. The CSO agreed the following modalities and mandate for the Sanctions Co-ordinator.

---

[4] CSCE/19-CSO/Journal No. 3, Annex 1.

Mandate The tasks of the Sanctions Co-ordinator will include:

(a) Oversight of sanctions to assess the implementation and effect of existing sanctions measures and to advise on measures to implement sanctions more effectively.

(b) To provide countries in the region with advice and assistance as requested. In particular to:

- provide technical advice, in co-operation with SAMs, on customs procedures to the local customs authorities;

- co-ordinate requests for further practical and technical assistance to apply sanctions and the response of donor countries to meet their requests;

- to liaise between and assist relevant authorities so that traffic denied transit through Serbia and Montenegro is ensured smooth passage by alternative routes through the neighbouring States;

- to help to develop procedures to facilitate the passage and verification of shipments exempted by the UN Sanctions Committee;

- to assist and give advice, based on prior rulings of the UN Sanctions Committee, to help to solve disputes on practical application of sanctions.

(c) To provide legal advice to enable neighbouring and other States to make full use of existing legislation or, where necessary, to advise on the need for new legislation, to ensure that they have effective legal powers to counter and prosecute violations of sanctions.

(d) To liaise with and between SAMs to assess their effectiveness and operational strength and to make recommendations concerning their activities.

(e) To bring to the attention of and consult with neighbouring and other States specific measures that they should take to improve their application of sanctions.

(f) To bring violations and suspected violations to the attention of the CSCE, the United Nations Sanctions Committee and concerned governments.

(g) To consult with concerned governments on investigation and prosecution of alleged violations of the sanctions.

(h) To report or provide advice on request to the CSO, representatives of participating States meeting in Vienna, the United Nations Security Council and Sanctions Committee, the co-Chairmen of the ICFY, the European Community Presidency and other appropriate bodies.

(i) To chair meetings of the EC-CSCE Sanctions Liaison Group in Vienna.

Composition The Sanctions Co-ordinator will be a senior, authoritative and respected figure. He or she will be supported by a small team including a legal adviser, a customs adviser and a secretary. One of the advisers will be designated as a deputy and will act in the co-ordinator's stead during absences from Brussels. All CSCE participating States will be eligible to nominate candidates for the post of Sanctions Co-ordinator or for places on his team. The Sanctions Co-ordinator will appoint members of his team from a list of candidates nominated by participating States.

Chain of Command The Sanctions Co-ordinator will report to the Chairman-in-Office at least once a month indicating difficulties which need to be addressed. The reports will then be immediately distributed to participating States by the CPC Secretariat. They may be discussed by the Sanctions Liaison Group or by participating States in the CSO Vienna Group.

The Sanctions Co-ordinator will at the same time present his reports to the President of the United Nations Security Council, the Chair of the United Nations Sanctions Committee, the co-Chairmen of the ICFY and the European Community Presidency, and to other appropriate bodies, as requested.

Location The Sanctions Co-ordinator will be co-located with the SAMCOMM Office in Brussels, so that he can work in close co-ordination with the SAMCOMM.

Travel The Sanctions Co-ordinator and members of his team will travel regularly to States in the region, and other States as necessary, to assess the implementation of sanctions, provide technical and legal advice and assess the operation of the SAMs. As required, he will travel to brief appropriate bodies on the implementation of sanctions, to advise on measures for the more effective implementation of sanctions and to chair the Sanctions Liaison Group.

Finance The host authority will provide office accommodation and equipment free of charge (including furniture, computers/word processors, photocopiers, telephone and facsimile facilities). Sending States will meet the direct costs of their nationals seconded as Sanctions Co-ordinator or as members of his team (including per diem and accommodation), and will provide their nationals with appropriate vehicles. Agreed common costs will be met by all CSCE participating States according to the CSCE scale of distribution.

Budget and Schedule of Payments A Budget of 1,600,000 ATS is established within the CPC Secretariat's budget to cover common costs for an initial six-month operating period with effect from the date of appointment of the Sanctions Co-ordinator.

The participating States will be requested by the CPC Secretariat to make their assessed contributions to cover the agreed common costs payable by 1 March 1993. Voluntary contributions will be welcomed.

Duration The Sanctions Co-ordinator will be appointed for an initial period of six months. Members of his team will serve for the same period.

Review Procedures The operation of the Sanctions Co-ordinator and his team, and other modalities, including duration, will be reviewed regularly by the CSO.

(...)

* * *

CSCE Mission to the Republic of Moldova[5]

The Committee of Senior Officials

Noted with appreciation the activities and the final report of Dr. Adam D. Rotfeld, Personal Representative of the Chairman-in-Office, as well as the earlier interim report with addenda and

1. Decided to establish a CSCE Mission to the Republic of Moldova in order to facilitate the achievement of a lasting, comprehensive political settlement of the conflict in all its aspects, based on the following understanding expressed by the parties to the conflict, and other interested parties, to the Personal Representative of the Chairman-in-Office:

- Consolidation of the independence and sovereignty of the Republic of Moldova within its current borders and reinforcement of the territorial integrity of the State along with an understanding about a special status for the Trans-Dniester region;

- An agreement on the withdrawal of foreign troops;

- Effective observance of international obligations and commitments regarding human and minority rights;

- Assistance in monitoring the implementation of agreements on a durable political settlement.

The Mission will assist the parties to the conflict in opening a political dialogue and entering into negotiations on a lasting political settlement. It will stand ready to assist the parties in their efforts to remove by diplomatic means the sources of conflict before violence results.

The Mission will be launched no later than 31 March 1993, for an initial period of six months. The question of a possible extension of the duration of the Mission beyond the initial period will be reviewed by the CSO.

2. Authorized the Chairman-in-Office, after appropriate consultations, to appoint a Head of Mission.

---

[5] CSCE/19-CSO/Journal No. 3, Annex 3.

3. Requested the Chairman-in-Office to consult the United Nations, and other international organizations with an active interest in contributing to the resolution of the conflict, on co-ordination and co-operation with the Mission. The Chairman-in-Office will report on the results of these consultations to the CSO Vienna Group.

4. Further requested the CSO Vienna Group to elaborate and approve by 15 March 1993, on a preliminary basis, the terms of reference and budget for the Mission, taking into account the recommendations of the Personal Representative of the Chairman-in-Office. The terms of reference and budget will be submitted to the CSO for final approval at its next Meeting. The CPC Secretariat is authorized to bill participating States immediately following the preliminary approval of the budget.

* * *

Decision on Georgia[6]

The Committee of Senior Officials,

Noting with satisfaction the initial progress achieved in the implementation of its decision of 6 November 1992,

Reiterating the urgent need for a lasting and comprehensive political solution to the conflicts in Southern Ossetia and Abkhazia,

Decides to extend the mandate of the Mission for a period of six months, with effect from 24 February 1993;

Authorizes the increase of the number of the members of the Mission by two additional diplomats and one additional military officer, with immediate effect;

Authorizes the Personal Representative to adjust the budget approved for the period December 1992 - February 1993 to the actual needs, not exceeding the authorized total costs;

Instructs the Financial Committee to examine the budget of the Mission for the period March - August 1993 and present it to the CSO Vienna Group for decision not later than 15 February 1993;

---

6 CSCE/19-CSO/Journal No. 3, Annex 4.

Urges participating States to transfer their contributions as early as possible, but in any case in time to ensure the financing of the Mission;

Requests the Chairman-in-Office and the Personal Representative of the Chairman-in-Office in Georgia to intensify contacts with the United Nations and other relevant international organizations, to elaborate recommendations on co-operation and co-ordination of their efforts for the establishment of a cease-fire and achievement of a political solution to the conflict in Abkhazia and to submit these recommendations to the next Meeting of the CSO.

THIRD EMERGENCY MEETING OF THE CSO

Prague, 26-29 April 1993

Statements on the Situation in Nagorny-Karabakh[1]

The Chairman announced that the following proposal, presented to the Meeting by him and by the Chairman of the Minsk Conference on Nagorno-Karabakh would be recorded in the Journal:

The Committee of Senior Officials received with deep concern reports of recent developments in the ongoing crisis concerning the conflict dealt with by the Conference on Nagorno-Karabakh and, in particular, the occupation of the Kelbajar district of the Republic of Azerbaijan. At the request of Azerbaijan, the Committee agreed to sit on an emergency basis.

The Committee noted that the continuation and new escalation of military actions further endangers security and stability in the entire region. The Committee called upon the parties to demonstrate the political will to solve all outstanding problems exclusively by peaceful means, thereby putting an end to the bloodshed.

The CSCE participating States reject territorial gains and other *faits accomplis* through the use of force, by whatever side. They view such actions as totally destructive also in terms of the negotiating process. They request the parties to reconfirm their commitment to abstain from them. They demand immediate and complete withdrawal of occupying forces from the Kelbajar and other recently occupied areas of Azerbaijan.

The CSCE participating States express their conviction that the carrying out of the above-mentioned steps, together with the de-escalation and ultimate cessation of military activities, will permit the CSCE peace process to resume its course under more favourable conditions. They request all concerned parties to take the necessary measures to ensure the free and unimpeded flow of emergency humanitarian aid to all populations affected by the conflict. They remain determined to pursue all negotiating efforts to ensure progress towards a peaceful settlement based on CSCE principles, commitments and decisions, to be achieved within the framework of the Minsk Conference process as established by the Ministers' decision of 24

---

[1] CSO/3-EM/Journal, paragraph 4. (Title added by the Editor.)

March 1992. They reconfirm their confidence to the Minsk Group and its chairman to renew the necessary contacts to this end.

The delegation of Turkey stated:

On 20 May last year Armenia vetoed a CSO decision calling for the withdrawal of its forces from the Lacin area of Azerbaijan. After a year, Armenia continues its illegal occupation of that region.

Today another proposal from the Chairman of the Minsk Group and the Chairman-in-Office calling for the withdrawal from the most recently occupied Azeri region, Kelbecer, was again rejected by Armenia. This Armenian rejection confirms that

(a) it is Armenia which is occupying the Kelbecer region;

(b) Armenia intends to continue its occupation of Azeri territory in pursuit of its expansionist designs.

The Acting Defence Minister of Armenia, Mr. Manukyan, was quoted in TASS on 7 April as stating 'The principle of non-violability of borders may apply to western countries whose borders are more or less solidly drawn up after two world wars. But this principle of non-violability of borders is not valid for Karabakh. The borders in the former Soviet Union have been established in a capricious manner and have to be corrected.'

With this mentality and clearly-stated position, the callous defiance of the CSCE community by Armenia today should not come as a surprise to anyone.

Armenia has turned down the text because it demands the immediate and complete withdrawal of occupying forces. Armenia is telling us that it will pursue its expansionist and aggressive policies.

Armenia has to realise that those who use force will see that force will be used against them. For the time being Armenia might be occupying Azeri territory, but as long as it continues to do that it will not have peace. Through its actions, it is engulfing itself with a widening conflict. Armenian actions constitute clear, gross and uncorrected violations of CSCE commitments. Its behaviour today is another confirmation of that.

On Monday when we started the Emergency Meeting I asked whether we are going to extend support to Azerbaijan which has asked for moral and political support from the CSCE in defence of our principles and values, whether we are going to condemn the violation of her sovereignty and territorial integrity, whether we are going to state that use of force will not be accepted to the international community or whether we are going to tell Armenia clearly and unambiguously that its policies are unacceptable to the international community.

Tonight, we cannot answer these questions affirmatively. A compromise text, which, because it is a compromise, does not fully reflect the gravity of Armenian violations was turned down by the perpetrator of these violations, despite overwhelming calls for its adoption. We can no longer permit Armenia to be the judge of it own violations. The time has come to avail ourselves of taking decisions without the consent of Armenia in accordance with Article 16 of the Prague Document. This conflict, in our view, can no longer be taken up in the CSCE with the participation of Armenia in our decisions.

The delegation of Azerbaijan stated:

Requesting the convening of an Emergency Meeting, the Azerbaijan Republic was proceeding from the really crucial critical situation caused by the aggression of the Republic of Armenia, and was expecting from the CSCE a really serious and strong decision, demanding from the Republic of Armenia the cessation of aggression and immediate withdrawal of all occupying Armenian forces from the territory of the Azerbaijan Republic. Unfortunately, as it had happened last year, on 18-20 May, when the Lacin region of Azerbaijan was occupied by Armenian forces, today the CSCE failed again to take a needed decision, which could help to restore the Minsk process, undermined by the aggression of the Republic of Armenia against Azerbaijan.

The Republic of Armenia by its aggressive actions and destructive position undermines all our peaceful efforts, and challenges the CSCE.

This critical situation demands extraordinary steps. In conformity with paragraph 16 of the Prague Document, and in view of clear, gross and uncorrected violations of relevant CSCE commitments by the Republic of Armenia, appropriate decisions and actions should be taken in the absence of the consent of the Republic of Armenia.

TWENTY-FIRST CSO MEETING

Prague, 26-28 April 1993

Statement by Albania on the question of Macedonia[1]

The Republic of Albania has blocked the consensus for admission to the CSCE of the Former Yugoslav Republic of Macedonia because of the failure of the Macedonian State to respect the human and national rights of the Albanians there in conformity with CSCE standards.

The Republic of Albania has welcomed since the very beginning the full membership of the former Yugoslav Republic of Macedonia in the United Nations. We believe that her membership in the United Nations has helped remove the vulnerability of this new State in the troubled region of the Balkans.

The Republic of Albania has recognized the Former Yugoslav Republic of Macedonia as an independent and sovereign State, demonstrating once again its unequivocal attitude to its well-defined policy of good-neighbourliness, making its contribution to promoting stability and enhancing security in the Balkans. Thus Albania has recognized and undertaken to respect the sovereignty and territorial integrity of that State.

We also reiterated our firm belief in the existence of that neighbouring State, as a premise for a closer co-operation with it.

But we are worried about the situation of the Albanians living in Macedonia, who make up more than one third of the whole population.

The constitutional exclusion of such a sizeable portion of the Albanian population from the very conception of the State is still an obstacle to be overcome. We accept the existence of the "Macedonian State", but we cannot accept "... Macedonia as a national State of the Macedonian people ...", as proclaimed in the preamble of the Macedonian Constitution. This denomination is incompatible with history as well as with recent and present realities. As such, it might give rise to a serious misunderstanding.

That exclusion in turn has brought about the alienation of the Albanian population from public life at large, including from such important and sensitive

---

[1] 21-CSO/Journal No. 3, paragraph 4. Editor's note: Albania made this statement at the occasion of the CSO decision to grant Macedonia observer status in the CSCE process.

sectors as the administration, police and army, economic management, education, the mass-media, etc.

The CSCE, for its part, lives in a community of common values, respect for which stands at its very foundation. Its human dimension is a substantial one, and as it has proved, closely linked with the other aspects of security in Europe.

The Albanians of Macedonia see in the CSCE precisely this equality and sameness of standards.

They also see the realization of their legitimate rights within the Macedonian State.

Hitherto, the machinery of the talks in Geneva has been set in motion although without any substantial results.

Under these conditions, the Republic of Albania agrees to give its consensus to grant the Former Yugoslav Republic of Macedonia the "silent observer" status.

The former Yugoslav Republic of Macedonia should concretely prove that it will work very seriously and constructively to fulfil the necessary conditions to be accepted in the CSCE as a fully-fledged participant.

We give the consensus for the "silent observer" status, having in mind the community of common values of the CSCE, the intention to have the doors open to dialogue and to exert its influence on Macedonia to improve the position of the Albanians there.

Every position of ours in the future will be conditioned on the improvement of the position of the Albanians in the former Yugoslav Republic of Macedonia.

This period of test, so to say, will give the CSCE, too, the possibility to set in motion all its mechanisms as soon as possible to make sure that the rights of the Albanians in that Republic are fully respected, and report back to the CSCE participating States.

The Republic of Albania will urge the parties concerned to intensify their efforts towards finding a quick solution to the existing problems, which would, on its part, bring about the necessary improvement in the situation of the Albanian population there.

Besides, it will, for its part, contribute to the creation of the necessary climate for the implementation of the well-known CSCE standards by this new State.

The Republic of Albania demonstrates, by this act, once again that it is firm on its position as an open, co-operative, constructive partner in the efforts of the international community towards a better world, towards enhanced stability and security in our troubled region."

* * *

Statement on Former Yugoslavia[2]

1. In Stockholm last December, the CSCE Council made clear that the moral and political authority of the CSCE was to be engaged fully in the search for a peaceful solution to the conflict in parts of the former Yugoslavia. The Ministers presented Serbia with a choice — either co-operate fully in a peaceful solution or face even more severe consequences.
2. Meeting directly following the rejection of the Vance-Owen peace plan by the Bosnian Serbs, the CSCE Committee of Senior Officials agreed that Serbia is making a fateful choice. Serbia continues to defy United Nations resolutions and stands against the will of the international community. Horrible fighting and unspeakable atrocities continue in Bosnia-Herzegovina. We were deeply concerned at the outbreak of fighting between Croats and Muslims in Central Bosnia, and we welcome the agreement concluded between them on 24 April. Violations of basic standards of human behaviour and of CSCE commitments continue unabated. Hundreds of thousands of persons have lost their homes. The very existence of the Republic of Bosnia-Herzegovina is threatened. The barbaric policy of ethnic cleansing is continuing in Bosnia-Herzegovina and many other parts of former Yugoslavia. The danger of spillover of the conflict has increased.
3. Such gross, continuing and uncorrected violations of humanitarian standards have to be prosecuted. Those responsible for war crimes and other atrocities will be held personally accountable. Progress towards an *ad hoc* international tribunal on war crimes is urgent. CSCE participating States have never sought to assign guilt to the Serbian people as a whole for this conflict. The responsibility for the future lies primarily with Serbian authorities.
4. Recent United Nations Security Council resolutions on implementing a no-fly zone over Bosnia-Herzegovina and strengthening economic sanctions are important steps. The Vance-Owen peace plan enjoys the full support of CSCE participating States as the basis on which peace can be

---

[2] 21-CSO/Journal No. 3, Annex 2.

established. In the absence of agreement on the Vance-Owen plan, CSCE participating States must continue consideration of even firmer measures. They accept the obligation to implement fully all United Nations decisions, including those on the relief of the needs of innocent victims in Bosnia-Herzegovina. They welcome the continued presence of United Nations peacekeeping forces and of EC monitors. These operations continue to make an essential contribution to the search for peace. They support the willingness of the North Atlantic Treaty Organization to enforce the no-fly zone and the action by WEU and NATO to enforce the embargo on the Adriatic Sea and their willingness to help implement the Vance-Owen plan. The CSO suggested that the convening of the Steering Committee of the ICFY at ministerial level could also be considered.

5. The CSCE framework continues to be an important means of pursuing this strategy of peace. Practices of ethnic cleansing must be stopped. Governments of the CSCE participating States will strengthen efforts to help ensure that the CSCE makes a full contribution to international efforts to end this horrible conflict. We will also continue to press for an end to brutal repression and for restoration of and respect for all rights to peoples of these regions. To that end, the Committee of Senior Officials has today adopted the following:

Steps within Bosnia-Herzegovina

6. The Committee of Senior Officials reaffirmed the commitment of participating States to support the sovereignty, territorial integrity and independence of the Republic of Bosnia-Herzegovina and to provide support for the pressing needs of its population. We will continue relief efforts and to support the important work of UNPROFOR and UNHCR. The Committee of Senior Officials drew attention to several steps of utmost importance which could be taken on the basis of existing United Nations decisions to provide urgent support to Bosnia-Herzegovina:
   - establish safe areas;
   - put heavy weaponry under international control;
   - place United Nations observers along the Bosnia and Herzegovina borders.

   Since the people of Bosnia-Herzegovina are threatened with extinction tougher measures under Chapter VII of the United Nations Charter are high on the international agenda. No option for further action under United Nations auspices is ruled out, including the lifting of the arms embargo against the Government of Bosnia-Herzegovina.

Economic Sanctions

7. With the adoption of United Nations Security Council resolution 820, our governments are committed to a substantial expansion of sanctions against

Serbia and Montenegro and to increase the economic pressure on Serbia by improving implementation by all of the existing sanctions and by providing comprehensive coverage of all river, rail and road crossings into Serbia and Montenegro. Transshipments on the Danube will only be permitted according to the terms laid down in this resolution. Strengthening of financial sanctions is a further essential step. The CSO endorsed the 22 April decision by the CSO Vienna Group to expand the size of Sanctions Assistance Missions and to increase technical assistance to States hosting Sanctions Assistance Missions. Participating States agreed to implement these decisions without delay and will take all possible measures to punish the violators. They will also consider publicizing the identity of serious violators. They welcome the WEU initiative to co-operate with riparian States in implementing the sanctions on the Danube. They recognize that countries of the region bear the brunt of the sanctions and that their specific needs for economic assistance should be considered. They also recognize that the possible risks for the security of these States should be taken into account.

Missions of long duration and the spillover mission

8. The CSCE missions of long duration to Kosovo, Sandjak and Vojvodina remain essential to prevent expansion of the conflict which the international community will not tolerate. The CSO stressed that CSCE Missions are an important element in the search for peace in the former Yugoslavia. The CSO reaffirmed the importance of increasing the size of these missions to levels authorized by the Council. The CSO Vienna Group is mandated to consider ways and means to improve the effectiveness of these missions in pursuit of their mandate. The CSO considered that the Memorandum of Understanding upon which the operation of these missions is based should be prolonged. The CSO reaffirmed the belief that a United Nations presence in Kosovo would be a positive step. The CSCE Spillover Mission to Skopje also continues to play an important role in preventing the spillover of the conflict.

* * *

Follow-up to Chapter VI of the Document of the Stockholm Council Meeting[3]

1. The CSO recalled the decisions of Ministers at Stockholm on behalf of a comprehensive CSCE strategy of early warning, conflict prevention and

[3] 21-CSO/Journal No. 3, Annex 3.

crisis management, integrating a broad range of methods and instruments. Requested by Ministers in Chapter VI of the Stockholm document to examine the issues involved in strengthening the CSCE's capabilities in this regard, the CSO took special note of the following:

- Organizational improvements already underway, including reinforcement of operational support for CSCE preventive diplomacy and peacekeeping missions;
- The initial activities of the High Commissioner on National Minorities;
- Experiences gained from various CSCE preventive diplomacy missions already in the field;
- Development of CSBMs in particular to prevent conflicts in the military field; and
- A new pattern of deepened consultations within the CSO Vienna Group on the root causes of conflict and on disputes which have arisen.

As part of this mandate, the CSO discussed objectives for further work by the CSO Vienna Group and, in particular, the seminars to be conducted by ODIHR and CPC to share experience and increase knowledge on CSCE early warning and peacekeeping.

2. Noting that tensions with a potential to develop into crises and conflict often have an important human dimension aspect, the CSO welcomed the intention of the ODIHR to hold its seminar on early warning in Warsaw. They instructed the ODIHR Director to accelerate planning on the seminar's modalities and agenda.

This seminar should be an occasion to review and to publicize the full range of CSCE activities in early warning, and to consider ways of enhancing CSCE's use of mechanisms and programmes for building democratic institutions and fostering human rights on behalf of preventive diplomacy.

3. The CSO welcomed the decision of the CPC/CC to hold the CPC's seminar on peacekeeping on 7-9 June 1993 in Vienna and the invitation extended to Ambassador Rene Nyberg of Finland to chair this seminar and noted the discussions underway in Vienna to prepare the agenda for this seminar. The CSO stressed the importance that all CSCE participating States be represented and take active part in this seminar.

Noting both the importance of preventive diplomacy and peacekeeping to the comprehensive CSCE strategy of early warning, conflict prevention and crisis management and the expectation of CSCE participating States that the CSCE should play a greater role in this regard, the CSO reaffirmed that the CSCE, while keeping its activities under regular review, should build upon experience and develop further its capabilities and instruments in this field.

The issues involved in achieving this objective deserve prompt discussion among CSCE participating States. To that end, the CSO tasked the CSO Vienna Group with further consideration of the CSCE's current activities and future potential in the field of preventive diplomacy and peacekeeping. As a conceptual aid to this effort, the CSO looked to the CPC seminar as an opportunity for informal and creative discussion, involving a broad spectrum of participants and reflecting the efforts on behalf of greater co-operation in peacekeeping underway in the UN Security Council, as well as within the NACC and other fora.

The CSO reaffirmed the importance of further exploring ways by which the CSCE can work closely in the field of preventive diplomacy and peacekeeping with the United Nations and with European and Transatlantic organizations or institutions such as NATO, WEU and the EC, and, as circumstances warrant, other international institutions and mechanisms, including the peacekeeping mechanism of the Commonwealth of Independent States (CIS).

The CSO noted that, in all of the CSCE's efforts at preventive diplomacy and peacekeeping, the willingness of CSCE participating States to provide both personnel and resources will continue to be essential. As new and potential requirements approach, the CSO reaffirmed the readiness of its members to back up their political commitments on behalf of the CSCE's preventive diplomacy and peacekeeping with specific contributions.

* * *

Financial Protocol established in accordance with Article 13 of the Convention on Conciliation and Arbitration within the CSCE[4]

Article 1
Costs of the Court

1. All the costs of the Court established by the Convention on Conciliation and Arbitration within the CSCE (hereinafter referred to as "the Convention") shall be met by the States parties to the Convention. Costs of conciliators and arbitrators shall be costs of the Court.

2. The obligations of the host State with respect to expenditures in connection with the premises and furniture for use by the Court, their maintenance, insurance and security, as well as utilities, shall be set out

[4] 21-CSO/Journal No. 3, Annex 4.

in an exchange of letters between the Court acting with the consent of and on behalf of the States parties to the Convention, and the host State.

Article 2
Contributions to the Budget of the Court

1. Contributions to the budget of the Court shall be divided among the States parties to the Convention according to the scale of distribution applicable within the CSCE, adjusted to take into account the difference in number between the CSCE participating States and the States parties to the Convention.

2. If a State ratifies or accedes to the Convention after its entry into force, its contribution shall be equal, for the current financial year, to one-twelfth of its portion of the adjusted scale, as established according to paragraph 1 of this Article, for each full month of that financial year which remains after the date on which the Convention enters into force in respect of it.

3. If a State which is not a party to the Convention submits a dispute to the Court pursuant to the provisions of Article 20, paragraph 2, or Article 26, paragraph 1 of the Convention, it shall contribute to the financing of the budget of the Court, for the duration of the proceedings, as if it were a party to the Convention.

For the application of this paragraph, the conciliation shall be presumed to commence on the day the Registrar receives notice of the agreement of the parties to set up a Commission and to end on the day the Commission notifies its report to the parties. If a party withdraws from the proceedings, these proceedings shall be considered as ended on the day of notice of the report specified in Article 25, paragraph 6 of the Convention. The arbitration proceedings shall be presumed to start on the day the Registrar receives notice of the agreement of the parties to establish a Tribunal and to end on the day the Tribunal renders its award.

Article 3
Financial Year and Budget

1. The financial year shall be from 1 January to 31 December.

2. The Registrar, acting with the concurrence of the Bureau of the Court, shall establish each year a budget proposal for the Court. The budget

proposal for the ensuing financial year shall be submitted to the States parties to the Convention before 15 September.

3. The budget shall be approved by the representatives of the States parties to the Convention. Consideration and approval of the budget shall take place in Vienna unless the States parties to the Convention otherwise agree. On approval of the budget for the financial year the Registrar shall request the States parties to the Convention to remit their contributions.

If the budget is not approved by 31 December the Court will operate on the basis of the preceding budget and, without prejudice to later adjustments, the Registrar shall request the States parties to the Convention to remit their contributions in accordance with this budget.

The Registrar shall request States parties to the Convention to make fifty per cent of their contributions available on 1 January and the remaining fifty per cent on 1 April.

4. Barring a decision to the contrary by the representatives of the States parties to the Convention, the budget shall be established in Swiss francs and the contributions of the States shall be paid in this currency.

5. A State which ratifies or accedes to the Convention after its entry into force shall pay its first contribution to the budget within two months after the request by the Registrar.

6. States which, without being parties to the Convention, have submitted a dispute to the Court, shall pay their contribution within two months after the request by the Registrar.

7. The year the Convention enters into force, the States parties to the Convention shall pay their contribution to the budget within two months following the date of deposit of the twelfth instrument of ratification of the Convention. This budget is preliminarily fixed at 250,000 Swiss francs.

Article 4
Obligations, Payments and Revised Budget

1. The approved budget shall constitute authorization to the Registrar, acting under the responsibility of the Bureau of the Court, to incur obligations and make payments up to the amounts and for the purposes approved.

2. The Registrar, acting under the responsibility of the Bureau of the Court, is authorized to make transfers between items and sub-items of up to 15 per cent of items/sub-items. All such transfers must be reported by the Registrar in connection with the financial statement mentioned in Article 9 of this Protocol.

3. Obligations remaining undischarged at the end of the financial year shall be carried over to the next financial year.

4. If so obliged by circumstances and following careful examination of available resources with a view to identifying savings, the Registrar is authorized to submit a revised budget, which may entail requests for supplementary appropriations, for the approval of the representatives of the States parties to the Convention.

5. Any surplus for a given financial year shall be deducted from the assessed contributions for the financial year following the one in which the accounts have been approved by the representatives of the States parties to the Convention. Any deficit shall be charged to the ensuing financial year unless the representatives of the States parties to the Convention decide on supplementary contributions.

Article 5
Working Capital Fund

A working capital fund may be established in case the States parties to the Convention deem it necessary. It will be funded by the States parties to the Convention.

Article 6
Allowances and Nominal Retainers

1. Members of the Bureau of the Court, of the Conciliation Commissions and of the Arbitral Tribunals shall receive, for each day on which they exercise their functions, a daily allowance.

2. Members of the Bureau of the Court shall additionally receive a nominal annual retainer.

3. The daily allowance and the nominal annual retainer shall be determined by the representatives of the States parties to the Convention.

Article 7
Salaries, Social Security and Pensions

1. The Registrar and any other registry staff appointed in accordance with Article 9 of the Convention shall receive a salary to be determined by the representatives of the States parties to the Convention.

2. The registry staff shall be limited to the strict minimum needed to ensure the operation of the Court.

3. The representatives of the States parties to the Convention shall ensure that the Registrar and the registry staff are afforded an adequate social security scheme and retirement pension.

Article 8
Travel Expenses

1. Travel expenses which are absolutely necessary for exercising their functions shall be paid to the members of the Bureau of the Court, of the Conciliation Commissions and of the Arbitral Tribunals and to the Registrar and the registry staff.

2. Travel expenses shall compromise actual transportation costs, including expenses normally incidental to transportation, and a daily subsistence allowance to cover all charges of meals, lodging, fees and gratuities and other personal expenses. The daily subsistence allowance shall be determined by the representatives of the States parties to the Convention.

Article 9
Records and Accounts

1. The Registrar, acting under the authority of the Bureau of the Court, shall ensure that appropriate records and accounts are kept of the transactions and that all payments are properly authorized.

2. The Registrar, acting under the authority of the Bureau of Court, shall submit to the States parties to the Convention, not later than 1 March, an annual financial statement showing, for the preceding financial year:

   (a) the income and expenditures relating to all accounts;

   (b) the situation with regard to budget provisions;

(c) the financial assets and liabilities at the end of the financial year.

Article 10
Audit

1. The accounts of the Court shall be audited by two auditors, of different nationalities, appointed for renewable periods of three years by the representatives of the States parties to the Convention.

Persons appearing or having appeared on the lists of conciliators or arbitrators or having received payment by the Court pursuant to Article 7 of this Protocol may not be auditors.

2. Auditors shall annually conduct audits. They shall, in particular, check the accuracy of the books, the statement of assets and liabilities, and the accounts. The accounts shall be available for the annual auditing and inspection not later than 1 March.

3. Auditors shall perform such audits as they deem necessary to certify:

(a) that the annual financial statement submitted to them is correct and in accordance with the books and records of the Court,

(b) that the financial transactions recorded in this statement have been effected in accordance with the relevant rules, the budgetary provisions and other directives which may be applicable, and

(c) that the funds on deposit and on hand have been verified by certificates received directly from the depositories or by actual count.

4. The Registrar shall give auditors such assistance and facilities as may be needed for the proper discharge of their duties. Auditors shall, in particular, have free access to the books of account, records and documents which, in their opinion, are necessary for the audit.

5. Auditors shall annually draw up a report certifying the accounts and setting forth the comments warranted by the audit. They may, in this context, also make such observations as they deem necessary regarding the efficiency of financial procedures, the accounting system and the internal financial control.

6. The report shall be submitted to the representatives of the States parties to the Convention not later than four months after the end of the financial year to which the accounts refer. The report shall be transmitted to the Registrar beforehand, so that he will have at least 15 days in which to furnish such explanations and justifications as he may consider necessary.

7. In addition to the annual auditing, auditors will at any time have free access to check the books, the statement of assets and liabilities, and accounts.

8. On the basis of the audit report, the representatives of the States parties to the Convention shall signify their acceptance of the annual financial statement or take such other action as may be considered appropriate.

Article 11
Special Disbursement Account

1. A special disbursement account may be established by the States parties to the Convention aimed at lowering the procedural costs for the States parties to disputes submitted to the Court which have difficulties paying these costs. It will be funded by voluntary contributions from States parties to the Convention.

2. A State party to a dispute submitted to the Court that wishes to receive funds from the special disbursement account shall file a request to the Registrar, with a detailed statement estimating procedural costs.

   The Bureau of the Court shall examine the request and forward its recommendations to the representatives of the States parties to the Convention which shall decide whether to grant this request and to what extent.

   After the case has been heard, the State having received funds from the special disbursement account shall address to the Registrar, for study by the Bureau, a detailed statement of procedural costs actually expended and shall proceed, if need be, with reimbursing the sums in excess of the actual costs.

Article 12
Decision Making

All decisions by the States parties to the Convention or their representatives under this Protocol shall be taken by consensus.

Article 13
Amendments

Amendments to this Protocol shall be adopted in accordance with the provisions of Article 35 of the Convention. The Bureau of the Court may address its opinion on the proposed amendments to the CSCE Secretariat for transmission to the CSCE participating States.

* * * * *

This Protocol, established in the English, French, German, Italian, Russian and Spanish languages, all six language versions being equally authentic, having been adopted by the Committee of Senior Officials at Prague, on 28 April 1993 in accordance with Article 13 of the Convention on Conciliation and Arbitration within the CSCE is deposited with the Government of Sweden.

TWENTY-SECOND CSO MEETING

Prague, 29-30 June 1993

Text on Nagorny-Karabakh[1]

The Committee of Senior Officials

- reiterates its deep concern at the continuation of the conflict dealt with by the Conference on Nagorno-Karabakh;

- welcomes the acceptance by all parties of a plan proposed to them by the Chairman of the Minsk Conference, the Honourable Mario Raffaelli, on behalf of nine countries of the Minsk Group, including a timetable of urgent steps to implement UN Security Council resolution 822;

- calls for the earliest possible entry into force of the plan;

- urges all parties to refrain from any action that may jeopardize the implementation of the plan;

- welcomes the intention of the Chairman of the Minsk Conference to carry out, together with a representative of the Chairman-in-Office, an early visit to the area on the basis of assurances by all parties of their readiness to implement the agreed plan, and in order to facilitate its implementation;

- urges the appropriate CSCE bodies to pursue actively the preparations currently under way for the sending of the CSCE Verification and Monitoring Missions to the area of conflict.

* * *

---

1 22-CSO/Journal No. 1, Annex 2. (Title added by the Editor.)

Report by the Chairman-in-Office on her visit to the newly admitted participating States of Central Asia[2]

The Committee of Senior Officials

- Welcomes the report by the Chairman-in-Office on her visit to the participating States of Central Asia, undertaken in accordance with the request of the Council at its Third Meeting in Stockholm;

- Welcomes the commitment to the CSCE in all its aspects which was expressed to the Chairman-in-Office by the leadership of all the five participating States in Central Asia;

- Stresses that the participation by the Central Asian States in the CSCE work and the establishment to that end of permanent representations in Vienna are matters of high priority and encourages other participating States to support the establishment of such representations;

- Requests the Chairman-in-Office to consult with those participating States that have embassies in the Central Asian CSCE States on practical arrangements to facilitate the transmission of information to and from the Central Asian participating States;

- Decides that the Programme of co-ordinated support for recently admitted participating States established in the Helsinki Document should contain, *inter alia*, a series of seminars to be arranged in Central Asian capitals over the period until the 1994 Budapest Review Conference;

- Requests the Secretary General to work out a suitable programme of regional seminars based on the outline in paragraph 22 of the report by the Chairman-in-Office and including, accordingly,

  a seminar on regional security issues organized by the CPC,

  a regional seminar on human dimension issues organized by the ODIHR and,

  subject to consultations by the Chairman-in-Office with interested participating States and international organizations, a seminar along the lines suggested by the Economic Forum on a topic of particular

---

[2] 22-CSO/Journal No. 1, Annex 3.

relevance to the process of transition to market economies in the region;

- Requests the ODIHR to explore in consultation with the Council of Europe ways and means to provide training and assistance to Central Asian States in their efforts to establish societies based on the rule of law;

- Further requests the ODIHR to explore the need for technical assistance in the fields of constitutional law, judicial structures and other relevant fields to other Central Asian States along the lines of assistance agreed to be provided to Tajikistan;

- Stresses the need for the involvement in CSCE seminars and other activities not only of government representatives but also of individuals outside government and of non-governmental organizations, in particular from the newly admitted States themselves;

- Requests the Secretary General to analyze the financial implications of providing Russian translations of additional documentation, in particular 'CSCE Communications';

- Recognizes with appreciation the work of the CSCE Communications Network Team in providing to Central Asian Governments end user stations for connection with the CSCE Communications Network and encourages the Project Leader to pursue his discussions toward this end;

- Endorses the view expressed in the report that the CSCE Parliamentary Assembly can make a significant contribution by extending its contacts to the parliaments of the Central Asian participating States;

- Requests the Secretary General to visit the participating States of Central Asia as a follow-up to the visit by the Chairman-in-Office;

- Requests the Chairman-in-Office to submit to the CSO or the CSO Vienna Group detailed proposals as required for the implementation of the measures outlined above.

* * *

Text on Georgia[3]

The Committee of Senior Officials heard the report of the Personal Representative of the Chairman-in-Office to Georgia and discussed the latest developments in Georgia, in the Autonomous Republic of Abkhazia and in the area of the Georgian-Ossetian conflict.

The CSO expressed its grave concern at the renewed violation of the cease-fire in Abkhazia and called on all parties concerned to cease immediately all hostilities and facilitate the early deployment of international military observers in the region. The CSO also urged all States of the region to exercise restraint and avoid any interference in the conflict.

The CSO endorsed the report of the Personal Representative and expressed its satisfaction with the activities of the CSCE Mission to Georgia. The CSO decided to prolong the mandate of the Mission for an additional six months and instructed the Financial Committee to submit a new budget for that period to the CSO Vienna Group for approval.

The CSO reiterated its conviction, as reflected in the mandate of the Mission, that the conflicts on the territory of the Republic of Georgia should be approached within the framework of international efforts of the United Nations and the CSCE working in close co-operation and with the authority of both organizations.

The CSO endorsed the proposal of the Personal Representative of the Chairman-in-Office to Georgia to hold two conferences under the auspices of the United Nations and the CSCE devoted to the resolution of these conflicts under United Nations and CSCE Chairmanship respectively. The CSO further authorized the Chairman-in-Office to invite United Nations participation in the activities of the CSCE Mission to Georgia and to offer CSCE participation in a United Nations operation in Georgia in accordance with the relevant statement of the President of the United Nations Security Council. Modalities for such participation should be developed by the Chairman-in-Office in co-operation with the United Nations.

The CSO requested the Chairman-in-Office to take urgent steps in order to ensure the speedy implementation of these decisions and keep CSCE participating States informed about all developments.

---

[3] 22-CSO/Journal No. 2, Annex 1. (Title added by the Editor.)

Text on Estonia[4]

The Committee of Senior Officials notes with concern the problems related to recent developments in the situation of the Russian-speaking population in Estonia, and in relations between Estonia and Russia. It urges both parties to demonstrate their abiding commitment to CSCE norms and principles. That commitment requires all parties to take steps conducive to dialogue and improved relations. The CSO requests the Chairman-in-Office to review with the Governments concerned progress achieved in this respect.

The Committee of Senior Officials paid special attention to problems related to the laws on local elections and on the status of aliens. It invites the High Commissioner on National Minorities to respond promptly, on behalf of the CSCE, to the request by the President of Estonia for an expert opinion from the CSCE on the law on the status of aliens.[5] The CSO supports the continued involvement of the High Commissioner in Estonia. It invites the Government of Estonia to take appropriate action in response to the recommendations of the High Commissioner on National Minorities contained in CSCE Communication No. 124.

The Committee of Senior Officials emphasizes the need for intensified efforts to promote integration and better understanding between the communities in Estonia. It underlines the vital importance of the work of the CSCE Mission to Estonia in this respect and requests the Head of Mission to encourage and promote practical steps intended to facilitate inter-communal dialogue. The CSO notes with satisfaction the announcement by the President of Estonia on the establishment of a Round Table of non-citizens and ethnic minorities. It requests the Head of the CSCE Mission to Estonia to explore with the Government of Estonia and with participants in the Round Table opportunities for co-operation with and assistance from the CSCE.

* * *

---

[4] 22-CSO/Journal No. 2, Annex 2. (Title added by the Editor.)

[5] Editor's note: The text of the letter, sent by the High Commissioner on National Minorities to the President of Estonia on 1 July 1993, is reproduced in the section "Documents of the High Commissioner on National Minorities" in the present volume (*infra* part V).

Text on the former Yugoslavia[6]

The CSCE participating States remain firmly committed to all CSCE principles and undertakings. These form the basis for their efforts to fully contribute to an end to the conflict in Bosnia-Herzegovina and Croatia.

The Committee of Senior Officials reaffirmed the commitment of the participating States to a durable and fair political solution based on the principles agreed by all parties at the London Conference including the sovereignty of the Republic of Bosnia-Herzegovina, the inviolability of its territorial integrity, respect for its pluralistic character, protection of human rights and the rights of national minorities and the democratic political rights of the peoples of Bosnia-Herzegovina, and the inadmissibility of acquisition of territory by force. Such a peace settlement has to find the free consent of all parties in Bosnia-Herzegovina.

They are determined to continue and strengthen the important role of the CSCE in containing the crisis and preventing its spillover to new areas, in supporting the implementation of the United Nations sanctions regime and in counteracting violations of human rights. In this context the Committee of Senior Officials has decided the following:

1. Missions of Long Duration

The Missions of Long Duration to Kosovo, Sandjak and Vojvodina provide an essential means of preventing conflict by fostering dialogue between the Serbian and non-Serbian populations of these areas. Any attempt to hamper the operation of the missions or to limit their presence would constitute a serious setback to efforts to try to bring an end to the tragic conflicts in the former Yugoslavia.

Acceptance by the authorities of the Federal Republic of Yugoslavia (Serbia and Montenegro) of their presence on a long-term basis is an important test of the willingness of these authorities to contribute to the goal of long-term peace and stability in the region and must not be predicated upon any other issue.

The CSO requested the Chairman-in-Office, together with the Troika, to maintain contact with the relevant authorities in the Federal Republic of Yugoslavia (Serbia and Montenegro) to ensure continuation of the Memorandum

---

6 22-CSO/Journal No. 2, Annex 3. (Title added by the Editor.)

of Understanding and improved efficiency of this important long-term contribution of the CSCE to the peace process.

Pursuant to the decision of the Stockholm Council Meeting in December 1992 to increase substantially the size of these missions and in order to ensure successful continuation of the work of the missions, the CSO tasked the Vienna Group to focus in particular on expansion of activities in Kosovo, Sandjak and Vojvodina and on identifying additional categories of personnel who may be assigned there as the operation evolves.

2. *Human Rights in Serbia*

The Helsinki Summit Declaration and other CSCE documents make clear that commitments undertaken in the field of the human dimension of the CSCE are matters of direct and legitimate concern to all participating States and do not belong exclusively to the internal affairs of the State concerned. A lasting peace cannot be achieved if democratic standards are not maintained everywhere in the former Yugoslavia.

The human rights violations in Serbia-Montenegro, in particular the imprisonment and beating of Vuk Draskovic and Danica Draskovic, have been condemned by the Chairman-in-Office and by CSCE participating States. The CSO demands the granting of international access to Vuk and Danica Draskovic and full clarification of the circumstances of their imprisonment and injuries.

The CSO decides to send a CSCE rapporteur mission to Serbia-Montenegro in accordance with paragraph 13, Chapter I of the Document of the Moscow Meeting of the Conference on the Human Dimension of the CSCE.

The tasks of the mission will be:

- to investigate fully reports of human rights violations in Serbia-Montenegro, in particular the beating and imprisonment of Vuk and Danica Draskovic and the reported banning of the Serbian Renewal Movement;

- to discuss the situation fully with government, opposition and other leaders;

- to give advice on possible solutions to the questions raised.

The mission's report shall be presented to the ODIHR for circulation to participating States no later than one week after completion of the visit. Its conclusions and recommendations will be discussed in the CSO Vienna Group.

In consultation with the Chairman-in-Office, the ODIHR is requested to identify rapporteurs and take necessary steps to facilitate immediate departure of the mission. In accordance with paragraph 14, Chapter I of the Moscow Document, the expenses for the mission will be covered by the participating States in accordance with the usual scale of distribution of expenses.

3. Implementation of United Nations Sanctions against Serbia-Montenegro

The Committee of Senior Officials examined the implementation of sanctions against Serbia-Montenegro. It called upon all participating States to ensure, in accordance with commitments under United Nations Security Council resolutions, the strictest implementation of the sanctions and urged those that pledged additional officers for the Sanctions Assistance Missions (SAMs) to deploy them as soon as possible.

The Committee took special note of the problems with enforcement of sanctions in the former Yugoslav Republic of Macedonia (FYROM), as outlined in the report of the SAM team leaders' 3 June meeting and the EC/CSCE Sanctions Co-ordinator's report of the 4 June Sanctions Liaison Group meeting. To help bolster sanctions enforcement in the FYROM, the Committee of Senior Officials decides to:

- Call on the participating States to substantially increase the size of the SAM in FYROM to possibly 70 in order to allow for an increase in the number of border crossings monitored and for 24-hour coverage of those crossings;

- Enhance the existing co-ordination of sanctions monitoring activities in FYROM. The Head of the Spillover Mission to Skopje should in close consultation with the EC/CSCE Sanctions Co-ordinator designate a diplomat of the Mission to handle sanctions issues on a full-time basis in close co-ordination with the SAM team leader, the Sanctions Co-ordinator's office and SAMCOMM;

- Task the Sanctions Co-ordinator to continue his efforts to enhance sanctions enforcement in the FYROM and to work for vigorous implementation of the above measures.

IV

DOCUMENTS

OF THE

CSCE PARLIAMENTARY ASSEMBLY

MADRID PARLIAMENTARY CONFERENCE

FINAL RESOLUTION CONCERNING THE ESTABLISHMENT OF THE CSCE PARLIAMENTARY ASSEMBLY

2-3 April 1991

The delegations of the Parliaments of countries participating in the Conference on Security and Co-operation in Europe, meeting in Madrid, on April 2nd and 3rd 1991,

Considering the provisions of the Paris Charter for a New Europe which, in recognition of the important role that parliamentarians can play in the CSCE process, calls for the establishment of a CSCE Parliamentary Assembly,

Considering that the aforesaid Assembly should meet the following criteria: structural simplicity (in view of the simplicity of the CSCE's political structures); plurality in its composition (reflecting the values of pluralistic parliamentary democracy); and willingness to use the resources of other European parliamentary institutions (including the Parliamentary Assembly of the Council of Europe, the Parliamentary Assembly of the WEU, the North Atlantic Assembly and, at a different level, the European Parliament - all of which must preserve their individual identities and organizational structures while maintaining close co-operative ties with the Assembly now being established).

Agree to establish within the framework of the Conference on Security and Co-operation in Europe a Parliamentary Assembly which shall function in accordance with the following rules of organization and operation:

1. The CSCE's Parliamentary Assembly will be composed of 245 parliamentarians representing participating countries. The number of members representing each country shall be as follows:

   A. Union of Soviet Socialist Republics and United States of America: 17

   B. Germany, France, Italy and United Kingdom: 13

   C. Canada and Spain: 10

D. Belgium, Netherlands, Poland, Sweden and Turkey: 8

E. Romania and Yugoslavia: 7

F. Austria, Czech and Slovak Federative Republic, Denmark, Ireland, Finland, Greece, Hungary, Norway, Portugal, Switzerland: 6

G. Bulgaria and Luxembourg: 5

H. Cyprus, Iceland, and Malta: 3

I. Liechtenstein, Monaco and San Marino: 2

The Holy See may send two representatives to the Assembly's meetings as guests of honour.

2. The CSCE's Parliamentary Assembly will hold a plenary annual meeting for a period of not more than five days. This meeting will normally be held during the first week of July in the capital or in another city of a State participating in the CSCE. The host country will provide the necessary support for the organization and conduct of the meeting.

3. There will be a Committee of Heads of Delegation composed of one representative from each country participating in the Assembly.

4. The purpose of the annual meeting of the Parliamentary Assembly will be:

   a) To assess the implementation of the objectives of the CSCE.

   b) To discuss subjects addressed during the meetings of the Council of Ministers for Foreign Affairs and the biennial Summit of Heads of State or Government.

   c) To initiate and promote whatever measures may further co-operation and security in Europe.

5. At its annual meeting, the Parliamentary Assembly may approve declarations, recommendations or proposals, or submit reports on subjects related to its activities. The decisions of the Assembly will be adopted by majority vote of its full membership. In special cases the

Committee of Heads of Delegation may determine that a specific agreement would require a two-thirds majority.

The Assembly will provide the Parliaments of States participating in the CSCE with regular reports of its work and will transmit its decisions to the Council of Ministers for its consideration.

6. The Committee of Heads of Delegation will be responsible for taking all decisions concerning the operation, organization and rules of procedure of the Assembly, as well as those concerning working methods, the establishment of new organs, the budget, secretariat, agenda, extraordinary meetings and place of meeting. Decisions of the Committee shall be reached by consensus.

7. The Assembly will have a small permanent secretariat whose budget, resources, mode of operation and headquarters will be established by the Committee of Heads of Delegation. Until such time as the inaugural meeting called for under the rule 11 is held, the General Secretariats of the Spanish Parliament will perform the customary duties of the secretariat of the Assembly.

8. The official languages of the Assembly will be English, French, German, Italian, Russian and Spanish.

9. In recognition of the acknowledged parliamentary experience of the international and supranational organizations mentioned in this Resolution, it was decided to propose to the first meeting of the Parliamentary Assembly that agreements should be reached to permit effective co-operation between these organizations and the Assembly, which might include according observer status.

10. The funding necessary for the operations of the Parliamentary Assembly will be apportioned amongst its members, as from the date of this Resolution, on the basis of an agreement reached by the Committee of Heads of Delegation at its first meeting.

11. The Parliamentary Assembly will hold its inaugural meeting during the first week of July 1992, in the city of Budapest. Exceptionally, after discussion within the respective Delegations, the Committee of Heads of Delegation may communicate the position of Delegations forming part of the Assembly, before the Helsinki follow-up meeting to be held in the Spring of 1992.

12. The Spanish Parliament, in its capacity as host of this inaugural meeting, will inform the Council of Ministers for Foreign Affairs of the CSCE of the decisions adopted.

13. Amendments to the rules set forth in this Resolution will be decided upon by consensus by the Committee of Heads of Delegation of the Parliamentary Assembly.

14. The delegations present at the Madrid meeting, the first official gathering of parliamentarians representing the Parliaments of the thirty-four signatory States of the CSCE, express their profound appreciation to the Spanish Government and Spanish Parliament for their initiative in organizing the Madrid meeting and for their outstanding contribution to the establishment of a permanent CSCE Assembly. The delegations express their particular gratitude to the President of the Spanish Congress of Deputies.

BUDAPEST DECLARATION OF THE CSCE PARLIAMENTARY ASSEMBLY

5 July 1992

We, parliamentary representatives of the CSCE participating States met in Budapest on July 3-5, 1992, as the parliamentary forum of the Charter of Paris to offer our advice to CSCE Ministers.

We welcome the representatives of the new CSCE participating States, sharing our principles and values.

We recognize that the management of change can only be successful if pluralist parliamentary democracy, respect for human rights, including minority rights, the rule of law, economic freedom and social justice gain deep roots in our countries and respect for these values is translated into everyday practice.

Aggressive nationalism, violation of minority rights, uncontrolled armed forces and the enormous difficulties accompanying the transition to market economy threaten the stability in the CSCE area and our objective to bring peace, democracy and prosperity to it.

The CSCE has returned to Helsinki after two decades to embark upon a new path full of opportunities and challenges. The CSCE Parliamentary Assembly wishes all success to the Meeting of Heads of Governments of the CSCE participating States to be held on July 9-10, 1992 and brings to their attention the following declarations and recommendations adopted by the CSCE Parliamentary Assembly:

Chapter I SECURITY QUESTIONS

The CSCE and European security

1. Security and stability in today's Europe are dependent on political, economic and environmental, as well as military factors. The major sources of instability are the deteriorating economic and social conditions in Central and Eastern Europe (CEE) as well as political and nationalist (ethnic) disputes which have resulted in several violent and bloody armed conflicts. Europe must find the means to deal with this endemic instability. The most urgent task is to assist the political and economic reforms now under way in CEE. The failure to improve

social conditions will ultimately undermine public support for democracy with serious consequences for the whole of Europe.

2. The deepening of democratic processes represents an essential factor in the reinforcement of European security. Human rights compliance represents an integral element of the European security system. There can be no secure system in any region where there is the violation of essential human rights, including those of national minorities.

3. The CSCE is the only European and transatlantic organisation both in terms of membership and mandate that is able to address the multiple sources of instability in Europe. However, the institutional structures and procedures of the CSCE must be further strengthened. In particular the CSCE must be given the procedures and means to act effectively in preventing and resolving conflict situations both within and between states. These means should include the ability to mandate clearly and precisely peace-keeping activities.

4. As the only institution that embraces all European and North American countries, and with its comprehensive mandate, the CSCE must represent the hope and the future as the framework in which Europe's security concerns can be addressed effectively. At the same time, the CSCE should make use of the organisational capabilities, experience, and infrastructure of regional organizations, such as the WEU, NATO, the EC, and the Peace-keeping Mechanism of the CIS.

5. Armed forces will continue to perform an important function in all countries. In view of the existing tension in many parts of Europe the size, structure and deployment of these forces could be a potential source of friction. It is understood, and in compliance with the CSCE principles and aims, that peace and security are established among all CSCE member States; therefore, it is necessary to withdraw without delay any troops or forces of any CSCE country which are stationed or occupy illegally part of another CSCE country, thus terminating such situation that may exist. Arms control has a key role to play in minimizing misunderstanding and encouraging mutual confidence. The new Forum for Security Cooperation (FSC) should build on the CFE Treaty and the existing CSBMs to further reduce and constrain the levels and types of armaments, increase security dialogue and develop cooperative measures that emphasize transparency and openness of military forces and activities.

6. Nuclear weapons are still kept but with roles that are now much more difficult to define; the traditional concept of nuclear deterrence is substantially diminished. All efforts must now be directed at preventing proliferation and ensuring that such weapons are at the lowest possible levels. A new and sensitive approach to the management, reduction, destruction, and elimination of nuclear weapons is an all-CSCE concern.

7. Constraining the proliferation of weapons and weapons technology demands more creative and cooperative action within a CSCE framework. With regard to nuclear and chemical weapons, cautious optimism is in order, though continued vigilance is essential. However, on the question of the proliferation of conventional weapons and technologies, serious dialogue must begin within the CSCE. The establishment of a Working Group of the FSC is recommended.

8. The reduction and restructuring of armed forces and the consequent contraction of defence industry are causing economic and social problems in all countries. These problems are particularly severe in countries in CEE. Western cooperation and assistance is urgently needed. In particular Western nations should give serious consideration to providing special assistance to the CIS countries in order to facilitate the speedy withdrawal of the former USSR forces from the Central and East European countries. In this context, the withdrawal of former USSR troops still remaining on the territories of the Baltic states without their consent has to be completed in the shortest terms and under international observation provided by the assisting countries. It must be also taken into account that a timely solution of the social and economic problems of military personnel is a necessary condition for maintaining stability during the withdrawal of military forces.

9. Democracy is the best guarantor of peace. It is essential that armed forces in all countries are subordinate to democratic civilian governments. Elected parliaments must have the ultimate authority and responsibility for the activities of the military forces.

10. The Parliamentary Assembly states that the present evolution of the situation regarding security in Europe demands a new examination of the objectives and procedures of the CSCE. It considers that it is necessary to go beyond the Charter of Paris and to envisage a security structure more coherent and more binding.

The Parliamentary Assembly wishes to transform the CSCE into a regional security organization as provided for in Chapter VIII of the United Nations Charter and to give it a legal base.

11. The deep-going political transformations in Central and Eastern Europe should in no way weaken the already achieved success of the CSCE process that has led to increased military security in Europe. Countries of the CSCE that have not yet ratified the CFE Treaty are urged to do so as soon as possible and fully implement it. Levels of military personnel (including paramilitary units) should be declared by all member States.

12. Parliaments and parliamentarians of the CSCE should participate more actively in the prevention, management and settlement of conflicts. When regional tensions arise, multilateral meetings of parliamentarians of countries concerned should be arranged to foster democratic and peaceful solutions. In this task, the assistance of the CPC in Vienna and ODIHR in Warsaw could be useful.

13. Prevention and containment of conflicts should continue to be the permanent task of the CSCE processes and structures. The idea of mandatory conciliation and arbitration should be encouraged, including the possibility of establishing a special forum or chamber for the purpose.

14. We wish that the CSCE continues its efforts in order to settle peacefully conflicts and establishes a convention which reinforces the conciliation and arbitration procedures.

15. The Committee acknowledges and appreciates the work of the North Atlantic Assembly in the preparation and functioning of the meeting of the Committee. The Committee looks forward to a continuation of this cooperation.

The presence of the former Soviet army in the Baltic countries

The CSCE Parliamentary Assembly:

1. Aware of the legitimate desire of the Baltic nations to live within sovereign states, and the incompatibility existing between this desire and the presence of foreign armed forces on their national territory;

2. Having in particular taken note of the results of the referendum as a result of which a great majority of Lithuanians declared themselves in favour of a withdrawal of ex-Soviet forces from their national territory;

3. Noting that some 130,000 ex-Soviet army soldiers are still stationed on the territories of the Lithuanian Republic, Estonia and Latvia;

4. Fearing that this situation could, with time, create tension between states of a nature to jeopardize peace and security in this part of Europe;

5. Having taken note of President Yeltsin's commitment to accelerate negotiations around the timing of retreat;

6. Aware of the internal economic and social problems caused within the Community of Independent States by a return to their home country of ex-Soviet armed forces, particularly with regard to housing;

7. Supporting the idea of a European political order within which all human rights and those of national minorities in these states are fully respected in accordance with the provisions of the UN Charter on Human Rights and all CSCE documents in this field.

Invites:

- the Russian government to finalize as soon as possible the return home of all ex-Soviet army forces present on the territories of the Baltic States;

- the governments of the member states of the Conference on Security and Cooperation in Europe to adopt all necessary measures with a view to granting financial assistance for the return home of these armed forces, and to negotiate the conditions with all concerned parties.

New mechanisms for CSCE peacekeeping

The CSCE Parliamentary Assembly:

1. Deplores the continuing violence and conflicts that are unfortunately occurring between members of the CSCE;

2. Considers that the CSCE must give priority to developing effective mechanisms for initiating peacekeeping operations capable of preventing conflict;

3. Recognising that the CSCE currently lacks the means to undertake such peacekeeping missions itself;

4. Urges the Council of Ministers to address urgently making collaboration arrangements with other multilateral organizations and individual member countries which have the means to undertake peacekeeping missions and which could respond to calls from the CSCE and establish the mechanism to begin working on the planning and coordination of peacekeeping efforts.

CSCE and environmental cooperation

The CSCE Parliamentary Assembly:

1. *Considering* that security means more than military security and that security has an environmental aspect;

2. *Aware of* the interdependence between the military and the environmental sectors and that military resources could be used in the fight for a better environment;

3. *Referring to* the report presented by the UN Secretary General to the UNCED.

Invites member countries and defence organizations to study the possibilities of - within the framework of the CSCE - integrating military-related resources into environmental strategies, using military means to strengthen the quick response capabilities for dealing with environmental emergencies, and using military means for environmental impact-assessment and decision-making.

Chapter II ECONOMIC QUESTIONS

Economic cooperation

1. We, the parliamentarians, assembled together from the CSCE participating States, representing our citizens, both men and women, and conscious of our many cultural, political, national and economical diversities, are committed to advance the interests of our peoples by

democratic means and international cooperation. As elected parliamentarians we recognise the fundamental importance of soundly based economic systems which will enable individuals freely to pursue their own interests.

2. We feel that a market economy, democracy and government by rule of law are elements that belong together and are inseparable values. We understand that the essential elements of a market economy are private ownership, contractual freedom, free competition, free trade unions, free formation of prices. Such a free and social market economy means an appropriate mix of public and private instruments and must respect social justice and take into account the ecological and welfare needs of the human being, working towards full employment.

3. We recognise in particular that the Europe under the CSCE must demand without delay the construction of an economic framework that will rapidly provide the essentials of democratic economic development.

4. Due to the growing interdependence of the national economies, it is more and more important to create the basic conditions for the reinforcement of European security, through the achievement of non-inflationary and environmentally-friendly economic growth, full employment and the dismantling of protectionist obstacles to the movement of capital, goods, people and ideas among CSCE participating States. In this context it is vital that the GATT negotiations should conclude rapidly with significant and positive results.

5. The recent efforts of the European Community and the EFTA member countries to create a European Economic Area constitute an important step towards the future integration of the new Central and Eastern European democracies. It is also essential that the CSCE participating States mutually open up their markets.

6. It is evident that the transition from a planned and controlled economic system to a free and social market economy is complex and is connected with considerable risks and dangers. Therefore it is essential to proceed in a responsible and balanced manner in order to avoid irreparable economic, social and ecological distortions.

7. Although we admit that the economic gap between the EC member states and the economies in transition of Central and Eastern Europe

and the countries of the CIS is still very wide - making their accession to the EC in the short term very difficult - we consider it essential that new association agreements with the Community be concluded and that existing ones be improved so as to institutionalise stronger European economic cooperation; it is urgent to eliminate the wide economic disparities between nations with very strong historic bonds on each side of Europe, though they have been apart in most of this century for ideological reasons.

8. On the other hand, the CSCE should make full use of the experience and competence of such institutions as the Council of Europe, the North Atlantic Assembly, the Organisation for Economic Cooperation and Development, the Economic Commission for Europe of the United States [*sic*] and the Commission of the European Communities with a view to introducing or strengthening market economies in Central and Eastern Europe and the countries of the CIS and to creating the instruments for cooperation and development.

9. In order to make relations between all CSCE participating States more effective and transparent, we invite the European Bank for Reconstruction and Development (EBRD), the Commission of the European Communities and other international and national bodies concerned (*e.g.* ECE-UN, OECD, IMF, World Bank, Chambers of Commerce) to present regular reports on plans and projects concerning cooperation with the CSCE economies in transition, wishing to develop free market economy without jeopardizing for too long the well-being of their populations. In order to increase the effectiveness of international aid and cooperation, the countries and organizations concerned should better coordinate their various assistance programmes.

10. Although the economic conjuncture is not very encouraging, since there are no firm signs yet of an economic upturn in the industrialised countries, we believe that the next G7 Summit to be held in Munich in July 1992 should decide on the various ways of helping Central and Eastern Europe and the countries of the CIS, notably with regard to practical measures (*e.g.* business and management courses, legal cooperation, privatisation, stock-markets, venture capital, investment guarantees, triangular forms of cooperation).

11. In order to promote balanced development in the CSCE countries in transition greater attention should be paid to setting up new forms of cooperation designed to improve the infrastructure - notably with

regard to communications - and increase these countries' capabilities in the field of public and private research. In this respect CSCE member governments should consider the conclusion of cooperation agreements.

12. Furthermore, we believe that the universities and technological institutes of EC and EFTA countries and the USA and Canada should set up joint cooperation programmes with similar institutions in the countries of Central and Eastern Europe and of the CIS.

13. We congratulate the Council of the CSCE on the setting up of an Economic Forum in the framework of the Committee of Senior Civil Servants and request to be associated with its work as the representatives of the parliaments of the CSCE member States.

14. We believe that the transition towards political and economic liberalisation in the CSCE countries in transition should be backed by special programmes in order to reduce the high risks of pollution they have to face, as a result of bad infrastructures and inadequate energy and industrial policies.

15. Finally, we invite each national parliament to devote every year a session or a debate to the state of progress in CSCE cooperation.

Chapter III HUMAN DIMENSION QUESTIONS

The human dimension

A.

The CSCE Parliamentary Assembly,

1. Stresses the importance of the parliamentary dimension of CSCE and the need for parliaments to follow the work more closely;

2. Expresses its concern that existing CSCE mechanisms such as the improved Moscow Mechanism on the Human Dimension are not sufficiently used;

3. Stresses the need to avoid unnecessary duplication and to make full use of the experience of existing organizations, and especially the Council of Europe;

4. Recognizes the valuable contribution of the Women's CSCE Seminar in Helsinki, held on 4-5 June 1992 and stresses the importance of the active participating of women in the work of the CSCE, including in its institutions;

5. Recognizes the important contribution to the Human Dimension made by NGOs;

6. Believes that the current situation in Europe urgently demands the strengthening of the CSCE Conflict Prevention Mechanism;

7. Urges the Council of Ministers to focus on concrete action and results by implementing existing provisions and making full use of existing mechanisms, ahead of the creation of new ones;

8. Requests the Council of Ministers to authorize the Office on Democratic Institutions and Human Rights to organize seminars on the development of democratic institutions, migration and the role of women in the political process.

B.

The CSCE Parliamentary Assembly,

1. Considers that the problems of minorities are the heart of the questions of human rights which concern all States and that in many regions of Europe conflicts concerning minorities are simmering, the eruption of which could seriously threaten peace in Europe;

2. Recognizes that in any case since the meeting of experts on national minorities in Geneva (1991), intervention to help national minorities is no longer considered an interference in the internal affairs of the State in question;

3. Welcomes the existing proposals for the establishment of an Office of a High Commissioner on National Minorities;

4. Believes that CSCE observer missions could form an efficient and appropriate means to give minorities a feeling of protection and alert the authorities of the countries concerned to their responsibilities towards minorities;

5. Recommends that the CSCE send observers, including parliamentarians active in CSCE matters, to Kosovo and Vojvodina and other threatened regions to monitor the protection of minorities. The CSCE should send observers before conflict erupts.

Chapter IV DECLARATION ON YUGOSLAVIA

Yugoslavia

The CSCE Parliamentary Assembly

A.

1. Strongly condemns continuing violence in the former Yugoslavia, in particular in Bosnia-Herzegovina. Although blame attaches to all parties, the greatest share falls to the leadership of Serbia and the Bosnian Serbs;

2. Condemns the continued violation of CSCE commitments by the authorities of Serbia and the denial of fundamental rights and freedoms of ethnic Albanians in Kosovo, and of Hungarian, Muslim and other minorities on the territory of Serbia, especially in Vojvodina, and of Montenegro;

3. Furthermore condemns the attacks on convoys and personnel of international humanitarian organizations trying to bring relief to the afflicted population in Sarajevo and other places in Bosnia-Herzegovina, and demands that violators of humanitarian law be held personally accountable for these violations;

4. Endorses Resolution 757 adopted by the UN Security Council on 30 May 1992 imposing sanctions on the Federal Republic of Yugoslavia (Serbia and Montenegro);

5. Estimates that the members of CSCE have to make all possible efforts to ensure that the United Nation's embargo against Serbia and Montenegro is respected and in order to bring their support to democratic forces in Serbia opposing the policy of the Government;

6. Estimates that in case these measures are not sufficient to obtain a ceasefire, further actions will have to be considered and carried out in order to have international law, human rights, and the rights of

minorities respected; and in order to protect the cultural heritage of humankind;

7. Endorses efforts of the Conference under Lord Carrington's chairmanship and expresses the desire that political negotiations be speeded up so as to solve the remaining legal questions;

8. Expresses support for all UN Security Council measures, including the deployment of peace-keeping forces, for effective delivery of humanitarian assistance and dismayed at continuing hindrance of humanitarian aid to Bosnia-Herzegovina;

9. Supports calls for Croatia and Serbia, as well as Croatian and Serbian militia to withdraw their armed forces to positions held prior to the outbreak of hostilities in 1991 and to seize hostile activities within or adjacent to UN protected areas;

10. Calls for the simultaneous withdrawal of all military units and paramilitary troops from all non-UNPA areas (so-called 'pink-areas'), occupied by Serbian forces;

11. Calls for the withdrawal of all occupation forces from the Dubrovnik area;

12. Calls on the UN peace-keeping forces (UNPROFOR) immediately to take control in the UNPA (United Nations Protected Areas) to enable the return of refugees to their homes;

13. Urges all parties and others concerned to honour their commitments to effect a complete cessation of hostilities and to implement the United Nations peace-keeping plan;

14. Expresses concern over the intolerable situation of the large number of displaced persons in the region;

15. Notes that the claim of Serbia and Montenegro to retain the status of the State of former Yugoslavia has not been accepted and should be resolved according to international law, in particular the Vienna Convention on State Succession;

16. Calls for the short-term recognition of all the former Yugoslavian Republics which correspond to the criteria of international law;

17. Urges all states to support relief efforts and to contribute generously to the planning and reconstruction of industries, farms and towns destroyed during the hostilities;

18. Calls upon CSCE Ministers to consider all necessary action to end the clear violations of the Paris Charter.

*****

B.

1. Expresses its deep astonishment and grave concern over the forceful displacement of the population of non-Serbian ethnic origin from Bosnia-Herzegovina forcing them to emigrate to neighbouring countries;

2. Recommends that an independent team of observers should be dispatched to the regions of armed conflicts in order to monitor the situation concerning refugee problems and in particular the information received about the forced displacement of non-Serbian ethnic minorities;

3. Invites the ODIHR (Office for Democratic Institutions and Human Rights) to monitor respect for the rights of persons in Croatia belonging to national minorities;

4. Invites all States and international organizations concerned to expand their humanitarian assistance to the neighbouring States of the former Yugoslavia which are the receiving countries of the ever-increasing number of refugees.

5. Urges the taking of concrete action that would permit the resettlement of Bosnian refugees, such as the establishment of safe havens within Bosnia-Herzegovina.

* * *

The CSCE Assembly acknowledges and expresses its appreciation for the work of the Parliaments of Hungary and Spain as well as of the Parliamentary Assembly of the Council of Europe and the North Atlantic Assembly which have provided invaluable assistance for the preparation and the running of this inaugural session in Budapest.

Resolution of the CSCE Parliamentary Assembly

With a view to stop the bloody flow from the Dniester banks, the CSCE Parliamentary Assembly:

1. Requires urgent cease-fire between the parties involved in the conflict from the Eastern part of the Republic of Moldova;

2. Asks immediate measures in the respect to obtaining the neutrality of the 14th Army of Russia, which is placed with no legal status on the territory of the Republic of Moldova, independent and sovereign state, member of United Nations, with a view to obtain, as soon as possible, its complete withdrawal.

3. Requires from the Council of Ministers of the CSCE to adopt proper measures in order to fulfil the above.

HELSINKI DECLARATION OF THE CSCE PARLIAMENTARY ASSEMBLY[1]

Helsinki, 9 July 1993

CHAPTER I POLITICAL AFFAIRS AND SECURITY

The CSCE Parliamentary Assembly,

1. *Aware* of the role that members of parliament can play in the process of maintaining peace and security in Europe based on the Charter of Paris;
2. *Convinced* that the holding of free elections, the establishment and strengthening of democratic and rule-of-law structures, as well as the respect of human and minority rights in all CSCE participating states will contribute considerably towards being able to reduce risks of conflict;
3. *Determined* to keep a close watch on the activities of government bodies in this field, and, to this end, develop its relations with the Chairman-in-Office of the Council and with the Secretary General of the CSCE;
4. *Considering* that contributing to the prevention, management and solution of crises caused by national, ethnic or religious tensions, as well as to the strengthening of cooperation between Member States, constitute therefore priority tasks of the CSCE;
5. *Recognizing* that at the Helsinki Summit in July 1992 the CSCE created a comprehensive set of instruments for early warning, conflict prevention and crisis management, involving rapporteur and fact-finding missions, mediation and conciliation efforts, observation and monitoring missions as well as the use of armed forces;
6. *Judging* that the inability of the CSCE and other international institutions to prevent and stifle the war and re-establish the peace in the former Yugoslavia is a consequence of the lack of political will among its members, and that to change the situation in the former Yugoslavia real implementation of resolutions of the Security Council, including military protection of safe areas, is as important as strengthening the CSCE institutions;
7. *Asking* the governments of CSCE member states to implement fully the UN resolutions and to strengthen CSCE institutions;
8. *Convinced* that justice and implementation of sanctions against Serbia and Montenegro require, in conformity with Article 50 of the United Nations

---

[1] CSCE (2) Plen. 15.

Charter, efforts to compensate for the economic difficulties of certain countries from the region in the strict application of these sanctions;

9. *Pointing out* that the CSCE is a regional arrangement under Chapter VIII of the United Nations Charter, which implies close coordination of its activities with those of the United Nations;
10. *Indicating its satisfaction* that certain measures, tending towards strengthening the CSCE, have already been taken, such as the creation of the function of Secretary General, the High Commissioner for National Minorities and the Forum for Security Cooperation;
11. *Convinced* nevertheless that the implementation of a system of collective security requires more than mere adaptation of institutions, and requires, in particular, a radical modification of the way the CSCE functions;
12. *Persuaded* that because of the disruptive element constituted by the lack of political control over the armed forces in numerous CSCE participating states, the development of democratic control over the armed forces of the former Warsaw Pact countries is urgently needed;
13. *Urges* the Council of Ministers to pursue a more active policy and in particular to adopt the following working principles so as to realize this objective:
    - greater speed in the decision-making process;
    - a decision-making procedure which no longer requires consensus or "consensus minus one";
    - an internal balance avoiding any supremacy or domination by a group of participating states;
    - strengthening internal institutional coherence;
14. *Encourages* the Secretary General, in conformity with these working principles, to coordinate the activities of all the current institutions of the CSCE and limit their geographical dispersion;
15. *Requests* the Secretary General to give thought to the effects on the objectives and procedures of the CSCE of the draft "For a Treaty of Stability of Europe" presented to the European Council in Copenhagen on 21 and 22 June 1993 and to submit his conclusions thereon to the meeting of the CSCE Council of Ministers to be held in Rome in December 1993;
16. *Requests* the Council of Ministers to set up a Council of Permanent Representatives with headquarters in Vienna, with the task of preparing for meetings of the Council and implementing and following-up the decisions of the Council;
17. *Invites* the Council of Ministers to consider setting up a CSCE security committee, based on an annual rotation system between representatives of Member States which would examine all subjects relating to peace keeping and peace enforcement;

18. *Requests* the Council of Ministers, and the Security Committee if it is established, to propose suitable confidence-building and security measures so that progress can be made in dismantling nuclear weapons in the former Soviet Union;
19. *Invites* the Council of Ministers to consider whether a defence counterpart to the CSO, including a subordinate permanent defence planning cell in the CPC, would promote the efficiency of CSCE conflict prevention and peacekeeping;
20. *Requests* the participating States of the CSCE to support in the competent international organizations the immediate implementation of effective measures to alleviate the economic problems of the countries most seriously affected by the United Nations sanctions against Serbia and Montenegro;
21. *Urges* the Council of Ministers to support the work of the High Commissioner for National Minorities and implement his recommendations accordingly;
22. *Urges* the Council of Ministers to actively support the negotiations on a code of conduct in the security field in order to strengthen the political and democratic control of armed forces;
23. *Emphasises* the need to develop political and administrative links with other international organisations operating in the security and cooperation field in Europe, in particular with the United Nations, the Atlantic Alliance, the Western European Union, the Council of Europe and the Commonwealth of Independent States;
24. *Advocates* a prompt implementation of the plan for establishment of a Conference on Security and Cooperation in the Mediterranean;
25. *Wishes* that the Conflict Prevention Centre destined to play a major role in the field of disarmament,
    - should have at its disposal all the information sent by States participating in the United Nations Register and, in consultation with other bodies, should formulate a programme for consideration by the Council of Ministers and Member States to limit the export of weapons from the CSCE countries to neighbouring regions and areas of tension;
    - should be charged with identifying the areas in which regional measures could be taken to prevent an armed conflict breaking out;
    - should make any proposals required to the Committee of Senior Officials, so that preventive measures may be negotiated and implemented with diligence;
26. *Requests* that a report should be submitted to it, concerning the capacities necessary for effective and vigorous action by the CSCE, as a regional arrangement under Chapter VIII of the United Nations Charter, in the field of peace keeping and peace enforcement;

27. *Wishes* to receive in good time all essential documents, and in particular the Annual Report which the Secretary General and other bodies of the CSCE submit to the Council or the Committee of Senior Officials;
28. *Requests* that a CSCE public affairs office be established under the Secretary General able to provide to the public all CSCE proposals, mission reports, implementation data, and agreements, and to increase awareness of CSCE activities in the entire CSCE region;
29. *Wishes* to be associated with missions to areas of tension or potential conflict, and with the actions of the High Commissioner on National Minorities;
30. *Welcomes* the conclusion of the Convention concerning Conciliation and Arbitration, *recommends* the signing and the ratification of the Convention and *invites* the Governments to complete this instrument in order to make it more effective;
31. *Emphasizes* the need to instruct members of the armed forces on international law regulations concerning human rights;
32. *Urges* parliaments and governments of the CSCE Parliamentary Assembly to ensure that sufficient financial and personal resources are made available to the CSCE so that it will be able to fulfil its function effectively;
33. *Determines* to strengthen its own efforts to contribute towards the development and strengthening of democratic structures in the CSCE participating states, since this is a particularly effective form of conflict prevention;
34. *Expresses satisfaction* about the decisions of the United States and Russia to prolong the nuclear weapons test moratorium and *supports* the aspiration of these countries to initiate negotiations on prohibition of nuclear tests;
35. *Considers* this initiative as a concrete step to preserve the Treaty on Non-Proliferation of nuclear weapons;
36. *Remains concerned*, despite substantial progress in the withdrawal of Russian troops from the Baltic region, over the continued presence of Russian military personnel and equipment in Latvia, Lithuania, and Estonia; *notes* that this presence constitutes an ongoing violation of the sovereignty of these states and, in keeping with basic principles of international law and recalling Article 15 of the 1992 Helsinki Summit Declaration, *strongly urges* the Russian Federation to conclude and implement, without further delay, appropriate bilateral agreements, including timetables, for the early, orderly and complete withdrawal of its troops from the territories of the Baltic States.

CHAPTER II ECONOMIC AFFAIRS, SCIENCE, TECHNOLOGY AND ENVIRONMENT

The CSCE Parliamentary Assembly,

1. *Having in mind,* human substance and sense of the whole economic transformation process in the reforming countries, mainly searching for a new quality of life and environment, broader definition of human dimension in development of mankind;
2. *Convinced of the* interdependencies among the three baskets of Helsinki and in particular the close relationship and synergy that exists among common security, human dimension and economic cooperation;
3. *Convinced that* the transition to a market economy system will be of decisive importance for the development and strengthening of democratic and rule-of-law structures in the countries of Central and Eastern Europe and the former Soviet Union;
4. *Referring to the fact that* there cannot be any uniform restructuring process in the reforming countries of Central and Eastern Europe and the former Soviet Union, resulting in reforms being in different stages of advancement;
5. *Realizing the fact that* standard methods, forms and models broadly used in the transformation process of the reforming countries could hardly lead to efficient and in many cases sufficient results because of the variety of their specific and unique extraordinary conditions;
6. *Recognizing* the necessity of identifying and transforming (as fast as possible) negative factors at least into neutral ones, neutral into positive, positive into intensive, intensive into optimal and for that last group of factors to create suitable conditions for their long-term stabilization;
7. *Recognizing that* the breakup of monopolistic production structures, the privatization of companies, as well as the liberalization of price formation and foreign trade are important elements of the economic reform process;
8. *Aware that* the restructuring of economies and the collapse of traditional Eastern markets initially led to a dramatic decline in industrial production;
9. *Aware of* the extensive losses and economic difficulties that certain European States meet with as a result of the strict application of UN sanctions against Serbia and Montenegro;
10. *Taking into account the fact that* in the course of the economic reform processes real-term wage levels declined drastically and the unemployment rate rose strongly in some countries;
11. *Referring to the fact that* the liberalization of foreign trade, in connection with very low labour costs in an international comparison and qualitative competitiveness in certain market segments, has led to an increase in

exports to the Western industrial countries, and that simultaneously the opening up of new Central and Eastern European markets has resulted in a foreign trade surplus of the Western countries; and *recalling* the need to establish equal and mutually advantageous relations between the Western industrial states and the reforming states of Central and Eastern Europe;

12. *In view of the fact that* a recovery with regard to trends in real-term income as well as an improvement in the difficult employment situation have emerged in some countries of Central and Eastern Europe and the former Soviet Union;
13. *In view of the fact that* the reforming countries of Central Europe in particular have made considerable progress in stabilizing their overall economic development;
14. *Welcomes* the fact that in all the reforming countries of Central and Eastern Europe and the former Soviet Union, the privatization of formerly government-owned companies and the founding of new private companies is an important part of the reform effort;
15. *Underscores the need* for increased international cooperation with a view to moving ahead with the difficult and time-consuming privatization of large government-owned companies and industrial complexes;
16. *Underscores* that the founding of new private companies, indispensable for a functionally viable market economy system, should be promoted by means of a specific policy on small and medium-sized companies;
17. *Refers* in view of the enormous capital requirement in the reforming countries of Central and Eastern Europe and the former Soviet Union to the importance of foreign investments in these countries;
18. *Notes* with regret recent decisions by the I.F.C. and the E.B.R.D. to withdraw from support of previously approved projects in Eastern Europe, especially when those withdrawals are based on a perceived softening of individual countries' economies and *urges* the financing institutions to recognize that their support of projects is needed even more now than previously as a catalyst to help create stability and growth;
19. *Underscores* that the investments of Western companies involving a transfer of know-how in addition to capital, can make an important contribution towards success of the economic restructuring process;
20. *Calls* upon the reforming countries, particularly the countries of the former Soviet Union, to encourage foreign investment by establishing as soon as possible the legal framework and guarantees to assure the safety of capital investments and the rights of ownership and profit repatriation;
21. *Calls* upon the reforming countries of Central and Eastern Europe as well as the former Soviet Union to adopt the necessary fiscal and monetary policies to control and lower the rate of inflation in their countries,

thereby promoting the financial stability necessary to attract foreign investment and protect the economic well-being of their populations;

22. *Urgently calls upon* those European countries which experience the drastic increase in unemployment connected with the restructuring process to undertake social and employment policy measures;
23. *Suggests* in this connection continuing the adaptation of social security systems to the new conditions, continuing to attach priority importance to the establishment of systems of financial support for the unemployed, and in the framework of an active employment market policy placing emphasis on providing career qualifications, job-creation schemes as well as the promotion of self-employment and regional mobility;
24. *Advocates* an active environmental policy, including internationally recognized safety standards at nuclear power facilities since in the current situation of radical change and crisis in the countries of Central and Eastern Europe and the former Soviet Union, the danger exists that short-term production and employment objectives will be conceded priority over protection of the natural environment;
25. *Warns against* the transfer of hazardous wastes and export of environmentally harmful technologies and products from other countries;
26. *Recommends* the establishment, at the next meeting of the Council of Ministers, of a new mechanism or institution, as appropriate, to coordinate the environmental protection policies of, and promote environmental cooperation between, all the participating States in order both to safeguard the natural environment and to protect the health and economic well-being of all peoples throughout the CSCE community;
27. *Welcomes* the conclusion of cooperation or association agreements between the reforming countries of Central and Eastern Europe and the European Community, which provide a necessary prospect for the political and economic integration of these countries in the European Community;
28. *Calls upon* the Western industrialized countries to eliminate existing trade barriers and other discriminating limitations on the access of these countries to the world markets of goods and services for the reforming countries and in this way contribute towards success of the market economy reforms in the countries of Central and Eastern Europe and the former Soviet Union;
29. *Appeals* to the Western industrialized countries to continue their technical assistance and financial measures for economic support of the countries of Central and Eastern Europe and the former Soviet Union, including the goal-oriented credits to countries of the former Soviet Union in order to buy energy resources and in so doing to contribute towards stabilization of the new democracies;

30. *Requests* all CSCE participating States to support the urgent introduction of effective measures aimed at assisting European countries most seriously affected by UN sanctions against Serbia and Montenegro to overcome their difficulties and to continue with their transition towards a market economy and a democratic society;
31. *Advocates* better coordination of support measures for the countries of Central and Eastern Europe and the former Soviet Union among the CSCE participating states;
32. *Appeals to* the parliaments of the CSCE participating states to intensify their efforts to support the transformation process in the countries of Central and Eastern Europe and the former Soviet Union;
33. *Underscores* the importance of economic cooperation between the Western industrial countries and the reforming countries of Central and Eastern Europe and the former Soviet Union in addition to the need for an exchange of information in economic matters within the framework of the responsible international organizations;
34. *Welcomes* the work carried out thus far by the CSCE Economic Forum, which gives the reforming countries an opportunity to describe their experience in connection with the transition to a market economy system and to look for solutions to problems together with the Western industrialized countries;
35. *Advocates* the regular attendance of the meetings of the CSCE Economic Forum by a member of the Economic Committee of the Parliamentary Assembly, and *encourages* the governments of CSCE participating States to include Members of Parliament in their delegations to meetings of the CSCE Economic Forum;
36. *Advocates* a regular information exchange with the CSCE Economic Forum;
37. *Suggests* continuing to deal regularly with the status of the economic reform process in the countries of Central and Eastern Europe and the former Soviet Union in the framework of the CSCE Parliamentary Assembly.

CHAPTER III DEMOCRACY, HUMAN RIGHTS AND HUMANITARIAN QUESTIONS

The CSCE Parliamentary Assembly,

A. *REFUGEES AND DISPLACED PERSONS*

1. *Considering* the role of parliamentarians in promoting and achieving respect for human rights;

2. *Recognizing* that displacement is often a result of violations of CSCE commitments and basic human rights;
3. *Noting*, in particular, the ongoing inter-ethnic violence in the former Yugoslavia, which has resulted in the most serious refugee crisis in Europe since World War II;
4. *Convinced* that the plight of refugees and displaced persons within the CSCE region requires the urgent attention and cooperation of all participating States and competent international organizations in a common effort to find equitable solutions;
5. *Reaffirms* the commitment of the participating States to the strict observance of the principles of the 1951 Geneva Convention and the 1967 New York Protocol relating to the Status of Refugees, notably including the principle of non-refoulement, and related human rights standards for the protection of refugees and displaced persons;
6. *Affirms* its commitment to extend the acceding to and observance of the Convention and the Protocol to all areas of the region;
7. *Recommends* that Member States do not demand an entry visa from asylum seekers originating from countries where owing to prevailing circumstances it is practically impossible for them to obtain one;
8. *Expresses* its willingness to promote actively joint responsibility for the protection of and assistance to refugees and displaced persons, and *encourages* the fullest cooperation with the International Organization for Migration, the UN High Commissioner for Refugees, and other organizations involved in migration and refugee issues, as well as with the human rights, development, and relief communities, both governmental and non-governmental, to find viable solutions to the pressing refugee challenges of today;
9. *Emphasizes* that such coordinated solutions should be based on recognition of the fact that the current situation in Europe concerns refugees as defined in the Convention and the Protocol, as well as displaced persons of broader categories in need of protection from violations of basic human rights;
10. *Condemns* the use of rape as an instrument of war and demands the cessation of the violence and trauma experienced by women and children who have been or will continue to be the victims of mass rape and forced pregnancy at the hands of their aggressors;
11. *Classifies* rape as a war crime, and urges that those responsible for these aggressions be held accountable before an international war crimes tribunal;
12. *Recognizes* that humanitarian aid is necessary and welcome and *urges* the participating States to support relief efforts designed to provide humanitarian assistance for those victims of rape, but nevertheless,

reaffirms the central issue that rape as a byproduct of conflict will not be tolerated and will incur the condemnation of the participating States;

13. *Recognizes* that the countries most vulnerable to migration are often among those least equipped to afford it, and *stresses* the need to pay due regard to sharing the burdens of protection and assistance, as well as to consider reorienting national resources and infrastructure for the handling of refugee problems in light of the interests of the CSCE region as a whole;
14. *Concurs* that, although refugee problems should, ideally, be solved in the immediate region of the country of origin, neighboring countries to the conflict areas should not be expected to bear solely the main burden of protecting and assisting refugees and displaced persons;
15. *Urges* close cooperation between CSCE and the UN High Commissioner for Refugees and other European structures to provide practical solutions within the region;
16. *Emphasizes* that measures must be taken by all member states to integrate fully those legal migrants and "resident foreigners" who will be staying permanently, including the granting of political rights and citizenship and *emphasizes* that refugees must be given the opportunity to return to their home country and to live in security there;
17. *Expresses* the wish that representatives of the Parliamentary Assembly will join CSCE missions sent to the centers of potential conflicts and tension, as well as the activities of the CSCE High Commissioner on National Minorities;
18. *Notes* the necessity of sending a CSCE observer mission to monitor the safe return of refugees to Tajikistan;

B. *MINORITIES ISSUES*

19. *Convinced* that violations of the rights of persons belonging to minorities are among the most urgent causes of instability and concern in our region;
20. *Deeply troubled* by ethnic tensions, civil unrest, flagrant disregard for the rule of law, and egregious human rights abuses in several of the newly admitted CSCE states, which have resulted in significant violations of CSCE human dimension commitments;
21. *Shocked* and *disturbed* by the recent wave of violence and terrorism by radical groups such as the PKK, including hostage-taking and bombing, which resulted in death and injury to innocent civilians;
22. *Considering* that prevention and settlement of the conflicts, caused by national or ethnic tension are one of the priorities of CSCE activities;
23. *Noting with serious concern* that a climate of intolerance and anti-foreigner sentiment is growing in many CSCE states, including those with

considerable democratic experience, resulting at times in violence or discrimination against immigrants, refugees, asylum-seekers, migrant workers, persons belonging to minorities, persons with disabilities, and others perceived as different or foreign;

24. *Concerned* about the situation in South-eastern Turkey and nearby areas with respect to the condition of minorities in the region;
25. *Considering* that the CSCE process should now contribute to finding a solution to the situation in South-eastern Turkey and closeby areas;
26. *Recommends* the CSCE Parliaments to appoint and coordinate delegations in order to send them to Turkey with the purpose to establish a permanent and close observation of the situation of the Kurdish population;
27. *Condemns unequivocally* all violations of human rights in CSCE member states, and particularly the atrocities committed against innocent civilian populations in several CSCE states;
28. *Recommends* the authorities of the Estonian Republic to adjust the Estonian legislation regarding the non-native population, so that it corresponds with the European standards, principles of CSCE and Council of Europe documents including the recommendations of the CSCE High Commissioner on National Minorities as well as the Council of Europe recommendations, and *hopes* that Estonian authorities will take all necessary steps to duly implement this law into practice;
29. *Calls on* the Estonian Republic and the Russian Federation to reopen active and constructive dialogue and negotiations on the basis of principles and commitments of CSCE on the whole complex of Russian-Estonian inter-state relations, including the issue of withdrawal of Russian troops from the territory of Estonia;
30. *Calls for* a concerted effort to strengthen existing mechanisms to advance the human rights objectives of the Helsinki process, including those relating to minorities issues, and to bolster the determination of participating states to use these mechanisms in a coordinated and committed fashion, as well as to demand accountability from participating States which fail to respect their CSCE commitments;
31. *Condemns* terrorism and violence in all forms as crimes against humanity and urges international cooperation to combat such terrorism and to bring about peaceful solutions to problems of minorities of all countries;
32. *Urges* all CSCE participating states to demand accountability from individuals found in violation of international humanitarian law through urgent and vigorous application of domestic laws and judicial processes, and *strongly supports*, in addition, the realization of the International War Crimes Tribunal established under United Nations Security Council Resolution 827, as well as the creation of a central register of war crimes

to be administered either by CSCE or by the United Nations in order to support the planned international war crimes tribunal;

33. *Welcomes* the creation of the office of the CSCE High Commissioner on National Minorities, and *urges* that a broad interpretation of the HCNM's mandate be applied, so that the HCNM might address the widest possible range of minority concerns within the CSCE region;
34. *Supports* the Parliamentary Assembly of the Council of Europe in its efforts for an additional protocol on the rights of national minorities in the European Convention on Human Rights;
35. *Hopes that* the forthcoming summit of Council of Europe Heads of State and Government (Vienna, 8 - 9 October 1993) will agree on an additional Protocol on the rights of minorities to the European Convention on Human Rights;
36. *Expresses its determination* to assist in the full implementation of relevant CSCE commitments in this area, including, inter alia, those relating to persons belonging to national minorities, women, human rights education, and promotion of tolerance and non-discrimination;
37. *Undertakes* to support by all means the full and immediate implementation of the provisions of the Final Document of the CSCE Conference in Moscow in 1991 indicating that true democracy must be founded on equal rights for men and women;
38. *Undertakes* to call a meeting of the female members of the CSCE at the next session of the Parliamentary Assembly;
39. *Invites* Member States to take positive measures aimed at increasing the participation of women in political life;
40. *Supports* the appointment of CSCE observer missions as an effective means of giving minorities a feeling of protection and of alerting the authorities of the countries concerned to their responsibilities towards minorities and *recommends* the attachment of members of the CSCE Parliamentary Assembly to these observer missions;
41. *Commends* the Office of Democratic Institutions and Human Rights (ODIHR) for the seminar on National Minorities held in May, 1993 in Warsaw and *urges* the Council of Ministers to provide additional resources to the ODIHR so that it could play a more active role;

C. *DEMOCRACY*

42. *Recognizing* the need for promotion of the development of democracy in the new democracies in Europe;
43. *Convinced* that there is a need for parliamentary technical assistance in connection with the establishing of multi-party democracy;

44. *Convinced* that monitoring of elections are not single events but part of a continuous process, including follow up actions for promotion of democracy;
45. *Taking into consideration* the division of work between the United Nations, the Council of Europe and the CSCE concerning monitoring of elections and promoting democratic development;
46. *Expresses its determination* to have monitoring of elections as an important task on the CSCE Parliamentary Assembly agenda;
47. *Considers* the establishment of a Parliamentary Commission for election monitoring;

D. *DUE PROCESS OF LAW*

48. *Expresses* its deep concern regarding the fate of citizens of the Republic of Moldova held captive and placed on trial by illegal authorities at Tiraspol in Eastern Moldova;
49. *Requests* all answerable authorities to ensure just proceedings for these detainees before an impartial, independent court established by law and in accordance with the constitution of Moldova, and treatment strictly complying with the principles of human rights shared by all CSCE states;

E. *OBSERVANCE OF INTERNATIONAL LAW ON HUMAN RIGHTS*

50. *Having regard to* the inadequacy of human rights instruments in time of armed conflicts, *reaffirms* the importance of respect for international law on human rights, and for the Geneva Convention and additional protocols in particular, invites all states to sign them and ratify them, and calls on the governments of participating States of the CSCE to consider attending the international conference for the effective protection of victims of war to be held in Geneva from 30 August to 1 September 1993;

F. *HIGH COMMISSIONER FOR NATIONAL MINORITIES - REPORT*

51. *Requests* the Council of Ministers to be held in Rome in November - December 1993 to give a new mandate to the High Commissioner for National Minorities to work out a report on the national minorities situation in CSCE participating States with regard to:
    a) The size of the minority according to direct census or census on people speaking the minority's language as "mother-tongue"; changes in the size of the minority - if possible - in the last 50 years;
    b) Legal guarantees of minority rights in the respective country;

c) The factual situation of a respective minority as represented by the total number of schools teaching in the minority's language, deputies of the minority in local and national parliaments, etc.

The report should be submitted to the next Parliamentary Assembly in 1994.

CHAPTER IV THE FORMER YUGOSLAVIA

The CSCE Parliamentary Assembly,

1. *Reaffirming* the provisions of its 1992 Budapest Declaration on Yugoslavia and of the Standing Committee statement issued earlier this year;
2. *Regretting* that fundamental CSCE principles have been severely violated in connection with the conflicts in former Yugoslavia, particularly in Bosnia-Herzegovina, as a result of the continuing threat and use of force as well as the practice of "ethnic cleansing". These serious violations of CSCE basic principles, for which Serbia and the Bosnian Serbs bear primary responsibility, but to which Croatia has also contributed, must not be tolerated by the international community;
3. *Deploring* the fact that the war in Bosnia-Herzegovina has resulted in organized, systematic, and pre-meditated war crimes and genocide, and threatens stability and security in Europe, especially in its Eastern and Central parts;
4. *Remaining* gravely concerned over the failure of the international community effectively to end the violence and genocide in Bosnia-Herzegovina;
5. *Believing* that the territorial gains in Bosnia-Herzegovina, achieved primarily as a result of continuing Serbian aggression, must not be accepted by the international community. Military aggression must never be rewarded by recognition of conquests made through the use of force. As such, the ultimate objective must continue to be that of annulling the territorial conquests made by Serbs and Croats;
6. *Convinced*, now that the Vance-Owen peace plan has failed, that the planned division of Bosnia-Herzegovina must be resolutely counteracted, a solution must be found to end the conflict in Bosnia-Herzegovina which will be equally acceptable to all national groups, i.e. the Bosnian Serbs, the Croats and the Moslems. There must be no approval of a solution imposed on the Moslems by the Serbs and Croats with reference to facts established by military means;
7. *Taking the view* that until such time as an internationally recognized solution can be found for former Yugoslavia as a whole, the sanctions

imposed against Serbia by the UN Security Council must be maintained with a view to achieving further international isolation of the Serbian aggressors and to motivating them to make concessions in the peace negotiations;

8. *Insisting* that those who unilaterally insist on facts brought about by force, in opposition to international peace efforts, must not receive any reconstruction assistance from the international community;
9. *Disturbed* by the growing number of displaced persons in Bosnia-Herzegovina, the decreasing resources available for their support and the potential requirements for their resettlement;
10. *Aware* that neither Bosnia-Herzegovina nor the neighbouring countries will be in a position to solve the growing refugee problem without intensive help from outside;
11. *Condemning* the brutal measures that have been recently taken against opposition forces in Serbia, including the brutal beating of opposition leader and fellow parliamentarian Vuk Draskovic;
12. *Welcoming* the decision of the Committee of Senior Officials to send to Belgrade a mission under the Mechanism agreed at the Moscow Meeting on the Human Dimension to investigate abuses of human rights and in particular the case of Mr. Draskovic and his wife;
13. *Echoing* the call of the Assembly's own delegation to the Former Yugoslav Republic of Macedonia (FYROM) and Kosovo and of the Committee of Senior Officials, for international access to Mr. and Mrs. Draskovic;
14. *Expressing* its deep concern over developments elsewhere in the former Yugoslavia, particularly where the possibility for spillover continues, including Kosovo and the FYROM;
15. *Aware* of the important role of CSCE Monitoring Missions in many parts of former Yugoslavia, and in particular, in the FYROM;
16. *Taking note* of the recent decision of the authorities of Serbia and Montenegro to refuse the continued presence of CSCE Monitoring Missions;

The Assembly,

17. *Urges* the participating States to undertake resolute action, without further delay, to:
    - support the disbanding and disarming of such irregular forces in Bosnia-Herzegovina with their weapons placed under effective international monitoring. In the event that such steps are not taken by irregular forces immediately, every effort, including the use of military air force, should be made to neutralize heavy arms in the hands of such forces;

- ensure the immediate, effective and unimpeded delivery of humanitarian aid to all civilian populations in Bosnia-Herzegovina, in keeping with international commitments and existing UN resolutions;
- ensure unimpeded access to all camps, prisons and detention centres maintained by irregular forces in Bosnia-Herzegovina by the International Committee of the Red Cross and other international humanitarian organizations and facilitate the release of all detainees from such facilities;

18. *Urges* the participating States not to recognize the incorporation of any of the territory of Bosnia-Herzegovina resulting from the threat or use of force, coercion or any other means inconsistent with international law and the Principles contained in the Final Act;
19. *Welcomes* efforts by the United Nations to investigate, prosecute, and try alleged war criminals responsible for war crimes and crimes against humanity in the former Yugoslavia and *urges* the participating States to provide adequate funding and support for these and related activities;
20. *Condemns* systematic and widespread rape and sexual abuse of women and girls of all ages in the former Yugoslavia and *strongly supports* the provision of assistance for the victims;
21. *Demands* that a spread of the conflict to bordering areas in the Balkans, such as Kosovo and the FYROM, must be prevented by the timely use of all the conflict-prevention mechanisms available to the international community;
22. *Condemns* the decision of the Government of the so-called Federal Republic of Yugoslavia to end the mandate of the CSCE Mission in Kosovo;
23. *Calls* upon the government of Yugoslavia (Serbia/Montenegro) to allow the CSCE long-term Missions in Kosovo, Sandjak and Vojvodina to continue their work in ensuring the prevention of spillover of conflict to the region and the observance of human rights, *requests* the Council of Ministers not to accept the ending of the CSCE Monitoring Missions and to ensure continued and expanding functioning of these Missions, and *affirms* its view that the withdrawal of the Missions can only impede the readmission of Serbia to the international community presaged by the Conclusions of the Stockholm Council Meeting;
24. *Recommends* the Council of Ministers to have a decision adopted by the UN Security Council which advocates all possible pressure to force the above government to accept the further activities of the CSCE within Kosovo;
25. *Concludes* that in view of the failure of the international community thus far to find a peaceful solution to the conflict, it has become clear that the

Mechanisms of the CSCE and other international organisations for conflict prevention and crisis management need to be strengthened;

26. *Requests* the Council of Ministers to continue the co-operation with UNPROFOR and to urge the competent UN authorities to enlarge UNPROFOR's mandate to monitor traffic and the content of vehicles and trains that pass the borders of the FYROM in the direction of Serbia and to stop traffic in violation of UN sanctions;
27. *Urges* all states to support relief efforts designed to provide humanitarian assistance to those in need;
28. *Recommends* the development of an overall European concept for defining the quota for all countries receiving refugees. The primary concern of such a concept must be "burden-sharing" in the context of assistance for the neighbouring countries, Croatia, Hungary, Austria, and with regard to humanitarian help for Bosnia-Herzegovina. Refugee movements from this European region to Asia are no solution in the long term;
29. *Requests* the Council of Ministers to direct the CSCE Secretary General to examine the plight of displaced persons in the former Yugoslavia and to report on measures that member states might take to resolve their problems.
30. *Calls* for the admission of the former Yugoslav Republic of Macedonia into the CSCE as a full participating State and urges those states which have not already done so to recognize that country.

Editors note: The Parliamentary Assembly at its Helsinki meeting in July 1993 also adopted the following resolution:

CSCE MISSIONS IN KOSOVO, VOJVODINA AND SANDJAK

The Parliamentary Assembly of the CSCE is most concerned that the Government of the Federal Republic of Yugoslavia has decided not to extend the mandate of the CSCE long term Missions in Kosovo, Vojvodina and Sandjak. If implemented, this decision means that the Government of the former Yugoslavia is isolating itself further from the international community. This also raises grave doubts about its intentions concerning the peace process and implementation of the CSCE principles.

The long term Missions have been able, in co-operation with the authorities and representatives of different communities, to promote the peace process and to help alleviate inter-ethnic tensions. It is essential that these Missions continue to do their valuable work. There are reasons to fear that tensions and violence will increase, if these Missions are closed.

The Parliamentary Assembly appeals to the Government of the Yugoslav Federal Republic to reconsider its decision and to secure the continuation of these Missions.

V

SELECTED DOCUMENTS

OF THE

CSCE HIGH COMMISSIONER

ON

NATIONAL MINORITIES

DOCUMENTS OF MISSIONS TO ESTONIA, LATVIA AND LITHUANIA[1]

His Excellency
Mr Trivimi Velliste
Minister for Foreign Affairs
of the Republic of Estonia

The Hague
6 April 1993

Dear Mr Minister,

Following my visits to Estonia on 12-13 January and 30-31 March 1993, I take the liberty of sending you, annexed to this letter, a number of recommendations concerning mainly the non-Estonian population of your country. I restrict myself to this question because I would go beyond my mandate if I would comment on other problems concerning your country. On the other hand, I can assure you that, in making these suggestions, I have been fully aware of the political and psychological background of many of the questions I am referring to. I think for instance of the long years Estonia suffered under Soviet occupation, the bitterness caused by what is perceived as a deliberate policy of Russification during those years, and your concerns about the continued, though greatly reduced, presence of Russian troops on you territory. I also recall the way you and your colleagues have repeatedly stressed the determination of the Estonian people firmly to establish its national identity in various fields. Finally, I have registered the concern felt by the Estonian Government about the situation of the Estonians living on the territory of the Russian Federation.

In making my recommendations, I am fully aware of the fact that there is no convincing evidence of systematic persecution of the non-Estonian population since the reestablishment of Estonian independence, and moreover, that there have virtually been no incidents pointing to interethnic violence. I am also pleased to note that during my visit I received repeated assurances from your Government that it was determined to fully respect its CSCE commitments, including those concerning minorities. I have written my recommendations in the hope that they may help you to accomplish the aim which your Government has repeatedly stressed of trying to find a formula for the problem of the non-Estonian population in your country in accordance with the international standards subscribed to by Estonia.

---

[1] CSCE Communication No. 124 (Prague, 23 April 1993). (Title added by the Editor.)

When I drafted my recommendations, my basic assumption has been that, though a number of non-Estonians have returned to their native country and more might follow, it would be unrealistic to expect that such a return will be on a massive scale. The great majority will probably prefer to stay in Estonia, partially because they have been living there for a long time or have been born there, and partially because they feel that they have no prospect of finding homes and jobs if they would move to the Russian Federation or any other CIS state.

Against this background, your Government is in my view, at least in theory, confronted with two completely contradictory options regarding the non-Estonian population of your country. The first is to try to assure in various ways a privileged position for its Estonian population. Apart from the fact that such a policy would scarcely be compatible with the spirit, if not the letter, of various international obligations Estonia has accepted, such a policy would, in my view, involve a considerable risk of increasing tensions with the non-Estonian population which, in turn, could lead to a destabilization of the country as a whole. In addition, it would have a strongly negative effect on relations between Estonia and the Russian Federation.

The alternative policy is to aim at the integration of the non-Estonian population by a deliberate policy of facilitating the chances of acquiring Estonian citizenship for those who express such a wish, and of assuring them full equality with Estonian citizens. In my view, such a policy would greatly reduce the danger of destabilization, because it would considerably enhance the chances of the non-Estonian population developing a sense of loyalty toward Estonia. Furthermore, such a policy would certainly not be incompatible with the wish of the Estonians to ensure and strengthen their political, cultural and linguistic identity.

I am fully aware that the policy I advocate does not only require an effort on the part of the Estonian Government, but equally a contribution on the part of the non-Estonian population. Adaptation to the reality of the reemergence of Estonia as an independent state requires that at any rate those who have not yet retired from work and who do not yet speak the Estonian language make a determined effort to master that language to such a degree that they are able to conduct a simple conversation in Estonian. In this way they would, without having to sacrifice their cultural or linguistic identity, provide a convincing proof of their willingness to integrate. The required psychological adaption to the reality of the reemergence of Estonia as an independent state would also be enhanced if it would be possible to ensure rapid implementation of paragraph 15 of the 1992 Helsinki Summit Declaration, calling for "the conclusion, without delay, of agreements, including timetables, for the early, orderly and complete withdrawal of foreign troops from the territories of the Baltic states."

Of course, I have noted that Estonian legislation opens the possibility for persons who have resided in Estonia for two years since 1990 to apply for Estonian citizenship, which can then be granted after a waiting period of one year. So far only a limited number of non-Estonians residing in Estonia have made use of this opportunity. I doubt, however, whether this is a sufficiently reliable indication of the potential interest of non-Estonians residing in Estonia in acquiring Estonian citizenship. Uncertainty about what the future might bring may play a role. But conversations I had with Russians living in Estonia also gave me the impression that, on the one hand, there was insufficient knowledge of the opportunities which the present Estonian legislation offers them and, on the other hand, where such knowledge does exist there are perhaps excessive fears that the language requirements might prove to be an insuperable obstacle. This, in turn, leads me to the following comments.

Recently, a law laying down Estonian language requirements for applicants for citizenship has been adopted. Even though this law does not completely exempt elderly people and disabled persons from language requirements, as I would have hoped, it does open the way for simplified language requirements for persons born before January 1st, 1930, and for certain categories of disabled persons. On the other hand, Estonian language requirements as laid down in Article 2 of the law are formulated in such a way that they could lend themselves to various interpretations. However, this problem can be remedied to a certain extent because Article 3, paragraph 1, makes it clear that the requirements and the contents of language examinations will be the subject of new government regulations. This would offer the Government the opportunity to ensure that the requirements will not be excessive. In this connection, I may recall that a knowledge of about 1500 words is usually considered to be sufficient to make oneself understood. It would also be important to open the opportunity to try again for those who failed the test for a first time and to ensure that examination fees do not constitute a prohibitive financial burden for applicants.

In my view, it could also greatly facilitate the relationship with the non-Estonian population, if the Estonian Government would decide to set up the office of a "National Commissioner on Ethnic and Language Questions". His or her main task would be to look into relevant complaints which in the view of the complainants have not been correctly dealt with, to signal possible diverging interpretations of the same laws by different authorities, and in a general sense, to act as a go-between to the Government and the community concerned. In this way, he or she could help to prevent tensions from arising or, of they already exist, to reduce or eliminate them. I would be willing to offer you any assistance you might find desirable in developing this idea.

In addition to the recommendations I have mentioned, you will find some others which are self-explanatory in the text which follows. Even though Russians constitute the largest non-Estonian population group in Estonia, I use the term "non-Estonian" in my recommendations in order to make it clear that they do apply equally to Russians and non-Russians amongst the non-Estonian population of your country.

My recommendations do not call for a drastic overhaul of existing legislation in Estonia. They do call, however, for a number of additional steps to be taken which might in my view help considerably in improving relations between the various population groups in Estonia.

Finally, permit me, Mr Minister, to thank you once again for the kindness shown to me during my visits to Estonia. You and your colleagues never tired from answering my questions!

Yours sincerely,

(Max van der Stoel)

* * *

Estonia - Conclusions and recommendations

1) In general, it is recommended that the Government consistently implement a visible policy of dialogue and integration towards the non-Estonian population, which should incorporate the following recommendations. In the High Commissioner's opinion, early government action in this regard is indispensable.

2) Taking into account Article 15 of the Universal Declaration of Human Rights, it is recommended that Estonia proceed to reduce the number of stateless persons permanently residing on its territory. To this end, the High Commissioner recommends the following (Recommendations 3 through 5).

3) Children born in Estonia who would otherwise become stateless should be granted Estonian citizenship, taking also into account Article 3, paragraph 6, of the Estonian Citizenship Act, Article 24, paragraph 3, of the International Covenant on Civil and Political Rights, and Article 7, paragraph 2, of the Convention on the Rights of the Child.

4) It is recommended that the Government, when implementing the law on Estonian Language Requirements for Applicants for Citizenship, should:
   a. ensure maximum publicity for the law and the government regulations to implement the law, especially amongst the Russian population;
   b. ensure, when implementing Article 3, paragraph 1, of the Law on Estonian Language Requirements for Applicants for Citizenship, that the risk of different interpretations and practices by the officials concerned is reduced to a minimum and that the ability to conduct a simple conversation will be considered sufficient;
   c. establish that those who fail the language test will have the opportunity to undergo another language test;
   d. implement Article 3, paragraph 3, in such a way as to amount to a waiver of all language requirements for persons born before January 1st, 1930, and disabled persons;
   e. ensure that the examination fees do not constitute a prohibitive financial burden for potential applicants.

5) A rejection because of a failure to meet the language or residency requirements should not preclude someone from applying again.

6) It should be made explicit that the requirement that applicants have a steady legal income in order to qualify for citizenship will not apply to unemployed people.

7) In view of Articles 1, paragraph 3, and 5, paragraph (d), of the International Convention on the Elimination of All Forms of Racial Discrimination, any discrimination on the ground of nationality or ethnicity should be avoided when enacting or implementing legal provisions concerning nationality, citizenship or naturalisation.

8) In the end, a number of persons will not qualify for citizenship nor have the status of permanent residents. The High Commissioner would recommend that humanitarian considerations and reasonableness be the guiding principles regarding those persons.

9) The use of the Estonian language in the internal affairs of private enterprises and organizations should not be made mandatory.

10) The Estonian Government should continue to enhance its efforts aimed at non-Estonian residents acquiring a reasonable level of knowledge of the Estonian language. More use should be made of the mass media, in particular television. The language education system existing in the Northeastern city of Kohtla-Järve should be studied with a view to its possible implementation elsewhere in Estonia.

11) The Government should continue its efforts at informing the non-Estonian population about the legislation, regulations and practical questions which concern citizenship, language requirements etcetera. The Government should also ensure that the Viruuma Information Centre can effectively contribute to informing the Russian population in the Northeast.

12) The office of a "National Commissioner on Ethnic and Language Questions" should be established, with the competence to take up any relevant complaint which he/she considers to require further attention with any government agency. He/she would also have to actively find out about uncertainties and dissatisfaction involving minorities, act speedily in order to help clarify grey areas in legislation and practice, answer to questions within a specified period of time (e.g. two months) and finally act as a go-between to the Government and the minorities in Estonia. He/she should focus his/her activities primarily on the Northeastern region of Estonia, specifically including in his/her activities the Estonian minority there.

    The National Commissioner should have the general confidence of all parties concerned. If it should prove impossible to find one person meeting this criterion, then a commission of three could be established to perform the same tasks (one Commissioner with two deputies, a triumvirate like many ombudsman offices are structured).

13) The Estonian Department for Minorities Questions should be made an independent body, so that it could act with more authority and credibility and work more effectively.

His Excellency
Mr Georgs Andrejevs
Minister for Foreign Affairs
of the Republic of Latvia

The Hague
6 April 1993

Dear Mr Minister,

Following my visits to Latvia on 15-20 January and 1-2 April 1993, I take the liberty of sending you, annexed to this letter, a number of recommendations concerning mainly the non-Latvian population of your country. I restrict myself to this question because I would go beyond my mandate if I would comment on other problems concerning your country. On the other hand, I can assure you that, in making these suggestions, I have been fully aware of the political and psychological background of many of the questions I am referring to. I think for instance of the long years Latvia suffered under Soviet occupation, the bitterness caused by what is perceived as a deliberate policy of Russification during those years, and your concerns about the continued, though greatly reduced, presence of Russian troops on your territory. I also recall the way you and your colleagues have repeatedly stressed the determination of the Latvian people firmly to establish its national identity in various field. Finally, I have registered the concern felt by the Latvian Government about the situation of the Latvians living on the territory of the Russian Federation.

I am fully aware of the fact that there is no evidence of persecution of the non-Latvian population since the reestablishment of Latvian independence, and moreover, that there have virtually been no incidents pointing to interethnic violence. My hope is that the ideas I am submitting to you - inspired as they are by the various CSCE documents to which Latvia, together with all other CSCE participating States, had subscribed - can contribute to the promotion of harmony and dialogue between the various population groups in your country.

When I drafted my recommendations, my basic assumption has been that, though a number of non-Latvians have returned to their native country and more might follow, it would be unrealistic to expect that such a return will be on a massive scale. The great majority will probably prefer to stay in Latvia, partially because they have been living there for a long time or have been born there, and partially because they feel that they have no prospect of finding homes and jobs if they would move to the Russian Federation or any other CIS state.

During my visits, I was told by officials of the Citizenship and Immigration Department that according to their estimates the number of non-Latvians that will have acquired Latvian citizenship before June and who will therefore be able to participate in the parliamentary elections scheduled for that month will not exceed 50%. As 98% of all non-Latvians have been living in Latvia for more than 5 years and 93% even for 16 years or more and as the prospects of finding jobs and apartments in the Russian Federation or other CIS republics have to be considered very small, it can be assumed that most of those who so far have not been able to acquire Latvian citizenship will sooner or later apply for it. This conclusion is supported by official data which show that per March 22nd out of a total of 617,443 persons registered as inhabitants of Latvia who are not Latvian citizens 593,008 want to acquire citizenship.

On the basis of my conversations, I assume that the Government of Latvia, confronted with this situation, will not decide to oblige this group or parts of it to leave the country. Although every Government has the right to remove from its territory persons whose continued presence could be damaging to vital interests of the state, it is also obvious that expulsions on a massive scale would be contrary to generally accepted international humanitarian principles and would, moreover, probably have very serious international repercussions.

From the point of view of harmonious interethnic relations, it would in my view also be undesirable that Latvia would insist on such high requirements for citizenship that a great number of applicants would not be able to meet them. As a consequence, the percentage of citizens of Latvian origin would be higher and that of citizens of non-Latvian origin lower then would be the case if Latvia would follow a more liberal line. However, the disadvantage of such a very strict policy would quite probably be that there would be considerable dissatisfaction amongst the very many who would then not have the chance of obtaining Latvian citizenship. Even though, as you pointed out in your speech before the UN Commission on Human Rights in Geneva on February 15, these persons would be free to choose their place of employment, to engage in professional activities and private enterprise, to receive pensions and unemployment benefits and to have access to health care and housing, they would not have the right to make their views known by participating in the election process.

Another solution would be that Latvia would restrict itself to requirements for citizenship which, broadly speaking, would not go beyond those used by most CSCE states. In my recommendations I have tried to elaborate this formula in somewhat greater detail. It is my opinion that such a policy would be the most effective way to ensure the loyalty of non-Latvians towards Latvia. I do understand that the Latvian Government feels the need, especially in the light of the demographic changes brought about in Latvia during the years of the Soviet period, to take measures to strengthen the Latvian identity. However, there are other instruments than the citizenship law to promote and strengthen the Latvian identity, especially in the cultural, educational and linguistic fields.

I am fully aware that the policy I advocate does not only require an effort on the part of the Latvian Government, but equally a contribution on the part of the non-Latvian population. Adaptation to the reality of the reemergence of Latvia as an independent state requires that at any rate those who have not yet retired from work and who do not yet speak the Latvian language make a determined effort to master that language to such a degree that they are able to conduct a simple conversation in Latvian. In this way they would, without having to sacrifice their cultural or linguistic identity, provide a convincing proof of their willingness to integrate. The required psychological adaptation to the reality of the reemergence of Latvia as an independent state would also be enhanced if it would be possible to ensure rapid implementation of paragraph 15 of the 1992 Helsinki Summit Declaration, calling for "the conclusion, without delay, of agreements, including timetables, for the early, orderly and complete withdrawal of foreign troops from the territories of the Baltic states."

In a policy aiming at the promotion of continued harmonious relations between Latvians and the non-Latvian population the most important element would, of course, be the passing of legislation which demonstrates that the Latvian Government is taking the interests of the non-Latvians living in Latvia fully into account. It would be especially conducive to harmonious relations if the present uncertainty amongst non-Latvians about the forthcoming legislation concerning their position in Latvia could be brought to an end as soon as possible. In this connection, I should like to mention the need for the speedy adoption of a citizenship law.

Experience shows that lack of information about government policies can lead to serious and perhaps often unnecessary misunderstandings. Against this background, I am making some recommendations concerning the problem of communication with the non-Latvian communities.

In my view, it could also greatly facilitate the relationship with the non-Latvian population, if the Latvian Government would decide to set up the office of a "National Commissioner on Ethnic and Language Questions". His or her main task would be to look into complaints by persons which, in their view, have not been correctly dealt with, to signal possible diverging interpretations of the same laws by different authorities, and in a general sense, to act as a go-between to the Government and the community concerned. In this way, he or she could help to prevent tensions from arising or, if they already exist, to reduce or eliminate them. I would be willing to offer you any assistance you might find desirable in developing this idea.

In addition to the recommendations I have mentioned, you will find some others which are self-explanatory in the text which follows. Even though Russians constitute the largest non-Latvian population group in Latvia, I use the term "non-Latvian" in my recommendations in order to make it clear that they do apply equally to Russians and non-Russians amongst the non-Latvian population of your country.

Finally, permit me, Mr Minister, to thank you once again for the kindness shown to me during my visits to Latvia. I was especially struck by the openness with which you and your colleagues answered my questions.

Yours sincerely,

(Max van der Stoel)

* * *

Latvia - Conclusions and recommendations

1) A new citizenship law should be speedily adopted, in order that the conditions for naturalisation be clearly defined.

2) Children born in Latvia who would otherwise be stateless should be granted Latvian citizenship taking into account Article 24, paragraph 3, of the International Covenant on Civil and Political Rights and Article 7, paragraph 1, of the Convention on the Rights of the Child, and the 1961 Convention on the Reduction of Statelessness.

3) As far as the requirement of a minimum period of residence in Latvia is concerned, such period should not exceed 5 years. This is the period

frequently adopted by states and in this case there do not seem to be good reasons not to adopt it. In terms of non-citizens eligible for citizenship, the difference between a 16, 10 of 5 years period of required residence is not great (93 percent, 96 percent an 98 percent respectively). Adopting a shorter period would also be a good decision for psychological reasons, since it would be seen as proof of the Government's determination to resolve the citizenship issue.

4) For those who are already residents of Latvia, the period of 5 years mentioned in Recommendation No 3 should be reckoned from the date they came to Latvia or were born there, whichever may be the case.

5) In order to reduce as much as possible the uncertainty prevailing in the non-Latvian communities, once applicants fulfil the legal requirements for citizenship they should be granted citizenship without delay and no further waiting period should be introduced.

6) If the new citizenship law would include a requirement that basic elements of the Constitution should be known, the requirement should be formulated in such a way that different interpretations are not possible. Generally speaking, the requirement that basic elements of the Constitution be known should not be a major obstacle to the acquisition of citizenship.

7) Whatever language requirements are chosen, they should not exceed the level of "conversational knowledge" which was required by the Supreme Council Resolution of 15 October 1991. The Government, administrative authorities and courts should be lenient in the application of this requirement as far as citizenship is concerned.

8) A clause exempting elderly persons (60 years and over) and disabled persons form language requirements when they apply for citizenship should be introduced.

9) It should be made explicit that any eventual requirement that applicants should have a steady legal income in order to qualify for citizenship should not apply to unemployed persons.

10) If certain persons would be explicitly excluded by law from acquiring citizenship, the law should stipulate that the validity of any allegation that a person would be the subject of such exclusion would, if denied, have to be established by court, in order to forestall any attempt at improper use of such provision.

11) In enacting or implementing legal provisions concerning nationality, citizenship or naturalisation, Articles 1 (3) and 5(d) of the International Convention on the Elimination of All Forms of Racial Discrimination, prohibiting any discrimination based on national or ethnic origin, have, of course, to be fully respected.

12) The effective and uniform implementation of the citizenship law should be assured by appropriate review or appeals procedure. A rejection of an application for citizenship, for instance because of a failure to meet language requirements, should not preclude the applicant from applying again. These procedures should be widely publicized.

13) In the end, a number of persons will neither qualify for citizenship, nor have the status of permanent residents. The High Commissioner would recommend that humanitarian considerations and reasonableness be the guiding principles regarding those persons.

14) The legislation on language should be made more precise. E.g. Article 7 of the Language Law of 5 May 1989, as amended on 31 March 1992, appears to require the use of the Latvian language in the internal affairs of all private enterprises and organizations. However, this had not been the intention of the legislator.

15) The Latvian authorities should enhance their efforts at helping non-Latvians to acquire a reasonable level of knowledge of the Latvian language. More use should be made of the mass media, in particular television.

16) The Government should enhance its efforts aimed at informing the non-Latvian population about the legislation, regulations and practical questions which concern citizenship, language requirements etcetera. An information brochure providing this information should be written in such a way that it can be comprehended even by persons with no more than a basic education. The brochure should be distributed in large numbers, not only to households but also to places where larger groups of non-Latvians can be expected, such as certain factories, associations and the like. Second, posters and placards could be positioned at public places and in streets, carrying the most important passages from the brochure or a summary of the main points.

17) The office of a "National Commissioner on Ethnic and Language Questions" should be established. The National Commissioner should be competent to take up any relevant complaint which he/she considers to require further attention with any government agency. He/she would have to actively find out about uncertainties and dissatisfaction involving minorities,

act speedily in order to clarify grey areas, answer to questions within a specified period of time (e.g. two months) and finally act as a channel for information and as a go-between to the Government and the minorities in Latvia.

The National Commissioner should have the general confidence of all parties concerned. If it should prove impossible to find one person who would meet this criterion, then a commission of three could be established to do the same thing (one Commissioner with two deputies, a triumvirate, like many ombudsman offices are structured).

18) In general, it is recommended that the Government consistently implement a visible policy of dialogue and integration towards the non-Latvian population, which should incorporate the above-mentioned recommendations. In the High Commissioner's opinion, early government action in this regard is indispensable.

The Latvian National Minorities department, which is currently part of the Ministry of Justice, should be made an independent body, so that it could act with more authority.

His Excellency
Mr Povilas Gylys
Minister for Foreign Affairs
of the Republic of Lithuania

The Hague
5 March 1993

Dear Mr Minister,

Allow me to thank you once again for hospitality you offered me during my visit to your country on January 21-23. The programme which was prepared for my visit offered me an excellent opportunity to get acquainted with the policies Lithuania is pursuing concerning especially the Russian and Polish minorities.

I was pleased to note that the problem of citizenship for members of the Russian and Polish minorities has been virtually resolved. The relationship between the various population groups seems on the whole to be harmonious, even though a number of desiderata remain unfulfilled. I did register complaints of the Polish minority concerning registration procedures for regional elections.

In this connection, I take the liberty to recommend to you the creation of the office of an Ombudsman, which could have as its main task to address in a non-judicial way complaints concerning administrative decisions and practices. The office of Ombudsman, as it has developed in the Scandinavian countries, could serve as a model. Serving the population as a whole, it could also play a useful role in addressing complaints concerning administrative decisions and practices relating specifically to members of the Russian and Polish minorities. I would be willing to offer any assistance you might find desirable in developing this idea.

Yours sincerely,

(Max van der Stoel)

COMMENTS BY ESTONIA, LATVIA AND LITHUANIA

Comments by the Ministry of Foreign Affairs
of Estonia on the Recommendations submitted by
H.E. Mr. Max van der Stoel,
CSCE High Commissioner on National Minorities

During the course of his two visits to Estonia, the CSCE High Commissioner on National Minorities held numerous meetings with members of the Government of Estonia, pertinent governmental authorities, representatives of ethnic minority groups and representatives of the non-citizen population[2], during which the High Commissioner demonstrated great knowledge and a clear understanding of the complex situation in our country. Based on the information acquired through these contacts, Mr. van der Stoel compiled what we deem to be a fair and accurate analysis of the current situation, together with valuable recommendations for its improvement it his letter to the Estonian Minister of Foreign Affairs, Mr. Trivimi Velliste.

Estonia fully supports the recommendation of the High Commissioner to take early action to improve a visible policy of dialogue between the Government of Estonia and the non-citizen population, a dialogue which will promote the full integration of this non-citizen population into Estonian society. The Estonian Institute of Human Rights, the existing CSCE Mission to Estonia, the Virumaa Information Centre and governmental and parliamentary commissions will continue to play an integral role in these efforts.

Estonia also recognizes the importance of drafting and implementing policies and legislation which will aid in the reduction of the number of stateless persons permanently residing on its territory, in conformity with Article 15 of the Universal Declaration of Human Rights.

Despite a consistent and deliberate Russification policy carried out by Soviet authorities during the occupation of Estonia, the Government of Estonia wishes to reiterate that discrimination against Russians or any other ethnic group living in Estonia is constitutionally and legislatively forbidden. The

---

[2] Estonian citizenship is not defined by ethnicity. Thus, wherever references are made to a "Russian-speaking population" or a "non-Estonian population", it must be kept in mind that there are about 100,000 ethnic Russian citizens of Estonia and numerous ethnic Estonians who are not citizens of the Republic of Estonia, or even Estonian-speaking.

previously privileged status of the Russian language has simply been revoked, an act which is perceived as "discrimination" by some circles.

The Government of Estonia would like to address Mr. van der Stoel's concern that any discrimination on the grounds of nationality or ethnicity should be avoided, in light of Articles 1, paragraph 3, and 5, paragraph (d) of the International Convention on the Elimination of All Forms of Racial Discrimination, by reaffirming Estonia's commitment to the policy of non-discrimination on the grounds of ethnic origin, citizenship or other distinctions as established in the 1992 Constitution. In particular, we would like to note that the 1938 Law on Citizenship and its subsequent amendments and regulations for implementation are consistent with this commitment. All decedents of Estonian citizens are automatically regarded to be citizens, irrespective of ethnic origin; no persons of any ethnic origin or of any previous citizenship are restricted from applying for naturalization.

Estonia also recognizes the importance of implementing the law on Language Requirements for Applicants for Citizenship in a fair manner and of providing a maximum amount of information on this issue. To this end, at the request of the Government of Estonia, the Council of Europe is providing expertise on the drafts of legal acts which regulate the implementation of language requirements.

In his letter, the High Commissioner recommends that persons who fail the language test required for citizenship be given the opportunity to re-take this examination. This opportunity is already available and no limitations are proposed in the drafts submitted for expertise.

Because Estonia recognizes the concerns regarding language requirements for the elderly and the disabled, considerably simplified examination procedures for persons born before January 1st, 1930, and disabled persons have been provided in the legislation.

In order to implement in a fair manner the language requirements and to promote integration into Estonian society, the Government of Estonia is seeking to enhance the possibilities for Estonian language training. All efforts are being made to develop an effectual system of language instruction with qualified instructors, effective teaching materials and methods and greater use of varying resources, including an expanded use of the mass media.

This effort includes providing better and more comprehensive information to the non-Estonian population on their rights and obligations, pertinent legislation and regulations as well as on practical matters concerning citizenship application, language instruction and examinations and other issues affecting their integration into Estonian society.

These efforts are, regrettably, constrained by our limited financial resources. We must, however, overcome these limitations. We welcome any suggestions or assistance which the international community might provide.

Although it should be noted that the Estonian Constitution already includes the post of ombudsman, the High Commissioner's recommendation for the establishment of the post of National Commissioner on Ethnic and Language Questions to review potential concerns and serve as a liaison between the population and governing structures has been met with a positive reaction by the relevant Estonian authorities. This recommendation merits further examination to determine how such an office could most beneficially be established in Estonia.

Once more, the Government of Estonia would like to take this opportunity to reiterate its thanks to Mr. Max van der Stoel for his attention and assistance to Estonia. We especially appreciate the High Commissioner's thoroughness and objectivity in these efforts. We firmly believe that his analyses and recommendations will significantly enhance the rapid and positive development of our country.

April 18, 1993

The Hon. Max van der Stoel
Office of the CSCE High Commissioner on National Minorities
Prinsessegracht 22
P.O. Box 20062
2500 EB The Hague
The Netherlands,

Dear Mr. van der Stoel,

The Republic of Latvia Ministry of Foreign Affairs presents its compliments to the Office of the CSCE High Commissioner on National Minorities and has the honour to refer to the following issue.

We appreciate the great interest expressed by the CSCE High Commissioner on National Minorities which is carried out in accordance with the relevant provisions of the Helsinki Document, 1992 and the Summary of Conclusions of the Stockholm Council Meeting, 1992, as well as your great personal interest, as expressed during your visit of April 1 & 2, 1992, concerning the current situation in Latvia which is a consequence of the long years which Latvia suffered under Soviet occupation.

The evaluations and suggestions which you have provided in your introductory letter and the attached conclusions and recommendations are carefully being examined by the respective Government institutions of Latvia.

Most of your conclusions appear to be reasonably grounded, especially those concerning the lack of a new citizenship law in Latvia. As you know, the current Latvia Supreme Council is a transitional parliament and has no legal mandate under the restored 1922 Latvia Constitution to change the body of Latvia citizenship through naturalization or other means. This legal mandate will be held by the newly-elected Saelma which is being elected on June 5 and 6, 1993. Thus, one of the most urgent tasks for the new Saelma will be to adopt a complete citizenship law which will include provisions for naturalization. Your recommendations will certainly be presented to the Saelma members.

Regarding the proposal for the establishment of a "National Commissioner on Ethnic and Language Questions" Office, it should be noted that this question involves careful examination and probably cannot be implemented until the new Government is formed. However, we would like to mention that the existing system of human rights protection in Latvia has not been exhausted and provides, in our opinion, sufficient avenues for problem-solving in this area.

We are confident that our further cooperation with the CSCE High Commissioner on National Minorities will be fruitful and valuable for all CSCE member states.

Please accept my highest considerations.

Sincerely yours,

Georgs Andrejevs
Minister for Foreign Affairs
Republic of Latvia

REPUBLIC OF LITHUANIA

Minister of Foreign Affairs

Vilnius, April 16, 1993

Dear Mr. Van der Stoel,

Thank you very much for your kind letter of 5 March 1993 as well as for the sympathetic evaluation of the situation in Lithuania. I hope your valuable opinion will produce a major impact in clarifying overall policies of the Baltic States with regard to national minorities and remove causes for unnecessary tensions.
Allow me to touch upon your suggestion concerning the creation of the office of an Ombudsman. I was particularly interested in this idea and after thorough considerations we have arrived to the following conclusions.

According to the Article 73 of the Lithuanian Constitution offices of Seimas controllers will be established with the mandate to "examine complaints of citizens concerning the abuse of powers by and bureaucracy of, State and local government officers (with the exception of judges). Controllers shall have the right to submit proposals to the court to dismiss guilty officers from their posts".

I could convey to your notion, that drafters of the Constitution were very impressed by Scandinavian experience of Ombudsmen activities, and this Article 73 is an attempt to reflect this experience in our presently reformed state governing system. Although differing in names of offices and varying in details of mandate, the idea of officials taking care of public complaints remains very much the same, corresponding thus to large extent to your suggestion.
The said Article 73 also sets forth that the powers of controllers shall be established by law. Due to immense amount of legislatory job, this law has not been adopted yet. Nonetheless, I am confident, that respective committees of Seimas will not allow it to be delayed, and, as soon as the first draft will appear, it will be my pleasure to send it to you for your comments.

Wishing you all the best in your difficult mission, I remain,

Sincerely yours,

Povilas GYLYS

COMMENTS BY THE RUSSIAN FEDERATION[3]

Comments on the Conclusions and Recommendations of the Mission of the CSCE High Commissioner on National Minorities, Mr. M. Van der Stoel, in Estonia and Latvia.

The work carried out by the Mission of the High Commissioner in Estonia and Latvia can be regarded as constructive. The "Conclusions and Recommendations" touch upon key problems which, as long as they remain unsolved, will continue to have a negative influence on the situation of the Russian-speaking populations in those countries. It is obviously not in the interest of Latvia and Estonia to send the Russian-speaking population back to its historical homeland; rather, they should help those who have linked their fate with the Baltic countries under new circumstances to adapt, they should promote the integration of ethnic Russians while allowing them to retain their identity.

Estonia

In Estonia, the chief barrier to the stabilization of inter-ethnic relations is the language law. The recommendations relating to the holding of language examinations at the level of simple conversations are therefore welcome. Their acceptance by the government of Estonia would enable an overwhelming majority of ethnic Russians to overcome this obstacle to obtaining citizenship.

Important also is the recommendation that citizenship should be granted to the children of parents who are not citizens of Estonia.

The recommendation not to apply to the unemployed the requirement of a steady legal income would also considerably reduce the number of Russians currently deprived of the possibility of applying for citizenship.

The proposal that the utmost clarity should be introduced in the interpretation of all laws and provisions relating to citizenship is also worthy of support. Indeed, local bureaucratic arbitrariness is the principal source of violation of the rights of non-indigenous populations.

---

[3] CSCE Communication No. 125/Add.1 (Prague, 26 April 1993).

Efforts by legislative bodies to clarify questions of citizenship and language, as recommended by the Mission, should also contribute to the creation of a better psychological climate in Russian-language circles.

The recommendation concerning the creation of a post of National Commissioner on Ethnic and Language Matters can also be regarded as constructive. This would provide persons whose rights have been infringed with an additional impartial channel for defending their interests.

Latvia

The main problem encountered by the Russian-speaking population in Latvia is the arbitrariness of the authorities in conducting the so-called registration of the country's inhabitants. Therefore, coupled with the proposed reduction of the qualifying period of settlement from 16 to 5 years, the recommendation whereby residence should be calculated from the date of arrival in Latvia would enable a large category of ethnic Russians to apply for citizenship.

The Mission's recommendation for improving the naturalization procedure constitutes a good basis for resolving this problem.

The recommendations concerning the granting of citizenship to children born in Latvia, the need to have a command of the Latvian language within the limits of the "conversational level" and the abolition of the requirement of a steady legal income in order to acquire citizenship should also be supported.

As a means of limiting potential abuses in the decision of questions of citizenship, it would be of great importance to provide for the possibility of appealing to the courts against action taken by the authorities.

As in the case of Estonia, implementation of the recommendation concerning the creation of a post of National Commissioner on Ethnic and Language Matters would contribute to a more effective resolution of national minority problems.

On the whole, the recommendations and conclusions of the Mission represent a good basis for dealing with problems affecting the interests of the Russian-speaking part of the population of Estonia and Latvia. The document is based on a realistic appraisal of the situation, shows balance and compromise, and rightfully refrains from introducing changes and additions as regards principles.

LETTER OF THE CSCE HIGH COMMISSIONER TO THE PRESIDENT OF ESTONIA[4]

Tallinn, July 1, 1993

His Excellency
Mr Lennart Meri
President of the Republic of Estonia

Dear Mr President,

With great interest I read the communique issued by your office on June 25. Please permit me to express my great appreciation for your decision to create a round table of non-citizens and ethnic minorities. In my view this round table could be an important instrument for promoting harmony between the various population groups in your country and for removing misunderstandings about governmental policies and intentions. It is also essential that it develops into a channel for drawing attention to specific concerns and problems facing non-citizens and ethnic minorities. Your announcement also opens the way to forward a number of problems for examination to the Council of Europe and the CSCE. As CSCE High Commissioner with a mandate to promote dialogue and mutual understanding between various population groups I am of course ready to help the round table in any way I can.

I was also very pleased to learn that you have decided to apply to the Council of Europe, the CSCE and other organizations for an expert opinion, in order to obtain an unbiased professional assessment of the law on aliens before taking a decision in favour or against the promulgation of this law. I see this as another indication that Estonia is trying to ensure that its legislation is in conformity with international norms.

I am aware that no state can do without a law on aliens. As you will undoubtedly agree, however, it is also important to keep in mind that the law raises a number of questions which are fundamental for the future of hundreds of thousands of residents in Estonia. Please allow me to make a number of comments on this aspect of the law. Knowing that other

---

[4] Editor's note: On 1 July 1993, the CSCE High Commissioner on National Minorities sent the following letter to the President of Estonia concerning the new law on aliens which was adopted by the Estonian Parliament in June 1993.

international organizations will give their expert opinion, I have not tried to give detailed consideration to various other aspects.

In my view, it is necessary not only to analyze the law on its purely legal merits, but also to consider its psychological effects on the Russian-speaking population of Estonia. Most of those belonging to this group have lived in your country for many years and have established their roots in Estonia. They prefer to continue to live in your country, and many of them have expressed their attachment to it by voting for its independence in the referendum. They were citizens of the former Soviet Union, living in Estonia. Now, under the new law, they would be considered to be aliens. This in itself inevitably causes emotions and concerns among them about what the future may bring, even to such an extent that it could lead to a destabilization of the country as a whole.

In my letter to Minister Velliste of April 7, 1993, containing a number of recommendations, I made a plea for a deliberate policy of facilitating the chances of acquiring Estonian citizenship for those who express such as a wish, and of assuring full equality with Estonian citizens for them. My hope is that you would use the first meeting of the round table to emphasize that non-Estonians who have legally resided in your country for more than two years and who want to acquire Estonian citizenship will be free to do so. Fears that the language requirement would be so high that only a restricted number of persons would be able to pass the test, could be laid to rest by making it clear that the ability to conduct a simple conversation in Estonian will be considered sufficient. In addition, I hope that the Government will announce concrete steps to implement the recommendations nos. 2-7 I made in my letter to Mr Velliste on April 7. It is my firm conviction that such a policy statement would be the best method to convince especially the Russian residents of Estonia that the Government of Estonia does want to offer the hand of friendship and cooperation to them, and does not intend to begin a process of expelling a large number of them, as many apparently fear. Such a statement would in my view be a logical complement to the assurance of the Estonian Government, in its comments to my recommendations, that it is in favour of a dialogue which will promote the full integration of the non-citizen population into Estonian society.

Turning to the text of the law itself, as adopted by the Riigikogu on June 21, I should like to stress at the outset that quite a number of its provisions can be found in the legislation of other CSCE states, such as those provisions denying residence permits to persons who have committed serious crimes or who are employed or have been employed by the intelligence services of another state. However, there are other articles that must be reconsidered, taking into account the fact that so many non-citizens have lived in Estonia for a considerable number of years. I should like to mention the following points:

1. Article 8, paragraph 4, in its present form leaves open the question whether for instance a Russian resident of Estonia has to prove that he or she has not managed in obtaining the passport of his or her country of origin before he or she can apply for an alien's passport. It seems preferable to formulate the article in such a way that any resident who has the right to residence permit in Estonia and who is not a citizen of another state can receive an alien's passport.

2. Article 9, paragraph 5, states that any alien who is lawfully sojourning in Estonia shall have the right to appeal a decision to refuse to extend or to prematurely terminate his or her residence permit. However, this right to appeal is not granted when the authorities refuse to issue a residence permit. I would hope that the right of appeal would also be granted in such cases. Also an appeals procedure seems to be justified to determine whether the conclusion of unlawfully sojourning is justified.

3. Article 12, paragraph 3, mentions 'employment of other lawful income sufficient to support himself or herself' as one of the conditions for receiving a permanent residence permit. This article has already led to serious concerns among the Russian population in Estonia, especially in areas where there is a high rate of unemployment. It could be interpreted as opening the door for expulsion of those who are unemployed and are no longer receiving unemployment benefits. There are even doubts whether unemployment benefits can be considered as 'lawful income'. I express the hope that the law will be amended in such a form that these fears are laid to rest.

4. Article 12, paragraph 4, subparagraph 2, stipulates that a residence permit will not be issued to any alien 'who does not respect the constitutional system and does not observe Estonia's legal acts'. No reference is made to any article of the Penal code; nor is it made clear that a court has to establish whether or not a person has not been respecting the constitutional system or has not observed Estonia's legal acts. It seems preferable, therefore, to delete this subparagraph, even more so because Article 12, paragraph 4, subparagraph 4, already contains a provision concerning criminal offences. Article 14, paragraph 2, subparagraph 2, would then also have to be deleted.

5. Article 12, paragraph 4, subparagraph 3, states that a residence permit shall not be issued to any alien 'who with his or her actions has compromised Estonia's national interests or international reputation'. This subparagraph, which does not mention specific criteria to be used, nor the need for a court to establish whether Estonia's national interest or international reputation has been compromised, and which seems to provide too much room for arbitrary decisions, ought, in my view, not to be maintained, at any rate not in its present form. Article 14, paragraph 2, subparagraph 3, would have to be adapted accordingly.

6. Article 12, paragraph 4, subparagraph 7, states that a residence permit shall not be issued to any alien 'who has served in a career position in the armed forces of a foreign state or has entered the reserve forces or retired from a career position in the armed forces of a foreign state, nor to his or her family members, who have entered Estonia in conjunction with the service or retirement of a member of such armed forces'. This subparagraph seems to open the door for the expulsion of a great number of Russians presently residing in Estonia. I, therefore, make a plea for reconsideration of this article. One formula would be to restrict its application to officers and their families who have been demobilized in Estonia after 1991. Article 14, paragraph 2, subparagraph 5, would then also have to be reformulated.

7. Article 20 deals with residence and employment permits for aliens who settled in Estonia prior to July 1, 1990. It seems, however, not clear which conditions, under Article 12 and 13, would apply for giving such permits to those persons. While, for instance, a requirement to have a lawful income in order to receive a residence permit may well be imposed for new immigrants, it is important to make clear that a person, who settled in Estonia prior to July 1, 1990, will not risk expulsion for the reason of being unemployed or for not being able to meet the criteria for Estonian citizenship.

8. Article 21 gives a key role to the local government in implementing the law. It seems desirable that measures are taken to ensure a uniform interpretation of the law.

In conclusion, I should like to repeat that I fully understand the need for a law on aliens. The main purpose of my comments is to suggest amendments, which, in my view, without affecting the structure and many of the provisions of the law, would help considerably to remove the tensions which have arisen about its contents. Against this background, I would appeal to you to decide not to promulgate the law in its present form.

Yours respectfully,

(Max van der Stoel)

DOCUMENTS CONCERNING THE HCNM MISSION TO SLOVAKIA AND BUDAPEST

Editor's note: Subsequent to his visit to Slovakia and Budapest in February 1993, the High Commissioner sent letters to the governments of Slovakia and Hungary, containing his proposals for follow-up activities. The texts of these letters as well as the corresponding CSO decisions are as follows:

His Excellency
Mr Milan Knazko
Minister for Foreign Affairs of the
Republic of Slovakia
BRATISLAVA

The Hague, 9 March 1993

Dear Mr Minister,

Allow me first of all to express my thanks for the way your ministry has assisted me during my visit to your country on February 14 - 18. I did regret that your illness made it impossible to continue the discussion we had when we met in Stockholm, but I hope that such an opportunity will present itself in the near future.

During my visit, I met with Prime Minister Meciar who indicated that the government of Slovakia would favour the creation of a team of minority rights specialists who would analyse both the situation of Hungarians in Slovakia and of Slovakians in Hungary. I got a similar positive reply from the Hungarian Prime Minister. These favourable reactions encourage me to submit to you the following proposals which I also send to the Hungarian government :

1)The CSCE High Commissioner on National Minorities will designate three persons who can be considered to be experts on national minority rights questions and to be completely impartial, to study both the situation of the Hungarian minority in Slovakia and the situation of the Slovak minority in Hungary, basing themselves on CSCE principles and commitments.

2)The experts will be appointed for a period of two years, which might be extended if both the governments of Slovakia and Hungary and the High Commissioner on national Minorities would consider this desirable.

3)During the two year period, the experts can pay a maximum of four visits. A visit will always include a visit to both states. The time to be spent in each country during a visit will not exceed seven days. The experts will be enabled to travel and communicate freely.

4)The experts will not include nationals or residents of either Slovakia or Hungary, or any expert against whom either of the two states has previously entered reservations. They will have to be nationals or residents of a state participating in CSCE, but they will not include more than one national or resident of any state.

5)After each visit, the experts will submit their advice and recommendations to the High Commissioner, who will decide whether and in what form the advice and recommendations will be communicated to the governments of Slovakia and Hungary. They will be non-binding. If the High Commissioner decides to make the advice and recommendations available to the CSO, the government concerned will have the opportunity to comment.

I would hope that your government can agree with these proposals. In my view agreement on this formula would be welcomed as an indication that the governments concerned are determined to deal with minority problems in a constructive way. In addition, it might serve as a model for dealing with minority questions in other parts of Europe.

If both governments agree, the CSCE Committee of Senior Officials will probably have to give its formal approval, both because it provides for an involvement of the High Commissioner, and also because decisions will have to be taken concerning the financing of the expert missions. As the next CSO meeting will already take place next month, I would greatly appreciate an early reply of your government to my proposals.

As I have discussed the idea of the monitors with Prime Minister Meciar during my visit, I send a similar letter to him. A copy is enclosed.

Yours sincerely,

(Max van der Stoel)

* * *

* * *

Editor's note: The Foreign Minister of Slovakia responded to the above letter of the High Commissioner by sending the following letter, dated 20 April 1993:

Bratislava, 20 April 1993

Dear Mr. Max van der Stoel,

The wave of political changes on the European continent after the end of the Cold War was followed by destabilization of the region. The process of democratization has brought to surface a number of problems and conflicts previously suppressed by political totalitarianism. In root of a majority of these conflicts lays problematic situation of persons belonging to national minorities. Consequently the situation of national minorities. Consequently the situation of national minorities has recently become a source of concerns, tensions, conflicts and instability.

Having in mind importance of this question, the Government of the Slovak Republic, when forming its independent policy, considered minorities topics one of the most important issues. Legal guarantee of rights of persons belonging to national minorities was reflected in the Constitution of the Slovak Republic and positive and constructive approach to minorities issues was made a main principle of the governmental policy.

An evidence of the importance attached to this topic was the invitation to visit Slovakia forwarded to you by then Slovak Minister of Foreign Affairs immediately after your appointment at the Stockholm Ministerial.

I was pleased that the invitation was met by your instant positive reaction resulting in your visit to Slovakia in February this year.

Even not having yet the opportunity to be acknowledged with conclusions of your visit, I take the liberty to express my deep belief that your activities significantly contributed to one common endeavours.

May I reaffirm the interest of my government to henceforth approach questions related to rights of persons belonging to national minorities in the utmost constructive way. I am sure that initiative originated by the Slovak Prime Minister Mr. Vladimir Meciar and further developed and elaborated by you, would become a positive example - a model - how to approach and deal with questions related to national minorities in other CSCE regions.

The Government of the Slovak Republic fully supports the idea of creating an impartial team of minority rights experts to study situation of national minorities in both, the Slovak Republic and Hungary. At the same time I suggest for your consideration a proposal not to draw attention of the experts only to problems of Hungarians and Slovaks respectively, but to study and analyze the complete governmental policy on national minorities, basing themselves on CSCE principles and commitments.

Allow me to express my hope that further questions (exact mandate of the team, its relation to the CSCE, organizational questions, financial applications etc.) could be considered and decided upon, in co-operation with the Hungarian side, in the shortest time.

Mr. High Commissioner, I am sure that our common activity will be a positive step to extending dialogue, mutual understanding and co-operation on this field with the final aim of strengthening relations among involved CSCE participating States and bodies.

Yours sincerely,

* * *

His Excellency
Mr Geza Jeszenszky
Minister for Foreign Affairs of the
Republic of Hungary
BUDAPEST

The Hague, 9 March 1993

Dear Mr Minister,

Allow me first of all to thank you for the way your ministry has seen to it that my visit to Budapest on 18 - 20 February was a most interesting and informative one. As you were on a journey, I was unable to discuss also with you an idea which, in principle, had the approval of Prime Minister Antall when I met him on February 19. My proposals are to create a team of minority rights specialists who would analyse both the situation of Slovakians in Hungary and of Hungarians in Slovakia. This idea was also positively received by the Prime Minister of Slovakia when I visited him on February 18. These favourable reactions encourage me to submit to you the following proposals which I also send to the government of Slovakia :

1) The CSCE High Commissioner on National Minorities will designate three persons who can be considered to be experts on national minority rights questions and to be completely impartial, to study both the situation of the Slovak minority in Hungary and the situation of the Hungarian minority in Slovakia, basing themselves on CSCE principles and commitments.

2) The experts will be appointed for a period of two years, which might be extended if both the governments of Hungary and Slovakia and the High Commissioner on national Minorities would consider this desirable.

3) During the two year period, the experts can pay a maximum of four visits. A visit will always include a visit to both states. The time to be spent in each country during a visit will not exceed seven days. The experts will be enabled to travel and communicate freely.

4) The experts will not include nationals or residents of either Hungary or Slovakia, or any expert against whom either of the two states has previously entered reservations. They will have to be nationals or

residents of a state participating in CSCE, but they will not include more than one national or resident of any state.

5) After each visit, the experts will submit their advice and recommendations to the High Commissioner, who will decide whether and in what form the advice and recommendations will be communicated to the governments of Hungary and Slovakia. They will be non-binding. If the High Commissioner decides to make the advice and recommendations available to the CSO, the government concerned will have the opportunity to comment.

I would hope that your government can agree with these proposals. In my view agreement on this formula would be welcomed as an indication that the governments concerned are determined to deal with minority problems in a constructive way. In addition, it might serve as a model for dealing with minority questions in other parts of Europe.

If both governments agree, the CSCE Committee of Senior Officials will probably have to give its formal approval, both because it provides for an involvement of the High Commissioner, and also because decisions will have to be taken concerning the financing of the expert missions. As the next CSO meeting will already take place next month, I would greatly appreciate an early reply of your government to my proposals.

Yours sincerely,

(Max van der Stoel)

* * *

DECISIONS OF THE CSO

Editor's note: The High Commissioner's first reports on his Missions to the Baltic States and Slovakia/Hungary were presented to the CSO in April 1993. On the issues raised the following decisions were taken in relation to the problems in the three Baltic states:

"The Committee of Senior Officials

- noted with appreciation the conclusions and recommendations by the CSCE High Commissioner on National Minorities upon the termination of his visits to Estonia, Latvia and Lithuania;
- noted with satisfaction the constructive comments to the conclusions and recommendations received from the participating States concerned;
- encouraged participating States to support implementation of the recommendations of the High Commissioner on National Minorities, for example by providing assistance to language education in Estonia, Latvia and Lithuania (...)".[5]

Concerning the situation in Slovakia the following decisions were taken:

"The Committee of Senior Officials

- noted with appreciation the proposal by the CSCE High Commissioner on National Minorities for the creation of a team of minority rights specialists to analyse the situation of the Hungarian national minority in Slovakia and of the Slovak national minority in Hungary;
- noted the constructive comments by the participating States concerned to this proposal;
- requested the High Commissioner on National Minorities to elaborate terms of reference for the team of minority rights specialists, in consultation with the participating States concerned;
- further requested the High Commissioner on National Minorities to refine his proposal by submitting an analysis of its financial implications to the CSO Vienna Group for approval not later than 31 May 1993 (...)".[6]

---

[5] 21-CSO/Journal No. 3(*), paragraph 5 (f).

[6] 21-CSO/Journal No. 3(*), paragraph 5 (g).

Editor's note: On the basis of the proposals from the High Commissioner, the CSO Vienna Group at its 14th meeting in Vienna on 27 May 1993 decided on the terms of reference and the financial implications of the establishment of a team of minority rights specialists to be sent to Slovakia and Hungary. The CSO Vienna Group decided that the costs of the project should be borne within the existing budget of the High Commissioner.[7] The terms of reference read as follows:

TERMS OF REFERENCE FOR A TEAM OF MINORITY RIGHTS EXPERTS TO BE SENT TO SLOVAKIA AND HUNGARY[8]

1(a) The CSCE High Commissioner on National Minorities will, in consultation with the participating states concerned, designate three persons who can be considered to be experts on national minority rights questions and to be completely impartial. Their task will be to study, in the light of the general policies towards minorities of each of the governments concerned, both the situation of the Hungarian minority in Slovakia and the situation of the Slovak minority in Hungary, basing themselves on CSCE principles and commitments.

(b) The role and the accountability of the High Commissioner will be governed by the appropriate paragraphs of Chapter II of the Helsinki Decisions of 10 July 1992.

(c) The experts will be appointed for a period of two years, which might be extended if both the governments of Slovakia and Hungary and the High Commissioner on National Minorities would consider this desirable.

(d) During the two year period, the experts can pay a maximum of four visits. A visit will always include a visit to both states. The time to be spent in each country during a visit will not exceed 9 days. The experts will be enabled to travel and communicate freely.

(e) The experts will not include nationals or residents of either Slovakia or Hungary, or any expert against whom either of the two states has previously entered reservations. They will have to be nationals or

---

[7] CSO Vienna Group, Journal No. 14, paragraph 4(a).

[8] CSO Vienna Group, Journal No. 14, Annex 1.

residents of a state participating in CSCE, but they will not include more than one national or resident of any state.

(f) Within fourteen days after each visit, the experts will submit a detailed report on their findings, an assessment of the follow-up given to earlier advice and recommendations made by the experts and/or the High Commissioner as well as their advice and recommendations to the High Commissioner.

(g) The High Commissioner will decide whether and in what form the advice and recommendations of the experts will be communicated to the governments of Slovakia and Hungary. They will be non-binding. If, after consultations between the High Commissioner and the Chairman-in-Office, it is decided to make the advice and the recommendations available to the CSO, the government concerned will have the opportunity to comment.

(h) When, after completion of the two year period, the report of the High Commissioner evaluating results will be sent to the CSO for consideration, his report will include a recommendation concerning a possible extension of the mandate of the team, taking into account paragraph 1(c) of the terms of reference.

2. The activities of the team can be described in more detail as follows :

(a) The members of the team will meet the representatives of the Hungarian minority in Slovakia and the Slovak minority in Hungary in order to hear their views about various aspects of their situation as a minority.

(b) The members of the team will meet with representatives of the Slovak government in order to hear their views, in the light of their general policies concerning minorities, about the question of the Hungarian minority in Slovakia, and with officials of the Hungarian government in order to hear their views, in the light of their general policies concerning minorities, about the question of the Slovak minority in Hungary.

(c) The members of the team will also meet with the members of the relevant Parliamentary commissions, academicians, NGOs and individuals in order to gather as broad as possible scale of opinions on both the government's minority policy and the assessment of the situation of the Hungarian and Slovak minority, respectively.

In order to facilitate the task of the team the CSCE High Commissioner on National Minorities will provide a briefing for the members of the team before their departure.

3. It is understood that a member of the staff of the CSCE High Commissioner on National Minorities will accompany the team on its journey, and that the governments of Slovakia and Hungary will provide the team with interpreters, drivers and transport in their respective countries.

VI

SELECTED REPORTS

OF

CSCE MISSIONS

REPORT OF THE RAPPORTEUR MISSION TO CROATIA[1]

September - October 1992

1 INTRODUCTION

The following is the report of the Rapporteurs (Corell-Türk-Thune) under the Moscow Human Dimension Mechanism mission to Croatia on 30 September - 5 October 1992.

The report contains a description of the background to the Rapporteur Mission (Section 2). After a description of their visit to Croatia (Section 3) the Rapporteurs make some general observations, in particular on the situation in the area (Section 4). Following that they give a short report on the facts concerning the human rights situation brought to their attention (Section 5). They then proceed to describe relevant national legislation etc. (Section 6) and to discuss questions of principle in relation to the prospect of attributing responsibility (Section 7). They also make proposals for a system for administration of collected information (Section 8) and deliberate on a competent jurisdiction (Section 9). They, furthermore, make other proposals, which they consider urgent (section 10). Their report also contains proposals for an extraordinary meeting of the Committee of Senior Officials and publication of the Report (Section 11). Acknowledgements and a few concluding remarks appear at the end of the Report (Sections 12 and 13). There are eight annexes to the Report.

The Rapporteurs wish to emphasize that the impressions of their short but intense visit to Croatia are very strong. Even if they were able to prepare themselves for the visit by reading some of the many documents that now exist concerning the situation in the former Yugoslavia, these documents were not able to convey the impressions which an on-site examination of the conditions makes. The Rapporteurs are also aware that they have only been able to make a preliminary examination. However, according to the rules a Rapporteur Mission is a mission of short duration: its report should be produced three weeks after the last Rapporteur has been appointed, or, they presume, after their mandate has been finalized if this occurs on a later date. The Rapporteurs, therefore, had no possibility of going deeper into the

---

[1] Editor's note: This Report is reproduced without the annexes. The chapters 10, 11 and 12 have also been omitted.

subject-matter. But they hope that their proposals will be of service for the future decision-making and the analysis which is necessary for laying down rules for further action.

This Report represents the unanimous opinion of the Rapporteurs.

2 BACKGROUND

2.1 Formation of the Rapporteur Mission

On 5 August 1992 the United Kingdom informed the Office for Democratic Institutions and Human Rights (ODIHR) in Warsaw that the United Kingdom, with the support of Italy, Portugal, Denmark, the United States, Greece, Spain, the Netherlands, Ireland and Germany, had decided to invoke the Moscow Human Dimension Mechanism with respect to Bosnia-Herzegovina and Croatia. Subsequently, ODIHR was informed that France and Belgium had also joined the supporting States.

The rules of the Moscow Human Dimension Mechanism are laid down in the Document of the Moscow Meeting of the Conference on the Human Dimension of the CSCE. The relevant provisions appear as Annex 1 to this report. The United Kingdom had invoked Paragraph 12 of the Document which allows for engaging this mechanism in case a participating State considers that a particularly serious threat to the fulfilment of the provisions of the CSCE human dimension has arisen in another participating State.

On 19 August 1992 the ODIHR was informed that the United Kingdom had appointed Ambassador Hans Corell, Under-Secretary for Legal and Consular Affairs, Ministry for Foreign Affairs of Sweden, as Rapporteur.

On 29 August 1992 the ODIHR informed the United Kingdom that the Republic of Bosnia-Herzegovina and the Republic of Croatia had appointed as Rapporteur for the mission to their respective countries Ambassador Helmut Türk, Deputy Secretary-General and Legal Advisor of the Federal Ministry for Foreign Affairs of Austria.

On 4 September 1992 Ambassador Corell and Ambassador Türk informed the ODIHR that they had on that day appointed Mrs. Gro Hillestad Thune, member of the European Commission of Human Rights from Norway, as the third Rapporteur for the mission to Bosnia-Herzegovina and to Croatia.

Consequently, the Moscow Human Dimension Mechanism in the present case was established and ready to enter into function on 4 September 1992. The participants in the Rapporteur Mission appear in Annex 2.

2.2 The Mandate

Originally, the mandate for this Rapporteur Mission was to enable investigation of reports of attacks on unarmed civilians in Bosnia-Herzegovina, especially in Sarajevo and Gorazde, and in Croatia.

Due to circumstances which prevailed after the initiation of the Mission, the mandate was further discussed among the initiators. On 28 September 1992 the mandate of the Mission was finalized. The Rapporteurs were informed through the Foreign and Commonwealth Office of the following mandate:

> "To investigate reports of atrocities against unarmed civilians in Croatia and Bosnia, and to make recommendations as to the feasibility of attributing responsibility for such acts.
>
> The additional mandate, depending on how much can be accomplished in the time available and in the light of any organisational difficulties which may arrive, is to visit areas which may be under threat of ethnic cleansing, and to investigate allegations of the arbitrary arrests of Serbs in Croatia."

Due to the time which had lapsed since the original contact with the Rapporteurs, in particular since Ambassador Corell was first approached, they had difficulties in performing their task as a whole immediately. Furthermore, the United Kingdom informed the Rapporteurs that the Foreign and Commonwealth Office would need some time to prepare a visit to Bosnia-Herzegovina in view of the security situation. In consultation between the United Kingdom, the ODIHR, and the Rapporteurs it was decided that the Rapporteur Mission should perform its task in two steps. It was thus decided that they should first visit Croatia, commencing on 30 September 1992, i.e. two days after the mandate was finalized. The visit to Bosnia-Herzegovina is being prepared for mid-November 1992.[2]

2.3 Coordination with other Missions

At its meeting in Prague on 16 to 18 September 1992 the Committee of Senior Officials invited the Rapporteur Mission to visit Bosnia-Herzegovina and Croatia as soon as possible and to consult the members of the Thomson Mission. The Rapporteurs note, however, that at that time they had not been given their final mandate.

---

[2] Editor's note: Due to security reasons this second visit has never taken place.

In view of this and other requests for coordination between this Rapporteur Mission and the Rapporteur appointed by the United Nations Commission for Human Rights, former Prime Minister Tadeusz Mazowiecki of Poland, and Sir John Thomson's Mission, appointed by the Committee of Senior Officials, Ambassador Corell had contacts with Mr. Mazowiecki's office in Geneva and had a telephone conversation with Sir John Thomson in Moscow.

During these contacts the Rapporteurs were informed that Mr. Mazowiecki planned to visit Bosnia-Herzegovina in early October 1992. It was made clear, furthermore, that the mandate of the present Rapporteur Mission was different from the mandate of the two other Missions, and that there would be little risk of duplication.

2.4 Relevant documents

There are by now a great number of reports and documents concerning the situation in the former Yugoslavia. The Rapporteurs have tried to study as many of them as possible. They should like to mention in particular the following:

- Report of the CSCE Mission to Bosnia-Herzegovina 29 August to 4 September, headed by Sir John Thomson

- Report on the situation of human rights in the territory of the former Yugoslavia submitted by Mr. Tadeusz Mazowiecki, Special Rapporteur of the Commission on Human Rights pursuant to paragraph 14 of Commission resolution 1992/S-1/1 of 14 August 1992 (E/CN. 4/1997/S-1/9:28/8-1992)

- Further report of the Secretary-General pursuant to Security Council Resolution 743 (1992) and 762 (1992) of 28 September 1992 (S/24600)

- War Crimes in Bosnia-Herzegovina: A Helsinki Watch Report - August 1992

- Submissions of Information to the United Nations Security Council by the US-Government in accordance with paragraph 5 of Resolution 771 (1992) of 22 September 1992.

3 VISIT TO CROATIA

During their Mission to the Republic of Croatia, the Rapporteurs visited Zagreb, Daruvar under Croatian authority in UNPA Sector West, as well as

Serb-controlled Pakrac in the same Sector. They also visited Serb-controlled Knin in UNPA Sector South and Vukovar and surrounding areas under the control of the Knin authorities in UNPA Sector East.

The Rapporteurs held discussions with numerous representatives of the Government of Croatia, the Knin authorities, UNPROFOR, UNHCR, ECMM, ICRC and representatives of Serbian and Croatian non-governmental organizations as well as academics. On the last day of their visit they were also received by the President of the Republic of Croatia. For the detailed programme see Annex 3.

The comprehensive programme was made possible thanks to careful coordination by the United States Embassy in Zagreb in cooperation with local authorities and international organizations. The extensive travels and visits outside Zagreb, furthermore, would have been impossible in the short time available without the very generous and efficient logistic support of UNPROFOR.

The Rapporteurs noted the forthcoming attitude of the Croatian Government and its willingness to take part in endeavours resulting from future decisions within the framework of the Moscow Human Dimension Mechanism.

4 GENERAL OBSERVATIONS

The bloodshed resulting from the disintegration of the Socialist Federative Republic of Yugoslavia prompted the United Nations to engage in a peacekeeping operation under which "United Nations Protected Areas" (UNPAs) were created in certain areas of the Republic of Croatia, that is Eastern Slavonia (Sector East), Western Slavonia (Sector West) and Krajina (Sectors North and South). The location of these areas appears on the attached map in Annex 4. These are areas in which Serbs constitute the majority or a substantive minority of the population and where inter-communal tensions have led to armed conflict.

It is the task of the United Nations Protection Force (UNPROFOR) to ensure that these areas are and remain demilitarized and that all persons residing in them are protected from fear of armed attack. The United Nations police monitors (UNCIVPOL) are to ensure that the local police forces carry out their duties without abusing human rights or discriminating against persons on the basis of nationality.

As the Secretary-General of the United Nations stated in his further report of 28 September 1992, pursuant to Security Council Resolutions 743 (1992) and

762 (1992), UNPROFOR is encountering increasing obstacles in its efforts to implement the United Nations Plan in the UNPAs. This was due to the failure of the parties, and principally of the Knin authorities and extremist forces in the UNPAs, to give UNPROFOR the full and continuing cooperation which it must have if it is to be able to carry out the tasks entrusted to it by the Security Council.

Through discussions with responsible officers of UNPROFOR the Rapporteurs gained the impression that the implementation of the United Nations Peace-keeping Plan ("Vance-plan") is, indeed, blocked at present. They came to the conclusion that there is little prospect for a major change in this respect in the foreseeable future, as the demilitarization of most of the UNPAs does not make real progress due to lack of cooperation by local Serb authorities.

At present, approximately one quarter of the territory of the Republic of Croatia remains under the control of ethnic Serbs, who seem to enjoy support by the Government in Belgrade. Of these territories Serb leaders have established the so-called "Republic of Serbian Krajina" with its "capital" in Knin ("Knin authorities"). These areas largely coincide with the UNPAs, with the exception of the Northern part of Sector West which is under Croatian authority.

The Knin authorities claim their "Republic" to be an independent State with its own parliament, government, legal system, currency, etc. Elections are planned in the regions controlled by them in mid-November to which the Rapporteurs, in principle, were invited as observers. Furthermore, there are reports that the Knin authorities are considering to join, at least economically, the territories they control in western Croatia with Serb-controlled areas in north-western Bosnia-Herzegovina.

In their conversations with the Rapporteurs, the representatives of the Knin authorities insisted that the talks were not taking place on Croatian territory. They are claiming the right to self-determination for the Serbs in Croatia through the establishment of their own State, claiming that they had been denied the status of a nation equal to the Croats under the new Croatian Constitution. They adamantly reject the status of a national minority, considering the legal provision on minority rights enacted by the Republic of Croatia as insufficient for safeguarding their national interests. The Rapporteurs at present saw little prospect that this attitude will change.

At the same time it has to be pointed out that the economic situation in these Serb-controlled areas is disastrous. The supply of electricity and water is frequently interrupted or non-existent. Thus, besides most serious violations of civil and political rights occurring in these areas, which will be described in Section 5 of this Report, the enjoyment of economic and social rights must be considered virtually non-existent by the generally accepted standards of the participating States of the CSCE.

In their conversations with the Rapporteurs, some representatives of the Knin authorities admitted that the level of respect for human rights in these areas under Serbian control was generally low because of current circumstances. The Knin authorities, however, claimed that the legal system established by them was functioning. They further denied that there existed a deliberate policy directed against non-Serbs. They also stated that serious human rights violations affecting Serbs were taking place in Croatia and even more so in Bosnia-Herzegovina, where atrocities against Serbs were committed particularly by Muslim forces.

The power of the Knin authorities was previously upheld by military units of the Yugoslav National Army (JNA) and Serbian "Territorial defence forces" (TDF). The JNA-forces have now been withdrawn and the TDF-units demobilized, according to the Vance-plan. However, the Knin authorities have instead renamed their military forces "Special Police", "Border Police" or "Multi Purpose Brigades'" made up of members of the JNA, TDF and Serbian irregulars, in order to evade the demilitarization of the UNPAs in conformity with the United Nations plan. The Knin authorities have so far not revealed the total strength of these forces, but according to UN estimates they might total 16,000 armed men.

At present these paramilitary forces constitute the power basis of the Knin authorities. Members of these "police forces" are reported to bear responsibility for assaults, "ethnic cleansing", robbery, murders and other criminal acts against the non-Serb population in the Serb-controlled areas of Croatia. As described by informed sources, the rule of law in these areas has widely been replaced by the "rule of the gun". The Serb "police forces" are seen as a great menace by the remaining non-Serb population in the self-proclaimed "Republic of Serbian Krajina".

Military and other supplies from Serbia and Montenegro are crucial for the continuing existence of the "Republic of Serbian Krajina", as also shown by the fighting over the control of a land-corridor from Serbia along the northern border of Bosnia-Herzegovina to the Serb-controlled Banja Luka-region of Bosnia and further on to the Krajina-region of Croatia.

The military situation along the confrontation line in the UNPAs is reported to have been generally stable during the last two months, except for some armed incidents. In Sectors North and West, inter-communal tension has reportedly decreased. However, tension appears to have increased in Sectors East and South, where reportedly numerous terrorist acts, predominantly against non-Serbs, have been committed under a state of near anarchy.

It was also reported that in certain areas under Croatian authority, cases amounting at least to indirect "ethnic cleansing" and terrorist acts against Serbs, such as the destruction of numerous homes belonging to members of that ethnic group, have taken place, although to a significantly lesser extent than in Serb-controlled regions. Arbitrary arrests of Serbs have also been reported in areas under the control of the Croatian Government. The competent Croatian authorities have assured the Rapporteurs that any form of criminal act, whoever it may be directed against, would be investigated and prosecuted according to the applicable legal provisions. They also strongly denied that any persons were arrested only because they are Serbs.

Regarding possible future military developments, there is great concern that with road communications hampered during the coming winter Serb forces will try to gain control over rail communication: from Banja Luka via Bihac in north-western Bosnia-Herzegovina and further on to Knin. The Muslim-dominated region of Bihac with a population in 1991 of some 250,000 people is today besieged by Serbian forces. According to different sources there is a serious risk of "ethnic cleansing" in this area, should it fall under Serbian control.

It was also indicated to the Rapporteurs that a major Serbian attack on Bihac might take place before the onset of winter. Besides great civilian casualties such a turn of events would lead to a major new influx of refugees to Croatia. There is a risk all together of about 500,000 new refugees coming from Bosnia-Herzegovina. In this connection, it has to be pointed out that there are already more than 2.1 million displaced persons or refugees on the territory of the former Yugoslavia, according to recent UNHCR estimates. It was indicated to the Rapporteurs that the humanitarian situation in Bosnia-Herzegovina, in particular in view of the lack of food supplies, was desperate and that it might lead to a catastrophe during the coming winter. International assistance might come too late for thousands of people.

There is, furthermore, great concern that Serbian forces in the Krajina region might resort to terrorist acts on a large scale. The Peruca High Dam, south east of Knin, was until recently held by Serbian "special police forces". These forces were withdrawn after negotiations with UNPROFOR. The dam is said to be in a bad condition and Serbian forces have reportedly mined the area. Even after UNPROFOR took over the control of the dam on 14 September 1992, a considerable number of Serbian forces are reportedly still deployed at close distance. There is great concern that the Knin authorities might threaten to destroy the dam, which would result in an ecological disaster and endanger the lives of 40,000-50,000 people living south of the dam. Another area of major concern is the many tons of explosives said to be stored near the Serb-controlled Zemunik airport, which, if detonated, could cause a seismic tremor endangering the historic town of Zadar and the surrounding area with a population in 1991 of some 135,000 people.

In the view of the Rapporteurs, it is obvious that the deployment of UNPROFOR in the areas concerned is a major factor in preventing a renewed armed conflict. The difficulties encountered with the implementation of the United Nations plan has understandably caused the Croatian Government profound disappointment. There is thus growing pressure regarding the return of refugees and displaced persons to their homes in the UNPAs. In the view of the Rapporteurs, however, such a return appears hardly feasible under present conditions as the security of the persons concerned could not be guaranteed. Furthermore, any violent incidents in this connection would carry a serious risk of renewed armed confrontation.

Unless a political solution with respect to the Serb-controlled areas of the Republic of Croatia can be found in the coming months, a withdrawal of UNPROFOR when its mandate expires would in the opinion of the Rapporteurs probably lead to new and massive bloodshed, including atrocities against the unarmed civilian population. Such a development might have dire consequences for the situation in the whole region.

5 THE HUMAN RIGHTS SITUATION IN CROATIA

5.1 Reports on atrocities against unarmed civilians

There are numerous reports regarding atrocities perpetrated against unarmed civilians as well as the practice of "ethnic cleansing" in the territory of the Republic of Croatia. Although responsibility for these grave violations of human rights and norms of international humanitarian law is to be attributed to both parties to the conflict, it appears that the scale and gravity of the crimes committed by the JNA, Serbian paramilitary groups such as the TDF, and the police forces of the Knin authorities, are by far the most serious. On the Serbian side, such violations of generally accepted international norms seem to form part of an officially tolerated or even supported systematic policy.

The means employed for the creation of "ethnically pure" areas are both direct and indirect. The most direct form consists of mass killings or forced deportations of the "undesirable" elements of the population. Furthermore, random killings, torture, death threats, and the subjection of civilians to cruel and inhuman conditions in detention camps are intended to create a general climate of terror, making it impossible for a specific ethnic group to remain in a given area. The indirect form of "ethnic cleansing" primarily consists of the destruction and confiscation of property and various forms of economic strangulation such as dismissal from employment of individuals belonging to a certain ethnic group. In such situations, deprivation of shelter and the means of livelihood compounded by a climate of fear, eventually force people to leave their towns and villages.

For the purpose of attributing responsibility, the reported violations in this section are categorized on the basis of acts committed either on the territory under the control of the Croatian Government or in areas presently under the control of the Knin authorities. This section of the Report does not intend to duplicate the work on the documentation of human rights violations already done by the Special Rapporteur of the United Nations Human Rights Commission, Mr. Mazowiecki, on the situation of human rights in the former Yugoslavia, or the reports of the Secretary-General on progress made by the United Nations Protection Force in the implementation of its mandate in Croatia under the United Nations peacekeeping plan. In this connection, reference may also be made to the comprehensive reports of non-governmental organizations such as Helsinki Watch in the documentation of atrocities in Croatia. Rather than providing an exhaustive enumeration of atrocities perpetrated against unarmed civilians, therefore, the following is intended only as a broad cross-section of such violations focusing on particularly notorious examples which were brought to the attention of the Rapporteurs.

5.2 Mass-killings and arbitrary executions

Territory under the control of the Croatian Government

The Rapporteurs received reports alleging the arbitrary execution of Serbs by Croatian forces. It was reported that in mid-November 1991, eighteen Serbian men from the village of Kip (near Daruvar in Sector West) were arrested by members of the Croatian Army and brought to the village of Marino Selo, where they were allegedly executed in December 1991. Despite reports by the press and numerous requests by the family of the missing, an official investigation has not yet been concluded by the Croatian authorities. It should be noted, however, that when this matter was raised during the meeting of the Rapporteurs with the Croatian Minister of the Interior, immediate instructions were given by him to the authorities to conduct a thorough investigation.

According to reports, the Croatian Army massacred approximately 150 civilians in the vicinity of the village of Pakracke Polje (Sector West) in November 1991. This incident was also reported in the Croatian press. It is not yet clear where the mass-grave is located. Despite appeals by the families of the victims, however, no information has been released by the Croatian authorities thus far although the matter is under investigation by the Ministry of the Interior. It has been alleged that the authorities are delaying the investigation because the Army is involved.

Areas presently under the control of the Knin authorities
There have been numerous reports of mass-killings of unarmed civilians the most serious of which appears to have occurred in the town of Vukovar (Sector East). According to several sources, between 2,000 and 3,000 unarmed civilians who disappeared after the fall of the city of Vukovar may have been executed by the combined forces of the JNA and Serbian irregular forces. There are allegations that there are between ten and fifteen mass-graves in Vukovar and vicinity. There appear to be clear indications concerning the specific location of three of these mass-graves. The Knin authorities, however, have refused access to these sites. The Rapporteurs were informed by competent experts that if the exhumation of these mass-graves does not take place before the coming winter (i.e. by November), it may be impossible to identify the victims and the cause of death.

5.3 Forced deportations and detention camps

Forced deportations on the basis of ethnic identity have taken place on numerous occasions, in particular by the Serbian side. In many cases, the deportees have been incarcerated in detention camps where they have been subjected to serious mistreatment. Such incidents have been amply documented. It has been reported that non-Serb prisoners in the Baranja region (Sector East) are subjected to forced labour on farms. Apart from detention camps as such, both sides have reportedly engaged in a policy of "hostage settlement". This practice involves the encirclement of an entire village and the use of the inhabitants as hostages in exchange for detainees held by the other party to the conflict. It was reported that the Serbian side has perpetrated such acts on numerous occasions. It was also reported that the Croatian army has held the inhabitants of several Serbian villages in Western Slavonia (northern part of Sector West) as hostages.

5.4 Areas under the threat of "ethnic cleansing"

Although "ethnic cleansing" is a *fait accompli* in many cases, ethnically mixed areas continue to exist. In most of these areas, however, specific ethnic groups are either presently undergoing the early stages of the ethnic cleansing process or are under imminent threat of expulsion or killings using the methods described above. Such situations are characterized by the destruction and confiscation of property, discriminatory dismissal from employment and a general policy of intimidation and harassment against a target ethnic group. The objective of these practices is to create a climate of terror and fear which, together with economic strangulation, leave the affected individuals with no alternative but to flee.

In the territory under the control of the Croatian Government the Serbian population is the sole target ethnic group. In areas under the control of the Knin authorities, however, other than the Croatian population, ethnic groups such as Muslims, Hungarians, Czechs, Slovaks and Ruthenians are also affected. It was also pointed out that while the destruction of Croatian homes occurred primarily during the armed conflict, most of the destruction of Serbian homes has taken place after the introduction of the Vance-plan, in order to prevent the return of Serbs. Other than eliminating the "undesirable" elements of the population through destruction of their homes, confiscated homes are also used to resettle refugees and displaced persons, primarily from Bosnia-Herzegovina, belonging to the "desired" ethnic group, in order to create ethnically "pure" areas.

Among the areas under threat of "ethnic cleansing" in the territory controlled by the Croatian authorities, the following were brought to the attention of the Rapporteurs: the area of Rijeka and Western Slavonia, particularly the region around Pakrac. As to areas under the control of the Knin authorities, the region of Baranja and areas in the region of the Dalmatian coast have been reported to be under threat of ethnic cleansing.

5.5 Destruction and confiscation of property

Territory under the control of the Croatian Government

It was reported that in numerous cases Serbian properties have been destroyed or confiscated in Croatia. It was reported that over 6,000 Serbian homes have been destroyed in the last 10 months. It was reported that in the region of Zadar (Dalmatian coast), on 2 May 1991 approximately 1,000 Croatians from Bibine (near Zadar) joined a group from Zadar and proceeded to systematically destroy and loot shops belonging to Serbs. It was also reported that a number of municipalities had lists of Serbian homes and properties to be destroyed. It was alleged, furthermore, that these lists were prepared by officials belonging to the HDZ party. In the region of Daruvar (Sector West) it was reported that between April and September 1992, 85 Serbian homes were destroyed or damaged.

Areas presently under the control of the Knin authorities
It was reported that most of the homes and property belonging to non-Serbs have already been destroyed or confiscated by the Knin authorities. Such acts, nevertheless, are allegedly still carried out. In September 1992, six elderly people from the village of Svinjarevci (Sector East) who were terrorized into abandoning their homes and who were desperately seeking to cross the line into Croatian-held territory, were informed by the "Internal Affairs Office" in Vukovar that in order to receive permission to leave the area they had to sign an official form stating that they were voluntarily leaving their homes. The Rapporteurs were particularly concerned about information received that the Knin authorities have enacted a law in November 1991 allowing for the confiscation of properties belonging to any individual who is considered an 'enemy of the Serbian Republic of Krajina'. In view of the fact that no effective judicial system exists in these areas, it is apparent that the sole purpose of such a law is to legitimize the arbitrary expulsion of non-Serbs from their homes.

5.6 Discriminatory dismissal from employment and harassment

Territory under the control of the Croatian Government
It was reported that significant numbers of Serbs have been arbitrarily dismissed from employment solely on the basis of their ethic origin. In particular, this has been the case in government offices and police departments. There are also numerous reported incidents of harassment against Serbs. It was reported, for example, that in March 1990, sixty members of the Serbian intelligentsia were pressured to leave Zadar through threatening letters signed by the HDZ party which stated that "we have had enough of Serbian Communist dictators, our time has arrived. You leave or you will have to behave as we want." The local police took no action to protect these individuals who subsequently received threatening telephone calls warning them that if they did not leave, their children would be killed and their wives would be raped. It was reported that most of these people were eventually dismissed from work. It was also reported that the children of Serbs have been threatened, both physically and psychologically, in their schools in certain areas.

It was pointed out by the Croatian authorities that in the former Yugoslavia, Serbs occupied a disproportionate number of jobs, particularly in the public sectors including the police because of their affiliation with the Communist

Party. They contend, therefore, that their dismissal from employment is not based on their ethnic origin, but rather a consequence of the establishment of democratic rule and the withdrawal of communist privileges.

Areas presently under the control of the Knin authorities
In these areas, it was reported that practically all Croats, as well as other non-Serbs, have been arbitrarily dismissed from employment, going on the basis of their ethnic origin. Non-Serbs, furthermore, are subjected to death threats and other serious forms of intimidation on a regular basis. It was pointed out that there are few such cases reported at present because of the fact that few non-Serbs remain in areas under the control of the Knin authorities.

5.7 Arbitrary arrests of Serbs in Croatia

There have been numerous reports involving the arbitrary arrests of Serbs in the territory under the control of the Croatian Government. It was reported that in most cases Serbs are accused of being "Chetniks" and charged with "rebellion against the State" pursuant to section 236(f) of the Criminal Code of Croatia, without any evidence whatsoever. While in police custody, furthermore, there have been reports of torture and mistreatment.

It was reported that the names of Serbian intellectuals have been published in Newspapers in the form of a "wanted" persons list. If they are located, therefore, they may be arrested. It was reported, furthermore, that legal action pursuant to section 236(f) of the Criminal Code of Croatia has been taken against some 20,000 Serbs, many of whom have been tried *in absentia*. It was alleged that as long as the name of an individual of Serbian origin appears on the list, no other evidence is necessary for his conviction.

According to figures of the Croatian authorities, 73% of the 20,071 persons prosecuted from August 1990 until June 1992 were charged under section 236(f) of the Criminal Code. It should be noted, however, that apparently, these proceedings shall be discontinued pursuant to Article 1 of the Law on Abolition. (See Annex 7)

6 RELEVANT LEGISLATION AND ADMINISTRATION OF JUSTICE

6.1 Relevant legislation

Constitutional Law
Article 134 of the Constitution of Croatia adopted 22 December 1990 stipulates that international treaties concluded, confirmed, and published in

conformity with the Constitution constitute an integral part of domestic law. (See Annex 5) Such international obligations, furthermore, prevail over domestic legislation in the event of inconsistency. The provisions of international treaties may only be abrogated on the basis of means contained in the treaty itself or in accordance with the general rules of international law. Similarly, with respect to the period prior to Croatian independence, the 1974 Constitution of Yugoslavia provided in article 210 that international treaties which have been promulgated shall be directly applied by domestic courts. (See Annex 5). Yugoslavia had ratified all the major international human rights instruments concluded under United Nations auspices, including the International Covenant on Civil and Political Rights; the Convention on the Prevention and Punishment of the Crime of Genocide; the Convention against Torture and other Cruel, Inhuman or Degrading Treatment and the Convention on the Elimination of All Forms of Racial Discrimination.

The Croatian Constitution does not contain any provision prohibiting the transfer of jurisdiction to an international judicial body. The Minister of Justice, furthermore, informed the Rapporteurs that he did not foresee any legal obstacles to a decision of this kind, provided that it would be approved by a competent national authority. It should be noted that the Constitution prohibits capital punishment. (See Annex 5).

In practice, however, it may often be difficult for prosecutors or courts to assess the precise scope of the provisions of international law, violations of which are not covered by the Law on Abolition. In order to assist the competent Croatian authorities in the interpretation of the relevant international legal norms, the granting of expert advice, possibly through an international expert commission, would be useful. The Croatian Government has indicated to the Rapporteurs that it would, in principle, be ready to accept such advice by a commission or in any other form.

Conclusions

Since an element of the present mandate is an assessment of the feasibility of attributing responsibility for atrocities committed against unarmed civilians, the Rapporteurs have considered the applicable law in the Republic of Croatia, including the prevailing situation after the entry into force of the Law on Abolition. The Rapporteurs conclude that the category of human rights violations which fall within the present mandate are punishable both under the law of the former Yugoslavia as well as under the law of the Republic of Croatia.

6.2 Administration of Justice

Criminal cases are investigated by the police under the supervision of an investigating judge. The decision to prosecute is taken by the Public Prosecutor. In addition to the Croatian Public Prosecutor, there are local prosecutors and military prosecutors. The Court system consists of three levels: Municipal Courts (a total of 99), District Courts (a total of 14) and the Supreme Court. In cases involving serious crimes, the court of first instance is the District Court. According to information received, such cases may be appealed to the Supreme Court. There are also six military courts operating at present. The decisions of these courts may be appealed to the District court, or, in serious cases, directly to the Supreme Court.

In the areas under control of the Knin authorities there also seem to be three levels of criminal courts. The Rapporteurs have not been in a position to obtain more specific information as to the functioning of the judiciary in this area. Furthermore, they have observed a substantial discrepancy between the system as explained by representatives of the authorities and the situation as it exists in practice.

The Rapporteurs have also made an effort to assess the effectiveness of the legal system in practical terms. They cannot but conclude that there are serious and important deficiencies so far as it may concern the effective protection of human rights in Croatia. In areas under the control of the Knin authorities and in the United Nations Protected Areas generally, the Rapporteurs have concluded that in practice, there is no functioning judicial system at this time. It appears that significant improvements must be made in order to protect the fundamental human rights of individuals. It is the opinion of the Rapporteurs furthermore, that such improvements require substantial international support and assistance.

7. ATTRIBUTING RESPONSIBILITY

7.1 Principles

From the mandate it appears that an important task of the Rapporteur Mission is to make recommendations as to the feasibility of attributing responsibility for atrocities against unarmed civilians in Croatia and Bosnia-Herzegovina. In the view of the Rapporteurs, such attribution is feasible. It will, however, be a major undertaking. One must foresee the compilation of large amounts of information as well as the need to allocate substantial resources in order to conduct investigations, trial and the administration of long-term prison sentences in a number of cases.

As a point of departure, the Rapporteurs should like to take the rules on criminal proceedings laid down in international law. It is evident that whatever suggestions are made, they must conform to these rules.

Article 6 of the European Convention on Human Rights lays down the following: In the determination of any criminal charge against him, everyone is entitled to a public hearing within a reasonable time by an independent and impartial tribunal established by law. This Article as well as Article 5, lay down further guarantees for the protection of persons charged with criminal offences. Similar provisions appear in Article 14 of the International Covenant on Civil and Political rights. It is evident that the guarantees laid down in these provisions must be observed.

An additional requirement follows from Article 2 of the Seventh Protocol to the European Convention on Human Rights. According to this provision, everyone convicted of a criminal offence by a tribunal shall have the right to have the conviction or the sentence reviewed by a higher tribunal. This right, however, may be subject to exceptions in cases in which the person concerned was tried in the first instance by the highest tribunal or was convicted following an appeal against acquittal. If an international criminal jurisdiction is contemplated, the obligations following from this provision must be examined.

According to Article 1 of the Sixth Protocol to the Convention on Human Rights, the death penalty shall be abolished. No one shall be condemned to such penalty or executed. There is, however, an exception in Article 2, which lays down that a State may make provision in its law for the death penalty in respect of acts committed in time of war or of imminent threat of war. The Rapporteurs would like to emphasize that it is in their opinion inconceivable that the CSCE should endorse the death penalty.

7.2 Collection of Information

The first step to be taken is the collection of information. Such collection has already taken place in various instances. (See Section 8)

In the view of the Rapporteurs it is important that the collection of information be performed in accordance with international rules. They have not been able to investigate further the possible existence of such rules. However, they wish to draw attention to the European Convention for the Protection of Individuals with regard to automatic processing of personal data.

7.3 Administration of Justice

Ever since the outbreak of the armed conflict in the former Yugoslavia and the first reports of alleged war crimes and crimes against humanity, there has been a growing demand for the establishment of an international tribunal to try the suspected war criminals. Before discussing this possibility, the Rapporteurs wish to emphasize that irrespective of which course is taken, it is necessary to apply a system which covers the entire proceedings from the outset until a convicted person is released from prison having served her sentence.

This means that it is necessary to have a law which covers the period of investigation and the preliminary measures that may have to be taken, such as detention on remand. There must also be rules on which law to apply when the case is examined by the court. Evidently, there must be rules on the formation of a court and the possibilities of appeal. Furthermore, there must be rules on the execution of sentences, containing e.g. provisions for the establishment of the date of release, possible leaves during the serving of the sentence, treatment in the prison, visits by relatives etc. If there is to be an international prison, this would require a special treaty and an agreement with the host State on accepting the prison on its territory. Other rules are also needed.

This information should suffice to indicate the complexity of an international effort in this case.

In determining the question of how to proceed, the Rapporteurs believe that it is necessary to identify the requirements which should be met by a criminal justice system in the present case. These requirements could be defined as follows:

- Suspects should be brought to justice as soon as possible.
- The justice system must comply with international norms.
- The system must be as cost-effective and accessible as possible.
- The persons sentenced must be treated according to the applicable standards for the treatment of prisoners and this should be done under international supervision.

If these conditions are to be met, it is necessary to investigate several options before a definite decision is taken. It may even be that it would be wise to investigate the possibilities of combining different possible solutions.

In this connection, the Rapporteurs would like to point to the fact that, even though this mandate only covers Bosnia-Herzegovina and Croatia, a possible proposal on their part will also inevitably have an impact on other missions to the former Yugoslavia.

8 PROPOSAL FOR A SYSTEM FOR ADMINISTRATION OF COLLECTED INFORMATION

A substantial amount of information on alleged criminal acts has been and is at present being collected. Considerable efforts to collect information have already been made by various organizations. The Rapporteurs consider that there is an urgent need to co-ordinate the efforts in a more systematic way. This is in particular so, since the Rapporteurs have observed frustration amongst persons serving in the various organizations because of the fact that there is no central and competent authority to whom they could forward the information. The Rapporteurs, therefore, see a need to institutionalize the collection of information and to entrust the responsibility for this collection to a particular organ on a more permanent basis.

In the view of the Rapporteurs, it is important that a thorough assessment of the necessary rules for a system for administration of collected information be made prior to any such centralized collection.

Before a system of this kind is introduced, it is necessary to lay down the reasons for it. In the opinion of the Rapporteurs, such a system should:

- make it possible to establish personal responsibility
- make it possible for victims or their relatives to participate and at the same time to ease their grief
- give the possibility for witnesses and organizations to deposit their statements or contributions in order to assist in the establishment of personal responsibility
- give a clear signal to the world that the international community is prepared to take action and to pursue such efforts
- save the possibilities for different options with respect to actions needed, in particular the bringing of suspects to justice.

From the above appears that there are many institutions where information is now being gathered. It is, however, an obvious interest that all these efforts are coordinated and that an efficient system is set up. Before such a vast collection of information is commenced, it is necessary to establish the rules according to which this information is to be treated.

It is not the task of the Rapporteurs to make proposals as to where this work is to be done. Irrespective of who is to be responsible, it is necessary to establish an authority with the responsibility for the administration of the information gathered. It is also necessary to lay down rules governing the right of access to this information. This is important in particular with respect to information deposited by persons who run the risk of being intimidated, if not worse, because of their deposition. In the view of the Rapporteurs, access to the information should only be granted to police officers and prosecutors engaged in the preparation of indictments against suspects. This means that rules on secrecy have to be laid down before any substantial gathering of information is commenced.

The Rapporteurs believe that it is also necessary, in particular, to establish the collection of information as an international enterprise. It may be possible to perform this work under the auspices of the United Nations (provided the necessary rules are laid down). If the registration is to take place elsewhere, it would be necessary to lay down the rules for such international cooperation.

The Rapporteurs foresee that the work to be performed in this context will be of considerable proportions. Thousands of incidents will be reported, thousands of people may make depositions, be they victims, the relatives of victims, witnesses or otherwise. It is also obvious that the preparation of the prosecution of suspects will take time; no effort should be spared, and prosecution may occur at a relatively late stage, depending on the results of the investigation and the rules on statutory limitation.

It is evident, therefore, that a system for administration of collected information must be managed by computers. Such a system should be elaborated with the participation of experienced police investigators, prosecutors, judges, military experts on humanitarian law, and computer experts. It may be that participating States can already provide ready-made systems in this field. The system should provide opportunities for cross references, the retrieving of data from full-text documents, etc. A special problem to be dealt with is the fact that it may not be sufficient to use the latin alphabet only. The possibilities of entering data in the cyrillic alphabet must also be examined.

The Rapporteurs are convinced that it is not sufficient that data are collected only through intermediaries. It should be possible for victims, witnesses, etc. to make their depositions directly. They see no reason why the system should deviate from normal procedure when crimes are reported at the national level.

The opening of the registration system for individuals will mean that a considerable amount of data will be submitted to the administrator. It is, therefore, necessary to organize this collection of data in a streamlined fashion, thus making it possible to feed the information into the computers with as little effort as possible. This means that some kind of form should be elaborated (in the latin and cyrillic alphabet). This form should be structured in such a way that registration could be made in a very simple way, while at the same time it would be possible to retrieve the data through the employment of cross references. To illustrate how such a form could be elaborated, the Rapporteurs would like to convey the following:

First, there should be a page containing information and instructions as to the completion of the form. The form itself should provide, *inter alia*, for the following items: name of depositor; plaintiff/witness/other; suspects, if any; the alleged violation; time; place.

The Rapporteurs are fully aware that many of the persons concerned will not be in a position to complete a form of the kind they contemplate. Some would be too frightened to submit information in this way, and others would not be able to do it without assistance. In the latter case, they could of course be assisted. In the former case, however, there is little one can do. Nevertheless, in view or the functioning of the system, it should gain confidence, which may entail more courage among the people concerned.

In many cases there will be no problem for people who want to make depositions to forward these to the administrator of the system. In other cases, e.g. in the UNPAs, it would be necessary to establish some kind of collection with the help of the international organizations operating in the area.

Proposed *action*:
In order to investigate the possibilities of establishing a system of the kind outlined, the Rapporteurs propose that a committee of experts be convened *immediately*. The committee could consist of two experienced police investigators, one prosecutor, one judge, one military expert, one expert on humanitarian law, and one computer expert. The Government of Croatia should be invited to appoint one expert to sit on the committee. Its mandate should be to propose, within a very short time, the necessary rules and the administrative and technical solutions, and to make an estimation of costs.

9 DELIBERATIONS ON A COMPETENT JURISDICTION

9.1 National courts

From Section 6.2 above, it appears that the court system in Croatia is structured in such a way that it would, in principle, be possible to use it for the purpose of bringing suspected war criminals to justice. Under present conditions, however, the Rapporteurs see no real possibility for an effective prosecution of war crimes and crimes against humanity at the national level. There are several reasons for this:

First, the Croatian courts are still in a transformation process from the court system under communist rule into a judiciary which would meet the prerequisites for courts in States operating under the rule of law.

Second, the antagonism which the Rapporteurs have experienced between Croats and Serbs as a result of the armed conflict is so intense at the moment, that it is unlikely that the courts in Croatia would be considered as impartial and independent by many of the persons concerned.

Third, the trials will inevitably mean that witnesses and other persons concerned will have to appear before the courts. In such cases, it can be assumed that persons from e.g. Serbia would hesitate to go to Croatia to appear as witnesses against suspected Croatian war criminals. The same would apply vice versa.

Fourth, the bringing to justice of suspected war criminals presumably encompasses persons of high level in the respective countries. In such cases, it could be argued that it is less appropriate that the administration of justice be entrusted to any of the parties to the conflict.

Fifth, a reassuring impression from the visit of the Rapporteurs to Croatia is that the Government of Croatia is, in principle, in favour of an international tribunal and would seem to be ready to coordinate with other States in order to establish such a jurisdiction. This issue is further discussed under Section 9.3 below. The Knin-authorities, however, indicated that they would not favour the creation of such an institution.

9.2 Establishment of an international criminal court

The possibility of establishing an international criminal court has been discussed for a long time. Many proposals have been forwarded, but so far these proposals have not been successful. The well-known Nuremberg and Tokyo tribunals should of course be mentioned in this connection. It should be borne in mind that these tribunals were set up under special regimes by the victors of the Second World War. The scope of the present report, however, does not allow for an elaboration of these experiences.

The material available on this topic is extensive. It may suffice in this connection to refer to the latest contribution of the International Law Commission (ILC) in the 1992 report on the work of its forty-fourth session. This report also contains the report of a working group set up by the ILC on the question of an international criminal jurisdiction.

The subject-matter has been on the agenda of the General Assembly of the United Nations for more than forty years. Even if there are at the moment some indications that progress can be made, the Rapporteurs are of the firm opinion that it will still take a considerable time before a permanent international criminal court can be established. There are several reasons for this. One important reason is that there is a linkage between the establishment of such a court and the applicable law. In spite of the efforts by the ILC over the past years, it has not been possible for the Commission to get further than a first reading of the relevant draft articles. The Rapporteurs expect that these provisions will be subjected to thorough scrutiny by Member States and that the Commission will not be able to present a final draft in the near future.

Although the Rapporteurs are very much in favour of the establishment of an international criminal court, they would now strongly advise against waiting for such a court to be established before action is taken against serious criminal acts committed in connection with the armed conflict on the territory of the former Yugoslavia.

The Rapporteurs, therefore, conclude that it will not be possible at present to entrust jurisdiction over the suspected war criminals in former Yugoslavia to an international criminal court of the kind contemplated in the work of the United Nations.

9.3 An International *ad hoc* Tribunal for certain crimes committed in the former Yugoslavia

As follows from the foregoing discussion, it remains to be examined whether an international *ad hoc* criminal jurisdiction would be feasible. The Rapporteurs believe that such an undertaking is feasible. However, many aspects remain to be considered. The Rapporteurs have examined some of these aspects and should like to mention the following as a basis for further considerations.

Applicable law

One of the most difficult issues to deal with in the establishment of an international criminal jurisdiction is the question of the applicable law. Even if the jurisdiction is described as international, it would still be dealing with a process which under ordinary circumstances would be a matter for national courts, namely adjudication of criminal cases.

A special feature in this connection is the principle *nullum crimen sine lege*. The meaning of this principle is that the alleged crime must have been punishable at the time it was committed. In other words, the suspect should have been under the obligation to observe the rule in question when he committed the act. Whether he in fact did know about the rule is of no relevance. The question in this connection is whether international instruments such as the 1948 United Nations Convention on the Prevention and Punishment of the Crime of Genocide would be a sufficient basis for action by an international jurisdiction. The same holds true of the 1949 Geneva Conventions and the additional Protocols of 1977. The characteristic of these instruments is that they require contracting States to provide penal sanctions for violations of certain provisions in the instruments in question. The instruments themselves, however, do not contain any provisions as to the punishments which should follow upon conviction. Such provisions ought, therefore, to be found in national laws.

If an international jurisdiction is set up, one option would be to formulate international provisions laying down the punishment which should follow upon the finding that a person is guilty of a crime against any of the provisions in question, e.g. the Geneva Conventions. Another solution is to examine whether the national legislation in force is a sufficient basis for legal action.

In this connection, the Rapporteurs have examined Articles 141 through 155c of the Penal Code of the Socialist Federal Republic of Yugoslavia (see Annex 6) as well as the corresponding provisions in the present Penal Code of Croatia. In our view these provisions provide a sufficient legal basis for the administration of justice with respect to suspected war criminals in the former Yugoslavia. It should in this respect be noted that Croatia has abolished the death penalty, which is prescribed in the Penal Code of the former Yugoslavia.

We emphasize that the examination of the Rapporteurs is a preliminary one, and that it would be necessary before any further action is taken to examine in greater depth the possibilities of applying the provisions in question. (See Section 6.1 and Annex 6).

Procedural Law

Another important matter is the procedural law which should be applied. The Rapporteurs have not been able to examine whether the procedural law of Croatia would provide rules which could be applied by an international jurisdiction. It is self-evident that many rules have to be laid down in the treaty establishing the jurisdiction. It is also self-evident that the court, in accordance with international practice, would have to establish its own rules of procedure. For further examination, however, it is necessary to investigate whether there are rules in the Croatian national legal system which could serve as a basis for measures that have to be taken by an international jurisdiction.

The establishment of a jurisdiction.

The normal procedure for the establishment of a jurisdiction (the Rapporteurs will use the term "court" in the following) is to conclude a treaty. This treaty would, in the present case, have to be agreed upon by the interested States.

The main purpose of the treaty should be to lay down the statute of the court. By becoming a party to such a treaty the States have to accept certain obligations. The most important would be that they have to contribute to the budget of the court. On the other hand, they may also be in a position to nominate judges to the court. Another matter to be examined is whether there are obligations with respect to holding accused persons in custody or providing means for imprisonment of convicted persons.

Another important matter is the composition of the court. The Rapporteurs assume that there will be numerous cases brought before the court. Therefore, it is to be expected that the court would have to work on a full-time basis. It is also necessary to lay down requirements for judges to serve on the court. As the Rapporteurs have already indicated (Section 7.1 above) it is necessary to examine whether Article 2 of the Seventh Additional Protocol to the European Convention of Human Rights requires that the treaty provide for an appeals court within the system.

Prosecution

Another equally important matter is the arrangement of the prosecutorial system. In this respect, there are different possibilities to be examined. These would all have to be studied in detail before any decision is taken. The Rapporteurs would, however, assume that a permanent prosecutorial institution would have to be established. This is particularly so because this is the organ which would have to take all preliminary measures such as deciding on which cases to bring forward, which preliminary measures to be taken, which investigation to be pursued, etc. The functions of the prosecutors would be to investigate alleged crimes, to collect information and to examine information available in the collection system, to examine the necessary evidence and to instigate the accusation and, finally, to act as prosecutor before the court.

The Rapporteurs have been informed that there are a number of cases in Croatia in which accused persons have been sentenced *in absentia*. We would, therefore, point out that Article 14 (3) (d) of the International Covenant on Civil and Political Rights stipulates that an accused person has the right to be tried in her presence. This means that all accused persons have to be brought before the court. As long as States are prepared to collaborate with the prosecutor there will be no problems in this connection. However, it will be necessary to examine the relation between the rules of the court and existing extradition systems.

Implementation of sentences

As the Rapporteurs have already indicated, it will be necessary to solve the question of where the sentences handed down by the court should be served. They recall that those condemned by the Nuremberg tribunal had to serve their sentences in a prison managed by the four Allied Powers. One way of solving this question would be, therefore, to establish an international prison. If the matter is pursued with efficiency the number of prisoners may be considerable. Another aspect is that prisoners would have to be treated according to the applicable international standards for the treatment or prisoners, which may influence the locaon of the prison.

In this respect, the Rapporteurs note that the Government of Croatia has expressed its willingness to consider international supervision concerning the execution of sentences in Croatian prisons. The possibility of such a system would have to examined. In this respect, it would be necessary to connect the national rules on parole, etc., with the provisions of the treaty.

Language

An additional question is the language which should be used. Since the court would be designed to deal with alleged crimes from a particular region, the languages of this region could be used as official languages of the court.

Summary

The foregoing discussion demonstrates that there is a viable possibility of establishing an international jurisdiction to deal with alleged war crimes and crimes against humanity committed in the former Yugoslavia. The review which the Rapporteurs have made is certainly not exhaustive. They are anxious to stress that the review is made only for the purpose of making an illustration of the problems which would have to be solved if an international jurisdiction were contemplated. There are no shortcuts, and an international jurisdiction must be set up to meet the highest standards of legal protection as well as efficiency. This examination would have to be made by experts in the field.

Proposed *action*:

In order to prepare a draft treaty establishing an international *ad hoc* tribunal for certain crimes committed in the former Yugoslavia we propose that a committee of experts from interested States be convened as soon as possible. The committee should be instructed to elaborate such a draft and to make an estimation of costs.

10 OTHER PROPOSALS

(...)

11 PROPOSAL FOR AN EXTRAORDINARY MEETING OF THE COMMITTEE OF SENIOR OFFICIALS - PUBLICATION OF THE REPORT

(...)

12 ACKNOWLEDGMENTS

(...)

13 CONCLUDING REMARKS

It is beyond any doubt that gross violations of human rights and norms of international humanitarian law, including war crimes and crimes against humanity have been committed in connection with the armed conflict in the former Yugoslavia. It is also common knowledge that every day atrocities continue to be committed. The evidence is overwhelming and undeniable. The international community cannot allow this horrifying situation to persist. In various fields, decisive measures should be taken to put an end to this tragic situation. One such field is the legal field.

One of the fundamental principles underlying the Charter of the United Nations, the Statute of the Council of Europe, and the documents of the CSCE is respect for the rule of law.

Over the past forty years efforts have been made in order to establish an international criminal court; so far, without tangible results.

This is, however, a historical moment with unprecedented opportunities. There is a willingness expressed by concerned States outside the area to contemplate action regarding the atrocities committed. But even more important is the indication of cooperation that has been made to the Rapporteurs by the Government of the Republic of Croatia. Within the near future, therefore, it should be possible to establish an international jurisdiction to deal with the individuals responsible for the crimes committed. The course of action which the Rapporteurs foresee should also make it possible to bring to justice criminals from other parts of the former Yugoslavia.The Rapporteurs already foresee cooperation on the part of Bosnia-Herzegovina which has repeatedly affirmed its commitment to the punishment of such atrocities (see the letter dated 10 August 1992 from the President of the Republic of Bosnia and Herzegovina to the Secretary-General of the United Nations, U.N. Doc. E/CN.4/1992/S-1/5 of 13 August 1992).

In the opinion of the Rapporteurs, the international community shares a common responsibility to bring to justice those who have committed crimes in connection with the armed conflict in the former Yugoslavia. The rules enshrined in the relevant international legal instruments should be enforced in order to punish those responsible and to demonstrate the determination of the international community to take action now - and in the future.

Vienna, 7 October 1992

Annex

Members of the Mission

Rapporteurs:
Ambassador Hans CORELL, Head of the Legal and Consular Department, Ministry of Foreign Affairs of Sweden

Ambassador Helmut TURK, Ministry of Foreign Affairs of Austria

Mrs. Gro HILLESTAD THUNE, Norway, Member of the European Commission of Human Rights

Assistants:

Mr. Jan NYBERG, First Secretary, Ministry of Foreign Affairs of Sweden

Ms. Birgit KOFLER, Legal Officer, Austrian Federal Ministry for Foreign Affairs

Mr. Payam AKHAVAN, Danish Centre of Human Rights

Interpreters:

Mr. Franjo SCHRUIFF, Austrian citizen

Ms. Gerlinde GREGORITZ, Austrian citizen

REPORT OF THE CSCE ODIHR MISSION ON THE STUDY OF ESTONIAN LEGISLATION

December 1992

I. Introduction

1. The Republic of Estonia on 28 September 1992 invited a CSCE mission of experts to study Estonian legislation and compare it, and its implementation, with universally accepted human rights norms.

2. The mission was invited under the provisions of Rule 4 in the Document of the Moscow Meeting of The Conference on the Human Dimension of the CSCE, according to which a participating State may request a CSCE mission "to address or contribute to the resolution of questions in its territory relating to the human dimension of the CSCE". This mission differs, however, from previous CSCE missions, and breaks new ground, because of the Estonian government request that the experts compare and contrast the Estonian situation not only to CSCE standards, but also universal norms.

3. From the resource list of experts maintained by the Office for Democratic Institutions and Human Rights, the Government of Estonia selected three individuals to serve as members of the mission. Professor Christian Tomuschat (Germany), Dr. Klaus Törnudd (Finland) and Professor Roman Wieruszewski (Poland). The Office was notified on 12 November that Professor Wieruszewski would be unable to take part in the mission because of other commitments.

4. The mission visited Estonia on 2-5 December 1992 in order to be able to draw further conclusions about the issues involved. They visited Tallinn, Tartu, Narva and Kohtla-Järve. They met with representatives of central and local authorities as well as with spokesmen for different groups and communities (for a full list of meetings, see Annex 2 to this report.)[1]

5. The members of the mission conclude that they had full and unimpeded access to all relevant sources of information. The government of Estonia facilitated their efforts in a spirit of total openness and frankness. The

---

[1] Annex not reproduced in the present volume.

members of the mission therefore wish to record their satisfaction with the unfettered cooperation which they received during their stay in Estonia. They also acknowledge the important contributions made by individuals from many groups and communities. Without their assistance, the mission could not have gained a clear picture of the prevailing conditions in Estonia.

II. Initial Observations

6. The participating States of the CSCE are committed to implement fully all the principles and provisions of the Final Act of the CSCE, of the Charter of Paris for a New Europe and of the other CSCE documents relating to the human dimension, including, in particular, the Document of the Copenhagen Meeting of the Conference on the Human Dimension of the CSCE. These documents refer, *inter alia*, to the International Covenants on Human Rights, adopted by the General Assembly of the United Nations in 1966, as normative models. The documents also reflect the determination of their relevant provisions regarding full respect for human rights and fundamental freedoms.

7. It is clear from the public debate that has taken place in recent months, that the principal issue concerning the implementation of human rights in Estonia has to do with the presence of a large number of individuals in the territory of the country who are not citizens of Estonia and who are not ethnic Estonians. The problems related to this issue as well as other problems are compounded by the current economic difficulties during a continuing period of transition from a centralized socialist economy (until recently largely controlled from Moscow) to an open, market-oriented economy.

8. Estonia is traditionally a multi-cultural society, where several ethnic and religious communities have lived together over the centuries. It should be emphasized at the outset that the mission found no evidence of deliberate discrimination among individuals on the basis of membership in ethnic, religious or language groups. Relations between individuals belonging to different groups in daily life were described as good by many spokesmen. A few historical observations are needed as background.

9. When the people of Estonia finally were able to take full responsibility for their own affairs through a democratic system of government, they were compelled to deal with all the consequences of the policies and practices of the former Soviet regime. Forced deportations of part of the ordinal population, as well as creation of new industries in certain parts

of Estonia within the context of all-Union industrial planning (partly for the huge military-industrial complex), without regard for the local availability of labour, led to the settlement of certain regions of the country with new population groups without any roots in the country. Until 1952, none of the surviving former inhabitants of Narva were even permitted to move back to that city, and Sillamäe remained until two years ago closed to outside visitors because of the establishment there of industries serving Soviet military needs.

10. To some extent the new settlers in Estonia have been a mobile population, of whom many have departed after a relatively short time, usually to be replaced by others much like migrant workers in other countries. Others, however, have settled down for good and have raised new generations in Estonian territory.

11. The next influx has been so large that the demographic composition of the population has changed drastically in comparison with 1940. At that time, the largest minority in the country was Russian, corresponding to some 8% of the whole population. The new population groups that are now found in Estonia comprise persons from many nationalities in the former USSR, but most of them are Russian-speakers.

12. The ethnic composition of the population in 1989 was roughly as follows:

Estonians	963000	61.5%
Russians	475000	30.3%
Ukrainians	48000	3.1%
Byelorussians	23000	1.5%
Finns	17000	1.1%
Others	35000	2.5%
Total	1561000	100%

13. The largest concentration of people belonging to the Russian or other non-Estonian language groups is found in north-eastern Estonia, in particular in the townships of Narva, Sillamäe and Kohtla-Järve, as well as in Tallinn.

14. The application of the Citizenship Act of 1938, as well as the dissolution of the USSR, have created a situation where many residents of the country are stateless. This is by no means a unique situation in various parts of the former USSR. The specific issue related to Estonian

citizenship and the requirements for naturalization will be discussed separately below.

III. General Legal Framework for the Protection of Human Rights

15. The Estonian Constitution, adopted by referendum on 28 June 1992, contains an entire chapter (Article 8 to 55) setting forth an extensive list of fundamental rights, liberties, and duties of the individual. Most of the entitlements are granted to everyone. Where the Constitution confines rights to Estonians, it sometimes (freedom of work, Article 29; freedom of commercial activity, Article 31; right to information, Article 44) specifies that, unless otherwise determined by law, the rights concerned shall also be enjoyed by non-Estonian citizens. Only rarely does the Constitution create preferential rights to the benefit of Estonians alone. Even access to public service is, in exceptional instances, open to non-Estonians (Article 30). The Constitution provides that certain categories of property may be reserved for ownership by Estonian citizens (Article 32, paragraph 3). Otherwise, however, the law provides for equal treatment of every human being, irrespective of nationality (Article 9, paragraph 1). Additionally, Article 12 states that there shall be no discrimination on account of nationality, language or political persuasion. The philosophy of the Constitution is thus in full harmony with the two International Covenants of the United Nations of 1966 and modern human rights standards in general. In certain respects, supplementary legislation is needed in order to give effect to the constitutional provisions or in order to deal with certain problems of implementation. Intensive legislative reform is in process in Estonia, and some of the relevant issues will be discussed in further detail below.

16. The Estonian Constitution characterizes its human rights provisions as directly enforceable law. According to Article 15, everyone has the right to appeal to a court of law if rights or liberties have been violated. In that respect, the tribunals are empowered to declare unconstitutional any law which would violate rights or liberties guaranteed by the Constitution. It should be observed, though, that little experience exists with the practical application of these provisions. The court system is presently in a stage of reform and renovation. Thus, of the many persons who appeared before the CSCE mission complaining about alleged violations of human rights, no one had thought to bring these allegations before a judicial body.

17. In 1991, Estonia acceded without reservations to the following international human rights instruments:

- Convention on the Prevention and Punishment of the Crime of Genocide (1948).
- International Convention on the Elimination of all Forms of Racial Discrimination (1966).
- International Covenant on Economic, Social and Cultural Rights (1966).
- International Covenant on Civil and Political Rights (1966).
- Optional Protocol to the International Covenant on Civil and Political Rights (1966).
- Convention on the Non-applicability of Statutory Limitations to War Crimes and Crimes against Humanity (1968).
- International Convention on the Suppression and Punishment of the Crime of Apartheid (1973).
- Convention on the Elimination of All Forms of Discrimination Against Women (1979).
- Convention Against Torture and Other Cruel, Inhuman or Degrading Treatment or Punishment (1984).
- International Convention against Apartheid in Sports (1985).
- Convention on the Rights of the Child (1989).

18. Estonia has not made a declaration in accordance with Article 41 of the International Covenant on Civil and Political Rights. No communications from individuals in Estonia have been addressed to the Human Rights Committee under the Optional Protocol of 1966.

19. As far as international treaties concluded by Estonia are concerned, the Constitution specifies that they take precedence over conflicting national laws and other legal acts (Article 123, paragraph 2). Additionally, Article 3, paragraph 1 stipulates that "universally recognized principles and norms of international law shall be an inseparable part of the Estonian legal system. Thus on an abstract level, one might draw the conclusion that any derogation from international standards is excluded *a priori*, since the relevant international standard would in each and every situation prevail over conflicting national rules. However, it should be recalled again that the judicial system is not yet fully operational. To date, there seem to exist no judgments which in fact apply any of the rights enunciated in the human rights treaties ratified by Estonia to an individual case. This may also be explained by the fact that to date such treaties have not been published in the Official Gazette of the country in a regular fashion. Like the Constitution itself, the basic human rights treaties should be officially brought to the knowledge of every citizen. It is only then they can deploy their full beneficial potential.

20. As already indicated, Estonia is presently in the process of reorganizing its courts. A Law on Courts, together with the Law on the Status of Judges, was adopted in October 1991. After establishing the new National Court, which is the highest judicial body in Estonia, district, country, city and administrative judges will be appointed. Every qualified jurist can submit an application. The Government hopes that by 1 July 1993 all posts will be filled. The procedures employed in reshaping the judicial system are fully in keeping with recognized international standards. It is obvious that Estonia, after regaining its independence as a sovereign State, had to adjust its judiciary to the tenets enshrined in its new Constitution. The faith and trust of the citizens in their courts had to be restored. For that purpose, personnel changes were necessary as well. It is gratifying to note, however, that none of the former judges have been excluded from applying for the new judgeships.

21. The judicial protection which the individual enjoys will in the future be strengthened by the activity of the Legal Chancellor. According to Articles 139 to 145 of the Constitution, the legal Chancellor has functions which closely resemble those of an Ombudsman in Scandinavian countries. However, to date the law which is intended to elaborate on the legal status of the Legal Chancellor has not been adopted. Accordingly, the office is still vacant.

IV. Citizenship

22. The issue of Estonian citizenship was discussed at virtually all of the meetings the mission had throughout its visit. It became clear that the current citizenship legislation is perceived as discriminatory by most representatives of the Russian-speaking population. According to this view, the conditions set forth for the acquisition of Estonian citizenship would create a segregated society and impose permanent restrictions on the civil rights of nearly 40% of Estonia's current residents. The opposite view was voiced by Estonian officials who emphasized in particular that the law on citizenship, which was re-enacted last February, includes - by international standards - extremely liberal naturalization procedures.

23. It appears that what could indeed be considered as liberal under conditions of continued statehood does not fully meet the requirements of a society whose ethnic composition has dramatically changed during 50 years of Soviet rule. The mission noted with some concern the expectation voiced by Estonian officials that a considerable share of the Russian-speaking population in their country would probably remain stateless for a long time - unless they become resident foreign citizens.

At the same time, it was equally concerned about the attitude of some Russian-speaking local authorities who had apparently done very little to prepare their populations for the changes brought about by the restoration of Estonian independence and to prepare them for citizenship.

24. The overwhelming impression was that of uncertainty, of ample "grey zones" still to be filled with more detailed legislation, and of a poor level of information on both sides. This is why, on the one hand, many of the fears voiced by Russian-speaking interlocutors with regard to the citizenship issue seemed exaggerated, and, on the other hand, some of the competent Estonian authorities visited by the mission appeared to underestimate the dimensions and the urgency of the problem.

25. An early attempt to deal with this question was made in the treaty on basic relations between the Republic of Estonia and the Russian Federation, concluded in January 1991. Under Article 3 of that Treaty, both parties undertook to guarantee to all those who then were citizens of the USSR the right to 'preserve or receive' the citizenship of Estonia or of the Russian Federation in accordance with their own free choice. The choice of citizenship shall according to Article 4 (3) in the Treaty be carried out in accordance with the legislation of the country of residence and a treaty on citizenship matters to be concluded between the parties.

26. For those who choose citizenship of Russia or of other states that have been established on the territory of the former Soviet Union, the procedure seems to be in principle relatively simple. Stateless persons who have formerly been citizens of the USSR can in most cases register with the Russian Embassy in Estonia as Russian citizens, and by October 1992 some 17,000 persons had done so. There are still difficulties with opting for the citizenship of certain other republics, which may not even have had the time to enact the required legislation, and reportedly the Russian authorities have not always been able to issue needed travel documents to their citizens. Those who wish to opt for Estonian citizenship have to follow the normal procedure established for naturalization in the Citizenship Act of 1938.

27. The relevant texts considered by the mission are:

- the *Law on Citizenship* of 1938 as valid on June 16, 1940, and re-enacted by the Supreme Council of the Republic of Estonia on February 26, 1992;

- the Supreme Council *Resolution on the Application of the Law on Citizenship* of February 26, 1992;

- the *Language Law* of the Estonian Soviet Socialist Republic adopted on January 18, 1989;

- the *Guidelines on the Application of Language Requirements* in the Estonian SSR issued by the ESSR State Committee on Labour and Social Affairs on July 14, 1989.

28. A more specific decree establishing temporary procedures for the application of language requirements under the Law on Citizenship, was mentioned by the Citizenship Department at the Ministry of Interior but was not made available to the mission.

29. In accordance with paragraph 17 (1) of the above-mentioned Supreme Council Resolution, a law specifying the required knowledge of the Estonian language as stipulated in the naturalization provisions of the Law on Citizenship was submitted to the Supreme Council earlier this year but was not adopted. New draft legislation on this subject is under preparation, but no project has yet been introduced to the newly elected *Riigikogu* (National Parliament).

30. The relevant provisions of the 1938 *Law on Citizenship* are as follows:

Article 6: Foreigners wishing to acquire Estonian citizenship by naturalization must fulfil the following requirements:

1) He or she must have attained the age of 18 years, or have obtained the consent of his or her parents or guardians for acquiring Estonian citizenship;

2) He or she must have permanently resided in Estonia at least two years prior to and one year after the date of application for Estonian citizenship;

3) He or she must know the Estonian language.

Article 7: The requirements foreseen by Article 6, Section 2 and 3, regarding duration of residence in Estonia and knowledge of the Estonian language waived in cases of:

1) Estonian nationals;

2) persons who provide particularly valuable service to the national defense or society of the Republic of Estonia or who are widely known for their talents, knowledge or work;

3) stateless persons, who, prior to the date of application for Estonian citizenship have permanently resided in Estonia for at least ten years.

31. The information to be provided by applicants (including knowledge of the Estonian language) is detailed in Article 11. Article 12 requires documentary proof of statements made pursuant to Article 11. Paragraph 16 of Resolution on the Application of the Law on Citizenship stipulates:

32. Applications for Estonian citizenship shall not be accepted from:

1) foreign military personnel in active service;

2) persons who have been in the employ of the security and intelligence organizations of the Union of Soviet Socialist Republics;

3) persons who have been convicted of serious criminal offenses against persons or who have a criminal record of repeated convictions for felonies;

4) persons lacking a legal steady income.

33. As expected, most of the criticism directed against the Citizenship Act focused on the language requirements under Article 6, paragraph 3. Contrary to some statements made by Estonian officials (apparently reflecting considerations on specific requirements yet to be introduced; the most common figure given was a minimum vocabulary of 1500 words), the present situation is that any applicant for naturalization not covered by special provisions such as those found in Article 7 (see above) must, as stipulated in the previously mentioned decree on temporary measures, provide either a proof of elementary, secondary or higher education in the Estonian language, or a certificate proving that he or she passed at least an E-level examination according to the 1989 Guidelines on the Application of Language Requirements. (see section VI on the Language Legislation).

34. The mission met with a number of ethnic Russians who had passed the grade "E" examination currently required for heads and senior staff of

organizations, enterprise directors and others according to the Language Act. It appears questionable whether this fairly high degree of language proficiency should be made conditional for naturalization under the circumstances prevailing in Estonia, and particularly in the predominantly Russian-speaking areas where there is hardly any opportunity to practice Estonian.

35. There is an obvious backlog for example in Russian-speaking cities of the Northeast. Only 2% of the Non-Estonians in Narva (who constitute 97% of the population), i.e. approximately 1,700 persons, have so far applied for Estonian citizenship, whereas approximately 3,000 already have obtained Russian citizenship (all figures provided by Narva City officials).

36. According to the Ministry of Foreign Affairs, 3,402 persons have been granted Estonian citizenship in all of the country as of 5 October 1992. Of them 2,706 are ethnic Estonians. 378 persons of non-Estonian origin were granted citizenship as they have provided services of particular value to Estonia. Furthermore, 318 ethnic non-Estonians who applied for citizenship prior to the elections to the Congress of Estonia in 1990 have also received citizenship without fulfilling the residence requirement. The present number of applications for Estonian citizenship given to the mission is 15,000.

37. Some 5,000 ethnic Non-Estonians had applied for citizenship prior to the constitutional referendum of 28 June 1992. A proposal to grant them the right to vote at the September 1992 Riigikogu elections was subsequently voted down. All permanent residents above 18 years, however, do have the right to vote in local elections according to Art. 150 of the Estonian Constitution. It remains to be determined whether (and under which conditions) they also have the right to be elected: if no solution is found, only about 6,000 persons would be eligible for any local political office in the city of Narva, for example, which has about 90,000 inhabitants.

38. The full extent of the provision excluding from citizenship "persons lacking a legal steady income" remains to be determined. It should be mentioned in this context that according to Estonian Trade Union Officials currently 10,000 permanent residents in Estonia are unemployed, and in addition 40,000 to 50,000 persons have been laid off by their employers without pay (while still being kept nominally on the lists of employees).

V. Immigration and Travel

39. Among the legislation yet to be passed by the Riigikogu is a law detailing the legal status of resident foreigners and stateless persons.

40. It is envisaged that stateless persons would eventually be granted aliens' passports by the Estonian authorities. For the time being, the validity of their present Soviet travel documents has been prolonged until autumn of 1993, while Estonian citizens have already been provided with regular passports.

41. This temporary solution did not seem to be known throughout the country: A factory director at Kohtla-Järve told the mission that, as of January 1993, he would no longer be able to travel abroad as the validity of his Soviet passport was about to expire. In addition, some countries seem to be reluctant to grant visas to bearers of old Soviet passports. Once the Estonian aliens' passports are introduced, it cannot be assumed that their bearers will enjoy the same travel privileges granted to Estonian citizens by other countries.

42. While there are no limitations for people to leave Estonia (2,000 Narva and 1,800 Kohtla-Järve residents have so far moved to Russia during 1992), the granting of permanent residence in Estonia (as in other places of the former Soviet Union) is subject to restrictions. The mission was told that currently the maximum of residence permits to be granted by the local authorities is set to 0.1 % of the number of inhabitants per year, i.e. about 90 for Narva, where reportedly 500 persons are on a waiting list for family reunification.

43. The Minister of Social Affairs stressed that exceptions from the quota regulation are being made for immediate relatives. She acknowledged, however, that in some cases marriages "have to wait" in order to make it possible for the authorities to ascertain that they are not "fictitious" marriages intended to circumvent the immigration restrictions. The situation again seems to be most serious in Narva due to its close relations with the neighbouring city of Ivangorod and the St. Petersburg district of the Russian Federation.

VI. Language Legislation

44. To understand the present language situation in Estonia, the historical facts briefly outlined above should be kept in mind. The national identity of Estonia is intimately linked to the Estonian language, which is not

spoken anywhere else in the world. The defence of this national identity is therefore a matter of high priority for the Estonian people. On the other hand, the presence of hundreds of thousands of residents, mostly Russian-speakers, must also be taken into account. At present, a large part of the Russian-speaking community has not yet acquired Estonian citizenship, but this issue will gradually have to be resolved, and it seems that Estonia will remain a country with a sizable linguistic minority.

45. This situation of course existed also during the Soviet period, but at that time the Russian-speakers in Estonia were part of the majority population of the USSR, and it was rather the ethnic Estonian population that experienced many of the problems of living as a minority. Today, the majority population in Estonia will have to adjust to the continuing presence of a Russian-language minority in the country, while the minority must adjust to the requirements of living as a loyal national minority in independent Estonia.

46. In this situation, Estonia could try to develop a comprehensive language policy that offers Russian-speaking citizens sufficient opportunities to fully identify with Estonia and live as loyal citizens of the country while using their own language. It would be logical at the same time to offer members of both language groups ample opportunities to learn the other language.At present the need is much greater for Russian-speakers to learn Estonian, since the ability to speak both languages is much more wide-spread among the members of the Estonian-speaking population. The mission has concluded that most members of the 'new' Russian-speaking population intend to remain in Estonia, and this is taken into account by the government.

47. For various reasons many Russian-speakers perceive the policy presently followed by the government as insufficient or unreasonable. This explains to a great extent the concerns expressed by some residents regarding the human rights situation in Estonia.

48. International human rights standards do not give exact guidelines for language policies. It is of course clear that mass expulsions of population groups are prohibited and are certainly not contemplated in Estonia. Language is also generally mentioned as a forbidden ground for discrimination and it is in fact clear that the mother tongue of an individual is not a valid ground for unequal treatment in Estonia. (For example, members or descendants of the "old" Russian-speaking minority in Estonia are automatically citizens of Estonia regardless of their ability to speak Estonian.)

49. The Language Act of 1989, which is still in force together with supplementary official instructions and guidelines, is based on the need to defend the rights of all to use the Estonian language in all spheres of public life. The law establishes Estonian as the single official language of the Republic and guarantees all individuals the right to "communicate and conduct his or her affairs in Estonian in all bodies of State authority and government, as well as in institutions, enterprises, and organization" (Article 2). The same right is guaranteed to all individuals as regards similar use of the Russian language (Article 3). The law acknowledges "the inalienable right of citizens of all other nationalities to use their native language and develop their vernacular culture, as well as the equality of all citizens before the law regardless of their native language" (preamble).

50. The law contains several provisions (Articles 5, 6, 7) which provide excellent protection to individuals wishing to use their own language as clients in services and trade or as subordinates in places of employment. The other side of the coin is that the law also requires certain levels of language ability of persons whose job requires communication with individuals (Article 4).

51. Although this law was enacted in 1989, it was reportedly not implemented effectively. The former Soviet regime did not enforce the law, and conditions for effective bi-lingualism were not created equally as regards the two language groups. In particular, Estonian was not taught in the Russian-language schools, while all Estonian-language schools did teach Russian.

52. The official guidelines for implementing the Language Act, also issued in 1989, establish six categories of language knowledge, from A to F. Category A requires a language knowledge corresponding to oral and written comprehension of 800 of the most common words and expressions. Category E corresponds to an ability to use the language in one's own profession, both orally and in written form, at a level which corresponds to the use of a vocabulary of some 2500 words. Category F is defined as full knowledge of the language. The guidelines indicate in great detail the jobs serving the public where the employees must show that they have passed the test for a certain level of language knowledge (for example level C for most retail sales and service jobs, levels D or E for persons in leading positions).

53. The Estonian government has established a network of 33 language centers in the whole country (*Eesti keelekeskus*), which test applicants

who want to prove their knowledge of Estonian. The tests are given by three-person boards. Until now, some 14,000 certificates have been issued in the country for all levels. The centers also arrange or help to arrange language training courses. State subsidies are available for local governments that want to arrange language training. Some companies provide language courses free of charge to their employees, but in other cases people have to pay them. The mission heard many complaints to the effect that there is a shortage of competent teachers and good teaching materials and that the language courses in many cases are expensive. More serious complaints were also heard questioning the justification for the language requirements or expressing fear that many persons would lose their jobs if they are unable to pass the test for the level required. In particular, many physicians and other specialists working in a totally Russian language environment as for example in Narva seem to feel no motivation to learn Estonian and pass the test.

54. While the Language Act represents a commendable effort to provide bilingual services to the population, efforts to establish common standards for employees, whether public or private, in the whole country irrespectively of local conditions go farther than normally is the case in multilingual countries. Estonia is not officially a bilingual state, since only Estonian is by law determined as the official language. In practice, however the country functions on the basis of bi-lingualism. The official gazette (*Riigi teataja*) is published in an equivalent Russian edition (*Vedomosti Estonskoj Respubliki*), in several localities the local government operates either in two languages or only in Russian, individuals can use either language in courts, etc. There is one full-service radio channel in Russian serving the whole country, and national TV offers news in Russian on weekdays as well as other Russian programs on Saturdays. Reportedly, the visibility of Estonian TV is for technical reasons not good in the Narva region, and the Estonian authorities recognize that this situation ought to be remedied and that the share of Russian-language programs in total TV programming ought to be increased. So far, the availability of several radio and TV channels with programs broadcast from Russia itself has made up for these shortages, but these programs, naturally, carry little news of Estonia.

VII. Property Rights

55. Various CSCE documents give guidelines for the enjoyment of property rights which are, however, prescribed in a general manner. In accordance with the Document of the Copenhagen Meeting of the Conference on the

Human Dimension of the CSCE everyone has the right to peacefully enjoy property either on his own or in common with others. No one may be deprived of his property except in the public interest and subject to the conditions provided for by law and consistent with international commitments and obligations. In accordance with the Charter of Paris for a New Europe everyone has the right to own property alone or in association and to exercise individual enterprise. The Document of the Bonn Conference on Economic Co-operation in Europe includes standards which touch upon property rights of citizens of other participating States from a slightly different angle.

56. In accordance with Article 32 of the Constitution of the Republic of Estonia the property rights of everyone are inviolable and enjoy equal protection. The law may however establish, in the public interest, categories of property in Estonia which are reserved for ownership by Estonian citizens. No property shall be expropriated without the consent of the owner except in cases of public interest, in accordance with procedures determined by law, and in exchange for equitable and appropriate compensation. When expropriation has been carried out without the consent of the owner, he shall have legal remedies to contest it.

57. The current legislation of Estonia gives foreigners and stateless persons the same rights with respect to private property as Estonian citizens, with the exception of areas where certain specific restrictions have been established. The most important restriction is that non-citizens do not as a rule have the right to own land. Such restrictions may be found in the legislation of other states as well and cannot be considered as violations of international standards.

58. The property reform in Estonia has been carried out in accordance with the Principles of the Property Reform Act, which was adopted in June 1991. This Act provides for restoration and compensation for property, privatization and creation of municipal property. More detailed legislation has been adopted and is currently being drafted in order to facilitate the privatization process and stimulate the economy.

59. The right of foreigners and stateless persons to make claims for restoration or compensation of property unlawfully seized during the Soviet period is restricted. Non-citizens who resided permanently in the territory of the Republic of Estonia in June 1991 (at the time of adoption of the relevant legislation) have the right to apply for restoration or compensation of their property regardless of their citizenship. The

persons who had property in Estonia and whose property was subsequently unlawfully seized but who lacked citizenship and now live outside of Estonia have no right to restoration or compensation of their property by virtue of law. Claims of such persons shall be settled by a treaty between the Republic of Estonia and the state of which the former owner is a citizen. Until now, no such treaties have been concluded with any state. Restrictions based on the citizenship and residence seem to have little practical significance to non-citizens who reside permanently in Estonia at the moment.

60. The Land Reform Act differentiates between cases where the right of ownership is restored and those where property is sold to a new owner, the last-mentioned falling under the concept of actual privatization. Former owners of land are entitled to restoration regardless of citizenship if they were permanent residents of Estonia in June 1991. Persons who do not have Estonian citizenship cannot participate in the actual privatization of land but may lease land property by agreements for a maximum time period of 99 years. This concerns permanent residents of Estonian as well as other foreigners, stateless persons and foreign legal persons. Foreigners and stateless persons may also fully participate in privatization of other forms of property, including especially the industrial privatization. The right to own land and own enterprises as stockholders gives non-citizens reasonable possibilities to run commercial businesses in Estonia.

61. The next phase of privatization includes residential dwellings. Any person who has worked in Estonia is entitled to one square meter of housing units for each working year. There is thus no discrimination contrary to the principle of equality which applies to all rights that satisfy basic social needs.

VIII. Economic, Social and Cultural Rights

62. The difficulties which Estonia presently has to grapple with concerning economic and social rights are not so much related to its legislation in this specific field. As already noted, the Constitution grants its rights generally to everyone. Where it deviates from that line, as in the case of the right to freely choose one's activity, profession and place of work (Article 29, paragraph 1), it must be read in conjunction with the International Covenant on Economic Social and Cultural Rights, which confers the right to work on "everyone" (Article 6). The right to work is a human right which may not be denied to any inhabitant of a country, irrespective of his nationality, language or political opinion. The mission

has not, however, been informed about any discrimination enacted by law. This applies also to the right of housing, recognized by Article 11 of the Covenant.

63. To be sure, the difficult economic situation of Estonia affects most economic and social rights. Unemployment has risen, due, in particular, to the need to adjust production lines to a market economy where there is no demand for military goods. Although unemployment seems to hit the Russian-speaking population in Estonia relatively harder than Estonians, this imbalance cannot be attributed to any policies of deliberate discrimination. Rather it results from divergent labour patterns. Mostly, the Russian-speaking population had their jobs in industrial undertakings that had to cut down their labour force in order to survive. On the other hand, Estonians were to a far greater extent active in the agricultural sector.

64. As far as social security is concerned, it would appear obvious that Russia and Estonia must conclude treaties regulating who has to assume the financial burden of old-age pensioners. It cannot be expected of Estonia that it shoulder that charge with regard to all of the persons in its territory, especially because many retired public servants chose Estonia as a country of residence.

65. The mission was informed that Estonia currently has no system of social assistance. After losing his job, a person is entitled to unemployment benefits for six months. Thereafter, he is totally left alone. Soup kitchens are organized during the winter, some shelter is provided, but these relief measures are not organized on a national scale and may not be available at all in rural areas. It must be acknowledged that Estonia simply cannot afford to establish an elaborate system of social assistance, given the fact that even employed persons now earn minimum wages which only suffice to cover their most basic needs. The Covenant on Economic, Social and Cultural Rights does not set forth a right to social assistance, but it recognizes the right of everyone to an adequate standard of living. The requirements of this guarantee vary according to the general level of well-being of a country. A rich country certainly has to provide more material assistance to a needy person than a country in difficult economic conditions. In any event, however, nobody must be left to starve or die from exposure to cold. Estonia should therefore strive to establish a system of minimum assistance to the benefit of those who are no longer entitled to unemployment benefits and who lack other income.

66. The most delicate issue is the effect of the language requirements stipulated by the Language Act of 1989 on the enjoyment of economic and social rights. In accordance with Article 5 of that law, everyone whose job requires communication with other people shall be subjected to certain requirements of language competence. It should be noted that this provision was enacted as a reaction to bitter experiences of the past when Estonian citizens found it difficult to be understood by persons whose services they urgently required. On the other hand, the International Covenant on Economic, Social and Cultural Rights states quite categorically that the rights which it guarantees shall be enjoyed by everyone without any discrimination on grounds of language (Article 2, paragraph 2). A similar reference to language as a forbidden ground of distinction is also to be found in the Estonian Constitution (Article 12, paragraph 1).

67. On the whole, the mission found no evidence supporting charges of discrimination against the Russian-speaking population. Many of the mission's interlocutors expressed genuine fears and anxieties about an unknown future. Still no substantiated complaints emerged. Similarly, trade union leaders contacted by the mission could not refer to any concrete case of allegations of discrimination based on language. To a great extent, therefore, the problems, as they are felt to exist, stem from a lack of information and could thus be easily remedied. Unfortunately, the Estonian administration itself could not always provide precise information on the requirements prescribed by law. In this respect also a general flexibility of the hitherto rather rigid language regime could have beneficial effects.

IX. Summary and Recommendations

68. The Constitution of Estonia as well as other laws examined by the mission meet the international standards for the enjoyment of human rights. Certain shortcomings need to be overcome by filling gaps in the legislation and by strengthening the judiciary and the administration. This process is under way.

69. There is also a need to improve the dissemination of information to the members of the whole population concerning their rights and duties. This problem, like many others encountered by the mission particularly in the economic and social field, could of course be more easily remedied, if more resources were available to the government.

70. The current situation of a large number of stateless residents of Estonia, most of whom are Russian-speaking former citizens of the Soviet Union, gives rise to some concern. Essentially, Estonian citizenship is acquired by birth from parents who held Estonian nationality according to the Citizenship Act of 1938. This means that all those who came to Estonia after the annexation of the country by the Soviet Union in 1940 can become Estonian nationals only by naturalization; the same applies to their descendants. While former citizens of the Soviet Union can obtain the citizenship of Russia, Ukraine, Belarus or of other republics corresponding to their nationalities, many individuals refrain from taking that step, because they do not want to become aliens in their country of residence where they feel at home.

71. The mission concurs with earlier findings to the effect that no international human rights instrument recognizes the right to a nationality as a human right enjoyed by everyone (cf. Report on Human Rights in the Republic of Estonia. Ad hoc Committee on Relations with Eastern Europe, Parliamentary Assembly, Council of Europe, Strasbourg 1991). Neither under Article 15 of the Universal Declaration of Human Rights nor under any of the CSCE documents is Estonia obligated to grant its citizenship to all residents without any preconditions. Estonia has not acceded to the Convention on the Reduction of Statelessness of 1961. However, international commitments flow from Article 24, paragraph 3, of the International Covenant on Civil and Political Rights, according to which every child has the right to acquire a nationality. By virtue of this provision, States are obligated to confer their nationality on any children who otherwise would remain stateless at birth.

72. It should be in the interest of Estonia itself to facilitate the integration of the large majority of the persons remaining in the country and to provide them with equal rights including citizenship as soon as possible. The mission therefore recommends the following specific measures in reference to citizenship:

- A law detailing language requirements for the acquisition of Estonian citizenship, significantly lower than the level currently required, should be adopted without further delay.

- Exceptions should be provided that would waive all language requirements for invalids and pensioners who fulfil the conditions of Article 7, paragraph 3 of the Citizenship Act.

- Steps should be taken to ensure that paragraph 16 (4) of the resolution of the Supreme Council of 26 February 1992 shall not be applied with respect to legal residents of Estonia who have lost their steady income due to unemployment.

- In full conformity with the Citizenship Act (Article 3, paragraph 6), it should be ensured that children born from former nationals of the USSR, who would otherwise be stateless, are registered as Estonian citizens.

73. According to longstanding CSCE standards, participating States are obligated to facilitate family reunification. Minor children must be able to live with their parents and spouses must be able to join one another. Although it is certainly legitimate to check whether a marriage is a real and not only a fictitious one, the mission recommends that Estonia review its legislation and practices with a view to ensuring that there are no inconsistencies with the standard of family reunification. There should be no waiting lists compelling family members to live separately for years.

74. Since freedom to leave one's country is an undisputed rule of international human rights law, Estonia should do everything in its power to grant every person lawfully resident within its territory a real opportunity freely to travel abroad and to return to Estonia. For that purpose, persons who are currently stateless should be provided with an alien's passport if they are no more holders [*of*] valid passports of the former Soviet Union.

75. Since the only viable and realistic assumption for the future is that Estonia will permanently have a linguistic minority of perhaps 25-40% of the total population, the cultural needs of the minority will need to be taken care of on a permanent basis. Within the limits of available resources, due attention should therefore be given to the cultural and educational needs of all language groups in the country as well as to facilities for the effective teaching of the Estonian language to all those who need to learn them.

76. The present language legislation may in certain respects require adaptation to the conditions of an independent State. For example, it is hardly the task of the State to lay down requirements for private employment contracts. If bilingual competence is necessary in a given situation, the potential employer will insist that any applicant possess the requisite qualifications. Language requirements for public service could be differentiated in different parts of the country, and transitional rules

could be liberally applied. Flexibility would alleviate tensions and help the Russian-speaking population to gain confidence in a future of peaceful cooperation between all groups living in Estonia. Particularly in those parts of the country where one language dominates the rights to security of employment should accordingly be weighed against the right of the public to service in either Estonian or Russian. Policy models for developing the language legislation can be found in countries that have given a generous treatment to migrant workers and in CSCE States that are historically multilingual (such as Canada, Finland, Switzerland).

* * *

Annex 1

MEMBERS OF THE MISSION

Experts
Christian Tomuschat, Professor, Faculty of Law, University of Bonn, Germany
Klaus Törnudd, Ambassador, Ministry of Foreign Affairs, Helsinki, Finland

Assistants
Ulrich Brandenburg, CSCE Division, Ministry of Foreign Affairs, Bonn, Germany
Päivi Kaukoranta, Legal and Human Rights Division, Ministry of Foreign Affairs, Helsinki, Finland

Executive Secretary
Jack Zetkulic, Deputy Director, CSCE Office for Democratic Institutions and Human Rights, Warsaw, Poland

RESPONSE TO THE REPORT OF THE CSCE ODIHR MISSION ON THE STUDY OF ESTONIAN LEGISLATION INVITED BY THE REPUBLIC OF ESTONIA

15 January 1993

The Government of Estonia would firstly like to use this opportunity to thank the CSCE ODIHR expert mission for their valuable contribution in determining the true situation regarding human rights in Estonia.

The initial draft of the mission's report has been carefully reviewed by the members of the Estonian Government, as well as by numerous officials dealing with the issues at hand.

The following is a compilation of remarks and comments which have been made regarding the report, which we kindly request be given due regard in finalizing the report of the mission's findings.

Comments

Point 14
We recommend that in lieu of the word 'stateless', the term 'foreign citizens' be used as these persons cannot be considered as stateless persons.

The term 'stateless person' is used in the Estonian Citizenship Law in the definition established in the Convention on the Status of Stateless Persons:

> "The term 'stateless persons' means a person who is not considered as a national by any State *under the operation of its law.*"

Estonia considers these persons as "citizens of the former Soviet Union". Also in accordance with Russian law former Soviet citizens cannot be considered as 'stateless persons' for at least two years.

Currently there are few persons resident in Estonia who can be considered as stateless in accordance with the convention's definition of the term. These are former Soviet dissidents, who were deprived of their Soviet citizenship on political grounds.

Point 15
In the second, third and fourth sentences, the term 'Estonian citizens' should perhaps be used instead of 'Estonians' and the term 'foreign citizens' should be used instead of 'non-Estonian citizens'.

Two different terms, 'citizenship' and 'nationality' are used in the text. In order to avoid any confusion, we suggest that the term 'citizenship' be used throughout.

Point 22
The sentence "... citizenship legislation is perceived as discriminatory by 'most' representatives of the Russian-speaking population ...' tends to contradict some recent opinion polls and we would like to suggest that it be replaced with 'many'.

Point 23
It would be appropriate to emphasize in the first sentence that Estonia, rather than being "a society whose ethnic composition 'has dramatically changed', is a country whose ethnic composition was forcibly altered and systematically changed as part of a policy of russification.

We feel that it is not effectual to state in the second sentence "... Russian-speaking population in their country would probably remain 'stateless' for a long time...", as this is primarily a question of not belonging to the Estonian citizenry, which does not automatically render them as stateless.

Point 34
We feel that there are no totally Russian-language regions in Estonia, since although the population of the city of Narva is primarily comprised of Russian-speakers, this region also includes rural areas, where the population is primarily Estonian-speaking.

Point 37
The article of the Constitution which is referred to is Article 156 (not 150).

Point 42
We feel that the comparison, in brackets, in the first sentence "as in other places in the former Soviet Union" should be re-worded as either "as in various places in the former Soviet Union" or "as in other states which *de facto* comprised the former Soviet Union", so that no confusion can arise regarding Estonia's status as an occupied, *de jure* existing state during the past 50 years.

Point 57
It should be emphasized that in fact no-one, including Estonian citizens, so far has the right to own land. The respective legislation is in the making.

Point 70
The term 'stateless residents' should be avoided in the first sentence, as this is referring to persons who are "citizens of the former Soviet Union". (cf. Point 14)

Point 72
We are pleased to inform the mission that on January 12, 1993, the Estonian Government presented a draft law "On Estonian Language Requirements for Applicants for Citizenship" to the Riigikogu (see Appendix). This will immediately be followed by a Government order which will specify the procedures and requirements for the language examinations. We will forward the translation of this document as soon as it has been adopted.

The Estonian Government wishes again to express its sincere gratitude for the mission's efforts during its visit to Estonia and in compiling this report. We thank the mission for its understanding of the local circumstances, and we hope that the comments forwarded in this Response will be reflected in the final report.

REPORT OF THE CSCE HUMAN DIMENSION MISSION TO MOLDOVA*

January - February 1993

I INTRODUCTION

1 Following informal contacts between the CSCE Office for Democratic Institutions and Human Rights and the Foreign Affairs Committee of the Parliament of Moldova, the ODIHR received on January 6, 1993, a Note Verbale from the Parliament of the Republic of Moldova requesting activation of the Human Dimension Mechanism under paragraph 4 of the Moscow document for an "investigation of current legislation and implementation of minorities rights and inter-ethnic relations on the territory of Moldova". In its Note Verbale dated January 7, 1993, the CSCE Office for Democratic Institutions and Human Rights informed the Parliament of the Republic of Moldova that, to comply with the agreed practice regarding the implementation of the Moscow Mechanism, it would need confirmation that the government of the Republic of Moldova supported the Parliament's initiative to activate the Mechanism.

2 On January 14, 1993, the CSCE Office for Democratic Institutions and Human Rights received a Note Verbale from the Ministry of Foreign Affairs of the Republic of Moldova fully supporting the initiative of the Parliament and appointing, from the resource list of experts/rapporteurs maintained by the Office, Professor Erik Siesby (Denmark) and Professor Paolo Ungari (Italy) as experts to the Mission (see annex 1 for a full description of the Mission's membership). The Mission was invited to visit Moldova from January 30 to February 4, 1993 (see schedule in annex 2). In its Note Verbale 7/93 dated January 15, 1993, the Office informed the CSCE participating States about the Mission.

3 The CSCE ODIHR sent Note Verbale 8/93 of January 18, 1993, to the Ministry of Foreign Affairs of Moldova confirming the dispatching of the Mission and informing of the full composition of the Mission. Three of the participants of the Mission had been visiting Moldova several times before. Prior to this visit, the members of the Mission had occasion to study several reports on the situation in Moldova, among them Dr. Adam D. Rotfeld's "Interim Report on the Conflict in the Left Bank Dniester Areas" and "Addendum 1 of the Interim Report".

---

* Reproduced without the Annexes.

4 The participants arrived in Chisinău on January 27, in order to attend an International Conference on Judicial Reform in Moldova, held between January 28 and 30. Mission experts and assistants presented papers for the conference. Prof. Siesby's paper dealt with the institution of ombudsman, a concept worth considering in the process of building a state based on the rule of law in Moldova. Prof. Ungari spoke about "Training of Judges and Human Rights". Mr. Almond focused on Penitentiary Systems in a democratic society and Mr. Weissman presented the latest political developments in Denmark as an example of rule of law and separation of powers.

II INITIAL OBSERVATIONS

5 The Republic of Moldova is a country of 33.700 km2, smaller than Denmark, bigger than Belgium. The population of 4,5 million equals the population of Norway. Moldova's present borders were determined by the Soviet Union, according to ethnic criteria. The major part of Moldova (formerly Romanian Bessarabia) became part of the Soviet Union as a result of the 'Molotov-Ribbentrop Pact' of August 23, 1939. The southern part of Bessarabia was transferred to the Ukraine S.S.R. A narrow peace of land east of the river Dniester which had been predominantly Romanian-speaking (see note 10), had a certain autonomy from 1924-1940 and was added to the Moldavian S.S.R.

6 Moldova is a multicultural and multilingual country. Romanian language and culture have been suppressed during the Soviet Regime. Political leaders, taking advantage of the comparative freedom at the end of the 1980's, gave Romanian language and culture the status these leaders felt they deserved. This development created a certain fear among the ethnic and linguistic minorities of an exaggerated 'Romanization'.

7 Three of the members of the Mission who had visited Moldova previously, have studied especially the situation of the Moldovan minorities and noted their concerns. During this Human Dimension Mission, an improvement of the relations between the Romanian-speaking majority and the minorities (i.e. Ukrainians, Russians, Gagauz and Bulgarians) was observed.

8 The most serious and dangerous problem is the relationship between the secessionist self-proclaimed "Dniester Moldovan Republic" and the Republic of Moldova. Even though the ethnic and linguistic composition of the Trans-Dniester population (Romanian-speaking 40%, Ukrainian 28,3% and Russian 25,5%) is different from that of Moldova, the main reason for the secessionist demands is not ethnic but political and ideological.

9 Ever since it was established, the "DMR" has been protected by the Russian 14th Army. Its powerful so-called "Republican Guard" has been equipped and trained by the 14th Army. Economically the "Dniester Moldovan Republic" is supported by the Russian Government with financial and material help. The problem which this secession republic has created for peace in Moldova can only be solved peacefully by negotiations in which Russia takes part.

10 The "Dniester Moldovan Republic" gradually evicted the Moldovan authorities following intensified clashes in Bender and Dubasari (April-May 1992). When Moldovan authorities attempted to rescue the police stations in Dubasari and later in Bender (June 1992), an armed conflict began which resulted in hundreds of dead and injured, destruction of hundreds of houses, and the displacement of thousands of persons from the conflict area. Although the bloodshed has stopped, elements of the conflict persist and tension is still high. Only a negotiated permanent political solution, in which Russia takes part, can avert the danger of renewed violence. It is the recommendation of the Mission that diplomatic action be taken without delay. In this regard, the Mission wishes to express its full support for a CSCE Mission to Moldova as proposed in the Final Report on the Conflict in the Left-Bank Dniester Areas of the Republic of Moldova by Dr. Adam Rotfeld, Personal Representative of the Chairman-in-Office, and as approved by the 19th Committee of Senior Officials in Prague (February 4, 1993). A proposal for extensive autonomy in the Trans-Dniester area which has recently been made by the Moldovan side will, in the opinion of the Mission, be a very valuable basis for the negotiations.

III THE MINORITIES OF MOLDOVA

11 *Ethnic-linguistic composition of the population of Moldova:*[1]

AREA	Total (1000)	Moldova (Rom.)	Ukr. %	Russian %	Gagauz %
Moldova	4,366	64,5 %	13,9	13,0	3,5
Left Bank	547	40	28,3	25,4	
rural	195	60	22	12,6	
urban	352	25,6	32,7	34,6	
Tiraspol	199	17,7	32,2	41,3	
Bender	138	29,9	25,1	41,9	

12 The "Ravnopravye-Edinstvo" (Movement for Equal Rights-Unity) criticized the Moldovan Government for ethnic discrimination and accused it of replacing leading Russian-speaking officials with ethnic Moldovans. Official statistics indeed show that the ethnic composition of higher civil servants and industrial managers in Moldova has changed from 1990 to 1992.

(%)	1990	1992
Moldovan	50.6	54.9
Ukrainian	23.5	21.5
Russian	14.4	12.7
Bulgarian	3.5	3.8
Gagauz	2.8	3.1

As could be expected, replacement of officials in leading positions since sovereignty and then independence has led to a higher percentage of ethnic Moldovans, but this percentage still is far lower than the proportion of Moldovans in the population (64.5%). There has been a decline in the percentage of Ukrainians and Russians and a certain rise in that of the smaller minorities in governmental positions (Bulgarian and Gagauz). These changes could, however, also be explained by political, social and ideological changes in the country, and are not necessarily the exclusive result of ethnic considerations. The Swedish institution of 'the

---

1 USSR Census of 1989.

Ombudsman against Ethnic Discrimination', mentioned in Professor Siesby's paper delivered at the conference held prior to the Mission, can be recommended as a measure to prevent job discrimination.

13 Another issue raised by the "Ravnopravye-Edinstvo" was that of schools. Russian schools were allegedly being transformed into Moldovan (Romanian) ones. The figures released by the Ministry of Education read as follows:

Medium Level Education

	1990/91	1991/92
Schools with instruction in Romanian	44,9%	47,2%
Schools with instruction in Russian	51,3%	43%
Mixed schools (Rom. + Russ.)	3,8%	9,8%

Higher Education

Students instructed in Romanian	45%	46,7%
Students instructed in Russian	54,6%	48,8%
Mixed classes	0,4%	4,2%

As the figures show, Russian as language of education is yielding to Romanian. The Mission does not consider the situation described by these figures to be alarming. Obviously, the official policy of encouraging the use of Russian has been abolished, while the incentive of Russian university degrees as an advantage in obtaining a job anywhere in the former Soviet Union has disappeared.

14 Official statistical material describes the education situation as follows:

LANGUAGE OF EDUCATION

(PERCENTAGE)

Area	Population Mol. / Non Mol.	Primary Schools Mol./Rus./Mixed	Preschool Education Mol./Rus./Mixed
Moldova		1032/429/132	614/1333/373
%	64,5 / 35,5	64,8/26,9/8,3	26,4/57,4/17
Left Bank		55/108/19	59/163/28
%	40 60	30,2/59,3/10,5	23,6/65,2/11,2
Tiraspol		1/24/0	1/49/1
%	17,7 82,3	4/96/0	2/96/2
Bender /Tighina		2/14/6	1/18/27
%	29,9 70,1	9,1/63,6/27,3	2,2/39,1/58,7

The low number of Moldovan schools and kindergartens represents a problem, especially against the background of the general political situation. The high proportion of mixed schools and kindergartens found for example in Bender/Tighina is generally considered as a tool of earlier russification.

IV GENERAL CONSTITUTIONAL AND LEGAL FRAMEWORK

15 *The Constitutional Issue*: Eighteen months after independence, Moldova does not have a constitution. Only a few amendments to the former Soviet Constitution have been passed to lay down a provisional basis for the political institutions and to adopt Romanian, in latin alphabet, as the official language. A draft constitution prepared in September by a mixed commission of Members of Parliament and experts exists but has not yet been discussed *in plenum* by the Parliament. So far, there is no resolution stipulating that the international instruments Moldova has acceded to (i.e. Universal Declaration of Human Rights, United Nations Pacts and Conventions, the International Covenant on Civil and Political Rights, all

CSCE Documents and in particular the Copenhagen Document) should form the basis of the constitution with regard to fundamental freedoms and individual rights. The Commission on Human Rights and Inter-ethnic Relations has however already adopted a Draft Law on Human Rights and a Declaration on Minorities. There is no doubt that the Parliament of Moldova is invested with constitution-making power with respect to the provisional determination of the State's structures, as it is demonstrated by the fact that the Parliament itself proclaimed the Sovereign Independence of Moldova, changed the official name of the Republic, drew up guidelines for the drafting of the constitution and passed laws of a quasi constitutional nature (laws on political parties, culture, languages, citizenship). However, the Parliament has not yet taken any initiative of its own to speed up the drafting of the constitution. This shortcoming, if persistent, constitutes a major obstacle to Moldova's admission to the Council of Europe, this in spite of official contacts in this regard and the recent talks in Paris of President Snegur of Moldova with President Mitterrand of France who promised France's support for Moldova's application. In general, the lack of constitution over the past eighteen months renders somewhat more unsettled Moldova's international relations as well as its foreign investments prospects.

16 *Recommendations*: Following various contacts and notably a meeting with the Presidium of the Parliament, the Mission is of the opinion that even before the application of the Constitution (including a possible referendum on the Constitution) and before the ensuing admission of Moldova to the Council of Europe, Moldova could accede to the European Convention on Human Rights while accepting the jurisdiction of the European Court of Strasbourg. This step would equally contribute to further anchor the new institutions of a free Moldova to the firm ground of international acceptance. It will also strengthen the image of the country among western democracies within the framework of the CSCE.

17 On August 31, 1989, the Constitution of the Moldavian SSR was amended by Art.70:

"The State Language of the MSSR is the Romanian Language. The State Language is used in the political, economic, social and cultural life and functions on the basis of the Latin alphabet. The MSSR assures the protection and development of the language of the Gagauz population, of which the largest part lives on the territory of the Republic. The Moldavian SSR assures on its territory the necessary conditions for the development and use of the Russian language as a language of communication among the nations of the USSR, as well as of other nationalities."

A law of the same date ("Law on the Use of Languages on the Territory of MSSR", see annex 3) provides in Art.2 that areas where the Gagauz constitute a majority there shall be three official languages: the State language (i.e. Romanian), Gagauz and Russian. Art.3 provides that the Russian language is the language of communication among the nations of the USSR and is used on the territory of the Republic side by side with the Romanian language as a language of communication between nationalities. According to Art.4, the State will respect the use of Ukrainian, Russian, Bulgarian, Ivrit, Yiddish, Gypsy languages in order to satisfy the national-cultural needs of these minorities. According to Art.5, the Language Law does not apply to relations between nations[2], as well as certain activities related to international commerce and communications. The citizens are, in accordance with Art.6, free to choose between Romanian and Russian in relation to State administration and public organizations, as well as with enterprises, institutions and organizations situated on the territory of Moldova. The Gagauz language may also be chosen in localities with significant population of Gagauz nationality. In localities where the majority belongs to another nationality than the rest of the state, the native language or another acceptable language may be used. Art.7 provides that persons who have positions in State administration and public organizations, enterprises, institutions and organizations, which bring them in contact with citizens (public health, education, culture, mass media, transport, telecommunications, trade, public services, municipal economy, law enforcement bodies, etc.), must know Romanian, Russian - and in areas with Gagauz population - also Gagauz, at a level necessary for their professional obligations.

18 *Comment on the Language Law*: Considering the linguistic composition of the population, these provisions satisfy the demands for respect of minority languages. In the Moldovan Parliament, both Romanian and Russian languages are used. Romanian is translated into Russian, whereas Russian is not translated into Romanian, as all members of Parliament understand and speak Russian. The only controversial provision is Art.7, which provides that certain persons who due to their line of work have contact with other citizens, shall know the language of the citizens at a level sufficient for their professional duties. Many Russian speaking persons therefore will have to learn Romanian. This demand is considered burdensome, especially by elderly people. Several leading Members of Parliament however have declared that the time limit for learning Romanian (January 1, 1995) should be extended. The demand, that certain persons, who through their work come into contact with citizens in a bilingual society, should master the citizens' language is justified for

---

2 Of the former USSR.

practical reasons and does not imply any inequality in relation with the major languages of Moldova. In order to avoid hardship to individuals who because of their age find it difficult to learn Romanian, it would be advisable to extend the time limit, as suggested by Members of Parliament. It is recommended that steps be taken to avoid administrative problems related to the necessary instruction in Romanian and corresponding language examinations. The Russian language, which until independence was the dominant language, must now yield to the Romanian language, the language of the majority of the population. This change, which takes place over a considerable period of time, cannot reasonably be criticized. For many purposes, Moldova is a bilingual country and to some extent even multilingual. An example of bilingualism are the street and place names, everywhere being indicated in both Romanian and Russian using the Latin and Cyrillic alphabets.

19 *The Citizenship Law*: The Law of June 5, 1991, immediately gives citizenship to:

1.- persons who lived on the territory before June 28, 1940, (when the Romanian province of Bessarabia was annexed by USSR) and their descendants who, at the time of the adoption of the law resided on the territory.

2.- persons who reside on the territory and were born there, or (at least) one of the parents (or ancestors) of whom were born on the territory - if they are not citizens of another state.

All other persons, who up to the adoption of the Declaration of Sovereignty of the Republic of Moldova, including the date of its adoption, June 23, 1990, have a permanent place of residence in the territory and a permanent job or other legal source of income, will have a year to decide whether to take Moldovan citizenship. The one year time limit has been extended to 18 months.

The Law furthermore contains rules of naturalization after 10 years of residence.

20 *Comment on the Citizenship Law*: The Law (see annex 4) is very liberal in extending Moldovan citizenship to practically everybody who had permanent residence on the territory at the time of sovereignty. There seem to have been certain administrative problems for persons who have wanted to opt for Moldovan citizenship but who have had no access to the necessary forms of government authorities. Some persons did not declare their citizenship fearing mobilization to the Army during the civil war of 1992. An extension of the time limit would be advisable in order to help such persons obtain citizenship. The population in the area controlled by the self-proclaimed "Dniester Moldovan Republic" would

have had serious problems had they declared Moldovan citizenship. For example, certain food stuffs in Bender are sold only to "citizens of the DMR". A "Citizen of the Republic of Moldova" stamp in an identity card can entail serious consequences for persons in the area controlled by the "DMR". After normalization of the situation, the citizenship situation of these persons must be resolved.

21 *The Law on Religious Freedom*: On 24 March, 1992, Moldova has adopted a Law guaranteeing religious freedom and confessional pluralism. Problems concerning the implementation of the Law have arisen especially regarding the official registration of the various denominations and of the Faculty of Theology of the State University of Chisinau. As far as the first issue is concerned, the Mission has received a letter from the bishop Petru Paduraru which criticizes the fact that the application for official registration presented by the Autonomous Metropolitan Church of Bessarabia (Old Style) on 28 October, 1992, notwithstanding the approvals given by the relevant Ministries, has not yet been accepted; the application took place within a context of the threat of violence aimed at the subordination of the Church to the Patriarchate of Moscow which is deemed by some as less devoted to the purity of the faith and more interested in furthering the hegemony of the Russian State over countries formerly belonging to the Soviet Union. In the meantime, the Moscow Patriarchate, departing from its normal hierarchy (Patriarch, Archbishop, Bishop), has appointed a Metropolitan for Moldova, thus acknowledging the existence of a Autocephalous Church in Moldova. There are even some Moldovan students in Theology who prefer studying in Romania (Bucharest and Iassy) rather than in Chisinau. As far as the Chisinau Faculty of Theology is concerned, there are reports of attempts to replace the incumbent dean with a candidate they considered less qualified but closer to the Moscow Patriarchate, thus resulting in a worsening conflict among students and the teaching staff.

22 *Recommendations*: The Mission is of the opinion that the State ought not to interfere directly or indirectly in religions and, should the work of a faculty of theology be hampered, the State should act in a spirit of fairness towards various churches and denominations existing in the society. Any wishes of churches to recognize an authority outside the country should be equally respected.

V THE SELF-PROCLAIMED "DNIESTER MOLDOVAN REPUBLIC"

23 The "Dniester Moldovan Republic" has created a serious situation for the relations between the populations of both sides of the Dniester River, and also between Romanian-speakers and speakers of Russian on the Left

Bank of Dniester. In August 1989, Russian-speaking workers of factories and plants on the Left Bank, apparently with the support of the 14th Army, resisted the endeavours of the Moldovan people to obtain independence, democratic reforms, the introduction of Romanian as a State language and the transition to Latin alphabet. A communist oriented organization, the OSTK[3] was formed. Strikes in protest against the proclamation of the Romanian as a State language to be used with the Latin alphabet, were organized by OSTK and the "Women's Strike Committees".

24 On January 28, 1990, a referendum on the autonomy of the Left Bank was held by the local authorities on the Left Bank. On September 2, 1990, the OSTK and other communist organizations held a congress at which the "Dniester Moldovan Soviet Socialist Republic (DMSSR)" was proclaimed. The aborted Moscow Coup on August, 1991, was supported by the "DMSSR" leadership. On August 27, 1991, the Parliament of the Republic of Moldova declared the Republic's independence. The "DMSSR" authorities eventually introduced a virtual mass media blockade, forbidding access of Moldovan media into the area under their control[4]. The tension began to increase, and small groups of Don Cossacks appeared on the scene, claiming to defend "this old Russian Land" or even the interests of the "Black Sea Cossack Nation"[5].

25 In order to take control of the territory of the Left Bank, the "DMSSR" proceeded with the eviction of Moldovan Police, Procuracy[6] and other local representatives of the central authorities of the Republic of Moldova. The OSTK's armed branch developed into the "Dniester Guard". Armed "Workers' Militia[7]" were formed. Supported by "Women's Strike Committees", the "Dniester Guard" forced several Moldovan police districts to leave the Left Bank. A few enclaves

---

3 "Obyedinyonnye Sovyety Trudovyh Kollektivov": United Councils of Labor Collectives.

4 Newspapers and books are prevented from crossing the "demarcation line"; Chisinău broadcast and TV are cut off.

5 President Yeltsin committed his Country not to allow armed groups to intervene in Moldova's affairs, and to ensure, that those already present on Moldovan territory would be removed, but the Cossacks are still there. According to information obtained by the Mission, some of the Cossacks now serve in the border guards and Customs Services of the "DMR".

6 Rus.: "Prokuratura". In the Soviet system the body acting as state prosecutors, investigation magistrates and law enforcement controllers.

7 Rus.: "Opolchenye".

controlled by the Moldovan Police still subsist today. The first armed incidents, resulting in dead and wounded, took place in early December, 1992, when the "Dniester Guard" attempted to take over the Dubasari Police Station. The "Bender[8] War" was also triggered by an attempt by the "Dniester Guard" to overrun Bender Police Station and the Moldovan attempt to bring Bender back under Moldovan control.

26 A serious conflict ensued, leaving behind hundreds of dead and wounded[9], as well as the destruction of several buildings in Central Bender. In the end, Bender was re-taken by the "DMR" army, apparently using tanks and artillery of the 14th Army. Serious fighting, resulting in scores of dead and injured and hundreds of destroyed houses, also took place around the Moldovan controlled areas in Dubăsari and Grigoriopol Raions, on the East Bank. The hostilities ended after an accord was signed by Moldovan President Mircea Snegur and Russian Federation President, Boris Yeltsin. A cease-fire ensued, but no durable political settlement was reached.

27 Among possible interests behind the creation of the self-proclaimed "Dniester Moldovan Republic" the following factors have been mentioned:

- A Russian interest in keeping a powerful military presence in the area;
- Interest in the "DMR" of the local communist power elite, connected with the national-political ideology attributed to the predominantly Ukrainian and Russian workers, in industrial areas;
- The interest of the Slav-speaking population to resist 'Romanisation'.

28 The Chairman of the Parliament of the self-proclaimed "DMR", Mr. Grigore Maracuţa, during his meeting with the Mission, emphasized that the history of the Left Bank was different from that of the rest of Moldova because the Left Bank had never been part of Romania, and had had an autonomous status between 1924 and 1940.[10] In his opinion, the right of the people of the Left Bank to self-determination, perceived as

---

8 Bender (Rom. Tighina), pop. approx. 160,000, whereof approx. 30% Moldavians, is on the Right Bank of Dniester. The town is, however, claimed as part of the "Dniester Moldavian Republic".

9 The number of casualties is not clear. The mission was given a figure of circa 860 persons killed, including combatants on both sides.

10 As "Autonomous Moldovian Soviet Socialist Republic" within Ukraine. The MASSR was, however, much larger than the present "DMR". Only the Western part, where the Moldovan ethnic element constituted the majority, was in 1940 merged with the rump Bessarabia to form the Moldovan Soviet Socialist Republic. No attempts seem to have been made on the side of the "DMR" to claim the remainder of the old MASSR, now belonging to Ukraine.

a human right, had been violated by the declaration of independence of Moldova. In his view, sufficient guarantees had not been given against a reunification of Moldova - including the Left Bank - with Romania. President Yeltsin and President Snegur had in a common declaration guaranteed that the Left Bank would not, against the wish of its people, be reunified with Romania. The Chairman of the "DMR" Parliament believed that the Constitution of Moldova ought to include such a guarantee. He also declared that the main obstacle for a re-unification of the Left Bank of Moldova proper with the rest of Moldova was the Romanization which allegedly had taken place in Moldova. This apparently was a reference to the new status of the Romanian language and the demand that certain persons, who until now only used the Russian language, in the future would also have to use Romanian in communicating with the public.

29 The Chairman of the "DMR" Parliament mentioned that Russia supported the Left Bank with 7,8 billion Roubles worth of goods and materials per year.

30 The Chairman of the "DMR" Parliament mentioned that "bilateral" commissions had been established between the two sides and he presented the Mission with copies of the two proposals for a political solution of the conflict between them. These were a "DMR" proposal for a "confederative" solution and a Moldovan proposal, according to which the Trans-Dniester area would enjoy local autonomy. The latter includes, *inter alia*, a provision about the population of the proposed Trans-Dniester Self-Administered Territory having the right to decide their future status, should the Moldovan State modify its status as an independent State.

31 At meetings with the Presidium of the Moldovan Parliament, Government Ministers and representatives of political parties, the Mission has asked whether proposals as those mentioned above could be subject to a referendum supervised by international organizations, e.g. the United Nations or the CSCE. The Presidium replied that a referendum could not possibly be held on the Left Bank before the withdrawal of the 14th Russian Army.

32 The Mission supports both conclusion of Dr. Rotfeld's Interim Report and Final Report that the search for a lasting political settlement in Moldova, involving the CSCE, should include an agreement on the withdrawal of the 14th Army as one of the pre-conditions for a political resolution of the conflict in the Trans Dniester area.

33 A Declaration by the Heads of State of Moldova, Romania, Russia and Ukraine, signed in Istanbul on June 25, 1992, called for negotiations between the Russian Federation and Moldova on the withdrawal of the 14th Army. Withdrawal, however, will hardly in itself create conditions

on the Left Bank which would make a fair referendum possible. Military units established by the "DMR" leadership, and the considerable arsenal now under the control of the 14th Army will still be an obstacle to a negotiated settlement. An overall inspection of the military potential on the Left Bank by a team of neutral military experts may be a first step to a lasting solution of the conflict.

34 A withdrawal of the Army and a removal of the threat which various military and paramilitary units of the "DMR" present to the peace in the area may be facilitated by a proposal by the Moldovan Government to give to the Left Bank local autonomy. This will satisfy the special needs of the population in the area, whose historical experience and ethnic composition somehow differs from those in the rest of Moldova.

35 *Visits to the Scenes of the Armed Conflict of June, 1992*: Reports in Russian, and western media have claimed that Bender was virtually destroyed by Moldavian heavy artillery and armour, resulting in many thousands of civilian casualties. The Mission visited Bender and found that the damage, still visible, inflicted on the town was not caused by heavy artillery. Most damage was done to the respective headquarters and barracks: Moldovan Police and the "Workers Detachment". The structure of the damaged buildings still remains (walls, floors and, to some extent, roof) and this could not possibly be the result of heavy artillery shells. It appears that the Moldovan side did not, and still does not, possess tanks and that both sides used mortar grenades. Civilian casualties seem to have been caused by the fierce fighting in the centre of town. Allegations, including those of the Russian Supreme Soviet, that Moldovans deliberately shelled residential areas seem highly questionable.

36 The Mission also visited the "front line" villages of Corjova and Cocieri on the Left Bank and found that damage apparently had been inflicted to houses apparently by mortar grenades fired by the "DMR" forces from nearby Dubasari. The Moldovan positions[11] were entrenched on the Dniester bank, relatively close to the villages. Many houses were destroyed and there were civilian casualties.

VI SITUATION REGARDING MINORITIES RIGHTS

37 *Human Rights Situation in the Areas Controlled by the "DMR"*:

37.1 The Mission was presented with a large number of allegations of human rights violations which are said to have taken place in the areas controlled by the "DMR", i.e. most of the Left Bank and the Bender enclave. The

[11] The Moldovan forces were mainly volunteers from the neighbouring villages.

Mission had for obvious reasons no possibility effectively to check these allegations. Their number and consistency give, however, cause for serious concern.

37.2 The media blockade - in fact the jamming of Moldovan TV and Radio by the "DMR" authorities - has been mentioned above. Residents of the area controlled by the "DMR" do not have access to any written or electronic media from Moldova, that can physically be stopped by the "DMR" authorities. Reversing the Moldovan language law described above, the "DMR Parliament" adopted its own language law, proclaiming Russian, Ukrainian and Moldovan as official languages. It also proclaims that the Moldovan language is to be written in Cyrillic. This further limits the access of the "DMR" residents to Moldovan and Romanian media and literature. It also attempts to perpetuate the old Soviet (actually Stalin's) theory of a Moldovan nation and culture distinct from the Romanian. This theory was used as a tool of ethnic and cultural oppression of the Romanians in the USSR and has no historical or linguistic merit. Its reconfirmation by law can only be perceived as a continuation by the "DMR" of the old Russian nationalist and cultural policy of the past. The Mission saw street names and road signs written only in Russian, and most activities in the "DMR" seem to be conducted in Russian, in spite of the fact that 40.1% of the residents declare Moldovan nationality and Moldovan (Romanian) as their mother tongue. In Tiraspol, there is only one Moldovan school with 800 students (approx. 35000 residents with Moldovan (Romanian) mother tongue of a total population of 199 000).

37.3 The Mission was told by a Moldovan schoolteacher residing on the Left Bank that teachers were removed because they resisted the reintroduction of the Cyrillic alphabet. Many allegations were related to the fact that employees at all levels were removed from work if they did not pledged allegiance to the "DMR". This seems to be the background for the mass displacement of about three quarters of the students and faculty of Tiraspol University, including the former pro-rector. While a majority of those who moved to Chisinau are ethnic Moldovans, there are also Russians and Ukrainians according to the University Administration. The Mission was handed the laws and decisions passed by the "Supreme Soviet" of the "DMR", which provides that persons opposed to the Cyrillic alphabet must be removed from their jobs."

37.4 At meetings with local authorities of the Moldovan-controlled enclave of Dubasary, the Mission heard allegations against the "DMR" authorities for apprehending and abusing persons who supposedly fought as volunteers on the Moldovan side in the armed conflict last summer. The Mission was told about deaths and torture.

37.5 A recurrent subject has been the elections and referenda held by the "DMR" on the Trans Dniester area on e.g. December 1, 1991. During a visit to a Moldovan village on the Left Bank, the Mission was told about armed elections campaigners bullying would-be voters to vote for the "DMR" leadership and to boycott the Moldovan presidential elections. Elections apparently were not held in the customary "Culture Houses" or schools. Buses from Tiraspol were used. Several persons told the mission that villages in which just a fraction of the residents had voted were declared by the "DMR" authorities to have voted 86% and more in support of the authorities.

37.6 A trial, held under the "DMR" authorities, is being prepared against five persons accused of terrorism. While investigating this issue, the Mission, the first of its kind to be permitted to visit in Tiraspol the prisoners charged with crime against the State for supporting Moldovan unity, acknowledges that the dialogue with the two detainees, chosen by the Mission from a list of six prisoners, was entirely free and without time-limit, albeit with two Trans-Dniestrian police officers attending and with the compulsory use of the Russian language. The Mission held also discussion with the lawyer of the prisoner who is considered to be the leader of the group (Ilascu). The Mission was able to confirm the good physical and mental health of the prisoners, but the two prisoners visited denounced a political plot by the police. They accused the police of using false witnesses, *agents provocateurs* and of smuggling military weapons - including chemical substances (Napalm) - into their home, to accuse them of the murder of two Trans-Dniestrian officials. The detainees denied the charge. They declared to be citizens of Moldova residing on the left bank of the Dniester River. They referred to some inhuman treatments in breach of international norms concerning Human Rights, hygienic conditions and confinement in prison, and with attempts of mixing psychotropic substance in their food. The detainees were aware that humanitarian organizations such as the International Red Cross and Amnesty International asked to see them but were turned down. They have no access to newspapers and exchanges of letters are *de facto* impossible. Starting in June 1992, Mr. Ilascu was several times tortured, beaten by masked men and threatened with the killing of his wife and children; six times he was blindfolded and his hands tied up; he was six times subjected to sham execution by guns firing empty bullets. Mr. Ilascu stated not to recognize the lawful existence of the Trans-Dniestrian Republic, which he describes as the 14th Army Occupation Regime, and, let alone, of the Court of Justice. The trial, initially scheduled for 8 February, 1993, by the Chairman of the Parliament, was postponed to a later date according to comments made by the Prosecutor and the defence lawyer Voyizan Ivan Ivanovic. The trial will be public and accessible to the international press.

37.7 The Mission is of the opinion that, either under the conditions of the cease-fire or a civil war/armed occupation, all international instruments on human rights in prisons plus the rights established by the CSCE Vienna Document of 1989 to allow Helsinki Watch Committees to monitor the compliance with the norms of the various CSCE Documents should be respected. The Mission believes that all kind of pressures on the detainees, as stated above, constitute not only a crime against humanity but also a move undermining the credibility of public trial held under such circumstances.

37.8 Serious allegations were made against "DMR" "Minister of National Security", supposed to be identical with a Soviet OMON officer wanted for several crimes by the Latvian Government.

38 *Gagauzia*:

38.1 The Gagauz, a Turkic people of Orthodox Christian religion, are mainly concentrated in certain districts in southern Moldova. In their particular area of compact settlement, the Gagauz account for 84% of the total population. Their total number is 153,000[12]. The Gagauz leaders declared independence in 1990, and have been defending the borders of the "Gagauz Republic", often supported by the "Dniester Moldovan Republic". Recently, the "Gagauz Republic", the "Dniester Moldovan Republic" and the "Republic of Abkhazia", three self-proclaimed states, have recognized each other and signed mutual assistance agreements, forming what could be called a "Secessionist Internationale".

38.2 In the last months, the atmosphere between Gagauzia and Moldova has improved to some extent. Unfortunately, proposals by Moldovan authorities, ensuring local and cultural autonomy for the Gagauz people, could not be finalized. Important seems to have been Turkish diplomatic and economic assistance. The alphabet could be used as an example. The Gagauz use mainly Russian language, Gagauz language was until now written in Cyrillic. The decision of the Moldovan Government to return to Latin alphabet was resisted by the Gagauz. When Turkey offered assistance in the effort to preserve the Gagauz language, the Latin alphabet was easily accepted, since it was no longer perceived as an expression of Romanization.

38.3 The improvement of the relations between the Gagauz and the Moldovan Government could have resulted in an agreement between the two sides on a draft law on the special legal status of Gagauz Yeri/Gagauzia. The

---

[12] USSR Census - 1989.

draft law however, signed by President Mircea Snegur and being now considered in Parliament, was recently rejected by the Gagauz.

38.4 According to the draft law, Gagauzia decides independently questions concerning its political, economic and cultural development. In the event of a change of the political status of the Republic of Moldova as an independent state or as a member of the United Nations, the people of Gagauzia have the right to determine their destiny independently. The highest official of Gagauzia, the Başkan, shall be confirmed by the President of the Republic of Moldova.

39 *The Bulgarian Minority*: Over the past two years, the overall situation of the Bulgarians in the Teraclia raion has improved. The difficulties encountered by the population there (43% Bulgarian, the remainder being Moldovan, Russian and Ukrainian) are no more acute than in the rest of the country. Whereas the representation of Bulgarians at local and national level was deemed satisfactory by the Bulgarians, the law on minorities was eagerly awaited. The decision to return to Bulgarian as a language of instruction in schools was successfully implemented, although the lack of books and suitably trained teachers is a real obstacle. The re-introduction of Bulgarian in schools was initially met with hostility since Bulgarians speak only Russian as a second language and thought that access to Romanian-speaking universities in Moldova would in practice be closed to them. Bulgarians hope that their culture will be preserved in a newly independent Moldova. They do not fear "romanization".

40 It was the impression of the Mission that the inter-ethnic relations in the areas controlled by the Moldovan authorities were relatively good. Apparently, the bulk of the Ukrainians and Russians have accepted the independent Moldovan State, while the Moldovan Government is showing an active interest in the status of minorities. It is also the impression of the Mission that Moldovans generally display tolerance and acceptance for persons belonging to other ethnic groups. Russian television is retransmitted and widely watched.

VII SUMMARY OF CONCLUSIONS AND RECOMMENDATIONS

41 In comparison with conclusions reached by some members of the Mission at previous visits to Moldova, the situation of minorities in Moldova, particularly in relation to the Romanian-speaking majority, has markedly improved. In all countries, however, there is a risk that ethnic, linguistic and religious minorities may be subjects to discrimination. In Moldova, where secessionist republics have been established and where some of the minorities seek support from neighbouring states, there are special reasons for doing the utmost in order to avoid discrimination, including

job-discrimination, of minorities. The Mission, therefore, *recommends* the introduction of the ombudsman institution for the prevention of discrimination of minorities.

42 The Mission regards the re-assertion of Romanian as the state language after 40 years of Russification as a legitimate move. The preservation of the Russian language as an inter-ethnic *lingua franca* and its use in administration constitutes, together with the protection of the languages of the minorities, a fair and realistic policy.

In order to avoid individual hardships, the Mission *recommends* that the time limit for learning the Romanian language imposed on persons who hold positions which require contact with the public be extended or applied in a flexible way.

43 Moldova's citizenship law is among the most liberal citizenship laws of all the newly independent republics of the former Soviet Union in the sense that citizenship is given to practically everybody who had permanent residence on the territory at the time of the sovereignty.

Certain persons have wanted to opt for Moldovan citizenship but have been prevented or discouraged from this option for administrative, technical or political reasons (see paragraph 20). The Mission *recommends* that measures be taken to allow these persons to obtain Moldovan citizenship.

44 Religious freedom has been guaranteed by the law of March 24, 1992. The Mission *recommends* that the State should not interfere either directly or indirectly in religious affairs.

45 The Mission *recommends* that the work on a democratic constitution for Moldova be speeded up in spite of difficulties caused by the secessionist republics. The constitution should contain provisions enabling Moldova to grant a degree of autonomy to areas whose population has a background different from that of the rest of the Moldovan population. It is recommended that the constitution be based upon international instruments concerning democratic principles, human rights and fundamental freedoms to which Moldova has acceded including all CSCE Documents.

46 Violations of human rights in the secessionist self-proclaimed republic east of Dniester have been reported to the Mission: clampdown on Moldovan written and electronic media by the Dniester authorities, the re-introduction of the Cyrillic alphabet for Romanian (Moldovan) language, the russification of everyday life, limited access to Moldovan schools, reports on torture and physical abuse, alleged fraud in the 1990 and 1991 elections and referenda.

47 The self-proclaimed "Dniester Moldovan Republic" is supported by the 14th Russian army and receives economic assistance from Russia. The withdrawal of the 14th army is a precondition for the resolution of the

problems created by this secessionist republic. The Mission *recommends* diplomatic action for the commencement of negotiations for a lasting solution of the problem. It is recommended that such negotiations - in which Russia should participate - be based upon a recent Moldovan proposal for extensive autonomy for the area east of Dniester. The Mission supports the CSCE Mission to Moldova as proposed in the Final Report on the Conflict in the Left Bank Dniester Areas of the Republic of Moldova by Dr. Adam Rotfeld, Personal Representative of the Chairman-in-Office, and as approved by the 19th Committee of Senior Officials.

48 The Mission *recommends* that the forthcoming Committee of Senior Officials of the CSCE, during its discussion of the present report and as part of a possible follow-up action to the Mission's observations, ask the CSCE Office for Democratic Institutions and Human Rights to serve as a venue for expert advice on a draft constitution for Moldova and the plans for a federation or confederation presented by the Moldovan and the "Dniester" side respectively (see annex 5 and 6) as well as a plan for similar autonomy for the Gagauz area. In this respect the Mission will welcome the involvement of the Council of Europe (in particular the European Commission for Democracy through Law) and of the United Nations (especially the members of the various past UN Missions to Moldova).

49 The Mission also *recommends* that personal contacts be established between this Mission and the CSCE Long-Duration Mission to Moldova in order to facilitate the exchange of information and ideas, and to ensure adequate co-ordination as well as a fruitful follow-up. Comments and advice on the documents handed to the Mission, as referred to in paragraph 48, will be forwarded to the CSCE Long-Duration Mission.

50 In carrying out its mandate as defined by the Republic of Moldova, the Mission was fully aware of the multiplicity of factors at stake in the issue of minorities in Moldova. Because humanitarian issues are very much a part of the sources of conflict in the region east of Dniester, the Mission had found it difficult to avoid addressing directly some of the issues connected with the armed conflict on the region east of Dniester. In doing so, needless to say, the Mission had no intention to infringe on the mandate of Dr. Rotfeld's Missions. The Mission would like to emphasize that the human rights issue is an integral part of the broader concept of security in Moldova, as indeed in the whole of Europe.

ANNEX

MEMBERS OF THE MISSION

Experts:

Professor Erik Siesby, former Professor of Law, University of Copenhagen, Chairman of the Danish Helsinki Committee.

Professor Paolo Ungari, Dean of the Faculty of Political Sciences of the LUISS University, President of the Commission of Human Rights.

Assistants:

Professor Mark Almond, lecturer in Modern History, Oriel College, Oxford.

Mr. Vladimir Weissman, Danish Helsinki Committee.

Executive Secretary:

Mr. Jacques Roussellier, Assistant to the Director, CSCE Office for Democratic Institutions and Human Rights.

REPORT OF THE RAPPORTEUR MISSION TO ALBANIA[1]

September 1991

Introduction

The Rapporteur Mission of the CSCE, which had been invited by the Government of the Republic of Albania at the CSCE Council of Berlin, on the occasion of Albania's admission to the CSCE, visited this country from 16 to 19 September 1991. The mission was composed of persons from some of the participating states, the CSCE institutions, the Council of Europe and the Commission of the European Community. (List of participants: Annex I)
The program of the visit had been prepared in consultation with the Albanian Government, who did everything possible to facilitate and assist the mission. In order to carry out their task, which included a wide range of contacts and visits to relevant institutions, the group split up in some cases into three or four teams, that eventually reported to the full Mission.
The Mission met with the President, with the Chairman of the National Assembly, with the Parties, with the Prime Minister, with several Ministers and Representatives of Government organs, with Trade-Union representatives, with representatives of human-rights groups, of churches and minorities and visited relevant institutions in Skhodra, Elbasani and Gjirokastra as well as on the way to and in the area of these towns. (Program: Annex II)[2]
The Mission gathered a good deal of first-hand information and got a comprehensive, up-to-date picture of the actual situation in the country. The attention of the Mission, along the lines of the three baskets of CSCE, was concentrated on human dimension, economic co-operation and security, the focus of the contacts being the human dimension as an expression of the three fundamental values named in the Charter of Paris: Human rights, Democracy and the Rule of law.

---

1 Editor's note: the Report on Albania was the first report of a mission of rapporteurs to a newly admitted CSCE participating state. It may serve as a example of a "CSCE country-report". Reports of the missions to other new CSCE states are not reproduced in the present volume.

2 Annex not reproduced in this volume.

General remarks

There can be little doubt on Albania's efforts towards the implementation of CSCE commitments. Through the radical reform of existing institutions and the creation of new ones, a comprehensive activity is being carried out by the various political forces in order to enhance the process of modernization and of democratization of the country.

The most important achievements of such activity, which are generally considered irreversible, can be briefly indicated in the following: a pluralistic political system with different parties; the acceptance of the general principles of a new Constitution (a draft of which is being discussed at present) that will ground democracy, the rule of law and the respect of human rights; a representative parliament that reflects the results of elections which have been, in general way, considered reasonably free; establishment of a free market economy (still in its initial stage); liberation of all political prisoners and the permission to any citizen to leave the country. Besides, some new non-governmental organizations have appeared that are carefully watching the democratic development and pressing at the same time for further progress.

Over against these and other positive achievements, some major shortcomings are still to be found in the new democratic framework, due to a number of hard-dying features of the past regime: the de-politicization of state structures is slow and difficult; at least part of the old security framework is still operative and a large part of the media, as well as other forms of expressions of modern societies, are broadly dominated by the government. But the transition from decades of a dictatorship withholding from the people even the most elementary human rights to full democracy can be expected to be neither easy nor rapid.

Human rights

Substantial work has been done, and is still being done, in the preparation and the adoption of juridical instruments aimed at sanctioning the rights of individuals and of groups and at preventing further abuses and oppression from institutions and people in power.

As a result of this, several provisions of the penal code and of the code of criminal procedure have been altered (giving, for example, right of defence to individuals during the penal proceedings) while other legal dispositions have been abrogated: this is the case, among others, of the law on deportation and 'internal exile' as an administrative measure, one of the gravest and massive human rights violations.

Other important measures have been taken to sanction freedom of thought, conscience and belief, as well as to abolish previous restrictions of movement both inside the country and when crossing the national borders.

As regards in particular freedom of religion or belief, there appear to be no more restrictions of any kind, except those which derive from the actual conditions of the former religious properties and organizations. Representatives of the catholic and of the orthodox churches as well as of the muslim community confirmed that the main present limitations on the exercise of religion comes from the lack of the most elementary facilities.

Freedom of expression and free circulation of information and ideas have been restored in Albania and there are no reported cases of infringement by the authorities. Nevertheless, much has still to be done in order to create appropriate conditions for a wide-spread enjoyment of these rights. Broadcasting is still within the old monopolistic structures and a new law needs to be adopted in order to introduce the necessary pluralism in programming and reporting. Written press suffers from difficulties in the access to a plurality of sources of information (there is only one state-run press agency).

Freedom of association and assembly as well as freedom of movement have also been fully restored, with some limitations due to practical reasons. However, the Mission could note in the course of its contacts a widespread feeling of concern, on behalf of all the emerging democratic forces in Albania, about the possibility of repressive action being undertaken at any time, both at group and individual levels, by the members of the former security police (that has been formally dissolved). The potential danger of anti-democratic activity by this organism, particularly in the field of violation of human rights, seems to be one of the main shadows of the general picture and has to be pointed out in that it was felt by all the interlocutors of the Mission not belonging to the former regime.

In the interview with the Head of the National Information Service, the Mission was told that this new entity has nothing to do with the previous secret police and that it will even help implementing CSCE principles. Nevertheless, despite its overall number having been reduced by two thirds and its concepts and methodologies being reshaped, it was admitted that 34 % of the old Segurimi staff form now the totality of the staff of the new Service. Indeed, the Head of the Service mentioned among the crimes for which the Service is competent those of 'sabotage' and 'severance of diplomatic relations' that appear to be concepts too large for proper legal control of police action. Against this background the law governing the activity of the National Information Service needs additional safeguards to be compatible with normal rule of law status.

The heavy inheritance of the past is inevitably hampering and slowing down progress in this field and many consequences of previous 'legal' violations of

human rights are still producing their negative effects in practice. One of the most impressive examples of such distortions is given by the number of persons who were sentenced to prison (sometimes for crimes which are no longer considered as such) with procedures without legal representation and advice; besides, they were sentenced for periods whose length is totally out of proportion with respect to the crime committed.
The general living conditions in Albanian prisons, especially as far as hygiene and medical treatment are concerned, are far from being acceptable. The working conditions in some broad sectors of economic production (especially heavy industry and mines) are by no means significantly better. The situation of the hospitals and the whole medical sector seems to be desperate.
A special case is represented by those citizens who recently fled the country and were eventually repatriated on the understanding of non-prosecution. While there seems to be no reported action on behalf of the authorities against the civilians - who were many thousands - sanctions were adopted with regard to members of the armed forces, on the ground that they had abandoned their post. To the members of the CSCE Mission who visited them in their quarters, a number of returned soldiers (who had fled to Italy) reported that they had been arrested at their return, detained for few days and interrogated, fearing possible trial and condemnation. Answers by commanding officers to questions from the Mission about possible punishment of the soldiers were vague and unclear.
A process of modernization and democratization is being carried out also in the armed forces, where the role of political commissaires has been abolished and a new program for re-education is being elaborated. On demand from the CSCE Mission about introducing alternative service for conscientious objectors, as required by the Vienna Concluding Document, the Minister of Defence declared that he would think over the problem which was completely new to him.

Democracy

Albania is now a parliamentary republic. A special commission, assisted by foreign experts and institutions (in particular the Council of Europe), is working at the text of a new constitution, whose basic principles have been embodied into the "law on the main constitutional provisions" recently adopted by the Peoples' Assembly. This law provides for separation between the executive, legislative and judicial powers.
Several parties and political organizations have been set up since the beginning of the year and play an active part in the life of the country. Opportunities for political parties are nevertheless unbalanced, as the Socialist Party - by far the most powerful and the heir of the party that bore

responsibility for the country's fate for 47 years - is somehow still in a dominating position.

Although both declaring their willingness to further progress in the democratization of the country, the views of the party in power and those of the opposition differ substantially as far as timing is concerned: new elections, more radical social and economic reforms and the complete dismantling of the old dictatorship structures (like the security organs) are urgently requested by the opposition, while a trend toward more restrictive, cautious and slow actions seems to characterize the line of the majority party.

Whatever will be the outcome of the political struggle, it appears that, as the present electoral system broadly favours in practice the government party, not only new elections but also some amendments of the electoral law are strongly needed, in view of both a fairer representation of the competing forces and of a sounder legitimacy and credibility of the institutions. Such amendments should include the withdrawal of the provisions which are discriminatory and declare illegal any party formed on an ethnic or religious basis.

It has to be noted, in this context, that the Greek minority living in the south of the country - namely in the only two regions recognized by the Albanian Government as minoritarian - is now represented in the People's Assembly: its possible exclusion from future national electoral campaigns would therefore be regarded as a step backward in the democratic process. The majority of party and government interlocutors, however, expressed to the CSCE Mission their reluctance to grant ethnic or religious minorities the right to full national representation.

From the contacts that the Mission had *in loco* with the representatives of the Greek minority it appears that the general situation has improved, with increasing respect for human and political rights (in the past a very high percentage of political prisoners were of Greek origin) and with their local authorities democratically elected. Problems of education in their own language have been reported. While a new comprehensive legislation on the structure and functioning of democratic local authorities is still in preparation (with the assistance of experts from West-European countries) the two communities in the region, Albanian and Greek, seem to go along well together. When the Mission raised the question of minorities in Albania it was confronted with the fate of ethnic Albanians in Kosovo. The Mission replied that the question was outside its mandate.

Rule of law

Substantive measures are already being taken with a view to establishing a modern system of law enforcement agencies; in particular, prosecution is being given the necessary independence and law enforcement bodies are said to have been put under appropriate control. It is intended to transfer responsibility for prison administration from the former Minister of Interior to the Minister of Justice. However, these developments deserve to be speeded-up.

In the frame of its extensive programme of legislative reform Albania will have to concentrate with a special care on rebuilding its judicial system.

The present judicial system, composed of two degrees of jurisdiction (district courts and either appellate or high court) is in need of urgent reform, both as regards the guarantees of the independence of the judges and the extension of the fields and matters subject to judicial control (ex. administrative acts, implementation of international treaties, constitutional review). The code of criminal procedure, where substantial improvements have already been introduced *de facto* (participation of defence lawyers), must be redrafted, and the penal code further adapted to international human rights standards.

Serious deficiencies have been inherited from the past as regards the legal profession. The profession of independent lawyers had been abolished in 1967, as well as the corresponding professional bodies, and contacts with lawyers abroad cut off. Relevant courses at the Law Faculty were cancelled. At present there are very few lawyers practising in court, in particular for defence in criminal matters (less than 150 all over the country) and they lack training, equipment, administrative facilities, contacts and communication.

An urgent appeal is made to governments, legal associations and relevant international organizations (such as the Council of Europe) to provide assistance and co-operation in order to rapidly develop a new legal culture, in particular as regards the re-establishment of a genuinely independent legal profession as well as the training of lawyers in all branches of the legal profession.

A special problem arises from necessary rehabilitation of former political prisoners as well as internal deportees and exilees. These have been freed, but are still discriminated against in many ways, in particular as regards the right to a job. The question also implies material and social consequences, for instance as regards housing of ex-prisoners and exilees wishing to return home, and their families. Representatives of the former political prisoners and deportees told the CSCE Mission about the discouraging difficulties they face to be 'cleared' of their alleged crimes and declared that they would begin a hunger strike. Probably due also to the pressure of the protest, the People's Assembly approved (after the departure of the Mission from Albania) a new law about rehabilitation of the former political prisoners and their financial compensation.

Economics

Albania exemplifies the link between democratic institutions and a market economy, referred to in the Document of the Bonn Conference and in the Paris Charter. The economic failure of the totalitarian regime was an important factor in its downfall, while the continued absence of any improvement in the economic situation seriously risks bringing discredit upon the pluralist institutions which have now been established in the country.

Albania's record in implementing the provisions of CSCE Second Basket must be seen against the background of a desperate economic crisis. Already the poorest country in Europe, Albania has seen both its agricultural and industrial production fall by half in the year to mid-1991. Only minimal supplies of both food and essential industrial inputs are available. As a result, effective unemployment approaches 35 %; the remaining workforce has lost confidence, and absenteeism is high. Working conditions, always very poor, have deteriorated further. Several thousands of Albanians have fled from economic hardship into neighbouring countries and many of them are still there.

On the financial side Albania has a relatively large external debt of some $ 500 M, most of which is due to arrears on short-term-credits. Foreign reserves are virtually exhausted, and exports have fallen to less than half their 1990 level. There is a large budget deficit, which with a sharp increase in money-supply presents a grave danger of inflation.

Under the previous regime, economic operations had proceeded without regard to the environment: but pollution as fortunately localised to the vicinity of large industrial installations. The main environmental threat is deforestation.

The new coalition government has shown vigour in tackling those problems by economic reforms aimed at achieving a market economy (and at the same time fulfilling CSCE provisions). In the short time available, only partial measures could be taken. All political parties agree on the need to privatize both agriculture and industry, but following lengthy Parliamentary debate, private ownership of land is still greatly limited. Price reform has begun with the raising of many prices for state purchases of food and the freeing of food prices on the open market.

One priority aim of the government, the attraction of foreign investment, has started with the adoption of legislation granting advantages for both joint ventures and wholly-owned enterprises. However, the absence of material resources and know-how makes it unrealistic to expect Albania to have fulfilled all the obligations concerning its legislative and administrative framework which figure in the Bonn document.

In these circumstances there can be no doubt about the urgent need for economic assistance for Albania from the outside world. This is not the place

to examine aid priorities, but it has to be noted that certain needs were repeatedly stressed by the CSCE Rapporteur Mission's interlocutors: food and means to distribute it; medical aid; technical assistance in economic and financial policy and legislation as well as in specific sectors; and funding for the import of agricultural inputs and for the privatization of SMEs.
In this context, special care should be given also to the needs in the field of education.
With an average age of the population of 26 years, the number of children and young people who will attend school or other educational establishments starting from autumn 1991 is approaching one million.
However, during the last months many school facilities have been seriously deteriorating (for example: out of 2,500 school buildings about 700 have been damaged or destroyed). There is an urgent need for new textbooks, eliminating former ideological bias, propaganda and lacunae. For this purpose the country lacks the necessary material, including paper. Urgent financial and intellectual assistance from governments and international institutions is required. In the longer term great efforts must be made in the field of training of teachers.
Coordination among potential donors, such as has already been initiated in the Group of 24, is clearly essential in order to ensure efficiency, eliminate duplication and avoid overburdening Albania with competing missions.

Security

A representative of the Rapporteur Mission - the Director of the Conflict Prevention Centre (CPC) - also had an exchange of views on security issues with the Minister of Defense and the Chief of General Staff. The Albanian authorities reported about the democratic reforms taking place in the armed forces and showed considerable interest in being able to live up to the relevant commitments of the CSBM regime, which followed Albania's accession to the CSCE.
The Director of the CPC illustrated the historic development of the CSBM regime and stressed in this context, the importance of the various commitments taken by the Government of Tirana following its acceptance of the Stockholm and Vienna Documents, *inter alia* notification of activities, exchange of military information, inspections and evaluation visits. The procedures for consultation and co-operation with regard to unusual military activities and hazardous incidents of a military nature were also discussed.
It was agreed that the Albanian delegation in Vienna would keep in contact with the Secretariat of the CPC and that the latter would assist the Albanian authorities in the implementation of their new commitments.

Conclusions

At the end of its stay in Albania the Mission had a long and comprehensive conversation with President Ramiz Alia.
The attention of the President was drawn to the fact that, while it has to be recognized that great efforts have been made and important results have been reached so far, more progress is still needed in some major areas.
Out of the general context the following particular points were raised, which might be essential for the good reputation of Albania:

- new judicial system and culture of law (on European standards);
- full re-habilitation of former political prisoners;
- disproportion between crime and sentence of common prisoners;
- new rules and new staff for National Information Service;
- rights for minorities to education in their own language and to proper political representation;
- publication and dissemination of CSCE documents.

It is the impression of the Mission that its message went through and that its concerns were fully understood.
President Alia committed himself to rapid compliance with the CSCE principles.
The Mission is also deeply convinced that Albania on its way towards implementation of CSCE-commitments needs further, more substantial, coordinated help from other CSCE participating states and from the competent European organizations.

ANNEX 1

List of participants

1. Amb. Wilhelm Höynck, Chairman of the CSO, Bonn
2. Mr Luchino Cortese, Director of the OFE, Warsaw
3. Mr Bent Rosenthal, Director of the CPC, Vienna
4. Mr Nils Eliasson, Director of the CSCE Secretariat, Prague
5. Mr Hans-Peter Furrer, Council of Europe, Strassbourg
6. Mr John Maslen, Commission of the European Community, Brussels
7. Prof. Christian Tomuschat, University of Bonn
8. Prof. Emmanuel Roucounas, University of Athens
9. Dr Pavel Hradecny, Institute of Eastern European History, Prague
10. Dr Heinrich-Wilhelm Beuth, MFA, Bonn
11. Mr Jack Zetkulic, Deputy Director of the OFE, Warsaw

INTERIM REPORT OF THE CSCE RAPPORTEUR MISSION ON THE SITUATION IN NAGORNO KARABAKH

February 1992

Introduction

The Rapporteur Mission to Azerbaijan and Armenia was established by the Deputy Prime Minister and Foreign Minister of the Czech and Slovak Federal Republic in his capacity as Chairman-in-Office of the Council of Ministers of the Conference on Security and Cooperation in Europe. This followed the decision of the Council of Ministers meeting in Prague on 30 and 31 January to take up the invitation of the Governments of the two Republics to send a mission to report on progress towards full implementation of CSCE commitments. The Mission was charged to submit an interim report on the situation in Nagorno Karabakh within twenty one days. The following is that report.

The Mission visited Moscow and then the Republics of Azerbaijan and Armenia from 12 to 18 February. The Chairman and some members visited Nagorno Karabakh on 17 February while other members spent the day at Agdam and a third group carried out a programme in Goris. A full list of participants in the Mission is attached at Annex A. A schedule of events is attached at Annex B[1].

The Mission would like to thank the authorities of the Russian Federation and of the Republics of Azerbaijan and Armenia as well as the local authorities in the Nagorno Karabakh area for their active cooperation and assistance which greatly facilitated its work. The Mission is also very grateful to the Government of the United States for the provision of an aircraft which greatly helped with the practical arrangements.

I. Evolution. The spiral of conflict

1. The emergence and escalation of the conflict

I.1.1. The conflict in Nagorno Karabakh forms part of a larger conflict in the region over the last four years, a conflict which has led to

---

[1] Annex B is not reproduced in the present volume.

large refugee flows, serious human rights violations, including mob violence killing hundreds of innocent civilians, and a legacy of animosity and images of the opposite side as the enemy in the minds of the people. The task now is not to apportion blame but to examine some of the factors which influenced the escalation of the conflict and then to consider ways in which the process could be reversed.

I.1.2. Several participants in, and observers of, the conflict point to deeper historical roots and the psychological effect of events of the past, whether events several thousand years old or events in the second and third decade of the present century. This report will not delve into these historical roots, but rather dwell on the prospects for resolving the conflict by peaceful means.

I.1.3. Events of the last four years coincided with the weakening and final dismantling of the power of the Communist Party of the Soviet Union. This process, which in turn contributed to the disintegration of the Soviet Union as a centralised political entity, gave birth to a nationalist revival which became a primary factor in the opposition, both to Communism as an ideology and to the power of "the Centre" i.e. organs of the State and the Party in Moscow.

I.1.4. Democratisation and national revival in the two republics were intertwined. Nationalism, however laudable from one perspective, has resulted in a rise in ethnic tension on both sides during the period of search for independence and democracy. It was aggravated by the political struggle between different political factions, both at the Centre and within each of the republics.

I.1.5. In 1988, the Armenian community in the autonomous region ('oblast') of Nagorno Karabakh in the Republic of Azerbaijan constituted some four fifths of the population there, the other fifth being Azeris. In the Armenian community, there was a long-standing resentment against the Centre due to serious limitations of cultural and religious freedom. By the beginning of 1988, there were almost no churches open and education in Armenian was impossible. This resentment was also directed against the Republic of Azerbaijan and unfortunately also in part against the Azeris living in the region itself.

I.1.6. It is alleged that, at the beginning of 1988, at a time of massive demonstrations in Stepanakert and Yerevan in favour of the attachment of the territory to Armenia, Azeris were being increasingly pushed out of Stepanakert and other Armenian-dominated centres in Nagorno Karabakh. Some took shelter in

Agdam. A march by demonstrators from Agdam, intended to be peaceful, led to the first shots in the conflict. Two Azeri youths were killed by these shots. Controversy exists as to who did the shooting; the Armenians hold that it was the militia but in Azerbaijan it was widely believed that they were killed by Armenians. These events caused a rapid rise in ethnic tension. It is also alleged that there was an increasing pressure on Azeris to leave Armenia itself during the same period, particularly in the Kafan region.

I.1.7. The Armenian community in Nagorno Karabakh, constituting a large majority of its inhabitants, controlled the elected bodies of the region. With the increasing possibility of a democratic majority exercising political power, the Soviet of the Nagorno Karabakh region was increasingly influenced by nationalist feeling both in that region and in Armenia. On February 20, Nagorno Karabakh voted for an attachment of the region to Armenia. To the Azeris this represented not only a challenge to the territorial integrity of Azerbaijan but also a serious threat to the Azeris of Nagorno Karabakh.

I.1.8. Refugee flows and mounting ethnic tension tragically gave rise to serious mob violence. The first serious mass killing of Armenians took place in Sumgait, north of Baku, during the last days of February 1988. Between 26 and 50 Armenians were brutally killed by the enraged mob. While it remains a matter of some controversy who were the actual instigators of the killings, there can be no doubt that the militia and the security forces were unacceptably passive and provided no protection for the victims. From that time on, a mass exodus of Armenians from Azerbaijan began. Some, but far from all, managed to sell their apartments and to leave under orderly conditions.

I.1.9. Obviously, this affected ethnic hostility in Armenia. Fear spread among the Azeris; women and children were moved to neighbouring Nakhichevan and to Azerbaijan in increasing numbers. Some nine months after the Sumgait events, the deportation or departure of the Azeris from Armenia was completed. How it was carried out remains a matter of some controversy. The delegation held interviews with Azeri refugees and also sought information on the issue in Armenia. There are conflicting allegations on the number of Azeris who where killed during the deportation; the Azeri refugees claim that more than 160 died from violence, while in Armenia it is claimed that the number did not exceed 25 and that those responsible have been prosecuted.

I.1.10. At least twice in 1988, Armenians in Ganja (Kirovabad) were victims of mob violence, and dozens were killed. As a result, all Armenians in the region left for Armenia. In August 1989, a bus carrying Azeris from Tbilisi to Jeblagh was destroyed by a bomb, undoubtedly placed there by Armenian militants. 23 Azeris were killed.

I.1.11. The most serious violence took place in Baku on January 13 and 14, 1990, involving the brutal killings of Armenians. Estimates of the number range from 60 to more than 100. Inadequate efforts have subsequently been made to determine who was responsible for the killings; there have been some difficulties in collecting the evidence. Clearly, however, there was an unacceptable passivity both by the militia and the Soviet forces stationed in Baku. The only aid given by the Soviet forces consisted in helping the remaining Armenians to leave Baku.

I.1.12. In the meantime, the fighting escalated inside and around Nagorno Karabakh. A particularly serious development took place in April and May 1991, when the Soviet army — with the participation of units from the Azerbaijan Ministry of Interior — deported Armenians from a number of villages in the region. The deportation was done with considerable violence.

I.1.13. Following the abortive coup in Moscow in August, the role of the Soviet army changed to one of neutrality. Subsequently, the Armenian community in Nagorno Karabakh and the neighbouring Shahumyan district proclaimed the establishment of an independent Republic of Nagorno Karabakh. This brought a strong response in Azerbaijan including the adoption by the National Assembly on 26 November 1991 of a resolution cancelling the autonomy of the region and placing it under direct Azerbaijani rule. Inside the region, however, the declaration of an independent republic was followed by the election of a new parliament and by a referendum confirming the declaration of independence by a vast majority, although the Azeri population boycotted the event. The proclamation was formalised on 6 January, 1992, by a resolution of the newly elected parliament. These acts are considered by the authorities of the Republic of Azerbaijan to be entirely anti-constitutional. In turn, the annulment of the autonomy of the region by the Azerbaijani National Assembly is also widely held to be unconstitutional within the Commonwealth of Independent States.

I.1.14. The situation in real terms — as will be shown in later parts of this report — is that the Armenian community, through its elected authorities, hold territorial control in major parts of

Nagorno Karabakh. But as an enclave within Azerbaijan, they are besieged on all sides. There remain only a few population centres inside the region where Azeri civilians are still holding out.

2. Position of the Republic of Azerbaijan

I.2.1. Azerbaijan sees the issue primarily as one of territorial integrity threatened by Armenian intentions to annex the region. Nagorno Karabakh is held to be Azerbaijani territory and the armed action by the Armenian community is seen as an unlawful use of force amounting to terrorism. The alleged participation of men coming from Armenia, and the support said to be given from that country to hostilities inside Nagorno Karabakh, is seen as unlawful interference in internal Azerbaijani affairs and in its efforts to maintain law and order.

I.2.2. In discussions with the mission, Azerbaijani officials deplored the mob violence in Sumgait, Ganja (Kirovabad) and Baku against Armenians, and claimed that a great number of criminal cases are under investigation or taken to court against persons suspected of being responsible. A number of convictions have allegedly been obtained. It is recognized, however, that complete investigation and prosecution, particularly for the Baku killings, are not complete. Evidence has been difficult to obtain from witnesses due to fear of reprisals.

I.2.3. On the other hand Azerbaijani representatives claimed that more than 160 were killed during the deportations of Azeris from Armenia, and that no proper legal prosecution of those guilty of murder and other atrocities has been carried out. The response in Armenia is that there were far fewer murders, probably around 25, and that legal action has been taken, leading to the conviction of some 55 Armenians who were found guilty. According to Azerbaijani representatives, no proper efforts have been made to deter other criminal or terrorist actions against Azeris in Nagorno Karabakh.

I.2.4. The Azerbaijani authorities hold that the cancellation of the autonomous status of Nagorno Karabakh by the Azerbaijani National Assembly (Supreme Soviet) is a justified response to the unconstitutional act of the proclamation of independence by the Armenian majority.

I.2.5. Since Azerbaijan sees Nagorno Karabakh as a part of Azerbaijan, it holds that there can be no question of negotiations on a level of parity between the authorities of the republic and representatives of the Armenian majority of Nagorno Karabakh. In discussions with the Mission it was stated, however, that more informal consultations would be possible. It was further stated that should the external involvement in Nagorno Karabakh end and the Resolution of 1990 about the incorporation of Nagorno Karabakh into Armenia be formally withdrawn, Azerbaijan would be willing to grant a degree of autonomy to the region. This would provide at least cultural autonomy, including the right to use the native languages and for both communities be educated in these languages, thus allowing the Armenians to have their own educational institutions. It would also include religious freedom for all including the Armenians whose churches have been closed and badly damaged during the last 70 years. This has subsequently been clarified in a letter from the Minister of Foreign Affairs of Azerbaijan to the Chairman of the Mission suggesting that local self-government should be granted to the region in cultural matters and in all other spheres save where its actions could threaten the security, economy or ecology of Azerbaijan.

3. Positions of the Republic of Armenia

I.3.1. The Armenian position has changed considerably during the last five years. Beginning in 1987, the main political opposition to Communist rule was formed by the nationalist movement, which rallied around the Karabakh committee, an organization aiming at the integration of Nagorno Karabakh into Armenia.

I.3.2. The strength of the nationalist movement grew quickly. Following elections in July 1990, the Armenian National Movement became the main political force forming the majority in Parliament. Armed groups had emerged on both sides, but in August 1990, after a tense but largely peaceful confrontation, the supremacy of Parliament was accepted by all sides. This helped to stabilize the situation and also made it possible to search for a modification of attitudes to the problem. Earlier in 1990, the Supreme Soviet of Armenia had accepted the demand by the Armenian community in Nagorno Karabakh for the incorporation of the region into Armenia. However, at a meeting with the President of the Parliament, Mr. Ararktasian, on February 18, 1992, the Mission was informed that the decision in 1990, concerning the incorporation of Nagorno Karabakh into Armenia was no longer valid and had been given no further legal effect. Mr. Ararktasian also stated that Armenia has no authority to determine the status of Nagorno Karabakh and that Armenia in this respect intends to comply with international law.

I.3.3. In the meeting with the President of Armenia the same day, the Mission was further informed that the main concern of Armenia, as an interested third party, was to contribute to a solution which ensured the security and the human rights of the people of Nagorno Karabakh, irrespective of their ethnic background, whether Armenian or Azeri. He insisted, however, that representatives of the people of Nagorno Karabakh must be actively involved in the processes by which this solution is found.

4. Positions of the Armenian community in Nagorno Karabakh

I.4.1. The Armenian community constitutes the great majority of Nagorno Karabakh and therefore controls the democratically elected bodies. As previously pointed out, on 20 February 1988 the Soviet of the region called for its integration into Armenia.

I.4.2. Following the changed political situation in the Soviet Union after the failed coup in August 1991, the Armenian community, through its elected representatives, declared Nagorno Karabakh, including the neighbouring Shahumyan district, independent.

I.4.3. As stated above, the declaration of independence was endorsed by a vast majority of the Armenian community. In the referendum [*it was*] boycotted by the Azeris. In the formal proclamation of the Republic of Nagorno Karabakh adopted on 6 January 1992 by the newly elected Parliament, it is alleged that the constitution and laws of the USSR in effect still give the right of autonomous regions and ethnic groups, living in compact areas within a republic, to determine their own political status in the case of a secession of that republic from the USSR. Consequently, the authorities elected by the Armenian majority consider continued military actions by Azeri self-defence forces and Azerbaijani military forces an act of aggression against what they now call the Republic of Nagorno Karabakh.

I.4.4. These authorities demand that they be included in any negotiations about the future status of the region.

5. Positions of the Azeri community in Nagorno Karabakh

I.5.1. Very little information is available on the positions taken by the Azeri community forming the minority in Nagorno Karabakh. They seek the protection of Azerbaijan in order to preserve their continued existence in the region. There have been consistent pressures during the last four years to make them move away. This pressure first started in the mixed population centres where Armenians were in majority, and later was applied to a number of purely Azeri villages.

I.5.2. Allegedly, several thousand Azeris were forced out of Stepanakert at the early stage of the evolution of the conflict during the first months of 1988. This pressure resulted in the first confrontations and killings. In the subsequent stages of the conflict, the Azeri inhabitants have found it necessary to remove women and children from most of the villages, due to fear of attacks. In only a few places (Shusha, and two nearby villages) does a civilian Azeri population still remain. Most of the Azeri refugees from Nagorno Karabakh, numbering approximately 20,000 are found in Agdam. Refugees in Baku from the village of Meylibeli told the Mission that their expulsion was preceded by the murder of some inhabitants and the Mission subsequently saw a funeral procession of some of the victims.

II. External views and proposals

1. The Russian Federation and the Republic of Kazakhstan

II.1.1. The conflict has been of great concern to the Commonwealth of Independent States. A Peace Mission was undertaken in September 1991 by Presidents Yeltsin of Russia and Nazarbayev of Kazakhstan. In a communique, this mission recognized that the central authorities of the USSR had been unable to handle the situation in a constructive way. On the contrary, it was found that from 1988 to 1991, serious mistakes had been made; leading to a sharpening of the antagonism between the two sides. In addition, it had led to a decrease in the level of confidence in the Union authorities.

II.1.2. The Yeltsin/Nazarbayev peace mission succeeded in obtaining agreement on a number of steps to be taken in a process towards peacemaking. These are found in what is called the Zheleznovodsk Communique, dated September 23, 1991. It was signed not only by Presidents Yeltsin and Nazarbayev, but also by President Mutalibov of Azerbaijan and President Ter-Petrosian of Armenia. The practical implementation of the steps agreed upon were to be achieved through negotiations involving observers and mediators. Some of these proposals are quoted here, because they contain constructive suggestions for ways in which a settlement may be achieved:

- With a deadline set for 1 January 1992, a ceasefire should be established; all anti-constitutional acts concerning Nagorno Karabakh by Azerbaijan and Armenia should be frozen: legally constituted bodies should be recognized and all groups should be removed from the region, with the exception of the Soviet armed forces, including those of the then USSR Ministry of the Interior. All other armed forces should be withdrawn, and their presence after the deadline should be considered illegal. Members of such groups still found active in the region should be prosecuted with the full rigour of the law.
- Observers were to be sent to the region to secure the cease-fire, neutralize the illegal forces, guarantee the security of all citizens living in the region of conflict and to secure normalization of the situation.
- Azerbaijan and Armenia undertook to guarantee the gradual return of all deported citizens beginning with those whose permanent homes are located in currently uninhabited villages. Assurances of the security of these citizens in their permanent residences were to be obtained through negotiations. Hostages should be freed immediately and those creating obstacles to this should be prosecuted.
- The Parties also undertook to secure the unhindered functioning of railroads, air transport and all means of communication. Free and mutually beneficial use of roads was also to be ensured through negotiations.
- One major factor in the escalation of the conflict being unreliable, often biased, and incomplete information, often generating rumours and exaggerated opinions about the activities of the other side, it was agreed that Russia and Kazakhstan should set up an information group to improve the availability of reliable and comprehensive information.
- Azerbaijan and Armenia were requested to enter into negotiations and the working group of observers was called upon to prepare proposals for the next stage of the negotiations.

II.1.3. The initiative by the presidents of Russia and Kazakhstan has suffered several setbacks. A serious blow came with the destruction of a helicopter carrying mediators and journalists over Nagorno Karabakh on 21 January 1992. Conditions in the region have also changed. Nevertheless, any future peace plan is likely to include most of the steps mentioned above, appropriately reformulated and involving the international community more generally.

2. Position of Turkey

II.2.1. Turkey takes considerable interest in the conflict, which affects peace and regional stability in its immediate neighbourhood. Turkey has sought to be a source of moderation and has stated that it will continue to exert its influence to effect a peaceful solution. Turkey considers that the problem is essentially one for the parties concerned to resolve but is prepared to consider what it can do to bring the conflict to an end and to ensure the application of all ten principles of the Helsinki Final Act throughout the region.

II.2.2. Turkey has, however, repeatedly asserted that there is a bias in the presentation of the situation by international media, particularly in the West. In its view, the loss of Azerbaijani lives is hardly ever reported even though, in Turkey's estimate, Azeri losses are much higher than those suffered by the Armenians. Among examples quoted are the passenger helicopters allegedly shot down by the Armenians. Turkey considers that delegations and non-governmental organizations which visit Armenia and Nagorno Karabakh do not make the same efforts to visit Azerbaijan and the Azeri-held territory of Nagorno Karabakh to hear the Azeri side of the story, including the tragedies that have befallen Azeri refugees.

3. Views of journalists

II.3.1. In Moscow on 13 February, the delegation had a meeting with a number of journalists who write on the conflict. While much useful information was obtained from this group — many have travelled extensively in the conflict area at the risk of their lives — they held differing views both on the facts and on the underlying causes.

II.3.2. There was broad agreement, however, that policies pursued by the Centre from 1988 to 1991 had been ambiguous and harmful. It was alleged that some of the central politicians had encouraged the majority in Nagorno Karabakh and the nationalists in Armenia to seek self-determination, whereas others had encouraged Azerbaijan to resist any change, emphasizing the principles of territorial integrity and non-intervention. In their view, both sides of the conflict had therefore — in their own ways and at various times — expected, and sometimes obtained, support for their views from the Centre. These double signals and consequent actions had made the conflict worse.

II.3.3. It was also generally recognized by the journalists that the activities of the Soviet (now Commonwealth) army in the deportation of Armenians from a number of villages in April and May 1991 had been a major element in the worsening of the conflict.

II.3.4. Great concern was expressed by many journalists over what they saw as a tendency by some members of the Soviet army to sell their weapons to the partisans in the conflict and even at times (and possibly for money) to take part in hostilities.

4. Report by non-governmental human rights organizations

II.4.1. The region has been visited by a number of missions on behalf of non-governmental organizations and by private individuals, aiming at investigating the situation on the spot. This resulted in a number of reports which deal with the factual situation, sometimes in great detail. Three reports will be referred to here.

II.4.2. In the report "Human Rights Violations in Armenia and Azerbaijan", published by Pax Christi Netherlands on 29 September 1991, a detailed description is given of the developments which led the Azeri population to flee or be deported from Armenia and the exodus of the Armenian population from Azerbaijan. The recommendations submitted in the report call e.g. for the establishment of a mixed commission to study mutual allegations, offer mediation and oversee the re-establishment of law and order in Nagorno Karabakh. The report also proposes to lift the economic, political and social isolation of the Armenian inhabitants in the area, and to lift the state of emergency in the region. It also proposes that the Azerbaijani authorities should offer proper compensation to the Armenian refugees from Azerbaijan, and that the Armenian authorities reconsider compensation for Azeri refugees from Armenia.

II.4.3. Several missions have been led by Baroness Cox. The first was an international delegation under the auspices of the First Andrei Sakharov Memorial Congress, undertaken from May 25-31 1991, which coincided with the most serious period of Soviet Army involvement prior to the unsuccessful coup in Moscow in August 1991. The violations carried out during those months are now generally recognised.

II.4.4. The second delegation led by Baroness Cox was under the auspices of Christian Solidarity International. The report on the last mission dates from 3-8 January 1992, dealing with the very serious situation which has arisen as a result of the violence by parties in conflict, affecting many innocent civilians. The mission report calls on the world community to render humanitarian assistance to the victims of the conflict. It also calls on the presidents of Russia, Kazakhstan, Armenia and Azerbaijan to ensure the enforcement of the Zheleznovodsk agreement. In contrast to Pax Christi Netherlands, the report recommends that the former Soviet forces in Karabakh should remain — at the request of either side — to prevent unprovoked attack and to help correct the present imbalance of forces. It also calls on the international community to recognize the results of the referendum of 10 December 1991 and the parliamentary elections of 28 December "as reflecting the will of the people of Karabakh".

III. Description of the current situation

1. The situation in the Stepanakert area and Shusha

III.1.1. Four members of the delegation visited Nagorno Karabakh on Monday 17 February. They visited both Stepanakert and Shusha. A cease-fire had been arranged and the journey was made by a helicopter of the Commonwealth forces at Ganja. The team met the authorities in both places and also visited the recently abandoned Azeri village of Meylibeli. They intended to visit the Armenian village of Karintak but had to abandon this plan because of time constraints. They had a distant view of the village and could appreciate both its remoteness and the difficulties and hardship created for the inhabitants of the countryside by the present conflict.

III.1.2. There was much evidence of destruction both in Stepanakert and to a lesser extent in Shusha. The team saw bodies of recent victims in the morgue of the hospital in Stepanakert which had been damaged by artillery or rocket fire. The director told the Mission that 17 people had been killed the night before. The Polyclinic in Shusha has also been struck by shell-fire. The authorities in Stepanakert stated that they consider Nagorno Karabakh to be fighting for its independence based on the right of self-determination. Nonetheless the population of the region wanted the quickest possible solution to the problem by peaceful means. They favoured direct talks between themselves and the Azerbaijan Republic but showed interest in the Valletta mechanism for the Peaceful Settlement of Disputes provided they themselves were represented in any negotiations which took place.

2. The situation in the Hadrut region of Nagorno Karabakh

III.2.1. Rapporteur Mission members also talked to the villagers of Tsor and Khotsaberd from the Hadrut region of Nagorno Karabakh as the villagers arrived by helicopter at the Armenian town of Goris. They reported that in May 1991 the population of some 14 villages in the Hadrut region was forcibly deported, mainly to Armenia. On 13 May 1991 the region was encircled by Soviet troops, while militia from the Azerbaijani Ministry of the Interior entered villages and started to load their inhabitants on buses for deportation. Some were asked to sign applications to leave. Those who refused to sign were cruelly beaten and some 30 were shot. Azeris from neighbouring villages joined in this. Property was destroyed and looted.

III.2.2. According to the villagers, the inhabitants of the remaining Armenian villages in the Hadrut region have since been subject to constant armed raids from Azeri territory. They witnessed several cases of murder by Azeri raiders where the victims were cruelly tortured and their bodies mutilated. Hadrut itself is under fire from Azeri forces and cannot receive air traffic from Armenia which is a vital source of food supplies to the region.

III.2.3. The villagers see these developments as a part of the policy of Azerbaijan to remove all Armenians from Nagorno Karabakh as has been the case in Nakhichevan.

3. The situation in Agdam

III.3.1. On 17 February part of the Mission visited the city of Agdam situated in Azeri territory immediately to the east of Nagorno Karabakh.

III.3.2. As there had recently been an important flow of refugees, the atmosphere in the city and in the larger refugee camps according to local authorities was very tense. The members of the delegation were consequently only permitted to visit a smaller refugee camp, the central hospital, a cemetery and a psychiatric hospital where two people were killed as a result of Armenian rocket assault. The conditions in the refugee camp were clearly unsatisfactory and the Mission was asked to send food, clothing etc. as soon as possible. The conditions in the hospital were better, even though there was said to be a shortage of medicine and medical equipment. Some refugees asked for helicopters to be made available to transport the dead bodies of their relatives from villages in Nagorno Karabakh.

III.3.3. The city had been hit a few times during the last weeks by rockets and artillery shells, but the damage shown to the delegation was limited and confined to the suburbs. Some small arms fire could be heard during the visit and according to the local authorities the positions of the Armenian forces were less than one kilometre from the city.

III.3.4. The local authorities also put the members of the delegation in contact with seven soldiers of the former Soviet army who had deserted in order not to be engaged in fighting against the Azeris and who said that they were very well treated by them. No armed Azeri fighters of any kind were seen.

4. The military situation

III.4.1. The information gathered from both sides about the escalation of the conflict was somewhat uncertain, and that relating to the size of the forces was mutually contradictory.

III.4.2. As far as the first point is concerned, the delegation has been left with the impression that in the period up to the failed coup in Moscow in August 1991 the Soviet forces played the most important role and were relied upon by the Azeri side. Smaller contingents of personnel from the Ministry of the Interior participated together with the Soviet armed forces. Generally speaking, they were on the offensive in the period April to June, attacking and destroying a number of Armenian villages in Nagorno Karabakh and deporting their inhabitants. At this time Azerbaijan itself had no regular army of its own but had a militia answerable to the Ministry of the Interior.

III.4.3. Since the beginning of 1992, however, Armenian forces have had an offensive role conquering many Azeri villages in the region. This has led to an increase in the number of refugees (according to Azeri information, about 20,000 Azeri refugees since the beginning of the year). Towards the middle of February fighting was particularly intensive around Shusha and Stepanakert. Shusha is located only a few kilometres from Stepanakert and commands the access to this city from the south-east, i.e. from Armenia.

III.4.4. Information about the relative size of the forces engaged in the fighting differs enormously according to whichever of the parties is providing it. As far as the general character of the fighting is concerned, it would seem to consist mainly of fairly sporadic actions accomplished by relatively small units, both regular and irregular. Furthermore, it seems to be generally recognized that the use of equipment belonging to the former Soviet forces is a major precondition for success. This equipment, including heavy equipment, is apparently stolen or bought (illegally) by both Armenian and Azeri fighters on a large scale. However, it would also seem that the more or less predominantly Armenian or Azeri nationality of the officers/draftees in some of the units of the former Soviet forces has played an important role in the way in which the equipment — at least in certain cases — has fallen into the hands of the fighters.

5. Unresolved issues concerning the refugees

III.5.1. There are large refugee populations on all sides — approximately 170,000 from Armenia in Azerbaijan, probably about 20,000 in Agdam from Nagorno Karabakh, and some 350,000 in Armenia from Azerbaijan including deportees from Nagorno Karabakh.

III.5.2. A peaceful solution will first require the voluntary repatriation of both Armenians and Azeris to Nagorno Karabakh. This will cause serious problems. Villages on both sides have been burned and looted. Secondly, steps will have to be taken to handle the refugee problems between Armenia and Azerbaijan. This involves issues such as the facilitation of voluntary repatriation under guarantees of security and full enjoyment of human rights as citizens of the country in which they lived, and compensation for property (movable of immovable) taken from them or destroyed.

III.5.3. Many Armenian refugees are presently in Moscow and other parts of the Commonwealth. Some complain of lack of co-operation by the Azerbaijan authorities in providing information about the place of burial of their relatives who were killed, and in restoring to them passports and documents, birth certificates, educational records and records of past employment, which were lost or destroyed when they had to flee. These are documents essential for them in order to obtain jobs, pensions and otherwise live a normal life. Azerbaijani authorities and representatives in the places where these refugees live, should urgently provide them with all assistance required.

IV. Conclusions

IV.1. The conflict in Nagorno Karabakh is now critical, involving great suffering for the population and risking serious instability in the region. Fighting has grown more intense, fuelled by the availability of arms from within and outside the region. There have been heavy flows of refugees throughout the area, many of whom require increased humanitarian assistance. Fundamental human rights have been violated by participants on both sides, including the rights of minority groups; and families on both sides have been unable to determine the fate of their relatives. The effects of the conflict have been felt throughout the region, as a result of the movement of refugees and the disruption of normal trading patterns.

IV.2. All parties in both countries attach great importance to their participation in the CSCE process, confirm their willingness to contribute to security and co-operation in Europe, and welcome CSCE involvement in resolution of their differences. The Mission believes that the interested parties could make productive use of CSCE instruments and institutions, including the Valletta mechanism for the Peaceful Settlement of Disputes in seeking a satisfactory resolution of the conflict. Advisory assistance may be necessary.

IV.3. The greatest urgency must be given to the establishment of a ceasefire and initiation of a dialogue among the interested parties. Both Armenia and Azerbaijan recognize the influential role which could be played by other countries in the region, especially the Russian Federation and Turkey, in encouraging this dialogue and facilitating any ensuing negotiations.

V. Recommendations

I

- that the CSO urge the interested parties to impose an immediate ceasefire on all forces in the Nagorno Karabakh area in conformity with the Zheleznovodsk communique of September 23, 1991
- that the CSO request that all CSCE participating states and all states in the region impose an immediate embargo on the transfer and transport of weapons and munitions to forces engaged in combat
- that the CSO urgently recommend that voluntary organizations with appropriate resources provide humanitarian assistance both to the

inhabitants of Nagorno Karabakh, and to the refugees on both sides of this conflict, including those from the Republics of Armenia and Azerbaijan

- that the CSO request that safe corridors be immediately established for the delivery of humanitarian assistance to the inhabitants of Nagorno Karabakh
- that the CSO request that all prisoners and hostages be exchanged immediately, if necessary under the auspices of the ICRC
- that the CSO request that the remains of all the dead be returned immediately to their families for respectful burial

II

- that the CSO request participating states in the region, in particular Kazakhstan and the Russian Federation, to continue their efforts to promote a process leading to a ceasefire and negotiation among the parties
- that the CSO strongly urge the continuation of dialogue among all interested parties, including the views of the inhabitants of Nagorno Karabakh. Such a dialogue could, if necessary, be informally pursued under the auspices of the CSCE Presidency at the earliest possible opportunity. Among the first issues to be discussed in this dialogue should be the question of observers to monitor the ceasefire, the re-establishment of normal trade relations and the establishment of an independent commission, including third parties, to review problems relating to the refugees
- the CSO call the attention of the interested parties to the possibility of using the CSCE mechanism for Peaceful Settlement of Disputes. In this connection the Presidency of the CSCE might be invited to form an international advisory commission on constitutional questions

III

- that the CSO decide upon the appropriate means for keeping the Nagorno Karabakh problem under review
- that, to this end, the CSCE participating states from the region which may be able positively to influence the situation, in particular Armenia, Azerbaijan, Kazakhstan, the Russian Federation and Turkey, be requested to report at subsequent CSO meetings on progress toward a peaceful settlement
- That the CSO foresee the possibility of additional missions to Nagorno Karabakh to monitor the evolving situation there

Annex A

List of Participants

Leader of the Mission
Karel Schwarzenberg, CSFR

Members
John J. Maresca, USA
Laurence O'Keeffe, UK
Asbjorn Eide, Norway
Arie Bloed, Netherlands
Luchino Cortese, Office for Democratic Institutions and Human Rights
Bent Rosenthal, Conflict Prevention Centre
Brig. Gen. William B. Davitte, USA
Roman Hronek, CSFR
Scott N. Thayer, USA
Vladimir Lomen, CSFR
Lucia Brabencova, CSFR

REPORT OF THE SECOND CSCE MISSION ON NAGORNO-KARABAKH

March 1992

I. Introduction

In accordance with the request of the eighth meeting of the Committee of Senior Officials, a second CSCE Mission visited Nagorno-Karabakh, Azerbaijan, and Armenia March 19-23, 1992. It was headed by the Chairman-in-Office of the Committee of Senior Officials, Mr. Jan Kubis. Representatives of Canada, the Czech and Slovak Federal Republic, the Netherlands, Norway, United Kingdom and the United States participated in the Mission. (Annex A contains a list of participants in the Mission. Annex B is the schedule of the Mission's activities.*)

The Mission expresses its appreciation to the authorities of the Republics of Armenia and Azerbaijan, as well as to the local authorities in the Nagorno-Karabakh area, for their active co-operation and assistance. The Mission also thanks the Government of Canada for the provision of an aircraft which greatly facilitated its work.

II. Meetings and Discussions

The Head of the Mission joined Mr. Cyrus Vance, personal representative of the United Nations Secretary-General, in Ganja on March 19. On March 20, they visited the Nagorno-Karabakh region. In the towns of Agdam and Stepanakert they, as heads of two separate Missions, held talks with the representatives of the conflicting sides, including senior elected authorities in Nagorno-Karabakh. It was agreed that this joint visit was an appropriate manifestation of the intention of the CSCE and UN to conduct complementary efforts towards a solution of the Nagorno-Karabakh conflict and that there is a need for further co-operation between the CSCE and the UN.

The Mission visited Baku on March 20 and 21. While there, they were received by the acting head of state of Azerbaijan, Mr. Jacub Mamedov, and Prime Minister Gasan Gasanov, as well as with Government officials and representatives of the opposition.

---

* Annex B is not reproduced.

In Yerevan March 22 and 23, the Mission met with President Levon Ter-Petrossian, as well as officials of the government and parliament of Armenia.

The visit of the Mission took place as a 7 day cease-fire brokered by Iran began. Despite reported violations, all sides expressed their commitment to maintaining it. The Mission was informed that Iranian points of contact had been stationed in Stepanakert, Agdam, and other locations. These developments gave the Mission the opportunity to discuss the objectives of its visit against a background that made it relatively easy for all parties to focus on the sort of measures that would be needed to sustain the cease-fire over the long-term.

The Head of the Mission met the Deputy Foreign Minister of Iran, Mr. M. Vaezi, on March 21 in Baku. They discussed the situation in Nagorno-Karabakh and modalities of the cease-fire established through Iran's mediation. Both agreed that every effort leading towards a lasting cease-fire as an essential step in a negotiated political settlement of the Nagorno-Karabakh conflict is welcome and expressed their interest in future contacts and co-operation.

III. Conclusions

A. Cease-fire

The implementation of an effective cease-fire is a high priority of the interested parties. The Mission was told by all interlocutors that the highly emotional and localized nature of this conflict made it very difficult for central authorities to ensure complete and immediate compliance with any cease-fire.

Although all of the interested parties expressed support for an initial cease-fire without pre-conditions, they pointed out that it could not be durable unless it led at an early stage to amelioration of other matters arising out of the conflict. In Baku, a key condition for an enduring cease-fire was the cessation of the delivery of arms and munitions to Nagorno-Karabakh, while in Yerevan a key condition was the lifting of the economic blockade of Armenia and Nagorno-Karabakh.

The Mission explored means of promoting both the effectiveness and durability of a cease-fire. In the area of effectiveness, it discussed the introduction of international liaison groups/observers. In the area of durability, the Mission suggested to each party that a goodwill gesture corresponding to a key concern of the other would give both parties a greater interest in making a cease-fire permanent. Responses indicated that the issues in the conflict are so complex and intertwined that only a 'package' of reciprocal gestures is likely to prove successful. The key elements of such a package include the cessation of weapon and munitions deliveries to forces engaged in combat, the lifting of all economic blockades, and humanitarian steps such as releases of prisoners and provision of medical supplies.

B. Chairman's Visit

All interested parties welcomed and will give full support to an early visit of the Chairman-in-office of the Council in order to discuss continued implementation of the present cease-fire and the possible contribution of confidence building measures to this end, as well as prospects for a comprehensive political settlement. They expressed the hope that international efforts to resolve the conflict could proceed in a co-ordinated fashion.

C. Observers

On the basis of its meetings and discussions, the Mission believes that the interested parties would welcome as a first step the establishment of CSCE liaison/observer groups in relevant areas. The purpose of the groups initially would be to establish a link between the interested parties and the CSCE.

As soon as practicable and in full co-operation with the interested parties, these groups would be augmented and converted into observer teams, and deployed to assist in monitoring the cease-fire on a local basis.

Full deployment of the liaison/observer teams could quickly involve upwards of 100 observers, plus support personnel. The budget of the CSCE does not envisage such expenditures. Therefore, consideration should be given, prior to a decision to proceed, to the issue of financing the liaison/observer teams.

In acknowledging the important role that could be played by observers, Armenian authorities stressed that a peacekeeping force would decisively restore confidence and establish a necessary guarantee for stability and peace in Nagorno-Karabakh.

IV. Recommendations

The Mission recommends, in addition to the recommendations contained in decisions of the Committee of Senior Officials and in the report of the first CSCE Mission to the area, that:

- the Chairman-in-Office act quickly at the present moment to visit the region and assist in the consolidation of a permanent and effective cease-fire which will preclude further bloodshed in the region.

- such a cease-fire be strengthened through agreement among the interested parties to lift economic blockades in the region.

- the Chairman-in-Office explore with all interested parties the development and implementation of mechanisms which will ensure an embargo on the transfer and transport of weapons and munitions to forces engaged in combat.

- the Chairman-in-Office seek specific commitments from the interested parties that all prisoners be released on a precise date agreed by all concerned.

- the Chairman-in-Office, after his visit to the region, contact key voluntary organizations and inform them of the types of humanitarian assistance most urgently required by the inhabitants of Nagorno-Karabakh, and by the refugees and displaced persons on both sides of the conflict, including those from the republics of Armenia and Azerbaijan.

- in order to contribute to the consolidation of the cease-fire, the CSCE despatch liaison/observer groups of 6-8 persons to Baku and Yerevan to establish a direct link among the parties and with the CSCE, and to lay the groundwork for the deployment of observer teams;

    - at least some of the personnel assigned to the liaison/observer groups have experience with UNTSO (Lebanon/Beirut) and/or UNIMOG (Iran/Iraq War);

    - in view of prevailing conditions in the area, CSCE arrange for all necessary administrative, logistic, and communications support (including fixed and rotary wing support as appropriate) for the observer group. Therefore, the CSCE must explore, on an urgent basis, the alternatives for providing such support.

- as soon as liaison/observer groups are established in Baku and Yerevan, an additional group should be deployed to Stepanakert. Observer teams should be deployed along the Armenia/Azerbaijan border and in other pertinent areas/locations as necessary.

- to ensure co-ordination among parties seeking to assist in the resolution of the conflict, the Chairman-in-Office after his visit inform all such parties as well as the participating States of progress achieved and maintain contact with them.

* * *

ANNEX A

PARTICIPANTS

Jan Kubis, Chairman, CSCE Committee of Senior Officials (Head of Mission)

Stephen Barrett, United Kingdom

Andrej Cima, Czech and Slovak Federal Republic

Col. Lewis Evans, Canada

Rudolf V. Perina, United States of America

Jaap Ramaker, Netherlands

Scott N. Thayer, United States of America

Gen. Martin Vadset, Norway

REPORT OF THE CHAIRMAN OF THE MINSK CONFERENCE

REPORT OF THE CHAIRMAN ON HIS MISSION IN THE AREA OF THE CRISIS

Helsinki, 17 May 1992

In my capacity as Chairman of the Conference on Nagorno-Karabakh, I visited the area from 4 to 11 May and had contacts with Government representatives and representatives of many of the parties interested in the Conference. I was accompanied by Ambassador Sica, Deputy Chairman of the Conference, Ambassador Armellini, Head of the Italian Delegation to the Helsinki FUM and a small number of Italian aides, as well as by a representative of the Chairman-in-Office of the CSCE and a representative of the UNHCR.

I had extensive talks in Moscow, Erevan, Tbilisi, Baku, Ankara and Minsk. Because of the abrupt burst of fighting on 7 May I had to stop in Agdam and could not visit Nagorno-Karabakh, but I had a meeting with representatives of that region the previous day in Erevan. I deemed it useful to seek also the views of the Iranian authorities, whose efforts for a solution to the crisis have resulted in the meeting organized in Teheran on 6 and 7 May. A complete list of my contacts is attached.

* * *

In *Moscow* Minister Kozyrev confirmed the Russian commitment to a successful outcome of the CSCE Conference. He also briefed me about further efforts at good offices that Russia is carrying out in other contexts, stressing the complementarity of these with the Conference and the CSCE process in general. We agreed to ensure adequate reciprocal information and all possible coordination.

In *Yerevan* I was asked to convene the Conference as early as possible. My attention was called to the conceptual linkage between the establishment of a durable cease-fire, the lifting of the economic blockade of Nagorno-Karabakh and the free flow of humanitarian relief. According to Foreign Minister Hovanissian, only a direct involvement of the people of Nagorno-Karabakh in the Conference would make them feel bound by the conclusions reached in Minsk. President Ter Petrossian expressed the view that on both sides there are 'uncontrolled elements' and, therefore, the effectiveness of a cease-fire should be guaranteed by peace-keeping forces.

The *Armenian* representatives of Nagorno-Karabakh, Melik Shek Nazarian and Manvel Sarkisian - whom I met in Erevan - illustrated their position as to the status of Nagorno-Karabakh, asking for the recognition of full parity in every diplomatic exercise aimed at solving the dispute. They mentioned, among others, participation in CSO. They took note of the ideas I was considering for the convening of the Conference.

In *Tbilisi* President Shevardnadze showed great concern for the recent developments, considering that the situation had been worsening in the last six months. He evoked the need of maintaining co-ordination among different initiatives, mentioning in particular the Caucasian regional dimension and recalling the decision, already taken in principle, of establishing a 'Consultative Caucasian Council'.

In *Teheran* I received information on the efforts by Iran for an improvement in relations between Armenia and Azerbaijan. Among their objectives, Vice Minister Vaezi pointed out the establishment of a 'framework of principles' between the two countries and the setting up of a mechanism for the enforcement of a cease-fire. The Iranian side suggested a co-ordination on the ground between CSCE monitors and their own.

In *Baku* I was asked to take into account internal circumstances, which made it difficult for Azerbaijan to engage effectively in a negotiation before end June. A strong expectation was expressed as to an international interest for the problem of refugees. Minister Sadykhov - whom I met while violent combats were going on in Shusha - protested against the deterioration of the military situation and hinted to an appeal to the International Court of Justice He complained about the fizzling out of the bilateral understanding signed in Teheran on 7 May. He considered that, in the light of the new situation, the convening of the CSCE Conference appeared more difficult and that, anyhow, the participation of representatives of Nagorno-Karabakh should be envisaged in the framework of the Azerbaijani Government's delegation.

In *Ankara* Turkish officials expressed their strong preoccupation for the worsening of the situation. They stressed the necessity of confidence building among parties, as a preliminary condition to a constructive negotiation. It was agreed that the present situation is characterized by mutual mistrust and that diplomatic initiatives are needed to overcome it. Turkey is particularly attached to safeguarding the basic principles of the CSCE, and expects them to be respected also in the organizational modalities of the Conference.

In *Minsk* Minister Kravchenko insisted on the urgency of setting up a cease-fire, as a basic element of an early convening of the Conference. Also, we extensively discussed concrete modalities and organizational matters connected with the preparation of the Conference and reviewed progress already made in this respect.

* * *

On the basis of the above mentioned contacts - as well as other made by Ambassador Sica and my aides - I would like to draw your attention to the following points:

1) from 7 May onwards, the situation in the field has considerably worsened. Armed clashes in the 'Latchin strip' risk changing the nature of the conflict;

2) in such a situation, ever greater is the need for a political forum where to address all the disputes; I am convinced that opportunities for a political solution still exist and should be explored to the fullest extent possible; all parties, even if on different assumptions, have declared their interest for the diplomatic exercise proposed by the CSCE;

3) under these circumstances, it is of the utmost importance that nobody works towards further 'faits accomplis', which in any case could not be recognized. Last week, I addressed an appeal to the Governments concerned, asking for self-restraint; I realize that activities by uncontrolled groups are possible, but I maintain that responsible behaviour of Governments is a key factor among the political conditions for the Conference;

4) an effective cease-fire is an important element of a mutually reinforcing process, which could allow the Conference to proceed towards a successful outcome, entailing i.a. a safe return for refugees and unhindered passage of humanitarian aid;

5) effective negotiations require that delegations attending the Conference operate on the basis of a full and flexible mandate;

6) at the same time, an early announcement of the convening of the Conference might play a role in the lessening of the tensions;

7) I think that convening the Conference should be possible on the basis of formulations which do not prejudge the answers to be given to

formal questions which will have to be addressed by the Conference itself. The peoples of Nagorno-Karabakh should be granted the possibility of expressing their views on the issues that concern them directly.

INTERIM REPORT OF THE CHAIRMAN OF THE MINSK CONFERENCE

presented by Ambassador Antonio Armellini Head of the Italian Delegation at the XIII Meeting of the Committee of Senior Officials

Helsinki, 29 June 1992

Mr. Chairman,

on behalf of the Rt. Hon. Mario Raffaelli, Chairman of the Minsk Conference, I would like to briefly report to this Committee on the further development of work undertaken in Rome in the framework of the preliminary emergency meeting of the Minsk Group. In addition to the session held from 1 to 5 June - on which Chairman Raffaelli reported to the XII CSO Meeting on 9 June 1992 - two additional sessions of the preliminary emergency meeting took place: one from 15 to 20 June, and the other starting today, always in Rome. In light of the fact that work will continue in the next days, the report submitted today by the Italian Chairmanship can only be a 'progress report' of a limited nature, it being understood that any political evaluation will have to be based on the outcome of the current session in Rome.

The second session of the preliminary emergency meeting, which took place - as stated above - from 15 to 20 June, highlighted the problems and the diplomatic positions of the various parties. The respective priorities were further elaborated upon, although all the obstacles which still prevent the prompt convening of the Minsk Conference could not be removed.

Parallel to the second session, there regretfully was a continuation of conflict on the ground. This led to accrued difficulties in the debate, which did not help common understanding. "Elected and other" representatives of Armenians of Nagorno-Karabakh did not participate in the second session, nor in the first one, to which both they were invited according to the terms stated in the conclusions of the CSCE Council of Ministers of the 24 March.

The dramatic confirmation - on the occasion of the second session of 15-20 June - of a continuing situation of fighting and conflict on the ground, can only lead us to underline once more the need to undertake all efforts to set in motion as soon as possible the peace process, through the early convening of the Minsk Conference. This is an objective on which the mandate given to the Chairman is based, and all parties participating in the meeting have firmly reiterated their commitment to its achievement.

Equally, the eleven States of the Minsk Group concur in underlining in this framework, and keeping in mind the above-mentioned need to accelerate by all means the peace process, the decisive importance of despatching CSCE observers to the region immediately, in conjunction with the opening of the Conference. Chairman Raffaelli, at the request of the above States, has transmitted to the Chairman of the Council of the CSCE a further appeal of the States of the Minsk Group that he nominate at the earliest the Head of the observers Mission, who should then with the shortest delay despatch a first "advance team".

In the course of the session which has begun this morning in Rome, the Chairmanship of the Conference intends to submit proposals which could help find an agreement for the hoped-for early convening of the Minsk Conference. In particular, we intend to verify once again the political will of all parties to proceed towards establishing the basic conditions to start the peace process in Minsk.

The Chairmanship hopes that the reaffirmation of this political will lead to positive results and intends to pursue all constructive efforts to achieve this goal. The Conference could thus open in Minsk within one week of the conclusion of the Rome meeting.

Mr. Chairman,

I feel I should underline to this Committee the great importance that the Italian Chairmanship attaches to such a possibility. Discussions held so far and the development of the different positions have confirmed the difficulty of existing problems; they have at the same time clearly shown that negotiation and consultation in the framework of the CSCE is the only realistic alternative to the degeneration of a conflict which, without advancing any solution, would risk to further worsen the already heavy burden of human suffering, mournings and destruction due to the crisis centred on Nagorno-Karabakh.

In establishing the Minsk Group, the CSCE has provided a precise signal of the political will of the 52 to endeavour to settle this crisis, without further recourse to arms but immediately promoting all measures, including those of a humanitarian nature, designed to facilitate normalisation and the prompt restoration of international legitimacy to the area.

This is an important effort, which the CSCE has undertaken under its own responsibility, fully aware of the need to translate in terms of real life and the development of peaceful societies, the principles and commitments undertaken by the new Europe, united by the values of democracy, rule of law, respect of human rights and fundamental freedoms. The Summit of 9-10 July will evaluate the results achieved and, if need be, provide at the highest political level an indication of what will be required to continue and strengthen the peace process. It is needed absolutely necessary for all the participants in the Minsk group, as well as for all the participants in the wider framework of the 52, to continue showing their firm will and strong determination to pursue the process of political negotiation to which they have solemnly and jointly committed themselves on the 24 March, here in Helsinki.

I thank you, Mr. Chairman.

VII

MISCELLANEOUS

TREATY ON CONVENTIONAL ARMED FORCES IN EUROPE[1]

Paris, 19 November 1990

The Kingdom of Belgium, the Republic of Bulgaria, Canada, the Czech and Slovak Federal Republic, the Kingdom of Denmark, the French Republic, the Federal Republic of Germany, the Hellenic Republic, the Republic of Hungary, the Republic of Iceland, the Italian Republic, the Grand Duchy of Luxembourg, the Kingdom of the Netherlands, the Kingdom of Norway, the Republic of Poland, the Portuguese Republic, Romania, the Kingdom of Spain, the Republic of Turkey, the Union of Soviet Socialist Republics, the United Kingdom of Great Britain and Northern Ireland and the United States of America, hereinafter referred to as the States Parties,

Guided by the Mandate for Negotiation on Conventional Armed Forces in Europe of January 10, 1989, and having conducted this negotiation in Vienna beginning on March 9, 1989,

Guided by the objectives and the purposes of the Conference on Security and Co-operation in Europe, within the framework of which the negotiation of this Treaty was conducted,

Recalling their obligation to refrain in their mutual relations, as well as in their international relations in general, from the threat or use of force against the territorial integrity or political independence of any State, or in any other manner inconsistent with the purposes and principles of the Charter of the United Nations;

Conscious of the need to prevent any military conflict in Europe,

Conscious of the common responsibility which they all have for seeking to achieve greater stability and security in Europe,

Striving to replace military confrontation with a new pattern of security relations among all the States Parties based on peaceful co-operation and thereby to contribute to overcoming the division of Europe,

---

1 Editor's note: Protocols, annexed to this Treaty, are not reproduced in the present volume.

Committed to the objectives of establishing a secure and stable balance of conventional armed forces in Europe at lower levels than heretofore, of eliminating disparities prejudicial to stability and security and of eliminating, as a matter of high priority, the capability for launching surprise attack and for initiating large-scale offensive action in Europe,

Recalling that they signed or acceded to the Treaty of Brussels of 1948, the Treaty of Washington of 1949 or the Treaty of Warsaw of 1955 and that they have the right to be or not to be a party to treaties of alliance,

Committed to the objective of ensuring that the numbers of conventional armaments and equipment limited by the Treaty within the area of application of this Treaty do not exceed 40,000 battle tanks, 60,000 armoured combat vehicles, 40,000 pieces of artillery, 13,600 combat aircraft and 4,000 attack helicopters,

Affirming that this Treaty is not intended to affect adversely the security interests of any State,

Affirming their commitment to continue the conventional arms control process including negotiations, taking into account future requirements for European stability and security in the light of political developments in Europe,

Have agreed as follows:

Article I

1. Each State Party shall carry out the obligations set forth in this Treaty in accordance with its provisions, including those obligations relating to the following five categories of conventional armed forces: battle tanks, armoured combat vehicles, artillery, combat aircraft and combat helicopters.

2. Each State Party also shall carry out the other measures set forth in this Treaty designed to ensure security and stability both during the period of reduction of conventional armed forces and after the completion of reductions.

3. This Treaty incorporates the Protocol on Existing Types of Conventional Armaments and Equipment, hereinafter referred to as the Protocol on Existing Types, with an Annex thereto; the Protocol on Procedures Governing the Reclassification of Specific Models or

Versions of Combat-Capable Trainer Aircraft Into Unarmed Trainer Aircraft, hereinafter referred to as the Protocol on Aircraft Reclassification; the Protocol on Procedures Governing the Reduction of Conventional Armaments and Equipment Limited by the Treaty on Conventional Armed Forces in Europe, hereinafter referred to as the Protocol on Reduction; the Protocol on Procedures Governing the Categorisation of Combat Helicopters and the Recategorisation of Multi-Purpose Attack Helicopters, hereinafter referred to as the Protocol on Helicopter Recategorisation; the Protocol on Notification and Exchange of Information, hereinafter referred to as the Protocol on Information Exchange, with an Annex on the Format for the Exchange of Information, hereinafter referred to as the Annex on Format; the Protocol on Inspection; the Protocol on the Joint Consultative Group; and the Protocol on the Provisional Application of Certain Provisions of the Treaty on Conventional Armed Forces in Europe, hereinafter referred to as the Protocol on Provisional Application. Each of these documents constitutes an integral part of this Treaty.

Article II

1. For the purposes of this Treaty:

(A) The term "group of States Parties" means the group of States Parties that signed the Treaty of Warsaw[1] of 1955 consisting of the Republic of Bulgaria, the Czech and Slovak Federal Republic, the Republic of Hungary, the Republic of Poland, Romania and the Union of Soviet Socialist Republics, or the group of States Parties that signed or acceded to the Treaty of Brussels[2] of 1948 or the Treaty of Washington[3] of 1949 consisting of the Kingdom of Belgium, Canada, the Kingdom of Denmark, the French Republic, the Federal Republic of Germany, the Hellenic Republic, the Republic of Iceland, the Italian Republic, the Grand Duchy of Luxembourg, the Kingdom of the Netherlands, the Kingdom of Norway, the Portuguese Republic, the

---

[1] The Treaty of Friendship, Co-operation and Mutual Assistance signed in Warsaw, 14 May 1955

[2] The Treaty of Economic, Social and Cultural Collaboration and Collective Self-Defence signed in Brussels, 17 March 1948

[3] The North Atlantic Treaty signed in Washington, 4 April 1949

Kingdom of Spain, the Republic of Turkey, the United Kingdom of Great Britain and Northern Ireland and the United States of America.

(B) The term "area of application" means the entire land territory of the States Parties in Europe from the Atlantic Ocean to the Ural Mountains, which includes all the European island territories of the States Parties, including the Faroe Islands of the Kingdom of Denmark, Svalbard including Bear Island of the Kingdom of Norway, the islands of Azores and Madeira of the Portuguese Republic, the Canary Islands of the Kingdom of Spain and Franz Josef Land and Novaya Zemlya of the Union of Soviet Socialist Republics. In the case of the Union of Soviet Socialist Republics, the area of application includes all territory lying west of the Ural River and the Caspian Sea. In the case of the Republic of Turkey, the area of application includes the territory of the Republic of Turkey north and west of a line extending from the point of intersection of the Turkish border with the 39th parallel to Muradiye, Patnos, Karayazi, Tekman, Kemaliye, Feke, Ceyhan, Dogankent, Gözne and thence to the sea.

(C) The term "battle tank" means a self-propelled armoured fighting vehicle, capable of heavy firepower, primarily of a high muzzle velocity direct fire main gun necessary to engage armoured and other targets, with high cross-country mobility, with a high level of self-protection, and which is not designed and equipped primarily to transport combat troops. Such armoured vehicles serve as the principal weapon system of ground-force tank and other armoured formations.

Battle tanks are tracked armoured fighting vehicles which weigh at least 16.5 metric tonnes unladen weight and which are armed with a 360-degree traverse gun of at least 75 millimetres calibre. In addition, any wheeled armoured fighting vehicles entering into service which meet all the other criteria stated above shall also be deemed battle tanks.

(D) The term "armoured combat vehicle" means a self-propelled vehicle with armoured protection and cross-country capability. Armoured combat vehicles include armoured personnel carriers, armoured infantry fighting vehicles and heavy armament combat vehicles.

The term "armoured personnel carrier" means an armoured combat vehicle which is designed and equipped to transport a combat infantry squad and which, as a rule, is armed with an integral or organic weapon of less than 20 millimetres calibre.

The term "armoured infantry fighting vehicle" means an armoured combat vehicle which is designed and equipped primarily to transport a combat infantry squad, which normally provides the capability for the troops to deliver fire from inside the vehicle under armoured protection, and which is armed with an integral or organic cannon of at least 20 millimetres calibre and sometimes an antitank missile launcher. Armoured infantry fighting vehicles serve as the principal weapon system of armoured infantry or mechanised infantry or motorised infantry formations and units of ground forces.

The term "heavy armament combat vehicle" means an armoured combat vehicle with an integral or organic direct fire gun of at least 75 millimetres calibre, weighing at least 6.0 metric tonnes unladen weight, which does not fall within the definitions of an armoured personnel carrier, or an armoured infantry fighting vehicle or a battle tank.

(E) The term "unladen weight" means the weight of a vehicle excluding the weight of ammunition; fuel, oil and lubricants; removable reactive armour; spare parts, tools and accessories; removable snorkelling equipment; and crew and their personal kit.

(F) The term "artillery" means large calibre systems capable of engaging ground targets by delivering primarily indirect fire. Such artillery systems provide the essential indirect fire support to combined arms formations.

Large calibre artillery systems are guns, howitzers, artillery pieces combining the characteristics of guns and howitzers, mortars and multiple launch rocket systems with a calibre of 100 millimetres and above. In addition, any future large calibre direct fire system which has a secondary effective indirect fire capability shall be counted against the artillery ceilings.

(G) The term "stationed conventional armed forces" means conventional armed forces of a State Party that are stationed within the area of application on the territory of another State Party.

(H) The term "designated permanent storage site" means a place with a clearly defined physical boundary containing conventional armaments and equipment limited by the Treaty, which are counted within overall ceilings but which are not subject to limitations on conventional armaments and equipment limited by the Treaty in active units.

(I) The term "armoured vehicle launched bridge" means a self-propelled armoured transporter-launcher vehicle capable of carrying and, through built-in mechanisms, of emplacing and retrieving a bridge structure. Such a vehicle with a bridge structure operates as an integrated system.

(J) The term "conventional armaments and equipment limited by the Treaty" means battle tanks, armoured combat vehicles, artillery, combat aircraft and attack helicopters subject to the numerical limitations set forth in Articles IV, V and VI.

(K) The term "combat aircraft" means a fixed-wing or variable-geometry wing aircraft armed and equipped to engage targets by employing guided missiles, unguided rockets, bombs, guns, cannons, or other weapons of destruction, as well as any model or version of such an aircraft which performs other military functions such as reconnaissance or electronic warfare. The term "combat aircraft" does not include primary trainer aircraft.

(L) The term "combat helicopter" means a rotary wing aircraft armed and equipped to engage targets or equipped to perform other military functions. The term "combat helicopter" comprises attack helicopters and combat support helicopters. The term "combat helicopter" does not include unarmed transport helicopters.

(M) The term "attack helicopter" means a combat helicopter equipped to imply anti-armour, air-to-ground, or air-to-air guided weapons and equipped with an integrated fire control and aiming system for these weapons. The term "attack helicopter" comprises specialised attack helicopters and multi-purpose attack helicopters.

(N) The term "specialised attack helicopter" means an attack helicopter that is designed primarily to employ guided weapons.

(O) The term "multi-purpose attack helicopter" means an attack helicopter designed to perform multiple military functions and equipped to employ guided weapons.

(P) The term "combat support helicopter" means a combat helicopter which does not fulfil the requirements to qualify as an attack helicopter and which may be equipped with a variety of self-defence and area suppression weapons, such as guns, cannons and unguided rockets, bombs or cluster bombs, or which may be equipped to perform other military functions.

(Q) The term "conventional armaments and equipment subject to the Treaty" means battle tanks, armoured combat vehicles, artillery, combat aircraft, primary trainer aircraft, unarmed trainer aircraft, combat helicopters, unarmed transport helicopters, armoured vehicle launched bridges, armoured personnel carrier look-alikes and armoured infantry fighting vehicle look-alikes subject to information exchange in accordance with the Protocol on Information Exchange.

(R) The term "in service," as it applies to conventional armed forces and conventional armaments and equipment, means battle tanks, armoured combat vehicles, artillery, combat aircraft, primary trainer aircraft, unarmed trainer aircraft, combat helicopters, unarmed transport helicopters, armoured vehicle launched bridges, armoured personnel carrier look-alikes and armoured infantry fighting vehicle look-alikes that are within the area of application, except for those that are held by organisations designed and structured to perform in peacetime internal security functions or that meet any of the exceptions set forth in Article III.

(S) The terms "armoured personnel carrier look-alike" and "armoured infantry fighting vehicle look-alike" mean an armoured vehicle based on the same chassis as, and externally similar to, an armoured personnel carrier or armoured infantry fighting vehicle, respectively, which does not have a cannon or gun of 20 millimetres calibre or greater and which has been constructed or modified in such a way as not to permit the transportation of a combat infantry squad. Taking into account the provisions of the Geneva Convention "For the Amelioration of the Conditions of the Wounded and Sick in Armed Forces in the Field" of 12 August 1949 that confer a special status on ambulances, armoured personnel carrier ambulances shall not be deemed armoured combat vehicles or armoured personnel carrier look-alikes.

(T) The term "reduction site" means a clearly designated location where the reduction of conventional armaments and equipment limited by the Treaty in accordance with Article VIII takes place.

(U) The term "reduction liability" means the number in each category of conventional armaments and equipment limited by the Treaty that a

State Party commits itself to reduce during the period of 40 months following the entry into force of this Treaty in order to ensure compliance with Article VII.

2. Existing types of conventional armaments and equipment subject to the Treaty are listed in the Protocol on Existing Types. The lists of existing types shall be periodically updated in accordance with Article XVI, paragraph 2, subparagraph (D) and Section IV of the Protocol on Existing Types. Such updates to the existing types lists shall not be deemed amendments to this Treaty.

3. The existing types of combat helicopters listed in the Protocol on Existing Types shall be categorised in accordance with Section I of the Protocol on Helicopter Recategorisation.

Article III

1. For the purposes of this Treaty, the States Parties shall apply the following counting rules:

All battle tanks, armoured combat vehicles, artillery, combat aircraft and attack helicopters, as defined in Article II, within the area of application shall be subject to the numerical limitations and other provisions set forth in Article IV, V and VI, with the exception of those which in a manner consistent with a State Party's normal practices:

(A) are in the process of manufacture, including manufacturing-related testing;

(B) are used exclusively for the purposes of research and development;

(C) belong to historical collections;

(D) are awaiting disposal, having been decommissioned from service in accordance with the provisions of Article IX;

(E) are awaiting, or are being refurbished for, export or re-export and are temporarily retained within the area of application. Such battle tanks, armoured combat vehicles, artillery, combat aircraft and attack helicopters shall be located elsewhere than at sites declared under the terms of Section V of the Protocol on

Information Exchange or at no more than 10 such declared sites which shall have been notified in the previous year's annual information exchange. In the latter case, they shall be separately distinguishable from conventional armaments and equipment limited by the Treaty;

(F) are, in the case of armoured personnel carriers, armoured infantry fighting vehicles, heavy armament combat vehicles or multi-purpose attack helicopters, held by organisations designed and structured to perform in peacetime internal security functions; or

(G) are in transit through the area of application from a location outside the area of application to a final destination outside the area of application, and are in the area of application for no longer than a total of seven days.

2. If, in respect of any such battle tanks, armoured combat vehicles, artillery, combat aircraft or attack helicopters, the notification of which is required under Section IV of the Protocol on Information Exchange, a State Party notifies an unusually high number in more than two successive annual information exchanges, it shall explain the reasons in the Joint Consultative Group, if so requested.

Article IV

1. Within the area of application, as defined in Article II, each State Party shall limit and, as necessary, reduce its battle tanks, armoured combat vehicles, artillery, combat aircraft and attack helicopters so that, 40 months after entry into force of this Treaty and thereafter, for the group of States Parties to which it belongs, as defined in Article II, the aggregate numbers do not exceed:

(A) 20,000 battle tanks, of which no more than 16,500 shall be in active units;

(B) 30,000 armoured combat vehicles, of which no more than 27,300 shall be in active units. Of the 30,000 armoured combat vehicles, no more than 18,000 shall be armoured infantry fighting vehicles and heavy armament combat vehicles; of armoured infantry fighting vehicles and heavy armament combat vehicles, no more than 1,500 shall be heavy armament combat vehicles;

(C) 20,000 pieces of artillery, of which no more than 17,000 shall be in active units;

(D) 6,800 combat aircraft; and

(E) 2,000 attack helicopters.

Battle tanks, armoured combat vehicles and artillery not in active units shall be placed in designated permanent storage sites, as defined in Article II, and shall be located only in the area described in paragraph 2 of this Article. Such designated permanent storage sites may also be located in that part of the territory of the Union of Soviet Socialist Republics comprising the Odessa Military District and the southern part of the Leningrad Military District. In the Odessa Military District, no more than 400 battle tanks and no more than 500 pieces of artillery may be thus stored. In the southern part of the Leningrad Military District, no more than 600 battle tanks, no more than 800 armoured combat vehicles, including no more than 300 armoured combat vehicles of any type with the remaining number consisting of armoured personnel carriers, and no more than 400 pieces of artillery may be thus stored. The southern part of the Leningrad Military District is understood to mean the territory within that military district south of the line East-West 60 degrees 15 minutes northern latitude.

2. Within the area consisting of the entire land territory in Europe, which includes all the European island territories, of the Kingdom of Belgium, the Czech and Slovak Federal Republic, the Kingdom of Denmark including the Faroe Islands, the French Republic, the Federal Republic of Germany, the Republic of Hungary, the Italian Republic, the Grand Duchy of Luxembourg, the Kingdom of the Netherlands, the Republic of Poland, the Portuguese Republic including the Islands of Azores and Madeira, the Kingdom of Spain including the Canary Islands, the United Kingdom of Great Britain and Northern Ireland and that part of the territory of the Union of Soviet Socialist Republics west of the Ural Mountains comprising the Baltic, Byelorussian, Carpathian, Kiev, Moscow and Volga-Ural Military Districts, each State Party shall limit and, as necessary, reduce its battle tanks, armoured combat vehicles and artillery so that, 40 months after entry into force of this Treaty and thereafter, for the group of States Parties to which it belongs the aggregate numbers do not exceed:

(A) 15,300 battle tanks, of which no more than 11,800 shall be in active units;

(B) 24,100 armoured combat vehicles, of which no more than 21,400 shall be in active units; and

(C) 14,000 pieces of artillery, of which no more than 11,000 shall be in active units.

3. Within the area consisting of the entire land territory in Europe, which includes all the European islands territories, of the Kingdom of Belgium, the Czech and Slovak Federal Republic, the Kingdom of Denmark including the Faroe Islands, the French Republic, the Federal Republic of Germany, the Republic of Hungary, the Italian Republic, the Grand Duchy of Luxembourg, the Kingdom of the Netherlands, the Republic of Poland, the United Kingdom of Great Britain and Northern Ireland and that part of the territory of the Union of Soviet Socialist Republics comprising the Baltic, Byelorussian, Carpathian and Kiev Military Districts, each State Party shall limit and, as necessary, reduce its battle tanks, armoured combat vehicles and artillery so that, 40 months after entry into force of this Treaty and thereafter, for the group of States Parties to which it belongs the aggregate numbers in active units do not exceed:

(A) 10,300 battle tanks;

(B) 19,260 armoured combat vehicles; and

(C) 9,100 pieces of artillery; and

(D) in the Kiev Military District, the aggregate numbers in active units and designated permanent storage sites together shall not exceed:

(1) 2,250 battle tanks;

(2) 2,500 armoured combat vehicles; and

(3) 1,500 pieces of artillery.

4. Within the area consisting of the entire land territory in Europe, which includes all the European island territories, of the Kingdom of Belgium, the Czech and Slovak Federal Republic, the Federal Republic of Germany, the Republic of Hungary, the Grand Duchy of Luxembourg, the Kingdom of the Netherlands and the Republic of Poland, each State Party shall limit and, as necessary, reduce its battle

tanks, armoured combat vehicles and artillery so that, 40 months after entry into force of this Treaty and thereafter, for the group of States Parties to which it belongs the aggregate numbers in active units do not exceed:

(A) 7,500 battle tanks;

(B) 11,250 armoured combat vehicles; and

(C) 5,000 pieces of artillery.

5. States Parties belonging to the same group of States Parties may locate battle tanks, armoured combat vehicles and artillery in active units in each of the areas described in this Article and Article V, paragraph 1, subparagraph (A) up to the numerical limitations applying in that area, consistent with the maximum levels for holdings notified pursuant to Article VII and provided that no State Party stations conventional armed forces on the territory of another State Party without the agreement of that State Party.

6. If a group of States Parties' aggregate number of battle tanks, armoured combat vehicles and artillery in active units within the area described in paragraph 4 of this Article are less than the numerical limitations set forth in paragraph 4 of this Article, and provided that no State Party is thereby prevented from reaching its maximum levels for holdings notified in accordance with Article VII, paragraphs 2, 3 and 5, then amounts equal to the difference between the aggregate numbers in each of the categories of battle tanks, armoured combat vehicles and artillery and the specified numerical limitations for that area may be located by States Parties belonging to that group of States Parties in the area described in paragraph 3 of this Article, consistent with the numerical limitations specified in paragraph 3 of this Article.

Article V

1. To ensure that the security of each State Party is not affected adversely at any stage:

(A) within the area consisting of the entire land territory in Europe, which includes all the European island territories, of the Republic of Bulgaria, the Hellenic Republic, the Republic of Iceland, the Kingdom of Norway, Romania, the part of the Republic of Turkey within the area of application and that part of the Union of Soviet Socialist Republics comprising the Leningrad, Odessa, Transcaucasus and North Caucasus Military Districts, each State Party shall limit and, as necessary, reduce its battle tanks, armoured combat vehicles and artillery so that, 40 months after entry into force of this Treaty and thereafter, for the group of States Parties to which it belongs the aggregate numbers in active units do not exceed the difference between the overall numerical limitations set forth in Article IV, paragraph 1 and those in Article IV, paragraph 2, that is:

(1) 4,700 battle tanks;

(2) 5,900 armoured combat vehicles; and

(3) 6,000 pieces of artillery;

(B) notwithstanding the numerical limitations set forth in subparagraph (A) of this paragraph, a State Party or States Parties may on a temporary basis deploy into the territory belonging to the members of the same group of States Parties within the area described in subparagraph (A) of this paragraph additional aggregate numbers in active units for each group of States Parties not to exceed:

(1) 459 battle tanks;

(2) 723 armoured combat vehicles; and

(3) 420 pieces of artillery; and

(C) provided that for each group of States Parties no more than one-third of each of these additional aggregate numbers shall be deployed to any State Party with territory within the area described in subparagraph (A) of this paragraph, that is:

(1) 153 battle tanks;

(2) 241 armoured combat vehicles; and

(3) 140 pieces of artillery.

2. Notification shall be provided to all other States Parties no later than at the start of the deployment by the State Party or States Parties

conducting the deployment and by the recipient State Party or States Parties, specifying the total number in each category of battle tanks, armoured combat vehicles and artillery deployed. Notification also shall be provided to all other States Parties by the State Party or States Parties conducting the deployment and by the recipient State Party or States Parties within 30 days of the withdrawal of those battle tanks, armoured combat vehicles and artillery that were temporarily deployed.

Article VI

With the objective of ensuring that no single State Party possesses more than approximately one-third of the conventional armaments and equipment limited by the Treaty within the area of application, each State Party shall limit and, as necessary, reduce its battle tanks, armoured combat vehicles, artillery, combat aircraft and attack helicopters so that, 40 months after entry into force of this Treaty and thereafter, the numbers within the area of application for that State Party do not exceed:

(A) 13,300 battle tanks;

(B) 20,000 armoured combat vehicles;

(C) 13,700 pieces of artillery;

(D) 5,150 combat aircraft; and

(E) 1,500 attack helicopters.

Article VII

1. In order that the limitations set forth in Articles IV, V and VI are not exceeded, no State Party shall exceed, from 40 months after entry into force of this Treaty, the maximum levels which it has previously agreed upon within its group of States Parties, in accordance with paragraph 7 of this Article, for its holdings of conventional armaments and equipment limited by the Treaty and of which it has provided notification pursuant to the provisions of this Article.

2. Each State Party shall provide at the signature of this Treaty notification to all other States Parties of the maximum levels for its holdings of conventional armaments and equipment limited by the Treaty. The notification of the maximum levels for holdings of

conventional armaments and equipment limited by the Treaty provided by each State Party at the signature of this Treaty shall remain valid until the date specified in a subsequent notification pursuant to paragraph 3 of this Article.

3. In accordance with the limitations set forth in Articles IV, V and VI, each State Party shall have the right to change the maximum levels for its holdings of conventional armaments and equipment limited by the Treaty. Any change in the maximum levels for holdings of a State Party shall be notified by that State Party to all other States Parties at least 90 days in advance of the date, specified in the notification, on which such a change takes effect. In order not to exceed any of the limitations set forth in Articles IV and V, any increase in the maximum levels for holdings of a State Party that would otherwise cause those limitations to be exceeded shall be preceded or accompanied by a corresponding reduction in the previously notified maximum levels for holdings of conventional armaments and equipment limited by the Treaty of one or more States Parties belonging to the same group of States Parties. The notification of a change in the maximum levels for holdings shall remain valid from the date specified in the notification until the date specified in a subsequent notification of change pursuant to this paragraph.

4. Each notification required pursuant to paragraph 2 or 3 of this Article for armoured combat vehicles shall also include maximum levels for the holdings of armoured infantry fighting vehicles and heavy armament combat vehicles of the State Party providing the notification.

5. Ninety days before expiration of the 40-month period of reductions set forth in Article VIII and subsequently at the time of any notification of a change pursuant to paragraph 3 of this Article, each State Party shall provide notification of the maximum levels for its holdings of battle tanks, armoured combat vehicles and artillery with respect to each of the areas described in Article IV, paragraphs 2 to 4 and Article V, paragraph 1, subparagraph (A).

6. A decrease in the numbers of conventional armaments and equipment limited by the Treaty held by a State Party and subject to notification pursuant to the Protocol on Information Exchange shall by itself confer no right on any other State Party to increase the maximum levels for its holdings subject to notification pursuant to this Article.

7. It shall be the responsibility solely of each individual State Party to ensure that the maximum levels for its holdings notified pursuant to the provisions of this Article are not exceeded. States Parties belonging to the same group of States Parties shall consult in order to ensure that the maximum levels for holdings notified pursuant to the provisions of this Article, taken together as appropriate, do not exceed the limitations set forth in Articles IV, V and VI.

Article VIII

1. The numerical limitations set forth in Articles IV, V and VI shall be achieved only by means of reduction in accordance with the Protocol on Reduction, the Protocol on Helicopter Recategorisation, the Protocol on Aircraft Reclassification, the Footnote to Section I, paragraph 2, subparagraph (A) of the Protocol on Existing Types and the Protocol on Inspection.

2. The categories of conventional armaments and equipment subject to reductions are battle tanks, armoured combat vehicles, artillery, combat aircraft and attack helicopters. The specific types are listed in the Protocol on Existing Types.

   (A) Battle tanks and armoured combat vehicles shall be reduced by destruction, conversion for non-military purposes, placement on static display, use as ground targets, or, in the case of armoured personnel carriers, modification in accordance with the Footnote to Section I, paragraph 2, subparagraph (A) of the Protocol on Existing Types.

   (B) Artillery shall be reduced by destruction or placement on static display, or, in the case of self-propelled artillery, by use as ground targets.

   (C) Combat aircraft shall be reduced by destruction, placement on static display, use for ground instructional purposes, or, in the case of specific models or versions of combat-capable trainer aircraft, reclassification into unarmed trainer aircraft.

   (D) Specialised attack helicopters shall be reduced by destruction, placement on static display, or use for ground instructional purposes.

(E) Multi-purpose attack helicopters shall be reduced by destruction, placement on static display, use for ground instructional purposes, or recategorisation.

3. Conventional armaments and equipment limited by the Treaty shall be deemed to be reduced upon execution of the procedures set forth in the Protocols listed in paragraph 1 of this Article and upon notification as required by these Protocols. Armaments and equipment so reduced shall no longer be counted against the numerical limitations set forth in Articles IV, V and VI.

4. Reductions shall be effected in three phases and completed no later than 40 months after entry into force of this Treaty, so that:

(A) by the end of the first reduction phase, that is, no later than 16 months after entry into force of this Treaty, each State Party shall have ensured that at least 25 percent of its total reduction liability in each of the categories of conventional armaments and equipment limited by the Treaty has been reduced;

(B) by the end of the second reduction phase, that is, no later than 28 months after entry into force of this Treaty, each State Party shall have ensured that at least 60 percent of its total reduction liability in each of the categories of conventional armaments and equipment limited by the Treaty has been reduced;

(C) by the end of the third reduction phase, that is, no later than 40 months after entry into force of this Treaty, each State Party shall have reduced its total reduction liability in each of the categories of conventional armaments and equipment limited by the Treaty. States Parties carrying out conversion for non-military purposes shall have ensured that the conversion of all battle tanks in accordance with Section VIII of the Protocol on Reduction shall have been completed by the end of the third reduction phase; and

(D) armoured combat vehicles deemed reduced by reason of having been partially destroyed in accordance with Section VIII, paragraph 6 of the Protocol on Reduction shall have been fully converted for non-military purposes, or destroyed in accordance with Section IV of the Protocol on Reduction, no later than 64 months after entry into force of this Treaty.

5. Conventional armaments and equipment limited by the Treaty to be reduced shall have been declared present within the area of application in the exchange of information at signature of this Treaty.

6. No later than 30 days after entry into force of this Treaty, each State Party shall provide notification to all other States Parties of its reduction liability.

7. Except as provided for in paragraph 8 of this Article, a State Party's reduction liability in each category shall be no less than the difference between its holdings notified, in accordance with the Protocol on Information Exchange, at signature or effective upon entry into force of this Treaty, whichever is the greater, and the maximum levels for holding it notified pursuant to Article VII.

8. Any subsequent revision of a State Party's holdings notified pursuant to the Protocol on Information Exchange or of its maximum levels for holdings notified pursuant to Article VII shall be reflected by a notified adjustment to its reduction liability. Any notification of a decrease in a State Party's reduction liability shall be preceded or accompanied by either a notification of a corresponding increase in holdings not exceeding the maximum levels for holdings notified pursuant to Article VII by one or more States Parties belonging to the same group of States Parties, or a notification of a corresponding increase in the reduction liability of one or more such States Parties.

9. Upon entry into force of this Treaty, each State Party shall notify all other States Parties, in accordance with the Protocol on Information Exchange, of the locations of its reduction sites, including those where the final conversion of battle tanks and armoured combat vehicles for non-military purposes will be carried out.

10. Each State Party shall have the right to designate as many reduction sites as it wishes, to revise without restriction its designation of such sites and to carry out reduction and final conversion simultaneously at a maximum of 20 sites. States Parties shall have the right to share or co-locate reduction sites by mutual agreement.

11. Notwithstanding paragraph 10 of this Article, during the baseline validation period, that is, the interval between entry into force of this Treaty and 120 days after entry into force of this Treaty, reduction shall be carried out simultaneously at no more than two reduction sites for each State Party.

12. Reduction of conventional armaments and equipment limited by the Treaty shall be carried out at reduction sites, unless otherwise specified in the Protocols listed in paragraph 1 of this Article, within the area of application.

13. The reduction process, including the results of the conversion of conventional armaments and equipment limited by the Treaty for non-military purposes both during the reduction period and in the 24 months following the reduction period, shall be subject to inspection, without right of refusal, in accordance with the Protocol on Inspection.

Article IX

1. Other than removal from service in accordance with the provisions of Article VIII, battle tanks, armoured combat vehicles, artillery, combat aircraft and attack helicopters within the area of application shall be removed from service only by decommissioning, provided that:

   (A) such conventional armaments and equipment limited by the Treaty are decommissioned and awaiting disposal at no more than eight sites which shall be notified as declared sites in accordance with the Protocol on Information Exchange and shall be identified in such notifications as holding areas for decommissioned conventional armaments and equipment limited by the Treaty. If sites containing conventional armaments and equipment limited by the Treaty decommissioned from service also contain any other conventional armaments and equipment subject to the Treaty, the decommissioned conventional armaments and equipment limited by the Treaty shall be separately distinguishable; and

   (B) the numbers of such decommissioned conventional armaments and equipment limited by the Treaty do not exceed, in the case of any individual State Party, one percent of its notified holdings of conventional armaments and equipment limited by the Treaty, or a total of 250, whichever is greater, of which no more than 200 shall be battle tanks, armoured combat vehicles and pieces of artillery, and no more than 50 shall be attack helicopters and combat aircraft.

2. Notification of decommissioning shall include the number and type of conventional armaments and equipment limited by the Treaty decommissioned and the location of decommissioning and shall be

provided to all other States Parties in accordance with Section IX, paragraph 1, subparagraph (B) of the Protocol on Information Exchange.

Article X

1. Designated permanent storage sites shall be notified in accordance with the Protocol on Information Exchange to all other States Parties by the State Party to which the conventional armaments and equipment limited by the Treaty contained at designated permanent storage sites belong. The notification shall include the designation and location, including geographic coordinates, of designated permanent storage sites and the numbers by type of each category of its conventional armaments and equipment limited by the Treaty at each such storage site.

2. Designated permanent storage sites shall contain only facilities appropriate for the storage and maintenance of armaments and equipment (e.g., warehouses, garages, workshops and associated stores as well as other support accommodation). Designated permanent storage sites shall not contain firing ranges or training areas associated with conventional armaments and equipment limited by the Treaty. Designated permanent storage sites shall contain only armaments and equipment belonging to the conventional armed forces of a State Party.

3. Each designated permanent storage site shall have a clearly defined physical boundary that shall consist of a continuous perimeter fence at least 1.5 metres in height. The perimeter fence shall have no more than three gates providing the sole means of entrance and exit for armaments and equipment.

4. Conventional armaments and equipment limited by the Treaty located within designated permanent storage sites shall be counted as conventional armaments and equipment limited by the Treaty not in active units, including when they are temporarily removed in accordance with paragraphs 7, 8, 9 and 10 of this Article. Conventional armaments and equipment limited by the Treaty in storage other than in designated permanent storage sites shall be counted as conventional armaments and equipment limited by the Treaty in active units.

5. Active units or formations shall not be located within designated permanent storage sites, except as provided for in paragraph 6 of this Article.

6. Only personnel associated with the security or operation of designated permanent storage sites, or the maintenance of the armaments and equipment stored therein, shall be located within the designated permanent storage sites.

7. For the purpose of maintenance, repair or modification of conventional armaments and equipment limited by the Treaty located within designated permanent storage sites, each State Party shall have the right, without prior notification, to remove from and retain outside designated permanent storage sites simultaneously up to 10 percent, rounded up to the nearest even whole number, of the notified holdings of each category of conventional armaments and equipment limited by the Treaty in each designated permanent storage site, or 10 items of the conventional armaments and equipment limited by the Treaty in each category in each designated permanent storage site, whichever is less.

8. Except as provided for in paragraph 7 of this Article, no State Party shall remove conventional armaments and equipment limited by the Treaty from designated permanent storage sites unless notification has been provided to all other States Parties at least 42 days in advance of such removal. Notification shall be given by the State Party to which the conventional armaments and equipment limited by the Treaty belong. Such notification shall specify:

   (A) the location of the designated permanent storage site from which conventional armaments and equipment limited by the Treaty are to be removed and the numbers by type of conventional armaments and equipment limited by the Treaty of each category to be removed;

   (B) the dates of removal and return of conventional armaments and equipment limited by the Treaty; and

   (C) the intended location and use of conventional armaments and equipment limited by the Treaty while outside the designated permanent storage site.

9. Except as provided for in paragraph 7 of this Article, the aggregate numbers of conventional armaments and equipment limited by the Treaty removed from and retained outside designated permanent storage sites by States Parties belonging to the same group of States Parties shall at no time exceed the following levels:

   (A) 550 battle tanks;

   (B) 1,000 armoured combat vehicles; and

   (C) 300 pieces of artillery.

10. Conventional armaments and equipment limited by the Treaty removed from designated permanent storage sites pursuant to paragraphs 8 and 9 of this Article shall be returned to designated permanent storage sites no later than 42 days after their removal, except for those items of conventional armaments and equipment limited by the Treaty removed for industrial rebuild. Such items shall be returned to designated permanent storage sites immediately on completion of the rebuild.

11. Each State Party shall have the right to replace conventional armaments and equipment limited by the Treaty located in designated permanent storage sites. Each State Party shall notify all other States Parties, at the beginning of replacement, of the number, location, type and disposition of conventional armaments and equipment limited by the Treaty being replaced.

Article XI

1. Each State Party shall limit its armoured vehicle launched bridges so that, 40 months after entry into force of this Treaty and thereafter, for the group of States Parties to which it belongs the aggregate number of armoured vehicle launched bridges in active units within the area of application does not exceed 740.

2. All armoured vehicle launched bridges within the area of application in excess of the aggregate number specified in paragraph 1 of this Article for each group of States Parties shall be placed in designated permanent storage sites, as defined in Article II. When armoured vehicle launched bridges are placed in a designated permanent storage site, either on their own or together with conventional armaments and equipment limited by the Treaty, Article X, paragraphs 1 to 6 shall apply to armoured vehicle launched bridges as well as to conventional

armaments and equipment limited by the Treaty. Armoured vehicle launched bridges placed in designated permanent storage sites shall not be considered as being in active units.

3. Except as provided for in paragraph 6 of this Article, armoured vehicle launched bridges may be removed, subject to the provisions of paragraphs 4 and 5 of this Article, from designated permanent storage sites only after notification has been provided to all other States Parties at least 42 days prior to such removal. This notification shall specify:

(A) the locations of the designated permanent storage sites from which armoured vehicle launched bridges are to be removed and the numbers of armoured vehicle launched bridges to be removed from each such site;

(B) the dates of removal of armoured vehicle launched bridges from and return to designated permanent storage sites; and

(C) the intended use of armoured vehicle launched bridges during the period of their removal from designated permanent storage sites.

4. Except as provided for in paragraph 6 of this Article, armoured vehicle launched bridges removed from designated permanent storage sites shall be returned to them no later than 42 days after the actual date of removal.

5. The aggregate number of armoured vehicle launched bridges removed from and retained outside of designated permanent storage sites by each group of States Parties shall not exceed 50 at any one time.

6. States Parties shall have the right, for the purpose of maintenance or modification, to remove and have outside of designated permanent storage sites simultaneously up to 10 percent, rounded up to the nearest even whole number, of the notified holdings of armoured vehicle launched bridges in each designated permanent storage site, or 10 armoured vehicle launched bridges from each designated permanent storage site, whichever is less.

7. In the event of natural disasters involving flooding or damage to permanent bridges, States Parties shall have the right to withdraw armoured vehicle launched bridges from designated permanent storage

sites. Notification to all other States Parties of such withdrawals shall be given at the time of withdrawal.

Article XII

1. Armoured infantry fighting vehicles held by organisations of a State Party designed and structured to perform in peacetime internal security functions, which are not structured and organised for ground combat against an external enemy, are not limited by this Treaty. The foregoing notwithstanding, in order to enhance the implementation of this Treaty and to provide assurance that the number of such armaments held by such organisations shall not be used to circumvent the provisions of this Treaty, any such armaments in excess of 1,000 armoured infantry fighting vehicles assigned by a State Party to organisations designed and structured to perform in peacetime internal security functions shall constitute a portion of the permitted levels specified in Articles IV, V and VI. No more than 600 such armoured infantry fighting vehicles of a State Party, assigned to such organisations, may be located in that part of the area of application described in Article V, paragraph 1, subparagraph (A). Each State Party shall further ensure that such organisations refrain from the acquisition of combat capabilities in excess of those necessary for meeting internal security requirements.

2. A State Party that intends to reassign battle tanks, armoured infantry vehicles, artillery, combat aircraft, attack helicopters and armoured vehicle launched bridges in service with its conventional armed forces to any organisation of that State Party not a part of its conventional armed forces shall notify all other States Parties no later than the date such reassignment takes effect. Such notification shall specify the effective date of the reassignment, the date such equipment is physically transferred, as well as the numbers, by type, of the conventional armaments and equipment limited by the Treaty being reassigned.

Article XIII

1. For the purpose of ensuring verification of compliance with the provisions of this Treaty, each State Party shall provide notifications and exchange information pertaining to its conventional armaments and equipment in accordance with the Protocol on Information Exchange.

2. Such notifications and exchange of information shall be provided in accordance with Article XVII.

3. Each State Party shall be responsible for its own information; receipt of such information and of notifications shall not imply validation or acceptance of the information provided.

Article XIV

1. For the purpose of ensuring verification of compliance with the provisions of this Treaty, each State Party shall have the right to conduct, and the obligation to accept, within the area of application, inspections in accordance with the provisions of the Protocol on Inspection.

2. The purpose of such inspections shall be:

   (A) to verify, on the basis of the information provided pursuant to the Protocol on Information Exchange, the compliance of States Parties with the numerical limitations set forth in Articles IV, V and VI;

   (B) to monitor the process of reduction of battle tanks, armoured combat vehicles, artillery, combat aircraft and attack helicopters carried out at reduction sites in accordance with Article VIII and the Protocol on Reduction; and

   (C) to monitor the certification of recategorised multi-purpose attack helicopters and reclassified combat-capable trainer aircraft carried out in accordance with the Protocol on Helicopter Recategorisation and the Protocol on Aircraft Reclassification, respectively.

3. No State Party shall exercise the rights set forth in paragraphs 1 and 2 of this Article in respect of States Parties which belong to the group of States Parties to which it belongs in order to elude the objectives of the verification regime.

4. In the case of an inspection conducted jointly by more than one State Party, one of them shall be responsible for the execution of the provisions of this Treaty.

5. The number of inspections pursuant to Sections VII and VIII of the Protocol on Inspection which each State Party shall have the right to conduct and the obligation to accept during each specified time period shall be determined in accordance with the provisions of Section II of that Protocol.

6. Upon completion of the 120-day residual level validation period, each State Party shall have the right to conduct, and each State Party with territory within the area of application shall have the obligation to accept, an agreed number of aerial inspections within the area of application. Such agreed numbers and other applicable provisions shall be developed during negotiations referred to in Article XVIII.

Article XV

1. For the purpose of ensuring verification of compliance with the provisions of this Treaty, a State Party shall have the right to use, in addition to the procedures referred to in Article XIV, national or multinational technical means of verification at its disposal in a manner consistent with generally recognised principles of international law.

2. A State Party shall not interfere with national or multinational technical means of verification of another State Party operating in accordance with paragraph 1 of this Article.

3. A State Party shall not use concealment measures that impede verification of compliance with the provisions of this Treaty by national or multinational technical means of verification of another State Party operating in accordance with paragraph 1 of this Article. This obligation does not apply to cover or concealment practices associated with normal personnel training, maintenance or operations involving conventional armaments and equipment limited by the Treaty.

Article XVI

1. To promote the objectives and implementation of the provisions of this Treaty, the States Parties hereby establish a Joint Consultative Group.

2. Within the framework of the Joint Consultative Group, the States Parties shall:

(A) address questions relating to compliance with or possible circumvention of the provisions of this Treaty;

(B) seek to resolve ambiguities and differences of interpretation that may become apparent in the way this Treaty is implemented;

(C) consider and, if possible, agree on measures to enhance the viability and effectiveness of this Treaty;

(D) update the lists contained in the Protocol on Existing Types, as required by Article II, paragraph 2;

(E) resolve technical questions in order to seek common practices among the States Parties in the way this Treaty is implemented;

(F) work out or revise, as necessary, rules of procedure, working methods, the scale of distribution of expenses of the Joint Consultative Group and of conferences convened under this Treaty and the distribution of costs of inspections between or among States Parties;

(G) consider and work out appropriate measures to ensure that information obtained through exchanges of information among the States Parties or as a result of inspections pursuant to this Treaty is used solely for the purposes of this Treaty, taking into account the particular requirements of each State Party in respect of safeguarding information which that State Party specifies as being sensitive;

(H) consider, upon the request of any State Party, any matter that a State party wishes to propose for examination by any conference to be convened in accordance with Article XXI; such consideration shall not prejudice the right of any State Party to resort to the procedures set forth in Article XXI; and

(I) consider matters of dispute arising out of the implementation of this Treaty.

3. Each State Party shall have the right to raise before the Joint Consultative Group, and have placed on its agenda, any issue relating to this Treaty.

4. The Joint Consultative Group shall take decisions or make recommendations by consensus. Consensus shall be understood to mean the absence of any objection by any representative of a State Party to the taking of a decision or the making of a recommendation.

5. The Joint Consultative Group may propose amendments to this Treaty for consideration and confirmation in accordance with Article XX. The Joint Consultative Group may also agree on improvements to the viability and effectiveness of this Treaty, consistent with its provisions. Unless such improvements relate only to minor matters of an administrative or technical nature, they shall be subject to consideration and confirmation in accordance with Article XX before they can take effect.

6. Nothing in this Article shall be deemed to prohibit or restrict any State Party from requesting information from or undertaking consultations with other States Parties on matters relating to this Treaty and its implementation in channels or fora other than the Joint Consultative Group.

7. The Joint Consultative Group shall follow the procedures set forth in the Protocol on the Joint Consultative Group.

Article XVII

The States Parties shall transmit information and notifications required by this Treaty in written form. They shall use diplomatic channels or other official channels designated by them, including in particular a communications network to be established by a separate arrangement.

Article XVIII

1. The States Parties, after signature of this Treaty, shall continue the negotiations on conventional armed forces with the same Mandate and with the goal of building on this Treaty.

2. The objective for these negotiations shall be to conclude an agreement on additional measures aimed at further strengthening security and stability in Europe, and pursuant to the Mandate, including measures to limit the personnel strength of their conventional armed forces within the area of application.

3. The States Parties shall seek to conclude these negotiations no later than the follow-up meeting of the Conference on Security and Co-operation in Europe to be held in Helsinki in 1992.

Article XIX

1. This Treaty shall be of unlimited duration. It may be supplemented by a further treaty.

2. Each State Party shall, in exercising its national sovereignty, have the right to withdraw from this Treaty if it decides that extraordinary events related to the subject matter of this Treaty have jeopardised its supreme interests. A State Party intending to withdraw shall give notice of its decision to do so to the Depositary and to all other States Parties. Such notice shall be given at least 150 days prior to the intended withdrawal from this Treaty. It shall include a statement of the extraordinary events the State Party regards as having jeopardised its supreme interests.

3. Each State Party shall, in particular, in exercising its national sovereignty, have the right to withdraw from this Treaty if another State Party increases its holdings in battle tanks, armoured combat vehicles, artillery, combat aircraft or attack helicopters, as defined in Article II, which are outside the scope of the limitations of this Treaty, in such proportions as to pose an obvious threat to the balance of forces within the area of application.

Article XX

1. Any State Party may propose amendments to this Treaty. The text of a proposed amendment shall be submitted to the Depositary, which shall circulate it to all the States Parties.

2. If an amendment is approved by all the States Parties, it shall enter into force in accordance with the procedures set forth in Article XXII governing the entry into force of this Treaty.

Article XXI

1. Forty-six months after entry into force of this Treaty, and at five-year intervals thereafter, the Depositary shall convene a conference of the States Parties to conduct a review of the operation of this Treaty.

2. The Depositary shall convene an extraordinary conference of the States Parties, if requested to do so by any State Party which considers that exceptional circumstances relating to this Treaty have arisen, in particular, in the event that a State Party has announced its intention to leave its group of States Parties or to join the other group of States Parties, as defined in Article II, paragraph 1, subparagraph (A). In order to enable the other States Parties to prepare for this conference, the request shall include the reason why that State Party deems an extraordinary conference to be necessary. The conference shall consider the circumstances set forth in the request and their effect on the operation of this Treaty. The conference shall open no later than 15 days after receipt of the request and, unless it decides otherwise, shall last no longer than three weeks.

3. The Depositary shall convene a conference of the States Parties to consider an amendment proposed pursuant to Article XX, if requested to do so by three or more States Parties. Such a conference shall open no later than 21 days after receipt of the necessary requests.

4. In the event that a State Party gives notice of its decision to withdraw from this Treaty pursuant to Article XIX, the Depositary shall convene a conference of the States Parties which shall open no later than 21 days after receipt of the notice of withdrawal in order to consider questions relating to the withdrawal from this Treaty.

Article XXII

1. This Treaty shall be subject to ratification by each State Party in accordance with its constitutional procedures. Instruments of ratification shall be deposited with the Government of the Kingdom of the Netherlands, hereby designated the Depositary.

2. This Treaty shall enter into force 10 days after instruments of ratification have been deposited by all States Parties listed in the Preamble.

3. The Depositary shall promptly inform all States Parties of:

   (A) the deposit of each instrument of ratification;

   (B) the entry into force of this Treaty;

(C) any withdrawal in accordance with Article XIX and its effective date;

(D) the text of any amendment proposed in accordance with Article XX;

(E) the entry into force of any amendment to this Treaty;

(F) any request to convene a conference in accordance with Article XXI;

(G) the convening of a conference pursuant to Article XXI; and

(H) any other matter of which the Depositary is required by this Treaty to inform the States Parties.

4. This Treaty shall be registered by the Depositary pursuant to Article 102 of the Charter of the United Nations.

Article XXIII

The original of this Treaty, of which the English, French, German, Italian, Russian and Spanish texts are equally authentic, shall be deposited in the archives of the Depositary. Duly certified copies of this Treaty shall be transmitted by the Depositary to all the States Parties.

CONCLUDING ACT

OF THE NEGOTIATION ON PERSONNEL STRENGTH OF CONVENTIONAL ARMED FORCES IN EUROPE

Helsinki, 10 July 1992

The Republic of Armenia, the Republic of Azerbaijan, the Republic of Belarus, the Kingdom of Belgium, the Republic of Bulgaria, Canada, the Czech and Slovak Federal Republic, the Kingdom of Denmark, the French Republic, the Republic of Georgia, the Federal Republic of Germany, the Hellenic Republic, the Republic of Hungary, the Republic of Iceland, the Italian Republic, the Republic of Kazakhstan, the Grand Duchy of Luxembourg, the Republic of Moldova, the Kingdom of the Netherlands, the Kingdom of Norway, the Republic of Poland, the Portuguese Republic, Romania, the Russian Federation, the Kingdom of Spain, the Republic of Turkey, Ukraine, the United Kingdom of Great Britain and Northern Ireland, and the United States of America, hereinafter referred to as the participating States,

Recalling the obligations undertaken in the Treaty of Conventional Armed Forces in Europe of November 19, 1990, hereinafter referred to as the CFE Treaty, and the important achievements attained in that Treaty,

In accordance with the obligation in Article XVIII of the CFE Treaty to continue the negotiations on conventional armed forces with the same Mandate and with the goal of building on the CFE Treaty and with the objective of concluding an agreement, no later than the Helsinki 1992 Follow-up Meeting of the Conference on Security and Co-operation in Europe (CSCE), on additional measures aimed at further strengthening security and stability in Europe,

Guided by the Mandate for Negotiation on Conventional Armed Forces in Europe of January 10, 1989, and having conducted negotiations in Vienna,

Having decided to limit and, if applicable, reduce, on a national basis, the personnel strength of their conventional armed forces within the area of application,*

Guided by the objectives and the purposes of the CSCE, within the framework of which these negotiations were conducted,

Looking forward to a more structured co-operation among all CSCE participating States on security matters and to new negotiations on disarmament and confidence and security building in accordance with their commitment in the Charter of Paris for a New Europe, and, accordingly, to the possibility, within the context of those new negotiations, for all CSCE participating States to subscribe to a common regime based upon the measures adopted in this Concluding Act, hereinafter referred to as the Act,

Taking into account the principle of sufficiency, and recalling the undertaking of the participating States to maintain only such military capabilities as are necessary to prevent war and provide for effective defence, bearing in mind the relationship between military capabilities and doctrines,

Recognising the freedom of each participating State to choose its own security arrangements,

Have adopted the following:

SECTION I SCOPE OF LIMITATION

1. Each participating State will limit, as specified in Section II of this Act, its personnel based on land within the area of application in the following categories of conventional armed forces:

   (A) all full-time military personnel serving with land forces, including air defence formations and units subordinated at or below the military district or equivalent level, as specified in Section I of the Protocol on Information Exchange of the CFE Treaty;

---

* The area of application of the measures adopted in this Act is the area of application of the CFE Treaty as defined in Article II, paragraph 1, subparagraph (B) of the CFE Treaty, taking into account the understanding specified in Annex A, paragraph 5 of the Final Document of the Extraordinary Conference of the States Parties to the Treaty on Conventional Armed Forces in Europe of June 5, 1992.

(B) all full-time military personnel serving with air and air defence aviation forces, including long-range aviation forces reported pursuant to Section I of the Protocol on Information Exchange of the CFE Treaty, as well as military transport aviation forces;

(C) all full-time military personnel serving with air defence forces other than those specified in subparagraphs (A) and (B) of this paragraph;

(D) all full-time military personnel, excluding naval personnel, serving with all central headquarters, command and staff elements;

(E) all full-time military personnel, excluding naval personnel, serving with all centrally-controlled formations, units and other organisations, including those of rear services;

(F) all full-time military personnel serving with all land-based naval formations and units which hold battle tanks, armoured combat vehicles, artillery, armoured vehicle launched bridges, armoured infantry fighting vehicle look-alikes or armoured personnel carrier look-alikes as defined in Article II of the CFE Treaty or which hold land-based naval combat aircraft referred to in the Declaration of the States Parties to the Treaty on Conventional Armed Forces in Europe with Respect to Land-based Naval Aircraft of November 19, 1990;

(G) all full-time military personnel serving with all other formations, units and other organisations which hold battle tanks, armoured combat vehicles, artillery, combat aircraft or attack helicopters in service with its conventional armed forces, as defined in Article II of the CFE Treaty; and

(H) all reserve personnel who have completed their initial military service or training and who are called up or report voluntarily for full-time military service or training in conventional armed forces for a continuous period of more than 90 days.

2. Notwithstanding the provisions of paragraph 1 of this Section, the following categories of personnel are not included within the scope of limitation specified in the Act:

(A) personnel serving with organisations designed and structured to perform in peacetime internal security functions;

(B) personnel in transit from a location outside the area of application to a final destination outside the area of application who are in the area of application for no longer than seven days; and

(C) personnel serving under the command of the United Nations.

3. If, after the date on which this Act comes into effect, any land-based formations or units are formed within the area of application which, according to their structure and armaments, have a capability for ground combat outside national borders against an external enemy, a participating State may raise in the Joint Consultative Group any issue regarding personnel serving with such formations and units. The Joint Consultative Group will consider any such issue on the basis of all available information, including information provided by the participating States concerned, with a view to determining whether the above-mentioned criteria are applicable to such formations and units; if such criteria are deemed to apply, the personnel serving with such formations and units will be included within the scope of limitation specified in this Act.

SECTION II NATIONAL PERSONNEL LIMITS

1. Each participating State will limit its military personnel based on land within the area of application in the categories of conventional armed forces specified in Section I, paragraph 1 of this Act so that, 40 months after entry into force of the CFE Treaty and thereafter, the aggregate number of such personnel will not exceed the number representing its national personnel limit as specified in this paragraph:

The Republic of Armenia**	
The Republic of Azerbaijan***	
The Republic of Belarus	100,000
The Kingdom of Belgium	70,000
The Republic of Bulgaria	104,000
Canada	10,660
The Czech and Slovak Federal Republic	140,000
The Kingdom of Denmark	39,000
The French Republic	325,000
The Republic of Georgia	40,000
The Federal Republic of Germany	345,000
The Hellenic Republic	158,621
The Republic of Hungary	100,000
The Republic of Iceland	0
The Italian Republic	315,000
The Republic of Kazakhstan	0
The Grand Duchy of Luxembourg	900
The Republic of Moldova****	
The Kingdom of the Netherlands	80,000
The Kingdom of Norway	32,000
The Republic of Poland	234,000
The Portuguese Republic	75,000
Romania	230,000
The Russian Federation	1,450,000
The Kingdom of Spain	300,000
The Republic of Turkey	530,000
Ukraine	450,000
The United Kingdom of Great Britain and Northern Ireland	260,000
The United States of America	250,000

2. For the purpose of recording changes to the information specified in paragraph 1 of this Section, the Government of the Kingdom of the Netherlands will distribute to all the participating States a revised version of the information in that paragraph.

** Editor's note: Armenia has not yet been able to decide on its limit.

*** Editor's note: Azerbaijan later on decided on a limit of 70.000. (Information from the Netherlands Ministry of Foreign Affairs.)

**** Editor's note: Moldova later on decided on a limit of 20.000. (Information from the Netherlands Ministry of Foreign Affairs.)

3. Each participating State may revise its national personnel limit in accordance with the provisions of Section III of this Act.

SECTION III REVISION PROCEDURES

1. A participating State may revise downward its national personnel limit by providing a notification of its revised limit to all other participating States. Such notification will specify the date on which the revised limit will become effective.

2. A participating State intending to revise upward its national personnel limit will provide notification of such intended revision to all other participating States. Such notification will include an explanation of the reasons for such a revision. Any participating State may raise any question concerning the intended revision. A revised national personnel limit will become effective 42 days after notification has been provided, unless a participating State raises an objection to such revision by providing notification of this objection to all other participating States.

3. If an objection is raised, any participating State may request the convening of an extraordinary conference which will examine the intended revision in the light of the explanations provided and seek to decide on a future national personnel limit. The extraordinary conference will open no later than 15 days after receipt of the request and, unless it decides otherwise, will last no longer than three weeks.

SECTION IV INFORMATION EXCHANGE

1. Each participating State will provide to all other participating States, in accordance with the provisions of this Section, the following information in respect of its personnel based on land within the area of application:

   (A) in respect of all personnel specified in Section I, paragraph 1 of this Act, the aggregate number;

   (B) in respect of all full-time military personnel serving with land forces, including air defence formations and units subordinated at or below the military district or equivalent level, as specified in Section I of the Protocol on Information Exchange of the CFE Treaty, the aggregate number and the number in each formation, unit and other organisation down to the brigade/regiment or equivalent level, specifying the command organisation, designation, subordination and peacetime location, including the geographic name and coordinates, for each such formation, unit and organisation;

(C) in respect of all full-time military personnel serving with air and air defence aviation forces, including long-range aviation forces reported pursuant to Section I of the Protocol on Information Exchange of the CFE Treaty, as well as military transport aviation forces, the aggregate number and the number in each formation, unit and other organisation of conventional armed forces down to the wing/air regiment or equivalent level, specifying the command organisation, designation, subordination and peacetime location, including the geographic name and coordinates, for each such formation, unit and organisation;

(D) in respect of all full-time military personnel serving with air defence forces other than those specified in subparagraphs (B) and (C) of this paragraph, the aggregate number and the number in each formation and other organisation down to the next level of command above division or equivalent level (i.e., air defence army or equivalent), specifying the command organisation, designation, subordination and peacetime location, including the geographic name and coordinates, for each such formation and organisation;

(E) in respect of all full-time military personnel of conventional armed forces, excluding naval personnel, serving with all central headquarters, command and staff elements, the aggregate number;

(F) in respect of all full-time military personnel of conventional armed forces, excluding naval personnel, serving with all centrally-controlled formations, units and other organisations, including those of rear services, the aggregate number and the number in each formation, unit and other organisation down to the brigade/regiment, wing/air regiment or equivalent level, specifying the command organisation, designation, subordination and peacetime location, including the geographic name and coordinates, for each such formation, unit and organisation;

(G) in respect of all full-time military personnel serving with all land-based naval formations and units which hold conventional armaments and equipment in the categories specified in Section III of the Protocol on Information Exchange of the CFE Treaty or which hold land-based naval combat aircraft referred to in the Declaration of the States Parties to the Treaty on Conventional Armed Forces in Europe with Respect to Land-Based Naval Aircraft of November 19, 1990, the aggregate number and the number in each formation and unit down to the brigade/regiment, wing/air regiment or equivalent level, as well as units at the next level of command below the brigade/regiment, wing/air regiment level which are separately located or independent (i.e., battalions/squadrons or equivalent), specifying the designation and peacetime location, including the geographic name and coordinates, for each such formation and unit;

(H) in respect of all full-time military personnel serving with all formations, units and other organisations of conventional armed forces specified in Section III of the Protocol on Information Exchange of the CFE Treaty, the number in each such formation, unit and organisation down to the brigade/regiment, wing/air regiment or equivalent level, as well as units at the next level of command below the brigade/regiment, wing/air regiment level which are separately located or independent (i.e., battalions/squadrons or equivalent), specifying the designation and peacetime location, including the geographic name and coordinates, for each such formation, unit and organisation;

(I) in respect of all personnel serving with all formations and units down to the independent or separately located battalion or equivalent level which hold battle tanks, artillery, combat aircraft or specialised attack helicopters as well as armoured infantry fighting vehicles as specified in Article XII of the CFE Treaty, in organisations designed and structured to perform in peacetime internal security functions, the number in each such formation and unit at each site at which such armaments and equipment are held, specifying the national-level designation of each such organisation and the location, including the geographic name and coordinates, of each site at which such armaments and equipment are held;

(J) in respect of all personnel serving with all formations and units in organisations designed and structured to perform in peacetime internal security functions, excluding unarmed or lightly armed civil police forces and protective services, the aggregate number and the aggregate number in each administrative region or equivalent;

(K) in respect of all reserve personnel who have completed their initial military service or training and who have been called up or have reported voluntarily for military service or training in conventional armed forces since the most recent exchange of information provided in accordance with this Section, the aggregate number, specifying the number, if any, of those who have been called up or have reported voluntarily for full-time military service or training in conventional armed forces for a continuous period of more than 90 days;

(L) in respect of all military personnel serving under the command of the United Nations, the aggregate number; and

(M) in respect of all military personnel, excluding naval personnel, serving with all other formations, units and other organisations of conventional armed forces, the aggregate number, specifying the designation of such formations, units and organisations.

2. In providing information on personnel strengths in accordance with this Section, each participating State will provide the peacetime authorized personnel strength, which will approximate the number of personnel serving within the area of application with each of the formations, units and other organisations specified in paragraph 1 of this Section.

3. The provisions of this Section will not apply to personnel who are in transit through the area of application from a location outside the area of application to a final destination outside the area of application. Personnel in the categories specified in paragraph 1 of this Section who entered the area of application in transit will be subject to the provisions of this Section if they remain within the area of application for a period longer than seven days.

4. Each participating State will be responsible for its own information; receipt of such information will not imply validation or acceptance of the information provided.

5. The participating States will provide the information specified in this Section in accordance with the formats and procedures to be agreed in the Joint Consultative Group.

6. Prior to the date on which national personnel limits become effective in accordance with Section II of this Act, each participating State will provide to all other participating States the information specified in paragraph 1, subparagraphs (A), (D), (E), and (G) to (M) of this Section, as well as the information on aggregate number of personnel in the categories specified in subparagraphs (B), (C) and (F) of that paragraph, in written form, in one of the official CSCE languages, using diplomatic channels or other official channels designated by them, in accordance with the following timetable:

   (A) no later than 30 days following entry into force of the CFE Treaty, with the information effective as of the date of entry into force of that Treaty; and

   (B) on the 15th day of December of the year in which the CFE Treaty comes into force (unless entry into force of that Treaty occurs within 60 days of the 15th day of December), and on the 15th day of December of every year thereafter, with the information effective as of the first day of January of the following year.

7. Beginning with the date on which national personnel limits become effective in accordance with Section II of this Act, each participating State will provide to all other participating States all the information specified in paragraph 1 of this Section in written form, in one of the official CSCE languages, using diplomatic channels or other official channels designated by them, in accordance with the following timetable:

   (A) on the date on which national personnel limits become effective in accordance with Section II of this Act, with the information effective as of that date; and

   (B) on the 15th day of December of the year in which the national personnel limits become effective in accordance with Section II of this Act, and on the 15th day of December of every year thereafter, with the information effective as of the first day of January of the following year.

8. The participating States will, at the first review of the operation of this Act in accordance with Section VII, paragraph 3 of this Act, consider issues relating to the adequacy and effectiveness of the disaggregation

of the information specified in paragraph 1, subparagraphs (B), (C) and (F) of this Section.

SECTION V STABILISING MEASURES

Notification of increases in unit strengths

1. Each participating State will notify all other participating States at least 42 days in advance of any permanent increase in the personnel strength of any formation, unit or other organisation which was reported in the most recent exchange of information at the brigade/regiment, wing/air regiment of equivalent level in accordance with Section IV of this Act when such increase equals 1,000 or more at the brigade/regiment level, or 500 or more at the wing/air regiment level, or equivalent levels.

Notification of call-up of reserve personnel

2. Any participating State intending to call up reserve personnel of its conventional armed forces based on land within the area of application will notify all other participating States whenever the cumulative total of the personnel called up and retained on full-time military service will exceed a threshold of 35,000.

3. Such notification will be provided a least 42 days in advance of such threshold being exceeded. As an exception, in the case of emergency situations where advance notification is not practical, notification will be provided as soon as possible and, in any event, no later than the date such threshold is exceeded.

4. Such notification will include the following information:

   (A) the total number of reserve personnel to be called up, specifying the number to be called up for more than 90 days;

   (B) a general description of the purpose of the call-up;

   (C) the planned start and end dates of the period during which such threshold will be exceeded; and

   (D) the designation and location of any formation in which more than 7,000 at the division or equivalent level or more than 9,000 at the army/army corps or equivalent level of the personnel so called up will serve.

Resubordination of units

5. After the first exchange of information in accordance with Section IV of this Act, a participating State intending to resubordinate formations, units or other organisations whose personnel are subject to limitation in accordance with Section I of this Act to a formation, unit or other organisation whose personnel would not otherwise be subject to limitation will notify all other participating States of the planned resubordination no later than the date on which such resubordination will become effective.

6. Such notification will include the following information:

   (A) the date on which such resubordination will become effective;

   (B) the subordination, designation and peacetime location of each formation, unit and organisation to be resubordinated, both before and after such resubordination will become effective;

   (C) the peacetime authorized personnel strength for each formation, unit and organisation to be resubordinated, both before and after such resubordination will become effective; and

   (D) the number, if any, of battle tanks, armoured infantry fighting vehicles, artillery, combat aircraft, attack helicopters and armoured vehicle launched bridges as defined in Article II of the CFE Treaty held by each formation, unit and organisation to be resubordinated, both before and after such resubordination will become effective.

7. Personnel serving with formations, units or other organisations resubordinated after the date on which national personnel limits become effective in accordance with Section II of this Act will remain subject to limitation in accordance with Section I of this Act until the date of the exchange of information in accordance with Section IV of this Act one year subsequent to the year in which such resubordination becomes effective, after which time the procedure specified in paragraph 8 of this Section will apply.

8. Forty-two days prior to the end of the one-year period specified in paragraph 7 of this Section, the participating State resubordinating such formations, units or other organisations will provide to all other participating States notification of the planned exclusion. Upon the request of any other participating State, the participating State resubordinating such formations, units or other organisations will provide all relevant information supporting such exclusion.

SECTION VI VERIFICATION/EVALUATION

1. For the purpose of evaluating observance of national personnel limits and the other provisions of this Act, participating States will apply Section VII and Section VIII of the Protocol on Inspection of the CFE Treaty and other relevant provisions of that Treaty, together with the provisions set out in this Section.

2. In the case of an inspection pursuant to Section VII of the Protocol on Inspection of the CFE Treaty, the pre-inspection briefing will include information on the number of personnel serving with any formation, unit or other organisation which was notified in the most recent exchange of information in accordance with Section IV of this Act and which is located at that inspection site. If the number of such personnel differs from the number of personnel notified in that most recent exchange of information, the inspection team will be provided with an explanation of such difference. The pre-inspection briefing will also include information on the number of personnel serving with any other formation or unit down to the brigade/regiment, wing/air regiment or equivalent level, as well as independent units at the battalion/squadron or equivalent level, in the categories specified in Section IV, paragraph 1, subparagraphs (B, (C) and (F) of this Act, which is located at that inspection site.

3. In the case of an inspection pursuant to Section VIII of the Protocol on Inspection of the CFE Treaty, the escort team will provide, if requested by the inspection team, information on the number of personnel serving with any formation, unit or other organisation which was notified in the most recent exchange of information in accordance with Section IV of this Act, which is located at that inspection site and whose facilities are being inspected. If the number of such personnel differs from the number of personnel notified in that most recent exchange of information, the inspection team will be provided with an explanation of such difference.

4. During an inspection pursuant to Section VII or Section VIII of the Protocol on Inspection of the CFE Treaty, inspectors may have access, consistent with the provisions of the Protocol, to all facilities subject to inspection at the inspection site, including those used by all formations, units and other organisations located at that inspection site. During such an inspection, the escort team will specify, if requested by the inspection team, whether a particular building on the inspection site is a personnel barracks or messing facility.

5. Inspectors will include in the inspection report prepared pursuant to Section XII of the Protocol on Inspection of the CFE Treaty information provided to the inspection team in accordance with paragraphs 2 and 3 of this Section in a format to be agreed in the Joint Consultative Group. Inspectors may also include in that report written comments pertaining to the evaluation of personnel strengths.

6. Evaluation of observance of the provisions of this Act will be further facilitated through confidence- and security-building measures that have been developed and that may be developed in the context of the new negotiations on disarmament and confidence and security building following the Helsinki Follow-up Meeting. In this context, participating States are prepared to join in considering ways and means to refine the evaluation provisions specified in the Vienna Document 1992.

SECTION VII REVIEW MECHANISMS

1. The participating States will review the implementation of this Act in accordance with the procedures set out in this Section, using the relevant bodies and channels within the framework of the CSCE process.

2. In particular, any participating State may at any time raise and clarify questions relating to the implementation of this Act within the framework, as appropriate, of the Joint Consultative Group. The participating States will consider in the context of the new negotiations on disarmament and confidence and security building which will be conducted following the Helsinki Follow-up Meeting, the role of the Conflict Prevention Centre in this regard, as appropriate.

3. Six months after the date on which national personnel limits become effective in accordance with Section II of this Act and at five-year

intervals thereafter, the participating States will conduct a review of the operation of this Act.

4. The participating States will meet in an extraordinary conference if requested to do so by any participating State which considers that exceptional circumstances relating to this Act have arisen. Such a request will be transmitted to all other participating States and will include an explanation of exceptional circumstances relating to this Act, e.g., an increase in the number of military personnel in categories listed in Section I of this Act in a manner or proportion which the participating State requesting such an extraordinary conference deems to be prejudicial to security and stability within the area of application. The conference will open no later than 15 days after receipt of the request and, unless it decides otherwise, will last no longer than three weeks.

SECTION VIII CLOSING PROVISIONS

1. The measures adopted in this Act are politically binding. Accordingly, this Act is not eligible for registration under Article 102 of the Charter of the United Nations. This Act will come into effect simultaneously with the entry into force of the CFE Treaty.

2. This Act will have the same duration as the CFE Treaty and may be supplemented, modified or superseded.

3. The Government of the Kingdom of the Netherlands will transmit true copies of this Act, the original of which is in English, French, German, Italian, Russian and Spanish, to all participating States, and bring this Act to the attention of the Secretariat of the CSCE and the Secretary General of the United Nations.

Wherefore, we have subscribed our signatures below:

Done at Helsinki, this tenth day of July, one thousand nine hundred and ninety-two, at the Meeting of the Heads of State or Government of the Participating States.

TREATY ON OPEN SKIES*

Helsinki, 24 March 1992

The States concluding this Treaty, hereinafter referred to collectively as the States Parties or individually as a State Party,

Recalling the commitments they have made in the Conference on Security and Co-operation in Europe to promoting greater openness and transparency in their military activities and to enhancing security by means of confidence- and security-building measures,

Welcoming the historic events in Europe which have transformed the security situation from Vancouver to Vladivostok,

Wishing to contribute to the further development and strengthening of peace, stability and co-operative security in that area by the creation of an Open Skies regime for aerial observation,

Recognizing the potential contribution which an aerial observation regime of this type could make to security and stability in other regions as well,

Noting the possibility of employing such a regime to improve openness and transparency, to facilitate the monitoring of compliance with existing or future arms control agreements and to strengthen the capacity for conflict prevention and crisis management in the framework of the Conference on Security and Co-operation in Europe and in other relevant international institutions,

Envisaging the possible extension of the Open Skies regime into additional fields, such as the protection of the environment,

Seeking to establish agreed procedures to provide for aerial observation of all the territories of States Parties, with the intent of observing a single State Party or groups of States Parties, on the basis of equity and effectiveness while maintaining flight safety,

Noting that the operation of such an Open Skies regime will be without prejudice to States not participating in it,

---

* Reproduced without the annexes in the present volume.

Have agreed as follows:

Article I
General provisions

1. This Treaty establishes the regime, to be known as the Open Skies regime, for the conduct of observation flights by States Parties over the territories of other States Parties, and sets forth the rights and obligations of the States Parties relating thereto.

2. Each of the Annexes and their related Appendices constitutes an integral part of this Treaty.

Article II
Definitions

For the purposes of this Treaty:

1. The term 'observed Party' means the State Party or group of States Parties over whose territory an observation flight is conducted or is intended to be conducted, from the time it has received notification thereof from an observing Party until completion of the procedures relating to that flight, or personnel acting on behalf of that State Party or group of States Parties.

2. The term 'observing Party' means the State Party or group of States Parties that intends to conduct or conducts an observation flight over the territory of another State Party or group of States Parties, from the time that it has provided notification of its intention to conduct an observation flight until completion of the procedures relating to that flight, or personnel acting on behalf of that State Party or group of States Parties.

3. The term 'group of States Parties' means two or more States Parties that have agreed to form a group for the purposes of this Treaty.

4. The term 'observation aircraft' means an unarmed, fixed wing aircraft designated to make observation flights, registered by the relevant authorities of a State Party and equipped with agreed sensors. The term 'unarmed' means that the observation aircraft used for the purposes of this Treaty is not equipped to carry and employ weapons.

5. The term 'observation flight' means the flight of the observation aircraft conducted by an observing Party over the territory of an observed Party, as provided in the flight plan, from the point of entry or Open Skies airfield to the point of exit or Open Skies airfield.

6. The term 'transit flight' means a flight of an observation aircraft or transport aircraft conducted by or on behalf of an observing Party over the territory of a third State Party en route to or from the territory of the observed Party.

7. The term 'transport aircraft' means an aircraft other than an observation aircraft that, on behalf of the observing Party, conducts flights to or from the territory of the observed Party exclusively for the purposes of this Treaty.

8. The term 'territory' means the land, including islands, and internal and territorial waters, over which a State Party exercises sovereignty.

9. The term 'passive quota' means the number of observation flights that each State Party is obliged to accept as an observed Party.

10. The term 'active quota' means the number of observation flights that each State Party has the right to conduct as an observing Party.

11. The term 'maximum flight distance' means the maximum distance over the territory of the observed Party from the point at which the observation flight may commence to the point at which that flight may terminate, as specified in Annex A to this Treaty.

12. The term 'sensor' means equipment of a category specified in Article IV, paragraph 1 that is installed on an observation aircraft for use during the conduct of observation flights.

13. The term 'ground resolution' means the minimum distance on the ground between two closely located objects observed as separate objects.

14. The term 'infra-red lined-scanning device' means a sensor receiving and visualizing thermal electro-magnetic radiation emitted by objects in the invisible infra-red thermal part of the optical spectrum due to the temperature of these objects in the absence of artificial illumination.

15. The term 'observation period' means a specified period of time during an observation flight when a particular sensor installed on the observation aircraft is operating.

16. The term 'flight crew' means individuals from any State Party who may include, if the State Party so decides, interpreters and who perform duties associated with the operation or servicing of an observation aircraft or transport aircraft.

17. The term 'pilot-in-command' means the pilot on board the observation aircraft who is responsible for the operation of the observation aircraft, the execution of the flight plan, and the safety of the observation aircraft.

18. The term 'flight monitor' means an individual who, on behalf of the observed Party, is on board an observation aircraft provided by the observing Party during the observation flight and who performs duties in accordance with Annex G to this Treaty.

19. The term 'flight representative' means an individual who, on behalf of the observing Party, is on board an observation aircraft provided by the observed Party during an observation flight and who performs duties in accordance with Annex G to this Treaty.

20. The term 'representative' means an individual who has been designated by the observing Party and who performs activities on behalf of the observing Party in accordance with Annex G during an observation flight on an observation aircraft designated by a State Party other than the observing Party or the observed Party.

21. The term 'sensor operator' means an individual from any State Party who performs duties associated with the functioning, operation and maintenance of the sensors of an observation aircraft.

22. The term 'inspector' means an individual from any State Party who conducts an inspection of sensors or observation aircraft of another State Party.

23. The term 'escort' means an individual from any State Party who accompanies the inspectors of another State Party.

24. The term 'mission plan' means a document, which is in a format established by the Open Skies Consultative Commission, presented by

the observing Party that contains the route, profile, order of execution and support required to conduct the observation flight, which is to be agreed upon with the observed Party and which will form the basis for the elaboration of the flight plan.

25. The term 'flight plan' means a document elaborated on the basis of the agreed mission plan in the format and with the content specified by the International Civil Aviation Organization, hereinafter referred to as the ICAO, which is presented to the air traffic control authorities and on the basis of which the observation flight will be conducted.

26. The term 'mission report' means a document describing an observation flight completed after its termination by the observing Party and signed by both the observing and observed Parties, which is in a format established by the Open Skies Consultative Commission.

27. The term 'Open Skies airfield' means an airfield designated by the observed Party as a point where an observation flight may commence or terminate.

28. The term 'point of entry' means a point designated by the observed Party for the arrival of personnel of the observing Party on the territory of the observed Party.

29. The term 'point of exit' means a point designated by the observed Party for the departure of personnel of the observing Party from the territory of the observed Party.

30. The term 'refuelling airfield' means an airfield designated by the observed Party used for fuelling and servicing of observation aircraft and transport aircraft.

31. The term 'alternate airfield' means an airfield specified in the flight plan to which an observation aircraft or transport aircraft may proceed when it becomes inadvisable to land at the airfield of intended landing.

32. The term 'hazardous airspace' means the prohibited areas, restricted areas and danger areas, defined on the basis of Annex 2 to the Convention on International Civil Aviation, that are established in accordance with Annex 15 to the Convention on International Civil Aviation in the interests of flight safety, public safety and environmental protection and about which information is provided in accordance with ICAO provisions.

33. The term 'prohibited area' means an airspace of defined dimensions, above the territory of a State Party, within which the flight of aircraft is prohibited.

34. The term 'restricted area' means an airspace of defined dimensions, above the territory of a State Party, within which the flight of aircraft is restricted in accordance with specified conditions.

35. The term 'danger area' means an airspace of defined dimensions within which activities dangerous to the flight of aircraft may exist at specified times.

Article III
Quotas

Section I. General provisions

1. Each State Party shall have the right to conduct observation flights in accordance with the provisions of this Treaty.

2. Each State Party shall be obliged to accept observation flights over its territory in accordance with the provisions of this Treaty.

3. Each State Party shall have the right to conduct a number of observation flights over the territory of any other State Party equal to the number of observation flights which that State Party has the right to conduct over it.

4. The total number of observation flights that each State Party is obliged to accept over its territory is the total passive quota for that State Party. The allocation of the total passive quota to the States Parties is set forth in Annex A, Section I to this Treaty.

5. The number of observation flights that a State Party shall have the right to conduct each year over the territory of each of the other States Parties is the individual active quota of that State Party with respect to that other State Party. The sum of the individual active quotas is the total active quota of that State Party. The total active quota of a State Party shall not exceed its total passive quota.

6. The first distribution of active quotas is set forth in Annex A, Section II to this Treaty.

7. After entry into force of this Treaty, the distribution of active quotas shall be subject to an annual review for the following calendar year within the framework of the Open Skies Consultative Commission. In the event that it is not possible during the annual review to arrive within three weeks at agreement on the distribution of active quotas with respect to a particular State Party, the previous year's distribution of active quotas with respect to that State Party shall remain unchanged.

8. Except as provided for by the provisions of Article VIII, each observation flight conducted by a State Party shall be counted against the individual and total active quotas of that State Party.

9. Notwithstanding the provisions of paragraphs 3 and 5 of this Section, a State Party to which an active quota has been distributed may, by agreement with the State Party to be overflown, transfer a part or all of its total active quota to other States Parties and shall promptly notify all other States Parties and the Open Skies Consultative Commission thereof.
Paragraph 10 of this Section shall apply.

10. No State Party shall conduct more observation flights over the territory of another State Party than a number equal to 50 per cent, rounded up to the nearest whole number, of its own total active quota, or of the total passive quota of that other State Party, whichever is less.

11. The maximum flight distances of observation flights over the territories of the States Parties are set forth in Annex A, Section III to this Treaty.

Section II. Provisions for a group of States Parties

1. (A) Without prejudice to their rights and obligations under this Treaty, two or more States Parties which hold quotas may form a group of States Parties at signature of this Treaty and thereafter. For a group of States Parties formed after signature of this Treaty, the provisions of this Section shall apply no earlier than six months after giving notice to all other States Parties, and subject to the provisions of paragraph 6 of this Section.

   (B) A group of States Parties shall co-operate with regard to active and passive quotas in accordance with the provisions of either paragraph 2 or 3 of this Section.

2. (A) The members of a group of States Parties shall have the right to redistribute amongst themselves their active quotas for the current year, while retaining their individual passive quotas. Notification of the redistribution shall be made immediately to all third States Parties concerned.

(B) An observation flight shall count as many observation flights against the individual and total active quotas of the observing Party as observed Parties belonging to the group are overflown. It shall count one observation flight against the total passive quota of each observed Party.

(C) Each State Party in respect of which one or more members of a group of States Parties hold active quotas shall have the right to conduct over the territory of any member of the group 50 per cent more observation flights, rounded up to the nearest whole number, than its individual active quota in respect of that member of the group or to two such overflights if it holds no active quota in respect of that member of the group.

(D) In the event that it exercises this right the State Party concerned shall reduce its active quotas in respect of other members of the group in such a way that the total sum of observation flights it conducts over their territories shall not exceed the sum of the individual active quotas that the State Party holds in respect of all the members of the group in the current year.

(E) The maximum flight distances of observation flights over the territories of each member of the group shall apply. In case of an observation flight conducted over several members, after completion of the maximum flight distance for one member all sensors shall be switched off until the observation aircraft reaches the point over the territory of the next member of the group of States Parties where the observation flight is planned to begin. For such follow-on observation flight the maximum flight distance related to the Open Skies airfield nearest to this point shall apply.

3 (A) A group of States Parties shall, at its request, be entitled to a common total passive quota which should be allocated to it and common individual and total active quotas shall be distributed in respect of it.

(B) In this case, the total passive quota is the total number of observation flights that the group of States Parties is obliged to accept each year. The total active quota is the sum of the number of observation flights that the group of States Parties has the right to conduct each year. Its total active quota shall not exceed the total passive quota.

(C) An observation flight resulting from the total active quota of the group of States Parties shall be carried out on behalf of the group.

(D) Observation flights that a group of States Parties is obliged to accept may be conducted over the territory of one or more of its members.

(E) The maximum flight distances of each group of States Parties shall be specified pursuant to Annex A, Section III and Open Skies airfields shall be designated pursuant to Annex E to this Treaty.

4. In accordance with general principles set out in Article X, paragraph 3, any third State Party that considers its rights under the provisions of Section I, paragraph 3 of this Article to be unduly restricted by the operation of a group of States Parties may raise this problem before the Open Skies Consultative Commission.

5. The group of States Parties shall ensure that procedures are established allowing for the conduct of observation flights over the territories of its members during one single mission, including refuelling if necessary. In the case of a group of States Parties established pursuant to paragraph 3 of this Section, such observation flights shall not exceed the maximum flight distance applicable to the Open Skies airfields at which the observation flights commence.

6. No earlier than six months after notification of the decision has been provided to all other States Parties:

(A) a group of States Parties established pursuant to the provisions of paragraph 2 of this Section may be transformed into a group of States Parties pursuant to the provisions of paragraph 3 of this Section;

(B) a group of States Parties established pursuant to the provisions of paragraph 3 of this Section may be transformed into a group of States Parties pursuant to the provisions of paragraph 2 of this Section;

(C) a State Party may withdraw from a group of States Parties; or

(D) a group of States Parties may admit further States Parties which hold quotas.

7. Following entry into force of this Treaty, changes in the allocation or distribution of quotas resulting from the establishment of or an

admission to or a withdrawal from a group of States Parties according to paragraph 3 of this Section shall become effective on 1 January following the first annual review within the Open Skies Consultative Commission occurring after the six-month notification period. When necessary, new Open Skies airfields shall be designated and maximum flight distances established accordingly.

Article IV
Sensors

1. Except as otherwise provided for in paragraph 3 of this Article, observation aircraft shall be equipped with sensors only from amongst the following categories:
   (A) optical panoramic and framing cameras;
   (B) video cameras with real-time display;
   (C) infra-red line-scanning devices; and
   (D) sideways-looking synthetic aperture radar.

2. A State Party may use, for the purposes of conducting observation flights, any of the sensors specified in paragraph 1 above, provided such sensors are commercially available to all States Parties, subject to the following performance limits:
   (A) in the case of optical panoramic and framing cameras, a ground resolution of no better than 30 centimetres at the minimum height above ground level, determined in accordance with the provisions of Annex D, Appendix 1, obtained from no more than one panoramic camera, one vertically-mounted framing camera and two obliquely-mounted framing cameras, one on each side of the aircraft, providing coverage, which need not be continuous, of the ground, up to 50 kilometres of each side of the flight path of the aircraft;
   (B) in the case of video cameras, a ground resolution of no better than 30 centimetres obtained at the lowest minimum height above the ground for any of the optical cameras specified in subparagraph (A) of this paragraph;
   (C) in the case of infra-red line-scanning devices, a ground resolution of no better than 50 centimetres at the minimum height above the ground level, determined in accordance with the provisions of Annex D, Appendix 1, obtained from a single device; and
   (D) in the case of sideways-looking synthetic aperture radar, a ground resolution of no better than three metres calculated by the impulse response method, which, using the object separation

method, corresponds to the ability to distinguish on a radar image two corner reflectors, the distance between the centres of which is no less than five metres, over a swath width of no more than 25 kilometres, obtained from a single radar unit capable of looking at either side of the aircraft, but not both simultaneously.

3. The introduction of additional categories and improvements to the capabilities of existing categories of sensors provided for in this Article shall be addressed by the Open Skies Consultative Commission pursuant to Article X of this Treaty.

4. All sensors shall be provided with aperture covers or other devices which inhibit the operation of sensors so as to prevent collection of data during transit flights or flights to points of entry or from points of exit over the territory of the observed Party. Such covers or other devices shall be removable or operable only from outside the observation aircraft.

5. Equipment that is capable of annotating data collected by sensors in accordance with Annex B, Section II shall be allowed on observation aircraft. The State Party providing the observation aircraft for an observation flight shall annotate the data collected by sensors with the information provided for in Annex B, Section II to this Treaty.

6. Equipment that is capable of displaying data collected by sensors in real-time shall be allowed on observation aircraft for the purposes of monitoring the functioning and operation of the sensors during the conduct of an observation flight.

7. Except as required for the operation of the agreed sensors, or as required for the operation of the observation aircraft, or as provided for in paragraphs 5 and 6 of this Article, the collection, processing, retransmission or recording of electronic signals from electro-magnetic waves are prohibited on board the observation aircraft and equipment for such operations shall not be on that observation aircraft.

8. In the event that the observation aircraft is provided by the observing Party, the observing Party shall have the right to use an observation aircraft equipped with sensors in each sensor category that do not exceed the capability specified in paragraph 2 of this Article.

9. In the event that the observation aircraft used for an observation flight is provided by the observed Party, the observed Party shall be obliged to provide an observation aircraft equipped with sensors from each sensor category specified in paragraph 1 of this Article, at the maximum capability and in the numbers specified in paragraph 2 of this Article, subject to the provisions of Article XVIII, Section II, unless otherwise agreed by the observing and observed Parties. The package and configuration of such sensors shall be installed in such a way so as to provide coverage of the ground provided for in paragraph 2 of this Article. In the event that the observation aircraft is provided by the observed Party, the latter shall provide a sideways-looking synthetic aperture radar with a ground resolution of no worse than six metres, determined by the object separation method.

10. When designating an aircraft as an observation aircraft pursuant to Article V of this Treaty, each State Party shall inform all other States Parties of the technical information on each sensor installed on such aircraft as provided for in Annex B to this Treaty.

11. Each State Party shall have the right to take part in the certification of sensors installed on observation aircraft in accordance with the provisions of Annex D. No observation aircraft of a given type shall be used for observation flights until such type of observation aircraft and its sensors has been certified in accordance with the provisions of Annex D to this Treaty.

12. A State Party designating an aircraft as an observation aircraft shall, upon 90-day prior notice to all other States Parties and subject to the provisions of Annex D to this Treaty, have the right to remove, replace or add sensors, or amend the technical information it has provided in accordance with the provisions of paragraph 10 of this Article and Annex B to this Treaty. Replacement and additional sensors shall be subject to certification in accordance with the provisions of Annex D to this Treaty prior to their use during an observation flight.

13. In the event that a State Party or group of States Parties, based on experience with using a particular observation aircraft, considers that any sensor or its associated equipment installed on an aircraft does not correspond to those certified in accordance with the provisions of Annex D, the interested States Parties shall notify all other States Parties of their concern. The State Party that designated the aircraft shall:

(A) take the steps necessary to ensure that the sensor and its associated equipment installed on the observation aircraft correspond to those certified in accordance with the provisions of Annex D, including, as necessary, repair, adjustment or replacement of the particular sensor or its associated equipment; and

(B) at the request of an interested State Party, by means of a demonstration flight set up in connection with the next time that the aforementioned observation aircraft is used, in accordance with the provisions of Annex F, demonstrate that the sensor and its associated equipment installed on the observation aircraft correspond to those certified in accordance with the provisions of Annex D. Other States Parties that express concern regarding a sensor and its associated equipment installed on an observation aircraft shall have the right to send personnel to participate in such a demonstration flight.

14. In the event that, after the steps referred to in paragraph 13 of this Article have been taken, the States Parties remain concerned as to whether a sensor or its associated equipment installed on an observation aircraft correspond to those certified in accordance with the provisions of Annex D, the issue may be referred to the Open Skies Consultative Commission.

Article V
Aircraft designation

1. Each State Party shall have the right to designate as observation aircraft one or more types or models of aircraft registered by the relevant authorities of a State Party.

2. Each State Party shall have the right to designate types or models of aircraft as observation aircraft or add new types or models of aircraft to those designated earlier by it, provided that it notifies all other States Parties 30 days in advance thereof. The notification of the designation of aircraft of a type or model shall contain the information specified in Annex C to this Treaty.

3. Each State Party shall have the right to delete types or models of aircraft designated earlier by it, provided that it notifies all other States Parties 90 days in advance thereof.

4. Only one exemplar of a particular type and model of aircraft with an identical set of associated sensors shall be required to be offered for certification in accordance with the provisions of Annex D to this Treaty.

5. Each observation aircraft shall be capable of carrying the flight crew and the personnel specified in Article VI, Section III.

Article VI
Choice of observation aircraft, general provisions for the conduct of observation flights, and requirements for mission planning

Section I. Choice of observation aircraft and general provisions for the conduct of observation flights

1. Observation flights shall be conducted using observation aircraft that have been designated by a State Party pursuant to Article V. Unless the observed party exercises its right to provide an observation aircraft that it has itself designated, the observing Party shall have the right to provide the observation aircraft. In the event that the observing Party provides the observation aircraft, it shall have the right to provide an aircraft that it has itself designated or an aircraft designated by another State Party. In the event that the observed Party provides the observation aircraft, the observing Party shall have the right to be provided with an aircraft capable of achieving a minimum unrefuelled range, including the necessary fuel reserves, equivalent to one-half of the maximum flight distance for the observed Party, as notified in accordance with paragraph 5, subparagraph (G) of this Section.

2. Each State Party shall have the right, pursuant to paragraph 1 of this Section, to use an observation aircraft designated by another State Party for observation flights. Arrangements for the use of such aircraft shall be worked out by the States Parties involved to allow for active participation in the Open Skies regime.

3. States Parties having the right to conduct observation flights may co-ordinate their plans for conducting observation flights in accordance with Annex H to this Treaty. No State Party shall be obliged to accept more than one observation flight at any one time during the 96-hour period specified in paragraph 9 of this Section, unless that State Party has requested a demonstration flight pursuant to Annex F to this Treaty. In that case, the observed Party shall be obliged to accept an overlap for the observation flights of up to 24 hours. After having

been notified of the results of the co-ordination of plans to conduct observation flights, each State Party over whose territory observation flights are to be conducted shall inform other States Parties, in accordance with the provisions of Annex H, whether or not it will exercise, with regard to each specific observation flight, its right to provide its own observation aircraft.

4. No later than 90 days after signature of this Treaty, each State Party shall provide notification to all other States Parties:
   (A) of the standing diplomatic clearance number for Open Skies observation flights, flights of transport aircraft and transit flights;
   (B) which language or languages of the Open Skies Consultative Commission specified in Annex L, Section I, paragraph 7 to this Treaty shall be used by personnel for all activities associated with the conduct of observation flights over its territory, and for completing the mission plan and mission report, unless the language to be used is the one recommended in Annex 10 to the Convention on International Civil Aviation, Volume II, paragraph 5.2.1.1.2.

5. The observing Party shall notify the observed Party of its intention to conduct an observation flight, no less than 72 hours prior to the estimated time of arrival of the observing Party at the point of entry of the observed Party. States Parties providing such notifications shall make every effort to avoid using the minimum pre-notification period over weekends. Such notification shall include:
   (A) the desired point of entry and if applicable, Open Skies airfield where the observation flight shall commence;
   (B) the date and estimated time of arrival of the observing Party at the point of entry and the date and estimated time of departure for the flight from the point of entry to the Open Skies airfield, if applicable, indicating specific accommodation needs;
   (C) the location, specified in Annex E, Appendix 1, where the conduct of the pre-flight inspection is desired and the date and start time of such pre-flight inspection in accordance with the provisions of Annex F;
   (D) the mode of transport and, if applicable, type and model of the transport aircraft used to travel to the point of entry in the event that the observation aircraft used for the observation flight is provided by the observed Party;
   (E) the diplomatic clearance number for the observation flight or for the flight of the transport aircraft used to bring the personnel in

and out of the territory of the observed Party to conduct an observation flight;

(F) the identification of the observation aircraft, as specified in Annex C;

(G) the approximate observation flight distance; and

(H) the names of the personnel, their gender, date and place of birth, passport number and issuing State Party, and their function.

6. The observed Party that is notified in accordance with paragraph 5 of this Section shall acknowledge receipt of the notification within 24 hours. In the event that the observed Party exercises its right to provide the observation aircraft, the acknowledgement shall include the information about the observation aircraft specified in paragraph 5, subparagraph (F) of this Section. The observing Party shall be permitted to arrive at the point of entry at the estimated time of arrival as notified in accordance with paragraph 5 of this Section. The estimated time of departure for the flight from the point of entry to the Open Skies airfield where the observation flight shall commence and the location, the date and the start time of the pre-flight inspection shall be subject to confirmation by the observed Party.

7. Personnel of the observing Party may include personnel designated pursuant to Article XIII by other States Parties.

8. The observing Party, when notifying the observed Party in accordance with paragraph 5 of this Section, shall simultaneously notify all other States Parties of its intention to conduct the observation flight.

9. The period from the estimated time of arrival at the point of entry until completion of the observation flight shall not exceed 96 hours, unless otherwise agreed. In case the observed Party requests a demonstration flight pursuant to Annex F to the Treaty, it shall extend the 96-hour period pursuant to Annex F, Section III, paragraph 4, if the additional time is required by the observing Party for the unrestricted execution of the mission plan.

10. Upon arrival of the observation aircraft at the point of entry, the observed Party shall inspect the covers for sensor apertures or other devices that inhibit the operation of sensors to confirm that they are in their proper position pursuant to Annex E, unless otherwise agreed by all States Parties involved.

11. In the event that the observation aircraft is provided by the observing Party, upon the arrival of the observation aircraft at the point of entry or at the Open Skies airfield where the observation flight commences, the observed Party shall have the right to carry out the pre-flight inspection pursuant to Annex F, Section I. In the event that, in accordance with paragraph 1 of this Section, an observation aircraft is provided by the observed Party, the observing Party shall have the right to carry out the pre-flight inspection of sensors pursuant to Annex F, Section II. Unless otherwise agreed, such inspections shall terminate no less than four hours prior to the scheduled commencement of the observation flight set forth in the flight plan.

12. The observing Party shall ensure that its flight crew includes at least one individual who has the necessary linguistic ability to communicate freely with the personnel of the observed Party and its air traffic control authorities in the language or languages notified by the observed Party in accordance with paragraph 4 of this Section.

13. The observed Party shall provide the flight crew, upon its arrival at the point of entry or at the Open Skies airfield where the observation flight commences, with the most recent weather forecast and air navigation information and information on flight safety, including Notices to Airmen. Updates of such information shall be provided as requested. Instrument procedures, and information about alternate airfields along the flight route, shall be provided upon approval of the mission plan in accordance with the requirements of Section II of this Article.

14. While conducting observation flights pursuant to this Treaty, all observation aircraft shall be operated in accordance with the provisions of this Treaty and in accordance with the approved flight plan. Without prejudice to the provisions of Section II, paragraph 2 of this Article, observation flights shall also be conducted in compliance with:
    (A) published ICAO standards and recommended practices; and
    (B) published national air traffic control rules, procedures and guidelines on flight safety of the State Party whose territory is being overflown.

15. Observation flights shall take priority over any regular air traffic. The observed Party shall ensure that its air traffic control authorities facilitate the conduct of observation flights in accordance with this Treaty.

16. On board the aircraft the pilot-in-command shall be the sole authority for the safe conduct of the flight and shall be responsible for the execution of the flight plan.

17. The observed Party shall provide:
    (A) a calibration target suitable for confirming the capability of sensors in accordance with the procedures set forth in Annex D, Section III to this Treaty, to be overflown during the demonstration flight or the observation flight upon the request of either Party, for each sensor that is to be used during the observation flight. The calibration target shall be located in the vicinity of the airfield at which the pre-flight inspection is conducted pursuant to Annex F to this Treaty;
    (B) customary commercial aircraft fuelling and servicing for the observation aircraft or transport aircraft at the point of entry, at the Open Skies airfield, at any refuelling airfield, and at the point of exit specified in the flight plan, according to the specifications that are published about the designated airfield;
    (C) meals and the use of accommodation for the personnel of the observing Party; and
    (D) upon the request of the observing Party, further services, as may be agreed upon between the observing and observed Parties, in order to facilitate the conduct of the observation flight.

18. All costs involved in the conduct of the observation flight, including the costs of the recording media and the processing of the data collected by sensors, shall be reimbursed in accordance with Annex L, Section I, paragraph 9 to this Treaty.

19. Prior to the departure of the observation aircraft from the point of exit, the observed Party shall confirm that the covers for sensor apertures or other devices that inhibit the operation of sensors are in their proper position pursuant to Annex E to this Treaty.

20. Unless otherwise agreed, the observing Party shall depart from the point of exit no later than 24 hours following completion of the observation flight, unless weather conditions or the airworthiness of the observation aircraft or transport aircraft do not permit, in which case the flight shall commence as soon as practicable.

21. The observing Party shall compile a mission report of the observation flight using the appropriate format developed by the Open Skies Consultative Commission. The mission report shall contain pertinent

data on the date and time of the observation flight, its route and profile, weather conditions, time and location of each observation period for each sensor, the approximate amount of data collected by sensors, and the result of inspection of covers for sensor apertures or other devices that inhibit the operation of sensors in accordance with Article VII and Annex E. The mission report shall be signed by the observing and observed Parties at the point of exit and shall be provided by the observing Party to all other States Parties within seven days after departure of the observing Party from the point of exit.

Section II. Requirements for mission planning

1. Unless otherwise agreed, the observing Party shall, after arrival at the Open Skies airfield, submit to the observed Party a mission plan for the proposed observation flight that meets the requirements of paragraphs 2 and 4 of this Section.

2. The mission plan may provide for an observation flight that allows for observation of any point on the entire territory of the observed Party, including areas designated by the observed Party as hazardous airspace in the source specified in Annex I. The flight path of an observation aircraft shall not be closer than, but shall be allowed up to, ten kilometres from the border with an adjacent State that is not a State Party.

3. The mission plan may provide that the Open Skies airfield where the observation flight terminates, as well as the point of exit, may be different from the Open Skies airfield where the observation flight commences or the point of entry. The mission plan shall specify, if applicable, the commencement time of the observation flight, the desired time and place of planned refuelling stops or rest periods, and the time of continuation of the observation flight after a refuelling stop or rest period within the 96-hour period specified in Section I, paragraph 9 of this Article.

4. The mission plan shall include all information necessary to file the flight plan and shall provide that:
   (A) the observation flight does not exceed the relevant maximum flight distance as set forth in Annex A, Section I;
   (B) the route and profile of the observation flight satisfies observation flight safety conditions in conformity with ICAO standards and recommended practices, taking into account

existing differences in national flight rules, without prejudice to the provisions of paragraph 2 of this Section;

(C) the mission plan takes into account information on hazardous airspace, as provided in accordance with Annex I;

(D) the height above ground level of the observation aircraft does not permit the observing Party to exceed the limitation on ground resolution for each sensor, as set forth in Article IV, paragraph 2;

(E) the estimated time of commencement of the observation flight shall be no less than 24 hours after the submission of the mission plan, unless otherwise agreed;

(F) the observation aircraft flies a direct route between the co-ordinates or navigation fixes designated in the mission plan in the declared sequence; and

(G) the flight path does not intersect at the same point more than once, unless otherwise agreed, and the observation aircraft does not circle around a single point, unless otherwise agreed. The provisions of this subparagraph do not apply for the purposes of taking off, flying over calibration targets, and landing by the observation aircraft.

5. In the event that the mission plan filed by the observing Party provides for flights through hazardous airspace, the observed Party shall:

(A) specify the hazard to the observation aircraft;

(B) facilitate the conduct of the observation flight by co-ordination or suppression of the activity specified pursuant to subparagraph (A) of this paragraph; or

(C) propose an alternative flight altitude, route, or time.

6. No later than four hours after submission of the mission plan, the observed Party shall accept the mission plan or propose changes to it in accordance with Article VIII, Section I, paragraph 4 and paragraph 5 of this Section. Such changes shall not preclude observation of any point on the entire territory of the observed Party, including areas designated by the observed Party as hazardous airspace in the source specified in Annex I to this Treaty. Upon agreement, the mission plan shall be signed by the observing and observed Parties. In the event that the Parties do not reach agreement on the mission plan within eight hours of the submission of the original mission plan, the observing Party shall have the right to decline to conduct the observation flight in accordance with the provisions of Article VIII of this Treaty.

7. If the planned route of the observation flight approaches the border of other States Parties or other States, the observed Party may notify that State or those States of the estimated route, date and time of the observation flight.

8. On the basis of the agreed mission plan the State Party providing the observation aircraft shall, in co-ordination with the other State Party, file the flight plan immediately, which shall have the content specified in Annex 2 to the Convention on International Civil Aviation and shall be in the format specified by ICAO Document No. 4444-RAC/501, 'Rules of the Air and Air Traffic Services', as revised or amended.

Section III. Special provisions

1. In the event that the observation aircraft is provided by the observing Party, the observed Party shall have the right to have on board the observation aircraft two flight monitors and one interpreter, in addition to one flight monitor for each sensor control station on board the observation aircraft, unless otherwise agreed. Flight monitors and interpreters shall have the rights and obligations specified in Annex G to this Treaty.

2. Notwithstanding paragraph 1 of this Section, in the event that an observing Party uses an observation aircraft which has a maximum take-off gross weight of no more than 35,000 kilograms for an observation flight distance not more than 1,500 kilometres as notified in accordance with Section I, paragraph 5, subparagraph (F) of this Article, it shall only be obliged to accept two flight monitors and one interpreter on board the observation aircraft unless otherwise agreed.

3. In the event that the observation aircraft is provided by the observed Party, the observed Party shall permit the personnel of the observing Party to travel to the point of entry of the observed Party in the most expeditious manner. The personnel of the observing Party may elect to travel to the point of entry using ground, sea, or air transportation, including transportation by an aircraft owned by any State Party. Procedures regarding such travel are set forth in Annex E to this Treaty.

4. In the event that the observation aircraft is provided by the observed Party, the observing Party shall have the right to have on board the observation aircraft two flight representatives and one interpreter, in addition to one flight representative for each sensor control station on

the aircraft, unless otherwise agreed. Flight representatives and interpreters shall have the rights and obligations set forth in Annex G to this Treaty.

5. In the event that the observing State Party provides an observation aircraft designated by a State Party other than the observing Party and the observed Party, the observing Party shall have the right to have on board the observation aircraft two representatives and one interpreter in addition to one representative for each sensor control station on the aircraft, unless otherwise agreed. In this case, the provisions on flight monitors set forth in paragraph 1 of this Section shall also apply. Representatives and interpreters shall have the rights and obligations set forth in Annex G to this Treaty.

Article VII
Transit flights

1. Transit flights conducted by an observing Party to and from the territory of an observed Party for the purposes of this Treaty shall originate on the territory of the observing Party or of another State Party.

2. Each State Party shall accept transit flights. Such transit flights shall be conducted along internationally recognized Air Traffic Services routes, unless otherwise agreed by the States Parties involved, and in accordance with the instructions of the national air traffic control authorities of each State Party whose airspace is transited. The observing Party shall notify each State Party whose airspace is to be transited at the same time that it notifies the observed Party in accordance with Article VI.

3. The operation of sensors on an observation aircraft during transit flights is prohibited. In the event that, during the transit flight, the observation aircraft lands on the territory of a State Party, that State Party shall, upon landing and prior to departure, inspect the covers of sensor apertures or other devices that inhibit the operation of sensors to confirm that they are in their proper position.

Article VIII
Prohibitions, deviations from flight plans and emergency situations

Section I. Prohibition of observation flights and changes to mission plans

1. The observed Party shall have the right to prohibit an observation flight that is not in compliance with the provisions of this Treaty.

2. The observed Party shall have the right to prohibit an observation flight prior to its commencement in the event that the observing Party fails to arrive at the point of entry within 24 hours after the estimated time of arrival specified in the notification provided in accordance with Article VI, Section I, paragraph 5, unless otherwise agreed between the States Parties involved.

3. In the event that an observed State Party prohibits an observation flight pursuant to this Article or Annex F, it shall immediately state the facts for the prohibition in the mission plan. Within seven days the observed Party shall provide to all States Parties, through diplomatic channels, a written explanation for this prohibition in the mission report provided pursuant to Article VI, Section I, paragraph 21. An observation flight that has been prohibited shall not be counted against the quota of either State Party.

4. The observed Party shall have the right to propose changes to the mission plan as a result of any of the following circumstances:
   (A) the weather conditions affect flight safety;
   (B) the status of the Open Skies airfield to be used, alternate airfields, or refuelling airfields prevents their use; or
   (C) the mission plan is inconsistent with Article VI, Section II, paragraphs 2 and 4.

5. In the event that the observing Party disagrees with the proposed changes to the mission plan, it shall have the right to submit alternatives to the proposed changes. In the event that agreement on a mission plan is not reached within eight hours of the submission of the original mission plan, and if the observing Party considers the changes to the mission plan to be prejudicial to its rights under this Treaty with respect to the conduct of the observation flight, the observing Party shall have the right to decline to conduct the observation flight, which shall not be recorded against the quota of either State Party.

6. In the event that an observing Party declines to conduct an observation flight pursuant to this Article or Annex F, it shall immediately provide an explanation of its decision in the mission plan prior to the departure of the observing Party. Within seven days after departure of the observing Party, the observing Party shall provide to all other States Parties, through diplomatic channels, a written explanation for this decision in the mission report provided pursuant to Article VI, Section I, paragraph 21.

Section II. Deviation from the flight plan

1. Deviations from the flight plan shall be permitted during the observation flight if necessitated by:
   (A) weather conditions affecting flight safety;
   (B) technical difficulties relating to the observation aircraft;
   (C) a medical emergency of any person on board; or
   (D) air traffic control instructions related to circumstances brought about by *force majeure*.

2. In addition, if weather conditions prevent effective use of optical sensors and infra-red line-scanning devices, deviations shall be permitted, provided that:
   (A) flight safety requirements are met;
   (B) in cases where national rules so require, permission is granted by air traffic control authorities; and
   (C) the performance of the sensors does not exceed the capabilities specified in Article IV, paragraph 2, unless otherwise agreed.

3. The observed Party shall have the right to prohibit the use of a particular sensor during a deviation that brings the observation aircraft below the minimum height above ground level for operating that particular sensor, in accordance with the limitation on ground resolution specified in Article IV, paragraph 2. In the event that a deviation requires the observation aircraft to alter its flight path by more than 50 kilometres from the flight path specified in the flight plan, the observed Party shall have the right to prohibit the use of all the sensors installed on the observation aircraft beyond that 50-kilometre limit.

4. The observing Party shall have the right to curtail an observation flight during its execution in the event of sensor malfunction. The pilot-in-command shall have the right to curtail an observation flight in the

event of technical difficulties affecting the safety of the observation aircraft.

5. In the event that a deviation from the flight plan permitted by paragraph 1 of this Section results in curtailment of the observation flight, or a curtailment occurs in accordance with paragraph 4 of this Section, an observation flight shall be counted against the quotas of both States Parties, unless the curtailment is due to:
   (A) sensor malfunction on an observation aircraft provided by the observed Party;
   (B) technical difficulties relating to the observation aircraft provided by the observed Party;
   (C) a medical emergency of a member of the flight crew of the observed Party or of flight monitors; or
   (D) air traffic control instructions related to circumstances brought about by *force majeur*.

   In such cases the observing Party shall have the right to decide whether to count it against the quotas of both States Parties.

6. The data collected by the sensors shall be retained by the observing Party only if the observation flight is counted against the quotas of both States Parties.

7. In the event that a deviation is made from the flight plan, the pilot-in-command shall take action in accordance with the published national flight regulations of the observed Party. Once the factors leading to the deviation have ceased to exist, the observation aircraft may, with the permission of the air traffic control authorities, continue the observation flight in accordance with the flight plan. The additional flight distance of the observation aircraft due to the deviation shall not count against the maximum flight distance.

8. Personnel of both States Parties on board the observation aircraft shall be immediately informed of all deviations from the flight plan.

9. Additional expenses resulting from provisions of this Article shall be reimbursed in accordance with Annex L, Section I, paragraph 9 to this Treaty.

Section III. Emergency situations

1. In the event that an emergency situation arises, the pilot-in-command shall be guided by 'Procedures for Air Navigation Services - Rules of

the Air and Air Traffic Services', ICAO Document No. 4444-RAC/501/12, as revised or amended, the national flight regulations of the observed Party, and the flight operation manual of the observation aircraft.

2. Each observation aircraft declaring an emergency shall be accorded the full range of distress and navigational facilities of the observed Party in order to ensure the most expeditious recovery of the aircraft to the nearest suitable airfield.

3. In the event of an aviation accident involving the observation aircraft on the territory of the observed Party, search and rescue operations shall be conducted by the observed Party in accordance with its own regulations and procedures for such operations.

4. Investigation of an aviation accident or incident involving an observation aircraft shall be conducted by the observed Party, with the participation of the observing Party, in accordance with the ICAO recommendations set forth in Annex 13 to the Convention on International Civil Aviation ('Investigation of Aviation Accidents') as revised or amended and in accordance with the national regulations of the observed Party.

5. In the event that the observation aircraft is not registered with the observed Party, at the conclusion of the investigation all wreckage and debris of the observation aircraft and sensors, if found and recovered, shall be returned to the observing Party or to the Party to which the aircraft belongs, if so requested.

Article IX
Sensor output from observation flights

Section I. General provisions

1. For the purposes of recording data collected by sensors during observation flights, the following recording media shall be used:
   (A) in the case of optical panoramic and framing cameras, black and white photographic film;
   (B) in the case of video cameras, magnetic tape;
   (C) in the case of infra-red line-scanning devices, black and white photographic film or magnetic tape; and
   (D) in the case of sideways-looking synthetic aperture radar, magnetic tape.

The agreed format in which such data is to be recorded and exchanged on other recording media shall be decided within the Open Skies Consultative Commission during the period of provisional application of this Treaty.

2. Data collected by sensors during observation flights shall remain on board the observation aircraft until completion of the observation flight. The transmission of data collected by sensors from the observation aircraft during the observation flight is prohibited.

3. Each roll of photographic film and cassette or reel of magnetic tape used to collect data by a sensor during an observation flight shall be placed in a container and sealed in the presence of the States Parties as soon as is practical after it has been removed from the sensor.

4. Data collected by sensors during observation flights shall be made available to States Parties in accordance with the provisions of this Article and shall be used exclusively for the attainment of the purposes of this Treaty.

5. In the event that, on the basis of data provided pursuant to Annex B, Section I to this Treaty, a data recording medium to be used by a State Party during an observation flight is incompatible with the equipment of another State Party for handling that data recording medium, the States Parties involved shall establish procedures to ensure that all data collected during observation flights can be handled, in terms of processing, duplication and storage by them.

Section II. Output from sensors that use photographic film

1. In the event that output from duplicate optical cameras is to be exchanged, the cameras, film and film processing shall be of an identical type.

2. Provided that the data collected by a single optical camera is subject to exchange, States Parties shall consider, within the Open Skies Consultative Commission during the period of provisional application of this Treaty, the issue of whether the responsibility for the development of the original film negative shall be borne by the observing Party or by the State Party providing the observation aircraft. The State Party developing the original film negative shall be responsible for the quality of processing the original negative film and producing the duplicate positive or negative. In the event that States

Parties agree that the film used during the observation flight conducted on an observation aircraft provided by the observed Party shall be processed by the observing Party, the observed Party shall bear no responsibility for the quality of the processing of the original negative film.

3. All the film used during the observation flight shall be developed:
   (A) in the event that the original film negative is developed at a film processing facility arranged for by the observed Party, no later than three days, unless otherwise agreed, after the arrival of the observation aircraft at the point of exit; or
   (B) in the event that the original film negative is developed at a film processing facility arranged for by the observing Party, no later than ten days after the departure of the observation aircraft from the territory of the observed Party.

4. The State Party that is developing the original film negative shall be obliged to accept at the film processing facility up to two officials from the other State Party to monitor the unsealing of the film cassette or container and each step in the storage, processing, duplication and handling of the original film negative, in accordance with the provisions of Annex K, Section II to this Treaty. The State Party monitoring the film processing and duplication shall have the right to designate such officials from among its nationals present on the territory on which the film processing facility arranged for by the other State Party is located, provided that such individuals are on the list of designated personnel in accordance with Article XIII, Section I of this Treaty. The State Party developing the film shall assist the officials of the other State Party in their functions provided for in this paragraph to the maximum extent possible.

5. Upon completion of an observation flight, the State Party that is to develop the original film negative shall attach a 21-step sensitometric test strip of the same film type used during the observation flight or shall expose a 21-step optical wedge onto the leader or trailer of each roll of original film negative used during the observation flight. After the original film negative has been processed and duplicate film negative or positive has been produced, the States Parties shall assess the image quality of the 21-step sensitometric test strips or images of the 21-step optical wedge against the sensitometric characteristics provided for that type of original film negative or duplicate film negative or positive in accordance with the provisions of Annex K, Section I to this Treaty.

6. In the event that only one original film negative is developed:
   (A) the observing Party shall have the right to retain or receive the original film negative; and
   (B) the observed Party shall have the right to select and receive a complete first generation duplicate or part thereof, either positive or negative, of the original film negative. Unless otherwise agreed, such duplicate shall be:
      (1) of the same format and film size as the original film negative;
      (2) produced immediately after development of the original film negative; and
      (3) provided to the officials of the observed Party immediately after the duplicate has been produced.

7. In the event that two original film negatives are developed:
   (A) if the observation aircraft is provided by the observing Party, the observed Party shall have the right, at the completion of the observation flight, to select either of the two original film negatives, and the original film negative not selected shall be retained by the observing Party; or
   (B) if the observation aircraft is provided by the observed Party, the observing Party shall have the right to select either of the original film negatives, and the original film negative not selected shall be retained by the observed Party.

Section III. Output from sensors that use other recording media

1. The State Party that provides the observation aircraft shall record at least one original set of data collected by sensors using other recording media.

2. In the event that only one original set is made:
   (A) if the observation aircraft is provided by the observing Party, the observing Party shall have the right to retain the original set and the observed Party shall have the right to receive a first generation duplicate copy; or
   (B) if the observation aircraft is provided by the observed Party, the observing Party shall have the right to receive the original set and the observed Party shall have the right to receive a first generation duplicate copy.

3. In the event that two original sets are made:
   (A) if the observation aircraft is provided by the observing Party, the observed Party shall have the right, at the completion of the observation flight, to select either of the two sets of recording media, and the set not selected shall be retained by the observing Party; or
   (B) if the observation aircraft is provided by the observed Party, the observing Party shall have the right to select either of the two sets of recording media, and the set not selected shall be retained by the observed Party.

4. In the event that the observation aircraft is provided by the observing Party, the observed Party shall have the right to receive the data collected by a sideways-looking synthetic aperture radar in the form of either initial phase information or a radar image, at its choice.

5. In the event that the observation aircraft is provided by the observed Party, the observing Party shall have the right to receive the data collected by a sideways-looking synthetic aperture radar in the form of either initial phase information or a radar image, at its choice.

Section IV. Access to sensor output

Each State Party shall have the right to request and receive from the observing Party copies of data collected by sensors during an observation flight. Such copies shall be in the form of first generation duplicates produced from the original data collected by sensors during an observation flight. The State Party requesting copies shall also notify the observed Party. A request for duplicates of data shall include the following information:
   (A) the observing Party;
   (B) the observed Party;
   (C) the date of the observation flight;
   (D) the sensor by which the data was collected;
   (E) the portion or portions of the observation period during which the data was collected; and
   (F) the type and format of duplicate recording medium, either negative or positive film, or magnetic tape.

Article X
Open Skies Consultative Commission

1. In order to promote the objectives and facilitate the implementation of the provisions of this Treaty, the States Parties hereby establish an Open Skies Consultative Commission.

2. The Open Skies Consultative Commission shall take decisions or make recommendations by consensus. Consensus shall be understood to mean the absence of any objection by any State Party to the taking of a decision or the making of a recommendation.

3. Each State Party shall have the right to raise before the Open Skies Consultative Commission, and have placed on its agenda, any issue relating to this Treaty, including any issue related to the case when the observed Party provides an observation aircraft.

4. Within the framework of the Open Skies Consultative Commission the States Parties to this Treaty shall:
   (A) consider questions relating to compliance with the provisions of this Treaty;
   (B) seek to resolve ambiguities and differences of interpretation that may become apparent in the way this Treaty is implemented;
   (C) consider and take decisions on applications for accession to this Treaty; and
   (D) agree as to those technical and administrative measures, pursuant to the provisions of this Treaty, deemed necessary following the accession to this Treaty by other States.

5. The Open Skies Consultative Commission may propose amendments to this Treaty for consideration and approval in accordance with Article XVI. The Open Skies Consultative Commission may also agree on improvements to the viability and effectiveness of this Treaty, consistent with its provisions. Improvements relating only to modification of the annual distribution of active quotas pursuant to Article III and Annex A, to updates and additions to the categories or capabilities of sensors pursuant to Article IV, to revision of the share of costs pursuant to Annex L, Section I, paragraph 9, to arrangements for the sharing and availability of data pursuant to Article IX, Sections III, and IV and to the handling of mission reports pursuant to Article VI, Section I, paragraph 21, as well as to minor matters of an administrative or technical nature, shall be agreed upon within the

Open Skies Consultative Commission and shall not be deemed to be amendments to this Treaty.

6. The Open Skies Consultative Commission shall request the use of the facilities and administrative support of the Conflict Prevention Centre of the Conference on Security and Co-operation in Europe, or other existing facilities in Vienna, unless it decides otherwise.

7. Provisions for the operation of the Open Skies Consultative Commission are set forth in Annex L to this Treaty.

Article XI
Notifications and reports

The States Parties shall transmit notifications and reports required by this Treaty in written form. The States Parties shall transmit such notifications and reports through diplomatic channels or, at their choice, through other official channels, such as the communications network of the Conference on Security and Co-operation in Europe.

Article XII
Liability

A State Party shall, in accordance with international law and practice, be liable to pay compensation for damage to other States Parties, or to their natural or juridical persons or their property, caused by it in the course of the implementation of this Treaty.

Article XIII
Designation of personnel and privileges and immunities

Section I. Designation of personnel

1. Each State Party shall, at the same time that it deposits its instrument of ratification to either of the Depositaries, provide to all other States Parties, for their review, a list of designated personnel who will carry out all duties relating to the conduct of observation flights for that State Party, including monitoring the processing of the sensor output. No such list of designated personnel shall include more than 400 individuals at any time. It shall contain the name, gender, date of birth, place of birth, passport number, and function for each individual included. Each State Party shall have the right to amend its list of

designated personnel until 30 days after entry into force of this Treaty and once every six months thereafter.

2. In the event that any individual included on the original or any amended list is unacceptable to a State Party reviewing the list, that State Party shall, no later than 30 days after receipt of each list, notify the State Party providing that list that such individual shall not be accepted with respect to the objecting State Party. Individuals not declared unacceptable within that 30-day period shall be deemed accepted. In the event that a State Party subsequently determines that an individual is unacceptable, that State Party shall so notify the State Party that designated such individual. Individuals who are declared unacceptable shall be removed from the list previously submitted to the objecting State Party.

3. The observed Party shall provide visas and any other documents as required to ensure that each accepted individual may enter and remain on the territory of that State Party for the purpose of carrying out duties relating to the conduct of observation flights, including monitoring the processing of the sensor output. Such visas and any other necessary documents shall be provided either:
   (A) no later than 30 days after the individual is deemed to be accepted, in which case the visa shall be valid for a period of no less than 24 months; or
   (B) no later than one hour after the arrival of the individual at the point of entry, in which case the visa shall be valid for the duration of that individual's duties; or
   (C) at any other time, by mutual agreement of the States Parties involved.

Section II. Privileges and immunities

1. In order to exercise their functions effectively, for the purpose of implementing this Treaty and not for their personal benefit, personnel designated in accordance with the provisions of Section I, paragraph 1 of this Article shall be accorded the privileges and immunities enjoyed by diplomatic agents pursuant to Article 29; Article 30, paragraph 2; Article 31, paragraphs 1, 2 and 3; and Articles 34 and 35 of the Vienna Convention on Diplomatic Relations of 18 April 1961, hereinafter referred to as the Vienna Convention. In addition, designated personnel shall be accorded the privileges enjoyed by diplomatic agents pursuant to Article 36, paragraph 1, subparagraph (b) of the Vienna Convention, except in relation to articles, the import

or export of which is prohibited by law or controlled by quarantine regulations.

2. Such privileges and immunities shall be accorded to designated personnel for the entire period between arrival on and departure from the territory of the observed Party, and thereafter with respect to acts previously performed in the exercise of their official functions. Such personnel shall also, when transiting the territory of other States Parties, enjoy the privileges and immunities accorded to diplomatic agents pursuant to Article 40, paragraph 1 of the Vienna Convention.

3. The immunity from jurisdiction may be waived by the observing Party in those cases when it would impede the course of justice and can be waived without prejudice to this Treaty. The immunity of personnel who are not nationals of the observing Party may be waived only by the States parties of which such personnel are nationals. Waiver must always be express.

4. Without prejudice to their privileges and immunities or the rights of the observing Party set forth in this Treaty, it is the duty of designated personnel to respect the laws and regulations of the observed Party.

5. The transportation means of the personnel shall be accorded the same immunities from search, requisition, attachment or execution as those of a diplomatic mission pursuant to Article 22, paragraph 3 of the Vienna Convention, except as otherwise provided for in this Treaty.

Article XIV
Benelux

1. Solely for the purposes of Articles II to IX and Article XI, and of Annexes A to I and Annex K to this Treaty, the Kingdom of Belgium, the Grand Duchy of Luxembourg, and the Kingdom of the Netherlands shall be deemed a single State Party, hereinafter referred to as the Benelux.

2. Without prejudice to the provisions of Article XV, the above-mentioned States Parties may terminate this arrangement by notifying all other States Parties thereof. This arrangement shall be deemed to be terminated on the next 31 December following the 60-day period after such notification.

Article XV
Duration and withdrawal

1. This Treaty shall be of unlimited duration.

2. A State Party shall have the right to withdraw from this Treaty. A State Party intending to withdraw shall provide notice of its decision to withdraw to either Depositary at least six months in advance of the date of its intended withdrawal and to all other States Parties. The Depositaries shall promptly inform all other States Parties of such notice.

3. In the event that a State Party provides notice of its decision to withdraw from this Treaty in accordance with paragraph 2 of this Article, the Depositaries shall convene a conference of the States Parties no less than 30 days and no more than 60 days after they have received such notice, in order to consider the effect of the withdrawal on this Treaty.

Article XVI
Amendments and periodic review

1. Each State Party shall have the right to propose amendments to this Treaty. The text of each proposed amendment shall be submitted to either Depositary, which shall circulate it to all States Parties for consideration. If so requested by no less than three States Parties within a period of 90 days after circulation of the proposed amendment, the Depositaries shall convene a conference of the States Parties to consider the proposed amendment. Such a conference shall open no earlier than 30 days and no later than 60 days after receipt of the third of such requests.

2. An amendment to this Treaty shall be subject to the approval of all States Parties, either by providing notification, in writing, of their approval to a Depositary within a period of 90 days after circulation of the proposed amendment, or by expressing their approval at a conference convened in accordance with paragraph 1 of this Article. An amendment so approved shall be subject to ratification in accordance with the provisions of Article XVII, paragraph 1, and shall enter into force 60 days after the deposit of instruments of ratification by the States Parties.

3. Unless requested to do so earlier by no less than three States Parties, the Depositaries shall convene a conference of the States Parties to review the implementation of this Treaty three years after entry into force of this Treaty and at five-year intervals thereafter.

Article XVII
Depositaries, entry into force and accession

1. This Treaty shall be subject to ratification by each State Party in accordance with its constitutional procedures. Instruments of ratification and instruments of accession shall be deposited with the Government of Canada or the Government of the Republic of Hungary or both, hereby designated the Depositaries. This Treaty shall be registered by the Depositaries pursuant to Article 102 of the Charter of the United Nations.

2. This Treaty shall enter into force 60 days after the deposit of 20 instruments of ratification, including those of the Depositaries, and of States Parties whose individual allocation of passive quotas as set forth in Annex A is eight or more.

3. This Treaty shall be open for signature by Armenia, Azerbaijan, Georgia, Kazakhstan, Kirgistan, Moldova, Tajikistan, Turkmenistan and Uzbekistan and shall be subject to ratification by them. Any of these States which do not sign this Treaty before it enters into force in accordance with the provisions of paragraph 2 of this Article may accede to it at any time by depositing an instrument of accession with one of the Depositaries.

4. For six months after entry into force of this Treaty, any other State participating in the Conference on Security and Co-operation in Europe may apply for accession by submitting a written request to one of the Depositaries. The Depositary receiving such a request shall circulate it promptly to all States Parties. The States applying for accession to the Open Skies Treaty may also, if they so wish, request an allocation of passive quota and the level of this quota.
The matter shall be considered at the next regular meeting of the Open Skies Consultative Commission and decided in due course.

5. Following six months after entry into force of this Treaty, the Open Skies Consultative Commission may consider the accession to the Treaty of any State which, in the judgement of the Commission, is able and willing to contribute to the objectives of the Treaty.

6. For any State which has not deposited an instrument of ratification by the time of entry into force, but which subsequently ratifies or accedes to this Treaty, this Treaty shall enter into force 60 days after the date of deposit of its instrument of ratification or accession.

7. The Depositaries shall promptly inform all States Parties of:
   (A) the date of deposit of each instrument of ratification and the date of entry into force of this Treaty;
   (B) the date of an application for accession, the name of the requesting State and the result of the procedure;
   (C) the date of deposit of each instrument of accession and the date of entry into force of this Treaty for each State that subsequently accedes to it;
   (D) the convening of a conference pursuant to Articles XV and XVI;
   (E) any withdrawal in accordance with Article XV and its effective date;
   (F) the date of entry into force of any amendments to this Treaty;
   (G) any other matters of which the Depositaries are required by this Treaty to inform the States Parties.

Article XVIII
Provisional application and phasing of implementation of the Treaty

In order to facilitate the implementation of this Treaty, certain of its provisions shall be provisionally applied and others shall be implemented in phases.

Section I. Provisional application

1. Without detriment to Article XVII, the signatory States shall provisionally apply the following provisions of this Treaty:
   (A) Article VI, Section I, paragraph 4;
   (B) Article X, paragraphs 1, 2, 3, 6 and 7;
   (C) Article XI;
   (D) Article XIII, Section I, paragraphs 1 and 2;
   (E) Article XIV; and
   (F) Annex L, Section I.

2. This provisional application shall be effective for a period of 12 months from the date when this Treaty is opened for signature. In the event that this Treaty does not enter into force before the period of provisional application expires, that period may be extended if all the signatory States so decide. The period of provisional application shall

in any event terminate when this Treaty enters into force. However, the States Parties may then decide to extend the period of provisional application in respect of signatory States that have not ratified this Treaty.

Section II. Phasing of implementation

1. After entry into force, this Treaty shall be implemented in phases in accordance with the provisions set forth in this Section. The provisions of paragraphs 2 to 6 of this Section shall apply during the period from entry into force of this Treaty until 31 December of the third year following the year during which entry into force takes place.

2. Notwithstanding the provisions of Article IV, paragraph 1, no State Party shall during the period specified in paragraph 1 above use an infra-red line-scanning device if one is installed on an observation aircraft, unless otherwise agreed, between the observing and observed Parties. Such sensors shall not be subject to certification in accordance with Annex D. If it is difficult to remove such sensor from the observation aircraft, then it shall have covers or other devices that inhibit its operation in accordance with the provisions of Article IV, paragraph 4 during the conduct of observation flights.

3. Notwithstanding the provisions of Article IV, paragraph 9, no State Party shall, during the period specified in paragraph 1 of this Section, be obliged to provide an observation aircraft equipped with sensors from each sensor category, at the maximum capability and in the numbers specified in Article IV, paragraph 2 provided that the observation aircraft is equipped with:
   (A) a single optical panoramic camera; or
   (B) not less than a pair of optical framing cameras.

4. Notwithstanding the provisions of Annex B, Section II, paragraph 2, subparagraph (A) to this Treaty, data recording media shall be annotated with data in accordance with existing practice of the States Parties during the period specified in paragraph 1 of this Section.

5. Notwithstanding the provisions of Article VI, Section I, paragraph 1, no State Party during the period specified in paragraph 1 of this Section shall have the right to be provided with an aircraft capable of achieving any specified unrefuelled range.

6. During the period specified in paragraph 1 of this Section, the distribution of active quotas shall be established in accordance with the provisions of Annex A, Section II, paragraph 2 to this Treaty.

7. Further phasing in respect of the introduction of additional categories of sensors or improvements to the capabilities of existing categories of sensors shall be addressed by the Open Skies Consultative Commission in accordance with the provisions of Article IV, paragraph 3 concerning such introduction or improvement.

Article XIX
Authentic texts

The originals of this Treaty, of which the English, French, German, Italian, Russian and Spanish texts are equally authentic, shall be deposited in the archives of the Depositaries. Duly certified copies of this Treaty shall be transmitted by the Depositaries to all the States Parties.

IN WITNESS WHEREOF the undersigned, duly authorized, have signed this Treaty.

DONE at Helsinki, this twenty-fourth day of March, one thousand nine hundred and ninety-two.

For the Federal Republic of Germany
For the United States of America
For the Republic of Belarus
For the Kingdom of Belgium
For the Republic of Bulgaria
For Canada
For the Kingdom of Denmark
For the Kingdom of Spain
For the French Republic
For the United Kingdom of Great Britain and Northern Ireland
For the Hellenic Republic
For the Republic of Hungary
For the Republic of Iceland
For the Italian Republic
For the Grand Duchy of Luxembourg
For the Kingdom of Norway
For the Kingdom of the Netherlands
For the Republic of Poland
For the Portuguese Republic
For Romania
For the Russian Federation
For the Czech and Slovak Federal Republic
For the Republic of Turkey
For Ukraine

The CSCE Declaration on the Treaty on Open Skies[1]

Helsinki, 24 March 1992

The Foreign Ministers of the participating States of the Conference on Security and Co-operation in Europe on the occasion of the signature of the Treaty on Open Skies have issued the following declaration:

- *Welcoming* the signing of the Treaty on Open Skies by the Foreign Ministers of the States concluding this Treaty,

- *Recognizing* the importance of the Open Skies regime for the security of States participating in the CSCE process,

- *Assessing* the Treaty as an important element in the process of enhancing security and confidence between members of the international community,

- *Reiterating* the importance of the principle of equal security for all their countries,

- *Noting* the interest expressed by a number of States not full participants in the negotiations, and believing that their adherence to the Treaty as well as signature by all the newly independent States, as mentioned in Article XVII of the Treaty, would enhance the effectiveness of the Open Skies regime,

1. *Recognize* the significant contribution to the Open Skies negotiations made by a number of participants in the CSCE who are not original signatories to the Treaty on Open Skies,

2. *Recognize* also that these States may participate, on the basis of the active and passive quotas they would hold as State Parties, in the implementation of the Treaty and that they may take part in discussions regarding practical arrangements for the regime which will continue in Vienna within the framework of the Open Skies Consultative Commission during the period of provisional application,

---

[1] See Journal No. 1 of the Helsinki 1992 Follow-up Meeting.

3. *Acknowledge* the interest of the States which are participants in the CSCE but not original signatories to the Treaty on Open Skies in information obtained through Open Skies observation flights,

4. *Welcome* the interest shown by States which are participants in the CSCE but not original signatories to the Treaty on Open Skies to accede to it as provided for by Article XVII of the Treaty,

5. *Call upon* all Parties to the Treaty to allow the accession of such interested States as soon as possible and to act, in all matters related to it, in the spirit of co-operation which the Treaty commands.

SELECTED BIBLIOGRAPHY

ACIMOVIC, L., Problems of Security and Cooperation in Europe (Alphen aan den Rijn 1981).

BARBERINI, G. 'La Dimensione Umana della CSCE', in: *Rivista internazionale dei diritti dell'uomo*, Vol. IV, No. 1, 1991, pp. 14-34.

BLOED, A., 'The CSCE as a New International Security Organization in Europe?", in: H. Fischer (Ed.), *The Changing CSCE* (Bochum 1993, forthcoming).

BLOED, A., 'A European System of Peaceful Settlement of Disputes?', in: *Polish Yearbook of International Law*, Vol. XVIII, 1989-1990 (Wroclaw-Warszawa-Krakow 1992), pp. 113-127.

BLOED, A., 'Monitoring the Human Dimension of the CSCE: In Search of its Effectiveness', in: A. Bloed et al. (Eds.), *Monitoring Human Rights in Europe. Comparing International Procedures and Mechanisms* (Dordrecht-Boston-London 1993), pp. 55-91.

BLOED, A. & DIJK, P. van (Eds.), *Essays on human rights in the Helsinki process* (Dordrecht/Boston/Lancaster 1985).

BLOED, A. & DIJK, P. van (Eds.), *The Human Dimension and the Helsinki Process; The Vienna Follow-up Meeting and its Aftermath* (Dordrecht-Boston-London 1991).

BLOED, A. & JONGE, W.J de (Eds.), *Legal Aspects of a New European Infrastructure* (Utrecht 1992).

BLOED, A., LEICHT, L., NOWAK, M. & ROSAS, A. (Eds.), *Monitoring Human Rights in Europe. Comparing International Procedures and Mechanisms* (Dordrecht-Boston-London 1993).

BORAWSKI, J., *From the Atlantic to the Urals: Negotiating Arms Control at the Stockholm Conference* (Washington, D.C. 1988).

BRETT, R., *The Challenges of Change; Report of the Helsinki Follow-up Meeting of the Conference on Security and Co-operation in Europe* (Essex 1992).

BUCHSBAUM, T.M., 'The Future of the Human Dimension of the CSCE', in: *Helsinki Monitor*, 1993, No. 2, pp. 5-24.

BUERGENTHAL, T. (Ed.), *Human Rights, International Law and the Helsinki Accord* (Montclair, N.Y. 1977).

BUERGENTHAL, T., 'The CSCE Human Rights System', in: *The George Washington Journal of International Law and Economics*, Vol. 25, No. 2, 1991, pp. 333-386.

CSCE: From Idea to Institution. A Bibliography (The Danish Institute of International Relations, Copenhagen 1993).

Commission on Security and Cooperation in Europe, *Beyond Process: The CSCE's Institutional Development, 1990-92* (Report prepared by the staff of the Commission, Washington, DC, December 1992).

Conflict Management Group, *Early Warning and Preventive Action inthe CSCE. Defining the Role of the High Commissioner on National Minorities* (A Report of the Conflict Management Group, Harvard Law School, Mass., USA, 1992).

CUTHBERTSON, I.M. (Ed.), *Redefining the CSCE: Challenges and Opportunities in the New Europe* (New York 1992).

DECAUX, E., *La Conférence sur la Sécurité et la Coopération en Europe (CSCE)* (Paris 1992).

DECAUX, E., 'La Réunion de Copenhague de la Conférence sur la Dimension Humaine de la CSCE', in: *Revue Générale de Droit International Public*, 1990, No. 4, pp. 1019-1034.

DECAUX, E. (Ed.), *Sécurité et coopération en Europe; Les texts officiels du processus de Helsinki (1973-1992)* (Paris 1992). (With extensive bibliography.)

DECAUX, E. & SICILIANOS, L.-A. (Eds.), *La dimension humaine de la Conférence de Sécurité et Coopération en Europe* (Paris 1993, forthcoming).

DIJK, P. van, 'The Implementation of the Final Act of Helsinki: The Creation of New Structures or the Involvement of Existing Ones?', in: *Michigan Journal of International Law*, 1989, Vol. 10, No. 1, pp. 110-126.

DIJK, P. VAN, 'The Relation between the European Convention on Human Rights and Fundamental Freedoms and the Human Dimension of the CSCE', in: *Helsinki Monitor*, 1991, Vol. 2, No. 4, pp. 5-14.

FERRARIS, L.V. (Ed.), *Report on a negotiation: Helsinki, Geneva, Helsinki 1972-1975* (Alphen aan den Rijn 1979).

GHEBALI, V.-Y., *Confidence-Building Measures within the CSCE Process: Paragraph by Paragraph Analysis of the Helsinki and Stockholm Régimes*, U.N. Institute for Disarmament and Research, Research Paper No. 3 (New York 1989).

GHEBALI, V.-Y., *La diplomatie de la détente: la CSCE, 1973-1989* (Brussels 1989).

HAM, P. van, *The EC, Eastern Europe and European Unity; Discord, Collaboration and Integration Since 1947* (London/New York 1993).

HELGESEN, J., 'Protecting Minorities in the Conference on Security and Co-operation (CSCE) Process', in: A. Rosas & J. Helgesen (Eds.), *The Strength ofDiversity; Human Rights and Pluralist Democracy* (Dordrecht-Boston-London 1992), pp. 159-186.

HERACLIDES, A., 'The CSCE and Minorities; The Negotiations behind the Commitments, 1972-1992', in: *Helsinki Monitor*, 1992, No. 3, pp. 6-18.

HERACLIDES, A., 'Helsinki-II and the Human Dimension: Normative Commitments, the End of an Era?', in: *Helsinki Monitor*, 1992, No. 4, pp. 65-76.

HERACLIDES, A., *Helsinki-II and its Aftermath. The Making of the CSCE into an International Organisation* (London/New York 1993).

HERACLIDES, A., *Conference on Security and Co-operation in Europe: The Human Dimension, 1972-1991* (London 1993, forthcoming).

HURLBURT, H., 'The CSCE Forum on Security Co-operation: Creating an Arms Control Negotiation for Post-Arms Control Europe', in: *Helsinki Monitor*, 1992, No. 4, pp. 21-32.

KOREY, W. *The Promises We Keep; Human Rights, the Helsinki Process, and American Foreign Policy* (New York 1993).

LEFEBER, R. et al. (Eds.), *The Changing Political Structure of Europe; Aspects of International Law* (Dordrecht-Boston-London 1991).

LEHNE, S., *The Vienna Meeting of the Conference on Security and Co-operation in Europe, 1986-1989: A Turning Point in East-West Relations* (Boulder 1991).

LEHNE, S., *The CSCE in the 1990s, Common European House or Potemkin Village?* (Vienna 1991) Laxenburg Paper No. 9.

LUCAS, M.R., *The Conference on Security and Cooperation in Europe and the Post-Cold War Era* (Hamburg 1990).

LUCAS, M.R. (Ed.), *The CSCE and the Evolution of a Pan-European Order of Security and Cooperation in the 1990s* (Baden-Baden 1993, forthcoming).

MARESCA, J.J., *To Helsinki. The Conference on Security and Cooperation in Europe 1973-1975* (Durham/London 1985).

MASTNY, V., *Helsinki, human rights and European security: analysis and documentation* (Durham 1986).

MASTNY, V. *The Helsinki Process and the Reintegration of Europe, 1986-1991: Analysis and Documentation* (London 1992).

MASTNY, V. & ZIELONKA, J. (Eds.), *Human Rights and Security; Europe on the Eve of a New Era* (Boulder etc. 1991).

McGOLDRICK, D., 'Human Rights Developments in the Helsinki Process', in: *International and Comparative Law Quarterly*, 1990, pp. 923-940.

McWHINNEY, E. et al. (Eds.), *From Coexistence to Cooperation; International Law and Organization in the Post-Cold War Era* (Dordrecht-Boston-London 1991).

NEUHOLD, H. (Ed.), *CSCE: N+N Perspectives: The Process of the Conference on Security and Co-operation in Europe from the Viewpoint of the Neutral and Non-Aligned Participating States* (Vienna 1987).

NEUHOLD, H. (Ed.), *The European Neutrals in the 1990s; New Challenges and Opportunities* (Boulder etc. 1992).

NEUHOLD, H. (Ed.), *The Pentagonal/Hexagonal Experiment; New Forms of Cooperation in a Changing Europe* (Laxenburg 1991).

Office for Democratic Institutions and Human Rights, *Handbook for human dimension mechanism experts/rapporteurs and election observers* (Warsaw 1993), 12 pp.

PENTIKÄINEN, M., *Human Rights Commitments within the CSCE Process: Nature, Contents and Application in Finland* (Helsinki 1992).

ROPERS, N. & SCHLOTTER, P., *Die Institutionalisierungsdebatte im KSZE-Prozeß: Geschichte, Modelle, Evaluation*, HSFK-Report No. 7 (Frankfurt am Main 1986).

ROPERS, N. & SCHLOTTER, P., *Die KSZE; Multilaterales Konfliktmanagement im weltpolitischen Umbruch. Zukunftsperspektiven und neue Impulse für regionale Friedensstrategien* (Frankfurt am Main, HSFK-Report 11-12/1992).

ROSAS, A. & HELGESEN, J. (Eds.), *Human Rights in a Changing East-West Perspective* (London 1990).

ROSAS, A. & HELGESEN, J. (Eds.), *The Strength of Diversity; Human Rights and Pluralist Democracy* (Dordrecht-Boston-London 1992).

SANTEN, H. VAN & RUIGROK, A., 'The Vienna Arms Control Negotiations', in: *Helsinki Monitor*, 1990, No. 3, pp. 7-15.

SCHELTEMA, G., 'CSCE Peacekeeping Operations', in: *Helsinki Monitor*, 1992, No. 4, pp. 7-17.

SCHLAGER, E.B., 'The Procedural Framework of the CSCE: From the Helsinki Consultations to the Paris Charter, 1972-1990', in: *Human Rights Law Journal*, Vol. 12, No. 6-7, 1991, pp. 221-237.

SCHRAMM, F.-K. et al. (Eds.), *Sicherheitskonferenz in Europa: Dokumentation 1954-1972* (Frankfurt am Main 1972).

SCHWEISFURTH, Th., 'Zur Frage der Rechtsnatur, Verbindlichkeit und völkerrechtlichen Relevanz der KSZE-Schlußakte', in: *Zeitschrift für ausländisches öffentliches Recht und Völkerrecht*, 1976, pp. 681-726.

SIZOO, J. & JURRJENS, R.Th., *CSCE Decision-Making: The Madrid Experience* (The Hague 1984).

TANJA, G.J., 'Peaceful Settlement of Disputes within the CSCE: Bridge over Troubled Water', in: *Helsinki Monitor*, 1993, No. 1, pp. 22-33.

WELLER, M., 'The International Response to the Dissolution of the Socialist Federal Republic of Yugoslavia', in: *American Journal of International Law*, Vol. 86, No. 3, July 1992, pp. 569-607.

ZAAGMAN, R.W., 'Helsinki-II and the Human Dimension: Institutional Aspects', in: *Helsinki Monitor*, 1992, No. 4, pp. 52-64.

ZAAGMAN, R.W., 'Helsinki-II and the Second Basket', in: *Helsinki Monitor*, 1992, No. 4, pp. 52-64.

ZAAGMAN, R.W., 'The CSCE High Commissioner on National Minorities: An Analysis of the Mandate and the Institutional Context', in: A. Bloed (Ed.), *The Challenges of Change: Helsinki-II and its Aftermath* (Dordrecht-Boston-London 1993, forthcoming).

ZAAL, H., 'The CSCE High Commissioner on National Minorities', in: *Helsinki Monitor*, 1992, No. 4, pp. 33-37.

INDEX

A

B

H

J

L

M

R

T

Y

Z